JIMMY SWAGGART BIBLE COMMENTARY

Luke

JIMMY SWAGGART BIBLE COMMENTARY

For prices and information please call: 1-800-288-8350
Baton Rouge residents please call: (225) 768-7000
Website: www.jsm.org • E-mail: info@jsm.org

Jimmy Swaggart Bible Commentary

Luke

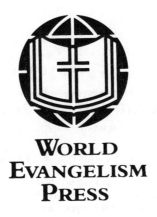

WORLD EVANGELISM PRESS

ISBN 978-1-941403-47-1

11-075 • COPYRIGHT © 2017 Jimmy Swaggart Ministries®
www.jsm.org

17 18 19 20 21 22 23 24 25 26 / LSC / 10 9 8 7 6 5 4 3 2 1

TABLE OF CONTENTS

———■———

INTRODUCTION

—■—

Many have claimed that Luke, the writer of the third gospel, which bears his name, was a Gentile. That may very well be true; however, I personally feel that Luke was Jewish, as were all the other writers of the Bible. The psalmist said, *"He shows His Word unto Jacob, His statutes and His judgments unto Israel"* (Ps. 147:19). One could take this passage to prove that every writer in the Word of God was Jewish.

Epiphanius and others mentioned that Luke was one of the 70 disciples (Lk. 10:17). Theophylact believed that Luke was one of the two disciples who met with the risen Jesus on their walk to Emmaus (Lk. 24:13, 18); however, there is no proof to substantiate these suppositions. They may be true, but they are uncertain.

A MARTYR

Gregory Nazianzen mentioned that Luke was among the martyrs. Nicephorus related the manner of his martyrdom—how that while ministering in Greece, he was hanged upon an olive tree.

He was called by the apostle Paul *"the beloved physician"* (Col. 4:14; II Tim. 4:11; Phile., Vs. 24). Having written the book of Acts, he referred to himself by the pronoun *"we"* (Acts 16:10-17; 20:5-15; 21:1-18; 27:1-28:16).

PHYSICIAN

The profession of physician in the early days of the empire was filled almost exclusively by those who had been set free by Rome. In other words, they were freed men. This calling implies a considerable amount of scientific knowledge and shows that Luke certainly belonged to the class of educated men.

As is obvious from the book of Acts, Luke was a close friend of the apostle Paul, and that would probably rate as an understatement. Exactly how this friendship began is not clear. Some feel that he became acquainted with Paul not too long after the apostle's conversion.

Among other places, as outlined in the book of Acts, it seems he was with or near Paul during the two years or more of Paul's imprisonment at Caesarea. Whenever Paul was sent under guard as a prisoner from Caesarea to Rome, Luke was evidently with him. Throughout the voyage, which ended in the memorable shipwreck, the subsequent stay at Melita, and on the voyage from Melita in the ship of Alexandria, we find the forms *"we"* and *"us"* used: *"And when we came to Rome"* (Acts 28:16); *"When the brethren heard of us"* (Acts 28:15).

THE MAN

During that long period of imprisonment at Caesarea, it is highly probable that Luke, acting under the immediate direction of Paul, made a personal investigation, searching out eyewitnesses of the events, which occasioned the gospel according to Luke. Less than 30 years had elapsed from the resurrection morning, so consequently, there would have been eyewitnesses still alive.

The book of Acts was quite probably written during the Roman imprisonment, which immediately followed the imprisonment at Caesarea. This was about A.D. 63-64.

It seems that this intimate friendship between Paul and Luke was for approximately 12 years, ending at Paul's death. How long before then the friendship existed, there is no way to know.

As Matthew presents Jesus as the *"King"* and Mark as the *"Servant,"* Luke presents Him as *"the Man,"* and one could say, *"The Man whose name is The BRANCH"* (Zech. 6:12).

Here, therefore, Jesus is especially presented as the friend of publicans and sinners, the Saviour of

Zacchaeus and the penitent thief, and the narrator of the parable of the prodigal son and of the story of the good Samaritan.

As the Son of Man, the Lord here appears at the center of a moral system much vaster than that which He filled as Israel's Messiah. He stands forth here as the Saviour of the world. Neither His titles nor His official glories engage the Spirit's thoughts so much as simply Himself as He was a man on the earth, walking in sinless fellowship with God. That was Jesus!

LUKE

Even though very little is known about Luke, it is interesting that God would have chosen and trained a physician to testify to and medically record the miraculous birth of Jesus, and to narrate the special discourses, actions, parables, and miracles that harmonize with His nature as man.

Williams says, *"The divine design in this gospel in grouping incidents together out of their chronological order so as to emphasize spiritual principles is one of the most striking peculiarities of the book."*

"Tell me the story of Jesus,
"Write on my heart every word;
"Tell me the story most precious,
"Sweetest that ever was heard.
"Tell how the angels in chorus,
"Sang as they welcomed His birth,
"Glory to God in the highest!
"Peace and good tidings on earth."

"Fasting alone in the desert,
"Tell of the days that are past,
"How for our sins He was tempted,
"Yet was triumphant at last.
"Tell of the years of His labor,
"Tell of the sorrow He bore,
"He was despised and afflicted,
"Homeless, rejected, and poor."

"Tell of the Cross where they nailed Him,
"Writhing in anguish and pain;
"Tell of the grave where they laid Him,
"Tell how He lives again.
"Love in that story so tender,
"Clearer than ever I see:
"Stay, let me weep while you whisper,
"Love paid the ransom for me."

THE
BOOK OF LUKE

■

(1) "FORASMUCH AS MANY HAVE TAKEN IN HAND TO SET FORTH IN ORDER A DECLARATION OF THOSE THINGS WHICH ARE MOST SURELY BELIEVED AMONG US."

The construction is:

1. The great system of salvation had been taught by the apostle Paul, and no other was to be admitted, no matter who preached it, no matter what the character or rank of the preacher, and no matter with what imposing claims he came.

2. It follows from this that the mere rank, character, talent, eloquence, or piety of a preacher does not, of necessity, give his doctrine a claim to our belief or prove that his gospel is true.

3. The truth is that great talents may be prostituted.

A DECLARATION

The phrase, *"Forasmuch as many have taken in hand to set forth in order a declaration,"* means there were many who were attempting to write accounts of the life and ministry of Christ, which proved to have no inspiration of the Holy Spirit and, consequently, were unreliable and, therefore, unsatisfactory. Actually, there were some 26 of these apocryphal or unreliable books called gospels or epistles. There were actually many others, which have not come down to us, but fell into the same category. The difference in these books and the books of the Bible is inspiration. The Bible books were inspired by the Holy Spirit, and the others were not, resulting in gross inaccuracies, etc.

The New Testament apocryphal books assume the truths of the four gospels. They

witness to the existence of the four gospels by quoting from them. They prove the existence of much material or other narratives before the four gospels were written. No doubt, hundreds of people wrote down facts and stories during the life of Christ that were later put in books supposed to be true of the life of Christ. However, the four gospels are the only ones counted authoritative by Christians, Jews, and heathen.

THE FOUR GOSPELS

The finding of these apocryphal documents confirms the good judgment of the church, which ultimately set apart the four gospels (Matthew, Mark, Luke, and John) from all others. Actually, as early as the second century, the four gospels were accepted without rivals.

All types of fanciful stories were written in these extra books, such as Jesus stretching lumber to the desired length, making one grain of wheat grow 800 bushels, making birds and animals of clay and giving life to them, etc.

In truth, none of this happened. Jesus did no miracle until after His anointing with the Spirit (Jn. 2:11).

These stories told of the boy Jesus are matched by those told of His sufferings, such as the Cross walking and talking, of Jesus coming out of the tomb so tall that His head was in the clouds, etc. None of these are worthy of truth and show why they were rejected from the Scriptures.

THE THINGS MOST SURELY BELIEVED

The phrase, *"Of those things which are most surely believed among us,"* proclaims the gospel as a narrative concerning facts fully established. It is built upon facts about the Lord Jesus Christ.

In essence, the declaration of these facts was proclaimed all over the world of that day, showing us that the early church took the Great Commission of Jesus very seriously, as we must do today as well (Mat. 28:18-20; Mk. 16:15-20).

There is widespread knowledge that before the close of the second century, the gospel of Jesus Christ pretty much covered the Roman Empire. For instance, before the middle of the second century, Justin Martyr wrote:

"There existed not a people, whether Greek or barbarian, whether they dwelt in tents or wandered about in covered wagons, among whom prayers were not offered up in the name of a crucified Jesus, to the Father and Creator of all things."

A few years later, while living in quite another part of the Roman world, Tertullian told the heathen that his brethren were to be found filling the camp, the assemblies, the palace, and the Senate.

Before the year 200, the well-known and voluminous writings of Irenaeus in Gaul, Clement in Alexandria, and Tertullian in Carthage, the capital of wealthy proconsular Africa, testified to the wide and general acceptance of the books composing the New Testament canon of Scripture.

In the last years of the second century, these books were universally received among Christians as authoritative and honored as Holy Scripture. Of course, among these books was the gospel according to Luke.

At the time Luke wrote his gospel, many attempts were being made to produce a connected history of the life and work of Jesus. Consequently, Luke's statement is in no way to censure these efforts but simply means they were incomplete. Actually, these accounts, whatever they were, could have well formed the basis of Luke's own gospel.

These of which we now speak are not the same as the apocryphal books just mentioned.

(2) "EVEN AS THEY DELIVERED THEM UNTO US, WHICH FROM THE BEGINNING WERE EYEWITNESSES, AND MINISTERS OF THE WORD."

The pattern is:

1. There is no record whatsoever that any of the twelve disciples ever opposed the gospel of Paul or opposed Paul in any manner.

2. There was one exception, the situation with Simon Peter, which was straightened out very quickly, and which Paul addresses in his epistle to the Galatians (Gal. 2:11-14).

3. However, there is some evidence that James, the brother of our Lord, who was the senior pastor over the church in Jerusalem, was not altogether in sync with Paul (Acts 21:20-24).

MUCH MATERIAL DELIVERED TO LUKE

The phrase, *"Even as they delivered them unto us,"* concerns those who were there and actually observed what took place.

Evidently, Luke made it known that he was going to write this account, which occasioned many coming to him with that which they had written themselves, or at least had personally observed.

"Which from the beginning were eyewitnesses, and ministers of the Word," probably concerned members of the *"12"* and the *"70,"* as well as others. No doubt, some of the women who were constantly with Jesus and His party also were among these groups. In other words, what Luke would write was not hearsay but actually eyewitness accounts.

As well, some of these individuals, such as the apostles and others, had been preaching the Word for years and had related these accounts over and over, which meant they had remembered the details exactly as they happened. As well, they were, no doubt, grandly helped by the Holy Spirit!

EYEWITNESS ACCOUNTS

What a thrill it must have been for Luke to hear these eyewitness accounts concerning the life and ministry of Christ. How so much the Spirit of God must have accompanied the telling of these wonderful experiences.

We presently sing the song, "Were You There When They Crucified My Lord?" or others similar. Of course, we were not there; however, those who related these accounts to Luke were there. They saw it with their eyes—the miracles, the ministry, the crucifixion, and the resurrection. Even as I dictate these words, I sense the presence of the Lord.

One day, the whole of the body of Christ will hear Christ personally relate these grand and glorious experiences of the miracles He performed and the great things done.

(3) "IT SEEMED GOOD TO ME ALSO, HAVING HAD PERFECT UNDERSTANDING OF ALL THINGS FROM THE VERY FIRST, TO WRITE UNTO YOU IN ORDER, MOST EXCELLENT THEOPHILUS."

THE GOSPEL ACCORDING TO LUKE

The phrase, *"It seemed good to me also,"* concerns the writing of these accounts, which was to be the book we now know as the gospel according to St. Luke.

The phrase, *"Having had perfect understanding of all things from the very first,"* means that he made absolutely certain of the reliability of these eyewitness accounts. The idea is not that he doubted their word, but that he made absolutely certain that he understood exactly what they said and wrote down the accounts correctly. Consequently, he did not rely on his memory and his narration of the experiences.

FROM THE VERY FIRST

The words, *"From the very first,"* have a double meaning:

1. It means that he took special pains to start at the beginning, which concerned Zacharias and Elisabeth, the father and mother of John the Baptist. Consequently, he goes into much greater detail than the other gospels.

2. The Greek word translated, *"From the very first,"* means, *"Another from above."* This implies inspiration as well as accuracy (II Tim. 3:16).

So, the gospel according to Luke is the result not only of painstaking devotion to accuracy but, as well, the inspiration of the Holy Spirit. Of course, the Holy Spirit inspired all the sacred writers.

THE ORDER

The phrase, *"To write unto you in order,"*

NOTES

referred to an orderly design, not necessarily in chronological order.

The phrase, *"Most excellent Theophilus,"* probably referred to a man of high rank in the Roman world of that day. Nothing is known of his history. The title by which he is addressed, we find several times applied to high Roman officials, such as Felix and Festus (Acts 23:26; 24:3; 26:5). Evidently, he was a Roman who had accepted Christ as his Saviour.

(4) "THAT YOU MIGHT KNOW THE CERTAINTY OF THOSE THINGS, WHEREIN YOU HAVE BEEN INSTRUCTED."

THAT YOU MIGHT KNOW

The phrase, *"That you might know,"* probably meant that Theophilus had heard many and varied stories concerning the life and ministry of Christ and was not certain as to the accuracy of some.

"The certainty of those things," means that this man could rely on what Luke told him because he had received his information from eyewitness accounts and, as well, was being helped greatly by the Lord.

Evidently, Luke strongly sensed in his heart that the Lord wanted him to write this account. It was a sense of purpose to a far greater degree than just a mere impression. All the evidence is that he had a mandate from the Lord respecting this all-important effort; consequently, his confidence was high because he was assured of the help of the Lord.

As well, the manner in which the events fell into place respecting individuals bringing him the accounts of what they had personally seen was a witness to Luke's spirit that this work was the will of the Lord.

"Wherein you have been instructed," concerns all the stories that Theophilus had heard. He would now be able to sort the facts from the fiction.

Whatever the occasion between Luke and Theophilus, this great gospel according to St. Luke," has helped millions to *"know"* the *"certainty of those things."*

(5) "THERE WAS IN THE DAYS OF HEROD, THE KING OF JUDAEA, A CERTAIN PRIEST NAMED ZACHARIAS, OF THE COURSE OF ABIA: AND HIS WIFE WAS OF THE DAUGHTERS OF AARON, AND HER NAME WAS ELISABETH."

THE MANNER OF THE WRITING OF LUKE

It is said that the first four verses of this gospel are written in pure classical language; the sentences are balanced almost with rhythmical accuracy. They are, it is stated, the words evidently of a highly-cultured mind, well versed in Greek thought.

However, with Verse 5, all of this changes, with Luke writing in the manner in which these experiences and information were given unto him. The information came from wonderful, simple people, and he would report it in the same manner. In this, it is easy to note that not only was the relating of these accounts to be absolutely accurate but, as well, that the very color and flavor were to be maintained.

HEROD THE GREAT

The phrase, *"There was in the days of Herod, the king of Judaea,"* pertains to *"Herod the Great."* The event concerning the birth of John the Baptist took place toward the end of his reign. Besides Judaea, his dominion included Samaria, Galilee, and a part of Perea.

Luke's description of him as *"king of Judaea"* is totally accurate in that the Roman Senate had, on the recommendation of Antony and Octavius, granted to him this title.

Spence says that it was a strange and sad state of things. The Land of Promise was ruled over by an Edomite, with the temple on Mt. Zion in his custody. Actually, by now, the entirety of Israel had been ruled by the Gentiles for some 600 years.

Spurning the clarion call of Jeremiah the prophet, Israel rebelled against God until her supremacy was taken away. The sacred writer said, *"But they mocked the messengers of God, and despised His words, and misused His prophets, until the wrath of the LORD arose against His people, till there was no remedy"* (II Chron. 36:16). At that time, the scepter of power was taken from the faltering hands of the kings of Judah and given to the Gentiles, where it has remained ever since.

ISRAEL

With their rebellion against Christ, which

was the crowning blow of all, Israel would lose everything. In A.D. 70, Titus, the Roman general, destroyed it all. Then their very reason to exist was lost, and consequently, they were made to wander as outcasts all over the world until finally becoming a nation again in 1948. Despite their abject failure, they will still fulfill the plan of God, finally accepting Christ at the second coming. So, when one reads of *"Herod, the king of Judaea,"* one is reading of the abject failure of Israel.

ZECHARIAH

The phrase, *"A certain priest named Zacharias,"* should actually be pronounced, *"Zechariah."* It means, *"Remembered of Jehovah."* Never was a man more aptly named.

For about 400 years, Israel had not heard the voice of a prophet. The Lord would now *"remember Israel"* and give to Zechariah and Elisabeth a son, who would be the first prophet after that long silence. As well, he would be the greatest prophet who has ever lived because of his introduction of *"the Lord Jesus Christ, King of Kings and Lord of Lords."*

The phrase, *"Of the course of Abia,"* pertained to the courses instituted by David for temple service. Each of the 24 courses performed their duties for one week (I Chron. 24:1). Then another group of priests would come in to do the same weekly service. Consequently, not any of the priests had to stay away from their homes very long.

ELISABETH

From Eleazar and Ithamar, the two surviving sons of the first high priest, Aaron, had descended these 24 families. Consequently, their forefathers had been carrying out these same duties for nearly 1,000 years, minus the approximate 70 years of the Babylonian dispersion. It continued until the fall of Jerusalem and the burning of the temple in A.D. 70.

According to Josephus, Zechariah was especially distinguished by belonging to the first of 24 courses or families.

The phrase, *"And his wife was of the daughters of Aaron, and her name was Elisabeth,"* means that both the husband and wife traced their lineage back to Aaron, the first high priest—a coveted distinction in Israel, as should be obvious.

However, we shall see that despite this honored distinction, Zechariah and Elisabeth placed little stock in their distinguished position, rather seeking and serving God for the righteousness that He alone could give.

(6) "AND THEY WERE BOTH RIGHTEOUS BEFORE GOD, WALKING IN ALL THE COMMANDMENTS AND ORDINANCES OF THE LORD BLAMELESS."

RIGHTEOUS

The phrase, *"And they were both righteous before God,"* tells us something remarkable about these people.

By this time, the Pharisees and religious leaders of Israel had become so lifted up within themselves that they actually thought that being a child of Abraham constituted salvation. Of course, as stated, those who held the coveted positions, as Zechariah and Elisabeth, generally thought very highly of themselves. Actually, their son, John the Baptist, would direct his attention to this, saying, *"And begin not to say within yourselves, we have Abraham to our father: for I say unto you, that God is able of these stones to raise up children unto Abraham"* (Lk. 3:8). To be sure, the religious leaders did not take too kindly to John declaring that they needed to repent.

And yet, there were some few in Israel at that time, as Zechariah and Elisabeth, who did not fall into this self-righteous group. Their righteousness was not self-righteousness but that imputed by the Lord.

"Walking in all the commandments and ordinances of the Lord blameless," although given by Luke, was sanctioned by the Holy Spirit and proclaimed a lifestyle of righteousness that not many had. What an honor to be called by the Holy Spirit *"blameless!"*

If the Holy Spirit, likewise, presently wrote an account of us, what would that account be?

(7) "AND THEY HAD NO CHILD, BECAUSE THAT ELISABETH WAS BARREN, AND THEY BOTH WERE NOW WELL STRICKEN IN YEARS."

NOTES

BARREN

The phrase, *"And they had no child,"* is said simply but with great portent.

The idea is that they desperately wanted children but had not been able to have any.

"Because that Elisabeth was barren," placed her in the same category as Sarah and Abraham (Gen. 11:30; 17:17).

In Israel, a childless house was looked on as a mark of divine displeasure, possibly the punishment of some grave sin. Consequently, and due to this, very few in Israel would have referred to Zechariah and Elisabeth as *"blameless."* However, God did!

The modern church, as well, is so prone to judge when it has little knowledge of the actual truth of the situation. This is at least one of the reasons Jesus said, *"Judge not, that you be not judged"* (Mat. 7:1).

As well, *"Man looks on the outward appearance, but God looks on the heart"* (I Sam. 16:7).

"And they both were now well stricken in years," means that Elisabeth was past the age of child bearing; consequently, John's birth was just as miraculous as that of Isaac (Rom. 4:17-21; Heb. 11:11).

(8) "AND IT CAME TO PASS, THAT WHILE HE EXECUTED THE PRIEST'S OFFICE BEFORE GOD IN THE ORDER OF HIS COURSE."

AND IT CAME TO PASS

The phrase, *"And it came to pass,"* is of far greater consequence than immediately meets the eye.

It referred not only to the time when Zechariah would go to Jerusalem, regarding his week of duties in the temple, but, as well, the passing of the entire 400 years of prophetic silence, which was now to be remedied. Even more so, it speaks of the way being prepared for the advent of Israel's Messiah, the Lord Jesus Christ. In other words, this is one of the most important moments in human history!

"That while he executed the priest's office before God," means that Zechariah took his duties very seriously before God. He considered that what he did was as *"unto the Lord."* In truth, and considering how the

Lord would use the father of John the Baptist, it was imperative that Zechariah be this type of man. To be sure, inconsistency, slothfulness, and little attention to duty will never characterize one used by God.

The phrase, *"In the order of his course,"* concerned, as stated, *"the course of Abia (Abijah)"* (I Chron. 24:10). Some think this was in the month of July. If that is so, Jesus was conceived six months later (Lk. 1:26), which would have been in January. Consequently, Jesus would have been born nine months later in October. It is fairly certain that He was not born on December 25th because shepherds were continuing to keep their flocks out at night, which would have hardly been the case in late December.

(9) "ACCORDING TO THE CUSTOM OF THE PRIEST'S OFFICE, HIS LOT WAS TO BURN INCENSE WHEN HE WENT INTO THE TEMPLE OF THE LORD."

THE CUSTOM

The phrase, *"According to the custom of the priest's office,"* means there were several duties that were to be performed.

"His lot was to burn incense when he went into the temple of the Lord," refers to something he probably had never done before.

There were approximately 20,000 priests in Israel at that time. Due to the *"burning of incense"* being the most coveted of all the priestly duties, the priests were chosen by the drawing of lots for the privilege of performing the sacred duty. Farrar conjectures that to enter that sacred spot would never happen to the same priest twice in his lifetime.

The first record of burning incense told of disobedience and, therefore, death (Lev. 10:1-2). The last told of unbelief but ultimately resulted in life—the birth of John the Baptist.

Among the Israelites, only priests were allowed to offer incense. The incense was burned upon the altar of worship, which sat immediately in front of the Holy of Holies (Ex. 30:1). It was burned every morning and every evening. The altar of incense was covered with gold, and the vessels that held the incense were, no doubt, covered with gold, as well.

Burning incense was one of the most prominent rituals in divine worship, which foreshadowed things to come.

THE GOLDEN ALTAR OF INCENSE

When Aaron and his sons were anointed, as is recorded in Exodus, Chapter 29, the sons were anointed with him, and not he with them. Aaron was a type of Christ, and everything in this is connected with Christ. His precious blood first had to be poured out before the Spirit could be poured forth, and sinners must first be washed from their sins in that precious blood before they can receive the Holy Spirit, which is done by faith. Thus cleansed and sanctified, worship at the golden altar of incense is possible, but not otherwise.

Having brought His people out of Egypt, God established the brazen altar outside the tabernacle, a type of the Cross of the Lord Jesus Christ, and the golden altar inside. He appointed a mediator in the form of the high priest to maintain relationship with Him in order that He might dwell among them.

The brazen altar, as stated, symbolized the Cross, which was the perfection of Christ's sacrifice for sin; the golden altar, the preciousness of His person. The altar itself spoke of Jesus. The wood and the gold prefigured His humanity and deity. The golden altar was crowned, and it had staves to bear it so as to be the day and night companion of a pilgrim people. The incense burned upon it spoke of Him. Aaron himself, in his robes of glory, pictured Him. The light of the golden lampstand foretold Him, who, being the light of that world that needs no sun, came into this world to be its light.

THE INCENSE

The incense was made of four principle spices—*"stacte, onycha, galbanum, and frankincense"* (Ex. 30:34). This perfume set out the spiritual and personal perfections of Christ.

When *"beaten very small,"* the perfume was offered to God. The minutest emotions of Christ's nature as a man were perfect, and all was *"of like weight"* in His sinless nature (Ex. 30:34).

The idea seemed to be that coals of fire

were to be taken from the brazen altar, which sat immediately in front of the temple, and placed on the golden altar, which sat in the Holy Place immediately in front of the Holy of Holies.

The coals of fire typified the judgment of God, which would ultimately come upon Jesus as He took the penalty for sin that we rightly deserve. As these coals of fire were placed on the golden altar, incense was poured over them, with the smoke and fragrance filling the Holy Place. This signified prayer and worship but, more than all, the intercession of Christ on our behalf, which could only be sanctified by Calvary.

THE LORD JESUS CHRIST

The Holy of Holies, which was separated by the veil from the Holy Place, was where God dwelt between the mercy seat and the cherubim. Sinful man could not approach Him in worship and prayer, which was signified by the incense, unless washed by the precious blood of Calvary. This was symbolized by the coals of fire taken from the brazen altar, which was a type of Calvary.

So, the burning of Incense, which had been done for nearly 1,600 years and always in anticipation of the One who was to come, was now to be done for the very first time in fulfillment of this coming event—the birth, life, ministry, death, and resurrection of Christ, who would fulfill all the types.

Due to what Christ did at Calvary and the resurrection, it is so easy to approach the Lord that we are even encouraged to do so (Heb. 4:16). Nevertheless, this privilege, as symbolized by the constant burning of incense upon the golden altar, did not come cheaply or easily. The miracle son of Zacharias and Elisabeth would be the very one who would introduce the glorious Redeemer. So, the burning of this incense was special in a way that is beyond the ability of man to fully comprehend.

(10) "AND THE WHOLE MULTITUDE OF THE PEOPLE WERE PRAYING WITHOUT AT THE TIME OF INCENSE."

AT THE TIME OF INCENSE

The phrase, *"And the whole multitude of the people were praying without,"* indicates

that the presence of the Lord covered the temple and its adjoining areas in a very special way. No doubt, the people wondrously sensed this presence and, consequently, were *"praying"* and worshipping.

Somebody suggested that among that praying crowd may very well have been the aged Simeon and Anna the prophetess (Lk. 2:25, 36).

The phrase, *"At the time of incense,"* was the time Gabriel appeared unto Zechariah.

As stated, this was to be the greatest time of incense ever known!

This time of incense symbolized the great host that had come before God all the preceding centuries, even thousands of years, asking Him for the Redeemer to be revealed. All of these prayers and petitions of which the incense symbolized were now about to be fulfilled.

When Zechariah walked into the Holy Place, little did he realize what was about to happen. As well, the people outside did not know what was about to transpire. However, it was truly to be a day of days, which would signify the beginning of the fulfillment of all the prophecies pertaining to the coming Messiah. True, this was not of Him, but the forerunner; however, the forerunner was given to *"prepare His way!"*

(11) "AND THERE APPEARED UNTO HIM AN ANGEL OF THE LORD STANDING ON THE RIGHT SIDE OF THE ALTAR OF INCENSE."

THE ANGEL OF THE LORD

The phrase, *"And there appeared unto him an angel of the Lord,"* referred to *"Gabriel"* (Lk. 1:19).

Angels are mentioned quite often in the gospel of Luke (1:11, 26; 2:9, 15, 21; 12:8; 15:10; 16:22; 22:43; 24:4, 23).

The word or name *angel* is used generically of "God, Christ, men, and certain spirit beings." One has to look at the context to ascertain to whom is referred. The word literally means *"messenger."*

The one referred to as *"Gabriel"* would fall into the class that is referred to as *"common angels,"* that is, if such a term can be used of such glorious beings.

As seems to be obvious in Scripture, such

angels have spirit bodies with spirit parts, such as hands, feet, eyes, heads, voices, mouths, hair, faces, and other parts that men have (Gen. 18:2, 4, 8; 19:1-22; Judg. 13:6). But yet, these *"body parts"* are spirit and not flesh, meaning they do not grow old or die.

As well, they have personal souls with emotions (Lk. 15:1-10); passions (Gen. 6:1-4; Jude 6-7); appetites (Gen. 18:8; 19:3); anger (Rev. 12:12), etc.

Also, they have personal spirits with intelligence and wisdom (II Sam. 14:20; 19:27; Mat. 24:36; Eph. 3:10); patience (Num. 22:22-35); meekness (II Pet. 2:11; Jude 9); modesty (I Cor. 11:10); holiness (Mk. 8:38); obedience (Ps. 103:20; Mat. 6:10); knowledge (Mk. 13:32; I Pet. 1:12), etc.

Angels can do anything men can do, including sin, which accounts for the one-third of the angels which fell with Lucifer.

They were created by Christ before the earth was created (Job 38:4-7; Ps. 148:2-5; Col. 1:16). They are not to be worshipped (Col. 2:18). They are organized into principalities, powers, and rulers with thrones (Rom. 8:38; Eph. 6:10-18; Col. 1:16; 2:18; I Pet. 3:22).

These beings carry out the wishes of God, at least those who serve Him. (As stated, one-third of the angels fell with Satan in his revolution against God some time in eternity past.)

TEN KINDS OF SPIRIT BEINGS

Besides God, there are 10 kinds of spirit beings spoken of in Scripture. They are:

1. SERAPHIM: (Isa. 6:1-7).

This is the only mention of these celestial beings in Scripture. They seem to have some association with the divine throne. These, as seen by Isaiah, were human in form but had six wings, a pair to shield their faces, another to conceal their feet, and a third pair for flight. They were stationed above the throne of God and appeared to have led in divine worship. One chanted a refrain, which Isaiah recorded, *"Holy, holy, holy, is the Lord of Hosts: the whole earth is full of His glory"* (Isa. 6:3).

So vigorous was this act of worship that the thresholds of the divine temple shook, and the Holy Place was filled with smoke.

NOTES

It seems their moral qualities were employed exclusively in the service of God, and their position was such that they were privileged to exercise an atoning ministry while, at the same time, extolling the ethical and moral character of God.

2. CHERUBIM: (Gen. 3:24; Ezek. 1:5-28; 8:1-4; 10:1-22).

In the Book, these beings were assigned to guard the Tree of Life in Eden. A similar symbolic function was credited to the golden cherubim, which were placed at either end of the mercy seat of the ark of the covenant (Ex. 25:18-22; Heb. 9:5). As stated, these were symbolic only.

In Ezekiel, Chapter 10, the chariot-throne of God, borne up by cherubim, becomes mobile. Representations of these winged creatures were also embroidered on the curtains and veil of the tabernacle and on the walls of the temple (Ex. 26:31; II Chron. 3:7).

Each of the cherubim had four faces and four wings. To what extent they were thought to be possessed of moral and ethical qualities is unknown. They were invariably in close association with God and were accorded an elevated position.

3. ZOA, OR LIVING CREATURES: (Rev. 4:5-6, 14; 6:1-8; 7:11; 14:3, 9-11; 15:7; 19:4).

These seem to be similar to the seraphim of Isaiah, Chapter 6, in that they also have six wings and also say, *"Holy, holy, holy Lord God Almighty"* (Rev. 4:8). As well, their position seems to be *"round about the throne"* (Rev. 4:6). However, the similarity ends there.

The *"living Creatures"* are *"full of eyes before and behind"* and, as well, seem to have four different kinds of faces, whereas the seraphim are not spoken of in that manner. However, they are very much involved in the worship of God.

4. SPIRIT ANIMALS: these are shaped like ones we have on earth (II Ki. 2:11-12; 6:13-17; Zech. 1:8-11; 6:1-8; Rom. 1:20; II Cor. 12:1-4; Rev. 19:11-21).

5. ARCHANGELS: these are chief angels who rule kingdoms and planets (Col. 1:15-18; I Thess. 4:16; Jude 9).

Included in these chief angels is *"Michael,"* the only one who is actually called an *"archangel,"* and is *"the prince of Israel"*

(Dan. 10:13, 21; 11:1; 12:1; I Thess. 4:16; Jude 9; Rev. 12:7-9).

The mighty angel *"Gabriel"* is not spoken of as an *"archangel,"* but as one *"who stands in the presence of God"* (Lk. 1:19). Consequently, he may even outrank Michael.

6. ANGELS: these are in the same category as the mighty angels just listed but do not rank nearly as high.

7. FALLEN ANGELS AND DEMON SPIRITS

"Lucifer," or the one we now refer to as Satan, who may have been the original ruler of planet Earth, it seems, is present pseudo-ruler of man's dominion on earth (Isa. 14:12-14; Ezek. 28:11-17; Mat. 4:1-11; Lk. 10:18; Eph. 2:2; Rev. 12:7-9).

As well, the *"unnamed princes of Persia and Grecia"* are powerful, evil angels, who ruled these areas (Dan. 10:13-11:1; Rev. 11:7; 17:8). Paul mentioned another group of spirit beings, *"For we wrestle not against flesh and blood, but against principalities, against powers, against the rulers of the darkness of this world, against spiritual wickedness in high places"* (Eph. 6:12).

The Greek scholars tell us that *"principalities"* constitute the highest rank of fallen angels. When we speak of angels being fallen, we're speaking of those who threw in their lot with Lucifer in his revolution against God some time in the dateless past.

The *"powers"* constitute more fallen angels, who serve Satan under the *"principalities."* Then we have *"the rulers of the darkness of this world,"* which the Greek scholars tell us, as well, are fallen angels, all ruling in the kingdom of darkness.

The last designation, *"spiritual wickedness in high places,"* they say, constitutes demon spirits.

We know that approximately one-third of the angelic host threw in their lot with Lucifer in his revolution against God (Rev. 12:4). As to exactly what their number is, we do not know. However, we do know that this revolution was a powerful factor in that it drew one-third of the angels, who now constitute the world of spiritual darkness.

8. DEMONS

The word *demon* is not actually found in Scripture but means "evil spirits."

NOTES

Demon spirits can possess people and cause all types of sickness. They do everything they can to work against man and God, and can even go out of and come back into men as they will unless cast out and rejected (Mat. 12:43-45).

Demon spirits are subject to Christ and believers by the atonement, the name of Jesus, and the Holy Spirit (Mat. 8:16-17; 12:28; Mk. 16:17; Lk. 10:17; Acts 19:15). Thousands of them can enter into and take possession of one man at the same time (Mk. 5:9). They must be discerned, tested, resisted, and rejected by believers (I Cor. 12:10; Eph. 4:27; 6:10-18; I Pet. 5:8-9; I Jn. 4:1-6).

Demons have more than ordinary intelligence (Mat. 8:29). As well, they have personalities (Lk. 8:26-33), but are disembodied (Mat. 12:43-45). Consequently, they seek a body to inhabit, whether human or animal (Mk. 5:1-18).

As to their origin, it is not known. We do know that God did not originally create them in this manner, but they became such after some type of rebellion against God, even before the creation of the Earth. Every record of anything created by God is always referred to as *"good"* (Gen. 1:31), and demon spirits certainly do not fall under the category of good.

As well, demon spirits are not fallen angels, as some suggest. Angels have spirit bodies and do not possess anyone.

It is my personal thought that demon spirits came from the civilization that was on this Earth before Adam and Eve and before the planet was destroyed by some type of upheaval. There is evidence that Lucifer, at that time, ruled this planet under God in righteousness and holiness. However, when he led his revolution against God, it caused the upheaval of this Earth. So, if Lucifer ruled this planet at that time, he had to have something to rule. What these creatures were, we do not know. At any rate, they threw in their lot with Lucifer in his revolution against God, and I personally believe this is where demon spirits originated. Let us say it again: God did not create them in this fashion.

9. DEMON LOCUSTS

These are found in Revelation 9:1-11. As well, these creatures serve and obey Satan.

They were not created in this fashion but became this way at a point in time, apparently, at the same time as the demon spirits.

10.   DEMON HORSEMEN

This is found in Revelation 9:12-21. As well, these also fall under the same category as the demon locusts.

THE RIGHT SIDE OF THE ALTAR OF INCENSE

The phrase, *"Standing on the right side of the altar of incense,"* is the side of propitiation, which, in effect, means that God accepts the sacrifice. Consequently, the *"right side"* was chosen for purpose (Mat. 25:33; Mk. 16:5; Jn. 21:6).

(12)   "AND WHEN ZACHARIAS SAW HIM, HE WAS TROUBLED, AND FEAR FELL UPON HIM."

THE ANGEL GABRIEL

The phrase, *"And when Zacharias saw him* (saw Gabriel),*"* expresses extreme startlement on the part of this priest.

"He was troubled, and fear fell upon him," expressed pretty well the reaction of most all at being placed in the presence of such a being.

The spirit world is very real, affecting all people, whether they know it or not, either in a negative or positive way. Of course, demon spirits from the world of darkness can only affect in a negative sense and, in one way or the other, come to *"steal, kill, and destroy"* (Jn. 10:10).

However, angels from God come either to bless or to warn. According to Scripture, we are surrounded by angels, although unseen (II Ki. 6:17; Ps. 34:7).

Angels were prominent during the Lord's earthly ministry and in connection with His death and resurrection. Their presence proves that the Messiah was not an angel, but the Lord of angels.

(13)   "BUT THE ANGEL SAID UNTO HIM, FEAR NOT, ZACHARIAS: FOR YOUR PRAYER IS HEARD; AND YOUR WIFE ELISABETH SHALL BEAR YOU A SON, AND YOU SHALL CALL HIS NAME JOHN."

FEAR NOT

The phrase, *"But the angel said unto*

NOTES

him, Fear not, Zacharias," proclaims that this appearance pertained to blessing. The fear and agitation of Zacharias, no doubt, was obvious. I cannot conceive that any other person would have acted any differently. Any contact with the other world of eternal light is something extraordinary, to say the least! It has not happened to many, and yet, this is the world in which all righteous souls will live forever.

As well, I cannot help but believe that when Gabriel said, *"Fear not,"* a great calming effect came over Zacharias. The fear does not so much derive from the glorious presence as the lack of spiritual knowledge in this area and, more particularly, the personal unworthiness of man. These beings, such as Gabriel, have never sinned and, consequently, are perfectly righteous.

The evidence seems clear that man was originally created even higher than the angels. The Scripture says, *"For You have made him a little lower than the angels, and have crowned him with glory and honor"* (Ps. 8:5).

The word translated *angels*, in the Hebrew is *Elohim*, and actually means "God" or "Godhead." In other words, the translators should have said, *"For You have created him a little lower than God"* or *"the God,"* i.e., Jehovah.

David then said, *"You made him to have dominion over the works of Your hands; You have put all things under His feet* (Ps. 8:6).

THE HEAD OF ALL OF GOD'S WORKS

This passage just quoted places man at the head of all of God's works—the heavens, including the sun, moon, stars, and the earth, and all living things. It makes him next to God in position and power over all creation, but it must be understood that man will never evolve into the status of godhood.

Thus, Adam was originally made higher than the angels, but by sin, he was brought very low and made subject to death. Now, man, in his lessened state (short of God's glory, Rom. 3:23) is below angels. Christ Himself was made lower for a time to take man's low place and to raise him again higher than angels, as he originally was.

Christ has been exalted to a place higher than angels or any other being except the Father (Eph. 1:21-23; Phil. 2:9-11; I Pet. 3:22).

Redeemed man is to be raised up to that exalted position with Him (Rom. 8:17-18; Eph. 2:6-7; 3:8-11; II Tim. 2:12; Heb. 2:5-11; Rev. 1:6; 5:10; 22:4-6).

So, this is the reason for the fear, even by righteous men, at the appearance of such beings. However, at the resurrection when redeemed man is glorified, he will then be once again elevated to his rightful place—higher than angels. Then, there will be no more fear as now expressed!

YOUR PRAYER IS HEARD

The phrase, *"For your prayer is heard,"* signifies two things:

1. The correct Greek translation should have been, "Was heard," implying that it was no longer offered because of their age, etc. No doubt, Zacharias and Elisabeth had sought the Lord earnestly for many years concerning the bearing of a child. However, the years had passed with their prayer not being answered, and now, due to age, they had given up.

2. When they sought the Lord, they possibly thought that God did not hear them, or else, did not desire that they have a child. No explanation came from the throne, only silence; however, their prayer was definitely heard, exactly as Gabriel announced.

What a lesson this should be to us.

Every prayer prayed in the will of God is always heard by the Lord. John wrote, *"And this is the confidence that we have in Him, that, if we ask anything according to His will, He hears us:*

"And if we know that He hears us, whatsoever we ask, we know that we have the petitions that we desired of Him" (I Jn. 5:14-15).

WILLING TO WAIT?

However, sadly, most modern believers are not willing to wait, which, at times, we are required to do exactly as Zacharias and Elisabeth. God's time is a part of His will, and consequently, delay does not mean denial.

Above all, the believer should keep believing and not falter. God is able! Not only

would they have a son, but he would be the greatest son who has ever been born, with the exception of Jesus Christ. What an honor! Actually, the Lord always gives us far more than we ask.

The phrase, *"And your wife Elisabeth shall bear you a son,"* seems to indicate that they had originally asked for *"a son."*

How old they were at this time is not known, but the Scripture says, *"They both were now well stricken in years"* (Lk. 1:7).

When nature is feeble, broken, and dead, it is then possible for God to act in power.

One can only shout, *"Hallelujah!"*

"And you shall call his name John," has the meaning, "Jehovah shows favor." John was one of the seven persons in the Bible named before his birth (Ishmael, Gen. 16:11; Isaac, Gen. 17:19; Solomon, I Chron. 22:9; Josiah—325 years before his birth, I Ki. 13:2; II Ki. 22:1; Cyrus—named 175 years before his birth, Isa. 44:28-45:1; John the Baptist, Lk. 1:13, 60-63; Jesus, Mat. 1:21).

In effect, the name *John* means "grace," and was an apt description of the one who would introduce the Lord of glory, the One who would bring *"grace and truth"* (Jn. 1:17).

(14) "AND YOU SHALL HAVE JOY AND GLADNESS; AND MANY SHALL REJOICE AT HIS BIRTH."

The overview is:

1. Any child born to godly parents and raised accordingly will always bring *"joy and gladness."*

2. Millions the world over have rejoiced at the birth of John the Baptist. Why?

3. While all other prophets pointed to the One who was to come, namely Jesus, it was John the Baptist who actually introduced Him.

JOY AND GLADNESS

The phrase, *"And you shall have joy and gladness,"* refers not only to Zacharias and Elisabeth but, as well, the whole of Israel. This would be the first prophetic voice in some 400 years. Israel's strength and power had always resided in their God-called prophets. The prophet's message, whether negative or positive, and whether heeded or not, always gave direction. It was, *"Thus saith the Lord!"*

The last prophetic voice had been that of Malachi, which concluded an approximate 1,600 year chain. Not having that voice, Israel had suffered greatly in the last 400 years. But now, the long silence was to be broken with the greatest prophetic voice Israel had ever heard because he would introduce the long-awaited Messiah.

The phrase, *"And many shall rejoice at his birth,"* included not only those in Israel but the entirety of the world for all time. The rejoicing would most of all be for the One he would introduce.

(15) "FOR HE SHALL BE GREAT IN THE SIGHT OF THE LORD, AND SHALL DRINK NEITHER WINE NOR STRONG DRINK; AND HE SHALL BE FILLED WITH THE HOLY SPIRIT, EVEN FROM HIS MOTHER'S WOMB."

The diagram is:

1. John the Baptist was great. In fact, Jesus said he was the greatest of all prophets because he introduced the Lord Jesus Christ.

2. His never drinking wine or strong drink means that he was a Nazarite from his mother's womb.

3. He was filled with the Holy Spirit, but yet, this was somewhat different than the baptism with the Holy Spirit, which we have had since the day of Pentecost (Acts 2:4).

GREAT IN THE SIGHT OF THE LORD

The phrase, *"For he shall be great in the sight of the Lord,"* constitutes the only true greatness. Regrettably, he would not be great in the eyes of the religious leaders of Israel. Actually, *"greatness"* from God is seldom recognized by the world or even the church. Sadly, most seek for greatness in the sight of man instead of God.

Greatness in the sight of God produces humility, while greatness in the sight of man produces conceit.

His greatness would come, as we have stated, because of his introduction of Christ. Anything connected with Jesus is great! Consequently, John the Baptist would be even greater than the mighty prophetic voice of Isaiah, etc., because Isaiah and others of the prophets only saw the Messiah at a distance. As stated, John would personally introduce

Him, hence, the greatness! So, the greatness was tied not to John, but rather his association with Jesus (Mat. 11:11).

A NAZARITE

The phrase, *"And shall drink neither wine nor strong drink,"* meant that he was a Nazarite.

The Nazarite had to abstain from intoxicating drinks in order that no spirit would control him other than that of Jehovah (Prov. 20:1).

As well, he was not to cut his hair during the time of consecration, which, in the case of John the Baptist, was the entirety of his life. Long hair on a man denoted weakness and, in essence, was meant to say that God was his strength.

Also, he must not go near a dead body, even that of his nearest relation. Death signified the terrible results of sin and was its perfect picture; consequently, the Nazarite, who was to epitomize life, must abstain from any association with death. There is, for example, the consecration of Samuel (I Sam. 1:11). Actually, in the Qumran text, I Samuel 1:22 ends with the words, *"A Nazarite forever all the days of his life."*

Chapter 6 of Numbers provides the fullest and most detailed account of the Nazarite.

THE HOLY SPIRIT

The phrase, *"And he shall be filled with the Holy Spirit, even from his mother's womb,"* has no reference to the Acts 2:4 experience, which had not yet come to pass.

The word *filled* in the Greek text means "to furnish or supply." It actually means that from his mother's womb, he was called and designated for a particular task.

As well, the Holy Spirit, even from his mother's womb, would furnish and supply direction, leading, and guidance. In other words, the Holy Spirit watched over him extensively, even as an infant, and with personal guidance once he reached the age of understanding.

Due to the significance of proclaiming the message of repentance to Israel, which was absolutely necessary respecting the coming of the Messiah, and above all, the introduction of the Messiah, there was an unusual or even a singular help given, which had never been afforded to another.

(16) "AND MANY OF THE CHILDREN OF ISRAEL SHALL HE TURN TO THE LORD THEIR GOD."

The exegesis is:

1. Considering this was the first true move of God in Israel in some 400 years, many gave their hearts to the Lord as a result of the ministry of John the Baptist.

2. He turned these Israelites *"to the Lord their God,"* and not to man, etc.

3. This is the basic reason that the religious leadership of Israel did not favor John, even as they did not favor Christ.

THE CHILDREN OF ISRAEL

The phrase, *"And many of the children of Israel,"* is used by Gabriel in an extremely endearing manner. God loved these people very much, even though at this time, they loved Him very little!

Actually, spiritually speaking, Israel was at an extremely low state at this time. The office of the high priest had long since ceased to follow the Aaronic lineage. It was now controlled by the Roman governor and, in essence, by Caesar; consequently, it was corrupt and wicked. Actually, much of the priesthood fell into this same category, with some few exceptions, such as Zacharias, etc. As stated, some 400 years had passed since the voice of the prophet had been heard in the land. As a consequence, spiritual declension was rife, but yet, with a great show of religion. The Pharisees pretty well controlled the religious life of Israel, with self-righteousness having reached an all-time high. No doubt, in the hearts of many, a hunger for God and His true ways abounded, but with precious little leadership to point the way.

TURNING TO THE LORD

The phrase, *"Shall he turn to the Lord their God,"* means that John the Baptist would point the way, and in no uncertain terms. It would be a time of revival in Israel, perhaps the greatest the nation had ever known, at least in this manner. However, this great turning to the Lord would little affect the religious hierarchy of the

NOTES

land. Its corruption would continue, even to the crucifying of the Lord, until they were ultimately destroyed in A.D. 70. Tragically, most organized religion has always been outside of and opposed to the moving and operation of the Holy Spirit.

(17) "AND HE SHALL GO BEFORE HIM IN THE SPIRIT AND POWER OF ELIJAH, TO TURN THE HEARTS OF THE FATHERS TO THE CHILDREN, AND THE DISOBEDIENT TO THE WISDOM OF THE JUST; TO MAKE READY A PEOPLE PREPARED FOR THE LORD."

The exegesis is:

1. John the Baptist would have the spirit and power of Elijah.

2. *"To turn the hearts of the fathers to the children,"* spoke of the patriarchs and prophets of old.

3. *"The disobedient to the wisdom of the just,"* refers to the fact that Israel was to be shown the right way.

4. *"To make ready a people prepared for the Lord,"* pertained to getting prepared for the advent of the Messiah.

THE SPIRIT AND POWER OF ELIJAH

The phrase, *"And he shall go before Him in the spirit and power of Elijah,"* had reference to Malachi 4:5-6. While John the Baptist would not be that prophet, still, he would have the same spirit and power! In effect, the statement is far more important than meets the eye.

It definitely lay within the possibility that John could be Elijah to the people, thereby, ushering in the kingdom age, if Israel had only accepted Jesus. However, with the rejection of Christ by the religious hierarchy, that wonderful and glorious opportunity was lost, thereby, destroying Israel and submitting the world to a continued rule of the Gentiles, which has not yet ended, even after nearly 2,000 years.

As well, it has been the cause of untold bloodshed, hatred, war, and want. Consequently, the fulfillment of Malachi 4:5-6 awaits the coming great tribulation called *"the time of Jacob's trouble."* Then, Elijah, who never died but was translated, will once again appear in Israel with one other witness, who will be Enoch, and will proclaim righteousness and, consequently, Jesus to that nation (Rev. 11:1-12).

THE HEARTS OF THE FATHERS TO THE CHILDREN

The phrase, *"To turn the hearts of the fathers to the children,"* spoke of the godly fathers of the past who had hearts of obedience and wisdom, i.e., Abraham, Isaac, Jacob, Joseph, Moses, Joshua, etc. In other words, the cry for righteousness in the hearts of these, who are long since past, would be presented in the present generation in Israel. The message of righteousness had not changed, and would not change.

THE WISDOM OF THE JUST

The phrase, *"And the disobedient to the wisdom of the just,"* concerned Israel, which had strayed from the Word of God, but now would be brought back to that perfect way, or at least proclaimed. There would be no excuse for Israel and the *"disobedient"* among these people because John would readily point the way. The *"just"* was God and His Word.

PREPARATION

The phrase, *"To make ready a people prepared for the Lord,"* meant preparation for the coming Messiah, who would be the Lord Jesus Christ.

When John began to preach, he quickly gained widespread fame as a preacher calling for national repentance. Actually, the message of repentance had to be preached before Christ could be introduced. It will have to be preached again before the second coming and will be done so by Elijah and Enoch. Crowds flocked to hear him, and many of his hearers were baptized by him in the Jordan, confessing their sins.

His attitude to the established order in Israel was one of radical condemnation. *"The axe,"* he said, *"is laid unto the root of the trees"* (Mat. 3:10; Lk. 3:9). He denounced the religious leaders of the people as a brood of vipers, and denied that there was any value in the bare fact of descent from Abraham.

A new beginning was necessary. The time had come to call out from the nation as a whole a loyal remnant who would be ready for the imminent arrival of the coming One and the judgment which He would execute. John thought and spoke of himself as a mere preparer of the way of this coming One, for whom he was unworthy, he said, to perform the lowliest service.

Whereas, John's own ministry was characterized by baptism with water, the coming One's ministry would be a baptism with the Holy Spirit and fire.

(18) "AND ZACHARIAS SAID UNTO THE ANGEL, WHEREBY SHALL I KNOW THIS? FOR I AM AN OLD MAN, AND MY WIFE WELL STRICKEN IN YEARS."

The synopsis is:

1. Zacharias asked the angel Gabriel what sign he would have as it regarded the birth of this coming child.

2. Actually, his question was that of unbelief.

3. He looked at the situation, his age, and the age of his wife Elisabeth, which caused doubt to arise in his heart.

UNBELIEF

The question, *"And Zacharias said unto the angel, Whereby shall I know this?"* presents, as stated, unbelief!

It seems strange that Zacharias, who was in the Holy Place alone respecting the offering of incense, would have needed more proof, considering that the angel Gabriel had suddenly appeared before him. This alone was of such magnitude that it defied description.

However, Zacharias did what most of us do—he doubted! It is very difficult for fallen man to believe God, even one as righteous as Zacharias. Perhaps the cry of the father with the demon-possessed son is relative to all of us, *"Lord, I believe; help Thou mine unbelief"* (Mk. 9:24).

Even once we believe, it seems that we have to be continually reinforced, or else, we will quickly lapse back into unbelief.

CIRCUMSTANCES

The phrase, *"For I am an old man, and my wife well stricken in years,"* proclaims Zacharias doing what all of us are so prone to do—looking away from the promises of God to our own deficiencies. If it is to be remembered, Moses functioned accordingly (Ex. 3:11; 4:1, 10).

It is so easy to look at circumstances and, thereby, to take one's eyes off God. With man, the impossibilities loom large; however, with God, all things are possible (Mat. 19:26; Mk. 9:23)!

(19) "AND THE ANGEL ANSWERING SAID UNTO HIM, I AM GABRIEL, WHO STANDS IN THE PRESENCE OF GOD; AND AM SENT TO SPEAK UNTO YOU, AND TO SHOW YOU THESE GLAD TIDINGS."

The order is:

1. Gabriel identified himself to Zacharias.

2. The phrase, *"Who stands in the presence of God,"* just might be the highest rank of all among angels.

3. The message was so important that was to be given to Zacharias that the angel Gabriel was dispatched to perform this service.

I AM GABRIEL

The phrase, *"And the angel answering said unto him, I am Gabriel,"* is the same one who had come to Daniel (Dan. 8:16; 9:21) and later was sent to Mary (Lk. 1:26).

Only four angels are named in Scripture: two righteous angels, Michael, the archangel, and Gabriel; and two fallen angels, Lucifer and Abaddon. This proves there are ranks among angels (I Thess. 4:16; Jude 9).

The phrase, *"Who stands in the presence of God,"* as previously stated, may well represent the mightiest and most powerful angel of all. Michael alone is called an *"archangel"* (Jude, Vs. 9); however, to *"stand in the presence of God,"* refers to a rank and position unequaled by anything else. As well, it seems the great tasks, as pertaining to Daniel, Zacharias, and the Virgin Mary, were appointed to Gabriel.

GLAD TIDINGS

The phrase, *"And am sent to speak unto you,"* refers to him being sent from the presence of God.

"And to show you these glad tidings," proclaims Gabriel as the special messenger of good news. When he came to Daniel, he told him of the restoration of Jerusalem; to Zacharias, as is here obvious, the announcement of the birth of the greatest

prophet who would ever live; and to Mary of Nazareth, the announcement of the birth of the Messiah.

On the other hand, Michael, the archangel, appears as the warrior of God.

The Jews had an ancient saying which said that Gabriel flew with two wings (symbolically), but Michael with only one. So, God is swift in sending angels of peace and of joy, of which blessed company Gabriel is the representative. However, the messengers of God's wrath and punishment, among whom Michael holds a chief place, come slowly. Such is the love of God.

In the very ancient book of Enoch, we read the names of four great angels: Michael, Gabriel, Uriel, and Raphael. The last two are not named in the Bible but are, no doubt, genuine. Actually, all the angels who are numberless have names.

(20) "AND, BEHOLD, YOU SHALL BE DUMB, AND NOT ABLE TO SPEAK, UNTIL THE DAY THAT THESE THINGS SHALL BE PERFORMED, BECAUSE YOU BELIEVED NOT MY WORDS, WHICH SHALL BE FULFILLED IN THEIR SEASON."

The overview is:

1. Because of unbelief, Zacharias would be stricken dumb and deaf until John the Baptist would be born.

2. It was because of the unbelief on the part of Zacharias.

3. Irrespective, Gabriel said that all he had spoken would be fulfilled at the appointed time.

JUDGMENT

The phrase, *"And, behold, you shall be dumb, and not able to speak,"* proclaims unbelief as exceedingly sinful. Zacharias asked for a sign and was given a painful one.

The Scripture seems to indicate that he was made deaf and dumb (Lk. 1:62).

"Until the day that these things shall be performed," proclaims the certitude of this coming action.

UNBELIEF

The phrase, *"Because you believed not my words,"* proclaims not only the present disposition of Zacharias, but almost the entirety of the world, including the church.

Unbelief springs from *"a want of faith and trust."* It is a state of mind and an expression of it. Unbelief toward Himself was the same sin of which Christ said that the Spirit would convict the world (Jn. 16:9). Unbelief in all its forms is a direct affront to the divine presence (I Jn. 5:10), which is why it is a heinous sin.

The children of Israel did not enter into God's rest for two reasons.

1. They lacked faith (Heb. 3:19).
2. They disobeyed (Heb. 4:6).

Unbelief finds its practical issue in disobedience.

THE CROSS OF CHRIST

In 1997, the Lord began to open up to me the great Message of the Cross, especially as it regards sanctification, in other words, how we are to live for God. At that time, my feelings were that if this message could just be given to the church world, how happy they would be.

However, I found to my dismay that this Message of the Cross did not meet with much approval from the church world. In fact, religious leaders plainly told me they did not believe it. So, I learned the hard way that unbelief is the characterizing sin of the human race, and even the church.

Why is it so hard to simply believe?

The truth, especially the Message of the Cross, exposes the hearts of men. It lays waste the wrong direction in which so many have given so much. Men do not like to be told that they are wrong in what they believe. As stated, they have placed their past, present, and future on the direction they have taken, and now, to be told that it is wrong does not set well.

Then again, circumstances play a tremendous role in all of this. Zacharias looked at the age of his wife Elisabeth and of himself and knew that they were long since past the time of conception and childbearing, so how could this be done? Of course, everything that God does pertains to the impossible. He is the God of the impossible.

Irrespective of religious leaders not believing the Message of the Cross, still, the Lord will herald this message throughout the entirety of the world. Thank God that despite religious leaders, many will accept and have their lives gloriously and wondrously changed.

IN DUE SEASON

The phrase, *"Which shall be fulfilled in their season,"* proclaims God's timetable.

As stated, many years before, the Lord heard the prayers of both Zacharias and Elisabeth concerning the birth of a son. Due to at least two things, He would not answer that prayer when it was first prayed. Those two reasons are as follows:

1. Due to their faith in God, the Lord would use them to bring into the world the greatest prophet ever known. Realizing that Zacharias was now registering unbelief, still, as far as his overall faith in God was concerned, it had never wavered. So, the delay was not because of lack of faith, but rather because of great faith. Even though because of their advanced age, they lost hope respecting the birth of a son, they did not lose faith in God.

The reader must understand that no one's faith is perfect, even as Zacharias' present unbelief portrays. Nevertheless, the intention of the Holy Spirit is to bring the believer's faith up to the level of the Word of God, and this He works at incessantly!

2. God's timing is an important part of His action. He has a *"season"* for everything, and the believer must be patient respecting that season. However, the waiting is never unproductive, at least if we will allow the Holy Spirit latitude within our lives. Isaiah said, *"But they who wait upon the LORD shall renew their strength; they shall mount up with wings as eagles; they shall run, and not be weary; and they shall walk, and not faint"* (Isa. 40:31).

(21) "AND THE PEOPLE WAITED FOR ZACHARIAS, AND MARVELLED THAT HE TARRIED SO LONG IN THE TEMPLE."

The construction is:

1. The people were waiting outside of the temple for Zacharias to come out and pronounce a blessing upon them.

2. They knew what time he should come out but marvelled that he took so long.

3. When he came out of the temple, he could not speak, even as Gabriel had pronounced.

The people perceived that something had happened, but due to not being able to speak, he was helpless to tell them.

THE BLESSING

The phrase, *"And the people waited for Zacharias,"* pertained to the usual custom of the priest finishing his duties and then coming out and pronouncing a blessing upon the people. Due to the fact that priests only were allowed into this sacred place, the people, believing he had been in the presence of God, always eagerly awaited this blessing. The group on this day, ever how large it was, was to be blessed more than they could ever begin to imagine, even though they did not know it at the time. They would know it when John would be born, which would be some nine months later.

The phrase, *"And marvelled that he tarried so long in the temple,"* means, as is obvious, that he stayed far longer than was the normal custom. They could not understand the reason for the long delay; however, the word *marvelled* does not show impatience, but rather anticipation. They were not to be disappointed but had to wait for some nine months until Zacharias would be able then to speak. Then, they would know that they had been privileged, at least those who were there, regarding this great thing that God would do.

(22) "AND WHEN HE CAME OUT, HE COULD NOT SPEAK UNTO THEM: AND THEY PERCEIVED THAT HE HAD SEEN A VISION IN THE TEMPLE: FOR HE BECKONED UNTO THEM, AND REMAINED SPEECHLESS."

The order is:

1. Due to his unbelief, Zacharias was now speechless and would remain so for some nine months.

2. The people knew that something had happened, but they didn't know exactly what.

3. Quite possibly, in sign language or some way, he related to them that something great had happened.

THE DUMBNESS OF ZACHARIAS AT THE HAND OF THE ANGEL GABRIEL

The phrase, *"And when he came out, he could not speak unto them,"* proclaims his dumbness at the hand of the mighty angel Gabriel.

The priest generally walked out and said to the waiting people, *"The LORD bless you, and keep you: The LORD make His face shine upon you, And be gracious unto you: The LORD lift up His countenance upon you, "And give you peace"* (Num. 6:24-26).

A VISION?

The phrase, *"And they perceived that he had seen a vision in the temple,"* probably referred to the possible glow on his countenance.

Zacharias had been face-to-face with one whose blessed lot was to stand forever in the presence of God. More than likely, that which he experienced lingered on his person and was obvious to the people.

The phrase, *"For he beckoned unto them, and remained speechless,"* probably refers to him conveying to them, possibly in writing, that he had, in fact, seen a vision. It is doubtful that he related many, if any, of the details at this time. However, when they finally did know, the blessing they would receive at being present at this event would exceed all expectations. As we have previously stated, there is definitely a possibility that Simeon and Anna were present that day, and nearly two years later, would see with their eyes the One to whom all of this was pointing (Lk. 2:25-38).

(23) "AND IT CAME TO PASS, THAT, AS SOON AS THE DAYS OF HIS MINISTRATION WERE ACCOMPLISHED, HE DEPARTED TO HIS OWN HOUSE."

The overview is:

1. Zacharias finished his duties at the temple.

2. He departed to his own house, but with a word from the Lord that would greatly bless Elisabeth.

3. It took many years for this prayer to be answered, but ultimately, it was answered.

THE DAYS OF HIS MINISTRATION

The phrase, *"And it came to pass,"* referred to the conclusion of the week of his duties.

"That, as soon as the days of his

ministration were accomplished," proclaims his faithfulness to his task.

I wonder what his fellow priests thought regarding his inability to speak. More so yet, did he relate by writing that he had seen and spoken with the angel Gabriel, or did he keep it to himself?

I think it is obvious that the news spread that he had had a vision, but I doubt that he related very much as to the particulars of the vision. He would want to wait and tell his wife first of all!

"He departed to his own house," would have indicated a time of unparalleled joy. What a message he would have for Elisabeth! That which they had sought for so very long, even giving up hope, was now about to happen, despite their advanced age. What a joyful moment between these two that must have been when he related by writing (Lk. 1:63) that which the angel had spoken unto him.

(24) "AND AFTER THOSE DAYS HIS WIFE ELISABETH CONCEIVED, AND HID HERSELF FIVE MONTHS, SAYING."

The format is:

1. Because of the touch from God, Elisabeth conceived despite her advanced age.

2. The five months in which she hid herself was, no doubt, to seek the face of the Lord as to what all of this really meant.

CONCEPTION

The phrase, *"And after those days his wife Elisabeth conceived,"* proclaims as coming to pass exactly what the angel Gabriel had foretold.

There is no way of knowing how old she was, just *"well stricken in years."* However, the Lord would renew her youth in order that this miracle child would be brought into the world. As the Lord brought forth the miracle child Isaac through Abraham and Sarah, who would begin the family through which the Messiah would come, likewise, the Lord brought forth another miracle child to announce that He has come (Jn. 1:29).

"And hid herself five months, saying," proclaims her fully realizing the magnitude of this moment.

Every indication is that she hid herself in

order to seek the face of the Lord regarding how this child was to be raised and how he was to be trained.

(25) "THUS HAS THE LORD DEALT WITH ME IN THE DAYS WHEREIN HE LOOKED ON ME, TO TAKE AWAY MY REPROACH AMONG MEN."

The diagram is:

1. The Lord heard the prayers of Zacharias and Elisabeth all the years for which they had sought God as it regarded a child.

2. It was a reproach in those days for a wife to not be able to conceive.

3. The Lord had a reason for the delay, which means that He wasn't interested in what people may have thought.

THE REPROACH

The phrase, *"Thus has the Lord dealt with me in the days wherein He looked on me,"* proclaims that during this five months, the Lord spelled out to her who her son would be and what he would do. Her task was very special, and every indication is that she carried it out exactly as the Lord demanded of her.

"To take away my reproach among men," proclaims her gratitude to the Lord, not only for doing this thing, but for making her the most blessed mother in the world, and for all time, other than Mary, the mother of our Lord.

Every indication is that in noting her barrenness, her neighbors had long since concluded that it was a judgment from God. How so wrong they were! As previously stated, this situation had been brought about not because of sin or wrongdoing in the lives of her and her husband, but rather because of right doing. The Holy Spirit said, *"And they were both righteous before God"* (Lk. 1:6).

(26) "AND IN THE SIXTH MONTH THE ANGEL GABRIEL WAS SENT FROM GOD UNTO A CITY OF GALILEE, NAMED NAZARETH."

The overview is:

1. The *"sixth month"* referred to six months since Elisabeth's conception.

2. Now, the angel Gabriel was sent from the throne of God to the home of Mary in the little town of Nazareth.

THE ANGEL GABRIEL

The phrase, *"And in the sixth month,"* refers to six months after Elisabeth had conceived; consequently, John was six months older than Jesus.

Matthew alludes to the birth of Jesus, but only Luke gives us the announcement of that birth as well as details concerning the actual event. More than likely, these details were provided to either Luke or Paul, or both, by Mary personally.

Other than the account given by Luke, fantastic stories have arisen concerning Mary, and mostly fostered and nurtured by the Catholic Church. However, these are utterly unknown to Scripture and should be ignored. It is wrong to be wise beyond what is written in the Word of God.

SENT FROM GOD

The phrase, *"The angel Gabriel was sent from God,"* concerns the announcement of the greatest event in human history, the coming birth of the Redeemer of man, the Lord Jesus Christ. This is the story of the incarnation as prophesied by Isaiah (Isa. 7:14; 9:6-7).

"Unto a city of Galilee, named Nazareth," pertains to where Jesus would be brought up.

Under Roman domination, Israel was divided into Judaea, Samaria, Peraea, and Galilee. Galilee comprised the territory of the tribes of Zebulun, Naphtali, and Asher. Josephus, the Jewish historian, tells us that this area was rich and populous and covered with flourishing towns. Nazareth is some 24 miles west of the Sea of Galilee.

It is said that at this time, or at least a little later, a Roman garrison was located near Nazareth, which, among other things, caused strict Jews to hold the place in scorn (Jn. 1:46).

So, it was at this place, ridiculed and despised, which God would choose for the upbringing of His Son. However, the glory of Jesus Christ easily erased that stigma and has given this little town fame unlike any other place in the world.

(27) "TO A VIRGIN ESPOUSED TO A MAN WHOSE NAME WAS JOSEPH, OF THE HOUSE OF DAVID; AND THE VIRGIN'S NAME WAS MARY."

The form is:

1. Mary was a virgin when Jesus was conceived in her womb, and done so by decree given by the Holy Spirit (Lk. 1:35).

2. She did not remain a virgin after the conception and birth of Jesus, for the Scripture tells us that Jesus had several brothers and sisters (Mat. 13:55-56).

3. The word *espoused* meant that Joseph was engaged to Mary to be married.

4. They were of the *"house of David,"* meaning they were in the lineage of David, of the tribe of Judah. In fact, Joseph went back to David through Solomon, while Mary went back to David through another son, Nathan.

THE VIRGIN

The words, *"To a virgin,"* in the Greek text is *parthenos,* which refers to a pure virgin who has never known a man and never experienced marriage relationship (Mat. 1:23; 25:1, 7, 11; Lk. 1:27; 2:36; Acts 21:9; I Cor. 7:25, 28, 34, 36, 37; II Cor. 11:2; Rev. 14:4). In Mary's case, it is plainly stated that she had never known a man (Lk. 1:34); and so, no one has a right to question the virgin birth.

In the Hebrew, the words are *"ha-alma,"* which means, *"The virgin—the only one who ever was, or ever will be a mother in this way."*

Some have contended that these original words, and especially the Hebrew text, simply mean any young woman, but this is blatantly untrue! It means only one who is a pure and undefiled virgin—any maid who has never known man.

In fact, some 750 years previously, Isaiah had prophesied, *"Behold, a virgin shall conceive, and bear a Son, and shall call His name Immanuel"* (Isa. 7:14).

THE HOUSE OF DAVID

The phrase, *"Espoused* (engaged) *to a man whose name was Joseph, of the house of David,"* proclaims, as stated, Joseph being in the direct lineage of David through Solomon. Actually, Mary was of the house of David, as well, but through another of David's sons, Nathan. If the Davidic throne had continued, Joseph would now be the king of Judah.

As recorded by Matthew, Joseph, at first, had difficulty accepting Mary's story concerning her conception but was given a dream by the Lord, which clarified the situation (Mat. 1:18-25). Luke does not mention this situation.

MARY

The phrase, *"And the virgin's name was Mary,"* is proclaimed in Luke, Chapter 3, and, as stated, to also be of the house of David.

Mary was a cousin of Elisabeth, the mother of John the Baptist (Lk. 1:36). It is said that her mother's name was Anne. It is also said that she surpassed the maidens of her own age and wisdom, and that there were many young men who sought her hand in marriage.

Scholars say that the absence of any mention of her parents in the Gospels suggests the thought that she was an orphan, and the whole narrative of the nativity presupposes poverty.

The name, *"Mary,"* is the same as *"Miriam"* or *"Marah."*

Unfortunately, Mary's name has been sullied because of the unscriptural devotion and even worship given to her by Catholicism. This exacerbated greatly due to the influence of the late John Paul II, who claimed that Mary appeared to him years ago, telling him he would be pope. I have no doubt that he did have some type of vision, but it was not of God, but rather of Satan. In other words, there was a familiar spirit, which claimed to be Mary, who spoke with this man who later became pope. There is no such thing as communication with the dead. Such is totally unscriptural.

Due to this error and many others regarding Mary in Catholicism, I think the following information about Mary would be helpful:

Incidentally, Pope John Paul II tried to have Mary positioned as a co-redemptress with Christ, making the Trinity then into a quadrinity. Wiser heads prevailed, and it was not done, but not for the lack of trying.

MARY, THE MOTHER OF GOD?

The Catholic people pray to Mary as mediatrix:

"Hail, Mary, full of grace, the Lord is with you. Blest are you among women and blest is the fruit of your womb, Jesus. Holy

NOTES

Mary, mother of God, pray for us sinners, now and at the hour of our death. Amen."

A former Catholic priest wrote:

"I can personally testify to the fact that the Jesus Christ I knew, loved, and served as a Roman Catholic is not the same Jesus Christ I know, love, and serve today. The Jesus I once knew was a wafer of bread and a cup of wine—and He had a mother called Mary who stood between Him and me. I couldn't get through to Him except through her, and He couldn't get through to me except through her."

"In other words, my religion back then was tantamount to—let's say—Buddhism or the Muslim religion. There was no difference objectively speaking, between me as a Catholic priest, and a Muslim priest, for example."

These words are sad, yet they describe the situation perfectly. How many times do we see bumper stickers that say: *"Can't find Jesus? Look for His mother!"*

Mary dominates every aspect of Catholic religious life. Unfortunately, this is opposite of biblical Christianity.

In these statements, we want to look at Mary as the Catholic sees her, Mary as the mediator between Jesus Christ and man and, as well, Mary as the Bible describes her.

MARY—AS THE CATHOLIC SEES HER

"My Queen and my Mother, I give myself entirely to you; and to show my devotion to you, I consecrate to you this day my eyes, my ears, my mouth, my heart, my whole being without reserve. Wherefore, good Mother, as I am your own, keep me, guard me, as your property and possession. Amen." (Prayer of consecration to Mary).

Catholics feel that Mary occupies a unique and tremendously influential position as a result of her role as Christ's human mother. They are taught that they can safely entrust all their problems to her. She provides the spiritual key to salvation of the soul and to receiving miraculous answers to prayers concerning more earthly problems.

Catholics are taught (although they will deny this) that Mary is to be given worship equal to God—and higher than that afforded the angels and saints. She is to be addressed as *"my mother."* Even casual observation of Catholics reveals that both conversations and services bring forth more references to the *"Blessed Virgin"* than to the Three Persons of the Holy Trinity. Obviously, the Catholic religion is strongly oriented toward veneration of Mary. She is called the following:

"The Mother of Divine Grace," "Help of Christians," "Ark of the Covenant," "Queen of Angels," "Morning Star," and *"Health of Heaven."*

The Catholic *"cult of Mary"* is based fundamentally on her sacred motherhood. The fourth century title bestowed on her by the church that would eventually become Catholic—*"Theotokos"* (Greek for *"Bearer of God"*)—was equivalent to *"Mother of God."*

The church evidently reasoned this way:

"Mary is the mother of Jesus. Jesus is God. Ergo, Mary is the mother of God."

Furthermore, Catholics state and believe that to deny honor to Mary is actually to deny the deity of Christ. Of course, if a person accepts this, he opens a floodgate of ensuing theological absurdities that must be accepted as logical developments of the original fallacy.

IS MARY THE MOTHER OF GOD?

No!

Mary is not the mother of God. Mary was the mother of the human being, Jesus. Mary served a biological function that was necessary to bring about a unique situation. The preexistent Son of God was to take on human form. As He walked the earth (in human form), He was very God and very man. His *"God"* component, if we are to use that term, had always been. While Mary was essential to harbor His developing human form for nine months, she had nothing whatsoever to do with His Godhood! To suggest such is ridiculous! Mary was, therefore, the mother of Jesus, the man. She was not by any stretch of the imagination the mother of God.

God has no mother! If one understands the incarnation, one understands that God, while never ceasing to be God, became completely man.

"Wherefore when He comes into the

world, He said, sacrifice and offering You would not, but a body have You prepared Me" (Heb. 10:5).

It was this body that God prepared for His Son—Jesus Christ—who would become man. Of necessity, He would be born into the world as are all other human beings, but with one tremendous difference:

"Therefore the Lord Himself shall give you a sign; Behold, a virgin shall conceive, and bear a Son, and shall call His name Immanuel" (Isa. 7:14).

This virgin was the little teenage maiden called Mary. She was to bring the Son of God into the world, but it was not God who would be born. It was *"The Man Christ Jesus"* (I Tim. 2:5).

THE ANNUNCIATION OF JESUS

The Bible tells us that the angel Gabriel was sent from God to a virgin named Mary.

"And the angel came in unto her, and said, Hail, you who are highly favoured, the Lord is with you: blessed are you among women" (Lk. 1:28).

Using this passage, the Catholic Church has altered the words to read, *"Hail, Mary, full of grace."* The church then interprets its own words by advancing the argument that since Mary was full of grace, she must have been the finest and holiest of all created beings. Further, Catholic doctrine concludes that through the grace bestowed on her, she received from God the degree of purity and holiness necessary to be worthy of serving in the role of mother of God.

Now, let us pause to examine for a moment the *"Hail, Mary,"* prayer, which is quoted in its entirety at the beginning of this article. Because this prayer is based (albeit loosely) on Scripture (Lk. 1:28), it seems to Catholics to place God's stamp of approval on the Catholic position in regard to Mary.

The *"Hail, Mary"* begins:

"Hail, Mary, full of grace, the Lord is with you. Blessed are you among women and blessed is the fruit of your womb, Jesus."

THE STUDY OF LANGUAGE

Language changes constantly. Word meanings change constantly. For example, a few

NOTES

years ago, a person who was *"gay"* was *"happy."* Today, a *"gay"* person is a *"homosexual,"* with the old definition having fallen completely out of usage.

By the same token, the word *blessed* has through usage taken on two meanings. *Blessed*—pronounced as one syllable—describes someone who has received a blessing. When someone is blessed, he has come suddenly into money, he has been cured of an illness, etc. On the other hand, when pronounced as two syllables (bless-ed), the word implies a person of superior spirituality or someone who is more saintly in moral character; for example, *"That bless-ed man returned my lost wallet and wouldn't even accept a reward."*

At the time the Bible was written (and when it was translated by the King James translators), the word *blessed* had only one meaning—referring to one who had received a blessing.

GRACE

Similarly, the word *grace* has come to have a meaning, as well, that is not the biblical definition. *Grace*—within Scripture—means a gift from God that is undeserved. Grace is a free gift from God with no preconditions or strings attached. However, today, *grace* has come to be used to imply an inherent human quality of goodness that is closely allied to bless-ed-ness.

So, the wording of the *"Hail, Mary"* prayer, taken in the context of today's language usage, appears to give scriptural support to Catholic contentions that Mary was eternally without sin. Turning to the actual words of Scripture, however, we receive a different picture. The angel Gabriel's actual words were:

HIGHLY FAVOURED

"Hail, you who are highly favoured, the Lord is with you: blessed are you among women" (Lk. 1:28).

Mary was unquestionably highly favored by God in that He chose her to receive this honor. As well, it was certainly a blessing to be singled out to hold such a distinctive position in the history of the world. However, all the rest of the words within this prayer simply were composed by the Catholic Church and have no basis in Scripture whatsoever.

MOTHER OF MY LORD

Delving further into this matter, we read where Mary's cousin, Elisabeth, said:

"And what is this to me, that the mother of my Lord should come to me?" (Lk. 1:43).

Here, Elisabeth called Jesus *"Lord."* She was talking about the unborn Holy Child then occupying Mary's womb. He definitely is Lord. He is called, *"The Lord Jesus Christ,"* many times within the Word of God.

However, once again, it must be emphasized that it was not God who was born of Mary, but it was the human child—the Lord Jesus Christ.

The unbiblical worship of Mary has its perverted foundation in the insupportable misnomer, *"Mother of God."* The correct scriptural description of Mary is the simple biblical expression, *"Mary the mother of Jesus"* (Acts 1:14).

THE IMMACULATE CONCEPTION

This erroneous (and confusing) term does not refer to the conception of Jesus Christ (as most non-Catholics and many Catholics believe). It refers to the conception of Mary in her mother's womb.

The Catholic Catechism says:

"The Blessed Virgin Mary alone, from the first instant of her conception, through the foreseen merits of Jesus Christ, by a unique privilege granted her by God, was kept free from the stain of original sin ... From the first moment of her conception she possessed justice and holiness, even the fullness of grace, with the infused virtues and the gifts of the Holy Spirit."

This doctrine, a total fiction with no scriptural support, was *"infallibly"* defined by Pope Pius IX as part of the *"Revealed Deposit of Catholic Faith"* in 1854. There was great opposition to this pronouncement at the time within the Catholic Church.

REPLACING THE PLAN OF SALVATION

The doctrine of the immaculate conception implies that for Mary to be born without original sin, her mother also had to be a sinless virgin. The only other alternative is that God granted her unique immunity to the all-pervasive original sin that is an inestimable element of the human condition.

To be frank, Roman Catholic theologians lamely defend their assertion of the immaculate conception by saying that, *"God could have done it,"* or *"It was fitting that He should do so—and therefore He did it."*

Of course, if God had decided on such a course, it would have meant that He was replacing the plan of salvation described in the Bible with a totally new concept. If this had happened, we would have a *"quadrinity"* instead of the *"Trinity."* God's Word then would have stated that the Godhead consists of God the Father, God the Son, God the Holy Spirit, and Mary the Mother of God. The Bible does not so state, so we can then conclude that this aberrant and ridiculous doctrine is not of God.

THE ORIGIN OF THE STATEMENT, "MARY, THE MOTHER OF GOD"

The veneration of Mary and the use of the term, *"Mother of God,"* originated about A.D. 381. It was officially decreed by the Council of Ephesus in A.D. 431. Actually, that which we now know as the Catholic Church came into being slowly. When the apostles died and those who followed them, little by little, the church began to lose it's way until it finally morphed into the Catholic Church, which, in fact, has continued to change over the years. It was in the early 600s that the first man, the Bishop of Rome, was actually named as the pope. His name was Damasus. The argument had been raging for a couple of centuries or more over who should occupy the top position and be referred to as pope, the Bishop of Rome or the Bishop of Alexandria. Rome finally won out.

The Catholic Church would try to make people believe that Peter was the first pope, meaning that the Catholic Church has always been. You can read the book of Acts and the Epistles in your Bible, and it is obvious that the early church was 180 degrees different from what is now known as the Catholic Church. The following is the gradual deterioration of the church, which finally came to be called the Catholic Church.

• As stated, the veneration of Mary and

the use of the term, *"Mother of God,"* originated about A.D. 381.

• It was made official by the Council of Ephesus in A.D. 431.

• Prayers began to be directed to Mary, as well as to other saints, about A.D. 600.

• The *"Immaculate Conception of Mary,"* was proclaimed by Pius IX in A.D. 1854.

• In 1931, Pope Pius XI reaffirmed the doctrine that Mary is the *"Mother of God,"* as if an infallible statement needs to be confirmed.

• In 1950, Pope Pius XII pronounced the doctrine of the *"Assumption of Mary."* This states that at the completion of her earthly life, Mary was bodily taken up into heaven without knowing death.

• Oddly enough, this mystical belief had been a peripheral precept within the Catholic Church since the Middle Ages but was only given official certification in 1950.

• There was a great deal of resistance to the issuance of this doctrine by Pius XII, but he insisted that it was his infallible right to declare such a *"fact."*

THE BABYLONIAN CULT

Fundamentally, the worship of Mary originated with the worship of *"the Queen of Heaven"*—a pagan deity. It seems that the Roman church—in altering its doctrines to conform to those formerly observed by conscripted pagans—saw that it would be politically desirable to supply the populous with a satisfying parallel figure within their newly-imposed Christian religion. Thus was Mary elevated to divine status.

The image of mother and child had been a primary object of Babylonian worship centuries before the birth of Christ. From Babylon, this spread to the ends of the earth. The original mother figure in this tableau was Semiramis—the personification of unbridled lust and sexual gratification. Once we begin to study the worship practices of heathen nations, we find amazing similarities embraced over wide areas and through long periods of time.

For instance:

• In Egypt, the mother and child are known as Isis and Horus.

• In India, Isis, and Iswara.

NOTES

- In Asia, Cybele and Edoius.
- In pagan Rome, Fortuna and Jupiter-puer.
- In Greece, Ceres with Plutus in arms.
- In isolated Tibet and in China and Japan, early Roman Catholic missionaries were stunned to find counterparts of the Madonna (the Italian name for the Virgin Mary) and her child being worshipped as devotedly as Rome itself.
- Shing Moo (the *"Mother of China"*) is represented with child in arms and with a halo around her head—exactly as if she had been painted by a Roman Catholic painter.

These nations all trace their common worship from Babylon—before its dispersion in the days of Nimrod. Thus, worship of Mary is Babylonian in origin. There is absolutely no suggestion of such worship in Scripture.

MARY AS THE MEDIATOR BETWEEN JESUS AND MAN

Mary is looked upon by the Catholic Church as an intercessor, a mediator, and a redemptress. Some Catholics say this is not a *"defined article of faith."* Others say it is. In any case, in practice, it is part and parcel of what is known as the *"Ordinary Teaching Authority"* of the church.

These titles signify that Mary is a universal intercessor—that is, she seeks God's favors for all mankind. They clearly imply that Mary is so intimately associated with our redemption that she may be considered as co-saviour with Christ, although subordinate to Him. Church doctrine further alleges that Mary *"mediates grace universally."*

What does this mean in plain language? Incredibly, the Catholic position is that no grace flows from God to any person without passing through the good offices of Mary!

Some church leaders state that doctrines concerning Mary were modified and tempered by the Second Vatican Council of 1962–1965. However, this is what Catholic priest Anthony Wilhelm stated in his book, *"Christ Among Us: A Modern Presentation of the Catholic Faith:"*

- On page 90: *"God the Son became a man through Mary His human mother,* whom we call the Mother of God. We can say that God has relatives, that God has a mother."
- On page 91: *"The 'hail, Mary' is one of the most ancient prayers of the Church ... 'Hail, Mary, full of grace.'*

"By these privileges, which God gave to Mary, we can see that He always prepares people for their roles in His plan."
- On page 367: *"We particularly honor Mary, the mother of Christ, because of her great role in God's plan of salvation. She was closer to Christ than anyone else."*
- On page 368: *"Mary is God's masterpiece. To honor her is to honor God, who made her what she is.*

"Because of Mary's great role, she was conceived without sin, remained sinless throughout her life, and was perpetually a virgin.

"We believe in Mary's assumption that she was taken into heaven, body and soul, at the end of her earthly life."
- On page 369: *"We give special place to Mary's intercession and sometimes consider her to be our 'spiritual mother.'"*
- On page 370: *"Mary is the model Christian, the preeminent member of the Church."*
- On page 371: *"Mary is particularly the model of our worship.*

"The devotion of the rosary has been a tremendous influence in helping hundreds of millions to pray."

MARY HAS NO ROLE

The Roman cult of Mary erects a barrier between the individual and the Lord. It confuses the Catholic believer's perception of the work and functions of the individual members of the Godhead. It robs Christ of His unique creatorship.

Rome's theologians insist that Mary's role and function is to lead souls to Christ; however, Jesus said:

"That which is born of the Spirit is spirit ... So is everyone who is born of the Spirit" (Jn. 3:6-8).

He further stated:

"No man can come to Me, except the Father who has sent Me draw him" (Jn. 6:43-44). Nothing is said about Mary.

So, according to the Bible, Mary has no role to play in the salvation of a soul.

I go back once again to our quote from a former Catholic priest:

"The Jesus I once knew was a wafer of bread and a cup of wine, He had a mother called Mary who stood between Him and Me."

Does his statement sound like he was *"led to Christ by Mary?"*

DO CATHOLICS WORSHIP MARY?

In scores of letters we have received, Catholics maintain that they do not worship Mary, but she only aids them in their worship of God.

However, when the Catholics attribute the immaculate conception to Mary, they are conferring divinity upon her by this claim. The term *worship,* as defined by Webster's New Collegiate Dictionary, is "reverence paid to a divine being and extravagant respect or admiration for, or devotion to an object of esteem." In ascribing the immaculate conception to Mary, the Catholic Church has, in effect, declared her divine and, thus, renders her worship that should be reserved only for deity. By their constant reference to her, worship is afforded.

Yes, Catholics do worship Mary. To be tragically concise, most Catholics do not understand the worship of God the Father or His Son Jesus Christ. The real focus and conception of their worship is directed to Mary. Of course, their perception of worshipping God is the worship of God through Mary. Everything must go through Mary to God—and everything must come from God through Mary, at least according to Catholic dogma.

MARY, AS THE BIBLE DESCRIBES HER

To be brutally frank, at least considering the Catholic position, there is very little mention of Mary within the Word of God.

MATTHEW

In Matthew, Chapter 2, we read of Mary's witnessing the adoration of the wise men. This chapter also recounts the event leading to the trip to Egypt. Then it gives the account of an experience from the childhood of Jesus and describes Mary's concern.

MARK

Mary is mentioned only briefly in this gospel: once as simply the mother of the carpenter Jesus (Mk. 6:3), and again as a family member (Mk. 3:32).

LUKE

Luke, Chapter 1, describes the visit of the angel Gabriel to Mary. The same chapter tells of Mary's visit to Elisabeth. We can conclude from the statements made by Mary that she had a wide-ranging knowledge of the Old Testament—which is a commentary on her spiritual perceptions.

Luke, Chapter 2, describes Mary as giving birth to the Lord Jesus Christ in the stable. She also pondered here the words of the shepherds as well as the incident when Jesus was 12.

JOHN

In John, Chapter 2, Mary asked Jesus to perform His first public miracle at Cana. Obviously, because of the confidence with which she approached the situation, she knew at least something of His potential. Oddly enough, in Mark, Chapter 3, Matthew, Chapter 12, and Luke, Chapter 8, it seems she at least harbored some confusion about His mission. John, Chapter 19, talks about how Mary stood at the foot of the Cross and observed with great sorrow the death of her Son—her Saviour and our Saviour, the Lord Jesus Christ.

ACTS

According to Acts 1:14, Mary was numbered among the 120 who tarried in the upper room, waiting for the enduement of power on the day of Pentecost. She, like other believers, needed the infilling of the Holy Spirit as power for service.

This is all the Bible reveals about Mary. Incidentally, in the Gospels, Jesus never did call her *"mother."* He addressed her as *"woman."* However, going back to the ancient Hebrew, this was not an expression of disrespect.

WHAT THE BIBLE ACTUALLY SAYS

When the angel Gabriel appeared to her,

as described in Luke, Chapter 1, he used the word *hail*. This simply means "hello" or "all joy," a salutation used to get a person's attention. He also used the phrase, *"Highly favoured,"* which means "blessed" or "endued with grace." As discussed earlier, these terms do not imply anything other than the person has received an unmerited favor.

Mary was highly favored. No doubt, hundreds of thousands (or even millions) of pious, young Israelite maidens had aspired through the centuries to be the one so highly favored. They had known from ancient prophecies that the *"Seed,"* the *"Redeemer,"* would be born to a Hebrew maiden. From Isaiah's prophecy, they further knew that she had to be a virgin.

"Therefore the Lord Himself shall give you a sign; Behold, a virgin shall conceive, and bear a Son, and shall call His name Immanuel" (Isa. 7:14).

Most importantly, the lineage had to come from the tribe of Judah and through David. Matthew gave the genealogy in the royal line through Solomon. In Luke, the royal line was given from Nathan, another son, through Heli, the father of Mary. Both lines were necessary in fulfilling prophecy.

God had cursed Jeconiah of the royal line and had sworn that no seed of his should ever sit on the throne of David and reign in Jerusalem (Jer. 22:24-30).

God had also sworn to David that his line (through Solomon) would forever sit on his throne (II Sam., Chpt. 7). The only way this could be fulfilled was for Jesus, the Son of David (through Nathan and Mary), to become legal heir to the throne of David through his stepfather, Joseph, of the kingly line (Lk. 1:32-33).

Jesus, as the foster son of Joseph and the firstborn of His family, became the legal heir to David's throne through Joseph. However, it must be remembered, the royal line in Matthew was given through Solomon, which culminated in Joseph. The royal line in Luke was given through Nathan, culminating in the father of Mary, Heli.

So, Mary, in the royal lineage through Nathan, David's son, became the mother of the Lord Jesus Christ.

Yes, Mary was highly favored!

As well, it certainly could be said that the Lord was with her and she would be blessed among many.

HANDMAIDEN OF THE LORD

Mary called herself *"the handmaid of the Lord"* (Lk. 1:38).

This shows the beautiful humility characterized by Mary and is a statement that might well be studied by Catholic theologians.

However, there is a tremendous difference between *"the handmaid of the Lord"* and *"Mother of God."*

By her own words, Mary refuted the Catholic doctrine of the immaculate conception:

"And my spirit has rejoiced in God my Saviour" (Lk. 1:47).

This statement totally discounts the theory of an immaculate conception and the Catholic contention that Mary was ever without sin. If God was her Saviour, which she readily admitted, then she must have needed salvation, which presupposes some history of normal human sin. No Scripture even hints that Mary was sinless. This false cult of Mary worship is another effort by Satan, who knows that one cannot completely accept Christ as long as one retains heretical concepts of Mary. Incidentally, Luke's statement in 1:28 quotes Gabriel's words as being, *"Blessed are you among women."* It does not say, *"Blessed are you above women."*

ACCORDING TO THE BIBLE, IS MARY AN INTERCESSOR AND A MEDIATRIX?

"Wherefore He is able also to save them to the uttermost who come unto God by Him, seeing He ever lives to make intercession for them" (Heb. 7:25).

Jesus Christ is our intercessor, at least in this manner. There is no hint or suggestion in the Word of God that Mary should or would occupy such a role. Whenever Mary is inserted into the role of intercessor (as she is by the Catholic Church) to intercede with her Son, Jesus Christ, on behalf of individuals on earth, this, in effect, robs Christ of the rightful position He earned through His tremendous sacrifice at Calvary. He paid the full price on the Cross with the shedding of His precious blood.

Christ alone is worthy to make intercession for us. Christ alone paid the price. Mary did not suffer and die on the Cross. She did not shed her blood. Neither does Christ need an assistant to motivate Him to intercede for the saints. He is perfectly capable of performing this duty Himself as He ever sits at the right hand of God making intercession for us.

IT IS CHRIST

"It is Christ who died, yea rather, that is risen again, who is even at the right hand of God, who also makes intercession for us" (Rom. 8:34).

We blaspheme when we imply that Jesus Christ would not satisfactorily accomplish His eternal work without persuasion from His earthly mother.

We blaspheme when we add to the Word of God:

"For there is one God, and one mediator between God and men, the Man Christ Jesus; who gave Himself a ransom for all" (I Tim. 2:5-6).

This states boldly that there is one God. We then are told further, in equally clear terms, that there is one mediator between God and man. Please note that fact well.

There are not two mediators, not three or four, just one! And then, if there is any confusion, the identity of that one mediator is revealed:

"For there is one God, and one mediator between God and men, the Man Christ Jesus" (I Tim. 2:5).

Why is He the mediator?

Again, Scripture spells it out clearly:

"Who gave Himself a ransom for all" (I Tim. 2:6).

Obviously, we blaspheme when we intrude Mary (or anyone else) into a mediatory role that is distinctively that of the Lord Jesus Christ alone. And, once again, there is no hint or suggestion in Scripture that any such role has ever been considered for her by God.

THE ROMAN CATHOLIC POSITION

The Roman Catholic position is that God the Father and His Son, Jesus Christ, are unreachable through normal human

efforts. By extension, they then propose that since Christ's mother is available, petitions delivered by her will not be ignored. Who would turn away his own mother if she came seeking a minor favor?

Thus, in Catholic tradition, when a person goes through the mother, he gets through more quickly and more surely. No doubt, Jesus will look with more favor on her request than on any delivered directly, hence, those bumper stickers: *"Can't find Jesus? Look for His Mother!"*

Such statements totally misinterpret the person of God and the incarnation, redemption, and plan of God for the human race. The apostle Paul said it well: *"Now the Spirit speaks expressly, that in the latter times some shall depart from the faith, giving heed to seducing spirits, and doctrines of demons;*

"Speaking lies in hypocrisy; having their conscience seared with a hot iron;

"Forbidding to marry, and commanding to abstain from meats, which God has created to be received with thanksgiving of them who believe and know the truth" (I Tim. 4:1-3).

In all of the early church, no statement is reported of an apostle referring to Mary as the *"mother of God."* There is no hint of prayers being offered to her or admonitions given to the saints to honor her beyond what the Bible suggests as normal deference.

Surely, if this great fabrication (and a fabrication it is) were valid, we would have at least a word from the early church concerning Mary.

The silence is deafening!

(28) "AND THE ANGEL CAME IN UNTO HER, AND SAID, HAIL, YOU WHO ARE HIGHLY FAVOURED, THE LORD IS WITH YOU: BLESSED ARE YOU AMONG WOMEN."

The pattern is:

1. The angel Gabriel addressed Mary.

2. He told her that she had been selected to be the mother of the Lord Jesus Christ.

3. She was blessed among women but not above women.

THE ANGEL GABRIEL

The phrase, *"And the angel came in*

unto her, and said," presents the greatest moment to date in human history, the announcement of the coming birth of the Lord of glory in the incarnation.

The phrase, *"Hail, you who are highly favoured,"* means, *"Much engraced,"* which signals what God freely does for an individual and, in this case, Mary (Eph. 1:6).

It is not *"full of grace"* as so fitted to bestow it upon others, as the Catholic Church teaches, but one who, herself meritless, had received signal grace from God.

The phrase, *"The Lord is with you,"* signals her position of humility.

"Blessed are you among women," as stated, did not say, *"Above women."*

Out of the countless women born into the world, she was chosen to be the mother of the human being, the Lord Jesus Christ. God, not Mary, was full of grace.

(29) "AND WHEN SHE SAW HIM, SHE WAS TROUBLED AT HIS SAYING, AND CAST IN HER MIND WHAT MANNER OF SALUTATION THIS SHOULD BE."

The form is:

1. Mary literally saw the angel Gabriel.

2. What he had to say to her greatly troubled her.

3. At the beginning, she really did not understand what he was saying.

THE SALUTATION

The phrase, *"And when she saw him, she was troubled at his saying,"* means it was a total disturbance and not a partial or light agitation.

The indication is twofold in that his glorious appearance and, as well, the manner in which he addressed her startled her.

"And cast in her mind what manner of salutation this should be," means that she in no way understood the reason that he addressed her as he did!

It seems that her reaction to the actual announcement, which was unique in the annals of human history, was of far less degree even than her reaction to the *"salutation."* Such, I think, shows tremendous consecration and faith in God.

(30) "AND THE ANGEL SAID UNTO HER, FEAR NOT, MARY: FOR YOU HAVE FOUND FAVOUR WITH GOD."

The overview is:

1. The angel Gabriel continued his statement, with it becoming more of a wonder as he continued.

2. Noting her agitation, he told her to, *"Fear not, Mary."*

3. He then told her, *"You have received grace from God."*

FEAR NOT

The phrase, *"And the angel said unto her, Fear not, Mary,"* proclaims basically the same words said to Zacharias.

"For you have found favour with God," should have been translated, *"You have received grace from God."* The sweetness and plentitude of the grace was not in Mary but in God. She was the unworthy object of that grace.

Grace is favor to the unworthy; patience is favor to the obstinate; mercy is favor to the miserable, and pity is favor to the poor.

(31) "AND, BEHOLD, YOU SHALL CONCEIVE IN YOUR WOMB, AND BRING FORTH A SON, AND SHALL CALL HIS NAME JESUS."

The construction is:

1. Gabriel told her that she would conceive in her womb.

2. She would have a baby—a little boy.

3. She was to call His name Jesus, which means *"Saviour."*

CONCEPTION

According to the Greek tense, the phrase, *"And, behold, you shall conceive in your womb,"* should have been translated, *"You shall forthwith conceived in your womb,"* meaning immediately!

There is a tradition that says this announcement was made to Mary on December 25th, and on that day, the Lord was conceived (not born). The same tradition says that He was born on September 29th; however, such is speculation!

Nevertheless, it is almost certain that December 25th was not the day of His birth due to the fact that when He was actually born, shepherds were in the field with their sheep overnight, which probably would not have been the case on December 25th (Lk. 2:8).

The phrase, *"And bring forth a Son,"*

proclaimed the incarnation, *"God manifest in the flesh, God with us, Immanuel."*

Approximately 800 years before, Isaiah had prophesied, *"For unto us a child is born, unto us a Son is given"* (Isa. 9:6).

"And shall call His name Jesus," portrays the Greek version of the Hebrew *Johoshua*, or the shortened *Joshua*. It means "Saviour" or "the salvation of Jehovah."

So, as the angel Gabriel told Zechariah to name his son John, which means, *"God gives grace,"* now, the same angel told Mary what to name her Son. In effect, He is the promised grace (Jn. 1:17).

(32) "HE SHALL BE GREAT, AND SHALL BE CALLED THE SON OF THE HIGHEST: AND THE LORD GOD SHALL GIVE UNTO HIM THE THRONE OF HIS FATHER DAVID."

The pattern is:

1. *"He shall be great,"* actually, the greatest of all.

2. *"He shall be called the Son of the Highest,"* meaning, *"The Son of God."*

3. He would be given the throne of His father David, which He will occupy in the coming kingdom age.

THE MOST HIGH

The phrase, *"He shall be great, and shall be called the Son of the Highest,"* actually means, *"The Most High,"* and refers to *"Jehovah!"*

It is ironic that this title given by the angel to the yet unborn child was the same title given to the Redeemer by the evil spirit in the case of the maniac of Gadara (Mk. 5:7). He was the Son of God, and consequently, demons knew Him, but the religious leaders of Israel did not know Him.

The phrase, *"And the Lord God shall give unto Him the throne of His father David,"* places Mary in the royal lineage, as suggested in Luke 3:23. This would be the fulfillment of that which was given to David by the Lord in II Samuel, Chapter 7. The Holy Spirit would refer to Jesus through the apostle Paul as *"the last Adam"* (I Cor. 15:45).

(33) "AND HE SHALL REIGN OVER THE HOUSE OF JACOB FOREVER; AND OF HIS KINGDOM THERE SHALL BE NO END."

The synopsis is:

1. This means the One whom Israel crucified will one day reign over all of Israel.

2. He will reign forever.

3. There will be no end to His kingdom.

WILL REIGN FOREVER

The phrase, *"And He shall reign over the house of Jacob forever,"* speaks of Israel, which, as of yet, has not come to pass but most surely shall! This *"reign"* will begin at the second coming and will continue, not only throughout the kingdom age but, as well, and as the Scripture says, *"Forever."* At His first advent, they would not own Him, but at His second advent, they will gladly own Him because He will then be their only hope, as He has always been their only hope.

HIS KINGDOM

The phrase, *"And of His kingdom there shall be no end,"* speaks of His rule and reign.

Man has ever attempted to rebuild the garden of Eden without the Tree of Life, i.e., the Lord Jesus Christ. Man has ever failed, as fail he must! Only when Jesus rules and reigns will the terrible problems that beset humanity be solved and eliminated. When the *"Prince of Peace"* comes back, all war will forever end (Isa. 2:4). This kingdom will be of *"judgment and with justice,"* which the world has never had before (Isa. 9:7).

When He reigns, which He will do personally, there will never be the danger of this government being overthrown. As stated, it will be *"forever."*

Even though Gabriel was speaking primarily of the fulfillment and totality of that kingdom, which will be spiritual, physical, and material, still, the spiritual kingdom has already come to the hearts and lives of millions. It is the *"kingdom of God,"* and it is centered in Jesus, this *"Son of the Highest."*

Four angelic statements about the wondrous child are made in Verses 32 and 33 and correspond to the four gospels.

(34) "THEN SAID MARY UNTO THE ANGEL, HOW SHALL THIS BE, SEEING I KNOW NOT A MAN?"

The exegesis is:

1. Mary now addressed the angel Gabriel.

2. She asked how such a thing could be.

3. She explained to him that she was not married, so how would this conception take place?

HOW SHALL THIS BE?

Mary exhibited far more incredulity over the salutation than she did the actual announcement. There seems to be no unbelief whatsoever. She seems to ask the question, "How shall this be, seeing I know not a man?" only to inquire about the method. I think the conclusion must be reached that this young lady, who was probably only about 16 or 17 years old at the time, was greatly consecrated to the Lord. Beginning with Verse 46, the worship exhibited portrays a spiritual depth far beyond her years.

I realize that many would argue that the worship portrayed in Verses 46 through 55 pertains to inspiration and, therefore, is not indicative of spiritual depth; however, that is only partly true.

The Holy Spirit, in an expression of this nature, seldom takes one beyond his spiritual maturity. So, even though her words were definitely inspired, still, they portray an excellence in the knowledge of the Word that is extremely rare.

Considering the statements made in these verses, it is almost certain that Mary was very much aware of the prophecy of Isaiah, *"Therefore the Lord Himself shall give you a sign; Behold, a virgin shall conceive, and bear a Son, and shall call His name Immanuel"* (Isa. 7:14).

WHAT DID MARY KNOW?

Mary knew she was of the kingly line of David through his son, Nathan, and that her betrothed, Joseph, was in the kingly line through Solomon. Actually, most every person in Israel knew their lineage all the way back to the sons of Jacob and, consequently, to Abraham. As well, all knew from the prophecies (Gen. 49:10; II Sam., Chpt. 7) that it was through the tribe of Judah that the Messiah would come. So, when the angel Gabriel made this great announcement, I personally do not think it was a great surprise to Mary.

The religious leaders of Israel had all of this information, even the approximate time the Messiah was to come, according to the prophecies of Daniel (Dan. 9:25-26). Consequently, they should have been ready and waiting for His appearance. However, they were not ready primarily because of their acute self-righteousness.

Likewise, the modern church should not be asleep concerning the near future. The Bible is very clear as to what is going to happen. And yet, the church, with some little exception, meanders in every direction, almost without purpose. The reason then is the reason now. There was very little true consecration to God then by the religious leaders of Israel as there is very little true consecration now! Consequently, there was very little study of the Word then and very little now.

Many, if not most, study the Word of God only to promote some erroneous doctrine.

Again we say it, "The religious leaders of Israel did not know, but this little teenage girl by the name of Mary knew!"

(35) "AND THE ANGEL ANSWERED AND SAID UNTO HER, THE HOLY SPIRIT SHALL COME UPON YOU, AND THE POWER OF THE HIGHEST SHALL OVERSHADOW YOU: THEREFORE ALSO THAT HOLY THING WHICH SHALL BE BORN OF YOU SHALL BE CALLED THE SON OF GOD."

The synopsis is:

1. Gabriel answered Mary's inquiry.

2. He, in essence, said that the Holy Spirit would decree this wonderful conception.

3. The power of God through the Holy Spirit would cause this to be brought to pass.

4. The child that would be born would be *"holy,"* and, as well, would be *"called the Son of God."*

THE HOLY SPIRIT

The phrase, *"And the angel answered and said unto her,"* pertains to her question, as is obvious.

The phrase, *"The Holy Spirit shall come upon you,"* has the same connotation as Genesis 1:2, *"And the Spirit of God moved upon the face of the waters."*

The phrase, *"And the power of the Highest shall overshadow you,"* has the same reference as, *"And God said, Let there be light: and there was light"* (Gen. 1:3).

In other words, God simply spoke the word concerning the conception in the womb of Mary, and it was done. We might say that He spoke the conception into existence exactly as He spoke light into existence. It very well could have happened, and, no doubt, did, even as the angel was speaking to her.

THE SON OF GOD

The phrase, *"Therefore also that holy thing which shall be born of you shall be called the Son of God,"* constitutes the incarnation, *"God becoming man."* Consequently, He would be very God and very man. In other words, fully God and fully man.

Many people misunderstand the incarnation, thinking that Jesus was half-God and half-man, etc.

The manner in which this was carried out portrays Him laying aside the expression of His deity while never losing possession of His deity. It is called the *"kenosis"* or *"self-emptying of Christ"* (Phil. 2:5-11).

The loss of the expression of His deity was so complete, with His humanity so obvious, that His fellow townspeople in Nazareth simply thought it absurd that He could be the Messiah (Mk. 6:1-5). They called Him the *"carpenter, the Son of Mary,"* while the angel Gabriel called Him *"the Son of God!"*

(36) "AND, BEHOLD, YOUR COUSIN ELISABETH, SHE HAS ALSO CONCEIVED A SON IN HER OLD AGE: AND THIS IS THE SIXTH MONTH WITH HER, WHO WAS CALLED BARREN."

The synopsis is:

1. The angel Gabriel had appeared to the husband of Elisabeth, Zechariah.

2. Elisabeth had miraculously conceived a son in her old age.

3. When Mary became pregnant, Elisabeth had already been pregnant for some six months. This means that John the Baptist was six months older than Jesus.

ELISABETH

The phrase, *"And, behold, your cousin Elisabeth,"* concerned her miracle, which it seems that Mary fully knew about. However, the word *cousin,* in the Greek text is

suggenes, which means, "countryman," and not necessarily a cousin in the sense of a blood relative. Elisabeth was of the tribe of Levi, which is clear from Verse 5, while both Joseph and Mary were from the tribe of Judah through David (Lk. 1:27). However, it is not impossible that Elisabeth was literally the blood cousin of Mary in that intermarriage between individuals of particular tribes was done at times, if not common.

"She has also conceived a son in her old age: and this is the sixth month with her, who was called barren," no doubt, encouraged the faith of Mary, that is, if such needed encouraging.

It is interesting that Gabriel mentioned the fact that Elisabeth had been *"barren!"* According to the next verse, it was said in order to proclaim the power of God, which knows no limitations.

(37) "FOR WITH GOD NOTHING SHALL BE IMPOSSIBLE."

The synopsis is:

1. God is almighty, meaning there is nothing He cannot do.

2. All of this means that God is a miracle-working God.

3. If He was a miracle-working God then, He is a miracle-working God now.

NOTHING SHALL BE IMPOSSIBLE

Gabriel said this for many and varied reasons but, most of all, that Mary would know that what was impossible with man was very much possible with God.

The word *impossible,* in this instance, means "that which is weak and unable to carry out that which is known to be right." God is not limited by such weakness. He is omnipotent, that is, all-powerful, and, consequently, able to do anything He says He will do.

Unfortunately, modern religious man has limited God through unbelief to such an extent that most of that which is referred to as *"Christianity"* is little more than an empty philosophy, *"The days of miracles are over,"* *"It passed away with the apostles,"* or *"It is not for this dispensation,"* ad infinitum.

There is not one hint in the Bible that God would cease such activity. He is a miracle-working God, has always been, and always shall be!

However, I feel that many honest hearts have been turned off by modern claims of miracles that have not happened! To be sure, the Lord does not need or desire false glory. Claiming He has done something when, in reality, nothing has been done is just as bad, if not worse, than the denial of His power. Much of that which claims to be miracles but, in reality, isn't, is only an effort to boost self in order to make people believe that certain individuals have great power with God, etc. These false claims, which seem to be abundant in certain circles, must be extremely grievous to the Lord. However, despite false claims or, conversely, denial of His power, *"He abides faithful"* (II Tim. 2:13).

THE GREEK WORDS FOR MIRACLES

A number of Greek words are associated with New Testament miracles. Each is linked with acts that clearly overrode what the people of the New Testament understood of natural law. Each produced wonder and the compelling conviction that the supernatural had been confronted.

Dynamis is often translated *miracle*. It is from a root meaning "power" and emphasizes that the miracle is a spontaneous expression of God's elemental power.

Semeion (used 77 times in the New Testament) indicates "sign." Its basic meaning is that of an authenticating mark or token. When it refers to a miraculous sign (Jn. 2:11; Acts 4:16, 22; I Cor. 1:22), it emphasizes the authenticating aspect of the miracle as an indication that supernatural power is involved.

Teras (used 16 times in the New Testament) is used only in the phrase, *"Signs and Wonders."*

WHAT MIRACLES ARE

The New Testament, particularly the Gospels, describes a number of miracles. These were performed by Jesus or by His followers. They are distinctive in several ways. First, in contrast with some contemporary reports of *"miracles,"* the New Testament miracles are not associated with spells or incantations. Jesus simply spoke or gestured, and the work was done. The power was in Jesus, not in a formula for magical

NOTES

control of the supernatural. Consequently, this eliminates all fortunetelling, crystal ball gazing, psychic readings, etc. In reality, these are from the world of darkness, which only steals, kills, and destroys, and are no miracles at all.

Second, the miracles carried out by Jesus and His disciples were not performed to punish in any way. Rather, Jesus' miracles were performed to rescue human beings from physical and spiritual forces that bound them. The gospel associated with Jesus is truly good news for humanity.

Third, in every way, the miracles provide testimony to Jesus' supernatural power and authority, and they witness to His ultimate victory.

The kingdom over which He rules will come at last, for neither hunger, sickness, madness, death, nor demons can stand before Jesus. All fall back before Him. Because Jesus will return someday, the ultimate fate of all of man's enemies is sealed.

THE MESSAGE OF MIRACLES

The essential message of miracles is, as we have stated, to deliver humanity. God has shown us His power and has proven that His power will be used to benefit us. We can trust Jesus fully. He is able, and He wills only our good.

However, there was also perhaps a surprisingly contemporary message to be found in miracles. Jesus was authenticated to follower and enemy alike as God's perfect man. Yet, the reaction of each group whom He confronted was different. His disciples saw in the miracles Jesus' glory, and they *"put their faith in Him"* (Jn. 2:11). However, His enemies did not do so. Both Nicodemus (Jn. 3:2) and the man born blind (Jn. 9:33) recognized and stated that God must be enabling Jesus to do miracles, but the Pharisees did not see (or refused to admit) this to be the case (Mat. 12:24; Jn. 9:34). This is reminiscent of Pharaoh. He was evidently convinced, but not converted, by the plagues on Egypt (Ex. 12:31).

The New Testament speaks of a future burst of miracles, both from God and Satan (Acts 2:17-21). Referring to Satan as history nears its end, God's final enemy will appear with *"all kinds of miracles, signs, and wonders"* (II Thess. 2:9). These will deceive *"those who are perishing"* (II Thess. 2:10), not those whose faith is anchored in the living and written Word of God.

FAITH AND MIRACLES

It is hardly surprising that the stories of miracles in the Bible or miracles performed presently do not produce faith today in those who are unwilling to accept Scripture's testimony about Jesus. It is faith that brings us to Scripture's vision of God as One who towers above the *"natural law"* that to the unconverted seems the ultimate reality. When God is seen as He really is, miracles—while they produce praise and wonder—hardly seem strange at all.

And yet, even though God is a miracle-working God (not was), still, miracles, except under the ministry of Jesus, were not common occurrences. Even in the miracle ministries of Elijah and Elisha, there were relatively few miracles performed, considering the long span of these ministries. But yet, the evidence is clear that God more or less performed miracles through the entirety of biblical history. He does the same today.

Some of the happenings in the Old Testament, such as God supernaturally aiding the armies of Israel, were not necessarily looked at as miracles, but yet, in reality, could not be truthfully defined as anything less (II Chron. 14:8-15; 20:17-25).

WHAT IS A MIRACLE

As well, I greatly suspect that the Lord does similar things presently, in whatever capacity, which are not construed as miracles but, in reality, are! While seeking to not give Him false glory, which He does not desire and, in fact, will not receive, at the same time, we must not fail to praise Him for things He actually does, which, in effect, are miracles if properly understood and analyzed.

In other words, it could not happen without God supernaturally intervening in whatever capacity. Such may not constitute a suspended law of nature, such as the Lord supernaturally helping the armies of Israel,

or other such incidents, but, still, His personal intervention is definitely a supernatural act.

A PERSONAL EXPERIENCE

To use our own ministry as an example, I have seen the Lord do things in these last several years that I think can be labeled as none other than miraculous.

To use just one example, in October 1991, when facing financial disaster, the Lord spoke to my heart while in prayer and told me that He would meet the financial needs of this ministry by the same method used to provide money to pay the taxes as inquired by Peter. Jesus told Peter, *"You go to the sea, and cast a hook, and take up the fish that first comes up; and when you have opened his mouth, you shall find a piece of money: that take, and give unto them for Me and you"* (Mat. 17:27).

As is obvious, this was a miracle! As well, it had to be one of the strangest fund-raising methods ever devised. However, that is the example the Lord gave me, telling me that in this manner, He would meet the needs of this ministry.

Looking back over these many years, I find that the Lord did exactly what He said He would do. Time and time again, we would come to the brink, but every time, the Lord, proverbially speaking, would help us to find money in the mouth of the fish. I feel that such can be interpreted as none other than miraculous.

At the same time, I cannot honestly say that a suspended law of nature has been involved, but I can definitely attest to supernatural intervention. In such cases, I personally feel we are spiritually and even scripturally remiss not to conclude such as *"miraculous."*

If the believing Christian will take stock of the entirety of his situation, be it spiritual, financial, or physical, I think he will, as well, be forced to come to the conclusion that the Lord supernaturally intervenes, oftentimes doing things that cannot be explained as other than *"miraculous."* The Bible encourages us to believe for such and to not fail to praise God when such happens (Mat. 18:18-19; 21:21-22; Mk. 11:22-24; Jn. 14:13-14; 15:7).

(38) "AND MARY SAID, BEHOLD THE HANDMAID OF THE LORD; BE IT UNTO ME ACCORDING TO YOUR WORD. AND THE ANGEL DEPARTED FROM HER."

The synopsis is:

1. Mary referred to herself as *"the handmaid of the Lord."*

2. She believed the word as given to her by Gabriel.

3. Gabriel departed, but only after delivering the greatest message man had ever known to date.

ACCORDING TO YOUR WORD

The phrase, *"And Mary said, Behold the handmaid of the Lord,"* beautifully portrays the humility of this young lady. Having referred to herself in such a manner, I think she would be greatly grieved at the unscriptural manner in which Catholicism has elevated her—even to the place of supposed deity.

The phrase, *"Be it unto me according to Your word,"* constitutes an amazing statement. Mary did not question the angel, nor did she register unbelief, it seems, in any manner. Spence said of her, "She gives this consent in a word that was simple and sublime, which involved the most extraordinary act of faith that a woman ever consented to accomplish."

As I have previously stated, I personally feel this did not come entirely as a shock to her. And yet, she stands almost alone in her faith—a faith, we might quickly add, which will soon be severely tested.

GABRIEL DEPARTS

"And the angel departed from her," constitutes the conclusion, at least to date, of the greatest event in human history, the announcement of the coming birth of the Redeemer. And yet, mighty Rome, which ruled the world at that time, would have given this announcement little credence or, if they had known it, believed it at all! The world at present has little or no record of what was taking place at that particular time regarding Rome and its vast worldwide interests, but it knows word for word what the angel Gabriel spoke to Mary.

Within itself, this should be a lesson to all. Even though certain things of this

world are necessary, still, it is the things of the Lord that are eternal, and nothing else!

(39) "AND MARY AROSE IN THOSE DAYS, AND WENT INTO THE HILL COUNTRY WITH HASTE, INTO A CITY OF JUDAH."

The structure is:

1. I believe Mary was impressed by the Holy Spirit at that time to go to the home of Zacharias and Elisabeth.

2. So, she went from Nazareth to a city of Judah, which tradition says was Hebron.

3. If that was the place, it was a distance of 100 miles or more. As to exactly how she got there, we aren't told.

LED BY THE HOLY SPIRIT

The account of Joseph, the betrothed of Mary, severely doubting her account of what the angel Gabriel had told her and the subsequent dream which cleared her, no doubt, took place immediately before the events of Verses 39 through 56.

The phrase, *"And Mary arose in those days,"* concerned the time immediately after the appearance of the angel Gabriel. These were momentous times, and she would seek the company of those who would have understanding as to her experience. To be sure, that would be precious few! The value of Christian fellowship is learned from Verses 39 through 56.

"And went into the hill country with haste, into a city of Judah," no doubt, refers to the area of Judaea. Tradition places the residence of Zacharias at Hebron. If so, this was a distance of approximately 100 miles or more. Exactly how Mary got there is not known. Quite possibly, friends were going there, and Joseph entrusted her to them. She would not have made the trip alone.

(40) "AND ENTERED INTO THE HOUSE OF ZACHARIAS, AND SALUTED ELISABETH."

The form is:

1. Evidently, the great happening of the angel Gabriel appearing to Zacharias while he was administering his duties in the temple was known to Mary.

2. It is understandable how that she desired to know exactly what Gabriel had said to Zacharias.

3. No doubt, the experience of Joseph in doubting what Mary told him, and then the subsequent dream given to him by the Lord verifying her experience, took place before she left for the home of Elisabeth.

ZACHARIAS AND ELISABETH

Mary, no doubt, made this journey and entered into the house of Zechariah according to the leading of the Holy Spirit. Inasmuch as Gabriel had mentioned Elisabeth to Mary and the miracle afforded her, this, no doubt, created a desire on the part of Mary to be with Elisabeth at this time.

There is no evidence that Mary related her situation to anyone other than Joseph, Zechariah, and Elisabeth. If, in fact, that is correct, it is wise that she did not. Things given to us by the Lord should, at times, unless directed otherwise by the Holy Spirit, be related to no one else, or only to those of like faith. The Holy Spirit through Paul said, *"Have you faith? Have it to yourself"* (Rom. 14:22).

Mary needed this companionship and encouragement, and the Lord provided it in Zacharias and Elisabeth.

"And entered into the house of Zacharias," means that she was welcomed wholeheartedly!

"And saluted Elisabeth," means that she told this dear lady all the things that the angel Gabriel had spoken to her.

(41) "AND IT CAME TO PASS, THAT, WHEN ELISABETH HEARD THE SALUTATION OF MARY, THE BABE LEAPED IN HER WOMB; AND ELISABETH WAS FILLED WITH THE HOLY SPIRIT."

The pattern is:

1. It is clear from this verse that Mary explained to Elisabeth and Zacharias exactly what had happened to her as it regarded the words of the angel Gabriel.

2. As Mary related this phenomenal experience, John the Baptist, in the womb of his mother Elisabeth, sensed and felt the presence of God.

3. At that moment, Elisabeth was filled with the Holy Spirit, which means, in essence, to verify what Mary had said. It does not carry the meaning of that which happened on the day of Pentecost, referring to Acts 2:4.

THE MOVING OF THE HOLY SPIRIT

The phrase, *"And it came to pass, that, when Elisabeth heard the salutation of Mary, the babe leaped in her womb,"* concerned the child being carried in the womb of Elisabeth even now six months, who was John the Baptist.

This does not mean that at this stage, the unborn child, John the Baptist, had the power of comprehension, etc. It simply means that at the mention of Jesus, the Holy Spirit moved upon this unborn child, who was actually called of God to serve as the introduction of Christ, and he reacted spontaneously to that moving and operation of the Holy Spirit.

"And Elisabeth was filled with the Holy Spirit," records this event taking place at the same time that the Spirit of God moved upon the child. It was a simultaneous action.

The word *filled,* in the Greek text, is *pletho* and means to "imbue, influence, or supply." It does not have the meaning as that which happened on the day of Pentecost, referring to Acts 2:4.

FILLED WITH THE HOLY SPIRIT!

Actually, at this time, no one could be baptized with the Holy Spirit as on the day of Pentecost and thereafter. John said, referring to Jesus and concerning the coming Holy Spirit in this realm, *"But this spoke He of the Spirit, which they who believe on Him should receive: for the Holy Spirit was not yet given; because that Jesus was not yet glorified"* (Jn. 7:39).

Elisabeth and her unborn son, who would be John the Baptist, were *"filled"* with the Holy Spirit, i.e., imbued with the Holy Spirit for a particular purpose and mission.

In Elisabeth's case, it concerned her being the bearer of this child. In John's case, his mission was as the prophet who would preach repentance to Israel and, above all, introduce Christ to the world as the Son of God. Actually, the Spirit of God came upon many in Old Testament times, empowering them for a special service because they had been called by God. David is a perfect example!

PRIVILEGES ...

When Samuel anointed David according to direction from the Lord, the Scripture says, *"And the Spirit of the LORD came upon David from that day forward"* (I Sam. 16:13). However, this still was not in the same capacity as the Acts 2:4 experience. Actually, Jesus proclaimed John the Baptist as the greatest man born of a woman up to that particular time because of his unique position of being called of God to introduce Christ (Mat. 11:11). However, almost in the same sentence, He further said, *"Notwithstanding he who is least in the kingdom of heaven is greater than he."*

By this, Jesus was referring to position and privileges in the fullness of the gospel, which all presently have, which those in John's position under the law did not and, in fact, could not have. John could only have a measure of the Spirit (Mat. 3:14; Jn. 1:15-17), but now, the least believer can have the fullness (Lk. 24:49; Jn. 7:37-39; 14:12-15; Acts 1:4-8; 2:38-39; 5:32; Eph. 3:19).

In Old Testament times, men, and only those with special callings, could have certain gifts of the Spirit, but now, the least believer may have any or even all of them (Mk. 16:15-20; Jn. 14:12-15; I Cor., Chpt. 12).

THE BAPTIZER WITH THE HOLY SPIRIT

Actually, there are many other blessings that the gospel presently promises under the dispensation of grace that were not available under the dispensation of law. It is all because of the Cross (II Cor. 3:6-15; Heb. 8:6; I Pet. 4:10-12).

In fact, John had much to do with the Holy Spirit, and the Holy Spirit had much to do with him. He was *"filled"* or furnished with the Holy Spirit even before he was born, with his mother experiencing the same help. As well, John introduced Jesus as the baptizer *"with the Holy Spirit, and with fire"* (Mat. 3:11).

So, even though John was not privileged to receive this wonderful experience himself, still, he was so close that he could introduce it in the person and power of the Lord Jesus Christ.

Also, if one is to notice, the Holy Spirit was

totally present and working in everything that pertained to Christ: the announcement of His birth (Lk. 1:35), the relating of this experience by Mary (Lk. 1:41), the prophecy given by Zacharias concerning the yet unborn Christ (Lk. 1:67), the prophecy given by Simeon concerning the baby Jesus (Lk. 2:25), the announcement of John concerning Jesus being the baptizer with the Holy Spirit (Mat. 3:11), and then, the Spirit of God coming upon and within Christ regarding His ministry (Lk. 3:22).

When we observe how the Holy Spirit played such a part in everything pertaining to Christ, and then observe how He plays almost no part at all in most churches presently, then the cause of spiritual declension becomes painfully obvious. Anywhere the Holy Spirit is present, Jesus will be glorified and lifted up. Where He is not present, men's philosophies are rather encouraged.

(42) "AND SHE SPOKE OUT WITH A LOUD VOICE AND SAID, BLESSED ARE YOU AMONG WOMEN, AND BLESSED IS THE FRUIT OF YOUR WOMB."

The synopsis is:

1. It was Elisabeth who spoke out here with a loud voice.

2. She pronounced a double blessing upon Mary, and it was sanctioned by the Holy Spirit.

3. She said, *"Blessed are you among women, and blessed is the fruit of your womb."*

4. This pertains to the incarnation, God becoming man.

JOY WITHIN HER SOUL

The phrase, *"And she spoke out with a loud voice,"* concerns the moving of the Holy Spirit on her heart, which produced this spontaneous reaction. It was loud because of the ecstasy and joy within her soul. What she would say would express the heartfelt cry of the ages respecting the coming of the Redeemer.

BLESSED ARE YOU AMONG WOMEN

If it is to be noticed, the phrase, *"And said, Blessed are you among women,"* did not say, *"Above women!"*

However, Mary was truly blessed in that

she was chosen by the Lord for this beautiful and wonderful privilege. Actually, her blessing would be such that she is unique in this position, with no other woman before or since having the privilege to do this thing because such will never be needed again.

THE FRUIT OF YOUR WOMB

The phrase, *"Blessed is the fruit of your womb,"* concerned Jesus Christ, for He truly was that *"fruit!"*

The incarnation, which means, *"God manifest in the flesh"* or *"God with us,"* was absolutely for man's redemption. Jesus would become the *"last Adam"* (I Cor. 15:45). As the first Adam was the representative man for the entirety of the human family because all were in his loins, his failure, which brought death, passed to all men (I Cor. 15:22).

Consequently, to redeem man from this fallen position, there had to be a last Adam. This was Jesus Christ, and to be the last Adam, He had to be born as a man, but yet, not by man. Had He been born by man, He would have been subject to the death penalty as all others because of original sin. However, due to the fact that He was not procreated as other men, exactly as the first Adam was not procreated, He was not born with sin as all others. As the last Adam, He became, as well, the representative man exactly as the first Adam had been. As the representative man, He acted on behalf of all. Consequently, His victory in all respects becomes our victory, at least to all who will exhibit faith in His name (Jn. 3:16).

So, He truly is blessed! As well, the word *blessed* should be pronounced *bless-ed,* which implies a person of superior spirituality, someone who is more saintly in moral character, and, in this case, perfect spirituality and character.

(43) "AND WHAT IS THIS TO ME, THAT THE MOTHER OF MY LORD SHOULD COME TO ME?"

The synopsis is:

1. Elisabeth was overjoyed that Mary would come to her for council and advice.

2. Mary is called, *"The mother of my Lord,"* and not the mother of God.

3. There is no doubt that Mary related to Elisabeth over and over again exactly what the angel Gabriel had said.

THE MOTHER OF MY LORD

The question, *"What is this to me?"* actually has a double meaning. It is as follows:

1. "Who am I that I should be privileged to associate in this glorious way with 'the mother of my Lord,' and more particularly, the 'Lord Himself?'"

2. "What does this all mean to me, or to the entirety of mankind, for that matter?"

The question, *"That the mother of my Lord should come to me?"* presents Elisabeth calling Jesus *"Lord"* by the Spirit of God.

The two words, *"My Lord,"* have a wealth of meaning! Spence said, "Not only did she bless the mother of the coming Messiah, but the Spirit opened her eyes to see who that coming Messiah really was."

The coming of the Messiah was spoken of constantly in Israel. However, even though a few of the prophets of the past undoubtedly had a correct view of who and what He would be, the truth was that most people had an entirely erroneous concept. By the time Jesus made His ministry debut, the idea that the Messiah would be a conqueror, ridding Israel of all her enemies and restoring her place and position of supremacy, was the prevailing thought at that time. It was gross error and no way matched up to proper scriptural interpretation, but still, it was the prevailing thought. This was the bitter fruit of acute self-righteousness.

THE LAWFUL SON OF THE HIGHEST

In their minds, they did not see the Messiah as God or the *"lawful Son of the Highest!"* This is the reason the Pharisees and religious leaders of Israel bridled at the idea that Jesus claimed deity. Their Messiah, which they imagined in their minds, could be controlled by men. Deity could not be controlled; consequently, they rejected Him out of hand.

Plumptre said, "The contrast leaves no room for doubt. She used the word 'Lord' in its highest sense. 'Great' as her own son was to be in the sight of the Lord, here was the mother of One yet greater, even the Lord Himself."

(44) "FOR, LO, AS SOON AS THE VOICE OF YOUR SALUTATION SOUNDED IN MY EARS, THE BABE LEAPED IN MY WOMB FOR JOY."

The synopsis is:

1. The *"salutation,"* as given by Mary, referred to the coming of the Messiah, the Lord of glory.

2. Elisabeth said that when that salutation was heard, *"The babe* (John the Baptist) *leaped in her womb."*

3. This was the Holy Spirit moving upon this unborn child.

THE SALUTATION

The phrase, *"For, lo, as soon as the voice of your salutation sounded in my ears,"* referred to the announcement by Mary and the actual fact as to what this salutation meant. It was, as stated, the coming of the Messiah, the Lord of glory, the Son of the Highest, even Jehovah wrapped in the habiliment of human flesh.

"The babe leaped in my womb for joy," concerned the response of the unborn John the Baptist to this announcement.

Once again we state that it was not that the unborn child could understand or comprehend, but rather the manifestation of the Holy Spirit that produced the response.

If this joy was expressed in an unborn child, how is it that we who are able to understand and comprehend should express less joy, especially considering what the Lord has done for us!

(45) "AND BLESSED IS SHE WHO BELIEVED: FOR THERE SHALL BE A PERFORMANCE OF THOSE THINGS WHICH WERE TOLD HER FROM THE LORD."

The diagram is:

1. It plainly tells us in this verse that *"Mary believed."*

2. She believed that everything she had been told by the angel Gabriel would come to pass exactly as he related it.

3. She recognized that the message Gabriel brought to her came straight from the throne of God.

I BELIEVE

The phrase, *"And blessed is she who believed,"* refers to Mary and her faith in that

NOTES

which was told her by the angel Gabriel. She did not question the word of the Lord and is here commended by the Holy Spirit through Elisabeth concerning her faith. *"Believing"* is the action part of faith. It is that which brings to pass that promised by faith.

The phrase, *"For there shall be a performance of those things which were told her from the Lord,"* means that what is said shall be done. The word is *"shall be,"* which is certitude of action. The Redeemer, at long last, was coming into the world, and doing so in order to redeem man. He could not be stopped by man or demon!

(46) "AND MARY SAID, MY SOUL DOES MAGNIFY THE LORD."

The overview is:

1. Mary now gave a great testimony of faith.

2. She magnified the Lord regarding what she had been told, and no wonder!

3. All of this tells us that Mary had an excellent knowledge of the Word of God and, as well, was deeply consecrated to the Lord. I think that should be obvious!

MAGNIFIES THE LORD

As we have previously stated, one can read Verses 46 through 55, which is referred to as *"The Magnificat,"* and easily determine that Mary had a tremendous knowledge of the Scripture and a spiritual depth that far surpassed most. Even though she was a teenaged girl, still, her consecration was exceptional!

It is ironic that she magnified the Lord while the Catholic Church erroneously magnifies her.

This *"Magnificat"* is actually a song and is in the tradition of the *"Song of Deborah"* (Judg. 5:1-31) and the *"Prayer or Song of Hannah"* (I Sam. 2:1-10).

(47) "AND MY SPIRIT HAS REJOICED IN GOD MY SAVIOUR."

The structure is:

1. Mary's spirit rejoiced in the Lord, and no wonder!

2. The statement, *"In God my Saviour,"* completely refutes and disproves the theory of the immaculate conception or the total absence of original sin in Mary.

3. If God was her Saviour, and she plainly said that He was, then she must have been

a sinner in order, therefore, to be saved.

IN GOD MY SAVIOUR

This statement of Mary, *"In God my Saviour,"* disproves, as stated, the theory of the immaculate conception or the total absence of original sin in Mary. If God was her Saviour, then she must have been a sinner in order, therefore, to be saved. Not one Scripture ever hints of such an idea—that Mary, or anyone else for that matter, was sinless, except the Lord Jesus Christ.

So, her rejoicing was in the fact that Jesus is God and would redeem her, as well as the entirety of mankind, at least those who will believe (Jn. 3:16). Consequently, the emphasis is placed on Jesus as *"Saviour."*

While He definitely is the healer and the provider of all good things, still, the emphasis must always be, as Paul said it, *"Jesus Christ, and Him crucified"* (I Cor. 2:2).

Sadly, in many charismatic circles, the emphasis is being shifted to other things, such as financial prosperity, etc. Even though the Lord is definitely a provider, such is all-dependent on Him as Saviour. As a result, the emphasis of the church must always be on the winning of souls, with everything else following in that train.

(48) "FOR HE HAS REGARDED THE LOW ESTATE OF HIS HANDMAIDEN: FOR, BEHOLD, FROM HENCEFORTH ALL GENERATIONS SHALL CALL ME BLESSED."

The pattern is:

1. The Holy Spirit through Mary says that despite the fact of her being of humble means, she was chosen by the Lord.

2. It is true that from then until now, *"All generations have called her blessed."*

3. However, we sin, and sin greatly, when we place Mary in the position of a mediator, as does the Catholic Church.

THE LOW ESTATE

The phrase, *"For He has regarded the low estate of His handmaiden,"* says several things:

• Mary's prayer or song is the highest order of worship, for it asks for nothing but only breathes out adoration and thankfulness for what is.

• Even though she was in the royal lineage of David, still, the throne of David was no more, except in Christ. Consequently, her estate was *"low,"* meaning that she had nothing of this world's goods, and she was recognized not at all by the religious elite of Israel. However, God recognized her, and in the highest way possible. Consequently, promotion does not come from man but from God. As some have well said, "If we look to man, we get what man can give, which is nothing. However, if we look to God, we get what He can give, which is everything." Mary looked to God!

BLESSED

The phrase, *"For, behold, from henceforth all generations shall call me blessed,"* is, in effect, a prophecy and has been fulfilled to the letter, and I do not speak of the erroneous contention of the Catholic Church.

As well, the word *blessed* is here a single syllable and simply means, *"A recipient of grace."* The word *blessed* in Verse 42, as stated, is a double syllable and should be pronounced *bless-ed,* which actually means, "The giver of grace," here received by Mary.

(49) "FOR HE WHO IS MIGHTY HAS DONE TO ME GREAT THINGS; AND HOLY IS HIS NAME.

(50) "AND HIS MERCY IS ON THEM WHO FEAR HIM FROM GENERATION TO GENERATION."

The structure is:

1. God is mighty, even almighty, and can do great things for all who believe Him.

2. However, we must never forget, *"Holy is His name."*

3. God extends mercy, but only on those who *"fear him from generation to generation."*

GOD IS ALMIGHTY

In the two verses just mentioned, Mary proclaims three principle divine attributes. They are as follows:

1. *"For He who is mighty has done to me great things"*: this speaks of God's attribute of power, which alone could bring about the virgin birth.

2. *"And holy is His name"*: this proclaims

His attribute of holiness and proclaims that it is bound up in *"His name."* His name is *"power"* (Mk. 16:17), *"healing"* (Mk. 16:17), *"comfort"* (Song of Sol. 1:3), and, as well, is *"holy!"*

His name is holy because it represents His character and nature. It represents the essence of His being; consequently, He is a thrice-holy God (Rev. 4:8).

3. *"And His mercy is on them who fear Him"*: the attribute of mercy is now introduced. Mary needed mercy exactly as all others. Mercy is a product of grace, and upon introduction of grace, it is always extended without fail!

FEAR OF GOD

However, mercy is tied to the *"fear of God."* There is no fear of God in self-righteousness; consequently, no mercy can be shown. The fear of God comes from a broken and contrite spirit, realizing that we are deserving of nothing good, but because of the grace of God, we are given all things. Upon that realization, mercy is always extended.

The phrase, *"From generation to generation,"* means that to those who truly fear Him, mercy will be extended, irrespective of the time frame, i.e., generation. The promise is forever!

All of this is wrapped up in the Redeemer, who Mary would have the privilege of bringing into the world. In effect, Jesus is the mercy of God.

(51) "HE HAS SHOWED STRENGTH WITH HIS ARM; HE HAS SCATTERED THE PROUD IN THE IMAGINATION OF THEIR HEARTS."

The overview is:

1. To those who fear Him, He will show His strength.

2. Conversely, the Lord is opposed to the proud, and in all circumstances.

3. Pride is the result of self-righteousness.

THE PROUD

The phrase, *"He has shown strength with His arm,"* proclaims the power of God and the manner in which it is used. It is described in Verses 51 through 53.

"He has scattered the proud in the imagination of their hearts," proclaims the

Messianic reversal of man's conception of what is great and little.

The idea is that the Lord ignored the proud self-exaltation of the religious elite of Israel and showered His attention on a little *"handmaiden."*

(52) "HE HAS PUT DOWN THE MIGHTY FROM THEIR SEATS, AND EXALTED THEM OF LOW DEGREE."

The structure is:

1. God is opposed to the proud.

2. He exalts the humble.

3. Faith expressed in anything other than the Cross of Christ always, and without exception, results in self-righteousness, i.e., pride.

EXALTATION

It is amazing that this young lady proclaimed almost the very words of the famous sermon her Divine Son preached some 30 years later in a village not far from Capernaum. He said, *"For every one who exalts himself shall be abased; and he who humbles himself shall be exalted"* (Lk. 18:14).

(53) "HE HAS FILLED THE HUNGRY WITH GOOD THINGS; AND THE RICH HE HAS SENT EMPTY AWAY."

The construction is:

1. They who hunger and thirst after righteousness shall be filled.

2. Those who trust in things other than the Lord will receive nothing from the Lord.

3. There will come a day that the mightiest of the mighty will need the Lord, but if they continue in their frame of mind of prideful attitude, they will receive nothing.

RIGHTEOUSNESS

The phrase, *"He has filled the hungry with good things,"* concerns those who hunger and thirst after righteousness (Mat. 5:6).

"And the rich He has sent empty away," refers to those who were *"rich, and increased with goods, and thought they had need of nothing"* (Rev. 3:17).

(54) "HE HAS HELPED HIS SERVANT ISRAEL, IN REMEMBRANCE OF HIS MERCY."

The overview is:

1. The Lord now fulfills the promises He made concerning the sending of a Redeemer into the world.

2. He did it because of His mercy.

3. Grace was a choice, and a choice made by the Godhead sometime in eternity past. However, once grace was chosen, as it regards dealing with man, then God had no choice but to extend mercy.

IN REMEMBRANCE OF HIS MERCY

The phrase, *"He has helped His servant Israel,"* concerns two things:

1. He remembered the promises He had made to the prophets. As such, He would bring the Messiah into the world.

2. As promised, He would be an Israelite. This would be done despite the fact that Israel had long since ceased to serve God, even though loudly proclaiming to do so. As a result, they would murder their Messiah.

The phrase, *"In remembrance of His mercy,"* means that it was not because of Israel's faithfulness, but because of God's mercy.

(55) "AS HE SPOKE TO OUR FATHERS, TO ABRAHAM, AND TO HIS SEED FOREVER."

The overview is:

1. The Lord gave promises concerning the coming Redeemer to the *"fathers,"* i.e., the prophets.

2. In a sense, it began with Abraham, even though the Lord gave such promises to some before Abraham.

3. In fact, the Lord is still giving promises as it regards events that are soon to take place, such as the rapture, etc.

PROMISES

This proclaims the value that God places on His promises and, as well, ends the song of Mary. It opened with magnifying the Lord and closed with the promises of God being remembered forever.

What a wonderful God we serve!

(56) "AND MARY ABODE WITH HER ABOUT THREE MONTHS, AND RETURNED TO HER OWN HOUSE."

The structure is:

1. Mary continued to abide with Elisabeth until John the Baptist was born.

2. She then returned to *"her own house"* in Nazareth.

3. However, due to her time spent with

Zacharias and Elisabeth, I feel that Mary was greatly encouraged in the Lord.

MARY

The phrase, *"And Mary abode with her about three months,"* means that she stayed there until John the Baptist was born. She had come in Elisabeth's sixth month (Lk. 1:26).

The phrase, *"And returned to her own house,"* refers to Nazareth.

It is claimed by some that Mary's condition of pregnancy was not known to Joseph at the time she went to the home of Elisabeth, consequently, with the events of Matthew 1:18 taking place after her return. However, I personally think it is almost certain that she informed Joseph immediately, with the events of Matthew 1:18 taking place while she was at the home of Elisabeth.

The expositors conclude that the statement, *"Her own house,"* means that she and Joseph had not yet come together as man and wife. If so, they claim she would have gone to Joseph's house. However, her informing Joseph of the situation had nothing to do with the actual time they were united in marriage.

This much is certain: If they were not united in marriage until some three months after the announcement by the angel Gabriel, this means that Jesus would have been born six months after their marriage. This seems highly unlikely, and it would have given rise to countless wagging tongues. Irrespective, it is known that during Jesus' ministry, He was, at least in a roundabout way, accused of being *"born of fornication"* (Jn. 8:41). Even though the religious leaders of Israel claimed that He was illegitimate, in reality, His birth was the only true legitimate birth there ever was.

At any rate, Mary would live with this stigma all of her life.

(57) "NOW ELISABETH'S FULL TIME CAME THAT SHE SHOULD BE DELIVERED; AND SHE BROUGHT FORTH A SON."

The construction is:

1. John the Baptist would now be born.

2. In the words of the Lord Jesus Christ, he would be the greatest prophet who ever lived.

3. That would be correct simply because while all the other prophets of the past pointed to the One who was to come, it was John who introduced Him.

ELISABETH

Many feel that Elisabeth, at this time, could have been in her 60s, or at least in her 50s. The Scripture uses the term, *"Well stricken in years"* (Lk. 1:7); however, the Lord had rejuvenated her youthfulness in that she conceived.

"And she brought forth a son," proclaims the greatest prophet who ever lived, the one who would be the mighty forerunner of the great King.

(58) "AND HER NEIGHBOURS AND HER COUSINS HEARD HOW THE LORD HAD SHOWED GREAT MERCY UPON HER; AND THEY REJOICED WITH HER."

The overview is:

1. Of course, with time, it was obvious that Elisabeth was pregnant.

2. Due to her age, this would have been the topic of great conversation.

3. As well, it seems that all who were acquainted with Zacharias and Elisabeth knew that the Lord was going to use this child in a mighty way, and so He did.

MERCY

The phrase, *"And her neighbours and her cousins heard,"* refers to the knowledge of the visitation of the angel Gabriel to Zacharias.

"How the Lord had shown great mercy upon her," means they believed what Zacharias had said because the proof was irrefutable. They were too old to have children, but yet, her condition was beyond question. Elisabeth would not bear the stigma that Mary would bear because John's conception was by the normal manner of procreation.

"And they rejoiced with her," means the entire area was very pleased and happy that this great thing was happening in the home and lives of Zacharias and Elisabeth.

(59) "AND IT CAME TO PASS, THAT ON THE EIGHTH DAY THEY CAME TO CIRCUMCISE THE CHILD; AND THEY CALLED HIM ZACHARIAS, AFTER THE NAME OF HIS FATHER."

NOTES

The overview is:

1. Little boy babies had to be circumcised on the eighth day after birth because it took that long for the properties of coagulation to be brought about in the blood of the baby. If it was circumcised before then, it would bleed to death.

2. Evidently, Zacharias had not mentioned that the little boy's name was to be John.

CIRCUMCISION

The phrase, *"And it came to pass, that on the eighth day they came to circumcise the child,"* was according to the command originally given to Abraham by the Lord (Gen. 17:10-12). This was a very solemn covenant, with dire penalties attached if broken. The uncircumcised Israelite was not covered by the covenant promise given to Abraham and was, therefore, lost.

The rite symbolized submission to God and belief in His covenant promise. However, God also required a *"circumcision of the heart"* (Deut. 10:16; 30:6; Jer. 4:4).

Circumcision did not bring salvation, as that came by faith. It was only a result of salvation and not the cause. The New Testament argues that Abraham was justified by faith even while he was uncircumcised years before the rite was given. Circumcision was a sign, *"A seal of the righteousness that he had by faith while he was still uncircumcised"* (Gen. 15:6; 17:10-27; Rom. 4:11).

The sign of circumcision was not carried over into the church because that which it represented, separation respecting the Jewish people, was fulfilled in Christ. Regrettably, many Hebrew Christians struggled to impose circumcision and, as well, the Mosaic law on Gentile Christians during the times of the early church (Acts 15:1). However, this was rejected at the Jerusalem Council (Acts 15:1-29).

Paul later wrote to the Corinthians, and I paraphrase, *"Was a man already circumcised when he was called? Therefore, he could not become uncircumcised. Was a man uncircumcised when he was called? If that is the case, he should not be circumcised, at least on religious grounds. Circumcision is nothing, and uncircumcision is nothing. Keeping God's commands is what counts"* (I Cor. 7:18-19).

THE EIGHTH DAY

Paul's point is that God has never been concerned for the symbol as the thing in itself. God cares about reality and, consequently, to what the symbol pointed. It is our heart response to Him that counts.

Thus, looking into the heart and examining those who have responded to Christ' gospel, the Bible says, *"It is we who are the true circumcision, we who worship by the Spirit of God, who glory in Jesus Christ, and who put no confidence in the flesh"* (Phil. 3:3).

In the law (Lev. 12:3), the Lord ordained that the little boy be circumcised on the *"eighth day"* after he was born. This had to do with the physical properties of his blood, etc. The medical profession does not hold to this standard presently because they now have a means to cause the blood to coagulate immediately.

Many years ago, almost all people died who were forced to submit to surgery. One medical doctor, while searching for the reason, found that God commanded in the law of Moses that the sick who were washed do so in *"running water"* (Lev. 15:13). He felt this command, and failure to obey it, was resulting in the tremendously high death rate among surgical patients.

At that time, the doctors did not wash their hands or instruments respecting surgery, etc. They reasoned that it was not necessary.

However, this particular medical doctor began to follow this command as given in Leviticus, and he noticed instantly that the death rate dropped because there was much less infection.

THE SUCCESS RATE

Actually, infection had been the cause of the high death rate. Whenever the hands of the surgeons and all of their operating instruments were constantly washed in running water, infection was instantly lowered, with future prospects of the patient greatly increasing.

It took him some time to get this adopted

NOTES

in the medical profession inasmuch as, regrettably, most of the doctors laughed at such a silly suggestion, as they put it. However, his success rate versus their failure rate soon became overly obvious, with his methods gradually being adopted until today, it is practiced universally.

Realizing that bacteria can multiply as much as 300 trillion times in 24 hours, we see the wisdom of the commands to wash in running water instead of stagnant water, as these physicians had been doing.

Through divine knowledge, Moses was thousands of years ahead of his time in bacteriological science, treatment of disease, sanitation, and health laws. This gave the Jews the benefit of wisdom concerning physical fitness that no other nation or people had at that time.

As a result of that command given thousands of years ago, modern medical science made a giant leap forward.

As well, going back only to the 1940s, or even later, many medical doctors exclaimed that tonsils served no purpose, etc. However, they have since found that the tonsils serve a tremendous purpose. They serve as a trap for all types of diseases, germs, infections, etc. Whereas, at that time, doctors routinely removed tonsils, now it is not done unless absolutely imperative.

Once again, the problem was evident of the creation thinking it knew more than the Creator. Regrettably, in matters spiritual and social, it continues to think such.

JOHN

The phrase, *"And they called him Zacharias, after the name of his father,"* presented the custom, which was to name the little boy on the day of his circumcision. The rabbis said this was because the names of Abram and Sarai were changed when God instituted circumcision (Gen., Chpt. 17).

However, it was very rarely that sons received the name of the father. So, for whatever reason, the neighbors seemed to desire that the custom be changed in this case, with the child being named after his father.

As well, this denotes that Zacharias had not related to the neighbors anything the angel Gabriel had told him. They did not know the child was to be named *"John."*

(60) "AND HIS MOTHER ANSWERED AND SAID, NOT SO; BUT HE SHALL BE CALLED JOHN."

The overview is:

1. As stated, neither Zacharias nor Elisabeth had made known what Gabriel had said respecting the name of the child.

2. Gabriel had stated that he was to be called John.

JEHOVAH GIVES GRACE

The phrase, *"And his mother answered and said, Not so,"* proclaimed another custom, which was that mothers among the Jews generally gave the children their names.

"But he shall be called John," was in obedience to what Gabriel had demanded. As stated, the name John meant *"Jehovah shows favor"* or *"Jehovah gives grace."* It was a fitting name for this one who would introduce Christ, who, in effect, was grace personified.

(61) "AND THEY SAID UNTO HER, THERE IS NONE OF YOUR KINDRED WHO IS CALLED BY THIS NAME."

The construction is:

1. The relatives and friends were confused as to why the child was to be named John.

2. They knew of no one in this family that was called John.

A DEPARTURE FROM CUSTOM

The neighbors were perplexed inasmuch as Zacharias and Elisabeth seemed to be departing from custom—the naming of a child after a relative or one of the greats of Israel. As well, names were often chosen to represent something good or bad that had happened in the family. And then, at times, the name was chosen by the Lord, as was the case here.

(62) "AND THEY MADE SIGNS TO HIS FATHER, HOW HE WOULD HAVE HIM CALLED."

The structure is:

1. Inasmuch as Zacharias could not speak, and it also seems evident that neither could he hear, they had to make signs to him as to what name the child would be given.

2. Zacharias would be stricken deaf and

dumb for a period of nine months simply because of unbelief.

3. However, before we criticize him, we had best ask ourselves, "If we were put under the same circumstances, would we have done any better or even as well?"

WHAT IS HE TO BE CALLED?

The phrase, *"And they made signs to his father,"* lets us know that Zacharias was not only rendered speechless because of his unbelief regarding the announcement by Gabriel, but he was deaf as well! Consequently, they had to use sign language for him to understand what was being asked.

"How he would have him called," portrays that Elisabeth had deferred to her husband Zacharias, and no wonder!

(63) "AND HE ASKED FOR A WRITING TABLE, AND WROTE, SAYING, HIS NAME IS JOHN. AND THEY MARVELLED ALL."

The synopsis is:

1. Unable to speak, Zacharias would have to write the information he desired others to have.

2. He wrote, *"Saying, His name is John."*

3. The group, ever how large it was, seemed to have been taken completely by surprise.

HIS NAME IS JOHN

The phrase, *"And he asked for a writing table,"* pertained to that which was in common use in those days.

These *"tables"* were of ivory or wood and coated with wax, and the letters were formed by a stylus made of gold, silver, brass, iron, ivory, or bone. One end was pointed for writing while the other end was smooth and round for erasing or smoothing out the wax so it could be used again.

Edges and backs of tablets were not waxed so that when two or more were put together, they would not be marred. Several tablets were sometimes put together at the backs by means of wire that served as hinges.

Letters, wills, and many documents of great length were written upon them. They could be bound by the outer edges with cords and fastened with a seal.

The phrase, *"And wrote, saying, His name is John,"* proclaims the obedience of

Zacharias, and that this child would ultimately introduce the bearer of grace and truth. That bearer was Jesus Christ (Jn. 1:17).

"And they marvelled all," could possibly indicate that, at that time, Zacharias could very well have related to them the appearance of the angel Gabriel to him some nine months earlier, and all that Gabriel had said.

(64) "AND HIS MOUTH WAS OPENED IMMEDIATELY, AND HIS TONGUE LOOSED, AND HE SPOKE, AND PRAISED GOD."

The synopsis is:

1. Immediately upon obedience, in other words, doing what the angel Gabriel had said to do, Zacharias was instantly able to speak and evidently could hear.

2. Realizing the glory of all of this, he began to praise God, as would be obvious.

PRAISING GOD

The phrase, *"And his mouth was opened immediately,"* speaks of his obedience in doing what the angel had demanded.

"And his tongue loosed, and he spoke, and praised God," lets us know that his tongue had formerly been used at the announcement of Gabriel to register unbelief. He now did that which he should have done at that time—praise God (Lk. 1:18).

This makes it painfully obvious to all just how much stock God places in our obeying His Word. Doubt and unbelief are the bane of the modern church. Regrettably, all have been afflicted with this malady at one time or the other. The Lord desires that we believe Him and not question His Word. To do so registers doubt in His ability to carry forth what He has promised. Considering that He is able to do all things, unbelief is an insult to His integrity.

As well, respecting God's Word, doubt and unbelief go back to the garden of Eden and constitute the foundation of original sin. Adam and Eve simply did not believe what God told them. They disobeyed Him by partaking of the fruit of the tree of which they had been told not to eat (Gen. 2:15-17).

(65) "AND FEAR CAME ON ALL WHO DWELT ROUND ABOUT THEM: AND ALL THESE SAYINGS WERE NOISED ABROAD THROUGHOUT ALL THE HILL COUNTRY OF JUDAEA."

The synopsis is:

1. When the people who lived nearby Zacharias and Elisabeth heard what had actually happened as it regarded the angel Gabriel, there was a certain fear, and rightly so, that became paramount.

2. As well, as is normal, this thing was talked up all through the *"hill country of Judaea."*

FEAR

The phrase, *"And fear came on all who dwelt round about them,"* further proclaims the fact that Zacharias told the people of the visitation of the angel Gabriel. They realized that a great thing was happening in their midst. While they did not understand the full portent of it all, still, they knew that God had spoken and that the child was destined for something great.

"And all these sayings were noised abroad throughout all the hill country of Judaea," meant that these things were constantly discussed in this area.

What Zacharias related to them was open very little to speculation. All knew that Zacharias and Elisabeth had long since passed the age of child-bearing; consequently, for her to conceive at this age was a miracle, to say the least. Considering that all of this had been brought about by the visitation of the mighty angel Gabriel, it placed a significance all out of proportion to normal thought. God was moving again in Israel! The 400-year prophetic drought was being broken. Once again they would hear, *"Thus saith the Lord."* Little did they realize what was actually about to happen!

(66) "AND ALL THEY WHO HEARD THEM LAID THEM UP IN THEIR HEARTS, SAYING, WHAT MANNER OF CHILD SHALL THIS BE! AND THE HAND OF THE LORD WAS WITH HIM."

The construction is:

1. Once again, God was moving in Israel. As stated, the 400-year prophetic drought was over.

2. Considering the manner of the birth of John the Baptist, they wondered *"what manner of child shall this be!"*

3. The voice of John the Baptist would be the greatest voice Israel had ever heard, or

the world for that matter, because He would introduce the Redeemer.

WHAT MANNER OF CHILD SHALL THIS BE!

The phrase, *"And all they who heard them laid them up in their hearts,"* spoke of what Gabriel had told Zacharias concerning John and what his ministry would be like, which pertained to Verses 15 through 17.

The exclamation, *"Saying, What manner of child shall this be!"* means they realized that something extra special was happening among them. They knew that John was destined to be special, even *"great,"* but at that time, they little knew that he would actually introduce the Messiah, which, in effect, spoke of the greatest moment in human history. Everything else pales by comparison.

"And the hand of the Lord was with him," is Luke's way of expressing all that would happen to John the Baptist through the entirety of his life.

It meant that even as a child, one could see the Lord at work with him. It was obvious to all!

(67) "AND HIS FATHER ZACHARIAS WAS FILLED WITH THE HOLY SPIRIT, AND PROPHESIED, SAYING."

The diagram is:

1. The statement, *"Filled with the Holy Spirit,"* is unique with Luke.

2. It meant that the Holy Spirit aided and helped them, even in a great way, for that which they were called.

3. Even though Zacharias *"prophesied,"* this does not mean that he stood in the office of the prophet, for he did not. But yet, God wondrously used him in this capacity at this time.

FILLED WITH THE HOLY SPIRIT

The phrase, *"And his father Zacharias was filled with the Holy Spirit,"* is unique with Luke. This same statement was made of John even before he was born (Lk. 1:15), and Elisabeth (Lk. 1:41), and now of Zacharias. It was also said of Mary, but in a little different way (Lk. 1:35).

It meant, as previously stated, that the Holy Spirit aided and helped them, even in a great way, for that which they were called. In the case of Zacharias, it would have pertained to his guiding hand regarding the upbringing of this all-important child. The same could be said for Elisabeth.

"And prophesied, saying," concerned what John the Baptist would do in his ministry.

PROPHECY

However, even though Zacharias prophesied, as stated, he did not stand in the office of the prophet, such as the prophets of old, or even his son John. While the Lord used him in this capacity at this particular time, there is little evidence that it continued, at least in this fashion. Many times the Lord uses believers in many and varied capacities, with them not really having the calling, as Zacharias, for that which is done. Being God, He has that prerogative and often uses it.

At times, a layman may be called on to preach, which he may do with the help of the Lord and, therefore, be a blessing. However, that does not mean that he has the calling of one of the fivefold ministry gifts (Eph. 4:11).

As well, considering the gift of prophecy (I Cor. 12:10), the bestowal of the manifestation of this gift by the Holy Spirit does not mean that person stands in the office of the prophet. In fact, all prophets have the gift of prophecy. All who have the gift of prophecy, however, are not prophets.

As well, any believer has the right to pray for the sick, which, at times, will result in healing; however, that does not necessarily mean they have the *"gift of healing"* (I Cor. 12:9).

The Lord condescends to use some people in various capacities, and regrettably they automatically assume more than is intended. While Zacharias prophesied by the unction of the Holy Spirit, still, there is no record that he considered himself a prophet.

(68) "BLESSED BE THE LORD GOD OF ISRAEL; FOR HE HAS VISITED AND REDEEMED HIS PEOPLE."

The construction is:

1. This is one of the prophecies of Zacharias.

2. He first of all blessed the Lord God of Israel.

3. He alluded to the fact that the Holy Spirit was now visiting Israel, and his son, John the Baptist, would be the forerunner. What an honor!

BLESS-ED

The phrase, *"Blessed be the Lord God of Israel,"* constitutes the beginning of this prophecy or song.

Once again, the word *blessed* is actually used as a double syllable, *bless-ed,* and means that God is full of grace, and actually the dispenser of grace.

At that time, Israel was the only nation in the world that knew God. The rest of the world lay in heathenistic darkness. However, it was God's will that the entirety of the world know of the great gospel message and have an opportunity to receive Christ. John the Beloved said (not John the Baptist) *"For God so loved the world,"* not just Israel (Jn. 3:16).

Sadly, Israel became so self-righteous that they excluded all others from the true gospel message but did strongly attempt to bring others into their self-righteousness. Concerning this misguided effort, Jesus said, *"Woe unto you, scribes and Pharisees, hypocrites! for you compass sea and the land to make one proselyte, and when he is made, you make him twofold more the child of hell than yourselves"* (Mat. 23:15).

It is tragic, but most modern church efforts fall into the same category. People are little won to Christ, but rather to a church, doctrine, philosophy, or religion. As Jesus, in essence, said, "They are in worse condition afterward than before." Rare is the preacher who truly brings people to Christ. Thank God for the ones who do!

REDEMPTION

The phrase, *"For He has visited and redeemed His people,"* refers to the long spiritual drought of some 400 years when the voice of the prophet was not heard in all of Israel. Even though it would be years before this little baby just born took his prophetic office, still, his very presence told Israel that the Holy One of Israel had again come to His people.

The word *"redeemed,"* no doubt, meant

NOTES

that Zacharias vividly remembered the words of the angel Gabriel, *"To make ready a people prepared for the Lord"* (Lk. 1:17). He would prepare the people for the Messiah. He also now knew the Messiah would be born of the Virgin Mary. This great redemption had long been a promise; now it was to be a reality!

(69) "AND HAS RAISED UP AN HORN OF SALVATION FOR US IN THE HOUSE OF HIS SERVANT DAVID."

The form is:

1. The *"horn of salvation"* referred to the Lord Jesus Christ.

2. He would come from the tribe of Judah, actually, from the family of David.

AN HORN OF SALVATION

The phrase, *"And has raised up an horn of salvation for us,"* referred to power and, in this case, the Lord Jesus Christ. So, this horn of salvation is another name given to Christ by the Holy Spirit.

A rabbinic writer said that God had given ten horns to His people: Abraham, Isaac, Jacob, Joseph, Moses, the law, the priesthood, the temple, David, and the Messiah. Spiritually speaking, they were all placed on the heads of the Israelites till they rebelled against God, and then they were cut off and given to the Gentiles.

"In the house of His servant David," signifies the Holy Spirit through Zacharias, referring back to the promise that God had made to David (II Sam., Chpt. 7). Zacharias knew that Mary and Joseph were in the direct lineage of David, the former through David's son, Nathan, and the latter through Solomon. So, the great prophecies of the past had been fulfilled and had come to fruition in the form of a little teenage *"handmaid of the Lord"* (Lk. 1:38).

(70) "AS HE SPOKE BY THE MOUTH OF HIS HOLY PROPHETS, WHICH HAVE BEEN SINCE THE WORLD BEGAN."

The synopsis is:

1. Zacharias was saying that the Lord *"spoke by the mouth of His holy prophets"* concerning these events that were now about to take place.

2. All of this was planned by God from the very beginning of time.

THE PROPHETS

The phrase, *"As He spoke by the mouth of His holy prophets,"* concerned all the Bible greats, such as Abel, Enoch, Noah, Abraham, Isaac, Jacob, Joseph, Moses, Joshua, Samuel, David, Isaiah, Jeremiah, Ezekiel, etc. All were Jewish!

The religious leaders of Israel would not accept this irrefutable evidence, even though Mary and Joseph met every scriptural specification. Their hatred for Jesus would know no bounds, with their opposition ultimately resulting in murdering Him.

Why?

The reasons then are the reasons now. He was not a product of their self-righteousness, and self-righteousness will never accept that which is not of their own making. As stated, that was true then, and it is true now. Self-righteousness, which spawns religion, specializes in control. These people could not control Jesus; therefore, what religion cannot control, it must destroy.

"Which have been since the world began," speaks of the time of Adam in the garden of Eden. It actually refers to Genesis 3:15. There the Lord gave the first promise regarding the coming Redeemer, of which Zacharias spoke.

(71) "THAT WE SHOULD BE SAVED FROM OUR ENEMIES, AND FROM THE HAND OF ALL WHO HATE US."

The direction is:

1. If it is truly of God, there will be enemies.

2. If it is truly of God, there will be hatred expressed toward it, which will mostly come from the world of religion.

SAVED FROM OUR ENEMIES

The phrase, *"That we should be saved from our enemies,"* could very well have been interpreted in a different light at that time. Rome was then the enemy of Israel; however, the Holy Spirit had much more in mind.

Plumptre said this: "What was transitory in the hymn vanished, and the words gained the brighter permanent sense which they have had for centuries in the worship of the church for the Lord Jesus Christ."

The expression as given by Zacharias

actually pertains to the spiritual evil agencies, which wove their ceaseless warfare against the soul of man. It was from these that the coming Deliverer would free His people.

The true *"enemies"* consist of Satan and his evil spirits, which constantly oppose the believer. Only Jesus can save from this power. Regrettably, the modern church, in defiance of this passage plus scores of others, has opted for humanistic psychology to *"save from their enemies."* However, poor, weak, and sinful man cannot even save himself, much less others!

THE SEVEN BENEFITS OF SALVATION

Those benefits are:

1. Deliverance from enemies (I Jn. 5:19).

2. Mercy from God (Eph. 1:4-9; Titus 3:4-5).

3. Justification by faith (Gal. 3:6-15).

4. Peace with God (Rom. 5:1-11; Eph. 2:14-18).

5. Holiness and righteousness (Eph. 4:24; Titus 2:11-12).

6. Reconciliation to God (II Cor. 5:14-21; Col. 1:20).

7. Light and guidance (Jn. 16:7-14; I Jn. 1:7).

The phrase, *"And from the hand of all who hate us,"* refers to those used by Satan to further his evil purpose. Even though it refers to any person, system, or government, more so, it refers to the apostate church. Satan uses this vehicle as he uses nothing else!

SPIRITUAL HINDRANCE

Actually, spiritual hindrance comes in two ways:

1. The world opposes the individual Christian and is actually his greater enemy. It beckons and bids with an alluring siren song. Primarily, this is what Paul was speaking of when he said, *"Wherefore come out from among them, and be you separate, says the Lord, and touch not the unclean thing; and I will receive you."*

He then said, *"And will be a father unto you, and you shall be My sons and daughters, says the Lord Almighty"* (II Cor. 6:17-18).

2. As the greatest enemy to the child of God is the world, the greatest enemy to the work of God is the apostate church.

The apostate church, which is far larger than the true church of Jesus Christ, will use any tactic at its disposal in order to silence truth. This is abundantly evident throughout the Bible and church history.

During the 1980s, possibly the greatest effort to hurt the true work of God was the *"unity of the body at any cost!"* In the 1990s, the apostate church took a different tact. However, I think the following thoughts on the unity of the body at any cost would be appropriate simply because, while this may not be the driving thrust at present, it has always been at least one of Satan's greatest trump cards, so to speak, to hinder the true work of God, and it remains so unto this day.

A STRONG DEMAND FOR UNITY AT ANY COST

Sometime ago, I received a unique distinction. A representative of the National Council of Churches cited me as the individual most responsible for disrupting the ecumenical movement in Louisiana. While he considered this an insult, I truly felt it was an honor.

As stated, despite the fact that Satan is not promoting this *"lie"* quite as stringently as in an earlier time, still, the strident plea for unity among the body of Christ at any cost continues to permeate the entire Pentecostal and Charismatic fellowships.

Are these efforts toward spiritual unity a complement to the Holy Spirit's program, or are they divisive?

I believe it is the compelling desire of the Holy Spirit to see unity within the body. However, I also think there is the preliminary problem of first defining *"the body,"* and then the further question of correction and sound doctrine.

It must be ever understood that unity must be based on truth, or else, there can be no unity.

OUR LORD'S LONGEST PRAYER

John, Chapter 17, supplies a transcription of the longest prayer by Jesus reported verbatim within the Word of God. Of course, He prayed *"all night"* at least once, and possibly much more, but there is no

NOTES

record of the actual words used during these times. Here, the specific prayer is reported, however, for our examination, and the very foundation of this prayer is unity within the body. He specifically mentions unity in five separate statements:

1. *"That they may be one, as We are"* (Jn. 17:11).
2. *"That they all may be one"* (Jn. 17:21).
3. *"That they also may be one in Us"* (Jn. 17:21).
4. *"That they may be one, even as We are One"* (Jn. 17:22).
5. *"I in them, and You in Me, that they may be made perfect in one"* (Jn. 17:23).

So, five times in this one prayer, Jesus mentioned unity within the body.

This unity within the body is at least one of the biggest problems within the church today.

NOW, WE SHOULD INTERJECT THIS THOUGHT:

The body of Christ is not a human organization arranged and supported by worldly powers. It is not sustained and nourished by secular influences.

The true church of the Lord Jesus Christ is the total company of true Christians of all times.

The Lord Jesus Christ (head of the church) said: *"For where two or three are gathered together in My name, there am I in the midst of them"* (Mat. 18:20).

THE STAMP OF THE HOLY SPIRIT

So, obviously there are thousands, perhaps tens of thousands, of churches without any national or international affiliation with an institutional religious denomination. The true church of the Lord Jesus Christ, whatever its affiliation, bears the stamp of the Holy Spirit—supplying His singular influence to produce faith, courage, and confidence in its faithful martyrs over the centuries.

The true church has carried a variety of names over the years. In God's view, it is made up of the sons of God. These sons can claim only one merit, and this is that they have obeyed their hearts. They have rejected the doctrines of men and accepted instead those God has revealed through His body. Even though the true body of Christ is the most powerful force on the face of the earth, yet, most of the time, it is weakened because of splintering within the body. That is at least one of the reasons Jesus said (five times, as recorded in John, Chapter 17) that we must seek unity among the brethren.

So, I think we conclude that this unity within the true body of Christ is of tremendous import.

IS IT POSSIBLE TO CREATE UNITY WITHIN THE BODY OF CHRIST?

One of the main reasons for the effectiveness of the early church was its cohesion. There was only one church. It had one basic belief supporting this foundational principle, and it reaped the rewards Jesus Christ had promised in Acts 1:8.

In its first 100 years—without the aid of the printing press, television, radio, airplane, or any of the communication devices now available—it evangelized most of the known civilized world. Even with the aid of all of our modern technological *"miracles,"* we have (sad to say) fallen far short of the goal of proper world evangelism.

Why?

I believe it is clear that the answer is today's lack of unity within the body of Christ. This is at least one of the most disruptive elements within the myriad organizations that claim to be the true branch springing forth from Christ's roots.

Sad to say, proper unity will not come about until Jesus Christ returns. The schisms seem to be deep; the differences are great. We should certainly endeavor (with certain reservations) to work toward unity in the body. This is important; however, we must also realize that it is never to be *"unity at any cost."* As we've already stated, let us say it again: "Unity must be based on truth, or else, it really isn't unity."

IS UNITY THE MOST IMPORTANT FACTOR IN CHRISTIANITY TODAY?

I would say that it is a most important factor. However, the elements involved in reaching this unity can be even more important. You see, it must be a unity based

on truth, i.e., the Word of God. If it is based on the Word of God, it will be approved by the Holy Spirit.

In light of the statement just made, truth becomes the single most important factor. We want unity, and we should (and will) strive for unity. However, unity, as stated, must be based on truth—and truth is the Word of God (Jn. 17:17). Unity cannot be obtained, at least sanctioned by God, if truth is compromised.

If we do not have unity based upon truth, we have no unity at all. We have an unacceptable compromise instead. We have diluted the Word. We have made a mockery of all for which Jesus died and for which the apostles spilled their own blood.

The bulk of the New Testament is not written to bring about unity; it is written to bring about truth. God in His omniscience knows that when truth is followed, it must bring about unity. So, when we get down to the fundamentals, the issue is not unity—it is truth!

TRUTH

Truth is the touchstone upon which we will sink or swim, live or die. God help us! It is on this issue that we are sinking and dying. Tragically, it seems that even in Pentecostal circles, truth is being sacrificed for unity. No preacher is called to preach unity. He is called to *"preach the Word,"* i.e., truth (II Tim. 4:2).

Unfortunately, the modern church is succumbing to the age-old problem of subjective truth. In other words, what is true for you may not be true for me. This means that truth is subject to anyone's interpretation. As stated, this is the basic problem of mankind.

The Bible proclaims objective truth, which means that truth is the same for all and for all time. In other words, truth, if it really is truth, cannot change because truth does not need to change. Facts may change, or the way one interprets facts may change, but truth never changes. The Bible speaks of truth in three ways:

1. Jesus is the truth (Jn. 14:6).
2. The Word is truth (Jn. 17:17).
3. The Holy Spirit is truth (I Jn. 5:6).

In other words, these mentioned do not merely contain truth, but actually are truth.

So, this means that truth is not a philosophy, which, within itself, is a search for truth, creed, theory, formula, or belief system. More particularly, it is a person, the Lord Jesus Christ, whether in the form of the living Word or written Word!

IS THE GOSPEL OF JESUS CHRIST ALWAYS POSITIVE AND ALWAYS A GOSPEL OF LOVE?

H.S. Ironside, long-time pastor of Moody Memorial Church in Chicago, said that it is impossible to be positive all the time while contending for truth. "To contend for all of God's truth," he continued, "necessitates some negative teaching … Any error, or any truth-and-error mixture calls for a definite exposure and repudiation. To condone such is to be unfaithful to God and His Word, and treacherous to imperiled souls for whom Christ died."

God help us!

I fear today that we don't really know what true love is. Does true love condone error? Does it embrace heresy? Does it approve sin?

No!

But this *"unity gospel"* forbids us to speak out against the evil specifically pointed out in God's Word. If one speaks out against sin, he is indicted for lacking love.

UNITY HEADQUARTERS?

To give an example, I will quote from a message delivered at Unity Headquarters in Lee's Summit, Missouri, by Robert Schuller:

"I talk a great deal to groups that are not positive … Even to what we would call fundamentalists … Who deal constantly with words like sin, salvation, guilt, and that sort of thing. So, when I am dealing with these people … What we have to do is make positive the words that have classically only had negative interpretations."

He also stated in *"Christianity Today"*: "I don't think anything has been done in the name of Christ and under the banner of Christianity that has proven more destructive to human personality, and hence, counterproductive to the evangelism enterprise than the often crude, uncouth, and un-Christian

NOTES

strategy of attempting to make people aware of their lost and sinful condition."

I would ask this question, "How does this we have just stated line up with the Word of God?" I think the answer to that is very obvious.

POSITIVE?

There are, sad to say, some Christian television networks and/or programs where guests are specifically cautioned against speaking negatively concerning Mormonism, Christian Science, Catholicism, etc. Everything must be *"positive."* By extension, anything that is positive they claim is love.

I wonder if these people have ever considered that there cannot be a positive without a negative?

Is it not to be realized that true love must not condone sin, nor does it embrace heresy? True love must also correct. If it doesn't, it isn't true love.

God is love. Still, there is a positive and a negative in all of God's dealings with man. Along with tenderness, gentleness, and compassion, there is also discipline and correction. There is always the potential for mercy, but inevitably, there is the confrontation with justice (Heb. 10:26-31).

Does the preacher fail to demonstrate love when he preaches against sin? Isn't he exhibiting love when he sternly rebukes the sinner?

"All Scripture is given by inspiration of God, and is profitable for doctrine, for reproof, for correction, for instruction in righteousness:

"That the man of God may be perfect, thoroughly furnished unto all good works" (II Tim. 3:16-17).

THE LORD HAD THREE BASIC APPROACHES TO MINISTRY

Jesus approached the public three distinct ways: the sinner, the worldling, and the religious leaders.

To those who were lost in sin (even the worst types of bondage), He had nothing but compassion and love.

"For God sent not His Son into the world to condemn the world; but that the world through Him might be saved" (Jn. 3:17).

However, for the worldling, He had nothing but sarcasm.

"And He said unto them, You go, and tell that fox (Herod), *Behold, I cast out demons, and I do cures today and tomorrow, and the third day I shall be perfected"* (Lk. 13:32).

For the *"religious"* crowd (self-righteous) He had nothing but scathing denunciation.

"Woe unto you, scribes and Pharisees, hypocrites! ... You serpents, you generation of vipers, how can you escape the damnation of hell?" (Mat. 23:29, 33).

While the Lord Jesus Christ was unquestionably positive, He was also negative—as I think we have demonstrated by Scripture.

Who would deny that He was the epitome of love? However, He also corrected.

I must say it again: "True love will not condone sin. It will not accept erroneous doctrine. It will be tender, compassionate, gentle, and long suffering, but at the same time, it will correct."

DIVIDING THE BODY?

The cry today, and possibly for all time, is that nothing must be done that will bring division to the body of Christ. Is this correct? Is divisiveness always bad? If it is, then we immediately have a problem with the Lord's teaching and ministry. He too caused a great deal of *"division."*

"Think not that I am come to send peace on earth: I came not to send peace, but a sword.

"For I am come to set a man at variance against his father, and the daughter against her mother, and the daughter-in-law against her mother-in-law.

"And a man's foes shall be they of his own household" (Mat. 10:34-36).

"Suppose you that I am come to give peace on earth? I tell you, No; but rather division:

"For from henceforth there shall be five in one house divided, three against two, and two against three" (Lk. 12:51-52).

"Therefore said some of the Pharisees, This man is not of God, because He keeps not the Sabbath day. Others said, How can a Man who is a sinner do such miracles? And there was a division among them" (Jn. 9:16).

Christ's teaching rightly divides truth from error, right from wrong.

DIVISION

Since it is impossible to have contradictory claims that are both true, there must be a *"division"* (a disagreement) between conflicting viewpoints. So, how do we know when division is good?

It is quite simple, really.

It is good when truth has been distinguished from error.

We are commanded to admonish and correct. Without admonishment and correction, we might have unity (absence of agreement), but we would be a far cry from what Christ expects for (and demands of) His followers.

"For the time will come when they will not endure sound doctrine; but after their own lusts shall they heap to themselves teachers, having itching ears;

"And they shall turn away their ears from the truth, and shall be turned unto fables" (II Tim. 4:3-4).

Sometime back, and which is indicative of what I say, several hundred ministers met in a particular city in America to discuss what was referred to as *"an exchange of ideas."* Most of the ministers were either Pentecostal or charismatic. Among them were the pastors of some of America's largest churches.

This group consisted primarily of Assemblies of God, a few Churches of God, and quite a number of charismatics. There was also a small number of Catholic charismatics present.

THE UNITY OF THE BODY?

I had the occasion to listen to some of the audio tapes of part of this meeting, with most of the discussion centering on *"the unity of the body."*

What I heard was shocking, to say the least, and totally contrary to the Word of God.

To be frank, and understanding that this meeting included a cross section of pastors, one would have to come to the conclusion that the Pentecostal message had been so compromised that it had reached the place that *"anything goes."* The bulk of the meeting (at least the part I heard) seemed to be devoted to appeasing the few Catholics present. Discussion was held at length as to how Communion could be taken with both the Catholics and the Protestants participating. (I think one must come to the conclusion presently that the word *Protestant* is somewhat ill-advised. There simply isn't much *"protesting"* anymore!)

We must never mind that the Catholic Church believes in the doctrine of transubstantiation, which claims that the bread actually turns into the body of the Lord Jesus Christ and the wine literally into His blood—and the claim that under Catholic doctrine, Jesus is sacrificed anew each time Catholics participate in the Mass.

CATHOLICISM

The Roman Catholic Church teaches that its *"Holy Mass"* is an expatiatory (sin-removing) sacrifice in which the Son of God is actually re-sacrificed on the Cross. According to their doctrine, Jesus literally descends into the priest's hands during the act of transubstantiation, wherein the elements of *"the host"* (the wafer) are physically transformed into the body, blood, soul, and divinity of Christ. This was defined as such by the Council of Trent—although inconsequential alterations were made in wording during the Second Vatican Council.

Further, the Catholic Church teaches that this repeated sacrifice of Christ can be specifically applied to the benefit of deceased souls. This is arranged by the living, who, by *"Mass cards,"* subsidize the *"expense"* of the Masses said for the deceased for this purpose.

CANON ONE

Canon One on *"the most Holy Sacrament of the Eucharist,"* reads:

"If anyone deny it, that in the Sacrament of the most Holy Eucharist are contained truly, really, and substantially, the body and blood, together with the soul and divinity of our Lord Jesus Christ, and consequently, the whole Christ, but says that He is only therein as in a sign, or in a figure, or virtue, let him be anathema."

In other words, any person who fails to accept the Catholic doctrine of transubstantiation is eternally lost. In the Roman Catholic minds, the Mass is a sacrament, which implies a sacrifice. This belief lies at the very heart of Catholicism.

Paul said:

"Wherefore whosoever shall eat this bread, and drink this cup of the Lord, unworthily, shall be guilty of the body and blood of the Lord.

"But let a man examine himself, and so let him eat of that bread, and drink of that cup.

"For he who eats and drinks unworthily, eats and drinks damnation to himself, not discerning the Lord's body" (I Cor. 11:27-29).

John said:

"Whosoever transgresses, and abides not in the doctrine of Christ, has not God. He who abides in the doctrine of Christ, he has both the Father and the Son.

"If there come any unto you, and bring not this doctrine, receive him not into your house, neither bid him God speed:

"For he who bids him God speed is partaker of his evil deeds" (II Jn., Vss. 9-11).

PURGATORY, CONFESSION TO THE PRIEST, PRAYING TO SAINTS?

Yes, some Catholics have truly been saved and truly baptized with the Holy Spirit. However, when we tell these Catholic Charismatics that it is perfectly proper for them to remain under false doctrine (grossly false), we not only do them a terrible disservice, we may well be working toward damning their souls to hell. That's a blunt statement, but it happens to be true.

We should love the Catholics, and all others for that matter, who are in false doctrine. We should pray for them. We should treat them with kindness and compassion, but we should also preach the truth to them. If we do not reveal the truth to them, how will they ever know the depths of their error?

The false doctrine now dominating the Pentecostal and Charismatic movements insists that nothing must cause dissension. *"Let the Holy Spirit take care of the problems!"* they say.

However, how does the Holy Spirit take care of these problems? He can do so only through honest preaching and teaching of the Word of God. What does Scripture say?

THE WORD OF GOD

"How then shall they call on Him in whom they have not believed? and how shall they believe in Him of whom they have not heard? and how shall they hear without a preacher?

"And how shall they preach, except they be sent? as it is written, How beautiful are the feet of them who preach the gospel of peace, and bring glad tidings of good things!

"So then faith comes by hearing, and hearing by the Word of God" (Rom. 10:14-15, 17).

The Holy Spirit can act only through the infallible Word of God. He can only function through truth. He expects the man of God to deliver the truth. He expects him to deliver it with compassion, love, and understanding, but, at the same time, he must deliver it!

According to the meeting I have mentioned and of which there have been many, they were, without exception, telling the Catholic charismatics, "Your doctrine is satisfactory; we can accept it."

Actually, the only condemnation was for those who dare to speak out against the compendium of errors that make up the foundation of the Catholic faith.

ACTUALLY, THERE
WAS SOME OPPOSITION

Among the hundreds at this particular meeting, I am sure some were in opposition to the ideas presented. However, they were either forbidden to speak or were afraid to stand up and voice their reservations.

Actually, one gentleman did stand and voice his reservation. He was evidently a Catholic priest, and he said, "Gentlemen, I am sorry that we cannot participate in any type of joint Communion service. The 'discipline' of our church does not allow it."

I thought it was somewhat ironic that the only voice of objection was from the Catholics themselves and not the Protestants.

The simple fact is, Catholicism is a

NOTES

mixture of Christianity and paganism. It has led untold millions down the path to hell, and millions more are on the way. As I have repeatedly mentioned, I thank God for the Catholics who have come to God and have been born again, and many have.

I thank God for those who have been baptized with the Holy Spirit. However, I maintain that the Spirit of God always adheres to truth and sound doctrine—which is the Word of God. If Catholic Charismatics do not forsake their pagan doctrines, they are destined for spiritual delusion and eventual loss of the tremendous spiritual gift they have received.

Yes, while there are Catholics who have genuinely been saved, they must come out of that false doctrine, that is, if they are to maintain their place in Christ.

And then, the question begs to be asked, *"Are we demonstrating love if we shelter them from the truth?"*

AM I BECOME YOUR
ENEMY BECAUSE
I TELL YOU THE TRUTH

As I listened to the tape sent to me concerning this meeting, I heard reference after reference to the Vatican—what the Vatican wanted and what the Vatican didn't want—and this from Pentecostal and Charismatic preachers.

The statement was emphatically made that, "The Vatican has moved much closer to our position."

Brethren, the Vatican has not moved at all. It is we who have moved closer to their position.

No, I am not *"picking on Catholics."* I would say the same things to the Protestant brethren. When false doctrine of any stripe is transplanted into the kingdom, it must be stripped of its camouflage.

However, there is something that should be addressed concerning this:

We may disagree on the nonessentials (such as sanctification, the pre-tribulation rapture, evidence of the infilling of the Holy Spirit, and a host of other matters), but we must never disagree on the essentials. By this I mean the universal, biblical basis for salvation.

Basically, even though most Pentecostal denominations disagree on the peripheral interpretations of Scripture, there is almost universal acceptance, at least among those who claim to believe the Bible, of the fact of salvation, which is faith and trust alone in the atoning sacrifice of Christ at Calvary. On the other hand, within Catholicism, the basis of salvation is not faith, but works. There is no way these can be reconciled.

SPEAKING IN TONGUES

We believe that speaking in tongues is the initial, physical evidence that one has been baptized with the Holy Spirit (Acts 2:4). We might also say that we do not believe a person has been baptized with the Holy Spirit unless that person speaks with other tongues.

As stated, it is the initial, physical evidence that one has received, and that is according to the Word of God.

However, the fact that God has baptized an individual with the Holy Spirit in no way implies that this individual has suddenly become a repository of infinite knowledge in that he is no longer capable of error. It simply means that this individual has been saved by the blood of Jesus and has evidenced faith to receive the infilling of the Holy Spirit.

As should be obvious, the Corinthian church had some problems. The apostle Paul wrote two books (I and II Corinthians) correcting the errors within this church. Yet, they had been baptized with the Holy Spirit with the evidence of speaking with other tongues.

The mere fact that they had been baptized with the Spirit, however, in no way led Paul to approve their erroneous doctrines or situations.

He strongly admonished them:

"Now I beseech you, brethren, by the name of the Lord Jesus Christ, that you all speak the same thing, and that there be no divisions among you; but that you be perfectly joined together in the same mind and in the same judgment" (I Cor. 1:10).

So, a few Catholics receiving the Holy Spirit in no way means their erroneous doctrines are approved by the Lord.

NOTES

WE MUST PREACH TRUTH

Paul did not hesitate to preach the truth. He had no alternative. Yet, to gain the *"acceptance"* of the Catholic hierarchy, it is claimed that we must abandon every standard and mute our voices.

I will say it again:

We should love them, we should pray for them, and we should treat them with all kindness and consideration, but we must tell them the truth! This is the same regarding all false doctrine of whatever stripe!

In good conscience, I cannot sit on a board or committee in company with Catholics who are still praying to Mary, who are still confessing to priests, and who are still attending Mass, thinking it delivers salvation to them. Even though they may speak in tongues and talk about some form of world evangelism, God cannot bless activities based on such false premises. In all honesty, there will be no world evangelization if it is to be delivered on a scaffolding doctrine.

God cannot bless error. He cannot bless teaching that is contrary to His Word, especially when they oppose the most basic of Christian tenets.

How can we join hands with those who believe in baptizing infants, thinking this act is responsible for their salvation? Brethren, these doctrines are of the devil. For there to be any type of Holy Spirit unity based on the Word of God, these evil, erroneous, wicked doctrines—born in hell for the express purpose of the loss of souls—must be abandoned and denounced.

TRUTH AT ANY COST

Yes, we may have disagreements in regard to peripheral doctrines. That is different. However, we must hold the line when it comes to the basic truth of salvation. If we don't, there could never be any ground for agreement.

What does this type of compromise do?

It tries to build unity from difference and harmony from discord, which is trying to mix darkness with light. It simply won't work.

I do have some knowledge in this area. Our television programming (24 hours a day, seven days a week) is aired in many countries of the world that are predominantly Catholic. I believe I can state without fear of contradiction that we have seen more Catholics brought to the Lord Jesus Christ than most any other ministry in the world. I think this number could well be into the tens or even hundreds of thousands.

How do we do this?

We do not do it by compromising the Word of God. We do it by loving these people and by being kind and compassionate toward them, but at the same time (and in no uncertain terms), we do our best to tell them the truth.

What kind of doctor would place a Band-Aid over a cancer? What kind of engineer would accept an improper mix of concrete for the bridge he was building? What kind of preacher would hide the gospel of Jesus Christ from those who walk in darkness?

Do we want unity of the body? Yes, but we do not want unity at any cost. However, we do want truth at any cost. Unfortunately, the two may well be mutually incompatible. *"Can two walk together, except they be agreed?"* (Amos 3:3).

(72) "TO PERFORM THE MERCY PROMISED TO OUR FATHERS, AND TO REMEMBER HIS HOLY COVENANT."

The pattern is:

1. Letting someone believe a lie without warning him, that is, if we truly know the way, is not mercy.

2. The holy covenant is the Word of God and must not be altered.

MERCY

The phrase, *"To perform the mercy promised to our fathers,"* proclaims Jesus as the bearer of that mercy. Actually, He is mercy! Tragically, Israel would not accept His mercy, and mercy rejected is wrath extended. That was true for Israel, and it is true even for the individual.

"And to remember His holy covenant," pertains to that promise to Abraham (Gen. 17:19). God calls it *"holy"* because any covenant He makes is holy!

(73) "THE OATH WHICH HE SWORE TO OUR FATHER ABRAHAM."

The overview is:

1. This oath is found in Genesis 12:3; 17:4; 22:16-17.

2. It was made or tendered toward Abraham.

3. One might say that Abraham is the father of all the faithful.

ABRAHAM

Abraham was named because, in effect, he was chosen by God to be the father of the Jewish people. These people had a special mission, and it was to a part of that mission that Zacharias spoke—the bringing of the Messiah into the world. That is the reason that Matthew began his book with the words, *"The book of the generation of Jesus Christ, the Son of David, the Son of Abraham"* (Mat. 1:1).

(74) "THAT HE WOULD GRANT UNTO US, THAT WE BEING DELIVERED OUT OF THE HAND OF OUR ENEMIES MIGHT SERVE HIM WITHOUT FEAR."

The diagram is:

1. When Zacharias delivered the word of our being delivered out of the hands of our enemies, he, no doubt, had only Israel in mind. However, the Holy Spirit included every single believer who has ever lived.

2. The idea is that we have the freedom to serve God without fear from authorities.

3. It is slowly, and sometimes not so slowly, coming to the place in America to where this great freedom is being lost.

DELIVERED OUT OF THE HAND OF OUR ENEMIES

The phrase, *"That He would grant unto us, that we being delivered out of the hand of our enemies,"* had a much wider distribution than Zacharias at that time could have understood.

Zacharias would probably have seen little further than Israel. However, the pronoun *"we"* speaks not only of Israel but its prophetic future, which is even yet to come, but, as well, every single believer who has ever lived. At that time, Zacharias could have little seen the church; however, the promise given here literally includes the church.

These *"enemies"* include the world, the flesh, and the Devil even though Zacharias may well have had something else in mind.

WITHOUT FEAR

The phrase, *"Might serve Him without fear,"* has a twofold meaning:

1. To *"serve without fear"* is one of the characteristics of salvation. Paul said, *"God has not given us the spirit of fear; but of power, and of love, and of a sound mind"* (II Tim. 1:7).

2. It speaks, as well, of the coming kingdom age when Israel will truly be restored to her rightful position in the world because of her sincere and true repentance, which will take place at the second coming. She will then accept this One born of Mary as her Saviour and Messiah. During this 1,000-year reign with Christ, every enemy will be put down, with the last enemy being defeated—death itself (I Cor. 15:26).

Zechariah's prophecy has to do with the statement of Paul, *"For He must reign, till He has put all enemies under His feet"* (I Cor. 15:25). This will be done in the coming kingdom age.

At that time, Satan will be locked in the bottomless pit, along with all of his minions of darkness (Rev. 20:1-3). Jesus Christ will be the Premier, not only of Israel, but also of the entirety of the world! He will be King of Kings and Lord of Lords. In every corner of the globe, men can then *"serve Him without fear."*

(75) "IN HOLINESS AND RIGHTEOUSNESS BEFORE HIM, ALL THE DAYS OF OUR LIFE."

The overview is:

1. The Lord alone can be described as *"holy."*

2. Our holiness as believers is that which is totally derived from Christ. We gain such by evidencing faith in Christ and what He did for us at the Cross.

3. Righteousness is simply that which is right. However, the definition is that which belongs to God and not man.

4. This will be brought about and cover the entirety of the world during the coming kingdom age *"all the days of our life,"* and our lives will then be forever.

HOLINESS AND RIGHTEOUSNESS

The phrase, *"In holiness and righteousness before Him,"* is meant to characterize

the character and nature of the believer. Although continuing in the realm of grace, in effect, the coming kingdom age will, as well, be the dispensation of holiness and righteousness. It is *"before Him"* now in spirit but will then be literally.

"All the days of our life," speaks of the Christian walk and what it is to be before the Lord, which is all made possible by the Cross.

In the coming kingdom age, life will not end except for rebels who refuse to obey the Lord.

As a result of the resurrection, all saints up to that time will have glorified bodies and, consequently, cannot die. As well, those who live on the earth in natural bodies will remain alive and healthy forever by partaking of the fruit that grows on the trees beside the river coming from the throne of God (Ezek. 47:12; Rev. 22:1-2). This will include many, plus children who will continue to be born.

(76) "AND YOU, CHILD, SHALL BE CALLED THE PROPHET OF THE HIGHEST: FOR YOU SHALL GO BEFORE THE FACE OF THE LORD TO PREPARE HIS WAYS."

The synopsis is:

1. The *"child"* here addressed is the yet unborn John the Baptist.

2. He would be *"called the prophet of the Highest"* because he would be the one to introduce Christ to the world.

3. John would serve as the forerunner in order to *"prepare His ways,"* which he definitely did.

TO PREPARE HIS WAYS

The phrase, *"And you, child, shall be called the prophet of the Highest,"* refers, as stated, to John the Baptist.

"For you shall go before the face of the Lord to prepare His ways," means that John the Baptist would be the mighty forerunner of the King about whom the prophets had written! That is the reason that John was called *"the greatest"* (Mat. 11:11).

Actually, the message that John would deliver to Israel in order to *"prepare His ways"* was the message of repentance. Before Jesus could make His debut, this message had to be preached. John preached it forthrightly without fear or favor, even to such an extent that it ultimately cost him his life, but not until he had finished his mission.

(77) "TO GIVE KNOWLEDGE OF SALVATION UNTO HIS PEOPLE BY THE REMISSION OF THEIR SINS."

The exegesis is:

1. The *"true knowledge of salvation"* would be delivered by John the Baptist to the people of Israel.

2. John, in essence, was constantly giving altar calls, so to speak.

3. In effect, he told them how to have their sins remitted, which was trust in the Lord.

KNOWLEDGE OF SALVATION

The phrase, *"To give knowledge of salvation unto His people,"* means that Israel was mistaken altogether in its conception of the salvation that they really needed.

Godet asked this question and gave this answer: "Why," he asked, "was the ministry of the Messiah preceded by that of another divine messenger? Because the very notion of salvation had been falsified in Israel, and had to be corrected before true salvation could be realized.

"A carnal and malignant patriotism had taken possession of the people and their rulers, and the idea of a political difference had been substituted for that of moral salvation.

"There was need then of another person, divinely authorized, to remind the people that perdition consisted not in subjection to the Romans, but in divine condemnation; and that salvation therefore was not tempered emancipation from Rome, but rather forgiveness of sins."

THE REMISSION OF SINS

The phrase, *"By the remission of their sins,"* constituted Israel's real need and, in fact, the need of the entirety of the human family for whom Jesus died.

Man thinks his problems lay elsewhere— a lack of education, improper environment, or economic disability. Of course, these things are problems; however, they are problems or symptoms caused by the real problem of sin. Only Jesus can deliver from sin.

Jesus was Jehovah and His descent to

NOTES

earth was not mainly to establish a perfect government but to deal with sins and their remission.

Jesus was truly a human being. He was physically born of a woman after the normal period of gestation. However, the child (Jesus) was not the seed of a man but of a woman mysteriously energized by the Holy Spirit (Gen. 3:15).

The Holy Spirit's great revelation in this third gospel is that a child should be conceived and born. Mary could not understand this, but she did not doubt it, although outside the order of nature.

Mary was willing to be the mother of the Great King, but not so much, it seems, the disciple of the despised Nazarene. The sword pierced her heart and revealed and judged its carnal thoughts. She shared these in common with Israel (Lk. 2:34-35). Yet, she looked upon Him whom she, as well as all of us, pierced (Jn. 19:25), and believed, and then joined the disciples (Acts 1:14).

In this, she personates the nation of Israel. It was the Lord's mother (Rev., Chpt. 12); it will look upon Him as the crucified One and believe (Rev. 1:7).

(78) "THROUGH THE TENDER MERCY OF OUR GOD; WHEREBY THE DAYSPRING FROM ON HIGH HAS VISITED US."

The exegesis is:

1. Our Lord coming to this world was because of the *"tender mercy of our God."*

2. *"The Dayspring"* is the Lord Jesus Christ.

3. While Jesus was most definitely human, He, as well, was most definitely God. As such, He came from heaven in order to redeem mankind, which necessitated the Cross.

THE DAYSPRING

The phrase, *"Through the tender mercy of our God,"* reveals that the sending of Jesus Christ, God's only Son, was strictly an act of mercy, and *"tender mercy"* at that, and not because of any merit on the part of mankind.

"Whereby the Dayspring from on high has visited us," concerns God becoming man, i.e., the incarnation.

The thought of picturing the advent of

the Messiah as a sunrise was a favorite one with the prophets of old.

The temple, whether Solomon's or Herod's, faced the east. When the sun rose, bursting above Olivet, its full force struck the temple, causing its pillars, which sat in front of the temple, to shine with a brilliance that defies description. It is this image in mind that Zacharias and the prophets had, but above all, that the Holy Spirit typifies. It is the symbol of darkness suddenly being turned to light, with Jesus being called *"the Dayspring,"* i.e., the springing up of day, dispelling the darkness! Only Jesus could do that.

(79) "TO GIVE LIGHT TO THEM WHO SIT IN DARKNESS AND IN THE SHADOW OF DEATH, TO GUIDE OUR FEET INTO THE WAY OF PEACE."

The structure is:

1. In Jesus alone there is light.

2. That light did shine in order to bring men out of darkness.

3. That darkness included *"the shadow of death,"* which always follows sin in some fashion.

4. Giving the light, He could then *"guide our feet into the way of peace."*

LIGHT

The phrase, *"To give light to them who sit in darkness,"* concerned not only Israel but the entirety of the world.

The *"darkness"* spoken of here concerns the absence of God from whom springs all light, hence, all true intelligence. This means that Mormonism, Islam, Buddhism, humanism, Shintoism, Confucianism, plus every other philosophy of man can only be concluded as darkness.

Only the Bible is light, which personifies Christ. Consequently, He said, *"I am the light of the world: he who follows Me shall not walk in darkness, but shall have the light of life"* (Jn. 8:12).

THE SHADOW OF DEATH

The phrase, *"And the shadow of death,"* is the fulfillment of Isaiah's prophecy, *"They who dwell in the land of the shadow of death, upon them has the light shined"* (Isa. 9:2).

The darkness spoken of here not only speaks of an absence of light but, as well, speaks of destruction because this darkness is spiritual death.

The phrase, *"To guide our feet into the way of peace,"* speaks of Jesus Christ being the only *"door"* to the Father (Jn. 10:7; 14:6).

WESTERN CIVILIZATION

Sometime ago, one of the Bass brothers of Texas, a billionaire, gave Yale University several millions of dollars to establish a chair respecting the study of western civilization. At the end of a period of time, Yale gave the money back, saying, "We do not know how to approach this subject," or words to that effect!

The reason they did not know or understand is because they were looking at it backwards. Bible Christianity established what is referred to as *"western civilization."* That does not mean the gospel of Jesus Christ is a western gospel for, in fact, it is for the entirety of the world.

It simply means that the West accepted the gospel more readily than those in the East, most of whom accepted the Eastern religions.

What is known as *"western civilization,"* by and large, began with the apostle Paul. On a particular missionary journey, the Scripture says, *"They assayed to go into Bithynia: but the Spirit suffered them not"* (Acts 16:7). Bithynia is in the northeastern part of modern Turkey, actually, Asia Minor.

During this time, Paul had a vision of a man, *"Saying, Come over into Macedonia, and help us"* (Acts 16:9). Macedonia is in Greece and to the west—the opposite direction from Bithynia. Several churches were ultimately established in this area—Corinth, Thessalonica, and Philippi, to name a few. It is said that the gospel ultimately went from there to Spain and then to Western Europe and to England. From England, it came to America. Actually, this nation was formed for the express purpose of being able to worship God in freedom.

Because of the gospel of Jesus Christ, western civilization came into being, which has provided America and other nations a standard of living and freedom that is the envy of the world.

Concerning any nation in the world, it probably can be said, "Much Bible, much prosperity and freedom; little Bible, little prosperity and freedom; no Bible, no prosperity and freedom."

THE SPREAD OF THE LIGHT

Consequently, the *"light"* spoken of here concerns not only spiritual light but, as well, economic and scientific light. If one is to notice, almost every invention known to mankind has come out of America or England—the two nations that have embraced this light to the greatest extent. (Canada could be included with America.) If the second coming of the Lord is delayed (which it will not be), and the spiritual decline in America continues, soon the economic and scientific decline will follow, which it already is, with this nation ultimately being destroyed. In fact, because of spiritual deterioration, England is already far along that path. Everything is tied to the *"light,"* i.e., the Lord Jesus Christ.

Regarding the great universities of the land, this means that the only depository of true wisdom in the world is found in the few copies of the Bible situated on the shelves of their libraries. It alone tells people how to live. Its standards are immutable whereas the standards of philosophers change almost by the day.

The idea is that man can be an excellent engineer, doctor, lawyer, chemist, scientist, etc., but if he does not know how to live, he has accomplished little! The Bible points to Jesus Christ, and He alone tells one how to live (II Pet. 1:3-4). Only the Bible presenting Jesus Christ and what He did for us at the Cross of Calvary can *"guide our feet into the way of peace."*

(80) "AND THE CHILD GREW, AND WAXED STRONG IN SPIRIT, AND WAS IN THE DESERTS TILL THE DAY OF HIS SHOWING UNTO ISRAEL."

The exegesis is:

1. John the Baptist was raised by his parents in an atmosphere of godliness.

2. As a result, he *"grew, and waxed strong in Spirit."*

NOTES

3. Upon becoming a young man, he spent his time in the deserts, *"till the day of his showing unto Israel."*

4. As stated, his was the first prophetic voice in some 400 years in Israel.

STRONG IN SPIRIT

The phrase, *"And the child grew,"* speaks of John the Baptist and his growing to manhood. Zacharias and Elisabeth, being up in years when the child was born, probably did not live very long after his birth. However, as long as they did live, it is certain that, as best as they could, they instilled in him the strange account of his birth and the exact words related to them by the angel Gabriel. Consequently, he *"grew"* by this principle.

"And waxed strong in Spirit," talks about the Spirit of the Lord.

Considering his excellent knowledge of the Word of God, these formative years were, no doubt, spent with the scrolls of the prophets, along with the wisdom books of psalms, etc.

HIS PREPARATION

The phrase, *"And was in the deserts till the day of his showing unto Israel,"* gives us almost nothing of his life. He remained there until he was 30 years of age before beginning his ministry because that was the fulfilling of the law (Num. 4:3).

Actually, what the Holy Spirit said of him was said, at least in part, of Jesus also (Lk. 2:40).

We are given very little information as to exactly how he was presented to Israel, or at least the beginning of his ministry. Luke simply wrote, *"The word of God came unto John the son of Zacharias in the wilderness"* (Lk. 3:2). This simply meant that the Lord told him it was time to make His ministry debut. As stated, he would have been 30 years of age.

The wilderness spoken of would have been the wilderness of Judaea. Some claim that his wilderness period was spent in association with the Qumran community or a similar Essene group; however, such must be treated with caution because there is little proof of that.

Knowing the errors that permeated almost all of Jewish religious life at that time, it is doubtful that he associated himself with any group of this nature. Inasmuch as his mission was designed totally by the Lord, his training would have been in the same capacity.

I personally feel he was alone much of this time, and the Spirit of God trained him and molded him for the greatest task known to humanity—the privilege of introducing the Son of God (Jn. 1:29). Actually, his ministry did not last very long, possibly about a year or a little longer. However, he accomplished his task.

"I must needs go home by the way of
　the Cross,
"There's no other way but this;
"I shall never get sight of the gates of
　light,
"If the way of the Cross I miss."

"I must needs go on in the blood-
　sprinkled way,
"The path that the Saviour trod,
"If I ever climb to the heights sublime,
"Where the soul is at home with God."

"Then I bid farewell in the way of the
　world,
"To walk in it nevermore;
"For the Lord says, 'Come,' and I seek
　my home,
"Where He waits at the open door."

CHAPTER 2

(1) "AND IT CAME TO PASS IN THOSE DAYS, THAT THERE WENT OUT A DECREE FROM CAESAR AUGUSTUS THAT ALL THE WORLD SHOULD BE TAXED."

They synopsis is:

1. In this chapter we will see the hand of God at work in a most obvious way.

2. As it had been from the very beginning, all of this was for the purpose of bringing the Son of God, the Redeemer of mankind, into the world.

3. All of this would culminate in a Cross, even as it was intended to be from the foundation of the world (I Pet. 1:18-20).

IT CAME TO PASS

The phrase, "And it came to pass," is a term used by Luke more so than any other writer in the Bible. It is used some 55 times in the books of Luke and Acts. It is used a number of times in the Old Testament but only 10 times elsewhere in the New Testament.

In the reckoning of time, the words, "In those days," would refer to A.D. 1 (In Latin A. stands for "Anno," meaning "year," with D. standing for "Domini," meaning "first."). So, all time is measured in respect to Christ. (B.C. stands for "Before Christ.")

The phrase, "That there went out a decree from Caesar Augustus," referred to Caius Octavius, the adopted son and successor of Julius Caesar. He reigned from 29 B.C. to A.D. 14, a time frame of some 43 years.

The title "Caesar" was the actual name of an aristocratic family that established ascendancy over the Roman Republic and with the triumph of Augustus (31 B.C.), kept it until Nero's death in A.D. 68. Its manner of government proved to be such a success that even with the elimination of the Caesarean family, their position was institutionalized and their name assumed by its incumbents.

One of the foundations of Caesar's power was his extended control of each province, embracing most of Rome's frontier forces. This would have included all of Israel, which came under the domain of Syria, as the next verse proclaims.

TAXES

The phrase, "That all the world should be taxed," is a figure of speech. The Greek word is *synecdoche*, which means, "A whole is put for a part," as in Genesis 6:17; II Samuel 6:5, 15; I Kings 11:16-17; Daniel 2:37-38, etc. Actually, it constituted only the part of the world of which it spoke or addressed.

One tradition says that Augustus had a quarrel with Herod, who was then king in Israel. The Roman Senate, advised by Anthony and Octavian, gave Herod the title "king of the Jews." It took him three years of fighting to make his title effective, but when he had done so, he governed Judaea for

33 years as a loyal friend and ally of Rome.

To punish Herod, this tax was imposed. However, the Holy Spirit would use this quarrel to fulfill the prophecy, which was given by Micah some 700 years before, that Jesus would be born in Beth-lehem (Mic. 5:2). This tax would demand that each person in Israel go back to the city of his ancestry, which, in the case of Joseph and Mary, was Beth-lehem.

History tells us that Herod the Great died in 4 B.C. This was the same Herod who murdered the babies two years old and under, according to Matthew, Chapter 2. With that being the case, the correct date of Herod's death should have been A.D. 1 or 2. Some think that Jesus may have been as much as two years old when this was done. There is really no discrepancy with the Bible because it does not give a date. However, to adjust the date given of Herod's death with the knowledge that Jesus was already born when this happened, it would mean either that the date of his death is wrong, or our present calendar is somewhat wrong.

There are some who claim that our calendar, which is referred to as the Gregorian calendar and was put together by Gregorian monks in the Middle Ages, is incorrect by several years. In fact, this argument has raged for quite some time. If, in fact, that is correct, this present year (as I dictate these notes) should be 2017 instead of 2013.

(2) "(AND THIS TAXING WAS FIRST MADE WHEN CYRENIUS WAS GOVERNOR OF SYRIA.)"

The synopsis is:

1. This Scripture has been the occasion of much controversy. However, perhaps our explanation will throw light on the subject.

2. Sometimes translations leave some things to be desired, and, of course, the entirety of the Bible has been translated from Hebrew and Greek into English.

3. However, this one thing is certain: when you hold the King James Bible in your hands, you can be certain that you are holding the pure, unadulterated Word of God.

CONTROVERSY

Controversy has raged over this Scripture because critics claim that "Cyrenius" (or

NOTES

called by some, "Quirinius") was not made governor of Syria until 10 or 12 years after the birth of Christ.

It is known that he was the Roman Consul in 12 B.C. and thus qualified to be a governor. From 12 B.C. to 4 B.C., the names of governors are recorded; however, from 4 B.C. to A.D. 4, a time frame of some eight years, the names are not given. It was during this time that the census took place, and who can disprove the inspired statement here that Cyrenius was governor during this time?

As well, the word first in this Scripture in the Greek text is protos and means "first, or before."

So, the verse could have been translated, "This census was before Cyrenius was governor of Syria," or, "Before the one made by Cyrenius."

Also, on the question of this alleged historical inaccuracy of Luke, it should be observed that none of the early opponents of Christianity, such as Celsus or Porphyry, impugn the accuracy of this account.

Spence says, "Surely, if there had been so marked an error on the threshold of this gospel, these adversaries of the faith, living comparatively soon after the events in question, would have been the first to call to attention this alleged error." I might quickly add that they did not do it simply because it was not error.

LUKE

As well, Luke, a man of obvious education and writing skills, would not have been so specific regarding this historical statement, especially considering that it could have been so easily disproved. It was never questioned until recent years because there was no reason to question it. Luke's statement was and is absolutely correct.

Regarding Cyrenius, he is mentioned by the historians Tacitus and Suetonius. He appears to have been originally of humble birth and, like so many of the soldiers of fortune of the empire, rose through his own merits to his great position. It is said that he was a gallant and true soldier but self-seeking and harsh with all.

For his Sicilian victories, the Roman

Senate decreed him a triumph. As well, when he died, he received the distinguished honor of a public funeral. That was in A.D. 21.

(3) "AND ALL WENT TO BE TAXED, EVERY ONE INTO HIS OWN CITY."

The pattern is:

1. As stated, this *"tax"* was a special tax and census levied on top of all the regular taxes, etc.

2. To ensure that all paid, one had to go back to the city of his ancestry, which, in the case of Mary and Joseph, was Beth-lehem.

3. The next verse tells us why.

(4) "AND JOSEPH ALSO WENT UP FROM GALILEE, OUT OF THE CITY OF NAZARETH, INTO JUDAEA, UNTO THE CITY OF DAVID, WHICH IS CALLED BETH-LEHEM; (BECAUSE HE WAS OF THE HOUSE AND LINEAGE OF DAVID.)"

The form is:

1. Joseph traced his lineage to David through Solomon.

2. Mary traced hers through Nathan, another son of David.

3. However, Solomon was in the kingly line, which, in essence, stated that had the Davidic throne continued, Joseph would now be king of Judah.

BETH-LEHEM

To pay this tax, Mary and Joseph were forced to go to Beth-lehem, called *"the City of David,"* because this was the birthplace of that famous king. From Nazareth, it was pretty close to 80 miles.

As we have stated, Joseph traced his lineage to David through Solomon, with Mary tracing hers through Nathan, another son of David. Solomon was in the kingly line and had the Davidic throne continued, Joseph would now be king of Judah. However, the old kingdom of David had been dismembered, conquered, and devastated. Because of sin on the part of succeeding kings after David, the throne was no more. It was at this moment in the power of Augustus Caesar because Israel had refused to walk in the law of the Lord. In fact, it had been in the power of the Gentiles since Nebuchadnezzar some 600 years before. So, the one who should have been the king of Judah was but a simple village carpenter.

Beth-lehem, to which they had to go to pay the tax, was a tiny village, probably only a few hundred in population, if that, and was actually called *"Beth-lehem Ephrathah,"* to distinguish it from another small village of the same name in another part of Israel.

THE PROPHET MICAH

Micah had prophesied about 700 years earlier, *"Though you be little among the thousands of Judah, yet out of you shall He come forth unto Me who is to be the ruler in Israel; whose goings forth have been from of old, from everlasting"* (Mic. 5:2).

How familiar Mary and Joseph were with this prophecy is not known. However, it is almost certain that both (especially Mary) at this time would have been very familiar with this prediction. If, in fact, that is the case, I wonder if Mary and Joseph ever discussed how this could be brought to pass—their being in Beth-lehem at the exact time of the birth of Jesus. In those days, especially for the poor, travel was very difficult. For a woman nine months pregnant, it was all but impossible!

CAESAR AND HEROD

However, little did they realize that several months past, a political situation was evolving, which would include Caesar and Herod. This situation would involve a tax and a census that demanded each family go back to its ancestral home. As well as the entire domain of Herod, it would involve Joseph and Mary and would fall at the exact time that Jesus would be born.

With Micah giving this prophecy some 700 years before, did this mean that God brought these things to pass by manipulating the wills of the individuals, whomever they may have been?

No! The Lord simply looked down through time and saw that these events would take place and through this foreknowledge, He gave the prediction through the prophet.

And yet, at the same time, if He so desires, God is, in fact, able to manipulate events wherever desired, which He does at times, without violating the free moral agency of man.

NOTES

(5) "TO BE TAXED WITH MARY HIS ESPOUSED WIFE, BEING GREAT WITH CHILD."

GREAT WITH CHILD

The phrase, *"To be taxed with Mary his espoused wife,"* means he had married Mary by now, possibly not long after the dream given him by the Lord (Mat. 1:18-21). By now, they probably had been married almost nine months.

The phrase, *"Being great with child,"* means that she was about to be delivered.

The journey must have been extremely difficult for her, with her either walking or, at most, riding a donkey. As is obvious, either way would have been extremely strenuous. As stated, it was a journey of approximately 80 miles.

One certainly cannot say that Joseph and Mary were shown any favoritism by the Lord even though they both were chosen by God for a unique task, and especially Mary. It would make possible the single most important event in human history—the death and resurrection of Jesus Christ, who would redeem fallen humanity. This so obviously flies in the face of modern teaching, which claims that if one has the proper confession, one can escape all the difficulties and vicissitudes of life. This example makes such false teaching seem insignificant by comparison.

(6) "AND SO IT WAS, THAT, WHILE THEY WERE THERE, THE DAYS WERE ACCOMPLISHED THAT SHE SHOULD BE DELIVERED."

THE DAYS WERE ACCOMPLISHED

The phrase, *"And so it was, that, while they were there,"* probably was in October as we have previously discussed, but almost certainly not in December.

The following verses tell us why:

"The days were accomplished that she should be delivered," concerned the most important delivery of a baby in human history. God would become flesh and, thereby, use this flesh, His human body, as a perfect sacrifice in order to deliver humanity, which He did at the Cross.

(7) "AND SHE BROUGHT FORTH HER FIRSTBORN SON, AND WRAPPED HIM IN SWADDLING CLOTHES, AND LAID HIM IN A MANGER; BECAUSE THERE WAS NO ROOM FOR THEM IN THE INN."

HER FIRSTBORN SON

The phrase, *"And she brought forth her firstborn Son,"* is meant to emphasize the fact that there were no other children up to this time. As well, it refutes the error, even gross error, of the Catholic Church, which claims that Mary had no other children and remained a virgin throughout her life. Actually, Jesus had four half-brothers, one might say, *"James, Joseph, Simon, and Jude,"* as well as two or three half-sisters (Mat. 13:55-56).

It was predicted by God that Mary would have other children, and the Messiah would have brothers. *"I am become a stranger unto My brethren, and an alien unto My mother's children"* (Ps. 69:8).

As well, His brethren are mentioned as not believing on Him until after the resurrection (Jn. 7:3-10; Acts 1:14). Also, James is called *"the Lord's brother"* (Gal. 1:19).

The Catholic Church claims that His brethren were cousins by another Mary and Cleophas. Their contentions are that Joseph was too old to have children of Mary or that he had children by a former marriage. All of this is false as nothing is mentioned in Scripture or history about these claims.

In fact, if Joseph did have children before Jesus was born, then Jesus could not be the legal heir to David's throne, which, by law, went to the firstborn.

So, the Catholic claims are spurious.

POVERTY

The phrase, *"And wrapped Him in swaddling clothes,"* pertained to the custom of that time.

The cloth was loosely wrapped all around the child with only its face uncovered. The cost of the material indicated the financial status and rank of the parents.

Even though the Scripture does not specifically state, still, every indication is that Joseph and Mary were very poor, and as a result, this material would have been very inexpensive.

The phrase, *"And laid Him in a manger,"* basically spoke of a feeding place for animals.

The Inn of Beth-lehem was of ancient duration, even being mentioned in Jeremiah 41:17.

This type of inn was for the poorest of the poor and offered little more than the shelter of its walls and roof.

To stable the animals, which most every traveler had during those times, either a cave or enclosure was used. In the case of Mary and Joseph, there are claims for both, even though the Scripture does not say. There would have been little difference in either, with a large cave affording a little more protection, but with the foul odor even worse.

Whichever it was, Joseph would have tried his best to make Mary comfortable among the animals on a bed of straw. Because of the many travelers coming to Beth-lehem for the same reason as Joseph and Mary, the stable would have been filled with animals. The scene would not have been pretty or pleasant to behold!

THE BABY CHILD JESUS

In the midst of the odor of barnyard waste and by the side of donkeys and horses, Mary delivered the baby child Jesus, the Lord of glory, God manifest in the flesh. Even though it was not a pretty picture to behold, still, one can be certain that angels were watching the move of every animal and affording a minute protection for the Saviour of mankind. As well, the glory of God must have accompanied this scene, turning the smelly stable into a place of glory.

Also, the Lord has turned many a hovel into a heaven! Millions have thought that a new house, a new car, or new clothes would satisfy the hunger of the heart, but they soon found that such did not and, in fact, cannot satisfy. Only proper union with Christ can bring a peace that passes all understanding. That is at least one of the reasons Jesus said, *"A man's life consists not in the abundance of things he possesses"* (Lk. 12:15).

NO ROOM IN THE INN

The phrase, *"Because there was no room for them in the inn,"* proclaims that God manifest in the flesh had come to earth, but yet, there was no room for Him there. So much the more wonderful and perfect is the love that brought Him here. He began His life in a manger, ended it on a Cross, and all along His ministerial way, had no where to lay His head!

The idea of there being no room in the inn seems to imply that Joseph dutifully inquired, with Mary's condition painfully obvious. However, none volunteered to give up their place in the inn, even though they, no doubt, had the opportunity to do so. What an eternal blessing someone would have gained had he taken this glorious privilege. However, to the unspiritual eye, Joseph and Mary looked like just two more exhausted, poverty-stricken travelers. Consequently, some undoubtedly heard the innkeeper dismiss them, probably gesturing toward the stables, but no one moved or spoke up to surrender his place. Tragically, it is the same story regarding the hearts of most of mankind. There is no room for Jesus. As it was then, so it is now!

We have briefly dealt with the time of the birth of Christ, which no one knows exactly; however, it is almost certain that it was not December 25th.

While it is certainly proper to celebrate the birth of Christ (on whatever day it may have been), Christmas, as we presently know it, needs some explanation.

ORIGINS OF THE CHRIST-MASS

We know that the apostles did not observe the day we do as Christ's birthday. Tertullian, writing in the middle of the third century, lamented the fact that Christians were beginning to observe the customs of the heathen in this regard. He said:

"Gifts are carried to and fro, New Year's Day presents are made with din, and sports and banquets are celebrated with uproar."

The church structure, full of pagans since the reign of Constantine, became so corrupt in its efforts to recruit even more to church membership that the heathen festival of December 25th was adopted and its name changed to *"Christ-mass."*

It is not known when this was officially done, but it was not observed as a ritual of the church before the fourth century.

Let us go back now and look at the origins of this wintertime pagan celebration.

A HEATHEN FESTIVAL

Christmas or Christ-mass was the direct adoption of a heathen festival observed on December 24th and 25th in honor of the son of the Babylonian queen, Astarte. Observed for centuries before Christ (a fact well documented), the Chaldeans called this *"Yule Day"* or *"Child Day."*

To find the origin of this festival, we must go all the way back to the city (nation) of Babylon, founded by Nimrod, the *"Mighty Hunter"* (Gen. 10:8-10).

Babylon was the seat of the first great apostasy against God after the flood. It was here that the Babylonian cult was instituted by Nimrod and his queen, Semiramis. Semiramis was Nimrod's mother and later his wife in an incestuous relationship. From this Babylonian cult is derived all kinds of worship, carried over today into various pagan religions, including the Christ-mass.

THE BABYLONIAN CULT

The Babylonian cult was a system claiming the highest wisdom and an ability to reveal divine secrets. It was characterized by the word *"mystery"* because of its system of claimed mysteries. Besides confessing to the priest at admission, a believer was compelled to drink of *"mysterious beverages,"* which, according to Salverte (Des Sciences Occultes, page 259,) was also a requirement for those who sought initiation into these mysteries.

Once admitted into the Babylonian mystery religion, men were no longer Babylonians, Assyrians, or Egyptians, but members of a mystical brotherhood over which was placed a supreme pontiff (high priest) whose word was final in all matters concerning the lives of the brotherhood (regardless of the country in which they lived). It was, therefore, a supernational organization.

The objects of worship were the supreme father, the incarnate female (Queen of Heaven), and her son. The last two were the only objects of worship in that it was believed that the supreme father did not interfere in mortal affairs (Nimrod III, page 239).

Actually, this system is believed to have had fallen angels and demons as its source. The object of the cult was to rule the world through its dogmas.

THE SPREADING OF THE BABYLONIAN CULT

During the days of Nimrod, this cult gained a deep hold over the whole human race, for there was only one language at that time, and all people were one homogeneous group. The Bible tells us that Nimrod gained the titles *"Mighty Hunter"* and the *"Apostate"* because of his innovative building of walled cities to free men from the ravages of wild beasts (which were then multiplying against mankind) and because of his leading men away from the idea of God, who was capable of interceding with wrath into the affairs of men. History records that he led people astray to such an extent that they drifted from the faith of their fathers.

From ancient history, it appears that these individuals became involved in the worship of the heavens through the zodiac (astrology) placed atop the Tower of Babel on the plains of Shinar. The end result was that God confused their language and scattered them throughout the earth.

It seems that this Babylonian system was one through which Satan planned to circumvent the truth of God. From Babylon, it spread to the ends of the earth—to the place where, Scripture records, Abraham was chosen of God to flee this idolatrous nation and thus preserve the truth of God. This would explain how so many different nations of the world are found to have common religious traditions interwoven into their cultures.

WORLDWIDE SATANIC ACTIVITY

Babylon continued to be the seat of worldwide satanic activity until it was conquered by Xerxes in 487 B.C. when the

Babylonian priesthood (the Chaldeans) was forced to move to Pergamos, which then became their headquarters.

Over the years, this cult gained power to the point that the Caesars absorbed the bulk of their principles and structure into their own pagan religion. Julius Caesar was made the supreme pontiff of the Etruscan Order in 74 B.C. Thereafter, Rome's religion became that of Babylon.

The Roman emperors continued to hold this office until A.D. 376 when the emperor Gratian (through Christian motivation) banned it; he saw that Babylonianism was idolatrous by nature. Religious matters then became somewhat disorganized until those in power decided once again to establish this position of apostasy.

ROMAN CHRISTENDOM

In A.D. 378, Damasus, bishop of the Christian church of Rome, was elected to fill this office. He had been bishop for 12 years, having been made such in A.D. 366. This was brought about through the influence of the monks of Mount Carmel, a college within the Babylonian religion founded by the priest of Jezebel and, incredibly, still in existence today within the Roman church.

So, in A.D. 378, the Babylonian system of religion became an official part of the Christian church, as it was then constituted. The bishop of Rome, who later became the supreme head of the organized church, was already supreme pontiff of the Babylonian Order.

All the teachings of pagan Babylon and Rome were gradually absorbed into the Christian religious organization. Soon after Damasus was made pontiff, the rites of Babylon began to come to the forefront. The worship methods of the Roman Catholic Church became Babylonian, and under Damasus (the supreme pontiff), heathen temples were restored and reestablished.

THE EFFECT UPON ORGANIZED CHRISTIANITY

The changes resulting from this union within the doctrines and practices of the Roman church did not come about all at once. The Roman church of today is purely

NOTES

a human institution. Its doctrines, which frequently stand in opposition to God's Word, were never taught by Christ or the apostles. They crept into the church over a long period of time.

It is evident to anyone who dispassionately examines the record that Babylonian rites and practices were inserted into the Roman Catholic Church when its major influence became the supreme pontiff of the Babylonian Order. In fact, many of today's pagan elements within the Catholic Church were taken directly from the Babylonian religion as founded by Nimrod and Semiramis.

THE WORSHIP OF SAINTS AND THE VIRGIN MARY

To understand the reasons behind all of this, we must examine the situation as it existed throughout Southern Europe toward the end of the fourth century. The official religion imposed by government edict was the Christian faith as then interpreted by the officials in Rome, but the mass of the population had followed the pagan religions for centuries. They, therefore, ostensibly accepted the Christian faith (out of necessity) but maintained observance of all the heathen deities, customs, and holidays. It was somewhat like the Haitians continuing in their voodoo while, at the same time, practicing Catholicism, which most do, or Brazilians practicing spiritism while also embracing Catholicism.

So, to gain a semblance of public compliance with the official religion of Christianity, it became apparent to the Roman powers that the simplest solution would be to absorb into their Christian format all the pagan elements demanded by the general population. Thus, the stage was set for a merging of the Christian and heathen religions.

The populace was accustomed to worshipping a number of gods of various origins and categories (fertility, success in battle, wisdom, etc.). To cater to this custom, a veneration of a wide roster of saints and holy men was instituted. Saints were considered to be lesser deities personally but who, nevertheless, carried the power to act as intercessors with God. Contrarily, the Bible states:

"There is one God, and one mediator between God and men, the Man Christ Jesus" (I Tim. 2:5).

PAGANISM

Places associated with various holy men were declared sacred, and pilgrimages were instituted. (This continues to happen to this day in the Catholic Church with pilgrimages to various places where the Virgin Mary is supposed to have been sighted, etc.) Relics of these officially designated *"saints"* were believed to have miracle-working powers. When Martin Luther first visited Rome, he expected to see a beautiful city dedicated to the glory of God. What he actually saw revolted and sickened him.

Wagons were coming into Rome to the so-called Holy See, carrying hundreds of bones and mummified body parts purported to be the remains of saints. Every church could become a holy shrine (that is, holier than other churches) if it contained one of these relics of a saint.

The worship of the Virgin Mary was set up three years after Damasus became head of the Babylon cult in A.D. 381. Because the Babylonian cult and the general populace worshipped the *"Queen of Heaven"* (along with her son), the Roman church saw that it would be politically expedient to supply them with a parallel figure within their new, officially imposed worship. Thus, Mary was elevated to divine status.

However, the image of mother and child had been a primary object of worship in Babylon for centuries before Christ was born. From Babylon, this had spread to the ends of the earth. The original mother in this tableau, as stated, was Semiramis, the personification of unbridled lust, licentiousness, and sexual gratification.

In studying the worship practices of other nations, we find an amazing similarity carried out through wide areas and over long periods of time.

These nations traced their common worship from Babylon before the dispersion in the days of Nimrod. Thus, we see that the worship of Mary is one of Babylonian derivation. There is no suggestion of such worship in Scripture.

NOTES

THE WORSHIP AND VENERATION OF IMAGES

Prayer to, and the worship of, images was decreed by the Second Council of Nice in A.D. 787. In the ninth century, certain emperors attempted to abolish this pagan practice, but it was so ingrained in the people (and the abolition so resisted by the monks) that the emperors gave up their efforts. In A.D. 869, a synod at Constantinople capitulated (bowed) to public demand, and image (idol) worship—a purely pagan, Babylonian practice—was officially endorsed by the Roman church.

PRIVATE CONFESSION TO A PRIEST

Confession to a priest had progressed from a small beginning in the second and third centuries to an elaborate system by the time of Pope Innocent III in A.D. 1215. It was not, however, officially endorsed until the Council of Trent in A.D. 1551. People were then compelled to confess to a priest at least once a year and do penance according to the degree of sins committed. Without this confession, no one had the right to the sacraments.

This was, of course, the same system Babylon had, which bound the people to the priest by fear of exposure or of retribution through divine wrath. This custom is still enforced today with forgiveness (salvation) coming from the absolution (forgiveness) of the priest and then the partaking of so-called Holy Communion.

THE SIGN OF THE CROSS

The sign of the Cross had its origin in the mystic *"Tau"* of the Babylonian cult. This came from the letter *"T,"* the initial letter of Tammuz (Ezek. 8:14), but better known in classical writings (and even today) as Bacchus. Bacchus was also known as *"the lamented one."* Actually, this was just one more name for Nimrod, the son of Cush. Even today, Bacchus lives on as the patron saint of such disgusting public homosexual orgies as are evident during the New Orleans Mardi Gras.

THE ROSARY

The rosary is also of pagan origin. It is used for the same magical purposes in

Romanism for which it was used in the Babylonian mysteries. Throughout the Middle East, it is common to see Arabs fingering their prayer beads as they sit contemplating in the public bazaars. However, Jesus specifically warned against the vain repetition of memorized prayer:

"When you pray, use not vain repetitions, as the heathen do: for they think that they shall be heard for their much speaking" (Mat. 6:7).

CELIBACY

Also borrowed from the Babylonian cult, the nuns are the reinstitution of the vestal virgins of pagan Rome (copied from Babylon).

Actually, just about all of the outstanding festivals of Romanism, such as Christmas, Easter, St. John's Day, Lady Day, Lent, etc., are Babylonian in origin and have been adopted (after application of a thin veneer of Christianity) into the Catholic Church, despite the fact that they have no relation to Christ or the Bible. None of these were celebrated in Christendom for the first century after Christ. As we have previously explained, they are of pagan origin and were later included into so-called Christian practice as an appeasement to public desires for their old pagan customs.

This is true of Lady Day, observed on March 25th. This is the supposed day of the miraculous conception of Mary. Among the heathen, this was observed as a festival in honor of Cybele (otherwise known as Semiramis and the mother of the Babylonian messiah, Nimrod). In Rome, Cybele was called Domina (or *"Lady"*), hence, the name, *"Lady Day."*

EASTER

It will, no doubt, come as a surprise to most Christians that Easter also springs from the fountain of Babylon. The word *Easter* has no Christian connections whatever since it is derived from *"Ishtar,"* the Babylonian title for *"the Queen of Heaven."* It was worship of this woman by Israel that was such an abomination in the sight of God (I Sam. 7:3; Jer. 44:18).

Round cakes imprinted with the sign

of the Cross were made at this festival, the sign being the sign of life within the Babylonian mystery religion. This day was observed centuries before Christ and is quite obviously involved in many of the customs connected with the modern celebration of Easter.

Eggs, which play a prominent part in celebrating Easter, were a fertility symbol in heathen nations. One of the fables has to do with "An egg of wondrous size that fell from heaven into the River Euphrates. The fish rolled it to the bank where doves settled upon it and hatched it, and out came Astarte (or Ishtar), the goddess of Easter."

The word *Easter* is used only one time in the Bible (Acts 12:4), and here, it is mistranslated. The Greek word here translated as Easter is translated as Passover at all other places within the Bible, and should be here, as well!

LENT

Lent (observed for the 40 days preceding Easter) is also derived from the Babylonian mysteries. It is observed today by devil worshipers in Kurdistan, who obtained it from the same source as Rome did: the Babylonian mystery religion. Both Easter and Lent were introduced into the church in A.D. 519.

A writer of this time (Cassianus) said that the observance of Lent had no existence as long as the church remained inviolate. At the same time of the year that Romanism observes it, heathens observe it as the prelude to an entirely different kind of religious observance (*"The Rape of Proserpine"*), which involves activities of unbridled lust. In their minds, the enforced morality of the Lent season only serves to sharpen their zeal for the degrading activities that follow.

A great many doctrines and heresies adopted by the Roman Catholic Church over a period of centuries actually came directly from pagan sources. Many of the practices thought of today as Christian are, in truth, heathen in origin.

"Now the Spirit (Holy Spirit) *speaks expressly* (pointedly), *that in the latter times* (the times in which we now live) *some shall depart from the faith* (Jesus Christ and Him

crucified), *giving heed to seducing spirits, and doctrines of demons;*

"Speaking lies in hypocrisy; having their conscience seared with a hot iron;

"Forbidding to marry, and commanding to abstain from meats" (I Tim. 4:1-3).

HERESIES

While we are on the subject of the major heresies introduced into Christianity through the romance of the Roman church with paganism, it is perhaps a good time to list here a general compilation of current religious practices that stem directly from pagan sources. These various traditions have been inserted into Christianity over a period of more than 16 centuries. Many of these practices were observed and followed over the years, but only at the times that they were officially adopted by church councils and then proclaimed by the pope did they become binding on all Catholics everywhere. These are the dates that will be used here, despite the fact that the traditions and usage might be older than otherwise appears.

At the Reformation in the 16th century, when Martin Luther redirected the world's attention (and conscience) to God's Word, these heresies were identified and repudiated as having no part in the worship of the Lord Jesus Christ as taught in the New Testament. Let us list and examine these heresies as they are observed within the Catholic Church today.

UNSCRIPTURAL PRACTICES

• Of all the human inventions taught and practiced by the Roman Catholic Church that are contrary to the Bible, the most ancient are the prayers for the dead and the sign of the Cross. Both of these began about three centuries after Christ, and there is no mention of either within the Word of God.

• Wax candles were introduced into churches about A.D. 320. These votive candles supposedly helped to bring about prayer requests when paid for and lighted in conjunction with prayer.

• Veneration of angels and dead saints began about A.D. 375.

• The Mass, as a daily celebration, was adopted in A.D. 349.

• The worship of Mary, the mother of Jesus, and the use of the term, *"mother of God,"* as applied to her, originated about A.D. 381. This was officially decreed in the Council of Ephesus in A.D. 431.

CONTINUED UNSCRIPTURAL PRACTICES

• Priests began to adopt distinctive costumes about A.D. 500.

• The doctrine of purgatory was first established by Pope Gregory the Great about A.D. 593.

• The Latin language, as the language of prayer and worship in the church, was imposed by Pope Gregory in A.D. 600. (This has since changed.) The Bible teaches that we are to pray to God alone and do so in the name of Jesus (Jn. 16:23). In the early church, prayers were never directed to Mary or to dead saints. This practice began in the Roman church about six centuries after Christ.

• The papacy is of pagan origin. The title of pope (Universal bishop or pastor) was given to the bishop of Rome about A.D. 600 from the Babylonian cult, as explained. Jesus did not appoint Peter to the headship of the apostles and, in fact, especially forbade such notion (Lk. 22:24-26; I Cor. 3:11; Eph. 1:22-23; Col. 1:18).

CONTINUED ERROR

• The kissing of the pope's feet began in A.D. 709. It had been a pagan custom to kiss the feet of emperors. The Word of God forbids such practices (Acts 10:25-26; Rev. 19:10; 22:8-9).

• The temporal power of the popes began in A.D. 750. Jesus expressly forbade such a practice, and He Himself refused any worldly kingship (Mat. 4:8-10; 20:20-28; Jn. 18:36).

• The worship of the cross, images, and relics was introduced in A.D. 787. Such practices are termed idolatry in the Bible and are severely condemned (Ex. 20:2-6; Deut. 27:15; Ps. 135:15).

• Holy water (water mixed with a pinch of salt and blessed by a priest) was authorized in A.D. 850.

• The canonization (official certification)

of saints was instituted by Pope John XV in A.D. 995. Actually, every believer and follower of Christ is referred to as a saint in the Bible, and, in fact, they become such at the moment of salvation (Rom. 1:7; I Cor. 1:2, etc.).

• The Mass was developed gradually as a sacrifice (of Christ on the Cross) and was made obligatory in the 11th century. The gospel teaches us that the sacrifice of Christ was offered once and for all, and is not to be repeated but only commemorated in the Lord's Supper (Heb. 7:27; 9:26-28; 10:10-14).

• The celibacy of the priesthood was decreed by Pope Hildebrand Boniface VIII in A.D. 1079. Jesus imposed no such rules, and neither did any of the apostles. On the contrary, Peter was married, and Paul stated that bishops (pastors within our terminology) were to have one wife and could have children (Mat. 8:14-15; I Tim. 3:5, 12).

MAN-MADE RULES

• The rosary (or prayer beads) was introduced by Peter the Hermit in A.D. 1090. This was copied from the Hindus and Muslims. The counting of prayers is a pagan practice and, as stated, is expressly condemned by Christ (Mat. 6:5-7).

• The inquisition (torture) of heretics (anyone disagreeing with the interpretations coming out of Rome) was introduced by the Council of Verona in A.D. 1184. Jesus, on the other hand, never taught the use of force to spread the gospel.

• The sale of indulgences, generally regarded as the purchase of forgiveness (for self or for deceased relatives) and a permit for indulging in sin, began in A.D. 1190. Christianity, as taught in the Bible, condemns such, and it was primarily a protest against this specific abuse that brought on the Protestant Reformation in the 16th century.

CONTINUED MAN-MADE RULES

• The dogma of transubstantiation was decreed by Pope Innocent III in A.D. 1215. According to this doctrine, the priest miraculously changes the communion wafer into the actual body of Christ, which he then

NOTES

proceeds to eat before the congregation. The gospel condemns such superstitious absurdities. It clearly stipulates that the act of Holy Communion is a memorial observation of the sacrifice of Christ. It contains no salvation, and neither is it meant to (Lk. 22:19-20; Jn. 6:35; I Cor. 11:26).

• The confession of sins to the priest at least yearly was instituted by Pope Innocent III at the Lateran Council in A.D. 1215. To the contrary, the Bible commands us to confess our sins directly to God (Ps. 51; Isa. 1:18; Lk. 7:48; 15:21; I Jn. 1:8-9).

• The adoration of the wafer (the host) was invented by Pope Honorius in A.D. 1220. The Roman Catholic Church thus worships a god made by hands. This is, by scriptural definition, idolatry and absolutely contrary to the Spirit of the gospel (Jn. 4:24).

• The Bible was labeled as a forbidden Book by the Catholic Church (as far as laymen were concerned) and placed in the index of forbidden books by the Council of Toledo in A.D. 1229. However, Jesus and Paul demanded that the Scriptures should be read by all (Jn. 5:39; II Tim. 3:15-17).

MORE FALSE DOCTRINE

• The scapular was invented by Simon Stock, an English monk, in A.D. 1287. This is a piece of brown cloth with a picture of the Virgin sewn onto it and is superstitiously believed to assure salvation, no matter the depth of a person's depravity, if worn next to the skin. This is superstition and fetishism of the most degrading kind!

• The Roman Catholic Church forbade the cup (as part of the Holy Communion) by instituting Communion via the host (wafer) alone in the Council of Constance in A.D. 1414. The gospel commands us to celebrate the Holy Communion with bread and grape juice (Mat. 26:27; I Cor. 11:26-29).

• The doctrine of purgatory was proclaimed as a doctrine of faith by the Council of Florence in A.D. 1439. There is not one word in the whole Bible suggesting that such a place as purgatory exists. Acceptance of the blood of Jesus completely cleanses of sin and leaves no sinful residue that must be burned off before we may enter the kingdom (Jn. 5:24; Rom. 8:1; I Jn. 1:7-9; 2:1-2).

• The doctrine of seven sacraments was affirmed in A.D. 1439. The gospel says that Christ instituted two sacraments, or perhaps they would be better referred to as ordinances: water baptism and the Lord's Supper (Mat. 26:26-28; 28:19-20).

ERROR LEADS TO MORE ERROR

• The Council of Trent (covering several years) in A.D. 1545 declared tradition to be of equal authority with the Bible. By *"tradition,"* it meant human opinions and their teaching. While there is room for interpretation of certain aspects of Scripture, there is never room for establishing traditions in opposition to Scripture. The Roman church is saying in this doctrine that when it chooses, it can do anything it wishes in opposition to Scripture and is in no way bound by Scripture. The Pharisees also believed, and Jesus condemned them with no room for misunderstanding because of their position on this issue (Mk. 7:7-13; Col. 2:8; Rev. 22:18).

• The immaculate conception of the Virgin Mary was proclaimed by Pope Pius IX in A.D. 1854. This doctrine has nothing to do with Mary's conception of Jesus by the Holy Spirit. It says instead that Mary was the only human ever born, except Adam and Jesus, without original sin. This implies, therefore, that Mary did not need a Saviour and that she was divine. To the contrary, the gospel states: *"There is none righteous, no, not one ... For all have sinned, and come short of the glory of God"* (Rom. 3:10, 23; 5:12).

• In 1931, Pope Pius XI reaffirmed the doctrine that Mary is *"the mother of God,"* a doctrine first decreed by the Council of Ephesus in A.D. 431. This heretical statement is contrary to Mary's own words.

In summary, an overwhelming percentage of the rites and ceremonies of the Roman Catholic Church are of pagan origin. Cardinal Newman, in his book, *"The Development of the Christian Doctrine,"* (Catholic), admits that "Temples, incense, oil lamps, votive offerings, holy water, holiday's and seasons of devotions, processions, blessing of fields, sacerdotal vestments, the tonsures of priests, monks, and nuns, and images, are all of pagan origin."

IS CHRISTMAS A PART OF THIS?

Christmas is looked upon in one of three ways:
1. The Biblical context
2. The framework of commercialism
3. The perspective of its heathen origins

If Christmas is observed in the way the Bible presents it, and if we celebrate it with the realization that, in all probability, Christ was not born on December 25th, and that we are celebrating His birth, irrespective of the day on which He was born, then I think we can celebrate it without being contrary to Scripture.

It is not wrong to give gifts to loved ones, but this should not, of course, be paramount or overindulged. Our greatest gift should be to the Lord Jesus Christ, and this should be our love and reverence.

As far as Christmas trees are concerned, I realize that most Christians put little weight to the religious significance of the tree itself, and it is probably little more than a harmless conformation to current customs. Realizing its pagan origins, however, we, no doubt, would all be better off if this custom had never been allowed to flourish as it has within our society.

Actually, the Christmas tree that we accept without question was well known in pre-Christian pagan times and was common to all tribes. According to one legend, on the eve of the day (December 24th), the yule log was cast into a tree, from which divine gifts appeared—presents from the gods to bless men in the new year. This tree was common in the days of Jeremiah, who expressly warned Israel to forsake this heathen custom (Jer. 10:1-9).

Of course, the tree of which Jeremiah spoke, and the manner in which it was used, was totally different than the present; however, the present tree does have its roots in that idolatrous, pagan custom. As stated, I think believers would be better off if this practice was eliminated.

THE TRUTH

To be sure, it is wrong to teach that Santa Claus (or Saint Nicholas) is real. No child should be taught myths about some mystical gift-giver. A child, from the time he is able to understand, should be taught the true meaning of Christmas, which should center on the observance of the birth of Christ and what He did in delivering humanity at Calvary's Cross and the resurrection.

THE CHRISTMAS STORY

A child should be taught the truth: no one knows the day Christ was born, but we celebrate His birth on this particular day in spirit because we are thankful to God for His gift beyond price—His Son, Jesus Christ (Jn. 1:1, 14; 3:16-17; Rom. 8:3; II Cor. 9:15).

On Christmas Day, it would be a fine thing if the whole family, particularly the children, would be afforded the opportunity to hear and discuss the Christmas story from the gospel of Luke. If this were done repeatedly, then our children would come to know the true meaning of this holiday we call *"Christmas."*

It is always Satan's desire to subvert the child of God from the simple truth of biblical worship. Sad to say, he has been successful in this over the years. Hundreds of millions of people are in heathenistic bondage to a superstitious system that is totally divergent from true salvation. According to the Holy Word of God, salvation comes only through a relationship with Jesus Christ.

Christmas can be beautiful when viewed within the context of God's Word. Otherwise, it becomes little more than a pagan holiday, which I fear has happened in the hearts and lives of the majority of people who attempt to celebrate Christmas. Instead of the frenetic pace of Christmas shopping, office parties, and holiday entertainment, if everyone would return to the Word for guidance at this season, and, in fact, every season, we could find that it is indeed possible to worship the Lord Jesus Christ in the beauty of holiness.

(8) "AND THERE WERE IN THE SAME COUNTRY SHEPHERDS ABIDING IN THE FIELD, KEEPING WATCH OVER THEIR FLOCK BY NIGHT."

SHEPHERDS

The phrase, *"And there were in the same country,"* referred to the area around Bethlehem where Jesus was born.

"Shepherds abiding in the field," pertained to the lowest caste in society at that time. In other words, shepherds were looked down upon, to say the least.

"Keeping watch over their flock by night," gives indication that December 25th was not the day on which Jesus was born.

Actually, it was very unusual for shepherds to keep their flocks in the open at night during the months of November through March. It was the custom to send flocks out after the Passover, which was in April, to stay until the first rain in October or November.

So, inasmuch as specific mention is made of the flocks being *"watched over by night,"* this pretty well tells us that December 25th would not be correct concerning the birth of Christ. In fact, it is probable that Jesus was born some time in October.

(9) "AND, LO, THE ANGEL OF THE LORD CAME UPON THEM, AND THE GLORY OF THE LORD SHONE ROUND ABOUT THEM: AND THEY WERE SORE AFRAID."

THE ANGEL OF THE LORD

The phrase, *"And, lo, the angel of the Lord came upon them,"* proclaims the fact that the Lord's birth was not trumpeted forth in lordly guise to priests and princes and the great ones of the earth, but rather to obscure shepherds.

"And the glory of the Lord shone round about them," tells of the glory accompanying the angel as he revealed himself to these humble shepherds.

"And they were sore afraid," proclaims this glory known among the Jews as the shekinah, which was the visible token of the presence of the Eternal. It appeared first in the bush before Moses, then in the pillar of fire and cloud that guided the desert-wanderings, and then in the tabernacle and the temple.

It appeared, as well, on Jesus on the Mount of Transfiguration. Again, it appeared on Jesus when, risen, He appeared to the Pharisee Saul (Paul) outside Damascus.

Of course, it became visible on the day of

NOTES

Pentecost when tongues of fire sat upon the heads of those who had gathered in obedience to the command of Christ (Acts 1:4).

Even the slightest degree of its manifestation brings awe, reverence, and even fear.

(10) "AND THE ANGEL SAID UNTO THEM, FEAR NOT: FOR, BEHOLD, I BRING YOU GOOD TIDINGS OF GREAT JOY, WHICH SHALL BE TO ALL PEOPLE."

GOOD TIDINGS OF GREAT JOY

The phrase, *"And the angel said unto them, Fear not,"* seems to be the standard statement to the reaction of those in the presence of God, which the angel manifested (Lk. 1:13; 2:10).

"For, behold, I bring you good tidings of great joy," proclaims that which salvation affords upon acceptance of Christ as one's Saviour. Actually, the angel was proclaiming to the shepherds that with the birth of Christ, the fulfillment of all the prophecies was taking place. Jesus would later refer to it as *"more abundant life"* (Jn. 10:10), while Peter referred to it as *"joy unspeakable and full of glory"* (I Pet. 1:8).

"Which shall be to all people," refers to Christ being given for the entirety of mankind. Consequently, there is no such thing as a *"western gospel," "eastern gospel,"* etc., but one gospel for the whole of mankind.

As well, *"All people,"* includes all races of red, yellow, brown, black, and white. None are excluded because Jesus died for all!

However, there will be no *"good tidings of great joy"* if someone does not tell any and all. The fact of this happening is of little consequence to anyone if he has no knowledge of it.

(11) "FOR UNTO YOU IS BORN THIS DAY IN THE CITY OF DAVID A SAVIOUR, WHICH IS CHRIST THE LORD."

THE SAVIOR

The phrase, *"For unto you is born this day,"* proclaims the incarnation, i.e., God manifest in the flesh, the Lord Jesus Christ. He was born of woman, a virgin, in order that He might be the last Adam, gaining back by His life, ministry, death, and resurrection what the first Adam lost (I Cor. 15:45).

"In the City of David," is Beth-lehem,

David's birthplace. Consequently, Jesus was not only a *"Son of David"* (Mat. 1:1), but, as well, was born in the *"City of David."*

"A Saviour, which is Christ the Lord," presents Jesus as the *"good tidings of great joy."* Consequently, this is a person, the Lord Jesus Christ, and not some religion with its creeds, doctrines, confessions, and outward forms.

The babe was not to become a king and a Saviour. He was born both. He was and is the Saviour; He was and is Christ; He was and is Jehovah.

The name *"Christ"* means *"the Anointed,"* consequently, fulfilling Luke 4:18-19.

(12) "AND THIS SHALL BE A SIGN UNTO YOU; YOU SHALL FIND THE BABY WRAPPED IN SWADDLING CLOTHES, LYING IN A MANGER."

THE SIGN

The phrase, *"And this shall be a sign unto you,"* concerned where they would find this baby, God manifest in the flesh.

The evidence is that the shepherds desired to see this baby and evidently asked where to find Him.

"You shall find the baby wrapped in swaddling clothes, lying in a manger," gives the description of His whereabouts.

I wonder what came to the minds of the shepherds as they attempted to contrast the glory of the appearance and announcement of the angles with this lowly manger. However, the glory of Christ was not in His surroundings and, in fact, never was, but rather, His person. Even though the Holy Spirit did not come upon Him until the beginning of His ministry, still, that did not mean that the Holy Spirit was not there. I personally believe that from the moment the Holy Spirit came upon Mary, thereby, decreeing the conception, He attended Christ from that very moment (Lk. 1:35).

(13) "AND SUDDENLY THERE WAS WITH THE ANGEL A MULTITUDE OF THE HEAVENLY HOST PRAISING GOD, AND SAYING."

PRAISING GOD

The phrase, *"And suddenly,"* proclaims a wonder that suddenly happened.

"There was with the angel a multitude of the heavenly host," does not necessarily proclaim their coming at that time, but only that the shepherds were able to see them and hear them at that particular time.

They had been there all the time.

"Praising God, and saying," presents sinless angels and not sinful men first praising Him on coming to earth, and yet, the angels needed no forgiveness.

Consequently, if they praise the Lord, how much more should we, who have experienced such glorious forgiveness and redemption, praise Him!

(14) "GLORY TO GOD IN THE HIGHEST, AND ON EARTH PEACE, GOOD WILL TOWARD MEN."

Three things are said here by the angelic host:

1. GLORY TO GOD IN THE HIGHEST

All glory must go to God for His great and marvelous salvation plan afforded to man. As stated, if the angels praise Him, how much more should we praise Him! The sadness is, most who call themselves believers never praise Him because they truly are not believers. If one is truly redeemed, one will truly praise Him.

2. AND ON EARTH PEACE

At that particular time, the Roman Empire was at peace all over the world. Consequently, the gates of the temple of Janus at Rome were closed, there being no need for the presence of the war god to guide and lead Rome's conquering armies.

Actually, there is evidence that during the entirety of the life of Christ, some 33 and one-half years, peace reigned. However, not long after the death, resurrection, and ascension of Christ, the gates of Janus were only too quickly thrown open again because of war. In A.D. 70, within sight of the spot where the shepherds beheld the multitude of the heavenly host, the awful conflagration of Jerusalem could be plainly seen, even with the shrieks and cries of the countless victims rending the air. There will not be peace on this earth until Jesus, who is the Prince of Peace, comes back.

3. GOOD WILL TOWARD MEN

Never has God willed otherwise. He seeks to convince men that He desires only their

good (Ps. 84:11; I Tim. 1:14; II Pet. 3:9).

God's glory in creation was high; in revelation, higher; but in redemption, the highest. His power was seen in creation; His righteousness, in law; but—His highest attribute—His love, as seen in the atonement.

(15) "AND IT CAME TO PASS, AS THE ANGELS WERE GONE AWAY FROM THEM INTO HEAVEN, THE SHEPHERDS SAID ONE TO ANOTHER, LET US NOW GO EVEN UNTO BETH-LEHEM, AND SEE THIS THING WHICH IS COME TO PASS, WHICH THE LORD HAS MADE KNOWN UNTO US."

The synopsis is:

1. God became man to do one thing, and that was to go to the Cross.

2. At the Cross, Jesus took all sin away, at least for all who will believe (Jn. 3:16).

3. There's only one place for sin, and that is at the Cross.

THE ANGELS

The phrase, *"And it came to pass, as the angels were gone away from them into heaven,"* proclaims them having visited these lowly shepherds while having ignored the high priest as well as the religious leaders of Israel.

Why?

There are several things to be learned from this. Some are as follows:

• *"God resists the proud, but gives grace to the humble"* (James 4:6). The religious leaders of Israel were eaten up with pride and would consequently experience no revelation from the Lord. The Lord says: *"To this man will I look, even to him who is poor and of a contrite spirit, and trembles at My Word"* (Isa. 66:2).

• Due to their pride and self-righteousness, these religious leaders of Israel would not have accepted the baby as the Messiah. The facts are, they did not accept Him, even when the evidence was irrefutable.

• Most, if not all, religions fall into the same category presently. It has no revelation from the Lord and, in fact, cannot!

At the turn of the 20th century, the Lord began to pour out His Spirit upon hungry hearts and lives even though many were uneducated. In fact, they were ridiculed and lambasted by the reigning religious order of the day. Nevertheless, this, the mighty baptism with the Holy Spirit with the evidence of speaking with other tongues, continued to fill hearts and lives until today, it has morphed into the greatest move of God on earth and, no doubt, ever, other than the ministry of Christ.

THE RELIGIOUS LEADERSHIP OF ISRAEL AND JESUS

The vaunted priesthood of Israel, along with all of its religious leaders, is gone, but the followers of the lowly Nazarene abound until they fill the earth.

The phrase, *"The shepherds said one to another, Let us now go even unto Bethlehem, and see this thing which is come to pass,"* represents them going to the *"house of bread"* to see the *"true bread"* Who has come from heaven.

"Which the Lord has made known unto us," proclaims one of the greatest honors in the whole of human history. Out of all the people on the face of the planet, the Lord would dispatch angels only to these lowly shepherds in exclusion of all others.

They had experienced something glorious in the appearance and announcement of the angels, but upon seeing the baby Christ, they would experience an even greater revelation, actually, the greatest of all!

I have to believe that the Lord's selection of this humble group was by no means random. I believe they were consecrated to God and loving Him with all of their hearts and, consequently, were privileged, even greatly so, to have this distinctive honor.

(16) "AND THEY CAME WITH HASTE, AND FOUND MARY, AND JOSEPH, AND THE BABY LYING IN A MANGER."

THE GREATEST HONOR OF ALL

The phrase, *"And they came with haste,"* refers to them following the directions as given by the angel in Verse 12.

Even though there must have been many mangers, or corrals, in the Beth-lehem area, still, there was probably only one inn of this nature, and so they readily knew where to go.

NOTES

"And found Mary, and Joseph," was probably only hours, if that, after Jesus was born. The accommodations were Spartan, to say the least! However, this is the manner in which God the Father desired to bring the Redeemer into the world.

Why?

PRIDE

Due to the manner in which man fell in the garden of Eden, pride became the crowning sin of the universe. It characterizes all that man is and does. Consequently, pomp and ceremony are the hallmarks of success and even religion.

So, if Jesus had come in splendor and glory, which He definitely could have, man may have been greatly impressed but would not have been redeemed. So, Jesus coming to this world as the epitome of humility, and surrounded by humility, portrayed the opposite of what man actually was—proud. Man is haughty, contentious, evil, angry, conceited, and self-serving. Actually, extreme selfishness, which marks humanity, is the child of pride; consequently, men are impressed by glitter and glamour. Therefore, to be saved, man has to humble himself, which he does not easily do. After conversion, the real battle begins—the subjugation of self. Jesus died on Cavalry to save man from sin and self. To be truthful, sin is far more easily handled than self.

SELF

So, the birth and lifestyle of Jesus was such because it could be no other way, that is, if man was to be redeemed. To be sure, such lifestyle did not save man. That could only come about by what was done at Calvary and the resurrection. Nevertheless, it would lay the groundwork for what conversion would do to the heart and life of the individual—a life of humility.

"And the baby lying in a manger," was the One who, some 33 years later, would die on the Cross of Calvary, thereby, delivering humanity—at least, all who will believe (Jn. 3:16).

As someone has well said, "The Lord died on Calvary not only to save man from sin but, as well, from self." Self-will has kept more people from being saved than anything else, and self-will has kept more believers from walking in victory than anything else. This is the reason the Cross is opposed. It shows what self really is, with all of its man-made plans, and exposes them to the glaring light of the presence of God, which religious man does not enjoy.

Abraham loved Ishmael, who was a work of the flesh, and man continues to love his Ishmaels.

(17) "AND WHEN THEY HAD SEEN IT, THEY MADE KNOWN ABROAD THE SAYING WHICH WAS TOLD THEM CONCERNING THIS CHILD."

The pattern is:

1. The phrase, *"And when they had seen it,"* should have been translated, *"And when they had seen Him."*

2. Theirs were the first human eyes to see Jesus after His birth, other than His foster father and His mother.

3. *"They made known abroad the saying which was told them concerning this child,"* names them as being the first preachers to proclaim His birth, as Mary Magdalene was the first to proclaim His resurrection. They related what the angel had told them to everyone who would listen. It was, to be sure, a joyous story to tell, and they told it with great joy.

(18) "AND ALL THEY WHO HEARD IT WONDERED AT THOSE THINGS WHICH WERE TOLD THEM BY THE SHEPHERDS."

The order is:

1. The phrase, *"And all they who heard it,"* means they were the very first ones to hear after the shepherds. What an honor!

2. *"Wondered at those things which were told them by the shepherds,"* referred to the appearance and announcement of the angels and, as well, their personal experience at seeing baby Jesus.

3. By now, Mary and Joseph had, no doubt, started back for Nazareth, with Mary well enough to make the journey.

(19) "BUT MARY KEPT ALL THESE THINGS, AND PONDERED THEM IN HER HEART."

The form is:

1. The phrase, *"But Mary kept all these*

things,"* referred to everything that had happened concerning the birth of Jesus, which included the announcement of the conception by the angel Gabriel, as well as her time with Elisabeth, and even the dreams of Joseph (Mat. 1:18-21). Now, the things the shepherds had seen and heard were added to the list.

2. *"And pondered them in her heart,"* means she thought about them almost constantly, and no wonder!

3. As she held this tiny baby in her arms, it is obvious that she knew who He was. Still, the magnitude at times may have been too much for her to comprehend, as it would have been for anyone.

(20) "AND THE SHEPHERDS RETURNED, GLORIFYING AND PRAISING GOD FOR ALL THE THINGS THAT THEY HAD HEARD AND SEEN, AS IT WAS TOLD UNTO THEM."

The diagram is:

1. The phrase, *"And the shepherds returned,"* refers to them going back to their flock. Who attended their sheep while they were gone, the Scripture does not say. As well, seeing the heavenly host was a wonderful thing. However, seeing Jesus, although only a baby at this time, would have been infinitely greater.

2. *"Glorifying and praising God for all the things that they had heard and seen, as it was told unto them,"* proclaims a Pentecostal meeting.

3. They had *"heard"* something, the greatest *"good tidings"* that had ever fallen upon the ears of man, which was the announcement of the birth of the Saviour. As well, they had *"seen"* something, which, in effect, was the heavenly host, and above all, *"the Lord Jesus Christ."*

4. Actually, this is the way it always has been. When people truly seek the Lord, they will always hear and see. The book of Acts is full of hearing and seeing. The Holy Spirit means for that to continue.

(21) "AND WHEN EIGHT DAYS WERE ACCOMPLISHED FOR THE CIRCUMCISING OF THE CHILD, HIS NAME WAS CALLED JESUS, WHICH WAS SO NAMED OF THE ANGEL BEFORE HE WAS CONCEIVED IN THE WOMB."

The overview is:

1. The birth of Christ presents the beginning of the greatest moment in human history to date.

2. He was born in a manger and would close out His ministry by dying on a Cross.

3. In fact, the Cross was the very reason that He came.

CIRCUMCISION

The phrase, *"And when eight days were accomplished for the circumcising of the child,"* proclaims, as previously stated, the law as enjoined in Mosaic commandments. Actually, Genesis, Chapter 17, gives an account of the covenant of circumcision as given to Abraham, which was carried over into the Mosaic system in connection with the Passover (Ex. 12:44).

As stated here, on the eighth day after birth, the little Hebrew boy was to have the fold of skin covering the end of his penis cut off. This rite was called *"circumcision"* and symbolized separation from the world and submission to God, as well as faith in His covenant promise.

However, circumcision, as water baptism or the Lord's Supper, in no way brought salvation but was only meant to serve as a sign or symbolism of salvation already attained through faith in the covenant as given by God. Every covenant given by God, either directly or indirectly, always referred to the coming Redeemer. It was faith in this Redeemer, namely the Lord Jesus Christ, and what He did for us at the Cross that brought salvation.

CIRCUMCISION AND SALVATION

To verify that circumcision did not bring salvation, Paul argued that Abraham was justified by faith even while he was uncircumcised, actually, years before the rite was given. Circumcision was a sign: *"A seal of the righteousness that he had by faith while he was still uncircumcised"* (Rom. 4:11).

The Jews in the New Testament had so associated circumcision with Moses that they had virtually forgotten its more fundamental association with Abraham (Acts 15:1, 5; 21:21; Gal. 5:2-3). Jesus had to remind them that it antedated Moses (Jn. 7:22).

NOTES

Circumcision was an Old Testament symbol that man was separated from the world unto God by covenant relationship. It also was intended as a perpetual witness to the deadly taint of imperfection and sin inherited by every child of man because of the fall in the garden of Eden.

Due to the virgin birth, Jesus was not tainted by original sin as all others, and, consequently, these rites were not necessary, at least as far as He was concerned; however, the mother devoutly submitted herself and her baby to the ancient customs, willingly obedient to the divine law under which she was born and hitherto had lived (Spence).

JESUS

The phrase, *"His name was called JESUS,"* proclaims the way in which His name was spelled and pronounced in the Greek, with Joshua being the correct manner in the Hebrew. The names (Jesus or Joshua) mean *"Saviour"* or *"God who is salvation."*

"Which was so named of the angel before He was conceived in the womb," concerned Gabriel being sent from God to announce to Mary the coming birth of Jesus and the manner in which He would be conceived. She was also told what He should be named (Lk. 1:26-31).

God's delights are with the sons of men, therefore, He became a man; and HE became, and is, our peace. So man could learn all of God in a man—that is, in the Man Christ Jesus (Col. 1:13-19) (Williams).

The Father might have chosen a loftier title for Jesus, for the highest titles are, in fact, His, but He passed them all by and selected a name that speaks of deliverance for a lost world.

Jesus was made of a woman under the law (Gal. 4:4). This fact is emphasized by His circumcision. The law is mentioned five times in this chapter, more often than in the rest of the book, and so confirms the statement in Galatians. To save man, justly doomed to death by the law, it was necessary that Christ should be born under the law.

(22) "AND WHEN THE DAYS OF HER PURIFICATION ACCORDING TO THE LAW OF MOSES WERE ACCOMPLISHED,

THEY BROUGHT HIM TO JERUSALEM, TO PRESENT HIM TO THE LORD."

The diagram is:

1. The phrase, *"And when the days of her purification according to the law of Moses were accomplished,"* speaks of 40 days after the birth of Jesus. It was 80 days in the case of a daughter (Lev. 12:1-6).

The birth of a child recalled the sin and disobedience of Eden and that woman was the instrument of that rebellion. Hence, after the birth of a boy, the mother was shut out of the temple for 40 days and in the case of a girl, as stated, for 80 days. During this time, she was not permitted to touch any hallowed thing.

2. *"They brought Him to Jerusalem, to present Him to the Lord,"* fulfilled Exodus 13:12; 22:29; 34:19; and Numbers 3:12-13; 18:15.

3. The presentation of *"Him to the Lord"* went back to the deliverance of the children of Israel from Egyptian bondage. With judgment having condemned to death all of the firstborn of the males in Egypt, including the firstborn of Israel, the latter were saved by the blood applied to the doorposts of the houses (Ex. 12:13). However, even though the firstborn were saved from death, they still belonged to the Lord and were to be presented to Him as a token of His rightful claim to them, as Mary and Joseph were doing (Num. 3:44; 18:15).

(23) "(AS IT IS WRITTEN IN THE LAW OF THE LORD, EVERY MALE THAT OPENS THE WOMB SHALL BE CALLED HOLY TO THE LORD.)"

The overview is:

1. The phrase, *"As it is written in the law of the Lord,"* refers to Exodus 13:2 and Numbers 18:15.

2. *"Every male that opens the womb shall be called holy to the Lord,"* refers to the firstborn only.

Why was every firstborn *"called holy to the Lord"*?

3. All firstborn males were to serve as a type of Jesus Christ, hence, called *"holy."* Anything that spoke of Jesus Christ, even the sacrifices, and especially the sacrifices, was referred to as *"holy"* or *"most holy!"* To be sure, the holiness was not in the person

or the sacrifice, but rather in Jesus.

4. Jesus is called, *"The image of the invisible God, the firstborn of every creature"* (Col. 1:15). This passage doesn't mean that Jesus was the first One who was born again, as some claim, but actually means that He is the Creator of all creation.

Wuest said, "The word 'firstborn' is 'prototokos.' The Greek word implied two things, "priority" to all creation, and "sovereignty" over all creation. In the first meaning we see the absolute pre-existence of the Logos. Since our Lord existed before all created things, He must be uncreated. Since He is uncreated, He is eternal. Since He is eternal, He is God. Since He is God, He cannot be one of the emanations from deity of which the Gnostic speaks, even though He precedes from God the Father as the Son.

"In the second meaning we see that He is the natural ruler, the acknowledged Head of God's household. The whole statement can be simplified by simply saying, to which we have already alluded, 'Jesus is Lord of creation because He is the Creator of all things.'"

(24) "AND TO OFFER A SACRIFICE ACCORDING TO THAT WHICH IS SAID IN THE LAW OF THE LORD, A PAIR OF TURTLEDOVES, OR TWO YOUNG PIGEONS."

The exegesis is:

1. The incarnation was but for one purpose, and that was to go to the Cross.

2. God is a Spirit and, therefore, cannot die. So, to die, He would have to become man, hence, the incarnation, God becoming man.

3. His body, His life, and His living, everything was prepared for Him for one purpose, and that was and is the Cross.

THE SACRIFICE

The phrase, *"And to offer a sacrifice according to that which is said in the law of the Lord,"* had to do with Leviticus 12:8.

This did not mean that every time a woman had a child she had sinned and needed to make atonement for her sin of childbirth. Her sorrow in conception simply reminded her of her original sin, a sin that deserved death, for which she could not atone, and for which a sacrifice had to be offered.

Having been saved from death in child-birth, though she deserved to die, a sacrifice was, therefore, commanded to be offered as soon as her days of separation were ended. The remembrance of sin was the true idea in the continued sacrifices until the Messiah should come (Heb. 10:3).

Now, if Christ is accepted as the substitute and Saviour, there is no more such remembrance of sins (Heb. 10:1-18). All the cleansings for sin, sickness, or any part of the curse otherwise, as these sacrifices represented, were ceremonial and, as stated, served to cause men and women to remember the terrible plight they were in due to the fall.

The real cleansing from sin had to be done, and was done, by faith in the coming Redeemer (Rom. 4:1-25; 5:1-11; Gal. 3:8-14; Eph. 2:1-8; Heb. 4:2; 11:1-40; I Pet., Chpt. 1), simply because the blood of bulls and goats could never take away sins (Heb. 10:4).

A FULFILLMENT OF ALL TYPES

When Jesus died on Calvary, He fulfilled all the types and made it unnecessary for such sacrifices to again be offered.

Actually, they will be offered again in the coming kingdom age, but only as a memorial of what Jesus did at Calvary.

The phrase, *"A pair of turtledoves, or two young pigeons,"* proclaimed that which could be offered in place of a lamb, providing the offerer could not afford the lamb.

This tells us that Mary and Joseph were poor, at least as far as this world's goods were concerned.

It also tells us that the Virgin Mary was not sinless, as claimed by the Catholic Church. If so, she would not have had to offer these sacrifices for her impurity.

As well, even though this sacrifice caused the woman and the man to remember how far they had fallen and that another fallen creature had been brought into the world (this did not apply to Jesus), still, the sacrifice of the lamb or the clean birds was, as well, a reminder that a Redeemer was coming.

I wonder if Mary and Joseph fully understood at this time that Jesus was actually that Redeemer and would fulfill all of that to which the sacrifices pointed.

(25) "AND, BEHOLD, THERE WAS A MAN IN JERUSALEM, WHOSE NAME WAS SIMEON; AND THE SAME MAN WAS JUST AND DEVOUT, WAITING FOR THE CONSOLATION OF ISRAEL: AND THE HOLY SPIRIT WAS UPON HIM."

SIMEON

The phrase, *"And, behold, there was a man in Jerusalem, whose name was Simeon,"* is proclaimed by some to be the son of the famous Hillel and the father of Gamaliel.

This Simeon, whether the same or not, became president of the Sanhedrin in A.D. 13.

Even though such is possible, it is very improbable due to the name Simeon being very common among the people. However, the Mishna, which preserved a record of the sayings and works of the great rabbis, completely passed by this Simeon who was president of the Sanhedrin, whether the same or not! Some think he was passed over due to his belief in Jesus of Nazareth.

At any rate, whether that Simeon or not, the Holy Spirit honored his faith by placing him and his experience in the Sacred Text. There could be no higher privilege!

"And the same man was just and devout," proclaims his consecration. This would have mattered little to the religious leaders of Israel, but it mattered much to the God of heaven.

The phrase, *"Waiting for the consolation of Israel,"* is a term describing the coming and ministry of the Messiah.

There was a general feeling among the more earnest Jews at this time that the advent of the Messiah would not be long delayed. How right they were! Actually, Daniel had almost pinpointed the time (Dan. 9:24-27).

THE HOLY SPIRIT

The phrase, *"And the Holy Spirit was upon him,"* proclaims two things:

1. His consecration was evident by the words, *"Just and devout."* Consequently, such can only be brought about by the Holy Spirit, and, as well, the Holy Spirit always accompanies true consecration. Without the Holy Spirit, such is impossible!

2. Also, the consecration of Simeon was channeled in the right direction and, consequently, scriptural. In other words, his every anticipation concerned the appearance of the Messiah. As well, his hunger, which was fueled by the Holy Spirit, produced a revelation of the Spirit, which will almost always follow such hunger.

Anything received by the believer from the Lord always comes by the Holy Spirit. Any consecration to the Lord will always mark a greater activity of the Holy Spirit in one's life. As well, the person will always be drawn closer to Jesus, for that is the business of the Spirit.

However, many, if not most, religious denominations believe in the Holy Spirit very little, or either ignore Him altogether. Consequently, there is almost nothing done for the Lord in these particular organizations, whatever they might be.

As well, even in Pentecostal denominations where the Holy Spirit is supposed to be given great latitude, He is little depended on anymore. Consequently, as the Israel of Simeon's day, precious few presently experience a genuine move of God.

(26) "AND IT WAS REVEALED UNTO HIM BY THE HOLY SPIRIT, THAT HE SHOULD NOT SEE DEATH, BEFORE HE HAD SEEN THE LORD'S CHRIST."

The exposition is:

1. Jesus died on Calvary not only to cleanse the sins of the unredeemed but, as well, to atone for the failures of the saints.

2. Forgiveness is as close as the confession of sin to the Lord (I Jn. 1:9).

3. When the Lord forgives, all is forgiven, never to be held against the person ever again.

THE REVELATION

The phrase, *"And it was revealed unto him by the Holy Spirit,"* pertains to several things:

1. As we have already stated, Simeon was extremely consecrated to the Lord, which, I think, is obvious.

2. Anything pertaining to God or His work that is revealed to any person is done so by the Holy Spirit. Paul said this, *"Now we have received, not the spirit of the world, but the Spirit which is of God; that we might know*

NOTES

the things that are freely given to us of God."

He then said, *"Which things also we speak, not in the words which man's wisdom teaches, but which the Holy Spirit teaches; comparing spiritual things with spiritual"* (I Cor. 2:12-13).

So, all revelation comes by and through the Holy Spirit! As well, such revelation will seldom come, if ever, without the consecration, as outlined in point one.

3. The same type of revelation is being given presently and, actually, has always been given to honest, earnest, and seeking hearts. While it is true that most of the modern church denies that such is presently done, such unbelief does not hinder the Holy Spirit from bringing revelation to honest, seeking hearts. However, as should be obvious, all revelation from the Holy Spirit will always coincide perfectly with the Word of God.

Sadly, there is much which claims to be a revelation of the Spirit but, in reality, is not! Just because someone says that God told him certain things does not necessarily mean it is so.

THE PROMISE

Many revelations are similar to that given to Simeon of old. He proclaimed that the Lord told him he would see the Messiah before he (Simeon) died. The only way the veracity of such a statement could be made was in it coming to pass, which it did!

However, even a prediction in the name of the Lord coming to pass does not necessarily mean that such prediction is of God. If the command or prediction is unscriptural, irrespective of it coming to pass, it is not of God. Moses said, *"If there arise among you a prophet, or a dreamer of dreams, and gives you a sign or a wonder,*

"And the sign or the wonder come to pass, whereof he spoke unto you, saying, Let us go after other gods, which you have not known, and let us serve them;

"You shall not hearken unto the words of that prophet, or that dreamer of dreams: for the LORD your God proves you, to know whether you love the LORD your God with all your heart and with all your soul" (Deut. 13:1-3).

THE WORD OF GOD

The Word of God is to always be the criterion.

"That he should not see death, before he had seen the Lord's Christ," presents a startling revelation.

Some claim that Simeon was very old; however, even though he may well have been, there is no proof of such.

There is an old and striking legend that speaks of this devout Jew being long puzzled and disturbed by the Messianic prophecy (Isa. 7:14), *"A virgin shall conceive."* At length, he received a supernatural intimation that he should not see death until he had seen the fulfillment of the strange prophecy given by Isaiah, the meaning of which he had so long failed to see.

At any rate, the revelation given to Simeon by the Holy Spirit was of such magnitude that it defies all description. To be able to look upon this One, who had been promised from the dawn of time, was a blessing of unimaginable proportions.

(27) "AND HE CAME BY THE SPIRIT INTO THE TEMPLE: AND WHEN THE PARENTS BROUGHT IN THE CHILD JESUS, TO DO FOR HIM AFTER THE CUSTOM OF THE LAW."

BY THE HOLY SPIRIT

The phrase, *"And he came by the Spirit into the temple,"* means that the Spirit of God impressed upon him strongly that particular day, and even that particular time, to go to the temple. The Spirit gave him the revelation and now superintended its fulfillment.

One cannot help but see the constant leading and guidance of the Holy Spirit in all of these activities, thus, proclaiming the absolute necessity of His presence, leading, and guidance in the heart and life of the modern believer (Jn., Chpt. 16).

"And when the parents brought in the child Jesus," proclaimed Him, as predicted (Mal. 3:1), coming suddenly to His temple. However, it was not with pomp and circumstance as the religious leaders expected, but as a baby with working class parents, and He was received by an obscure company of Simeon and Annas—His hidden ones—the poor of the flock.

As well, Malachi 3:1 speaks of the triumphant entry that took place immediately before His crucifixion (Mat. 21:1-11).

The phrase, *"To do for Him after the custom of the law,"* meant, as stated, that He was subject to the law of Moses. Paul said, *"But when the fullness of the time was come, God sent forth His Son, made of a woman, made under the law.*

"To redeem them who were under the law, that we might receive the adoption of sons" (Gal. 4:4-5).

KEEPING THE LAW

In effect, Christ was the only One who actually kept the law. All others failed, even Moses, and, therefore, came under the curse of the law (Gal. 3:13). The curse of the law was death.

However, with Christ fully keeping the law and, thereby, satisfying its demands, upon simple faith in Him, the believer is automatically granted His perfection as a perfect law-keeper. He was our substitute, and as the representative man, was able to do what no other man ever did. He satisfied the claims of heavenly justice and, as well, broke the grip of sin that Satan had on humanity.

This is the reason that God is sore displeased with believers who attempt to go back under law, thereby, attaching their salvation to their efforts. Why should any believer try to do such when, in effect, no one has ever succeeded in keeping the law except Christ? Inasmuch as He perfectly kept the law, simple faith in Him and what He did grants us the victory of His accomplishment. Consequently, for a believer to attempt to attach law to his walk with God, in effect, says that Jesus did not succeed, thereby, calling Him a liar. Consequently, Paul said, *"Let God be true, but every man a liar"* (Rom. 3:4).

(28) "THEN TOOK HE HIM UP IN HIS ARMS, AND BLESSED GOD, AND SAID."

The pattern is:

1. The phrase, *"Then took he Him up in his arms,"* proclaims Simeon, the first on record, to have *"seen and handled"* the

"*Word of Life,*" other than Mary and Joseph.

2. Quite possibly, and no doubt, there were other parents there with their children to undergo the purification process. However, the Holy Spirit must have singled out Mary, Joseph, and Jesus. When this happened, Simeon probably asked Mary and Joseph if he could hold the child! Inasmuch as the Holy Spirit was moving in the entirety of this situation, Mary and Joseph knew this was of the Lord and gladly consented.

What must this man have thought when he picked up baby Jesus?

3. "*And blessed God, and said,*" simply means that he had great thanksgiving in his heart for the Lord allowing him this great and glorious privilege. Consequently, he "*blessed God,*" or praised the Lord. It means his entire being was filled with praise and thanksgiving, and no wonder!

(29) "LORD, NOW LET YOU YOUR SERVANT DEPART IN PEACE, ACCORDING TO YOUR WORD."

The form is:

1. The phrase, "*Lord, now let You Your servant depart in peace,*" insinuates that it had been a number of years since the Lord had revealed to Simeon that he would actually, personally, see "*the Lord's Christ.*" The implication is that he had tarried long for this moment.

2. Faith not only has to claim the promise but, as well, has to stay the course. I am afraid that the modern church, especially in the last few years, has been led down a different path. If faith's answer is not immediate, many soon give up, falling by the wayside. In scriptural reality, such is not true faith. For faith to be faith it must stay the course.

3. As well, Simeon felt that inasmuch as he had now seen the Lord's Christ, there was nothing else in life that could really matter. Therefore, he was now ready "*to depart in peace.*"

3. The phrase, "*According to Your word,*" means that all of this, the promise of him actually seeing the Messiah, and now the promise becoming a reality, had all been "*according to Your word.*"

5. What a tremendous blessing that this man's experience and testimony would be

forever written in the Bible—all because of faith in God's word!

(30) "FOR MY EYES HAVE SEEN YOUR SALVATION."

The pattern is:

1. Simeon did not have to ask Mary who the child was or inquire as to the wonders of His birth. He recognized Him at once by inspiration as Jehovah's anointed and said, "*My eyes have seen Your salvation.*"

2. He personally possessed that salvation, for he took Him into his arms, and that possession conquered death and banished all its terror.

3. This passage tells us that God's salvation is not a philosophy, theory, formula, doctrine, or religion, but instead, a person, the Man Christ Jesus.

4. Millions try to find salvation in the church, but it is not to be found. The church did not die on Calvary to purchase man's redemption. Jesus Christ did that! Consequently, He and He alone is salvation (Jn. 3:16).

(31) "WHICH YOU HAVE PREPARED BEFORE THE FACE OF ALL PEOPLE."

The pattern is:

1. The phrase, "*Which You have prepared,*" means that salvation is all of God and none of man! This is at least one of the reasons that God will not tolerate man adding his puny little selfish works to the finished work of Jesus Christ.

2. "*Before the face of all people,*" opens the door of salvation to every human being on the face of the earth, regardless of color, nationality, or country.

3. Considering what God did in the sending of His Son and the great price He paid, it is our business to tell this great story to the whole of humanity.

(32) "A LIGHT TO LIGHTEN THE GENTILES, AND THE GLORY OF YOUR PEOPLE ISRAEL."

The form is:

1. Preachers who refuse to preach the Cross are, in fact, refusing to preach the gospel.

2. What Jesus did at the Cross is actually the gospel, the meaning of the new covenant.

3. The Cross is where Satan and all of his

cohorts were totally and completely defeated (Col. 2:14-15).

THE GENTILES

The phrase, *"A light to lighten the Gentiles,"* is basically a quote from Isaiah 42:6.

However, despite the fact of this prophetic announcement by Isaiah, and Simeon further proclaiming this great truth, it was perhaps the hardest lessons the apostles and first teachers of the faith had to master— this full, free admission of the vast Gentile world into the kingdom of their God. It actually took a divine rebuke for the apostles to concede such a doctrine (Acts 10:18; 11:18). It was over this that controversies raged in the early church (Acts, Chpt. 15; Gal., Chpt. 2).

Why was this simple truth of the gospel going to the Gentiles so difficult to grasp and carry out?

It is actually a spirit of self-righteousness, which desires to exclude all, except a select few. Some modern religious denominations follow suit, claiming that unless one is associated with their group, one cannot be saved. Sometime ago, I heard a preacher exclaim over radio that to be saved, one must be baptized in water. However, he added, even that was not enough, as he exclaimed that a certain baptismal formula must be adhered to. He then added the crowning clincher of all! Not only must the individual be baptized in water according to a particular formula, one, incidentally, that had been made up by men, but the individual had to be baptized in that preacher's tank in his church.

We may possibly smile at such foolishness. However, it is actually no more foolish than claiming that one must be a Baptist to be saved, or a Methodist, a Pentecostal, etc. And yet, the church world is full of such absurdities.

Consequently, it seems that we have not progressed so very much from the days of the early church.

THE GLORY

The phrase, *"And the glory of Your people Israel,"* nevertheless, was not recognized by Israel as such.

NOTES

Israel had been raised up for the very purpose of bringing the Messiah into the world. This was their privilege and their glory. And yet, when the time came, they did not even know who He was. Worse still, they murdered Him!

As well, Jesus Christ is the glory of the church. However, in too many church circles, He has been pushed aside, if recognized at all, and even denied in some cases.

The Catholic Church places Mary ahead of Jesus, the Lord of glory! Many Methodists, Presbyterians, and Lutherans presently deny His virgin birth or even that He is the Son of God. As well, and too often, even in the Pentecostal and Charismatic circles, He is little more than someone to use in order to obtain *"things."*

Whether they realize it or not, most Baptists deny Him, as well as many holiness groups, simply because they deny the Holy Spirit with which He baptizes.

God help us!

Jesus is the only light, and yet, the modern church holds up psychology as the answer to the ills of man. He is the only glory, and yet, we parade our buildings and such like before the world instead of Him!

(33) "AND JOSEPH AND HIS MOTHER MARVELLED AT THOSE THINGS WHICH WERE SPOKEN OF HIM."

The pattern is:

1. Exactly how much Joseph and Mary had related to others concerning what they now knew about this baby is not known. However, Zechariah and Elisabeth knew, as well as all of those to whom the shepherds had spoken (Lk. 2:17). Quite possibly, the information related by the shepherds had reached the ears of Simeon inasmuch as Beth-lehem was only a short distance from Jerusalem and the temple. Irrespective, the scriptural evidence is that he came to the temple this day strictly by the bidding of the Holy Spirit (Lk. 2:27).

2. The word *marvelled* relates to their surprise at the tremendous statements made by Simeon concerning this child. Of course, as the Holy Spirit had led him this far concerning his beholding the Messiah, the Holy Spirit would now speak through

him in prophecy concerning the work of the Messiah.

3. Incidentally, if one is to notice, Luke wrote *"Joseph and His mother,"* and not, *"His father and mother."* Of course, the reason is obvious! Joseph was only our Lord's foster father.

(34) "AND SIMEON BLESSED THEM, AND SAID UNTO MARY HIS MOTHER, BEHOLD, THIS CHILD IS SET FOR THE FALL AND RISING AGAIN OF MANY IN ISRAEL; AND FOR A SIGN WHICH SHALL BE SPOKEN AGAINST."

The exposition is:

1. The Cross of Christ must ever be the object of faith for the saint.

2. In fact, the Cross of Christ covers the entirety of the Bible.

3. That's the reason that Paul said, *"We preach Christ crucified"* (I Cor. 1:23).

BLESSED

The phrase, *"And Simeon blessed them,"* refers only to Joseph and Mary and not Jesus. While Christ blesses all, none are qualified to bless Christ! Sometimes the word *blessed* is used in the sense of *praise,* which then becomes not only acceptable but desirable.

"And said unto Mary His mother," refers to her only and not Joseph. Whether Simeon knew at this stage about the virgin birth is not known; however, the Holy Spirit, who knows all things, called Simeon to address his words exactly as they should have been. Mary was related to Jesus while Joseph was not, at least in a literal sense. By lineage, Joseph was related through David, but not by blood.

The phrase, *"Behold, this child is set for the fall and rising again of many in Israel,"* has come to pass in totality, and shall yet come to pass in totality!

Israel fell because of her rejection of Jesus Christ as her Lord, Saviour, and Messiah, while a few rose, which was actually the beginning of the early church.

In totality, Israel suffered its most horrible fall of all in A.D. 70, with the destruction of Jerusalem by Titus. However, her greatest fall is yet to come when she will come close to extinction at the hands of the Antichrist, whom she, at first, will think is the Messiah.

And yet, at the second coming when Israel will finally accept Jesus Christ as Lord and Master, then the world will witness a *"rising again of many in Israel,"* almost like one from the grave.

THE SIGN

The phrase, *"And for a sign which shall be spoken against,"* as well, has been fulfilled to the letter.

For nearly 300 years, the name of Jesus of Nazareth and His followers was a name of shame among both the Romans and Jews. Romans, such as Tacitus, Suetonius, and Pliny, spoke against the name of Jesus with intense bitterness.

As well, the Jews referred to Jesus as *"the deceiver," "that man,"* or *"the hung."* These were common expressions used in the great rabbinical schools which flourished in the early days of Christianity.

Even today, the name of Jesus is referred to either with great love or hatred. Men who have agreed in nothing else have agreed in hating Christ.

Why?

Jeremiah gave us the answer. He said, *"The heart is deceitful above all things, and desperately wicked: who can know it?"* (Jer. 17:9).

The heart of Jesus Christ was and is absolutely pure; consequently, the darkness hated and hates His light.

Paul said, *"There is none righteous, no, not one:*

"There is none who understands, there is none who seek after God."

He went on to say, *"Their throat is an open sepulcher; with their tongues they have used deceit; the poison of asps is under their lips:*

"Whose mouth is full of cursing and bitterness:

"Their feet are swift to shed blood:

"Destruction and misery are in their ways" (Rom. 3:10-16).

It is called the total depravity of man. Be it known that it applies to every single person in the world, other than those who have made Jesus the Lord of their lives and, consequently, have had His righteousness imputed unto them.

EVIL

As well, education, culture, money, breeding, or power cannot change this evil, wicked condition. Men do not merely exhibit evil, they are evil. The only power on earth that can change that evil is the power of the crucified, resurrected Christ. Faith in Him and Him alone can set the captive free from this death of sin.

That is the reason they hated Him and continue to hate Him!

The only thing that is keeping this world on a half-way even keel is the saints of God, who are *"the salt of the earth"* and *"light of the world"* (Mat. 5:13-14).

THE MEDIA

That is the reason the world is going to go downhill fast during the time of the coming great tribulation when the Antichrist makes his debut. The rapture of the church will take every blood-bought, blood-washed believer out of this world, leaving precious little restraint against the forces of wickedness (I Thess. 4:16-17; II Thess. 2:6-8).

Due to having quite a bit of experience with the media, I have noticed in my own personal ministry the manner in which the opposition works against the true body of Christ.

The world system, which is energized by Satan, has no love for anything that pertains to God. However, if one is to notice, if any good thing is said by the media about anything religious, it will, most all of the time, be in favor of the Catholic Church.

If any words of praise are still forthcoming at this stage, it will be reserved for the denominational churches such as the Baptist, Methodist, etc.

For Spirit-filled believers, the media has no good word, irrespective of what may be done.

SCHOOLS

In the 1980s, Jimmy Swaggart Ministries built some 40 schools in the little country of Haiti. These were very simple affairs, which handled about 300 to 500 children each, and only went through the sixth grade. We also served a hot meal at

noon each day. However, this was the only schooling to which most of these children had access. These schools cost us approximately $50,000 each to construct, plus the monthly upkeep for the teachers and hot meals each day.

A lady by the name of Judy Woodruff, who then worked, I believe, for public television, and now works, I think, for CNN, did a television documentary on our work in Haiti.

Despite the fact that we had built some 40 schools over the island, giving an elementary education to approximately 15,000 children, she reported that we had built only one school in Haiti. These were schools, I might quickly add, that could be easily found. She claimed that it was built in a wealthy part of the city of Port-au-Prince, and only the children of wealthy were allowed to attend. If I remember correctly, this *"documentary"* was aired in 1985 or 1986.

PUBLIC TELEVISION

This was portrayed over public television in Seattle, Washington, with the entire flavor of the program, as would be obvious, proclaiming us as charlatans and cheats.

We sent the proof of the schools we had built to the manager of this respective television station, and to his credit, he did air a retraction; however, the point is this:

This woman had no regard for the truth! She did not care that thousands of children were being educated and given at least a helpful start in life. Rather than admit that we were doing this type of work, which should have been commendable to anyone, she would do all she could to destroy us, and whatever happened to the children was of no consequence.

Regrettably, it seemed that many felt that way! That is why Paul said, *"With their tongues they have used deceit; the poison of asps is under their lips"* (Rom. 3:13).

Were one to ask these people the reason for their attitude and spirit, I am not certain they would be able to give a definitive answer. However, I know what the answer is; their true hatred, if the truth is known, is against Jesus Christ.

(35) "(YES, A SWORD SHALL PIERCE THROUGH YOUR OWN SOUL ALSO,)

THAT THE THOUGHTS OF MANY HEARTS MAY BE REVEALED."

The pattern is:

1. Jesus came for one purpose, and that was to go to the Cross.

2. For the fallen sons of Adam's lost race to be redeemed, the price had to be paid.

3. That price was the Cross.

THE SWORD

The phrase, *"Yes, a sword shall pierce through your own soul also,"* basically pertained to the rejection of Jesus' ministry by the religious leaders of Israel and, ultimately, His crucifixion on the Cross.

No doubt, the time of Jesus' childhood and His growing into manhood were Mary's happiest times. Especially considering that He was the only perfect child who ever lived and that it exemplified itself in His daily demeanor and lifestyle, this must have been a source of untold blessing for Mary. However, with the advent of His ministry, that soon ended. The anger was so intense against Him, even in His hometown of Nazareth, that there was no way Mary could escape the brunt of this oppression.

The phrase, *"That the thoughts of many hearts may be revealed,"* presents the very purpose of the gospel of Christ. With Mary's own heart being carnal, as all others, she had to come under the rays of this great light, and her soul had to feel the piercing of the divine sword of the Word of God. As we have stated, she was willing to be the honored mother of the King of Israel (Lk. 1:32), but she was unwilling to be the despised disciple of the hated Nazarene (Mk. 3:21, 31). Natural grief pained Mary's heart at Cavalry, but this dread sword, as we have stated, had to pierce her soul, also.

THE GOSPEL OF JESUS CHRIST

Mary was indeed blessed as the chosen vessel of the incarnation, but women who follow Jesus are more blessed (Lk. 11:27).

The gospel of Jesus Christ alone penetrates the hearts of men, for this is where the true problem resides.

At the dawn of time, Adam and Eve fell because they did not take the Word of God seriously. The very first words that Satan

said, using the faculties of the serpent, were, *"Has God said?"* (Gen. 3:1). He was attempting to replace the Word of God with something else, which he was successful in doing. He has been doing the same thing ever since; consequently, the blight of the human family, even from that earliest day, has been what is referred to as *"subjective truth."* In other words, truth according to this erroneous thinking is whatever one wants it to be or whatever one says it is. In effect, this is the cause of all human problems.

The Bible proclaims *"objective truth,"* which is truth that does not change, either by time, race, or circumstances.

For instance, in the beginning of creation, God perfected a system of laws or truths that are immutable. This pertains to both scientific and social. Fortunately, man cannot change the scientific truths that are found in the laws of mathematics as originally created by God. He must abide by these truths, even in the total sense, or else, buildings will fall, airplanes will not fly, bridges will not hold, etc.

SPIRITUAL LAWS

However, in the social sense, man has changed these laws, which are just as immutable as in the scientific realm, and has brought upon himself untold harm. He has inserted the drivel of evolution in place of creationism, called abortion pro-choice instead of murder, which it rightly is, and replaced the foundation of the Word of God, with its immutable rules for life and godliness, with humanistic psychology.

All of that is subjective truth, which means that truth has been perverted to the extent that it is whatever community standards say it is. That is the reason many marriages do not work, education little works, and wars begin. Men have taken the objective truth of the Word of God, which never changes, and replaced it with their own subjective truth, which, in reality, is no truth at all and changes with the wind. The results are disaster.

The Word of God, in the person of Jesus Christ, reveals the thoughts of men's hearts. In this revelation, one of two things is brought about. Men become angrier and seek to kill the messenger, as they did in the crucifixion of Christ, or else, they repent. Regrettably, the latter is not usually the case.

(36) "AND THERE WAS ONE ANNA, A PROPHETESS, THE DAUGHTER OF PHANUEL, OF THE TRIBE OF ASER: SHE WAS OF A GREAT AGE, AND HAD LIVED WITH AN HUSBAND FOR SEVEN YEARS FROM HER VIRGINITY."

ANNA, THE PROPHETESS

The phrase, *"And there was one Anna, a prophetess, the daughter of Phanuel,"* presents this dear lady as a preacher of the gospel. The silly idea that God does not, or cannot, call women to preach has no scriptural foundation whatsoever, as should be glaringly obvious! In the Bible, the first woman to prophesy was Rachel (Gen. 30:24), even though she is not called a prophetess.

Actually, the Lord uses women exactly as He uses men.

In Acts 21:8-9, it is clear that Philip's four daughters were prophetesses, that is, they were evangelists like their father. This is in perfect accord with Joel 2:28-29, which was fulfilled in the early church (Acts 2:16), and with Acts 2:17-18, which is being fulfilled in these last days.

In Romans, Chapter 16, we have record of a number of women servants of the Lord in various churches. Phoebe (Vss. 1-2), Priscilla (Vss. 3-5), Mary, Tryphena, Tryphosa, Persis, and Julia (Vss. 6-15) are mentioned as laborers in the Lord.

In Philippians 4:2, Paul mentions Euodias and Syntyche as being leaders of the church at Philippi.

As well, and as we have alluded to, women were used of God in Old Testament times as prophetesses and preachers (Ex. 15:20; Judg. 4:4; II Ki. 22:14; II Chron. 34:22; Neh. 6:14; Isa. 8:3).

While it is true that all of the disciples chosen by Christ were men, still, that does not preclude God from calling women to preach. All the disciples were men because man was created first by God and is actually under Christ, the federal head of the human family (Eph. 5:23).

NOTES

As well, all of these men were Jews, but that did not mean that God could not call Gentile men as preachers, which He has by the multitudes.

In effect, Simeon represented men concerning the recognition and worship of Christ, even as a baby, as Anna represented women. No favoritism or partiality was shown to either one by the Holy Spirit.

THE TRIBE OF ASER

The phrase, *"Of the tribe of Aser,"* referred to Asher.

Most Jews at this time knew their tribal affiliation even though the tribal boundaries were no longer adhered to as they had been at the beginning. Rebellion against God had resulted in 10 of the tribes breaking off and forming the northern kingdom called Israel, Samaria, or Ephraim.

Of the 13 tribes, Benjamin stayed loyal to Judah, which formed the southern kingdom called Judah. Inasmuch as Simeon was a part of Judah, they probably remained loyal to Judah as well! The tribe of Levi, which was the priestly tribe, did accordingly.

During the time of Hezekiah, which was about 800 years before Christ, the northern kingdom of Israel was destroyed by the Assyrians and was never restored. About 200 years later, at about 600 B.C., the southern kingdom of Judah was destroyed by the Babylonians. They were taken captive as the northern kingdom had been, but were restored about 70 years later. However, with that restoration, many of the tribes of the northern kingdom came back, as well, but not as a nation.

TRIBAL BOUNDARIES

Consequently, even though all of the tribes were represented in Israel during the time of Christ, due to Roman occupation, there were no tribal boundaries as there once had been.

As is known, in A.D. 70, Jerusalem was destroyed along with the temple, which contained all of the genealogical records of all of the families in Israel. As a result, Jews presently have no idea, except maybe with some small exceptions, as to their particular tribe.

Some may ask how this would have any bearing on events at present. It has almost none! However, the prophet Ezekiel predicted in the last eight chapters of his book that the tribal boundaries, at least after a fashion, will be restored, with Israel once again being the premier nation in the world. Actually, it will be the priestly nation of the world. This will be in the coming kingdom age.

This is important in the sense that Israel must be restored to her rightful place and position, as previously ordained by God, before the entirety of the world can be blessed as it will be at that time. That is at least part of the reason that David said, *"Whither the tribes go up, the tribes of the Lord, unto the testimony of Israel, to give thanks unto the name of the Lord.*

"For there are set thrones of judgment, the thrones of the house of David."

He then said, *"Pray for the peace of Jerusalem: they shall prosper who love you.*

"Peace be within your walls, and prosperity within your palaces" (Ps. 122:4-7).

Luke states, regarding Anna, *"She was of a great age, and had lived with an husband seven years from her virginity."* This means that her husband died seven years after they were married.

(37) "AND SHE WAS A WIDOW OF ABOUT FOURSCORE AND FOUR YEARS, WHICH DEPARTED NOT FROM THE TEMPLE, BUT SERVED GOD WITH FASTINGS AND PRAYERS NIGHT AND DAY."

The pattern is:

1. The phrase, *"And she was a widow of about fourscore and four years,"* means that it had been 84 years since her husband had died. This means she was over 100 years old, probably between 115 and 120.

2. *"Which departed not from the temple,"* means that for some time she had literally lived in the temple, probably being provided a small room or chamber and being assigned some small task.

3. *"But served God with fastings and prayers night and day,"* notes her wonderful consecration to the Lord. Consequently, she would be rewarded by having the privilege of seeing and recognizing the Messiah, even as a baby. To both her and Simeon, there could have been no higher honor. To think

of coming to the end of one's life and being rewarded by the Lord in this fashion would be the absolute ultimate, to say the least. And yet, most of the people in the world of that day would have had no interest whatsoever in such a privilege.

4. It is the same presently. Most of humanity has absolutely no idea of that which is of true value. Most spend their lives on *"vanity and vexation of spirit,"* which means "empty nothings!"

5. Most of the world does not know Jesus and, consequently, has absolutely no idea as to the total satisfaction He brings to the human heart. As well, it is satisfaction and fulfillment that cannot be derived from any other source.

(38) "AND SHE COMING IN THAT INSTANT GAVE THANKS LIKEWISE UNTO THE LORD, AND SPOKE OF HIM TO ALL THEM WHO LOOKED FOR REDEMPTION IN JERUSALEM."

The form is:

1. The phrase, *"And she coming in that instant gave thanks likewise unto the Lord,"* proclaims the Holy Spirit revealing unto her, as well, that this child was indeed the Messiah. Consequently, upon this revelation, she *"gave thanks unto the Lord."*

2. *"And spoke of Him to all them who looked for redemption in Jerusalem,"* means that she related her experience at seeing Christ to all those who were truly looking for the Messiah, at least those who were privileged to come in contact with her.

3. Thus, two witnesses, the one a man and the other a woman, testified to the fulfillment of Malachi 3:1. They both loved the courts of Jehovah's house, and He met them there.

(39) "AND WHEN THEY HAD PERFORMED ALL THINGS ACCORDING TO THE LAW OF THE LORD, THEY RETURNED INTO GALILEE, TO THEIR OWN CITY NAZARETH."

THE LAW OF THE LORD

The phrase, *"And when they had performed all things according to the law of the Lord,"* referred to the law of Moses. Actually, the law of Moses is referred to in several different ways:

"The book of the law of God" (Josh. 24:25-26; Neh. 8:1-13; 9:3; 10:29); *"The book of the law of Moses"* (Josh. 8:31; 23:6); *"The law of God and the law of Moses"* (Acts 13:39; Rom. 7:22-25; Heb. 10:28); *"The law of commandments and handwriting of ordinances"* (Eph. 2:15; Col. 2:14-17); *"The statutes ... Ordinances ... And the law and commandments which God wrote"* (Ex. 24:12; II Ki. 17:34-37; II Chron. 14:4); *"The whole law ... By the hand of Moses"* (II Ki. 17:13; 21:8; II Chron. 33:8; Gal. 5:3); and *"Moses and the Old Testament"* (Acts 15:21; II Cor. 3:6-15; Heb. 8:6-9:10).

All are one and the same—the law of Moses.

MADE UNDER THE LAW

As well, this phrase tells us exactly how particular Mary and Joseph were regarding the law of Moses under which they lived. Actually, it was necessary that Jesus fulfill the law in every single respect, which He did! As we have stated, *"When the fullness of the time was come, God sent forth His Son, made of a woman, made under the law,*

"To redeem them who were under the law, that we might receive the adoption of sons" (Gal. 4:4-5).

In other words, Jesus, that is, if He was to redeem humanity, must fulfill the law in every respect, not breaking it in even one point. He did fulfill the law in every respect, which no other had ever done!

"They returned into Galilee, to their own city Nazareth," implies this would be their home regarding the upbringing of Jesus, with the exception of the short time spent in Egypt.

Some time now, or up to some months later, was when the wise men visited the house of Mary and Joseph in Nazareth and gave gifts to Jesus. (Incidentally, the wise men did not visit Jesus at Beth-lehem, as many believe, but rather at Nazareth (Mat. 2:11)).

Almost immediately upon the departure of the wise men, the Lord appeared to Joseph in a dream and told him to quickly flee into Egypt because Herod was seeking to kill *"the young child"* (Mat. 2:13-15).

Exactly how long Joseph, Mary, and Jesus remained in Egypt is not known; however,

NOTES

it was probably only a few months due to Herod dying shortly thereafter (Mat. 2:20). Actually, Jesus could have been as much as two years old when taken into Egypt.

Luke does not mention the visit of the wise men or the flight into Egypt as Matthew does not mention the shepherds!

Whereas Matthew dealt with situations sometimes after the birth of Christ, Luke dealt with those things surrounding the birth and almost immediately thereafter. Luke, as well, dealt with the only incident that took place in Jesus' formative years, as we will now study.

(40) "AND THE CHILD GREW, AND WAXED STRONG IN SPIRIT, FILLED WITH WISDOM: AND THE GRACE OF GOD WAS UPON HIM."

THE FORMATIVE YEARS OF JESUS

The phrase, *"And the child grew,"* concerns the formative years spent in Nazareth. Due to Jesus being without original sin, He would have grown up without sickness of any nature. This means that He never had a cold, a fever, a toothache, a headache, etc. In fact, He would not have died, nor could He have died, had He not laid down His own life. Not being born of the seed of man, He was not subject to the debilitating effects of the fall; consequently, He was void of sickness or any effects of death.

It is well nigh impossible for us to fully grasp or understand the full magnitude of these statements. No one, other than those who looked upon Christ, has ever seen man as God originally made him. They only see the results of the fall, which is destructive beyond comprehension, even affecting those who are truly born again.

Everything presently is stunted by death, which is a result of the fall. From the moment a child is born, the effects of death begin to work on his physical organs as well as his mental faculties. Death covers everything and is actually the last *"enemy"* that will be defeated. This will take place at the conclusion of the kingdom age (I Cor. 15:25-26). This is the very reason Jesus came! Paul said, *"And when all things shall be subdued unto Him* (unto Jesus), *then shall the Son also Himself be subject unto Him*

(God the Father) *who put all things under Him* (under Jesus), *that God may be all in all"* (I Cor. 15:28).

STRONG IN SPIRIT

The phrase, *"And waxed strong in spirit,"* concerned His personal spirit, which communed constantly with God the Father. This is evident from Verse 49.

The phrase, *"Strong in spirit,"* should be said, at least in some measure, about all believers, but instead, most of the time, the opposite is recorded. Of course, it is impossible for the unbeliever to nurture his spirit at all because he has no access to God. On the other hand, the believer has constant access, that is, if he is truly baptized with the Holy Spirit according to Acts 2:4. The more I study the Word of God, the more I come to the conclusion that the baptism with the Holy Spirit is not an option but an absolute necessity—that is, if one is to truly worship God in Spirit and in truth (Jn. 4:24). Jesus did not suggest that one be baptized with the Holy Spirit but, actually, *"commanded"* it (Acts 1:4).

One nurtures one's spirit through prayer, study of the Word of God, and praise to the Lord. As well, one must be certain that one's faith is exclusively in Christ and the Cross. The object of our faith is very, very important. In fact, this is the only faith that God will recognize—that which is anchored solely in His finished work (Rom. 6:1-14; 8:1-11; I Cor. 1:17-18, 23; 2:2; Col. 2:10-15).

These privileges cannot be properly carried out to a successful conclusion without the help of the Holy Spirit. While every believer truly has the Holy Spirit, which is afforded at conversion and definitely is of inestimable help, still, without being baptized with the Spirit according to Acts 2:4, the full potential of the Holy Spirit can never be realized in one's life.

FILLED WITH WISDOM

The phrase, *"Filled with wisdom,"* concerned the Word of God. There is every evidence that Jesus began studying the Bible from the time He learned to read.

Every little Jewish boy began his instruction and training at approximately 5 years

NOTES

old. The synagogues were mostly used for this purpose. Their textbook was the Bible, and, of course, we are speaking of the Old Testament, with parts of it being committed to memory. The Bible governed, or at least was supposed to govern, every facet of Jewish life. Unfortunately, by the time of Christ, the Bible was misinterpreted, misconstrued, and misapplied.

While Jesus underwent all of this instruction, still, His learning basically came from the Holy Spirit. This is what was said of Him:

"O how I love Your law! it is my meditation all the day … I have more understanding than all my teachers, for Your testimonies are my meditation. I understand more than the ancients, because I keep Your precepts … I have not departed from Your judgments: for You have taught me" (Ps. 119:97-102).

So, we learn from this that the Holy Spirit taught Him and due to His sinlessness and devotion to the Word, He knew more than all His teachers, or even the ancients, i.e., the prophets of old, and was, consequently, *"filled with wisdom."*

THE GRACE OF GOD

The phrase, *"And the grace of God was upon Him,"* constituted *"enabling grace."* It was the grace of God that enabled Him to be what He should be. Just because He was sinless and was God manifest in the flesh, it did not mean that He automatically knew the Word or all things about God. In effect, He had to learn as others learned, subject to the ordinary growth and development of human knowledge. However, His sinlessness and total consecration enhanced the learning process. Still, it was all made possible by the grace of God.

Actually, because of what Jesus did at Calvary and the resurrection, this same grace of God is available to all! This is that of which Paul was speaking when he spoke of the Lord saying to him, *"My grace is sufficient for you"* (II Cor. 12:9).

(41) "NOW HIS PARENTS WENT TO JERUSALEM EVERY YEAR AT THE FEAST OF THE PASSOVER."

The form is:

1. The word *went* means that they were

accustomed to going, for they were godly people and desired to carry out the commandments of the Lord. The law commanded this trip to Jerusalem at Passover every year (Deut. 16:1).

2. Even though the Passover alone is being spoken of here, the law required the attendance of all men at the three great feasts—Passover, Pentecost, and Tabernacles (Deut. 16:16). Even though the Mosaic ordinance was binding only upon men, still, the wives generally accompanied their husbands, even with the children.

3. Passover took place in April, so this was the time of this incident. Pentecost took place 50 days later, with the Feast of Tabernacles taking place in October.

(42) "AND WHEN HE WAS TWELVE YEARS OLD, THEY WENT UP TO JERUSALEM AFTER THE CUSTOM OF THE FEAST."

The overview is:

1. The phrase, *"And when He was twelve years old,"* refers to the age at which time every Jewish boy became *"a son of the law."* At this time, Joseph would have fulfilled the law by paying five shekels in redemption money (Num. 3:47; 18:16), which gave him the legal right of father, claiming the obedience of Verses 48 through 51.

2. When a Jewish boy was 3 years old, he was given the tasseled garment directed by the law (Num. 15:38-41; Deut. 22:12).

At 5 years old, he usually began to learn portions of the law under his mother's direction. This was begun by her and continued in the synagogue under other teachers.

When the boy was 13 years old, he wore for the first time the phylacteries, which the Jew always put on at the recital of the daily prayer. The phylacteries were small containers in which were placed four passages (Ex. 13:1-16; Deut. 6:4-9; 11:13-21), which were written by hand on small pieces of parchment. The men attached the phylacteries to leather straps by which they were fastened to the left hand and the center of the forehead before morning prayers, whether in the home or in the synagogue.

3. The Holy Spirit gives us only one glimpse of Christ between birth and manhood, which is recorded in these verses.

NOTES

At the age of 12, the Jewish boy, in effect, was looked at as a man. Consequently, this will explain some of the actions of Jesus at this age and some of the statements made about Him.

4. *"They went up to Jerusalem after the custom of the feast,"* means that Jerusalem was where the feast was held and, in fact, must be held. This was where the temple was located, and these feasts could not be properly celebrated without some things done at that structure.

(43) "AND WHEN THEY HAD FULFILLED THE DAYS, AS THEY RETURNED, THE CHILD JESUS TARRIED BEHIND IN JERUSALEM; AND JOSEPH AND HIS MOTHER KNEW NOT OF IT."

THE FEASTS

The phrase, *"And when they had fulfilled the days,"* pertained to seven days, which actually incorporated three feasts: the *"Feast of Unleavened Bread,"* which typified the perfect life of Jesus, the *"Feast of Passover,"* which typified Christ dying on the Cross, and the *"Feast of Firstfruits,"* which typified His resurrection.

The *"Feast of Unleavened Bread"* was meant to serve as a symbol or type of the unblemished, spotless life of the Lord Jesus Christ. In other words, during this particular seven days, all bread was to be without leaven, which is a form of corruption or rot. As well, it typified the perfect body of Christ used as a sacrifice and, thereby, offered at Calvary.

As stated, the Passover, symbolized His death on Calvary.

The *"Feast of Firstfruits"* symbolized His resurrection. So, as Mary and Joseph celebrated this week of feasts, I wonder if they realized that Jesus, then 12 years old, was, in reality, the fulfillment of these feasts that had been carried out for nearly 1,600 years.

THE CHILD JESUS

The phrase, *"As they returned, the child Jesus tarried behind in Jerusalem,"* presents a scene that is immensely interesting, to say the least.

The word *child* in the Greek text is *pais* and means "a servant." Inasmuch as Jesus was now a *"son of the law,"* He was, as well, old enough to be the *"servant of Jehovah,"* which He was!

This was probably the first time Jesus had been to Jerusalem and, consequently, the first time He had seen the temple.

"And Joseph and His mother knew not of it," presents something understanding only to the Jewish mind.

Inasmuch as He was now 12 years old and looked at as an adult, He would have been treated accordingly. Consequently, He probably was pretty much left to Himself during the days of the feasts. As He had now come of age, His mother and Joseph would have trusted Him to have conducted Himself responsibly, which He did. This was the custom in those days because of the strict upbringing of the child. So, when Mary and Joseph left with other friends on the trip back to Nazareth, the fact that Jesus was not with them at that time aroused no concern. They felt He was with another group, which would all join together after leaving Jerusalem.

(44) "BUT THEY, SUPPOSING HIM TO HAVE BEEN IN THE COMPANY, WENT A DAY'S JOURNEY; AND THEY SOUGHT HIM AMONG THEIR KINSFOLK AND ACQUAINTANCE."

The overview is:

1. The phrase, *"But they, supposing Him to have been in the company,"* referred to the several groups which had come from Nazareth to the feasts. They were not concerned, thinking Jesus was surely in one of these groups.

The phrase, *"Went a day's journey,"* refers to the custom at that time.

2. An ordinary day's journey was 18 to 30 miles, but it was the custom with all caravans to travel only three to eight miles the first day. That way, if anything was forgotten or left behind by mistake, one could return quickly to get it in time to rejoin the company the next day.

3. The first stopping place of most travelers was at Beeroth, now el-Bireh, about six miles north of Jerusalem.

4. *"And they sought Him among their kinsfolk and acquaintance,"* refers to this stopping place where all the groups returning to Nazareth were to join.

NOTES

5. When He did not show up at this designated meeting area, they began to quickly inquire among the groups if Jesus had been seen. He was nowhere to be found!

(45) "AND WHEN THEY FOUND HIM NOT, THEY TURNED BACK AGAIN TO JERUSALEM, SEEKING HIM."

The composition is:

1. The phrase, *"And when they found Him not,"* refers to a diligent search. It also speaks of concern and anxiety.

2. *"They turned back again to Jerusalem, seeking Him,"* speaks of both Joseph and Mary returning.

(46) "AND IT CAME TO PASS, THAT AFTER THREE DAYS THEY FOUND HIM IN THE TEMPLE, SITTING IN THE MIDST OF THE DOCTORS, BOTH HEARING THEM, AND ASKING THEM QUESTIONS."

JESUS AND THE TEMPLE

The phrase, *"And it came to pass, that after three days they found Him in the temple,"* probably refers to the third day after originally leaving Jerusalem. They spent the first day traveling from Jerusalem to the designated meeting point. Upon not finding Jesus, they then journeyed back to Jerusalem the next day. That probably took a great part of the morning, with the rest of the day being used to search for Him, but to no avail. Finally, on the third day, they found Him in the temple. They should have known to look there first, but thinking that a 12-year-old boy would have little interest in the temple, they looked there last. Had they been thinking correctly, they would have known this was the place where He would have been.

Actually, everything in the temple had been designed by Him before the incarnation, with the plans faithfully delivered by the Holy Spirit to David (I Chron. 28:11-12). Solomon would carry out the actual work of constructing the temple, which would be the most expensive building ever constructed. It would be destroyed by the Babylonians about 600 years before Christ. After the dispersion, Zerubbabel built another edifice to take its place but of far simpler design, but yet, leaving the two main rooms the same size. Herod's temple, which Jesus was now in, was magnificent, to say the least! It was built on the same spot as the other two.

SITTING IN THE MIDST OF THE DOCTORS

The Scripture gives us very little indication as to how much Jesus knew at this particular time concerning His role as Messiah. However, He definitely knew some things, as this account reveals.

"Sitting in the midst of the doctors," could well have included, and no doubt did, the most famous scholars of that day.

Among the famous doctors (rabbis) then living and teaching in Jerusalem was the famous Hillel, who was then very aged. We are told that he was verging on his one-hundredth year. Also living and teaching in Jerusalem were his almost equally illustrious rival, Shammai; Gamaliel, the teacher of Saul of Tarsus; and Simeon, the son and successor of the vaunted Hillel. Among others, these may well have been some of the men whom the boy questioned at this Passover.

The Lord, as a youth, did not dispute with the doctors but asked questions of them and listened to their answers.

QUESTIONS

Verse 47 says they also asked Him questions.

The phrase, *"Both hearing them, and asking them questions,"* was probably carried out in one of the three synagogues located in the temple enclosure. There the great doctors of the law would meet and discuss this all-important subject. Most always, a crowd would gather, listening intently to the discussion. Jesus had probably spent much of His time in the temple during the entirety of the past seven days, and by now, some 10 days. As well, His participation in this discussion could very well have gone on for several days.

More than likely, He had come upon the group in His investigation of the temple and had, no doubt, listened for quite some time.

A QUESTION!

Edging to the front of the crowd, at some point, He must have ventured a question—a question so deep in its searching

NOTES

penetration that it immediately aroused the attention of the famous doctors of the law. Soon they drew Him into their very midst, with Him actually becoming a part of the proceedings.

What a sight that must have been: These most famous doctors of the Mosaic law with this 12-year-old boy sitting in their midst and with most of the attention directed toward Him. Did they even have an inkling as to who He was? Did they even briefly realize that the Lord of glory, the Creator of all things, was sitting in their very midst?

Some even think that Nicodemus, who, years later, would come to Jesus by night, may have been in this meeting. If so, he was to never forget this moment and would later accept Christ as his Saviour and his Lord.

(47) "AND ALL WHO HEARD HIM WERE ASTONISHED AT HIS UNDERSTANDING AND ANSWERS."

The synopsis is:

1. This would have referred not only to the great doctors of the law but, as well, to the audience that stood nearby, which was considerable.

2. The word *astonished* in the Greek text refers to amazement to such an extent that one is beside oneself. It means "out of wits" or "beyond comprehension." In truth, His *"understanding and answers"* were far beyond that of these learned doctors.

3. In other words, neither the people nor the learned teachers could believe their ears at such wisdom coming from a child. However, what they did not know or realize was that God, His Father, had been His personal instructor (Isa. 50:4). As well, the indication from Isaiah is that God literally whispered into the ear of Jesus, even at that young age, His Word and its understanding.

4. Jesus had earthly teachers, but He was always far ahead of them (Ps. 119:97-104).

(48) "AND WHEN THEY SAW HIM, THEY WERE AMAZED: AND HIS MOTHER SAID UNTO HIM, SON, WHY HAVE YOU THUS DEALT WITH US? BEHOLD, YOUR FATHER AND I HAVE SOUGHT YOU SORROWING."

The synopsis is:

1. The phrase, *"And when they saw Him, they were amazed,"* means that before

speaking to Him, they undoubtedly heard the exchange of questions and answers between Him and the doctors of the law. His answers amazed them, as well! It would seem from this statement that He had not exhibited such knowledge at home but had purposely held Himself in reserve.

2. The question, *"And His mother said unto Him, Son, why have You thus dealt with us?"* presents a question she should not have asked! She of all people knew Him and should have known all the time that He was in the temple. Little else would have held interest for Him.

Of course, we have no way of knowing, but the possibility does exist that Jesus did this purposely and was led by the Holy Spirit to do so in order to awaken Mary and Joseph to His true mission and purpose, even though it would not truly begin until He was 30 years of age.

4. *"Behold, Your father and I have sought You sorrowing,"* will enjoin a gentle rebuke from Jesus. Mary used the phrase, *"Your father,"* and Jesus gently reminded her in the next verse as to who His Father actually was. Legally, Joseph was His father, but only in the foster sense.

5. While it was true that they had been very concerned about Jesus' whereabouts, this entire scenario portrays, as stated, that they should not have been. They should have instantly known where His interest was at all times. However, they too often first thought carnally rather than spiritually, whereas He always thought spiritually. As such carnal thinking brought sorrow then, it brings sorrow now!

(49) "AND HE SAID UNTO THEM, HOW IS IT THAT YOU SOUGHT ME? DO YOU NOT KNOW THAT I MUST BE ABOUT MY FATHER'S BUSINESS?"

The overview is:

1. The question, *"And He said unto them, How is it that you sought Me?"* is actually a very gentle rebuke within itself! He is gently reminding them that they should have known who He was and His mission. Regrettably, they seemed to have forgotten it. Most probably, this entire scenario was engineered by the Holy Spirit for that very reason.

2. The question, *"Do you not know that I must be about My Father's business?"* is another gentle rebuke, as stated, concerning who His Father really was! It was not in any way meant to demean Joseph, who seems to have conducted himself with dignity and aplomb, but to once again bring to the fore that which had been slowly covered—the true identity of His person.

3. It is beautiful that this, *"I must be about My Father's business,"* was His first recorded utterance, with the words, *"It is finished,"* being His last before His crucifixion (Jn. 19:30).

What was His Father's business?

John answered that question by saying, *"For this purpose the Son of God was manifested, that He might destroy the works of the Devil"* (I Jn. 3:8).

4. The *"works of the Devil"* are to *"steal, kill, and destroy"* (Jn. 10:10). The Father's business is to destroy these works, which Jesus did at Calvary. He broke the bondage of sin and darkness in which Satan had held men captive. As well, He satisfied the heavenly courts of justice in paying the price that was owed with His own precious blood (I Pet. 1:19).

(50) "AND THEY UNDERSTOOD NOT THE SAYING WHICH HE SPOKE UNTO THEM."

The form is:

1. How is it that they did not understand?

2. They should have understood, for they had had seven testimonies as to who He was. These were Matthew 1:20; Matthew 2:1; Luke 1:26; Luke 1:43; Luke 2:9; Luke 2:29; and Luke 2:36. He was their God and Creator, and so Mary should not have spoken to Him as she did.

(51) "AND HE WENT DOWN WITH THEM, AND CAME TO NAZARETH, AND WAS SUBJECT UNTO THEM: BUT HIS MOTHER KEPT ALL THESE SAYINGS IN HER HEART."

SUBJECT UNTO HIS PARENTS

The phrase, *"And He went down with them, and came to Nazareth,"* refers to the city being about 1,500 feet lower than Jerusalem respecting altitude.

The phrase, *"And was subject unto them,"* concerned the next 18 years.

He was conscious of who He was. Just as that consciousness caused Him in John 13:1 to wash the feet of the disciples, so it here caused Him to return with His reputed parents to Nazareth and to become subject to them. Joseph was legally His father according to Hebrew law (Lk. 3:23), but only in the sense of being a foster father.

The question has been asked as to why this scene with the doctors of the law was not repeated in the next 18 years since He may have returned to Jerusalem to keep the many feasts.

The only answer is that it was not repeated because the Holy Spirit did not desire such.

For that 18 years between his twelfth birthday and the advent of His ministry at 30 years of age, He appears to have lived and toiled as a carpenter at Nazareth. Actually, it seems that inasmuch as Joseph was not mentioned again, the possibility exists that he died sometime during this 18 years. As a result, Jesus, as the eldest, would have taken responsibility for the family.

PLANNED BY THE HOLY SPIRIT

Justin Martyr, who lived about 150 years after Christ, spoke of the ploughs and yokes that Jesus made and fashioned with His own hands during that particular time.

In this atmosphere at Nazareth, the Holy Spirit could teach and instruct more so than in the ritualism and rabbinical discussions at Jerusalem. This we do know: everything He did was planned and designed by the Holy Spirit, which He was quick to follow.

The phrase, *"But His mother kept all these sayings in her heart,"* refers to all that pertained to Jesus.

Even though the angel Gabriel had not used the word *Messiah,* still, he had said enough that she should have known exactly who and what Jesus was (Lk. 1:32). However, despite these wondrous things, Jesus was totally human, so much so that Mary seemed to forget at times exactly who He was, despite Him being without flaw or failure.

(52) "AND JESUS INCREASED IN WISDOM AND STATURE, AND IN FAVOUR WITH GOD AND MAN."

WISDOM AND STATURE

The phrase, *"And Jesus increased in wisdom and stature,"* refers to His instruction from the Holy Spirit continuing, even above and beyond that exhibited to the doctors of the law.

"And in favour with God and man," means that He perfectly kept the law of God and did perfectly the will of God. As a result, the people of Nazareth thought highly of Him and continued to do so until He made His ministry debut in this city. Then, the *"favour"* turned to hate. While they thought very highly of Him as a local young man because of His godly lifestyle, still, they were not willing at all to accept Him as the Messiah. This was a different story entirely! In their minds, the Messiah would be one of splendor and glory and not a mere carpenter as Jesus was.

As the city fathers of Nazareth misunderstood Jesus, many do the same presently. They did not understand the incarnation, and many little understand it now.

THE SELF-EMPTYING OF CHRIST

However, such is no longer a mystery when we understand the true *"kenosis,"* or self-emptying of Christ. He retained His divine nature but limited Himself to human attributes and powers during the days of His flesh so that He could be a true example of a sinless human being overcoming sin and being anointed with the Spirit to defeat Satan (Phil. 2:5-11; Heb. 2:10-18; 4:14-16).

That His power came by the Spirit baptism and not by natural attributes and powers is one of the clearest doctrines of Scriptures (Isa. 11:1-2; 42:1-5; 61:1-2; Mat. 3:16-17; 12:28). He proved to men that by the same Spirit anointing, they could do His works, as well, even as He promised (Mat. 18:18; Mk. 16:15-20).

Jesus repeatedly said He could do nothing of Himself (Jn. 8:28). What do all these Scriptures mean if they do not mean what they say? Could not the Holy Spirit gifts accomplish through Christ all that He did? As God, with divine power and attributes, would He need an anointing of the Spirit to do these works? If He did them because He was God, then how does He expect believers to do them?

If He did them by the Spirit that He has also promised to all believers, then He has a right to expect His followers to carry on His work the way He did (Matt. 17:20-21; 21:22; Mk. 9:23).

"I can see far down the mountain,
"Where I wandered weary years,
"Often hindered in my journey
"By the ghosts of doubts and fears,
"Broken vows and disappointments
"Thickly sprinkled all the way.
"But the Spirit led unerring,
"To the land I hold today."

CHAPTER 3

(1) "NOW IN THE FIFTEENTH YEAR OF THE REIGN OF TIBERIUS CAESAR, PONTIUS PILATE BEING GOVERNOR OF JUDAEA, AND HEROD BEING TETRARCH OF GALILEE, AND HIS BROTHER PHILIP TETRARCH OF ITURAEA AND OF THE REGION OF TRACHONITIS, AND LYSANIAS THE TETRARCH OF ABILENE."

DETAIL AS GIVEN BY LUKE

The phrase, *"Now in the fifteenth year of the reign of Tiberius Caesar,"* spoke of the stepson of the Emperor Augustus, whom he succeeded. At about this time, Tiberius retired to the Island of Capri while his lieutenants continued to rule absolutely in his name. His rule was a byword for evil and tyranny. He reigned from 14 B.C. to A.D. 37, consequently, covering the entire span of Jesus' life and ministry.

Actually, all the men listed in this verse were wicked and infamous. The earth was given into the hands of the wicked, and the people were like their rulers regarding evil.

Some 600 years before, Judah had forfeited her position as the titular head of the nations under God, with that authority passing into the hands of Gentiles where it has remained ever since. Jesus called it *"the times of the Gentiles"* (Lk. 21:24), which will continue until the second coming (Rev., Chpt. 19).

The phrase, *"Pontius Pilate being governor of Judaea,"* proclaims him also referred to as a procurator. In Judaea, this civil functionary was also military commander. Consequently, this double office gave the person, in this case, Pilate, a higher rank and title.

Pilate was a weak man, who allowed a mob to crucify the innocent Christ, which made it doubly worse by him knowing that Jesus was innocent. He did this to appease these hypocrites, thinking to save himself when, in reality, he destroyed himself.

HEROD

The phrase, *"And Herod being tetrarch of Galilee,"* is the one known as *"Antipas."* He was a son of Herod the Great and reigned for more than 40 years. He was eventually deposed by the Roman authorities and banished to Gaul. During his tenure in office, Galilee was the most flourishing and densely populated portion of Israel. It occupied all the center of Israel and the rich plain of Esdraelon.

"And his brother Philip tetrarch of Ituraea and of the region of Trachonitis," presented another son of Herod the Great and brother of Herod Antipas. He ruled the area northeast of the Sea of Galilee. This included Caesarea Philippi, which was actually built by him.

(The word *tetrarch* meant "ruler of a fourth part," but actually came to be used of all governors.)

"And Lysanias the tetrarch of Abilene," referred to the district now known as southern Lebanon.

After Luke gave the accounts of the birth of John the Baptist and Christ, including the one example of Jesus at 12 years old, he now reverted back to his style of writing with which he began. It seems that he attempted to preserve as closely as possible the exact words of the accounts of the experiences as related in most of Chapters 1 and 2, consequently, changing his style somewhat. He continued this method through the entirety of this book plus the book of Acts. That he was a man of education is obvious. That he wrote in two different styles, as in the salutation and the beginning of this chapter, is also obvious.

However, the actual narrating of the accounts given to him respecting the actual experiences of Christ and others proclaims him reverting to simplicity so as not to change the meaning in the slightest. No doubt, in many cases, he reported the very words as they were given to him. This was probably carried through by all the gospel writers, but in Luke, it is more obvious than the others.

ATTENTION TO DETAIL

Because of Luke's attention to detail, no doubt, desired by the Holy Spirit, we have an excellent knowledge of the ruling political order of Israel, even as it was governed by Rome.

As well, considering the attention to detail, I think it would be understandable that Luke did not make a mistake regarding when Cyrenius was governor of Syria (Lk. 2:2).

Chapter 3 opens with the mention of Caesar, the emperor of the world, at least the world of that day, but closes with the genealogy of the true King of Glory, the Lord Jesus Christ. The juxtaposition of this face-off has continued ever since between worldly rulers and Christ. Some few have had sense enough to acquiesce to Him, and even if in the smallest way, are blessed abundantly, with America and Canada being prime examples. To those who have opposed Him, they have ultimately been destroyed, even as mighty Rome was ultimately destroyed.

(2) "ANNAS AND CAIAPHAS BEING THE HIGH PRIESTS, THE WORD OF GOD CAME UNTO JOHN THE SON OF ZACHARIAS IN THE WILDERNESS."

The pattern is:

1. Anna and Caiaphas, the high priests of Israel at that time, were anything but godly. In fact, they were acutely wicked.

2. The Word of God now came to John the Baptist but did not come to these high priests.

3. John the Baptist, it seems, lived much of his younger life in the wilderness, at least until it was time for him to be introduced to Israel as the first prophet in the last 400 years.

NOTES

THE OFFICE OF THE HIGH PRIEST

The phrase, *"Annas and Caiaphas being the high priests,"* presents a unique arrangement.

This office of high priest, which had begun with Aaron according to the will of God, had now ceased to be spiritual and was more political than anything else. Actually, the office was ruled by Rome, with Rome choosing whomsoever they desired, meaning that the high priests, whomever they were, were no longer sons of Aaron. Rome, as stated, chose whomsoever they desired to fill this office.

Annas, the father-in-law of Caiaphas, had been deposed some 15 years previously by the Roman procurator, Valerius Gratus. Despite him being *"fired"* by this Roman official, he apparently continued to be regarded as legitimate high priest by the great majority of the people. Since his being forced to step down, four high priests had been promoted in succession to the chief office; however, at this stage, his son-in-law now occupied the position.

Annas, although not daring to defy Roman authority, did continue to fill the office of president of the vaunted Sanhedrin.

So, even though Caiaphas was legally the high priest, still, he deferred to his father-in-law, Annas, who was still looked at by the people as the legitimate high priest.

THE WORD OF GOD

The phrase, *"The word of God came unto John the son of Zacharias in the wilderness,"* seems to be the formula for the prophetic call (Gen. 15:1; I Sam. 15:10; II Sam. 7:4; 24:11; I Ki. 6:11; 13:20; 16:1; 17:2; 18:1). John was the last and greatest of the prophets who operated under the old covenant.

However, even though this formula was used of John and others who preceded him, it was not used in connection with Jesus, for, in fact, He was the Word of God.

The inference of Verse 2 is that despite Israel's saddened spiritual condition and the rulership of the Gentiles, still, God did not cease relations with His people. He continued to speak unto men as unto John the Baptist.

How long John had been in the wilderness at this time is not known. By now his parents were probably both dead and probably had been so for some years. John was now 30 years old.

THE WILDERNESS

As Jesus had spent His formative years in the little village of Nazareth, John had spent his in the wilderness. Both places were, in a sense, places of seclusion. There, God prepared both of them for their ultimate tasks.

Exactly where this wilderness was, Luke does not state, but it must have been near the Jordan River. Now would begin the voice of the prophet, which would break the silence of some 400 years. It was to be the greatest moment in Israel's long history, especially considering that John would introduce the Messiah.

However, Israel was spiritually blind at this time and, consequently, could not "see," "know," or "hear." Therefore, they missed the greatest visitation of God ever and, actually, all that to which the prophets had pointed and spoken. Their rejection of both John and Jesus, and especially Jesus, would seal their doom, not only as a nation but, as well, of any purpose and place in the plan of God for nearly 2,000 years. Only now are they coming back, being prepared for the fulfillment of the great promises that will soon take place, but yet, continuing in their blindness, and will do so until the second coming.

(3) "AND HE CAME INTO ALL THE COUNTRY ABOUT JORDAN, PREACHING THE BAPTISM OF REPENTANCE FOR THE REMISSION OF SINS."

The diagram is:

1. John's preaching was fiery and very passionate.

2. He preached the baptism of repentance, which is what Israel desperately needed to do.

3. Therefore, he introduced water baptism, which was not to forgive and cleanse sins, but as a result of their repentance.

THE BAPTISM OF REPENTANCE

The phrase, "And he came into all the country about Jordan," concerned the Jordan

River and the place of his ministry. However, it was not a singular spot, with this district being 150 miles in length. So, he probably changed locations a number of times but remained close to the Jordan River.

"Preaching the baptism of repentance for the remission of sins," says to us a number of things:

• The message of repentance had to be preached before Christ could be introduced.

• In the Greek text, preaching has the idea, at least concerning John, of being highly animated, consequently, vigorous, powerful, and filled with passion and feeling. Israel had seldom, if ever, seen anything of this nature in its long history. John's preaching would have been extremely anointed, calling people to repentance. His scathing words, no doubt, held the people spellbound. As stated, this was a completely new experience for Israel.

• The type of repentance preached by John was somewhat different in that it was personal. Heretofore, the message of repentance, although called for by the prophets of old, was more so of a national approach. John's call was personal, which made it different. His message, although intended to have a national effect, was meant more so to deal with the individual personally. Israel had never experienced anything quite like this, at least on this scale.

• The baptism of repentance spoke of water baptism, which was carried out as a result of repentance already enjoined, instead of the cause.

• True repentance occasioned remission of sins, which is what the gospel is all about. The problem is sin, and the solution is the Saviour. There is no other!

THE MESSAGE

This message must have hit like a sledgehammer at Israel because they in no way reckoned themselves as being in need of repentance. In their minds, they were God's chosen people. They were the people of the Book and the people who had given the world the prophets.

While it was true that they were looking for the Messiah, their expectation of Him was that He would deliver them from the

NOTES

hated Gentile oppressor. They had no conception of their true state—their hypocrisy, their formalism, or their total ignorance of all true worship of God.

Unfortunately, that describes, as well, much of the present church in America.

One Chinese preacher, upon visiting the United States, was asked the question as to what he thought about the churches here.

His answer is most revealing. He said, "It's amazing how well the church can do in America without God."

Even the chosen disciples of our Lord little understood or grasped the Master's true mission until the Cross and the passion belonged to history. Only then did they realize why He truly came. It was to deliver Israel and the whole of humanity of a far greater plague than mere Gentile oppression. He came to set humanity free from the captivity of sin.

The very word *repentance* not only insinuates, but plainly says, that an individual is going in the wrong direction and must do an about-face. This was hard for these pious Israelites to swallow! For them, the children of Abraham, to admit being rank sinners was not easy for them to do and, in fact, could not have been done without the convicting power of the Holy Spirit, which characterized John's ministry.

WHAT IS TRUE REPENTANCE?

True repentance says to God, "I am wrong, and You are right!" Repentance says, "I deserve no mercy or grace, and, in fact, I am worthy of death, but I beg of You, please, have mercy on me!" This was the type of repentance demanded by the Holy Spirit through John.

As well, and as stated, water baptism, at least in this fashion, was brand new to Israel. It was something they had never witnessed or seen. It was not practiced among the Jews, and neither was it used in respect to pagan proselytes converting to Judaism.

The symbol of their repentance, as stated, was to be this baptism in water, which typified purification—a purification already enjoined by their repentance.

Josephus, writing for the Jews, said, "John enjoined upon the Jews first to cultivate virtue and to put in practice righteousness toward one another, and piety toward God, and then come to his baptism, for thus only would the baptism be acceptable to God."

Some foolishly claim that *repentance* is an Old Testament doctrine and has no place in the new covenant. However, Paul said, even if the ministries of John and Jesus are to be ignored, *"And the times of this ignorance God winked at* (Old Testament Times)*; but now commands all men everywhere to repent"* (Acts 17:30).

Actually, of the seven churches of Asia, Jesus demanded repentance of five of them (Rev. 2:5, 16, 21; 3:3, 19). So, the idea that repentance basically only applies to Old Testament times is foolish indeed!

This which Paul and our Lord said does not sound like a message with an expiration date on it, as claimed by some. In truth, both repentance and faith are required for one to be saved. Paul also said, *"Testifying both to the Jews, and also to the Greeks, repentance toward God, and faith toward our Lord Jesus Christ"* (Acts 20:21).

Repentance toward God is required because it is against God that we have sinned. Consequently, one must confess that he has sinned against Him, which is called repentance.

As well, one must have faith in that which Jesus did at Calvary. Admittedly, one may not understand much about it, but he must believe, at least in some loose way, that Jesus died for him, that is, if he is to be saved.

(4) "AS IT IS WRITTEN IN THE BOOK OF THE WORDS OF ISAIAH THE PROPHET, SAYING, THE VOICE OF ONE CRYING IN THE WILDERNESS, PREPARE YOU THE WAY OF THE LORD, MAKE HIS PATHS STRAIGHT."

The overview is:

1. This word given by Isaiah was partially fulfilled in John the Baptist but will be totally fulfilled in the coming ministry of Elijah (Mal. 4:5-6).

2. *"The voice of one crying in the wilderness,"* of course, addressed John the Baptist. So, Israel was not in the dark.

3. The way was clear: preparation and straight paths.

THE VOICE OF ONE CRYING IN THE WILDERNESS

The phrase, *"As it is written in the book of the words of Isaiah the prophet,"* is found in Isaiah 40:3-5. Consequently, John's message was completely scriptural.

"Saying, The voice of one crying in the wilderness," was the prediction some 800 years before of the ministry of John the Baptist. Consequently, Israel should not have been lacking in knowledge of this ministry. However, few truly knew the Word of God, and consequently, few truly understood the purpose of John.

John's ministry had been completely predicted by Isaiah, with the exception of water baptism, with even it being mentioned casually. Isaiah said, *"Wash you, make you clean; put away the evil of your doings from before My eyes"* (Isa. 1:16).

However, even the water baptism was not the central focus of John's ministry, with that being the preaching of the message of repentance. It was called, *"The beginning of the gospel of Jesus Christ, the Son of God"* (Mk. 1:1).

The phrase, *"Saying, The voice of one crying in the wilderness"* was done thusly, at least in part, because Israel was now a *"spiritual wilderness."* Consequently, the location of John's training and ministry was indicative of what Israel truly was; and yet, in their self-righteousness, they in no way saw this.

PREPARATION

The phrase, *"Prepare you the way of the Lord, make His paths straight,"* symbolized that which the gospel does when accepted in the hearts and lives of people. This is repentance! Through humble, broken contrition, the *"way of the Lord"* is prepared that salvation may come in. It is not that the individual merits salvation by such action, but that he makes it possible for the Lord to perform His word as a result of this action.

God's way is straight and never deviates. That is what is meant by objective truth. It never changes. The ways of Satan are crooked and with no design or purpose, or else, the wrong purpose.

The presentation of the true gospel has a way of preparing things and making things straight. Actually, it is impossible for it to come about otherwise! Consequently, we need preachers, such as John the Baptist, who are touched by a holy fire from the altar and, consequently, have the tongue of the pen of a ready writer.

(5) "EVERY VALLEY SHALL BE FILLED, AND EVERY MOUNTAIN AND HILL SHALL BE BROUGHT LOW; AND THE CROOKED SHALL BE MADE STRAIGHT, AND THE ROUGH WAYS SHALL BE MADE SMOOTH."

The overview is:

1. The Cross of Christ appeals to man's need.

2. Every other way appeals to man's pride.

3. Any direction other than the Cross of Christ always and without exception concludes in self-righteousness.

PROPER INTERPRETATION OF THE WORD

The phrase, *"Every valley shall be filled, and every mountain and hill shall be brought low,"* refers to the proper interpretation of the Word of God, which produces proper lives.

Men have a tendency to ignore certain parts of the Word, consequently, making a valley, while overemphasizing other parts, making a mountain. Consequently, it is difficult to follow or traverse.

Whenever it is properly interpreted and properly proclaimed, the low places are filled and the high places are brought low, consequently, making it much easier to understand and, therefore, to apply to one's life.

"And the crooked shall be made straight, and the rough ways shall be made smooth," proclaims the Word of God now being interpreted as it should be and was intended to be—straight and smooth. It does the same to one's life when properly applied.

Not knowing or understanding the Bible, most do not realize that it is also the greatest common sense Book in the world. Not properly interpreted or understood, its common sense is lost! So, the ministries of John the Baptist and Jesus properly interpreted the Word of God, which meant this was the very first time most of the people had truly heard the Word as it ought to have been explained and delivered.

For instance, the Pharisees by and large ruled the religious thinking of Israel. They had so twisted the Bible until it had become bloated (a mountain) or, conversely, a pit (valley).

As an example, a woman was not allowed to comb her hair on the Sabbath for in doing so, she might move a dust particle, and that would be construed as plowing, which was forbidden on the Sabbath. That was only one of hundreds of such silly rules.

Jesus ignored these rules and properly interpreted the Word of God, which infuriated the Pharisees.

(6) "AND ALL FLESH SHALL SEE THE SALVATION OF GOD."

The pattern is:

1. The true meaning of this Scripture is that Israel would literally *"see"* the Lord Jesus Christ, their Messiah, who is *"the salvation of God."*

2. As well, the gospel would be presented to all whereas, heretofore, the poor and unlearned, who made up the greater part of Israel, were left out. That is one of the reasons the Scripture says, *"The poor have the gospel preached to them,"* and *"the common people heard Him gladly"* (Mat. 11:5; Mk. 12:37).

3. In the twisting of the gospel by the Pharisees, little attention was paid to its true purpose, which was good news given to man, but instead, that they (the Pharisees) be shown as clever and deep. Consequently, most of the common people didn't even bother to listen to them simply because they did not understand what they were saying. Even if they had understood, it would not have made any sense.

4. However, when John the Baptist and Jesus began to preach, the presentation was powerfully anointed by the Holy Spirit and, therefore, was easy to understand and straight to the point. As well, the great truths that had been hidden were now revealed, even where a child could understand them.

(7) "THEN SAID HE TO THE MULTITUDE WHO CAME FORTH TO BE

NOTES

BAPTIZED OF HIM, O GENERATION OF VIPERS, WHO HAS WARNED YOU TO FLEE FROM THE WRATH TO COME?"

The form is:

1. The Cross of Christ is the means, and the only means, by which we receive all of the wonderful things from God.

2. Consequently, Jesus Christ and Him crucified must ever be the object of our faith.

3. The story of the Bible is the story of Christ and His finished work.

WATER BAPTISM

The phrase, *"Then said he to the multitude who came forth to be baptized of him,"* presents a startling revelation.

As stated, water baptism was completely new to Israel. Especially considering that the voice of John was the first prophetic voice in some 400 years, it made many of the people eager to be baptized by him. From John's tone and direction, we know the Holy Spirit pointedly addressed the shallowness of the commitment of many of the people, especially the Pharisees and Sadducees. John bluntly told them that water baptism was not mere ritual in which they could formally engage, but rather something else entirely. Consequently, their curiosity led them straight into the fiery, burning, and scathing demands for repentance.

THE PREACHING OF
JOHN THE BAPTIST

The question, *"O generation of vipers, who has warned you to flee from the wrath to come?"* was commented on by Farrar. He said, "Let it be borne in mind that only teachers of transcendent holiness, and immediately inspired by God with fervency and insight, may dare to use such language."

One certainly could not accuse John of attempting to curry favor!

As well, with him using words such as *vipers*, the Holy Spirit was informing Israel, and especially its religious leadership, exactly what He, the Lord of glory, thought of them! Even though little was said at the moment, the Pharisees and Sadducees rejected the message and God's description of them.

They harbored a hate that would manifest itself in not lifting a voice on John's behalf when he was ultimately arrested and executed by Herod.

As they heard the words, *"Wrath to come,"* little did they realize its true application. It referred to two things:

1. The coming destruction by the Romans in A.D. 70 of their temple, city, and nation.

2. The ultimate loss of their souls by the judging hand of God because of their rejection of His Son and their Saviour.

THE WRATH OF GOD

Many presently claim that in this day of grace, the wrath of God no longer applies. However, while it is true that we are living in the day of grace, still, God's wrath against sin and rebellion has not changed because it cannot change.

While it is true that the wrath of God was poured out on Jesus at Calvary, who, in effect, took our place, still, God's wrath is mollified only by faith exhibited in Christ and what Christ did for us at the Cross. If such faith is lacking, and it is woefully lacking in today's world, Paul said, *"The wrath of God is revealed from heaven against all ungodliness and unrighteousness of men, who hold the truth in unrighteousness"* (Rom. 1:18).

This is the reason for destructive weather, disease, plagues, and destruction of whatever sort. While Satan may be the instigator of these things (Jn. 10:10), still, he can only do what God allows him to do.

Exactly as wrath was manifested in Old Testament times, it is manifested presently! Against Old Testament wrath, faith in the covenant alone stayed the hand, exactly as faith in Jesus does now, which actually are one and the same.

John warned Israel, even from the highest to the lowest, because the Holy Spirit was the instigator of such warning. How successful is the Holy Spirit in getting preachers to warn men presently?

The answer is simple: not very! The reason is simple, as well! Most that do, at least in one way or the other, come to the same end as John.

THE WARNING

Sadly, most modern preachers who deny the power of the Holy Spirit are busy telling their congregations what the Lord won't do instead of what He will do. Sadder still, many preachers who claim to believe in the Holy Spirit are busy telling congregations how God will make them rich. Very precious few are warning anyone!

Even as I dictate these words, I can literally feel the brooding of the Holy Spirit as He cries for the warning to be sounded. The reason is obvious.

Even though many modern preachers are busily proclaiming that we are about to enter into the kingdom age, or else, have already done so, the truth is, in the very near future, the world is facing an outpouring of the wrath of God as it has never known before. It's called the great tribulation. The Scripture says, *"For the great day of His wrath is come; and who shall be able to stand?"* (Rev. 6:17). This speaks, as stated, of the coming great tribulation, which Jesus said, *"Such as was not since the beginning of the world to this time, no, nor ever shall be"* (Mat. 24:21).

However, as it was not a popular message then, it is not a popular message now!

(8) "BRING FORTH THEREFORE FRUITS WORTHY OF REPENTANCE, AND BEGIN NOT TO SAY WITHIN YOURSELVES, WE HAVE ABRAHAM TO OUR FATHER: FOR I SAY UNTO YOU, THAT GOD IS ABLE OF THESE STONES TO RAISE UP CHILDREN UNTO ABRAHAM."

FRUITS WORTHY OF REPENTANCE

The phrase, *"Bring forth therefore fruits worthy of repentance,"* in effect, is saying that water baptism would do them no good unless first, the fruits of repentance were obvious.

What did he mean by that statement?

It actually referred to a changed life. The gospel of Jesus Christ, of which this was the forerunner, changes men's lives. If it doesn't, it is not the gospel. It makes drunkards sober, harlots holy, and drug addicts free, in other words, as stated, it effects a great change. Greed and pride give way to unselfishness and humility. Hate turns to love!

NOTES

True repentance brings about these changes, and not water baptism. This is, in essence, what John was saying.

So, if they expected water baptism to carry out this task without a change of heart, which, as stated, could only be brought about by repentance, they were sadly mistaken. It is the same presently!

Water baptism, the Lord's Supper, joining the church, turning over a new leaf, etc., fall under the same heading as the admonition of John; those things cannot change a person's heart. Only the power of God registered on a repentant heart can truly work a miraculous change.

REPENTANCE

By and large, we have directed our attention to what repentance does instead of what repentance is.

The call for repentance on the part of man is a call for him to return to his creaturely (and covenant) dependence on God. Such calls, even as that exhibited by John, make it clear that the evil God intends as a consequence of one's sin is not malicious or vindictive, but rather is intended to bring the person to repentance. He who commits evil finds further evil willed by God, but he who repents of his evil finds a God who repents of His judgment.

To say it another way, when man removes himself by his self-will from God's direction and care, he finds that the God-willed consequence of his evil is more evil (Gen. 6:6; I Sam. 15:11, 35; II Sam. 24:16; Jer. 18:10). However, whoever repents, even at the eleventh hour, finds a God of mercy and love, and not of judgment (Jer. 18:8; 26:3, 13, 19; Jonah 3:9).

So, in both Testaments, the note of remorse and feeling sorry are definitely evident in repentance, but it is much more than that. It is a turning around, a complete alteration of the basic motivation and direction of one's life. To be sure, the individual cannot do that within himself, with only God and His power able to carry out this task. Nevertheless, the person must be willing for this to happen.

Repentance means acknowledging that one has no possible claim upon God and

submitting oneself without excuse or justification to God's mercy (Lk. 18:13). In the ministry of Jesus, the *"turn around"* in previous values and lifestyle is highlighted by the encounter with the rich young man (Mk. 10:17-22) and Zacchaeus (Lk. 19:8). Above all, Matthew 18:3 makes it clear that to convert is to become like a child, that is, to acknowledge one's immaturity before God, one's inability to live life apart from God, and to accept one's total dependence on God.

GOD'S GIFT AND MAN'S RESPONSIBILITY

It is clear from Acts 5:31 and 11:18 that no difficulty was felt in describing repentance both as God's gift and man's responsibility.

As well, the Scripture is replete, and even emphatic, that not only must unbelievers repent, but Christians, at times, also need to repent (II Cor. 7:9; 12:21; James 5:19; I Jn. 1:5-2:2; Rev. 2:5, 16, 21; 3:3, 19).

As previously stated, the Scripture teaches that repentance is owed to God because it is God who has been offended by man's sin. Added to that, faith must be exercised toward the Lord Jesus Christ in order for a person to be saved. Consequently, to bring about salvation, repentance is joined with faith (Acts 20:21).

"And begin not to say within yourselves, We have Abraham to our father," proclaims John striking boldly at the very root of Jewish pride.

Israel had come to the place that they believed that simply by being born a Jew guaranteed one's salvation, except in certain cases, such as publicans. It could be referred to as nationalistic salvation.

They had so engrossed themselves in such religious pride that they expressed such extravagant expressions as: "Abraham will sit at the gates of hell, and will not permit any circumcised Israelite of decent moral character to enter it"; or "A single Israelite is worth more in God's sight than all the nations of the world"; or "The word was made for Israel's sake." Incredibly, this arrogance grew as their earthly fortunes became darker and darker.

Long ago, the great Hebrew prophets had warned the diluted race that their election would profit them nothing if they failed in their duties to their God and their neighbor.

Regrettably, many modern churches have fallen into the same spiritual trap as Israel of old, thinking that by being born a Baptist, Methodist, Catholic, or Pentecostal, such ensures salvation. As there was no salvation inherently in Israel, even though elected by God, likewise, there is no salvation in the church. Salvation is only in Christ, and Christ alone, which takes in, as well, what He did at Calvary's Cross.

GENTILES

The phrase, *"For I say unto you, That God is able of these stones to raise up children unto Abraham,"* is, in a sense, exactly what God did!

Paul said, *"Know you therefore that they which are of faith, the same are the children of Abraham"*; and, *"If you be Christ's, then are you Abraham's seed, and heirs according to the promise"* (Gal. 3:7, 29).

At this time (the time of John's message), the hearts of the Gentiles were as hard as the *"stones."* However, they would prove to be not as hard as the hearts of the Jews. Consequently, when the gospel was presented to the Gentiles, many accepted, and in reality, tens of millions down through the centuries have accepted Christ.

It was God's will all along for the gospel to go to the Gentiles. Israel was to be that witness; however, Israel refused to give it to others and actually refused to accept it themselves. Consequently, the wrath that John had just mentioned came upon them, where it remains unto this day. However, the early church, at least in its beginning, was made up entirely of Jews. Thankfully, spearheaded by Peter and Paul, the gospel was then taken to the Gentiles, who did accept it.

(9) "AND NOW ALSO THE AXE IS LAID UNTO THE ROOT OF THE TREES: EVERY TREE THEREFORE WHICH BRINGS NOT FORTH GOOD FRUIT IS HEWN DOWN, AND CAST INTO THE FIRE."

The exegesis is:

1. The phrase, *"And now also the axe is laid unto the root of the trees,"* presents a solemn statement indeed!

NOTES

2. The *"trees"* spoke of Israel, and the *"axe"* spoke of the judgment of God. He did not say that the axe was then severing the roots, but that it was poised to do so, that is, if certain things were not done.

3. As well, the *"root"* represented the very foundation of Israel as a nation. Consequently, the Lord was speaking through the prophet the destruction of the entirety of the nation unless repentance was forthcoming. Regrettably, that repentance was not forthcoming, and the axe commenced its severing of the root in A.D. 70, when Titus destroyed Jerusalem and the temple. Over 1 million Jews died in that holocaust. As well, the temple was totally destroyed, making it impossible for Judaism to continue. The nation was lost, as well!

5. John's words are so plain that it was virtually impossible for the people, and especially the religious leaders of Israel, not to know exactly what he was talking about. Being the first prophetic voice in some 400 years, and especially being the forerunner of the Messiah, they should have understood that each and every word he uttered was of vast significance. However, their self-righteous unbelief would not allow them to heed the warning.

The phrase, *"Every tree therefore which brings not forth good fruit is hewn down, and cast into the fire,"* applied not only to Israel but is, in effect, a law of God that applies even to the individual person.

6. The sole purpose of the believer is to bear fruit. Following John, Jesus plainly said, *"Every branch in Me that bears not fruit He takes away"* (Jn. 15:2).

7. As well, the *"taking away"* is always in the realm of judgment, hence, the *"wrath"* of Verse 7.

8. As we have already stated, let not the reader think that this applied only to Israel of old, with the church being exempt. It applies just as much to the modern church as it did Israel. In fact, the Holy Spirit through Paul said that if the church followed in the footsteps of Israel, *"Being ignorant of God's righteousness, and going about to establish their own righteousness, have not submitted* (and refusing to submit) *themselves unto the righteousness of God,"* they would

be *"cut off"* (Rom. 10:3; 11:22). I'm afraid that the church has already done that.

WHAT DID JOHN MEAN BY FRUIT?

Concerning fruit, Matthew, Chapter 7, and Luke, Chapter 6, report Jesus' explanation to His followers that true character is recognized in a person's acts. "The good man brings good things out of the good stored up in his heart, and the evil man brings evil things out of the evil stored up in his heart."

There is only one way the believer can bring forth good fruit, and that is that his faith is anchored squarely in Christ and the Cross. The Cross of Christ, referring to what Jesus there did, opens the door for all of these good things that God gives us and all the things that we can then do as believers. With our faith anchored squarely in the Cross of Christ, the Holy Spirit, who works exclusively within the parameters of the finished work of Christ, is then free to work mightily on our behalf (Rom. 6:1-14; I Cor. 1:17-18, 23; 2:2; Col. 2:10-15).

FRUIT OF THE FLESH AND FRUIT OF THE SPIRIT

If our faith is in anything other than the Cross of Christ, that means we are functioning through the flesh and not by the Spirit. The *"flesh,"* as Paul used the word, portrays that which is indicative to human beings. In other words, it speaks of our motivation, education, willpower, talent, ability, personal strength, etc. Those things, within themselves, aren't wrong; however, if we try to live for God by those means, in other words, to bring forth fruit by those means, we will fail every single time.

The way that the believer functions according to the Holy Spirit is that he places his faith exclusively in Christ and the Cross. With that being done, the Holy Spirit, who works exclusively through the sacrifice of Christ, will work mightily on our behalf, helping us to bring forth the *"fruit of the Spirit."* Otherwise, it is bad fruit (Rom. 8:1-11; Gal., Chpt. 5).

The very purpose of salvation is that one may bear much fruit. If salvation is possessed, fruit will be brought forth. So, the

fruit not being present tells us that salvation is not present, or else, the believer is sowing to the flesh, and if such, the believer will reap corruption. Paul, in Chapter 8 of Romans, deals with this conclusively.

If we are to live a victorious life, we can only do so by walking after the Spirit. Otherwise, it is failure. There are four players, one might say, in this scenario:

1. The believer
2. The Holy Spirit
3. The Cross of Christ
4. Faith: The Cross of Christ, without fail, must be the object of our faith, and the Cross of Christ alone the object of our faith. I'm sure the believer understands that we aren't speaking of the wooden beam on which Jesus died, but rather what He there accomplished. In other words, the Cross of Christ is the means by which everything is given to us by the Lord. It is the Cross that has made, and does make, it all possible.

(10) "AND THE PEOPLE ASKED HIM, SAYING, WHAT SHALL WE DO THEN?"

The composition is:

1. This question, as asked by the people, shows that inasmuch as John's message was powerfully anointed by the Holy Spirit, it struck conviction in the hearts of the hearers.

2. As should be obvious, John's preaching was not a psychological or philosophical discourse, and neither was it a motivational clinic.

3. This modern foolishness is an abomination in the eyes of God. The Holy Spirit gave John the message, and John delivered the message without softening or compromising it in any manner. This is the only type of preaching that will bring people to God. Anything else is no more than any other secular effort, which brings no spiritual help whatsoever.

(11) "HE ANSWERED AND SAID UNTO THEM, HE WHO HAS TWO COATS, LET HIM IMPART TO HIM WHO HAS NONE; AND HE WHO HAS MEAT, LET HIM DO LIKEWISE."

The synopsis is:

1. John's answer has no reference to the doing of these things as the cause of salvation, but rather the result.

In effect, he is saying that if one is truly serving the Lord, such kindness and generosity will be evident in his daily life, even in practical ways, and especially in practical ways.

2. This was not a new message. Some 700 years before, the prophet Micah said, *"He has shown you, O man, what is good; and what does the LORD require of you, but to do justly, and to love mercy, and to walk humbly with your God?"* (Mic. 6:8).

3. People who claim salvation but exhibit no fruit of that salvation are merely playing word games. They may profess, but they do not possess. Again we emphasize, these things do not produce salvation, but salvation definitely produces these things.

As well, it does not mean for one to give a *"coat"* to another who will not work, is lazy, shiftless, and expects others to take care of him. The same could be said for the *"meat,"* etc. Paul plainly said, *"That if any would not work, neither should he eat"* (II Thess. 3:10).

4. The Holy Spirit through John is speaking of those who are truly in need through no fault of their own.

(12) "THEN CAME ALSO PUBLICANS TO BE BAPTIZED, AND SAID UNTO HIM, MASTER, WHAT SHALL WE DO?"

The order is:

1. The phrase, *"Then came also publicans to be baptized,"* represented, at least in the eyes of other Jews, the worst type of individuals in Israel.

2. These were tax-collectors who had gained such a position by purchasing the right from Rome or being appointed in some way. Consequently, they enjoyed Roman protection. As a result, as stated, they were hated by other Jews.

3. The question, *"And said unto him, Master, what shall we do?"* means they had been placed in another class by other Jews. Actually, the Pharisees believed that a publican could not be saved. As well, they not only believed such, but they made their ideas very much known. In effect, this question was asked with that in mind, that is, if they actually could be saved.

(13) "AND HE SAID UNTO THEM, EXACT NO MORE THAN THAT WHICH IS APPOINTED YOU."

NOTES

The overview is:

1. John treated them no differently than he did the Pharisees who claimed to be so religious. The message was the same to all. All needed to repent, and if all would come to God and come God's way, they would receive the benefits from such action.

2. This must have infuriated the Pharisees, knowing that John placed all on the same level, in effect, in the same category, whether Pharisee or publican.

3. John did not command the tax-gatherers and soldiers to abandon their calling. Despite what the Pharisees said, it was not unlawful in the sight of God, that is, if they were honest in their dealings.

4. John merely demanded that in gathering of taxes they stay within the guidelines laid down by Rome, i.e., *"appointed you."* Actually, Jesus chose a publican, Matthew, as one of His disciples. As well, Matthew wrote the very first book in the new covenant.

(14) "AND THE SOLDIERS LIKEWISE DEMANDED OF HIM, SAYING, AND WHAT SHALL WE DO? AND HE SAID UNTO THEM, DO VIOLENCE TO NO MAN, NEITHER ACCUSE ANY FALSELY; AND BE CONTENT WITH YOUR WAGES."

The construction is:

1. Many have asked the question as to who these soldiers were, considering that Israel had no army. Consequently, the possibility definitely exists that these men could have been Gentiles. At any rate, the instructions were the same.

2. Whereas one thing was said to the publicans, three things were said to the soldiers:

a. *"Do violence to no man"*: This did not mean that violence was wrong under any and all circumstances, but merely that they were not to engage in violence for the sake of violence just because they had the power to do so, as many soldiers did. They must not terrify any man with the view of extortion or plunder.

b. *"Neither accuse any falsely"*: This has the idea of bribery. People would be falsely accused in order to get them to pay a certain amount of money in order that the accusation be dropped. John proclaimed that this must stop!

c. *"Be content with your wages"*: This

tells us that the first two commands had to do with extortion of money in some way. They were to cease all such activity and be content with what they were normally paid.

3. The idea is that if they truly had salvation, this would be the result of that salvation.

4. Spence said, "These men, both publicans and soldiers, are not bidden by this inspired prophet of the Highest to change their way of life, but only its manner."

5. John, in effect, is saying, "Would you indeed wash and be clean in the eyes of the all-seeing? Then, in that profession of yours, remember, be scrupulous, be honest."

(15) "AND AS THE PEOPLE WERE IN EXPECTATION, AND ALL MEN MUSED IN THEIR HEARTS OF JOHN, WHETHER HE WERE THE CHRIST, OR NOT."

The structure is:

1. The phrase, *"And as the people were in expectation,"* proclaims the fact that Israel was looking for the Messiah at this particular time. Actually, Daniel the prophet had prophesied concerning His coming and had pretty well pinpointed the time (Dan. 9:23-26).

2. The phrase, *"And all men mused in their hearts of John, whether he were the Christ, or not,"* was the talk of the entire region.

3. John's ministry was so unique and different that people quickly fastened to the idea that he, indeed, may be the long-awaited One!

4. If the people had truly known the Word of God, they would have known that John was not the Messiah. Micah had prophesied that the Messiah would be born in Beth-lehem (Micah 5:2). As well, he had prophesied, along with Jacob of old, that the Messiah would come from the tribe of Judah (Gen. 49:10). John was not born in Beth-lehem, nor was he of the tribe of Judah, but rather of the tribe of Levi. People come to foolish conclusions about the things of God simply because they do not know their Bible.

(16) "JOHN ANSWERED, SAYING UNTO THEM ALL, I INDEED BAPTIZE YOU WITH WATER; BUT ONE MIGHTIER THAN I COMES, THE LATCHET OF WHOSE SHOES I AM NOT WORTHY TO UNLOOSE: HE SHALL BAPTIZE YOU WITH THE HOLY SPIRIT AND WITH FIRE."

The structure is:

1. In Romans, Chapters 4 and 5, the Holy Spirit through Paul proclaims to us the work of the Cross as it regards salvation. It is referred to as *"justification by faith."*

2. Chapters 6, 7, and 8 of Romans proclaim to us the part the Cross plays as it regards the sanctification of the saint.

3. The Cross opened up the way to the Holy of Holies, so to speak, which means that the Holy Spirit can now permanently abide in the heart and life of the individual believer (Jn. 14:16-17).

ONE MIGHTIER THAN I

The phrase, *"John answered, saying unto them all, I indeed baptize you with water,"* is the beginning of his answer to the inquiry respecting his being the Messiah or not!

The idea is that he could baptize with water, which was merely symbolic, for it could not purify them. That remained for the true Messiah. John was merely the forerunner to prepare the way for this coming One.

Actually, that is all any man can do, or any church for that matter. Preachers or believers can point the way, but Jesus is *"the way."*

As well, all the ceremony of the church, no matter how beautiful, is merely symbolic of the One who alone can truly change one's life.

The phrase, *"But One mightier than I comes,"* if anything, is an understatement. Jesus alone has entered the strong man's (Satan's) house and spoiled his goods, as well as his house (Mat. 12:29). Jesus is God, and nothing is impossible with God (Lk. 1:37).

As well, it was the Cross of Christ that entered the strong man's house and spoiled his goods (Col. 2:10-15).

UNWORTHY

The phrase, *"The latchet of whose shoes I am not worthy to unloose,"* places John, as all men, in the rightful position relative to the Lord Jesus Christ.

The task of performing such a duty was assigned to the lowliest slave in a household. The roads then were not paved, and the feet of the people became very dusty. When a visitor came, the slave would remove the shoes and wash the feet. John was saying that when the Messiah came, which would be shortly, that he (John) would not be worthy to perform even this menial task—the washing of the Messiah's feet. As well, there is another truth represented in this statement.

The Holy Spirit through the prophet tells us that humility is the required principle in the life of the believer in order to be baptized with the Holy Spirit.

In years of dealing with tens of thousands, I have noted that pride is the greatest factor in hindering believers from being baptized with the Holy Spirit. It will not let them yield in any capacity. Therefore, it is very difficult for them to receive this which Jesus alone can give—the baptism with the Holy Spirit. Even though it takes a certain amount of *"breaking"* in order to be saved, still, it takes even more to be baptized with the Holy Spirit. It is as if the Lord is saying that He does not expect much out of the unbeliever, as should be obvious, but He does expect certain things from the believer. So, He will save a person who exhibits even the slightest degree of faith, whereas He expects much more from one who is saved.

BAPTIZED WITH THE SPIRIT

The phrase, *"He shall baptize you with the Holy Spirit and with fire,"* presents a subject that John the Baptist probably little understood. John the Beloved would later say, *"For the Holy Spirit was not yet given; because that Jesus was not yet glorified"* (Jn. 7:39).

What the Holy Spirit inspired John the Baptist to say was fulfilled in Acts 2:4, and has resulted from then until now in multiple millions experiencing this gift from on high. Actually, it is said that some 500 million have been baptized with the Holy Spirit with the evidence of speaking with other tongues since the turn of the 20th century.

The Holy Spirit desired that John make this statement in order that believers may know and understand that the very purpose of salvation is that the believer may become *"an habitation of God through the Spirit"* (Eph. 2:22).

Even though salvation, of necessity, is the single most important thing that could ever happen to a person, still, if it stops there, all that God wants to do in the human heart and life can never be realized. The believer is to be made into the *"image of the heavenly"* (I Cor. 15:49). This is done by the Holy Spirit and cannot be done without the Holy Spirit.

BAPTISM

Many in the modern church claim that one receives the Holy Spirit at salvation, with nothing else to be received. It is certainly true that the believing sinner definitely does receive the Holy Spirit at salvation, for it is the Holy Spirit who regenerates the believer. However, as wonderful as that is, it is not the baptism with the Spirit of which John was speaking. That of which John was speaking concerned the baptism of power and fire, which comes with the Acts 2:4 experience.

The word *baptize* is a far stronger word than those things done by Jesus Christ and through the Holy Spirit at salvation. Baptism implies an immersion, even a saturation if you will! Some have called it the doctrine of interpenetration.

It can probably be best described by the union of the man and his wife in the marriage bond. The Scripture says of that union, *"And they shall be one flesh"* (Gen. 2:24).

Even though that union speaks of the flesh, the union of the Holy Spirit and the believer in the baptizing process is a spiritual union, as would be obvious.

So, the believer who fails to be baptized with the Holy Spirit is, in effect, stopping the very purpose of his salvation. Two things become quickly obvious:

1. SPIRITUAL GROWTH

Spiritual growth is seriously hindered in the life of a believer if such a believer does not go on and be baptized with the Holy Spirit, which will always be accompanied by the speaking with other tongues (Acts 2:4). As a result, relationship with Christ little advances. Things of the Spirit are shut off, with the person remaining by and large in a carnal state. Without the baptism with the Holy Spirit, there is very little *"growing in grace, and in the knowledge of our Lord and Saviour Jesus Christ"* (II Pet. 3:18).

2. WORK FOR GOD IS SERIOUSLY HINDERED

As well, without the baptism with the Holy Spirit, all work for God is severely hindered. While there can be much religious machinery and, consequently, much religious activity, still, it will mostly all be man induced and not of the Spirit. In fact, such characterizes most churches. They are a beehive of activity, with almost all the effort expended in man-made activities. There is no leading of the Spirit and, consequently, no revelation of the Spirit. So, despite all the activity, very little is truly done for the Lord.

That is the reason Jesus *"commanded"* His followers to be baptized with the Holy Spirit before they set out to do anything on His behalf (Acts 1:4). And, yes, that command is just as much for us today as it was the followers of Christ 2,000 years ago.

Also, the word *fire,* as it is attached to the Holy Spirit, in no way is meant to be punitive, but rather to purify. It is to be *the flame of purification.* This is symbolized by the coals of fire taken from off the altar and laid on the mouth of Isaiah the prophet (Isa. 6:6-7).

Even in the lives of the holiest of believers, there is far more self or dross than one realizes. The Holy Spirit will burn this out if given the opportunity.

Regrettably, most of the modern church doesn't even believe in this of which John spoke, and even those who do give the Holy Spirit little opportunity to do the things He desires to do. So, much of the time, Satan wins on both counts.

There are 10 emblems of the Holy Spirit given in the Bible. Each emblem is meant to symbolize a particular work of the Spirit in the heart and life of the believer.

TEN EMBLEMS

1. Fire: this is, as stated, for purification and refining (Ps. 104:4; Isa. 4:3-4; Mal. 3:1-4; Mat. 3:11; Jn. 2:17; Acts 2:3).

2. Dove: gentleness, harmlessness, and comforting power (Lk. 3:22; Jn. 1:32-33).

3. Water: life-giving and infinite power (Jn. 7:37-39).

4. Wind: resurrection power (Ezek. 37:9; Jn. 3:8; Acts 2:2).

NOTES

5. Oil: consecration and anointing power (Ps. 45:7; Isa. 61:1-3; Lk. 4:16-21; Heb. 1:9; James 5:14-16).

6. Seal: redemptive and keeping power (Eph. 1:13; 4:30; I Pet. 1:5).

7. Earnest: ownership and guarantee of power (II Cor. 1:22; Eph. 1:13-14).

8. Rain: life-giving and quickening power (Ps. 1:2; Hos. 6:3; 10:12; Joel 2:23-32; Zech. 10:1; James 5:7).

9. Dew: refreshing and invigorating power (Ps. 72:6; Hos. 14:5).

10. Gift: joyful, gracious, and liberating power (Acts 2:38-39; 4:31-33; II Cor. 3:17-18; Heb. 1:9).

(17) "WHOSE FAN IS IN HIS HAND, AND HE WILL THOROUGHLY PURGE HIS FLOOR, AND WILL GATHER THE WHEAT INTO HIS GARNER; BUT THE CHAFF HE WILL BURN WITH FIRE UNQUENCHABLE."

The exegesis is:

1. Living for Christ means that I accept what He did for me at the Cross.

2. This means that I am as safe as He is Himself, that is, if I continue with my faith in the finished work of Christ.

3. When we speak of the Cross, we aren't speaking of the wooden beam on which Jesus died, but rather what our Lord accomplished at Calvary.

THE MANNER OF THRESHING

The phrase, *"Whose fan is in His hand,"* begins the illustration of the threshingfloor of old. The Holy Spirit through John used this example, which is an apt description of what the Holy Spirit does within one's life.

The manner of threshing pertained to grain being piled on the threshingfloor and then trampled under the feet of oxen or by other instruments in order to separate the grain from the husks.

To complete the separation process, a worker took a wooden pitchfork of sorts and threw the grain up in the air. Another worker would wave a large fan at the grain thrown in the air, which would blow the light husks to the side while the grain fell back to the floor.

The wheat would then be gathered into baskets while the husks, which were over to the side of the threshingfloor, would at times be burned.

The Holy Spirit likens Himself to the man with the *"fan in His hand."* It is the business of the Spirit of God to get the dross out of one's life. Most, if not all the time, the fan symbolizes a judgment or trial of sorts. To be frank, the entirety of this process involves spiritual violence.

Men, even godly men, do not separate from the flesh easily. While we are very willing to make it very religious, we are not very willing to be separated from it. Consequently, almost all of the time the believer has to be pushed into a process not of his liking in order for this separation to be made.

THE PURGING OF THE FLOOR

"And He will thoroughly purge His floor," is meant to convey the fact that the process requires force in order that it be brought about. The word *purge* means to "cleanse perfectly."

The idea, as it pertains to the spiritual, refers to the work of the Holy Spirit in separating self-will from God's will. As we have said a number of times in these volumes, sin, as loathsome as it is, can be handled rather quickly by simple faith in Christ and what He did for us at the Cross. However, we must remember, our faith, which is so very, very important, must at all times have as its object the Cross of Christ. The reason is simple: this is where Jesus atoned for all sin and triumphed over Satan and all of his cohorts of darkness (Col. 2:10-15).

And yet, the sanctification of the self-life is very difficult. It is the business of the Holy Spirit to root out the works of the flesh, which is jealousy, envy, malice, lust, pride, self-will, etc., and replace those things with the fruit of the Spirit, which is *"love, joy, peace, long-suffering, gentleness, goodness, faith, meekness, and temperance"* (Gal. 5:22-23). This is what the purging process is all about.

GATHERING THE WHEAT

The phrase, *"And will gather the wheat into His garner,"* in the spiritual sense, refers to the finished work of the Holy Spirit.

NOTES

Every semblance of the flesh, or more particularly, self-will, must be rooted out of the life, with nothing left but the work of the Spirit. Once again, this is done by the believer ever placing his or her faith in the Cross of Christ, referring to what He there did.

Especially considering that the Holy Spirit through John uses this type of illustration as an example, to which we have alluded, this portrays to us that the process is, at times, painful. However, even though it is painful to the flesh, it is invigorating to the spirit.

As one biblical example among many, the question might be asked as to why the Lord allowed Saul to torment David for so long. The Lord, having the power to do whatever, could have easily changed the situation in many different ways. And yet, He allowed this persecution to continue for years, even to the point that David was not even sure if he would survive it.

The Lord allowed Saul to persecute David because such was needed to drive David to his knees, which was all a part of the purging process. Even though Saul was of Satan, and used of Satan, the Lord, nevertheless, used it for His own purpose. He does the same with us presently in many different ways.

JOB

Job is another example. His book explains why good men are afflicted. It is in order for their sanctification. It is interesting that this difficult question should be the first taken up and answered in the Bible, because Job is probably the oldest book in the Bible.

Williams says, "In the book of Job we find that the discovery of the worthlessness of self is the first step in Christian experience, as in the Song of Solomon, we find the very opposite, the worthfulness of Christ. However, the 'worthfulness of Christ' cannot be reached until the 'worthlessness' of self is realized."

Understanding that, it becomes more obvious as to why the Lord would use such a godly man as Job to present this great truth.

It is evident that all unbelievers need to be brought to the end of themselves, but that a man who feared God, who was perfect, and who hated evil should also need this comes as a surprise to most believers.

In all of this, as we have stated, God uses Satan, calamity, and even sickness at times to be His instruments in creating character and making men partakers of His holiness. Such were the instruments, but the hand that used them was God's. The facts of these biblical examples explain to believers (such as Job, David, Paul, and others) who are conscious of personal integrity, why calamities, sorrows, and at times, even diseases are permitted to afflict them. It is all a part of the sanctification process, as John the Baptist here brings out.

THE POSITION AND THE CONDITION

Every believer is given the position of sanctification at conversion. This is automatic in Christ and constitutes a part of one's salvation. It is actually as the Lord looks at the believer, which is, in effect, perfect. Still, the sanctification process continues. Our *"position"* of sanctification is outlined in I Corinthians 6:11, while our *"condition"* of sanctification is outlined in I Thessalonians 5:23. Consequently, the entire process speaks of the Holy Spirit attempting to bring our condition, which is what we are at present, up to our position, which is what we are because of our faith in Christ. In effect, it is a lifelong process.

THE BURNING OF THE CHAFF

"But the chaff He will burn with fire unquenchable," in the spiritual sense refers to all of the old carnal life, i.e., self-will being completely done away with, in effect, burned.

The Holy Spirit is telling us by this word He gave to John that either these works of self-will can be burned here, or they will be burned there, i.e., the judgment seat of Christ. There our motives will be judged, and that which is not strictly Christ will be burned, in effect, destroyed. This is that of which Paul was speaking when he said, *"If any man's work shall be burned, he shall suffer loss: but he himself shall be saved; yet so as by fire"* (I Cor. 3:15). As stated, this is speaking of the judgment seat of Christ.

He was speaking of the works done through self-will and wrong motivation. Such will not stand the acid test when the believer stands at the judgment seat of Christ. So, the Holy Spirit does it here, that is, if we will allow Him to do so, or else, as stated, He will do it there. At the judgment seat of Christ, rewards may be lost because of wrong motivation, etc.; however, the soul will not be lost because that was settled at Calvary.

A PERSONAL EXPERIENCE

In 1983, we conducted a citywide crusade in Guatemala City, Guatemala. The meeting was to be conducted in the stadium in the city. The stadium seated approximately 50,000 people. The Lord gave us a tremendous meeting, with the stadium jammed to capacity, and with many, many souls saved. We were on television in Guatemala, with the program translated into Spanish, which covered most of that country.

We arrived in the city about three days before the meetings were to begin. I generally did this so I could use the extra time to pray, study, and get the mind of the Lord for the crusade.

The time element of which I wish to speak was on a Wednesday night. We had arrived in Guatemala City that afternoon. After getting settled in the hotel, Frances and I retired for the evening at about 10 p.m. Being tired from the long trip, I went to sleep almost immediately but awakened about 1 a.m.

I arose and went into the next room and shut the door so as not to disturb Frances. I almost immediately began to seek the Lord respecting the coming crusade, as well as other matters. The Spirit of God began to move mightily upon me, with something happening that is relative to this of which John spoke.

I believe the Lord gave me a vision that night. At any rate, I saw what I'm about to relate to you with such vividness that I will never forget it.

THE THRESHINGFLOOR

I saw in my vision the threshingfloor piled high with grain, even though I did not see the purging process. I did see the man with a pitchfork-like instrument throwing the grain in the air, and the man with the fan in his hand creating a breeze, which blew the husks to the side of the threshing-floor. Actually, the husks were piled up all around the threshingfloor.

I did not see what happened to the grain, but I assume that it had been gathered, leaving only the husks. Actually, the vision was directed toward the husks and its burning.

As I watched the flames lick at the husks with them being consumed, I knew this was the part of the vision that the Lord was making real to me.

The husks were no more joined to the grain and were not even on the threshing-floor any longer. So, I asked the Lord why it was necessary for the husks to be burned because in the vision, it seemed that this was attended to with great diligence.

NOTHING OF THE FLESH MUST REMAIN

I could very well understand the absolute necessity for its separation from the grain and, as well, its separation even from the thresh-ingfloor. However, it seemed to me that the husks presented no more problems, so I was not sure as to the reason for the burning.

The Lord spoke to me and said, "The husks are burned because there must be absolutely nothing left of the old life. The flesh, with all its self-will, must be eliminated, with no trace left."

When the Lord spoke these words to me, the Spirit of God came on me greatly, and I remember standing in the middle of the room sobbing.

The sanctification process, which would be stepped up greatly in my life before too very long, was to be, I believe, the fulfillment of this vision given to me by the Lord.

To be sure, it has been extremely violent, so much so, at times, that I was not sure I would survive; however, a passage is given in Isaiah which reflects on that statement.

The Spirit through the prophet said, *"Bread corn is bruised; because he will not ever be threshing it, nor break it with the wheel of his cart, nor bruise it with his horsemen"* (Isa. 28:28).

This Scripture, as I explained in the commentary on that particular verse, is somewhat a question. *"Is bread corn bruised?"* The answer is, "No."

The farmer will not continue always

threshing it or crunching it with his cart wheel and with his horses. If he did so, it would destroy it. Therefore, he does it only enough to separate the grain from the husks.

This Scripture tells us that even when the rougher mode of threshing is employed, there is moderation in its employment. Care is taken not to injure the grain. Here, the main meaning of the entire parable appears.

ADAPTED TO OUR STRENGTH

The afflictions that God sends upon His people are adapted to our strengths and to our needs. In no case are they used to crush and injure; only such violence is used that is required to detach the bread corn from the husks. Even when the process is severe, still, the bread corn is not bruised.

So, we have the promise, *"As your days, so shall your strength be"* (Deut. 33:25).

As well, I think one can say, at least in one form or the other, this process is unending. It will continue and, in fact, must continue until *"this corruptible must put on incorruption, and this mortal must put on immortality"* (I Cor. 15:53).

It is incredible, but this work of the Spirit, which, in effect, must take place in the life of every believer, is little understood or even accepted by the modern church. Such is looked at mostly as failure when all the time it speaks of victory.

Actually, the true body of Christ has been affected in a negative way by the modern confession message. Basically, this message claims that all difficulties, problems, and trials can be dispensed with, that is, if the proper confession is made, etc. While a proper confession is certainly important, the idea that this purging process can be eliminated in that manner, or even should be eliminated, is facetious indeed! It has produced a crop of unsanctified Christians.

(18) "AND MANY OTHER THINGS IN HIS EXHORTATION PREACHED HE UNTO THE PEOPLE."

The structure is:

1. This could, no doubt, be said about both John and Christ, as well as Paul, and all others whose messages are printed in the Bible.

2. What we are given is what the Holy

Spirit wanted given and, no doubt, provides the basic ingredients of what was said.

(19) "BUT HEROD THE TETRARCH, BEING REPROVED BY HIM FOR HERODIAS HIS BROTHER PHILIP'S WIFE, AND FOR ALL THE EVILS WHICH HEROD HAD DONE."

The pattern is:

1. The phrase, *"But Herod the tetrarch,"* referred to the son of Herod the Great, called Herod Antipas. He reigned over Galilee and Perea 4 B.C. to A.D. 39. He is the one who killed John the Baptist.

2. *"Being reproved by him for Herodias his brother Philip's wife,"* pertained to John saying publicly that this marriage between Herod and Herodias was not lawful. This woman was both niece and wife to Philip and Herod, who were brothers, being the daughter of Aristobulus, son of Herod the Great.

3. She first married Philip, her uncle, by whom she had Salome. Later, she left him to live publicly with Herod, who had been previously married to the daughter of Aretas, king of Arabia Petra.

4. Later on, Aretas made war on Herod and destroyed his army, which Josephus said was judgment on him for murdering John the Baptist.

5. The phrase, *"And for all the evils which Herod had done,"* does not actually proclaim what was done, other than what was mentioned, but the evil must have been greatly pronounced. This is the one that Jesus referred to as *"that fox"* (Lk. 13:32).

6. He was a great builder, having built the city of Tiberias on the Sea of Galilee in A.D. 22, and named it in honor of Emperor Tiberius. It is the only city remaining presently among the many that once ringed the lake. Israel had forsaken God; consequently, those who ruled over them were despots. Someone has well said that the leadership of a nation mirrors the people.

(20) "ADDED YET THIS ABOVE ALL, THAT HE SHUT UP JOHN IN PRISON."

The form is:

1. John was placed in the fortress of Machaerus on the border of Arabia north of the Dead Sea.

2. Some would claim that John was not wise in publicly naming the sin of Herod.

However, every indication is that the Holy Spirit desired that he do this, even though He certainly knew what would happen to John. John, consequently, was not put in prison for a lack of wisdom, but instead, for obeying God.

3. This proclaims the fact that a God-called preacher is not a *"career"* preacher. Neither does he temper his message to the times or, above all, to curry favor with the rich and famous. The message is, *"Thus saith the Lord,"* and neither its content nor to whom it is directed matters.

4. While it is true that this brave preacher of the gospel paid the penalty for his splendid courage, the main thing is he obeyed God. Spence said, "Like so many of earth's great ones, he passed through pain and agony to his eternal rest."

Luke did not go into detail concerning the death of John the Baptist, as did Matthew, but only mentioned it.

(21) "NOW WHEN ALL THE PEOPLE WERE BAPTIZED, IT CAME TO PASS, THAT JESUS ALSO BEING BAPTIZED, AND PRAYING, THE HEAVEN WAS OPENED."

Four things are said in this verse:

1. NOW WHEN ALL THE PEOPLE WERE BAPTIZED

Inasmuch as Jesus was present at this baptismal service, it shows His relationship with the people. He was the Lord of glory, the Creator of all things, but yet, He purposely placed Himself on our level. There is no hint in the four gospels that He placed Himself aloft or distant. He was a man among men.

This portrays the spirit of humility, which is lacking in so many of us who name the name of Christ. However, even though He accepted worship because He is God, still, he ate the same food, wore the same clothing, lived in the same humble manner, and associated with the same people—the humble, unassuming, common people.

2. IT CAME TO PASS, THAT JESUS ALSO BEING BAPTIZED

Jesus was baptized to testify of His death, burial, and resurrection, which are typified by the baptismal process. As well, in a spiritual sense, it testifies the same for the believer.

Whenever the believer accepts Christ as his Saviour, the old man dies, hence, the going out into the water.

The act of putting the believer under the water in baptism is a symbol of the burial of the old man—the unsaved person that once was.

The bringing the believer out of the water in the baptismal act is symbolic of the resurrection of the new man in Christ, the born-again believer.

As well, water baptism does not cleanse from sin and in no way is meant to convey that impression. It is, *"The answer of a good conscience toward God,"* meaning that it is the result or a symbolism of a work already done in the heart, and not the cause of that work.

The word *also* proves that baptism in water is not to remit sins, but that it is for the same purpose that Christ was baptized—to testify of the death, burial, and resurrection of Christ. If it was to remit sins, then Christ *"also"* had His sins remitted, but if it was not to remit His sins, which it was not because He had no sins, then the sins of men are not remitted by it, as well! (I Pet. 2:21-23).

3. PRAYING

This is the first of seven times that Luke records the praying of Jesus (Lk. 3:21; 5:16; 6:12; 9:18, 28; 11:1; 22:41-44). His praying was to accentuate the nature of Christ as man. He prayed as being dependent, and as He moved among the people, as being related. This means that as John brought Him up out of the water, He came up praying.

This is the first mention of what, no doubt, had been, and would continue to be, a strong prayer life in the heart of the Master. Even though Jesus was God and never ceased to be God, still, He emptied Himself of His attributes of deity in His incarnation. Consequently, during this time of some 33 years, He was also very man, i.e., total and complete man. Thus, He had to pray and seek the face of the heavenly Father exactly as we do. Actually, He set the example for us for life and ministry. Therefore, the prayerlessness of most Christians is the opposite of the Christlike life. As someone has said, *"If Jesus had to pray, and He certainly did, then what about us?"*

4. THE HEAVEN WAS OPENED

Heaven had been closed to man since the fall. It meant that fellowship that Adam had with God before the fall was stopped of necessity, which was because of man's sin.

Jacob had a dream of the open heavens, with *"a ladder set up on the earth, and the top of it reaching to heaven"* (Gen. 28:12).

The fact that the ladder began on earth and reached to heaven portrayed the truth that salvation would have to be effected by Jesus coming to this earth and paying the price for man's redemption, which would, in turn, open heaven. The fall took place on earth; consequently, the redemption would have to take place on earth, which it did! The song says:

"Jesus opened up the way,
"The way to heaven's gate."

In brief, the fall so crippled man that there was no way he could reach God on his own. Conversely, God had to reach man, which He did, in the sending of His Son, Jesus Christ. Now the heavens are open, *"And let him who is athirst come. And whosoever will, let him take the water of life freely"* (Rev. 22:17).

(22) "AND THE HOLY SPIRIT DESCENDED IN A BODILY SHAPE LIKE A DOVE UPON HIM, AND A VOICE CAME FROM HEAVEN, WHICH SAID, YOU ARE MY BELOVED SON; IN YOU I AM WELL PLEASED."

THE HOLY SPIRIT

Several things are said in this verse, which are actually a continuation of the previous verse. Therefore, we will continue:

"And the Holy Spirit descended in a bodily shape like a dove": This passage relates to us, as in many other places, that the Holy Spirit is a person separate from the Father and separate from the Son and, as well, is God, as is the Father and the Son. It is the Trinity.

As well, I think this passage also informs us that the Holy Spirit has a spirit body.

With the use of the word *body*, many believers automatically think of the human body. That is not what is meant, for the Holy Spirit is not human. Luke wrote the words *bodily shape* because that is what was told him, and they are the words sanctioned by the Holy Spirit Himself. Therefore, we must conclude that the Holy Spirit has a bodily shape although a bodily shape that is spirit and not flesh.

As well, Luke did not say this bodily shape was a dove, but *"like a dove."*

The dove was a symbol for gentleness exactly as the fire was a symbolism of purity in Verse 16. The Holy Spirit is not made of fire, and neither is He a dove.

INTO CHRIST

"Upon Him": The actual word used in the Greek text is *eis* and means literally "into," and should have been translated, *"The Holy Spirit descended in a bodily shape like a dove into Him."* This means it was not merely upon Him. This was the signal for His threefold ministry of the prophet, priest, and king to begin. The Holy Spirit would enable the Messiah to discharge the duties connected with these offices (Lk. 4:16-19).

As well, when we think of the Holy Spirit coming into Jesus, and into any believer for that matter, we must not think in the physical but in the spiritual. The Holy Spirit being God and Spirit can easily make the human body His temple, as He actually does, and as with Jesus, become one in spirit.

Incidentally, the Lord did not begin His public ministry until He was first filled with the Holy Spirit. If our Lord needed the Holy Spirit to carry out His work, I certainly think that we should understand that we desperately need the Holy Spirit to help us carry out our work.

MY BELOVED SON

"And a voice came from heaven, which said, You are My beloved Son": this presents the Trinity, the *"Holy Spirit descending,"* the *"voice of God from heaven,"* and *"the Son to whom the voice speaks."*

Respecting the words, *"My beloved Son,"* the Greek has the pronoun of the second person *Su,* literally, *"As for you, in contradistinction to all others."* In other words, the Messiah is the unique Son of God. We believers are sons of God, but only by adoption (Rom. 8:15). Even though we are sons of God, we have a different relationship to the Father than does the Son. The Messiah claimed to be the Son of God in a unique

way, for He said that God was His own private, personal, unique Father. The Greek word is *idios,* which speaks of one's own private, unique, absolute possession (Jn. 5:18). The order of the Greek words are, *"As for You, You are My Son, the beloved One."* An equal emphasis is laid upon the fact that Messiah is the Son of God and that He is the beloved Son.

The particular word for love here is *agape,* which, in the classics, spoke of a love called out of one's heart by the preciousness of the object loved. The Son of God is infinitely precious to God the Father. This love is called out of the Father's heart by the preciousness of the Son.

IN YOU I AM WELL PLEASED

The expositors say that the way it is given in the Greek text means that the Father has always been pleased with the Son, is pleased with Him now, and will always be pleased with Him. It is a delight that never had a beginning and will never have an end.

In a limited sense, another beautiful thought is brought out in this text:

Upon acceptance of the Son as divine and as the Saviour of mankind, then the individual personally is placed *"in Christ"* (Jn. 14:20). Consequently, the Father proclaiming His being well pleased with the Son, at the same time, says the same identical thing about every believer.

So, upon acceptance of Christ, the Father, in essence, says, "This is My beloved Jimmy Swaggart (or your name if you are saved) in whom I am well pleased."

Irrespective of all religious works, He is not pleased whatsoever unless one is totally in Christ, which can only be carried out by our faith being exclusively in Christ and the Cross. The Cross of Christ is the means, and the only means, by which all of these wonderful things are given to us from God. The Cross of Christ alone has made it possible.

And yet, the Father being pleased is centered on Christ and not the believer. Consequently, it is only when the believer is in Christ, which can only be done by the means of the Cross, that the acclamation is given.

This means that the church holds no saving grace, and neither do its sacraments; only

Christ, and more particularly, only Christ and Him crucified (I Cor. 1:17-18, 23; 2:2).

UNDERSTANDING THE TRINITY

The word *trinity,* as such, is not found in the Bible; however, in its simplest form, trinity means three (I Jn. 5:7).

Many claim that the doctrine of the Trinity cannot be understood. While it is certainly true that man presently has an elementary knowledge of God, still, I think most of the difficulties are because of not properly interpreting the Bible.

And yet, the essence of God cannot be fully comprehended by any man. John said, *"No man has seen* (fully comprehended) *God at any time"* (Jn. 1:18). God is infinite. Man is finite. God is immortal and almighty. Man is mortal, meaning that he is dying and is limited, as well. The Bible calls this gap between the awesomeness of God and the lack of comprehension of man, as it regards God, a *"mystery"* (Eph. 3:9). Of course, God has revealed Himself to us by the Holy Spirit and through His Word so that we can know Him, at least as far as is presently possible.

I believe, consequently, we can understand the Trinity. We just won't be able to completely know Him or absolutely understand His mysteries (at least not until the resurrection). The bottom line is that when we come to doctrines like the Trinity, we can admit to the limitations imposed by mystery without escaping our responsibility to know and understand the truth that has been revealed. We must not let the mystery of God's supremacy become an excuse for ignorance.

BIBLE TEACHING ON THE TRINITY

The Bible's teaching on the Trinity, we believe, is clear. The Word teaches that there is a Divine Trinity, and I believe that in this Divine Godhead, there are three separate and distinct persons. Yet, there is only one God. There are not three Gods, only one.

Some people conclude that the Father, the Son, and the Holy Spirit are all one and the same—just different names for the same person. Actually, they are not. These people take I John 5:7 (*"For there are three who bear record in heaven … And these three*

are one") to mean one in number when this is not what is meant at all. In the original Greek text in which the New Testament was written, the word *one* means "one in unity." Jesus prayed, *"Holy Father, keep through Your own name those whom You have given Me, that they may be one, as We are"* (Jn. 17:11). Jesus did not mean that every member of the body of Christ would physically inhabit one physical body. What He did pray was that we would be one in unity, one in desire, one in purpose, and one in design.

He used the term again when He said, *"That they may be one, even as We are one"* (Jn. 17:22). If we read this casually without effort of study, we may miss the thrust. Jesus used the plural pronoun *they* and then asked that they may be one. It is only possible to make several people into one when we speak of unity, and, of course, this is what is meant here.

INDIVIDUALLY AND SEPARATELY IN SCRIPTURE

The Father, the Son, and the Holy Spirit are spoken of individually and separately in Scripture. There is one God, the Father, one Lord Jesus Christ, and one Holy Spirit (I Cor. 8:6; Eph. 4:3-6). There are three separate persons in divine plurality and divine individuality. The Father is called God; the Son is called God; and the Holy Spirit is called God. Individually, they are each God, and collectively, they are one God in perfect essence and unity.

SEPARATE THINGS SAID

There are things said of each person of the Deity as to position, office, and work that could not be said of the other members of the Godhead. For example, the Father is the head of Christ (I Cor. 11:3); the Son is the only begotten of the Father (II Jn. 3); and the Holy Spirit proceeds from the Father (Jn. 15:26).

God said, *"Man is become as one of us"* (Gen. 3:22), with the pronoun *us* proving plurality of persons. Two persons of the Trinity are spoken of in Genesis 19:24—one on earth and one in heaven. In Mark, Chapter 1, three are represented at Jesus' baptism.

1. God the Holy Spirit descended on God the Son like a dove.

2. And then, God the Father spoke from heaven.

3. Later, Jesus would say, *"For David himself said by the Holy Spirit, The LORD said to my Lord, You sit on My right hand, till I make Your enemies Your footstool"* (Mk. 12:36). Here again, the three persons of the Trinity are revealed.

THE MYSTERY OF THE TRINITY

The mystery of the Trinity comes about by people trying to force three separate personalities into one person because they refuse to recognize the true meaning of the word *one* as referring to unity in the Scriptures as it pertains to the Trinity. Mankind itself could be just as great a mystery if we try to define all men as only one person. You can think of God the Father, God the Son, and God the Holy Spirit as three different persons in much the same way you would think of any three other people. The only difference is that these three persons share the same essence or being.

In heaven, we will see all three members of the Godhead: God the Father, God the Son, and God the Holy Spirit. We are told of the great vision the mighty prophet Daniel had when he saw God the Father and God the Son (Dan. 7:13-14). Jesus again and again used the pronoun *He* when referring to the Holy Spirit, denoting that the Holy Spirit is a person (Jn., Chpt. 16).

SYMBOLS?

Even though men have seen symbols of the Holy Spirit (Mk., Chpt. 1; Rev. 5:6), but never the Holy Spirit Himself, I still believe that when we get to heaven, we shall see God the Holy Spirit as well as God the Father and God the Son. The closest anyone came to seeing the Holy Spirit is the description given by Luke in this very verse on which we are offering commentary.

There is a word used by some theologians called *anthropomorphism*. This word basically means the effort of God to portray Himself to mankind in ways that man can understand and not truly the way He actually is. In other words, He speaks of Himself in human ways, such as having hands, arms, etc., when, in reality, He does not have these

members. Consequently, were that true, this would mean the account given to us in Daniel, Chapter 7, is not really the way God is. I do not believe this. Were that the case, I think that would be dishonest. I believe God told us the truth in His Word exactly as it is and exactly as He meant for us to believe it. Consequently, when Moses said he saw God, I believe Moses actually saw God and not some *"form"* that God took for Himself just so that He could appear to Moses. I believe the way Moses saw God is the way God actually looks.

THE BIBLE

If we are to take the Bible at face value, which we are certainly meant to do, I believe that when we get to heaven, we will see a real figure encased in light, sitting upon a real throne. I believe His Son, Jesus Christ, our Redeemer, will be sitting by His side in the same human body (albeit in a glorified state) that He had while on this earth. I believe the nail scars in the Master's hands will be there forever and forever. I also believe, as previously mentioned, that we will see the Holy Spirit.

I believe the books of the Bible, from Genesis through Revelation, as written by the prophets and apostles of old, were given to mankind by God Almighty. I believe the Bible is the Word of God, and I believe God said exactly what He meant and meant exactly what He said. When Genesis says that God appeared to Abraham, I believe God appeared to Abraham and that Abraham saw Him and talked with Him (Gen. 17:1; 18:1; compare Ex. 6:3).

When the Bible said that God appeared to Moses (Ex., Chpts. 3; 4; 32; 33; Lev., Chpt. 8; Deut. 31:15), I believe that God appeared to Moses and that Moses saw Him and talked with Him.

When Daniel (Dan, Chpt. 10), Ezekiel (Ezek., Chpts. 1; 8) and others (for example, Isa., Chpt. 6; Rev., Chpt. 1), described God, I believe they described Him precisely as they looked upon Him with actual physical vision; and I believe God looks just the way they said He did.

BELIEVING THE BIBLE

I believe the understanding of the Trinity,

though shrouded in mystery, is basically simple if we will only choose to believe what the Bible reveals concerning it. To believe the Word of God totally and without reservation concerning the eternal Godhead will illumine a person's understanding of the matter and alleviate all confusion. For a certainty, in heaven, all will be understood, if not now. *"For now we see through a glass, darkly; but then face to face: now I know* (believe) *in part; but then I shall know even as also I am known"* (I Cor. 13:12).

(23) "AND JESUS HIMSELF BEGAN TO BE ABOUT THIRTY YEARS OF AGE, BEING (AS WAS SUPPOSED) THE SON OF JOSEPH, WHICH WAS THE SON OF HELI."

The synopsis is:

1. We must understand that the Cross of Christ was not an incident, not an accident, not an execution, and not an assassination. It was a sacrifice.

2. No man could have killed Jesus Christ. He had the power to lay down His life Himself, and He had the power to take it up again (Jn. 10:17-18).

3. In fact, the Cross was planned from before the foundation of the world (I Pet. 1:18-20).

JESUS

The phrase, *"And Jesus Himself began to be about thirty years of age,"* represented the age at which priests, under the law, entered into their work (Num. 4:23; I Chron. 23:3).

Jesus was the Son of the law; therefore, He would keep the law in every respect.

"Being (as was supposed) *the Son of Joseph,"* should have been translated, *"Being by legal adoption the Son of Joseph."* Jesus was actually the Son of God and the Son of Mary, but the Son of Joseph only by legal adoption.

The phrase, *"Which was the son of Heli,"* referring to Joseph, portrays the double relationship of Joseph as was ordained in Numbers, Chapter 36. The man who married the daughter of a father having no son became the son of that father and inherited his property.

Hezron (I Chron. 2:21-23), and others in the Old Testament, illustrate this law.

Hezron married the daughter of Machir, and his sons were reckoned to belong to Machir. Hence, by birth, Hezron was of the tribe of Judah; by marriage, of the tribe of Manasseh.

In obedience, therefore, to the law of Numbers, Chapter 36, Mary married her cousin Joseph. Accordingly, Joseph had two fathers, one by nature, the other by law.

Thus was Jesus, as man, descended from Adam, the first man.

THE LINEAGE OF CHRIST

So, from this text, we learn that Mary had no brothers and, therefore, in Jewish thinking, her husband Joseph became the son of her father Heli. Actually, it is little different today in Gentile circles. The husband of the daughter is called the son-in-law of the daughter's father and mother. Actually, it could be translated and still be correct, *"Son-by-law,"* which would basically mean the same, at least in that sense, as the old Jewish law.

Matthew traced the lineage of Christ through Joseph, hence, through Solomon to David, which was the kingly line; whereas, Luke traced the genealogy through Mary to Nathan, another of David's sons. Consequently, the lineage of Jesus was perfect through both Joseph and Mary to David, through whom the Messiah must come and, in fact, did come (II Sam., Chpt. 7), and then, on back to Adam.

As well, as we have stated, the genealogy of Christ was unquestioned, even by His most strident enemies, because the records of every family were kept in the temple, as well as individually in each family. Josephus, the Jewish historian wrote, "I relate my genealogy as I find it recorded in the public tables."

THE GENEALOGY

To show how impeccable these records were, some 70 years after Christ, the grandchildren of Jude, the reputed half-brother of the Lord, a son of Joseph, were summoned to Rome and appeared before the emperor Domitian as descendants of the old royal house of David.

As well, the reason for inserting the name of Joseph at the beginning of this narrative, even though it is not his genealogy but rather that of Mary, is because women are not reckoned in genealogies. Consequently, Joseph, the son-in-law, or as thought of then, the legal son of Heli, Mary's father, naturally took the place of Mary in this genealogy of the natural line of Jesus Christ back to Adam.

As is the rule of genealogies, the natural line always begins with the man himself and goes backward as far as can be. However, in a royal line, as in Matthew, Chapter 1, it begins at the source of the dynasty and ends with himself, thus, Matthew's genealogy beginning with David.

THE MOST IMPORTANT NAMES IN THE WORLD

As the Bible student knows, all of these names are extremely important respecting the lineage of Christ because in order to redeem man, Christ had to be a true Son of Adam while, at the same time, being a true Son of God, which He was! As well, that lineage had to go through David because it was to David that the promise was made by the Lord that through his family the Messiah would come (II Sam., Chpt. 7). In order to pay the price for man's redemption, Jesus had to be a true man but, at the same time, not contaminated by the fall as all men are, hence, the virgin birth.

So, the tedious account of these names constitutes the single most important group of names in the history of the world. In other words, there is no way that one could fully comprehend the magnitude of this significance simply because they were necessary in order to bring the Redeemer into the world.

Satan's plan for the fall of man was very crafty. Inasmuch as the seed of all humanity was in the loins of Adam, consequently, Adam acted for all. Hence, with his fall, all fell. As well, Jesus, the last Adam, acted for all. As a result, all who believe in Him have eternal life (I Cor. 15:21-22). In the former, all fell and died whereas, in the latter, all are made alive, at least those who believe (Jn. 3:16).

(24) "WHICH WAS THE SON OF MATTHAT, WHICH WAS THE SON OF LEVI, WHICH WAS THE SON OF MELCHI, WHICH WAS THE SON OF JANNA, WHICH WAS THE SON OF JOSEPH,

(25) "WHICH WAS THE SON OF MATTATHIAS, WHICH WAS THE SON OF AMOS, WHICH WAS THE SON OF NAUM, WHICH WAS THE SON OF ESLI, WHICH WAS THE SON OF NAGGE,

(26) "WHICH WAS THE SON OF MAATH, WHICH WAS THE SON OF MATTATHIAS, WHICH WAS THE SON OF SEMEI, WHICH WAS THE SON OF JOSEPH, WHICH WAS THE SON OF JUDAH,

(27) "WHICH WAS THE SON OF JOANNA, WHICH WAS THE SON OF RHESA, WHICH WAS THE SON OF ZOROBABEL, WHICH WAS THE SON OF SALATHIEL, WHICH WAS THE SON OF NERI."

The pattern is:

1. Verse 27 contains that which is concluded to be an error by some expositors. I am speaking of the phrase, *"Which was the son of Zorobabel, which was the son of Salathiel."* I Chronicles 3:19 says that *"Pedaiah"* is the father of Zerubbabel. It is spelled a little differently in I Chronicles simply because it is in the Hebrew whereas the name in Luke is in the Greek. So, how do we clear this up?

2. The following presents what I feel could explain it:

a. Salathiel and Pedaiah could be the same person, for many Bible characters had several names.

b. If they were brothers, Zerubbabel could be the real son of Salathiel, as stated in Matthew 1:12 and Luke 3:27, and be the legal son of Pedaiah when the real father died (Deut. 25:5-6).

c. Zerubbabel could have been the son-in-law of Pedaiah, as Joseph was of Heli, and as we have commented on.

3. One thing is certain: If there had been the least flaw in the claim and genealogy of Christ through Joseph and Mary, the Jews and the heathen would have found it and brought it to everybody's attention. That within itself is proof that the genealogy was as indisputable then as it is now.

4. Both the Davidic lines—that of Solomon and Nathan—united in Zerubbabel by the marriage of Salathiel to the daughter of Neri of Nathan's line. Neri, no doubt, died without having a son, thus, the two branches of David were united in Zerubbabel and Christ,

and became the heir to the blood rights and privileges of the whole house of David.

(28) "WHICH WAS THE SON OF MELCHI, WHICH WAS THE SON OF ADDI, WHICH WAS THE SON OF COSAM, WHICH WAS THE SON OF ELMODAM, WHICH WAS THE SON OF ER,

(29) "WHICH WAS THE SON OF JOSE, WHICH WAS THE SON OF ELIEZER, WHICH WAS THE SON OF JORIM, WHICH WAS THE SON OF MATTHAT, WHICH WAS THE SON OF LEVI,

(30) "WHICH WAS THE SON OF SIMEON, WHICH WAS THE SON OF JUDA, WHICH WAS THE SON OF JOSEPH, WHICH WAS THE SON OF JONAN, WHICH WAS THE SON OF ELIAKIM,

(31) "WHICH WAS THE SON OF MELEA, WHICH WAS THE SON OF MENAN, WHICH WAS THE SON OF MATTATHA, WHICH WAS THE SON OF NATHAN, WHICH WAS THE SON OF DAVID."

The synopsis is:

1. *"Nathan"* was the older brother of Solomon (I Chron. 3:5), and is not mentioned in Old Testament Scriptures nearly as much as the line of Solomon. However, it is given here because Mary's genealogy goes back to David through Nathan, as Joseph went back to David through Solomon.

2. As we have repeatedly said, this was absolutely imperative if Jesus was to be the proper Redeemer, thereby, the last Adam, and would purchase back with His own precious blood that which the first Adam lost.

3. Even though every name is of great significance in this genealogy, still, there are certain names that stand out, representing a move of God, which, in essence, charted the course for the whole of humanity. Zorobabel, as we have stated, is one of those names.

4. However, without a doubt, the name *David* would stand out the greatest in the whole of the genealogy from Adam to Christ. There are reasons for that:

a. It was through David and his family, of the entirety of the Hebrew people, through whom the Messiah would come (II Sam., Chpt. 7). However, He would not only be the Messiah of Israel, but even more importantly, the Redeemer of the whole of

humanity, at least those who will believe (Jn. 3:16).

b. As a result of Jesus coming through the Davidic line, He would be called the *"Son of David!"* There is no higher honor that could be given to any name than that. While it is true that Jesus is also called the *"Son of Abraham"* (Mat. 1:1), still, the name of David comes first, and that, by design.

5. So, even though the prophecies had stated that the Messiah, and the Redeemer of the world, was to come through the family of Abraham (Gen. 12:3) and through the tribe of Judah in that family (Gen. 49:10), until God spoke to David (II Sam., Chpt. 7), no one knew which part of Judah. The tribe of Judah was very large at that time, probably numbering several hundreds of thousands of people.

(32) "WHICH WAS THE SON OF JESSE, WHICH WAS THE SON OF OBED, WHICH WAS THE SON OF BOOZ, WHICH WAS THE SON OF SALMON, WHICH WAS THE SON OF NAASSON."

The exegesis is:

1. As important as the name of David is, at least as it refers to the Messiah, other names listed in this passage are of great significance, as well, and not only because they lead to David.

2. Boaz, here spelled *"Booz,"* was the husband of Ruth the Moabitess. Thus, a Gentile had a part in the great lineage of Christ.

3. As well, Rahab, the harlot who married *"Salmon,"* was a Gentile and figured prominently in this genealogy. This shows us two things: the grace of God and the power of faith. Rahab and Ruth, although Gentiles outside the covenant and promises, nevertheless, had faith in God, and the Lord honored that faith by making them a part of the greatest lineage in the history of man. God always honors faith in His name and Word, irrespective of where it is found.

4. The serious Bible student knows that Rahab married Salmon when the children of Israel first came into the Promised Land (Mat. 1:5). As well, it is known that the time of Ruth was during the judges (Ruth 1:1); therefore, it would have made it impossible for Salmon to be the son of Boaz due to the time span. Consequently, some names were

left out, with the idea seeming to be to prove the lineage and not necessarily incorporate every name. However, the Scripture is correct in that the Jews referred to any individual as the *"son of,"* irrespective of how many times removed.

(33) "WHICH WAS THE SON OF AMINADAB, WHICH WAS THE SON OF ARAM, WHICH WAS THE SON OF ESROM, WHICH WAS THE SON OF PHARES, WHICH WAS THE SON OF JUDA."

The overview is:

1. *"Judah"* figures prominently in this section.

2. It was through the tribe of Judah that the Messiah would come and, in fact, did come (Gen. 49:10).

3. Let us say it again: the greatest thing that ever happened to planet Earth was God becoming man, hence, the incarnation, and doing so for the purpose of going to the Cross to, thereby, redeem the fallen sons of Adam's lost race.

(34) "WHICH WAS THE SON OF JACOB, WHICH WAS THE SON OF ISAAC, WHICH WAS THE SON OF ABRAHAM, WHICH WAS THE SON OF THARA, WHICH WAS THE SON OF NACHOR."

The structure is:

1. Of course, as is obvious, this Scripture carries the heavy weights of the great plan of God, hence, the phrase, *"The God of Abraham, Isaac, and Jacob."* Through these men came the entirety of the Jewish people, with Abraham as the fountainhead. He was called out of Ur of the Chaldees by God for the express purpose of a people being brought out of his loins, through whom would come the Messiah.

2. Actually, Abraham was a Gentile and, thus, an idol-worshipper when the Lord spoke to him (Josh. 24:2-3).

3. The names *"Abraham, Isaac, and Jacob"* stand out so prominently because these men virtually walked alone. They had nothing but their faith to sustain them. They had no church to attend, no saints with whom they could fellowship, and no Bible, with the exception of the Word of God, which had been handed down by word of mouth from Adam's time, a period of some 2,000 years. In effect, they and their little group

constituted the only people on the earth at that time who served God. Even by the time of Jacob when he went into Egypt, there were only 70 people counting the children.

(35) "WHICH WAS THE SON OF SARUCH, WHICH WAS THE SON OF RAGAU, WHICH WAS THE SON OF PHALEC, WHICH WAS THE SON OF HEBER, WHICH WAS THE SON OF SALA,

(36) "WHICH WAS THE SON OF, WHICH WAS THE SON OF ARPHAXAD, WHICH WAS THE SON OF SEM, WHICH WAS THE SON OF NOE, WHICH WAS THE SON OF LAMECH."

The construction is:

1. At the moment that Jesus died on the Cross, the price was paid.

2. This means that the sin debt on all individuals, whomever they might have been, was canceled, providing they expressed faith.

3. That means that anyone who registers faith in Christ and what He did for us at the Cross is instantly saved, i.e., *"justified"* (Rom. 5:1).

CAINAN, SHEM, AND NOAH

These three names stand out prominently in Verse 36.

To take the last first, Noah was used of God mightily in the building of the ark at the time of the flood.

There were two things about Noah:

1. He was a *"just man,"* meaning that he did strive to follow the Lord.

2. He was *"perfect"* in his generations, meaning that his immediate family was the only family on earth who, at that time, had not been corrupted by the mixture of fallen angels and women, which produced the giants (Gen. 6:4, 9). This was an effort by Satan to corrupt the entirety of the human family in order that it might be impossible for the Messiah to come, consequently, fulfilling Genesis 3:15.

SHEM AND CAINAN

"Shem" (pronounced here *"Sem"*) was the brother of Ham and Japheth, all sons of Noah, from whom sprang the entirety of the human family. As known, this took place after the flood, with them and their wives the only ones left alive on earth. Through Shem

would come the Messiah (Gen. 9:26; 10:21-32).

"Cainan" being here mentioned is not a mistake in the text, as some have claimed, because he is in the lineage of Ham and not Shem. However, he is, no doubt, a son-in-law of Arphaxad, while at the same time, the son of Ham. Cainan was Ham's youngest son. He is the one who sinned against his grandfather Noah, and not his father Ham, and consequently, was cursed.

To be sure, it was not just the looking on the nakedness of his grandfather that incurred such a solemn curse (Gen. 9:25). Even though no one is exactly certain as to what was done, there is indication that he may have committed a homosexual act on Noah (Gen. 9:20-23).

The Scripture says, *"And Noah awoke from his wine, and knew what his younger son* (grandson) *had done unto him"* (Gen. 9:24). If all that Cainan had done was to look upon his grandfather's nakedness, there is no way that Noah could have known of such. Whatever it was, it was obvious when he awoke.

Whatever Cainan's action was, it was sufficient for Satan's purpose. The deep schemes of Satan (Rev. 2:24) were planned either to prevent the birth of the Messiah or to bring it about by satanic cooperation and, thus, destroy its redemptive nature.

SATAN

The precedence given to Shem, as he was the firstborn of Noah (Gen. 5:32), disclosed him as the depository of the promise of Genesis 3:15. It was necessary, therefore, to repeat, in his case, the action of Genesis 6:2 from which Noah was called *"perfect,"* i.e., without blemish is his pedigree (no union of women and fallen angels). Satan found that agent in Cainan.

He first introduced him into the family of Shem, as we have stated, by a marriage with a daughter of Arphaxad, which secured a legal right of inheritance similar to Joseph's marriage with Mary, which made him the heir of Heli. Secondly, he influenced Cainan so as to bring upon him the doom of Genesis 9:25, as he energized Jehoiakim (Jer. 36:30) in order to make impossible the promise to David (Ps. 132:11).

NOTES

Thus, by this double action, with Cainan as his instrument, Satan made him (as Jehoiakim was) the depository of the promise, even as Luke shows, and then impelled him to an action in order to make impossible the performance of the promise. If it be objected that Cainan's assumed marriage with Arphaxad's daughter is not recorded in the pedigree, it can be replied that neither is Joseph's with Heli's daughter. The omissions denote harmony and not discrepancy.

It is, of course, quite true that just as Satan, in his opposition to God and to Christ, overthrew with an *"apple"* (Song of Sol. 8:5) the divinely-appointed head (Adam) of *"the world"* that then was, so did he with a *"grape"* overthrow the head of *"the world"* that now is, namely Noah (Gen. 9:20-21). It is suggested that Noah's drunkenness was a minor purpose, but that the major purpose was the Canaanite scheme.

THE CANAANITES

Cainan, therefore, having a legal title by his marriage into the family of Shem, took possession of Israel and Zion under satanic impulse; for it is possible that the adversary foreknew that both were purposed by God for the advent of the Messiah. This supposition would, therefore, help to explain Abraham's and Isaac's divine instinct in guarding against marriage with Canaanites (Gen. 24:3; 28:1); and also would shed light upon the command to Israel by God to utterly destroy the Canaanites (Deut. 12:1, 3).

The cunning and malignity of Satan in his opposition to Christ is seen in the murder of Abel, the act of Cainan, the retardation in the births of Isaac and Jacob, the introduction of Pharaoh, of Abimelech (twice), and of Hagar. The attempted murder of Isaac by Ishmael, of Jacob by Esau, both before and after his birth, by the misconduct of Judah and David, and by the massacres of Pharaoh, Athaliah, of Haman, and Herod must be included, as well, and in the expulsion of Jehoiakim's descendants from the throne of Jehovah at Jerusalem.

That Cainan could be a son of Arphaxad, i.e., his heir, and at the same time, a son of Ham is illustrated more than once in the Scriptures, as has already been pointed out.

For example, Jair was *"the son of Manasseh,"* but was begotten by Judah; Attai was *"the son of Sheshan,"* but was born of Jarha; Moses was *"the son of Pharaoh's daughter,"* but was born of Amram; Hiram was of the tribe of Naphtali, but also of the tribe of Dan; and Joseph, Mary's husband, was *"the son of Jacob"* and also *"the son of Heli."*

He, as a son by descent from Jehoiakim, could not sit on the throne of David, but as the son-in-law and heir of Heli by his marriage with Mary, divinely legalized by Numbers, Chapters 28 and 36, he could, by the execution of a deed, adopt Mary's child as his son and vets in him all his titles to the kingdom. This he did, as is shown in the force of the words *"the son of"* in Luke 3:23.

Mary was by descent a daughter of David (Lk. 1:27, 32) and, consequently, was born of Heli, and *"perfect"* (Gen. 6:9) in her generations from Shem through Sala and Nathan, Solomon's older brother. Her child, therefore, as born of her and legally adopted by Joseph, united in His person both the Davidic and Adamic claims to the throne of the world. He, by His resurrection, is, and remains, its only legal sovereign. This pure descent through Nathan and Sal defeated Satan's efforts to make impossible through Cainan and Jehoiakim the advent of the Redeemer promised in Genesis 3:15.

Putting all these facts together, it is urged that the insertion of Cainan's name in the pedigree of Luke, Chapter 3, is not an error but a moral and historical necessity, and as important and necessary as the inclusion of Jehoiakim's name in the pedigree of Matthew, Chapter 1. And so, it will appear that Genesis 9:24 illumines and interprets Luke 3:36, and that this seeming inaccuracy is an instance of the law of subsequent narration.

Some expositors believe that Cainan and Cainan are different men, but their reasoning's lie outside of the sacred text.

(The information regarding Cainan and the genealogy was derived from the writings of George Williams).

Up until Noah, a period of approximately 1,600 years, only three men are recorded as having lived for God: Abel, Enoch, and Noah. However, there is some indication that Lamech, Noah's father, was also a believer. The naming of his son Noah, which means *"rest or comfort,"* lends some credence to the thought that Lamech may have known the Lord.

(37) "WHICH WAS THE SON OF MATHUSALA, WHICH WAS THE SON OF ENOCH, WHICH WAS THE SON OF JARED, WHICH WAS THE SON OF MALELEEL, WHICH WAS THE SON OF CAINAN."

The exegesis is:

1. In this Scripture, Enoch is the principal figure. He stands out as a giant for God, especially at a time when the whole world was delving deep into spiritual wickedness.

The Scripture tells us that Enoch began to serve God at 65 years of age. It then said, *"And Enoch walked with God: and he was not; for God took him"* (Gen. 5:21-24). This means that he was translated so that he did not see death.

2. It seems that the birth of Methuselah had something to do with the revelation of the Lord, which changed Enoch's life. It is clear at this time that he did receive a revelation from God, for he named his son *"Methuselah,"* which means, "When he is dead it (the flood) shall come." He also foretold the second coming of Christ to destroy the ungodly (Jude, Vs. 14).

3. The life of Methuselah is the longest earthly life on record. His father, Enoch, still lives in heaven and will again live on earth and die as one of the two witnesses (Rev. 11:3-11).

Methuselah lived 969 years and was allowed to live so long because of the grace of God. Having foretold that when his life ended, the flood would come, the Lord gave man extra time to repent, as portrayed in the long life of Methuselah. Regrettably, man did not repent, and consequently, the world was deluged by the flood.

4. The *"Cainan"* of Verse 37 is different than the *"Cainan"* of Verse 36.

(38) "WHICH WAS THE SON OF ENOS, WHICH WAS THE SON OF SETH, WHICH WAS THE SON OF ADAM, WHICH WAS THE SON OF GOD."

The structure is:

1. When Cain was born, Eve thought he was the promised Redeemer of Genesis 3:16 because she said, *"I have gotten a man from*

the LORD" (Gen. 4:1). She used the covenant name *"Lord,"* thinking this was the One, and God was keeping His covenant.

2. However, she was to find that Cain was to be anything but the coming Redeemer, actually a murderer (Gen. 4:8).

She didn't realize, even as many do not realize presently, that sinful man cannot produce anything that God can use. If it is of God, it must be totally from God.

3. Consequently, when Seth was ultimately born to Adam and Eve, she had given up hope, saying, *"For God, said she, has appointed me another seed instead of Abel, whom Cain killed"* (Gen. 4:25).

4. By using the name *"God"* and not *"Lord"* as she had with Cain, Eve had ceased to believe. She felt that God was no longer true to His covenant promise of Genesis 3:15. Because of a lack of faith, little did she know or realize but Seth, the very son she dismissed, was actually the one through whom the promised Redeemer would come, as outlined in Verse 38, although it would be approximately 4,000 years before Jesus actually came.

5. Adam was *"the Son of God"* by creation and not by the born-again experience. Actually, he was the only one who could be of God in this sense. All others are born of men.

6. In fact, it was God's original intention, as proven by Verse 38, that it was the intention of the Lord that all babies who were born would be born sons and daughters of God. However, due to the fall, that was stopped. It will, no doubt, be possible once again during the coming perfect age (Rev., Chpts. 21-22).

"The Saviour is waiting to enter your
    heart,
"Why don't you let Him come in?
"There's nothing in this world to keep
    you apart,
"What is your answer to Him?"

"If you'll take one step toward the
    Saviour, my friend,
"You'll find His arms open wide;
"Receive Him, and all of your dark-
    ness will end,
"Within your heart He'll abide."

CHAPTER 4

(1) "AND JESUS BEING FULL OF THE HOLY SPIRIT RETURNED FROM JORDAN, AND WAS LED BY THE SPIRIT INTO THE WILDERNESS."

The overview is:

1. The phrase, *"And Jesus being full of the Holy Spirit returned from Jordan,"* refers to the time immediately after His water baptism.

2. The words, *"Full of the Holy Spirit,"* are used to describe the anointing of the Holy Spirit in various measures upon men. In Christ's case, He received the Spirit without measure, or in all fullness, which no other human being has ever done (Jn. 3:34; Acts 10:38).

3. In the case of others in Old Testament times, the Holy Spirit could not come into them to dwell permanently simply because the blood of bulls and goats could not take away sins (Heb. 10:4). Thank the Lord, the Cross of Christ remedied that situation, for it took away all sin, at least for all who will believe. Now, the Holy Spirit comes into the believer at conversion, there to abide forever (Jn. 14:16).

4. After the day of Pentecost, all were filled with the Holy Spirit, at least those who sought for such, of which Jesus serves as the example (Acts 2:4; 4:8; 31; 6:3-8; 7:55; 9:17; 11:24; 13:9, 52).

5. Jesus served as our example of life and ministry. He did not perform His great works by deity, but rather as a man full of the Holy Spirit. As deity, He needed nothing to do anything. As man, He needed the Holy Spirit as we definitely and desperately need the Holy Spirit.

6. The phrase, *"And was led by the Spirit into the wilderness,"* speaks of great urgency by the Spirit. Actually, Mark used the phrase, *"The Spirit driveth Him"* (Mk. 1:12).

7. This did not speak of reluctance on the part of Christ to enter into this stage of His life and ministry, but rather the urgency and haste of the Holy Spirit to get things started.

8. Jesus did not (like Simon Peter [Lk.

22:33]) seek temptation. He was *"led"* into it by the Spirit.

9. The Scripture does not say exactly where this wilderness was; however, most expositors feel it was near Jericho.

(2) "BEING FORTY DAYS TEMPTED OF THE DEVIL. AND IN THOSE DAYS HE DID EAT NOTHING: AND WHEN THEY WERE ENDED, HE AFTERWARD HUNGERED."

The synopsis is:

1. The Cross is the reason that Jesus came.

2. While everything Christ did was of utmost significance, still, His overriding destination was the Cross.

3. The Cross of Christ is the means, and the only means, by which we receive from God.

FORTY DAYS

The phrase, *"Being forty days tempted of the Devil,"* refers to being tempted for the entirety of this time.

The *"forty days"* mentioned here is quite prominent in Scripture. Moses was alone with the Lord some 40 days on Horeb. As well, Elijah fasted for 40 days in the wilderness before the vision and the voice came to him (I Ki. 19:8).

Forty years was the period, as well, of the wanderings of the chosen people.

Why 40 days?

The Scripture really does not give us any clue; however, is it possible that this was the length of time that Adam and Eve walked in innocence before the fall? In other words, is the number *"40"* God's probationary number?

The Devil is here spoken of as a real being and not a mere influence or force as claimed by some!

SATAN

Satan was created as Lucifer, which means "light bearer," and carries a number of names in the Old and New Testaments. These include the Devil, the Serpent, the accuser of the brethren, and the ruler of the kingdom of the air.

The Hebrew word is *Satan,* which means "adversary." The Greek is *Satanas,* which

NOTES

carries the same meaning. The common name of Satan in the New Testament is *Diabolos* (Devil), meaning, "One who slanders or accuses."

Both Testaments reveal Satan as God's adversary and the enemy of mankind. Passages taken to refer to Satan (Isa. 14:12-15; Ezek. 28:11-19), with New Testament references, provide insight into his history and destiny.

ONCE A POWERFUL ANGEL

Satan was a powerful angel in God's original creation and served Him in righteousness and holiness for an undetermined period of time. His pride (Isa. 14:12-15; I Tim. 3:6) and warped desire to take God's place introduced sin into the universe. Satan's initial rebellion included the defection of many angels and will ultimately lead to the expulsion of that host from heaven (Rev. 12:4).

SATAN AND HIS POWER

Satan was the power influencing the serpent in Eden, and thus, he was an instrument in mankind's fall, by which he introduced sin's corruption into the human race. Satan still exercises great power in the world. He is called the *ruler of the kingdom of the air* in Ephesians 2:2, and is at work in all who are disobedient to God.

Despite his powers and the devices he uses to deceive humanity, Satan was decisively defeated in every confrontation he had with Jesus, and especially at the Cross (Mat. 4:1-11; Lk. 11:13-22; 13:10-16; Col. 2:10-15).

SATAN'S DEFEAT

The New Testament foretells a day when Satan will lead another great rebellion, working through individuals he empowers, namely the Antichrist, etc. (II Thess., Chpt. 2).

However, the final destiny of this evil being is fixed. Following yet another final attempt to overthrow the Lord (Rev. 20:7-9), which will be at the conclusion of the kingdom age, Satan will be thrown into the lake of burning sulfur, as Revelation portrays hell to be, *"Tormented day and night forever and ever"* (Rev. 20:10).

FASTING FORTY DAYS AND FORTY NIGHTS

The phrase, *"And in those days He* (Jesus) *did eat nothing,"* speaks of the Lord fasting for 40 days and nights.

Adam faced Satan, who used the serpent in a garden—and with plenty to eat. Jesus faced Satan in a wilderness—and with nothing to eat.

Why did Jesus have to fast?

It was the wants, passions, and desires of the flesh that caused Adam and Eve to fall in the garden of Eden. Satan suggested that they would be as gods if they partook of the forbidden fruit. Thus, the groundwork was laid for the sin of the *pride of life*.

The pride of life questions God's Word, in effect, saying it is not true (Gen. 3:2-5).

The next step was easier, which was *the lust of the eyes*. The Scripture says, *"And when the woman saw that the tree was good for food"* (Gen. 3:6).

The next and final step was *the lust of the flesh*. *"She took of the fruit thereof, and did eat, and gave also unto her husband with her; and he did eat"* (Gen. 3:6).

Thus was laid Satan's method of temptation, which has varied very little though the ages. He questions God's Word, enticing man to *look* and then to *take*. All of this, as stated, was through the flesh i.e., wants, passions, and desires.

Fasting helps subdue the flesh but, within itself, cannot overcome sin. It was at the Cross where all sin was addressed, and it is faith in Christ and what He did for us at the Cross that gives us victory over sin. Fasting will definitely help but, within itself, cannot bring about victory over the world, the flesh, and the Devil.

The flesh of man must be defeated with the regenerated spirit of man made supreme. If the flesh rules, sin will always result (Rom. 8:1-11).

The spirit of man is energized only by the Spirit of God. Even though Jesus would suffer greatly in the flesh in the wilderness experiences, at the same time, He would be greatly invigorated in His spirit.

NOTES

FASTING AND THE BELIEVER

As Jesus set the example, fasting should be a part of our Christian experience as well! However, it should not be a means to an end within itself, for the simple doing without food is of little spiritual consequence. Fasting will not force God's hand, and neither will it change His mind. Fasting is meant to help subdue the illicit desires of the flesh, but with the Cross of Christ and our faith in that finished work, that is where sin should be addressed.

No particular guidelines are laid down in the New Testament regarding how long one should fast or how often. The Scripture merely says concerning Paul, *"In fastings often"* (II Cor. 11:27).

Concerning the church at Antioch and the ministries of Paul and Barnabas, the Scripture says, *"As they ministered to the Lord, and fasted"* (Acts 13:2). It does not say how long, but it was probably about a day.

Acts, Chapter 27, should not be taken as an example of fasting because the indication is that it had little to do with spirituality, but it had to do with the storm that made it difficult, if not impossible, to suitably prepare food in the ship.

The believer should fast as he feels the Lord leads him to and leave it at that.

The phrase, *"And when they were ended, He afterward hungered,"* is normal in a prolonged fast.

Some claim that the ordinary bodily wants of Christ were suspended during these 40 days and nights; however, there is no indication in the Scripture of such, but rather the opposite! Jesus faced the rigors of a 40-day fast exactly as anyone else. More than likely, it was more difficult than for anyone else instead of less, especially considering that Satan opposed Him greatly for the entirety of this time.

(3) "AND THE DEVIL SAID UNTO HIM, IF YOU BE THE SON OF GOD, COMMAND THIS STONE THAT IT BE MADE BREAD."

The synopsis is:

1. The phrase, *"And the Devil said unto Him,"* means that Satan actually appeared to Him.

2. As well, some claim that these

temptations were all in vision and were not literal. The Scripture indicates otherwise! Why could not Satan literally appear before Him as the Scripture plainly says he did?

3. The phrase, *"If You be the Son of God,"* should have been translated, *"Since You be the Son of God,"* for Satan was not questioning who Jesus was! He knew beyond the shadow of a doubt that Jesus was the Son of God.

4. The phrase, *"Command this stone that it be made bread,"* would not seem to be much of a temptation to most; however, Satan knew exactly what he was doing.

5. The temptation was designed to gratify the flesh. Jesus was hungry, and there was no food. Since He had the power to turn stone to bread, why not do it?

6. One could say that every single temptation levied at the believer follows this course—a gratification of the flesh.

7. More importantly, the temptation was structured to pressure Christ into using His power outside of the will of God, in other words, for personal use. The model for success in the life of Christ was His astute following of the wishes of His heavenly Father. He would later say, *"The Son can do nothing of Himself, but what He sees the Father do"* (Jn. 5:19). So, Satan tempted Jesus to use His power for His own benefit exclusive of the will of God.

That is one of the reasons that believers are given little power; they tend to use it for themselves and not according to the will of God.

(4) "AND JESUS ANSWERED HIM, SAYING, IT IS WRITTEN, THAT MAN SHALL NOT LIVE BY BREAD ALONE, BUT BY EVERY WORD OF GOD."

THE ANSWER OF OUR LORD

The phrase, *"And Jesus answered him,"* constitutes the Word of God taken from Deuteronomy 8:3.

"Saying, It is written," proclaims the weapon of the Word used by Christ to overcome Satan. It is our weapon as well! However, it is not to be used as a magic talisman. In other words, one cannot quote the Scripture over and over thinking to force God's hand, as some are wont to do.

Satan's appeal to Christ was a twisting and perversion of the Word of God. Jesus simply answered him according to what the Word actually said.

Tragically, most believers little know the Bible, taking someone else's word for it.

Men believe all types of false doctrine simply because they do not know the Word of God, or else, they know it but do not believe it. Everything that is done should be done according to the Bible. It is the greatest common sense Book in the world. It alone holds the answer to all things that pertain to *"life and godliness"* (II Pet. 1:3-4).

For instance, our politics should be based on what the Word of God says about the issue. As well, our direction should be according to the Word of God. While we may listen to what so-called religious leaders might say, still, if they contradict the Bible, they are to be ignored and the Bible to be followed. It should never be, *"My church says ..."* but rather, *"My Bible says ...."* Anytime we leave the Word of God for whatever reason, we suffer greatly.

JESUS AND THE WORD

The entirety of Jesus' life up to this point had been spent learning the Word. The psalmist said this about Him, *"O how I love Your law! it is my meditation all the day"* (Ps. 119:97). So, if we use any defense other than *"it is written,"* referring to the Word of God, we are sowing the seeds of our own destruction.

LIVING BY THE WORD OF GOD

The phrase, *"That man shall not live by bread alone, but by every word of God,"* is the basic truth for all humanity.

The physical body has to have bread for physical nourishment and sustenance. As well, the spirit of man has to have the Word of God for spiritual sustenance. It is just as important, and more so, than the former.

Tragically, almost the entirety of the world attempts to live on bread alone! Sadly, even much of the church falls into the same category. In the physical sense, our daily food is lovingly attended and prepared. Too oftentimes, the Word of God is given short shift, if at all! The idea is this:

As physical food is a daily habit, the Word of God must be a daily habit as well. The believer should set aside a portion of each day to be spent in the Bible.

THE STUDY OF THE WORD OF GOD

The Bible should be read from cover to cover, beginning at Genesis and going straight through to the book of Revelation. I would caution the reader that whatever you have, it must be a word-for-word translation, such as the King James. Others that are thought-for-thought translations are not really the Bible but, actually, just religious books.

The Bible tells a story, and the story cannot be properly followed if it is not properly read and studied. While it is certainly proper to pick up the Bible and read at random, still, it is not proper to do so on a continuing basis. If we treated every other book in this fashion, we would have little idea as to what the writer was talking about; likewise, the Bible!

As Jesus here speaks, read the Bible daily, and that means seven days a week. One should set aside a few minutes each day for this all-important task.

The believer should pray that the Lord will open his understanding and that the Holy Spirit will reveal to him the lesson that is needed. I have personally read the Bible completely through some 51 times, and each time, the Spirit of God gives me things I had not previously known. Inasmuch as the Bible is the Word of God, it can be said to be alive and, therefore, constantly operative.

As well, one should avail oneself of material that helps explain the Bible, such as these commentaries.

The understanding of the Bible, which the Lord certainly desires that we do, is the greatest source of spiritual growth there is. Actually, spiritual growth is impossible without the Word of God. As we live by bread in the physical sense, as well, we live in the spiritual sense by the Word of God. If one is not doing that, one is not truly living!

(5) "AND THE DEVIL, TAKING HIM UP INTO AN HIGH MOUNTAIN, SHOWED UNTO HIM ALL THE KINGDOMS OF THE WORLD IN A MOMENT OF TIME."

The composition is:

1. The phrase, *"And the Devil, taking Him up into an high mountain,"* constitutes that which was literally done. There is no evidence that it was in vision only, except for the world kingdoms.

2. The phrase, *"Showed unto Him all the kingdoms of the world in a moment of time,"* is that of which Jesus was very familiar.

3. If one is to notice, while the account of these temptations (as given in Matthew and Luke) are identical regarding their beginning, thereafter, they differ. In Matthew, the temple was second with the mountain being third. Here, the mountain is second with the temple being third.

4. In Matthew, the order is historical, while in Luke, it is dispensational. Matthew presents Jesus as the Messiah coming to His temple and then as Son of Man reigning over the earth. However, in Luke, the Holy Spirit places Jesus' relation to the earth in the foreground and His connection with Israel in the background. This was done by design.

5. In Matthew, Jesus is presented as King, which He must be for Israel before He can be for the world, hence, the temple first. In Luke, Jesus is presented as man and, therefore, the kingdoms of the world would be first with Israel last. So, the order is not confusion, but rather design.

(6) "AND THE DEVIL SAID UNTO HIM, ALL THIS POWER WILL I GIVE YOU, AND THE GLORY OF THEM: FOR THAT IS DELIVERED UNTO ME; AND TO WHOMSOEVER I WILL I GIVE IT."

The synopsis is:

1. The phrase, *"And the Devil said unto Him, All this power will I give You, and the glory of them,"* proclaims Satan's method of operation.

2. He had captured many kings by the offer of a part of the glory of earthly dominion, and he now tried to capture the heart of the carpenter of Nazareth by the offer of the whole. However, the object of that heart was God and His will and not earth and its glory. He did not despise the throne of the earth, but He would only have it as His Father's gift, and never from Satan.

3. As well, Jesus did not contradict Satan respecting the power and glory of kingdoms. Actually, they do belong to Satan— the pain, sickness, suffering, and heartache of this present world, hence, man's inhumanity to man!

4. *"For that is delivered unto me,"* referred back to the garden of Eden when Satan gained such authority because of the default of Adam and Eve. God gave them the dominion of the earth, and they in turn gave it to Satan, one might say, by default (Gen. 1:28; 3:7; PS. 8:4-6; II Cor. 4:4).

5. The phrase, *"And to whomsoever I will I give it,"* means that Satan is now the pseudo-ruler of the world (Jn. 12:31; II Cor. 4:4; Eph. 2:1-3; Rev. 13:2, 7); however, that he has absolute autonomy is wrong. He is able to give rulership to certain people, which he often does, but only by the permission of the Lord. We learn this from Daniel, Chapter 10. Certain kings were to be moved out of the way, with others taking their place. There is every evidence that Satan did not desire this, but he had no choice in the matter. While it is true that both rulers would be wicked, still, the change was necessary in order for Bible prophecy to be fulfilled.

(7) "IF YOU THEREFORE WILL WORSHIP ME, ALL SHALL BE YOURS."

SINLESS AMBITION

Every evidence is that Satan knew the rulership of the entirety of the world had been promised to Jesus by the heavenly Father. Consequently, this temptation was something more than *"offering to One who had lived as a village carpenter the throne of the world."*

Spence said, "It appealed to his ambition certainly, but in Jesus' case it was a high, pure, sinless ambition. His ambition was righteousness, and that it fill the earth, replacing the deadly woe of sin. For only then can man truly know what Jesus and prosperity truly are."

THE WORSHIP OF SATAN

The phrase, *"If you therefore will worship me,"* proclaims Satan's condition. He wanted worship because he wanted to be God. Isaiah 14:12-14 proclaims this.

NOTES

Consequently, he presented to Jesus a shortcut, which, in effect, was a lie. To govern a world plagued by sin and shame, resulting in pain, poverty, sickness, and death, would be an undesirable gift.

Some claim that Satan's temptation had little merit inasmuch as there was no chance that Jesus would do this thing. However, there was far more plausibility than one realizes.

Satan wanted a number of things. Above all, he wanted to stop Calvary, actually, the very reason for which Jesus came. So, he would cut straight through to the offer of the kingdoms of the world, but with the price tag attached, which was worship of him.

THE BIG LIE

The phrase, *"All shall be Yours,"* was as usual a lie! But yet, the world has fallen for this lie from the beginning of time. Adam and Eve fell for it, and millions, if not almost all, continue to do so unto this hour. However, it has no means within its power to give man what man truly needs but can only offer a weak substitute, if that!

Morrison said, and with some validity, as he parrots Satan's thoughts as they were said to Jesus: "I am indeed the prince and god of this world. Its kingdoms and their glory are at my disposal. I could at once open up Your way to the highest honors that a universal conqueror and a universal sovereign could desire. I could gather at once around You a host of devoted Jewish troops; I could pave their way for victory after victory, until at no distant period the whole Roman Empire, and indeed the whole world, should be subject to Your sway. Only abandon the wild chimera of putting down sin ad making all men fanatical and holy; fall in with my way of things; let the morals of the world alone, more especially its morals in reference to God; work with me and under me, and all will go well. But if You refuse this offer, look out for determined opposition, for incessant persecution, for the most miserable poverty, and for every species of woe."

(8) "AND JESUS ANSWERED AND SAID UNTO HIM, GET THEE BEHIND ME, SATAN: FOR IT IS WRITTEN, YOU SHALL WORSHIP THE LORD YOUR

GOD, AND HIM ONLY SHALL YOU SERVE."

The order is:

1. The phrase, *"And Jesus answered and said unto him,"* addresses itself to worship as the first addressed itself to desire. Men desire the wrong thing—the opposite of the Word of God—and worship the wrong thing—that which is proposed by Satan.

2. *"Get thee behind Me, Satan,"* constitutes a statement that must be made more than once (Mat. 16:23; Eph. 6:10-18; James 4:7; I Pet. 5:7-8).

3. *"For it is written, You shall worship the Lord your God, and Him only shall you serve,"* is quoted from Deuteronomy 6:13; 10:20.

While it is true that Jesus will ultimately receive the total inheritance, He will only receive it at the hands of His heavenly Father. As well, it would not be won by any short-cuts but by a slow and painful process—by self-denial, self-sacrifice, and self-surrender.

(9) "AND HE BROUGHT HIM TO JERUSALEM, AND SET HIM ON A PINNACLE OF THE TEMPLE, AND SAID UNTO HIM, IF YOU BE THE SON OF GOD, CAST YOURSELF DOWN FROM HENCE."

THE TEMPTATION OF PRESUMPTION

The phrase, *"And he brought Him to Jerusalem,"* was literally done and was not a mere vision.

"And set Him on a pinnacle of the temple," is said by some to have been over 300 feet above the Kedron Valley below.

"And said unto Him, If You be the Son of God, cast Yourself down from hence," should have been translated, *"Since You are the Son of God."* Satan had no doubt that Jesus was the Son of God.

In this scenario, we learn something about temptation and the power of Satan. It could be argued as to why Jesus even allowed Himself to be taken to the pinnacle of the temple.

Neither temptation nor its ingredients hold any sin. The sin comes about only in yielding.

For instance, many men (or women) have been strongly tempted to drink alcoholic beverage. The temptation could even include the driving by the bar where such

NOTES

could be purchased. It could even include parking the automobile in front of the place and sitting there fighting the temptation, as many have no doubt done. However, the person sins only if he yields in obtaining the drink and imbibing it.

THE ARGUMENT

Of course, many would make the statement that the person is wrong to even drive beside the place, wherever it may be, and above all, to park there, at least if that is what is done. However, such is the power of temptation. As stated, the same person can argue that Jesus should not have gone to the pinnacle of the temple, but He did go, and He did not sin by doing so.

People who argue such are either hypocritical, or else, they have never truly been opposed by Satan. I suspect the latter is the case. They don't give Satan enough trouble for him to bother with them to this degree. While none of us can claim the measure of temptation that Jesus underwent, still, to those who are truly causing Satan damage, the powers of darkness can be brought to bear to an alarming degree.

A dear preacher proclaimed the following in a message many years ago. I think it is worth repeating:

• When you hear something negative about a fellow believer, understand that you are only hearing gossip, and it should be treated accordingly. Unfortunately, Satan loves to lie on Christians, and some Christians, unfortunately, love to believe it.

• Even if you think you know the truth about a certain situation that has involved failure, still, please remember that you have little understanding of the spiritual warfare involved. Consequently, judgment should be left in the hands of God, who alone is qualified.

• If you were placed in the same circumstances and faced the same powers of darkness, would you have done any better, or even as well?

SELF-RIGHTEOUSNESS

Self-righteous men, at least if they dared, would take Jesus to task for allowing Himself to be taken to the place of temptation. They would question how Satan could have *"brought Him"* (Jesus) *to Jerusalem."* They would have lampooned the powers of darkness that drove Him to the pinnacle of the temple, claiming that if He was really who He said He was, He would not have allowed such action. Only self-righteous hypocrisy would dare think such things, and yet, it is thought and said every day about those who are truly called of God and are truly following Him, even those whom the Lord has powerfully anointed.

If one truly understands the power of Satan (and he does have power), then one understands the ingredient of this type of temptation. While the Lord, through the power of the Holy Spirit, definitely had power over Satan, still, it was not a situation that could easily be disposed. Satan is real! His power is real! As well, the temptation is real! No one has to yield, but in so doing, it is always the fault of the individuals. Still, the matter is never as simple as some make it out to be.

Some have suggested that all temptation is the result of lust, quoting James 1:14, *"But every man is tempted, when he is drawn away of his own lust, and enticed."* While it is certainly true that all lust is followed by temptation, it is not true that all temptation is preceded by lust. Jesus did not have lust, and yet, He was greatly tempted, as is obvious here. Some are tempted, and tempted greatly, simply because they are a great threat to Satan, as Jesus was!

(10) "FOR IT IS WRITTEN, HE SHALL GIVE HIS ANGELS CHARGE OVER YOU, TO KEEP YOU:

(11) "AND IN THEIR HANDS THEY SHALL BEAR YOU UP, LEST AT ANY TIME YOU DASH YOUR FOOT AGAINST A STONE."

The synopsis is:

1. The phrase, *"For it is written,"* is misquoted from Psalms 91:11-12.

2. For the phrase, *"He shall give His angels charge over You, to keep You,"* to have been complete as the psalmist used it, *"In all Your ways,"* should have been added. These are the *"ways"* of God, which will guarantee the protection of God; however, Satan did not add that simply because

what he was proposing was not God's ways.

3. *"And in their hands they shall bear You up,"* is quoted correctly, however, only to continue the misquote in the remainder of the verse.

4. The phrase, *"Lest at any time You dash Your foot against a stone,"* has the words added, *"At any time,"* which are not in the original text. Consequently, the Word of God is subtly changed by Satan.

5. Here, Satan claims unlimited protection in all circumstances, even disobeying God by using the words, *"At any time,"* which the Lord did not originally give.

6. This tells us that Satan knows the Word of God very well, and to his own advantage, he subtly changes it to make it say something it originally did not say. So, if the believer does not know the Word as he should, he is grist for Satan's mill, so to speak.

7. As well, if one is to notice, Satan did not dare quote Verse 13 in Psalm 91, for it predicts his destruction by the Lord Jesus Christ.

(12) "AND JESUS ANSWERING SAID UNTO HIM, IT IS SAID, YOU SHALL NOT TEMPT THE LORD YOUR GOD."

The exegesis is:

1. The phrase, *"And Jesus answering said unto him,"* is taken from Deuteronomy 6:16.

2. *"It is said, You shall not tempt the Lord Your God,"* expresses the sin of presumption.

3. Presumption is an attitude or belief dictated by probability. In other words, God's Word is not probable but certain. Consequently, when someone steps out on what he claims to be the promises of God but, in reality, is only presumption, that person is going to fail. It amounts to tempting God, which is sin.

(13) "AND WHEN THE DEVIL HAD ENDED ALL THE TEMPTATION, HE DEPARTED FROM HIM FOR A SEASON."

The pattern is:

1. To satisfy the broken law, God demanded that a perfect life be given, which is the reason that God became man.

2. God cannot die, and if justice was to be completely satisfied, a perfect life had to be offered.

3. Due to original sin, no human being could qualify; therefore, the Lord would have to pay the price Himself. He would do so by becoming man.

WAS IT POSSIBLE FOR JESUS TO HAVE SINNED?

The phrase, *"And when the Devil had ended all the temptation,"* only speaks of this particular time.

"He departed from Him for a season," means that he would return, which he, no doubt, did again and again.

Matthew closes his account of this incident by relating how angels came and ministered unto Jesus. Luke does not mention this episode.

Of course, the question is asked regarding this temptation, *"Was it truly possible for Jesus to actually sin and, thereby, fail?"*

Only those who do not properly understand the incarnation would ask such a question. Yes, it was possible for Jesus to yield to the temptation, thereby, sinning, and, thereby, failing. Were it not, Satan would have been wasting his time.

Of far greater significance, Jesus had to be perfectly human in His combat with Satan. As well, He could not use any attributes of deity, only what you and I have access to, namely the Holy Spirit. If it were possible for Adam to sin and fall, which he did, then it was possible for Jesus as the *"last Adam"* to sin and fall, which, thankfully, He did not!

TEMPTATION

The Scripture says concerning Jesus, *"But was in all points tempted like as we are, yet without sin"* (Heb. 4:15). While it was certainly impossible for God to sin, it was not impossible for the human Jesus to sin. The fact that He did not guarantees us our victory in living an overcoming, victorious life.

Temptation is allowed by God in order to prove or test what is within the individual. However, God cannot be blamed when someone fails to respond in a godly way under pressure (James 1:13-15).

The source of human failure is to be found not in the situation that God permits,

but in *his own evil desire* (James 1:14). The temptation itself, although evil, cannot be transferred unless yielded to. The evil that emerges comes from within the human personality.

Jesus showed us the way to victory, and actually, the victory demonstrated by Jesus is available to us. This is God's way of escaping failure, which points to a total reliance on Christ and what He did for us at the Cross.

It should be remembered that God has not permitted the test or temptation in order to entrap us. God does, however, use difficult situations in our lives. As we remain close to Him, we find His way of escape, and our godly response to pressure demonstrates the genuineness of our faith.

However, at the same time, we are to never seek temptation in some foolhardy attempt to prove to ourselves that our faith is real. Rather, we should follow Jesus' guidance and when we pray, say, *"Lord, help us not to be led into temptation"* (Mat. 6:13; 26:41; Mk. 14:38; Lk. 11:4; 22:40-46). There are tests enough ahead for each of us without our seeking them out. When they come, it is good to know that we can turn to the Lord and expect Him to rescue us.

WHAT IS THE WAY OF ESCAPE PREPARED FOR US BY THE LORD?

There is only one answer for sin, just one. That answer is the Cross of Christ. It was at the Cross that all sin was addressed, and Satan was totally defeated. Paul said:

"So Christ was once offered to bear the sins of many; and unto them who look for Him shall He appear the second time without sin unto salvation" (Heb. 9:28).

He also said, *"For then must He often have suffered since the foundation of the world: but now once in the end of the world has He appeared to put away sin by the sacrifice of Himself"* (Heb. 9:26).

So, if we look for help in any direction except the Cross of Christ, no such help will be forthcoming.

Paul said: *"There has no temptation taken you but such as is common to man: but God is faithful, who will not suffer you to be tempted above that you are able; but will with the temptation also make a way to escape, that you may be able to bear it"* (I Cor. 10:13).

WHAT IS THAT WAY OF ESCAPE?

Every believer should look at this verse, which precedes the last one just given. Paul also said: *"Wherefore let him who thinks he stands take heed lest he fall"* (I Cor. 10:12).

There is only one way of escape as it regards temptation. We are to look exclusively to Christ and the Cross and understand that it was at the Cross where all sin was addressed, handled, and atoned. If the believer tries to overcome temptation any other way, he is destined for failure. He might overcome for awhile, but ultimately, he will fail.

Now, let's look at the Scripture just quoted:

We must understand that all temptation comes from the powers of darkness, which are far more powerful than we are. We need to understand that. That's the reason that Paul also said, *"We wrestle not against flesh and blood"* (Eph. 6:12). In other words, what the child of God is up against is a far greater power than our personal willpower or resolve. We must understand that. That's the reason that it is so foolish to think that humanistic psychology can stem the tide of these powers of darkness.

WHAT EXACTLY IS THE CHILD OF GOD FACING?

The Holy Spirit through the apostle tells us what we're facing. They are:

PRINCIPALITIES: These are very powerful fallen angels, who work under Satan. They have devised the kingdom of darkness, and to be sure, they are mighty—but not mightier than the Holy Spirit.

POWERS: these are also fallen angels who answer to the principalities.

RULERS OF THE DARKNESS OF THIS WORLD: These again are fallen angels who answer to the powers. They are of the group that fell with Lucifer when he led his revolution against God in eternity past. Of course, as the reader knows and understands, Satan is a fallen angel as well. More than likely, he is the wisest angel that God ever created (Ezek. 28:12).

SPIRITUAL WICKEDNESS IN HIGH PLACES: according to the Greek scholars, these are demon spirits.

There is very little evidence, if any at all, that humanity deals with the fallen angels, but rather with demon spirits. Then again, the possibility exists that the *"messenger of Satan"* that was allowed to hinder Paul, as it regards the *"thorn in the flesh,"* could well have been a fallen angel instead of a demon spirit (II Cor. 12:7).

However, irrespective of whether it was a fallen angel or demon spirits that were allowed to hinder Paul, the fact is, within ourselves, we simply do not have the power, the ability, or the strength to overcome these things. We must have the help of the Holy Spirit.

THE HOLY SPIRIT

The Holy Spirit works exclusively within and through the finished work of Christ (Rom. 8:2). In other words, what Jesus did at the Cross atoned for all sin, which gives the Holy Spirit the legal means to function as He does. Before the Cross, the Holy Spirit could not come into the hearts and lives of believers to abide permanently. He did come into some, such as prophets, etc., to help them carry out their mission, and then He would leave. The reason that He could not come into their hearts and lives, and we speak of the time before the Cross, was because *the blood of bulls and goats could not take away sins* (Heb. 10:4).

So, that means the sin debt remained, which limited the Holy Spirit as to what He could do. However, when Jesus died on the Cross, thereby, paying the sin debt, this made it possible for the Holy Spirit to come into the heart and life of the believing sinner immediately upon conversion, which He definitely does. He comes to abide forever. Paul said:

"For the preaching of the Cross is to them who perish foolishness; but unto us who are saved it is the power of God" (I Cor. 1:18).

Where is the power?

There is no power in the Cross per se, and I speak of that wooden beam. There was really no power in the death of Christ per se, for Jesus died in weakness (II Cor. 13:4).

However, it was a contrived weakness. In other words, Jesus had the power to do whatever He so desired. He could have called 12 legions of angels to His side in a moment had He so desired, but He didn't because He came to die, which means to offer up Himself as a perfect sacrifice, which He did.

With that being done, all sin was atoned, which means that the Holy Spirit can use His power on our behalf to do what needs to be done.

For the believer to have the benefit of this power, our faith must be exclusively in Christ and the Cross. With that being done and our faith maintained in Christ and the Cross, the Holy Spirit will do for us what we cannot do for ourselves. That is the way of escape that the Lord has outlined for us.

(14) "AND JESUS RETURNED IN THE POWER OF THE SPIRIT INTO GALILEE: AND THERE WENT OUT A FAME OF HIM THROUGH ALL THE REGION ROUND ABOUT."

THE POWER OF THE SPIRIT

The phrase, *"And Jesus returned in the power of the Spirit into Galilee,"* concerns the beginning of His ministry. Even as I write these words, I sense the presence of God. From 40 days and nights of fasting and His tryst with Satan, Jesus may have looked thin and emaciated; however, in spirit, He was powerful beyond belief. Never had the Holy Spirit had such a temple in which to dwell. Never has He had one since!

As the *"power of the Spirit"* was His strength, likewise, it is our strength. For the individual without the Holy Spirit, there is no power. We are speaking of the baptism with the Holy Spirit that is always accompanied by the speaking with other tongues. This verse tells us that, and it should be obvious to all. As well, the Holy Spirit is not an automatic operation in the life of the believer, though He definitely is present. Neither is His working automatic in the life of the Spirit-filled believer. That is a matter of consecration, dedication, and humble submission to the Lord, as the 40 days and nights of fasting proclaimed in the life of Jesus. His example is meant for our instruction.

NOTES

THE FAME OF JESUS

Unfortunately, most of the church, whether of the Pentecostal or non-Pentecostal variety, takes the Holy Spirit for granted. The non-Pentecostal thinks that the power of the Holy Spirit is automatic upon conversion. The Pentecostal too often thinks that one is full of the Holy Spirit if he speaks in tongues. Neither is correct! A powerless church testifies to that fact. The church is powerless because believers are powerless.

After the 40 days and nights of temptation, which probably occurred near Jericho, Jesus went back into Galilee where would occasion most of His ministry.

The phrase, *"And there went out a fame of Him through all the region round about,"* concerned the mighty miracles being performed, which actually began with the changing of the water to wine at Cana (Jn. 2:1-11).

Thus would begin the greatest ministry the world had ever known—the ministry of the Son of God. Consequently, this *"region round about"* would witness a display of the miracle-working power of God as had never been seen in human history.

(15) "AND HE TAUGHT IN THEIR SYNAGOGUES, BEING GLORIFIED OF ALL."

The pattern is:

1. The Cross, by no stretch of the imagination, is a hidden symbol in the Word of God.

2. The Cross of Christ is the glaring centerpiece of the proclamation of the gospel all the way from Genesis 1:1 through Revelation 22:21.

3. It takes an acute deception to miss this glaring fact.

THE MESSAGE

Jesus taught in the synagogues in all the towns and villages in Galilee. At this early stage in His ministry, He had not ministered in them all, but the ones in which He ministered witnessed a portrayal of the Word of God totally unlike anything they had ever heard. Heretofore, the scribes and Pharisees mostly argued over the Word or attempted to present some hypotheses, which were little understood by the people. The message, as presented by Christ, was clear, concise, understandable, to the point, and freighted with Holy Spirit power. The people understood exactly what He was saying and, as well, understood it easily, with the exception of some of the parables. Also, His messages warmed their hearts, touched their souls, and gladdened their spirits. For the first time, many of them, if not all, heard the Word of God preached under the anointing of the Holy Spirit, which was unlike anything ever heard.

The phrase, *"Being glorified of all,"* concerned the beginning days of His ministry, which would sadly change very shortly. The animosity directed toward Him by the scribes, Pharisees, and Sadducees would know no bounds and, in fact, would not let up until they put Him on the Cross.

(16) "AND HE CAME TO NAZARETH, WHERE HE HAD BEEN BROUGHT UP: AND, AS HIS CUSTOM WAS, HE WENT INTO THE SYNAGOGUE ON THE SABBATH DAY, AND STOOD UP FOR TO READ."

The form is:

1. Everything in Old Testament times pointed to the Cross.

2. This speaks of every ceremony, every ritual, every law, and every sacrifice of the Mosaic law.

3. Even the tabernacle with all of its sacred vessels pointed to Jesus in either His intercessory work, mediatorial work, or atoning work, with all made possible by the Cross.

NAZARETH

The phrase, *"And He came to Nazareth,"* is used in such a way by the Holy Spirit to denote the terrible thing that would follow. The men of Nazareth, with their violent antagonism (which we are about to consider), were only a few months in advance of the balance of the nation in their rejection of the Messiah.

After the temptation, Jesus journeyed to Capernaum, passing by Nazareth. Having taught and wrought there, He retraced His steps and visited Nazareth. He never

revisited it. The particulars of this visit are related by Luke only.

"Where He had been brought up," makes vivid the fact that Jesus was a man.

The phrase, *"And leaving Nazareth,"* found in Matthew 4:13, has nothing to do with ministry in Nazareth, but simply means that Jesus left His home in Nazareth and came and dwelt in Capernaum.

Jesus lived in Nazareth for about 30 years. Consequently, everyone in the little village knew Him.

For this 30 years, He had said nothing about His coming mission and ministry; consequently, He *"increased in wisdom and stature, and in favour with God and man"* (Lk. 2:52).

Only when He claimed to be the fulfillment of the prophecies concerning the Messiah did they turn on Him. Had they known the Bible as they should, they would not have made the worst mistake any people ever made.

AS WAS HIS CUSTOM

"And, as His custom was, He went into the synagogue on the Sabbath day, and stood up for to read," tells us something personally about Jesus.

As we would say in today's terminology, His custom was to attend church every single week, and even more often. Then it was on Saturday because it was under the old Jewish law. Now it is on the first day of the week, Sunday, the day our Lord rose from the dead. So, if this was His custom, it should be our custom in one way or the other as well!

At this ministry (Jimmy Swaggart Ministries), we encourage believers to find a church where the Cross is preached. However, if such cannot be found, and sadly, in most places there aren't any, we encourage them to make Family Worship Center their church. How can they do that?

They can do that by tuning in with us, whether by television, the Internet, or even radio, as untold thousands do every service. We have had thousands join Family Worship Center Media Church, and they look at our church as their church, which they should. It is far better to do that than to attend a church where the gospel is not really preached.

As it regards the synagogues of Jesus' time, children at the age of 5 years were admitted when their instruction began. At 13, their attendance was a part of the legal life of the Jew. They not only met every Sabbath but usually on Monday and Tuesday, as well as other special occasions.

Synagogues were operated somewhat differently than the temple, with the priests and Levites having no recognized position in this local worship.

If any stranger was present who was known to be competent, it was not unusual for the ruler of the synagogue to ask him to read and to expound a passage in the law or the prophets.

Due to the fact that Jesus had been raised in this little village and that His fame had preceded Him, the place was, no doubt, filled to capacity, with no room to seat the people, and with many, many people outside trying to hear.

(17) "AND THERE WAS DELIVERED UNTO HIM THE BOOK OF THE PROPHET ISAIAH. AND WHEN HE HAD OPENED THE BOOK, HE FOUND THE PLACE WHERE IT WAS WRITTEN."

The synopsis is:

1. The phrase, *"And there was delivered unto Him the book of the prophet Isaiah,"* either proclaimed Him asking for this particular scroll, or as some have suggested, this was the passage that was supposed to be expounded on regarding this particular Sabbath. Either way, it was that which the Holy Spirit wanted.

2. As the life and ministry of Jesus is analyzed, it quickly becomes obvious that He based everything He did on the Word of God. It alone was His foundation. In other words, it was not something referred to once in awhile but, actually, was the basis of all activity. This should be a lesson for us!

3. The phrase, *"And when He had opened the book, He found the place where it was written,"* did not mean that He had a problem finding it but that He simply turned to it. He was extremely familiar with the Word of God. This was what we now know as Isaiah 61:1, along with the first part of Verse 2.

(18) "THE SPIRIT OF THE LORD IS UPON ME, BECAUSE HE HAS ANOINTED ME TO PREACH THE GOSPEL TO THE POOR; HE HAS SENT ME TO HEAL THE BROKENHEARTED, TO PREACH DELIVERANCE TO THE CAPTIVES, AND RECOVERING OF SIGHT TO THE BLIND, TO SET AT LIBERTY THEM WHO ARE BRUISED."

The exegesis is:

1. Counting Verse 19, as well, there are seven directives given in these two verses concerning the work of the Lord Jesus Christ. They are:

a. The Spirit of the Lord is upon Me

b. Because He has anointed Me to preach the gospel to the poor

c. He has sent Me to heal the brokenhearted

d. To preach deliverance to the captives

e. And recovering of sight to the blind

f. To set at liberty them who are bruised

g. To preach the acceptable year of the Lord.

2. In this great statement, every problem that confronts humanity is addressed.

3. This means that there is no room for humanistic psychology.

THE SPIRIT OF THE LORD IS UPON ME

This is at least one of the most powerful passages in the entirety of the Word of God. It not only gives the prospective ministry of Jesus, but it is meant to serve as an example for all preachers of the gospel. This, as given here, outlines the functions of the Lord Jesus Christ, not only in His earthly ministry but, as well, for all time. These things He alone can do!

As we have stated, these passages are some of the most important in the Bible as it concerns man's condition. This completely eliminates man's foray into humanistic psychology.

Sometime back, one preacher said that modern man is facing some problems that are not addressed in the Bible and, therefore, he needs the help of humanistic psychology. What a ridiculous statement! Peter said, and I quote directly from The Expositor's Study Bible, both text and notes:

"Grace and peace be multiplied unto

NOTES

you through the knowledge of God, and of Jesus our Lord (this is both sanctifying grace and sanctifying peace, all made available by the Cross),

"According as His divine power has given unto us all things (the Lord with large-handed generosity has given us all things) that pertain unto life and godliness (pertains to the fact that the Lord Jesus has given us everything we need regarding life and living), through the knowledge of Him who has called us to glory and virtue (the 'knowledge' addressed here speaks of what Christ did at the Cross, which alone can provide 'glory and virtue'):

"Whereby are given unto us exceeding great and precious promises (pertains to the Word of God, which alone holds the answer to every life problem): that by these (promises) you might be partakers of the divine nature (the divine nature implanted in the inner being of the believing sinner becomes the source of our new life and actions; it comes to everyone at the moment of being 'born again'), having escaped the corruption that is in the world through lust. (This presents the salvation experience of the sinner and the sanctification experience of the saint)" (II Pet. 1:2-4).

Now, either the Lord did exactly what He said He would do, or else, He didn't tell the truth. I know He told the truth. So, once again, that leaves no room for humanistic psychology.

The phrase, "The Spirit of the Lord is upon Me," contains a clear definition of the Trinity. The "Holy Spirit" is spoken of, with the name "Lord" referring to God the Father, and with the pronoun "Me" referring to Christ as the One anointed.

THE MAN, CHRIST JESUS

As well, we learn again of the absolute necessity of the person of the Holy Spirit in carrying out the work of God. As a man, in fact, "the man, Christ Jesus," He had to have the Holy Spirit in order for this work be done. It would not have been possible otherwise.

Actually, Jesus did not even begin His ministry until He was first filled with the Holy Spirit.

Concerning this, Luke also said, "Now when all the people were baptized (were being baptized), it came to pass, that Jesus also being baptized (this was to testify of His death, burial, and resurrection, of which water baptism is a type), and praying (as He came up out of the water, He came up praying), the heaven was opened (heaven had been closed to man since the fall; through Jesus it would now open),

"And the Holy Spirit descended in a bodily shape like a dove upon Him (the Holy Spirit is a person, the third person of the Godhead, separate from the Father and the Son), and a voice came from heaven, which said (the voice of God the Father), You are My beloved Son (literally, 'as for You,' in contradistinction to all others); in You I am well pleased (God is pleased with us only as long as we are in Christ)" (Lk. 3:21-22).

Incidentally, the Greek word translated upon at the beginning of Verse 22 should have been translated within. The Holy Spirit literally came into the Lord Jesus Christ. I might quickly add that never before or since has the Holy Spirit had such a perfect vessel to occupy than the physical body, mind, soul, and spirit of the Lord Jesus Christ.

THE POWER OF THE SPIRIT

To be sure, the needs that presented themselves then present themselves now and, as then, can only be remedied by the power of the Holy Spirit. Without the Holy Spirit, the church, no matter its wealthy accouterments, is no more than any other meeting, and for whatever purpose. However, if empowered by the Holy Spirit, it becomes a living dynamo, which is what Christ intended for His church to be (Mat. 16:18-19).

To make less of the Holy Spirit than we should is the sin of the church. To make more of the Holy Spirit than we should is nearly impossible! If the Holy Spirit is given His rightful place, Jesus will always be promoted and glorified (Jn. 16:12-15).

HOW THE HOLY SPIRIT WORKS

It is the Cross of Christ that gave and gives the Holy Spirit the legal means to do all that He does within our hearts and lives (Rom. 8:2).

Before the Cross, due to the fact that the blood of bulls and goats could not take away sins, the Holy Spirit was very limited as to what He could do. This meant that the sin debt was still upon the believers, even the greatest. Consequently, when believers in Old Testament times died, they could not go to heaven because of this very problem. They were taken down into paradise where they were comforted. Still, they were captives of Satan (Eph. 4:8).

However, when Jesus died on the Cross, He atoned for all sin and defeated Satan, all fallen angels, and demon spirits. Our Lord could then liberate all those in paradise from that place and the dominion of Satan and take them to heaven. Now, since the Cross, when the believer dies, his soul and spirit instantly go to be with the Lord Jesus Christ in heaven.

As well, before the Cross, the Holy Spirit could only come into the hearts and lives of a few people, such as prophets, etc., to help them carry out the task assigned them. When that task was completed, the Holy Spirit would leave.

Now (Jn. 14:16-17), the moment any person accepts Christ, the Holy Spirit comes into him to abide forever.

Please consider the following:

• Jesus Christ is the source of all things we receive from God (Jn. 1:1, 14, 29; Col. 2:10-15; Rom. 6:1-11).

• The Cross of Christ is the means, and the only means, by which all of these things are given to us (I Cor. 1:17-18, 23; 2:2).

• While Jesus is the source, and the Cross is the means, this means that our faith (this is very, very important) should ever have the Cross of Christ as its object. Of course, we aren't speaking of the wooden beam on which Jesus died, but rather what He there accomplished for us (Rom. 6:1-11; I Cor. 2:2; Gal. 6:14; Col. 2:10-15).

• With our faith properly placed with the Cross of Christ as its object, then the Holy Spirit, who is God, will do great and mighty things for us and with us (Rom. 8:1-11; Eph. 2:13-18).

As we have stated, the Cross of Christ is what gives the Holy Spirit the legal means to do all that He does. This means that He

NOTES

will not work outside of the parameters of the Cross.

THE ANOINTING

The phrase, *"Because He has anointed Me,"* concerns a spiritual anointing and not a physical anointing, as was common in the Old Testament. It refers to a special appointment or commission by God that sets the person apart (Acts 4:27; 10:38; II Cor. 1:21; Heb. 1:9).

Jesus is here identified as the ultimate Anointed One, the One who will ultimately rule as king over a restored Davidic kingdom, which will be during the coming kingdom age. This conviction is expressed in Jesus' title, *Christ.* This is not a name but a title that means "the anointed."

Consequently, the anointing of the Holy Spirit actually belongs to Christ.

Even though this anointing is given to all who God calls for service in any capacity, still, it is anointing that is given at the discretion of Christ. As stated, the anointing is His, and the Holy Spirit gives it only at the direction of Christ (I Cor. 12:11; Mat. 3:11; Jn. 16:14).

As an aside, the idea that poor, mere mortals can bestow anointing upon someone is foolishness indeed! The Lord alone dispenses that which He so desires.

VARIOUS CALLINGS

Paul said, *"And He gave some, apostles; and some, prophets; and some, evangelists; and some, pastors and teachers"* (Eph. 4:11).

With these callings of various ministries, an anointing of the Holy Spirit automatically follows. As well, any Spirit-filled believer who so desires can have gifts of the Spirit, that is, if he will only desire and seek such gifts (I Cor. 12:31; 14:1), which are automatically followed with an anointing. However, the fivefold calling of apostles, etc., can only be delegated by the Lord. In other words, the believer cannot pray to be an apostle, a prophet, etc., with that prerogative belonging only to the Lord. The Scripture says, *"And He gave."*

THE DEGREE OF ANOINTING

Even though the anointing of the Holy

Spirit is automatic respecting these callings and gifts, still, the degree of the anointing is predicated on one's consecration, dedication, and relationship with the Lord. Many individuals are truly called of God for various ministries but have little anointing simply because there is little consecration. The anointing flows more or less through the believer according to his relationship with Christ. So, even though the anointing automatically follows the calling or gift, still, its operation depends much on one's daily walk before God. It is not that such is earned, for these things are all gifts of God, but it is simply that the vessel be prepared for use.

WITH THE ANOINTING

Only with the anointing of the Holy Spirit can these attributes of ministry listed by Christ be carried out. If these things do not occur, it means the anointing is not present because the Holy Spirit is either absent or given little latitude to work. If the Holy Spirit has the required latitude and the degree of consecration as it ought to be, these tremendous attributes of ministry will follow. It is impossible to be otherwise. Jesus listed them; consequently, there is no reason to be in doubt as to what they are:

TO PREACH THE GOSPEL TO THE POOR

The word *poor* would have probably been better translated *meek* as it is translated in Isaiah 61:1. It speaks of those who are humbled to receive the gospel and has nothing to do with one's financial status. As well, this is far more important than meets the eye because it addresses itself to pride and self-sufficiency, which is man's real problem.

Due to the fall, man thinks he can surely solve his social, emotional, domestic, financial, and even spiritual problems. Actually, this is the basis for humanistic psychology. It thinks it has the answers when, in reality, it has no answer at all.

So, for men to receive the gospel, much, if not most of the time, it has to be a time of crisis in their lives that has humbled them, or else, dire circumstances of one sort or the other.

When Jesus said that He was anointed, and we should be anointed to *"preach the*

NOTES

gospel to the poor," what type of gospel was He addressing?

In short, the gospel is *Jesus Christ and Him crucified* (I Cor. 1:17). In fact, the entirety of the story of the Bible is the story of Jesus Christ and Him crucified. It brings good news to all who will heed its clarion call. It is the answer for man's problems. Man's problem is sin, and the solution is Christ and what He did for us at the Cross. According to Paul's teaching, which was given to him by the Holy Spirit, we must never separate Christ from the Cross. To do so, we are left with *another Jesus, another spirit, and another gospel* (II Cor. 11:4).

When we speak of Jesus and the Cross, we aren't speaking of the wooden beam on which He died, but rather what He there accomplished. Jesus is no longer on a Cross. He is seated by the right hand of the Father, making intercession for all the saints of God. In other words, His work at the Cross has been totally accepted by God the Father (Heb. 7:25). Jesus came to this world to go to the Cross. That was His mission, His work, and that which had been planned from before the foundation of the world (I Pet. 1:18-20).

TO HEAL THE BROKENHEARTED

The *"heart,"* as referred to here, has nothing to do with the physical organ in our bodies, but rather refers to the seat of our emotions, feelings, and passions. It is somewhat a combination of the activities of the soul and the spirit of man.

The word *broken* means to be crushed into pieces, shattered, and broken beyond repair. In other words, there is no earthly remedy for this condition. As well, if the truth be known, this terrible malady affects the far greater majority of the human family, irrespective of race or nationality.

Such is caused by the terrible condition in which man finds himself due to the fall. Much of the world goes to bed each night wondering how they will find food for the next day. Others are tormented by the terrible ravages of the bondages of darkness, such as alcohol, drugs, nicotine, hate, etc., which can make life a living hell. Actually, the loved ones of people caught in these webs of deceit are affected just as much or more. Their lives also are tormented. All produce a broken heart. As we have repeatedly stated, and will continue to state, only Jesus can heal the broken heart because only He has the power to do so.

TO PREACH DELIVERANCE TO THE CAPTIVES

Jesus Christ does not treat people; He delivers them. The word *deliverance*, as used here, carries several meanings. It means to be unchained and unshackled; however, it also means to "pardon, forgive, and set at liberty." This is a work that only Christ can do and, in fact, does constantly! However, much of the modern church no longer believes in deliverance by the power of God, which can only come by that method, but instead, refers to the psychological way.

The method of deliverance is by the Cross—always by the Cross. This is where Jesus atoned for all sin, broke the power of sin, and defeated all principalities and powers of evil, meaning that whatever our problem is, He addressed it at the Cross (Col. 2:10-15).

Every drunkard that's ever been set free, every gambler that's ever been delivered from that bondage, every person that's ever been delivered from pornography and all the evils of immorality, and every deliverance period, whatever the problem, have all been set free by the Lord Jesus Christ, and millions have.

Muhammad has never set one soul free, not one! The same can be said for Confucius, Joseph Smith, and anyone or anything else. It is the Lord Jesus Christ alone who sets the captive free because it is Christ who paid the price at Calvary's Cross. Let us say it again: whatever the problem in one's life, and I mean whatever, the statements made here by Christ in Luke 4:18-19, address themselves to every single problem of humanity, excluding none and including all.

THE PSYCHOLOGIZING OF THE FAITH

The following statements are derived from a small booklet, *"The Psychologizing of the Faith,"* by Bob Hoekstra. Some of what is said is what I have been

NOTES

proclaiming for several years, often incurring the wrath of almost the entirety of the world of religion. Thankfully, some few are beginning to see the light and return to the Bible, which I know holds all the answers to everything pertaining to life and godliness (II Pet. 1:3-4).

THE REDEFINING PROCESS

"A subtle and deadly process is at work in the church today in which the Christian faith is being 'psychologized.' This work speaks of the redefining of the Christian faith by the intrusion of psychological thinking into the church of the Lord Jesus Christ. It is related to secularism and humanism running rampant in much of the world over recent decades. The secularists (those who have no regard for God or His Word) are attempting to remove God from our thinking and our values. The humanists (those who believe that man has the solution to all things within himself) are at the same time trying to establish man as the source of all values and all necessary adequacy. These perspectives on life have helped establish psychology as a cultural religion for multitudes of people.

"Unfortunately, many people would view psychology's influential position as an inevitable result of living in an enlightened scientific age; however, only a minor portion of psychological theory is capable of scientific verification (repeated experiments where the same results are always brought about, thus indicating factors that God built into creation as He made it). Actually, the overwhelming portion of psychological theory is philosophical in nature, meaning that it cannot be proved scientifically, or any other way. It amounts to an attempt to explain man (who he is, why he is here, how to develop him, how to solve his problems, how to meet his needs, and how to help him get where he thinks he needs to go). It is a philosophy of life with man at the center and with man as his own basic hope. Colossians 2:8 gives a strong warning about the philosophies of man.

THE WEAKENING OF THE CHURCH

"Along with all of these developments in

the thinking of the world, the church has for decades been weakening in its calling to be salt and light; consequently, instead of us affecting the world as we are supposed to be doing, the world is affecting the church. Instead of the people of God telling the world about Him and about His ways in all things, the world is now teaching the church the ways of man, as worldly thinking makes increasing inroads into the church.

"This process is bringing us a new vocabulary and a new way of thinking about God and man. Actually, this means we are being given a new theology that is in conformity to this world. In this worldly theology, the Word of God is not forsaken altogether; however, the Scriptures get twisted and tortured in order to protect and propagate this new message. Fundamental elements of 'the faith once and for all, delivered to the saints' (Jude 3) are given a new, popular, earth-bound, psychological meaning. Many of us believers are convinced that the church desperately needs a warning call to come back to the Lord and to His Word.

SIN AND ITS EFFECT

"The question must be asked as to what is going on in much of the church world today concerning the basic problem of man and God's basic remedy. Instead of sin, man's problems now are dysfunctionalism or co-dependency or victimization or various types of 'nonphysiological diseases and disorders.' This sort of psychologized thinking in the church is redefined in new, inadequate humanistic terms what man's problems are all about.

THE CONCEPT OF DYSFUNCTIONALISM

"This concept is a prime example. Man observes or learns of a troubled family, and decides to call it dysfunctional. That is, this particular family is not functioning in a manner that we or the participants would desire. In that sense, however, 'All have dysfunctioned and have fallen short of their desired level of human functionality.' Consequently, we can understand where such a term comes from.

"It is attempting to describe some actuality in human experience; however, it is using the wrong standard, and it does not go deep enough in its analysis. As a standard, dysfunctionalism says that I cannot function in a manner that I desire, or others did not function toward me in a manner that I desired. The true standard, however, is what God desires, and He says that 'All have sinned and fallen short of the glory of God.'

CO-DEPENDENCY IS ANOTHER PSYCHOLOGICAL WORD

"Co-dependency also is inadequate as a diagnosis of man's problem. Certainly people can wrongfully attempt to find meaning for their lives by becoming dependent upon helping others who are wrongly dependent upon drugs, alcohol, or whatever. The problem is not that we are sacrificing for others, in fact, the Lord called us to lay down our lives for one another (I Jn. 3:16). Jesus tells us that greatness in His kingdom is measured in servanthood (Mat. 20:25-28). The problem is that we either serve self or we serve others out of self-interest.

"The remedy is to learn to serve others by the grace of God and for the glory of God.

VICTIMIZATION IS ANOTHER WORD

"Victimization is another insufficient term that people often turn to in trying to understand their deepest problems. It explains, and often justifies our shortcomings as being a consequence of wrongs done to us, so we thereby find justification for our condition and/or place blame on others. While everyone has been wrongfully treated in some way, and at the same time has wrongfully treated others; still, we cannot build a relationship with God on the basis of 'They made me this way.' Neither can we relate to others on the basis of blame. The problems that we can deal with before God are our wrongs against Him and against others. We can find that His remedy is forgiveness, cleansing, transformation, and reconciliation between God and man.

IS SIN A DISEASE?

"Another psychologized evaluation of man's needs is seen in trying to turn every aspect of sin and carnality into a disease or a disorder. So we are now treating

alcoholism as a disease, and the disorder of compulsive eating in the same manner, instead of dealing spiritually with the sins of drunkenness and gluttony.

"The Scriptures do not deny that we can have physiological needs, like chemical imbalances. God's Word does not disallow medical treatment for physical problems; however, this does not mean that we can turn the spiritual problem of sin into mental or emotional diseases, and then treat them by drugs and individual or group therapy.

"The ultimate problem that man faces is sin. Only God can deal with sin. Sadly, the problem of sin is being psychologically redefined in many churches today, or ignored altogether!

SELF AND SELF-ESTEEM

"The church once followed the Scriptures in calling people to deny self. Today, and because it has been by and large psychologized, it is urging people to esteem self.

"Self-esteem, one of the great new doctrines of the world, has become the rage of many churches, leaders, and authors. The tragedy of this philosophy is that it undermines true discipleship. Actually, it is the complete opposite of what the Word of God teaches. Denying self and esteeming self are two opposite directions. One is humility, and the other is pride. One is God's way, and the other is man's way.

"Some have asked what should be used to replace this false gospel of self-esteem. The answer is simple! 'Christ esteem' (Heb. 11:26).

"Self-esteem means to hold self in high regard. Following Jesus, we are to learn increasingly to hold Him in high regard. We are to get caught up in His greatness, love, provision, mercy, goodness, grace, power, and work on our behalf. Another way to say it is that we can get all caught up in His sufficiency.

THE TRUTH IS, MOST PREACHERS NO LONGER BELIEVE THE BIBLE.

"Many, many churches no longer believe in the inspiration or authority of the Word of God, so they cannot be expected to proclaim its sufficiency; however, many preachers

NOTES

who claim to hold to the inspiration and authority of the Word also declare by their actions the insufficiency of the Word. Many of these are teaching people to turn to the uninspired theoreticians of the world to get the final, sufficient answers for life. Those who have studied the social sciences (or more accurately, the behavioral philosophies) are now viewed as those who have the sufficient answers for man.

"The new creed in all of this is 'All truth is God's truth.' It reasons that since God created all things and since God is truth, any truth found anywhere must have its source in God.

"This thinking tends to place the ramblings of man on the same level as the divinely-inspired truth of God's Word; therefore, the message of a psychological theorist can be brought into the ministry of the church and integrated into the message for God's people, which is done everyday.

"These individuals assume that these 'experts' who have studied man have valid insights into humanity.

NO INSIGHT INTO HUMANITY

"However, the truth is, these individuals have no insight into humanity. They may know something of the symptoms of the problems that plague mankind, but they have no knowledge as to the cause or the cure. What happens in this process is that we end up greatly overestimating man's wisdom, while we tragically underestimate God's wisdom. The two end up on a common level, and people grab a little bit of each, thinking they are getting the best of all truth, when in reality, they are getting nothing. The Word of God will not mix with the foolish ramblings of man. To attempt to do so only leaves a watered-down gospel, instead of a Christianized psychology.

"This 'other truth' is man's best guess about what is going on in an arena that he cannot really see, the heart, soul, mind, and inner man. Man cannot look into this arena, which only God can see. When he tries to do so, he gets nothing but confusion, because the heart is deceitful. God is the only One who can do such, and He is not guessing at what is taking place.

6

"He declares the way He made man, how man fell, what the resultant problems are, and what He has provided to make man whole inside. He has declared all of this to us in His Word.

"If we integrate, or attempt to do so, human philosophies or theories into these matters of divine revelation, we are polluting God's truth. We are offering a new, unworkable, psychologized faith to people for their lives and their walk with God. It is an undermining of the sufficiency of God's Word. This is a major aspect of the psychologizing of the Christian faith."

LIFE'S PRESENT PROBLEMS

"Many church leaders are presently saying that life's problems are too complex today for these old-fashioned approaches of the Bible and the Holy Spirit. Thereby, they are declaring the inadequacy of the Holy Spirit to meet the needs of people's lives or to accomplish the purposes of God. They thereby demonstrate intellectual answers instead of spiritual answers found only in the Bible. Much of the church world has opted for intellectualism.

"While God certainly places no premium on ignorance, still, the intellectual way is man's conceived way, which claims that man's mental capacities can solve his problems. So, we end up trading off the power of the Holy Spirit for the weakness of human theories and philosophies. The church tends to forget that the Holy Spirit alone can reveal spiritual matters and make them real in our lives.

"Actually, all of these theories of man from behavioral philosophies represent man's best attempt to help man become what man wants to be, using man's own resources and his own best effort. This is a world apart from 'The faith, once for all delivered to the saints.' God has His ways to make of us all that He wants us to become. It is, 'Not by might (human might) nor by power (human power), but by My Spirit, saith the Lord of Hosts' (Zech. 4:6). We need the Holy Spirit controlling our minds and revealing to us 'the mind of Christ' (I Cor. 2:16).

NOTES

THE MODERN CHURCH IS NOT SEEKING TO KNOW GOD, BUT INSTEAD, TO KNOW SELF

"Peter told us that God's divine power has given to us all things that pertain to life and godliness. He also said that all of this is 'Through the knowledge of Him,' meaning Christ Jesus (II Pet. 1:3).

"That is an amazing and glorious statement. God has exerted His power to make available to those who are in Christ Jesus all things that pertain to living life His way, as well as all that is necessary for growing in godliness.

"The more that we get to know the Lord, the more we avail ourselves of all that He has provided for the necessary needs of life and godliness. We thereby discover personally what His Word declares, that His provision includes everything that we need. This is a foundational truth of the faith.

"Instead, churches have been so psychologized, that the new cry of the church is like that of the world; not to know God, but to know yourself. Instead of urging and assisting people along a path of knowing God, many are turning people to personal introspection through all kinds of sophisticated new 'tools of ministry,' as they are called. Self-evaluation tests, temperament analysis tests, and personal preference inventories abound in the programs of the modern church. Though these tools may seem to bring about useful information, in truth, they do not. What we really need to know about ourselves is already revealed in the Word of God.

"Those who are seeking to know God will learn His evaluation of man. His evaluation is what we ultimately must have, not only because it is the only reliable perspective, but also because it is a part of getting to know our Lord.

THE LOVE OF GOD

"Instead of urging people to love God, to love others, and to be alert to the dangers of self-love, many modern churches now instruct people in what could be called the 'self-love myth.' That is the myth which says we must learn to love ourselves first *before we can learn to love others properly.*

"How has this come into the modern church? It has borrowed psychology, attempting to add this foolish drivel to the Word of God, and because it sounds good to the human ear.

"It is true that many people experience failure; however, to be told by some church leader that they are really suffering from a lack of proper self-love, can only lead that person into further difficulties.

"To remedy this situation, these false teachers say that time and attention must be given in order to learn to love ourselves properly. This usually means that psychological therapy or a self-help recovery program will have to be undertaken, and another group of believers are off on a self-centered quest, perhaps hoping someday they will master self-love enough that they can begin to learn to love others a bit. God comes up last, if at all!

"The truth is, that if we will properly love God as we ought to, and as we are commanded to do, and then love others as we already love ourselves, the problem will be solved. There is nothing in the Word of God that tells one to learn to love themselves. As well, to involve oneself in such a fruitless quest, reverses the priority laid down in the Word of God, that we are to first of all love God, and then our neighbors, with no mention concerning any efforts to love oneself (Mat. 22:35-40).

DECEIVED BY THE SERPENT'S CRAFTINESS

"One of Paul's concerns for the early church was that she might be enticed to drift away from the God-ordained simplicity that pertains to Christ. His concern was related to the craftiness of our enemy: 'But I fear, lest somehow, as the serpent deceived Eve by his craftiness, so your minds may be corrupted (or led astray) from the simplicity that is in Christ' (II Cor. 11:3).

"In the garden, Eve succumbed to subtle trickery, not some obvious frontal attack on her relationship with God. By enticing the church to follow after psychological insights and theories, the enemy of our souls may have unleashed one of his craftiest tactics

NOTES

ever. It all sounds so scientific, so wise, so beneficial, so justifiable, so compatible with the things of Christ. It all appears to supply those contemporary perspectives and sophisticated remedies that man assumes are not available in the 'ancient writings of the prophets and apostles.' What could they know, they say, about dysfunctionalism or co-dependency, or clinical depression, or being the mate of an alcoholic?

JESUS CHRIST

"The message of the Scriptures is that the whole kingdom of God is wrapped up in Jesus Christ. That is the simplicity. Follow Him, and what He did for us at the Cross, and He changes us! Follow Him, and all the fullness is in Him! Follow Him, and we are complete in Him (Col. 2:10). Follow Him, and find everything that pertains to life and godliness (I Pet. 1:18-20). Follow Christ and we will grow in a fruitful, useful, purposeful life as we become instruments in the hands of Almighty God (Rom. 6:1-14). It is all found in following Jesus (Lk. 9:23; 14:27). That is the simplicity, the lack of complication; however, it is not simplistic in the sense of lacking sufficient substance.

"If one thinks the simplicity in Christ indicates inadequacy on His part, then one greatly underestimates who Jesus is and what He has done. If we told a fish that all it needed was simply the ocean, and the fish felt that we were being too simplistic, then we would know that the fish was unfamiliar with, or was underestimating the resources of the ocean. Christ is far deeper than the deepest ocean. In fact, we are offered in the person and work of Jesus, 'The unsearchable (unfathomable) riches of Christ' (Eph. 3:8). People saying that they need more than the simplicity of Christ is like a fish saying it needs more than the ocean! The depths of the riches of Christ can never be exhausted or be shown as insufficient.

THE DECEIT AND FUTILITY OF HUMAN PHILOSOPHY

"Paul warned us in Colossians 2:8, 'Lest any one cheat you (or, take you captive) through philosophy and empty deceit, according to the tradition of men, according

to the basic principles of the world, and not according to Christ.' We are to watch out for and sound the alarm about these perspectives on life. We are not to welcome them into the church. We are not to integrate them into our message and ministry. This certainly includes the psychological theories of man.

"This warning and prohibition applies no matter how well educated, intended, popular, or influential in the church a leader might be. Beware, lest anyone captivate your thinking through any of these matters. Philosophy is man's way of viewing man and life, and how to help and/or change people. Empty deceit involves humanly-contrived ways of thinking that originate in spiritual deception and therefore are not built upon true godly realities.

"The tradition of man is another area of dangerous enticement, because it is merely man passing onto man that which seems to be useful or desirable. Closely related to these traditions are the basic principles of the world which represents the contemporary, conventional wisdom and accepted procedures of society.

"Jesus said, 'My kingdom is not of this world' (Jn. 18:36). How can we mix the wisdom of the kingdom of man with the kingdom of God? God's pronouncement on the wisdom of this world is given in I Corinthians 3:19-20, 'For the wisdom of this world is foolishness to God. For it is written, He catches the wise in their own craftiness; and again the Lord knows the thoughts of the wise, that they are futile.' God says man's wisdom is foolishness.

PSYCHOLOGICAL THEORETICIANS

"All of these psychological theoreticians who have intrigued the church in our day seem so brilliant when measured against other humans. However, before God, they are foolish, because they did not learn from God, but rather from their own vain imaginations.

"Also, the Lord is fully aware of the thoughts of the wise, or those who think themselves wise. He knows all about the theories of those who possess special measures of human genius, like Freud, Adler,

Jung, Maslow, Fromm, Rogers, etc. He says their thoughts are futile. That word means useless, vain, and empty. They are of no value to God in developing His kingdom and building the lives of His people, nor to anyone else for that matter! Only Jesus Christ, His ways and His truth are to guide and shape our lives.

"The preacher of the gospel, and all believers for that matter, are called to proclaim the Word of God, not man's theories; and psychology is man's theory in totality, and contains no part of God's wisdom, which is found only in His Word."

THE GODLESS PHILOSOPHY OF PSYCHOLOGY

It is refreshing, as we have stated, and which we have just given in the above paragraphs, to find some who at long last are speaking out against this godless philosophy of psychology, which has made such inroads into all sectors of the modern church.

Jesus Christ does not treat people; He delivers them. Never before in human history has His deliverance been so needed because so many are held captive. To be sure, this *"captivity"* is not only in the realm of alcohol or drugs but, as well, in racism, prejudice, hate, pride, jealousy, etc. One of the greatest bondages of all, and perhaps the greatest, is religion, with much of the world held in its prison maw. Hundreds of millions need deliverance from religion just as much as alcoholics do from alcohol, etc.

Incidentally, the word *religion* refers to the efforts of man to reach God by man's own methods or to better himself in some way. In other words, it is not of God.

The word *captives* has the meaning of "prisoner of war." In other words, these individuals are spiritual captives, taken prisoner by Satan. The captivity in which he holds them, which includes almost all of humanity, cannot be broken by any of man's ingenious devices, philosophies, or efforts.

The war spoken of and the captives addressed are not such because of environment, association, or lack of education. While those things certainly play a part in our lives and can increase or decrease whatever problem is already there, still, the real problem is the lies and deceit of Satan. Most of the world believes it and are taken captive. Only Jesus Christ can effect the release of such captives (Rom. 6:1-14; I Cor. 1:17-18, 23; 2:2; Col. 2:10-15).

THE RECOVERING OF SIGHT TO THE BLIND

The word *blind* as used here does not speak of physical blindness, but rather spiritual blindness. It speaks of one who has become spiritually blind as the result of pride and conceit. This answers to most of the world. That is the reason Jesus mentioned preaching the gospel to the meek or poor.

Without the gospel being preached and anointed by the Holy Spirit, it is impossible for those who are blind in this manner to ever see. In effect, a blind person cannot see anything. Consequently, for preachers to attempt to deal with people intellectually is a waste of time. While this is certainly not a plea for ignorance, still, it is a plea that we understand man's problem, which is sin, and man's solution, which is Jesus Christ and Him crucified.

When the gospel is preached in all of its power, the Holy Spirit takes it to the very heart of the one in question and reveals to him his lost condition, i.e., blindness, and consequently, the cure, which is Christ and the Cross. Only then can the scales fall from his eyes.

TO SET AT LIBERTY THEM WHO ARE BRUISED

The word *bruised* means "to be crushed."

The word *liberty* means "to pardon," which means that whatever has happened to the person has brought about a prison within his life. Much of the world falls into this category. It speaks of sin, shame, failure, etc.

Such can definitely be caused by present problems but can also be caused by abuse suffered as a child, etc.

The terrible problems that some children have to go through, including abuse in every form, at times leave the person scarred, i.e., bruised.

The world of psychology attempts to deal with such by encouraging the dredging up

NOTES

of these incidents, whether by suggestion, hypnosis, etc. Actually, this particular type of counseling has encouraged at times the confession of things that never really happened. However, even if it did happen, the talking and spilling it out, which is all psychology can do, only exacerbates the problem.

Jesus alone can heal these memories, etc. The person is to give such to Him and believe that He is able to handle the situation, whatever it may be.

BITTER WATERS

As well, if this type of abuse includes ill treatment by others, which it almost always does, then the person must forgive those who have done this thing against him. That doesn't mean he has to go and take up residence in the house with them once again, but it does mean that in Christ they have to forgive them for what they have done, irrespective of how bad it may have been.

Then, they are to *forget those things which are behind, and reach forth unto those things which are before,* which is the very opposite of the teaching of psychology (Phil. 3:13).

There is a beautiful *"type"* of this in the Old Testament.

The children of Israel, after being delivered from Egyptian bondage, found themselves in the wilderness at a place called *"Marah."* Actually, the very word means "bitter." Consequently, the waters were unfit to drink.

The *"wilderness"* is a type of this world, made so by sin and rebellion against God. The *"bitter waters"* symbolize exactly what we are talking about, the problems that come about in life, even as a child, which cause bitterness of the soul. This, as stated, creates a *"prison"* in the heart and life of the individual.

The Scripture says that Moses *"cried unto the LORD,"* regarding these bitter waters. At that stage, the *"LORD showed him a tree,"* which is a type of the Cross of Calvary, symbolizing all that Jesus did for humanity on that dark day.

Moses was instructed to cast this tree *"into the waters."* After this was done, the Scripture says, *"The waters were made sweet."*

The Lord then gave further commands to Moses and closed His statement by saying, *"For I am the LORD who heals you"* (Ex. 15:22-26).

If one is to read this account carefully in Exodus, it was water the people wanted and not healing; however, the Lord would use this occasion to teach them a tremendously valuable lesson.

HEALING

The problems of life are many, and some are extremely acute, even to the degree of destroying one emotionally and spiritually. However, no matter how difficult the problems may be, Jesus Christ is the answer, and through the person and agency of the Holy Spirit, He can bring about healing in one's life. Too many times, healing is limited only to a physical problem, which it definitely does include.

However, it goes much further than that, including the healing of one's emotions, the healing of one's spirit, and the healing of the memories, taking in all of the extremely bitter experiences of life, whatever they may be and whenever they may have happened. Jesus literally *"sets at liberty them who are bruised."*

The sadness is, as we have stated, the modern church is advocating psychology, which actually holds no remedy whatsoever, but only makes a bad matter worse.

(19) "TO PREACH THE ACCEPTABLE YEAR OF THE LORD."

The exegesis is:

1. The *"Year of the Lord"* actually refers to the *"Year of Jubilee,"* which came every 50 years.

2. It is said that on this very day that Jesus read these words in the synagogue was the very day which began the Year of Jubilee.

3. It was also the *"Great Day of Atonement,"* which came every year, but also at the beginning of the fiftieth year, denoting this all-important occasion. However, Israel, at the time of Christ, no longer kept the Great Day of Atonement simply because there was no ark of the covenant in the Holy of Holies in the temple due to it having been lost in the invasion of Nebuchadnezzar some 600 years earlier. The ritual of the atonement could not be carried out without the ark.

4. On this first day of the Year of Jubilee, according to the law of Moses, all mortgages were canceled, all servants released, and all bondages of men annulled. Debts were forgiven, and lands reverted to the original owners. The new start in business at the end of Jubilee was based on another year of release 50 years in the future.

5. So, this particular Year of Jubilee, which was little adhered to by present Israel, was meant to serve originally as a type of One who would come and set the captives free. Jesus Christ was, in effect, the *"forever"* of Jubilee and, as well, the Great Day of Atonement.

(20) "AND HE CLOSED THE BOOK, AND HE GAVE IT AGAIN TO THE MINISTER, AND SAT DOWN. AND THE EYES OF ALL THEM WHO WERE IN THE SYNAGOGUE WERE FASTENED ON HIM."

The synopsis is:

1. The phrase, *"And He closed the book,"* referred to the scroll containing the writings of Isaiah.

2. *"And He gave it* (the scroll) *again to the minister, and sat down,"* portrays the custom of that time. The chair of the speaker or preacher was placed near where the lesson or Scripture was read. Upon reading the text, as Jesus did, the speaker would then sit in the chair and deliver his discourse.

3. Synagogues were built with one end facing Jerusalem. The men sat on one side of the building and the women on the other.

4. At the end of the building sat a replica of the ark of the covenant, in which were kept scrolls of the Bible as it then was (Genesis through Malachi).

5. As cumbersome as scrolls were, it seems that the only ones used in the synagogues were those used by the speaker and maybe one or two more for reference by the synagogue leaders.

6. *"And the eyes of all them who were in the synagogue were fastened on Him,"* represented a moment far exceeding anything these people had ever known. Their curiosity was high, especially considering that Jesus had lived in their midst for about 30 years. As well, as stated, they had heard the accounts

of His miracles, which, in effect, were the greatest the world had ever known, and by far. So, they wondered what He was going to say, with every eye *"fastened on Him."*

(21) "AND HE BEGAN TO SAY UNTO THEM, THIS DAY IS THIS SCRIPTURE FULFILLED IN YOUR EARS."

The pattern is:

1. The phrase, *"And He began to say unto them,"* constituted a discourse that was startling and evidently something they did not expect to hear.

2. *"This day is this Scripture fulfilled in your ears,"* means that every prophecy given by the prophets of old concerning the coming of the Messiah was fulfilled in Christ. He, in effect, was saying, *"I am the Messiah!"*

3. If one is to notice, in the reading of this passage from Isaiah 61:1-2, the Lord stopped in the middle of Verse 2 because the day of vengeance is yet future.

4. This shows how a prophecy given can pertain to two particular times, even in the same sentence. The first part of Verse 2 from Isaiah proclaims the coming of the Messiah, while the last part of the verse and sentence speak of the coming great tribulation, which has not even yet come to pass, even after nearly 2,000 years. That is the reason it is of such necessity that the Word of God be properly *divided* (II Tim. 2:15).

(22) "AND ALL BEAR HIM WITNESS, AND WONDERED AT THE GRACIOUS WORDS WHICH PROCEEDED OUT OF HIS MOUTH. AND THEY SAID, IS NOT THIS JOSEPH'S SON?"

The form is:

1. The phrase, *"And all bear Him witness,"* means that all understood exactly what He said, but as the record will show, all did not believe Him.

2. *"And wondered at the gracious words which proceeded out of His mouth,"* means that we are only given a small portion of the things He said.

3. The question, *"And they said, Is not this Joseph's son?"* refers to the fact that they could not equate these gracious words with the carpenter they had known for about 30 years.

4. They could not understand how He was so eloquent, so knowledgeable in the

Scriptures, and, as well, how He experienced such tremendous anointing of the Holy Spirit, which, no doubt, stirred the hearts of all who were present.

5. The fact that they would refer to Him as *"Joseph's son"* means that very few, if any, of them at this time, knew of the circumstances of His birth. If they did know, they had dismissed it long ago as little more than a fairy tale!

6. Furthermore, the idea that a carpenter's son, especially one they had known all His life, would claim to be the Messiah was, to their ears at least, beyond belief!

7. The problem of recognizing Christ for who He is is just as acute presently as then. The world meets His claims with the same astonishment as His townspeople. Sadly and regrettably, much of the church does the same.

8. Now, as then, people do not know the Word of God, or else, if they do claim to know it, do not believe it.

(23) "AND HE SAID UNTO THEM, YOU WILL SURELY SAY UNTO ME THIS PROVERB, PHYSICIAN, HEAL YOURSELF: WHATSOEVER WE HAVE HEARD DONE IN CAPERNAUM, DO ALSO HERE IN YOUR COUNTRY."

The pattern is:

1. The phrase, *"And He said unto them, You will surely say unto Me this proverb, Physician, heal Yourself,"* proclaims Him knowing the thoughts and probably referred to a saying that was quite common among the Jews at that time. It meant simply, *"What You have done for others, do for Yourself."*

2. In this case, *"Whatsoever we have heard done in Capernaum, do also here in Your country,"* meant, *"Whatever miracles You performed there, perform here!"*

3. However, due to the things He would momentarily say, they became so incensed at Him that, according to Mark, they would not even bring the seriously sick to Him (Mk. 6:5). So, no miracles were performed because of their unbelief.

4. Actually, their petition for miracles was not sincere anyway! They were simply being sarcastic and then, very shortly thereafter, would turn violent.

(24) "AND HE SAID, VERILY I SAY

UNTO YOU, NO PROPHET IS ACCEPTED IN HIS OWN COUNTRY."

The form is:

1. Jesus was speaking of far more than the little village of Nazareth. He was speaking of the entirety of Israel, and, in fact, it holds true for all time and in every place.

2. In effect, by giving them the illustration He did concerning the two Gentiles who received from the Lord, He was telling them who, in fact, would receive Him.

3. As we will see, at the mention of Gentiles receiving from the Lord, they were incensed at such a thing, even though it had happened, and they knew it to be true.

(25) "BUT I TELL YOU OF A TRUTH, MANY WIDOWS WERE IN ISRAEL IN THE DAYS OF ELIJAH, WHEN THE HEAVEN WAS SHUT UP THREE YEARS AND SIX MONTHS, WHEN GREAT FAMINE WAS THROUGHOUT ALL THE LAND."

The structure is:

1. The phrase, *"But I tell you of a truth,"* even though brief, will proclaim in no uncertain terms Israel's problem of self-righteousness resulting from pride and her consequent dearth of the Spirit. The statements made here would infuriate the people of Nazareth just as they infuriate the modern church.

2. Israel had become so sectarian that they believed they were the only ones who could be saved when, in reality, they were the very ones not saved, at least, most of them. To be sure, this truth espoused so long ago is just as apropos now as then!

3. The phrase, *"Many widows were in Israel in the days of Elijah,"* speaks of the prophet Elijah.

4. *"When the heaven was shut up three years and six months, when great famine was throughout all the land,"* proclaims the time of Ahab and a time of great wickedness concerning the northern kingdom of Israel. Sin shuts heaven up tight just as much now as then. The account of this is found in I Kings, Chapter 17. These were illustrations well known in Israel during the time of Christ.

(26) "BUT UNTO NONE OF THEM WAS ELIJAH SENT, SAVE UNTO SAREPTA, A CITY OF SIDON, UNTO A WOMAN WHO WAS A WIDOW."

NO FAITH

The phrase, *"But unto none of them was Elijah sent,"* tells a complete story within itself.

During this time of famine and starvation, as would be obvious, there were many widows in destitute condition among God's chosen people. However, the Holy Spirit directed Elijah to none of them.

Why?

There was no faith on their part. They had turned their backs upon the God of Israel, although continuing to proclaim themselves as His children. However, in their heart of hearts, they did not believe. Regrettably, this is not the first instance of such an occasion, with Israel and the church plagued by this spiritual malady.

At this time (2013), one could say that as a whole, the modern church has never had such little faith.

How do I know?

If it's not faith in Christ and the Cross, then it's not faith that God will recognize (Rom. 6:1-14; 8:1-11; I Cor. 1:17-18, 23; 2:2; Gal. 6:14; Col. 2:10-15).

Faith always and without exception is based on the Word of God. If the people know the Word and believe the Word, there is great faith. To be sure, the story of the Bible is the story of Jesus Christ and Him crucified. So, if believers claim to know the Word and ignore the Cross of Christ, Jesus plainly said that they could not be His disciples (Lk. 9:23; 14:27). As stated, God will not honor faith that's not anchored squarely in Christ and the Cross. To divorce Christ from the Cross is to present *"another Jesus"* (II Cor. 11:4).

The problem now is basically the same as was the problem then. The people then were supposed to put their faith in what the sacrifices represented, which was the Cross. Even though they would not have understood at that time anything about a Cross, still, in the mind of God, that's what the sacrifices represented. Unfortunately, even as is being done now, what the sacrifices represented was ignored, with the sacrifices themselves completely ignored. In fact, the people of the northern kingdom of Israel could not even offer up sacrifices simply because this could be done only at the temple. So, one might say in modern vernacular, they were without the help and safety that the Cross of Christ provides.

THE WIDOW WOMAN

The phrase, *"Save unto Sarepta, a city of Sidon, unto a woman who was a widow,"* speaks of a Gentile city and woman. In other words, the Lord bypassed His chosen people and went to a Gentile who was outside the covenants and the promises.

Even though this woman possibly knew little of God, still, when the message was presented to her, she accepted whereas Israel refused. God knows the hearts of people, and He works accordingly!

(27) "AND MANY LEPERS WERE IN ISRAEL IN THE TIME OF ELISHA THE PROPHET; AND NONE OF THEM WAS CLEANSED, SAVING NAAMAN THE SYRIAN."

The structure is:

1. The phrase, *"And many lepers were in Israel in the time of Elisha the prophet,"* is said in the same sense as the widows of Verse 25. This is found in II Kings, Chapter 5.

2. *"And none of them was cleansed, saving Naaman the Syrian,"* once again refers to another Gentile.

3. None of the lepers in Israel were cleansed, as none of the widows were fed, all for the same reason, the disbelieving of God's Word.

4. What makes this so sad is that the people of Israel were the very ones who were supposed to know the Word of God and, consequently, believe the Word of God. They were the people of the covenants and the promises. They were God's chosen. However, God cannot bless faithlessness in His chosen any more than He can in the heathen. The requirements are the same for all—a strict adherence to the Word of God and faith that God will do what He has said He will do.

5. It is amazing that of all the widows in the land of Israel, not one went to the prophet Elisha and asked him to pray for them or to implore the Lord on their behalf.

6. Even though there were many lepers

NOTES

in Israel, not a single one went to Elisha and asked for healing. Think of it: two of the greatest prophets who ever lived, who saw more miracles than any other prophets, and yet, they were little consulted or even respected, at least, in accordance with who and what they were.

7. Is it any different now? The modern church opts for psychologists or entertainment, with the true men of God being all but ignored, if not outrightly opposed and persecuted.

(28) "AND ALL THEY IN THE SYNAGOGUE, WHEN THEY HEARD THESE WORDS, WERE FILLED WITH WRATH."

THE SYNAGOGUE

The phrase, *"And all they in the synagogue,"* speaks of the great crowd that had come this day to hear Jesus.

As this will show, it is quite possible for the church to be the most wicked place in town. If Jesus had gone into a place of ill repute, such as surely existed at that time, and had preached the same message, more than likely, it would have been accepted by some, or at least not opposed. However, in the church, they wanted to kill Him.

And yet, most of these people who attended the synagogue would have never dreamed of committing some of the sins of the flesh that were rampant then (and now). But yet, they would attempt to kill the Lord of glory.

How can the two be reconciled?

The truth is this: Most of the church now, as then, is corrupt even to the place of killing the Lord of glory, that is, if such a thing were possible. However, they kill Him everyday in other ways. Consequently, the true believer must seek the face of the Lord earnestly concerning where he or she attends church. The horrible truth is that many, if not most, churches exist for the purpose of killing the Lord instead of lifting up the Lord. They do it by disavowing or ignoring His Word and having little or no faith in His name.

The truth is, if the church is not preaching the Cross, whatever it is they are preaching, it is not the gospel. Paul said:

"Christ sent me not to baptize, but to

preach the gospel: not with wisdom of words, lest the Cross of Christ should be made of none effect" (I Cor. 1:17).

In this one passage, we are unequivocally told exactly what the gospel of Jesus Christ is. It is Jesus Christ and Him crucified.

However, the majority of the churches in the world today never mention sin, never mention the Cross, never mention the shed blood of Jesus Christ, etc. Their excuse is, *"It might offend some people."* Paul addressed that as well. He said:

"We preach Christ crucified, unto the Jews a stumblingblock, and unto the Greeks foolishness" (I Cor. 1:23).

In other words, the apostle was saying that he knew that the preaching of the Cross was a stumblingblock to the Jews, and he also knew that as it regarded the Gentiles, they thought it was foolishness. Both found it difficult to accept as God a dead man hanging on a Cross, for such Christ was to them.

Nevertheless, Paul preached the Cross, and the reason is obvious: there is no other hope for humanity.

THAT WHICH JESUS SAID

The phrase, *"When they heard these words,"* concerns the message preached by Jesus that day. They heard it, and they rejected it! Even in the days of the apostle Paul, they continued to rebel against the true Word of God until Paul said, *"We turn to the Gentiles"* (Acts 13:46).

Regarding the modern church at the present, the Holy Spirit has left entire denominations because of their unbelief. He then turns to hungry hearts, whomever they are, and wherever they are. Such is generally among the poor, who are broken in spirit and will gladly accept the Lord.

Spiritual pride is a terrible thing because it always harbors self-righteousness. This is exactly what the people in Nazareth had and, in fact, almost the entirety of Israel.

WRATH

The phrase, *"Were filled with wrath,"* is generally the response of unbelief. Such is seldom content to walk away but must silence the voice that has spoken the truth.

Unless there is revival in the modern

NOTES

church, at least to some extent, this wrath is going to be felt by all true believers, as some of us have already felt it.

The world of religion demands control as it regards those who are under their sway. The religious leadership of Israel wanted to control Jesus. This they could not do simply because they were ungodly. Now, think of it!

The Pharisees, who were the greatest enemies of Christ, had excellent reputations all over Israel. But yet, they hated the Lord of glory and, in fact, demanded His crucifixion and did everything they could to bring it about.

You must understand that reputation is what people think you are while character is what God knows you are. The truth is, religion has sent more people to hell than all the vices of the world put together.

Religion is that which is devised by man, which claims in some way to reach God or to better oneself. It does neither!

We encourage our followers all over the world that if there isn't a good church in their community that preaches the Cross, they should join Family Worship Center Media Church. They can worship with us in all of the services as it comes into their homes, whether by television, radio, or satellite. At this stage, we have well over 100 a week who join. The only requirement is that they be born again, and we take their word for that.

While church might be many things, its direct purpose is to preach the gospel. If it succeeds in everything else and fails in that, then it is a waste of time. We feel that those who associate themselves with Family Worship Center Media Church will be fed the proper Word of God. Consequently, they can live a victorious life and make heaven their eternal home. Nothing is more important than that.

(29) "AND ROSE UP, AND THRUST HIM OUT OF THE CITY, AND LED HIM UNTO THE BROW OF THE HILL WHEREON THEIR CITY WAS BUILT, THAT THEY MIGHT CAST HIM DOWN HEADLONG."

THE ANGER OF THE CROWD

The phrase, *"And rose up, and thrust Him out of the city,"* means that they bodily seized Him and took Him by force out of the synagogue and out of the city. This was their response to their own Messiah, God's only Son, and their and our only Saviour. However, they did not know it because they refused to know it.

"And led Him unto the brow of the hill whereon their city was built," was a place where He had, no doubt, gone hundreds of times to be alone with His heavenly Father.

As this Scripture indicates, this hill runs like a horseshoe around the little town of Nazareth. At the present time, it has had a large piece sliced out of it and taken for its bauxite.

As I have related elsewhere in these volumes, I visited this very hill once. At least, it seems to be the only one that would fit this description because it ends in an abrupt cliff, over which they intended to push Jesus to His death. Standing on this hill, one is able to see many of Israel's historical sites. Spread out in front is the valley of Megiddo, where numerous battles have been fought in the past, and where the battle of Armageddon will commence in the future.

Across that valley is Mount Gilboa where Saul and Jonathan were killed by the Philistines.

To the left and close to the Mediterranean is Mount Carmel where Elijah called down fire from heaven. At one's back, as he faces these sites, is the mountain where it is thought the transfiguration took place.

THEY DESIRED TO KILL HIM

The phrase, *"That they might cast Him down headlong,"* presents Nazareth, His own village, as the first to seek His death.

Such a scene is little possible for us to comprehend. Why were they so angry?

Several things aroused their anger. First of all, at least in their minds, He was no more than Joseph's son. As such, He was a peasant, and they surely did not envision their Messiah as being a peasant.

Secondly, His preaching infuriated them because He spoke of the Gentiles receiving from God, with Israel shut out. So, in their minds, He insulted them by His claim of being the Messiah and infuriated them by placing the Gentiles in a favored position.

So, they would kill Him by pushing Him headlong over the cliff. It was a mob out of control. Such has always been the response of most of the world and most of the church to the Lord.

(30) "BUT HE PASSING THROUGH THE MIDST OF THEM WENT HIS WAY."

The exposition is:

1. The phrase, *"But He passing through the midst of them,"* leaves us no clue as to how it happened, but only that it happened. Quite possibly, the power of God was so strong on Him that at some point in time, they had to turn Him loose. It seems they were then powerless to do anything else, with Him walking through their midst and leaving. How it must have grieved His heart!

2. *"Went His way,"* proclaims Him never to return. Most expositors agree that Jesus only visited His hometown one time. He never went back! His way was not their way. Consequently, there was no reason to return.

3. Some believe that Luke may have derived his information directly from Mary, or at least from some in her intimate circle. Luke gives no hint whatsoever regarding her feelings or the attitude of Jesus' half-brothers and sisters at this time. However, we do know that His brothers were very much opposed to Him during His earthly ministry (Jn. 7:5). This must have caused great grief, as well, on His part.

4. However, no demonstration of human hatred could dry up the founts of compassion that an infinite wealth perpetually welled up in His breast. He returned to the lake's shore, and as He went, all the power of the enemy and all the sad outward effects of sin disappeared before Him.

5. Incidentally, at least two of His brothers (James and Jude) served Him wondrously after the resurrection. They both wrote the books in the New Testament that bear their names.

(31) "AND CAME DOWN TO CAPERNAUM, A CITY OF GALILEE, AND TAUGHT THEM ON THE SABBATH DAYS."

CAPERNAUM

The phrase, *"And came down to Capernaum, a city of Galilee,"* was where He had made His headquarters some weeks earlier.

It would remain His home for the some three and one-half years of His public ministry. As well, many, if not most of His disciples, came from this area.

It is said that in Jesus' day, this little town was a flourishing area and a center of manufacturing. It lay on the high road, which led from Damascus and the Syrian cities to Tyre, Sidon, and Jerusalem. It was also on the great caravan road, which led from the East to the Mediterranean, thereby, making it a focal point from all directions. Hence, it was very much suited to be a center of far-reaching ministry, of which even many Gentiles came in contact with the ministry of our Lord.

Josephus tells us that the name *Capernaum* originally belonged to a fountain, which, if so, would have beautifully typified the ministry of Christ. Zechariah prophesied, *"In that day there shall be a fountain opened to the house of David"* (Zech. 13:1), which was rejected on His first advent but will be accepted on the second.

Josephus also spoke of the mildness of the climate in Capernaum, with this little city first being a health resort, and finally becoming a flourishing center of trade, which it was during the time of Christ.

Situated immediately beside the Sea of Galilee, which is about seven miles wide and 14 miles long, it was, no doubt, a place of great beauty.

THE AREA SELECTED BY THE HOLY SPIRIT

My first time to see Capernaum was the occasion of our first trip to Israel. Coming from Nazareth, we topped the range of hills that separates the valley of Megiddo from the Sea of Galilee area. I had the driver stop while Frances and I, along with the others, got out of the vehicles and looked at this panorama spread before us. Almost all of it could be seen from our vantage point. Only one city remains today on the shores of Galilee—the city of Tiberias. I don't think it would be possible for me to fully express my feelings as to exactly how I felt that day. I knew that the Lord of glory, the Creator of all things, had especially selected this spot to serve as the headquarters of the ministry

of His Son and my Saviour. It left me in awe and in tears. It was in Capernaum, plus other cities that did ring the western Galilee shore, where He performed most of His miracles. It was on the Sea of Galilee where other great events took place. Even now, I weep as I dictate these words. If one has never known the lowly Galilean, one would not know of the things of which I speak. However, if one has experienced the touch of His hand, spiritually speaking, one will never be the same again. Then He becomes all in all; consequently, anything and everything He does becomes the single most important thing that ever has been.

Were He a mere man, even freighted with ever so much ability, still, such would excite little lasting impression. However, considering that He was not only man but also God, He then is of eternal consequence.

HE TAUGHT THEM

The phrase, *"And taught them on the Sabbath days,"* spoke of their synagogues in Capernaum. Even though only a few heeded His message, still, at least they did not oppose Him as they did in Nazareth. How wonderfully blessed they were to have this distinct honor and privilege of being able to listen to the Lord of glory as He opened the Word. I wonder how many of them fully knew exactly how blessed they actually were.

(32) "AND THEY WERE ASTONISHED AT HIS DOCTRINE: FOR HIS WORD WAS WITH POWER."

ASTONISHMENT

The phrase, *"And they were astonished at His doctrine,"* had to do with the manner in which He explained the Scriptures. They were accustomed to the scribes attempting to impress the people by their supposed lofty knowledge, which treated the Scriptures in such a way that it made it difficult, if not impossible, to understand them. And now, Jesus came preaching simply the gospel, dealing with profound subjects, but in such a simple way that even a child could understand what He was saying. It was something they had never known and were now privileged to hear.

"For His word was with power," concerned the anointing of the Holy Spirit, which He had claimed in His address in Nazareth (Vs. 18). In other words, He preached and taught under the anointing of the Holy Spirit in a manner they had never experienced. Consequently, not only did He rightly divide the Word of Truth, even making it easy to understand, but His words, as well, carried such power in them that people were moved to tears or to joy, or both! Actually, this is the same anointing that He desires to give His preachers at present, that is, if we will only believe.

PENTECOSTALS

The first generation of Pentecostals of the 20th century knew and understood the anointing of the Holy Spirit possibly as no one else has since the days of the early church. I had the privilege of sitting under the ministry of some few of these stalwarts of the faith. Even though that fledgling Pentecostal group in those early days was from the wrong side of the tracks, had little education and no money, still, God used it to touch the world.

The second generation of Pentecostals came along, with some few of us continuing to know what the anointing is and seeking the Lord earnestly for it. As such, God helps us to touch a great part of this planet with the gospel. In some of our crusades, entire nations have been touched by the power of God. In 1987, I believe it was, in our crusade in Santiago, Chile, according to the stadium attendants, some 28,000 people answered the altar call that Sunday afternoon. Scores of other cities all over the world experienced the same move of the Holy Spirit in these meetings. The Spirit of God moved in mighty ways.

PREACH JESUS

When I first began to conduct these meetings, the Lord spoke to my heart and told me that I must preach Jesus, especially to these crowds. Consequently, that was my message! I preached Jesus in every conceivable way possible as the answer to all of our troubles and problems, irrespective of what they might be. I still do!

NOTES

However, certain things took place during this time, with my generation, in effect, saying, *"We do not want the anointing of the Holy Spirit."* Of course, there were exceptions to that, but generally, it was the rule. As such, my generation lost the anointing, and I'm afraid that this modern Pentecostal generation is Pentecostal in name only, actually not even knowing what the anointing of the Holy Spirit really is. Hence, they fall for fads and any type of phenomenon in the spirit realm, not really knowing if it's of God or not!

Even though the miracles of Christ were the greatest the world had ever known, still, it was His preaching and teaching that pointed men to God and contained such power. It is that which our modern preachers must also have *words with power,* meaning the "power of the Holy Spirit" if we are to touch this generation for God. These words given by this power brought such life to the listeners as to be beyond description. As it did then, it will do now! As well, as we shall see, that *"word"* translated into great deliverances for all who were there.

(33) "AND IN THE SYNAGOGUE THERE WAS A MAN, WHICH HAD A SPIRIT OF AN UNCLEAN DEVIL, AND CRIED OUT WITH A LOUD VOICE."

The synopsis is:

1. The phrase, *"And in the synagogue there was a man, which had a spirit of an unclean devil (demon),"* presents two things:

a. This man who was demon possessed came to church, which is where he should have come. Are our modern churches open to such? Why did he come?

b. In his tormented state, he heard that Jesus was there, and that such preaching and miracles were taking place as the world had never known or seen. Therefore, he came. Sadly, the world is filled with such, and their only hope is Jesus. However, if Jesus is not in the church, there will be no deliverance.

2. He was gloriously and wondrously delivered by the power of God. Jesus was the only answer then, and Jesus is the only answer now! However, sadly, such demented souls are now referred to the psychologists.

The reason is simple! The modern church has no power to set these captives free.

3. My prayer is that God will give such Holy Spirit power to His preachers, or to any who believe for that matter, that such will once again become the norm in the modern church.

4. The phrase, *"And cried out with a loud voice,"* proclaims the voice of this demon spirit using the vocal chords of the man. The awful torment in which this man lived could never be fully comprehended unless experienced. God forbid that!

(34) "SAYING, LET US ALONE; WHAT HAVE WE TO DO WITH YOU, THOU JESUS OF NAZARETH? ARE YOU COME TO DESTROY US? I KNOW YOU WHO YOU ARE; THE HOLY ONE OF GOD."

DEMON SPIRITS

The phrase, *"Saying, Let us alone,"* refers to the fact that Jesus alone has power over these spirits of darkness. As well, those who carry His name and use it as they're told enjoy the same results (Mk. 16:17).

Demons exist now as then. Even though no one knows for sure their origin, it is for certain that they were not created by God in this manner. Some expositors believe (which I happen to agree) that demons are the spirits of those who inhabited the earth (whatever type of creation they were) before Adam and Eve and at the time of the fall of Lucifer. Very little information is given on this subject, if any; therefore, any statement on this particular is speculation at best.

However, of this, one can be sure: demon spirits are real and exist now as then. They are the cause of much of the problems and troubles which afflict this world. They seek to possess human beings and can even possess children (Mat. 17:14-18). However fearsome demons may be, the person who walks with Jesus has nothing to fear.

Even though the ministry of Jesus was characterized by Him casting out countless demons, after His death and resurrection, with Him returning to heaven, little demonic activity is reported in the Epistles. Acts 5:8 and 19 mention evil spirits. The Epistles portray them, but only in a vague way. There is some teaching on them, but only in passing.

NOTES

DOCTRINES OF DEMONS

Paul warns that demonic beings are the spiritual realities behind the facades of idolatry. In I Timothy 4:1, he suggests that demons distort truth and encourage the spread of twisted doctrines of their own. Aside from brief views of increased demonic activity at history's end, given in the book of Revelation, this is all that the New Testament has to say about demons, other than the Gospels!

Of particular note regarding the Epistles' comparative silence on the demonic is the fact that in the many passages that deal with Christian life and ministry, none speak of demons. There are no guidelines for exorcism. There are no warnings against demon possession. There is no hint of terror or awe and no suggestion that we should fear or pay special attention to these unseen evil powers, even though they most definitely do exist.

THE VICTORY WON BY JESUS AT CALVARY

Why this silence? I think it is for several reasons:

First of all, even though there was much demonic activity in the time of Christ, as one would know, this was before His death at Calvary and His resurrection. At Calvary and the resurrection, demon powers were totally and completely defeated (Col. 2:14-15). This great victory was of far greater magnitude than the victories won by Christ in His earthly ministry. Then, demon spirits were defeated on a singular, personal basis; however, the victory that Christ won at Calvary incorporated the whole of the world of darkness.

In other words, every power of darkness was broken, with total victory awarded to the Lord Jesus Christ. Paul spoke of this when he said, *"And having spoiled principalities and powers, He made a show of them openly, triumphing over them in it"* (Col. 2:15).

He also said, *"That at the name of Jesus every knee should bow, of things in heaven, and things in earth, and things under the earth;*

"And that every tongue should confess

that Jesus Christ is Lord, to the glory of God the Father" (Phil. 2:10-11).

Consequently, since Calvary and the resurrection, every demon spirit bows at the mention of the name of Jesus, knowing they are totally and completely defeated.

However, this does not mean that they are inoperative because in the lives of unbelievers, they are very operative, even controlling entire nations, but no believer need ever fear them if he follows Jesus.

VICTORY OVER DEMON SPIRITS

To be sure, if demon spirits had the power and authority to act now as they did before Calvary, the church would be in serious straits. However, their power and authority are broken, at least as far as the child of God is concerned. What authority they do presently have is a pseudo-authority, which means authority that believers, either directly or indirectly, allow them to have. Wherever believers go, sooner or later, demon spirits disappear, or else, are greatly lessened in their influence. This is the reason that the taking of the gospel to the world is so very important. Not only does it bring about the salvation of lost souls, but, as well, it stifles the demonic activity in each particular life, area, and nation. It does not mean that all such activity ceases, but that it is greatly hindered and weakened, if not completely cast out, as a result of Spirit-filled believers. Even the very presence of the faith-filled child of God makes a vast difference.

This does not mean that demon spirits have no effect, for they certainly do. Actually, Paul also said, *"Put on the whole armor of God, that you may be able to stand against the wiles of the Devil.*

"For we wrestle not against flesh and blood, but against principalities, against powers, against the rulers of the darkness of this world, against spiritual wickedness in high places" (Eph. 6:11-12).

PRINCIPALITIES, POWERS, RULERS OF THE DARKNESS, SPIRITUAL WICKEDNESS IN HIGH PLACES

The Holy Spirit through Paul gave us four designations in this statement. The

Greek scholars say the meaning is as follows:

1. PRINCIPALITIES: these are fallen angels of the highest rank, who threw in their lot with Lucifer in his revolution against God sometime in the dateless past.

2. POWERS: these are also fallen angels but of lesser rank than the principalities and, thereby, serving the world of spiritual darkness under them.

3. RULERS OF THE DARKNESS OF THIS WORLD: this also speaks of fallen angels, who aid both the principalities and powers in Lucifer's opposition to God.

4. SPIRITUAL WICKEDNESS IN HIGH PLACES: these, so say the Greek scholars, are demon spirits.

Individuals cannot be possessed by angels, for they have spirit bodies; however, demon spirits most definitely can oppress and even possess individuals and even animals.

Paul is telling us here that not only do these fallen angels and spirits of darkness of different ranks oppose us on an individual basis, but, as well, these are the great hindrances to the great work of God all over the world. This can only be stifled by the power of God in the name of Jesus. Everything the believer does for God will be opposed by these various ranks of evil spirit beings. However, even though it is a fight, our heavenly Naphtali has already wrestled them to the mat, so to speak, which leaves us with not nearly as much opposition as it would have been otherwise.

That is the reason the church is wasting its efforts in trying to change the nation by the political process. It was never intended to do that and cannot, therefore, be blessed by God in this endeavor. It sounds good to the carnal ear, but it is not scriptural.

The business of the church is to oppose the Devil, not politically, even though we may certainly have some voice there, but most of all, in the spiritual sense. This is done by Holy Spirit praying and preaching of the gospel and Holy Spirit power in the use of the name of Jesus.

WHAT HAVE WE TO DO WITH YOU

The question, *"What have we to do with You, Thou Jesus of Nazareth?"* portrays the total separation of the Spirit world of light from the spirit world of darkness. The two cannot join, at least with any type of harmony.

The question, *"Are You come to destroy us?"* can only be answered in the affirmative. John said, *"For this purpose the Son of God was manifested, that He might destroy the works of the Devil"* (I Jn. 3:8).

What Jesus did at Calvary and the resurrection will ultimately be finished at the conclusion of the kingdom age when the last enemy will be defeated, which is death (I Cor. 15:26). Then, *"God may be all in all"* (I Cor. 15:28), which means there will be no vestige of evil left anywhere in the world or among men. One can only shout, *"Hallelujah!"*

The phrase, *"I know You who You are; the Holy One of God,"* proclaims the demons knowing, but seemingly, most of the modern church not knowing!

Jesus Christ is God! He alone is the *"door"* to the Father (Jn. 10:9; 14:6).

If Jesus is the *"Holy One of God,"* then Muhammad is not, and neither is any other man! Please note the following:

• The only way to God is through Jesus Christ (Jn. 14:6).
• The only way to Jesus Christ is through the Cross (Lk. 14:27).
• The only way to the Cross is a denial of self (Lk. 9:23).

(35) "AND JESUS REBUKED HIM, SAYING, HOLD YOUR PEACE, AND COME OUT OF HIM. AND WHEN THE DEVIL HAD THROWN HIM IN THE MIDST, HE CAME OUT OF HIM, AND HURT HIM NOT."

COME OUT OF HIM

The phrase, *"And Jesus rebuked him, saying, Hold your peace, and come out of him,"* proclaims Jesus not needing or desiring accolades or recognition from Satan or his cohorts.

Jesus came to set captives free. He came to destroy the works of Satan, which are the cause of all the heartache, suffering, pain, and death in this world. There can be no amalgamation of any sort between this light and that darkness. There will never be a reconciliation between God and Satan, consequently, laying to rest the false doctrine

NOTES

of Ultimate Reconciliation. This doctrine teaches that everything will ultimately be reconciled to God, even Satan, fallen angels, and demon spirits. There is no hint in the Word of God of such action, but rather, the very opposite!

The earth and its inhabitants have been seized by Satan, and it is the business of the Lord Jesus Christ to overcome this darkness. That He has done, and that He is doing! Consequently, it is the business of the church to follow His lead. In other words, the only power against the demon forces of darkness that plague mankind is the Spirit-filled church. Regrettably, the church presently is not too Spirit-filled; consequently, there is presently very little true work being done for the Lord.

THE EFFORTS OF MEN

Much of the energy of the modern church is being spent in political forays; for instance, the so-called Christian coalition, which joins together Catholics, Protestants, and anyone else for that matter, with the idea of changing the political spectrum of America. This sounds good, as we have stated, to the carnal ear. However, irrespective of the tens of millions of dollars spent, which should go to world evangelism, the words of the prophet Jeremiah rather apply, *"For they have healed the hurt of the daughter of My people slightly, saying, Peace, peace; when there is no peace"* (Jer. 8:11).

These efforts are the efforts of men, and be they ever so religious will effect no change. However, if the power of the Holy Spirit is allowed to have His way instead of man's way, other words of Jeremiah will also be brought to bear: *"Heal me, O LORD, and I shall be healed; save me, and I shall be saved: for You are my praise"* (Jer. 17:14).

Man's ways bring a false healing, while God's way brings a true healing.

Some may argue that these modern methods are opposing the powers of darkness and, consequently, are of God! However, the answer to that is simple:

MAN'S REAL PROBLEM

To oppose Satan by the power of man's ingenuity or by means not stressed in the

Word of God will bring no lasting results. To be sure, these modern political methods of the church are not scriptural.

However, to oppose Satan according to the Word of God and by the power of the Holy Spirit brings the desired results.

Jesus could have very easily used His power to oppose Rome and all of its wickedness; however, He never did that.

Why?

He did not do it because the Roman Empire was not man's real problem. Sin was the real problem that affected humanity then, and sin is the real problem that effects humanity now. If the so-called Christian Coalition was 100 percent successful in its political efforts to place men and women of their choice in political power, the situation in America would change precious little, if at all. Once again, the word *slightly,* as used by Jeremiah, would apply. There may be a slight improvement but not enough to notice.

GOD'S WAY

However, when God's way is enjoined, the demon possessed man does not merely have a different *"mayor"* in Capernaum, but rather, he has a brand-new life, with the demon powers of hell forever gone from his mind, soul, and spirit. I will ask this question:

"What good would it have done this man if Jesus had led a political party to 'clean up' Capernaum, thereby, replacing certain corrupt individuals with others?"

To be sure, such a move would have probably gone to the support of the majority of the people in Capernaum, with them hailing Jesus as the great deliverer. However, the man would not have been delivered, or anyone else for that matter.

Consequently, this scenario of Jesus setting the captive free in Capernaum is a perfect example of what the church ought to be instead of what it is. Even though multiple tens of millions of dollars are presently spent, with a great percentage of the church world backing these efforts, the final conclusion will be that for all the money spent and all of the efforts made, the *"nation"* will still be *"demon possessed."*

NOTES

DELIVERANCE

Satan little cares if we do things our way, irrespective of how good it may seem to the religious eye. He trembles only when we do things God's way. He knows that our way will set no captives free, so he does not fight that which is proposed by religious man, but fights with all of hell's strength that which is proposed by God. The reasons are obvious.

The phrase, *"And when the devil (demon) had thrown him in the midst, he came out of him, and hurt him not,"* proclaims the deliverance of this man according to the word of Jesus. No matter what our religious platitudes may be, Satan only responds to that name of Jesus. Modern thought, as we have been stating, belittles the preaching of the gospel and the power of God, and exalts ceremony, irrespective of the direction it may take. The eternal Son of God was wholly a preacher and a deliverer. This fact and the opposition of Satan to such proclamation of the gospel demonstrates its importance.

(36) "AND THEY WERE ALL AMAZED, AND SPOKE AMONG THEMSELVES, SAYING, WHAT A WORD IS THIS! FOR WITH AUTHORITY AND POWER HE COMMANDS THE UNCLEAN SPIRITS, AND THEY COME OUT."

WHAT A WORD IS THIS!

The phrase, *"And they were all amazed, and spoke among themselves, saying, What a Word is this!"* presents something the people had never seen before. Thankfully, they did not oppose Him as they did in Nazareth and would later do in Jerusalem. Then again, they never did really fully accept Him either!

"For with authority and power He commands the unclean spirits, and they come out," proclaims the people understanding exactly what Jesus had done. They recognized His authority and power.

Jesus possessed authority over every demon of darkness, irrespective of how strong they may have been, and power to make them do what He desired. The reason is simple; Jesus was very man and also very God. The apostle Paul in Colossians 2:9 recognizes these two natures—deity and humanity—residing in the person of Jesus of Nazareth. He says, *"In Him dwells all the fullness of the Godhead bodily."* As well, the word *Godhead* is found in Acts 17:29 and Romans 1:20.

At the same time, Jesus never performed one single miracle or cast out one single demon by the power of deity, but only as a man filled with the Holy Spirit. As someone has well said, *"While in the incarnation, He laid aside the expression of His deity, but He never for a moment lost possession of His deity."*

JESUS AS GOD

In the statements given by Paul, he declares how much of God may be known from the revelation of Himself that He has made in nature, yet, it is not the personal God whom any man may learn to know by these aids. He can only be fully known by the revelation of Himself in His Son, but only His divine attributes—His majesty and glory.

Paul is declaring that in the Son, there dwells all the fullness of absolute Godhead. They were no mere rays of divine glory that gilded Him, lighting up His person for a season with splendor, but not His own, but He was and is absolute and perfect God. In speaking of Jesus of Nazareth in His incarnation, Paul is, in essence, saying: *"In Him there is at home, permanently, all the fullness of absolute deity in bodily fashion"* (Col. 2:9). That is, in the human body of Jesus of Nazareth, there resided permanently at home all that goes to make deity what it is. It was absolute deity clothed with a human body, but yet, not used, as previously stated, in the performing of His miracles and the casting out of demons. That was done, as also stated, by the power of the Holy Spirit.

(37) "AND THE FAME OF HIM WENT OUT INTO EVERY PLACE OF THE COUNTRY ROUND ABOUT."

The exegesis is:

1. The phrase, *"And the fame of Him went out,"* means that He was the topic of most all conversations.

2. The things done by Him were so great, so powerful, and so miraculous, actually, such as the world had never seen before.

3. Jesus Christ is God!

(38) "AND HE AROSE OUT OF THE SYNAGOGUE, AND ENTERED INTO SIMON'S HOUSE. AND SIMON'S WIFE'S MOTHER WAS TAKEN WITH A GREAT FEVER; AND THEY BESOUGHT HIM FOR HER."

THE HEALING OF PETER'S WIFE

The phrase, *"And He arose out of the synagogue, and entered into Simon's house,"* seems to suggest that Peter's house was the headquarters of Jesus during His three and one-half years of public ministry.

I have seen the ruins of Capernaum, as have many. Archaeologists have uncovered what they believe to be the site of the synagogue and even where it is thought Peter's house stood. It is very near the Sea of Galilee.

The phrase, *"And Simon's wife's mother was taken with a great fever,"* proclaims Luke's medical expertise. The word *great* was a well-known technical term used for certain types of fevers.

The fact was that she had been sick for sometime with this fever, actually, unable to stand on her feet. Whatever it was, it was of far greater degree than a mere temporal malady. The implication is that it could have been life-threatening.

THEY TOOK HER PROBLEM TO JESUS

The phrase, *"And they besought Him for her,"* means, as is obvious, that they took the problem to Him.

If the whole world sought Jesus for their problems, irrespective of the type, how much better each and every situation would be! However, sadly, even most of the church seeks anything and everything but Jesus, despite the fact that He said, *"Come unto Me"* (Mat. 11:28-30).

Some may argue that they too would take it to Jesus if He were here in person; however, that was far more difficult then than one might imagine. Even though the disciples had no difficulty getting to Him, as here observed, still, the crowds were so large at times that it was well nigh impossible for some people to get a personal audience (Mk. 5:27-28). So, it is easier to take a problem to Him now even than it was when He was here personally.

The Word of God implores us over and over again to do just that—take our problems to the Lord—which we can do in prayer (Mat. 21:22; Mk. 11:24; Jn. 14:14; 15:7).

A PERSONAL EXPERIENCE

In October 1991, the Lord gave me instructions to begin two prayer meetings a day, morning and evening. This would be with the exception of service times and Saturday morning. For over 10 years, a group of us faithfully met together to seek the Lord, and I still personally hold to such prayer times.

My grandmother taught me to pray. When I was 8 years old, during the summer months when not in school, I would be in one or two prayer meetings every day, with the exception of Sunday. One may wonder what in the world an 8-year-old child would find enticing about prayer meetings.

The Lord saved me when I was 8 years old and baptized me with the Holy Spirit with the evidence of speaking with other tongues a few weeks later. Also, in those prayer meetings, even at such a tender age, I knew that I would be an evangelist. At times, the power of God would be so great in those prayer times that I would literally go unconscious. I would awaken sometime later, thinking it had been only a few minutes when it had been a few hours.

My grandmother taught me the value of prayer, and I can hear her now as she would say, *"Jimmy, God is a big God, so ask big!"* That little statement has helped me to touch much of this world for the cause of Christ.

In fact, no Christian can have a proper relationship with the Lord unless he has a prayer life. I don't care how busy that one is, if one will set aside a few minutes each day, even if it's only 15 minutes, and hold true to that time, one will find that everything will go better. Let me say it again:

No believer can have a proper relationship with the Lord without having a proper prayer life.

This doesn't mean that such earns us something from God. We must ever understand that God has nothing for sale. Everything He has is a gift. However, when it comes to prayer, I need to talk over a lot of

NOTES

things with the Lord, and He needs to talk over a lot of things with me.

Most of my prayer time is spent in praise and worship, thanking Him for all that He has done, is doing, and shall do.

FAITH

The believer should have faith that God will hear and answer prayer. As well, the answer may not come immediately and, in fact, may be years in coming, but it will come. The Lord uses the intervening time to work out things in our lives that need to be addressed. Unfortunately, many believers go before the Lord once or twice and if there is not an immediate answer, they soon lose heart and quit. This evidences that there is no real faith to start with. So, faith will not only believe God, it will, as well, stay the course.

The believer should take everything to the Lord in prayer and seek His leading and guidance respecting the entirety of his life and work.

PRAY TO THE FATHER IN THE NAME OF JESUS

One should enter into prayer by addressing the heavenly Father because He is the one to whom we should pray (Jn. 16:23). Actually, we should pray to Him in the name of Jesus. Consequently, even though we are to constantly praise Christ, all petitions should be addressed to the Father.

Immediately upon going to prayer, the believer should enter with praise. Actually, the psalmist said, *"Enter into His gates with thanksgiving, and into His courts with praise: be thankful unto Him, and bless His name"* (Ps. 100:4).

Of course, the *"gates"* and *"courts"* spoken of by the psalmist pertained to the temple of old. Since Jesus fulfilled all the old law, the temple part no longer applies. However, the *"thanksgiving"* and *"praise"* definitely do apply inasmuch as the writer of Hebrews said, *"Let us therefore come boldly unto the throne of grace, that we may obtain mercy, and find grace to help in time of need"* (Heb. 4:16).

Actually, much, if not most of our time before the Lord, should be spent in thanksgiving and praise. Then, we should take our petitions to the Lord, whatever they may be and in whatever category. As stated, we should pray about everything.

Also, it is very important in our prayer time that we allow the Holy Spirit to deal with our hearts in whatever capacity He desires. At least one of the reasons that many believers do not pray is because there is wrongdoing in their lives, which they do not desire to stop, and which prayer would automatically reveal. In other words, it is well nigh impossible to pray, and continue to pray, and not forsake wrongdoing of any nature. The Holy Spirit automatically calls attention to such. So, before progress can be made, this thing must be confessed before the Lord and forsaken (I Jn. 1:9).

To be sure, if one truly seeks the Lord, the Holy Spirit will constantly probe the heart and call to attention things that need to be dealt with. This is the reason prayer is so very important.

Admittedly, prayer is hard work. The Devil will do everything within his power to take our minds off the Lord onto other things. Sometimes we are so tired that we cannot seem to concentrate. Irrespective, if we will persist and persevere, we will find ourselves greatly strengthened as time goes by. In fact, every believer ought to have a prayer life through the entirety of his earthly sojourn.

Please understand that when we pray, we are speaking to someone who can do anything. Knowing and understanding that should greatly increase our confidence.

A GUARANTEE

In giving the few statements we have on prayer, I want to say something that I believe I can guarantee:

As we have already stated, if you, the reader, will set aside a little time each day for prayer, even if it's only 15 minutes, and habitually do such every day and not allow this habit to be broken, you will find yourself growing stronger in the Lord and getting closer to Him, with your relationship with Him greatly improving. As well, you will see your life begin to change. Then, also, in taking your petitions to the Lord,

NOTES

you will begin to see Him operate within your life, bringing to pass things that you thought were impossible. However, it takes a prayer life for all of this to happen.

The book of Psalms is not only a songbook, it is also the greatest prayer book in the Bible. It best captures the warmth and intimacy of prayer that grows out of the believer's relationship with God. Consequently, it ought to be studied in that light, as well as all of its other directions. Of course, we who live in New Testament times come to the Father through the Son, accompanied by the guidance of the Holy Spirit, which was not the case in Old Testament times. However, everything else is basically the same.

You've heard it said, and it is true, *"God answers prayer!"*

(39) "AND HE STOOD OVER HER, AND REBUKED THE FEVER; AND IT LEFT HER: AND IMMEDIATELY SHE AROSE AND MINISTERED UNTO THEM."

The synopsis is:

1. The phrase, *"And He stood over her,"* is terminology that would have been employed by a medical doctor, which Luke was!

2. *"And rebuked the fever,"* indicates that he took authority over this sickness. Matthew and Mark say that He touched her while Luke does not mention this.

3. The word *rebuked* means to "censure, admonish, or charge." So, in actuality, Jesus was addressing the demon spirit causing the fever.

4. This does not mean that every single sickness is caused by a demon spirit. However, inasmuch as sickness is a part of the curse and not originally intended by God, we know that demon spirits are the author of sickness per se. The expression of sickness, however, is found in environment, improper diet, heredity, etc.

As well, for a demon spirit to cause sickness in a believer, or anyone for that matter, it does not mean that the person is demon possessed. Probably, the right word here would be *"oppressed"* (Acts 10:38). Demon possession is far more serious and comes from within. No believer can be demon possessed. Demon oppression comes from without and, at one time or the other, has troubled every single believer who has ever lived.

5. The phrase, *"And it left her,"* refers to the evil spirit that was causing this physical malady to instantly leave, which caused the fever to instantly subside.

6. The phrase, *"And immediately she arose and ministered unto them,"* speaks of an instant recovery, even with her preparing an evening meal. This is how quickly the Lord can do things. This lady was desperately ill and then a moment later, due to the power of God, she was instantly well. No convalescence or slow recovery, but rather an immediate recovery.

7. One can well imagine the joy that filled that home after this incident. If Jesus will be allowed to come into any home, the results will be as miraculous and instantaneous.

(40) "NOW WHEN THE SUN WAS SETTING, ALL THEY WHO HAD ANY SICK WITH DIVERS DISEASES BROUGHT THEM UNTO HIM; AND HE LAID HIS HANDS ON EVERY ONE OF THEM, AND HEALED THEM."

THE SABBATH

The phrase, *"Now when the sun was setting,"* had to do with the ending of the Sabbath. The Sabbath began on Friday night at sundown, ending Saturday night at sundown. The Jews reckoned the beginning of their day at sundown instead of midnight as we now do.

Inasmuch as it was improper to carry out much activity during the hours of the Sabbath, the people would have waited for the sun to set in order to bring the sick to the house of Peter.

One noted atheist referred to this Scripture concerning the sun setting and remarked that this proved the Bible was not true. *"Anyone knows,"* he said, *"that the sun is stationary and does not move."* However, his own speech betrays him.

I am positive that he does not personally respond to the setting of the sun as a particular position of the rotation of the earth, which it actually is, but as the eye sees it and Luke reported it.

The saying, *"Setting of the sun,"* is not unscientific. It really refers to where the sun sits and the rotation of the earth in its

present position to it. So, as usual, the atheist did not know what he was talking about!

DIVERS DISEASES

The phrase, *"All they who had any sick with divers diseases brought them unto Him,"* probably referred to many, if not most in the city, who were in that condition. The words *"divers diseases"* referred to all types of diseases.

"And He laid His hands on every one of them, and healed them," has a little different reference than Peter's mother-in-law, even though He laid His hands on her as well. As stated, it seems that He then dealt with the spirit behind the fever while, with these people, He dealt directly with the sicknesses.

The laying on of hands is a doctrine of both Testaments. Touching or laying on of hands is found some 40 times in the New Testament. It is seen in connection with healings performed by Jesus and the apostles (Mat. 9:17; Mk. 6:5; 8:23; Lk. 13:13; Acts 28:8). As well, it is seen in Jesus' act of blessing the children (Mat. 19:13, 15). It is also referred to in the context of receiving the baptism with the Holy Spirit (Acts 8:17; 9:17; 19:6).

It is also used in its association with the ordination of individuals for special tasks or for offices. This use is found in Acts 6:6; 13:3; I Timothy 4:14; and II Timothy 1:6. However, we should take note that these acts of ordination were performed by different groups: the apostles (Acts, Chpt. 6), the prophets and teachers in Antioch (Acts 13:3), local church elders (I Tim. 4:14), and Paul (II Tim. 1:6). In no case was the transfer of one's office or ministry in view, so no case for apostolic succession can be made from these New Testament references.

LAYING ON OF HANDS

So, the idea of laying on of hands, as it was carried through in the early church, is meant to be carried over even unto the present. It signifies authority, and in this case, authority that comes from God. It finds its foundation or roots in Jesus sitting at *"the right hand of God"* (Acts 2:33-34; 5:31; 7:55-56; Rom. 8:34; Eph. 1:20; Col. 3:11; Heb. 1:3, 13; 8:1; 10:12; 12:2; I Pet. 3:22).

Signifying the completion of the redemption process, Jesus exercised the full power of God and used it on behalf of His church, evidenced, at least in part, by the laying on of hands.

Jesus even now is, *"Far above all rule and authority, power and dominion, and every title that can be given, not only in the present age, but also in the one to come"* (Eph. 1:21).

In effect, and as someone has said, *"We are to be His hand extended."*

(41) "AND DEVILS ALSO CAME OUT OF MANY, CRYING OUT, AND SAYING, YOU ARE CHRIST THE SON OF GOD. AND HE REBUKING THEM SUFFERED THEM NOT TO SPEAK: FOR THEY KNEW THAT HE WAS CHRIST."

The pattern is:

1. The phrase, *"And devils (demons) also came out of many,"* speaks of deliverances other than the healings. This should accompany the modern church as well! Tragically, many do not even believe that evil spirits exist, and if they do believe such, do not believe the church enters into the picture, referring rather to the psychologists. Irrespective, Jesus said, *"These signs shall follow them who believe; In My name shall they cast out devils (demons)"* (Mk. 16:17).

2. The word *many* does not mean that Jesus failed to cast some out, but rather that the total number, which included all who came, constituted many.

3. The phrase, *"Crying out, and saying, You are Christ the Son of God,"* speaks of these spirits having personalities and intelligence. How did they know Him so readily?

4. They knew Him not just from the incarnation but, as well, from His divine glory. It is sad that demons knew who He was, but the religious leaders of Israel did not know Him. It has not changed at all presently.

5. Demons know the Word of God, and they also know exactly what is of God and not of God, even though many, if not most believers, don't!

6. *"And He rebuking them suffered them not to speak,"* was for several reasons.

a. First, He rebuked them exactly as He rebuked the fever of Verse 39.

b. Secondly, He wanted no testimony from them whatsoever. If men would not believe the Word of God as to its testimony regarding Him, He did not want them accepting Satan's word in this regard, or any other regard for that matter.

7. *"For they knew that He was Christ,"* means there was absolutely no doubt!

(42) "AND WHEN IT WAS DAY, HE DEPARTED AND WENT INTO A DESERT PLACE: AND THE PEOPLE SOUGHT HIM, AND CAME UNTO HIM, AND STAYED HIM, THAT HE SHOULD NOT DEPART FROM THEM."

The overview is:

1. The phrase, *"And when it was day,"* refers to daylight and means that He probably ministered all night, healing the sick and casting out demons.

2. *"He departed and went into a desert place,"* referred to a desired place of solitude and privacy. He probably desired to be alone with His heavenly Father for a period of time to renew His strength; however, that was not to be.

3. *"And the people sought Him,"* could very well have referred to other sick who had been brought, as well as the desire of simply wanting to be near Him, which is certainly understandable.

4. *"And came unto Him,"* means they sought Him until they found Him. This could have been several hundreds or even several thousands of people.

5. *"And stayed Him, that He should not depart from them,"* refers to the fact that they desired that He spend all His time in Capernaum and not go elsewhere.

6. It must be understood that this is before the opposition of the scribes and Pharisees. Upon the advent of this malady, the ardor of the people would cool somewhat. Actually, the religious leaders would bitterly oppose Him.

(43) "AND HE SAID UNTO THEM, I MUST PREACH THE KINGDOM OF GOD TO OTHER CITIES ALSO: FOR THEREFORE AM I SENT."

THE KINGDOM OF GOD

As we shall see, the phrase, *"And He said unto them,"* constitutes the basic fundamentals of the gospel, at least as far as its propagation is concerned.

"I must preach the kingdom of God to other cities also," suggests several things:

• The gospel must be proclaimed to the entirety of the world to the people who do not know Jesus, or else, as far as they are concerned, He died in vain. The gospel has the effect of not only causing souls to be saved, but of subduing many, if not most demon spirits. So, it has a mediating influence on everything. This refers not only to the spiritual but, as well, to the economical and physical sense. In other words, there is not so much sickness where the gospel of Jesus Christ reigns. Part of that is because of the hold of demon spirits being broken, or at least seriously weakened.

So, this means that there is not nearly as much true gospel being preached in America, Canada, and, as well, the balance of the world as there once was, thereby, bringing about an increase in crime, diseases, and general declension of all kinds.

THE METHOD

• The *"kingdom of God"* refers to a method and plan of salvation, victory, power, healing, and prosperity, which rules every part and particle of a person's life. It has now come in the spiritual sense, which affects greatly, as stated, all else. However, it will come in totality at the second coming of Christ, which will commence the beginning of the kingdom age.

So, the kingdom of God is not a mere philosophy, but is rather wrapped up in a person, the Lord Jesus Christ. When a person accepts Him as his Lord and Saviour, he enters into the kingdom of God. It is a way of life that directs every aspect of one's existence. As we have stated, the only way into it is through Jesus Christ (Jn. 10:9).

PREACHING

• This kingdom of God must be preached, thereby, proclaiming God's method. The word *preach* means "to announce good news."

The best examples of preaching by the early church are found in sermons recorded in Acts, especially two by Peter (Acts

2:14-41; 3:11-26) and two by Paul (Acts 13:16-43; 17:22-31).

The common elements in these messages reveal basic truths that were preached as believers in the early church set about evangelizing the world: Jesus, the historical person, was crucified and raised in accordance with Scripture; He, the promised Messiah, must be received by faith with repentance.

As well, the preaching is to be a public proclamation of Christianity to the non-Christian world. It is not religious discourse to a closed group of initiates, but open and public proclamation of God's redemptive activity in and through Jesus Christ. The current popular understanding of preaching as biblical exposition and exhortation has tended to obscure its basic meaning.

As someone has said, *"Preaching proclaims truth, while teaching explains truth."* So, this of which Jesus speaks rather means the proclamation of truth. Men must have the truth presented to them before they can understand the truth, hence, preaching.

There is a divine compulsion attached to preaching, as is evidenced by Christ in Verse 43. As well, Peter would say, *"We cannot but speak the things which we have seen and heard"* (Acts 4:20).

PREACHING THE GOSPEL

"Woe to me if I do not preach the gospel," cries the apostle Paul (I Cor. 9:16). Consequently, preaching is not the relaxed recital of morally neutral truths; it is God Himself breaking in and confronting man with a demand for decision. As well, this sort of preaching meets with opposition. In II Corinthians 11:23-28, Paul lists his sufferings for the sake of the gospel.

Another feature of apostolic preaching is its transparency of message and motive. Since preaching calls for faith, it is vitally important that its issues not be obscured with eloquent wisdom and lofty words (I Cor. 1:17; 2:1-4). Paul refused to practice cunning or to tamper with God's Word, but sought to commend himself to every man's conscience by the open statement of the truth (II Cor. 4:2).

The radical upheaval within the heart and consciousness of man, which is the new birth, does not come about by the persuasive influence of rhetoric or eloquence, but by the straightforward presentation of the gospel in all its simplicity and power.

The nature of preaching is not only to herald the good news, but in its proclamation of the kingdom of God, God's kingly rule is to be proclaimed as over all, with Jesus, as stated, as its door. That is primary. Only secondly does it refer to a realm or people within that realm.

It is the idea of God's eternal power through Jesus Christ invading the realm of evil powers and winning the decisive victory. *"For this cause was Christ manifested."*

THE LORD JESUS CHRIST

When we move into the Epistles, we note a significant change in terminology. Even though the kingdom of God is mentioned several times, still, we find Christ as the content of the preached message. This is variously expressed as *"Christ crucified"* (I Cor. 1:23), *Christ raised* (I Cor. 15:12), *"The Son of God, Jesus Christ"* (II Cor. 1:19), or *"Christ Jesus the Lord"* (II Cor. 4:5). This change of emphasis is accounted for by the fact that Christ is the kingdom.

This means that the death and resurrection of Jesus Christ was the decisive act of God whereby His eternal sovereignty was realized in human history. With the advance of redemptive history, the apostolic church could proclaim the kingdom in the more clear-cut terms of decision concerning the King. To preach Christ is to preach the kingdom.

The apostolic message was, *"A proclamation of the death, resurrection, and exaltation of Jesus that led to an evaluation of His person as both Lord and Christ, which confronted man with the necessity of repentance, and promised the forgiveness of sins"* (R.H. Mounce).

THE REVELATION OF THE LORD

True preaching is best understood in terms of its relation to the wider theme of revelation. Revelation is essentially God's self-disclosure apprehended by the response of faith. Since Calvary is God's supreme self-revelation, the problem is,

NOTES

"How can God reveal Himself in the present through an act of the past?" The answer is, *"Through preaching,"* for preaching is the timeless link between God's redemptive act (we speak of the Cross of Christ) and man's apprehension of it. It is the medium through which God contemporizes His historic self-disclosure in Christ and offers man the opportunity to respond in faith (J.R.W. Stott).

"For therefore am I sent," proclaims the example for all of the church.

In other words, God did not send His Son for just a select few, but rather for all of mankind. As well, we were not saved in order to store up this salvation within ourselves, but we rather are a *"debtor"* to all others (Rom. 1:14), meaning that we must take the gospel to all others.

(44) "AND HE PREACHED IN THE SYNAGOGUES OF GALILEE."

The diagram is:

1. This proclaims Him doing exactly what He said—going to other places in Galilee.

2. Even though Jesus was sent for the entirety of the world, still, His personal ministry was basically confined to Israel. There was a reason and purpose for this.

3. It was through Israel that the Messiah must come and, consequently, to Israel that the gospel must first be preached. It was God's will that they accept it and then give it to the entirety of the world.

4. Regrettably, they did not accept it and were shut out. However, the early church, constituted, of course, of the ones who did accept it, was then given instructions by the Holy Spirit to take the gospel to the Gentiles, which was begun by Peter (Acts, Chpt. 10). However, Paul became the chief proponent of the proclamation of the all-important message to the Gentiles, calling himself, *"The apostle of the Gentiles"* (Rom. 11:13).

5. The thrust and content of the message has not changed from the days of the early church until now and, in fact, will not change until the coming of the Lord. Then, instead of the message being, *"He is coming,"* it will rather be, *"He has come"* (Rev. 22:20).

As well, let all understand that unless the preacher preaches the Cross, in essence, he is not preaching the gospel, for the gospel is the Cross of Christ. When we speak of the Cross, we aren't speaking of the wooden beam on which Jesus died, but rather what He there accomplished. For everything, and I mean everything that we receive from the Lord, the Cross of Christ is the means, and the only means, by which these things are given to us.

"I can see far down the mountain,
"Where I wandered weary years.
"Often hindered in my journey
"By the ghosts of doubts and fears,
"Broken vows and disappointments
"Thickly strewn all the way,
"But the Spirit led unerring
"To the land I hold today."

CHAPTER 5

(1) "AND IT CAME TO PASS, THAT, AS THE PEOPLE PRESSED UPON HIM TO HEAR THE WORD OF GOD, HE STOOD BY THE LAKE OF GENNESARET."

The exegesis is:

1. The phrase, *"And it came to pass, that, as the people pressed upon Him to hear the Word of God,"* proclaims several things:

a. Modern thought belittles preaching and exalts ceremony. The eternal Son of God was wholly a preacher. This fact and the opposition of Satan to preaching demonstrate its importance.

b. The Word of God is the only revealed truth in the world today and, in fact, ever has been. That means there is no truth in Islam, Buddhism, Hinduism, Confucianism, spiritism, atheism, Mormonism, Catholicism, etc.

c. Inasmuch as it is the Word of God, every believer should make it a lifelong pursuit. It should be a daily habit until the stories, illustrations, experiences, miracles, and general thrust are as familiar as firsthand knowledge. The believer ought to know far more about the Bible than he does anything else in the world.

d. Jesus preached the Word of God as the people had never heard it by opening

its truths, which had so long been hidden by the scribes and Pharisees. As well, He preached it with such an anointing of the Holy Spirit that whatever He said greatly warmed the hearts of the listeners.

2. The phrase, *"He stood by the lake of Gennesaret,"* refers to the Sea of Galilee. It is also called the Sea of Tiberias (Jn. 21:2) and the *"Sea of Chinnereth"* (Num. 34:11; Deut. 3:17; Josh. 12:3; 13:27). It is about seven miles wide and approximately 14 miles long.

(2) "AND SAW TWO SHIPS STANDING BY THE LAKE: BUT THE FISHERMEN WERE GONE OUT OF THEM, AND WERE WASHING THEIR NETS."

The overview is:

1. The phrase, *"And saw two ships standing by the lake,"* spoke of only two among the many. Some authorities state that there were as many as 4,000 ships on Galilee at that time. Actually, the Galilee area was the most prosperous in Israel, with the lake at that time being ringed by towns, at least on the northern and western sides. Josephus stated that approximately 250,000 people lived in the area.

2. *"But the fishermen were gone out of them, and were washing their nets,"* signifies two things:

a. Peter, Andrew, James, and John had fished all night, which was the normal time for fishing, and had caught nothing.

b. They had given up and were now washing their nets, signifying that any further effort was futile; however, as we shall see, they were reckoning without Jesus.

(3) "AND HE ENTERED INTO ONE OF THE SHIPS, WHICH WAS SIMON'S, AND PRAYED HIM THAT HE WOULD THRUST OUT A LITTLE FROM THE LAND. AND HE SAT DOWN, AND TAUGHT THE PEOPLE OUT OF THE SHIP."

The structure is:

1. The phrase, *"And He entered into one of the ships, which was Simon's,"* proclaims Him borrowing this vessel to serve as a platform or pulpit. The crowds had pressed the shoreline to hear Jesus speak and, as well, to see Him heal the sick. They were pressing so close that they were undoubtedly pushing Him into the water. So, Jesus evidently waded out into the water to where Peter's

vessel was anchored, climbed on board, and asked to borrow the ship for a short time for a preaching platform.

2. *"And prayed him that he would thrust out a little from the land,"* means that he probably pushed out 10 to 15 feet to where the people could not wade out, and Jesus would have opportunity to speak to them without being interrupted.

3. Even though the account concerning the call of these four is now given by Luke, still, they were not strangers to Jesus. Andrew and John had definitely been followers of John the Baptist and possibly even Peter and James as well!

4. They very well could have been present at the baptism of Jesus (Jn. 1:29-46). This had been before the 40 days and nights of fasting. Therefore, their call probably came about 60 to 90 days after Jesus' baptism in the river Jordan.

5. The phrase, *"And He sat down, and taught the people out of the ship,"* represents the manner in which teaching and preaching was carried out in those days. They sat down to preach and teach.

(4) "NOW WHEN HE HAD LEFT SPEAKING, HE SAID UNTO SIMON, LAUNCH OUT INTO THE DEEP, AND LET DOWN YOUR NETS FOR A DRAUGHT."

THE LORD JESUS

The phrase, *"Now when He had left speaking,"* as is obvious, proclaimed the end of His message. How wonderful it must have been to have had the privilege of standing there that day and hearing the Son of God. And yet, there is coming a day when all believers for all time will be able to sit at the feet of Jesus just as this crowd of old. How wonderful it will be to hear Him speak of all things He has done, including the creation and, above all, that which pertains to the redemption of man. As Fanny Crosby wrote a long time ago:

"I shall see Him face-to-face,
And tell the story, saved by grace."

"He said unto Simon," immediately places Peter in the position of leadership regarding the disciples. While it is quite true that he made some mistakes, some of which were of a very serious nature, still,

Simon Peter was undoubtedly one of the greatest men of God who ever lived. And yet, Jesus did not choose him or the others for the qualities they had but for what He could make of them. However, it is obvious that they did have a tender heart that was pliable before God, which could be molded and, in fact, desired to be molded according to the will of God. This must be true in any and every person for them to be used by God.

LAUNCH OUT INTO THE DEEP

The phrase, *"Launch out into the deep, and let down your nets for a draught,"* probably came as a surprise to these fishermen. They had fished all night, which was actually the time to catch fish, and had taken nothing. Peter and the others probably mused, "How does this man think that fish can now be caught?" especially considering that He was not a fisherman and that they, who were professional fishermen, had fished all night with no success. However, they were to find that Christ had the same power over the fish of the sea as He had over the frogs, flies, lice, and locusts of Egypt. As well, Jesus had borrowed the boat and now would repay these men for their kindness. One should take a lesson from this:

The Lord never asks anything of anyone but that He gives back, even in kind, so much more than what He asks.

How wonderful it is to give to God exactly as Peter and the others did, knowing that He will bless abundantly. And yet, our giving is not to be on that premise. We are to give because we love Him, and for that purpose alone. To be sure, if that is our attitude, our spirit, and our way, God will most definitely bless it just as He did Peter and the others regarding the great catch of fish that He gave them. The Lord will never owe anyone anything. Always remember that. It's us who owe Him everything, and never Him owing us. If He asks something of us, He will always return it many times over.

(5) "AND SIMON ANSWERING SAID UNTO HIM, MASTER, WE HAVE TOILED ALL THE NIGHT, AND HAVE TAKEN NOTHING: NEVERTHELESS AT YOUR WORD I WILL LET DOWN THE NET."

SIMON PETER

The phrase, *"And Simon answering said unto Him,"* proclaims another stage in the lesson that would be taught here. Actually, everything Jesus did was a lesson not only for His disciples, but for all men, for all time.

Lessons are slowly and gently taught in the school of God. Simon was first asked to push out a little from the land. He obeyed. There was no danger in that. He was then asked to launch out into the deep where human aid could not reach, where man could sink, and where he was wholly cast upon God for both safety and sustenance, but where the big fish could be caught.

So, what was about to happen was far more than a mere payment for a kindness. It was meant to serve as a great lesson of faith, which it did!

The phrase, *"Master, we have toiled all the night, and have taken nothing,"* proclaims the inability of man in comparison to the ability of God.

The title *"master"* means "commander," and not merely a teacher. It speaks of one who has great authority.

Consequently, in using this title of Jesus, Peter was acknowledging Christ as the master of the fish and the sea, but yet, his (Simon's) inability to comprehend what the Lord was going to do.

WHERE PETER STOOD, WE SOONER OR LATER STAND, AS WELL

Peter registered the lack of comprehension for the others as well! He was a fisherman, and Jesus was not. Consequently, he did not understand how fish could now be caught, especially considering that it was the very worst time to catch fish, i.e., during the day.

In living for Christ, one will quickly come to this place where Peter stood. In the natural we simply do not see how it can be done, and I speak of whatever the need may be. In the natural the problem is oftentimes impossible. However, faith in Christ demands that we place the matter in His hands, knowing that He is able to do all things, irrespective of what they might be. This is at least a part of the great lesson of faith taught in these

simple passages. As well, for all of man's efforts in his toiling to solve the problems of this planet, he has reaped pretty much what Peter here said, *"Nothing."*

NEVERTHELESS AT YOUR WORD

The phrase, *"Nevertheless at Your word I will let down the net,"* proclaims an act of faith that was to characterize the lives and ministries of all the disciples, and not for them only, but for all who truly follow Jesus.

Upon the command of Christ, they had probably gone several hundred yards out into the Sea of Galilee. It was probably the area that Peter and the others had just fished, throwing their nets over the side time and time again, actually, all night long, but without any favorable results. Now, Jesus went back to what was probably the same area they had fished and told them to once again throw their nets over the side, which seemed to them to be a futile gesture.

Peter's words proclaim that there was doubt in his heart but, at the same time, his using the title *"master"* proclaimed a great faith in Christ. Such is the heart of even the strongest believer.

The battle between doubt and faith constantly rages. Circumstances point to the opposite of what God says, and feelings and flesh give way to doubt while the spirit cries to God in faith. It is the age-old struggle! And yet, the spark of faith is so powerful that if given even small opportunity, it will grow and overcome all doubt. The person has to learn that with Jesus in the boat (the boat of life), anything is possible!

The idea of this text is that Peter would not have bothered himself to let down that net for the word of anyone else other than Jesus. So, he used the phrase, *"Your word!"*

There is nothing more important than God's Word. The Scripture says, *"For You have magnified Your Word above all Your name"* (Ps. 138:2).

(6) "AND WHEN THEY HAD THIS DONE, THEY INCLOSED A GREAT MULTITUDE OF FISHES: AND THEIR NET BROKE."

The diagram is:

1. Whether the fish were already there or the Lord summoned them is beside the

point. What was done must be construed as a miracle.

2. At His word, although uttered silently, the fish were there, and at His word, Peter let down the net. As a result, the catch was so great that the net, as strong as it was, began to break.

3. Some have claimed that Jesus used the word *nets* and that Peter, being skeptical, only let down one net. However, that is incorrect.

4. The word *net* or *nets* can be used either way, in the singular or plural, both meaning the same. In fact, a fishing net is made up of many nets; consequently, it can be referred to either way. The evidence is that Peter used the net they had been using all night long.

(7) "AND THEY BECKONED UNTO THEIR PARTNERS, WHICH WERE IN THE OTHER SHIP, THAT THEY SHOULD COME AND HELP THEM. AND THEY CAME, AND FILLED BOTH THE SHIPS, SO THAT THEY BEGAN TO SINK."

The form is:

1. The phrase, *"And they beckoned unto their partners, which were in the other ship, that they should come and help them,"* referred to James and John.

2. There is a possibility, but not likely, that the other ship followed them out. The evidence seems to be that either Peter or Andrew shouted across the water, whatever the distance may have been, *"That they should come and help them."*

3. *"And they came, and filled both the ships, so that they began to sink,"* proves that the net Peter threw over the side was all the net they had. In fact, it must have been a huge net, or it would not have been able to catch so many fish as to fill both the ships beyond their ability to carry. This was a miracle of outstanding proportions. As stated, this proclaims the ability of the Lord up beside that of man. As is obvious, there is no comparison!

4. Was there an immediate reason that Jesus performed this miracle, other than the obvious lesson of faith?

5. As we have stated, there is some indication in Chapter 1 of John that Jesus had already extended an invitation to these men

NOTES

to follow Him. Yet, they proposed to return to their fishing, possibly wondering how they would make a living for their families if, in fact, they were to follow Jesus!

6. Such is the insensibility of the carnal nature to the divine voice, and such is its incurable propensity to earthly things! Pentecost, however, made them victorious over their natural inclination.

7. Perhaps Jesus was showing them in the performing of this miracle that they needed to have no fear. Such is indicated in the following verses.

(8) "WHEN SIMON PETER SAW IT, HE FELL DOWN AT JESUS' KNEES, SAYING, DEPART FROM ME; FOR I AM A SINFUL MAN, O LORD."

The exegesis is:

1. The phrase, *"When Simon Peter saw it,"* proclaims the effect of this lesson as not to give Simon high thoughts of himself but low thoughts. Such is ever the effect of a manifestation of divine power and grace upon the conscience of fallen man.

2. *"He fell down at Jesus' knees, saying, Depart from me; for I am a sinful man, O Lord,"* proclaims that this miracle revealed the hidden unbelief of Simon's heart, for, without a doubt, when casting the net, he said to himself, "We shall catch nothing."

3. The Lord Jesus never rebuked His disciples for manifesting or expressing too lofty conceptions of Him. On the contrary, their confession of His deity and Godhead was grateful to His spirit.

4. Actually, Peter using the name *"Lord"* acknowledges the deity of Christ (I Cor. 12:3).

(9) "FOR HE WAS ASTONISHED, AND ALL WHO WERE WITH HIM, AT THE DRAUGHT OF THE FISHES WHICH THEY HAD TAKEN."

The synopsis is:

1. The phrase, *"For he was astonished, and all who were with him,"* concerned the tremendous miracle that had just taken place and their reaction to it.

2. *"At the draught of the fishes which they had taken,"* means that if they had once had doubt concerning Jesus' ability of provision, those questions had been answered abundantly so.

3. It seems that the disciples were just

now beginning to comprehend, at least to a certain degree, just who Jesus actually was.

(10) "AND SO WAS ALSO JAMES, AND JOHN, THE SONS OF ZEBEDEE, WHICH WERE PARTNERS WITH SIMON. AND JESUS SAID UNTO SIMON, FEAR NOT; FROM HENCEFORTH YOU SHALL CATCH MEN."

JAMES AND JOHN

The phrase, *"And so was also James, and John, the sons of Zebedee, which were partners with Simon,"* concerned the entirety of this fishing partnership. Zebedee, the father of James and John, was about to lose the main people of his organization; however, what a privilege for Jesus to have chosen his two sons, as well as Peter and Andrew. There is no record that Zebedee complained. Also, one can feel assured that the Lord, who was able to perform such miracles, would see to it that Zebedee's loss would, in effect, not be a loss at all. Other people were, no doubt, immediately secured, with Zebedee being abundantly blessed.

FEAR NOT

The phrase, *"And Jesus said unto Simon, Fear not,"* means that Simon, of all the men, was affected the most.

All of a sudden, Jesus is no longer just an itinerant preacher, as may possibly have been the previous thoughts of Peter, but rather He was God. Spence said, "The very fish of his native lake, then were subject to this strange holy man!" Consequently, he was not only astonished at what had happened, but fear gripped him as well.

Trench said, "Finding as it does its parallel in almost all manifestations of a divine or even an angelic presence, it (this awful fear) must be owned to contain a mighty and instructive witness for the sinfulness of man's nature, out of which it comes to pass that any near revelation from the heavenly world fills the children of men, even the holiest among them, with terror and amazement, yes, sometimes with the expectation of death itself."

This is the first recorded instance of Jesus using the words, *"Fear not,"* to His disciples.

The last instance of these reassuring words being spoken by the Redeemer was after the ascension when He appeared to John on the Isle of Patmos, when John could not bear the sight of the glorious majesty of his risen Lord (Rev. 1:17).

A FISHER OF MEN

The phrase, *"From henceforth you shall catch men,"* elevates them to being fishers of men and constitutes their call to discipleship and as apostles.

There is some evidence that this incident is different from the illustrations given in Matthew and Mark concerning the call of this four (Mat. 4:18-22; Mk. 1:16-20). It can be explained in two ways:

1. Matthew and Mark are telling the same story, while Luke is telling another story altogether of an entirely different happening. It is quite possible that Jesus called them exactly as Matthew and Mark explained it, with these four not quite turning loose of the fishing business at the beginning, wondering how they were going to take care of their families. That could very well have happened, with Jesus giving them this final call and it accompanied by this great miracle. If that is the way it happened, they were now convinced and would follow unreservedly.

2. All three incidents could well have been identical, with Matthew and Mark only relating some of the things that happened, with Luke giving the balance.

Even though this is certainly possible, I personally feel the former explanation is probably closer to what actually took place.

(11) "AND WHEN THEY HAD BROUGHT THEIR SHIPS TO LAND, THEY FORSOOK ALL, AND FOLLOWED HIM."

The pattern is:

1. The phrase, *"And when they had brought their ships to land,"* regards them doing this in a manner that had never been done previously. The Lord of glory was now on board, and that which had just transpired would forever change their lives.

2. The phrase, *"They forsook all, and followed Him,"* means they did so immediately.

3. This is a requirement of the gospel (Mat. 19:27-30). It means a willingness

to follow God regardless of the price; however, it never means to forsake responsibility. Even these men still retained their own homes, families, and responsibilities (I Tim. 5:8). The main idea is to put God first (Mat. 22:37; Lk. 14:16-27).

4. The things that recently transpired caused each of these men to believe that Jesus was truly the Messiah. Even though their faith would be tested in the future, there seems to be no doubt at the present that they were all in agreement on this fact. He was God manifest in the flesh.

5. Even though following him involved suffering, sacrifice, persecution, and ultimate martyrdom, still, the journey would lead to dizzying heights. Even though the 12 disciples would have their names inscribed on the 12 foundations of the New Jerusalem, still, the greatest glory of all, even accounting for all the other rewards, is the privilege of following Him. He is ever the objective.

6. In the fall of 1991, the Lord instructed me to begin two prayer meetings a day, which I did. The only thing He told me was, "Seek Me not so much for what I can do for you, but rather for who I am."

Clement of Alexandria wrote so long ago:
"Fisher of men, the blest,
"Out of the world's unrest,
"Out of sin's troubled sea,
"Taking us, Lord, to Thee;
"Out of the waves of strife,
"With bait of blissful life;
"Drawing your nets to shore,
"With choicest fish, good store."

(12) "AND IT CAME TO PASS, WHEN HE WAS IN A CERTAIN CITY, BEHOLD A MAN FULL OF LEPROSY: WHO SEEING JESUS FELL ON HIS FACE, AND BESOUGHT HIM, SAYING, LORD, IF YOU WILL, YOU CAN MAKE ME CLEAN."

The form is:

1. How do I actually have faith in Christ and the Cross?

2. You are to just simply believe that Jesus Christ is the source of all things we receive from God, while the Cross of Christ is the means, and the only means, by which these things are given to us.

3. We are to believe that!

LEPROSY

The phrase, *"And it came to pass, when He was in a certain city, behold a man full of leprosy,"* referred to leprosy being all over the man's body, in other words, the last stages!

Leprosy, as it is described in the Old Testament, was considered to be a type of sin, with its bearer cursed by God.

The leprosy spoken of was probably the *lepra vulgaris,* called "white leprosy" or "dry tetter."

This disease first appears in reddish pimples, the surface of which becomes white and scaly, spreading in a circular direction, and covering large parts of the body. Even though very unsightly, it could last for years and then disappear. Upon such occasion, the individual was to show himself to the priest and be pronounced clean of leprosy.

However, the disease oftentimes did not disappear, partially covering the entire body, becoming raw and open, and emitting corruption. In these stages, which describes the leper at hand, body extremities, such as fingers, nose, etc., could be literally eaten away and actually fall off. The evidence is that this man who approached Jesus was in that state. In other words, there was no chance of his leprosy disappearing. In fact, had he not met Jesus, it would shortly have killed him.

SIN

As stated, with leprosy being a type of sin and portraying the terrible results of sin, the picture is aptly drawn of its awful effects. As there was no earthly cure for leprosy in these stages, likewise, there is no cure for sin other than Jesus. Man has devised all types of ways to cover the sinful sores, and even to ameliorate the smell of the corruption; however, he has not succeeded in any way in curing the disease itself. He merely treats the symptoms.

The phrase, *"Who seeing Jesus fell on his face,"* proclaims this man recognizing who Jesus was and that He was able to cleanse him of this dreaded malady.

Him falling on his face portrays him realizing his dire condition as well as the power of Christ. I believe he knew he was in the presence of deity.

Even though the physical position has little to do with it, still, the sinner must humble himself before Christ if he is to receive the great benefit.

IF YOU WILL …

The phrase, *"And besought Him, saying, Lord, if You will, You can make me clean,"* means that the man expressed doubt about the willingness of Jesus, considering that this disease was leprosy. He knew He had the power to do so, but the leper wasn't sure if He really would do it.

This seems to be Jesus' first encounter with leprosy; consequently, the man had, no doubt, heard of Jesus performing many other miracles and healing many sicknesses, but not leprosy. Considering that all Jews thought of this disease as a curse of God, the man was not certain what Jesus would do. All others threw stones at him, and quite possibly, at least in his thinking, Jesus might do the same.

From him using the title *"Lord,"* I think he knew that Jesus was the Messiah. He knew He had the power, but he wasn't sure if He had the will.

What must have been going through his mind when he made this request? This was it! If Jesus did not heal him, he would die. As well, if Jesus does not save the sinner, he will die in his sins. There is no other remedy!

(13) "AND HE PUT FORTH HIS HAND, AND TOUCHED HIM, SAYING, I WILL: BE THOU CLEAN. AND IMMEDIATELY THE LEPROSY DEPARTED FROM HIM."

THE HAND OF JESUS

The phrase, *"And He put forth His hand, and touched him, saying, I will: be thou clean,"* proclaims the greatest word that ever fell upon the ear of this man. The answer was instant in its forthcoming proclamation.

The structure of the sentence in the Greek text tells us that as Jesus was reaching forth His hand to touch the man, He, at the same time, was saying, *"I will,"* which brought about instant healing. In other words, the man was not touched in order to heal him; he was already healed before Jesus touched him. Jesus touched him to show the people who must have been standing

NOTES

nearby that the man was already cleansed of his leprosy. Actually, the Levitical law forbade a Jew to touch a leper. Our Lord lived under this law and obeyed it. This means that the first kind touch of a human hand this leper ever experienced was the gentle touch of the Son of God. One must shout, "Hallelujah!"

IMMEDIATELY

The phrase, *"And immediately the leprosy departed from him,"* pronounces the same manner in which the sinner is cleansed. Salvation comes immediately upon faith in Christ.

One moment the man was a leper, and the next moment he was perfectly cleansed, never again to be afflicted by this dreaded malady. The sinner is identical!

One moment he is lost without God, on his way to an eternal darkness, and then the next moment, after faith in Christ, he is instantly cleansed, with his name being inscribed in the Lamb's Book of Life, never again to be bound by the horrible bondage of sin, at least if he continues to trust Christ.

In the two words, *"I will,"* the Lord forever lays to rest His questioned willingness to save and to heal all who come to Him.

Many have thought that they were too wicked for Jesus to save them; however, the portrayal of this leper in the last stages of this loathsome disease, which was meant to portray the horror of sin, tells us that the Lord can and will save to the uttermost (Heb. 7:25).

The degree of sin is of no consequence. The Lord does not patch up the old, hence, attempting to repair the damage that is done, but rather makes new (II Cor. 5:17).

THE PRECIOUS BLOOD OF CHRIST

Wuest said, "In the divine economy, sanctification precedes justification, because the subject must be cleansed, which sanctification does, before the subject can be legally justified" (I Cor. 6:11).

As well, in John 1:12, justification precedes regeneration, because mercy is given only on the basis of justice satisfied.

"So, the sinner recognizes the Lord Jesus as the one who through His outpoured blood on the Cross procured for sinful man a legal right to the mercy of God, he then becomes the recipient of regeneration and of all the other parts of salvation."

While the believing sinner does not know or even understand that these things are going on, still, they are taking place in heaven at the moment of one's redemption. It is all a work of God.

SANCTIFICATION AND JUSTIFICATION

As we have stated, sanctification cleanses the filthy sinner, and it is done so by the washing of the precious blood of Jesus. This is carried out by faith, which sets the person apart as now belonging only to God. This happens in a moment's time as one exhibits faith in Christ and what He did.

Justification instantly follows, which is a legal work declaring the sinner clean, and it will stand up in the court of heaven. Then the person enters into regeneration simply because he has a legal right to become one born of God, and because he has put his trust in the name of Jesus and what Christ accomplished at Calvary. As we have stated many times, it is the doctrine of substitution and identification. Jesus became our substitute, and we identify with Him.

A young man once had difficulty understanding the plan of salvation. It seemed the more the preacher explained it, the more confused the boy became.

With an appointment to keep, the preacher had to leave, but he lent the boy his Bible and pointed out Isaiah 53:6 to him.

It reads: *"All we like sheep have gone astray; we have turned every one to his own way; and the LORD has laid on Him the iniquity of us all."*

He told the young man, "Go in at the first 'all' and come out at the last 'all'!"

When the preacher came back the next day, the boy met him with a smile, returned his Bible, and stated, "I understand it now, and I have given my heart to Jesus."

(14) "AND HE CHARGED HIM TO TELL NO MAN: BUT GO, AND SHOW YOURSELF TO THE PRIEST, AND OFFER FOR YOUR CLEANSING, ACCORDING AS MOSES COMMANDED, FOR A TESTIMONY UNTO THEM."

THE CHARGE

The phrase, *"And He charged him to tell no man,"* actually meant that he was not to testify of his healing until he had first gone to the priest, thus obeying the law of Moses. The word *charged* is strong, meaning, "to do so sternly, even threateningly." There was a reason for this, which we will see:

The phrase, *"But go, and show yourself to the priest,"* was done for several reasons:

MESSIAHSHIP

Jesus made no claim to being the Messiah, at least openly, but rather performed all the things that the prophets said that the Messiah would perform.

To be sure, a fake messiah would have constantly shouted from the housetops his claims, but Jesus simply did the works of healings and miracles that the prophets had foretold.

TO FULFILL THE LAW

When this former leper went to the priests and told them how he was healed, which they could verify, this, in essence, told these priests that Jesus was the Messiah. By the Lord telling the former leper to do what he did, this fulfilled the law and offered the testimony that Moses commanded in such cases (Lev. 14:4, 10, 21-22).

So, we realize that everything that Christ did had a purpose behind it that was far more than the act itself, whatever that was. Now, even though they would not accept it, the priests had irrefutable proof that Jesus was the Messiah.

POPULARITY

At a point in time, the people wanted to make Jesus king. He didn't want that, so He shunned all popularity, all of which He did not need.

However, at a point toward the end of His ministry, He no longer told His disciples to *"tell no man,"* as He previously had done (Mat. 8:4; Mk. 8:26, 30, Lk. 5:14; 8:56; 9:21).

A TESTIMONY

The phrase, *"And offer for your cleansing, according as Moses commanded, for a testimony unto them,"* proclaimed Jesus caring for the man even more than other things. Had he not done this (Mk. 1:43-45), the possibility existed that the authorities would not accept his healing, even though it was obviously evident. Regrettably, the former leper disobeyed Christ; however, it is hard to fault him considering the tremendous joy he must have felt. Nevertheless, considering the stern charge given by the Lord, he should have been more responsible.

(15) "BUT SO MUCH THE MORE WENT THERE A FAME ABROAD OF HIM: AND GREAT MULTITUDES CAME TOGETHER TO HEAR, AND TO BE HEALED BY HIM OF THEIR INFIRMITIES."

THAT WHICH JESUS DID

The phrase, *"But so much the more went there a fame abroad of Him,"* proclaims (as Mark recorded) this leper telling everyone far and wide what had happened to him. There were scores of others who had been healed, who did the same thing. We are only given a representative number of illustrations respecting all the things Jesus did. John the Beloved testified to that when he said, *"And there are also many other things which Jesus did, the which, if they should be written every one, I suppose that even the world itself could not contain the books that should be written"* (Jn. 21:25).

Due to the miracles, the crowds were massive, numbering at times perhaps between 20,000 and 30,000 people. When one considers that every single person who was ill in any way was healed by the power of God, it is easy to comprehend His great fame. There were, no doubt, healings and miracles of such magnitude that they defied description! As well, not a single one was turned away, but all received that for which they came.

GREAT MULTITUDES

The phrase, *"And great multitudes came together to hear, and to be healed by Him of their infirmities,"* respects two needs:

1. *"To hear"*: As we have alluded, His preaching and teaching were such as the people had never heard previously. Through Him, the Word of God became a living thing. He never engaged in any theological

NOTES

hair-splitting, but rather opened up the Scripture to where people could easily grasp and understand what He was saying, even about complex matters. As well, the anointing of the Holy Spirit rested upon each and every word He spoke, which again, was something else the people had never experienced. As a result, as He ministered, they, no doubt, wept, but for joy. They laughed, but with relief. They were moved, but toward righteousness.

2. *"To be healed"*: the *"infirmities"* here spoken of pertained to physical, mental, and even moral weaknesses or flaws.

In this text we see Jesus opposing every power of darkness. He came to destroy the works of Satan and, consequently, met these works, and even more importantly, their instigator, on all fronts. What a joy those meetings must have been!

One can imagine the roads filled with happy people praising God. They had just attended His meetings and had been healed and delivered by the mighty power of God. What a time it must have been!

(16) "AND HE WITHDREW HIMSELF INTO THE WILDERNESS, AND PRAYED."

The overview is:

1. His praying proclaimed His perfection as a man born under the law and dependent upon God.

2. Thus, His deity appears in Verse 13 and His humanity in Verse 16.

3. If the divine evangelist felt the need of prayer and spiritual retirement in the midst of an overwhelming successful ministry, how much more do His servants. He also prayed at His baptism, His transfiguration, and many other times recorded in the four gospels.

(17) "AND IT CAME TO PASS ON A CERTAIN DAY, AS HE WAS TEACHING, THAT THERE WERE PHARISEES AND DOCTORS OF THE LAW SITTING BY, WHICH WERE COME OUT OF EVERY TOWN OF GALILEE, AND JUDAEA, AND JERUSALEM: AND THE POWER OF THE LORD WAS PRESENT TO HEAL THEM."

The overview is:

1. The phrase, *"And it came to pass on a certain day, as He was teaching,"* no doubt, pertained to Capernaum, and probably at Peter's home. It didn't really matter where

He was, the crowds thronged Him, and the house, as is here obvious, was filled with people.

2. *"That there were Pharisees and doctors of the law sitting by,"* pertained to the two leading classes of religious leaders in Israel.

3. Some claim that there were only about 7,000 Pharisees in Israel at that time. However, by and large, they ruled the religious life of Israel. Even though a few of them, it seems, became followers of the Lord, mostly, they were the most strident enemies of Jesus.

4. The doctors of the law probably pertained to the scribes, who, in effect, were the pastors of the people and were supposed to be experts in the law of Moses. As events prove, their expertise was mostly man endowed and not of the Spirit. In other words, they really did not know the true spirit of the law of Moses, even though they loudly professed to do so.

5. *"Which were come out of every town of Galilee, and Judaea, and Jerusalem,"* proclaims just how widespread His fame had become. Now the great opposition would begin!

6. This opposition was almost exclusively centered in the religious leaders of Israel. As such, they were the greatest hindrance to the true work of God then, and so it is presently.

7. *"And the power of the Lord was present to heal them,"* presents a picture that is difficult to put into words.

8. The implication is that sick people were being healed without Jesus even addressing their sicknesses or infirmities. The best way it could be described is the Spirit of God was literally emanating from Him to such an extent that no sickness or disease could stand up under it. In other words, His mere presence brought the healing, even while He was teaching on other subjects. What a moment that must have been!

(18) "AND, BEHOLD, MEN BROUGHT IN A BED A MAN WHICH WAS TAKEN WITH A PALSY: AND THEY SOUGHT MEANS TO BRING HIM IN, AND TO LAY HIM BEFORE HIM."

The synopsis is:

1. The phrase, *"And, behold, men brought in a bed a man which was taken with a palsy,"* concerns four men, as Mark testifies, who were, no doubt, bearing the man on a litter. As we shall see, these four exhibited a tremendous faith, which would result in this man not only being healed but being saved as well!

2. This proves to be a perfect example of believers bringing unbelievers to Jesus. They came to Jesus because He was the only source of such help, as He is the only source presently. In addition, without the assistance of these men, it would not have been possible for this man, as sick as he was, to get to Jesus. As well, it is not possible for unbelievers on their own to get to Jesus without believers bringing them. Being spiritually blind, they do not know who He is, or where He is. The tragedy is that most believers little know either!

3. *"Palsy,"* as a description of his disease, is apt. It spoke of a type of paralysis, which hindered the man from walking. As well, every unbeliever, at least in a spiritual sense, is a paralytic. As a result, he has to be helped by any scriptural means at one's disposal.

4. *"And they sought means to bring him in, and to lay him before Him,"* speaks of the normal hindrances to faith, but despite these hindrances, faith will find a way. We shall see exactly the extremes that their faith would take them. It is a wonderful illustration!

(19) "AND WHEN THEY COULD NOT FIND BY WHAT WAY THEY MIGHT BRING HIM IN BECAUSE OF THE MULTITUDE, THEY WENT UPON THE HOUSETOP, AND LET HIM DOWN THROUGH THE TILING WITH HIS COUCH INTO THE MIDST BEFORE JESUS."

The exegesis is:

1. The phrase, *"And when they could not find by what way they might bring him in because of the multitude,"* means that the doorways and windows were blocked by scores of people who could not get in because of the mass of people inside and outside. In other words, every way, at least regarding these routes, was blocked.

2. *"They went upon the housetop,"* was not nearly as difficult then as now.

3. Most, if not all the houses in those

days, at least in that part of the world, had a flat ceiling or roof and could be easily reached by outside stairs.

4. Many of the houses of that time also had a square place on the roof that was open in summer to give light and air to the house, but it was closed with tiles during the rainy season, which this evidently was.

5. *"And let him down through the tiling with his couch,"* means they had to pry up the tiling, which was probably a composition of mortar, tar, ashes, and sand that had been rolled hard and placed over the opening. It would have taken some doing to dislodge this material.

6. *"Into the midst before Jesus,"* seems to imply that this opening had been made almost directly above Jesus. I wonder what Peter thought (as it was his house), and the others, as well, at all this commotion going on immediately above them. Evidently, it did not take them too long to effect an opening and to let down the man, probably with ropes, into the *"midst before Jesus."* What an unorthodox way, but how so very much it was rewarded.

(20) "AND WHEN HE SAW THEIR FAITH, HE SAID UNTO HIM, MAN, YOUR SINS ARE FORGIVEN YOU."

HE SAW THEIR FAITH

The phrase, *"And when He saw their faith,"* is a startling and yet beautiful statement.

"Their" refers to the four men who carried the sick man, dug up the roof, and let him down into the room. Their actions were the visible evidence of their faith. Maybe the paralytic had faith to be healed, but the faith referred to here was that evidenced by the strenuous actions of the men.

When Jesus presently looks at us, what does He see? Does He see faith or doubt? This statement plainly tells us that faith can be seen, meaning that faith always has corresponding action of some sort.

FAITH IN GOD

In the Gospels, one vital fact is made clear in Jesus' words about faith: A lack of trust in the God in whom we have faith closes off life's possibilities. When we fail to believe

(faith is believing and is actually the action part of faith), we do not experience the full range of God's activity (Mat. 21:22). When we trust, we open up our future to a full experience of God's power in and through us (Mat. 17:20; 21:21; Lk. 7:9-10). All things are possible to the one who believes.

FAITH IN MIRACLES

Even though miracles are real and probably occur much more frequently than people realize, still, our faith in Jesus does not come through an observation of miracles. Faith is born as we learn about Jesus, find out what He said, and put our trust in Him. We then go on to deeper faith and active reliance on the power and presence of God. As we trust, our life opens up to all sorts of possibilities. Miracles follow faith. Believing, we experience God at work in our lives.

It is to be ever remembered that even though miracles definitely are the result of faith, faith is seldom, if ever, the result of miracles.

INTELLECT AND THE HEART

In Christian faith, knowing and believing are linked. We respond to testimony about Jesus with our intellects as well as with our hearts. As an example, John's gospel looks at two kinds of testimony. There is the testimony of Jesus' miracles and the testimony of Jesus' words.

At times these two lines of testimony enhance each other. Thus, the Twelve, who are already committed to Jesus, saw the miracle at Cana (Jn. 2:11) and found their belief in Jesus strengthened. It is not unusual to find that many of the observers of Jesus' works were moved to some kind of belief or faith, even though such doesn't have the impact that some are made to believe. The testimony of His miracles was compelling (Jn. 7:31; 11:45; 12:11). Yet, others who saw the same signs chose not to believe, rejecting Jesus against the mountain of evidence of the Lord's works (Jn. 10:38; 14:11).

In John we see that the testimony provided by miracles and signs forced observers to take Jesus seriously, but signs and miracles alone did not bring about saving faith, even as it very seldom ever does.

THE LIMITING OF GOD'S POWER DUE TO LACK OF FAITH

It is possible to have saving faith, as many have in Christ, and yet, limit His power, as many do! When we put our trust in Jesus, the Son of God, we enter a relationship with one who is Lord and whose ability to act in our world is without limitations. And yet, due to false teaching, many simply do not believe God regarding the things that are needed, such as finances, healing, or a host of other things, despite the fact that Jesus repeatedly told us to believe Him for these things (Mat. 21:22; Mk. 11:22-24; Jn. 14:14; 15:7).

The faith walk is the most exciting life that one could ever live. Of course, we speak of faith in God and His promises. Respecting the believer and the Lord, the entire theme of the Bible is relationship. This relationship proclaims and even demands that man look to God for his total sustenance. This speaks of every walk of life, be it spiritual, physical, or economical. In other words, the believer must trust the Lord to lead him in every facet of life, thereby, trusting Him to meet his every need.

PRESUMPTION

However, our faith is to never lead to presumption, which, in effect, takes the role of leadership away from God and places it in the hands of the individual.

An example of presumption is presented in the temptation of Christ by Satan that He throw Himself off the pinnacle of the temple (Lk. 4:9-11), simply because the Scripture said, *"For He shall give His angels charge over You, to keep You in all Your ways. They shall bear You up in their hands, lest You dash Your foot against a stone"* (Ps. 91:11-12). Incidentally, Satan misquoted it, on which we have already commented in Chapter 3. However, Jesus related to Satan that doing such would be presumption simply because it would fall under the order of tempting God, considering that God had not told Him to do this.

In effect, many have done this in other ways, such as denying medical help or refusing to earn a living, claiming that their faith would sustain them, etc. All of this is presumption, has no basis in Scripture, and certainly is not faith in God.

YOUR SINS ARE FORGIVEN

"He said unto Him, Man, your sins are forgiven you," proclaims that the wretched physical condition of the sick man was due to his sinful life. Yet, Jesus treated him with the utmost of kindness.

The word *forgiven,* as used here and as it is commonly used presently, does not adequately convey what has actually transpired.

Whenever we say that we have forgiven someone who has wronged us, by that we mean that any feeling of animosity we may have had has changed to one of renewed friendliness and affection. In other words, we do not hold the wrong done against us against the person anymore, but so far as the act itself is concerned, we cannot do anything about it. It has been done, and it cannot be removed from the one who committed the wrong, at least by man.

However, whenever God forgives someone, He deals with the act of wrong in such a way that the sinner who appropriates the Lord Jesus as Saviour has his sins put away in two ways.

1. They are put away on a judicial basis by the outpoured blood of Christ. He paid the penalty the broken law required and, thus, satisfied divine justice.

2. On the basis of that, God removes the guilt as well as the spiritual penalty of that sin from the believing sinner and bestows a positive righteousness, Jesus Christ Himself, in whom this person stands justified forever. That is what is meant by Bible forgiveness in the case of God and a believing sinner and is referred to as *"justification by faith."*

(21) "AND THE SCRIBES AND THE PHARISEES BEGAN TO REASON, SAYING, WHO IS THIS WHICH SPEAKS BLASPHEMIES? WHO CAN FORGIVE SINS, BUT GOD ALONE?"

The diagram is:

1. The question, *"And the scribes and the Pharisees began to reason, saying, who is this which speaks blasphemies?"* speaks of Jesus in the sense of being a man only and not God also!

2. Were that the case, they would have

been right concerning the blasphemies. Inasmuch, however, as Jesus was and is God manifest in the flesh, they were woefully incorrect.

3. Regarding the question, *"Who can forgive sins but God alone,"* Wuest said, "There was a hostile atmosphere in the room, and our Lord sensed it. What they thought in their hearts was expressed on their faces, in their actions, and in their very personalities."

4. For a dissertation on the claims of Catholic priests claiming to forgive sins, please see our commentary on Mark, Chapter 2.

(22) "BUT WHEN JESUS PERCEIVED THEIR THOUGHTS, HE ANSWERING SAID UNTO THEM, WHAT REASON YE IN YOUR HEARTS?"

The overview is:

1. The phrase, *"But when Jesus perceived their thoughts,"* refers to the fact that even though the spirit in the room was charged with their disbelief and accusations concerning His statement, still, the Holy Spirit revealed to Him what they were actually thinking.

2. The question, *"He answering said unto them, What reason ye* (do you reason) *in your hearts?"* was not meant to ask for information but to call attention to the fact of what He already knew.

3. Doubt and unbelief always begin in the heart, even as faith. Even though the intellect is definitely involved, it is the seat of passions (the heart) that fuels the intellect. One could say the heart, which, incidentally, has nothing to do with that physical organ in this case, is an amalgamation of the spirit and soul of man.

4. To prove what we are saying, faith really does not have its source in the intellect because many, if not all, believe many things they do not fully understand. Actually, the power of knowing (the intellect) is distinguished from the power to feel and to will.

5. So, the thoughts (intellect) of these scribes and Pharisees were expressed after they had already willed in their hearts, erroneously so we might quickly add, that Jesus had blasphemed.

(23) "WHETHER IS EASIER, TO SAY,

YOUR SINS BE FORGIVEN YOU; OR TO SAY, RISE UP AND WALK?"

The pattern is:

1. The idea of the question as posed by Christ is that God alone could do both—forgive and heal! One was just as hard as the other, actually, impossible as far as man is concerned. Even modern doctors with the aid of medical science do not claim to heal. They are only able to dispense particular drugs, etc., in order that the human body may be placed in a position to more quickly heal itself. While particular drugs can kill particular germs, that is the extent of the ability.

3. Actually, in this verse, Jesus linked the physical malady to the moral malady. Man fell morally in the garden of Eden, which caused him to also fall physically. That is the reason medical science, even with all its vaunted technology, can never totally eliminate sickness and disease, at least within its own ability. It is treating the symptoms and not the real cause. By that I speak of original sin, which is the cause of original sickness.

2. Unfortunately, modern man, as always, seems to think he has the answer to man's dilemma, in whatever capacity. It is ironic, but the present failed social programs were looked at only a short time ago as the answer to the ills of humanity. Regrettably, the latest program presently being touted as the great answer will, in just a short time, join the failed so-called solutions of the past. It doesn't matter what that program may be or to what it may be directed. Whatever the problem, Jesus is not only the solution but, actually, the only solution. However, the world, as the scribes and Pharisees of old, does not appreciate Jesus because its deeds are evil (Jn. 3:19).

(24) "BUT THAT YOU MAY KNOW THAT THE SON OF MAN HAS POWER UPON EARTH TO FORGIVE SINS, (HE SAID UNTO THE SICK OF THE PALSY,) I SAY UNTO YOU, ARISE, AND TAKE UP YOUR COUCH, AND GO INTO YOUR HOUSE."

The form is:

1. The phrase, *"But that you may know that the Son of Man has power upon earth to forgive sins,"* is Jesus' answer to the reasoning of the scribes.

2. The word *power* is used in the sense of "delegated authority." It means that God the Father has delegated authority to the Son of Man, who is the Son of God, to forgive sins.

3. Some may argue that He did not have to have that authority from the Father inasmuch as He is deity as well! However, even though it is certainly true that as God, He did not need such authority, still, as man, He did have to have authority from the Father, which was clearly given.

4. *"(He said unto the sick of the palsy,) I say unto you, Arise, and take up your couch, and go into your house,"* instituted a command of such power that it defies proper description. Jesus proved His deity. He did not do so by argument or even by theological hair-splitting, but rather by His action.

4. The man's physical condition was obvious to all, and his spiritual condition was obvious to Christ as well.

5. If the spoken word could bring instant healing to this man, which it did, likewise, the spoken word forgave his sins. As stated, God alone could do either.

(25) "AND IMMEDIATELY HE ROSE UP BEFORE THEM, AND TOOK UP THAT WHEREON HE LAY, AND DEPARTED TO HIS OWN HOUSE, GLORIFYING GOD."

The exposition is:

1. The phrase, *"And immediately he rose up before them,"* records an instant deliverance. As well, upon proper faith in Christ, one's sins are *"immediately"* taken away.

2. *"And took up that whereon he lay,"* refers to him at first being attached to the bed, but now the bed was attached to him. In other words, the bed had previously taken him prisoner, but due to the power of Christ and the spoken word one might say, he now took the bed prisoner.

3. Such is the power of God! It took Moses with his explosive temper and made him the meekest man on earth. It took a hate-filled fanatic by the name of Saul and made him the love-filled apostle by the name of Paul. It took an impulsive Simon Peter and made of him a veritable rock. This is the only power that can really and truly change a human being.

4. *"And departed to his own house, glorifying God,"* speaks of a happy man. He had

come being carried on a bed, and he now returned home, instead, carrying the bed. He had come a sinner and left a saint. He had come sick and left well! No wonder he glorified God, i.e., gave praise unto Him!

(26) "AND THEY WERE ALL AMAZED, AND THEY GLORIFIED GOD, AND WERE FILLED WITH FEAR, SAYING, WE HAVE SEEN STRANGE THINGS TODAY."

The synopsis is:

1. The phrase, *"And they were all amazed,"* means in a sense that they were left speechless, at least as far as the former accusations were concerned. The truth was incontestable and was actually carried out before their very eyes. Consequently, they had no further argument.

2. *"And they glorified God,"* refers to all, even the scribes and Pharisees.

3. *"And were filled with fear,"* proclaims the reason they glorified God. They were fearful to not do so. In other words, what was done (the healing of this man, as well as the forgiveness of sins) was undoubtedly the work of deity.

4. *"Saying, We have seen strange things today,"* referred to the fact that the miracle of healing substantiated the forgiveness of sins. It was strange in the sense that they had never seen or even heard of such. In fact, such had never happened in all of human history, at least in this fashion. While it was certainly true that God had previously forgiven sin and had healed people, He had not done so in the form of the Messiah.

(27) "AND AFTER THESE THINGS HE WENT FORTH, AND SAW A PUBLICAN, NAMED LEVI, SITTING AT THE RECEIPT OF CUSTOM: AND HE SAID UNTO HIM, FOLLOW ME."

THE PUBLICAN

The phrase, *"And after these things He went forth, and saw a publican named Levi,"* speaks of Matthew, who wrote the book that bears his name.

Wuest said, "Levi was sitting at the toll gate on the Great West Road from Damascus to the Mediterranean. This was also the customs office at Capernaum, the landing place for the many ships that traversed the Sea of Galilee or coasted from town to town.

Matthew was a tax collector who collected toll for Herod Antipas. Being in the employ of the Roman government, which bled its subject for taxes, these tax collectors were hated and despised by the Jews, and consequently, classed with traitors and sinners."

Inasmuch as the Galilee district, according to Josephus, was the most prosperous part of Israel at that time, and considering that Capernaum was its principle city, Matthew quite possibly could have been at least one of, if not the most powerful, tax-collectors in all of Israel. These tax-collectors were called *"publicans."*

TAX COLLECTORS

These particular positions as tax collectors were obtained by collaboration with Rome. In order to secure a necessary amount of money to pay for the occupation forces and to add to Caesar's coffers, as well as the local reigning monarch, Herod in this case, districts in every country subjugated by Rome were at times sold to the highest bidder. Even though Rome had several methods, this was one of the most often used.

Rome would place a certain levy on each district, consisting of a base amount, and then open the position for bids. Whoever rendered the highest bid, which had to be as much as the base amount, was awarded the district. They could then charge, up to a certain point, as much as they desired regarding taxes, which occasioned many of these tax collectors growing rich.

The phrase, *"Sitting at the receipt of custom,"* means that Matthew was sitting on an elevated platform or bench, which was the principle feature of the toll office. The individual sitting at this receipt of custom had the power, delegated to him by Rome, to collect taxes in pretty much any fashion he desired. Caravans were stopped on this major road, and taxes were charged somewhat like a toll, with the tax collector having the authority to personally inspect the merchandise, etc.

ISRAEL

Israel thought of herself as the premier nation in the world, even though they were then ruled by Rome. They looked at themselves as God's elite, consequently, looking

NOTES

down on all Gentiles. As a result, one can well imagine the hatred they had for an individual who would sell out to Rome, which the tax collectors did. As far as they were concerned, such a person was beyond the pale of salvation.

In view of the stigma attached to this position, many publicans hired others to take their place, at least as far as the actual collections were concerned. However, it seems that Matthew had little regard for what anyone thought, publicly occupying this position himself.

FOLLOW ME

The phrase, *"And He said unto him, Follow Me,"* pronounces the invitation that Jesus extended to this man.

Considering his occupation, why did Jesus do this?

First of all, this was not the first time Jesus had seen Matthew. As well, it certainly wasn't the first time that Matthew had seen Jesus, with the Masters' fame known to all and probably the topic of most conversations. It is even possible that Jesus had previously had dialogue along with some association with Matthew.

Jesus extended this invitation to Matthew because the Holy Spirit told Him to. He looked beyond Matthew's occupation, even deep down into his heart. He, no doubt, saw that this man was turned off by the present religious scene of hypocrisy and self-righteousness. However, He also knew that there was a hunger in Matthew's heart for a deep walk with God, despite his occupation.

Actually, there was nothing spiritually wrong with the position that Matthew now held, that is, if he treated people fairly, which he probably did. The real wrong was in the attitude of the religious leaders of Israel, who, in their self-exalted positions, felt free to condemn others such as Matthew. They would also condemn Christ!

The invitation extended to this tax collector was more than a command. When Jesus issued the summons, it was like a king, sovereign in his demands, summoning one to him. Matthew, no doubt, recognized this authority in Jesus' voice and, as well, was moved upon greatly by the Holy Spirit.

Also, the words, *"Follow Me,"* would have probably been better translated, *"Follow with Me."* Jesus welcomed him to a participation in His companionship. As well, it was not in Indian-file nature, with one following another, but a side-by-side walk down the same road. Also, this same type of invitation is given, in essence, to every believer.

(28) "AND HE LEFT ALL, ROSE UP, AND FOLLOWED HIM."

The form is:

1. Mackintosh said, "The holiness of God's dwelling-place, and the ground of His association with His people, could never be regulated by the standard of man's conscience, no matter how high the standard might be."

2. "There are many things which man's conscience would pass over—many things which might escape man's cognizance—many things which his heart might deem alright, which God could not tolerate;"

3. "Which, as a consequence, would interfere with man's approach to, his worship of, and his relationship with, God."

HE LEFT ALL

The phrase, *"And he left all,"* means that he was leaving everything behind, including his tax collector's position with all of its luxury, etc., and was willing to undergo any privation and want respecting his new-found life in Christ. That which Matthew did is required of all believers.

Unfortunately, the modern invitation is quite different than that extended by Christ. The modern method is to promise all types of rewards and riches in this present life; however, such is not true Christianity.

While it is true that the Lord definitely blesses people, and the reward of eternal life is held out to all, still, it is demanded that when one follows Christ, his own personal wants and ambitions must be laid aside in favor of that which is desired by Christ.

It is not my will, but Your will be done (Mat. 6:10). To be sure, at times this life lived for Christ may include persecution and even privation; however, whatever the Lord allows in one's life is done for purpose and reason. Paul said that he had, *"Learned, in whatsoever state I am, therewith to be content."*

He also said, *"I know both how to be*

abased, and I know how to abound."

He then said, *"I can do all things through Christ who strengthens me,"* which meant he could abound or suffer need, whichever was the case (Phil. 4:11-13).

When Paul was asked to produce his credentials, he said, *"Are they ministers of Christ? (I speak as a fool) I am more; in labours more abundant, in stripes above measure, in prisons more frequent, in deaths oft.*

"Of the Jews five times received I forty stripes save one.

"Thrice was I beaten with rods, once was I stoned, thrice I suffered shipwreck, a night and a day I have been in the deep" (II Cor. 11:23-25).

MATTHEW ROSE UP AND FOLLOWED JESUS

In the following verses, Paul continued to speak of other hardships, etc. While the Lord may not ask all of this of all believers, He definitely does ask some of all believers.

As stated, this is a far cry from the modern invitation, but yet, it is the biblical way and is actually that which God demands of all.

So, how in the world could the Lord get people to follow Him, even as He did Matthew, considering what it would involve?

There is a hunger in every heart that can only be supplied by the Lord. To satisfy that hunger, some are willing to undergo anything, even leaving all, as Matthew. To be sure, even as Matthew, considering what one receives in Christ, no price is too high to pay.

The phrase, *"Rose up, and followed Him,"* was the greatest decision Matthew ever made, and, as well, it is the greatest decision anyone could ever make.

In this quest for eternal life, there is no alternative. Jesus is the only answer. As well, when Jesus is made Lord of one's life, no other person or philosophy is needed. He is all in all!

(29) "AND LEVI MADE HIM A GREAT FEAST IN HIS OWN HOUSE: AND THERE WAS A GREAT COMPANY OF PUBLICANS AND OF OTHERS WHO SAT DOWN WITH THEM."

The exegesis is:

1. The phrase, *"And Levi made Him a*

great feast in his own house," speaks of the fact that Matthew was a person of consideration and position.

2. *"And there was a great company of publicans and of others who sat down with them,"* spoke of a group of people who were probably not even allowed in the synagogues. Evidently, most all had heard about the decision of Matthew to leave the tax collecting business and to wholly follow Jesus. Due to the fact that Jesus' fame was spread abroad everywhere, it seems that Matthew's fellow tax collectors were happy for him.

3. There is no indication that anyone of this group of individuals felt that Matthew was making a mistake. As well, these people had drawn a kind word from Jesus, which they had not gotten from any religious leaders.

(30) "BUT THEIR SCRIBES AND PHARISEES MURMURED AGAINST HIS DISCIPLES, SAYING, WHY DO YOU EAT AND DRINK WITH PUBLICANS AND SINNERS?"

SCRIBES AND PHARISEES

The phrase, *"But their scribes and Pharisees murmured against His disciples,"* proclaimed the religious leaders of the area being very much opposed to what Jesus was doing. In their self-righteousness, they would not have even remotely considered having a meal with any of these people, much less treating them in a friendly fashion. They felt they had to constantly show their disapproval.

As well, self-righteousness pretty much makes up its own definition of sin. They looked at themselves as very holy and the tax collectors as the wickedest of the wicked.

While it was certainly true that some of these tax collectors were, no doubt, of that stripe, the tax collecting had nothing to do with it.

Despite the impeccable reputations had by the scribes and Pharisees, and the very bad reputations had by the publicans, which is what people thought, the Lord saw it totally differently.

Jesus never chose any of the scribes or Pharisees to be His disciples because of the obvious reasons. They really did not

know the Lord, and because of their acute self-righteousness, their hearts could not be changed. The ones He did choose were chosen not so much for what they were but because of what He knew He could make of them because of a yielded heart.

THOSE WHOM GOD CHOOSES

I am afraid that the modern church too often sees as Israel of old instead of as God sees. It is doubtful that a single religious leader in Israel would have even remotely thought of choosing people such as Matthew and others. Actually, as is obvious, such was abhorrent to them. And yet, Jesus chose them!

It has little changed from then until now. Those whom God chooses, the church seldom does. Conversely, those whom the church chooses, God seldom does!

The question, *"Saying, Why do you eat and drink with publicans and sinners?"* was asked because such was considered to be a terrible sin. However, these were *"sins"* constituted by the scribes and Pharisees and not God. Religious people consider it a great sin for someone not to obey religious, man-made rules, but that's not what God says! He says, *"You shall worship the Lord your God, and Him only shall you serve"* (Mat. 4:10).

(31) "AND JESUS ANSWERING SAID UNTO THEM, THEY WHO ARE WHOLE NEED NOT A PHYSICIAN; BUT THEY WHO ARE SICK."

BUT THEY WHO ARE SICK

The phrase, *"And Jesus answering said unto them,"* is the beginning of the confrontation, which will only exacerbate during the entirety of the ministry of Christ. Despite the wisdom of His answers, the religious leadership of Israel never seemed to grasp the source, which was God. This proclaims the fact, as we have stated, that doubt and unbelief do not actually begin with the intellect but, basically, in the heart. Were it intellect alone, they would have instantly seen the sheer intelligence of His answers.

The phrase, *"They who are whole need not a physician; but they who are sick,"* was one of the favorite themes of the early church. It went beyond the self-righteousness of a religious elite and included the moral waifs and strays, which is actually the true target of Christianity. I will give you an idea of what I speak.

AN EXAMPLE

A lovely young lady and her young son, who were the victims of a divorce, began attending Family Worship Center sometime back. She shared not in the blame, even according to the husband, I am told.

At any rate, the pastor of another church she was attending in Baton Rouge called her in after the divorce and told her that she might be happier elsewhere. She asked what she had done inasmuch as none of this was her fault, even as the pastor knew, for he was well aware of the entire situation.

He actually gave her no reason, I am told, but continued to insist that she go elsewhere to church.

I know that particular pastor, and I felt the lady was relating to me the situation exactly as it happened.

Of course, she was welcome to attend Family Worship Center and be a part of our church congregation, where she continues unto this day. Rather than feeling as if we are doing her a favor, we feel that she is a great blessing to this church.

If the church is not the haven for those in trouble, then what is?

Jesus was not at the feast given by Matthew and surrounded by publicans and sinners because He enjoyed that kind of company, for He did not. There was probably sin all about Him, and His righteous, sensitive soul shrank back from it; however, He was there to reach their souls for salvation.

Church is not a perfect place and never will be as long as human beings inhabit it. As well, being kind and gracious to someone doesn't mean that one is condoning sin. Actually, the greatest problem in the church today and, in fact, always has been, is not the sins of the flesh, as despicable as they may be, but rather the sin of self-righteousness, as is evidenced here by the scribes and Pharisees.

The association with publicans and sinners was not the Pharisees' problem, but

NOTES

rather their black hearts, which were more wicked in the sight of God even than the ones they were condemning. They crucified Christ, so how wicked is that?

(32) "I CAME NOT TO CALL THE RIGHTEOUS, BUT SINNERS TO REPENTANCE."

THE MISSION OF CHRIST

The Pharisees and scribes were denying Jesus the very reason for which He came. While it was certainly true that some few people in Israel were then living for God because of His grace, and could be referred to as righteous, still, most did not come under that banner. Even more particularly, very few Gentiles the world over knew God; consequently, the mission of Christ was twofold:

1. TO BRING THE GOSPEL TO ISRAEL

Even though most in Israel had come to believe that because they were Israelites, therefore, sons and daughters of Abraham, this constituted their salvation.

In other words, it was a nationalistic salvation. John the Baptist addressed himself to that by saying, *"Begin not to say within yourselves, We have Abraham to our father: for I say unto you, That God is able of these stones to raise up children unto Abraham"* (Lk. 3:8). So, the awful truth was that most of Israel, despite their great religiosity, was, in fact, lost! They were lost primarily because of their religious leaders who led them astray (Mat. 9:36). So, He came that they may hear the true gospel and, thereby, be saved.

2. THE GOSPEL FOR THE ENTIRETY OF THE WORLD

What Jesus did in His first advent opened up the gospel not only to Israel, which they would not accept, but to the entirety of the world, i.e., Gentiles (Jn. 3:16).

Israel had pretty much closed off the gospel to Gentiles. They would not accept it themselves, and they tried to shut the door to the balance of the world. In fact, Gentiles were thought of as *"dogs."* Consequently, their self-righteousness permeated everything, especially their extremely negative attitude toward all others not exactly of their stripe. Actually, this is what self-righteousness does!

If a Gentile came in, which some did, they were forced to submit not only to the law of Moses but to a plethora of man-made laws, as well. Consequently, Jesus said of them, *"Woe unto you, scribes and Pharisees, hypocrites! for you compass sea and land to make one proselyte, and when he is made, you make him twofold more the child of hell than yourselves"* (Mat. 23:15).

So, Jesus came not only to Israel, but that these sinners (Gentiles) may be brought to repentance.

The beginning of the fulfillment of this took place with Peter's visit to the household of Cornelius (Acts, Chpt. 10), and then was greatly enlarged and carried out by the ministry of the apostle Paul.

As I have been addressing myself to the publicans and the Pharisees, and the objection of the latter to the former, I think it would be proper to include a statement regarding *"reputation"* and *"character."* Over Israel at that time, the Pharisees had an impeccable reputation, while the publicans had the very opposite. However, as we have alluded, let's look at this as God sees it.

WHAT IS THE DIFFERENCE BETWEEN REPUTATION AND CHARACTER?

Reputation is what people think you are, and character is what God knows you are.

WHAT IS REPUTATION?

Webster says that reputation is the "overall quality or character as seen or judged by people in general."

It was said of Jesus, *"But made Himself of no reputation, and took upon Him the form of a servant, and was made in the likeness of men"* (Phil. 2:7).

As all Bible students know, the above passage refers, as stated, to Christ. Does it mean that Jesus did not have a good reputation?

Of course, the statement actually refers to what is called "the kenosis of Christ," which means the self-emptying of Christ when He, as God, became man. In other words, it refers to the incarnation.

In doing that, Jesus divested Himself of the glory that He had with the Father and took upon Himself the form of man. The

difference between what He had been (God), with all of the attendant glory, and now what He became (although continuing to be God but minus the glory) is staggering indeed! Actually, there is no way the mind of man can comprehend what He gave up to redeem humanity.

As creature, we are very limited in our knowledge regarding the glory of the Creator. Therefore, our comprehension is limited to say the least!

Yet, at the same time, according to Isaiah, Chapter 53, Jesus had no reputation at all among His own people. Of course, the fault was not His but theirs.

The religious leaders of Israel did all they could to destroy His reputation, whether with lies, half-truths, or outright fabrications.

WHAT THEY SAID OF HIM

First of all, Jesus wore the stigma of His virgin birth all of His life. In other words, the religious leaders of Israel simply did not believe it, instead, spreading the story that He was born of fornication (Jn. 8:41). Actually, the accusations they made in this regard are too sordid for me even to repeat here. Never mind that they were totally untrue, He lived with this stigma or reputation.

As well, He was a peasant and not of the aristocracy; therefore, this class distinction placed Him in a category lower than many others in Israel, especially the religious elite. That is the reason they asked, *"From where has this man these things? and what wisdom is this which is given unto Him, that even such mighty works are wrought by His hands?"*

They then went on to say, *"Is not this the carpenter, the Son of Mary?"* The Scripture then says, *"And they were offended at Him"* (Mk. 6:2-3).

So, Jesus did not have a good reputation at all among the religious leaders of Israel, who continually tried to poison the people's minds against Christ, even though in truth and in fact, His life was impeccably perfect.

This shows us that a person can have a bad reputation and, at the same time, have an excellent character, which, in fact, characterized Christ. Sometimes reputation equals character, but most of the time, it doesn't.

OTHER THAN CHRIST

Of course, Christ was perfect whereas no other human being can lay claim to this quality. In other words, all others fall short.

In the eyes of God, and only His eyes matter, no human being has a good reputation. What He knows about us is not hearsay, rumor, prejudice, or bias, but rather the knowledge of God, which is omniscient, that is, all-knowing.

Consequently, He had pronounced all as falling short of the glory of God (Rom. 3:23). Then He said, *There is none righteous, no, not one*" (Rom. 3:10), which referred to righteousness within themselves and not righteousness that God gives. He then went on to list what man is, which is not at all a pretty picture (Rom. 3:10-18).

Thankfully, the Lord can change an individual, wash away all sin, and make him a new creation in Christ Jesus (II Cor. 5:17).

REPUTATION ACCORDING TO THE WORLD

The world looks at reputation in an entirely different manner than God looks at it.

The world sets standards varying according to culture and says they define a good reputation. However, regardless of such standards, the Lord will not accept them.

In the eyes of the world, education, and especially money, go a long way toward affording a good reputation for an individual, irrespective of what his character may be. In this context, it is alright to drink alcoholic beverages, but just don't overdo it. It is alright to gamble, but just don't overdo it. It is alright to lie, providing you don't get caught in it. Actually, in the reputation afforded by the world, almost anything goes, providing one does not get caught or overdo it. So, as far as the world is concerned, it is not so much what is done, but the stupidity of being caught in the act or taking to extreme that which is important. This would pertain to stealing, dishonesty, immorality, or any other devious act.

In other words, the world has a code of conduct by which it operates, and if that code is upheld, the individual is labeled as one with a good reputation.

REPUTATION IN THE CHURCH

Unfortunately, the church judges reputation pretty much as the world does.

For the most part, most religious denominations take the position that they are not too concerned with what their preachers do unless they get caught. So, the code of the church, at least regarding reputation, is pretty much the same as the world's. This is sad but, regrettably, true!

Unfortunately, the church is very political. It should not be, but it is! As a result, it conducts its business in a political sense instead of the spiritual. In other words, it is very much concerned about its reputation. Therefore, anything that tends to bring any type of reproach on its reputation is looked at with great displeasure. In fact, very little is done to carry forth the biblical admonition regarding restoration, which is supposed to be the very foundation of the church.

If wrongdoing is committed and then repented of and put away, according to the Bible, the matter is to be dropped there. However, if the church is embarrassed in any way, the matter, regrettably, is not dropped there. The Word of God is set aside in favor of what makes the church look good in the eyes of the world.

At that stage, far too often the church engages in character assassination, which means slandering a person with the intention of destroying public confidence in him or her. In other words, it tries to further destroy his or her reputation.

So, even in the church, reputation means what people think of the individual, whether it is true or not.

WHAT IS CHARACTER?

Character, as stated, is what a person really is, whether good or bad. It is their nature, which can be judged by two things alone, with Jesus saying them very succinctly:

"And you shall love the Lord your God with all your heart, and with all your soul, and with all your mind, and with all your strength: this is the first commandment.

"And the second is like, namely this, You shall love your neighbour as yourself" (Mk. 12:30-31).

The love of God and one's fellowman, if accomplished, is character. To be sure, only the Lord can develop such character. Man is helpless to bring about love for God on his own or to love his neighbor.

A PERFECT CHARACTER

Of course, perfection is only in Christ. As stated, no human being, at least within himself, or even those close to God, is perfect. In fact, every single believer has had to ask the Lord for forgiveness time and time again. Actually, such is so predominant within our lives that the plea for forgiveness is included in what we refer to as the Lord's Prayer (Mat. 6:9-13).

This does not mean that a Christian habitually sins, but it does mean that there are flaws, faults, and failures of one kind or the other, even in the best of believers, which require the mercy and grace of God.

As one Baptist preacher said, and rightly so, "Without the constant intercession of Christ, we wouldn't last an hour." He is right!

As well, it is not right for a fellow believer, or anyone else, to look at a roll of film, so to speak, of a person's life and judge him on only a few bad frames taken out of the whole. Even though David did something wrong, as serious and wicked as the act was that he committed, it was not what David truly was!

Abraham went down into Egypt and lied about his wife, greatly endangering the great plan of God for the redemption of humanity. That was a grievous sin, but that's not what Abraham truly was!

Simon Peter denied the Lord, which was a grievous sin, but that's not what Peter truly was!

The list is endless. However, even though individuals have different viewpoints concerning the reputation of these people, these acts did not portray their true character. Their true character was excellent because the Lord made it so.

THE CHURCH AND CHARACTER

It is the business of the church, ideally speaking, to see things as the Lord sees them. In other words, the church is to look through spiritual eyes, not carnal eyes.

When God does something, such as

justification by faith, it is irrevocably done. For the church not to recognize God's plan of redemption is a grievous sin indeed, even greater than what was done by the individual it has censured, whoever and whatever that may have been. Everything must be looked at scripturally, or not at all.

IN SUMMARY

Reputation, as stated, is what people think of someone, whether true or not. Character is what a person really is and what God knows about the individual. Reputation may be identical to character, as stated, but not necessarily so. It is possible for an individual to have an excellent character and a sorry reputation, or a sorry character and an excellent reputation.

Concerning the reputation of another, the question should be asked by every believer, "Have I hurt that person's reputation or helped it?"

There is nothing that believers can do about another's character except pray for him. Only God can make character; however, there is much that believers can do relative to one's reputation that will either help or hurt.

Too many Christians engage in whispering, which means to carry out accusation against others, whether true or false, blasting their reputation by clandestine gossip (Rom. 1:29). To be sure, this hurts their reputation, but it does not hurt their character. Whatever their true character is remains the same irrespective of what others say about them.

JUDGING!

Paul said, *"Speak evil of no man,"* which speaks of their reputation (Titus 3:2).

Jesus said, *"Judge not, that you be not judged,"* which speaks of judging one's motives, which has to do with one's reputation (Mat. 7:1).

James said, *"There is one Lawgiver, who is able to save and to destroy: who are you who judges another?"* (James 4:12).

In other words, James is saying that God is the only one who is qualified to judge another, and no human being can claim such qualification.

NOTES

Again, this has to do with affecting one's reputation, for the word *judging*, in this instance, means to "sentence, censure, or punish." If we ignore the law of God and attempt to judge others in this fashion, at the same time, we will probably speak evil of them.

In doing so, their reputation is hurt or hindered. That will not really hurt them, but it will hurt the influence they could have. Even though reputation is important, the most important thing by far is one's character. As stated, only God can make a suitable character.

Concerning reputation, a great British poet said it well:

"I am sore wounded but not slain,
"I will lay me down and bleed a while,
"And then rise up to fight again."

(33) "AND THEY SAID UNTO HIM, WHY DO THE DISCIPLES OF JOHN FAST OFTEN, AND MAKE PRAYERS, AND LIKEWISE THE DISCIPLES OF THE PHARISEES; BUT YOURS EAT AND DRINK?"

"And they said unto Him, Why do the disciples of John fast often, and make prayers, and likewise the disciples of the Pharisees," presents the disciples of John joining forces with the Pharisees.

Evidently, John's disciples had not heard their leader right when they sided with the Pharisees. He had called the Pharisees a brood of vipers; however, his disciples here joined with the Pharisees in criticizing Jesus.

Why would John's disciples have done this?

The reasons are probably varied and many. John practiced a stern asceticism, which meant a separation of any and all things that pertained to luxury, comfort, etc. He undoubtedly required the same of his followers, that they should imitate his example.

The Holy Spirit desired this of John for purpose and reason. As his message was to be one of repentance, his life was to be lived in the same manner because this was what God was demanding of Israel in preparation for the Messiah, who was Jesus.

MORE ABUNDANT LIFE

Once Jesus was introduced, the Lord's way of life, His presence at feastings and merry-makings, His consorting with publicans, even His choice of one of them as His disciple and friend, no doubt, surprised and disturbed not a few of the followers of John (Spence). However, they were confusing some things:

First of all, John's lifestyle, as demanded by the Holy Spirit, had nothing to do with his salvation, or anyone else for that matter. It was merely to serve as a symbol, which it did!

Likewise, Jesus eating with the publicans and living a lifestyle totally opposite of John was, as well, ordained by the Holy Spirit and had nothing to do with one's salvation. It was meant to serve as a symbol, which it did.

As the symbol of John's life was to serve as one of repentance, the symbol of Jesus' lifestyle was to serve as one of more abundant life, which is the fruit of repentance. That is the reason Jesus said, *"For John came neither eating nor drinking, and they say, He has a devil* (demon).

"The Son of Man came eating and drinking, and they say, Behold a man gluttonous, and a winebibber, a friend of publicans and sinners. But wisdom is justified of her children" (Mat. 11:18-19).

This means that both ways, John's and that of Jesus, were right, and for the reasons stated.

The continuing of the question, *"But yours eat and drink?"* referred to what the disciples of Jesus were doing in comparison to the disciples of John. That reason is given by Jesus in the next verse.

(34) "AND HE SAID UNTO THEM, CAN YOU MAKE THE CHILDREN OF THE BRIDECHAMBER FAST, WHILE THE BRIDEGROOM IS WITH THEM?"

The overview is:

1. The object of all that is done by the believer, whether it be fasting or feasting, is Jesus. He alone is the focal point of all. Consequently, the fasting done previously under the old covenant was in relationship to His coming, which speaks of the first advent, and, as is obvious, because He was not with them at that time.

2. Actually, the law of Moses only

appointed one fast day a year—that on the solemn Day of Atonement (Lev. 16:29; Num. 29:7).

3. After the exile, the one fast was increased to four a year, but the prophets gave no sanction to the added ritual (Zech. 7:1-12; 8:19), meaning that it was not something instituted by the Lord, but it was man-devised.

4. By the time of Jesus, the Pharisees had increased the fasting to two days a week—Mondays and Fridays. It is evident that the Lord Himself never observed or even approved of these fasts of the Pharisee sect. Such was the product of self-righteousness (Spence).

5. Now that Jesus has come (speaking of the first advent), fasting should be done as a request or petition for His soon second coming.

(35) "BUT THE DAYS WILL COME, WHEN THE BRIDEGROOM SHALL BE TAKEN AWAY FROM THEM, AND THEN SHALL THEY FAST IN THOSE DAYS."

The overview is:

1. Christ was made sin for us *"that we might be made the righteousness of God in Him"* (II Cor. 5:21).

2. He took our position with all its consequences in order that we might get His position with all its consequences.

3. He was treated as sin (a sin offering) upon the Cross that we might be treated as righteousness in the presence of infinite holiness.

4. Jesus had to pass through three hours of darkness while on the Cross that we might walk in everlasting light.

THE CHURCH AGE

The phrase, *"But the days will come, when the bridegroom shall be taken away from them,"* took place about three years later. The structure of the sentence proclaims several things:

• Jesus would be rejected.

• The rejection would be violent, resulting in His crucifixion.

• As a result, God would take His Son away from Israel, with them basically wandering as outcasts for nearly 2,000 years now.

NOTES

The phrase, *"And then shall they fast in those days,"* refers to the period of time of now nearly 2,000 years called the *"church age,"* and does not refer to Israel at all. In other words, the fasting will be done by those in the church, made up mostly of Gentiles.

Also, no rules for fasting are laid down, with the spirit of it being that it must ever proceed from the impulse of a sorrow-stricken heart, and must be no penance or duty imposed by authority. Least of all must it be regarded as pleasing in the eyes of the Almighty or, in any sense, a substitute for the practice of the higher virtues really loved of God—justice, mercy, and truth.

WHEN JESUS COMES BACK

Consequently, as the fasting phrase bears out, even though the purpose of fasting by the modern believer may be for many reasons, the primary reason should be that Jesus is not now here, and the world situation will not be improved at all until He is here. Jesus is the key to everything, be it prosperity, cessation of war, social justice, or above all, spiritual blessings. Even though believers since the day of the early church have had an earnest, or down payment, of the kingdom of God, mostly summed up in the spiritual part, still, that points to what actually is coming when Jesus personally reigns from Jerusalem over the entirety of the world. Our fasting is, in part, that this will happen soon.

When He comes back, as He certainly shall, joy, prosperity, and feasting will then be the order of the entirety of the world, as evidenced by the feast at the home of Matthew.

Because of not properly interpreting the Word of God, the disciples of John, at least in this instance, joined hands with the Pharisees, who hated Christ. Thankfully, the evidence is that they did not remain in this posture for long.

This should be a lesson to all: That an improper interpretation of the Word of God can result in one joining hands with the enemies of God. I think it should be obvious that none are immune; consequently, consecration to the Word is demanded of all.

(36) "AND HE SPOKE ALSO A PARABLE UNTO THEM; NO MAN PUTS A PIECE OF A NEW GARMENT UPON AN OLD; IF OTHERWISE, THEN BOTH THE NEW MAKES A RENT, AND THE PIECE THAT WAS TAKEN OUT OF THE NEW AGREES NOT WITH THE OLD."

The form is:

1. "The full assurance of sin put away ministers, not to a spirit of self-confidence, but to a spirit of praise, thankfulness, and worship."

2. "It produces, not a spirit of self-complacency, but of Christ-complacency, which blessed be God, is the spirit which shall characterize the redeemed throughout eternity."

3. "It does not lead one to think little of sin, but to think much of the grace which has perfectly pardoned it, and of the blood which has perfectly canceled it."

(The three points are by C.H. Mackintosh).

THE PARABLE

The phrase, *"And He spoke also a parable unto them,"* presents a common way in that time to impart information or instruction.

"No man puts a piece of a new garment upon an old," was the introduction of the new covenant, which would take the place of the old. Jesus was very discretely telling His audience that He was the fulfillment of the old, and, as well, He was going to introduce something new.

However, it does not mean that the old was bad, but only that it had served its purpose. It was now worn and torn with use, with much of the use being error, as evidenced by the Pharisees.

So, He had not come to patch the old, but rather to introduce the new.

THE NEW COVENANT

The phrase, *"If otherwise, then both the new* (new covenant) *makes a rent, and the piece that was taken out of the new agrees not with the old,"* proclaims the fallacy of attempting to foster off the old (the old covenant) any longer upon the people, especially considering that Jesus was the fulfillment, and consequently, its task was done and completed.

As well, there is no way the new would

NOTES

agree with the old simply because the new was a brand-new concept based upon a finished work, whereas the old only pointed to such. The description was very apt, irrespective of whether the people understood it or not.

Even despite the fact of Jesus telling His disciples these things, which seemed to be so easy to understand, still, the old was not given up easily. Some in the early church, despite these very words of Christ, attempted to do exactly what He said not to do—put a piece of new garment upon an old. Along with the grace of God, which was part and parcel of the new covenant, some attempted to add the old law as well! This is what the first council at Jerusalem was all about, as recorded in Acts, Chapter 15.

As well, this is what Paul was speaking of when he said, *"Stand fast therefore in the liberty wherewith Christ has made us free, and be not entangled again with the yoke of bondage"* (Gal. 5:1).

He was speaking of attempting to mix the old and new covenants. The new agrees not with the old.

THE MODERN HEBRAIC MOVEMENT

In the recent past, the church has seen an increase in this attempt of trying to mix the old and new covenants. It cannot scripturally or spiritually be done.

I speak of preachers advocating that people purchase prayer shawls, which are supposed to help them get through to the Lord better and bring some type of blessing. To be factual, there was no prayer shawl under the old covenant, with that being something that men devised. In other words, it didn't come from God.

We must understand that Jesus totally and completely fulfilled the entirety of the old covenant, meaning that it's not binding on modern believers. The old law is not acceptable in any capacity. In fact, Paul plainly said that if we try to institute the law in any fashion, then we are placing ourselves *"under the curse"* (Gal. 3:10).

He also referred to it as *"another gospel."* He said:

"I marvel that you are so soon removed from Him (the Holy Spirit) *who called you into the grace of Christ* (made possible by

the Cross) *unto another gospel* (anything which doesn't have the Cross as its object of faith)" (Gal. 1:6).

The apostle continued by saying, *"For by the works of the law shall no flesh be justified"* (Gal. 2:16).

(37) "AND NO MAN PUTS NEW WINE INTO OLD BOTTLES; ELSE THE NEW WINE WILL BURST THE BOTTLES, AND BE SPILLED, AND THE BOTTLES SHALL PERISH.

(38) "BUT NEW WINE MUST BE PUT INTO NEW BOTTLES; AND BOTH ARE PRESERVED."

The exposition is:

1. "It is impossible that anyone can gaze on the Cross—can see the place where Christ died—can meditate upon the sufferings which He endured—can ponder on those three terrible hours of darkness, and at the same time think lightly of sin.

2. "When all these things are entered into, and the power of the Holy Spirit, there are two results which must follow, namely an abhorrence of sin in all its forms, and a genuine love for Christ, His people, and His cause" (Mackintosh).

NEW WINE

The phrase, *"And no man puts new wine into old bottles* (old wineskins)," is the same thing said in another way. They were illustrations, incidentally, which His hearers readily understood, whether they understood the meaning or not, although they should have!

The *"bottles"* spoken of here would have probably been better translated *"skins."*

There was no such thing as glass in those days, for the technology had not yet been devised; consequently, liquid was held in what one may refer to as bottles made of lambskins or vessels made of clay.

"Else the new wine will burst the bottles (wineskins), *and be spilled, and the bottles shall perish,"* referred to new wine being placed into old skins, which were cracked and parched. If the wine (grape juice) was not drunk immediately, fermentation would set up, resulting in the old skins bursting. As stated, it was symbolism readily understood by all Jews.

NEW WINESKINS

The phrase, *"But new wine must be put into new bottles* (new wineskins)," referred to the new covenant not being attached to the old covenant at all.

Consequently, as Spence said, "His doctrine must be entrusted to no Rabbi of Israel, fettered by a thousand precedents, hampered by countless prejudices, but to simple un-prejudiced men, who would receive His teaching, and then pass it on pure and unadulterated to other simple, truthful souls—men earnest, loyal, devoted, like His fisher-friends of Gennesaret, or His publican-followers of Capernaum."

Jesus would later say, *"I thank you, O Father, Lord of heaven and earth, that You have hid these things from the wise and prudent, and have revealed them unto babes"* (Lk. 10:21).

"And both are preserved," means that the church will be preserved if this is done, but not be preserved if not done.

As well, it means that any believer who attempts to live by law, in other words, attempts to please God by one's own strength and efforts, will find that he is not preserved, i.e., kept. He must live by the grace of God, which refers to enabling grace, giving one the liberty to live a holy life.

Unfortunately, despite the experience of thousands of years, many in the modern church are still attempting to patch up the old garments or put new wine into old bottles. In that, there is no preservation, only loss! And yet, I suspect that every single believer has fallen into this trap at one time or the other.

(39) "NO MAN ALSO HAVING DRUNK OLD WINE STRAIGHTWAY DESIRES NEW: FOR HE SAYS, THE OLD IS BETTER."

The structure is:

1. What did Jesus mean by this?

2. He meant that man prefers the old wine of ordinances, rules, regulations, and laws rather than the new wine of the gospel. Why?

3. Due to the fall, there is something in man that desires to somehow effect his own salvation, irrespective of the fact that it cannot be done. Actually, the world and the

church are full of it. Men attempt to effect a righteousness with good works. The Catholic Church is made up entirely of this fallacy, with many Protestants following suit.

4. Somehow it makes one feel good to know that one has done good things, and somehow that is equated with salvation, but never by God.

5. It is very difficult for man, especially religious man, to admit that all the good things he has done, or all the bad things he has not done, in no way effects his salvation, and that the good man must throw himself at the feet of Jesus and ask for grace the same as the bad man. That doesn't sit well with self-righteousness.

6. Many would blanch at the idea that Mother Teresa, for all her good works, had to trust Jesus alone for salvation, with all these good works, even as noble as they might have been, playing no part at all, just the same as the vilest of the vile. However, that is exactly the way it is and the way it must be. It's called *"justification by faith,"* which means that it's not justification by works of any nature.

"Is there a heart that is waiting,
"Longing for pardon today?
"Hear the glad message we bring you,
"Jesus is passing this way."

"Coming in love and in mercy,
"Quickly now unto Him go;
"Open your heart to receive Him,
"Pardon and peace He'll bestow."

"Listen, the Spirit is calling,
"Jesus will freely forgive,
"Why not this moment accept Him?
"Trust in God's mercy and live."

"He is so tender and loving,
"He is so near you today;
"Open your heart to receive Him,
"While He is passing this way."

CHAPTER 6

(1) "AND IT CAME TO PASS ON THE SECOND SABBATH AFTER THE FIRST, THAT HE WENT THROUGH THE CORN

NOTES

FIELDS; AND HIS DISCIPLES PLUCKED THE EARS OF CORN, AND DID EAT, RUBBING THEM IN THEIR HANDS."

THE SABBATH

The phrase, *"And it came to pass on the second Sabbath after the first,"* refers to the regular Saturday Sabbath that followed the special Sabbath, which began the feast regardless of what day of the week it fell on.

Every Saturday was the Sabbath, which actually began at sundown on Friday. However, the Jews also had other Sabbaths, which fell on other days of the week, depending on what day a special feast began, such as the Passover, etc.

"That He went through the corn fields," probably referred to wheat and not Indian corn as we know it, for that did not then exist in that part of the world (Jn. 12:24). It was probably the time of the year of the Feast of Pentecost, which possibly referred to the first Sabbath.

The seven major feasts came at the time of the harvest.

• The three Feasts of Unleavened Bread, Passover, and Firstfruits all came together during the first part of April and were at the time of the barley harvest.

• Fifty days after Passover was the Feast of Pentecost, which was at the time of the wheat harvest.

• The three Feasts of Trumpets, Atonement, and Tabernacles came during October and were at the time of the fruit harvest.

"And His disciples plucked the ears of corn, and did eat, rubbing them in their hands," pertained to them pulling stalks of wheat and rubbing the pods with the grains briskly back and forth in their hands, which shed the husks. They would then eat it raw, which was quite common at that time. The idea was that as they were walking through the wheat field, they would pluck the stalks or heads of grain, etc.

Some have attempted to construe this as poverty on their part; however, this is incorrect, at least in the case of several of them who had been successful businessmen, such as Peter, Andrew, James, John, and Matthew.

(2) "AND CERTAIN OF THE PHARISEES SAID UNTO THEM, WHY DO YOU

THAT WHICH IS NOT LAWFUL TO DO ON THE SABBATH DAYS?"

The overview is:

1. The phrase, *"And certain of the Pharisees said unto them,"* means from the Greek text that the Pharisees kept prodding Jesus and the disciples by asking the question over and over again until Jesus finally responded. Knowing that His answer would of necessity be confrontational, it seems that He attempted to avoid the discussion but was unable to do so due to their persistence.

2. *"Why do you that which is not lawful to do on the Sabbath days?"* was unlawful only in their eyes and not God's. There was actually nothing in the law of Moses restricting this.

3. Around the original Sabbath law of Moses, 39 prohibitions had been laid down in the oral law. Around these 39, a vast number of smaller rules had grouped themselves, which were all devised by man and not God. However, they had come to equate their own man-made rules with those originally given by God, placing all in the same category. Man's great sin is adding to or taking away from the Word of God. As acute as it was then, as acute as it is now!

(3) "AND JESUS ANSWERING THEM SAID, HAVE YOU NOT READ SO MUCH AS THIS, WHAT DAVID DID, WHEN HIMSELF WAS HUNGRY, AND THEY WHICH WERE WITH HIM."

The exposition is:

1. The phrase, *"And Jesus answering them said,"* refers generally as always to Christ resorting to Scripture. Most all of their arguments or accusations were from man-made rules, while His answers always came from Scripture.

2. The question, *"Have you not read so much as this, what David did, when himself was hungry, and they which were with him?"* is derived from I Samuel 21:3-6.

3. Jesus chided the Pharisees for not knowing this illustration of David in I Samuel, which readily applied itself to their question. However, even if they had read it, which they, no doubt, had, self-righteousness would have seen only what it desired to see. It reads the Word of God with the idea of making it fit its preconceived notions instead of allowing the Word of God to mold one's notions and ideas.

(4) "HOW HE WENT INTO THE HOUSE OF GOD, AND DID TAKE AND EAT THE SHEWBREAD, AND GAVE ALSO TO THEM WHO WERE WITH HIM; WHICH IT IS NOT LAWFUL TO EAT BUT FOR THE PRIESTS ALONE?"

The diagram is:

1. The phrase, *"How he went into the house of God,"* refers to the tabernacle at Nob, which was only a short distance from Jerusalem.

2. *"And did take and eat the shewbread, and gave also to them who were with him,"* pertained to the hallowed bread, which, since it had evidently just been baked, meant it was the Sabbath.

3. The conclusion of the question, *"To them who were with him; which it is not lawful to eat but for the priests alone?"* was intended for that purpose, but it was broken in the case of David as necessity overrode rulings, even though those mentioned by Jesus were the legitimate law of Moses.

(5) "AND HE SAID UNTO THEM, THAT THE SON OF MAN IS LORD ALSO OF THE SABBATH."

WHO WAS THIS MAN JESUS?

The phrase, *"And He said unto them,"* refers to a statement so startling in concept that it must have struck terror into the hearts of those who opposed Him.

Who was this man Jesus?

Everyone knew Him to be a carpenter out of despised Nazareth. And yet, He spoke as if He were something else entirely!

"That the Son of Man is Lord also of the Sabbath," means that He is Lord and master of this particular day, for He was the one who gave it to Israel to commemorate their deliverance from slavery in Egypt (Deut. 5:15).

The word or title *"Lord"* is the august title of God, who we know as Jehovah, and thus speaks of deity. Wuest says, "The Creator is Lord of creation, and Lord of the Sabbath which He brought into being for the sake of Israel."

So, this statement by Jesus, in effect, declares Him to be God. As should have been obvious, it was not an idle boast. Everything backed up what He said:

THE PROOF OF JESUS AS THE SON OF GOD

• His genealogy was perfect as a Son of David, which they could have easily checked and, no doubt, did. The prophecy was that the Messiah would come through the family of David (II Sam., Chpt. 7).

• His miracles were astounding and spoke of that which the Messiah would do (Isa. 11:2; 29:18; 35:5-6; 61:1).

• The gospel He preached was exactly that which the Messiah should bring, as also prophesied by Isaiah (Isa. 11:2; 42:1-5; 60:1-3; 61:1-2).

So, there was no excuse for them not to know who He was!

The old Jewish Sabbath, which was Saturday, is not now kept by Christians for the following reasons:

THE JEWISH SABBATH IS NO MORE

• Neither God nor Christ made the Jewish Sabbath a part of the new covenant. If they had, it would be somewhere in the New Testament as the other nine commandments actually are.

• Of all the words of Jesus on earth, only four references are made of the Sabbath (Mat. 12:8; 24:20; Mk. 2:27-28; Lk. 6:5). He merely taught that it was lawful to do good on this day, and that no day is lord of man. He did not once command any particular observance of any definite day.

• The old Jewish Sabbath was part of the contract between God and Israel and a token and sign of that covenant (Ex. 20:8-1; 31:13-18; Ezek. 20:12-20). This contract was not made with men before Moses (Deut. 5:2-3), or with Gentiles and the church (Deut. 4:7-10; Rom. 2:14). The reason is that the Sabbath did not refer to Gentiles and the church.

• The fourth commandment (the keeping of the Sabbath) was the only one of the 10 that was a ceremonial law and not a moral law. Its sole purpose was to commemorate the deliverance from Egyptian bondage when Israel had no rest (Deut. 5:15). It was only a type of future and eternal rest (Col. 2:14-17; Heb. 4:1-11; 10:1). It was natural

NOTES

for it to be left out of the new contract when the reality of *"rest"* came, who was Jesus, of which it was a shadow (Mat. 11:28-29; Col. 2:14-17). The physical and spiritual benefits of a rest day can be realized on any other day as well as on Saturday.

• The fourth commandment was the only one that could degenerate into a mere form without affecting the morals of men, as it actually did! All other commandments concerned moral obligations of men. It is the only one of the 10 that could be done away with and still have a moral law for men.

• God foretold and promised that He would do away with the old Jewish Sabbath (Isa. 1:10-15; Hos. 2:11).

• The prophets predicted that God would abolish the old and make a new covenant (Isa. 42:6; 49:8; 59:21; Jer. 31:31-40; 32:37-44; Ezek. 36:24-38). That this referred to the New Testament is clear in Matthew 26:28; Rom. 11:25-29; and Hebrews 8:8-12; 10:16-18.

• In no passage is it stated that men should keep the Jewish Sabbath to commemorate the old creation rest. It was to commemorate the deliverance from Egypt (Deut. 5:15). This was what they were to *"remember"* (Ex. 20:8).

• It is the only commandment that could be and has been broken without breaking a moral law. Israel marched on that day (Lev. 23:5-11; Num. 33:3; Josh. 6:12-16); set up the tabernacle on that day (Ex. 40:1, 17, with Lev. 23:5-11); searched Cainan on that day (Num. 13:25); and made war on that day (Josh. 6:12-16; I Ki. 20:29; II Ki. 3:9). David and others broke it and were blameless (Mat. 12:2-5).

• The New Testament permits Christians to keep any day, with it being one of the doubtful things not covered by commandment in the new covenant (Rom. 14:1-13; Gal. 4:9-11; Col. 2:14-17). The day early Christians observed, not by commandment but by choice, was the first day (Sunday) because it was on Sunday that Jesus rose from the dead (Jn. 20:1, 19; I Cor. 16:2).

THE FOLLOWING LISTS TEN REASONS CHRISTIANS KEEP SUNDAY

1. To commemorate the resurrection

and the finished work of Christ in His victory over death, hell, and the grave, which took place on Sunday (Mat. 28:1; Mk. 16:9; Jn. 20:1).

2. The Lord's manifestations to His disciples after His resurrection were on Sunday (Mat. 28:1; Mk. 16:9; Jn. 20:1, 19, 26).

3. Christ ignored completely the old Jewish Sabbath. The first day is the prominent day after the resurrection (Mat. 28:1; Mk. 16:9; Jn. 20:1, 19, 26).

4. The outpouring of the Holy Spirit came on Sunday. Pentecost was the first day after seven Jewish Sabbaths (Lev. 23:15-21; Acts 2:1). Thus, both Christ and the Holy Spirit manifested themselves to the church on this day, completely ignoring the Jewish Sabbath.

5. Neither Christ nor any apostle commanded believers to keep the old Jewish Sabbath or any other day, but they did command all men not to be bound by any particular day (Rom. 14:5-6; Gal. 4:9-11; Col. 2:14-17). Sin is sin whenever it is committed. It is transgression of the law that constitutes sin (I Jn. 3:4), not the day on which it is done. Anything sinful on Saturday or Sunday is sinful on every other day. If it is not sinful on Monday, Tuesday, etc., it is not sinful on Sunday.

6. Although no set day is commanded in the New Testament to be kept, and we speak of the book of Acts and the Epistles, those in the early church did keep Sunday as their day of worship because this was the day Christ rose from the dead (Mat. 28:1; Mk. 16:9; Jn. 20:1, 19, 26; Acts 20:7; I Cor. 16:2; Rev. 1:10).

7. Typology of the old covenant made Sunday a day of worship:

a. The Jewish Sabbath was a changeable Sabbath, changing at Pentecost every year to one day later until each day of the week was observed every seven years. Pentecost was the first day after the seventh Sabbath (Lev. 23:15-21).

b. The Feast of Firstfruits came on Sunday, typifying the resurrection (Lev. 23:9-14; Mat. 28:1; Jn. 20:1).

c. The Feasts of Unleavened Bread and Tabernacles also were observed on at least one Sunday, and perhaps two, being seven and eight days long (Lev. 23:6-36).

NOTES

8. God honored Sunday by giving the law on that day (Ex. 12:2-18; 19:1, 3, 11; Lev. 23:3-6).

9. God again honored Sunday when giving the book of Revelation to John, which closed out the canon of Scripture (Rev. 1:10).

10. Constantine and the pope did not change the Sabbath from Saturday to Sunday, as some claim.

(6) "AND IT CAME TO PASS ALSO ON ANOTHER SABBATH, THAT HE ENTERED INTO THE SYNAGOGUE AND TAUGHT: AND THERE WAS A MAN WHOSE RIGHT HAND WAS WITHERED."

THE SABBATH

The phrase, *"And it came to pass also on another Sabbath, that He entered into the synagogue and taught,"* probably pertained to several weeks later than the Sabbath previously mentioned.

If one is to notice, the Lord addressed the issue of one doing necessary things on the Sabbath, such as the plucking of the corn, and now He addressed the help that can be given to others on this particular day. Both incidents are grouped together by Luke, no doubt, to impress upon the reader the true purpose of the Sabbath—that it was made for man, and not man for it.

It is obvious that the Pharisees, as well as the scribes, had completely forgotten the true intent of the law, which was meant to help people, but instead, made it a burden grievous to be borne. Unfortunately, many attempt to do the same with Christianity.

A PERSONAL EXPERIENCE

Years ago in a meeting in Florida, after the service that particular night, a man and his wife came up on the platform. He immediately began to berate me because I had not preached on *"holiness."* After talking with him a few moments, I found that his idea of holiness pertained only to women, and more specifically, how long their hair should be, also their sleeves, and, of course, that they wear no makeup at all.

I looked over at his wife, who had said nothing, and noticed her bedraggled appearance, and instantly felt sorry for her.

This man's spirit was awful because, as

the Pharisees of old, he really did not know Jesus. His *"religion"* was made up of rules and regulations, which he had devised himself. Consequently, he set about to force all others to subscribe to his particular brand of holiness, which, in effect, was no holiness at all!

As well, years ago, Frances and I preached a meeting in a particular church in Ohio, which had some peculiar rules and regulations. The pastor had determined that a woman who wore a pin (jewelry) that cost more than $2.98 was unholy. As usual, with these types of things, the rule was his and not God's. Actually, such is silly, but strangely enough, seems to always have some adherents.

Man loves to devise his own holiness, sanctification, or salvation. It makes him feel very religious when, in effect, all such foolishness, as the Pharisees, has nothing to do with God, but rather is man's silly self-righteousness.

The phrase, *"And there was a man whose right hand was withered,"* set the stage for what Jesus would do next.

(7) "AND THE SCRIBES AND PHARISEES WATCHED HIM, WHETHER HE WOULD HEAL ON THE SABBATH DAY; THAT THEY MIGHT FIND AN ACCUSATION AGAINST HIM."

THE SCRIBES AND THE PHARISEES

The phrase, *"And the scribes and Pharisees watched Him,"* means they kept watching so as to find something for which they could accuse Him.

If one is to notice, Jesus paid no attention whatsoever to the silly rules made up by men concerning the Sabbath, or any other time. He did the right thing, irrespective of what they liked or did not like.

It is amazing and somewhat amusing to watch modern pastors do that which they know to be wrong in order to appease denominational figureheads. Anytime preachers bow to that which is unscriptural, they have weakened their message and relationship with the Lord to that extent. Either the Lord is the head of the church, with His Word serving as the foundational guidelines, or else, man is the head. There cannot be two heads!

WHETHER HE WOULD HEAL ...

The phrase, *"Whether He would heal on the Sabbath day,"* meant that their rules and regulations were far more important to them than people.

In effect, their religion was the very opposite of that which had been given by God. The law of Moses was given to help men and not to be a burden. These people made a burden out of the law, which made serving God a chore rather than the abundant life it was intended to be.

In these descriptions as given by Luke, one finds a perfect description of man-devised religion. Man serves it instead of it serving man.

In truth, the law of Moses said no such thing as to what these men had devised! These were strictly man-made rules, which had no foundation in the Word of God, and were, therefore, specious.

A PERSONAL EXPERIENCE

The other day, a preacher remarked to me that he happened to see a copy of the constitution and bylaws of a particular Pentecostal denomination. It was sitting beside a copy of the Bible. The former was about three or four times thicker than the Bible, with him calling attention to this fact. Little by little, this particular Pentecostal denomination had become centered in man-made rules and regulations. This means they had long since departed from the Bible.

Actually, sometime back, some folk who were members of this particular denomination stopped by Family Worship Center on a given Sunday morning. They were on their way to their biannual meeting. My wife noticed the women were wearing no jewelry of any kind.

While they were at this particular convention, a new rule was passed allowing women to wear jewelry, etc. The same people stopped by Family Worship Center on their way back. This time, the women had on all types of jewelry. It was now alright to do so because their man-made rule had been changed.

However, truth does not change. If it was previously a sin, irrespective of what type of rule men made or struck down, it was still a sin.

To be sure, whether the women wore jewelry or not was of no consequence, at least in a spiritual sense. However, their obeying some church rule that had no foundation in the Word of God was wrong. In all of the four gospels, we find Jesus completely ignoring all man-made rules and regulations and doing whatever He set out to do, irrespective of what these religious leaders thought about it. That should be the attitude and action of all believers presently.

THE WORD OF GOD

If something is plainly condemned in the Word of God, or even the spirit of such action is condemned, the believer should not associate with it. However, it should be done because the Word of God says it and not because of what men say. The Word of God must ever be the criterion for all things. At the moment the believer yields to the silly unscriptural rules of men, ever how small or ridiculous they may be, the Word of God is compromised. We either follow Him in all, or we follow Him not at all! Regrettably, most preachers are following men and not God.

ACCUSATIONS

The phrase, *"That they might find an accusation against Him,"* tells us what their religion was all about. Jesus was setting people free while they were accusing. Actually, religion can only accuse; it cannot deliver anyone.

Self-righteousness lifts a person up so high in his own pride that he can feel comfortable, even as these Pharisees, in accusing God. Of course, they would have denied doing such because they did not believe Jesus was God. However, their unbelief had no bearing on the truth of the matter. He was and is God!

It is regrettable and sad that most modern religious denominations have become so busy accusing that they have little time for anything else. They have to protect their rules and regulations; consequently, no time is left for the work of God.

(8) "BUT HE KNEW THEIR THOUGHTS,

AND SAID TO THE MAN WHICH HAD THE WITHERED HAND, RISE UP, AND STAND FORTH IN THE MIDST. AND HE AROSE AND STOOD FORTH."

JESUS KNEW WHAT THEY WERE THINKING

The phrase, *"But He knew their thoughts,"* means that the Holy Spirit told Him what they were thinking. Regarding the modern gifts of the Spirit, it would presently be called *"the word of knowledge"* and *"discerning of spirits"* (I Cor. 12:8-10). Actually, Jesus exhibited all the gifts of the Spirit, with the exception of *"tongues"* and *"interpretation,"* with these two being absent because He had not yet been glorified (Jn. 7:39).

Many Spirit-filled believers exhibit one or more of these gifts, which ought to be resident in every Spirit-filled life.

The Spirit of the Lord knows everything, and exactly as He informed Christ, He will, as well, at times, do the same with modern believers if they will only believe and trust Him.

THE WITHERED HAND

The phrase, *"And said to the man which had the withered hand, Rise up,"* proclaims Jesus completely ignoring the fault-finding Pharisees who were there to accuse Him.

"And stand forth in the midst," means that what was done was carried out for all to see. He had no regard for what the skeptics thought. He would not compromise the Word or the way of the Lord.

The phrase, *"And he arose and stood forth,"* has the connotation of expectation.

It is said that this man's exact petition was preserved in the early church and referred to many times. It is as follows, as he stood before Jesus:

"I was a mason earning my livelihood with my own hands; I pray Thee, Jesus, restore me to health, in order that I may not with shame beg my bread."

What a beautiful plea, and one which Christ would not reject!

(9) "THEN SAID JESUS UNTO THEM, I WILL ASK YOU ONE THING; IS IT LAWFUL ON THE SABBATH DAYS TO DO

GOOD, OR TO DO EVIL? TO SAVE LIFE, OR TO DESTROY IT?"

The structure is:

1. The phrase, *"Then said Jesus unto them, I will ask you one thing,"* has to do with Christ discerning the thoughts of the scribes and the Pharisees, his bitter critics, and responding accordingly.

2. The question, *"Is it lawful on the Sabbath days to do good, or to do evil? to save life, or to destroy it?"* concerns the very ingredient of His mission and what Christianity is actually all about!

3. To have the power to do good and not do it, consequently, is to do evil.

4. As well, to have the power to save a life and not do it is, in effect, to destroy it.

5. Also, the entirety of this scenario places everything in its proper perspective. Jesus was on one side, with the religious Pharisees and scribes on the other. The former was interested in saving life, while the latter was interested only in preserving their rules, and they had no regard whatsoever for the crippled man. So, we are given a picture as to who Christ is and what religion is! Regrettably, the far greater majority of the world has opted for religion when, in reality, it has no regard for men, and it certainly cannot deliver them.

RELIGION AND CHRISTIANITY

Religion is not biblical Christianity, and conversely, biblical Christianity is not religion.

Religion is that which is devised by men, which means it was not devised by God, and claims to reach God or to better one in some way. It is not of God, and because it is not of God, it really cannot help anyone. In fact, religion enslaves more people than all the alcohol and drugs in the world today. Billions, and I mean literally billions, are ensnared in religion and will ultimately lose their souls.

In fact, the Jews had turned the law of Moses, which was devised by God, into a religion, meaning that they had so changed it and tortured its meaning until it no longer was what it once was. Millions have done and are doing Christianity the same way. They've made a religion out of it, which

concerns itself with rules and regulations that have no bearing on anything, at least that which is good.

Bible Christianity has only two ceremonies, and they are freighted with great meaning. They are water baptism and the Lord's Supper. Both, in a sense, refer to Christ and the Cross. The first is to emulate that which was done at Calvary, and the second is that we not forget that which was done.

(10) "AND LOOKING ROUND ABOUT UPON THEM ALL, HE SAID UNTO THE MAN, STRETCH FORTH YOUR HAND. AND HE DID SO: AND HIS HAND WAS RESTORED WHOLE AS THE OTHER."

The synopsis is:

1. The phrase, *"And looking round about upon them all,"* means that He looked at all of them with an astute gaze. Mark said, *"With anger, being grieved for the hardness of their hearts"* (Mk. 3:5).

2. They did not answer His question simply because they could not answer.

3. *"He said unto the man, Stretch forth your hand,"* no doubt, presented a hand that was withered and unusable.

4. *"And he did so: and his hand was restored whole as the other,"* means that before their very eyes, a miraculous healing took place, with the hand being made completely whole.

5. This should have caused everyone, especially these religious leaders, to have fallen on their faces, crying to God for mercy. However, it is impossible to show a blind man anything. Being spiritually blind, these scribes and Pharisees were unable to properly see what had actually happened.

(11) "AND THEY WERE FILLED WITH MADNESS; AND COMMUNED ONE WITH ANOTHER WHAT THEY MIGHT DO TO JESUS."

The order is:

1. God came in the flesh to take sin away, which He did at the Cross, and not to accomplish something for Himself. He needed nothing!

2. The Cross of Christ is the central event in time and eternity and the answer to all of the problems of both.

3. The Cross is not the Cross of man, but rather the Cross of God.

MADNESS

The phrase, *"And they were filled with madness,"* constitutes their reaction to this great miracle. It is unthinkable! They had no regard whatsoever for the plight of this poor man, but only for their petty rules.

The word *madness* has to do with far more than mere anger. It pertained to their minds and could probably be said to be a form of insanity. When people depart from the Word of God, they do not think correctly, which is actually the cause of all the problems in the world. This madness speaks of folly, and folly of the worst kind.

"And communed one with another what they might do to Jesus," spoke of hearts actually filled with murder. Mark said that the Pharisees joined with the Herodians, who were normally bitter enemies, in order that they might find a way to kill Jesus. It is astounding that they would kill Him simply because He had healed a man on the Sabbath.

Religion is never content to simply oppose something. It must, as well, seek to destroy it. It is especially incensed, as here, at that which it cannot control, for control is the name of the game in religion. Men love to control other men, and religious men love to control other men most of all.

THE WORLD OF RELIGION

Men will do things in a group that they never would do while alone. Consequently, religious organizations, as here, will do almost anything and will justify it on the basis that they all agreed.

Presently, great segments of the modern church, at least regarding preachers, grow incensed at someone being healed, claiming such has passed away. It is the same spirit that characterized the Pharisees of so long ago.

Other segments of the church will not recognize what is done if they have not placed their seal of approval upon the one who has done it, irrespective of how obvious and wonderful it may be!

The question must be asked, "Did these religious leaders actually think that Jesus was a deceiver?"

Perhaps the answer to that will never be known. However, I personally think they were not nearly as concerned about Him being a deceiver as they were about control slipping away from them as people saw the miracles that Jesus did. They would do anything to protect the control they had over people's minds, even to the point of killing Jesus. Regrettably, it has little changed presently, if at all!

(12) "AND IT CAME TO PASS IN THOSE DAYS, THAT HE WENT OUT INTO A MOUNTAIN TO PRAY, AND CONTINUED ALL NIGHT IN PRAYER TO GOD."

PRAYER

The phrase, *"And it came to pass in those days, that He went out into a mountain to pray,"* tells us several things.

• What mountain this was is not stated. It could very well have been one of the hills near Capernaum and, no doubt, was.

• It was virtually impossible for Him to have any privacy except in a place of this nature. The crowds were clamoring for Him in respect to their sick being healed, or for whatever purpose. As well, due to the fact that most of His praying was done in a secluded place of this nature, and I refer to the countryside, perhaps His desire in this capacity was that He may be among nature. This was His creation, and as such, it was beautiful. Perhaps He felt a greater kindred spirit there than in a house, etc. However, that in no way means that it is mandatory for all people who pray to follow suit. Actually, the location has little to do with it, if anything.

• As I think the record will show, Jesus prayed constantly. The inference is that not only did He seek these times of seclusion where He could be alone with the heavenly Father but, as well, while He walked from town to town in His evangelistic work, He at times would walk ahead of the disciples where He would constantly pray and meditate on the Word. Of course, He was not able to do this much due to the constant petition of people desiring healing, etc. Nevertheless, the Scripture says concerning Jesus,

"O how I love Your law! it is My meditation all the day" (Ps. 119:97).

A STUDY IN THE WORD

To be sure, this constitutes a degree of study in the Word that is unheard of presently. I realize that many would exclaim that Christ would have done that, but such would not be necessary for Christians. This is where people go wrong, at least if they believe that.

The study of the Word of God is the single most important thing in the life of the believer. It alone holds all the answers to life's problems. One might say that it is the road map for life and living and the blueprint for eternity.

If every believer will take it upon himself to make the study of the Bible a lifelong project, he will find, as Jesus, 1,000 percent improvement in every facet of life and living. In the studying of the Bible, the believer must have every intention of mastering its contents, at least as far as is humanly possible, by asking the Lord to help in this extremely profitable endeavor.

Jesus was going to engage in an extremely important exercise, the choosing of His most intimate 12, the disciples; consequently, He would make it a thorough examination in prayer. This should be a lesson to us.

Regrettably, many believers make their own plans and then ask God to bless them. To say the least, that is wrong.

The believer is to seek God about everything, no matter how little or large it may be, and then allow Him to do the selecting and make the choice, with His blessings then guaranteed.

In my prayer life, and I've always had a strong prayer life, I have learned this lesson over and over. Seek God about everything. Ask Him His will. Let Him know that you desire nothing else and, in fact, will accept nothing else, and will not move until He gives direction. If one will do this, one will find a leading and direction that is absolutely phenomenal. As well, foolish directions and mistakes will not be made, especially considering that the Lord is charting the course.

Jesus set the example for us, and it is incumbent upon all of us to follow.

NOTES

PRAYING ALL NIGHT

The phrase, *"And continued all night in prayer to God,"* proclaims the exact opposite of most of that taught by modern faith teachers.

Of course, there would be exceptions to what I say; nevertheless, the idea of *"praying through"* is totally contrary and foreign to most modern believers. Actually, and as alluded to, most faith teaches do not even believe in such a thing as praying through. Consequently, their followers, of which there seem to be many, are little led by the Holy Spirit.

Praying through exactly as Jesus did, and as is here recorded, means seeking the face of God until one has a clear-cut direction of what should be done. Sometimes it can be done in an all-night session, as here recorded, or even much shorter, and then sometimes it requires much longer.

The idea is not that it is difficult for God to answer, but that we have to be brought to the place we should be spiritually in order for the Lord to properly give us the directions He desires. No, Jesus was certainly not lacking in consecration or in obedience, but quite possibly, evil spirits endeavored to hinder, so he sought and needed direction. This often happens and means the believer, above all, should not give up but should press through, irrespective of the time taken, until the answer is forthcoming.

There were quite a number of disciples following Jesus at this time; nevertheless, the Holy Spirit desired a particular 12 to be chosen out from this number. He wanted those who had a heart toward God in a very strong way and could be molded into that which the Lord desired.

Again, what an example for us!

Paul said, *"Even so the things of God knows no man, but the Spirit of God"* (I Cor. 2:11).

So, we have to really seek God in order to know what the Spirit wants, even as Jesus did!

(13) "AND WHEN IT WAS DAY, HE CALLED UNTO HIM HIS DISCIPLES: AND OF THEM HE CHOSE TWELVE, WHOM ALSO HE NAMED APOSTLES."

HE CHOSE TWELVE

The phrase, *"And when it was day, He*

called unto Him His disciples," referred to quite a number, possibly even a hundred or more.

The phrase, *"And when it was day,"* referred to the next morning after the all-night vigil with God. He now had the mind of the Spirit and knew exactly what to do and who to choose.

"He called unto Him His disciples," no doubt, meant the entire group, which could have numbered, as we have stated, as many as a hundred or more.

"And of them He chose twelve," were those selected by the Holy Spirit.

As previously stated, these were not selected necessarily because of who they were, but because of hearts that hungered after God and could be pliable according to the will of God. Basically, this is the criterion respecting every call of God concerning those He uses. The Lord little looks at the outward, but rather the heart. Is it a heart that seeks after God? Is it a heart that desires to be changed, because all need to be changed! To be sure, at the time of the choosing in whatever capacity, the attributes are little present but have to be molded and made by the Holy Spirit. This takes time, as experience proves.

When Jesus chose these men by the guidance of the Holy Spirit, they were crude, carnal, walking after the flesh, and little understanding the purpose of God. However, they were willing to be molded into the image of the heavenly and, as such, could be used of God.

APOSTLES

The phrase, *"Whom also He named apostles,"* literally means "those who were sent on a special mission."

Even though the Lord would call other apostles, with others named in the New Testament and thousands since then, still, none will ever be in the capacity of the original Twelve (Eph. 4:11).

Why 12?

Even though they were to represent, at least in a sense, the 12 tribes of Israel, still, 12 is God's number respecting government. In other words, God's government is a perfect government and something man has

little had. That is the reason 12 tribes of Israel were chosen, 12 apostles, 12 foundations to the New Jerusalem, 12 gates, etc. (Rev. 21:12-21; 22:1-2).

At least one of the reasons the world has suffered greatly is because it has had the government of man instead of the government of God. Naturally, God's government is perfect, consequently, guaranteeing fair and equitable treatment to all.

The closest that man has known of God's government is the law of Moses, which was given to Israel. Even though it only pertained to those particular people, and they little adhered to it as a whole, still, it brought untold blessing and prosperity. (The Gentile world had no part in this government.)

As well, a few governments of man presently have been greatly influenced by Christianity, such as America and Canada, the U.K., Australia, Brazil, etc., and they have received untold blessings. However, when Jesus comes back (the second coming), the government of the world will then be on His shoulder (Isa. 9:6), and *"Of the increase of His government and peace there shall be no end, upon the throne of David, and upon His kingdom, to order it, and to establish it with judgment and with justice from henceforth even forever. The zeal of the LORD of Hosts will perform this"* (Isa. 9:7).

At that time, and we speak of the coming kingdom age, which will last for a thousand years, these 12 apostles will play a great part in this government of God.

WHAT IS AN APOSTLE?

An apostle is an authorized messenger of God, sent for a specific purpose and calling, with a specific message, and is backed up by the authority of God. His mission in some way and to a certain extent, whatever the purpose or designation, affects the entirety of the body of Christ, that is, the true body.

During the time of Israel in the Old Testament, it was prophets who were used of God to guide the spiritual destiny of the nation. That's the reason so many of them were killed. Many times, Israel simply did not like their message.

At the present time, under the new covenant, the prophet continues to be a minister of righteousness, which seeks to pull the church into shape, but the first place has been taken by the apostle. There were no apostles under the old covenant, with that being reserved for the new covenant.

Paul referred to himself constantly as *"an apostle,"* and more particularly an apostle to the Gentiles (Rom. 1:1, 13). Consequently, the things he did affected the entirety of the work of God, as well as the entirety of the body of Christ, and for all time. The same could certainly be said for the original Twelve, plus others called, as referred to in the book of Acts and the Epistles. While their work may not have equaled that of the apostle Paul, still, it definitely was of vital significance.

So, if we are to use the Bible as our definition, I think we will find in the book of Acts and the Epistles that those designated as apostles literally served as the spearhead of the early church and, therefore, in some way affected its doctrine and direction. While it may be true that we presently do not have much information on these other apostles, other than the Twelve, or Paul, still, inasmuch as their designation was given by the Holy Spirit, we must come to the conclusion that their work was of vital significance to the entirety of the body of Christ.

MISSIONARY?

Many have claimed that the modern designation of apostle is *"missionary."* However, even though some few missionaries through history definitely would have fallen into this category, still, the far greater majority would not.

I wish to emphasize again that while the modern designation of apostle may not be given to particular individuals, still, that is of little consequence if God, in fact, has called them for such. It would refer to ones whose ministries have a worldwide impact on the body of Christ, whether they are known or not, and because of the contribution made regarding purpose or direction of the work of God.

As previously stated, the one who is truly a God-called apostle is known for a particular message that the church needs, and which the Holy Spirit designates. We look

at Paul, and his message was the message of grace. One might even say that Paul was "an apostle of grace." Those who were with Paul probably could be given the same designation inasmuch as their message was the same.

While others may preach the same message, and do so with authority, still, it will not be with the same authority as the apostle who has been called of God for that particular direction. One might say that there is such a thing as an apostle of faith, of grace, of repentance, of the Cross, etc.

ARE APOSTLES STILL BEING CALLED TODAY?

We are told in Ephesians 4:11 that God is still continuing to put apostles in the church, as well as prophets, evangelists, pastors, and teachers.

Many people have the original Twelve in their minds, not realizing that there were a number of others referred to as apostles in the book of Acts, as well as the Epistles. However, it must be quickly stated that none will ever be called again as the original Twelve. These walked with Jesus personally for some three and one-half years. Of course, that is no longer possible. As well, due to the special designation of the original Twelve (with Judas being replaced by Matthias) and being personally selected by Christ, no others can ever enter into that particular role. Nevertheless, there were others who were called to be apostles, and who continue to be called unto this present hour (Barnabas, Acts 13:1-3; 14:4, 14; I Cor. 9:5-6; Gal. 2:9; Andronicus, Rom. 16:7; Junia, Rom. 16:7; Apollos, I Cor. 4:6-9; James, the Lord's brother, Gal. 1:19; 2:9; Silas, I Thess. 1:1; 2:6; Timothy, I Thess. 1:1; 2:6; Titus, II Cor. 8:23; Epaphroditus, Phil. 2:25; Paul, Gal. 1:1; 2:8).

WHAT IS THE AUTHORITY OF THE APOSTLE?

There is no higher God-given, spiritual authority than the calling of the apostle. Actually, it is the apostle who is the de facto leader of the church. It has always been that way. However, one must understand that apostles aren't appointed by other men and aren't elected by popular ballot, but strictly by a call of God.

As we have attempted to bring out, it is by and large, but not altogether, to these individuals that the Holy Spirit speaks, who literally guide the direction of the church. However, this calling is never to be a position of lordship, but rather of humility.

Some Charismatics have attempted to designate certain individuals as apostles, claiming they have authority over particular cities, areas, or groups of preachers. In other words, so-and-so is the apostle of New York, etc. None of that is scriptural and holds no biblical validity. All such designations are man-devised and are not to be obeyed by anyone. A true apostle will not use his authority in this manner, will desire no place and position, will not expect others to pay him deference, etc. While all of these things are extremely prominent in the modern church and, in fact, always have been, they are all man-induced, man-directed, and have no relationship to the Lord. Men love to lord it over others, and religious men love this most of all. Consequently, it is very easy for one man, or a group of men, to designate an individual as an apostle, or whatever! However, that is not God's doings and, as stated, holds no scriptural validity.

AUTHORITY

The authority possessed by the apostle is never wielded as such. It simply means that God has called a person as an apostle and, accordingly, will give him guidance and direction in certain particulars, which, if heeded, will affect the entirety of the body of Christ in a positive way. Sadly, it is little heeded presently, with man far too often usurping authority over that which is called by God.

However, if one will look back in church history, one will see that every major step forward taken by the church was instituted by men, such as Luther, Wesley, Whitefield, and Finney, to name a few. In more modern times, one could speak of Wigglesworth, Garlock, Trotter, etc. As well, there are many who are nameless, at least as far as notoriety or fame is concerned, but yet, are called of God as an apostle and have

contributed greatly toward the work and thrust of God. One will look in vain for any contribution made by religious denominations simply because such does not figure in the plan of God. While some have been greatly used in particular denominations, still, God used the men or women. It had little to do with the denomination or organization with which they were associated.

SPIRITUAL AUTHORITY

Actually, the question of *"spiritual authority"* is the great battlefield of the church.

Every believer in the world has spiritual authority, with, of course, some, such as apostles, having much more, which is all given by God. However, the following must be noted and noted carefully:

This authority is to never be used against other people in any capacity. It is to be used against demon spirits, along with every other power of darkness in the spirit world. That's where the spiritual authority begins, and that's where the spiritual authority ends.

Unfortunately, in this modern age, some have tried to claim that denominational heads have spiritual authority, and unless you do exactly what they say do, no matter how unscriptural it might be, you are rebelling against spiritual authority. No, there is no such thing as a man or woman having spiritual authority over another. You won't find such in the Word of God. Again let us state that while all do have spiritual authority, and while some have much more than others, still, always and without fail, that authority is to be used against Satan, demon spirits, and all powers of darkness.

Jesus said: *"You know that the princes of the Gentiles exercise dominion over them, and they who are great exercise authority upon them.*

"But it shall not be so among you: but whosoever will be great among you, let him be your minister;

"And whosoever will be chief among you, let him be your servant:

"Even as the Son of Man came not to be ministered unto, but to minister, and to give His life a ransom for many" (Mat. 20:25-28).

He also said, *"And these signs shall follow*

them who believe; In My name shall they cast out devils (demons)*"* (Mk. 16:17).

And then, Paul said, *"For we wrestle not against flesh and blood, but against principalities, against powers, against the rulers of the darkness of this world, against spiritual wickedness in high places"* (Eph. 6:12).

He also said, *"For though we walk in the flesh, we do not war after the flesh: (For the weapons of our warfare are not carnal, but mighty through God to the pulling down of strongholds;) Casting down imaginations, and every high thing that exalteth itself against he knowledge of God"* (II Cor. 10:3-5).

Let us state it again: You will look in vain in the book of Acts and the Epistles for preachers exercising authority over other people. It simply does not exist because it's not of God.

Unfortunately, some denominations tend to think that their officials elected by popular ballot hold some type of spiritual authority that individuals must obey. Millions are in hell today because of that very idea.

I love my brother in the Lord and will do whatever it is he may ask, providing it's scriptural. However, the only thing I as a believer and you as a believer owe any other believer is love (Rom. 13:8).

Some are fond of using a threat against someone that they do not particularly like by saying, "They are in rebellion against spiritual authority." They are simply meaning that the individual will not obey what has been demanded that he or she must do, whatever it is. Let us state it unequivocally:

The Bible is the handbook for life and living and for discipline. Whatever is scriptural, that I will obey; otherwise, I not only will not obey such, but I must not obey such. To do so is to go against the Word of God, which no sane believer desires to do.

Unfortunately, men love to lord it over others, and religious men love this most of all.

God-called apostles leave the control in the hands of the true head of the church, who is Jesus. All too often denominational heads do the very opposite by taking the leadership of the church into their own hands and, as stated, will do anything within their power to maintain that control. Actually,

NOTES

this was the great controversy between Jesus and the religious leaders of Israel.

They saw control (authority) slipping out of their hands into the hands of Christ; consequently, they killed Him. Unfortunately, that same spirit thrives presently.

(14) "SIMON, (WHOM HE ALSO NAMED PETER,) AND ANDREW HIS BROTHER, JAMES AND JOHN, PHILIP AND BARTHOLOMEW,

(15) "MATTHEW AND THOMAS, JAMES THE SON OF ALPHAEUS, AND SIMON CALLED ZELOTES,

(16) "AND JUDAS THE BROTHER OF JAMES, AND JUDAS ISCARIOT, WHICH ALSO WAS THE TRAITOR."

THE DISCIPLES

• *"Simon"*: The changing of Simon's name to *"Peter,"* which means *"Cephas,"* or literally, *"A mass of rock,"* portrays what Jesus would do for this man. In other words, He would take someone who was impetuous, and in some ways weak, and instill within him a power and fortitude that would make him an entirely different man. He can and will do the same for any and all who will believe Him. It is believed that Peter was crucified, actually, upside down.

• *"Andrew"*: He was one of, if not the first believer, of the Twelve. And yet, for some unexplained reason, Andrew did not occupy the position of intimacy shared by Peter, James, and John. He was the brother of Peter.

Tradition says that both Peter and Andrew were of the tribe of Reuben. It is said that Andrew evangelized Scythia, becoming Russia's patron saint, and that he was stoned and crucified in Greece, or Scythia.

• *"James"*: His name in the Hebrew was *"Jacob,"* and he was the brother of John and the son of Zebedee. He was one of the three most intimate with Jesus and the first martyr among the apostles (Acts 12:1-2).

Tradition says that he was of the tribe of Levi through his father and of Judah through his mother, consequently, of both the priestly and royal house. It is said that he preached in India with Peter and later in Spain, becoming the patron saint of Spain.

• *"John"*: His name means "Jehovah

is gracious." It seems in some way that he (and James) was a kinsman of the high priest (Acts 4:6). He wrote five of the New Testament books: the gospel of John, I, II, and III John, and Revelation.

With his brother James being the first of the apostles to die, John was the last. Tradition says he was the only one of the Twelve to die a natural death. Tradition also says he died at Ephesus, with the actual words used of him, "Fell asleep at Ephesus."

It is said that when he became too old to walk, probably nearing a hundred years old, he was carried to the church services, repeating again and again, "Little children, little children, love one another."

As James, he was the son of Zebedee, and his mother's name was Salome. Some think that Salome was the sister of Mary, the mother of Jesus. If, in fact, that is the case, James and John were cousins of Jesus on His mother's side. John's parents would appear to have been well-to-do, for his father, a fisherman, had *"hired servants"* (Mk. 1:20); and Salome seems to have been one of the women who provided for Jesus out of their means (Mk. 15:40; Lk. 8:3).

THE LIST

• *"Philip"*: This apostle was called to follow Jesus on the day following the call of Andrew and Peter and was instrumental in bringing Nathanael to Jesus (Jn. 1:43-46). His home was Bethsaida (Jn. 1:44); this was the Bethsaida of Galilee (Jn. 12:21) and also the hometown of Andrew and Peter.

The references to him in the New Testament tell of his inability to suggest to Jesus how to supply the food for the 5,000 (Jn. 6:5), his bringing the Greeks to Jesus (Jn. 12:21), and his request of Jesus to see the Father (Jn. 14:8). Some also suggest that Philip was the brother of Nathanael.

• *"Bartholomew"*: This is another name for Nathanael. He is supposed to have preached in Syria, Phrygia, and India, finally being tied to a cross head down, beaten to death, and beheaded by King Astyages in Armenia.

• *"Matthew"*: The tax collector was the son of Alphaeus, which means he may have been the brother of James, who was

NOTES

referred to as *"James the less,"* to distinguish him from James the son of Zebedee. Some think that Matthew, James, and Judas (not Iscariot) were brothers, which seems to be indicated in the text.

• *"Thomas"*: He is also called *"Didymus."* As well, many have referred to him as "doubting Thomas" because he doubted, but on the same basis, we can call all the apostles doubters and unbelievers (Mat. 28:17; Mk. 16:11-14; Lk. 24:11, 25, 41; Jn. 20:27).

Thomas is supposed to have labored in India and made many Christian converts. It is said that idol-priests tortured him with red hot plates and then cast him into an oven, which had no effect on him. They then pierced him with spears while in the furnace until he died. Jerome says that his body, unconsumed, was buried at a town called Calamina.

• *"James the son of Alphaeus"*: As stated, he was known as *"James the less"* to distinguish him from James the son of Zebedee. The word *less* meant that he was either younger or smaller in stature. As stated, he may have been the brother of Matthew and was definitely the brother of Judas (not Iscariot). He was also thought to have been a cousin of Jesus, which would have meant that Matthew and Judas (not Iscariot) were also cousins of Jesus. Luke 24:10 says that Mary, the wife of Cleophas, was his mother. She was also the sister to Mary, the mother of Jesus. Actually, the mother of James, the sister of Mary, the mother of Jesus, was named *"Maria."*

THE LIST CONTINUES

• *"Simon called Zelotes"*: He was also called *"the Canaanite."* Before coming to Christ, he had been a zealot, a member of a Jewish party that rebelled against the Romans. Tradition says that Zelotes was killed by crucifixion in Syria. Some even think he was also the brother of James, Matthew, and Judas (not Iscariot), which, if so, would have meant that four brothers were apostles of Christ.

• *"Judas the brother of James"*: he was also called *"Lebbaeus"* and *"Thaddaeus."*

• *"Judas Iscariot, which also was the traitor"*: In the apostolic band, Judas was treasurer (Jn. 13:29). He was also branded by John as a thief (12:6). Evidently, he pilfered the money that was entrusted to him.

Judas was the traitor of all traitors. The last hours of his life proclaimed the fruit of such direction. He committed suicide.

Some have claimed that Judas was a devil from the very beginning and was predestined to do what he did; however, the Scripture does not bear that out. Three guiding principles ought to be stated as a preliminary to all such considerations.

WAS JUDAS ALWAYS A TRAITOR?

1. We ought not to doubt the sincerity of the Lord's call of Judas. Jesus, at the beginning, viewed him as a potential follower and disciple. No other presupposition does justice to the Lord's character and His repeated appeals to Judas.

2. The Lord's foreknowledge of him does not imply foreordination that Judas must inexorably become the traitor.

3. There is evidence that Judas followed Jesus wholeheartedly at the beginning. He was even given power to heal the sick and cast out demons as the other disciples. Nevertheless, other impulses ultimately took over until his commitment to Christ waned, weakened, and ultimately died.

He leaves the gospel story *a doomed and damned man* because he chose it so, and God confirmed him in that dreadful choice.

(17) "AND HE CAME DOWN WITH THEM, AND STOOD IN THE PLAIN, AND THE COMPANY OF HIS DISCIPLES, AND A GREAT MULTITUDE OF PEOPLE OUT OF ALL JUDAEA AND JERUSALEM, AND FROM THE SEA COAST OF TYRE AND SIDON, WHICH CAME TO HEAR HIM, AND TO BE HEALED OF THEIR DISEASES."

OTHERS THAN THE TWELVE

The phrase, *"And He came down with them, and stood in the plain,"* refers to Him coming down from the mountain where He had *"continued all night in prayer to God."* The Twelve evidently were with Him.

"And the company of His disciples," referred to the large number of other followers besides the Twelve. As Jesus traveled

NOTES

from place to place, there is a possibility that from 50 to 100 people were with Him most of the time. Luke later recorded that Jesus *"appointed other seventy also,"* as well as the Twelve, sending them out to do evangelistic work (Lk. 10:1, 17).

"And a great multitude of people out of all Judaea and Jerusalem, and form the sea coast of Tyre and Sidon, which came to hear Him," no doubt, represents the crowd to whom Jesus gave the famous discourse known as the Sermon on the Mount. Luke, as we shall see, related some of it, but not nearly to the detail as did Matthew (Mat., Chpts. 5-7).

THE SERMON ON THE MOUNT

What this multitude would hear this day would be the greatest message that had ever fallen upon human ears. The Sermon on the Mount bridged the old and new covenants. As well, it was the foundation of the new covenant and presented the ideal respecting relationship to God and man. The truths represented were so revolutionary that they would make Bible Christianity the foundation of all principle and life. Not only has nothing ever equaled this before or since but, in fact, has not even come close.

The Sermon on the Mount is not philosophy, but rather a person—the Man Christ Jesus. To divorce the message from the Man only leaves a philosophy, which within itself can change nothing. Coupled with Christ, it becomes the most powerful change agent known to humanity—a change from bad to good. Unfortunately, Christ has been divorced from much of Christianity, leaving nothing but a moralist philosophy, which within itself is little better than other worldly offerings.

The phrase, *"And to be healed of their diseases,"* refers, as is obvious, to the many who desperately needed healing and were not disappointed.

The manner in which this Scripture is given tells us that not only were there Jews in this great multitude but, as well, Gentiles, including Romans, Greeks, and even Phoenicians from Tyre and Sidon. Incidentally, they were all treated alike, with grace and dignity.

(18) "AND THEY WHO WERE VEXED WITH UNCLEAN SPIRITS: AND THEY WERE HEALED."

The synopsis is:

1. The word *vexed* in the Greek text is *ochleo* and means "to harass" (Acts 5:16).

2. The idea of this verse is that *"unclean spirits"* cause particular types of sicknesses among the people. As we have previously stated, this does not mean that all sicknesses are directly caused by evil spirits, but it definitely does mean that some are.

3. *"And they were healed,"* has reference to the fact that the physical damage done by these unclean spirits was immediately assuaged. The following, which is an abbreviated form of the Sermon on the Mount, gives instructions that if followed, can keep these things from happening ever again.

(19) "AND THE WHOLE MULTITUDE SOUGHT TO TOUCH HIM: FOR THERE WENT VIRTUE OUT OF HIM, AND HEALED THEM ALL."

TOUCHING JESUS

The phrase, *"And the whole multitude sought to touch Him,"* presents a startling picture. The power of God emanated from Him to such an extent that the multitudes soon learned that a mere touch would effect their healing or deliverance, irrespective of its degree.

"For there went virtue out of Him, and healed them all," respects all being healed with no exceptions. To adequately portray this happening would literally be impossible. One can well imagine the shouts of praise and glory to God when instant healing came upon those who were blind, deaf, paralyzed, etc. It was a sight and a scene that the world had never experienced in all of its history.

As well, this tells us that the message of Christ, which is given in the following verses, cannot be divorced from the person of Christ. Unfortunately, much of the Christian world has attempted to present the philosophy of Christianity, which is only a moralist philosophy and, in fact, cannot change anyone or anything. Jesus is the power behind the message. To divorce the message from Him leaves a powerless

NOTES

gospel. Unfortunately, many churches have set Christ aside in one way or the other.

WHO IS JESUS?

Many claim that Jesus was a good man but not the Son of God. As such, they deny Him any involvement.

Others claim Him as Saviour but deny Him as baptizer with the Holy Spirit. As such, the power that accompanies the gospel is absent, thus, producing powerless lives, of which churches are filled.

Others accept Him as Saviour and baptizer with the Holy Spirit but deny Him as coming King, at least as the Scriptures proclaim! This group, which is quite large, somewhat proclaims the political message, believing that proper men and women voted into office will usher in the millennium. Such is foolishness, to say the least, and outright blasphemy at worst!

As Jesus alone is the Saviour and alone the baptizer with the Holy Spirit, He alone as coming King will transform this world. It will not be with the help of anyone, even the church. Daniel described it perfectly when he said, *"Forasmuch as you saw that the stone was cut out of the mountain without hands, and that it broke in pieces,"* which referred to the kingdoms of this world (Dan. 2:45). The *"stone"* is Jesus, and the phrase, *"Without hands,"* means that man will have no part in that which He will do at the second coming.

(20) "AND HE LIFTED UP HIS EYES ON HIS DISCIPLES, AND SAID, BLESSED BE THE POOR: FOR YOURS IS THE KINGDOM OF GOD."

THE POOR

Some have maintained that this account given by Luke is not the same as the Sermon on the Mount given by Matthew. They say this message was given in the plain, while the Sermon on the Mount was given while Jesus sat on a mountain. However, those two statements constitute no discrepancy. The *"plain"* of St. Luke was simply a level spot on the hillside and was, as Matthew stated, on the mountain. Matthew's account, which is far more detailed, took three chapters, while Luke, giving an abbreviated version, is contained in one chapter. Both the account of Matthew and Luke are one and the same.

The phrase, *"And He lifted up His eyes on His disciples, and said,"* means it was addressed primarily to the disciples but, no doubt, overheard by many of the multitude.

BLESSED

The phrase, *"Blessed be the poor: for yours is the kingdom of God,"* is the first beatitude and is basically the same as that of Matthew, but with the two words, *"in spirit,"* eliminated. Nevertheless, the meaning is the same.

Jesus was not actually speaking to those who are economically poor, but rather to those who know and understand that within themselves, they are morally and spiritually bankrupt. This would have been very difficult for the religious leaders of Israel to accept, especially considering that they thought very highly of themselves inasmuch as they were the people chosen by God. As such, they looked on the Gentiles as *"dogs."* So, for them to admit that within themselves they were morally and spiritually bankrupt was a threshold that most were not prepared to cross. And yet, this very first beatitude is the rudiment of all salvation.

If man thinks he deserves the grace of God, he automatically forfeits the grace of God. Man must see himself exactly as he actually is and as God sees him.

Naturally, all born-again believers have been imbued with an imputed righteousness, which, in effect, makes one highly moral and spiritual. However, this is none of the doings of man, but all of God. As stated, it is imputed righteousness, which means that it is something given by God to an undeserving person.

THE KINGDOM OF GOD

As well, the kingdom of God and the kingdom of heaven, as used by Matthew, are basically the same and are actually interchangeable.

The kingdom of God speaks of a king whose name is Jesus. While all believers now have the kingdom of God in their hearts, the totality of this kingdom, which is spiritual, physical, and material, will not

take place until the second coming. Then Jesus will reign personally from Jerusalem and establish this kingdom in every sense, which will last forever.

There are nine beatitudes given by Matthew while there are only four given by Luke.

(21) "BLESSED ARE YOU WHO HUNGER NOW: FOR YOU SHALL BE FILLED. BLESSED ARE YOU WHO WEEP NOW: FOR YOU SHALL LAUGH."

THE HUNGER FOR RIGHTEOUSNESS

The phrase, *"Blessed are you who hunger now,"* corresponds with Matthew's, *"Hunger and thirst after righteousness"* (Mat. 5:6).

When a believer begins to hunger for God, for a certainty he will find Him.

It is somewhat easy to tell in a local church just who hungers after the Lord, and who doesn't! Those who truly hunger never miss a service, at least if possible for them to attend, and they endeavor to put God first in everything. Regrettably, these seem to be in the minority.

The phrase, *"Blessed are you who weep now: for you shall laugh,"* corresponds with Matthew's, *"Blessed are they who mourn: for they shall be comforted"* (Mat. 5:4).

As in Matthew, the word *weep* has nothing to do with the normal problems of life, but rather the knowledge that no matter how close one tries to live for God, the flaws and inconsistencies in even the most consecrated Christian life seem to be many. Regrettably, this does not seem to bother many; however, to those who truly love God, these things are a sore grievance.

Nevertheless, upon seeing ourselves as we really are, which causes consternation, we have His promise that He will comfort us, giving the joy of salvation, i.e., laughter.

(22) "BLESSED ARE YOU, WHEN MEN SHALL HATE YOU, AND WHEN THEY SHALL SEPARATE YOU FROM THEIR COMPANY, AND SHALL REPROACH YOU, AND CAST OUT YOUR NAME AS EVIL, FOR THE SON OF MAN'S SAKE."

HATRED

The phrase, *"Blessed are you, when men shall hate you,"* must have the phrase, *"For the Son of Man's sake,"* attached to it to understand its true meaning. Many are disliked, and justly so, because of their character faults, but only those can rejoice who are disliked because they belong to Jesus and testify for Him.

"And when they shall separate you from their company," speaks of being ostracized. This will happen more so in churches than anywhere else.

When individuals are baptized with the Holy Spirit with the evidence of speaking with other tongues, they will be politely, or not so politely, told to go elsewhere if they are attending a church that does not believe in this experience.

Now it is the Message of the Cross. Oddly enough, when Christians embrace this message, which every believer most definitely should, they will sometimes be told to leave their churches that they have attended for many, many years. Others will be ostracized by their families.

Why?

How in the world could the Message of the Cross cause that much opposition?

WHY IS THE MESSAGE OF THE CROSS OFFENSIVE?

The main reason is that it exposes self-righteousness, which means it lays bare works religion and efforts of the flesh. Men do not enjoy being told that what they're doing is of no benefit. We are speaking of their labor, etc., in other words, what they are doing to try to earn their salvation. The truth is, most do not really understand that they are trying to earn anything from the Lord, but actually, this is what is happening. The Cross of Christ exposes all of that, lays it bare, and lets the individual know that this is wrong. People do not like to be told that they are wrong. They do not like to be told they are heading in a wrong direction, especially when they have put their time, talent, thinking, and money into this false direction.

So, when someone comes along and says, "I'm sorry, but what you're doing is not going to help you," and that the "Cross of Christ is the only answer," it doesn't set very well.

NOTES

A CASE IN POINT

Millions bought the book, *The Purpose Driven Life.* Another book was written that captivated many in the Pentecostal world, which stated unequivocally that if one will fast 21 days, then one can get rid of the sin problem, etc.

While fasting is definitely scriptural, at least if it's done correctly, fasting is not the answer for sin. The Cross of Christ, and the Cross of Christ alone, is the answer for sin. Paul said:

"But this man (the Lord Jesus Christ), *after He had offered one sacrifice for sins forever, sat down on the right hand of God"* (Heb. 10:12).

The great apostle also said, *"And you, being dead in your sins and the uncircumcision of your flesh, has He quickened together with Him, having forgiven you all trespasses; Blotting out the handwriting of ordinances that was against us, which was contrary to us, and took it out of the way, nailing it to His Cross; And having spoiled principalities and powers, He made a show of them openly, triumphing over them in it"* (Col. 2:13-15).

Plainly and unequivocally, the Holy Spirit through the great apostle tells us in no uncertain terms that the Cross of Christ is the answer for sin and, in fact, is the only answer for sin.

The message that we believe the apostle Paul taught is ensconced in his epistles and is so very, very important. Paul was selected by the Holy Spirit to be the master builder of the church. I think his message can be summed up in the following:

• Jesus Christ is the source of all things we receive from God (Jn. 1:1, 14, 29; 14:6; Col. 2:10-15).

• With Jesus as the source, the Cross now becomes the means, and the only means, by which all of these great things are given to us by the Lord (I Cor. 1:17-18, 23; 2:2; Rom. 6:1-14).

• With Jesus as the source and the Cross as the means, then the object of our faith, which is so very, very important, must be Christ and the Cross (Rom. 6:1-14; I Cor. 2:2; Gal. 6:14; Col. 2:15).

• With Jesus as the source, the Cross as the means, and the Cross of Christ the object of our faith, meaning that this is the imprint of the Word of God, then the Holy Spirit will grandly help us (Rom. 8:1-11; Eph. 2:13-18; Gal., Chpt. 5).

REPROACH

The phrase, *"And shall reproach you,"* is something that is going to happen to the believer by both the world and the apostate church, that is, if one truly follows the Lord. The name of Jesus is a reproach to the world and to religion; consequently, those who bear that name and carry it proudly suffer reproach.

The phrase, *"And cast out your name as evil,"* is the very opposite of that which the flesh desires. All enjoy others thinking well of them; however, true followers of the Lord will not be lauded and praised, but rather reviled.

The phrase, *"For the Son of Man's sake,"* is the key to this persecution. Even though one's church, a particular doctrine, etc., may be the target, still, the real cause for the bitter opposition is the name of Jesus.

As we have stated, only four beatitudes are stated by Luke, while nine were given by Matthew. Why the difference?

Matthew presented Christ as king; consequently, the totality of the message germinates in the heart of the believer but will see its full fruition in the coming kingdom age.

Luke presented Jesus as man. As such, the basic fundamentals are given. For instance, Matthew spoke of the meek inheriting the earth, which can only happen in the coming kingdom age. Other beatitudes, which Luke did not mention, fall into the same category. While the spirit of those particular beatitudes is definitely present in the believer, its full fruition is not, and, in fact, cannot be, at least in totality, until the coming kingdom age.

FOUR FUNDAMENTALS

However, the four fundamentals, which inculcate themselves in the salvation experience, are here presented by Luke:

1. The individual must understand, as stated, that he is morally and spiritually bankrupt and as such, contains no salvation within himself. Matthew addressed this, as well, and Luke repeated it because it is absolutely imperative for one to understand this if one is to be saved. Only Jesus can supply what is needed.

2. There must be a hunger and thirst for righteousness, which will result in one's consecration, and which Matthew mentioned as well.

3. Despite whatever consecration one might have, still, the believer must be conscious of his continued flaws and failings. By that, we do not mean open, practiced sin, but rather the foibles of self-will, etc., which bring about mourning.

4. For the one who truly knows the Lord, persecution will follow.

If Luke's presentation is understood in this light, then the omitting of certain beatitudes becomes clear. It definitely was not an oversight on Luke's part in the writing of this, but the way in which the Holy Spirit designed it, and for purpose and reason.

(23) "REJOICE YE IN THAT DAY, AND LEAP FOR JOY: FOR, BEHOLD, YOUR REWARD IS GREAT IN HEAVEN: FOR IN THE LIKE MANNER DID THEIR FATHERS UNTO THE PROPHETS."

The exegesis is:

1. The phrase, *"Rejoice ye in that day, and leap for joy,"* proclaims the purpose and reason for the joy. If the action of Verse 22 is not present, the possibility may definitely exist that one is not truly saved. However, such negative action for His name's sake proclaims to the heart of the believer the veracity of one's salvation. Consequently, joy, and even great joy, is the result of that knowledge.

2. *"For, behold, your reward is great in heaven,"* insinuates that there will not be much reward here. So much of the so-called modern faith teaching, which, in reality, is no faith at all, is proven false.

In effect, Jesus is saying that if one is looking for His reward here, that means he is not truly living for God. Treasures are laid up in heaven, not on earth.

3. *"For in the like manner did their fathers unto the prophets,"* presents a common denominator. The persecution of the saints

happened to the greatest of prophets; consequently, the modern believer, that is, if he truly follows the Lord, can expect the same.

(24) "BUT WOE UNTO YOU WHO ARE RICH! FOR YOU HAVE RECEIVED YOUR CONSOLATION."

WOE

The idea of Verse 24 and the *"woe"* it contains speaks of those who trust in riches. Riches within themselves are not evil, only their misuse.

Spence said, "Prophets and apostles, as well as the Son of God, never ceased to warn men of the danger of misusing wealth and power; but at the same time they always represented these dangerous gifts as gifts from God, capable of a noble use, and, if nobly used, they pointed out these gifts would bring to the men who so used them a proportional reward."

Actually, the believer is warned not to seek riches for the sake of riches. Paul said, *"But they who will be rich fall into temptation and a snare, and into many foolish and hurtful lusts, which drown men in destruction and perdition."*

He then said, *"For the love of money is the root of all evil: which while some coveted after, they have erred from the faith, and pierced themselves through with many sorrows"* (I Tim. 6:9-10).

And yet at the same time, riches can come to some even as a blessing from God, and if so, the following should be done:

DANGERS

One must understand the dangers that lurk in the accumulation of wealth. The tendency is always present to believe that one is special because of such riches. Nothing could be further from the truth! If the believer is blessed by riches, it is certainly not because he is special but because God is special. One should never fail to understand that.

RICHES

Riches must never be used to force one's will on others, such as churches or preachers, in an attempt to force one's way. Money must be given with no strings attached simply because one loves God. To attempt to

force a preacher or church in a certain direction by the threat of not giving, or to sway with much giving, is an attempt to manipulate the Spirit of God. Such is wicked and will not only not bring the blessings of God, but rather will bring His judgment.

THE PURPOSE

If God does give riches, one should always understand the purpose for which they are given. It is certainly proper for one to take care of one's family, even with a serious penalty attached if this is not done (I Tim. 5:8). Having done that, one's riches, should they come one's way, should be used for the furtherance of the gospel.

As well, the furtherance of the gospel must not be the perpetuation of one's name, which speaks of pride, etc. The idea is never personal glory but the furtherance of the kingdom.

It is tragic, but money given by individuals, especially those who give large sums, at times is given with the wrong motive in mind. Acts, Chapter 5, gives a strong warning, to say the least, against this. It should be heeded!

The believer should have one thing in mind regarding his giving, and that is souls being brought to Christ. Regrettably, much of that and, in fact, most of that given to what proposes to be the work of the Lord is oftentimes anything but the work of the Lord. Jesus told us to check the fruit, and if this is not done, our money could be wasted (Mat., Chpt. 7).

(25) "WOE UNTO YOU WHO ARE FULL! FOR YOU SHALL HUNGER. WOE UNTO YOU WHO LAUGH NOW! FOR YOU SHALL MOURN AND WEEP."

The overview is:

1. The idea of this verse pertains to supposed self-sufficiency, which plagues a great part of the human family.

2. The lyrics of a famous song, "I Did It My Way," portrays the feeling of much of the world.

3. They refuse to admit they need God!

(26) "WOE UNTO YOU, WHEN ALL MEN SHALL SPEAK WELL OF YOU! FOR SO DID THEIR FATHERS TO THE FALSE PROPHETS."

NOTES

The composition is:

1. The false prophets have always had men singing their praises and do so no less today. However, it is because they are telling men what they want to hear instead of what God wants them to hear.

2. Church members find no opposition from the world, while those who have a true relationship with Christ are met with all types of opposition. As stated, the offense is the Lord Jesus Christ!

3. If one is to notice, there are four beatitudes and there are four woes. The woes correspond to the opposite of the Beatitudes.

• The *"poor"* and *"rich"* of the first beatitude and woe do not necessarily speak of financial lack or the opposite. While it certainly can include that, it speaks more so of the attitude of the individual. Humility is honored by God, while pompous pride is rejected.

• The *"hungry"* and the *"full"* are here contrasted. The former realize their need for God while the latter realize no need at all, at least in the spiritual sense.

• The *"weeping"* and *"laughing"* are here contrasted, representing the knowledge of one's true condition versus the *"fool,"* who has no idea of the acute danger he is facing.

• The last beatitude speaks of persecution for those who truly follow Jesus, while the last *"woe"* speaks of those who are lauded and applauded by the world.

Consequently, it is easy to contrast the two groups. In many cases, all claim to follow the Lord, but Jesus plainly delineates the two.

(27) "BUT I SAY UNTO YOU WHICH HEAR, LOVE YOUR ENEMIES, DO GOOD TO THEM WHICH HATE YOU."

WE MUST HEAR

The phrase, *"But I say unto you which hear,"* refers to the fact that many would refuse to *"hear."*

Every vestige of what is right and what is wrong comes from the Bible. In other words, every law in the world, at least that which is right, irrespective of what society it is, has its foundation in the Bible, actually, the Ten Commandments, whether realized or not. It is when men leave the standard of the Word of God and make up their own rules that the system breaks down, hence, the abortion rulings by the Supreme Court, which have stained America's hands with blood.

As well, the teaching of evolution in the public school system and the psychologizing of the nation (and the world for that matter), both secular and religious, have taken the nation away from the Word of God. The results are murder, an exploding crime rate, no respect for law and order, plus a generation that has no feelings for anything or anyone. It is all because the nation will not *"hear!"*

THUS SAITH THE LORD

By using the phrase, *"But I say unto you,"* Jesus places Himself in the position of deity; consequently, it is the same as *"thus saith the Lord"* in the Old Testament.

The people were accustomed to hearing the scribes allude to this teaching or that teaching, splitting theological hairs over something they knew little or nothing about. Jesus alluded to nothing, except directly to the Word, or else, as here, announced the Word. There was no halting, stumbling, or equivocation.

"Love your enemies, do good to them which hate you," begins the most revolutionary lifestyle ever known in the history of man. It is so revolutionary, in fact, that it is impossible to carry out, other than by the power of the Holy Spirit. And yet, this which Jesus said is the ideal and is actually what a believer should be and do.

(28) "BLESS THEM WHO CURSE YOU, AND PRAY FOR THEM WHICH DESPITEFULLY USE YOU."

BLESS THEM WHO CURSE YOU

The phrase, *"Bless them who curse you,"* has the emphasis on the word *bless* and means "to speak well of." How can one speak well of an individual who is cursing him, i.e., speaking harmfully?

One can pray that the Lord will deal mercifully with that particular individual and help him to see the right way, or thoughts to that effect. The idea is to get away from the *"kind for kind"* spirit that characterizes the world. In other words, "Do it to them if they do it to you." Jesus turned all of this on its head, which is totally foreign to the thinking of the world.

"And pray for them which despitefully use you," was carried out by Jesus on the Cross when He prayed for His murderers. Stephen actually did the same (Acts 7:60).

Some people misunderstand these commands as given by Christ, thinking they contradict the Old Testament, which says, "Eye for eye, tooth for tooth, hand for hand, foot for foot" (Ex. 21:24). However, there is no contradiction!

This of which Jesus spoke pertains to one's personal dealings with another. That given in the law of Moses concerned the judicial position, which must be taken by civil authorities. Actually, the principle of all law in the world is based on the Old Testament law of Moses, which demands commensurate punishment.

THE INTENT OF THE HOLY SPIRIT

There is no record in the Old Testament of someone having his eye gouged out due to the guilty party maliciously blinding the eye of another. We are speaking of a time frame that covered about 1,600 years, at least as it regards the law of Moses. However, whatever type of punishment the guilty suffered, whether the payment of money or service, was to be commensurate, at least as far as possible, with the loss experienced by the innocent victim. This was the intent of the Holy Spirit, on whose foundation all law is based.

If one is to notice, there were four beatitudes, four woes, four laws of love, followed by four laws of retaliation, followed by four principles of the Golden Rule, and then four laws of mercy, concluding with four laws of justice.

"Four" is believed by some to be God's number of completion, i.e., fourfold, or the same on all sides. So, what Jesus is saying is the sum total of these great divine principles. Nothing of any consequence can be added, and neither should anything be taken away. Amazingly enough, these divine principles, which form the basis of Bible Christianity, are said in so few words.

THE BIBLE

If man attempted to devise something of this nature, he would be totally unable to do so. Even if he tried, his efforts would fill volumes, consequently, so cumbersome as to be unintelligible.

In fact, if one studies the style in which Christ taught, one finds that the most complex of subjects are reduced to utter simplicity, even down to a few words, as here, but without losing any meaning whatsoever. This speaks of wisdom such as no man ever had, even Solomon, for Jesus said of Himself, "Behold, a greater than Solomon is here" (Lk. 11:31).

Men would deny Him this wisdom inasmuch as He did not deal with the great questions of science. However, the mission of Christ concerned how man lived instead of the way man lived. Men have learned how to harness the atom, plus a host of other secrets of science, but other than Jesus, man does not know how to live. Jesus taught men how to live, which can only be done by His saving grace. That alone contains the true purpose of life, actually giving man a reason for living (Jn. 10:10).

It is tragic that men stumble from one catastrophe to another and try one foolish way after the other, all without success, when the true purpose and meaning for living is found as close as their Bibles. However, the Bible, sadly and regrettably, is given little credence, with Jesus given even less, if possible!

(29) "AND UNTO HIM WHO SMITES YOU ON THE ONE CHEEK OFFER ALSO THE OTHER; AND HIM WHO TAKES AWAY YOUR CLOAK FORBID NOT TO TAKE YOUR COAT ALSO."

The order is:

1. The phrase, "And unto him who smites you on the one cheek offer also the other," is meant to serve as a principle and not to be taken literally. For example: the Lord, Himself, did not offer Himself to be stricken again (Jn. 18:2-23), but firmly, though with exquisite courtesy, rebuked the one who struck Him.

2. Paul, as well, followed the same principle (Acts 23:3). The principle is that one should not seek retaliation.

3. The phrase, *"And him who takes away your cloak forbid not to take your coat also,"* holds a tremendous secret if understood.

4. Inasmuch as tax collectors were backed by Rome in those days, they had the power to do pretty much whatever they desired, within certain limits. Consequently, Jesus is saying that if the *"cloak"* is demanded, give it over without argument, or even the *"coat,"* as well, if demanded! The idea is that if one demands his rights too loudly, the loss could be even greater than the cloak and coat.

5. Actually, this one law of retaliation addresses itself to the demands of many, even modern Christians, concerning their rights. Our rights are to be hidden in Christ and, as here stated, little protected, at least by the individual, with some exceptions. Giving up one's rights in Christ then allows the Lord to defend the individual. It is a matter of self or Christ! Regrettably, too many believers are resorting to courts of law when the matter should be left to the Lord.

(30) "GIVE TO EVERY MAN WHO ASKS OF YOU; AND OF HIM WHO TAKES AWAY YOUR GOODS ASK THEM NOT AGAIN."

The composition is:

1. The phrase, *"Give to every man who asks of you,"* speaks of those truly in need. It does not refer to rewarding one's slothfulness. In fact, Paul said, *"That if any would not work, neither should he eat"* (II Thess. 3:10).

2. Actually, all of these laws of retaliation must be understood in that spirit. Our Lord, for instance, did not offer Himself to be stricken again (Jn. 18:22-23), but firmly, though with exquisite courtesy, rebuked the one who struck him. Actually, Paul, as stated, did the same thing (Acts 23:3).

3. Even though we have addressed ourselves briefly to the subject of *"rights,"* stating that they should be left to Christ, still, there are situations when a Christian should demand his rights. For instance, Paul, as a Roman citizen about to be condemned to the Jewish court, demanded his right to, *"Stand at Caesar's judgment seat, where I ought to be judged"* (Acts 25:10).

NOTES

4. *"And of him who takes away your goods ask them not again,"* proclaims two things:

a. Unselfishness that ought to characterize every believer.

b. Trust in God that He will reimburse that which is lost.

However, at the same time, it is the principle that is to be understood rather than the act itself.

(31) "AND AS YOU WOULD THAT MEN SHOULD DO TO YOU, DO YE ALSO TO THEM LIKEWISE."

The exegesis is:

1. This is the verse that is referred to as the *"Golden Rule."* It is also a teaching of the law (Lev. 19:18).

2. This does not mean that we are to give all that we have to another, for we would not expect him to do this for us. If we so expected it, we would be condemned of gross covetousness of what belongs to another, and this itself is contrary to the law and the gospel. We are not to covet anything that belongs to another (Ex. 20:17; Deut. 5:21; Rom. 13:9; I Cor. 5:11; 6:9-11; Eph. 5:5).

Therefore, that which belongs to the other cannot be expected from him. The main idea is that of rendering justice, mercy, and love to all men as prescribed by the law and the gospel.

(32) "FOR IF YOU LOVE THEM WHICH LOVE YOU, WHAT THANK HAVE YOU? FOR SINNERS ALSO LOVE THOSE THAT LOVE THEM."

The synopsis is:

1. The idea is that Jesus loved us when we were unlovable (Rom. 5:8). Inasmuch as He did this for us, we are to do the same for others who do not love us and, in fact, at least in some cases, hate us. Within one's own abilities, such is impossible. However, upon conversion to Christ, the God kind of love is given to the believer. In the Greek text, it is called *"agape."*

2. In essence, this type of love is what motivates the taking of the gospel to the world. When the church begins to weaken spiritually, its love follows suit, and the sacrifice of taking the gospel to those who have never heard has less and less priority.

3. The closer to Christ, the greater is the

love. The greater the love, the greater is the burden to tell others.

(33) "AND IF YOU DO GOOD TO THEM WHICH DO GOOD TO YOU, WHAT THANK HAVE YOU? FOR SINNERS ALSO DO EVEN THE SAME."

The overview is:

1. Augustine observed that the ordinary rule of man is to return good for good and evil for evil.

2. Then, beneath this, there is the returning of evil for good, which is devilish; while above it, there is the returning of good for evil, which is divine—and this is what is commanded for the followers of Jesus.

(34) "AND IF YOU LEND TO THEM OF WHOM YOU HOPE TO RECEIVE, WHAT THANK HAVE YOU? FOR SINNERS ALSO LEND TO SINNERS, TO RECEIVE AS MUCH AGAIN."

The diagram is:

1. The world pretty well operates on the basis of these "sinners." In other words, you scratch my back, and I'll scratch yours!

2. As we have stated, the Sermon on the Mount was the most revolutionary message that man had ever heard, and continues so unto this hour.

3. This is the ideal for believers, but sadly, precious few follow its concepts. However, for the few who do, this world is made immeasurably better. Nevertheless, the fulfillment of these commands awaits the coming kingdom age when Jesus rules supremely from Jerusalem, with the world filled with glorified saints and people who desire to follow Christ. Then, the full weight of these glorious commandments will take effect.

(35) "BUT LOVE YE YOUR ENEMIES, AND DO GOOD, AND LEND, HOPING FOR NOTHING AGAIN; AND YOUR REWARD SHALL BE GREAT, AND YOU SHALL BE THE CHILDREN OF THE HIGHEST: FOR HE IS KIND UNTO THE UNTHANKFUL AND TO THE EVIL."

The exegesis is:

1. The phrase, "But love ye your enemies," once again epitomizes Christ who prayed for His murderers, even while He hung on the Cross.

2. The phrase, "And do good, and lend," speaks of two things:

NOTES

a. "Do good": The only people in the world who truly do good are those who truly follow Christ. I will venture to say that every vestige of good in this world comes from this source. If one will look at the nations ruled by the religious fervor of Islam, Buddhism, Shintoism, Confucianism, atheism, etc., one will find little regard for one's fellowman. A few enjoy the bounty, while all others suffer in abject poverty. Such is the world!

b. "And lend": this has the idea of being generous with our money, time, and abilities.

The phrase, "Hoping for nothing again," presents a paradox to the unbeliever. How could we call it lending if it's not to be repaid?

Solomon gave the answer to that a long time ago. He said, "He who has pity upon the poor lends unto the LORD; and that which he has given will He pay him again" (Prov. 19:17).

3. The phrase, "And your reward shall be great," proclaims God giving His word that if such is done (lending [giving] to the poor), He will see to it that the return will be abundant. Consequently, it is left up to the believer as to exactly how much he trusts the Lord to do this. Jesus said that the return would be "great!"

4. "And you shall be the children of the highest," means that we are to be like our heavenly Father.

5. "For He is kind unto the unthankful and to the evil," portrays what He does, and what we ought to do as well!

(36) "BE YE THEREFORE MERCIFUL, AS YOUR FATHER ALSO IS MERCIFUL."

MERCY

Once again, as He is, we are to be!

No one has a right to mercy. When we understand this fact and its implication, we gain a deeper appreciation of God's goodness to us. Mercy is not merely something that God chose to give us. Mercy is a quality that God expects in us, for those who live close to the Lord are to reflect His character.

MERCY PROVIDED AND EXPERIENCED

According to Romans, Chapters 9 and 11, God's mercy is the basis for His action. This does not take away from love as the primary motivation in providing salvation. However, in context, Paul emphasizes that God was responding to the need of the helpless and was not moved by any merit on the part of those He chose to love. The New Testament continues to affirm that mercy has been provided for the believer: God, who is rich in mercy, made us alive with Christ, even when we were dead in transgressions (Eph. 2:4-5). In His great mercy He has given us new birth into a living hope (I Pet. 1:3). Actually, He saved us, not because of righteous things we have done, but because of His mercy (Titus 3:5).

THE EXPRESSION OF MERCY

There can be no doubt that mercy has been provided for every believer and that the salvation we enjoy is a vivid expression of the mercy of God. Moreover, His mercy is designed to transform our experience. On a few occasions, the New Testament links *"mercy and peace"* (I Tim. 1:2; II Tim. 1:2; II Jn. Vs. 3; Jude Vs. 2). Each of these occurrences comes in a letter designed to encourage those living in difficult times. When stress fills our lives, knowledge of God's mercy fills us with peace.

IN BOTH TESTAMENTS

In both Testaments, mercy is compassion as expressed to meet human need. The focus in both is on God's mercy to human beings. In the final analysis, God is the only one truly able to meet our needs. He is the one on whom we must depend.

Those who know Jesus have received mercy, and continue to experience God's mercy. We follow the example of those men and women of the Gospels who came to Jesus, acknowledged Him as Lord, and cried out to Him for mercy in their time of need.

Because in mercy God has brought us to life in Jesus, we too can show mercy to those around us, providing in our own compassion a witness to the loving mercy of God.

GRACE AND MERCY

Somewhere in eternity past, God, by deliberate choice, made grace the principle on which He would deal with man. Grace must be a choice, or else, it cannot be grace.

NOTES

However, once grace was chosen, mercy, which is a natural product of grace, must be extended. In other words, upon choosing grace, God had no choice but to extend mercy.

Inasmuch as grace has been shown to us in ever abundant amounts, as well, we have no choice, that is, if we are to follow Christ, but to also show mercy to others. So, this statement by Christ is not a suggestion but a command. As well, the true believer cannot pick and choose to whom he will show mercy, but must show mercy to all.

(37) "JUDGE NOT, AND YOU SHALL NOT BE JUDGED: CONDEMN NOT, AND YOU SHALL NOT BE CONDEMNED: FORGIVE, AND YOU SHALL BE FORGIVEN."

JUDGE NOT, AND YOU SHALL NOT BE JUDGED

These statements of Christ hit at the very heart of Jewish thought and life and do no less today! The religious leaders of Israel were quick to judge entire groups of individuals in a very censorious way. The judging was based upon particular practices of outward show of religion. If people did not meticulously keep the myriad of man-made religious laws, they were quickly judged as being unrighteous, etc.

Presently, the outward externals may not be as rigidly pronounced; however, the judging spirit is no less predominant now than then.

It is so easy to judge a situation resulting from externals when, in reality, one knows very little, if anything, about the person's heart. In doing this, one is almost all the time wrong in the judgment he makes.

In Romans 2:1-3, Paul speaks passionately of passing judgment on others. He warns that at whatever point you judge the other, you are condemning yourself. To pass judgment implies the assumption of a moral superiority that we simply do not possess. Consequently, no human being is able to judge others without becoming vulnerable to the same judgment.

IS IT EVER RIGHT FOR A BELIEVER TO JUDGE ANOTHER?

No!

It is never proper to judge one's motives

or his heart. Only God is qualified to do such a thing (James 4:11-12).

However, having said that, it is proper to judge the fruit and, actually, the believer is called upon to do so.

Jesus said, *"Judge not according to the appearance, but judge righteous judgment"* (Jn. 7:24).

Without going into detail, Jesus was saying that at times, appearances are deceiving. In fact, they can be deceiving in either direction. In some cases, an individual can appear outwardly to not be right with God when, actually, the opposite is true. As well, the opposite can well be the case; consequently, the believer is called upon to judge righteous judgment.

HOW CAN ONE JUDGE RIGHTEOUS JUDGMENT

The Word must be adhered to in all situations. It is not what the denomination or others say, or even what prevailing opinion may be, but only what the Word of God says. This alone is to be our criterion.

If something is obviously unscriptural, it must be judged accordingly; however, if it seems to be scriptural, or else, one is not certain, Jesus said, *"You shall know them by their fruits"* (Mat. 7:16).

The word *know,* while not pertaining directly to judging, does apply to the principle in this case. It means to make a full investigation in order that one may have proper knowledge upon which to base a judgment concerning the fruits of another.

CONDEMN NOT

"Condemn not, and you shall not be condemned": At that time, this would have pertained to the Pharisees condemning as sinners beyond the pale of mercy whole classes of their fellow countrymen—publicans, Samaritans, and the like. Spence said, "This resulted in undue estimate of themselves."

Does this mean that a believer should condone open practicing of sin in the lives of other believers?

No! It does not mean that at all; however, it does mean that while the sin is judged and condemned, that is as far as it should go.

The individual himself (or herself) is not to be condemned.

In I Corinthians, Chapter 5, a leader in the church at Corinth was openly living in sin by cohabiting with his stepmother (I Cor. 5:1). This sin was judged and condemned by Paul, with the admonishment by that apostle that the church at Corinth must do the same. Consequently, the individual was given a choice to repent, ceasing all such activity, or be disfellowshipped (I Cor. 5:2). As Verse 5 in that chapter proclaims, this was done not to destroy the person but to help him.

II Corinthians, Chapter 2, proclaims that the man did repent, that is, if it is the same person in question.

Even disfellowshipped, should such have occurred, Paul warned that the church was to *"count him not as an enemy, but admonish him as a brother,"* meaning that while the sin was condemned, the individual wasn't (II Thess. 3:15).

COUNTING HIM AS A BROTHER?

Counting him as a brother simply means that every scriptural effort is to be made to bring the person to a state of repentance, which the Holy Spirit, as well, is attempting to do. Upon such repentance, the incident is to be forgotten, with the person enjoying full restoration privileges (Gal. 6:1).

The reason for this admonishment by Christ becomes crystal clear, that is, if one properly sees himself as he should:

• There but for the grace of God go I!

• Being guilty ourselves of past infractions, we have no right to condemn others.

• Inasmuch as God has shown great mercy to us, we must do the same to others.

• The true love of God will demand that we do these things, and if they are not done, it shows that the love of God is not in us.

FORGIVE, AND YOU SHALL BE FORGIVEN

The idea is, and a rather stern idea at that, that if we don't forgive, we cannot be forgiven our sins.

Forgiveness is demanded by the Lord on the part of the believer; however, our actions toward the forgiven one are predicated on his present spiritual state.

If an individual truly repents (of whatever the situation), the individual is to be treated as if the infraction was never committed (Gal. 6:1). That is the manner in which the Lord treats us and the manner in which He demands that we treat others.

Some would demand proof of the sincerity of repentance. Of course, total sincerity is absolutely necessary if true repentance is to be engaged. That should go without asking. Nevertheless, it should be obvious as to whether the individual is sincere. These things are fairly observable.

The believer is commanded to forgive even though the individual does not ask for forgiveness and, in fact, does not cease the wrongdoing. However, in this case, fellowship could not be resumed, and for the obvious reasons. Still, the forgiveness must be entertained simply that no ill will arise in our hearts.

(38) "GIVE, AND IT SHALL BE GIVEN UNTO YOU; GOOD MEASURE, PRESSED DOWN, AND SHAKEN TOGETHER, AND RUNNING OVER, SHALL MEN GIVE INTO YOUR BOSOM. FOR WITH THE SAME MEASURE THAT YOU METE WITHAL IT SHALL BE MEASURED TO YOU AGAIN."

GIVE, AND IT SHALL BE GIVEN UNTO YOU

The idea of this fourth command is that God's people be givers instead of judges. Many have taken this passage to refer only to money. While it certainly includes that, still, the great idea is that we are to give the person the benefit of the doubt without judging him. As well, we should give them love instead of condemning them. Also, forgiveness falls into the category of "giving."

To forgive, a person has to give grace, mercy, and compassion. That is the reason, as someone has said, "To err is human, to forgive is divine."

The phrase, "Good measure, pressed down, and shaken together, and running over, shall men give into your bosom," constitutes a remarkable promise.

MEN SHALL GIVE ...

If one is to notice, it says that men shall give instead of God shall give. Even though,

as stated, it certainly does refer to money, to a far greater degree, however, it refers to things that are far more important. To give grace is truly God-like! If such is done, the Lord gives us the promise that, as a rule, such will be returned to us accordingly.

The idea is, as is obvious, that it takes great principle for one to give grace. It takes no principle at all to give condemnation; however, whatever is given will be returned. Of that one can be sure!

The phrase, "For with the same measure that you mete withal it shall be measured to you again," is a law of God that everyone should take into consideration at all times.

The idea of the entirety of these laws of justice is, even though these graces are man-instituted, and of necessity must be man-instituted, still, they are God-appointed and, therefore, God-upheld!

If people stop to consider that whatever they do is going to be measured to them again, and they really believe that Jesus meant what He said, conduct toward others would, no doubt, greatly improve.

(39) "AND HE SPOKE A PARABLE UNTO THEM, CAN THE BLIND LEAD THE BLIND? SHALL THEY NOT BOTH FALL INTO THE DITCH?"

The pattern is:

1. The phrase, "And He spoke a parable unto them," concerns a very simple analogy that was readily understandable by all. Some of Jesus' parables were designed to somewhat hide their true intent. However, others, as these, were meant to make the subject crystal clear, which they evidently did.

2. The question, "Can the blind lead the blind?" refers to false religious leaders. The idea is that irrespective of the effort made, there will be no true illumination. Blind teachers can only impart error.

3. The question, "Shall they not both fall into the ditch," speaks of the ultimate destination of both teacher and student.

(40) "THE DISCIPLE IS NOT ABOVE HIS MASTER: BUT EVERY ONE WHO IS PERFECT SHALL BE AS HIS MASTER."

The pattern is:

1. The phrase, "The disciple is not above his master," means that they become as

their masters, i.e., teachers. Hence, the disciples of Catholicism, Mormonism, Christian Science, etc., become as wholly deluded as their teachers.

2. The phrase, *"But every one who is perfect shall be as his master,"* would have been better translated, *"But every one who has been perfected in this false doctrine shall be as his master."*

3. The fruit of the Spirit is the product of the teaching of the Spirit. Modern teaching denies this and claims that self-sacrifice, kindness, good temper, and benevolence spring out of human nature and have no fundamental relationship to a correct interpretation of the Word of God.

4. There can be an imitation of the fruit of the Spirit, as a paper rose may be so like a real one as to be indistinguishable from it. However, a bee will make no mistake! The only power that will make men really love one another is the doctrine of the Bible, which says, *"Walk in love as Christ also loved us."* Teaching love on any other principle is vain.

(41) "AND WHY BEHOLD THOU THE MOTE THAT IS IN YOUR BROTHER'S EYE, BUT PERCEIVE NOT THE BEAM THAT IS IN YOUR OWN EYE?"

The structure is:

1. The question, *"And why behold the mote that is in your brother's eye"* pertains to mote hunting and was pandemic among the Pharisees of Jesus' day. These individuals constantly inspected others, attempting to catch them in the slightest infraction of some man-made law or regulation. They were continuously doing this with Jesus, claiming He had broken a law, which, in effect, was of their own making. The record shows that Christ paid no attention whatsoever to man-made rules and regulations. He was interested only in what the Word of God said and constantly called people's attention to that source.

2. The continuance of the question, *"But perceive not the beam that is in your own eye?"* proclaims the fact that an individual has enough wrong with himself, which should require constant introspection, that he not have time to look for *"motes"* in the eye or person of another.

3. At the same time, many people

misunderstand these passages, thinking that contending for the faith is an abrogation of this commandment of Christ. However, it is perfectly proper, and even commanded in the Word, that truth be preached, which will, of necessity, point out error (Jude, Vs. 3). However, that is vastly different than attacking someone personally.

(42) "EITHER HOW CAN YOU SAY TO YOUR BROTHER, BROTHER, LET ME PULL OUT THE MOTE THAT IS IN YOUR EYE, WHEN YOU YOURSELF BEHOLD NOT THE BEAM THAT IS IN YOUR OWN EYE? THOU HYPOCRITE, CAST OUT FIRST THE BEAM OUT OF YOUR OWN EYE, AND THEN SHALL YOU SEE CLEARLY TO PULL OUT THE MOTE THAT IS IN YOUR BROTHER'S EYE."

THE QUESTION

To clarify the issue, I will separate the question Jesus asked into two parts. *"Either how can you say to your brother, Brother, let me pull out the mote that is in your eye?"* opens up a panorama of questions.

What makes us think we are qualified to judge another? James addressed himself to this under the guidance of the Holy Spirit (James 4:12). In effect, James said, "Who do you think you are, thinking you are qualified to judge someone else?" And yet, we have all done it, treading on this dangerous ground.

To do so places us in the position of conducting ourselves as God, which, in effect, is satanic.

Not being God, we have little idea as to the actual circumstances in any situation. It is not a question of failing to recognize the wrong in others, which definitely does exist oftentimes, but that we must be very careful as to how we address it, if at all. In other words, at all times, as Jesus said, we must *"judge not,"* *"condemn not,"* and then we must *"forgive."*

No, this in no way means that responsible action is not to be taken against unconfessed continued sin. However, even then, only those who are truly spiritual must undertake the effort, and only with the idea in mind of restoring the individual instead of punishing him. Punishment is always left to God, and only to God (Rom. 12:19; Gal. 6:1).

WHAT IS THE BIBLICAL METHOD OF RESTORATION?

Paul said:

"*Brethren, if a man be overtaken in a fault, you who are spiritual, restore such an one in the spirit of meekness; considering yourself, lest you also be tempted*" (Gal. 6:1).

What does it mean to be "*spiritual*"?

This speaks of those who understand the sanctification process, which pertains to the Cross of Christ. In other words, the spiritual one must understand that Jesus Christ is the source of all things we receive from God, while the Cross of Christ is the means, and the only means, by which all of these good things are given to us. With that being the case, we must place our faith exclusively in Christ and what Christ did for us at the Cross. Then and only then can the Holy Spirit, who works exclusively within the framework, so to speak, of the finished work of Christ, help us. To be sure, that is the only way that we are going to gain victory over the world, the flesh, and the Devil.

So, such a one who understands these things should tell the believer who has stumbled and failed why the failure came about. It is because the individual has placed his or her faith in works, etc., in other words, his faith was moved from Christ and the Cross to something else. This curtails the Holy Spirit and sets the believer up for failure.

The one who has stumbled must be told that he or she must return to the path of faith, which is Jesus Christ and Him crucified.

That is God's method of restoration, and His only method of restoration. It does not include punishment, for no person is qualified to do such a thing. It includes only instructions as to how the situation can be rectified, which is to pull the person back to Christ and the Cross.

FALLEN?

As well, it must always be understood that irrespective of what is done, as long as a person continues to trust Jesus, he is not fallen (I Jn. 1:9). Were that not the case, every single believer in the world would be in a fallen state. It is only when an individual refuses to repent, consequently, failing to continue

his trust in Christ, that he is to be labeled as "*fallen.*" The first case is found in Galatians 5:4, where Paul said, "*Christ is become of no effect unto you, whosoever of you are justified by the law* (or at least attempt to be justified in that manner); *you are fallen from grace.*" Regrettably and sadly, much of the church falls into that position.

The second case is found in Revelation 2:5, where Jesus said, "*Remember therefore from where you are fallen, and repent, and do the first works; or else I will come unto you quickly, and will remove your candlestick out of his place, except you repent.*" This was because the church had left their first love (Rev. 2:4). These are the only two cases in the New Testament that speak of the "*fallen.*"

Once again, this would include much, if not most of the church.

YOUR OWN EYE

So, as stated, the Holy Spirit through the Word of God, which must be the criterion for all things, never labels as fallen anyone who continues to trust Christ. In fact, that should be obvious to even the most elementary Bible student.

The conclusion of the question as asked by Jesus, "*When you yourself behold not the beam that is in your own eye?*" pulls the inspection to introspection. In other words, the person starts looking at himself as he should and finds plenty of things wrong that need to be attended to, rather than trying to find things wrong with others. In street terminology, Jesus is saying, "Heal yourself before you try to heal others." By that, we speak of the judging and condemnation of others. As well, the insinuation is that we will find so much wrong with ourselves that it will be a full-time job dealing with that, with no time left for finding fault with others.

Again we emphasize that this has nothing to do with the preaching of the gospel, which definitely does point out the sins of individuals, but rather deals with personal faultfinding.

HYPOCRITE

The words, "*Thou hypocrite,*" tell us what the faultfinding individual actually is.

The word *hypocrite* actually denotes

someone acting out the part of a character in a play. In Greek drama the actors held over their faces oversized masks painted to represent the character they were portraying. In life the hypocrite is a person who masks his real self while he plays a part for his audience.

What is it that characterizes the religious hypocrite?

• A hypocrite does not act spontaneously from the heart but with calculation to impress observers (Mat. 6:1-3).

• A hypocrite thinks only of the external trappings of religion, ignoring the central, heart issues of love for God and others (Mat. 15:1-21).

• A hypocrite uses spiritual talk to hide base motives (Mat. 22:18-22).

Jesus' warning to such, which includes hypocrites of every age, is *"woe unto you"* (Mat. 23:13-16, 23, 25, 27, 29).

TO SEE CLEARLY

The phrase, *"Cast out first the beam out of your own eye, and then shall you see clearly to pull out the mote that is in your brother's eye,"* simply means for one to take care of oneself first. As stated, if that is done as it ought to be done, the person will then see clearly and will realize that he has no room or right to condemn others.

The problem with most believers is that they do not see clearly how bad their own personal problem actually is!

(43) "FOR A GOOD TREE BRINGS NOT FORTH CORRUPT FRUIT; NEITHER DOES A CORRUPT TREE BRING FORTH GOOD FRUIT."

The synopsis is:

1. The unfortunate thing as it regards the Christian experience, which has been with us from the time of the garden of Eden, is the problem of self-righteousness.

2. The believer can have the righteousness of God only by believing in what Christ has done at the Cross.

3. With that being done, and continuing to be done, the righteousness of God is freely imputed to the believing sinner.

GOOD FRUIT AND CORRUPT FRUIT

The phrase, *"For a good tree brings not*

forth corrupt fruit," is the method delineated by Jesus for separating the good from the bad.

He has just spoken of all types of professors of religion, some loudly claiming all types of righteous things, whom Jesus calls *"hypocrites,"* but not so easily discernable among other believers. Therefore, He tells us how to discern those who are real and those who aren't.

In effect, He is saying that no matter what the claims, one must judge the fruit.

"Neither does a corrupt tree bring forth good fruit," says the same thing in a different way.

Let us look at *"corrupt fruit"* and *"good fruit."*

What is corrupt fruit?

• In short, it is anything that is not scriptural.

• If it's not scriptural, it is that which is man-induced, irrespective of its religiosity. If it is man-induced, as stated, no matter how religious, it will accomplish no work for God. There may be much machinery, much activity, and much religiosity, but when it's all said and done, no lives will be changed, no souls saved, no bondages broken, no sick bodies healed, and no believers baptized with the Holy Spirit, no matter the claims.

To be sure, among the corrupt fruit, the claims abound, but with no factual or scriptural validity.

CLAIMS

Unfortunately, many believers are fooled by such claims and pour millions of dollars into schemes that have no foundation in the Lord or His Word. I will give a brief example:

Sometime back, I received a letter from a lady, who enclosed a donation. She said that she wanted to help with our television coverage in Russia to get the gospel to these people. I very much appreciated her help; however, she also stated in her note that she was supporting another alleged ministry that was covering Russia with the gospel by television.

The sad fact was, this particular television ministry, although claiming to all and sundry that they were, in fact, reaching all of Russia with the gospel of Jesus Christ by television, in truth, did not even have a television program in Russia. To be sure, the claims were grandiose but without any truthful foundation whatsoever.

So, the believer should have enough spiritual discernment to not believe everything he is told, but rather to ask a few questions and, above all, seek the Lord for guidance. Devils, even though parading as angels of light, are not too hard to spot if the believer will use the common sense with God's work as he or she does with other things.

I think it should be obvious that any support of *"corrupt fruit"* is not only not aiding the work of God, but rather the work of Satan. It is a shame, but most money and efforts in the realm of Christendom go to support corrupt fruit.

WHAT IS GOOD FRUIT?

It is that which is generated by the Holy Spirit and is always scriptural. What do we mean by this?

If God tells a person to do something, and he carries it out, it will always generate *"good fruit,"* which translates into souls saved, lives changed, sick bodies healed by the power of God, bondages broken, and believers baptized with the Holy Spirit.

As well, the fruit of the Spirit, which is *"love, joy, peace, longsuffering, gentleness, goodness, faith, meekness,"* and *"temperance,"* will be developed as the result of a good fruit ministry (Gal. 5:22-23).

As well, this good fruit will be obvious and can be easily substantiated.

Sometime back, one of the supporters of our ministry stated that he desired to go to Africa to see for himself the work we were carrying out there respecting food for the hungry, the propagation of the gospel, etc. We strongly encouraged him to do so, which he did. Actually, he made several trips.

He came back, stating, "Brother Swaggart, if every person could see that work, and see what is actually being done with the money they give, you would never again have to plead for funds."

While most do not have the ability to take such a trip, still, the point I wish to make is that if many donors to many alleged

ministries went to the site where the proposed work is supposed to be carried out, they would find little or nothing. Thank the Lord that this is not always the case, but too often, it is.

The sadness is, most believers, influenced by hype and having little spiritual discernment, little know which is the good tree or the corrupt tree. Actually, this is the real problem in Christianity.

Naturally, the corrupt tree is not going to advertise itself as corrupt fruit, but is going to do everything within its power to make people believe it is good fruit. So, it is left up to the believer to check out the fruit, to ascertain if it is good or bad. Most do not, trusting their denomination to make the choice for them, or else, are influenced by appearances, none of which has any scriptural validity!

(44) "FOR EVERY TREE IS KNOWN BY HIS OWN FRUIT. FOR OF THORNS MEN DO NOT GATHER FIGS, NOR OF A BRAMBLE BUSH GATHER THEY GRAPES."

The pattern is:

1. The phrase, *"For every tree is known by his own fruit,"* proclaims God's standard. It is not as much the amount of fruit, but rather the quality of fruit. As well, the words *"own fruit"* mean that God judges a person individually, and not according to the religious denomination to which he or she belongs, or even a particular church.

2. *"For of thorns men do not gather figs, nor of a bramble bush gather they grapes,"* means several things:

a. False doctrine, no matter how well presented, is not going to bring forth good fruit. This means that Catholicism, Mormonism, Buddhism, Hinduism, Confucianism, atheism, spiritism, or other such like philosophies cannot bring forth any good fruit, irrespective of the favorable publicity or how much the world may acclaim it as such.

b. As it applies to particular religious beliefs, likewise, it applies to the individual. The idea is this:

3. It doesn't matter how much a thorn bush or bramble bush is dressed up, publicized, and made to appear righteous, it will bring forth no good fruit.

Likewise, a good tree may have some

problems and may need some purging and pruning, as Jesus outlined in John, Chapter 15, but, still, it will ultimately bring forth good fruit because that's the kind of tree it is.

4. So, it really doesn't matter what man says it is. It matters what it actually is and is judged accordingly by God. As well, there is no excuse, as Jesus brings out, for one not to be able to properly define the fruit.

5. Too oftentimes, men support a corrupt tree because they are corrupt themselves. Conversely, many support a good tree because that's what they are.

(45) "A GOOD MAN OUT OF THE GOOD TREASURE OF HIS HEART BRINGS FORTH THAT WHICH IS GOOD; AND AN EVIL MAN OUT OF THE EVIL TREASURE OF HIS HEART BRINGS FORTH THAT WHICH IS EVIL: FOR OF THE ABUNDANCE OF THE HEART HIS MOUTH SPEAKS."

The exegesis is:

1. The phrase, *"A good man out of the good treasure of his heart brings forth that which is good,"* refers to the fact that all of this, whether good or evil, begins in the heart.

2. The actual meaning is that irrespective of what happens to a good man, even as David of old, ultimately, his heart will produce good treasure.

3. *"And an evil man out of the evil treasure of his heart brings forth that which is evil,"* once again specifies that the evil begins in the heart.

4. This means that no matter how much the evil is dressed up, lauded, or praised, and even thought by some or many to be good, ultimately, the evil treasure will come forth. It may take awhile on both counts, the good or the evil, but ultimately, the heart will produce what is there.

5. The phrase, *"For of the abundance of the heart his mouth speaks,"* says two things:

a. The heart is the seat of either good or evil. If it is good, this means the Lord has changed the heart from its evil ways, even though it may take awhile for the externals to fall into line. However, ultimately they will.

b. If one carefully listens to what is said, no matter how it is religiously flowered,

the telltale signs of evil will show themselves. A good heart cannot produce bitter water, while an evil heart cannot produce sweet water.

6. How is one to know, especially considering that all evil terminology is designed to deceive?

7. Once again, we come back to the Word of God. If the believer knows the Word, as all are commanded to do, it will be obvious. Conversely, if one does not know the Word, he will be easily deceived, hence, so many being presently deceived.

(46) "AND WHY DO YOU CALL ME LORD, LORD, AND DO NOT THE THINGS WHICH I SAY?"

The pattern is:

1. The beginning of the question, *"And why do you call Me, Lord, Lord"* means that all will call Him *"Lord,"* even though they have an evil heart. So, we have the spectacle, as I have repeatedly stated, of the true prophet and the false prophet, all espousing the same *"Lord."*

2. The conclusion of the question, *"And do not the things which I say?"* draws us back to the Word of God.

3. The true prophet, i.e., true believer, will attempt with all his or her strength to obey the Word. Others seek to twist and turn the Word, as the Pharisees of old, in order that they may not do what He says but what they or others say.

(47) "WHOSOEVER COMES TO ME, AND HEARS MY SAYINGS, AND DOES THEM, I WILL SHOW YOU TO WHOM HE IS LIKE."

The form is:

1. The phrase, *"Whosoever comes to Me,"* refers to the first step, which means accepting Christ as one's Saviour. Consequently, Jesus proclaims Himself as God.

2. *"And hears My sayings,"* constitutes the Word of God, both the Old and New Testaments. Of course, many things in the Old Testament have been fulfilled, especially the law of Moses. Nevertheless, there are many things in the Old Testament that are just as appropriate for the present as they were when originally given. Actually, the entirety of all civil law in the world, irrespective of the nation, creed, or race, is based on nine

of the Ten Commandments. Only the fourth commandment, *"Remember the Sabbath day, to keep it holy,"* is not included in the new covenant. As well, it is the only commandment that did not have a moral content. In effect, as we have previously stated, this commandment was specifically between God and Israel only and had no bearing on the rest of the world. Consequently, it is not included in the new covenant.

3. Of course, as should be obvious, all of the new covenant (New Testament) is apropos for any and all.

4. So, it is absolutely imperative that every believer hear, and continue to hear, *"My sayings,"* i.e., the Word of God.

5. The phrase, *"And does them,"* takes us to the third step.

Man must not only come to Christ and hear the Word, but, as well, he must do the Word. Regrettably, many, if not most, of the Christian community, little hear the Word of God, and even fewer still attempt to do it.

6. The phrase, *"I will show you to whom he is like,"* proclaims the end result of one who hears and does the Word.

7. Incidentally, this is the criterion for the entirety of the world, consequently, for all mankind, and for all time.

(48) "HE IS LIKE A MAN WHICH BUILT AN HOUSE, AND DIGGED DEEP, AND LAID THE FOUNDATION ON A ROCK: AND WHEN THE FLOOD AROSE, THE STREAM BEAT VEHEMENTLY UPON THAT HOUSE, AND COULD NOT SHAKE IT: FOR IT WAS FOUNDED UPON A ROCK."

The overview is:

1. The phrase, *"He is like a man which built an house,"* proclaims another parable, one readily understood by all.

2. This refers, at least as Jesus portrays it, to the entirety of the life's work of an individual in whatever capacity. Regrettably, many do not build much of a house; however, for those who do build a house, at least a house that will stand, it must be built on the principles laid down by Christ. Actually, Christ is that principal.

3. *"And digged deep, and laid the foundation on a rock,"* concerns the rock of the Word of God.

4. *"And when the flood arose, the stream*

beat vehemently upon that house," does not say that maybe a flood will come, but that for certain it shall!

5. Unfortunately, much of the teaching in the last few years on what purports to be faith has attempted to project an erroneous doctrine, claiming that if the proper confession is tendered, all vicissitudes of life can be eliminated. The Bible does not teach that!

6. Irrespective of how close a person lives to God, how consecrated that individual may be, or even how much faith that person may have, the flood is going to come and, to be sure, exactly as Jesus said, it will be *"vehement,"* i.e., strong with every attempt to destroy.

7. Actually, the Bible rather teaches the greater the faith, the greater the opposition, i.e., floods.

8. *"And could not shake it: for it was founded upon a rock,"* refers, as is obvious, to the indestructibility of this house because the foundation is laid on a rock.

9. As well, it must be understood that irrespective of the difficulties or problems that arise, irrespective of the vicissitudes of life, and irrespective of how severe it all may be, this house will not fall.

10. The key is the Word of God and one's adherence to it, which necessitates a very close relationship with Christ, as should be obvious!

(49) "BUT HE WHO HEARS, AND DOES NOT, IS LIKE A MAN THAT WITHOUT A FOUNDATION BUILT AN HOUSE UPON THE EARTH; AGAINST WHICH THE STREAM DID BEAT VEHEMENTLY, AND IMMEDIATELY IT FELL; AND THE RUIN OF THAT HOUSE WAS GREAT."

The exegesis is:

1. Even at the risk of being overly repetitious, we want to continue to proclaim the fact that every single thing that comes to us is by and through the Cross of Christ.

2. The Cross of Christ is to ever be the object of our faith.

3. With this done, the Holy Spirit will then work mightily within our hearts and lives, overcoming the law of sin and death.

HOLDING TO THE WORD OF GOD

The phrase, *"But he who hears, and does*

not," refers to one who has come to Christ and has even heard the Word of God, but, in effect, does not do the Word of God, which characterizes many, if not most.

So, even though a person is in Christ and has heard the Word, as important as it may be, such does not guarantee future blessing. He must, as well, obey the Word. This completely refutes the unscriptural doctrine of Unconditional Eternal Security.

Some may claim that this refers to people who know about Christ and have even heard the Word but will not accept it. However, the proper structure of the original language by the using of the words, *"Come to Me,"* refers to accepting Christ as one's Saviour.

Actually, the entirety of this scenario is said in another way in the *"parable of the sower"* (Mat. 13:18-23).

PARABLE OF THE SOWER

Some, as Jesus explained in that parable, indeed heard the Word and accepted it but, due to particular situations, fell by the wayside. So, it is not just those who say, *"Lord, Lord … But he who does the will of My Father which is in heaven"* (Mat. 7:21).

The phrase, *"Is like a man that without a foundation built an house upon the earth,"* refers to most of the world that builds upon that which looks like a foundation but, in reality, is not. This means that the Word of God is not one of several foundations, *but is the only foundation.* That is the reason nations and empires crumble.

Just the other night, I saw a documentary on one of the richest families in America. Even though the money numbered into the billions of dollars, still, the misery and heartache experienced by the family members were beyond description. It was because there was no *"foundation!"* That is the reason the mighty Soviet Empire crumbled, as well as every other empire that has ever existed.

That is the reason America is presently facing problems to which it has no solution—it has forsaken the Word of God. No matter how big, rich, large, or powerful it may be, without that foundation of the Word of God, ultimately, it will fall.

NOTES

THE FLOOD

The phrase, *"Against which the stream did beat vehemently, and immediately it fell,"* once again refers to the inevitable *"flood!"*

"And the ruin of that house was great," means the greater the house, the greater the ruin. Whether little or large, and no matter how large, without Christ, it will ultimately fall. As we have stated, even though it speaks of individuals, the principle holds true for mighty empires as well!

Egypt was once the greatest nation on the face of the earth, but today, she is but a drowsy sexton of ancient tombs.

THE FOUNDATION

The house built upon the sand, according to all outward observance, looked identical to the one that was built on the rock. You couldn't tell the difference in looking at them; however, there was a difference, and a great difference at that. One was built on the rock, and the other was built on the sand. So, when the flood came, as it always will sooner or later, the one built on the rock stood the test, while the one built on the sand crumbled and fell.

For hundreds of years, mighty Assyria laid claim to the world, at least the world of that day. However, at the present time, it is difficult to even find the ruins of its capital city, Nineveh.

Where is mighty Babylon? She was the head of gold of Daniel's interpretation. Sometime back, amidst the ruins of Babylon, a boy found a bronze seal. On it were inscribed the words, "The bearer of this seal has the same authority as the king of Babylon." The power of ancient Babylon was now held in the hands of a dirty urchin boy.

Where today is mighty Rome that ruled the world for nearly a thousand years? Her Caesars are organ grinders, and her mighty generals are peanut vendors!

Once, the armada of Spain sailed the seven seas. Today, Spain sits like a drowsy beggar watching the hands of a broken clock.

Mighty England once ruled half the world, with most of civilization saying, "Hail

Britannica." Today, the sun has set on her mighty empire.

Is America following suit?

Every empire fell because they built their house on sand, and ultimately, the flood swept them away. America is great because, as one philosopher said, "America is good!"

He then said, "When America ceases to be good, America will cease to be great!"

America, sad to say, is losing her way. We have slapped the face of God by making same-sex marriages legal. We are killing millions upon millions of babies by abortion, which means the earth is stained with the blood of those infants. The nation is no longer content to exist in its sin; now it wants to confront God, which it is doing. The sad fact is according to the following:

The problem is because the church has lost its way. The gospel is little being preached anymore. The Cross of Christ, which alone holds back the judgment of God, is little preached at this particular time. So, without a revival in the nation of America, wreckage will be the end result.

To be frank, every past empire has been built on sand and ultimately fell; however, one is coming, which will be built entirely on the solid rock, and that solid rock is Jesus Christ. That awaits the second coming! He will come, and of that, one can be certain because the Bible tells me so (Rev. 22:20).

"The Cross upon which Jesus died,
"Is a shelter in which we can hide,
"And its grace so free is sufficient for me,
"And deep is its fountain; as wide as the sea."

"Tho' millions have found Him a friend,
"And have turned from the sins they have sinned.
"The Saviour still waits to open the gates,
"And welcome a sinner before it's too late."

"The hand of my Saviour is strong,
"And the love of my Saviour is long.
"Through sunshine or rain,
"Through loss or in gain,

"The blood flows from Calvary,
"To cleanse every stain."

"There's room at the Cross for you,
"There's room at the Cross for you.
"Tho' millions have come,
"There's still room for one,
"Yes, there's room at the Cross for you."

CHAPTER 7

(1) "NOW WHEN HE HAD ENDED ALL HIS SAYINGS IN THE AUDIENCE OF THE PEOPLE, HE ENTERED INTO CAPERNAUM."

THE SAYINGS OF CHRIST

The phrase, *"Now when He had ended all His sayings in the audience of the people,"* refers to the Sermon on the Mount, the same as related by Matthew in Chapters 5 through 7. As we have alluded, some have claimed that Luke's account is an entirely different message than that of Matthew. However, I think the evidence points otherwise.

"He entered into Capernaum," concerned His headquarters, but more importantly, it was very near the mountain on which He gave this all-important message. As well, Matthew gives the same statement concerning Capernaum, and then, as Luke, he relates the healing of the centurion's servant. Therefore, every evidence points to both accounts being the same although, as commented on previously, Luke's account is abbreviated, and for reason.

Spence said, "The Sermon on the Mount was the foundation of all that Jesus was to do and teach. It spoke of the kind of reign He was inaugurating over the hearts of men, its stern rebuke of the dominant religious teaching of the day, its grave prophetic onlooks—all marked as the great manifesto of the all-great Master."

A LIFELONG STUDY

One could make a lifelong study of this all-important message and never begin to plumb its depths. It states what man is to be like, and above all, what he must be like, that is, if he is to enjoy that which God originally intended. As we have said repeatedly, the world with its creation, along with man, has never been viewed as God originally created them. Jesus let us know in St. John 10:10 what Satan has done to this creation. He steals, kills, and destroys, thus, the hallmark of his sinful, wicked reign, with all of its attendant misery.

However, Jesus then added in that great verse, *"I am come that they might have life, and that they might have it more abundantly."* Still, the observation of that more abundant life has only been observed in part, with its total fulfillment yet to come, but come it shall!

"He entered into Capernaum," refers to Him going back to this city after the Sermon on the Mount.

When one thinks of the wonderful things that Jesus did at Capernaum, and would have done in His hometown but for the stubbornness and gross unbelief of the people, one stands amazed. Of course, He will do the same for any and all who will give Him the opportunity, but sadly, so few do!

(2) "AND A CERTAIN CENTURION'S SERVANT, WHO WAS DEAR UNTO HIM, WAS SICK, AND READY TO DIE."

The pattern is:

1. *"And a certain centurion's servant"*: Referring first to the centurion, he was an officer in the Roman army. He would probably have been the equivalent of a modern captain. He was in charge of 100 soldiers, hence, centurion. In all the accounts given in the four gospels, this centurion's faith stands out as one of the most remarkable in history, intended by the Holy Spirit to serve as a lesson for all who follow Christ. As we shall see, it will be one of only two occasions where Jesus marvelled, this one of faith and the other of unbelief (Mk. 6:6). It is especially revealing, considering that this centurion was a Gentile.

2. *"Who was dear unto him, was sick, and ready to die,"* is spoken of a little differently by Luke, who was a physician, than by Matthew (Mat., Chpt. 8). Matthew mentioned that it was a particular type of paralysis, which caused considerable pain, and as Luke added, had taken him to the point of death.

(3) "AND WHEN HE HEARD OF JESUS, HE SENT UNTO HIM THE ELDERS OF THE JEWS, BESEECHING HIM THAT HE WOULD COME AND HEAL HIS SERVANT."

The structure is:

1. The phrase, *"And when he heard of Jesus,"* probably would have been better translated, *"And when he had heard about Jesus."*

2. As we shall see, this man was very much involved in the worship of God according to the law of Moses, even though he was a Gentile. So, he was not a novice concerning Jehovah. Inasmuch as Jesus was the topic of most every conversation, someone evidently related to him the healing power of Christ.

3. The original translation sounds as if he had not known of Jesus; however, that is not the case. I think one could say without fear of exaggeration that everyone by now knew about Jesus. The problem was, by the man being a Gentile, he probably thought that Jesus would not heed his request concerning the healing of his servant. However, the proper translation of the text shows us that somebody evidently related to him that Jesus did not discriminate whatsoever. Therefore, he now took steps to get to Christ.

4. *"He sent unto Him the elders of the Jews,"* means that he felt they probably had more sway with Christ than he as a Gentile would have. Little did he know who Christ actually was! Had he known, there would have been no hesitation on his part whatsoever.

5. *"Beseeching Him that He would come and heal his servant,"* speaks of desperation. As stated, the man was dying.

6. Many people came to Jesus. One came for a son, another for a daughter, and another for himself or herself, but here is the only instance of a master coming for a slave. In addition, this master was a Gentile—a Roman centurion in the army of Caesar. When the servant fell sick, he did not turn him out of doors, as many masters then did, but he hastened to the Great Physician on his behalf.

(4) "AND WHEN THEY CAME TO JESUS,

THEY BESOUGHT HIM INSTANTLY, SAYING, THAT HE WAS WORTHY FOR WHOM HE SHOULD DO THIS."

The order is:

1. The phrase, *"And when they came to Jesus, they besought Him instantly,"* presents the Jews beseeching Jesus on behalf of the centurion.

2. However, the manner in which they besought Jesus was totally ignored by the Lord. The elders of the Jews sought to impress upon Jesus the worthiness of the centurion. The centurion himself pleaded no merit, taking the position of utter unworthiness of even having Jesus come to his home.

3. Jesus did not regard either plea, but saw the great faith of the centurion in recognizing that He had power to merely speak a word where He was, and the servant of the centurion would be healed.

4. The phrase, *"Saying, That he was worthy for whom He should do this,"* pictures the basis on which most people expect an answer to prayer.

5. As the Jews sought to impress Jesus with this man's good works, likewise, many seek to impress God with the good things they have done or the bad things they have not done.

6. Prayer is not answered on this basis. In fact, there is nothing that man can do in order to earn favor with God. Such is impossible! As stated, the basis for answered prayer is faith in God and His Word. This alone moves God, not these little things of supposed merit.

(5) "FOR HE LOVES OUR NATION, AND HE HAS BUILT US A SYNAGOGUE."

A GOOD CHURCH WHERE THE SPIRIT OF GOD IS PREVALENT

The phrase, *"For He loves our nation,"* has much greater reference than to mere geography.

Being a Roman, if, in fact, he was, he had only known of the pagan worship of many gods. None of this, as it never can, filled the ache and void in his heart, as resides in all hearts. When he was given the assignment to be stationed in Israel, and more particularly, near the city of Capernaum, it is

NOTES

anyone's guess as to what his thoughts were. However, it was to be the greatest thing that would ever happen to him. To think that he would be stationed in the exact place where the earthly headquarters of the Son of God was is the greatest thing that could ever happen to any human being.

Likewise, anyone who has the privilege of being able to attend a good church where the Spirit of God is prevalent is blessed indeed! Despite the proliferation of Christianity around the world, believe it or not, these types of churches are rare. However, as most in Capernaum did not appreciate Who was in their midst, likewise, many today do not appreciate good churches, even if they are privileged to attend one. Thank God, this Gentile did not fall into this category.

A HUNGER FOR GOD

While stationed near Capernaum, the centurion evidently became acquainted little by little with the worship of the true God. Even though there is no record that he became a full-fledged proselyte, still, he seemed to be a frequent visitor to the synagogue and a true worshipper of God.

Gentiles who attended Jewish synagogues and who did not become full-fledged proselytes were referred to as *"strangers,"* and were allotted a particular place to sit at the rear of the building, but only as observers.

"And he has built us a synagogue," evidently means that the man was wealthy and had restored their existing structure, or else, built a new one entirely. For him to have done this proclaims his devotion to the God of Israel.

I have personally seen the site in the ruins of Capernaum where this synagogue is supposed to have been. Even though the ruins above the ground are not original, with earthquakes having destroyed what was once there, or even if the foundation is not original, still, the agreement seems to be that the site is correct. It is located only a short distance from the Sea of Galilee. It was in this synagogue where Jesus delivered a man of *"an unclean demon,"* and possibly performed many other miracles.

(6) "THEN JESUS WENT WITH THEM. AND WHEN HE WAS NOW NOT FAR

FROM THE HOUSE, THE CENTURION SENT FRIENDS TO HIM, SAYING UNTO HIM, LORD, TROUBLE NOT YOURSELF: FOR I AM NOT WORTHY THAT YOU SHOULD ENTER UNDER MY ROOF."

THE RESPONSE OF OUR LORD

The phrase, *"Then Jesus went with them,"* concerns the elders of the Jews who had been sent by the centurion.

Matthew says the centurion came personally; Luke here states that he came by deputation. Both statements are true, for his messengers represented him. Also, the word *"him,"* as is given in Verse 9, supports the belief that the centurion followed his messengers, and in his anxiety for his servant, repeated the message he had given them to deliver. The scenario seems to be as follows:

THE SCENARIO

First, Jairus sent the elders of the Jews with the message.

Then it seems that he sent other friends with another message as is outlined in Verse 6.

With this group evidently near his house and possibly standing immediately outside, the centurion himself came out, approached Jesus, and made statements to Christ that occasioned Jesus' statement about the man's great faith. As stated, there is no discrepancy.

"And when He was now not far from the house, the centurion sent friends to Him," which may have meant that when Jesus consented to come, which was at the request of the elders of the Jews, someone evidently ran and told the centurion that Jesus was on His way. At this stage, he sent friends to Jesus with a particular message.

"Saying unto Him, Lord, trouble not Yourself," probably referred to the thought on the centurion's part that the elders of the Jews may not have related to Jesus that he (the centurion) was a Gentile.

"For I am not worthy that You should enter under my roof," is the message the friends were sent to deliver.

This Gentile readily knew that most Jews thought of Gentiles as no more than dogs.

Even though he was respected very highly (even by the elders of the Jews) because of the reasons given, still, he had no idea what Jesus would think. So, he wanted Him to know beyond the shadow of a doubt exactly who he was, a Gentile, who was not a part of the great covenant between Jehovah and His people.

(7) "WHEREFORE NEITHER THOUGHT I MYSELF WORTHY TO COME UNTO YOU: BUT SAY IN A WORD, AND MY SERVANT SHALL BE HEALED."

The form is:

1. The phrase, *"Wherefore neither thought I myself worthy to come unto You,"* seems to be the time that the centurion came out himself. As stated, the party (including Jesus) was nearing the centurion's home, with him coming out to meet them and taking up the conversation.

2. *"But say in a word, and my servant shall be healed,"* proclaims a level of faith that is seldom, if ever, equaled by anyone in the Bible, at least of this nature. He asked for no outward sign, no touch, no contact, and not even a handkerchief or apron (Acts 19:12). The word the Master would speak would be enough.

3. Spence said that Martha would later say, "'I know whatsoever You will ask of God, He will give it to You' (Jn. 11:22), in effect, speaks amiss." Even though Christ did take directions from the Father concerning everything, still, Jesus was actually the source of blessing because as well as being man, He was also God.

(8) "FOR I ALSO AM A MAN SET UNDER AUTHORITY, HAVING UNDER ME SOLDIERS, AND I SAY UNTO ONE, GO, AND HE GOES; AND TO ANOTHER, COME, AND HE COMES; AND TO MY SERVANT, DO THIS, AND HE DOES IT."

The structure is:

1. The phrase, *"For I also am a man set under authority, having under me soldiers,"* proclaims the meaning of spiritual authority, and from a Gentile at that!

2. While every believer has spiritual authority, some have greater authority than others.

3. The origin of this authority always is God.

WHAT IS SPIRITUAL AUTHORITY?

Even though the centurion was speaking of civil or military authority, still, the meaning is the same respecting spiritual authority, which is delegated power. Even though this Roman centurion had power, to which he here refers, still, the power did not originate with him, but rather with the governmental structure of the Roman Empire headed up by Caesar. Likewise, in the sense of spiritual power, it does not originate with the individual who wields it, but rather has its source in God.

Recognizing and understanding authority, this military officer realized that the authority Jesus derived from God was so complete that He was able to exercise control even over diseases. Jesus spoke and acted with full divine authority and authorization.

THE AUTHORITY OF JESUS CHRIST

The authority Jesus possessed during the incarnation was derived from the Holy Spirit (Lk. 4:18). However, after He was glorified (after Calvary and the resurrection), the power now resides exclusively in Him (Mat. 28:18).

The very freedom of action in teaching and healing the people by Jesus stunned and disturbed the Jewish authorities, as well as all the people in Israel (Mk. 1:22, 27; Lk. 4:32-36). Instead of constantly referring to tradition as the authority for His actions, Jesus relied on His own unmistakable aura of power. When Jesus scandalized His listeners by pronouncing the sins of a paralyzed man forgiven, He proved His authority to do so by healing him so *that you may know that the Son of Man has power* (authority; freedom of action) *on earth to forgive sins* (Mat. 9:6-8; Mk. 2:10; Lk. 5:24).

Despite the greatest display of miracles the world had ever known, at the end of Jesus' ministry on earth, He was still being challenged by the religious leaders who were unwilling to accept Him as God's Son and messenger (Mat. 21:23-29; Mk. 11:28-33; Lk. 20:2-8).

Unfortunately, this contest did not conclude at that time. Many modern, so-called, religious leaders still refuse to accept authority

as delegated by God. Spiritual authority is given by God; it does not come by ballot.

Unfortunately, some officials in particular denominations think that because of their occupying some religious office, this means that they have added spiritual authority, and they are to be obeyed, irrespective as to what they demand. Nothing could be further from the truth.

HOW FAR DOES TRUE SPIRITUAL AUTHORITY EXTEND?

The Scriptures teach and assume that in a world warped by sin, governing authorities are a necessity, as should be obvious (Rom. 13:1-7).

In a philosophical and theological sense as freedom of action to control or limit the freedom of action of others, do Christian leaders really have authority within the church?

The issue is an important one and deserves much study and debate. However, a number of observations should be made to help us think about this issue.

For instance, Jesus delegated authority to His disciples (Mk. 3:15; 6:7; Lk. 9:1; 10:19), but this was authority over demons and diseases. No passage suggests freedom to exercise control over other human beings. In fact, the freedom of choice of those to whom these disciples came is clearly protected (Mk. 6:11; Lk. 10:8-12).

This is so important that we must say it again:

While every saint in the world has spiritual authority, and while some definitely have more than others, still, that authority is never over other human beings, but always and without exception, it is over Satan, demon spirits, etc. You won't find anything in the Bible that is otherwise.

NOT SO WITH YOU

One incident reported in the Synoptics is especially significant. Matthew, Chapter 20; Mark, Chapter 10; and Luke, Chapter 22, all tell of a heated debate among the disciples over which of them would be greatest. Jesus took that opportunity to instruct them on leadership and its character within the church. Each passage reports that Jesus said, *"You know that the rulers of the Gentiles lord over them, and their high officials exercise authority over them."* In each passage, Jesus bluntly ruled out this kind of leadership authority for them: *"Not so with you!"*

The alternative that Jesus spelled out is a servant leadership, and we might quickly add, a servant is a far cry from a ruler!

It is fascinating to compare these three passages and to note that one of them uses *exousia* to indicate the authority exercised by secular officials. The other two (Mat. 20:25; Mk. 10:42) use *katexousiazo,* and it is found only here in the New Testament. The latter word means "authority over," but it also implies a tendency toward whatever compulsion is required to gain compliance.

These passages suggest strongly that whatever authority Christians or even leaders may have, their freedom of action does not include the right to control the actions and choices of their brothers and sisters in the Lord.

THE USE OF APOSTOLIC AUTHORITY

The apostle Paul was deeply aware of the fact that as an apostle, he did have authority. He spoke of it in II Corinthians 10:13. He told the Corinthians that the Lord gave him authority with a specific purpose: For building you up, not for tearing you down (II Cor. 10:8; 13:10). In II Corinthians, Chapter 13, Paul spoke of his concern not to be harsh in my use of authority (II Cor. 13:10).

The context shows that the Christians in Corinth refused to admit that Christ was speaking through this servant leader.

It is almost impossible to conceive of such, especially considering that Paul had planted the Corinthian church, and most of these people had been saved under his ministry. However, this attitude and spirit show what can happen to believers when they leave the Word of God and begin to respond favorably to error.

How could they do this, considering who Paul was?

PAUL

In effect, Paul was the Moses of the New Testament, having been given the meaning of the new covenant of grace, as Moses had been given the law. As well, he wrote a little

over one-third of the New Testament. It is obvious, also, that he, under Christ, was the spearhead of the move of God in the early church, and was responsible, as well, for extending the frontiers of the gospel, with a burden equaled by no one else.

Why was this not obvious to the saints at Corinth?

False teachers had come in, attempting to mix law with grace, and in order to successfully do this, they had to denigrate the person and ministry of Paul as well. This they did, and with obvious success! Deception is a powerful weapon in the hands of Satan. If believers do not stay on fire for God, ensuring their close relationship with Christ, all, even the strongest, are susceptible to this effort by the evil one.

Although this must have hurt Paul greatly, he did not respond by threatening. Neither did he try to manipulate or coerce. He simply reminded them that Christ is not weak in dealing with you, but is powerful among you (II Cor. 13:3).

JESUS AS THE HEAD OF THE CHURCH

Paul had no need to resort to manipulation, coercion, or threats because Jesus was alive and acting as head of the church. Jesus remained powerful among His people and was free to exercise His authority in disciplining ways. Paul relied on Jesus to bring about a response to the words that He, Jesus, had given Paul to speak to the Corinthians.

These passages, and studies of Paul's style of leadership, suggest strongly that in the church, God limits the authority given to so-called leaders. The leaders' authority is not an authority to control, but an authority to help the believer use his or her freedom to respond willingly to the Lord.

IN SUMMING UP

Our primary insight into the nature of authority, as is obvious, comes from the New Testament. There we see it portrayed as unrestricted freedom of action. God has unlimited authority, which He exercises as He chooses to direct or permit. Jesus demonstrated His deity by proving that His own freedom of action was likewise unlimited.

Although Jesus delegated authority to His disciples, their freedom of action did not involve a right to manipulate or to coerce other persons. In fact, Jesus never acted in this way Himself. He did not compel, but rather invited His hearers to obey.

When Jesus taught His disciples about how authority would be experienced in the church, He specifically ruled out the kind of power-based authority that is exercised in the secular world for personal gain or glory. Jesus gives Christian leaders authority to build up believers, not to enslave or smother them. Built up in the faith, Christians will freely choose to be obedient to Jesus as living Lord, which is what Christianity is actually all about.

(Some of the notes on spiritual authority were derived from the teaching of Lawrence Richards.)

THE WORD OF THE CENTURION

The phrase, *"And I say unto one, Go, and he goes; and to another, Come, and he comes; and to my servant, Do this, and he does it,"* proclaims military authority enjoyed by this Roman centurion and, as well, typifies the authority possessed by Christ.

Respecting any and all beings in the spirit world, including righteous angels as well as the unrighteous variety, along with demon spirits, and even sickness, disease, and bondage caused by these evil spirits, Jesus exercised full authority. He, as well, has authority over the entirety of the human family but, as stated, little used it in that capacity, rather dealing with individuals to follow willingly. Actually, God does not force individuals to do anything, although He deals with them strongly! In fact, most of the world disregards His admonitions, with only a few believers truly responding in the manner in which this centurion described.

When the Lord says *"go,"* we should go!

When the Lord says *"come,"* we should come!

When the Lord says *"do thus and so,"* we should do thus and so!

If Caesar could expect such obedience from his pagan soldiers, should not the Lord expect at least the same from His followers?

NOTES

(9) "WHEN JESUS HEARD THESE THINGS, HE MARVELLED AT HIM, AND TURNED HIM ABOUT, AND SAID UNTO THE PEOPLE THAT FOLLOWED HIM, I SAY UNTO YOU, I HAVE NOT FOUND SO GREAT FAITH, NO, NOT IN ISRAEL."

THE HUMANITY OF CHRIST

The phrase, *"When Jesus heard these things, He marvelled at him,"* records one of the two instances when Jesus marvelled, with the other being at unbelief (Mk. 6:6).

This proclaims the humanity of Christ because as deity, He would not marvel at anything. The word *marvel* means to register astonishment.

It is further remarkable that God's people registered unbelief, as at Nazareth, which caused Jesus to marvel, and this Gentile, who was outside the covenant, registered a degree of faith not seen in God's chosen.

Why?

Faith comes by hearing and obeying the Word of God, and will accrue to all who meet the criteria, irrespective of whom they may be! When a person ceases to believe the Word and, consequently, ceases to obey the Word, irrespective of past experiences or covenants, as the Israel of Jesus' day, the results will always be the same—unbelief. The degree of unbelief of the Word, as Nazareth, determines the degree of rebellion against God. Everything is predicated on the Word of God. To adhere to it registers faith. To depart from it brings about the opposite result.

AN EXAMPLE

The phrase, *"And turned him about, and said unto the people that followed Him,"* refers to Jesus using the centurion's faith as an example of the faith He desired among all believers. Consequently, He addressed the people accordingly.

"I say unto you, I have not found so great faith, no, not in Israel," records this man as not only having faith, but great faith!

How could this centurion have this great faith, seeing that he had little access to the Word of God?

The record seems to be clear that he had more access than one at first might think

(Lk. 7:5). In building a synagogue for the people of Capernaum, he, no doubt, attended regularly, thereby, hearing the Word of God. As well, he possibly had copies of the various scrolls himself.

At any rate, what little of the Word he knew, he believed, which is all that is necessary to generate faith.

Coming down to the bottom line, every spiritual failure, of whatever kind, can ultimately be traced to a failure to believe and act upon the Word. The Word must not only be the standard but, as well, must be the interpreter. In other words, the Word rightly divided interprets itself (II Tim. 2:15).

FAITH

Faith is clearly one of the most important concepts in the whole of the New Testament. Everywhere it is required and its importance insisted upon. Faith means abandoning all trust in one's own resources. Faith means casting oneself unreservedly on the mercy of God. Faith means laying hold on the promises of God in Christ, relying entirely on the finished work of Christ for salvation, and on the power of the indwelling Holy Spirit of God for daily strength. Faith implies complete reliance on God and full obedience to God, which can only be done through His Word.

As well, it should be noticed that only two things caused Jesus to marvel, unbelief and faith, which means He completely ignored all the things at which most men marvel. For instance, He did not marvel at the beautiful buildings of the temple!

This means that the modern church gets very excited over things to which God gives little notice. Only unbelief and faith, with all their attendant results, both negative and positive, are the occasion for astonishment respecting our Lord.

(10) "AND THEY WHO WERE SENT, RETURNING TO THE HOUSE, FOUND THE SERVANT WHOLE WHO HAD BEEN SICK."

The exegesis is:

1. The phrase, *"And they who were sent,"* probably referred to the friends of Verse 6.

2. *"Returning to the house,"* refers to them going back after the Word of healing

NOTES

had been spoken by Jesus. Even though Luke does not mention what Jesus said, Matthew records Him saying, *"Go your way; and as you have believed, so be it done unto you"* (Mat. 8:13).

3. *"Found the servant whole who had been sick,"* was what they expected to find and is exactly what they did find. Whatever the sickness was, because of the faith of the centurion, at the command of Christ, the man was instantly healed.

4. If the world only understood exactly who Jesus is and that He alone is the answer to all of life's problems, the world situation would be instantly and drastically improved. However, unbelief prevails, even in the church, to such an extent that Christ is given little latitude in the hearts and lives of most!

5. The word *whole* not only implies healing for his sick body but, as well, implies salvation for the soul.

(11) "AND IT CAME TO PASS THE DAY AFTER, THAT HE WENT INTO A CITY CALLED NAIN; AND MANY OF HIS DISCIPLES WENT WITH HIM, AND MUCH PEOPLE."

The diagram is:

1. The phrase, *"And it came to pass the day after, that He went into a city called Nain,"* refers to an approximate 21-mile journey, which was an average day's travel. Immediately after healing the centurion's servant, Jesus, plus many disciples, left for Nain, possibly spending the night along the way.

2. As Luke is the only one who records this incident, quite possibly Jesus went to Nain for the express purpose of raising this young man from the dead. We know that whatever He did was guided and directed totally by the Holy Spirit; therefore, His journey to this little city was by design. What a blessed day for Nain!

3. *"And many of His disciples went with Him, and much people,"* which could have numbered a party of several hundred. Many wanted to be near Jesus, and no wonder!

(12) "NOW WHEN HE CAME NIGH TO THE GATE OF THE CITY, BEHOLD, THERE WAS A DEAD MAN CARRIED OUT, THE ONLY SON OF HIS MOTHER, AND SHE WAS A WIDOW: AND MUCH

PEOPLE OF THE CITY WAS WITH HER."

The overview is:

1. The phrase, *"Now when He came nigh to the gate of the city,"* refers to the entrance where this miracle took place. To be sure, it was to be a miracle of astounding proportions!

2. *"Behold, there was a dead man carried out, the only son of his mother, and she was a widow,"* refers to the normal manner of burying the dead at that time, which was always outside the towns, villages, and cities. The Jews believed that to touch a corpse or a tomb was the occasion of defilement and made the person ceremonially unclean. Therefore, all tombs, with some few exceptions, were outside the city limits.

3. *"And much people of the city was with her,"* denotes that the woman and the son evidently were well known, even though it seems not people of means.

(13) "AND WHEN THE LORD SAW HER, HE HAD COMPASSION ON HER, AND SAID UNTO HER, WEEP NOT."

The structure is:

1. The phrase, *"And when the Lord saw her,"* is rare in the Gospels, with *"Jesus"* being the usual term; however, it is stated that Luke and Paul both wrote in this manner because they always thought of Jesus *"as the Lord risen form the dead, enthroned in heaven."*

2. It is thought that Luke wrote this book not earlier than A.D. 60, and that this title of *"Lord"* had probably become the usual term by which the Redeemer was known among His own.

3. The phrase, *"He had compassion on her,"* portrays the love of God, as is obvious!

4. *"And said unto her, Weep not,"* has reference to what He was about to do. In other words, He was telling her that her cause for weeping was over as this young man was about to be raised to life.

5. Only Jesus can dry the tears from the eyes of the world, which, to be sure, run copiously! But sadly, many will not allow Him the opportunity, and dispensationally, due to the fall, the veil of sorrow will not be lifted until Jesus comes again. Then, He will *"wipe away all tears from their* (our) *eyes"* (Rev. 21:4).

(14) "AND HE CAME AND TOUCHED THE BIER: AND THEY WHO BEAR HIM STOOD STILL. AND HE SAID, YOUNG MAN, I SAY UNTO YOU, ARISE."

THE TOUCH

The phrase, *"And He came and touched the bier,"* referred to a wooden frame on which the dead was laid, wrapped in folds of linen. As well, a cloth was laid over the face, with the entire apparatus being carried on the shoulders of four men.

As we have alluded, it was unlawful for the living to touch a corpse or even the frame on which it was lying. Those who had no choice but to do so, as those who prepared the corpse and carried the frame, had to go through a ceremonial cleansing process, which had to do with the law of the red heifer (Num. 19:2-17).

The heifer symbolized Christ. It was spotless externally and without blemish internally. It was free from any bondage whatever. It was a female, and it was to be red. Christ, in His humanity, was spotless within and without. He was gentle as a woman, and He was never in bondage to any sin. The law had no claim on Him as a debtor, and He robed Himself with the red earth of manhood.

The heifer was to be led forth without the camp and there slain. So was Christ led of the Spirit to Calvary where He offered up Himself.

The blood of the heifer is mentioned only once, and that is in Numbers, Chapter 19. So Christ was once offered. It needed not that a heifer should be slain each time the cleansing process was offered—its ashes sufficed.

Purification from the defilement of touching the dead was effected by an application of the ashes of the burnt heifer with running, i.e., living water.

THE CROSS OF CHRIST

Christ's death need not be repeated, as the Catholics and others teach, in order to effect the forgiveness of the daily sins of the celestial pilgrim. It only needs that the meaning and perfection of His death, typified by the burnt ashes, should be effectively applied to the conscience by the living Spirit, which was symbolized by the running water. The sense of forgiveness and cleansing is then enjoyed.

Accidentally touching a bone, even though it was many years old, defiled and procured exclusion from the camp. Restoration was only possible after an application of the ashes of the heifer on the third day and on the seventh day.

The three days prior to the first purging fastened on the conscience the hatefulness of sin to God. The four days prior to the second and final application of the ashes and running water instructed the conscience as to the perfection of the purge and the wonders of the grace that provided it.

A PERFECT SALVATION

Possibly the third day pointed to the resurrection of Christ; the seventh day to His return in glory. During the first period, only an imperfect sense of the fullness of His sacrifice was possible, but in the coming, glorious, seventh day, there will be a perfected consciousness of this fullness.

However, to enjoy this perfect salvation on the seventh day, it must be appropriated on the third.

At evening after the seventh day, the defiled person was pronounced clean. The preciousness of Christ's atoning blood and its sufficiency to cleanse from all sin speaks with special sweetness to the heart and conscience at evening when life is closing and the shadows of death are about to fall.

The presence of death in a house defiled everything in a house except a covered vessel. The Christian pilgrim necessarily comes in contact with death every day, i.e., with that which defiles, but he escapes defilement if he is a *"covered vessel,"* that is, if he lives under the covering of the Holy Spirit.

With death being the ultimate result and final symbolism of sin, the law of the red heifer, symbolizing Christ, made it possible for the terrible effects of death to be stricken from the obedient believer.

TOUCHING THE BIER

So now, the astonished onlookers were amazed that one such as Jesus, the teacher

of Nazareth, the miracle-worker, should commit so strange an act, purposely defiling Himself. However, what they did not realize was, that perfect life, which was Jesus, could not be defiled simply for the reason that His touch would bring the dead to life. Consequently, His touching of this bier portrayed His touching and defeating death itself in order that it may have no more stranglehold over the child of God. Because of what He did at Calvary and the resurrection, one can shout as Paul, *"Death is swallowed up in victory."*

Consequently, *"O death, where is your sting? O grave, where is your victory?"* (I Cor. 15:54-55).

"And they who bear him stood still," referred to the astonishment of these people at the action of Jesus. There is no doubt that all there knew who Jesus was even though they had little understanding as to what He was! So, in astonishment, they *"stand still."* In His presence, everything must stop, including death.

ARISE

The phrase, *"And He said, Young man, I say unto you, Arise,"* presents the startling announcement of Christ. He raised one who had just died (Lk. 8:49-56), one being carried to burial (Lk. 7:12), and one dead four days (Jn., Chpt. 11). Several things are said in Verse 14:

• There is no evidence that any faith was present on the part of the mother. Of course, being dead, the young man could not have faith.

This symbolizes the unregenerate sinner who little knows or understands anything about God, or having faith for that matter, but simply believes to some small degree. The evidence is that even though this mother portrayed little faith, if any, there is no record of unbelief either!

• The words, *"Young man,"* symbolize death that cuts men off at about the time they have enough knowledge to make at least some sense of life. It is said that Einstein pleaded for five more years of life, feeling that during this time, he could unlock some of the secrets of the universe. What is 70 or 80 years in the light of eternity?

This terrible debilitating result of death was brought on by the fall, but as Jesus here portrays, will ultimately be defeated.

• The words, *"I say unto you,"* proclaim the deity of Christ. Only God could do such a thing as raise the dead, and that by a simple word!

As the song says:

"When He speaks, the tempter's pow'r is broken,

"When He speaks, the dark clouds roll away."

• The word *arise* speaks of the resurrection of the soul as well as the coming resurrection of the body. At salvation, one is literally raised from spiritual death, and at the resurrection of life, here portrayed by Christ, the sainted dead will come forth (I Thess. 4:13-18).

(15) "AND HE WHO WAS DEAD SAT UP, AND BEGAN TO SPEAK. AND HE DELIVERED HIM TO HIS MOTHER."

The diagram is:

1. The phrase, *"And he who was dead sat up, and began to speak,"* proclaims a miracle, as is obvious, of astounding proportions.

2. It is generally assumed that our Lord only raised three persons from the dead—this young man of Nain, the little daughter of Jairus, and Lazarus of Bethany; however, such an assumption is purely arbitrary.

Augustine, who lived about 350 years after Christ, said, "Of the numerous persons raised to life by Christ, three only are mentioned as specimens in the Gospels."

From this statement by Augustine, it seems that it was common knowledge in those days that only a small part of what Jesus actually did respecting miracles, etc., was actually given to us in the four gospels. John himself said, *"And there are also many other things which Jesus did, the which, if they should be written every one, I suppose that even the world itself could not contain the books that should be written"* (Jn. 21:25).

3. What must have been the reaction of the crowd that day at the city gate of Nain when this young man who had been dead, which was obvious to all, suddenly, because of the touch of Jesus, *"Sat up, and began to speak"*?

4. Williams said, "The Prince of Peace is stronger than the king of terrors; and death is not so mighty as the sinner's friend."

5. This, as the other occasions of Jesus raising someone from the dead, is an example of what will happen in the resurrection.

6. *"And He delivered him to his mother,"* proclaims far more here than meets the eye.

7. The idea refers to a presentation of sorts, with the mother standing in utter awe at what had transpired, and Jesus presenting her son to her, now vibrantly alive and healthy, which, without a doubt, was beyond comprehension.

(16) "AND THERE CAME A FEAR ON ALL: AND THEY GLORIFIED GOD, SAYING, THAT A GREAT PROPHET IS RISEN UP AMONG US; AND, THAT GOD HAS VISITED HIS PEOPLE."

FEAR

The phrase, *"And there came a fear on all,"* is a normal reaction to such a display of the mighty power of God. This was something that precious few people in human history had ever seen, the raising of one from the dead.

"And they glorified God," means that they knew this mighty miracle had been carried out by the power of God. There was no doubt about that!

The phrase, *"Saying, That a great prophet is risen up among us,"* is right and wrong at the same time. Spence said, "The sublime humility of the great wonder-worker failed to persuade the bulk of men and women with whom He came in contact. They could not look on this quiet rabbi-physician, Who gently put all state and pomp and glory aside, as the divine Messiah."

Why?

Once again, it was unbelief, pointing to a failure to know or properly interpret the Scriptures. While it was true that Israel was looking for a Messiah at this particular time according to the prophecies of Daniel and others, still, Jesus did not fit their imagined perception of what the Messiah would be like. They were looking for a conqueror who would come in royal majesty, overthrow Rome, and make Israel once again the leading nation in the world.

SPIRITUAL BLINDNESS

While there are many Scriptures that actually do point to this coming phenomenon, which will definitely happen, still, Israel was woefully unprepared in a spiritual sense for this for which they longed. To have made them master of the world would have made them a worse tyrant even than Rome, for there is no evil like religious evil. Had they carefully studied Isaiah, Chapter 53, plus many other passages in the Scriptures, they would have known Who this meek and lowly person actually was. The proof was abundant, but they could not see it because of their spiritual blindness.

Jesus was a great prophet and in that, they were correct; however, He was also priest and king, but of that, He was denied.

While it was true that they desired to make Him king, still, it was the wrong type of king. They wanted to use His miracles for their benefit instead of having their lives changed. Their self-righteousness, especially among their religious leaders, would not admit their dire spiritual need. Sadly, we have many today who seek to do the same thing, to use God instead of Him using them.

"And, That God has visited His people," proclaims a truth, but in far greater degree than they imagined.

They were speaking of the great spiritual drought of some 400 plus years since the days of Malachi, the last prophet of Israel. This spiritual drought was now over but in a way they never dreamed or imagined. John had introduced Jesus as the Messiah, but the religious leaders of Israel had totally ignored his introduction. Despite the miracles, signs, and wonders, they ignored Jesus as well!

(17) "AND THIS RUMOUR OF HIM WENT FORTH THROUGHOUT ALL JUDAEA, AND THROUGHOUT ALL THE REGION ROUND ABOUT."

The structure is:

1. The rumor spoken of here pertained to the debate as to who He really was! Some actually did believe He was the Messiah, but that number little included the religious leaders of Israel.

NOTES

Why?

2. Religion specializes in two things, money and control. There is little record of any financial dealings on the part of Christ, but to care for 12 men and their families, plus others, the amount would have been considerable. Most of all, the religious leaders were losing control of the people.

3. Religion demands total loyalty. At the first, despite the popularity of Christ, there was little breach. However, as the doctrines of Christ more and more began to contradict the false teaching of the Pharisees and scribes, the breach became wider and wider. Finally, open war was declared, with most of the synagogues in Israel closed to Christ during the last year of His ministry. It is ironic that the Lord of Glory was not welcome in His own church; however, it is little different at present, with many, if not most, modern churches the same as the Jewish synagogues of old!

(18) "AND THE DISCIPLES OF JOHN SHOWED HIM OF ALL THESE THINGS."

The pattern is:

1. John the Baptist was now in prison. It seems that his disciples had free access to him and, no doubt, even as the Scripture says, outlined to him all the wonderful things being done by Jesus. However, it seems what they told John puzzled him!

2. As stated, they, no doubt, recounted the miracles they had witnessed and all the gracious words they had heard. However, they heard nothing about Roman rule or anything concerning Herod Antipas, who had wrongfully shut John up in prison. Actually, there was little political bent to the message of Jesus whatsoever.

Evidently this puzzled John, with him seemingly having at least some of the thoughts that others had concerning what the Messiah would be like. Many things, such as the miracles and messages, were exactly what the Messiah would do; however, other things, at least according to their ideas, seemed to be missing.

(19) "AND JOHN CALLING UNTO HIM TWO OF HIS DISCIPLES SENT THEM TO JESUS, SAYING, ARE YOU HE WHO SHOULD COME? OR LOOK WE FOR ANOTHER?"

The form is:

1. The phrase, *"And John calling unto him two of his disciples sent them to Jesus,"* constituted a mission that has left many questions unanswered.

2. The questions, *"Are You He who should come? or look we for another?"* have been looked at in two different ways.

3. Some of the expositors of old have claimed that John, while never doubting Jesus himself, watched his disciples begin to waiver and sent them to Jesus in order that their doubts may be quelled.

4. However, others believe that the questions of John were prompted by his own wavering faith—a faltering, no doubt, shared by his own disciples. Jesus' answers, as we shall see, seem to fit the latter case.

5. Spence said, "It is thus ever the practice of Holy Scripture; while it tenderly and lovingly handles the characters of its heroes, it never flinches from the truth. We see God's noblest saints, such as Moses and Elijah (John's own prototype) in the Old Testament, Peter and Paul in the New Testament, depicted in this Book of Truth with all their faults; nothing is hid. Only one flawless character appears in its storied pages—it is only the Master of Peter and Paul who never turns aside from the path of right."

(20) "WHEN THE MEN WERE COME UNTO HIM, THEY SAID, JOHN BAPTIST HAS SENT US UNTO YOU, SAYING, ARE YOU HE WHO SHOULD COME? OR LOOK WE FOR ANOTHER?"

The form is:

1. The phrase, *"When the men were come unto Him, they said, John Baptist has sent us unto You,"* presented in symbolic form a mission on which many have embarked. The investigation into the claims of Christ has involved in one way or the other a great part of the human family. Even if it is in a negative way, as in the Muslim religion, still, Christ is presented, with men forced to make a decision. Regrettably, most reject His claims and His person.

2. All unbelievers are deceived, and even some believers to a certain degree. The deception is so complete and, therefore, total that it is very difficult for one to be brought to the place of receiving Christ, even though the

NOTES

Word is truthfully presented and the Holy Spirit truly convicting. While there would be exceptions to this, as a whole, it is so! Hence, *"Few there be that find it"* (Mat. 7:14).

3. The questions, *"Are You He who should come? or look we for another?"* proclaims John's disciples faithfully delivering the message to Christ exactly as John had requested.

4. Even though John may have temporally doubted, no criticism is in order, as the answer of Christ projects!

(21) "AND IN THAT SAME HOUR HE CURED MANY OF THEIR INFIRMITIES AND PLAGUES, AND OF EVIL SPIRITS; AND UNTO MANY WHO WERE BLIND HE GAVE SIGHT."

A SPIRIT OF INFIRMITY

The phrase, *"And in that same hour He cured many of their infirmities,"* proclaims, as Luke described it, the first of the threefold classification of these maladies.

The Greek word for *infirmities* is *astheneia* and refers to "want of strength" or "weakness." In other words, no specific disease was attached to the individual, but yet, the person was constantly sick or sickly. As well, some actually had a spirit of infirmity, which was definitely caused by demon spirits, although most did not fall into this category (Lk. 13:11).

The words, *"And plagues,"* referred to particular diseases. The Greek word is *mastix* and means "a whip or scourge." The idea is that the person is plagued by a disease of some nature, which affects the body in the same manner as someone whipping or scourging it. As would be obvious, it is not a very pleasant situation. This is the second classification.

The phrase, *"And of evil spirits,"* refers to both demon possession and demon oppression. As well, demon spirits could very well be involved in the first two classifications, although not every time.

TO THE BLIND HE GAVE SIGHT

The phrase, *"And unto many who were blind He gave sight,"* refers to the effects of a disease that had caused blindness, which necessitated the healing of the disease and the miraculous restoration of that which had been damaged, in this instance, eyesight. In other words, it was a miracle! However, the word *miracle* could probably be used for all of these situations, as it refers to an intervention by the Lord.

All of these great things were being done at the same time the disciples of John approached Jesus. They, no doubt, stood and watched as these miracles were performed. As well, considering the display of the power of God, the entirety of this setting was freighted with the glory of God. In other words, the praises to God must have filled the air as people were instantly healed by the Master's touch. Some were, no doubt, laughing, while others were crying—crying not for sorrow but for joy! It was a scene such as humanity had never witnessed in all of its history, and in truth, has not witnessed since. What it must have been like is impossible to describe.

Not a single one who came for healing went away without that healing, irrespective of how bad his situation. All were healed and all were delivered!

Even as I sit here dictating these words, I sense the presence of God. I can imagine what it must have been like. Some who had been sick for years, and even at the point of death, were suddenly completely healed! Blinded eyes were opened! The demon possessed were instantly set free! Diseases with obvious results were instantly dispelled, with the individual made every whit whole.

WHAT MUST IT HAVE BEEN LIKE?

In one's mind, one can see parents bringing a child to Jesus, a child even at the point of death. Patiently they wait their turn, and then finally, they are standing before the Creator of the ages. In many cases, without a word, He extends His hand and touches the child, and the moment that glorious touch is manifested, instant healing takes place. One moment the child is sick and dying, and the next moment completely well!

One can see the smile on the child's face as it realizes in its body that it is healed. One can look at the parents' faces, as tears roll down, as they attempt to thank the Lord for what He has done.

NOTES

As someone has said, and said it well, "About all one can do for the great things done for him by Jesus is to simply say, 'Thank you!'"

The scene I have attempted to describe, no doubt, happened thousands of times over, and in every description. Think of it! Not a single person who came to Him left unhealed or undelivered. This is what was observed by the disciples of John the Baptist. What a story they would have to tell!

(22) "THEN JESUS ANSWERING SAID UNTO THEM, GO YOUR WAY, AND TELL JOHN WHAT THINGS YOU HAVE SEEN AND HEARD; HOW THAT THE BLIND SEE, THE LAME WALK, THE LEPERS ARE CLEANSED, THE DEAF HEAR, THE DEAD ARE RAISED, TO THE POOR THE GOSPEL IS PREACHED."

The overview is:

1. The phrase, *"Then Jesus answering said unto them,"* proclaims Him not answering their question until everyone around Him had received their healing or deliverance.

2. *"Go your way, and tell John what things you have seen and heard,"* were things never seen and heard by any previous generation. And yet, the religious leaders of Israel refused Him!

3. The phrase, *"How that the blind see,"* was a fulfillment of the prophecies of Isaiah 29:18; 35:5. Incidentally, Jesus quoted Isaiah more than He did any other prophet.

4. The phrase, *"The lame walk,"* was a fulfillment of Isaiah 35:6; 61:1.

5. The phrase, *"The lepers are cleansed,"* was a fulfillment of Isaiah 61:1.

6. The phrase, *"The deaf hear,"* was a fulfillment of Isaiah 29:18; 35:5.

7. The phrase, *"The dead are raised,"* was a fulfillment of Isaiah 11:2.

8. The phrase, *"To the poor the gospel is preached,"* was a fulfillment of Isaiah 11:2; 42:1-5; 60:1-3; 61:1-2.

9. John would have been very familiar with these passages. As well, it tells us of the great prophetic part played by Isaiah in the ministry of Christ, for, as stated, Jesus quoted or referred to him more than any.

10. Miracles as miracles did not accredit Jesus to be the promised Messiah. What did accredit Him was that He worked the

miracles predicted of Him in the Scriptures, and as given. Actually, the false prophet will work amazing miracles, as well, proving that doing such is not really a reliable verification (Rev. 13:13).

11. It is sad that Israel refused the miracles of Christ, although scriptural, and obviously so, but yet, will accept the miracles of the Antichrist, although unscriptural, and obviously so! (Jn. 5:43; Rev. 13:14).

(23) "AND BLESSED IS HE, WHOSOEVER SHALL NOT BE OFFENDED IN ME."

The overview is:

1. The phrase, *"And blessed is he,"* begins this mild rebuke regarding John's questions and is actually given in the form of a beatitude.

2. *"Whosoever shall not be offended in Me,"* is actually a plea that John (or whoever) would not find an occasion of stumbling in the manner in which Christ had actually come. They wanted a victorious conqueror to overthrow Rome. In fact, Jesus was a victorious conqueror, but over the powers of darkness, which were a far greater despot than Rome. Israel's problem was not Rome, but rather sin, which is the problem of all! It was this stranglehold that Jesus came to break, which He did break. By referring to the miracles of healing and the poor having the gospel preached to them, Jesus was referring John strictly to the Scripture. In effect, He was saying, "Look to the Word of God and forget the assumptions, which are man-devised."

3. The mention of the gospel being preached to the poor was that which the Scripture proclaimed, and that with which John would have been greatly familiar, especially considering that it was these same people who responded to his ministry.

4. John's disciples would have especially noticed the poor class of people who basically made up the great crowds that came to hear Jesus. Actually, it was a new experience in the world's story, this tender care for the poor. No heathen teacher of Rome, Athens, Alexandria, or the Far East had ever cared to make this vast class of unprofitable hearers the objects of their teaching. The rabbis of Israel cared nothing for them. In fact, in the Talmud, we often find the poor spoken of with contempt.

NOTES

5. However, John knew that this speaking to and consorting with the poor would be one of the marked characteristics of the Messiah when He came.

6. Such is still the mark of Jesus presently. If it isn't, with the poor gradually shoved aside, then it means the gospel of Jesus Christ is being preached less and less.

(24) "AND WHEN THE MESSENGERS OF JOHN WERE DEPARTED, HE BEGAN TO SPEAK UNTO THE PEOPLE CONCERNING JOHN, WHAT WENT YOU OUT INTO THE WILDERNESS FOR TO SEE? A REED SHAKEN WITH THE WIND?"

The composition is:

1. The phrase, *"And when the messengers of John were departed, He began to speak unto the people concerning John,"* referred especially to those who had heard the questions posed by John's disciples. Jesus did not want the people to think less of John because of these questions; consequently, He would ask some questions of His own.

2. The question, *"What went you out into the wilderness for to see?"* refers to much of Israel responding to the message and ministry of John the Baptist when it first began. A new wind was blowing over Israel. In fact, the prophetic voice had not been heard in Israel since Malachi, a period of some 400 years.

3. Jesus was saying to these people that they did not make the trip into the wilderness for nothing! They had heard that God was once again speaking through a man, and they wanted to hear the message. They were not disappointed! Jesus called attention to this fact.

4. The question, *"A reed shaken with the wind?"* referred to the reedy banks of Jordan. These reeds had little strength and would bend with the slightest wind. It was obvious that John was anything but that. Although his faith had failed him for a moment perhaps, still, he was no wavering reed.

(25) "BUT WHAT WENT YOU OUT FOR TO SEE? A MAN CLOTHED IN SOFT RAIMENT? BEHOLD, THEY WHICH ARE GORGEOUSLY APPARELLED, AND LIVE DELICATELY, ARE IN KINGS' COURTS."

The structure is:

1. The question, *"But what went you out for to see?"* was probably asked in response

to the mumblings that may have occurred respecting the questions of John's disciples. Consequently, Jesus hammered home His statements in the form of questions, which called attention to what John really was.

2. Among other things, Jesus was saying that a man should not be judged on one momentary lapse. But yet, that is exactly the way many judge.

3. If the truth be known, every single believer who has ever lived, even the giants of the faith, has wavered momentarily in one way or the other. Possibly it was known only to God, but nevertheless, it happened, and probably more times than one.

4. The believer should take a lesson from this and not be so judgmental. The prophet wavered, the people murmured (that is, if they did!), and, as we shall see, Jesus gave (concerning John) the most glowing testimony of any man who has ever lived. It should be a lesson to us!

5. The question, *"A man clothed in soft raiment?"* proclaims that John had denied himself the normal comforts and pleasures. His life was lived for one thing: to do the will of God.

6. In fact, the austere life was designed by the Holy Spirit to serve as a symbol of what Israel needed to do. Israel had grown soft and effeminate, with financial prosperity becoming her goal instead of God. John's lifestyle and appearance were a witness to the entirety of the nation that they desperately needed to repent.

7. The phrase, *"Behold, they which are gorgeously appareled, and live delicately, are in kings' courts,"* in effect, is stating that had John compromised his message, he would have been Herod's preacher. Instead, he was Herod's prisoner.

(26) "BUT WHAT WENT YOU OUT FOR TO SEE? A PROPHET? YES, I SAY UNTO YOU, AND MUCH MORE THAN A PROPHET."

The diagram is:

1. The questions, *"But what went you out for to see? A prophet?"* in effect, answered what was asked. It is obvious that the people went to see a prophet, but Jesus, by His next statement, was to take them even to a higher scale regarding John.

2. The phrase, *"Yes, I say unto you, and much more than a prophet,"* was, in fact, a startling statement!

3. What could be more, even much more, than a prophet?

4. This one statement placed John in a category all to himself. At that moment the people may have thought less of him, but not God!

(27) "THIS IS HE, OF WHOM IT IS WRITTEN, BEHOLD, I SEND MY MESSENGER BEFORE YOUR FACE, WHICH SHALL PREPARE YOUR WAY BEFORE YOU."

The structure is:

1. The phrase, *"This is he, of whom it is written,"* once again referred the people back to the Word of God. The Word was always the standard that Jesus used and the standard that all must use presently and forever.

2. *"Behold, I send My messenger before Your face, which shall prepare Your way before You,"* was quoted from Malachi 3:1, a passage with which, no doubt, the hearers were very familiar. Several things are here said:

a. The One initially speaking was God the Father. He said, *"I send."*

b. The messenger is John the Baptist, whom Jesus now identified as fulfilling this great prophecy.

c. The words, *"Before Your face,"* referred to Jesus. Consequently, the Lord announced himself as the coming angel of the covenant. Even though the Son of Man may not have openly declared Himself as such, still, it was enough that by the thrice-repeated, *"Your face," "Your way,"* and *"Before You,"* He signified that He was marked out and referred to by the Father. Consequently, there was no excuse for anyone not knowing who He was!

d. The preparation of Your way would be done by John the Baptist. As the forerunner, he introduced Christ, and now that his mission was done, he would soon be called to glory. Actually, Herod would execute him in a very short time.

3. If one is to notice, two persons of the Trinity were referred to here because Jehovah was not speaking of Himself, but Jehovah was speaking to Jesus, hence, the form, *"Before You."*

(28) "FOR I SAY UNTO YOU, AMONG

THOSE WHO ARE BORN OF WOMEN THERE IS NOT A GREATER PROPHET THAN JOHN THE BAPTIST: BUT HE WHO IS LEAST IN THE KINGDOM OF GOD IS GREATER THAN HE."

The overview is:

1. The phrase, *"For I say unto you, Among those who are born of women there is not a greater prophet than John the Baptist,"* places this man in a greater position than all the prophets who preceded him.

How could this be?

2. All the other prophets, as great as they were, such as Isaiah, only pointed to the distant future and said, in essence, "He is coming," referring to the Messiah. John had the privilege of not just pointing to Him in some distant time, but actually announcing, *"Behold, the Lamb of God,"* or, in essence, "Behold, He is here!" That privilege, and a privilege it was, even beyond the magnitude of comprehension, was John's alone.

3. *"But he who is least in the kingdom of God is greater than he,"* presents such a startling statement that it has been a source of controversy ever since.

4. However, there seems to me no need for confusion. Jesus was merely referring to the greater position and privileges enjoyed and entertained in the fullness of the gospel than was John's position under law in introducing the Messiah, who was to bring the fullness of blessing and grace to men (Jn. 1:16-17).

5. This is what Paul was addressing when he said, *"But now has He obtained a more excellent ministry, by how much also He is the mediator of a better covenant, which was established upon better promises"* (Heb. 8:6).

6. John could only have a measure of the Spirit (Mat. 3:14; Jn. 1:15-17), but now, the least believer can have the fullness (Lk. 24:49; Jn. 7:37-39; 14:12-15; Acts 1:4-8; 2:38-39; 5:32; Eph. 3:19).

7. Men could only have certain gifts of the Spirit in Old Testament days. Now, the least believer may have them all (Mk. 16:15-20; Jn. 14:12-15; I Cor., Chpt. 12). Many are the blessings the gospel promises now that could not have been given to anyone before Christ (II Cor. 3:6-15; Heb. 8:6; I Pet. 1:10-12).

NOTES

8. John could only announce that the kingdom of God was at hand (Mat. 3:2). This meant that it was now ready to be introduced, which, of course, would come through Christ. As we have stated, even though John was privileged to introduce it, still, he was not privileged at the time to enjoy it as all were able to do after Calvary and the resurrection. Calvary was the new covenant, with the old law lasting up unto that moment (Heb. 10:10-18).

(29) "AND ALL THE PEOPLE WHO HEARD HIM, AND THE PUBLICANS, JUSTIFIED GOD, BEING BAPTIZED WITH THE BAPTISM OF JOHN."

The overview is:

1. The phrase, *"And all the people who heard Him, and the publicans, justified God,"* means that the people pronounced God just in showing mercy to penitent sinners by honoring John's ministry.

2. *"Being baptized with the baptism of John,"* referred to John declaring them all to be sinners, and, therefore, those who submitted to the baptism of repentance confessed that their judgment was just.

3. *"And the publicans,"* is placed here for a particular reason. As is known, the publicans were tax collectors, and as such, were declared by the religious leaders of Israel to be outside the covenant, in other words, unable to be saved. However, John opened his baptism to all, including the publicans, which infuriated the Pharisees and lawyers mentioned in the next verse. The idea that John said these had to repent the same as these publicans caused them to reject John's message.

However, many of the publicans accepted John's offer of repentance and, in turn, justified God in His demand that they repent. In other words, they saw themselves as God saw them, which repentance demands, to which the Pharisees and scribes would not submit.

(30) "BUT THE PHARISEES AND LAWYERS REJECTED THE COUNSEL OF GOD AGAINST THEMSELVES, BEING NOT BAPTIZED OF HIM."

PHARISEES AND LAWYERS

The phrase, *"But the Pharisees and*

lawyers rejected the counsel of God against themselves," means that they refused to admit they needed to repent. How so like the modern church! That bad men need to repent is readily understood, but that good men need to repent is not understood at all!

This passage does not mean that none of this class accepted John's baptism, but that, as a whole, they came not to his baptism.

Spence said, "The result of the refusal of these powerful and learned men to hear the reformer's voice was that John's mission failed to bring about a national reformation." In effect, this is the same problem that has always prevailed.

If the religious leaders will not accept the ways of God, or at least enough of them to bring about a national move, generally, as here, the greatest move will fail. People are like sheep, and as a result, they follow the wrong shepherd most of the time.

"Being not baptized of him," means that they refused his baptism simply because they refused to admit that they needed to repent, even as these publicans.

This has ever been the problem of much of mankind. That all must come alike is of no difficulty to the publican types, but great difficulty to those who consider themselves God-fearing and morally good. Actually, the Pharisees and scribes were the moralists of their day. They were not just religious but, in effect, very religious. As such, they became very lifted up in their self-righteousness. As a result, they rejected John's message and killed Jesus Christ. That is how moral they really were.

MORALISTS

Actually, most in the modern-day church could only be labeled as *"moralists."* They belong to a church and do their duty respecting particular charitable events. They subscribe to a particular code of conduct and call themselves *"Christians."* The truth is, most of these individuals have never had a salvation experience. They have never made Jesus Christ their Lord and Saviour. He is known to them as a historical figure. By their particular code of conduct and their belonging to a particular church, they would label that as *"accepting Him,"* when,

NOTES

in reality, they have never truly had a heart experience with God.

So, the idea to these people, as those of old, that they need to repent is foreign to their ears and mostly rejected.

In my many years of evangelistic work, I have seen some few of these people yield to the convicting power of the Holy Spirit and accept Jesus Christ as Saviour. However, that number has been small. Of the many who have come to Christ under our ministry, it has mostly been those who, proverbially speaking, had their backs to the wall so to speak. With nowhere to turn, they turned to Jesus as the publicans of old.

(31) "AND THE LORD SAID, WHERE UNTO THEN SHALL I LIKEN THE MEN OF THIS GENERATION? AND TO WHAT ARE THEY LIKE?"

THIS GENERATION

The question, *"And the Lord said, Where unto then shall I liken the men of this generation?"* now proclaims judgment. The generation which He was then addressing had been singularly blessed with two great divine messages. The one was delivered by the eminent servant of God, John, about whom He had been speaking in such glowing, earnest terms. The other message was His own. In effect, no generation before or since has ever seen a move of God such as this. *"Unto whomsoever much is given, of him shall much be required"* (Lk. 12:48).

As a result of this generation spurning this clarion call, a little over 35 years later, it would suffer total destruction. The Roman 10th Legion under Titus laid waste Jerusalem, slaughtering over 1 million people.

A RECKONING ...

Is America likewise facing a reckoning?

If the spiritual declension continues, which it certainly shall unless revival is forthcoming, America is definitely facing judgment. In effect, the judgment is already commencing, with crime increasing to alarming proportions and, as well, with the weather patterns wreaking havoc in many areas.

I fully believe the Bible teaches that all of these things are tied somewhat to the spiritual condition of the people, which greatly affects any nation, and the spiritual condition of the people is greatly tied to the Cross of Christ or the lack thereof.

In other words, the modern church is not preaching the Cross. It's preaching everything except the Cross. The Message of the Cross holds back judgment. It will not stay all judgment, but it most definitely will have a mediating influence, that is, if it is preached.

That's why I believe that the Sonlife Broadcasting Network is so very important. Our message is the Message of the Cross. In other words, we preach the Cross, and that, no one can deny.

WHAT ARE THEY LIKE

The question, *"And to what are they like?"* will be answered in the following statement.

When people lose their way with God, as the following Scriptures prove, several things begin to happen:

• Such people no longer have the spiritual discernment to recognize the Lord and His work; consequently, they easily follow any false shepherd.

• Whatever the Spirit of God does, and in whatever direction, is unacceptable to these people.

• The plague of deception grips such individuals, causing spiritual blindness, which causes the Holy Spirit to bring upon them a just judgment. If men want darkness, it will be given them!

(32) "THEY ARE LIKE UNTO CHILDREN SITTING IN THE MARKETPLACE, AND CALLING ONE TO ANOTHER, AND SAYING, WE HAVE PIPED UNTO YOU, AND YOU HAVE NOT DANCED; WE HAVE MOURNED TO YOU, AND YOU HAVE NOT WEPT."

The pattern is:

1. The phrase, *"They are like unto children sitting in the marketplace, and calling one to another,"* presents Jesus using an illustration that was familiar to all the people.

2. *"And, saying, We have piped unto you, and you have not danced; we have mourned to you, and you have not wept,"* in effect, proclaims the two methods used by the Lord to reach Israel, but both to no avail!

3. Bishop Wordsworth said, and paraphrasing the words of Jesus, "You were angry with John because he would not dance to your piping, and with Me because I will not weep to your dirge; John censured your licentiousness, I rebuke your hypocrisy; you vilify both, and reject the good counsel of God, who has devised a variety of means for your salvation."

(33) "FOR JOHN THE BAPTIST CAME NEITHER EATING BREAD NOR DRINKING WINE; AND YOU SAY, HE HAS A DEVIL."

The form is:

1. The phrase, *"For John the Baptist came neither eating bread nor drinking wine,"* refers to John's austere lifestyle spent in the desert apart from the ordinary joys and pleasures of men, and little sharing even in these things termed *"the necessities of life."* As we have stated, his lifestyle was directed by the Holy Spirit and was meant to picture the destitute spiritual condition of Israel, which could only be changed by repentance in sackcloth and ashes, proverbially speaking.

2. *"And you say, He has a devil* (demon),"* presented the response of the religious leaders of Israel to the message of John demanding repentance.

3. One of Satan's favorite ploys is to have professing believers brand anything not of their choosing as *"of the Devil!"* Consequently, many in the modern church proclaim the baptism with the Holy Spirit with the evidence of speaking with other tongues (Acts 2:4) as being of the Devil.

4. Likewise, and using myself as an example, many so-called Pentecostal leaders have labeled our own efforts as no more than *"showmanship"* or a *"nice act."* And this, I might quickly add, is despite multiple thousands of people coming to Christ, with satanic bondages being broken and other thousands being baptized with the Holy Spirit. In effect, they were referring to the Holy Spirit and that which He does as little more than an act!

5. As with Israel of old, such is dangerous business!

(34) "THE SON OF MAN IS COME EATING AND DRINKING; AND YOU SAY, BEHOLD A GLUTTONOUS MAN, AND A

WINEBIBBER, A FRIEND OF PUBLICANS AND SINNERS!"

The pattern is:

1. The phrase, *"The Son of Man is come eating and drinking,"* referred to the lifestyle of Jesus as being totally opposite of that of John.

2. The idea, as presented by the Holy Spirit, is that Israel should have repented under the preaching of John, which they were intended to do, and which would have occasioned great joy respecting the ministry of Christ. In other words, as should be obvious, the Holy Spirit designed both lifestyles.

3. *"And you say, Behold a gluttonous man, and a winebibber,"* was not what Jesus was, but what they said He was. These religious leaders also said that He performed His miracles by the power of Satan.

4. The truth is, He was not a gluttonous man or a winebibber!

5. *"A friend of publicans and sinners,"* for a change, pronounced something truthful of Jesus. He was a friend to these groups, and thankfully so. However, being their friend did not mean that He condoned or partook of their lifestyles. In fact, it was not condoned; however, love does not have to condone something for love to be shown.

(35) "BUT WISDOM IS JUSTIFIED OF ALL HER CHILDREN."

The form is:

1. The idea of this verse is that both methods tendered by the Holy Spirit to reach Israel were wise and right.

2. However, neither method was accepted by Israel; therefore, Israel went to her doom!

3. All of this shows us the efforts of the Holy Spirit to try to turn men from judgment to salvation, but most of the time, it is to no avail.

(36) "AND ONE OF THE PHARISEES DESIRED HIM THAT HE WOULD EAT WITH HIM. AND HE WENT INTO THE PHARISEE'S HOUSE, AND SAT DOWN TO MEAT."

The structure is:

1. The phrase, *"And one of the Pharisees desired Him that He would eat with him,"* constitutes the enemy of the *"wisdom"* mentioned in Verse 35. This incident is peculiar to Luke.

NOTES

2. The Pharisee invited the Lord to his table evidently in order to belittle and insult Him, for he refused Him the customary courtesies of a host to a guest, and forced Him to find a place for Himself as best He could.

3. The Lord did not resent this studied insult. He gently took a place, probably near the door, and waited for the honor that comes from above. It was quickly sent. The glory of Christ's person and the majesty of His deity were both demonstrated, and wisdom's child—the woman—justified her Lord.

4. Being in the early part of Christ's ministry, the relations between the Lord and the dominant parties in Israel had not yet reached a state of positive hostility.

5. Even though this very invitation was probably extended to Christ in order that He may be studied by this Pharisee, at this time they had not yet declared Him a public enemy and blasphemer.

6. As well, He may well have been influenced in a positive way by Christ, and would seek this opportunity to learn more about this man Who was different than anyone he had ever met.

7. *"And He went into the Pharisee's house, and sat down to meat,"* implies that Jesus was given no prominent place at the table and, as stated, that He had to find seating for Himself.

8. Quite probably, Simon the Pharisee knew he was watched that day, and that among his guests were men who would report every action of his on that occasion to the leaders of his party in Jerusalem. Consequently, his cold, almost total lack of courtesy toward the Master was probably the result of his fear of man and of man's judgment.

9. In those days, meals were not undertaken in the modern manner of sitting on a chair at a table, but rather reclining on a couch, with one's elbows on a table and his feet, unsandaled, stretched out on the couch behind.

10. It seems to us presently a difficult way to eat a meal; however, meals then were quite different than now. Then it was a time of fellowship, enjoyment, and relaxation, which served a purpose of far greater degree than merely satisfying hunger. So, the insult tendered toward Christ (referring to

the Pharisee's neglect of his guest) was of far greater degree than mere lack of courtesy.

(37) "AND, BEHOLD, A WOMAN IN THE CITY, WHICH WAS A SINNER, WHEN SHE KNEW THAT JESUS SAT AT MEAT IN THE PHARISEE'S HOUSE, BROUGHT AN ALABASTER BOX OF OINTMENT."

THE WOMAN

The phrase, *"And, behold, a woman in the city, which was a sinner,"* was not Mary Magdalene, as some have suggested, for this was in Nain (Lk. 7:11-35), not Magdala on the Sea of Galilee. Who the woman was, we are not told, and it really does not matter. As well, what type of sinner she was is of no consequence either.

From the way Luke describes her, she evidently was someone known throughout the city of Nain, with her lifestyle being one of shame.

"When she knew that Jesus sat at meat in the Pharisee's house," tells us several things:

Due to the miracles Jesus was continually performing, His whereabouts were constantly known. He had just raised the widow's son from the dead, plus having healed countless other diseases, and was, no doubt, the talk of all of Nain. During all of these conversations, she heard that Jesus was at this particular house.

There is even a possibility that she had heard the words of Jesus when He pleaded with sinners, *"Come unto Me, all you who labour and are heavy laden, and I will give you rest,"* which immediately followed the discourse concerning John the Baptist, and was recorded by Matthew but not by Luke (Mat. 11:28-30). Whatever the case, she now came to Jesus!

THE ALABASTER BOX OF OINTMENT

This woman's situation is the same the world over. They must know and hear about Jesus, especially considering that He is not only the answer but, in reality, the only answer. Paul said, *"How shall they hear without a preacher?"* and *"how shall they preach, except they be sent?"* (Rom. 10:14-15).

So, I think it should be obvious that priority with God is the taking of His Word to the

NOTES

entirety of the world. Nothing must stand in the way of this all-important task. This is the calling of Jimmy Swaggart Ministries, to take the gospel to the world by television, and that's what we are attempting to do. I believe the Lord has told me to put the programming in every city of the world that will accept it. I realize that is a tall order, but that is what the Lord has instructed that we do and what we are attempting with all of our might and strength to do.

The phrase, *"Brought an alabaster box of ointment,"* is said to have been made in and named from Alabastron, Egypt, where soft marble is found. Vessels were called *"alabaster"* that were also made from other materials. They were of various shapes and sizes; the average held about a pint.

The word translated *ointment* was used for any kind of sweet-smelling vegetable essence, especially that of the myrtle. Exactly why she brought this, and what she felt she would do with it upon coming, is anyone's guess. However, we shall soon see that for which it was used, and which the Holy Spirit through Luke carefully notes.

It is said that this type of ointment was very expensive and much used by wealthy Roman ladies. What the cost represented to this woman is not known; however, she would use it in the holiest of purposes.

(38) "AND STOOD AT HIS FEET BEHIND HIM WEEPING, AND BEGAN TO WASH HIS FEET WITH TEARS, AND DID WIPE THEM WITH THE HAIRS OF HER HEAD, AND KISSED HIS FEET, AND ANOINTED THEM WITH THE OINTMENT."

WEEPING

The phrase, *"And stood at His feet behind Him weeping,"* represents an act of repentance. As we have stated, more than likely she had heard Him in the last few hours and had been brought under great conviction for her sinful lifestyle. Sensing that He held the answer to the craving in her heart, which her sin had never satisfied and, in fact, could not satisfy, she now sought out Jesus, seemingly determined to approach Him at any cost.

In these Oriental feasts in those days, the

houses were often left open and uninvited strangers frequently passed in through the open courtyard into the guest chamber and looked on. Presently, such would be impossible and, as well, undesirable. However, in those days, there was a great class distinction in society. For certain individuals, such as Simon the Pharisee, who was, no doubt, wealthy, to have the lower class stand at a respectable distance and observe the opulence and wealth that was at time employed on these occasions was a matter of pride. These onlookers would then go out and tell others how grand and glorious such an occasion was, which boosted the reputation of one such as Simon.

DESPERATION

Consequently, for this woman to break protocol, in fact, come into the very dining hall itself, and stand at the feet of Jesus portrayed her desperation and, therefore, determination. What she did was unusual and for the reasons stated; however, her persistence and risk would prove to be the greatest thing she ever did.

Now that she had found Jesus and had even gained His presence, why was she weeping?

The presence of God often elicits weeping as a response. The heart is greatly touched and moved, and for a variety of reasons. It is somewhat a mixture of sadness and joy— sad because of failure and joy because of the work being carried out in the heart by Christ.

I personally believe that the moment she came into His presence, she realized that He, and He alone, could change her life. She sensed that which millions have sensed, and which millions have received. It is called *"the gift of God,"* which is *"eternal life"* (Rom. 6:23). All of this is *"through Jesus Christ our Lord."*

Accepting Christ is not a cold, intellectual decision, although it certainly does affect the intellect. It goes much deeper than merely one's mind, down to the very recesses of the soul. Consequently, one believes with the heart (Rom. 10:9-10).

THE WASHING OF HIS FEET

The phrase, *"And began to wash His*

feet with tears," presents more than just the shedding of a few tears. The woman must have been sobbing, almost if not uncontrollably.

The presence of God does not affect all in this manner, but it does affect many, this evangelist included.

I suspect that it is very difficult with anyone to properly explain what happens in the heart, in fact, in the entirety of one's being during these times of consecration. It is as if the Lord cleanses the soul to such an extent that a oneness with Christ is brought about, which can hardly happen any other way. This type of brokenness typifies a yielding to the Lord, which gives occasion to the Holy Spirit to perform His invaluable work. To be sure, this is the greatest therapy there is and, in fact, the only true therapy there is.

As I have previously mentioned, countless times Frances and I have come to our morning or nightly prayer meetings with such a heavy load that it would defy description. In some of these times of prayer, the Holy Spirit would so move, and in the very manner here presented, that it seemed as if the very fountain of my heart would be broken up.

At these times the problems often were not relieved, but the care of those problems was relieved. Without these constant times, I do not see how we could have stood, or could presently stand. This is the reason that prayer and yielding to the Lord is so very, very important. Admittedly, every prayer time does not result in this of which I speak; however, it does oftentimes, which is actually the salvation of my life—the yielding to the Holy Spirit.

So, this is not for sinners only but for believers as well. Amazingly enough, when the Holy Spirit begins to move, the effect on believers and unbelievers is generally the same, especially if all are yielding to Christ.

KISSING HIS FEET

The phrase, *"And did wipe them with the hairs of her head, and kissed His feet,"* constituted an act that was not as strange then as it would seem now.

It is stated that this was a custom among

the Jews, Greeks, and Romans. It was a mark of affection and reverence. It was practiced by supplicants in making an important request and by conquered people as a token of subjection and obedience.

So, by this act, she was telling Jesus that she yielded to His mastery, in effect, accepting Him as the Messiah. He was now her Lord and Master, but in a way she had never known before.

Slaves, at times, did this (washed one's feet with ones tears) to their masters, so, in effect, she was telling Jesus that because of what He had done for her, she would be His slave from here forward. Actually, Paul, in essence, did the same thing (Eph. 3:1).

Of course, this was all done in the heart, with, as of yet, no words having passed between Jesus and this woman.

THE OINTMENT

The phrase, *"And anointed them with the ointment,"* spoke of His feet.

In those days, and at such a gathering, the duty of the host was to assign someone to wash the feet of the guests. Most roads were unpaved and with most wearing little more than sandals, their feet became dirty. Upon coming to a gathering of this nature and immediately upon entering the house, the person assigned this task was to remove the sandals from the feet of the guest and then wash the feet of the dust and grime of the road.

The insult tendered to Christ by Simon the Pharisee ignored Jesus in disrespect, with no one washing His feet. Consequently, the Holy Spirit would attend to this common courtesy ignored by Simon, causing Jesus' feet to be washed with the tears of this woman and then anointed. There is evidence that the other guests were not treated so harshly by Simon.

As a sinner washed and anointed His feet, likewise, sinners gave Him the only crown He wore—a crown of thorns. As the songwriter said, "His Kingdom Was In Hearts Alone!"

(39) "NOW WHEN THE PHARISEE WHICH HAD BIDDEN HIM SAW IT, HE SPOKE WITHIN HIMSELF, SAYING, THIS MAN, IF HE WERE A PROPHET, WOULD HAVE KNOWN WHO AND WHAT MANNER

NOTES

OF WOMAN THIS IS WHO TOUCHES HIM: FOR SHE IS A SINNER."

THE PHARISEE

The phrase, *"Now when the Pharisee which had bidden Him saw it,"* refers to the action of this woman. There is evidence that her weeping had been very quietly carried out, with her being as unobtrusive as possible. However, after a period of time, the Pharisee saw her and noted carefully her actions.

"He spoke within himself, saying," means that he reasoned in his own mind and concluded that Christ did not know what kind of woman this was. In other words, he was judging both Christ and the woman, and very wrongly we might add. Judgment on appearances only is almost always wrong. And yet, so few are spiritual enough not to commit this sin, for sin it is!

A PROPHET?

The phrase, *"This man, if He were a prophet,"* portrays the fact that Simon the Pharisee had noted all the great miracles performed by Christ, but yet, had not made up his mind if He was genuine or not! In no way had he even remotely come to the conclusion that Jesus might be the Messiah, only *"if He were a prophet?"*

As we have repeatedly stated, all the things that really pointed to the Messiah, which were abundantly given in the Scriptures, were obvious in Christ but ignored by these unbelievers. The Jews had envisioned a Messiah who would use his power to overthrow Rome and make Israel the leading nation in the world once again as in the days of Solomon.

Their view was completely unscriptural, but yet, a view held by almost all of the religious elite. So, knowing this man was a peasant from the despised town of Nazareth, in Simon's mind, He could not be the Messiah. This little incident with the weeping woman only goes to prove what he had already thought.

WHAT MANNER OF WOMAN

The phrase, *"Would have known who and what manner of woman this is who touches Him: for she is a sinner,"* proclaims the judgment made by this man of both Jesus and the woman. He was wrong on both counts.

Jesus did know what manner of woman this was; however, this is the very reason He came.

Religion is untouchable. In its self-righteousness, it wants nothing that will embarrass it. To the contrary, Jesus accepts any and all who come to Him. In reality, which speaks of the eyes of God, Simon the Pharisee, which the Holy Spirit is very careful to delineate, was in far worse spiritual condition than this poor woman. And yet, this Pharisee had an impeccable reputation in the city, while the reputation of this woman, as is obvious, was not too good to say the least.

No! This does not mean that all who profess salvation are like Simon the Pharisee and, therefore, worse than a woman of the streets, if, in fact, that is what she was. It does mean that many fall into that category, and, as well, God looks on the heart while man judges from appearances.

Also, whatever the woman had been, the moment she touched Jesus, her heart was totally changed, which, in effect, would change her life. So, it was not a vile woman who touched Jesus, but rather one who had been so in the past but no longer was.

This proclaims to all how quickly the grace of God can change an individual. However, all self-righteous Pharisees, as Simon, would, no doubt, demand a long period of penance, or some such trial period, before her testimony could be accepted, if ever. Jesus accepted her immediately, and if the truth be known, she was probably never accepted by the religious establishment.

I wish it were possible to say that the situation has presently changed; however, it is doubtful that it has changed at all.

(40) "AND JESUS ANSWERING SAID UNTO HIM, SIMON, I HAVE SOMEWHAT TO SAY UNTO YOU. AND HE SAID, MASTER, SAY ON."

The overview is:

1. The phrase, *"And Jesus answering said unto him, Simon, I have somewhat to say unto you,"* concerns the answer of the Lord to this attitude and should be heeded by all because it is meant for all.

2. The Holy Spirit told Jesus what the man was thinking.

3. *"And he said, Master, say on,"* is laced with sarcasm and little expects the words of wisdom he will receive. He has already revealed the unbelief of his heart by using the words of Verse 39, *"This man, if He were a prophet."*

(41) "THERE WAS A CERTAIN CREDITOR WHICH HAD TWO DEBTORS: THE ONE OWED FIVE HUNDRED PENCE, AND THE OTHER FIFTY."

The structure is:

1. The phrase, *"There was a certain creditor which had two debtors,"* refers to a moneylender who had loaned different sums of money to two individuals. This type of business was provided by the law but regulated strictly to assure justice (Ex. 22:25-27; Lev. 25:14-17, 35-37; Deut. 23:19-20; 24:6-17).

2. Actually, all debts were to be forgiven to brethren every seven years under the Mosaic law but not to strangers (Ex. 21:2-6; Deut. 15:1-3). Christian lending is on a different basis (Mat. 5:42; Lk. 6:34).

3. This illustration used by Jesus was something well-known in Jewish life and would have been readily understood by all present.

4. *"The one owed five hundred pence, and the other fifty,"* would have been the equivalent of $30,000, and $3,000 in today's value.

(42) "AND WHEN THEY HAD NOTHING TO PAY, HE FRANKLY FORGAVE THEM BOTH. TELL ME THEREFORE, WHICH OF THEM WILL LOVE HIM MOST?"

The pattern is:

1. The phrase, *"And when they had nothing to pay,"* means that when the debt was due, the two debtors could not pay no matter if the debt was large or small.

2. The phrase, *"He frankly forgave them both,"* refers to the creditor writing off the debts.

3. Jesus was likening the creditor to God and the two debtors as sinners in debt to God. Irrespective of the amount, it was a sum they could not even begin to hope to pay. They were both sinners before God and both equally insolvent in His eyes. Whether the debt was much or little was to the

almighty creditor a matter of comparative indifference—He frankly forgave them both (better said, "He freely forgave of His generous bounty").

4. *"Tell Me therefore, which of them will love him most?"* now comes to the point illustrated by the parable.

5. In the mind of Jesus, the larger debt pictured the terrible catalogue of sins, which the penitent woman acknowledged she had committed. The smaller pictured the few transgressions of which even the Pharisee might have confessed to having been guilty.

6. It should be understood that Jesus was appealing to this man on his own level. Without a doubt, God would have judged it the other way around, with the sins of this man the blacker of the two.

7. So, even on the level of the Pharisee, he would be forced to admit the rightness of the action of Christ plus the response of this dear woman.

(43) "SIMON ANSWERED AND SAID, I SUPPOSE THAT HE, TO WHOM HE FORGAVE MOST. AND HE SAID UNTO HIM, YOU HAVE RIGHTLY JUDGED."

The synopsis is:

1. The phrase, *"Simon answered and said, I suppose that he, to whom He forgave most,"* constitutes the only answer that could be obviously given.

2. *"And He said unto him, You have rightly judged,"* in effect, judged himself.

3. Now Jesus would call to task the actions of this self-righteous bigot.

(44) "AND HE TURNED TO THE WOMAN, AND SAID UNTO SIMON, DO YOU SEE THIS WOMAN? I ENTERED INTO YOUR HOUSE, YOU GAVE ME NO WATER FOR MY FEET: BUT SHE HAS WASHED MY FEET WITH TEARS, AND WIPED THEM WITH THE HAIRS OF HER HEAD."

The synopsis is:

1. The phrase, *"And He turned to the woman,"* records the first instance of Jesus acknowledging the woman in any way.

2. The question, *"And said unto Simon, Do you see this woman?"* places the woman in an entirely different light than the manner in which she was spoken of by Simon. In effect, how many millions has the Lord

spoken of just as this as a trophy of grace!

3. *"I entered into your house, you gave Me no water for My feet,"* proclaims the studied insult now being noted. The reader should take into account the entirety of this scenario as it portrays the heart action of all, whether good or bad. As we have stated, it was the custom for a servant to wash the feet of guests upon arrival, which Simon had neglected to do with Jesus.

4. *"But she has washed My feet with tears, and wiped them with the hairs of her head,"* proclaims the Holy Spirit rebuking the insult of this man by this act of courtesy being carried out in the most beautiful and wonderful way. Even if Simon had seen to it that a servant washed the feet of Jesus, there would have been no kindness in the action, only courtesy. However, this Pharisee did not bother with even this most common of courtesies.

5. While the world, or even most of that which calls itself church, gives Jesus little honor as here, multiple tens of millions, who are drawn by the Holy Spirit, praise and worship Him as the Lord of Glory and the Saviour of their souls. Consequently, this scenario is a perfect picture of the church as a whole, which gives Jesus little credence, if any at all, and the true regard and worship He receives at the hands of those who have felt His glorious touch.

6. As well, if we attempt to portray Christ outside of the Cross, we have just negated the very reason He came.

(45) "YOU GAVE ME NO KISS: BUT THIS WOMAN SINCE THE TIME I CAME IN HAS NOT CEASED TO KISS MY FEET."

The form is:

1. The phrase, *"You gave Me no kiss,"* was, as well, a custom that men greeted each other with a kiss on the cheek (Gen. 27:7; 29:13; 33:4; 45:15; 48:10; Ex. 4:27; 18:7; I Sam. 20:41; Lk. 15:20; Acts 20:37).

Also, this common courtesy, while, no doubt, extended to others, was not extended that day to Jesus.

As we have stated, the possibility definitely existed that this man's actions would be reported to other Pharisees in Jerusalem. Consequently, in front of these eyes, he must portray a cold distance.

2. Unfortunately, this practice did not die with the Pharisees of old. I have marvelled as I have watched modern preachers do the same with my own person, concerned that someone might report to denominational heads that they had shown me an act of kindness of some sort. As a result, they had to make certain that nothing but coldness was extended, and it was because of man fear.

Such is not Christianity! Such is religion, pure and simple. It serves men instead of God.

3. The phrase, *"But this woman since the time I came in has not ceased to kiss My feet,"* has a meaning far greater than meets the eye.

4. Simon would not kiss the face of Jesus, denoting, at least of Christ, His kingship. However, the Holy Spirit had the woman to kiss the feet of Jesus, denoting His authority, power, and rule (Lk. 10:19).

(46) "MY HEAD WITH OIL YOU DID NOT ANOINT: BUT THIS WOMAN HAS ANOINTED MY FEET WITH OINTMENT."

The pattern is:

1. The phrase, *"My head with oil you did not anoint,"* presented another custom of that day.

2. Anointing with olive oil mixed with fragrant and costly spices was customary in the coronation of kings (II Ki. 11:12), installing high priests (Ps. 133:2), and an act of courtesy and hospitality toward guests (Deut. 28:40; Ps. 23:5; 92:10; 105:15).

3. As well, this particular scenario had a spiritual application in that Simon, by not anointing the head of Jesus, in effect, was saying that he did not believe that Jesus was the Messiah, i.e., the head.

4. *"But this woman has anointed My feet with ointment,"* has the same connotation as the last phrase in the previous verse. With the Holy Spirit having this woman anoint the feet of Jesus, He was saying by symbolism that despite what Simon believed, or the whole of the religious elite of Israel for that matter, Jesus was anointed by the Holy Spirit as the Messiah (Lk. 4:18).

5. Whether Simon fully understood what Jesus was saying is anyone's guess! Actually, in his spiritual state of attempting to please man and God, he would conclude by pleasing no one.

NOTES

(47) "WHEREFORE I SAY UNTO YOU, HER SINS, WHICH ARE MANY, ARE FORGIVEN; FOR SHE LOVED MUCH: BUT TO WHOM LITTLE IS FORGIVEN, THE SAME LOVES LITTLE."

FORGIVEN

The phrase, *"Wherefore I say unto you, Her sins, which are many, are forgiven,"* was a statement of startling proportions to all who were present that day. Who is this man Who can forgive sins?

In essence, Jesus was performing that which only the Messiah could actually do, which Simon had denied and Jesus now declared. When He said these words, what the woman had already felt now became a reality. She was forgiven of all her sins, which only God could do.

The phrase, *"For she loved much,"* does not mean that she was forgiven because she first evidenced love. The last verse tells us that her faith caused her to be saved, as it causes all to be saved!

What is wanting in order to love much is not sin but the knowledge of it.

SHE LOVED MUCH

Salvation is a heart experience as this example portrays. Her salvation was probably brought about in the following manner:

Already sickened by her present lifestyle, she came in search of Christ, and those who truly search for Him will truly find Him. The moment she came into His presence, her heart reached out to Him. This was expressed in her repentance, which was portrayed, at least in this instance, through her emotion. She began to weep and, as stated, for probably a mixture of sadness and joy. At that moment she was saved without her actually uttering a word. To be sure, the confession, no doubt, quickly followed (Rom. 10:9-10).

Jesus announcing that her sins were forgiven was the result of an act already performed. Her loving much, which was expressed in her acts of kindness of washing His feet with her tears and anointing His head with ointment, was a result of what He had already done. Consequently, she loved much!

FORGIVEN SINS

The phrase, *"But to whom little is forgiven, the same loves little,"* does not mean that Simon and others like him only have a few sins to be forgiven, but that they will little admit, as this woman, that their sins are many. Consequently, most of their sins, which they will not admit to because of their self-righteousness, are not forgiven.

Though this Pharisee was very religious, his life, in fact, was disfigured with censoriousness, narrowness, harshness, and pride—the many faults of his class.

As we have stated, the Lord implied in His sad irony that the little forgiveness that Simon had received was his own fault, for he did not think in his self-righteousness that he had any need to be forgiven. Therefore, he loved little, which was obvious in his treatment of Christ. Regrettably, much, if not most of the church world, falls into that same category.

Religious self-righteousness, resulting from religious pride, can never admit its true state but must always hold up the façade of self-righteousness.

(48) "AND HE SAID UNTO HER, YOUR SINS ARE FORGIVEN."

The form is:

1. The phrase, *"And He said unto her,"* means that He had made the announcement of her sins being forgiven to Simon and others in the room but not directly to her. Now He spoke directly to her!

2. *"Your sins are forgiven,"* is said without any attachment. In other words, no penance was required and no religious works counseled. It was done, a finished work!

3. As well, it should be quickly added that this woman was saved without water baptism. Even though this ordinance is important, and every true believer will engage in such after conversion, still, the act within itself of water baptism plays absolutely no part whatsoever in the salvation process. That, as we have stated, is by faith alone.

(49) "AND THEY WHO SAT AT MEAT WITH HIM BEGAN TO SAY WITHIN THEMSELVES, WHO IS THIS WHO FORGIVES SINS ALSO?"

The pattern is:

1. The phrase, *"And they who sat a meat with Him began to say within themselves,"* portrays the exclamation of all the guests at His telling the woman that her sins were forgiven.

2. The question, *"Who is this Who forgives sins also?"* refers to the fact that only God can forgive sins. This should have told them, and, in fact, did tell them, that He was the Messiah.

3. In such a case, to forgive sins, as the Lord alone can do, means that not only are the sins forgiven, but the stain is washed clean so to speak, meaning there is no trace of the sin left.

(50) "AND HE SAID TO THE WOMAN, YOUR FAITH HAS SAVED YOU; GO IN PEACE."

FAITH

The phrase, *"And He said to the woman,"* now proclaims the cause of her salvation, which was her faith in Christ. This, as well, was a rebuke to Simon the Pharisee and others like him who were trying to earn their salvation by their religious works, as does much, if not most, of the modern church.

God's will is that the guiltiest who believe upon the Son of His love should enjoy assurance of salvation and the conscious forgiveness of sin.

Jesus did not say to the woman, "Your love has saved you," or "Your tears have saved you," but rather, *"Your faith has saved you."*

PEACE

The phrase, *"Go in peace,"* should have been translated, *"Go into peace."*

The peace that one receives upon the acceptance of Christ is that which comes as a result of the enmity between God and man being taken away.

Man fell because he sinned against God. In other words, God did not wrong man; man wronged God! As a result of this wrong, an enmity developed in man's heart, which means hatred against God. There is a perpetual war with God in the heart of the unbeliever, which necessitates the absence of peace. Unredeemed man, never having had peace, does not really realize this terrible loss. As well, the word *enmity*, which means "hatred," refers not only to man hating God, but God hating the sin and rebellion in man, which has brought about this terrible condition.

To remedy this terrible situation, at least to those who will believe, Jesus Christ, by His death at Calvary, restored to man the peace that was lost. Consequently, Paul said, *"For He is our peace* (meaning Jesus), *who has made both one* (made Jew and Gentile one and God and man one), *and has broken down the middle wall of partition between us* (the sin and its penalty which caused the rupture)."

MAKING PEACE WITH GOD

Paul then said, *"Having abolished in His flesh* (Jesus' death at Calvary) *the enmity* (hatred), *even the law of commandments contained in ordinances* (abolished the law that pointed out man's sin); *for to make in Himself of twain one new man* (neither Jew nor Gentile, but one in Christ), *so making peace* (He took away the sin and penalty that was causing the war)" (Eph. 2:14-17).

Upon acceptance of Christ, the enmity and hatred stops, which means the war has stopped, with peace being instantly given.

Without a doubt, the peace that instantly comes upon acceptance of Christ is the greatest thing of all. It takes place in one's spirit, and the person knows that he is saved, hence, the term, *"Making peace with God."* The only thing that can destroy this peace or take it away is sin.

Sin, which caused the offence against God to begin with, if committed after salvation, continues to function in the same manner as in the beginning. That is the reason a heavy weight returns to the believer if sin is committed and not confessed with repentance engaged (I Jn. 1:9). However, the moment proper confession to the Lord is made, the peace returns!

This woman who came to Jesus that day had never known true peace, as no unbeliever has ever known peace. However, despite her many sins and because of her faith in Christ, she left with peace while Simon the Pharisee, although very religious, had no peace at all because he did not know God despite his claims.

*"Just as I am, without one plea,
"But that Your blood was shed for me,
"And that You bid me come to Thee,
"O Lamb of God, I come! I come!"*

*"Just as I am, and waiting not,
"To rid my soul of one dark blot,
"To Thee whose blood can cleanse each spot,
"O Lamb of God, I come! I come!"*

*"Just as I am, tho' tossed about
"With many a conflict, many a doubt,
"Fightings and fears within, without,
"O Lamb of God, I come! I come!"*

*"Just as I am, poor, wretched, blind;
"Sight, riches, healing of the mind,
"Yes, all I need, in You to find,
"O Lamb of God, I come! I come!"*

*"Just as I am, You will receive,
"Will welcome pardon, cleanse, relieve,
"Because Your promise I believe,
"O Lamb of God, I come! I come!"*

CHAPTER 8

(1) "AND IT CAME TO PASS AFTERWARD, THAT HE WENT THROUGHOUT EVERY CITY AND VILLAGE, PREACHING AND SHOWING THE GLAD TIDINGS OF THE KINGDOM OF GOD: AND THE TWELVE WERE WITH HIM."

PREACHING

The phrase, *"And it came to pass afterward,"* as is obvious, refers to the events of the previous chapter. However, it signals a change in the ministry of Jesus as His schedule now becomes extremely heavy, with Him, along with others, going to various towns and villages throughout Galilee.

"That He went throughout every city and village, preaching," presents the opposite of religious man, who magnifies sacraments and ceremonies and belittles preaching. God magnifies preaching. It pleases Him by the foolishness of preaching to save men. Christ preached incessantly and so did the apostle Paul, the Twelve, the seventy, etc.

Satan does not fear ceremonies, but he greatly fears preaching.

When preaching weakens, the church automatically begins to weaken as well! Preaching for the sake of preaching, however, is of little consequence. The preacher must be full of the Holy Spirit, with such obtainable only by a deep consecration to the Lord, which can only come about by constant prayer and study of the Word. As well, if he is to be effective, the preacher must understand the Cross of Christ not only as it relates to salvation but, as well, to sanctification. As stated, if the believer doesn't understand the Cross relative to sanctification, such a believer does not know how to live for God. This spells spiritual disaster! Unfortunately, precious few preachers have a prayer life, study the Word, and understand the Cross, and precious few preachers see any spiritual results.

THE KINGDOM OF GOD

The phrase, *"And showing the glad tidings of the kingdom of God,"* speaks of healings, miracles, and deliverances. As well, it speaks of the cheer brought to those who receive the gospel message. It is truly glad tidings!

It is impossible for the true gospel of Jesus Christ to be heeded by anyone and them not be immeasurably bettered. It stands alone in the midst of all the religions of the world in bringing such positive results. One would think that surely everyone would desire such benefits, which include eternal life. However, *"Few there be that find it"* (Mat. 7:14).

Man is spiritually blind and cannot, at least on his own, even begin to grasp what the gospel actually is without a revelation by the Holy Spirit. Even then, he is so deceived that often, if not most of the time, he turns it aside, refusing to believe it, and rather believes a lie.

The kingdom of God is the gospel of Jehovah's King, the Lord Jesus Christ. It is a dispensational term and refers to Messiah's kingdom on earth. It was offered by both John and Jesus (Mat. 3:2; 4:17; 10:7). Sadly, it was rejected and, thus, was postponed until Christ comes to set up the kingdom, which will take place at the second coming

(Mat. 11:12, 20-24; 27:22-25; Lk. 19:11-27; Acts 1:6-7; 3:19-26).

A CONFESSION OF FAITH IN JESUS CHRIST

The kingdom of God is now in the realm of profession (Mat. 13:11-17, 30, 38-43, 47-50), which pertains basically to the spiritual, but at the second coming, will include the physical and material as well!

One enters this kingdom by confession of faith in the Lord Jesus Christ; consequently, the entrance qualification is the *"born-again"* experience (Jn. 3:3).

The phrase, *"And the Twelve were with Him,"* actually means that the Twelve remained with Him constantly. There were, no doubt, numerous others, as well, even as the next verses proclaim, with many of them coming and going.

(2) "AND CERTAIN WOMEN, WHICH HAD BEEN HEALED OF EVIL SPIRITS AND INFIRMITIES, MARY CALLED MAGDALENE, OUT OF WHOM WENT SEVEN DEVILS."

CERTAIN WOMEN

The phrase, *"And certain women,"* presents something totally unique to the ministry of Jesus. By His actions, as are here obvious, He made these women fellow-heirs with men of the kingdom of heaven. Consequently, it is now obvious that they would no longer occupy on earth their old inferior and subordinate position. In fact, out of all the religions of the world, Christianity is the only one that truly gives equal status to women. Not only did His public ministry portray this, but, as well, Calvary and the resurrection ratified this acceptance. It is proven by Mary Magdalene having been given the privilege of being the first human being to herald the resurrection of the Lord (Mk. 16:9-10).

MARY MAGDALENE

The phrase, *"Which had been healed of evil spirits and infirmities,"* proclaims them being drawn to Jesus for many and varied reasons, but most of all, because they had been delivered and healed. Consequently, some of these, if not many, traveled in the party at times, offering their assistance any way it could be used.

Incidentally, the phrase, *"Healed of evil spirits,"* actually means, "Healed of that which had been caused by evil spirits."

The phrase, *"Mary called Magdalene, out of whom went seven devils (demons),"* is about all the information we have concerning the deliverance and salvation of this woman who figures so prominently in the Gospels.

The name *Magdalene* means "of Magdala," a little town near Tiberias, located close to the Sea of Galilee.

What had been the occasion of her demon possession (seven demons) is not stated; however, this much is sure: The torture she suffered before her deliverance must have been terrible to say the least. However, when she was set free by the power of God, she fell into the category of the woman of the previous chapter, "Who loved much, because she had been forgiven much."

(3) "AND JOANNA THE WIFE OF CHUZA HEROD'S STEWARD, AND SUSANNA, AND MANY OTHERS, WHICH MINISTERED UNTO HIM OF THEIR SUBSTANCE."

PROMINENT WOMEN

The phrase, *"And Joanna the wife of Chuza Herod's steward,"* is believed to be the family whose dying son was healed by Jesus. Chuza is referred to as the nobleman of Capernaum (Jn. 4:46). It is said that several of Herod's court were believers, with Manaen referred to some years later, who was the foster-brother of Herod and a notable Christian (Acts 13:1).

If, in fact, Joanna was the mother of the child healed in John, Chapter 4, one can well imagine the love this woman and her husband had for Jesus. No wonder she wanted to do what she could to serve Him. And yet, aren't all of us in the same category? He has done so much for us; therefore, we should be quick to respond to do whatever we can for Him.

"And Susanna, and many others," must reflect a woman of means; however, nothing else is known of her. What is meant by the word *many* is not known. It probably

NOTES

referred to 15 or 20, or even more, of both men and women who were people of note doing all they could to minister to the needs of Christ.

MINISTERED UNTO CHRIST

The phrase, *"Which ministered unto Him of their substance,"* gives us a clue as to how Christ and His many workers received their support. To be frank, irrespective of how large the party was that traveled with Jesus, which could have easily numbered 100 or more, finances were no problem.

Of the thousands who were healed of every disease imaginable, it stands to reason that many of these people would have been extremely generous. However, this we do know: Jesus never used His miraculous power to supply His daily needs. His power was used exclusively for the salvation, deliverance, and healing of others.

What an example!

It should be mentioned, as well, that true disciples, now as then, always minister to Him; mere professors do not.

It should be quickly added that even though the good deeds of these women and others were recorded nearly 2,000 years ago, still, they are known presently all over the world.

Whatever is done for Christ, irrespective of how small, has an eternal consequence.

Inasmuch as the Holy Spirit had Luke to mention these particular women, we know it was done for purpose. It must have been difficult for these women to face the scorn and contempt of the religious leaders of Israel, yet, they were faithful to the end. It was not a woman who sold the Lord for 30 pieces of silver. It was not a woman who forsook Him and fled, and neither was it a woman who thrice denied that she knew Him.

However, it was women who wailed and lamented when He was led forth to be crucified; it was women who stood to the last by His Cross; and it was women who were the first to visit His tomb on the resurrection morning.

(4) "AND WHEN MUCH PEOPLE WERE GATHERED TOGETHER, AND WERE COME TO HIM OUT OF EVERY CITY, HE SPOKE BY A PARABLE."

MANY PEOPLE

"And when much people were gathered together, and were come to Him out of every city," refers to the tremendous throngs that came for healing or out of curiosity. Considering the astounding miracles He was performing at this time, even to the raising of the dead, it is no wonder that thousands thronged to Him. And yet, these giant crowds were to raise the ire of the religious leaders of Israel to such an extent that open opposition would now begin. They felt that they were losing control of the people, and consequently, they would do anything within their power to stop this loss, even to murdering the Lord of Glory.

Those who truly follow the Lord never look at the body of Christ as belonging to them, even though they feel totally responsible for it. Preachers who are truly godly know that Jesus is the true head of the church, and we are but undershepherds. As such, we exercise no control whatsoever over others, and neither do we desire to do so. We know that even though they have the privilege of planting and watering, still, it is God who gives the increase (I Cor. 3:6). We ought to never serve as *"lords over God's heritage"* (I Pet. 5:3).

RELIGION

However, religion is different! Its devotees, not truly knowing the Lord even though great profession is made, feel they must control the hearts and minds of the people. Denominational heads too often fall into this category. Consequently, if they see anything, such as Jesus, that seems to be a threat to their control, they will do anything to eliminate that threat, and I mean anything!

That is the reason religion is probably Satan's greatest strategy. I think one could say without fear of contradiction that more people have lost their souls through religion than all the vices put together.

When the early church ultimately apostatized, finally degenerating to what is presently known as the Catholic Church, it did all it could to maintain total control, even to the killing of tens of thousands who would not bow to the pope.

It took the Reformation to break that stranglehold on humanity. In fact, religious control was what brought about the Dark Ages. Even then, it was only a short time before a Protestant state church developed in many countries, just as it had been a Catholic state church.

RELIGIOUS DENOMINATIONS

That stranglehold was broken, at least in part, by the ministries of such men as John and Charles Wesley, Finney, and others. However, most of these great moves that saw hundreds of thousands brought to Christ ultimately degenerated into denominations, with all the denominational hierarchy, which again demands control.

At the present time, and possibly for all time, most preachers, as well as the people, serve a religious denomination instead of the Lord.

Many would disagree with that statement; however, if any preacher of the gospel, or any layman for that matter, bows to any ruling that is unscriptural, he has ceased to serve the Lord and instead serves man.

For instance, during the ministry of Jesus, He was little welcome in most of the synagogues the last year of His public ministry. It is almost impossible to conceive of such a thing, but yet, that's what happened! The rulers of these synagogues had a choice. They could ignore the religious leaders and welcome Jesus or else submit to the demands of the religious leaders. Of course, had they ignored their religious leaders, they would have had to pay the price. To be sure, the price was high.

EXCOMMUNICATION

They would have been excommunicated from their own synagogue and, in fact, every other synagogue in Israel. In effect, they would have been shut off from the religious and public life of Israel. Many, no doubt, resolved in their minds that they would not jeopardize themselves and their families on behalf of this one preacher called Jesus. However, the moment they made that decision (which almost all did), they sold their principles and their salvation. They were now men-servers instead of servers of God.

Modern preachers too often do the same. Instead of looking at the principle, they look at the person and make their decision accordingly. Consequently, they compromise the Word of God and their allegiance to Christ, plus, they sacrifice the leading of the Holy Spirit. Either the Holy Spirit leads, or man leads. One cannot have both!

Sometime back, as we have previously stated, the general superintendent of the largest Pentecostal denomination in the world sent a letter to all the district superintendents of that denomination. I happened to see a copy of that letter. It requested that they "preach on the Holy Spirit" because it had been brought to their attention that very few people, if any, were being baptized with the Holy Spirit in their respective churches.

Why were precious few people being baptized with the Holy Spirit in this particular denomination?

UNSCRIPTURAL

It is because the preachers, in effect, had yielded to that which was unscriptural instead of standing up for that which many knew was right. As a result, by their decision, they said that they were followers of men instead of the Holy Spirit. Therefore, most operation of the Holy Spirit in this particular denomination has ceased.

Actually, that which I have just addressed took place about 20 odd years ago. The situation now is far, far worse! In fact, it is rare now for a person to be baptized with the Holy Spirit in an Assembly of God church, a Church of God church, a Four Square church, etc. As stated, one can be led by the Holy Spirit or led by men, but he cannot be led by both.

As it regards the problem this general superintendent was addressing, it was not their lack of preaching on the Holy Spirit, which, no doubt, was a problem, but rather who was recognized as the actual head of the church, Christ or man?

Actually, this is the battle that every believer fights constantly. Is Jesus Christ Lord, or do other things take His place? Someone has well said, "Jesus is Lord of all or not Lord at all!"

NOTES

THE PARABLE

The phrase, *"He spoke by a parable,"* constituted a new way of teaching. Actually, the parable of the sower seems to have been the first given and was recorded by Matthew, Mark, and Luke. In effect, this parable is the foundation of all parables. Of course, the question of why Jesus deliberately chose to change the manner of His teaching must be asked.

The Sermon on the Mount, for instance, contains little if anything of the parable form. However, despite its simplicity, the people seemed to little understand what He said, forming altogether false views of the kingdom He described to them. Consequently, He changed His manner of teaching.

Parables were a common form of teaching and were simply the use of a story or illustration designed to be interesting and to present a message. It was a way to proclaim truth in very simple form, which could be easily remembered.

And yet, a parable could be given in such a way that its real meaning was not easily arrived at, which it seems Jesus often did. This was for purpose.

Jesus had a message to deliver, and yet, the opposition by the Pharisees and Sadducees was increasing almost daily. There is nothing more volatile than a Holy Spirit anointed message. Consequently, had He continued speaking clearly and plainly, the situation may have quickly become incendiary, with the people demanding that He be made king. Actually, it came close to that anyway (Jn. 6:15). Even though He definitely was a king and, in fact, *the King,* still, His kingly position was not that which they desired. They wanted another type of king altogether.

THE MANNER OF THE PARABLES

Jesus did not come to this earth to foment a revolution. He came to deliver man from the clutches of sin, and to do that, He must destroy the powers of darkness. Consequently, His mission was not political in any way but totally spiritual. The changing of His teaching and preaching style to parables made the impact of His message much less volatile and actually made them much easier to remember. However, His shading the meaning at times was done for purpose, as we have already stated.

The parables had a tendency to confuse His opposers and to enlighten those who were truly His followers. The merely curious would not inquire further, with the truly seeking heart continuing to push in until the answer was forthcoming.

So, the parables served two purposes:

1. Lessening the immediate volatility of His messages

2. Turning off the merely curious while enlightening the true followers. As someone said, "He used the parable way of teaching almost as a fan to separate the wheat from the chaff."

(5) "A SOWER WENT OUT TO SOW HIS SEED: AND AS HE SOWED, SOME FELL BY THE WAY SIDE; AND IT WAS TRODDEN DOWN, AND THE FOWLS OF THE AIR DEVOURED IT."

The structure is:

1. The phrase, *"A sower went out to sow his seed,"* represented something that all the listeners readily understood.

2. This was the manner of planting crops in those days and is still the manner in some places. Actually, when I was a little boy, I would watch my dad sow mustard seed in the same identical way. He would take handfuls of seed and walk over the plowed ground. He would sling his hand as he walked and let the seed fall until the entirety of the ground was covered.

3. The phrase, *"And as he sowed, some fell by the way side,"* referred to an area that had not been prepared for the seed. The listeners would have easily understood that as well.

4. The phrase, *"And it was trodden down, and the fowls of the air devoured it,"* concerns only some of the seed and not all of it.

(6) "AND SOME FELL UPON A ROCK; AND AS SOON AS IT WAS SPRUNG UP, IT WITHERED AWAY, BECAUSE IT LACKED MOISTURE."

The construction is:

1. Beside that which fell by the wayside and that which was trodden down, as well

NOTES

as that which was devoured by the fowls of the air, some fell on ground that was very shallow, with rock just below the surface.

2. *"And as soon as it was sprung up, it withered away, because it lacked moisture,"* means that the ground was so shallow that the roots could not grab hold because of the rock. Inasmuch as the roots could not go down into the soil where the moisture was, the plant soon withered away.

3. All of this is symbolic of the gospel of Jesus Christ and man's response to that gospel.

(7) "AND SOME FELL AMONG THORNS; AND THE THORNS SPRANG UP WITH IT, AND CHOKED IT."

The diagram is:

1. The phrase, *"And some fell among thorns,"* pertains to good ground, but yet, the competition of the thorns would prove to be a debilitating factor.

2. *"And the thorns sprang up with it, and choked it,"* refers to the thorn vines intertwining themselves around the plant until the plant was destroyed even though it had good ground.

3. So we see that there is always a hindrance to the gospel.

(8) "AND OTHER FELL ON GOOD GROUND, AND SPRANG UP, AND BEAR FRUIT AN HUNDREDFOLD. AND WHEN HE HAD SAID THESE THINGS, HE CRIED, HE WHO HAS EARS TO HEAR, LET HIM HEAR."

A HUNDREDFOLD

The phrase, *"And other fell on good ground,"* means ground that was not full of rocks or thorns.

"And sprang up," refers to the bountiful growth because of the suitability of the soil. *"And bear fruit an hundredfold,"* presents a tremendous harvest, as should be obvious.

"And when He had said these things, He cried, He who has ears to hear, let him hear," proclaims the reason for teaching in parables.

EARS TO HEAR

Many did not have ears to hear because their hearts were hardened. Some few did, and they changed the world!

Why would one hear and another not hear?

From this question, men have devised the unscriptural doctrine of an unbiblical understanding of predestination, claiming that some are predestined to be lost while others are predestined to be saved. Consequently, at least according to this erroneous teaching, there is nothing either party can do within themselves, for the matter has already been settled.

PREDESTINATION

While predestination is definitely a biblical doctrine, still, its correct interpretation is required.

There are some things predestined by God, and those things cannot be changed. They include, among other things, the first advent of Christ, with His death on Calvary and His resurrection. It, as well, includes the rapture of the church, the second coming, and the kingdom age.

These things, plus much we have not named, were and are predestined by God, and nothing can change it, be it man or demon.

However, there is nothing in the Bible that speaks of some individuals being predestined to be lost while others are predestined to be saved. The teaching of the Scripture from Genesis through Revelation is *"Whosoever will"* (Rev. 22:17). In other words, while the plan is predestined, who will be in the plan is left up to the individual. The Lord will deal with such people, speak to them, and move upon them, but He will never force the issue.

Actually, God is *"not willing that any should perish, but that all should come to repentance"* (II Pet. 3:9); however, it is up to the choice or free will of the individual to come or not to come to repentance.

LACK OF OPPORTUNITY

Many would claim that great numbers in the world have little choice in the matter simply because no one has bothered to bring the message of redemption to them. That is true! However, that has nothing to do with their status, only the lack of opportunity.

The Lord told the prophet Ezekiel to

NOTES

warn the people; however, if the prophet failed to warn them, no provision was made for them otherwise, as no provision, in fact, could be made in that regarded. Concerning that, the Lord said:

"When I say unto the wicked, You shall surely die; and you give him not warning, nor speak to warn the wicked from his wicked way, to save his life; the same wicked man shall die in his iniquity; but his blood will I require at your hand" (Ezek. 3:18).

In other words, as stated, there is no provision of salvation for anyone who does not accept Christ as his Saviour, irrespective of the opportunity or lack thereof. However, great condemnation is tendered toward the church that allows that individual to remain in spiritual ignorance. The Scripture plainly says, *"His blood* (the fate of the unredeemed) *will I require at your hand* (the hand of the church)." So, it is incumbent upon the church to get the gospel to every person in the world that they may have an opportunity to either accept or reject the gospel.

IS SUCH A PROGRAM FAIR?

It is fair as far as is possible for anything to be. Millions of people die each year of hunger in this world, and one might ask, "Is that fair?" As well, over a period of time, millions die for the want of a particular type of medicine. Is such the fault of the victim?

The far greater majority of the time, it is not their fault, but they still die.

IS IT GOD'S FAULT?

If one is to be fair and honest, one cannot lay a finger of blame upon God. He has done all that heaven can do in the giving of His only Son in order that the world may be saved. As well, He gave the Holy Spirit to enable believers to take the gospel to the entirety of the world; consequently, God has done everything that He can do. The fault lies with believers and not with God, thus, Jesus said, *"He who has ears to hear, let him hear."* That applies to believers and unbelievers.

Paul said, *"How shall they hear without a preacher?"*

He then said, *"And how shall they preach, except they be sent?"* (Rom. 10:14-15).

We believe that God has given a mandate to this ministry (Jimmy Swaggart Ministries), and that mandate is the entirety of the world. That's the reason we are doing everything within our power to make the gospel of Jesus Christ, the Message of the Cross, available to every human being on the face of the earth. Will we be able to do that? Probably not, but we've got to try. I cannot stand before God, and neither can you, without having done all that was humanly possible to reach that next soul with the gospel of Jesus Christ. We are responsible! And so, every believer should ask himself the question, "Am I doing all that I can do?"

The Sonlife Broadcasting Network is an excellent vehicle for carrying out the mandate of the Lord. We go into hundreds of millions of homes all over the world, and we are doing everything within our power to go into even more. We must! The eternal souls of men are at stake. Unfortunately, most of the money given for that which purports to be the gospel is not the gospel. It's one of Satan's imitations. God help us!

Only that which is truly scriptural will be anointed by the Holy Spirit. For sinners to be saved and for lives to be changed, the Word of God has to be anointed, and the unsaved soul has to be placed under conviction, all by the power of the Holy Spirit. Unfortunately, there isn't much Holy Spirit in most presentations of that which claims to be the gospel.

(9) "AND HIS DISCIPLES ASKED HIM, SAYING, WHAT MIGHT THIS PARABLE BE?"

The exegesis is:

1. Matthew related that this parable was spoken from a boat moored close to the bank. He also related other parables that were, no doubt, given at that time.

2. However, Luke only mentioned this one parable, possibly because he wished to mark this example as the first of this new kind of teaching.

3. The question, *"What might this parable be?"* proclaims the story being understood perfectly well, but not its meaning. Therefore, they now sought the meaning.

(10) "AND HE SAID, UNTO YOU IT IS GIVEN TO KNOW THE MYSTERIES OF

NOTES

THE KINGDOM OF GOD: BUT TO OTHERS IN PARABLES; THAT SEEING THEY MIGHT NOT SEE, AND HEARING THEY MIGHT NOT UNDERSTAND."

THE MYSTERIES OF THE KINGDOM OF GOD

The phrase, *"And He said, Unto you it is given to know the mysteries of the kingdom of God,"* actually pertains to any and all who seek to know the Lord and have a deeper understanding of His Word.

In the ordinary sense of the word, a mystery implies knowledge withheld; however, Jesus is saying that the scriptural significance to these mysteries is about to be revealed, at least to those who hunger and thirst after righteousness.

Among the ancient Greeks, the *"mysteries"* were religious rites and ceremonies practiced by secret societies into which anyone who so desired might be received. Those who were initiated into these mysteries became possessors of certain knowledge, which was not imparted to the uninitiated, and were called "the perfected" (I Cor. 2:6-16).

In the realm of the gospel, what are these mysteries?

WHAT ARE THESE MYSTERIES?

• The resurrection of the saints, both living and dead, was somewhat of a mystery to Old Testament saints. They understood that there was to be a resurrection, but exactly how this was to be brought about and what it would entail was a *"mystery"* (I Cor. 15:51-57).

• The blindness of Israel is a mystery, especially considering all the great promises of God given to them (Rom. 11:25-26). This should be a lesson to us that the ways of the Lord can be lost. In fact, the Holy Spirit through Paul said to us that if the church follows the way of Israel and rejects the righteousness of God and, thereby, tries to establish our own righteousness, we, as Israel, will also *"be cut off"* (Rom. 10:3; 11:22).

• The grace of God, as it resides in the church, was a mystery to Old Testament saints until it was revealed to the apostle Paul (Eph. 3:1-4).

The mystery that the Gentiles should be

partakers with the Jews in the gospel and be in the same church, so to speak, was completely unknown to Old Testament saints but, as stated, was revealed to the apostle Paul (Col. 1:26-27).

• It is a mystery as to why the Lord has allowed Satan to continue so long; however, Revelation 10:7 tells us that soon this *"mystery of God should be finished."*

These are but a few of *"the mysteries of the kingdom of God,"* which were revealed to some of the apostles in the early church.

BUT TO OTHERS IN PARABLES

The phrase, *"But to others in parables,"* proclaims the sad fact that most of Israel did not want to be disturbed from their earthly hopes, loves, and fears. They preferred not to be healed as God would heal them.

Jesus then spoke His parables with the intention of veiling His divine story from the careless and indifferent.

Godet said, "The veil which the parables threw over truth became transparent to the attentive mind, while it remained impenetrable to the careless."

SEEING BUT YET DO NOT SEE

The phrase, *"That seeing they might not see, and hearing they might not understand,"* pertained to a willful blindness and lack of comprehension.

Morrison stated, "It is the sinner's deeply rooted wish that he should not see and understand, and the sad explanation of this wish is given by Mark—the sinner is afraid lest he should be prevailed to turn, 'lest at any time they should be converted'" (Mk. 4:12).

WILLFUL BLINDNESS

A willful blindness resulted in a judicial blindness. In other words, he who wills rebellion receives further rebellion, and it is ordained of God that he should do so (Mat. 13:12).

Conversely, it is willed by God that he who wants righteousness will receive more righteousness (Mat. 5:6).

Many have attempted to take Verse 10, also, and claim that it means that some are predestined to be saved while others are predestined to be lost; however, a mere cursory

examination of the text reveals the fallacy of that idea.

These individuals are not forced into blindness or lack of comprehension, but rather, they desire it that way, and God has structured His message in such a way that if they so desire that, then ample opportunity will be given for such a course.

What we are reading is a fearful thing! It places the blame squarely on the individual involved, once again leaving it to *"whosoever will"* (Rev. 22:17).

(11) "NOW THE PARABLE IS THIS: THE SEED IS THE WORD OF GOD."

The pattern is:

1. The phrase, *"Now the parable is this,"* pertains to its explanation as requested by the disciples. A sincere answer will always be given by the Lord to an earnest, seeking heart.

2. The phrase, *"The seed is the Word of God,"* pertains to that which must be sowed.

3. This means that the sowing of any other type of seed is a fruitless gesture. Regrettably, most of that which is presently being sowed behind modern pulpits constitutes psychology or other philosophies and is not the Word of God.

4. Considering all preachers and priests in the Protestant and Catholic churches, it should be obvious that the Word of God is not the criterion for most in their proclamation. Were it so, the Catholic Church and many, if not most, Protestant churches would cease to exist immediately.

5. However, false doctrine exists and even flourishes because the majority of people desire something that does not affect their lifestyle or their sin. Consequently, they flock to false teachers because they have itching ears that desire to hear that which makes them feel comfortable.

(12) "THOSE BY THE WAY SIDE ARE THEY WHO HEAR; THEN COMES THE DEVIL, AND TAKES AWAY THE WORD OUT OF THEIR HEARTS, LEST THEY SHOULD BELIEVE AND BE SAVED."

The composition is:

1. The phrase, *"Those by the way side are they who hear,"* refers to them hearing the true Word of God.

2. The phrase, *"Then comes the Devil,*

and takes away the Word out of their hearts," proclaims two things:

a. Satan will always oppose the Word of God anywhere it is preached.

b. The *"Word"* is taken out of their hearts because this group desires that it be taken out, as the Jews of Jesus' day.

3. *"Lest they should believe and be saved,"* means that it is impossible for them to be saved unless they believe the Word. Also, it is impossible for individuals to be saved if they are listening to error. As well, as stated, Satan will not oppose error because, in effect, he is the author of such.

(13) "THEY ON THE ROCK ARE THEY, WHICH, WHEN THEY HEAR, RECEIVE THE WORD WITH JOY; AND THESE HAVE NO ROOT, WHICH FOR A WHILE BELIEVE, AND IN TIME OF TEMPTATION FALL AWAY."

The form is:

1. *"They on the rock are they, which, when they hear, receive the Word with joy,"* thusly proclaims a great beginning, which characterizes many.

2. *"And these have no root, which for a while believe, and in time of temptation fall away,"* proclaims some deep-seated, sinful desire within their hearts, which is described by Jesus as a rock, which in a short time causes their falling away.

3. This, as should be obvious, completely refutes the erroneous doctrine of unconditional eternal security. These individuals are true believers for awhile; however, they do not last simply because the Word is not allowed to take root within their hearts.

(14) "AND THAT WHICH FELL AMONG THORNS ARE THEY, WHICH, WHEN THEY HAVE HEARD, GO FORTH, AND ARE CHOKED WITH CARES AND RICHES AND PLEASURES OF THIS LIFE, AND BRING NO FRUIT TO PERFECTION."

The overview is:

1. The phrase, *"And that which fell among thorns are they,"* once again proclaims a good start, even a healthy plant; however, the *"thorns"* ultimately choke it to death.

2. *"Which, when they have heard, go forth, and are choked with cares and riches and pleasures of this life,"* proclaims Satan

NOTES

using the world and the vicissitudes of life to bring about the spiritual demise of these so affected.

The following is among that of which Jesus spoke:

• *"Cares"*: From the Greek text, the word means "to draw in different directions, or to distract." This is meant to wear down an individual's faith and, regrettably, often succeeds.

Someone has said that every attack by Satan is designed but for one purpose, and that is to destroy, or at least seriously weaken, our faith in God.

Conversely, everything the Lord allows is meant to strengthen our faith in God. In essence, everything is a test of faith, which the Lord desires that we use according to His Word and, thereby, be strengthened.

• *"Riches"*: such within itself is not sin; however, if we allow riches to turn our faces away from God to our own abilities, which this suggests, then the riches become a stumblingblock.

• *"Pleasures of this life"*: The word, as it is here used, speaks of the gratification of sinful desires. It also speaks of the world and its constant allurement to the believer. At times, the pleasures may not be wrong, but if we allow them to pull us away from total concentration on the Lord, they then become sin.

3. *"And bring no fruit to perfection,"* actually means that there is a beginning of fruit, but it does not go ahead and ripen and is, therefore, unusable. In other words, they come very close and, as well, fall into the same category as the previous group who believes for awhile and then falls away.

(15) "BUT THAT ON THE GOOD GROUND ARE THEY, WHICH IN AN HONEST AND GOOD HEART, HAVING HEARD THE WORD, KEEP IT, AND BRING FORTH FRUIT WITH PATIENCE."

The diagram is:

1. The phrase, *"But that on the good ground,"* constitutes the fourth group, who will bring forth fruit to perfection, i.e., fruit to maturity.

So, this description tells us that most who hear the gospel, even though at first accepting it, will not endure unto the end.

2. *"Are they, which in an honest and good heart,"* tells us that the problem is with the heart and not with the circumstances. In other words, the heart that is not honest before God will allow circumstances to drag it down.

3. *"Having heard the Word, keep it, and bring forth fruit with patience,"* tells us several things:

a. Hearing the Word is not enough; one must keep it as well!

b. As in the natural, it takes time for fruit to develop; likewise, it takes time for the Christian to bring forth spiritual fruit, hence, patience.

(16) "NO MAN, WHEN HE HAS LIT A CANDLE, COVERS IT WITH A VESSEL, OR PUTS IT UNDER A BED; BUT SETS IT ON A CANDLESTICK, THAT THEY WHICH ENTER IN MAY SEE THE LIGHT."

The overview is:

1. The phrase, *"No man, when he has lit a candle, covers it with a vessel, or puts it under a bed,"* means that the method of teaching used by Christ (referring to the parables) is not meant to hide truth from sincere, inquiring hearts, but rather the very opposite. In fact, Jesus' explanation of the sower, which He had just given them, showed them how really simple and adapted to everyday life His teaching was.

2. *"But sets it on a candlestick, that they which enter in may see the light,"* refers to the type of teaching in which Jesus was now engaged, and that it was designed to appeal to the honest, seeking heart. He wants men to see the light. Actually, this is His very purpose in coming, that men may know the truth, and that the truth will set them free.

(17) "FOR NOTHING IS SECRET, THAT SHALL NOT BE MADE MANIFEST; NEITHER ANYTHING HID, THAT SHALL NOT BE KNOWN AND COME ABROAD."

The composition is:

1. The phrase, *"For nothing is secret, that shall not be made manifest,"* addresses itself to the mysteries of the gospel. Even though there were mysteries in the past, and for rightful purpose, still, the explanation of those mysteries is about to be revealed and, in fact, has already been revealed.

2. Most every religion in the world has secret words of knowledge known only by the devotees; however, Christianity has no secrets whatsoever. Incidentally, Christianity is not a religion but a relationship.

3. *"Neither anything hid, that shall not be known and come abroad,"* means that every mystery will be revealed and, in fact, has been because the very purpose of the gospel is that all may see the light.

4. The only reason there were mysteries in the past concerning the plan of God is because it was not time for these things to be brought to pass; however, most, if not all the mysteries, have now been revealed.

5. Consequently, the idea of hiding any part of the gospel is foreign to what the gospel is all about. Men cannot be saved unless they hear the gospel, i.e., see the light. God is *"not willing that any should perish, but that all should come to repentance"* (II Pet. 3:9), which negates all false teaching of one predestined to be lost or saved.

(18) "TAKE HEED THEREFORE HOW YOU HEAR: FOR WHOSOEVER HAS, TO HIM SHALL BE GIVEN; AND WHOSOEVER HAS NOT, FROM HIM SHALL BE TAKEN EVEN THAT WHICH HE SEEMS TO HAVE."

The structure is:

1. The phrase, *"Take heed therefore how you hear,"* refers not only to what is heard, but how it is heard.

2. Consequently, the hearing of the gospel is the single most important thing that could happen to anyone. The following tells us what will happen, as to how it is heard.

3. *"For whosoever has, to him shall be given,"* constitutes a divine law that whoever accepts truth and is honestly wanting the whole truth and nothing but the truth will be given truth.

4. *"And whosoever has not, from him shall be taken even that which he seems to have,"* also constitutes a divine law that whosoever is dishonest and evasive of truth, and who seeks for excuses not to accept and obey it, will revert to darkness and fallacy in the extreme.

(19) "THEN CAME TO HIM HIS MOTHER AND HIS BRETHREN, AND COULD NOT COME AT HIM FOR THE PRESS."

HIS MOTHER AND HIS BROTHERS

The phrase, *"Then came to Him His mother and His brethren,"* refers to those of His immediate family.

The Catholics and others claim that Jesus did not have any brothers or sisters and that Mary had no other children.

MARY HAD OTHER CHILDREN

• It is plainly stated that Jesus had four brothers (half-brothers), James, Joseph, Simon, and Jude. He had at least three half-sisters also—*"Are not His sisters here with us?"* These are referred to as *"His own kin"* and *"His own house."* Also, the phrases, *"His mother ... His brethren ... His sisters"* are used in the plain literal sense of them (Mat. 13:55-56; Mk. 6:3-4).

• Jesus is called Mary's *"firstborn"* (Mat. 1:25; Lk. 2:7). The natural inference is that she had other children.

The Greek *prototokos* is used only in Romans 8:29; Colossians 1:15-18; Hebrews 1:6; 11:28; 12:23; and Revelation 1:5, of the first of many others. Had Jesus been Mary's only Son, the word would have been *monogenes,* which occurs in Luke 7:12; 8:42; and 9:38; of human parentage of the "only son," "only daughter," and "only child," and of the Lord Jesus as *"the only begotten of the Father"* (Jn. 1:14, 18; 3:16, 18; I Jn. 4:9).

• It was predicted by God that Mary would have other children, and the Messiah would have brothers:

"I am become a stranger unto My brethren, and an alien unto My mother's children" (Ps. 69:8-9).

• *"His mother and His brethren"* are mentioned as following Him to Capernaum and seeking to hinder His work (Mat. 12:46-50; Mk. 3:31-35; Lk. 8:19-21; Jn. 2:12). The children of some other woman would not be following Mary as His brethren.

• *"His brethren"* are mentioned as not believing on Him until after the resurrection (Jn. 7:3-10; Acts 1:14).

• James is called *"the Lord's brother"* (Gal. 1:19).

• The natural meaning of *"His brethren"* would have never been questioned but for the fact of pagan corruption in the church—in seeking to raise Mary from a mere *"handmaid of the Lord"* (Lk. 1:38) to that of mother of God and to invest her with divine powers as a goddess.

MARY

Thus, the way was prepared for identifying her with the goddess of paganism, who is supposed to be the mother of a divine son, and who is yet a virgin.

So, it is said by the Catholic Church and others that Mary had no other children and that His brethren were cousins by another Mary and Cleophas, that Joseph was too old to have children of Mary, or that he had children by a former marriage. All of this is false as nothing is mentioned in Scripture or history about these claims.

If Joseph did have children before Jesus was born, then Jesus could not be the legal heir to David's throne, which, by law, went to the firstborn.

As well, from the time that Pope John Paul II was selected as pope until he died, Mary worship was increased dramatically. This man claimed that Mary appeared to him some years ago, promising he would be pope. Consequently, he said that he owed his position to Mary; therefore, Mary worship was encouraged as never before.

As well, Mary is supposedly appearing to all types of people around the world.

Is this really Mary?

No! It was not Mary who appeared to Pope John Paul II or any of the other appearances to whomever.

While it is certainly possible that Pope John Paul II and others may have had a real vision, it was not and is not of Mary, but rather of a demon spirit impersonating her, called *"a familiar spirit"* (Lev. 19:31; 20:6, 27; Deut. 18:11; I Sam. 28:3; II Ki. 21:6; 23:24; I Chron. 10:13; II Chron. 33:6; Isa. 8:19; 19:3; 29:4).

The phrase, *"And could not come at Him for the press,"* refers to His family coming to Him, but when they arrived, the crowd was so large that they simply could not get to Him.

(20) "AND IT WAS TOLD HIM BY CERTAIN WHICH SAID, YOUR MOTHER AND YOUR BRETHREN STAND WITHOUT, DESIRING TO SEE YOU."

NOTES

WHY DIDN'T THE BROTHERS OF JESUS BELIEVE IN HIM DURING HIS EARTHLY MINISTRY?

The phrase, *"And it was told Him by certain which said,"* implies that they told others who they were and that they desired to see Jesus. Consequently, the news filtered through the crowd, finally getting to Jesus.

"Your mother and Your brethren stand without, desiring to see You," proclaims much more than meets the eye.

Even though there is little knowledge regarding Mary's thoughts and feelings at this time, at least concerning His acceptance, the Scripture is clear respecting His brothers. John said, *"For neither did His brethren* (brothers) *believe in Him"* (Jn. 7:5). It was only after the resurrection that James and Jude accepted Him for who and what He really was (I Cor. 15:7; Gal. 1:19). Actually, James became the senior pastor of the church in Jerusalem.

Why didn't His brothers believe in Him during His earthly ministry?

We are given the answer in the next verse. They simply did not believe the Word of God concerning Him. This is the cause of all error! If men do not believe the Word of God, they are left to their own prejudice and bias, hence, the reason for the condition of the world.

BESIDE HIMSELF?

His mother and His brothers were now desiring to see Him but, actually, for the wrong reason. There is some evidence that His own brothers thought He was *"beside Himself,"* in other words, insane! (Mk. 3:21).

First of all, despite all the evidence to the contrary, they simply did not believe that He was the Son of God. He had grown up with them and despite the fact that His life was perfect, still, their hearts were evil, and they refused to see His perfection. Either that, or they did see it, and it angered them, which is probably the case.

And then, the opposition was now beginning on the part of the Pharisees and Sadducees, in other words, the religious leaders of Israel. They probably were legitimately concerned about where this

would lead. It was obvious what His townspeople thought of Him since they tried to kill Him on His only appearance in that city (Lk. 4:16-30).

To be sure, it has never been easy to accept and follow Christ. All who do so do it at the expense of the world. As well, there is also a good chance that relatives and loved ones will be totally opposed, bringing a rupture into the family. They hated Him, and they will hate all His followers (Jn. 15:18).

(21) "AND HE ANSWERED AND SAID UNTO THEM, MY MOTHER AND MY BRETHREN ARE THESE WHICH HEAR THE WORD OF GOD, AND DO IT."

The structure is:

1. The phrase, *"And He answered and said unto them,"* presents a principle that places God first in all things.

2. *"My mother and My brethren* (brothers) *are these which hear the Word of God, and do it,"* bluntly and plainly proclaims allegiance to God as even more solemn than family ties. In addition, He was proclaiming that, though holy and binding, they must not be allowed to stand in the way of plain, unmistakable duty to God. So, once again we have the statement that not only must one hear the Word of God, but, as well, one must do the Word of God.

3. How many believers presently put the Word of God ahead of all things?

4. I am afraid the answer is "not many!" Many, if not most, do place family, religious denominations, the making of money, or a host of other things ahead of God.

5. The first criterion for all things is, "Is it scriptural?"

6. As well, Jesus proclaimed the qualifications for entrance into the family of God. As such, it holds true not only with Him and the body but, as well, even between believers.

7. Many, if not all believers, are far closer to their true brothers and sisters in the Lord than they are even to their unsaved family members. As stated, the Word of God is the criterion, and Jesus is the bond.

(22) "NOW IT CAME TO PASS ON A CERTAIN DAY, THAT HE WENT INTO A SHIP WITH HIS DISCIPLES: AND HE SAID UNTO THEM, LET US GO OVER

UNTO THE OTHER SIDE OF THE LAKE. AND THEY LAUNCHED FORTH."

The pattern is:

1. The phrase, *"Now it came to pass on a certain day, that He went into a ship with His disciples,"* institutes a mission that is a portrayal of what He did to redeem humanity.

2. *"And He said unto them, Let us go over unto the other side of the lake,"* refers in a sense to His coming to this world of sorrow, bondage, and heartache. As well, I remind the reader that He said, *"Let us go over unto the other side of the lake,"* not, "Let us go out into the middle of the lake and be destroyed by a storm."

3. *"And they launched forth,"* constitutes their doing so at His command. However, it was not to be an uneventful trip. Satan would do everything he could to stop it, exactly as he continues to make every effort presently.

(23) "BUT AS THEY SAILED HE FELL ASLEEP: AND THERE CAME DOWN A STORM OF WIND ON THE LAKE; AND THEY WERE FILLED WITH WATER, AND WERE IN JEOPARDY."

The form is:

1. The phrase, *"But as they sailed He fell asleep,"* proclaims being exhausted from healing and delivering, as well as teaching. This portrayed His humanity.

2. *"And there came down a storm of wind on the lake,"* proclaims Satan evidently attempting to take advantage of the disciples being in the middle of the lake while Jesus was asleep.

3. From the Greek text, the *"storm of wind"* represents a "furious storm or hurricane." It was not a single gust of wind or even steadily blowing wind, but rather a storm breaking forth from black thunder clouds and furious gusts, with floods of rain, and throwing everything upside down, as such a storm will do.

4. *"And they were filled with water, and were in jeopardy,"* means that the waves were throwing themselves into the boat, and were repeatedly doing so. They were actually in danger of sinking and were in jeopardy of losing their lives.

(24) "AND THEY CAME TO HIM, AND

AWOKE HIM, SAYING, MASTER, MASTER, WE PERISH. THEN HE AROSE, AND REBUKED THE WIND AND THE RAGING OF THE WATER: AND THEY CEASED, AND THERE WAS A CALM."

JESUS

The phrase, *"And they came to Him, and awoke Him,"* refers to them not doing so until the danger was acute.

As well, His being able to sleep in this thunderous action tells us something about His person. There was never any worry, care, or anxiety about Him. He always exhibited a perfect faith that never waned or weakened, even in the face of the direst circumstances, as now; consequently, there was absolutely no fear within His heart and life. As such, His sleep was deep and immensely restful.

One could probably say that no human being, no matter how close to God one may be, can sleep with such soundness as did Jesus. Even the most consecrated are not totally free from worry or care, seeing that all of us have an imperfect faith.

MASTER, DO YOU NOT CARE THAT WE PERISH?

The phrase, *"Saying, Master, Master, we perish,"* is recorded by Mark as saying, *"Master, do You not care that we perish?"* Matthew records the statement as, *"Lord, save us: we perish"* (Mat. 8:25).

All statements were, no doubt, uttered, with each apostle recording only a part of what was actually said.

One can well imagine just how bad the storm was when even these men who had seen many storms were alarmed.

JESUS REBUKED THE STORM

The phrase, *"Then He arose, and rebuked the wind and the raging of the water,"* refers to a spirit behind the storm attempting to kill the disciples. I am sure that Satan knew that Jesus could not be killed, but he also knew the disciples were very mortal; however, with Jesus in the boat with them, even asleep, there was no way this ship was going down.

Some have attempted to use the account of this storm as Satan having authority over the weather, etc. However, to do such denies the omnipotence of God. Satan was, no doubt, the instrument in this case, but still, he could only do what God the Father allowed him to do. In fact, every single incident which happens to the child of God is either caused or allowed by the Lord. While it is true that He certainly does not cause things such as the storm, at the same time, He definitely does allow it, for Satan cannot do anything otherwise.

While Satan means it for our destruction, as should be obvious, the Lord means it for our good, whatever it may be. In fact, the Lord never does anything but that it is for the good of all concerned. James said, *"Every good gift and every perfect gift is from above, and comes down from the Father of lights, with whom is no variableness, neither shadow of turning,"* meaning that He will never change from this principle (James 1:17).

PEACE, BE STILL

The phrase, *"And they ceased, and there was a calm,"* records Mark saying that He said, *"Peace, be still"* (Mk. 4:39).

In effect, Jesus said to the storm, "Hush!"

Instantly, the storm ceased! That is how quickly Jesus can change a situation. One moment the storm is raging, and the next moment there is a calm. No power on earth can even begin to approach such authority. Of all the human beings who have ever lived, none has even remotely approached His power, authority, and total control over all things. Even the secular history of that particular time testifies to His miracle-working power. So, why do not men serve Him?

As we have repeatedly stated, the world is deceived. It thinks up is down and down is up. It thinks black is white and white is black. It thinks darkness is light and light is darkness. It thinks evil is good and good is evil.

A perfect example is homosexuality. Many, if not most of the powers that be, entertain the idea that homosexuality is good. It's the way that God made these people, so what's wrong with it?

God did not make individuals to be homosexual. They become that way after a period of time.

NOTES

HOMOSEXUALITY

Please understand that anything that God says is wrong is wrong, and He most definitely says that homosexuality is wrong (Gen. 18:20; 19:4-5; Lev. 20:13; 18:22; I Cor. 6:9; I Tim. 1:10; Deut. 23:17-18; I Ki. 14:24; 15:12; II Ki. 23:7; Rom. 1:26-27; Jude 7; Rev. 22:15).

Let's see why God says it is an abomination.

• Thirty percent of all homosexuals attempt suicide. Only three and one-half percent of heterosexuals do so.

• The life expectancy of a homosexual is only 42 years old. In fact, only two percent live past 65. The life expectancy of a heterosexual male is 75 years old.

• As it regards AIDS, 46 percent of homosexual males contract AIDS.

Anything that God tells us in His Word is wrong is all for our good. It's when men think they know more than God that the trouble begins to arise.

You can look at every empire of the past, and three things were pandemic in these empires when they finally rotted from within and fell. Those three things were:

1. Pedophilia
2. Incest
3. Homosexuality

Passing laws that make same-sex marriages legal and that homosexuality is a good thing doesn't change the reality. When educators attempt to make children in our public schools believe that homosexuality is normal, they aren't doing those kids a favor, not at all! Those who buy into that lie will die at an early age and will live a life of misery. Laws cannot take away the guilt, and guilt ultimately kills.

INSANITY

As well, there is a form of insanity about the deception that plagues the human race. It inculcates itself in every form and facet of one's life. Within himself, man cannot assuage this malady. It can be overcome only by the power of the Holy Spirit as He makes the Word of God real to one's life. Then, as the soul yields to Christ, the terrible shell is broken, with the prisoner going free. In fact, the entire plan of redemption proclaims the prisoner being loosed from the prison cell (Isa. 42:7).

The storms that arise in life and, in fact, come to every life, can be assuaged only by Christ. There is no other answer! Sadly, men attempt to treat this terrible malady by rehabilitation, counseling, therapy, or a host of other things, all to no avail. Jesus alone can bring the calm, and it is a peace that passes all understanding (Phil. 4:7).

(25) "AND HE SAID UNTO THEM, WHERE IS YOUR FAITH? AND THEY BEING AFRAID WONDERED, SAYING ONE TO ANOTHER, WHAT MANNER OF MAN IS THIS! FOR HE COMMANDS EVEN THE WINDS AND WATER, AND THEY OBEY HIM."

WHERE IS YOUR FAITH?

The question, "And He said unto them, Where is your faith?" proclaims the answer to be Christ concerning all the storms of life.

He was telling them that while He would not be with them forever in a physical sense, He definitely would be with them in a spiritual sense, hence, faith. In practical terms, what was He saying?

He was not saying that faith can stop all storms before they start, but He was saying that faith in God will see us through these storms, and will even stop some of them at the point of their fiercest intensity, as here. Above all, our faith will help us to come out stronger in the end than at the beginning. As we have stated, Satan designs such for our destruction while the Lord allows such for our spiritual betterment.

What type of faith is Christ speaking of in this text?

Faith in God is not merely accepting certain things as true, but rather trusting a person and what that person has done at the Cross. Of course, that person is Christ.

THE OBJECT OF OUR FAITH!

The object of faith must always be Christ and what He did for us at the Cross. The writer of Hebrews said, "Looking unto Jesus the author and finisher of our faith" (Heb. 12:2).

If the believer tries to claim faith in Christ and, at the same time, ignores or denies the

NOTES

Cross of Christ, such a believer is serving another Jesus, whether he realizes it or not. Paul said that when we eliminate the Cross or deny the Cross, we are left with "another Jesus," "another spirit," and "another gospel." In fact, He said to the Galatians the following:

"I marvel that you are so soon removed from Him (the Holy Spirit) who called you into the grace of Christ (made possible by the Cross) unto another gospel (anything which doesn't have the Cross as its object of faith):

"Which is not another (presents the fact that Satan's aim is not so much to deny the gospel, which He can little do, as to corrupt it); but there be some who trouble you, and would pervert the gospel of Christ (once again, to make the object of faith something other than Christ and the Cross).

"But though we (Paul and his associates), or an angel from heaven, preach any other gospel unto you than that which we have preached unto you (Jesus Christ and Him crucified), let him be accursed (eternally condemned; the Holy Spirit speaks this through Paul, making this very serious).

"As we said before, so say I now again (at some time past, he had said the same thing to them, making their defection even more serious), If any man preach any other gospel unto you (anything other than the Cross) than that you have received (which saved your souls), let him be accursed (eternally condemned, which means the loss of the soul).

"For do I now persuade men, or God? (In essence, Paul is saying, 'Do I preach man's doctrine or God's?') or do I seek to please men? (This is what false apostles do.) for if I yet pleased men, I should not be the servant of Christ (one cannot please both men and God at the same time)" (Gal. 1:6-10).

THE GIFT INSTEAD OF THE GIVER

Too often, the object of faith is the gift instead of the giver. The Lord told Abraham, "I am your shield, and your exceeding great reward" (Gen. 15:1). In other words, He was telling the Patriarch that his reward was not the gift, in this case Isaac, but rather the giver, who was the heavenly Father. Abraham was guilty of doing what all of us probably have done, possibly several times, in getting our eyes on the gift instead of the giver.

If there is a fault in the modern faith community, that is it. The gift (for whatever we are believing God) becomes paramount, with the Lord merely being used to arrive at this particular conclusion. We must understand that everything is designed by the Lord, even the increase of our faith, for one purpose, and that is to draw the individual close to Him. Consequently, things are not, and must not be, the object of our faith, but rather Christ Himself and what He did for us at the Cross.

As stated, Christ and the Cross must never be separated. Of course, this does not mean that Christ is still on the Cross. In fact, He is seated by the right hand of the Father in heaven, meaning that His work is finished and complete. However, we must never forget that it is the Cross of Christ that is the means of all things we receive from the Lord, and I mean all things.

While faith in God and His Word will definitely get things and do things for the believer, still, the object of the Holy Spirit is not these *"things,"* but rather the Lord Jesus. Sadly, almost all of the books printed on faith point to things rather than Christ— "How to have faith for healing," "How to have faith for financial success," "How to have faith for your needs to be met," etc. I don't believe I've ever seen a book or an article entitled, *"How to Have Faith to be Drawn Closer to Christ."*

In 1991, the Lord impressed upon me to begin two prayer meetings a day, with the exception of service nights. This we did and continued it for some 10 years, which I still continue personally regarding my own prayer life. At the very outset, the Lord said to me:

"Do not seek Me so much for what I can do, but rather for Who I am."

At the beginning, I didn't quite understand what the Lord was saying to me; however, little by little, it began to make sense as to what the Lord was speaking. That's why Paul said while imprisoned in Rome:

"That I may know Him, and the power of His resurrection, and the fellowship of His

NOTES

sufferings, being made conformable unto His death" (Phil. 3:10).

In truth, if one places Christ and the Cross as the object of one's faith as the Holy Spirit intends, the other things will come. That is at least one of the reasons the Scripture says, *"Seek ye first the kingdom of God."*

WHERE IS YOUR FAITH?

As well, the question, *"Where is your faith?"* as asked by Jesus, could have been asked, "Where or what is the object of your faith?"

Let us say it again because it is so very, very important:

Where is your faith? Better yet, what is the object of your faith?

Many Christians would immediately answer, "The Word of God is the object of my faith," "The Lord is the object of my faith," etc. These answers are correct, but as many answers, that which says too much, in effect, says nothing.

The entirety of the story of the Bible is the story of Jesus Christ and Him crucified. That's the entire thrust of the Word of God. So, when one has his or her faith in Christ and the Cross, then one has one's faith in the Word of God. If we ignore the Cross of Christ, this then puts us on the road to spiritual adultery (Rom. 7:1-5).

The modern church has a modicum of understanding respecting the Cross of Christ and salvation. In fact, the words "Jesus died for me" are possibly the greatest words that could ever be penned or spoken. However, when it comes to the Cross of Christ and one's sanctification, sadly and regrettably, the modern church has absolutely no understanding whatsoever.

In fact, virtually the entirety of the Bible, at least 99 percent, is given over to telling believers how to live for God. It all comes to a head in the book of Romans, and more specifically, Chapters 6, 7, and 8. This should be obvious inasmuch as the Bible is for believers and not for unbelievers. In fact, unbelievers don't understand it whatsoever.

WHAT MANNER OF MAN IS THIS?

The phrase, *"And they being afraid wondered,"* pertains to His person. The disciples had accepted His Messiahship but had a most inadequate view of the same. They evidently did not recognize all the implications which that office carried with it.

The exclamation, *"Saying one to another, What manner of man is this!"* takes them to a level they had not heretofore attained.

When one considers that all things are possible with God and that Jesus is God, one begins to realize that there is absolutely no limit to what God can do.

After the storm had instantly subsided at the command of Jesus, the Twelve stood transfixed on the deck of the ship. They were exclaiming one to another not only the awesome power it took to cause a storm to cease immediately, but more importantly, what kind of person Jesus was, who could bring such a thing about in a moment's time! In other words, what was done was astounding, but more importantly, the One who did it was more so. Consequently, this thing brought about in the hearts of these disciples was exactly what the Holy Spirit wanted. He wanted the attention to be focused on Jesus instead of what He had done. The reasons are obvious:

JESUS

• Men love to play God, especially religious men. This is perhaps one of the greatest temptations for any faith-filled believer. We forget that it is God who charts the course and not we ourselves.

• Keeping our eyes focused on Jesus and the Cross as the object of our faith always demands that we seek His will and not our will. This is paramount.

• If the object of faith is Jesus and what He did for us at the Cross, only that which He desires will be brought into being. That is at least one of the great objectives of the Holy Spirit. He wants us to think like Christ, conduct ourselves like Christ, and desire only what Christ desires. When we become completely one with Him, then the purpose is one, which is extremely important in our spiritual growth.

THE WIND AND THE WATER OBEY HIM

The phrase, *"For He commands even the winds and water, and they obey Him,"*

proclaims His total control not only over demon spirits and sickness but, as well, the elements. In effect, He commands any and all, and it must be done. He is the Creator!

In that context, if that is so, many would say, "Why doesn't He command all the evil in the world to stop, including poverty, sickness, etc.?"

THE OMNIPOTENCE OF GOD

Demons and elements are one thing, but the free moral agency of man is something else. While God surely could command all evil to immediately cease in the universe, if, in fact, He did it in this manner, He would not achieve the end results that will be best for all. With God being omniscient, omnipotent, and omnipresent, He can do anything. However, according to His creation, and the end result He desires in that creation, He is limited in the things He can do, that is, if the end result is to be what He desires.

As well, God will never do anything that's against His nature, His character, or His being itself. God is a thrice-holy God, meaning He cannot abide sin in any form. So whatever He does must be in keeping with His nature of pure holiness.

WHAT DOES GOD DESIRE?

He desires that men truly and freely love Him. This, in turn, means that they will love each other, which, due to its very nature, cannot be forced. Love has to be of one's free choice and volition or else it is not love. So, to obtain this in man, Jesus Christ had to come and die on Calvary and pay the price for man's sins and, thereby, redeem him, that is, if man will only believe (Jn. 3:16). When this is done, man is *"born again,"* which, in a sense, means that he is regenerated (Jn. 3:3). Through redeemed man, God is getting, and will get, what He desires, which will be for the good of all.

In order to bring this about, a period of time must lapse with evil and Satan allowed free course, at least up to limits, for man must continue to make a choice just as he did in the garden of Eden. Regrettably, he failed there, but from that time, many have not failed, at least in that sense. In other words, even though all of mankind is a product of the fall and, therefore, sinful and wicked, still, many have partaken of the Tree of Life, which is Jesus Christ. They have had the terrible bondage of sin broken within their lives, which was a product of the fall.

THE TREE OF LIFE

Originally, if man had partaken of the Tree of Life in the garden in his unregenerate state, the problems brought about would have been overwhelming. In other words, an Adolph Hitler or a Joseph Stalin would have lived forever. Had that happened, the world would have been destroyed a long time ago (Gen. 3:22-24).

The true *"Tree of Life,"* to which we have alluded, is the Lord Jesus Christ. When men partake of Him, they are gloriously and wondrously changed, which is bringing, and will bring, that which God desires. It is found in Revelation, Chapters 21 and 22. It will ultimately be achieved, and then all evil will be banished, never to return.

(26) "AND THEY ARRIVED AT THE COUNTRY OF THE GADARENES, WHICH IS OVER AGAINST GALILEE."

The composition is:

1. The phrase, *"And they arrived at the country of the Gadarenes,"* is on the eastern side of the Sea of Galilee. We know He went there for the purpose of delivering the maniac of Gadara, but His mission, no doubt, included far more as well!

2. What He could and would have done in this entire area would have been astounding, but as we shall see, the civic leaders did not want Him. Consequently, all of that which could have been done was not done, which is the case in most hearts and lives.

3. *"Which is over against Galilee,"* refers to the part of Decapolis, which, in itself, was quite large and bordered the Sea of Galilee on the southern tip and the eastern side.

(27) "AND WHEN HE WENT FORTH TO LAND, THERE MET HIM OUT OF THE CITY A CERTAIN MAN, WHICH HAD DEVILS LONG TIME, AND WORE NO CLOTHES, NEITHER ABODE IN ANY HOUSE, BUT IN THE TOMBS."

A CERTAIN MAN

The phrase, *"And when He went forth to

NOTES

land, there met Him out of the city a certain man,"* means the man was at least part of, if not the main reason, for Jesus coming to the eastern side of the Sea of Galilee. The community had given up on this *"certain man,"* but Jesus would set him free.

"Which had devils (demons) *long time, and wore no clothes, neither abode in any house, but in the tombs,"* is, whether one believes it or not, a perfect description of the human family who Christ came to save, of which this is an example. It is as follows:

A SYMBOL OF THE WORLD

"Which had devils (demons) *long time"*: Satan is the god of this present world and the prince of the powers of the air (II Cor. 4:4; Eph. 2:2). The *"powers of the air"* refers to this world being infested by demon spirits that actually control entire nations and most of the people. That does not mean all people who are not believers are demon possessed, but it definitely does mean that all are strongly demon influenced. As a result, the world is bathed in blood, sickness, darkness, hate, poverty, superstition, etc. The only power against this is the name of Jesus and the power of the Holy Spirit (Mk. 16:15-18; Acts 1:8).

The world thinks that education or environment is the answer to these problems. While these things certainly play their part, still, it is only a minor part, with the power of Jesus Christ, as illustrated in the account of this demoniac, being the only real solution.

MEN HOLD NO SOLUTION

Men never seem to learn, and that includes the church. In 1992, when the Republicans swept into power, controlling both Houses of Congress, millions, including the church, were acclaiming this as the answer. I stood before our congregation at Family Worship Center and told them that in four years or less, many would be demanding the ouster of the present incumbents, claiming that others could better get the job done. That's exactly what happened!

These problems cannot be solved by man. In fact, they are far more acute than any man realizes. They are so acute, in fact, that it takes divine intervention for any type of change for the good to be made.

So, man, and even the church, may resent me comparing this maniac of Gadara to the human family as a whole; however, I personally think it is an apt description, with the evidence being borne out almost everyday.

Luke mentioned that this man had been in this state a long time, which perfectly characterizes the human family. To be sure, if man could solve these problems, he would have done so a long time ago.

THE INFLUENCE OF THE BIBLE

Yes! There have been some improvements in the world; however, it is only because of the influence of Bible Christianity. Take that away, and the world would have long since destroyed itself. That is how critical the situation really is. Jesus called believers *"salt"* and *"light"* (Mat. 5:13-14). This means it is the light given by the Holy Spirit through believers and the salt, which is a preservative generated by believers, that have kept this world going. That and that alone is the answer to any and all prosperity, freedom, and illumination in this world.

NAKED TO THE JUDGMENT OF GOD

"And wore no clothes": This was certainly speaking in the literal sense; however, it, as well, is speaking of the spiritual. Man is naked to the judgment of God because of him being in rebellion against God. The only answer to this is the Cross of Christ!

When Adam and Eve fell, the Scripture says, *"And they knew that they were naked"* (Gen. 3:7). This referred to the physical, but more than all, it referred to the spiritual. Adam and Eve, and all who would follow them, would be naked to the judgment of God. This has been assuaged only by Jesus Christ and what He did for us at the Cross, and man's acceptance of Him as Saviour and Redeemer.

This judgment is absolutely necessary because God is unalterably opposed to sin and all that pertains to Satan and the kingdom of darkness. The reasons are obvious; Satan steals, kills, and destroys (Jn. 10:10). So, there is a war being fought in the spirit world between light and darkness, which

NOTES

spills over into the physical, domestic, material, and financial. That is why Jesus came to *"destroy the works of the Devil"* (I Jn. 3:8).

DEATH

"Neither abode in any house, but in the tombs": Death strangles everything man touches because man carries death with him as a result of the fall. So, in effect, he does not abide in the house of God, but rather in the tombs. Death hovers over everything like a cloud, and, in effect, it is a shroud.

Man knows something is not right, but he will not believe the Word of God as to the cause or the cure. Hence, the Egyptians built the largest tombs on the face of the earth in the form of pyramids because they believed there was an afterlife. In fact, much of the world believes in a false hope called *"reincarnation,"* which is not taught in the Bible because it does not exist. All of this is because man knows that death is an aberration.

In truth, God never intended that man would die; consequently, he originally created man that he should live forever. It was the fall that brought on death, first in the realm of spiritual death, which is separation from God. This ultimately brought on physical death, with the ultimate degeneration of all things.

THE MISSION OF CHRIST

Part of the mission of Christ was not only to redeem man from sin but from death, and in every form. He became the firstfruits of that redemption when He went to the Cross and then on the third day, walked out of the tomb, which was on the resurrection morning. At that moment, death was dealt a blow, which took Satan's victory out of the grave and the sting out of death (I Cor. 15:55-56).

At the conclusion of the coming kingdom age, death, as the *"last enemy,"* will be totally destroyed, bringing man back to his original creation (I Cor. 15:24-26).

Once again, as Jesus crossed this lake, in the incarnation He has crossed the great divide between God and the fallen sons of Adam's lost race, with Him coming to set the captive free. As He did it then, He does it now, and will ultimately do it for all, at least those who believe.

"*Oh the grace that drew salvation's plan,*
"*Oh the love that brought it down to man,*
"*Oh the mighty gulf our God did span,*
"*At Calvary.*"

(28) "WHEN HE SAW JESUS, HE CRIED OUT, AND FELL DOWN BEFORE HIM, AND WITH A LOUD VOICE SAID, WHAT HAVE I TO DO WITH YOU, JESUS, YOU SON OF GOD MOST HIGH? I BESEECH YOU, TORMENT ME NOT."

WHEN HE SAW JESUS

The phrase, "*When he saw Jesus, he cried out, and fell down before Him,*" proclaims the spirit world of darkness, with all its attendant destructive spirits, as being obedient and subservient to the Lord Jesus Christ. His crying out was in fear, for it was the demon speaking through the man, and his falling down before Jesus was an acknowledgment of Him as Lord and Master.

It is amazing that the demons instantly recognized Jesus for who and what He was, but the religious leaders of Israel did not know. As well, this should be a lesson to all of mankind, and especially the church.

These demon spirits will not bow down to the political process, no matter how well intentioned. Neither will they bow down to education or prosperity, but only before the Lord Jesus Christ. Consequently, Satan works overtime to get the church off on sidetracks. As someone has said, "The great battle in the church has always been between the 'good' and the 'best.'"

While it may be good for the church to be successful in having certain individuals elected to high political office, still, it is not the best. God has called the church for one particular purpose, and that is to herald His gospel far and wide, in other words, to preach Jesus Christ and Him crucified. That is the mission of the church, and when it gets off into other things, it is always without power because the Holy Spirit will never honor such. It is only the Word of God preached, testified, and proclaimed in all of its glory in the mighty name of Jesus that will

NOTES

set the captive free. Nothing else will suffice.

THE HOLY SPIRIT

Satan never trembles or bows before politicians, educators, scientists, psychologists, or professional preachers for that matter. He only trembles and bows before someone, be it man or woman, who is full of the Holy Spirit and knows how to use the mighty name of Jesus. Even as I dictate these words, I sense the presence of God. That is why the Lord told the prophet Zechariah a long time ago, it is "*Not by might* (human might), *nor by power* (human power), *but by My Spirit, says the Lord of Hosts*" (Zech. 4:6). When will the church ever learn this?

The church thinks if a man has a doctorate, and especially if that doctorate is in psychology, he is certainly equipped to meet the needs of humanity. The truth is, he is not only not equipped to meet their needs, but he will actually do them harm by keeping them from the only power that can set them free, which is the power of God. My words are strong, but they are true. Satan trembles before nothing but that name.

WHAT HAVE I TO DO WITH YOU, JESUS?

The question, "*And with a loud voice said, What have I to do with You, Jesus, You Son of God Most High?*" proclaims these spirits, as stated, knowing exactly who Jesus was! He was not just "*Jesus,*" or "*Jesus, You Son of God,*" but, as well, "*Jesus, You Son of God Most High!*"

Why doesn't all of mankind know exactly who Jesus is just as these demons?

They do not know because Satan has them blinded, and, as well, they choose to stay blind because they love their sins.

The phrase, "*I beseech You, torment me not,*" proclaims them knowing and realizing that Jesus had the power to do with them whatever He desired. There was no argument about that in this arena, which this testimony proves.

Matthew mentions two demoniacs, with Mark and Luke mentioning only one. In fact, there were two, with one being more prominent than the other, hence, him alone being mentioned by Mark and Luke.

Matthew records them asking the

question, *"Are You come here to torment us before the time?"* (Mat. 8:29).

BEFORE THE TIME

They knew that a particular time had already been judged by God as the time of their being locked away in the lake of fire (Rev. 20:10). As well, Jesus said of the Holy Spirit that He would *"reprove the world of sin, and of righteousness, and of judgment … Of judgment, because the prince of this world is judged"* (Jn. 16:8, 11), meaning that a time has been set for the doom of Satan and all his followers. In effect, these spirits were requesting that they not be consigned to the lake of fire before that particular time.

It should be understandable from this encounter as given by Matthew, Mark, and Luke, that the outcome of this conflict is not in doubt at all! Satan is totally and completely defeated. It is only a matter of time until he is locked away forever.

Praise God!

(29) "(FOR HE HAD COMMANDED THE UNCLEAN SPIRIT TO COME OUT OF THE MAN. FOR OFTENTIMES IT HAD CAUGHT HIM: AND HE WAS KEPT BOUND WITH CHAINS AND IN FETTERS; AND HE BROKE THE BANDS, AND WAS DRIVEN OF THE DEVIL INTO THE WILDERNESS.)"

THE UNCLEAN SPIRIT

The phrase, *"For He had commanded the unclean spirit to come out of the man,"* speaks of the head spirit or demon, who was the leader of all the others, a great host, as we shall see.

The word for *commanded* in the Greek text is *epitasso* and means "to charge," as in a military command. It has the idea of a superior and in this case, Jesus giving the orders, which much be obeyed.

So, Jesus did not merely request that this spirit come out, but rather charged him to do so, which placed the authority of omnipotence behind the command. This proclaims the various ranks in the spirit world, with Jesus being the Most High!

The phrase, *"For oftentimes it had caught him,"* refers to this spirit, or spirits, taking control of this man and giving him

superhuman strength, as we shall see. Actually, this is the way many superhuman feats are done that seem to have little or no explanation. Even though the man was demon possessed at all times, he was not always taken over completely regarding this superhuman strength, but only on special occasions.

CHAINS AND FETTERS

The phrase, *"And he was kept bound with chains and in fetters,"* means that others attempted to restrain him but to no avail. Apparently, he was very destructive!

The chains and fetters represent the ultimate of man's pitiful efforts to help someone of this nature, or any type of problem for that matter. When one looks at these efforts, he is also looking at modern-day psychology. As that psychological method did not help then, neither does it help now!

Humanistic psychology is a product of man, and unredeemed man at that, and we might quickly add, grossly unredeemed. This means that there is nothing that can benefit man that can come from such a source. But yet, the modern church has embraced humanistic psychology in totality. Let me quickly make this statement:

Man cannot believe in the Cross of Christ and humanistic psychology at the same time. It's impossible. Either one cancels out the other. So, where does that leave the modern church?

It leaves the modern church unable to help anyone. Please understand that Satan does not bow before higher education, or anything else of the world, but only the power of the Holy Spirit. When something is embraced, such as humanistic psychology, and done so by the church, in effect, that leaves that church without the power of the Spirit. This means that there is no one saved, no one baptized with the Holy Spirit, no one healed, and no one delivered. That's the state of the modern church.

Yes, there are a few people saved, as it regards some churches that are affiliated with these denominations, but after a period of time, the Holy Spirit will serve notice that all ties must be severed with such organizations. One cannot serve God and mammon at the same time.

DRIVEN OF THE DEVIL

The phrase, *"And he broke the bands, and was driven of the Devil into the wilderness,"* records the strength he had, plus Satan driving him.

This proclaims to us that evil is not a mere abstract or the absence of good. Evil is headed by the Prince of Darkness, Satan himself. Under his command is a host of demon spirits and fallen angels. With those helpers, he controls the world of darkness that opposes God but ultimately is doomed to destruction, even as we have already stated. Nevertheless, even though Satan already knows this, he is determined to bring down with him every human being he possibly can.

The word *driven* in the Greek text is *elauno* and means "to drive on or impel." It is the same thing as the power of wind upon ships. In other words, this man had long since passed the place to where he had any exercise of willpower. He was totally taken over by Satan and had no choice but to do what Satan desired. To be frank, millions are in this same state in one way or the other.

If one wants to see the conclusion of the powers of darkness upon a human heart and life, this passage adequately describes it. This is Satan's payoff. He promises all types of things, exactly as he did to Adam and Eve in the garden, but, in fact, he is a liar and the father of it (Jn. 8:44). Every one of his followers is in some stage of this destruction, whether physically or mentally.

THE SPOILING OF SATAN'S GOODS

While it is true that Satan elevates some, at least for a period of time, in order to snare others, which he is very successful in doing, still, he works his entire scheme on a worldwide basis in order to achieve his ultimate goal, which is to steal, kill, and destroy (Jn. 10:10).

As we have repeatedly stated, only Jesus has been able to enter this strongman's house because He is stronger than Satan. Two thousand years ago He did so and *"spoiled his* (Satan's) *goods,"* and actually *"spoil* (spoiled the entirety of) *his house,"* which was done at the Cross (Mat. 12:29; Col. 2:10-15).

NOTES

As well, the word *wilderness* in the Greek text is *eremos* and means a "desolate, deserted, and lonely place." Such characterizes the state of all mankind that does not know God. As the songwriter said, "This world is a wilderness," which has been made so by Satan. Satan drives men into this wilderness of loneliness, heartache, and disappointment. It is a world without God! However, praise God, Jesus invaded this wilderness, and He has come but for one purpose, and that is to deliver humanity and restore what Satan has taken and stolen.

(30) AND JESUS ASKED HIM, SAYING, WHAT IS YOUR NAME? AND HE SAID, LEGION: BECAUSE MANY DEVILS WERE ENTERED INTO HIM."

WHAT ARE DEMON SPIRITS AND WHERE DO THEY COME FROM?

The question, *"And Jesus asked him, saying, What is your name?"* proclaims these demons as personalities.

• The Jews taught that these spirits were the spirits of evil men who were dead, with their spirits now entering into others; however, there is no scriptural reference to such. Actually, the Scripture teaches that the moment evil men die, their souls and spirits immediately go to hell (Lk. 16:23-25).

• Some scholars feel that demon spirits originated with a pre-Adamic creation, who actually threw in with Lucifer in his original rebellion against God. It is believed that this was an intelligent creation of some nature, originally created by God as holy and true, and occupied this earth before Genesis 1:2. I share this view, as well!

• Some believe that demon spirits are fallen angels; however, no angel, fallen or otherwise, is disembodied, as are demon spirits. Therefore, that is immediately ruled out.

• This we do know: God did not originally create these spirits in this evil manner. They became that way after rebellion against Him of some nature, which probably falls into the category of the pre-Adamic creation, as we have stated.

• Although believers can definitely be influenced and even oppressed by demon spirits, which can definitely cause physical problems as well as emotional problems, believers cannot be demon possessed. The body is the temple of the Holy Spirit, and as such, cannot be at the same time a temple of demon spirits (I Cor. 3:16).

• As we have stated, demon spirits greatly influence every unbeliever and probably have far more control than is realized, with possibly many more being demon possessed. Due to the power of the spirit world, be it holy or unholy, everyone is greatly influenced by either the Spirit of God or demon spirits. Knowing there are only a few who are truly led by the Holy Spirit, this means that the far greater majority of the human population is greatly influenced or totally controlled by demon spirits, hence, the war, pain, sickness, suffering, poverty, superstition, heartache, etc.

• The only power on earth that can successfully oppose these spirits of darkness is Spirit-filled believers who know how to use the mighty name of Jesus (Mk. 16:17). Regrettably, there are not many believers who truly fall into this category.

• One day, even as this illustration in Luke, Chapter 8, portrays, the entirety of the world and mankind will be free of Satan, fallen angels, and demon spirits. Actually, they will be locked away with their master, first of all in the bottomless pit, and then eternally in the lake of fire (Rev. 20:1-3, 10).

"And he said, Legion: because many devils (demons) were entered into him," refers to approximately 6,000. That this many demons could infest one human being is startling to say the least.

WHAT CAUSES DEMON SPIRITS TO ENTER INTO A PERSON?

The occasions are probably varied and many. Anyone who does not know Jesus as his personal Saviour is subject to demon possession. Having no divine protection, all such individuals, as stated, are definitely influenced, even more or less controlled. However, I think the record will show that all people who are truly demon possessed will at the same time be insane to one degree or the other. While many may not be insane enough to be institutionalized, still, traces of insanity will, I think, always surface at one time or the other.

I think we could say that this man who Jesus delivered was altogether insane, and constantly. However, most demon possession would not be that severe.

So, any unbeliever is subject to demon possession because of having no protection from the Lord.

IS THERE SUCH A THING AS TERRITORIAL SPIRITS?

Inasmuch as Mark recorded these demons beseeching Jesus that "He would not send them away out of the country," I think this tells us that there are certain areas where demon spirits enjoy more so than others (Mk. 5:10).

As well, it is obvious that Satan operates his kingdom of darkness in a very prescribed manner (Dan. 10:12-13).

However, none of this has much bearing on the child of God. Whatever ranks or designations Satan has for his kingdom of darkness is of little consequence to the child of God because all are subject to the name of Jesus, irrespective of the territory or area.

IS THERE SUCH A THING AS A PARTICULAR TYPE OF DEMON SPIRIT THAT OPERATES IN FAMILIES?

I definitely believe there is! However, the moment that person comes to Christ, that hold by the powers of darkness is broken. So, the answer is Jesus, irrespective of how the demons operate.

There is an element that is referred to presently as "the family curse." This teaching claims that if somebody in the family many years ago did something bad, the demon spirit or spirits that caused it can come down to the immediate person and cause him terrible problems, even though he is saved and Spirit-filled.

That is not so!

While there definitely are spirits of darkness that work in every type of situation and cause all types of problems in families, the moment a person gets saved, he becomes a new creation in Christ Jesus, with old things passing away and all things becoming new (II Cor. 5:17).

If it is to be noticed, it states, and I quote again, "Old things are passed away," and that means all old things, irrespective of how evil or wicked they were.

To claim that a person who is truly saved by the blood can have demon spirits tormenting them, which requires a preacher to cast this thing out, etc., is making a mockery of what Jesus did at the Cross. You won't find anything in the Bible that corresponds with such thinking.

This teaching of the *"family curse"* is derived from an erroneous interpretation of the following passage. It says:

"You shall not bow down yourself to them, nor serve them: for I the LORD your God am a jealous God, visiting the iniquity of the fathers upon the children unto the third and fourth generation of them who hate Me" (Ex. 20:5).

However, we must quickly state that if people continue to walk a path that is ungodly, evil spirits most definitely can cause all types of problems, but if it is to be noticed, it says, *"Of them who hate Me."*

Then it also says, *"And showing mercy unto thousands of them who love Me, and keep My commandments"* (Ex. 20:6).

As well, the Scripture plainly says, *"The soul that sins, it shall die. The son shall not bear the iniquity of the father, neither shall the father bear the iniquity of the son: the righteousness of the righteous shall be upon him, and the wickedness of the wicked shall be upon him"* (Ezek. 18:20).

Now, that refutes the *"family curse"* spectacle about as clearly as it can be refuted.

WHY DO CHRISTIANS AT TIMES HAVE PROBLEMS

There are many reasons, too many, in fact, to try to answer. However, probably the greatest problem of all is that believers do not understand the Cross of Christ as it regards life and living. They have a modicum of understanding respecting the Cross as it regards salvation but none at all as it regards sanctification, in other words, how we live for God on a daily basis.

When the believer places his or her faith in anything except Christ and the Cross, this opens the door for Satan to cause all types of problems. It was at the Cross where Satan was totally and completely defeated.

NOTES

It was at the Cross that all sin was atoned. It was at the Cross where the victory for the child of God was won. So, if the believer will place his or her faith exclusively in Christ and the Cross, and maintain it exclusively in Christ and the Cross, many of these problems will be overcome.

The reason is simple. The Holy Spirit, who is God, works exclusively within the parameters of the finished work of Christ. When we place our faith in anything other than Christ and the Cross, this greatly hinders the Holy Spirit in the help that He can give to us. However, when we place our faith exclusively in Christ and the Cross, then the Holy Spirit, who can do anything, will work mightily on our behalf, and we will begin to see many of these problems cleared up (Rom. 6:1-14; 8:1-11; I Cor. 1:17-18, 23; 2:2; Gal. 6:14; Col. 2:10-15).

Satan hates the Cross because it was there where he was totally and completely defeated. All salvation comes through the Cross. All working of the Holy Spirit comes through the Cross! All victory comes through the Cross! All healing comes through the Cross! In fact, whereas Jesus is the source of all things we receive from God, the Cross of Christ is the means, and the only means, by which all of these things are given to us. So, that means that Satan fights the Cross as nothing else. However, if you the believer will place your faith exclusively in Christ and what He has done for you at the Cross, you will find the Holy Spirit working on your behalf, and doing so mightily. Many of the problems will begin to clear up.

(31) "AND THEY BESOUGHT HIM THAT HE WOULD NOT COMMAND THEM TO GO OUT INTO THE DEEP."

The pattern is:

The word *deep* is an interesting word and refers to *"the bottomless pit"* (Rev. 20:1-3). Several things are said here:

a. The pleading of these demons with Jesus showed their acquiescence to Him in all matters.

b. It is obvious that He has total authority over all spirits of darkness and can command them to do whatever He desires. He is exactly as the demons said, the *"Most High"* (Lk. 8:28).

c. These spirits know they have an ultimate destination, the bottomless pit and ultimately the lake of fire, and seem to fear that Jesus could consign them there at any time, hence, their request. Whether this is correct, this premature judgment is not scripturally known.

d. This *"bottomless pit,"* or as referred to here as the *"deep,"* is *"in the heart of the earth"* (Mat. 12:40; Eph. 4:9). Actually, this is where hell is located, with all of these areas being a part of that domain (Deut. 32:22; Job 11:8; PS. 16:10; 63:9; Prov. 9:18; Isa. 14:9; 66:22-24; Ezek. 31:14-18; 32:18-24; Lk. 16:19-31).

(32) "AND THERE WAS THERE AN HERD OF MANY SWINE FEEDING ON THE MOUNTAIN: AND THEY BESOUGHT HIM THAT HE WOULD SUFFER THEM TO ENTER INTO THEM. AND HE SUFFERED THEM."

DID JESUS HAVE THE RIGHT TO DO WHAT HE DID?

The phrase, *"And there was there an herd of many swine feeding on the mountain,"* is recorded by Mark as being *"about two thousand"* in the herd (Mk. 5:13).

"And they besought Him that He would suffer them to enter into them," proclaims the necessity of evil spirits inhabiting a body, whether human or animal. However, as we shall see, their request did them little good because the hogs seemed to be able to tolerate these demon spirits even less than the man.

The phrase, *"And He suffered them,"* means He permitted them to do so.

Considering that these hogs were worth upward of $75,000 in 2013 money and were owned by others, many have asked the question if Jesus had the right to do what He did by allowing these spirits to go into the hogs, causing them to destroy themselves.

Of course, we know that everything Jesus did <u>was</u> right, not just because He did it, but because, in fact, it <u>was</u> the right thing to do.

This area on the eastern side of the Sea of Galilee was known as *"the Decapolis"* or *"the area of ten cities."* It had been colonized, at least in part, by the Romans immediately after the conquest of Syria some 60 years before Christ. As a result, most of the Jews who lived there were considered to be Hellenistic, which means they spoke the Greek language and pretty much adopted the Roman way of life, etc.

WRONG DIRECTION

Eating pork or even raising hogs was strictly forbidden in the Mosaic law; however, some claim that the law did not forbid the breeding and raising of such animals for sale to the Romans, etc. Irrespective, it seems to me that the raising of swine would be a violation of the spirit of the law, if not the letter.

As to Jesus allowing these spirits to go into the herd of swine, it is highly likely that He wished to show His indignation at the flagrant disregard of the Mosaic law. The herd was an open disobedience to the divine injunctions respecting swine, which was shown by the presence of so many of these animals pronounced unclean by the Mosaic law under which these Jews were professedly living, or should have been living.

At any rate, as the Lord of Glory, He definitely had the right to do what He did, quite possibly, even using the incident as a way to bring the owners to Himself, which it did, but sadly, to no avail! Job said, *"The LORD gave, and the LORD has taken away; blessed be the name of the LORD,"* which, as well, should be the spirit of all (Job 1:21).

(33) "THEN WENT THE DEVILS OUT OF THE MAN, AND ENTERED INTO THE SWINE: AND THE HERD RAN VIOLENTLY DOWN A STEEP PLACE INTO THE LAKE, AND WERE CHOKED."

The overview is:

1. The phrase, *"Then went the devils (demons) out of the man, and entered into the swine,"* refers to these demons doing exactly what the Lord told them to do.

2. *"And the herd ran violently down a steep place into the lake, and were choked,"* proclaims the habitation of these spirits as being of short duration due to the animals going berserk and killing themselves by running into the sea.

3. This must have been quite a sight, with some 2,000 hogs suddenly going berserk!

(34) "WHEN THEY WHO FED THEM

SAW WHAT WAS DONE, THEY FLED, AND WENT AND TOLD IT IN THE CITY AND IN THE COUNTRY."

The overview is:

1. The phrase, *"When they who fed them saw what was done, they fled,"* probably means they saw everything, the discharge of the demons from the maniac and their entrance into the swine. As well, as fearful at the loss of their charge was, they were probably terrified at this exhibition of power by Jesus.

2. *"And went and told it in the city and in the country,"* means they told what had happened not only to the owners, but to any and all who would hear them.

3. Even though they could not see these spirits of darkness, they definitely could feel what had happened.

(35) "THEN THEY WENT OUT TO SEE WHAT WAS DONE; AND CAME TO JESUS, AND FOUND THE MAN, OUT OF WHOM THE DEVILS WERE DEPARTED, SITTING AT THE FEET OF JESUS, CLOTHED, AND IN HIS RIGHT MIND: AND THEY WERE AFRAID."

SITTING AT THE FEET OF JESUS

The phrase, *"Then they went out to see what was done,"* concerns not only the owners but others as well!

"And came to Jesus, and found the man, out of whom the devils (demons) *were departed,"* must have been a startling sight. This was the man they had attempted to bind with fetters and chains, but to no avail. This was the man they knew to be insane and demon possessed. And yet, there was absolutely no doubt that the demons had departed. The following passages tell us how:

"Sitting at the feet of Jesus," proclaims Jesus teaching this former demoniac, with him eagerly absorbing the Word of God. To be sure, no man ever had a greater teacher.

The word *clothed* refers to the total opposite of his former condition of nakedness. However, he was not only clothed with garments but, as well, and more importantly, with salvation. Quite possibly, one or more of the disciples shared with him some of the extra clothing they had in the ship.

HIS RIGHT MIND

The phrase, *"And in his right mind,"* means he was perfectly sound in mind. Thus, God can do in one moment what it takes man months and years to do and, in fact, cannot do!

I will venture to say that no one who does not know Jesus Christ as Saviour and Lord, irrespective of his educational or intellectual background, is totally in his right mind. I realize that is a very sweeping statement, but I believe it to be true!

Paul said, *"For God has not given us the spirit of fear; but of power, and of love, and of a sound mind"* (II Tim. 1:7).

FEAR

The phrase, *"And they were afraid,"* proclaims their response to Christ. They were afraid of Him because of an exhibition of such power, as was obvious, in the sudden and miraculous change of this man. They knew what the man had been and, as stated, had probably tried to restrain him themselves. They knew how hopelessly insane he was, even to cutting himself with stones, etc. They had heard the screams in the night and knew everything, at least that a human being could know, about this man's terrible condition. And yet, they now observed him totally delivered and in his right mind.

As well, considering the great herd of swine that ran into the sea after the demons were allowed to go into them, these people realized they were confronting a power that was greater than anything they have ever seen or heard.

(36) "THEY ALSO WHICH SAW IT TOLD THEM BY WHAT MEANS HE WHO WAS POSSESSED OF THE DEVILS WAS HEALED."

1. The phrase, *"They also which saw it told them by what means,"* implies that the hog-herders were nearby when the demoniac was delivered and seemingly witnessed the whole thing.

2. The phrase, *"He who was possessed of the devils* (demons) *was healed,"* means they gave a blow-by-blow account to the owners of the hogs, plus others.

(37) "THEN THE WHOLE MULTITUDE

OF THE COUNTRY OF THE GADARENES ROUND ABOUT BESOUGHT HIM TO DEPART FROM THEM; FOR THEY WERE TAKEN WITH GREAT FEAR: AND HE WENT UP INTO THE SHIP, AND RETURNED BACK AGAIN."

THEY DESIRED THAT JESUS LEAVE

The phrase, *"Then the whole multitude of the country of the Gadarenes round about besought Him to depart from them,"* presents one of the saddest episodes in the gospels. They felt they could not keep both the Saviour and their swine, and of the two, they preferred the swine!

The Gadarenes took no interest in the salvation of a fellow creature from Satan's power, but they viewed the loss of their property with deep concern. Regrettably, they have many successors today.

It seems that the deliverance of people from the power of alcohol, drugs, or whatever for that matter, excites little interest even among most Christians, while other things cause great excitement.

These Jews were so close to eternal life, even with the evidence sitting before them in the form of this man totally delivered, but yet, they missed it. So close, but yet so far!

GREAT FEAR

The phrase, *"For they were taken with great fear,"* constituted fear that should have brought them to the Lord because of the great power exhibited, but instead, they responded in the opposite manner. They were not alone in this type of response.

How many have I seen come into our meetings, even into Family Worship Center, and for the first time in their lives sense the convicting power of the Holy Spirit, but instead of it causing them to turn to the Lord, which it is designed to do, they would run away. Such is out of fear as well!

Most people, even those who attend church, have never sensed the presence of God in any form because the Lord is not present in their churches, whatever type they may be. Consequently, when they feel the Spirit of God the first time, it brings a certain amount of fear, which it is supposed to do, but with many responding wrongly.

Why?

As these Jews of old, they prefer their sin to the Saviour. Consequently, millions prefer to attend a church where, as stated, the Lord is not present, and where conviction of sin is not a factor.

JESUS LEFT, NEVER TO RETURN

The phrase states, *"And He went up into the ship, and returned back again,"* and we may quickly add, never to return. Where He is not wanted, He does not stay!

The opportunity, as far as the Gadarene district was concerned, was gone forever. Within 40 years, this district was the scene of one of the terrible calamities of the great Roman War. The result was ruin!

It is said that back in the 1800s, this very district, which preferred its hogs to Christ, was, in fact, infested with wild, fierce hogs. As a result, the land was plowed up by these wild hogs in search of roots on which they live.

They wanted the hogs, and they got the hogs!

What a sorry trade! And yet, a trade, we must quickly add, that characterizes most of the world, and for all time. Think of what these people missed!

Every sick person in the entirety of their midst would have been gloriously healed. Everyone bound by demon spirits would have been delivered. As well, salvation, the most important and glorious gift of all, would have been given to all who would have believed. It would have changed their lives for time and eternity, and for a thousand times the better.

(38) "NOW THE MAN OUT OF WHOM THE DEVILS WERE DEPARTED BESOUGHT HIM THAT HE MIGHT BE WITH HIM: BUT JESUS SENT HIM AWAY, SAYING."

The exegesis is:

1. The phrase, *"Now the man out of whom the devils* (demons) *were departed besought Him that he might be with Him,"* proclaims the very opposite of his countrymen, which is quickly noted by the Holy Spirit.

2. It is no wonder that this man desired to be with Jesus. His life had been a veritable hell on earth before this moment, and now, miracle of miracles, he was gloriously

free, and above all, free forever! The demon spirits would never return. The King of glory had demanded they leave, which also constituted a demand that they never return. The deliverance was complete!

3. His reaction, as all, at least those who truly know Jesus, is to be constantly with Christ. Only those who did not know Him did not want to be with Him. How so much this spirit continues unto this very hour.

4. Using my own unworthy person as an example, I observe many, some in the church and some out of it, who speak very negatively, and even very harshly of my person, when, in fact, they know next to nothing about me, only some opinion they have formed due to some gossip. One can understand the world doing such, but it is little understandable as to believers following suit. Perhaps they still have so much of the world in them that they cannot think in a spiritual sense, only in the carnal.

5. Due to Calvary and the resurrection, and Jesus presently being glorified through the person and agency of the Holy Spirit, Jesus is now with every believer constantly, at least as much as they will allow Him to be. This is one of the great benefits of the new covenant, a benefit we might quickly add that is beyond the pale of our comprehension.

6. The phrase, *"But Jesus sent him away, saying"* constitutes a denial regarding his request, but yet, with a mission to perform. A mission, we may quickly add, that he carried out with great distinction.

(39) "RETURN TO YOUR OWN HOUSE, AND SHOW HOW GREAT THINGS GOD HAS DONE UNTO YOU. AND HE WENT HIS WAY, AND PUBLISHED THROUGHOUT THE WHOLE CITY HOW GREAT THINGS JESUS HAD DONE UNTO HIM."

The synopsis is:

1. The phrase, *"Return to your own house, and show how great things God has done unto you,"* constitutes a commission not only for this man but for all believers. The songwriter said:

"It was a great thing, that He did for me.

"It was a great thing, that He set me free.

"Jesus died on Calvary,

NOTES

"That the whole wide world may see,

"It was a great thing, that He did for me."

To be sure, anything done by the Lord for anyone is a great thing. However, at least on the surface, what Jesus did for this man was so great that is beggars description. And yet, He has done the same for millions.

"And he went his way," proclaims him doing so with no reluctance whatsoever, and even with great joy.

While it was true that the Lord denied his request, still, what He commissioned him to do was even greater. I am persuaded that if the Lord does say "no" to any of His children, the alternative He proposes, as here, will always be far greater than what was denied.

"And published throughout the whole city how great things Jesus had done unto him," does not tell us exactly which city, but does proclaim this man's success.

2. He was probably well known in the city, therefore, had a ready audience wherever he stopped, as many were interested in hearing his great story, even as they should have been.

3. The word *published* in the Greek text is *kerusso* and means "to proclaim, to preach." Think of it!

4. The day before, this man was a demon-crazed maniac, possessed by at least 6,000 demons, and totally insane. Twenty-four hours later or less, he was an evangelist for the Lord Jesus Christ, preaching and proclaiming up and down every street and to all who would listen what Jesus had done for him. Only the miracle-working power of God could carry out such a notable and instant change. And yet, much of the church has traded that for the mindless drivel of humanistic psychology. God help us!

5. The personal testimony, which actually constituted this man's preaching, is the greatest witness of all. Actually, there is no testimony like that which Jesus has done for an individual. It is proof that is undeniable, and in this case, a miracle. What a ministry he must have had!

(40) "AND IT CAME TO PASS, THAT, WHEN JESUS WAS RETURNED, THE PEOPLE GLADLY RECEIVED HIM: FOR THEY WERE ALL WAITING FOR HIM."

282

The synopsis is:

1. The phrase, *"And it came to pass,"* refers to the time it took to cross the lake from the eastern shore.

2. The phrase, *"That, when Jesus was returned,"* refers to Capernaum.

3. *"The people gladly received Him: for they were all waiting for Him,"* constitutes what could have been the whole of Israel had the religious leaders only accepted Him. Of course, all the people flocking to Him was one of the very reasons they would not accept Him. They were jealous of His fame, and above all, of His touch with God. They attempted to pass it off by claiming that He was in league with Satan and carried out His miracles by the power of demon spirits. In doing such, they blasphemed the Holy Spirit, consigning themselves to an eternal darkness and destroying their nation with them.

4. Concerning the reception given to Jesus, the idea seems to be that other ships had spotted Him returning and informed the city of His imminent return. Consequently, scores, perhaps even thousands, were eagerly awaiting the arrival of His ship. The sick were there to be healed, along with others to be delivered. To be sure, notable miracles would be carried out today, even to the raising of the dead. The moral is, if people *"gladly receive Him,"* great things always happen.

(41) "AND, BEHOLD, THERE CAME A MAN NAMED JAIRUS, AND HE WAS A RULER OF THE SYNAGOGUE: AND HE FELL DOWN AT JESUS' FEET, AND BESOUGHT HIM THAT HE WOULD COME INTO HIS HOUSE."

THE RULER OF THE SYNAGOGUE

The phrase, *"And, behold, there came a man named Jairus, and he was a ruler of the synagogue,"* proclaims that the Galilee enthusiasm for Jesus was by no means confined to the poorer part of the population, or even to the more careless and thoughtless. Jairus, in fact, was a fair representative of the wealthy and highly orthodox Jew. As well, he was held in high esteem by his fellow Jewish citizens.

During Jesus' time, synagogues were scattered all over Israel. It is said that there were over 400 in Jerusalem alone. Every town

or city had one or more. Jesus ministered in these synagogues constantly until He was no longer welcome, which constituted approximately the last year of His ministry.

The importance of the synagogue for Judaism cannot be overestimated. More than any other institution, it gave character to the Jewish faith. Here, Judaism learned its interpretation of the law.

In the synagogue, there was no altar. Prayer and the reading of the Torah (law) took the place of the sacrifice. In addition, this place performed important social functions. It was a gathering point and a meeting place where the people could congregate whenever it was necessary to take counsel over important community affairs.

THE MODEL OF THE TEMPLE IN JERUSALEM

It was required that synagogues be built on high ground or above surrounding houses. In all probability, they were constructed on the model of the temple in Jerusalem.

There was a portable ark in which the scrolls of the law and the prophets were kept. It faced the entrance to the building. On fast days, the ark was carried in a procession. Before the ark and facing the worshippers were the *"chief seats"* (Mat. 23:6) for the religious and governing leaders of the synagogue. The law was read from a platform.

The seats near the reading desk were the more honorable. It is said that a platform stood in the middle of the house so that the person who read the law, or any who would speak words of exhortation to the people, might stand upon it, and all might hear him. Men and women were seated apart.

The Great Synagogue of tradition may have been organized by Nehemiah about 400 B.C. It is said to have consisted of 120 members, who occupied themselves with the study of the law of Moses and transmitted it. The Sanhedrin succeeded it.

The congregation of the synagogue in each area was governed by elders who were empowered to exercise discipline and punish members. Punishment was by scourging and excommunication. The chief officer was the ruler of the synagogue. He supervised the service to see that it was carried on in accord with tradition. Thus did Jairus fill this position in Capernaum.

"And he fell down at Jesus' feet," proclaims his recognition of Jesus as to who He actually was, the Messiah, and his desperation regarding his daughter.

"And besought Him that He would come into his house," proclaims his level of faith. The centurion said, *"Speak the word only,"* while Jairus sought the immediate presence of Christ at his daughter's side.

(42) "FOR HE HAD ONE ONLY DAUGHTER, ABOUT TWELVE YEARS OF AGE, AND SHE LAY A DYING. BUT AS HE WENT THE PEOPLE THRONGED HIM."

The exegesis is:

1. The phrase, *"For he had one only daughter, about twelve years of age, and she lay a dying,"* proclaims the acuteness of the situation.

2. The condition of the girl had probably been very serious the past 24 hours; however, Jesus was not present, being on the other side of the lake. Consequently, with the situation growing more desperate by the hour, the moment Jesus set foot on the western shore, Jairus implored Him, as illustrated here, to come quickly.

3. *"But as He went the people thronged Him,"* referred to the massive crowd and the many who needed healing as well.

(43) "AND A WOMAN HAVING AN ISSUE OF BLOOD TWELVE YEARS, WHICH HAD SPENT ALL HER LIVING UPON PHYSICIANS, NEITHER COULD BE HEALED OF ANY."

The structure is:

1. The phrase, *"And a woman having an issue of blood twelve years,"* probably referred to a female disorder, which seemed to rupture constantly. Due to this sickness, Leviticus 15:19 declared this woman to be ceremonially unclean.

2. It is worthy of note that the girl was *"twelve years old,"* while the woman had been sick *"twelve years."*

3. While the sameness of these numbers may be mere coincidence, still, *"twelve"* represents God's order of government. If His government had been clung to instead of what man presently had, the girl would not have been at the point of death or the woman sick,

for there would be no death or sickness. In the coming kingdom age, and forever, God's government will once again be supreme, guaranteeing prosperity in every capacity such as man has never known before.

"Which had spent all her living upon physicians, neither could be healed of any," was recorded by Luke, a physician himself (Col. 4:14). Mark implies that these particular physicians knew they could not help her but treated her solely for the money. There is even the intimation that whatever type of treatment they gave her, it not only did not help her, but made the situation worse (Mk. 5:26).

At any rate, as there was no earthly remedy for her sickness, there is no earthly remedy for sin. However, there is a remedy, as we soon shall see!

(44) "CAME BEHIND HIM, AND TOUCHED THE BORDER OF HIS GARMENT: AND IMMEDIATELY HER ISSUE OF BLOOD STANCHED."

CAME BEHIND JESUS

The phrase, *"Came behind Him,"* was probably for several reasons. The crowd was large, and if she had desired to personally speak with Jesus about her sickness, due to the press of the people, this had now become virtually impossible. However, while the throng definitely was a factor, due to her being ceremonially unclean, she was not even supposed to be in this crowd. The Levitical law said that whosoever touched her, or that she touched, would be unclean until nightfall (Lev. 15:19). So, she was faced with a dilemma, and what was she to do?

Tradition says that she lived out of town, and this might be the last time she would have the opportunity to be in the presence of Jesus. So, she evidently reasoned within her mind that she must take her chances and do whatever possible to receive healing, irrespective of the consequences. She was dying anyway, and she had nothing to lose by what she was about to do.

JESUS

She had already reasoned in her heart, no doubt instigated by the Holy Spirit, that if she could but touch Him, even the end of the blue tassels that hung upon the shawl thrown over His shoulder, she would be immediately whole. Furthermore, if she was behind Him, quite possibly, He would not know it, and she would be healed without her infraction being noticed.

There is also evidence from Mark 5:27-28 that she had not even heard of Jesus before this present time. This seems difficult to comprehend; however, the Greek text does bear it out.

Upon arriving in Capernaum, for whatever reason, the talk seemed to be nothing but Jesus. Consequently, in a short time, she would have known of His healing power. Therefore, the moment the news came that He was expected shortly, as quickly as possible, she went to His expected place of arrival, and so did hundreds, if not thousands, of others.

Even though the text does not bear it out, the presence of God must have emanated from Him to such an extent that faith instantly detected it. Quite possibly, others were being healed as well. At any rate, faith built within her heart, and irrespective of the difficulties, faith will always find a way.

TOUCHING JESUS

The phrase, *"And touched the border of His garment,"* pertained to one of the four tassels that formed part of the Jewish mantle, one of these so arranged as to hang down over the shoulder at the back. It was this one that the sufferer's fingers grasped. The blue of the tassel, which was worn by most men, reminded Israel that their help came from above and of their duty to keep the law (Num. 15:28-41; Deut. 22:12).

Some have claimed that she was a Gentile and lived in Caesarea Philippi; however, every indication is that she was Jewish, especially considering that she seemed to understand the spiritual value of this blue tassel.

The phrase, *"And immediately her issue of blood stanched,"* is stated by Mark that *"she felt in her body that she was healed of that plague"* (Mk. 5:29).

Whatever it was, she knew she was healed, and beyond the shadow of a doubt. Mark also said, *"And straightway the fountain of her blood was dried up,"* meaning that the

NOTES

flow did not merely stop, but rather what was causing it was completely healed. In other words, it was a permanent cure, something she would never be troubled with again. Of all the physicians she had sought, she had now come to the right one.

(45) "AND JESUS SAID, WHO TOUCHED ME? WHEN ALL DENIED, PETER AND THEY WHO WERE WITH HIM SAID, MASTER, THE MULTITUDE THRONG YOU AND PRESS YOU, AND YOU SAY, WHO TOUCHED ME?"

The exegesis is:

1. The question, *"And Jesus said, Who touched Me?"* startled Peter because many were touching Jesus; however, He was not speaking of the many but of this lone individual.

2. How could He distinguish her touch from all the others? As well, what was different about her touch from the others? For Him to have noticed it in particular, there had to be something different. The difference was faith!

3. While there were scores touching Him out of curiosity, and with others not really knowing why they touched Him, this one was different because of the faith she exhibited. This means that one can literally feel faith! It also means that faith literally pulls from God that which is needed. In fact, I think one could say without fear of contradiction that it is the only commodity to which He responds. If one cannot please Him without faith, then everything displeases Him that is faithless (Heb. 11:6).

4. As well, we learn from this that what Jesus did for people in the realm of healing was not without price. To fully explain it, I think would be impossible; however, with each healing, there must have been a drain on Him in the physical, emotional, and spiritual sense. We do know that at certain times, He was so physically exhausted from healing the sick that He could hardly stand. The Greek text in Mark 4:36 bears that out.

5. *"When all denied,"* refers to whoever was standing close to Jesus. It seems they did not exactly know what He was talking about.

6. The question, *"Peter and they who were with Him said, Master, the multitude throng You and press You, and You say, Who*

touched Me?" is actually as much an exclamation as it is a question.

7. Peter affirmed that scores were thronging and pressing Jesus, with them, it seems, having difficulty keeping any semblance of order. Consequently, Jesus' question perplexed them.

(46) "AND JESUS SAID, SOMEBODY HAS TOUCHED ME: FOR I PERCEIVE THAT VIRTUE IS GONE OUT OF ME."

POWER HAS GONE OUT OF ME

The phrase, *"And Jesus said, Somebody has touched Me,"* speaks of a distinct type of touch other than the grabbing, striking type.

"For I perceive that virtue is gone out of Me," speaks of power. In other words, power went out of Him the moment the woman touched Him in faith. Several things can be learned from this:

It is possible for anyone to touch the Lord even though He has not touched you. What do we mean by that?

Jesus did not touch this woman; she touched Him. In that, we are given a very valuable lesson.

As an example, whenever individuals go forward for prayer in church (or wherever), if healing comes, or whatever, that is the same as the Lord touching us. However, if we do not receive what we have gone for following that course, there remains, as this woman of old, another alternative. We can touch the Lord.

We must first make certain that our faith is in Christ and what He did for us at the Cross. This is very, very important! We must then establish a prayer session time each day, even if it's only 15 or 20 minutes. We must be faithful to that, thanking the Lord for what He has done for us, and then stating our need and petition to Him. We have His promise that if we truly need certain things, in whatever capacity, if it is His will, He will do it. Luke, Chapter 11, especially bears this out.

FAITH

Jesus, in the incarnate state as a human being, although never ceasing to be God, still did not know this woman was in the crowd or even that she existed. And yet, by

touching Him, she received her healing.

This tells us that faith in God is such a powerful factor that it can effect a tremendous result, even though Jesus did not even know she was there.

Many believers do not understand exactly how God looks at faith. Actually, our association with Him is based entirely on faith. One could say without fear of contradiction that no other attribute is held so highly by God. Actually, every single thing that comes into motion in our relationship with the Lord is activated by faith.

However, when we speak of faith, we are not speaking of presumption. Many have mistaken the two. Faith in God is not a credit card to purchase anything we so desire but, in effect, the things He desires. The idea is that our relationship with Him is to be so close that we will only desire what He desires.

We learn from this scenario that true faith in God, even though faced with terrible obstacles, exactly as this woman of old, will not allow those circumstances or difficulties to hinder. Such faith in God refuses to look at the obstacles, but rather keeps its eyes fastened on the object, which should always be Jesus and what He did for us at the Cross (Heb. 12:2).

(47) "AND WHEN THE WOMAN SAW THAT SHE WAS NOT HID, SHE CAME TREMBLING, AND FALLING DOWN BEFORE HIM, SHE DECLARED UNTO HIM BEFORE ALL THE PEOPLE FOR WHAT CAUSE SHE HAD TOUCHED HIM AND HOW SHE WAS HEALED IMMEDIATELY."

The structure is:

1. The phrase, *"And when the woman saw that she was not hid,"* means that she evidently was trying to hide.

"She came trembling," was probably for several reasons.

2. First of all, it must have startled her that Jesus would stop, in essence, calling for her. Mark said, *"He looked round about to see her who had done this thing,"* meaning that He knew it was a woman who touched Him (Mk. 5:32). Consequently, I think her fear was normal and something to which any of us would have responded in a similar manner.

3. As well, she knew that according to Levitical law, she was unclean, and as a

consequence, was not supposed to be in this crowd, much less touching Him. She knew that the Levitical law stated that not only was she unclean, but all who touched her were unclean; consequently, her fear that caused the trembling could well have been caused by this knowledge.

4. *"And falling down before Him,"* proclaims her stepping out from the crowd and falling on her knees at His feet.

5. *"She declared unto Him before all the people for what cause she had touched Him,"* meant that she explained her sickness to the extent that all knew she had been ceremonially unclean. She withheld nothing!

6. *"And how she was healed immediately,"* relates that she told Jesus, which was heard by all, how that *"she felt in her body that she was healed of that plague"* (Mk. 5:29). She may have been greatly concerned, which she, no doubt, was, about her being unclean due to her sickness, but she also knew that she was healed. So, in effect, she was no longer unclean because of her contact with Jesus.

How many millions who were filthy with sin have touched Him, and each and every one came away totally and completely clean!

(48) "AND HE SAID UNTO HER, DAUGHTER, BE OF GOOD COMFORT: YOUR FAITH HAS MADE YOU WHOLE; GO IN PEACE."

DAUGHTER

The phrase, *"And He said unto her, Daughter,"* proclaims a wonderful and beautiful statement.

At first she was referred to as *"a woman"* (Vs. 43), and now she is referred to as *"daughter,"* drawing our attention to several things:

• He now claimed her as His own.

• He made her a part of the family of God and did so by referring to her as *"daughter."*

• She was not only healed physically but spiritually as well. As someone has said, "Yesterday she was one of the Devil's nobodies, and now she is one of heaven's somebodies!"

"Be of good comfort," addressed itself to her fear concerning her previous uncleanliness. She needed to have no fear that anyone would judge her unclean now because

all evidence of her uncleanness was gone. This is a perfect picture of redemption in Christ.

"Your faith has made you whole; go in peace," refers to the pipeline that brought her healing from the Lord.

As well, it must be hurriedly said that if her faith made her whole, it will do the same for all who will believe. God is no respecter of persons. What He did for her, He will do for all (Acts 10:34).

The peace here given means that not only was the woman healed physically, but she was healed spiritually, as well, meaning that she was now saved.

There is a beautiful spiritual application in this illustration. It is as follows:

CHAINED

The woman was chained: This speaks of being chained by sickness, and from the context, sin as well! She is typical of all the world that is chained by the maladies of darkness. In effect, all unbelievers are in a spiritual prison, which spills over into every other facet of their lives. Even though these were chains on this woman that could not be seen by the physical eye, nevertheless, they were chains. As well, the entirety of the world is chained by alcohol, drugs, jealousy, envy, immorality, sickness, disease, fear, religion, etc. Only Jesus, as here, can break those chains.

CHANGED

The woman was changed: This was done by the miracle-working power of God. Regrettably, the world turns to its own sources, which, in effect, can change nothing. Sadly, the church follows suit far too often. Psychology has become the great change agent at the present; however, it cannot really change anything.

Only faith in God and the miracle-working power of Christ can truly change a person. As this woman was instantly changed by touching Jesus, so have multiple millions of others been changed.

The testimonies we have received into our office over the years number into the hundreds of thousands, if not millions, and are so remarkable that they defy description.

That, and that alone (Jesus Christ and Him crucified) is the answer.

CLAIMED

The woman was claimed: She was not only changed but was claimed into the family of God. She was given a new life and even a new status. She was now a child of God and, consequently, a member of the greatest family on earth.

Incidentally, tradition says the name of this woman was Veronica. Eusebius, who lived about 350 years after Christ, is said to have seen the house in which this woman lived. It was at Caesarea Philippi, or Paneas as it was sometimes called, and had on its door on a stone pedestal two brazen statues. One represented a woman kneeling and the other a man with his cloak over his shoulder and his hands stretched out toward the kneeling woman, representing Jesus.

It is also stated that this same woman gave the handkerchief to wipe the face of Jesus as He carried the Cross up to Calvary.

(49) "WHILE HE YET SPOKE, THERE CAME ONE FROM THE RULER OF THE SYNAGOGUE'S HOUSE, SAYING TO HIM, YOUR DAUGHTER IS DEAD; TROUBLE NOT THE MASTER."

The synopsis is:

1. The phrase, *"While He yet spoke,"* referred to Jesus speaking to the kneeling woman who had just been healed.

2. Knowing how critical the condition of his daughter actually was, Jairus must have been extremely anxious at this delay.

3. *"There came one from the ruler of the synagogue's house,"* represents a message that would be given to Jairus, which would be awful to say the least!

4. *"Saying to him, Your daughter is dead; trouble not the Master,"* realized his worst fears. The little girl was dead!

5. Spence related as to while sufferers and their friends and the Lord's disciples in countless instances asked Him to put forth His power in cases of disease and sickness, neither friend nor disciple ever asked Him to raise the dead to life. To the last, despite what they had seen, none, until after the resurrection, could persuade themselves that He was, indeed, the Lord of death as well as of life.

NOTES

(50) "BUT WHEN JESUS HEARD IT, HE ANSWERED HIM, SAYING, FEAR NOT: BELIEVE ONLY, AND SHE SHALL BE MADE WHOLE."

FEAR NOT

The phrase, *"But when Jesus heard it,"* speaks of the announcement of death, with Him not perplexed at all about it.

"He answered him, saying, Fear not," in essence, says, "Despite death, everything is going to be all right."

Some have said that love descends rather than ascends. Hence, parents love their children more than children their parents. So, God loves man, but man does not love God. The gospels do not record small children coming to Jesus on behalf of their parents, but cases of parents coming to Him on behalf of their children are frequent, as with Jairus.

"Believe only, and she shall be made whole," demands a level of faith that is astounding to say the least.

And yet, the raising of someone from the dead is really not that much different than the opening of a blind eye, restoring hearing to a deaf ear, or feeding thousands with a little bread and fish. As well, the instantaneous quieting of the elements, the waves and the wind, is another example. All require the miracle-working power of God, as does the raising of someone from the dead. Jesus' purpose for raising the dead was severalfold:

THE LORD OF LIFE

• Jesus was the Lord of life, and as such, had mastery over death. This meant that in every domain where Satan held sway, as death, it still had as its highest authority Jesus Christ. While Satan definitely had latitude in many areas, still, in all things he must ultimately answer to Christ.

• As the Lord of life, Jesus had the power to raise one from the dead, which He at times did. In fact, there is no record that He ever met a funeral procession that He didn't break it up. He did so by raising the dead.

• He raised some from the dead in His earthly sojourn to illustrate that He would raise all from the dead in the resurrection, at least those who believed on Him. In other words, this which Jesus did was an earnest of that which He will do when the trump sounds.

• His raising the dead and proving that He was the Lord of that world, as well, also portrayed that death would one day be totally abolished. So it shall (I Cor. 15:24-28; Rev. 21:4). The command of Christ to *"believe only"* proclaims to all that there is no problem, no matter how severe, that He cannot solve. With Jesus, it is never too late!

(51) "AND WHEN HE CAME INTO THE HOUSE, HE SUFFERED NO MAN TO GO IN, SAVE PETER, AND JAMES, AND JOHN, AND THE FATHER AND THE MOTHER OF THE MAIDEN."

The exegesis is:

1. The phrase, *"And when He came into the house,"* refers to the home of Jairus. It had been a house of death but now will be a house of life.

2. *"He suffered no man to go in, save Peter, and James, and John, and the father and the mother of the maiden,"* represents the first time these three disciples had been singled out.

a. In the raising of the girl from the dead, these three saw the power of God.

b. In the transfiguration, these three saw the glory of God (Lk. 9:28).

c. In His passion, these three saw His sufferings (Mat. 26:37).

3. As well, there were seven in the room, counting the mother, the father, and the girl who was dead.

"Seven" is God's number of perfection. While the number was now imperfect due to the girl being dead, which represents the death of the sons and daughters of Adam, Jesus, by His power, would make it perfect, portraying the coming resurrection and the ultimate perfection of all things.

4. In other words, God's creation, although presently imperfect because of sin, will one day be made perfect, as symbolized by the raising of this girl from the dead.

(52) "AND ALL WEPT, AND BEWAILED HER: BUT HE SAID, WEEP NOT; SHE IS NOT DEAD, BUT ASLEEP."

The composition is:

1. The phrase, *"And all wept, and bewailed her,"* represents the paid mourners who had already been called and were now engaging in their ritual (Mat. 9:23).

2. *"But He said, Weep not; she is not dead, but asleep,"* is actually the way believers, such as was this child, are referred to in death. No, this does not teach *"soul sleep"* as some claim.

3. Soul sleep teaches that the body, soul, and spirit of believers sleep after death until the resurrection; however, this is not taught in the Bible.

4. While it is true that the body does sleep, in effect, going back to dust, the soul and the spirit of the sainted dead immediately go to be with the Lord Jesus at death (Phil. 1:20-24).

5. As well, if one were to see the soul and the spirit, which are different but yet indivisible, that person would be as recognizable as before death. Such is proven in the transfiguration when Moses and Elijah, while with Jesus, appeared to Peter, James, and John (Lk. 9:28-30).

6. While Elijah, having been translated, had never died, Moses had been dead for about 1,600 years. Consequently, the three disciples only saw the spirit and soul of Moses, whose appearance was very similar to what he had been in his life on earth. Elijah, having been translated, still retained his earthly body, which he still has, but will be changed with all others at the coming resurrection.

7. Actually, due to the fact that Jesus had not yet been glorified when the daughter of Jairus died, her soul and spirit went down into paradise, from where she would now be brought back upon Jesus raising her from the dead. Moses would have been there as well! (Lk. 16:19-31).

(53) "AND THEY LAUGHED HIM TO SCORN, KNOWING THAT SHE WAS DEAD."

The construction is:

1. The phrase, *"And they laughed Him to scorn,"* was done for two reasons:

a. They knew the child was dead and not in a swoon as some have later claimed. They had no understanding of the word *sleep* as He was using it, referring to all believers.

b. Knowing who He was and thinking that He thought she was merely asleep, although very ill, they were laughing, thinking He was going to be very surprised when He found her not sleeping but dead. In other words, they were ridiculing Him, claiming that while He might be able to heal the sick, He certainly could not do anything with one who had died.

2. How surprised they were to be!

The phrase, *"Knowing that she was dead,"* left no doubt in their minds as to her state.

(54) "AND HE PUT THEM ALL OUT, AND TOOK HER BY THE HAND, AND CALLED, SAYING, MAID, ARISE."

The diagram is:

1. The phrase, *"And He put them all out,"* is strong, meaning that the Lord had to use pressure to make these individuals leave. The word from the Greek text is *ekballo* and means "to throw out." Wuest says, "It must have been very close to a forceful ejection as in the case of the cleansing of the temple."

Bengel says, "This was an exhibition of wonderful authority in the house of a stranger. Jesus was really Master of the house."

2. The phrase, *"And took her by the hand,"* refers to a strong grip.

3. The word *took* in the Greek text is *krateo* and means *"to get possession of, to become master of, to take hold of."*

4. Jesus was master of the entirety of the situation, including the house, the paid mourners, the parents, His disciples, and above all, the dead girl. There was no doubt as to Who was in authority!

5. The phrase, *"And called, saying, Maid, arise,"* continues the exhibition of this authority.

6. Somewhere down in paradise, the soul and spirit of this girl heard the command and somehow knew it pertained to her. Since the beginning of the ministry of Jesus, this was probably not new to those in paradise, with some new arrivals not staying very long. As we have stated, even though the Scriptures only record three were raised from the dead, it is undoubtedly correct that Jesus raised others, perhaps many others as well!

(55) "AND HER SPIRIT CAME AGAIN, AND SHE AROSE STRAIGHTWAY: AND HE COMMANDED TO GIVE HER MEAT."

The overview is:

1. The phrase, *"And her spirit came again,"* demonstrates the separate existence of the spirit as independent of the body, to which we have just alluded. Her spirit and soul were once again reunited with her body, with the body instantly coming alive.

2. *"And she arose straightway,"* is said by Mark, *"The damsel arose, and walked."*

3. What a wonder it would have been to have stood nearby and witnessed this glorious moment. How must these parents have felt, seeing their daughter was restored to them healthy and alive!

4. *"And He commanded to give her meat,"* proclaims that she was not just a spirit but flesh, bone, and blood, exactly as she had been, but minus the sickness that killed her.

(56) "AND HER PARENTS WERE ASTONISHED: BUT HE CHARGED THEM THAT THEY SHOULD TELL NO MAN WHAT WAS DONE."

The exposition is:

1. The phrase, *"And her parents were astonished,"* means they did not know what to say or do. They were transfixed to the spot, actually, barely able to move, if at all. No wonder!

2. *"But He charged them that they should tell no man what was done,"* means that Jesus sought neither publicity nor admiration.

3. His appeal was to the heart and to the conscience. His mission was to bring people to repentance and to the forgiveness of sins. Apart from this consciousness of sin against God and the need of pardon, there can be no understanding of the person and work of the Lord Jesus Christ.

4. To work great miracles, and yet, seek to hide them is foreign to human nature. Men love admiration and publicity, and shallow streams make the most noise.

*"I hear Your welcome voice, that calls
  me, Lord,
"To You for cleansing in Your precious
  blood,
"That flowed on Calvary."*

*"Tho' coming weak and vile, You do
  my strength assure;
"You do my vileness fully cleanse,
"Till spotless all and pure."*

"Tis' Jesus calls me on to perfect faith
　and love,
"To perfect hope, and peace and trust,
"For earth and heaven above."

CHAPTER 9

(1) "THEN HE CALLED HIS TWELVE DISCIPLES TOGETHER, AND GAVE THEM POWER AND AUTHORITY OVER ALL DEVILS, AND TO CURE DISEASES."

THE TWELVE

The phrase, *"Then He called His twelve disciples together,"* represents the Twelve, as He had many others also.

The word *called* speaks of a divine call and, of necessity, has its origin in heaven. There is nothing man can do to instigate this call, and neither can he add to it or subtract from it. As well, no other person, religious denomination, or secular government may govern this call. This commission is from the Lord, and the Lord alone can give directives.

To be sure, Satan will seek to hinder this call or stop it altogether through man fear or self-will. Even though other things are used by the evil one, his greatest effort of control is through religious denominations. They will seek to tell one where to preach, when to preach, and at times, even what to preach. If such is yielded to in the slightest, the Lord has ceased to be the director of that particular ministry in favor of man; consequently, all anointing, leading, and guidance by the Holy Spirit ceases. The Holy Spirit controls all or not at all. While He is very patient and forgiving, if such erroneous course is followed, ultimately, He will leave. Regrettably, that is the case in most ministries.

POWER AND AUTHORITY

The phrase, *"And gave them power and authority over all devils* (demons), *and to cure diseases,"* represents only the beginning in the New Testament program. He has been doing the same ever since, at least for those He has called and those who will

NOTES

dare to believe Him. He said, *"And these signs shall follow them who believe"* (Mk. 16:17). Please allow this question:

If this was normal in the New Testament church, should it not be normal presently?

It most definitely should be normal in churches today. The book of Acts is the pattern for the church, whether then or now. If it is not the pattern, then it is church in name only, with the Holy Spirit having no part in its proceedings. To justify such a condition, many are the excuses:

• "The days of miracles passed away with the apostles."

• "Healing is not in the atonement."

• "When the last book of the Bible was finished by John, all miracles and gifts of the Spirit stopped."

Of all various churches on the spiritual landscape, for the most part, it is only the Pentecostal and Charismatic variety that claim to continue to believe in these great gifts of God, and sadly, only a small percentage of those do. While most all in these particular camps may claim to believe accordingly, their actions prove otherwise.

So, in truth, only a small percentage seeks to carry on the program as laid down by the Lord Jesus Christ.

IS THIS AUTHORITY OVER PEOPLE OR SPIRITS OF DARKNESS?

Jesus Christ is the only one who can give this type of power and authority. If one is to notice, it is power and authority over all demons and not over other people. As we have addressed elsewhere in this volume, such exercised authority over other people is never from God.

The word *power* in the Greek text is *dunamis* and means "ability and might," "mighty works," or "mighty deeds."

Then, the disciples had an outside source for this power, who was Jesus. Now, it is an inside source who is the Holy Spirit (Acts 1:8). Actually, the word *power* in Acts 1:8 means "reproducing dynamo," or, in essence, something from within that does not have to have an outside source.

DELEGATED POWER

Authority means "delegated power" or

"the right to exercise power." The Greek word is *exousia*.

The power constituted the ability to do what needed to be done, in this case, to cast out demons and heal diseases, with the authority constituting control over Satan's kingdom of darkness. Whatever these disciples said do, the demons had to obey simply because the power and authority of Christ were behind these 12. A short time later, the Lord was to send out 70 others also (Lk. 10:1).

It is strange that in those days, the doubters, who were the Pharisees, said that Jesus could heal, but He could not forgive sins. Now they say that He can forgive sins, but He cannot heal. To say that He will not heal is the same as saying that He cannot heal.

I believe the greatest move of God the world has ever known is yet to come, but it will come shortly. In this move will be fulfilled the great prediction of Christ, *"He who believes on Me, the works that I do shall he do also; and greater works than these shall he do; because I go unto My Father"* (Jn. 14:12).

(2) "AND HE SENT THEM TO PREACH THE KINGDOM OF GOD, AND TO HEAL THE SICK."

THE KINGDOM OF GOD

The phrase, *"And He sent them to preach the kingdom of God,"* refers to the fact that preaching is primary and, therefore, the foundation of miracles and healings.

As well, they were to preach the kingdom of God and not a gospel of their own making.

What does it mean to preach the kingdom of God?

It simply refers to the rule and authority of God, which is to rule within our lives, and, therefore, will overcome the powers of darkness. It is a literal kingdom inculcating itself in every facet of our lives, be it spiritual, physical, or economical. When the sinner comes into this kingdom, thereby becoming a believer, he takes upon himself an entirely different allegiance and culture— the culture of the Bible. That does not mean he is not to obey secular government, for he is, unless it violates the Word of God within his heart.

HEALING THE SICK

The phrase, *"And to heal the sick,"* always constituted a part of these missions. It continued all the days of the early church and does so unto the present, at least for those who are truly God-called. If one is to notice, three things are done in these two verses. They are:

1. *"He called"*: as stated, this is His prerogative.

2. "(He) *gave"*: all of that given comes from Him and not man.

3. *"He sent"*: He alone is to give the leading and directives.

However, even though corresponding power continues to be given to all who believe, this in no way means apostolic succession. The Catholic Church claims such succession and so do many Protestants. Such does not exist!

In the Pentecostal denomination with which I was formerly associated, there is a group of men elected by popular ballot which forms a hierarchy at its very top. These men are the governing or ruling body of that particular denomination. While I have no idea as to the thinking of all of these men, I do know that at the time of my association, some of them thought of themselves in the realm of apostolic succession. In other words, they thought that they were the successors to the original twelve apostles in exactly the same manner, at least regarding this point, as the priesthood of the Catholic Church.

As well, the other major Pentecostal denominations function in the same manner. I have no idea how they divide the two in their thinking, but each probably thinks the other is bogus, etc. In fact, it is all bogus, that is, if one desires to adhere to the Scriptures. As we have stated, there is no such thing as an apostolic succession, at least according to the Bible.

SPIRITUAL DECLENSION

When these things come about, irrespective of the religious organization in which they are ensconced, it is a sure sign of spiritual declension. In the book of Acts and the Epistles, which are the criteria for the church, one will find no apostolic succession, religious denomination, hierarchy, or religious headquarters. All of those things are man-made and, therefore, not Spirit-directed. It was this spirit, and we must quickly add, promoted by Satan, that Jesus had more difficulty stamping out than anything else. Hours before His crucifixion, the apostles were arguing among themselves over *"which of them should be accounted the greatest"* (Lk. 22:24). At that stage, Jesus taught them the servant principle, which its leaders must have, irrespective of whom they may be (Lk. 22:24-27). Unfortunately, religious men love to *"lord"* it over others, and strangely enough, many enjoy being *"lorded over."* It absolves them of all responsibility, at least that is what they think.

Jesus Christ is the head of the church, the shepherd and bishop of our souls. All who serve under Him in any leadership capacity (according to his calling) serve as undershepherds and are to never exercise lordship authority over others. Jesus said, *"But so shall it not be among you"* (Mk. 10:43).

DENOMINATIONS AND DENOMINATIONALISM

There is nothing scripturally wrong with forming a denomination or being a part of a denomination. Ideally, if it functions according to the Word of God, it can provide a tremendous help to the furtherance of the kingdom all over the world. However, those who occupy the various man-made offices must understand that this is administrative only and is not a scriptural office. As far as ministers are concerned, there are really only five offices in the church. They are apostles, prophets, evangelists, pastors, and teachers (Eph. 4:11).

However, when the leaders of a denomination, as well as those who are associated with it, begin to think that belonging to that denomination gives some type of spiritual authority and makes one superior to all others, then denominationalism is beginning to creep in.

Denominationalism is a great deal like racism, which believes that one race is superior to the other. Then such a denomination ceases to be of help to the kingdom of God

and actually becomes a hindrance. Unfortunately, most denominations (I won't say all), after a period of time, tend to drift into denominationalism.

If one looks at the Word of God, one doesn't find any denominations in the book of Acts and the Epistles. Actually, one doesn't even find a headquarters church, etc. As well, one doesn't find a hierarchy in the book of Acts. Each church was independent. While they sought and received help from the apostles, especially the apostle Paul, their autonomy was never imposed upon. That's the way it should be now, at least if we desire to be scriptural. However, there is something in man that loves to control other men, and religious men most of all love to control other men. Unfortunately, there are many who like to be controlled because they think this absolves them of responsibility, but it doesn't!

Every person is going to be judged according to their adherence to the Word of God. They will not be able to put the blame on others. The soul that sins, it shall die!

(3) "AND HE SAID UNTO THEM, TAKE NOTHING FOR YOUR JOURNEY, NEITHER STAVES, NOR SCRIP, NEITHER BREAD, NEITHER MONEY; NEITHER HAVE TWO COATS APIECE."

The pattern is:

1. The phrase, *"And He said unto them,"* concerns itself with very important instructions concerning those who have been called by God.

"Take nothing for your journey, neither staves, nor scrip, neither bread, neither money," means that when the person is called, he should go.

2. Some have the idea that they are to wait until certain things come to pass, such as the making of so much money to ensure support, that certain financial things be handled, etc., before a full-time commitment. While all these things certainly are important, still, the important thing is to obey God. If He calls someone and then opens the door, He means for that call to be obeyed immediately, at least to the extent that one is able to do so. If such is not done in this manner, it shows a lack of trust in God. The idea behind the statement as

given by Jesus is that God is able to meet all needs and supply whatever is required.

3. His call is the same as a military command. If a command is given by a general that certain things are to be done, no one under that general has the right to countermand those orders or reinterpret them. They are to be carried out exactly as given, and forthwith. To be sure, the Lord conducts His business in the same manner.

4. The phrase, *"Neither have two coats apiece,"* is the same as above but with a little different twist.

The idea is that one may not have suitable clothing, or whatever, and that this problem must be rectified before one can obey. Once again, the Lord is saying that His command is to be obeyed immediately, irrespective of these problems. It is a matter of trust. Will God supply our needs, whatever they may be, or will He not?

(4) "AND WHATSOEVER HOUSE YOU ENTER INTO, THERE ABIDE, AND THENCE DEPART."

The pattern is:

Several things are said in this verse. They are as follows:

1. It was an honor and a privilege for anyone to entertain any individual called of God and sent on a special mission, as here described.

2. The insinuation is that the blessing of God will rest upon such a house if they aid and abet those called of God for such a mission.

3. If such a house does not treat a man of God accordingly, the blessing will be withdrawn, which speaks, in essence, of judgment in one form or the other.

(5) "AND WHOSOEVER WILL NOT RECEIVE YOU, WHEN YE GO OUT OF THAT CITY, SHAKE OFF THE VERY DUST FROM YOUR FEET FOR A TESTIMONY AGAINST THEM."

REJECTION

The phrase, *"And whosoever will not receive you,"* speaks of whoever falls into that category, be it a single house or the entirety of a city. This speaks of anyone sent by God with the true message of Jesus Christ.

As an example, when our television

programming is placed on a cable system, or wherever, we are there because the Lord has told us to be there. In other words, we have a direct mandate from the Lord respecting evangelism in this manner.

From that moment, every person who is within the listening radius of the programming will be held responsible in the judgment for this opportunity. While it may be true that many in this listening radius pay little attention to the programming, if any at all, or possibly do not even know it is on the air, still, in the far greater majority of the cases, they will be held responsible just the same. The idea is that the opportunity is there. Many do not know it is available because they have no interest in anything that pertains to God. Consequently, the visitation comes and ultimately goes without them even knowing it existed. Still, as stated, they are responsible for the opportunity not taken because of lack of interest.

THE DIRECTION TAKEN

The phrase, *"When ye* (you) *go out of that city,"* refers to the Lord's visitation at such a place. Of all the things happening in that particular city, in the eyes of God, this visitation is the single most important. However, most would not share that thought, and if called to their attention, it would be met with mockery. Nevertheless, in no way does the negative reaction of such a city negate the significance of what has happened—a visitation from the Lord.

As well, in the judgment, every single person who was in the listening radius of our programming, as stated, will answer to God, as well as every godly preacher over television or in any other capacity.

In the mind of God, because of the importance of the eternal soul, nothing can be as important as this. So, three things are at stake, the presentation of the gospel, its acceptance, or its rejection.

FOR A TESTIMONY AGAINST THEM

The phrase, *"Shake off the very dust from your feet for a testimony against them,"* refers to another startling fact.

Despite there being a myriad of preachers in the world, only a few (very few) truly preach the gospel of Jesus Christ. Even though there are a myriad of churches in many cities, only a few truly have and truly present the gospel.

As an example, years ago a friend of mine presented the testimony of a dear African brother who received a visitation from an angel, telling him to go to the coast and turn right, and there he would find the Lord.

That was all the information given, and the angel did not even state what church it would be.

In a part of Africa where there were no missionaries at that time, and not going into detail as to how he had heard about the gospel in the first place, he had prayed earnestly regarding how to be saved. This visitation was the answer to that prayer.

He immediately set out, literally running physically during the day and resting a little at night. After several days, he arrived in the city of Monrovia, Liberia. After arriving at the city, he stopped at the first church that he saw, but the angel appeared again and told him "no." This happened several times before he happened upon the church pastored by my friend. The angel appeared again and said, "This is the one!" That's when he broke into the building like someone possessed. Brother Trotter said that when he first came in, people were astonished at his display of emotionalism. However, once they heard his story, then they understood the reason for his joy.

He gave his heart to Christ, was baptized with the Holy Spirit very shortly after, stayed in Bible school for some three months, if I remember correctly, and then went back to his home area and won many souls to Christ.

However, the point I wish to make is, church after church where he stopped, the angel appeared to him and said "no," meaning he couldn't get saved there if he wanted to. Sadly and regrettably, that's the condition of most churches in the world presently. There were possibly hundreds of churches in that particular city, with the possibility definitely existing that the only church having the gospel was the one to which the angel pointed. That is the same in every city.

NOTES

In fact, there are many cities, despite having many churches, where not one truly preaches the gospel. In other cities, there may be only one or two. Any city that is privileged to have several is blessed indeed!

The gospel refused always heralds judgment in one form or the other, whether for a single person or the entirety of an area.

(6) "AND THEY DEPARTED, AND WENT THROUGH THE TOWNS, PREACHING THE GOSPEL, AND HEALING EVERYWHERE."

The form is:

1. Whatever towns these were, they had the privilege of being visited by an emissary from the Lord, in this case, the twelve apostles.

2. In fact, this indigenous area saw terrible judgment about 35 years later because of their refusal to repent.

3. God's method is *"preaching the gospel, and healing."* Anything less is not truly the gospel.

(7) "NOW HEROD THE TETRARCH HEARD OF ALL THAT WAS DONE BY HIM: AND HE WAS PERPLEXED, BECAUSE THAT IT WAS SAID OF SOME, THAT JOHN WAS RISEN FROM THE DEAD."

The composition is:

1. The phrase, *"Now Herod the tetrarch heard of all that was done by Him,"* pertained to Jesus.

2. According to Spence, this was Herod Antipas, the son of Herod the Great. His mother's name was Malthrace. After his father's death, he became tetrarch or prince-ruler of Galilee, Peraea, and of a fourth part of the Roman province of Syria.

3. His first wife was the daughter of Aretas, a famous Arabian sheik, spoken of by Paul as king of the Damascenes (II Cor. 11:32).

4. He divorced this princess and immediately contracted an incestuous and adulterous marriage with his niece Herodias, the beautiful wife of his half-brother Philip.

5. Philip was not a sovereign prince, and it was probably for motives of ambition that Herodias deserted Philip for the powerful tetrarch Herod Antipas.

6. It was owing to his fearless remonstrances against this wicked marriage that

John the Baptist incurred the enmity of Herodias, who was only satisfied with the head of the daring preacher who dared to attack her brilliant, wicked life.

7. The phrase, *"And he was perplexed, because that it was said of some, that John was risen from the dead,"* presented a terrifying spectacle to the hurting conscience of Herod, who had murdered John.

8. Normally, Herod was probably inclined to the Sadducee creed, which believed in neither angel nor spirits; however, these erroneous beliefs were no defense against his hurting conscience.

(8) "AND OF SOME, THAT ELIJAH HAD APPEARED; AND OF OTHERS, THAT ONE OF THE OLD PROPHETS WAS RISEN AGAIN."

The diagram is:

1. The phrase, *"And of some, that Elijah had appeared,"* was equally discomforting.

2. As well, Ahab and Jezebel had slain the Lord's prophets. As a result of their barbaric action, both Ahab and Jezebel met a sordid and untimely death, which was well known, even at this late date.

3. Also, there was a rooted expectation among the Jews that Elijah would reappear again on earth and that his appearance would herald the advent of the Messiah. They were right, but they were early by the time frame of approximately 2,000 years.

4. Realizing this, and knowing that the crime committed by himself and Herodias was very similar to that of Ahab and Jezebel, everything fueled his fear, especially the miracles performed by Jesus.

5. The phrase, *"And of others, that one of the old prophets was risen again,"* served only to continue to fuel the driving fear that plagued this monster.

(9) "AND HEROD SAID, JOHN HAVE I BEHEADED: BUT WHO IS THIS, OF WHOM I HEAR SUCH THINGS? AND HE DESIRED TO SEE HIM."

The overview is:

1. The phrase, *"And Herod said, John have I beheaded,"* is not said in bravado or scorn, but rather of fear. Even though Herod had not seen the actual beheading, he had seen the head brought in on a platter, with all its ghastly overtones. It was a

scene he could not shake from his mind, and instead of its terror lessening, it rather increased with the passing of time.

2. The question, *"But Who is this, of whom I hear such things?"* is again asked with fear. The things he heard constituted the miracles performed by the Lord. While they brought joy to those on whom they were performed, they brought nothing but fear to this man.

3. It, no doubt, had come to his ears that God would visit him with judgment because of his terrible deed. He had probably laughed it off, but the stinging conscience would not let it die.

4. The phrase, *"And he desired to see Him,"* referred to Jesus.

5. In fact, this desire would be gratified, but not at the present. He did see Him on the day of the crucifixion when Pilate sent Him to Herod for judgment; however, Herod, satisfying himself that this was not John the Baptist risen from the dead, declined any more involvement, sending Jesus back to Pilate. Wicked though he was, he would not be responsible for shedding that blood. He would leave that to the Jews.

6. To be sure, that judgment would be sure and swift, coming approximately 35 years later, with the whole of Jerusalem and the temple completely destroyed and over 1 million Jews dying in that carnage.

7. What men want, they generally get, but they must pay the price.

(10) "AND THE APOSTLES, WHEN THEY WERE RETURNED, TOLD HIM ALL THAT THEY HAD DONE. AND HE TOOK THEM, AND WENT ASIDE PRIVATELY INTO A DESERT PLACE BELONGING TO THE CITY CALLED BETHSAIDA."

The structure is:

1. The phrase, *"And the apostles, when they were returned, told Him all that they had done,"* concerned the great victories that had been won over the powers of darkness respecting healings and deliverances, all done in the name of Jesus.

2. *"And He took them, and went aside privately into a desert place belonging to the city called Bethsaida,"* referred to Bethsaida Julias, situated on the northeastern shore of the Sea of Galilee. It was only a

short distance from Capernaum, with Jesus and His disciples cutting across the corner of the lake.

3. This city had been recently beautified by Herod Philip and named after the daughter of Caesar Augustus.

4. The crowds and the excitement of the multitude about Jesus were now at their height. Thousands were flocking to His side, their interest, no doubt, fueled by many things, with the miracles and Him being the prospective Messiah certainly not the least.

5. As well, the crowds at this particular time were swelled by the Passover pilgrims who had just arrived in Capernaum on their way to the Feast at Jerusalem. They would be anxious to hear the great Galilean prophet, Whose name just then was on every tongue.

7. Nearby this small city was a secluded plain where Jesus probably proposed to spend some time in rest. As well, the recent death of John the Baptist, no doubt, only added to the hectic stress that compelled Him to seek seclusion, at least for a short time. However, as we shall see, it was not to be!

(11) "AND THE PEOPLE, WHEN THEY KNEW IT, FOLLOWED HIM: AND HE RECEIVED THEM, AND SPOKE UNTO THEM OF THE KINGDOM OF GOD, AND HEALED THEM WHO HAD NEED OF HEALING."

The synopsis is:

1. The phrase, *"And the people, when they knew it, followed Him,"* means they were actively seeking His whereabouts and immediately, upon receiving that information, proceeded to seek Him out.

2. *"And He received them, and spoke unto them of the kingdom of God,"* refers to a kind reception and, as well, instruction given concerning the plan of God.

3. What must have been their feelings as they heard this man, the incarnate Son of God, expound on the things only glimpsed by the prophets of old! How their hearts must have warmed as they heard Him speak. For the first time, to most if not all of them, the Word of God became crystal clear. No longer were they listening to the muddled confusion of the Pharisees and scribes who:

a. Did not know the Word of God; and,

b. Purposely complicated what little they

did know in order to make themselves seem intellectual and scholarly.

4. The phrase, *"And healed them who had need of healing,"* proclaims the continuing of His method to preach the gospel and heal the sick.

(12) "AND WHEN THE DAY BEGAN TO WEAR AWAY, THEN CAME THE TWELVE, AND SAID UNTO HIM, SEND THE MULTITUDE AWAY, THAT THEY MAY GO INTO THE TOWNS AND COUNTRY ROUND ABOUT, AND LODGE, AND GET VICTUALS: FOR WE ARE HERE IN A DESERT PLACE."

THE TWELVE

The phrase, *"And when the day began to wear away, then came the Twelve, and said unto Him,"* pointed to honest concern the disciples had for the great crowd. There could easily have been as many as 10,000 to 15,000 people present.

"Send the multitudes away, that they may go into the towns and country round about, and lodge, and get victuals," presents the disciples thinking in normal terms, in no way expecting the miracle Jesus was to perform. To be frank, He was ever surprising them!

As we have said repeatedly, every miracle performed by Christ was not only for the benefit of the individual(s) but, as well, was meant to serve as a broader spiritual lesson, of which this miracle is no exception.

SEND THE MULTITUDE AWAY?

The multitudes had come to Jesus, and Jesus would show His disciples, plus all others who would read the account of this great happening, that He could meet every need of anyone, irrespective of its nature. In fact, He alone could meet these needs. Unfortunately, as a whole, the modern church limits Him or excludes Him altogether. Very few actually teach and believe that He meets every need. Most modern preachers do exactly as the disciples of old thought to do, *"Send the multitude away."* Presently, they are sent to psychologists, therapists, counselors, etc. In fact, the modern church has become one great referral system; consequently, the Jesus now presented (if presented at all) is a watered-down, emaciated, weak, forlorn, philosophic figure of the past, who little applies to the modern, technological present. Actually, many so-called Christian psychologists claim that modern man faces problems that the Bible does not address; therefore, according to them, something else is needed, with psychology being the modern answer.

Such is blasphemy!

THE DESERT PLACE

The modern church finds itself in this condition because of unbelief. There is little relationship with Christ; consequently, most modern preachers little know Him.

"For we are here in a desert place," was true then and is true now concerning this world. The spiritual thirst of man cannot be slaked by anything the world has to offer. Concerning that, it is a desert place!

It is understandable that the world does not know this, with the people continuing to cast about, attempting to find a solution where there is no solution; however, it is inexcusable for the church not to know this.

The major emphasis of the church must be on Christ and His Word; however, little attention is given to His person in prayer or His Word in study. Unfortunately, He cannot be known any other way.

(13) "BUT HE SAID UNTO THEM, GIVE YE THEM TO EAT. AND THEY SAID, WE HAVE NO MORE BUT FIVE LOAVES AND TWO FISHES; EXCEPT WE SHOULD GO AND BUY MEAT FOR ALL THIS PEOPLE."

The synopsis is:

1. The phrase, *"But He said unto them, Give ye* (You give) *them to eat,"* proclaims that which they could not do within themselves. And yet, in the spiritual sense, this is something they would later do and, in fact, had already begun. They would give the world the Bread of Life, which is Jesus.

2. Likewise, this command is given not only to the Twelve, but to all, and especially those distinctly called by Christ.

3. As well, if anything else is given other than Jesus, who is the embodiment of the written Word, the craving hunger will never be satisfied. Regrettably, most of that given from behind modern pulpits is not the Word of God, but rather the traditions or

NOTES

philosophies of men. Paul said, *"Preach the Word"* (II Tim. 4:2).

"And they said, We have no more but five loaves and two fishes; except we should go and buy meat for all this people," presents two alternatives:

a. They had five loaves and two fish, but they had no idea as to how this little could be of service.

b. The other alternative, at least in their thinking, was to purchase food for 10,000 or more people. This would have required a great sum of money, plus, it would have probably been difficult to find that much food, even in Bethsaida Julias.

(14) "FOR THEY WERE ABOUT FIVE THOUSAND MEN. AND HE SAID TO HIS DISCIPLES, MAKE THEM SIT DOWN BY FIFTIES IN A COMPANY."

The overview is:

1. The phrase, *"For they were about five thousand men,"* was other than the women and children.

2. Some have surmised that there probably were not many women and children present; however, due to the nature of this meeting, with many coming for healing and deliverance, there were probably just as many women as men and, no doubt, a great number of children as well. So, the total number was at least 10,000 more!

3. *"And He said to His disciples, Make them sit down by fifties in a company,"* is said by Mark to be hundreds and fifties (Mk. 6:40). There is no discrepancy, with both figures being correct.

4. With a crowd this size, it was advantageous to seat them in sections of 50 in some areas, with other areas in sections of 100.

5. Everything that is done in this scenario is done for purpose by the Holy Spirit. The ranks of fifties and hundreds signified a systematic order. It is extremely clear in the Word of God that everything done by the Lord is systematic and with purpose. In other words, His government is perfect. It is only when man leaves God's government or ways, which he has done almost to a man, that he finds himself in terrible trouble. God has a divine order for everything, and it is up to the believer to ascertain that order, which is given in the Word of God.

(15) "AND THEY DID SO, AND MADE THEM ALL SIT DOWN."

The form is:

1. The phrase, *"And they did so,"* proclaims the disciples carrying out the orders of the Master. As well, this is a picture of the systematic approach that the church should take respecting world evangelism or, for that matter, anything that pertains to the work of God.

2. *"And made them all sit down,"* sounds somewhat harsh in the English translation, but the original text leaves the idea of expectation.

3. In other words, the people were anticipating that Jesus was about to do something special even though, at least at the time, they had no idea what it would be. They were not to be disappointed!

(16) "THEN HE TOOK THE FIVE LOAVES AND THE TWO FISHES, AND LOOKING UP TO HEAVEN, HE BLESSED THEM, AND BROKE, AND GAVE TO THE DISCIPLES TO SET BEFORE THE MULTITUDE."

FIVE LOAVES AND TWO FISH

The phrase, *"Then He took the five loaves and the two fishes,"* proclaims that which the disciples said they had.

It is said that the loaves were made of barley, which was the ordinary food of the poorest in Israel, with the two fish being dried, as was the common custom of the country. The fish were usually eaten with the bread and was very nutritious, with the bread containing much roughage and mineral content.

As well, this represents Jesus taking what we have, whatever it may be and as little as it may be, and using it for His glory. This should be a lesson to all!

With His miracle-working power, which He is here portraying, He can do anything with what we have, irrespective of the amount or content. Many believers are bemoaning the fact of what little they have, of whatever nature, while that is not the problem at all. It really doesn't matter what we have. We are to have faith in Him to take the little bit we have, whatever it is, as is surely represented by the five loaves

and two fish, and believe Him to multiply it exactly as He multiplied the loaves and the fish. Once we understand that, everything takes on a brand-new complexion. As He takes it (whatever it is) into His hands, anything becomes possible.

HE BLESSED IT

The phrase, *"And looking up to heaven, He blessed them,"* proclaims that all blessings, help, and sustenance come from above. Our answer is not in other men but in God.

The words, *"And broke,"* signify the beginning of the miracle. As He began to break the bread, the multiplication process began to come into effect. As to how He did it, we are not told. Even the evangelists did not try to explain it; they just related it. They evidently did not ask Him; they only saw it, participated in it, and related it to us just as they saw it in its simple grandeur. Spence said, "Neither disciples nor crowds seem at first to have grasped the stupendous nature of the act."

John did relate that when it began to dawn on the people exactly what had happened, they wished to take Him by force and make Him king (Jn. 6:15).

In fact, how did Jesus perform this miracle?

Miracles simply refer to an intervention by God and surpass the ability of nature. The miracle may be obvious, as it is here, or it may not be obvious at all. Nevertheless, if God has intervened in order to answer prayer, or in whatever capacity, it is a miracle. To be sure, if one can explain it, it is not a miracle.

GIVEN TO THE MULTITUDE

If the believer carefully analyzes, at least as far as is possible, that which is done by the Lord, one will find that God performs far more miracles than one dare realize. In fact, God is constantly answering prayer, at least for those who believe. The trouble is, most who call themselves believers, in fact, believe little, if anything at all. Most entire religious denominations hardly believe that God answers prayer whatsoever of any nature. They do not believe that He reveals Himself in any capacity but that living for God is little more than joining a church. With these people, there is no relationship with Christ whatsoever. In fact, most of them are not even truly saved.

The phrase, *"And gave to the disciples to set before the multitude,"* was the order then and is the order now. God gives Jesus to His people to give to a hurting world, and this we must do, for this is the only spiritual sustenance that can be given. To be sure, there is no spiritual sustenance in Islam, Mormonism, Catholicism, Hinduism, Buddhism, or any of the religions of the world.

As well, there is a spiritual order laid out in this scenario, which we have given in other volumes, but is so important that it bears repeating.

HE TOOK

This speaks of Christ taking us from sin to salvation in the born-again experience.

HE BLESSED

Immediately after conversion, it seems that the Lord pours upon the new convert a cornucopia of blessings. It is almost like a little child asking his rich parent for something, and it is given on request.

AND DID BREAK

And then, it seems that all of a sudden, the blessings stop or else are greatly slowed, with the believer entering into a breaking process, which at times seems to be unbearable. The entire process pertains to the believer being taught to be led by the Spirit instead of leaning on flesh. To say the least, it is not pleasant, but yet, happens to all, at least if they are to be used by God.

AND GAVE

Christ will only give to a hurting world that which is totally led and guided by the Holy Spirit, hence, the necessity of the breaking process. To be sure, many have attempted to give *"their"* abilities and talents but found that the Lord had little or no use for such, and, in fact, such can never bless anyone. That which is given must be totally of the Spirit and by the Spirit.

(17) "AND THEY DID EAT, AND WERE ALL FILLED: AND THERE WAS TAKEN UP OF FRAGMENTS THAT REMAINED TO THEM TWELVE BASKETS."

THEY WERE FILLED

The phrase, *"And they did eat, and were all filled,"* naturally pertains to the physical, but even more importantly, the lesson it portrays concerns the spiritual and that one can only be *"filled"* as he partakes (eats) of Christ. In effect, this is what Jesus was meaning when He said, *"Except you eat the flesh of the Son of Man, and drink His blood, you have no life in you"* (Jn. 6:53). This was a figure of speech that spoke of believing fully on Christ and, thereby, accepting what He did for us at the Cross of Calvary (Jn. 6:63).

In fact, the entire scenario of Chapter 6 of John proclaims to us the fact that we died with Christ, were buried with Christ, and rose with Him from the dead (Rom. 6:3-5).

The partaking of Christ alone will satisfy the human heart. The spiritual craving in man, which should be obvious to all and was placed there at creation by God (Gen. 2:7), can be satisfied only by God. He does so through His Son, the Lord Jesus Christ, and what He did for us at the Cross.

That is the reason a person attempting to survive on the bare necessities of life can find joy, happiness, and fulfillment in Christ, with the billionaire, who does not know Christ, unable to do so despite all the money he or she might have.

THE FRAGMENTS

The phrase, *"And there was taken up of fragments that remained to them twelve baskets,"* points to several meanings:

• What God blesses always concludes with much more than when it began!

• The number 12 is no accident in that it portrays God's government, which always guarantees ample provision, and more.

• The number 12 pertained to the twelve apostles and showed them that ample provision was made for each.

Incidentally, this miracle is the only one in the entire Galilean ministry that is told by all four evangelists.

As well, in the performing of this miracle, there is no record that Jesus took fish from the lake, etc., but that He used what He had and multiplied it.

There is a law called *"Hamilton's law,"* which states that anything constructed must be made out of materials depleted somewhere else. In other words, for every house that is built, etc., trees have to be cut down to provide the lumber, with sand and rock taken from the earth to make the brick, etc. A gain is a loss somewhere else.

However, this law, as is here obvious, does not apply to Jesus. There is no record that He depleted resources elsewhere in order to perform this miracle.

This tells us that while man is depleting the resources of this earth, in the coming kingdom age, Jesus will not deplete such, but rather will replenish them by His miracle-working power. That is at least one of the reasons His economy is of such wondrous magnitude!

(18) "AND IT CAME TO PASS, AS HE WAS ALONE PRAYING, HIS DISCIPLES WERE WITH HIM: AND HE ASKED THEM, SAYING, WHOM SAY THE PEOPLE THAT I AM?"

PRAYER

The phrase, *"And it came to pass as He was alone praying,"* proclaims Luke skipping over a variety of incidents and discourses told at greater or lesser length by the other evangelists. Evidently the Holy Spirit desired that Luke omit certain things in order that He might place emphasis in other areas little touched at all by the other evangelists.

Some eight times Luke alludes to Jesus praying, which should serve as a lesson to us. As a man in the incarnation, He sought His heavenly Father exactly as we must do. As well, the frequency in which this is mentioned should point out to us the necessity of prayer and fellowship with the Lord. And yet, tragically, most Christians pray little, if at all!

WHY PRAYER?

Prayer is communication. In other words, when the believer prays, he is communicating with the heavenly Father, and the heavenly Father has opportunity then to communicate with the believer. That within itself opens up a vista of opportunity

NOTES

that defies description. To be able to talk to someone of the magnitude of God opens up all possibilities; therefore, the believer should take full advantage of this great and glorious opportunity exactly as Christ.

COMFORT

In 1991, the Lord instructed me to begin two prayer meetings a day (morning and night), with the exception of service nights. That we did and continued it for some 10 years, which I still personally do.

I do not mention this with any thought or idea in mind that such merits favor with God because it does not! I say it merely that I may be able to properly explain what I am talking about.

I doubt that very many people in the world have had to undergo what Frances and I were forced to experience in those years. Of course, our detractors, of which there seemed to be many, would instantly retort by saying that it was all my fault. Naturally, any wrongdoing on the part of anyone is the fault of the individual. That is a given. However, the erroneous and un-Christlike action of others is not my fault but the fault of that particular individual, or persons, whomever they might be. God does not give a license to anyone to mistreat others. That is done only because of promotion by the powers of darkness.

At any rate, without these prayer meetings, there was no way that we could have survived. Actually, many pointed toward our joy, which, incidentally, was from the Lord, and claimed that we were not taking the matter seriously, or any other type of false assumption they may have chosen to propose. The truth is, the Lord has sustained us by His grace.

DAVID

Countless times, with much of the church world joining hands with the secular world in attempting to destroy us, the problems have been so overwhelming as to be insurmountable, at least as far as human ability is concerned. In every way that one could look, financially, physically, and spiritually, scores of times the situation looked hopeless. I could say with David, *"I looked on my* right hand, and beheld, but there was no man who would know me: refuge failed me; no man cared for my soul."

However, David also said, *"I cried unto You, Oh LORD: I said, You are my refuge and my portion in the land of the living.*

"Attend unto my cry; for I am brought very low: deliver me from my persecutors; for they are stronger than I."

And then, *"Bring my soul out of prison, that I may praise Your name: the righteous shall compass me about; for You shall deal bountifully with me"* (Ps. 142:4-7).

I have lived these passages, and I know exactly what they mean, at least as far as a poor human can know. Countless times in prayer, as I have laid difficulties and problems before the Lord, quite possibly the problem did not go away, but the <u>care</u> of that problem instantly went away as it was laid on Christ.

Many times, Frances and I walked into one of these prayer meetings, gathering with the few who were there, with the weight of the world on our shoulders, but after a short season of prayer, we would leave as if we were floating on clouds. The Spirit of God had come down in the meeting and had helped us to soar above all the difficulties and problems. This is a therapy and strength the world knows nothing about, and sadly, most of the church is little acquainted with it either.

A SEVERE PROBLEM?

Upon reading this, many believers will think in their hearts that if they have a severe problem, they too will resort to the Lord; however, they think that their situation does not register such need, and, therefore, such frequency of prayer is little necessary. Such thinking is totally wrong.

I have always had a strong prayer life, and if I had not had that prayer life at a time of crisis, I would not have known what to do. However, due to the fact that such consecration was already there, it was no problem to continue it, and even increase it.

No! If we take the position that prayer is only for crisis times, then we miss the point altogether. While it definitely is for crisis times, still, it is for all times. To say the same

NOTES

thing in another way: if we do not have a constant prayer life all the time, when the crisis comes, as it usually does in the lives of most, we will not then make prayer the sustenance and strength it really is.

FREQUENCY?

Understanding the frequency with which Luke expressed or called attention to the prayer life of Christ, we should understand that the Spirit of God is attempting to relate something to us that is very important.

It is not that one earns something from God by the amount of time he or she prays. That is not the idea at all! The idea is that we as believers need this constant communication, and we really cannot satisfactorily have it outside of prayer. While it is true that the believer can communicate with the Lord constantly in an impromptu manner, still, it is not true that the believer can have a deep personal communication with the Lord in that manner. That requires prayer or else Jesus would not have engaged Himself accordingly.

If one thinks about prayer on a frequent basis, or as I have mentioned above concerning our prayer meetings, most would probably shrink back in their spirit, feeling that such is a bit much or else not required, or something in which they do not delight in partaking. This type of thinking is engaged simply because the individual does not know or realize what true prayer is.

GUIDANCE AND DIRECTION

Admittedly, prayer is hard work. However, its benefits far outweigh any effort we make. I actually look forward with great anticipation to my time of prayer each day, sometimes as much as three times a day. I do so because it is a time of great refreshing and rejoicing in the Lord. Admittedly, some of the prayer times do not result in great movings of the Holy Spirit. At times it seems that very little is accomplished; however, I know in my heart that these times are just as productive as the times when God moves in a great way. Therefore, I do not allow the difficult times to discourage me.

Jesus prayed often because He needed constant direction from the Father. Don't we need the same?

In prayer, the Lord leads me as to what I should do. He gives me guidance and direction. As well, He deals with problems in my own immediate life, helping me to overcome them. He calls attention to things I had not formerly seen, but yet, things which need attention and which are spiritually debilitating. This can only come about through prayer; therefore, prayer is a time of consecration. We consecrate our will and our desires to the Lord, desiring only His will.

LET'S LOOK AT CONSECRATION

Without a proper prayer life, there is no way that proper consecration to the Lord can be engaged. Actually, I believe that proper consecration is impossible without a proper prayer life. That is the reason not much consecration is seen in most Christians. They simply do not pray; consequently, the Lord has little opportunity to deal with their hearts concerning things that need to be addressed.

Consecration is something that requires daily attention. If daily attention is required, and it certainly is, then daily supplication before the Lord is required as well.

COMMUNION WITH THE LORD

Besides all the other benefits of prayer, communion with the Lord is undoubtedly the most prized benefit. Just to be able to talk to Him and feel His presence is a glory and healing that nothing else can replace. To be sure, the Lord wants this even more than we do. This is epitomized in the Song of Solomon.

It says, *"You who dwell in the gardens, the companions hearken to your voice: cause me to hear it"* (Song of Sol. 8:13).

This proclaims the shepherd bridegroom, who typifies Christ, saying, "Your companions in the vineyard hear Your voice. That is good, but speak to Me, cause Me to hear it!"

Such is Christ's complaint today. Many speak to their companions in testimony in the necessary ordering of Christian service, but they neglect private prayer and secret communion.

The Lord wants to hear our voice! This is the second time He has requested such, emphasizing the strong desire (Song of Sol.

NOTES

2:14). While it is true that others needed to hear her story, still, more than all, He says, *"Cause me to hear it."*

I wonder how much our blessed Lord is saying the same thing to His church but without much response! Today's church, sadly, is not a praying church. Therefore, the communion and fellowship that can only be attained by doing so, which gives us spiritual health so grand that it is unexplainable, is little engaged.

TO HEAR OUR VOICE?

That He would even want to hear our voice is beyond our pale of understanding. What do we have to say to Him that could be of interest? Quite possibly, it is not so much what we say, but the love with which we say it!

Years ago I heard the great Pentecostal preacher, A.N. Trotter, say, "The Holy Spirit interprets every single word, sigh, groan, or exclamation that comes from the heart of the child of God."

I never forgot that. In some way it helped me to understand the measure of communion and fellowship that He, our Lord, longs to have with us.

The phrase, *"His disciples were with Him,"* spoke of the Twelve.

The question, *"And He asked them, saying, Whom say the people that I am?"* is asked for several reasons.

Much had happened since the feeding of the thousands with the five loaves and two fish, which was at the height of our Lord's popularity. The defection, which the Master had foreseen when He commenced His parable-teaching with the sad story of the sower, had begun. Many had fallen away from Him. Spence says, "The enthusiasm for His words was rapidly waning; the end was already in sight."

In view of all of this, and especially concerned about what the disciples thought, He would begin first of all with what the people thought. What were they saying about Him? Whom did they say He was?

The question was not asked because of a desire for self-glory. It was rather asked with the idea in mind that if they did not know who He was, they would never know. With all the miracles that had been performed, and with all the proof that had been given, there was no reason that they not know He was the Messiah.

As well, their not knowing it, which most did not, would bring about their destruction, and horribly so!

Consequently, His question, or rather the answer to it, held grave consequences!

(19) "THEY ANSWERING SAID, JOHN THE BAPTIST; BUT SOME SAY, ELIJAH; AND OTHERS SAY, THAT ONE OF THE OLD PROPHETS IS RISEN AGAIN."

THE ANSWER GIVEN BY HIS DISCIPLES

The phrase, *"They answering said,"* concerns itself with the popular beliefs concerning Christ, erroneous beliefs we must quickly add, that portrayed a sad misinterpretation of the Scripture. The entire scenario of this error was brought about by the people not understanding the Word of God.

Without a doubt, this was the fault of the scribes and Pharisees, but still, the final responsibility would always be left up to the individual. This situation is, regrettably, no less acute today.

Concerning the great cardinal doctrines of the Word of God, most little understand because of sitting under false teachers and not properly studying the Word of God for themselves.

Properly understanding the Word of God has a lot to do with one's consecration or lack thereof, which always points to self-will. If the consecration is not where it ought to be and self-will replaces God's will, there will always be, at least for the most part, a false interpretation or misinterpretation of the Bible.

WHO IS JESUS

The name *"John the Baptist"* concerned those who thought Jesus was John raised from the dead. It was a strange answer, this report of the popular belief concerning Jesus. Actually, it was a form of reincarnation, which the Bible does not teach, and which is therefore false.

"But some say, Elijah," also presented a false belief.

Considering that Malachi had pointed to the fact that Elijah would one day reappear

NOTES

(Mal. 4:5), and, in fact, those were the last words of that prophet, it gave occasion to this error.

Then, the two miracles of creating the loaves and fish for a great famishing crowd especially suggested this idea. Elijah had performed a similar miracle respecting the widow of Sarepta and her son, with the cruse of oil and the barrel of meal that failed not (I Ki. 17:14). So, many concluded that Jesus was Elijah!

The phrase, *"And others say, that one of the old prophets is risen again,"* was also a popular concept in Israel.

Jeremiah would be a good example of *"one of the old prophets."* Tradition had already asserted that the spirit of that great one had passed to Zechariah; consequently, was not it possible that Jesus was Jeremiah, especially considering that they were similar? Jeremiah's family turned on him, as did the family of Jesus. Likewise, His hometown of Nazareth did the same, as did the hometown of Jeremiah.

As well, Jeremiah wept over Jerusalem, as Jesus would do the same. So, the similarity was there.

THE BIBLE

Tradition says that Jeremiah had hidden the ark of the covenant, as well as the altar of incense, somewhere in the mountain where Moses died by the *"kiss of God."* So, would not Jeremiah return to tell where the ark and altar actually were?

When people drift from the revealed Word of God, they always come up with fables that seem to have some weight of Scripture but, in reality, do not! As we have stated, such ideas proclaim a misunderstanding of the Scripture.

As we have already alluded, the Bible does not teach reincarnation, and neither does it teach the transmission or migration of one's spirit to another.

While it is true that Elijah will definitely come back to this earth, it is also true that he has not yet died but was rather translated (II Ki. 2:11).

Actually, Elijah, along with Enoch, who, as well, was translated and did not see death, will return to earth in the coming great

NOTES

tribulation addressed by Jesus. There they will minister in Jerusalem until almost the close of that period and will then be killed, raised from the dead, and raptured to glory (Mat. 24:21; Rev. 11:3-12).

No, Jesus was none of those, but rather the Son of the living God, in fact, God manifest in the flesh.

(20) "HE SAID UNTO THEM, BUT WHOM SAY YOU THAT I AM? PETER ANSWERING SAID, THE CHRIST OF GOD."

WHOM DO YOU SAY THAT I AM

The question, *"He said unto them, But whom say you* (do you say) *that I am?"* now poses the question. While it was certainly important what Israel thought, it was even more important what the disciples thought, who had been Jesus' constant companions since the beginning of His ministry. They were to form the nucleus of the early church. If they had a wrong conception, the entirety of the great plan of God would be placed in jeopardy.

CHRIST OF GOD

The phrase, *"Peter answering said, The Christ of God,"* proclaimed the correct answer.

"Christ" is actually a title, and it means "anointed," or more perfectly, "the Anointed," which all of Israel knew and understood to refer to the Messiah. In other words, there would never be another anointed such as Christ was anointed.

If one is to notice, the Pharisees and the religious leaders of Israel never referred to Jesus by that name, which means "Saviour" or "Christ," which means, as stated, "the Anointed." They only referred to Him by the title of *"rabbi"* or *"teacher"* because they did not believe He was the Messiah.

A MYSTERY OVER AND ABOVE

However, the disciples had not come to this confession easily. They knew Jesus was entirely unlike all other rabbis. Spence said, "He was looked at by the disciples as the master of masters, and a mystery over and above." In other words, He was totally unlike any other human being they had ever seen in that He was perfect in character and nature.

As well, even though He had alluded to the fact of His being the Messiah, still, He had pretty much left them to observe for themselves, and as Spence again said, "They had been observing." However, along with the great miracles and the perfect character, as well as fitting all the prophetic profile, they were also witnesses of the great humiliation, in that He was rejected by all. They had difficulty reconciling the two.

How could He be the conquering Messiah and at the same time be so humiliated? Even up unto the end, they could not grasp the conception of a suffering Messiah. The passion and the Cross tended to deepen their gloom, with them falling once again into unbelief. It needed the resurrection to complete the education of their faith.

FAITH

As well, we learn from this that no believer, even the disciples of old who walked shoulder-to-shoulder with Christ, comes to faith, or rather full-blown faith, instantly. The Scripture says that we *"grow in grace, and in the knowledge of our Lord and Saviour Jesus Christ"* (II Pet. 3:18).

We are to walk in the light as light is given unto us. If we fail to do this, spiritual regression is the result, which can, if continued, cause a person to lose his soul. This is a principle that applies not only to the individual but to entire religious denominations.

For instance, as we previously alluded, some of the so-called, old-line denominations were formerly used greatly by the Lord. However, since being given the light of the Holy Spirit and by and large rejecting it, most have ceased to have any present effectiveness for the Lord. As light is given, light must be entered into or else it is lost. Actually, as this very occasion suggests, the entirety of the nation of Israel was lost because they would not believe Christ and walk in the light that was freely given unto them. As Israel, so is all!

(21) "AND HE STRAITLY CHARGED THEM, AND COMMANDED THEM TO TELL NO MAN THAT THING."

The pattern is:

1. Why did Jesus command such a thing of His disciples?

2. He knew that Israel had already rejected Him. Consequently, for the disciples to spread far and wide this truth of His Messiahship would have only fanned the flames of hatred of Him even more by the religious leaders. It was even now becoming almost intolerable, and one can well imagine what would have happened had Peter's confession been widely known.

3. Also, even though the people may have rallied at the beginning to such a confession, still, they were for the most part looking for the wrong kind of Messiah. They wanted a victorious Messiah who would overthrow Rome, thereby, once again making Israel the premier nation in the world. They were by no means looking for a suffering Messiah and, consequently, would have soon turned on Him as He did not fit their self-conceived profile.

4. Regrettably, we must remember that at least in a sense, Israel was the church of that day. As well, most of that church did not truly know God, as most of the modern church does not know God presently.

(22) "SAYING, THE SON OF MAN MUST SUFFER MANY THINGS, AND BE REJECTED OF THE ELDERS AND CHIEF PRIESTS AND SCRIBES, AND BE SLAIN, AND BE RAISED THE THIRD DAY."

THE SON OF MAN

The phrase, *"Saying, the Son of Man must suffer many things,"* is never mentioned apart from the glory that follows the sufferings.

What did He suffer?

He suffered the rejection of His family, hometown, and, in effect, all of Israel. As well, in this rejection, He suffered great humiliation.

Even though great crowds thronged to His side, still, He was treated as no more than a peasant. He was not even given the honor of being a great prophet or a great teacher, much less the honor that belonged to the Son of God!

As well, the religious leaders of Israel were not satisfied to just merely reject Him, they also hated Him with a passion that defies all description. Their hatred was actually fueled by Satan himself.

WHAT HAD HE DONE TO DESERVE SUCH HATRED AND REJECTION?

That page is blank, for He had done nothing. Actually, they did not hate Him for what He had done, for He had done only good, but rather because of who He was. It was not that He claimed such position, for He actually claimed nothing, at least in a public sense.

So, their hatred was purely hatred that came from a sinful, wicked nature in their own hearts that was responding to His altogether perfect and pure character because His nature was perfect.

In other words, had you asked them why they hated Him, they could not have answered, or else if they tried to answer, the accusation would have been altogether false and, thereby, without foundation. Actually, the situation has not changed.

REJECTION

Presently, the world hates the true follower of Christ, and it's for reasons they do not really know.

"And be rejected of the elders and chief priests and scribes," concerned the entirety of the religious leadership of Israel. It is sad that the church of that day rejected Him, and it is sadder still that the modern church follows suit.

As Jesus closed out His message to the seven churches of Asia, which, by symbol, refers to all churches and for all time, He is found at the last not inside the church, but rather outside knocking on the door, attempting to come in, but little wanted or desired (Rev. 3:20-22).

It is easily understood as to why the world would reject Christ but not so easy respecting the church. In truth, Rome played into Israel's bloody hands by crucifying Christ, but still, it was Israel who truly crucified Him. How could they, who were supposed to know, not know, and how is it so similar to the present?

Satan's greatest effort is not in the realm of vice or sins of the flesh, as evil as they may be, but rather in the field of religion.

Religion is that which is man devised and, consequently, not of God. It is what Israel had succumbed to and what characterizes much of the modern church.

THE ORIGIN OF RELIGION

(The following is derived from the writings of Bernard Rossier, Ph.D.)

The noun *religion* is found only five times in the Bible, and four of the five times it is used in a negative way. First, we see the word as part of Paul's testimony before King Agrippa: *"Which (Jews) knew me from the beginning, if they would testify, that after the most straitest (strictest) sect of our religion I lived a Pharisee"* (Acts 26:5). Paul obviously was talking about his life before becoming a Christian.

He did the same thing when he wrote to the Galatians: *"For you have heard of my conversation (lifestyle) in time past in the Jews' religion, how that beyond measure I persecuted the church of God, and wasted it"* (Gal. 1:13). Both the Greek verb for *persecuted* and the one for *wasted* are imperfect tense verbs, so they speak of continuous actions in the past. Paul continued by saying, *"And profited in the Jews' religion above many my equals in my own nation, being more exceedingly zealous of the traditions of my fathers"* (Gal. 1:14).

James, the Lord's half-brother, also employed the word *religion* twice. *"If any man among you seem to be religious, and bridles not his tongue, but deceives his own heart, this man's religion is vain"* (James 1:26). The prepositional phrase, *"If any man (anyone among you) seem(ed) to be religious,"* comes from a condition of the first class in the Greek language, so it constitutes a statement of fact about someone who really thinks he or she is religious.

THE ONLY POSITIVE EXAMPLE IN SCRIPTURE

As previously mentioned, the fifth example of the utilization of the term *religion* is the only positive example in Scripture. *"Pure religion and undefiled before God and the Father is this, To visit the fatherless and widows in their affliction, and to keep himself unspotted from the world"* (James 1:27). As you can see, James equated genuine religion to a living relationship with

NOTES

God, which is demonstrated by scriptural works. Possibly, the word *religion* given by James would have been better translated *spirituality*.

Why is it that the word *religion* is not found more in the written Word of God? Both the epistle of James and the letter to the Galatians were written very early in the history of the New Testament church. In fact, James probably was the first New Testament letter written. It was most likely some time after the year A.D. 45. We can see that Christianity still was closely connected with Judaism at that time. In James 2:2, *"For if there come unto your assembly a man with a gold ring, in goodly apparel, and there come in also a poor man in vile raiment,"* the word *assembly* comes from the Greek noun for *synagogue*. Hence, believers still were worshiping in Jewish synagogues.

As well, the church at this early stage was mostly concentrated in Jerusalem.

THE EARLY CHURCH

It is believed by some that Galatians was probably Paul's first epistle. It was most likely written around A.D. 48-49, just shortly before the church council, which we read about in Chapter 15 of the book of Acts. Why do we emphasize the early dates for James and Galatians? It is to show that the early church soon abandoned the use of the word *religion* because of its negative connotations. With some exceptions, this word apparently came to stand for a substitute for the real thing, a relationship with the Lord.

If one will trace the concept of religion throughout the Bible, one will find that this is exactly what religion always has been: a substitute for the real thing. By this we mean that the Devil himself interjected religion into the affairs of humans to provide them with a false security, which helps them to reject a real relationship with God. This means that religion was foisted onto humans from an external source, and it began in the garden of Eden.

SATAN: A RELIGIOUS CREATURE

Satan is able to trick people because they do not recognize him as an extremely religious creature. How do we know that he has always been religious? We know this because of what the Bible says about him. *"You* (Lucifer) *are the anointed cherub who covers; and I have set you so: you were upon the holy mountain of God; you have walked up and down in the midst of the stones of fire"* (Ezek. 28:14).

In the phrase, *"The anointed cherub who covers,"* the last word contains the idea of guarding something, so the phrase could be translated, *"You are the anointed cherub who guards." "I have set you so,"* indicates that God Himself ordained for Lucifer to guard something. The logical question is, "What was he assigned to guard?" I believe the context in Ezekiel, Chapter 28, indicates that he was assigned to guard the worship that was directed to God.

SATAN'S WAYS—
THE FIRST STEP

Hence, this creature was assigned the greatest responsibility that any created being ever could have. What happened? It seems that he decided to direct the worship to himself. *"You were perfect in your ways from the day that you were created, till iniquity was found in you"* (Ezek. 28:15). If our conclusion is correct, it should make it a little bit easier to figure out what the Devil was doing in the garden of Eden with reference to our first parents, Adam and Eve. The bottom line relates to the fact that he still was attempting to direct worship to himself. Actually, this reveals the whole basis of religion: it is Satan's way of diverting worship from God to himself.

Please look at the way the Devil approached Eve. *"Now the serpent* (the mouthpiece of Satan) *was more subtle than any beast of the field which the LORD God had made. And he said unto the woman, Yes, has God said, You shall not eat of every tree of the garden?"* (Gen. 3:1). As one can see, there really is nothing untrue about Satan's question. Therefore, the first step in establishing religion among humans was to refer to God's Word so the religion would appear to be from God. It is true that nearly all error rides into the church on the back of truth.

THE SECOND STEP

The second step in establishing religion

NOTES

among humans was to take the confrontational tact. How did the Devil do this? He did it by changing God's command into a question, *"And the LORD God commanded the man* (Adam), *saying, Of every tree of the garden you may freely eat:*

"But of the Tree of the Knowledge of Good and Evil, you shall not eat of it: for in the day that you eat thereof you shall surely die" (Gen. 2:16-17). Look at the subtle difference between the Lord's clear command and Satan's crafty question, *"Yes, has God said, You shall not eat of every tree of the garden?"*

You see, both the command and the question are true. Even Eve recognized this fact. *"And the woman said unto the serpent, We may eat of the fruit of the trees of the garden:*

"But of the fruit of the tree which is in the midst of the garden, God has said, You shall not eat of it, neither shall you touch it, lest you die" (Gen. 3:2-3). The fact that Eve added the incorrect phrase, *"Neither shall you touch it,"* indicates here carelessness regarding God's command. He always means exactly what He says because He always has an important reason behind what He says. Please do not be afraid to take God at His Word! Instead, be afraid of not taking Him at His Word!

THE THIRD STEP

Satan's third step was denial of the Lord's clear Word. *"And the serpent said unto the woman, You shall not surely die:*

"For God does know that in the day you eat thereof, then your eyes shall be opened, and you shall be as gods, knowing good and evil" (Gen. 3:4-5). *"As gods"* would be better translated as *"like God."* A major subtlety comes in the use of the word *die.* God meant spiritual death while the Devil meant physical death.

Another major subtlety comes in the invitation for Adam and Eve to become like God. This is the heart of religion because it attempts to remove the difference between God and man, between the Creator and the creature. Hence, Satan basically told Eve that she and Adam could be masters of their own destiny, or that they could direct to themselves part of what they were directing to God. Here we see one of the clear foundations of religion: from the human standpoint, it diverts the glory of God to man. This is exactly why religion always stems from human works in one way or another.

THE REASON RELIGION DOES NOT WORK

This also is the reason humanistic psychology does not work. It claims that humans can solve their own problem. Actually, what we see in this biblical passage reveals the very opposite. *"And the eyes of them* (Adam and Eve) *both were opened, and they knew that they were naked; and they sewed fig leaves together, and made themselves aprons"* (Gen. 3:7). The garments of human works may make people feel satisfied in their own eyes, but these garments never will suffice with God.

This is what we see in the next verse. *"And they heard the voice of the Lord God walking in the garden in the cool of the day: and Adam and his wife hid themselves from the presence of the Lord God amongst the trees of the garden"* (Gen. 3:8). Human works only deal with the symptom, not with the real problem. In this case, the nakedness of Adam and Eve was the symptom, but sin was the problem. As one person put it, "Adam and Eve were nude long before they realized they were naked." Their nakedness, not their nudeness, made them hide from God. *"And he* (Adam) *said, I heard Your* (God's) *voice in the garden, and I was afraid, because I was naked; and I hid myself.*

"And He said, Who told you that you were naked? Have you eaten of the tree, whereof I commanded you that you should not eat?" (Gen. 3:10-11).

UNBELIEF

Hence, it was the sin of not taking God at His Word (which is unbelief) that caused the problem. Unbelief also caused Adam to sin by blaming Eve (*"And the man said, The woman whom You gave to be with me, she gave me of the tree, and I did eat"* [Gen. 3:12]), and it caused Eve to sin by blaming the Devil (*"And the Lord God said unto the woman, What is this that you have done? And the woman said, The serpent beguiled me, and I did eat"* [Gen. 3:13]). Actually,

Adam and Eve should have taken full responsibility for their sins. Sin was not dealt with until God promised a Saviour (*"And I will put enmity between you* [Satan] *and the woman* [Eve], *and between your seed and her seed; it* [Jesus] *shall bruise your head, and you shall bruise His heel"* [Gen. 3:15]), and God slew an innocent victim and provided a blood offering for Adam and Eve (*"Unto Adam also and to his wife did the Lord God make coats of skins, and clothed them"* [Gen. 3:21]).

THE DIVERSION OF RELIGION

There is one more foundation of religion that needs to be mentioned: It really is directed toward the Devil and its final analysis. I mean by this that he deceives people into thinking that accepting his methods will benefit them when actually, his goal is to get them to serve him. This is, of course, what always happens with religion, at least to a degree.

By this strident statement, I mean that religion always hurts its participants because it diverts them from enjoying a true relationship with God.

Unfortunately, most of that which calls itself church is no more than religion.

THE CRUCIFIXION OF CHRIST

The short phrase of Verse 22, *"And be slain,"* refers to the crucifixion of Christ. The inference is that these *"elders and chief priests and scribes"* would be guilty of His death. In fact, He would die at their hands. So, here we have the church killing their very Lord whom they should be praising.

"And be raised the third day," spoke of His resurrection, but sadly, a truth that was totally lost on the disciples, as their future behavior at that event clearly shows.

As well, we learn from this that the Cross was not dependent on the resurrection, but rather the resurrection was dependent on the Cross. In other words, if Jesus accomplished at the Cross that which He set out to do, the resurrection was not in doubt. However, if Jesus had failed to atone for even one sin, then He could not have been raised from the dead because *"the wages of sin is death"* (Rom. 6:23).

Evidently, the disciples did not know what Jesus was addressing, or else they simply did not believe Him. It seems that His language was clear enough, but it also seems that their thinking was so grounded in the reign of the victorious Messiah, in which, incidentally, they would share a high and lofty position, that they really did not hear what He was saying. This points to the terrible seed of unbelief.

This unbelief carried right through the crucifixion and the resurrection, which kept them from recognizing Him when they actually did see Him, which was immediately after the resurrection.

They were, in effect, making up their own religion as billions have done. Thank God, that ultimately did change, but not until after the resurrection and the presentation of incontrovertible proof.

(23) "AND HE SAID TO THEM ALL, IF ANY MAN WILL COME AFTER ME, LET HIM DENY HIMSELF, AND TAKE UP HIS CROSS DAILY, AND FOLLOW ME."

IF ANY MAN WILL COME AFTER ME

The phrase, *"And He said to them all,"* presents the doctrine of self-denial, which is the very opposite of the modern false doctrine of self-esteem.

As well, it seems that this message was delivered by Jesus not only to His immediate disciples, but also to a great crowd that had evidently gathered.

"If any man will come after Me," is the beginning of an invitation that is totally unlike any invitation that has ever been given.

The great religions of the world open their doors wide and make it very easy to join, promising all sorts of benefits. Jesus here presents the very opposite. There is no promise, at least in this invitation, of the proverbial pot of gold at the end of the rainbow. Actually, there was no dangling carrot whatsoever!

While in other places He did proclaim the great reward of eternal life, as well as the glorious rest that comes to the true follower of Christ (Mat. 11:28-30; Jn. 3:16), He does not mention these things here.

Why?

LET HIM DENY HIMSELF

Considering the astounding miracles He was constantly performing and the recent desire of the people to make Him king, He knew their coming to Him would be because of wrong motives, that is, if they did not perfectly understand what following Him actually meant. Therefore, He left off the great reward while extolling the heavy price tag.

How so unlike much of the modern church, which promises instant riches to all followers of Christ.

The phrase, *"Let him deny himself,"* means "to forget oneself, lose sight of oneself and one's interest." It speaks of entrance into a new state of condition. It could be translated, *"Let him at once begin to lose sight of himself and his own interest, and take up his cross."*

As well, the phrase means that the believer is to deny himself of his own actions, efforts, and abilities at trying to live this life and overcome sin. It simply cannot be done in that fashion. One can overcome only by placing one's faith exclusively in Christ and the Cross. This is the denying of self.

SELF

As we have repeatedly stated in these volumes, when man fell in the garden of Eden, he fell from the lofty height of total God-consciousness to the far lower level of acute self-consciousness. Hence, whereas man was supposed to be conscious only of God, which is the epitome of all life, he instead is conscious only of self, hence, the preening and exaltation of self.

As a result, man is ever attempting to improve self. It is his major pastime. Unfortunately, a great part of the modern church has bought into this lie, and a lie it is.

The world of humanistic psychology is built on the premise of self-improvement. It claims that man can improve self by following certain prescribed methods, etc. However, as should be obvious, all such efforts are doomed to failure. Man cannot improve self because such is the same as the patient treating the patient. Sin cannot deliver from sin, as sickness cannot heal sickness. Consequently, all of man's self-improvement programs are doomed to failure. This includes, as well, the old lie of Satan under a new covering called *"self-esteem."*

Whether man's problem is low self-esteem or high self-esteem, the problem is still self. Making him feel good about himself is not going to change the end results.

The answer that Jesus gave to self is a denial of self, which is the total opposite of pampering, petting, and promotion of self by humanistic psychology.

HOW DOES ONE DENY ONESELF?

We've already addressed this, but due to the fact that this is so very, very important, please allow a continued statement.

We have to understand that we cannot be what we ought to be in Christ, what we ought to do for Christ, and what we ought to have in Christ by our own machinations and ability. It simply cannot be done that way. So, our Lord tells us that we must deny self, meaning that we must deny our own abilities, personal strength, talents, education, motivation, etc.

We are to understand without question that we can only be what we ought to be as we understand the Cross of Christ. Paul told us what to do with self in Romans, Chapter 6.

We are to understand that when we came to Christ, whenever that was, we actually died with Him, were buried with Him, and were raised with Him in newness of life (Rom. 6:3-5). This means that not only do we deny our own abilities, but we are to understand that what we are and what we must be can only be found in Christ and what He did for us at the Cross.

Having done this, we now understand that self, or *"our interest,"* is not the issue, but rather the interest of Christ. Christ becomes foremost and all in all. It must be His will in all things and not self-will.

This is demanded by Christ because He knows that self is man's real problem and that all improvement of self is doomed to failure. Therefore, self must be hidden in Christ and His Cross if it is to find its true potential.

Actually, this is the great battleground of the believer. It is the battle between self (the flesh) and the Spirit (Holy Spirit).

With all the problems that beset humanity, self is always at the center. It is this struggle that is the great struggle.

This is where self-righteousness comes into play. Religious man attempts to cover up his evil self by good works of religion, which make him think that he is righteous when, all the time, it is a promotion of self instead of Christ.

HOW DOES ONE KNOW THAT SELF IS DEFINITELY HIDDEN IN CHRIST?

In truth, most all believers claim to be hidden in Christ, but their spirits and attitudes proclaim something altogether different.

Let it quickly be understood that if the believer doesn't understand the Cross of Christ, not only as it refers to salvation but, as well, our sanctification, such a believer will never know victory. In other words, although saved, such a believer simply does not know how to properly live for God. We must understand the following:

• The Lord Jesus Christ is the source of all blessings from God (Jn. 1:1-3, 14, 29; 14:6, 20).

• Understanding that Christ is the source, we must then understand that the Cross of Christ is the means, and the only means, by which we receive all of these wonderful things from the Lord (Rom. 6:1-14; Col. 2:10-15).

• Understanding that Christ is the source, and the Cross is the means, then we must understand that the Cross of Christ must always be the object of our faith. Of course, when we speak of the Cross, we aren't speaking of the wooden beam on which Jesus died, but rather what He accomplished at the Cross (I Cor. 1:17-18, 23; 2:2; Col. 2:13-15).

• With our faith properly placed in Christ and what He did for us at the Cross, the Holy Spirit, who works exclusively within the framework of the finished work of Christ, will then work grandly on our behalf (Rom. 8:1-11; Eph. 2:13-18).

With the believer believing and understanding what we have just said, then self is easily handled. However, it's when the faith of the believer is directed at something other than Christ and the Cross that he brings upon himself or herself real problems, which means that self cannot be properly addressed in that fashion.

HIDDEN IN CHRIST

When one is truly in Christ, hurts and slights are of little consequence. There is no self-promotion, with the attitude being that God will promote as He so desires.

When one is truly hidden in Christ, all religious politicking comes to a halt. For example, hours before the crucifixion, the disciples of our Lord were in strife among themselves, *"Which of them should be accounted the greatest"* (Lk. 22:24). Regrettably, this did not end with the disciples but continues in too many hearts and lives even unto this hour.

Self properly hidden in Christ does not promote self. Self properly hidden in Christ does not take hurts and slights personally, committing them rather to the Lord. Self properly hidden in Christ has no personal agenda but daily seeks the will of God in all matters.

No! It is not a high self-esteem that man needs, but a high Christ-esteem that is sorely needed.

TAKE UP HIS CROSS DAILY, AND FOLLOW ME

The phrase, *"And take up his Cross daily, and follow Me,"* presented a message to Jesus' listeners that was startling to say the least.

First of all, the Cross was no unknown image to the Jews. Spence said, "The gloomy procession of robbers and of rebels against Rome, each condemned one bearing to the place of death, the Cross on which he was to suffer, was a sadly familiar image outside of most towns and villages." Consequently, Jesus could not have said anything that would have been more repulsive to the ears of these Jews.

As well, the word *daily* is peculiar to Luke. It, with the word *all*, which the spirit of the text proclaims, teaches that no person is excused and no day excepted. Hence, the apostle Paul said, *"I die daily"* (I Cor. 15:31); for he daily bore the shame and hatred that resulted from following Jesus.

NOTES

The Cross was the instrument of death, and here it speaks of death to self as it is hidden in Christ. Unfortunately, the Message of the Cross is no more desired today than then.

HOW DOES ONE TAKE UP THE CROSS DAILY?

We must understand what Jesus was talking about. As we have already alluded, the very mention of the word *cross* to the Israel of Jesus' day would be alarming to say the least. However, the truth is the very opposite.

Every blessing that we have in the Lord, every answer to prayer, all the communion we have with the Lord, and all prosperity in every capacity, all and without exception are made possible by the Cross of Christ.

Suffering?

Yes! But it's Jesus who suffered and not ourselves. Unfortunately, most believers have a totally erroneous idea of what Jesus was talking about regarding taking up the Cross daily. They think it means suffering.

So, whenever some poor person has a car wreck and is laid up in the hospital for several weeks, Christians are wont to say, "That's his cross that he has to bear."

No! It is not his cross; it is only a car wreck.

As we said in a previous paragraph, the Cross of Christ is the means by which all of these blessings are given to us by the Lord.

HOW DOES THAT HAPPEN?

Before the Cross, animal blood was the best that humanity had, and it was woefully insufficient. In fact, the blood of bulls and goats could not take away sins (Heb. 10:4). So, due to the fact that the sin debt still hung over the heads of every single individual, even the Bible greats of the Old Testament, this meant that the Holy Spirit could little help in those days. As well, before the Cross, when a believer died, his soul and spirit did not go to heaven, but rather down into paradise (Lk. 16:19-31).

However, when Jesus went to the Cross and atoned for all sin, past, present, and future, at least for all who will believe, this broke the back of Satan so to speak. Sin is the legal means that Satan has to hold man captive. With that legal means removed, he has no more right to hold anyone captive. If he does, and sadly, he is doing such all over the world, even among believers, it's because the individual will not avail himself or herself of the great victory that Christ has won. In other words, it must be that the Cross of Christ is not the object of our faith, but rather something else.

As we have alluded, the modern church has a modicum of understanding regarding the Cross of Christ respecting salvation but no understanding at all respecting sanctification. The truth is, virtually all of the material given to us by the apostle Paul is telling us how to live for God. In fact, over 99 percent of the Bible from Genesis 1:1 through Revelation 22:21 is given over to telling believers how to live for the Lord. It all culminates in Christ and what He did at the Cross.

"Daily" is used by Christ, and it was the Lord who said this, in effect, meaning that a consecration of sorts must be made each day as it regards taking up the Cross.

Yes, the Cross was a place of death, but it was also a place of the greatest blessings that man has ever known, all made possible by Jesus Christ and what He accomplished at that place of death. As we've already stated, every single thing we receive from God (He only gives us good things) is made possible by the Cross. We must dedicate our hearts and our lives to what Jesus did at the Cross, even on a daily basis. It is somewhat like we renew our faith daily. It is not that we lose faith daily, but it is that we gain more and more faith, but in the correct object, which is the Cross of Christ.

This word *daily* lets us know exactly how important all of this is. In other words, we are not speaking of a trifling thing. We are speaking of the single most important aspect of our life and living, and actually of eternity, and I speak of the Cross. Consequently, Paul said the following:

"Therefore we ought to give the more earnest heed to the things which we have heard (actually refers to the New Testament Message of the Cross), *lest at any time we should let them slip* (In the Greek text, it carries the idea of a ring slipping from a finger.

Regrettably, the church presently has let the Message of the Cross slip, and as a result, the church hardly knows where it's been, where it is, or where it is going)*" (Heb. 2:1).

In effect, our Lord said in Luke 14:25-27 that if one did not deny oneself and take up the Cross daily to follow Christ, such *"cannot be My disciple."* So, we are speaking here of something that is tremendously important.

(24) "FOR WHOSOEVER WILL SAVE HIS LIFE SHALL LOSE IT: BUT WHOSOEVER WILL LOSE HIS LIFE FOR MY SAKE, THE SAME SHALL SAVE IT."

WHOSOEVER WILL SAVE HIS LIFE SHALL LOSE IT

The phrase, *"For whosoever will save his life shall lose it,"* proclaims the bedrock of Bible Christianity and the very opposite of that touted by the world.

Spence says, "The Greek word here rendered 'life' signifies the natural animal life, of which the main interests are centered in the earth."

Spence went on to say, "If a man grasps at this shadow, quickly passing earthly life, he will assuredly lose the substantial enduring heaven-life."

The idea is that if we place our life into Christ, which is done at conversion when we died with Him, was buried with Him, and rose with Him, meaning that we lose our life to Him, then we will find it. Otherwise, it will be lost. One can only do this by the method and means of the Cross. It simply cannot be done otherwise.

Wuest says, "God has so created man that he does not find complete rest and satisfaction until his entire being is swallowed up in the sweet will of God."

He went on to say, "Our Lord is not here giving the terms upon which God will give salvation, for the denial of self never saved a soul from sin. Only Jesus' blood can do that."

Jesus was here giving the real purpose of life, which is a life hidden in God through Jesus Christ (Jn. 14:20).

FOLLOW ME

If one is to notice, Christ emphatically used the phrases, *"Come after Me," "Follow Me,"* or *"For My sake."* Outside of Christ, one cannot

---

NOTES

find God. Jesus is the door, in effect, *"the way, the truth, and the life"* (Jn. 10:9; 14:6).

Some have claimed that this was Jesus' philosophy of life. However, philosophy is basically man's search for truth. Jesus Christ was not searching for truth. In fact, He is truth. His way is not one of several ways but, in fact, the only way.

Once again, this entire statement goes back to a denial of self. Man thinks by aggrandizing self, which is the epitome of selfishness, and which characterizes the world without God, he will save himself. However, he finds to his amazement that money, riches, fame, popularity, or a hundred and one other things that could be named, do not find one the life he seeks. And yet, despite total failure, others keep trying.

Conversely, this losing of life, i.e., self, in Christ carries out the very opposite of what man normally thinks. Even though he is losing his life, he finds to his amazement that it is something he definitely needs to lose, and then he is given new life in Christ.

Let us say it again: such life cannot be found outside of Christ and the Cross. It is only in Christ, by Christ, and through Christ.

(25) "FOR WHAT IS A MAN ADVANTAGED, IF HE GAIN THE WHOLE WORLD, AND LOSE HIMSELF, OR BE CAST AWAY?"

The synopsis is:

1. The beginning of the question, *"For what is a man advantaged?"* proclaims Jesus introducing profit and loss; however, the ultimate profit and loss is one's soul!

2. The conclusion of the question, *"If he gain the whole world, and lose himself, or be cast away?"* proclaims the worth of the eternal soul.

3. The truth is, no one has ever gained the whole world, with most gaining nothing! However, even if one could, all such gain would be temporal, where the salvation of the soul is eternal.

4. Considering the seriousness of this question, why is it that men will not accept Christ, especially considering the incontrovertible proof of His Lordship?

5. As we have repeatedly stated, deception is the culprit. Men are deceived. In fact, and also in the Words of Jesus, only a few are truly saved or will be saved (Mat. 7:14).

(26) "FOR WHOSOEVER SHALL BE ASHAMED OF ME AND OF MY WORDS, OF HIM SHALL THE SON OF MAN BE ASHAMED, WHEN HE SHALL COME IN HIS OWN GLORY, AND IN HIS FATHER'S, AND OF THE HOLY ANGELS."

JESUS

The phrase, *"For whosoever shall be ashamed of Me and of My words,"* places Christ squarely in the place and position of Saviour and Lord.

The contention has always been with Christ. There is little or no controversy respecting God in the sense that He is not easily understood or even explained. To most people, as stated, God is just an abstract. Even though He is the first person of the Godhead, still, the contention in the minds of people is not with Him, even though indirectly it is! The real contention is with Jesus Christ. The Jews refuse to accept Him as the Messiah while the Muslims claim that He definitely was a great prophet but not the Son of God.

Millions of modernists claim Him to have been a good man but deluded respecting His part in the Godhead. It is difficult to understand how He could be a good man and deluded at the same time!

Robertson says, concerning the words *"whosoever shall be ashamed,"* that "this is not a statement concerning the future conduct of a person, but about the person's present attitude toward Jesus. The present conduct of the individual now determines Christ's future conduct with reference to that person."

The Greek word for *ashamed,* as used here, is *epaischunomai* and means "to have a feeling of fear or shame which prevents a person from doing the thing he knows he should do."

Why would anyone be ashamed of Jesus, considering who He is and what He has done for humanity!

TRUTH

The truth is, most do not know who Jesus really is or what He actually has done! Then again, many do know, at least up to a point, but they simply do not want to give up their sin. However, the major thrust of this statement is that many will not serve Christ simply because they are ashamed of the reproach it brings to do so.

The phrase, *"Of Him shall the Son of Man be ashamed,"* speaks of the second coming. As such, Jesus was actually referring to the judgment of the nations, which will take place very soon after the second advent (Mat. 25:31-46), even though it also refers to the sole individual.

This particular judgment, as outlined in Matthew, Chapter 25, pertains a great deal to the treatment of Israel by the nations. This simply means that God keeps His promises. He has promised Israel certain things, and even though the fulfillment of those promises has been delayed by Israel's rejection of Jesus Christ and the resultant blindness, still, those promises will ultimately be kept. A large segment of the modern church denies these promises to Israel, claiming that Israel is no more, with no restoration forthcoming. Consequently, according to this passage, they are placing themselves in serious jeopardy with the Lord.

THE SECOND COMING

The phrase, *"When He shall come in His own glory, and in His Father's, and of the holy angels,"* speaks of the second coming.

There are three glories in the world of light: the glory of the Father; the glory of the Son of Man; and the glory of angels.

In effect, the Lord was saying that He will return as almighty judge. That judgment will take place with the nations, as stated, and then, ultimately, for all unsaved at the great white throne judgment (Rev. 20:11-15).

Incidentally, the great white throne judgment will take place immediately after the thousand year kingdom age.

Along with the proclaimed coming judgment, the idea is also expressed by Jesus that if individuals were ashamed of Him due to the manner of the incarnation and His rejection (at least in part because He was a peasant), this will be wondrously changed at His second coming when He will come with glory such as the world has never known

before. The idea is that if one accepts Him in His humiliation, Christ will accept that person in His glory. The opposite holds true upon rejection.

(27) "BUT I TELL YOU OF A TRUTH, THERE BE SOME STANDING HERE, WHICH SHALL NOT TASTE OF DEATH, TILL THEY SEE THE KINGDOM OF GOD."

The pattern is:

1. The phrase, *"But I tell you of a truth,"* proclaims a preview of the glory of which He has just spoken.

2. *"There be some standing here, which shall not taste of death, till they see the kingdom of God,"* simply meant that Peter, James, and John would see the glory of God before they died. Actually, this would happen in just a few days as they witnessed the transfiguration of Christ.

3. It should be stated, as well, that the believer has only seen the spiritual side of the kingdom of God, and that very dimly (I Cor. 13:12). We have not yet seen the glory of that kingdom but most certainly shall in the coming kingdom age when Jesus will personally rule and reign from Jerusalem over the entirety of the earth (Rev., Chpt. 19).

(28) "AND IT CAME TO PASS ABOUT AN EIGHT DAYS AFTER THESE SAYINGS, HE TOOK PETER AND JOHN AND JAMES, AND WENT UP INTO A MOUNTAIN TO PRAY."

The synopsis is:

1. The phrase, *"And it came to pass about an eight days after these sayings,"* has Mark saying *"six days"* (Mk. 9:2). There is no discrepancy.

The phrase in Mark is exclusive, which means all the days and time are not included in the statement.

2. In Luke the Greek phrase is inclusive, meaning that two more days of time elements were counted, which Matthew and Mark did not include.

3. *"He took Peter and John and James,"* represents these three singled out again.

4. The first time this was done, they saw His power when the daughter of Jairus was raised from the dead. Now they would see His glory.

5. Why these three in preference to the others? We know that the Lord is no

respecter of persons; therefore, everything He does is for purpose and reason.

6. Quite possibly these three had a greater hunger for God than the others. As a result, that hunger would be addressed by Jesus taking them into a deeper expression of His work and will. There could well have been, and no doubt was, greater faith on their part, and God always rewards faith.

7. This does not mean they were perfect, as the text plainly shows. Actually, they were still very immature. However, the Lord never deals with us on what we presently are, but what He is able to make of us as we yield to His will. God seldom works from what is but from what can be as individuals yield to Him.

8. The phrase, *"And went up into a mountain to pray,"* records by Luke the first of three things not mentioned by Matthew or Mark:

a. Went up to the mountain to pray.

b. Was transfigured while praying.

c. Conversation was of His decease.

9. The word *pray* tells us that it was in a prayer meeting where the transfiguration took place. This should show us how important prayer is and, as well, the frequency in which it was engaged by Christ.

(29) "AND AS HE PRAYED, THE FASHION OF HIS COUNTENANCE WAS ALTERED, AND HIS RAIMENT WAS WHITE AND GLISTERING."

THE PRAYER LIFE OF CHRIST

The phrase, *"And as He prayed, the fashion of His countenance was altered,"* means that it took on a glow that was obvious to all. As well, the glory He was now experiencing did not come from without but from within. The idea is of giving outward expression of one's inner character, with the outward expression coming from and being truly representative of that inner character of Jesus.

On the outward, the disciples and others saw only the peasant from Galilee, clad in homespun garments, the son of the carpenter of Nazareth. However, now that outward expression was changed. Out from within the inmost being of the Son of God, there shone that dazzling glory of the essence of deity that He possesses co-eternally with

God the Father and God the Spirit. It shone right through the clay walls of His humanity and through the clothing He wore. It was the same dazzling radiance that the angels saw in His preincarnate state (Phil. 2:6), but given through His physical body, not in the sense of the spiritual, only as in the case of the angels.

"There was no borrowed radiance, even from the heavens, which might shine on the Lord Jesus. This effulgence of glory came from within, and was an inherent possession of the Lord of Glory" (Wuest).

HIS RAIMENT

The phrase, *"And His raiment was white and glistering,"* proclaims that this inward glory turned those homespun, peasant garments into a thing of such beauty that it was absolutely indescribable.

Spence said, "The earthly robes were so beautified by contact with this divine light that human language is exhausted by the evangelists to find terms and metaphors to picture them. Matthew describes them as 'light,' while Mark said they were as 'white as snow,' while Luke likens them to 'flashing lightning.'"

Even though Jesus was not a part of the aristocracy of Israel but, in fact, was a peasant, a class despised by this religious aristocracy, He is now shown for who and what He really is.

The idea is that we are not serving a peasant, even though that form was necessary in the incarnation, but rather the Lord of Glory. It is a glory of such magnitude, as we have stated, that it is difficult, if not impossible, to describe.

(30) "AND, BEHOLD, THERE TALKED WITH HIM TWO MEN, WHICH WERE MOSES AND ELIJAH."

TWO MEN

The phrase, *"And, behold, there talked with Him two men,"* expresses those of whom Peter, James, and John were not aware because they had been asleep. How long this prayer meeting had gone on before this happening, we are not told. It is certainly possible that the disciples were exhausted after the climb up the mountain, and possibly after many hours of dealing with thousands of people who needed healing and help.

As well, the tremendous expression of the power of God as it emanated from Christ, which resulted in the transfiguration, could have had a numbing effect on these three. At any rate, they were suddenly awake, possibly awakened by the voices. *"Behold"* proclaims a sudden realization of what was happening.

MOSES AND ELIJAH

The phrase, *"Which were Moses and Elijah,"* proclaims an astounding experience to say the least. Moses had been dead for about 1,500 years, and Elijah, having been translated, had never died, having been in heaven for about 900 years. Some expositors say the transfiguration portrayed the following:

• The transfigured Lord Jesus is the Messiah glorified in the millennium.

• This entire projection is an anticipatory picture of the millennium.

• Peter, James, and John are Israel, cleansed, and restored at the second advent.

• Moses represents the law and, consequently, all who died in the faith, looking forward to the coming promise, who was Christ.

• Elijah represents grace. All, whether under law or grace, who truly trusted Christ, share the same benefits. There is no difference.

• The thousands fed by Christ with the five loaves and two fish point to the Gentile nations in the millennium, the recipients of the ministry of Israel.

THE SOUL AND THE SPIRIT

As well, and to which we have previously alluded, Moses is a perfect example of the soul and spirit of a person without the physical body, for Moses, as stated, had been dead for about 1,500 years. Elijah, also as stated, had not died due to the translation, and he still maintained his original physical body.

This tells us that the inner man of the soul and spirit is very similar to the outer man portrayed in the physical body and can speak and move exactly as Moses did here. At the resurrection, Moses will be given a

NOTES

glorified body, along with Elijah, as will every saint of God, dead or alive (I Cor. 15:51-57). As well, this puts to rest the erroneous doctrine of soul sleep, which teaches that the soul and the spirit sleep at death and will do so until the resurrection. It is true that the physical body sleeps in the dust of the earth, and actually goes back to dust, but the soul and the spirit either go to heaven or hell, depending on their salvation or the lack thereof.

(31) "WHO APPEARED IN GLORY, AND SPOKE OF HIS DECEASE WHICH HE SHOULD ACCOMPLISH AT JERUSALEM."

GLORY

The phrase, *"Who appeared in glory,"* pertains to Moses and Elijah. Everything that pertains to God is bathed in glory exactly as here described; however, the glory that emanated from them was in no way to be compared with the glory that came from Christ. Their glory was that which came from without, actually from God the Father, while the glory of Christ came from within Him because He is God, the second person of the Godhead.

HIS DECEASE

The phrase, *"And spoke of His decease which He should accomplish at Jerusalem,"* proclaims the topic of this conversation, which, according to the Greek text, had been going on for some time. Williams said in respect to that, "If saints in glory delight to speak of Christ's atoning death, how much more ought sinners on earth."

Actually, the doctrine of the atonement is the theology of heaven. In that glory, Elijah learned the lesson that he failed to learn on earth, that salvation is by grace and not by law. Christ redeems men from the curse of the law by suffering Himself in atonement for that curse, i.e., the wrath of God.

As well, Christ's death did not merely happen. He *"accomplished"* it; therefore, He was God.

Years ago, I heard A.N. Trotter say, "Any believer who goes beyond the Cross backslides."

It took me awhile to understand what he had said. He was meaning that every single thing given to the child of God comes through Calvary. But for Calvary, the believer could not be baptized with the Holy Spirit, could not be healed, could not have communion with the Lord, could not have answers to prayer, and, in effect, couldn't have his sins taken away (Jn. 1:29).

THE CROSS OF CHRIST

That's the reason Paul said, *"For I determined not to know anything among you, save Jesus Christ, and Him crucified"* (I Cor. 2:2).

This is also the reason he said, *"But God forbid that I should glory, save in the Cross of our Lord Jesus Christ, by whom the world is crucified unto me, and I unto the world"* (Gal. 6:14).

This is what makes the modern faith ministry so dangerous in many respects, its failure to understand the value of the Cross and our everyday walk before God. To speak of Calvary as "the greatest defeat in history" and to speak of it as "past miseries," insinuating that songs about the Cross should be eliminated from our worship, shows a complete misunderstanding of the Scriptures. As well, it is a misunderstanding about something so important as the very heart of the gospel.

The truth is, every believer gets in through the Cross of Christ, and concerning his walk before God, remains in in the same manner. Jesus won complete victory over Satan and his cohorts at Calvary, with that victory given to us at conversion, and also after conversion in our daily walk. In other words, it is the emulation of the death of Christ on the Cross that defeats self after conversion.

Let us say it again:

• Jesus Christ is the source (Jn. 1:1-3, 14, 29; Col. 2:10-15).

• The Cross of Christ is the means (Rom. 6:1-14; Gal. 6:14).

• The object of our faith must be the Cross (I Cor. 1:17-18, 23; 2:2; Col. 2:14-15; Phil. 3:17-19).

• With our faith properly placed, the Holy Spirit will then work mightily for us (Rom. 8:1-11).

(32) "BUT PETER AND THEY WHO WERE WITH HIM WERE HEAVY WITH SLEEP: AND WHEN THEY WERE AWAKE, THEY SAW HIS GLORY, AND THE TWO MEN THAT STOOD WITH HIM."

The diagram is:

1. The phrase, *"But Peter and they who were with him were heavy with sleep,"* proclaims their disposition apparently after the prayer meeting had begun.

2. *"And when they were awake, they saw His glory, and the two men who stood with Him,"* proclaims them, as stated, awakening to behold the glory of the transfiguration.

3. As well, this portrays to us how the child of God will die, by simply going to sleep in Jesus and awakening in heaven in His presence, as well as the Bible greats of old! What a glorious thought!

(33) "AND IT CAME TO PASS, AS THEY DEPARTED FROM HIM, PETER SAID UNTO JESUS, MASTER, IT IS GOOD FOR US TO BE HERE: AND LET US MAKE THREE TABERNACLES; ONE FOR YOU, AND ONE FOR MOSES, AND ONE FOR ELIJAH: NOT KNOWING WHAT HE SAID."

The overview is:

1. The phrase, *"And it came to pass, as they departed from Him,"* pertains to Moses and Elijah disappearing from the scene, leaving only Jesus plus the three.

2. *"Peter said unto Jesus, Master, it is good for us to be here,"* proclaims the apostle discussing something about which he knew nothing. There is no record that Peter was addressed, so there was really no need for him to say anything.

3. The phrase, *"And let us make three tabernacles,"* could be a clue to what Peter was thinking.

4. He was continuing to think, even at this stage, that Jesus was going to usher in the kingdom at any time. Then with the appearance of Moses and Elijah, he probably thought this great time was about to begin. Having, no doubt, studied the prophet Zechariah and knowing that the Feast of Tabernacles will continue in the millennium, this may have been the reason for his suggestion (Zech. 14:16).

5. *"One for You, and one for Moses, and one for Elijah: not knowing what he said,"*

proclaims Peter placing these two on the same par with Christ, which was not looked at favorably by God. Even after the transfiguration and seeing Christ in all His glory, Peter still did not fully realize who Jesus really is, even though he did know in part.

(34) "WHILE HE THUS SPOKE, THERE CAME A CLOUD, AND OVERSHADOWED THEM: AND THEY FEARED AS THEY ENTERED INTO THE CLOUD."

The exegesis is:

1. The phrase, *"While he thus spoke, there came a cloud, and overshadowed them,"* proclaims God's response to Peter. The cloud was the same as that which led the children of Israel in the wilderness wanderings (Ex. 40:34-38). Such was quite different than this mere tent or small tabernacle that Peter suggested.

2. *"And they feared as they entered into the cloud,"* spoke of Peter, James, and John, and not Jesus. There was no fear in Him, as should be obvious.

3. This tells us that this was no ordinary cloud. In fact, it contained all the presence and preeminence of Jehovah. As such, it must have been an awesome sight and feeling.

(35) "AND THERE CAME A VOICE OUT OF THE CLOUD, SAYING, THIS IS MY BELOVED SON: HEAR HIM."

A VOICE OUT OF THE CLOUD

"And there came a voice out of the cloud," was the voice of God the Father.

"Saying, This is My beloved Son: hear Him," proclaims the rebuke to Peter's folly.

While Mark used the same phraseology, Matthew said, *"This is My beloved Son, in whom I am well pleased; hear ye Him"* (Mat. 17:5). This is no discrepancy, with the meaning not changed, inasmuch as each evangelist seldom gave the same account, with one or more reporting at times more than the other. Actually, we are only given a fragment in any of the accounts concerning all the experiences of what actually happened and what actually was said. However, everything reported was exactly what was said, even if only a part was given.

THIS IS MY SON, THE BELOVED ONE

The Greek text, in which it was originally written, says, *"This is My Son, the beloved One."* Consequently, two things are here said:

1. The Messiah is God's Son.

2. He is the beloved One. Wuest says, "The Greek word used for 'beloved' is 'agapao,' and speaks of a love called out of one's heart by the preciousness of the person loved, and in this case Christ."

The words, *"Hear Him,"* actually say, "Be constantly hearing Him."

The idea is that He, the Lord Jesus Christ, is the One to be listened to and not the others, who are but minor subjects, at least in comparison to Christ.

Consequently, this shoots down the Catholic theory of hearing Mary or any other dead saints. This should tell the Catholic Church that to place anyone on a par with Christ, or anywhere close, is doing terrible disservice to the person of Christ.

Also, even though I deeply appreciate the advice and counsel of any true brother or sister in the Lord, still, the final authority will always be *"Him!"* To be sure, Satan will move heaven and earth to get the fellow apostles of Peter, plus anyone else for that matter, to listen to others instead. The command, *"Hear Him,"* must ever resound within our hearts and lives, and may that sound never dim.

(36) "AND WHEN THE VOICE WAS PAST, JESUS WAS FOUND ALONE. AND THEY KEPT IT CLOSE, AND TOLD NO MAN IN THOSE DAYS ANY OF THOSE THINGS WHICH THEY HAD SEEN."

The pattern is:

1. The phrase, *"And when the voice was past, Jesus was found alone,"* proclaims the fact that the voice did not come from a physical body, for there was no one with Jesus when the cloud lifted except the three.

2. *"And they kept it close, and told no man in those days any of those things which they had seen,"* was proclaimed by Mark as Jesus *"charged them that they should tell no man what things they had seen"* (Mk. 9:9).

3. The words, *"In those days,"* mean that these three did not relate the account of this incident until after the resurrection. I suspect that after the resurrection, and especially after Pentecost, all of these grand and glorious experiences began to become much

more understandable to the apostles, especially with the Holy Spirit constantly with them and giving them divine guidance.

(37) "AND IT CAME TO PASS, THAT ON THE NEXT DAY, WHEN THEY WERE COME DOWN FROM THE HILL, MUCH PEOPLE MET HIM."

The order is:

1. The phrase, *"And it came to pass, that on the next day, when they were come down from the hill,"* means that this great visitation and transfiguration had probably taken place during the night. As well, it probably lasted far longer than the limited account that is given by the evangelists.

2. *"Much people met Him,"* implies that they were waiting for Him, probably having been told by the nine that Jesus should come down from the mountain at any time.

3. Only Jesus could meet the need, whatever that need might be.

(38) "AND, BEHOLD, A MAN OF THE COMPANY CRIED OUT, SAYING, MASTER, I BESEECH YOU, LOOK UPON MY SON: FOR HE IS MINE ONLY CHILD."

The diagram is:

1. The phrase, *"And, behold, a man of the company cried out,"* represents the man with the demon possessed son.

2. Mark mentions the scribes berating the other disciples about the time Jesus and the three arrived. Luke did not mention it.

3. *"Saying, Master, I beseech You, look upon my son,"* presents the man appealing to the only One in the world who could help him. The record will show that the disciples had tried and failed. His appeal was a heart-wrenching cry of desperation.

4. Apparently, one could look at the child and tell that his situation was critical, hence, the plea, *"Look upon my son."*

5. *"For he is mine only child,"* is peculiar to Luke. He is the only one who mentioned that this poor tormented boy was an only child.

6. One can well imagine the hopes held for this boy by his parents. And then, to realize at some particular time that he was not normal and seeing him steadily grow worse must have broken their hearts.

(39) "AND, LO, A SPIRIT TAKES HIM, AND HE SUDDENLY CRIES OUT; AND IT TEARS HIM THAT HE FOAMS AGAIN,

AND BRUISING HIM HARDLY DEPARTING FROM HIM."

THE EVIL SPIRIT

The phrase, *"And, lo, a spirit takes him,"* proclaims the boy to be demon possessed. Jesus did not contradict him regarding the cause of the problem, and He proved that the diagnosis was correct by casting the demon out.

We are not told how old the child was; however, the same word *child* was used for Jesus in Luke 2:43, stating that He was 12 years old. Consequently, this boy was probably within two or three years either way of the same age.

It is difficult for many to understand how a child could be demon possessed. But yet, this account shows us that such definitely can happen. In fact, some of the gruesome things children are presently doing, even down to the age of six, can probably only be understood in the realm of demon possession, or at least strong demon influence. As I dictate these words, a judge is attempting to make the decision as to whether a 6-year-old boy can be tried for a gruesome murder he has committed. It should go without saying that a 6-year-old child does not have the maturity or understanding to be tried in a court of law as an adult in this fashion. So, what is to be done with situations of this nature?

CHILDREN

Having established biblically that children can be demon possessed, one must wonder at the circumstances that would bring about such.

I think one can safely say that no child is born demon possessed, but for a few, which seem to be more and more all the time, this thing can come about, it seems, as young as 4 or 5 years old.

The environment in which children are raised has probably never been worse in history. Television is piping into the home a constant barrage of demonic activity, appealing especially to children. I speak of cartoons, of which many are pure witchcraft or else lean heavily in that direction. MTV is another example that has a great influence, perhaps the greatest of all on the preteens and early teens. This is freighted with a glorification of heavy rock music, which, within itself, contains tremendous demonic activity. As well, gross immorality is championed as the *"norm"* and fed as a steady diet to the viewer. Actually, most regular television programming can be said to be little better.

MUSIC

And then, of course, the rock music has long since been a vehicle for demon activity, which has probably caused more destruction among teenagers than anything known in human history. Just yesterday, in watching the local news, it showed a 16-year-old handcuffed in the backseat of a police car, who had just killed his mother and seriously wounded his father. It was said that he had been playing a song by a particular rock group which glorified the murdering of parents. They were asking the question, even before the police car pulled away, if this song had anything to do with what the boy did!

Looking at his face as he peered through the window of the car, one could easily detect demonic activity. Yes, I think it is a foregone conclusion that the type of music he was listening to definitely had a bearing on what he did. There is demonic activity in all of these things mentioned, plus even much of the so-called *"regular"* television programming.

With this type of thing coming into the far greater majority of the homes in America, and the world for that matter, it is not a wonder that little children are committing murder, but that it is not happening more often.

THE HOME AND SCHOOLS

The educators bemoan the fact that our schools are failing, along with the rise in juvenile delinquency, even of the worst stripe, but never seeming to realize the cause. Hundreds of billions of dollars are being spent on inane ideas that have no effect whatsoever. I continue to speak of our public schools.

This is the reason that if it is humanly possible, parents ought to enroll their children in a Christian school. Otherwise,

they are literally playing with the souls of their children.

Please allow me to say it again: Jesus is not just one of several answers; He is the only answer to these problems.

As well, a child born and raised in a Christian home where Bible values are the standard is immune from these dread things of which we mention. Solomon said as much, *"Train up a child in the way he should go: and when he is old, he will not depart from it"* (Prov. 22:6).

"And he suddenly cries out," speaks of this demon spirit suddenly taking control of the boy, even though occupying him constantly.

"And it tears him that he foams again, and bruising him hardly departing from him," means that these convulsions were constant occurrences. Mark records how this spirit *"has cast him into the fire, and into the waters, to destroy him"* (Mk. 9:22).

So we see that this demon spirit was attempting to kill this boy, which he had come close to doing any number of times.

There is no way that one can imagine the torture this child was going through or the heartache these parents were suffering.

(40) "AND I BESOUGHT YOUR DISCIPLES TO CAST HIM OUT; AND THEY COULD NOT."

THE DISCIPLES

Why couldn't the disciples cast this demon out, especially considering that Jesus had recently given *"them power and authority over all devils* (demons), *and to cure diseases"* (Lk. 9:1)?

Luke doesn't refer to it, but Mark refers to them asking *"Him privately, Why could not we cast him out?"* (Mk. 9:28).

Jesus told them, *"This kind can come forth by nothing, but by prayer and fasting"* (Mk. 9:29).

Robertson says that the emphasis in the Greek text is on their "prayerlessness," rather than their "lack of fasting." Actually, there is no record that they fasted at all during the three and a half years of Jesus' public ministry.

Of what kind of prayer is Jesus speaking?

The Greek word for *"prayer"* in Mark 9:29 is *proseuche* and means to "pray earnestly."

PRAYER

This does not refer to the type of prayer that was prayed over the boy by the disciples attempting to cast out the demon. It refers to times spent alone with God, with one entreating the face of the Lord in intercession. In other words, these battles are won in the spirit world before the actual occurrence. Many times in our prayer meetings, of which I have previously spoken, the Holy Spirit will take me into a spirit of intercession to where I will actually feel the helplessness and lostness of a lost soul. It is as if everything in me cries out for their deliverance, even though I am not normally praying for any particular person. I have noticed that when this happens, a short time later, we will receive letters from individuals who were watching the television programming of SonLife Broadcasting Network and were saved and delivered out of the worst type of bondage.

I believe this is what Jesus was addressing, and the intercession in which the Holy Spirit helps me and others to engage is definitely a factor in the deliverance of these people.

Actually, this is the type of prayer that has ushered in every move of God that has taken place in history. And yet, it is so little engaged presently by the modern church that most have no idea as to that of which we speak.

However, I do not believe this was lost upon the apostles, for they said in the earliest days of the early church, *"But we will give ourselves continually to prayer, and to the ministry of the Word"* (Acts 6:4).

(41) "AND JESUS ANSWERING SAID, O FAITHLESS AND PERVERSE GENERATION, HOW LONG SHALL I BE WITH YOU, AND SUFFER YOU? BRING YOUR SON HITHER."

FAITHLESS AND PERVERSE GENERATION

The phrase, *"And Jesus answering said, O faithless and perverse generation,"* was spoken to the whole of Israel. What a contrast to the glorious scene on the Mount of Transfiguration and this horrible spectacle below. The former is a type of heaven, while the later is a type of this pitiful, pathetic

NOTES

world. One is conscious only of God, with the other conscious only of the terrible effects of sin.

Israel at this time was faithless, but on top of that, she was perverse, which means "turned aside," and in this case, "turned aside from the Word of God," which caused the faithlessness.

Even though Jesus was addressing that particular generation, I wonder if He would not say the same at present! Most modern *"disciples"* do not even believe in demon possession or that Jesus is the very Son of God. Most do not believe in prayer or the power of God in any capacity.

So, the demon possessed go undelivered, the sick unhealed, and the sinner unsaved.

Many of the old-line churches believe little or nothing anymore, while the Pentecostal and Charismatic varieties, who claim to believe all of the Bible, instead are busily chasing one fad after the other, with few truly saved and delivered. So, I think the statement applies at present as well.

HOW LONG SHALL I BE WITH YOU?

The question, *"How long shall I be with you, and suffer you?"* portrays a human exasperation on the part of Jesus. This entire statement pertains not only to His disciples but, as well, the crowd looking on that day, and for that matter, the entirety of Israel.

One would have to say at this stage, as far as Israel's acceptance was concerned, the ministry of Christ was a failure, at least for the time. Actually, there is no other conclusion that can be reached. The religious elite of Israel were becoming more hostile toward Him by the day. The people, not having proper spiritual leadership respecting their religious leaders, were actually as sheep with no shepherd. Jesus said as much (Mat. 9:36).

It is almost inconceivable that such would be (this dark tragedy, the failure of the ministry of Christ), but that is what happened. As a result, Israel was totally destroyed and has wandered as an outcast all over the world for nearly 2,000 years, only finally becoming a nation once again in 1948. Even now, their darkest days are just ahead.

And yet, at the same time, even though His ministry to Israel failed, that directed toward the planting and building of the church did not fail. The church sprang from His ministry. He said, *"Upon this rock I will build My church; and the gates of hell shall not prevail against it"* (Mat. 16:18). As well, it is *"a glorious church, not having spot, or wrinkle, or any such thing; but that it should be holy and without blemish"* (Eph. 5:27). This can be said because as Jesus was the true Israel, He is also the true church. As the true Israel, national Israel will one day be brought back to Him because in the ultimate, He cannot fail!

BRING YOUR SON HERE

The phrase, *"Bring your son hither (here),"* indicates that the boy was being restrained a short distance away. As this child would be totally and completely delivered from the demon powers of darkness, Israel likewise could have been delivered in totality. That goes for anyone else as well! Jesus alone is the answer!

In a sense, the failure of the disciples is the failure of the church, even the true church. These men loved the Lord, and of that, one does not doubt. As well, they had been very successful at other times in bringing healing and deliverance to those in need while, at this time, experiencing failure. The true church follows the same pattern. At times, it is close to God, and great miracles are performed through the body, while at other times, there is failure, as here recorded.

Until the coming kingdom age, things will not be exactly as they ought to be. Even then, certain corrections are going to have to be made, at least with Israel, as symbolized by Peter's outburst on the Mount of Transfiguration.

(42) "AND AS HE WAS YET A COMING, THE DEVIL THREW HIM DOWN, AND TORE HIM. AND JESUS REBUKED THE UNCLEAN SPIRIT, AND HEALED THE CHILD, AND DELIVERED HIM AGAIN TO HIS FATHER."

THE DEMON

The phrase, *"And as he was yet a coming, the devil* (demon) *threw him down, and tore him,"* represents this demon's last effort to

hurt this child, knowing that he would have to obey Christ.

At this stage, Mark records some information (no doubt given to him by Peter as an eyewitness) that Luke does not mention.

According to Mark, Jesus told the man that his faith played a part in this, which by now had, no doubt, been seriously weakened by the failure of the disciples. Jesus said to him, *"If you can believe, all things are possible to him who believes"* (Mk. 9:23).

In this, we are led to understand that what the Lord does for us demands faith on our part. Actually, this was the only thing He ever demanded of anyone. He never one time pointed out sin within lives, even though it is positive that many, if not most, suffered such. As well, He never chided anyone about their lack of consecration, etc., at least where healing or deliverance was concerned. The only requirement seemed to be faith, hence, the sweeping promise just given.

FAITH

Spence said, "Then the poor Father, won by the divine goodness manifest in every act and word of Jesus, stammered out that pitiful, loving expression, re-echoed since in so many thousand hearts, 'Lord, I believe; please help my unbelief.'"

Spence went on to say, and beautifully so, "If Jesus accepted and rewarded that trembling, wavering faith in Him, will He reject ours?"

The answer is a resounding "No!" If there is even a flicker of faith, it will be rewarded, as here.

The phrase, *"And Jesus rebuked the unclean spirit, and healed the child, and delivered him again to his father,"* is recorded by Mark with more detail and portrays Jesus saying, *"You dumb and deaf spirit, I charge you, come out of him, and enter no more into him"* (Mk. 9:25).

In Mark's account, the word *charge* in the Greek text is "epitasso" and is used as a military term. It is the same as a superior officer, in this case, a general or field marshal, giving orders to a mere private. In other words, there is no doubt that it will be obeyed.

Consequently, a Word from the Great Master was sufficient, and the spirit that had brought the cruel curse and bondage of madness into the boy was instantly cast out, and the cure was complete.

AND HEALED THE CHILD

The words, *"Healed the child,"* mean that whatever physical damage the demon had caused, the boy's body was instantly healed. Consequently, when Jesus presented the boy to his father, the child was completely whole in every respect.

Somewhat imagining the terrible suffering the parents had gone through respecting this child, and considering that he was their *"only child,"* one can, as well, imagine the joy that must have filled this father's heart upon this boy being made completely whole. Their going home that day was without a doubt the greatest journey they had ever made.

Of course, not being there, we have little real knowledge as to what actually happened. However, one can well imagine that as the father and his son walked home, their joy must have known no bounds. The father would probably cry awhile and then praise awhile. The boy undoubtedly joined him.

Even though the mother is not mentioned, if she were still alive, which in all likelihood she was, her joy must have been overwhelming when she greeted their arrival. What a story they had to tell! What a story millions have to tell! In a way, this boy's deliverance was typical of the salvation of all. While the situation may not be that severe, in many lives it is even worse; however, Jesus has never met one who He could not save or deliver.

(43) "AND THEY WERE ALL AMAZED AT THE MIGHTY POWER OF GOD. BUT WHILE THEY WONDERED EVERY ONE AT ALL THINGS WHICH JESUS DID, HE SAID UNTO HIS DISCIPLES."

The composition is:

1. The phrase, *"And they were all amazed at the mighty power of God,"* presents the astonishment that was always present at the outstanding healings and deliverances of Christ. The problems of many of these people were so obvious that the healings and deliverances were beyond question.

Blinded eyes were instantly opened, lepers were instantly cleansed, and the most debilitating sicknesses were instantly healed. This case of the demon-possessed boy, while extreme, was no more extreme than scores of others. As well, all knew that these things were brought about by *"the mighty power of God,"* even though the religious leaders refused to accept the incontrovertible proof.

2. *"But while they wondered every one at all things which Jesus did, He said unto His disciples,"* portrays the idea coming up once again of Him being the triumphant Messiah and, therefore, being made king.

3. Jesus, knowing their thoughts, once again told them, as recorded in the next verse, of the terrible fate that awaited Him. Spence says, "They must remember there was no earthly crown or human sovereignty for Him."

(44) "LET THESE SAYINGS SINK DOWN INTO YOUR EARS: FOR THE SON OF MAN SHALL BE DELIVERED INTO THE HANDS OF MEN."

The pattern is:

1. The phrase, *"Let these sayings sink down into your ears,"* concerned that which they did not want to hear.

2. *"For the Son of Man shall be delivered into the hands of men,"* was actually no different than what He had said several days before (Lk. 9:22).

3. Regrettably and sadly, Satan does most of his evil work through the church.

(45) "BUT THEY UNDERSTOOD NOT THIS SAYING, AND IT WAS HID FROM THEM, THAT THEY PERCEIVED IT NOT: AND THEY FEARED TO ASK HIM OF THAT SAYING."

A LACK OF UNDERSTANDING

The phrase, *"But they understood not this saying, and it was hid from them, that they perceived it not,"* must be answered by "Why?"

In other words, why did they not understand Him, especially considering how simple His statement was?

It was not purposely hidden from them, but was rather hidden because of their unbelief. They were the reason it was hidden and not because Jesus purposely, in some mysterious way, made it impossible for them to comprehend.

Seeing all of these miracles and, as well, being recipients of His great wisdom, even greater than Solomon's (Mat. 12:42), the apostles mapped out a regimen which they felt Jesus was to follow. This included the overthrow of Rome, the supremacy of Israel, and, as well, exalted positions for themselves. They believed this fully, which was error. Consequently, this error blinded them to the true mission of Christ, which was the redemption of mankind. So, their thoughts were so directed toward their own interpretation that they could not really grasp or understand anything said that pointed to the opposite.

UNBELIEF

Unbelief is powerful in that it refuses to believe the clear, plain, written Word of God, consequently, devising its own way. Much, if not most of the modern church world, is in this trap. If anything is done or believed outside the Word of God, unbelief is the natural and immediate result. It is man's way versus God's way!

"And they feared to ask Him of that saying," means that what He had said did not line up with their thinking. As well, they were so geared to their own vision of what the Messiah would be like that communication, for whatever reason, had broken down.

Why did they fear to ask Him?

There would have been no fear had their thinking and direction been right. They strongly sensed that the things He was saying were not exactly what they had in mind, at least regarding the immediate future. So they feared to press the issue.

(46) "THEN THERE AROSE A REASONING AMONG THEM, WHICH OF THEM SHOULD BE GREATEST."

The order is:

1. This *"reasoning,"* which referred to thoughts and imaginations, would soon degenerate into *"strife,"* and for the same reason (Lk. 22:24).

2. The disciples could not understand the simple fact of the coming sufferings of Christ, but they were perfect in understanding that there would have to be leadership

NOTES

in this new move of God, and each wanted to be the leader.

3. Actually, this spirit, *"Which of them should be greatest,"* was the cause of all the misinterpretation of His words, along with the erroneous conclusions. Likewise, if one could pull back the cover on all of self-will, irrespective of the religious cloak under which it hides, one would probably find that self-aggrandizement is the reason for most erroneous beliefs. People simply are not willing to become a servant. Self-will demands self-exaltation, the very opposite of what Jesus said in Verses 23 and 24.

Most church fights are caused by someone wanting his way, in effect, wanting to be *"greatest."* Even though there certainly would be exceptions, still, I think if the truth be known, this problem would be the culprit in the far greater majority of cases.

4. When man fell in the garden of Eden, as we have stated many times, he fell from total God-consciousness to the far lower level of self-consciousness. As such, every effort is made to promote self. Regrettably, the problem is just as pandemic in the church as it is in the world, hence, symbolized in these very verses. So, the believer will find the desire to be greatest as one of his biggest problems. The total opposite is what Christ demands and what the following verses portray.

(47) "AND JESUS, PERCEIVING THE THOUGHT OF THEIR HEART, TOOK A CHILD, AND SET HIM BY HIM."

THE THOUGHT OF THEIR HEART

The phrase, *"And Jesus, perceiving the thought of their heart,"* refers to the Holy Spirit revealing to Him this of which the apostles were engaged. Actually, Christ only knew what any other human knows and finds out by observation, etc., with the exception of that which the Holy Spirit told Him, which was considerable, as would be obvious.

Was this thought of their heart sinful?

Yes, it was! Anything that is not according to the revealed will of God is sinful, as should be obvious. That is the reason it is incumbent upon the child of God to find the will of God and do it. Paul said, *"And be not conformed to this world: but be you transformed by the renewing of your mind, that you may prove what is that good, and acceptable, and perfect, will of God"* (Rom. 12:2).

I think it should be obvious from this very text that God is little interested in what is referred to as a *"permissive will,"* but will accept only His perfect will.

The phrase, *"Took a child, and set him by Him,"* is said by some to refer to Peter's home and the child as one of his. Clement of Alexandria especially mentions that this apostle had children.

Mark adds the note that Jesus folded His arms around the little fellow in loving fondness (Mk. 9:36).

WHY DID JESUS USE A CHILD AS A SYMBOL OF THIS GREAT TRUTH?

If, in fact, this little boy did belong to Peter, such an incident as that embrace would never have been forgotten by the father and would, of course, have been related to Mark.

Spence says, "By this action the Lord answers the silent questioning thought of the worldly Twelve. The child stands as a type of the humble and childlike disciple, and such a disciple is the greatest; he is so honored by God that he stands on earth as the representative of Christ, and of God Himself."

Why did Jesus use a child as a symbol of this great truth?

• A child is defenseless, forced to depend on someone else to protect it. The Lord desires that we not defend ourselves, but rather look to Him for support and defense.

• A little child has no ambition to succeed, especially at the expense of others, which is so characteristic of adults. Jesus tells us that the key to greatness is not in service to self, but rather to others, which is peculiar to Bible Christianity alone.

• A little child holds no grudges. If there is an altercation, in a few minutes' time, it is forgotten. As well, Jesus demands that we forgive readily.

• A little child does not know whether it is rich or poor. It is taken up with other things entirely. Even though riches are the driving ambition of many, Jesus tells us to take no thought for tomorrow, exactly as a little child.

NOTES

• A little child loves supremely, irrespective of the flaws of the one it loves. Such love is given by God to those who truly know Him. It is called the "God kind of love."

(48) "AND SAID UNTO THEM, WHOSOEVER SHALL RECEIVE THIS CHILD IN MY NAME RECEIVES ME: AND WHOSOEVER SHALL RECEIVE ME RECEIVES HIM WHO SENT ME: FOR HE WHO IS LEAST AMONG YOU ALL, THE SAME SHALL BE GREAT."

RECEIVING JESUS

The phrase, *"And said unto them, Whosoever shall receive this child in My Name receives Me,"* has the idea of service to others.

Many, if not most, help others because they hope to get something in return. To help a child, one must do so strictly out of love because a child cannot return the favor. This is the type of love the Lord expects of us. He wants us to do things for others without any thought of return simply because we love them. This is the manner in which God sent His Son.

Man has absolutely nothing that God needs, or even wants, other than love, which must be given freely. Many times we preachers will make the statement, in effect, that God has a great investment in us. No! God has not invested anything in us because investments expect a return.

God has done everything for the human family solely on the basis of love. In fact, love must be given or it is not love. It cannot be invested.

RECEIVING JESUS IS RECEIVING GOD

The phrase, *"And whosoever shall receive Me receives Him who sent Me,"* means that when one receives Christ, one receives God who sent Him.

The idea is that when one helps others, loves others, and does for others without any thought of return, he is conducting himself as God.

Jesus conducted Himself as a child, at least in this respect, with no worldly or earthly ambitions. He was not angling to be king over Israel and the world. Likewise, He did not come to make men rich in worldly goods. While it is true that He had great power, even almighty power, still, He never used it for Himself but always for others. So, the idea of His disciples, or anyone for that matter, following Him strictly for worldly gain misses the point altogether for serving Him. At this stage, that is exactly what the apostles were doing, and sadly, it is exactly what many modern Christians are doing!

While it is true that Jesus will one day be all of these things, King, even King of Kings, still, those things had little to do and have little to do with the moment of redemption. A powerful lesson is taught here. If we overlook or misunderstand it, we will forfeit who Jesus really is and what Christianity really is.

THE LEAST AMONG YOU

The phrase, *"For he who is least among you all, the same shall be great,"* sums up all that Christ has said.

The idea is not greatness as the world counts greatness, but rather as God looks at such.

Jesus is speaking of humility.

Trench said, "The work for which Christ's gospel came into the world was no less than to put down the mighty from their seat, and to exalt the humble and meek."

The idea springs out of and rests upon the sense of personal unworthiness and agrees with the fact that the sinless Lord laid claim to this grace, saying, *"I am meek and lowly in heart"* (Mat. 11:29).

The thought is that we are all creatures, thereby, created by God, meaning that we began with nothing and must receive all things from God. Thus, the grace of humility belongs to the highest angel before the throne, being as he is a creature the same as we.

Consequently, in the human nature of Christ, He set the pattern of all humility and all creaturely dependence; and it is only as a man that Christ thus claims to be meek and lowly in heart. His human life was a constant living in the fullness of His Father's love; consequently, He evermore, as man, took the place of the creature in the presence of its Creator. He is ever the example!

UNNOTICED BY OTHERS

The idea, as Jesus is explaining this to

NOTES

His disciples, is *to habitually do the just and righteous thing in a quiet way unnoticed by others.*

As well, true humility is a product of the Holy Spirit in the yielded believer and in no way can have its source in the heart of man. As we have stated, the only self-description that even fell from the Lord's lips was, *"I am meek and lowly in heart."* Paul said that this explains the mind of Christ, which must be in us as well (Phil. 2:3). Peter also spoke of the humility that he learned at the feet of Christ as being that particular virtue that makes all the other Christian graces what they should be (I Pet. 5:5).

Respecting the wrongs done to us by others, a perfect example is that of David when Shimei cursed and flung stones at him at the time of Absalom's rebellion (II Sam. 16:11). David felt it was just for him to suffer these things, however unjustly the other might inflict them.

Why did David lift no hand to defend himself or even punish Shimei when the other was plainly in the wrong?

DAVID

The idea is that David knew himself as a sinner among sinners. This knowledge of his own sin taught him to endure meekly the provocations with which others might provoke him, and not to withdraw himself from the burdens that their sin might impose upon him.

In other words, David saw himself as having wronged God exactly as Shimei was doing wrong to him. Consequently, as David wanted God to show grace unto him, likewise, he would show grace unto this foul-mouthed man; however, there was a difference.

David recognized and repented of his sin, while Shimei never did. Nevertheless, David lifted no hand against this man, even though he had the power to do so, leaving it in the hands of God.

If this lesson of wrongs done to us by others can only be looked at in the light of our wrongs done to God, desiring that God treat us kindly, we will in turn treat them kindly as well.

Someone has said, "Humility has to do

with one's estimate of oneself, meekness with one's attitude toward the dealings of God and man with respect to oneself, and gentleness with one's treatment of others."

All of this characterizes what Jesus was teaching respecting the child.

(49) "AND JOHN ANSWERED AND SAID, MASTER, WE SAW ONE CAST-ING OUT DEVILS IN YOUR NAME; AND WE FORBAD HIM, BECAUSE HE FOL-LOWETH NOT WITH US."

JOHN

The phrase, *"And John answered and said,"* proclaims the only instance in the four gospels where John said something directly. He was referred to several times as one of the three who seemingly was closer to the Master than any, but he was not very vocal, as Peter was.

His character seemed to be fiery and impetuous although, at the same time, reserved and retiring. However, ultimately, he would become a teacher of the Master's love and would be referred to as *"John the Beloved."*

"Master, we saw one casting out devils (demons) *in Your name; and we forbad him, because he followeth not with us,"* may have been spurred by Jesus' statement, *"Whosoever shall receive this child in My name receives Me."*

It seems that John and others had sternly forbidden one not of their company to use the name of Jesus, and now Jesus seemed to place His seal of approval on such by the manner in which He spoke concerning the child. From hearing this statement by Christ, John evidently felt that they had done wrong in this matter, which they had!

Even though John and some of the other disciples did this thing out of ignorance, still, this problem greatly persists even unto this hour.

SECTARIANISM

This is the sin of sectarianism, which, in essence, means "the exclusion of all others, outside of a particular group."

In fact, many religious denominations believe that if you are not associated with them, you are not saved, or else, at the best,

a second-class Christian, as if there were such a thing. A particular religious denom-ination comes to mind at present, which espouses the thought, in one way or the other, that if an individual is truly right with God, he will be a part of their organization. If he is not, that means that something is wrong with the person in some manner. Such thinking is not only unscriptural, but facetious to say the least!

Most of the laity has absolutely no idea of the control that many religious denom-inations attempt to exert in one way or the other over its followers. It is control exer-cised to such an extent that if the preacher does not obey their man-made rules exact-ly as they desire, they will do everything within their power to destroy that person's ministry.

In other words, they are not satisfied to just merely excommunicate the individ-ual. They must, they feel, set about to sys-tematically destroy that person's ministry, and they will use any tactic at their dis-posal, and I mean anything! It is the same spirit evidenced by the disciples when they attempted to stop the man from casting out demons in the name of Jesus *"because he followeth not with us."* Of course, the next verse will tell us Jesus' answer to that; how-ever, let's take the scenario to its conclusion as many modern denominations attempt to do. For the sake of properly explaining the situation, let's say that the disciples would not listen to Christ, but instead, began to do the following:

AN EXAMPLE

Let's say that this man was not doing anything wrong, which seems to be the case, but simply was not following with the disciples, and for that reason alone, they would set about to systematically destroy him. Not only would they demand that he cease all ministerial activity of any nature, but they would assign people to follow him in order that they may report if he, in fact, continued to cast out demons in the name of Jesus.

As well, they would write letters to every synagogue in Israel, telling them not to have this man in any capacity in any synagogue.

In other words, he was not welcome in any synagogue, even to worship. Along with that, they would put out any report they could, whether true or not, to demean his character and to destroy any influence he may have had among the people. In other words, every effort would be made that was humanly possible, and every action taken, to keep him from using the name of Jesus in order to deliver people.

Let's say, as well, for the sake of explanation, that this man was seeing scores of people delivered by the power of God. The testimonies were far and wide of people who were totally bound by the powers of darkness, but were wondrously and gloriously set free as a result of him using the mighty name of Jesus to set them free. Irrespective of that, the disciples were ignoring the tremendous number of people who were hearing from this man, and who were being set free by the power of God. They were demanding that he cease all such activity, and then were doing everything within their power to stop him, short of taking his life.

The reason?

BECAUSE HE FOLLOWS NOT WITH US

I think it becomes crystal clear that if we seriously consider this scenario, which, incidentally, happens constantly, such activity is not only not of God, but is rather satanic. The very spirit of such action is so foreign to the grace of God and so opposed to that which is of the Lord that I think one could say without any fear of scriptural contradiction that the disciples would no longer be of God, but instead, would be fighting God. Actually, the Pharisees were doing exactly that, with the disciples entering into that destructive spirit.

Let's see what Jesus said, for that is the only thing that really matters.

(50) "AND JESUS SAID UNTO HIM, FORBID HIM NOT: FOR HE WHO IS NOT AGAINST US IS FOR US."

FORBID HIM NOT

The phrase, *"And Jesus said unto him, Forbid him not,"* is straight and to the point and needs very little explanation.

No effort is to be made to hinder anyone from attempting to do the work of God. Let's look at that a little closer.

There are many men who I personally feel are not preaching the truth, and others who I feel are not particularly honest. Nevertheless, even though I will not turn my pulpit over to such individuals, still, in no way am I to seek to stop their ministry. That is between them and God. He is perfectly able to take care of His work and His own.

As an example, Judaizers were coming into the church at Corinth, attempting to undermine Paul, even demeaning his gospel of grace. Paul very strongly contended for the faith, fully espousing the true gospel, which exposed their error greatly. Still, he never called them by name one time or sought to destroy them, even though they were preaching a false message and, consequently, attempting to destroy the true work of God.

JESUS CHRIST, THE HEAD OF THE CHURCH

Paul desired that the people at Corinth, as well as elsewhere, know the Word of God well enough that they would turn a deaf ear to these deceivers. If they would do that, which they eventually did, these false teachers would have to withdraw of necessity. Actually, this is exactly what happened!

Several things are said here:

• Jesus Christ is the head of the church and not man. As well, He is an active head and not passive, as some indicate.

• Even though we must guard against false teachers, still, even that, as the example we've given of Paul, is to be done in the right way. There must never be an attempt by a believer to destroy the character or ministry of someone else, even though there may be strong disagreement. We must leave that person in the Lord's hands.

• Even though a debilitating thing may be true about a fellow believer, such is not to be spread or gossiped, but rather every effort made to bring the person to repentance by prayer and love.

• If a person desires to continue in sin, refusing to repent, while that person must be disfellowshipped, still, he is not to be treated as an enemy, and every attempt is to be made to bring him back (II Thess. 3:15).

• If a wrong has, in fact, been committed, and the person has truly repented, that individual is to be accepted and fully restored instantly, with the past being forgotten (II Cor. 2:6-9; Gal. 6:1).

WHO DO YOU THINK YOU ARE?

• No so-called religious leader has any control whatsoever, at least from a scriptural standpoint, over another person's ministry. While they may agree or disagree, still, the individual's ministry is between him and God.

• Never, under any circumstances, is one believer allowed to punish or chastise another believer. No one has that right but God. Actually, James said, *"There is one Lawgiver, who is able to save and to destroy: who are you who judges another?"* (James 4:12). In other words, James is saying "Who do you think you are, thinking you are qualified to chastise or punish another?" As we have stated, certain individuals may have to be disfellowshipped, but that is as far as it should go (I Cor., Chpt. 5).

WHAT DO WE MEAN BY DISFELLOWSHIPPED?

• It means what it says. If a person is openly sinning and refusing to repent, there is no basis for fellowship between a believer who loves God and such a person. It would mean that if such a person is holding an office in the church, he should be stripped of that office and allowed no place in that capacity. However, even that doesn't mean that such a person could not attend church. In most circumstances, it should be desired that he attend church so that the Holy Spirit may deal with his heart in order to bring him to a place of repentance. In fact, and as we have already stated, the individual should not be counted as an enemy but admonished as a brother, with every effort made to bring the person to a place of repentance. Under no circumstances are efforts to be made to close the door for the person's return, or must any silly man-made rules be fostered off upon the individual. If the Bible is not to be our standard, then what is to be the standard?

FOR HE WHO IS NOT AGAINST US IS FOR US

The heading presents a far-reaching truth.

The complaint of the disciples was not so much the man using the name of Jesus, but that he was not directly associated with their group.

It was obvious that the ministry of Christ was affecting far more people than just the immediate disciples, hence, the extended ministry.

Spence says, according to the Words of Jesus, that "no earthly society, however holy, would be able to exclusively claim the divine power inseparably connected with a true and faithful use of His name."

However, the major problem with religious denominations, and which has always existed, is the control they attempt to exert over their followers, even to blatantly violate this command of our Lord.

For instance, some years ago, a pastor of one of the local churches in Baton Rouge demanded that we take a preacher off our radio station, which was owned by Jimmy Swaggart Ministry, for the reason that he had a divorce in his background.

Actually, the man was not local and had a nationwide ministry. Scripturally, however, it did not really matter whether he was local or not.

I refused to take the man off the air for the simple reason that I believe I would have been unscriptural in doing so.

First of all, I had no knowledge whatsoever of his circumstances. As well, I was not his judge and am sternly forbidden in the Word of God to act accordingly (James 4:11-12).

NOT CHRISTLIKE

The attitude this local pastor showed was not Christlike and portrayed exactly that of which I speak. While this pastor certainly had the right to approve or disapprove this man's ministry, as well as close his pulpit to him if he so desired, he had no right whatsoever to reach out beyond his church, attempting to hurt and harm this man's ministry by having him taken off the air. To be frank, that spirit is of Satan. The idea is, if we don't like you, we will destroy you. I do not know whether the man was right or wrong respecting his divorce problem. If he was wrong, the attitude of this particular pastor constituted him doing even worse than the brother he was condemning.

As should be obvious, such attitude stems from self-righteousness and is strongly disapproved by the Lord. Actually, not being Christlike stems from Pharisaism and is what ultimately crucified the Lord.

(51) "AND IT CAME TO PASS, WHEN THE TIME WAS COME THAT HE SHOULD BE RECEIVED UP, HE STEADFASTLY SET HIS FACE TO GO TO JERUSALEM."

The synopsis is:

1. The phrase, "And it came to pass, when the time was come that He should be received up," is filled with meaning, as should be obvious.

2. This particular "time" probably involved itself in the approximate six months between the Feast of Tabernacles, which came in October, to the Passover, which came in April.

3. Spence said, "These last months were occupied by the Master in a slow progress from Capernaum, through those parts of Galilee hitherto generally unvisited by Him, gradually making His way toward the capital, which we know He reached in time for the Passover Feast, during which He was crucified."

4. However, there is evidence that Jesus did visit Jerusalem one time during this period in December. It was at the Feast of Dedication, which was appointed by Judas Maccabaeus, and was not really a feast of the Lord (Jn. 10:22-24).

5. Actually, this particular time had been in the mind of God since before the foundation of the world (I Pet. 1:20; Rev. 13:8).

6. Even though Jesus came for several reasons, with the offering of the kingdom to Israel certainly not being the least, still, His overriding purpose was the redemption of mankind, which would require His death on the Cross.

7. The phrase, "He steadfastly set His face to go to Jerusalem," is in fulfillment of the prophecy of Isaiah, "Therefore have I set My face like a flint" (Isa. 50:7).

(52) "AND SENT MESSENGERS BEFORE HIS FACE: AND THEY WENT, AND ENTERED INTO A VILLAGE OF THE SAMARITANS, TO MAKE READY FOR HIM."

The form is:

1. The phrase, "And sent messengers before His face," referred to His disciples or others, who went to make preparation for them to spend some time, at least one night, in this village.

2. "And they went, and entered into a village of the Samaritans, to make ready for Him," constituted a particular type of people who were descendants of the pagans that settled in the land at the time of the captivities. They intermarried with the few Jews who remained in the land (II Ki. 17:24-34).

3. When the Jews returned from Babylonian exile, these Samaritans sought to be allowed to share in the rebuilding of the temple, and then to be admitted as Jews to share in the privileges of the chosen people. Their wishes, however, were not complied with.

4. They were actually hated by the Jews, and this bitter hatred is noticed in the New Testament (Jn. 4:9). As well, in the synagogues, these Samaritans were cursed as a people and claimed to have no access to God.

5. In response, they erected a rival temple on Mt. Gerizim, adopting the Pentateuch as the sole sacred book.

6. They taught that the Messiah was no greater than Moses, would appear 6,000 years after creation, would live 110 years, and would lead men to the true faith.

7. Jesus repudiated this erroneous belief by saying to the Samaritans, "You worship you know not what: we know what we worship: for salvation is of the Jews" (Jn. 4:22).

However, He in no way shared in the hatred of these people by the Jews, and on more than one occasion, we find Him dealing gently and lovingly with them.

(53) "AND THEY DID NOT RECEIVE HIM, BECAUSE HIS FACE WAS AS THOUGH HE WOULD GO TO JERUSALEM."

The overview is:

1. The phrase, "And they did not receive Him," presented the greatest mistake they ever made. The Lord of Glory would come into their midst, which would have

brought them salvation and healing, but He was refused.

2. Why?

3. *"Because His face was as though He would go to Jerusalem,"* proclaimed the reason.

4. As stated, the argument was bitter between the Jews and the Samaritans, with this village evidently more bitter than some of the others. Due to this religious argument, they missed the Lord of Glory.

5. How many actually do miss the Lord simply because some particular teaching is not exactly according to their doctrine?

6. Sadly, this small village in Samaria is not the exception, but rather the rule. Many people actually serve a doctrine exactly as these Samaritans of old, and the Jews for that matter, instead of Christ. Consequently, they are unable to see the Lord because of their bias and prejudice. Millions fail to receive the baptism with the Holy Spirit for that very reason. It is not according to their particular doctrine, so it is rejected.

7. When those religious heads made the decision in that village to reject Christ, they did not know or understand what they were actually doing. Surely they knew of Jesus and were well aware of His power to heal sicknesses and perform miracles. As well, there were surely many in this village who needed healing. However, due to this bias, they would not be healed, delivered, or saved. In effect, they allowed their religion to take them to hell, as all religion ultimately does!

(54) "AND WHEN HIS DISCIPLES JAMES AND JOHN SAW THIS, THEY SAID, LORD, WILL YOU THAT WE COMMAND FIRE TO COME DOWN FROM HEAVEN, AND CONSUME THEM, EVEN AS ELIJAH DID?"

JAMES AND JOHN

The phrase, *"And when His disciples James and John saw this,"* probably proclaims the two sent to the village by Jesus seeking accommodations.

The question, *"They said, Lord, will You that we command fire to come down from heaven, and consume them, even as Elijah did?"* speaks of the incident in II Kings 1:8-15.

Jesus would show that their proposed

NOTES

solution to this problem was satanic to say the least! It should be a tremendous lesson for all!

Why did they propose such a thing?

They truly loved Jesus and were hurt deeply that He was insulted in this manner, even denied access to the village. As a result, it angered them greatly, with their response, however, reducing them to a level no higher than these Christ-rejecters.

Their spirit, at least at this time, was very similar to many modern Christians. That is the reason God cannot give much power to many because, as is obvious, they would use it to destroy people instead of saving them. Actually, most churches do destroy people instead of saving them.

The man who was casting out demons in the name of Jesus was stopped by the disciples *"because he followeth not with us."* Now, they wanted to incinerate this village because they had rejected Christ. When people begin to play God, as the disciples were here doing, the control demanded quickly degenerates into the spectacle of desiring that Jesus call fire down from heaven. It must ever be understood that religious men will do anything in the name of the Lord, and justify themselves in doing so, just as the Pharisees would crucify Christ.

RELIGION

Hundreds of thousands, if not millions, have lost their lives down through the centuries because they would not bow their knee to the pope. As well, Catholics have not always been the culprit in the case, with some Protestants following suit at times. Even though the law of the land in most countries presently prohibits such, still, this same spirit continues to exercise as much control as is legally possible. As such, the believer should be very particular about where he attends church and seek the Lord earnestly as to His will in the matter. Regrettably, the leadership in many churches and religious denominations has the same spirit as James and John had at that time and are restrained only by civil law.

I realize that most would think that I am overstating the case; however, if anything, it is being understated.

This spirit is carried by many, if not most religious people in the world, and I'll give you examples.

THE MUSLIM RELIGION

If anyone in the Muslim religion converts to Christianity, most of the time that person is killed. That is religion!

As I have related elsewhere in these volumes, sometime ago, I had the occasion to have lunch with a Jewish writer. He stated that some of the rhetoric used by some of the leading evangelicals alarmed him greatly. I shocked him somewhat when I answered that it alarmed me as well.

If they had their way, which, thankfully, the Constitution of the United States prohibits, some, if not many of the religious denominations, organizations, and particular churches, would stop every preacher in the land who did not subscribe to their particular way or adhere to their particular doctrine. They would shut up every church, not allow any preacher to preach, and stop anything that disagrees with them in any way. As stated, the only thing that prohibits such is the law of the land.

These individuals are not satisfied to have the freedom to preach the gospel as they see fit. At the same time, they desire to stop any and all who do not subscribe to their particular tenets of faith. This is the same spirit that the disciples were then portraying but, thankfully, was later changed by the Holy Spirit.

Williams said, "Zeal without knowledge, and failure to rightly divide the Word of Truth, cause well-meaning men to greatly err."

This incident and John being surnamed *"a son of thunder"* shows that his natural temperament was very different from what it became afterward. The transforming power of grace may be observed in him. One might say that he sinned against the Spirit of the gospel three times (Mat. 20:21; Lk. 9:49, 54).

(55) "BUT HE TURNED, AND REBUKED THEM, AND SAID, YOU KNOW NOT WHAT MANNER OF SPIRIT YOU ARE OF."

The structure is:

1. The phrase, *"But He turned, and rebuked them,"* is the same Word used by

Jesus when He rebuked evil spirits (Mat. 17:18). The spirit of the disciples at that time and demon spirits were all the same, hence, they were both rebuked accordingly.

2. *"And said, You know not what manner of spirit you are of,"* portrays them operating in the spirit of the Devil. The disciples did not yet fully understand the true mission of Jesus. Christianity is not to be propagated by force.

3. This spirit stemmed from their erroneous idea that Jesus was going to then become king of Israel, consequently, overthrowing Rome, with Israel once again taken to lofty heights. One can see exactly how this kingdom would be, that is, if they had total control. They would burn up anyone who disagreed with them.

4. To be outside of the will of God, as these men were at this particular time, portrays a course that is diametrically opposed to the way of the Lord. Such a course will always be accompanied by demon spirits in one way or the other. To be sure, there are far more religious spirits at work, which this was, even than those associated with the common vices.

5. We should not allow this lesson to be lost upon us. These men were with Jesus constantly and were actually His hand-picked disciples. In other words, they were chosen by the Holy Spirit. They loved God, and of that, there is no doubt. However, self-will kept intruding into the will of God because of purposely dividing the Word in a wrongful way. Actually, very few people are ignorant for the sake of ignorance, but rather because of self-will.

6. The moral is, if these men, who were the protégés directly of Christ, could fall into this type of spirit, how easy is it for others of us to do the same!

7. This spirit can only be controlled and defeated by the individual denying himself, and taking up his Cross daily, and following Jesus (Lk. 9:23).

(56) "FOR THE SON OF MAN IS NOT COME TO DESTROY MEN'S LIVES, BUT TO SAVE THEM. AND THEY WENT TO ANOTHER VILLAGE."

The overview is:

1. The phrase, *"For the Son of Man is not come to destroy men's lives, but to save*

them," proclaims the true mission of Christ. In fact, He had the power to do anything of this nature if the heavenly Father had so desired. Actually, when He was arrested in the garden of Gethsemane, He said, *"Thinkest thou that* (Do you not think that) *I cannot now pray to My Father, and He shall presently give Me more than twelve legions of angels?"* (Mat. 26:53).

2. Jesus used His power to heal, deliver, save, and help, but never to destroy. Neither He nor the Father desired to do such a thing. As well, if His children truly follow Him, they will conduct themselves as their Lord.

3. Incidentally, the apostle John, at a later period in his life (Acts 8:25), preached the gospel in a very different spirit in many villages of the Samaritans.

4. *"And they went to another village,"* constituted the greatest moment this village would ever know. Even though we are given no information, it is positive that Jesus healed all their sick and delivered all those who would come to Him. Such He will do with all who welcome Him.

(57) "AND IT CAME TO PASS, THAT, AS THEY WENT IN THE WAY, A CERTAIN MAN SAID UNTO HIM, LORD, I WILL FOLLOW YOU WHITHERSOEVER YOU GO."

The diagram is:

1. The phrase, *"And it came to pass, that, as they went in the way,"* concerned their continuing on their trip toward Jerusalem.

2. *"A certain man said unto Him, Lord, I will follow You whithersoever* (wheresoever) *You go,"* proclaimed this man, according to Matthew, as being a scribe (Mat. 8:19).

3. The scribes were, in effect, the pastors of the people of Israel. They were very closely aligned to the Pharisees and were normally very difficult to reach with the gospel. It is sad, but these individuals were supposed to be the teachers of the law for Israel. Tragically, they did not even know the Lord when He came. How similar to so many presently.

4. The natural heart is either too forward (Vs. 57), too backward (Vs. 59), or too undecided (Vs. 61).

5. These incidents proclaim the veracity of the parable of the sower. Many make a start but soon fall by the wayside.

NOTES

(58) "AND JESUS SAID UNTO HIM, FOXES HAVE HOLES, AND BIRDS OF THE AIR HAVE NESTS; BUT THE SON OF MAN HAS NOT WHERE TO LAY HIS HEAD."

The overview is:

1. *"And Jesus said unto him, Foxes have holes, and birds of the air have nests,"* proclaims the Father's natural care over His creation.

2. *"But the Son of Man has not where to lay His head,"* proclaims that Christ, one of the three members of the Godhead who created all things, was reduced by His own choice to that of the lowest of creation for man's sake. The implication regarding this scribe is that he had not counted the cost, and when revealed, did not desire to pay the price.

3. This statement by Christ is a far cry from the modern greed gospel, which promises that if believers have enough faith, they can be millionaires. This tells us that money and the things it can buy, even though necessary for the child of God, is not priority.

4. To follow Christ, the believer must be willing to forsake all and, in fact, do without all. Still, Christ has promised that if such consecration is forthcoming, He will guarantee the necessities of life (Mat. 6:19-21, 25-34).

(59) "AND HE SAID UNTO ANOTHER, FOLLOW ME. BUT HE SAID, LORD, SUFFER ME FIRST TO GO AND BURY MY FATHER."

The composition is:

1. The phrase, *"And He said unto another, Follow Me,"* presents a different appeal than the last. There, the man asked if he could follow, whereas here, Christ extended that invitation. What precipitated the call is not known! However, something in the man's heart, which the Lord evidently saw, proclaimed a desire for God. Nevertheless, it was a desire not realized.

2. *"But he said, Lord, suffer me first to go and bury my father,"* proclaims the cares of this life robbing him of preeminence with Christ. In other words, he placed other things first.

(60) "JESUS SAID UNTO HIM, LET THE DEAD BURY THEIR DEAD: BUT GO THOU AND PREACH THE KINGDOM OF GOD."

The exegesis is:

1. The phrase, *"Jesus said unto him, Let the dead bury their dead,"* was not meant to show disrespect for the dead or a shirking of responsibility. It did speak of priority. Christ speaks to all things.

2. In fact, there is no record in the Word of God that Christ ever demanded any shirking of responsibility, but rather the very opposite. It wasn't the idea of burying his father, but rather of placing such things first.

3. *"But go thou* (you go) *and preach the kingdom of God,"* means that he was one of the few called to preach and, consequently, was desperately needed. As stated, there were plenty to perform the other tasks but precious few to perform the work of God.

4. As well, this passage definitely could have a spiritual meaning, referring to false teachers, who, by their error, cause the spiritual death of many. The God-called preacher is not to waste his time trying to set all error straight, but is rather to preach the truth, which will serve as its own defense.

(61) "AND ANOTHER ALSO SAID, LORD, I WILL FOLLOW YOU; BUT LET ME FIRST GO BID THEM FAREWELL, WHICH ARE AT HOME AT MY HOUSE."

EXCUSES

The phrase, *"And another also said, Lord, I will follow You,"* is another scenario of which we have no knowledge except this given here; however, the Holy Spirit gave us this for a reason.

It is not important as to the circumstances that led up to these invitations by Christ or the desire on the part of the individual. The idea is to portray the reasoning of the heart, which too often, as here, is divided and, therefore, not acceptable!

"But let me first go bid them farewell, which are at home at my house," once again proclaims other situations demanding attention that keep the would-be believer from following Christ.

These excuses are but several of myriad, and yet, incorporate within themselves the basic excuses of all.

The first one was not willing to pay the price.

The second did not realize the high office

of his call. He felt that surely the burying of a father took preeminence over Jesus.

The third made his call a part of his everyday lifestyle. In other words, Jesus had to stand in line with the others.

HOW MUCH DOES THIS APPLY TO MODERN CHRISTIANS?

The Holy Spirit is here portraying to us the single-minded purpose that must be paramount in the lives of every believer if they are to follow Christ as they should. As well, Jesus is not speaking only of preachers, but for all who would follow Him.

To most modern Christians, living for God is a Sunday affair, if that! They feel that if they attend church on this particular day, this constitutes real consecration. In fact, most have precious little relationship with Christ, if any at all, with Him little figuring in their everyday affairs.

It should be obvious from these passages exactly what Jesus demands. It is total allegiance and total consecration.

In almost every church, the large crowd assembles on Sunday morning, with most not bothering to come during the midweek service or on Sunday nights, that is, if their church even has a Sunday night service. As someone has said, "Only those who truly love God and the paid staff show up on Wednesday nights."

(62) "AND JESUS SAID UNTO HIM, NO MAN, HAVING PUT HIS HAND TO THE PLOUGH, AND LOOKING BACK, IS FIT FOR THE KINGDOM OF GOD."

The overview is:

1. The phrase, *"And Jesus said unto him,"* notes a touch of sarcasm, and yet, a profound truth.

2. The words, *"No man,"* refer to every single believer. In other words, as stated, none are excluded. The price is the same for all!

3. *"Having put his hand to the plough,"* presents a statement drawn from agricultural imagery and, in this case, refers to one beginning to live for God. In other words, he is a sincere, genuine believer.

4. *"And looking back,"* constitutes those who allow the cares of life, riches, or other things to deter them from obeying God. Consequently, they fall by the wayside.

5. Williams said, "Attachment to Christ and to His service must be unconditional."

6. *"Is fit for the kingdom of God,"* means that God can only use those who do not look back, but rather press forward.

7. Myriad are those who have looked back and lost their way.

8. This, as should be obvious, completely refutes the unscriptural doctrine of unconditional eternal security, which teaches once saved, always saved, irrespective of the lifestyle.

"Softly and tenderly Jesus is calling,
"Calling for you and for me;
"See, on the portals He's waiting and
watching,
"Watching for you and for me."

"Why should we tarry when Jesus is
pleading,
"Pleading for you and for me?
"Why should we linger and heed not
His mercies,
"Mercies for you and for me?"

"Time is now fleeting, the moments
are passing,
"Passing from you and from me;
"Shadows are gathering, deathbeds
are coming,
"Coming for you and for me."

"O for the wonderful love He has
promised,
"Promised for you and for me;
"Though we have sinned, He has
mercy and pardon,
"Pardon for you and for me."

CHAPTER 10

(1) "AFTER THESE THINGS THE LORD APPOINTED OTHER SEVENTY ALSO, AND SENT THEM TWO AND TWO BEFORE HIS FACE INTO EVERY CITY AND PLACE, WHITHER HE HIMSELF WOULD COME."

THE APPOINTMENT
OF SEVENTY MEN

The phrase, *"After these things the Lord*

appointed other seventy also," proclaims a great spiritual truth.

Why 70?

This was the number of the elders of Israel who were chosen at the command of God by Moses (Num. 11:16).

Whether these men came from each tribe is not known. Actually, if six per tribe had been chosen, the number would have been 72. Therefore, we know that was not the method. These were men whom Moses knew to be elders of the people and officers over them. So, it is probable that representation from each tribe was not the purpose, but rather 70 trusted men, irrespective of the tribe.

The purpose was that the Spirit of God that was upon Moses, who, at least in this instance, was a type of Christ, would be taken from him and distributed to the seventy. They would then be able to function, at least in part, in the same manner as Moses.

Jesus would here appoint this seventy in much the same manner. They would be given of the Spirit of God that rested on Jesus and would then do the same works that He had been doing (Lk. 10:17-20).

So, the seventy is God's number representing His Spirit-anointed ministry.

THE CROSS

This was foreshadowed by Israel's presence at Elim almost immediately after being delivered from Egypt (Ex. 15:27). This was near the bitter waters of Marah where Moses had been instructed by the Lord to throw a tree into those waters. The tree typified Calvary, which would make the bitter waters sweet (Ex. 15:22-26).

At this time, the Lord not only healed the waters, which symbolized the bitter waters of this world, but, as well, gave the great covenant to Israel, *"For I am the LORD who heals you"* (Ex. 15:26). So, we have the entirety of the plan of God for the human family wrapped up in these few passages.

After this, they journeyed to *"Elim, where were twelve wells of water"* (Ex. 15:27). This symbolized the twelve tribes of Israel, who gave the world the prophets and the twelve apostles, which constitute the foundation of the church, with *"Jesus Christ Himself being the chief corner stone"* (Eph. 2:20).

As well, Jesus had sent out the Twelve sometime before on the same mission.

TWELVE WELLS OF WATER AND SEVENTY PALM TREES

In addition to the *"twelve wells of water"* at Elim, there were *"threescore and ten palm trees."* These 70 palm trees represent the ministry, which speaks of all God-called preachers who are supposed to have the power of Christ, which, as stated, rests on the foundation of the apostles and prophets (Ex. 15:27).

While there can never be another 12 as the original *"Twelve,"* still, the number 70 represents an unending number of God-called preachers. As well, the 70 had the same anointing as the Twelve.

This tells us also that the anointing of the Holy Spirit actually belongs to Christ (Lk. 4:18), and it is dispensed by Him to those He calls through the agency and person of the Holy Spirit.

So, as the anointing was upon Moses, likewise, it was on Christ. Also, as it was taken from Moses and given to the 70, it is now taken from Christ and given to all whom He calls, represented by the 70.

The word *appointed* has the idea of being singled out in order that it might be made known whom the Lord has chosen.

Also, the word carries the idea of not only the one chosen but, as well, what he (or she) is chosen to do. In other words, the person is appointed and given his mission, and then he is given the power to carry it out.

Inasmuch as Christ is the One who appoints, as well, those whom He appoints must never be subjected to control by other men. While the prayers, advice, and counsel of others may certainly be requested, still, those appointed belong strictly to Christ and are to be led exclusively by the Holy Spirit and not by man.

SENT THEM TWO AND TWO

The phrase, *"And sent them two and two before His face into every city and place,"* is for the following reasons:

• To help each other in tests, loneliness, and discouragements (Eccl. 4:9-12; Rom. 15:14).

NOTES

• To lift up when one fails and to be a balance in success (Eccl. 4:9-10; 12:9-10; Gal. 6:1).

• To strengthen in weakness when burdened (Rom. 15:1-5; Gal. 6:2).

• For unity in prayer (Mat. 18:19).

• For protection in attacks (Deut. 32:30; Eccl. 4:12).

• For confirmation of preaching (Deut. 17:6; 19:15; Mat. 18:16).

The phrase, *"Whither* (Where) *He Himself would come,"* spoke of places where Jesus was scheduled to come, with these appointed ones going in before Him.

As well, the entirety of this verse speaks of ministers of the gospel going all over the world to where they are sent by the Holy Spirit, and their ministering before the coming of the Lord. So, even though this method served a practical purpose, and continues to do so, still, it is well served as a broader picture of the entirety of the plan of God respecting the occupation till He comes.

PERSONAL

God has called this ministry (Jimmy Swaggart Ministries) for the entirety of the world. I realize that's quite a statement, but I know it to be true. The reason that we must go on television everywhere in the world that the door will be opened is because the Lord has told us to do so.

As well, as the Lord has called us to be sent, He has called you to do the sending. In one sense of the word, your role is just as important as my role, plus all the preachers in this organization. God calls some to be sent, and He calls others to do the sending. Both are equal in His sight. Without me being called of God, it would do you no good to send us. Due to the fact that I am called of God to do what I'm doing, He has called you, as well, to do the sending. It is an awesome responsibility, but yet, when we obey the Lord, we then have a part in unprecedented blessings.

(2) "THEREFORE SAID HE UNTO THEM, THE HARVEST TRULY IS GREAT, BUT THE LABOURERS ARE FEW: PRAY YE THEREFORE THE LORD OF THE HARVEST, THAT HE WOULD SEND FORTH LABOURERS INTO HIS HARVEST."

THE HARVEST

The phrase, *"Therefore said He unto them, The harvest truly is great, but the labourers are few,"* proclaims the need then and now!

The emphasis here placed on the bringing of souls to Jesus tells us that this is priority with God.

Is it priority with the believer?

The structure of the sentence tells us that the harvest is ever ready. In other words, it was not, nor would it be, a seasonal thing. But yet, there were few laborers, i.e., true workers for the Lord. Many claim salvation and, in fact, have truly been saved, but they seem to express little concern for proclaiming the greatest story ever told.

Who are these laborers?

In truth, every single believer is to be a laborer in the harvest; however, most are not. Why?

It is the problem of self-will, which always pulls inward. In other words, the believer is very concerned for himself, hence, the growth of the greed message. Millions have been led to believe that they can confess the right things and be rich. It is all done under a cloak of religion and, therefore, at least in this warped message, justifiable.

THE BAPTISM WITH THE HOLY SPIRIT

True Christianity always has at its heart service to others. Jesus proclaimed this constantly. As well, when one is baptized with the Holy Spirit, the gift is given basically for two great purposes:

1. To draw one nearer to Jesus Christ, thereby, understanding how to truly worship God, with Jesus becoming bigger and bigger in one's life (Jn. 16:12-15).

2. To give one power to do the works of Christ respecting the deliverance of others and bringing others to Jesus (Acts 1:8).

When people truly are following the Lord, they will conduct themselves exactly as Christ and Paul, along with the early church.

Christ came to bring men to God, which is evident in all of His ministry.

Likewise, the thrust of the early church was not a selfish greed message or a selfish emotional high, but rather a superhuman effort to take the gospel to lost regions.

So, as then, even now, *"The labourers are few."*

The phrase, *"Pray ye* (You must pray) *therefore the Lord of the harvest,"* proclaims to us two very important aspects of this all-important effort of world evangelism: Christ presents prayer as the foundation principle of the greatest work on earth—the harvest of souls, and the type the type of prayer addressed here is intercessory prayer.

Sadly, this is a type of prayer seldom engaged at the present time but is always active in any move of God, and is actually the instigator of such a move.

WHAT IS INTERCESSORY PRAYER?

Probably the greatest example of the intercessory prayer is found in Genesis 18:23-33. This is the account of Abraham interceding for his nephew Lot when God was about to destroy Sodom and Gomorrah where Lot resided. It seems that the intercession of Abraham alone saved his nephew.

As well, we must quickly add that Abraham quit asking before God quit giving. That is a tremendous statement and should not be passed over quickly.

A believer who has a prayer life of any nature will find the Holy Spirit at times interceding through him for a particular area of the world, for particular people, or even maybe one family, as Abraham. I realize that many would understand this to mean interceding for a close loved one; however, intercession, as given by the Holy Spirit, goes much further than that.

As alluded to, I believe every single move of God that has taken place in the world has always been preceded somewhere by intercessory prayer. The Holy Spirit has laid something on someone's heart (or maybe the hearts of many), with them interceding respecting that which the Holy Spirit desires. The believer must understand and remember that God has allowed His people to enter into His great plan in many and varied ways. It is done with our faith, giving, witnessing, and intercessory prayer.

However, the other side of that coin is, if God's people are so shallow that they cannot hear the Lord, this means the Holy Spirit cannot get through to such people. In that case, whatever the Lord desires to be done is not done. Please understand, as well, that if we don't do our part, then God is limited as to what He will do. As stated, He has given us the privilege and the responsibility of having a great part to play in His work.

PREDESTINATION

I believe that every single believer on the face of the earth is predestined by God for certain things—things that are mighty and wonderful. Unfortunately, most believers never realize their full potential. It is because of self-will or a lack of consecration and dedication. In fact, the reasons are many; but please understand that the Lord will never force the issue. He will speak, move, and even proclaim, but He will never force one to do what one ought to do. The truth is, due to the reasons given and many not given, only a small percentage of believers will realize their full potential in Christ. As also stated, the reasons are many; however, if you as a believer can understand that, God has great things for you. I don't care who you are or what your past has been, none of that makes any difference. He has great plans for you, but those plans will be realized only on your consecration to Him, or not realized due to that lack of consecration.

INTERCEDING

When this burden comes, it weighs heavily on the heart of the individual, with him spending much time interceding before the Lord as the Holy Spirit reveals certain needs around the world. As well, this type of prayer may continue for a period of months or even years before the answer finally comes. Nevertheless, the believer must not discontinue, lose heart, or be swayed by outward circumstances, but rather persevere until the answer comes, which it most assuredly will.

Actually, some people have been given such a burden that they seek God for great lengths of time and even die without seeing its fulfillment. However, ultimately, that intercession will bring forth fruit, sometimes

NOTES

even years after the Holy Spirit has laid it on the hearts of particular individuals.

So, if the Lord does such a thing, which He most assuredly shall if there is even a modicum of consecration, the believer must not allow circumstances, events, doubt, discouragement, or the sarcasm of other believers (regrettably) to hinder his continuing in this all-important effort.

This is the manner in which the harvest is gathered. God lays a burden on the hearts of particular people, and they intercede, sometimes not even for a particular place but just for a move of God in general.

THE SPIRIT WORLD

All of these things are played out in the spirit world long before they come to fruition in the natural. This is evidenced by Daniel's intercession as outlined in Chapter 10 of his book. The Holy Spirit had placed upon his heart a burden concerning particular world governments, and he was interceding for that. However, the great Grecian Empire for which he was interceding did not come about until many years after Daniel's death.

When one considers the magnitude of that of which we are speaking (the rise and fall of great empires), then one begins to understand how tremendously significant all of this is.

For instance, when the mighty Soviet Union fell, I think heaven will ultimately reveal that this great happening was brought about because of the intercessory prayer of believers all over the world. Many of these, no doubt, were in the Soviet Union, with others being elsewhere. Nevertheless, it was not U.S. policy that brought this about inasmuch as the State Department was taken completely by surprise at these momentous happenings.

Actually, about 30 days before the fall, I overheard one of America's leading political commentators state that such would ultimately happen but would not come to pass for about a hundred years or more. It happened in 30 days! As stated, I definitely believe it was the intercessory prayer of believers around the world, however many there were, who brought this about.

Whether it is for a single person, a close loved one, or a world empire, the *"prayer of a righteous man avails much"* (James 5:16).

GREATLY HINDERED IN THE LAST FEW YEARS

The modern faith message, at least as a whole, greatly demeans such scriptural activity, claiming that intercessory prayer is not needed, with things instead being brought about by confessing them into existence.

However, even though confession is definitely important, still, nowhere in Scripture does it state that such a thing can be done. Such error proclaims a complete misunderstanding of the Word of God. While proper confession definitely plays an important part, still, it is intercessory prayer, coupled with this great attribute, that brings about the change in the spirit world. This is what defeats demon spirits.

HOW IS THIS DONE?

Demon spirits along with fallen angels seek to hinder the plan of God from coming about in any and all circumstances. Actually, this constitutes war and is described as spiritual warfare (Eph. 6:11-18).

Paul closed out this great dissertation regarding the battle with demon spirits and fallen angels by saying, *"Praying always with all prayer and supplication in the Spirit, and watching thereunto with all perseverance and supplication for all saints"* (Eph. 6:18).

Paul is speaking of intercessory prayer.

Actually, in Ephesians, Chapter 6, Verses 19 and 20, he was admonishing the believers at Ephesus to pray for him that he may be able to properly proclaim the gospel. So, he was asking for intercessory prayer on his behalf, which he felt he desperately needed.

Whenever the believer begins to pray in the Spirit respecting the burden given by the Holy Spirit, tremendous things happen in the spirit world. Inasmuch as God has given the believer tremendous latitude, authority, and responsibility in this arena, that which He (God) does or does not do is predicated on what is done by the saints. If there is no burden of prayer, in other words, no intercessory prayer, the great things the

Lord desires to do in the realm of revival and otherwise are simply left undone. In effect, the Lord must find someone who is willing to cry to Him in order that these things be brought to pass.

It is not that God cannot do it without us. Actually, He does not need us at all. The idea is that He has allowed us to have a part in that which He does, and a very important part I might quickly add. What a privilege this is, and yet, a privilege entertained by so few.

JESUS CHRIST, THE LORD OF THE HARVEST

Christ is the One who designates the way this harvest is to be gathered. He calls certain people for certain places and lays a burden of prayer on particular hearts and lives for certain things.

This means that no committee or religious denomination can serve in this capacity, even though many erroneously attempt to do so.

As an example, the denomination with which I was formerly associated years ago had one of the greatest missions programs in the world. God touched hearts and lives regarding particular parts of the world, and these people went to these distant places, with God doing great and mighty things at times. This particular fellowship (for it was then a fellowship and not a denomination) was instrumental in helping to get this done; however, little by little the situation began to change. At the present time, very little credence is given regarding the particular place to which individuals claim God has called them. Generally, they are sent to where some committee thinks they ought to go.

As well, at present their qualifications are pretty much decided by psychological evaluation. In other words, the Holy Spirit has little if anything to say about where these people go or why they go. As a result, they are mostly man-led at present, with very little actually being done for the Lord.

This means that Jesus Christ is no longer Lord of the harvest in that particular domain, but instead, men have usurped His position. As such, the Holy Spirit will have no part in that which is man-directed. Consequently, very little is done for God, even though there is much religious machinery in motion, with many erroneously thinking that much is being done.

LABOURERS INTO HIS HARVEST

The phrase, *"That He would send forth labourers into His harvest,"* proclaims His direction and leading. He is the one who sends the laborers and not man. This is done in many ways.

It is done with many who give primarily of their money in order that this might be carried out. They are to be led and directed by the Holy Spirit in this. Sadly, the far greater majority of funds supposedly given for world evangelism little go to take the gospel to hurting souls, but rather to man-instituted projects or the bloated religious bureaucracy.

Others are called to pray, and that is what we mean by "intercessory prayer."

Others are actually called as preachers of the gospel, with others sending the ones who are called. Paul places both the preacher who is sent and the believers who do the sending on the same level of importance (Rom. 10:15).

A PERSONAL EXAMPLE

On July 1, 1985, on a Monday morning at about 7 a.m., the Lord did something that involved our ministry and, as well, was meant for the entirety of the world.

Actually, this was my custom every morning: I would drive my car to a particular place that was near some railroad tracks about a half mile or more from our house. I would sit in the car for awhile studying the Word, and then I would walk down the tracks praying. Little did I realize what would happen.

As I finished studying, I then proceeded to walk down the tracks, praying as I went. All of a sudden, everything changed around me. As far as the eye could see in every direction, it seemed that the world had turned into an ocean of cotton. After the vision ended, and it was a vision, I remembered the words of our Lord when He said, *"Say not ye* (Do not say), *There are yet four months, and then*

comes harvest? behold, I say unto you, Lift up your eyes, and look on the fields; for they are white already to harvest" (Jn. 4:35).

Then I looked to my left, and I saw the worst storm that I had ever witnessed coming out of the east. The heavens had turned an inky black, with jagged forks of lightning cutting through the heavens.

I looked into the distance, and I could see two or three mechanical cotton pickers attempting to gather the harvest. I knew that if this harvest wasn't gathered immediately, the storm was going to destroy it all.

I believe this harvest pictures the last great move of God in this respect before the coming great tribulation. The great tribulation will come out of the east (Rev. 16:12).

THEN THE LORD SPOKE TO ME

He said to me, "Put the telecast in every city in the world that will accept it. I will hold back the storm for a period of time until the work can be accomplished." He then said, "Don't fail me." Then He said, "I have called other ministries for particular localities, but I've called this ministry (Jimmy Swaggart Ministries) for the entirety of the world."

I did my very best to obey the Lord as He had said, but events came to pass that made it impossible for me to finish the task, even though we tried with all of the effort that we had.

Then in 2011 while in prayer, the Lord helped me to relive that scene all over again. When it was completed in my heart, He spoke to me, saying, "The commission that I gave you in 1985 is still in force now. Place the programming in every city in the world that will accept it, and as I told you in 1985, I will hold back the storm for awhile until it can be done."

That's the reason for our urgency! That's the reason for our haste! In fact, that's the reason for what we do. I must not be disobedient to the heavenly vision. Please understand this:

For this that the Lord has called us to do, He has, as well, called you. The Lord calls some to be sent, even as He has me, and He calls others to do the sending, even as He has you. We must not fail Him! Too much is at stake, in fact, more than any of us could even begin to imagine. The harvest truly is white and the laborers are few.

(3) "GO YOUR WAYS: BEHOLD, I SEND YOU FORTH AS LAMBS AMONG WOLVES."

The pattern is:

1. The phrase, *"Go your ways,"* respects those the Lord has called, and for all time. It refers to now as then. These *"labourers"* have a distinct commission from the Lord, and that commission is to be obeyed.

2. *"Behold, I send you forth as lambs among wolves,"* presents something not ordinarily done. No shepherd deliberately sends his sheep among wolves, but this shepherd can because He is almighty to save. It actually relates to Psalm 23.

3. However, the protection is not automatic but requires faith on the part of the one so commissioned.

4. Inasmuch as Christianity is not to be propagated by the sword, the protection is afforded solely from the Chief Shepherd, making Christianity totally unlike the religions of the world.

5. Regrettably, the wolves mentioned here spring mostly from the religious type. In fact, the secular wolves, symbolized by Rome, were not nearly as vicious as the religious wolves, i.e., Pharisees. The same holds true presently!

(4) "CARRY NEITHER PURSE, NOR SCRIP, NOR SHOES: AND SALUTE NO MAN BY THE WAY."

The exegesis is:

1. The entirety of this passage is meant to emphasize that nothing must hinder the commission from being carried out.

2. The phrase, *"Carry neither purse,"* does not refer to a declaration of poverty, but that one is to go when called and not wait until a certain amount of money is amassed. Neither does it mean that it is improper to have or raise funds, but only that no time is to be lost in attempting to gather more funds.

3. As well, such does not refer to missionaries securing support. It only refers to individuals with a call of God not trusting God to meet their needs and, consequently, delaying the carrying out of the call for an extended period of time, or possibly not going at all.

NOTES

4. The words, *"Nor scrip,"* pertain to a leather provision bag of travelers and shepherds.

5. As well, such is not actually condemned, but the thought is projected that one should not attempt to engage in unnecessary business affairs as well as answer the call. In fact, Paul would later say, which was probably taken from this very statement by Christ, *"No man who wars entangles himself with the affairs of this life; that he may please Him who has chosen him to be a soldier"* (II Tim. 2:4).

The words, *"Nor shoes,"* actually refer to a second pair of shoes. As well, such did not mean that having two pairs (or even several pairs) was wrong, but that one is not to fail in the call, claiming that he does not have proper clothing, or in modern terminology, proper transportation.

"And salute no man by the way," does not refer to normal courtesies, which every Christian should extend, but that no person is to be allowed to stop one from the carrying out of this Great Commission.

None of these statements are meant to be taken literally, only that the significance of the call is presented, and that it must not be stopped or hindered.

(5) "AND INTO WHATSOEVER HOUSE YOU ENTER, FIRST SAY, PEACE BE TO THIS HOUSE."

The synopsis is:

1. The phrase, *"And into whatsoever house you enter,"* proclaims the invitation extended. No believer is to impose on others but at all times accept only when invited.

2. *"First say, Peace be to this house,"* proclaims the blessing promised by the Lord to any who aid and abet those He has called and are attempting to carry out their commission.

3. The *"peace"* here promised by the Lord is, in fact, a blessing of unparalleled proportions. First of all, it refers to prosperity and means that God will bless such a house in a financial sense.

4. It also refers to quietness and rest, which speaks of a cessation of hostility. Regrettably, many homes do not have such peace and are troubled by dissension and rebellion; however, the presence of such

a God-called one will command the spirit world of hindrance to subside.

5. It also means to "set at one again," which speaks of agreement.

6. Consequently, one can see just how important this blessing of peace actually is.

7. As well, this promise, as given by Christ, extends to every house that merely supports a God-called man or woman. This means that every believer who attends a church and supports that particular ministry falls into this category. Consequently, which church or ministry one supports is very important. Many are not God-called and, therefore, experience no blessing.

(6) "AND IF THE SON OF PEACE BE THERE, YOUR PEACE SHALL REST UPON IT: IF NOT, IT SHALL TURN TO YOU AGAIN."

THE SON OF PEACE

The phrase, *"And if the son of peace be there,"* actually refers to one who desires the blessings of the Lord attempting to serve in any capacity possible. It is one who truly understands the significance and priority of the call of God on the life of an individual. He is to aid and abet in that call, thereby, referred to by Jesus as *"the Son of peace."*

What a beautiful phrase!

Regrettably, the sons of peace are not as plentiful as one would desire.

The phrase, *"Your peace shall rest upon it,"* means that the son of peace is the recipient of peace because he fully understands the role he is playing respecting the help extended to God's called ones.

IT SHALL TURN TO YOU AGAIN

The phrase, *"If not, it shall turn to you again,"* proclaims that any hindrance in this all-important task stops the blessings of God from being extended to that person or area.

Any nation that has a sizable number of God-called ones will experience peace to the extent that these *"ones"* are helped and not hindered.

For instance, upon her rejection of Christ, Israel attempted to stamp out the early church and, consequently, saw the peace of God withdrawn from that nation. Actually, it was withdrawn to such an extent

NOTES

that it was completely destroyed in A.D. 70.

A PERSONAL EXPERIENCE

In 1992, some of the governmental leaders of the African country of Zaire requested that we place our telecast on their network in their nation. We did this almost immediately, with the program translated into French, inasmuch as Zaire is a French-speaking country.

They told me that their country was in deep trouble, and they felt the only solution was the gospel of Jesus Christ. They actually aired the program daily for a period of time even though they were only furnished one program a week.

About two years later, several government officials from various African French-speaking countries visited our office in Baton Rouge, Louisiana.

After all the greetings were extended, the government official from Zaire spoke to me, stating that he felt his country had been saved from what looked like certain anarchy because of our telecast and, actually, because of the gospel we preach. He said, "Brother Swaggart, had it not been for your telecast, I believe that what happened in Rwanda, with the loss of some 500,000 lives, would have taken place in Zaire as well."

Many may doubt that statement; however, I believe it to be true. The gospel has that kind of power!

This country desired the gospel, and consequently, God's peace rested upon it exactly as Jesus said!

(7) "AND IN THE SAME HOUSE REMAIN, EATING AND DRINKING SUCH THINGS AS THEY GIVE: FOR THE LABOURER IS WORTHY OF HIS HIRE. GO NOT FROM HOUSE TO HOUSE."

The structure is:

1. The phrase, *"And in the same house remain, eating and drinking such things as they give,"* certainly applied to a single house but, more importantly, applies to the field of ministry assigned by the Lord. In modern terms, the idea would be that total diligence is to be given to the ministry, making do with whatever finances are afforded. Too many times preachers become entangled with the things of this world,

attempting to increase their salaries. While these things in themselves may not be sinful or wrong, still, they can be a hindrance to the devotion of one's total life and being to the ministry. Such is not to be!

2. The phrase, *"For the labourer is worthy of his hire,"* is quoted by Paul in I Timothy 5:18. It is stated to be *"Scripture."*

3. Inasmuch as the preacher is to be satisfied with that which is given, on the other hand, the *"house"* or *"church"* should realize the worth of such a God-called one and attempt to meet his needs (within reason) in order that he may devote full attention to the work at hand. To be sure, it is not a gift as the Lord says he is worthy of his hire.

4. *"Go not from house to house,"* in effect, meant that early church pioneers were not to go from place to place seeking better accommodations, but to be satisfied with what they were offered.

5. In modern terms, it refers to preachers seeking better churches simply because they pay more money. Money is never to be the object, with the call of God only dictating place and position.

(8) "AND INTO WHATSOEVER CITY YOU ENTER, AND THEY RECEIVE YOU, EAT SUCH THINGS AS ARE SET BEFORE YOU."

WHEREVER!

The phrase, *"And into whatsoever city you enter,"* concerns the taking of the gospel of Jesus Christ to the world. It also has reference to the Holy Spirit leading God's man or woman to a particular place. In other words, the Spirit of God chooses the place instead of the individual.

The greatest thing that could ever happen to a city anywhere in the world is for the gospel of Jesus Christ to be brought to that place.

In 1939, the gospel was brought to our little town. Two women came, stretched a tent, and began to preach. As a result of that meeting, a small church was built where, eventually, most of my family came to Christ.

There were other churches in our small city, but I seriously doubt a single one of them preached the gospel. So, until the gospel came, as mentioned, our town probably

did not have a single church where a person could truly accept Christ.

GOD'S METHODS

Maybe I cannot actually remember it, being only 4 years old, but it seems that I can recall the first service we were in. My dad played the violin and had been invited to come and play in the "church orchestra." The orchestra consisted of an upright piano, guitar, and another brother who played the violin. My dad carried his violin wrapped in a pillow case simply because he could not afford a violin case. He had never been in church in his life.

It seems that I remember him walking upon the platform with his violin under his arm. He was to play in the church orchestra that night even though he had never heard a single Christian song in all his life; however, that night was to change our lives.

Once again, I am not certain, but it seems that the first song was:
"I have found a friend in Jesus,
"He's everything to me,
"He's the fairest of ten thousands to my soul."

Even though my parents were not saved that night, they did begin on the road that would ultimately lead to their salvation a short time later. As stated, that was in 1939. I was 4 years old. In 1943, at 8 years of age, Jesus Christ came into my life, with an experience that has stood the test unto this particular time.

Yes! When Jesus was brought to our city and to our house, the whole world changed.
"Oh happy day, Oh happy day,
"When Jesus washed my sins away."

RECEIVE

The phrase, *"And they receive you,"* also implies by its structure that at times the man or woman of God will not be received. Actually, a certain village in Samaria would not receive Jesus, exactly as we studied in the previous chapter. Consequently, all that the gospel could have given was eternally lost. Thank God for those who do receive the man of God.

"Eat such things as are set before you," actually leans in several directions:

• The man of God, though called of God and, thereby, signally honored, still is to conduct himself in the same manner as all others. The puffed-up, egotistical spirit is foreign to those who truly follow after the Spirit.

This is a problem among many Charismatic preachers. They desire to be treated in a kingly fashion, with someone opening the door for them, helping them with their coats, or other silly things, which should not be a part of the man of God.

• As well, the phrase points to the workman being worthy of his hire. Those who are kind enough to furnish the meal, or whatever, are not to think that such is a gift, but all should understand that whatever the man of God receives, he has earned it.

• If the fare is meager, irrespective as to how meager, the preacher of the gospel is to say nothing about it, but instead, be thankful.

Such statements as given by Christ must seem somewhat mundane to the unspiritual eye. However, in reality, Jesus is dealing with the very motivation and heart position of those He has called. Most of the time, people's actions are motivated by the condition of their heart. So, the obedience or disobedience to these simple commands shows what the person really is.

(9) "AND HEAL THE SICK WHO ARE THEREIN, AND SAY UNTO THEM, THE KINGDOM OF GOD IS COME NIGH UNTO YOU."

HEAL THE SICK

The phrase, *"And heal the sick who are therein,"* proclaims the tremendous blessing that comes to all who eagerly and kindly accept those whom God sends.

The word *heal* not only refers to the sick, but, as well, it has the connotation of the word *servant.* In other words, the man or woman of God is to be a servant serving the people. It means that prayer for the sick and their healing are a part of what the God-called one has to offer. It is to be done with a servant spirit and not as of some great one.

As well, the word *sick* from the Greek text has the idea not only of one being sick physically but spiritually. Only the gospel

NOTES

of Jesus Christ can ameliorate such a condition. So, it refers not only to the physical but the spiritual also.

THE KINGDOM OF GOD

"And say unto them, The kingdom of God is come nigh (near) *unto you,"* refers to the power of God and the tremendous change it brings about in hearts and lives, all made possible by the Cross of Christ.

When a person comes to Christ, he comes into the kingdom of God and, consequently, the economy of God. Even though he continues to be in the world, he is no longer of the world. Salvation brings one into God's program, which touches every facet of one's life. It deals with our employment, home, marriage, family, and activities of every sort. It actually proclaims a way of life that is totally different from anything else in the world. The person becomes enamored with Jesus Christ and with God's Word, which fulfills every need, be it spiritual, physical, mental, or material. In other words, it is a brand new culture.

As an example, I am an American citizen living in the United States of America. As such, I obey the laws of the land and do my best to make a contribution to the community; however, my allegiance first of all is to Christ. He comes before everything. If the law of the land violates the law of God, I must refuse to obey the law of the land. As well, I must understand that I will have to pay the consequences, whatever they are. Nevertheless, God comes first in everything and fills every other void as well!

JOINING THE CHURCH ...

Consequently, merely joining a church, as many do, has absolutely no bearing on entering into the kingdom of God. One enters this kingdom by being born again, which is the total requirement (Jn. 3:3).

The religion of Islam has attempted to emulate Bible Christianity but without any success whatsoever. It has words that are not the Word of God, consequently, there is no power. Conversely, the kingdom of God is not in word only *"but in power"* (I Cor. 4:20; II Tim. 1:7). This power, and this power alone, can change one's life. Neither Islam nor any other religion in the world changes anything but for the worse.

(10) "BUT INTO WHATSOEVER CITY YOU ENTER, AND THEY RECEIVE YOU NOT, GO YOUR WAYS OUT INTO THE STREETS OF THE SAME, AND SAY."

The overview is:

1. The phrase, *"But into whatsoever city you enter,"* begins exactly as Verse 8 but takes the opposite direction.

2. *"And they receive you not,"* means, as is obvious, that some places will not receive the gospel.

3. However, it is very important that even though they do not receive, they have the opportunity to hear.

4. *"Go your ways out into the streets of the same, and say,"* proclaims that the gospel must not be forced on anyone. That which is not desired is not to be given. Islam is spread by the sword. Christianity is not to function in that capacity at all.

(11) "EVEN THE VERY DUST OF YOUR CITY, WHICH CLEAVES ON US, WE DO WIPE OFF AGAINST YOU: NOTWITH-STANDING BE YE SURE OF THIS, THAT THE KINGDOM OF GOD IS COME NIGH UNTO YOU."

THE DUST

The phrase, *"Even the very dust of your city, which cleaves on us, we do wipe off against you,"* has to do with the coming great white throne judgment (Rev. 20:11-15).

The idea is that the record is carefully kept that this city, wherever it may have been, was visited by God; therefore, they have no excuse. This is how carefully the Holy Spirit records each and every visitation. In other words, the very dust of their city that clings to the shoes of the man of God is to be used as a witness against the place.

THE KINGDOM OF GOD HAS COME NEAR

The phrase, *"Notwithstanding be ye* (you be) *sure of this, that the kingdom of God is come nigh* (near) *unto you,"* presents a strong argument by the Holy Spirit. It is actually an argument that is irrefutable, which says, in effect, that the Lord offered them the kingdom but to no avail.

From this we learn how insistent the Holy Spirit is that every person have the opportunity to hear the gospel, whether they accept it or not. As we have stated previously, the reason is clear. The whole of humanity will one day stand before God, with many, no doubt, saying, "I am condemned to eternal perdition, but I never had an opportunity to even hear the gospel, much less to accept or reject!"

Considering what God has done in the giving of His only Son to save the human family, and then for the church to show precious little inclination in this all-important task, but rather run from one fad to the other, casts the Lord in a very bad light. One day, every believer will have to stand before God and give account of exactly what he did to help take the gospel to the world. It is one thing for an area to have the opportunity to hear the gospel and then reject it and quite something else altogether to not have any opportunity at all.

THE GOSPEL OF JESUS CHRIST

I personally feel that the responsibility of the believer in the taking of the gospel to lost humanity is going to be the area of the greatest accountability. Many things that we think are so important will probably be little discussed, but it will rather be this for which Jesus died—the salvation of lost humanity.

To be sure, every single believer is to have a part in this all-important task. Even though only a few may actually go, still, every single believer can pray and give. Consequently, the praying and giving is incumbent upon all. There is no excuse, at least for these two responsibilities.

(12) "BUT I SAY UNTO YOU, THAT IT SHALL BE MORE TOLERABLE IN THAT DAY FOR SODOM, THAN FOR THAT CITY."

The overview is:

1. The phrase, *"But I say unto you,"* places Christ in the position as judge. Now He is Saviour; then He will be the judge of all humanity.

2. *"That it shall be more tolerable in that day for Sodom, than for that city,"* concerns itself with opportunity.

3. Sodom had very little opportunity,

other than the ministries of Abraham and Lot, and Lot's ministry was hopelessly compromised.

4. So, we are given to understand that every city in the world evangelized by a man or woman of God, if rejected, will be judged far more severely even than the notorious city of evil, Sodom.

5. What will the cities of America and Canada say when they stand before God after having so many opportunities? Actually, the only cities on earth that have had more opportunity are those visited by Jesus in His earthly ministry. Consequently, He will now address that.

(13) "WOE UNTO YOU, CHORAZIN! WOE UNTO YOU, BETHSAIDA! FOR IF THE MIGHTY WORKS HAD BEEN DONE IN TYRE AND SIDON, WHICH HAVE BEEN DONE IN YOU, THEY HAD A GREAT WHILE AGO REPENTED, SITTING IN SACKCLOTH AND ASHES."

The exegesis is:

1. The phrase, *"Woe unto you, Chorazin! woe unto you, Bethsaida!"* proclaims two cities where mighty works were performed by Jesus.

2. In this account, we are led to believe that Jesus did many great and wonderful things that are not recorded in the gospels because there is no record of Him doing anything in Chorazin. However, He says here that mighty works had been done in this city, plus Bethsaida.

3. It is said that the ruins of Chorazin have been discovered near Capernaum.

4. The phrase, *"For if the mighty works had been done in Tyre and Sidon, which have been done in you,"* speaks of two cities on the Mediterranean in the present country of Lebanon. As should be obvious, they were Gentile.

"They had a great while ago repented, sitting in sackcloth and ashes," proclaims the terrible rebellion of the cities of Israel against Christ. Jesus plainly said that if the Gentile cities of *"Tyre and Sidon"* had had the opportunity of His ministry as the cities of Israel, they would have repented, and grandly so.

5. Spence says, "A great theological truth is urged in this saying of the Master. Men

will be judged not only for what they have done or failed to do, but their opportunities, their circumstances, their chances in life, will be, before they are judged, strictly taken into account."

(14) "BUT IT SHALL BE MORE TOLERABLE FOR TYRE AND SIDON AT THE JUDGMENT, THAN FOR YOU."

JUDGED AT CALVARY

As we have already stated, men will answer to God not only for acts committed but for opportunities as well.

Of what kind of judgment is Jesus speaking?

In effect, every human being who has ever lived has been judged or will be judged.

Those who have already been judged are those who have accepted Christ as their Saviour and, in effect, were judged in Christ when He suffered the judgment of God on the Cross in our place. Consequently, all who have placed their trust in Him will never be judged for sin or sins because they have been judged in Him (II Cor. 5:17-19).

THE JUDGMENT SEAT OF CHRIST

This judgment will take place in heaven, and the judge will be the Lord Jesus Christ.

At this judgment seat, no believer will ever be judged for his sins inasmuch as that has already been done in Christ. However, we will be judged as it regards our motivation and our faithfulness, or the lack thereof. While believers may lose all or part of our reward because of wrong motivation and a lack of faithfulness, we will not lose our souls (I Cor. 3:11-15; II Cor. 5:10).

THE GREAT WHITE THRONE JUDGMENT

Every unbeliever will appear at the great white throne judgment as outlined in Revelation 20:11-15. They will be *"judged every man according to their works."* In other words, every single thing done is written down in books in heaven.

However, the record of the things done only serves to show their guilt and has nothing to do with one's salvation or the lack thereof. Works, good or bad, do not constitute salvation; only faith in Christ does.

After being shown a record of their works, they will also be shown the Book of Life and that their name is not written therein. All will then be *"cast into the lake of fire."*

This judgment will take place on earth, and Christ will be the judge. This means that every unsaved person on the face of the earth will face Christ. You will face Him at the judgment seat of Christ or the great white throne judgment, but face Him you will.

JUDGMENT—A BIBLE DOCTRINE

The idea of a judgment is foreign to the thinking of most people. Actually, even most believers little comprehend such, with most preachers ignoring this doctrine; however, it is ignored at one's peril.

At least one of the major causes for such unbelief is because the entirety of the world has been so psychologized to one extent or the other.

The Bible claims that all are responsible for their own sins and life and will be judged accordingly. Psychology claims that the individual is not responsible, with the blame being placed on environment, abuse as a child, etc. Consequently, the idea that men will one day stand before God and be judged accordingly is foreign to the thinking of a psychologized world and church. Nevertheless, it will happen.

If this were preached behind most pulpits, quite possibly, men would think twice before they commit some particular acts. In fact, if every believer understood this concerning the judgment seat of Christ, perhaps they might order their lives somewhat differently.

Man's sins will either be covered and washed away here by the blood of Jesus, which is done upon faith in Him and what He did for us at the Cross, or else, man will face those sins at the judgment bar of God.

Man has a choice!

As well, this passage tells us that there will be degrees of punishment in the judgment, as stated, by the Master Himself.

Blackest were the sins of Sodom, Tyre, and Sidon, and yet the sin of rejecting the gospel is the greatest of all sins.

(15) "AND YOU, CAPERNAUM, WHICH ARE EXALTED TO HEAVEN, SHALL BE THRUST DOWN TO HELL."

CAPERNAUM

The phrase, *"And you, Capernaum,"* constituted a city situated on the western shore of the Sea of Galilee. This was the small city chosen by the Holy Spirit to be the earthly headquarters of the Son of God during His earthly ministry.

Capernaum was near a most copious spring, which was actually called *"Seven Springs."* These were warm springs that were high in mineral content and served as a healing spring of a sort where the sick and afflicted came to bathe. In one way it was an apt description and symbolism of the greatest one of all who would be the healer of all mankind, the Lord Jesus Christ.

It is said that this entire western shore of the Sea of Galilee was lined with heavily populated towns and villages. Actually, this was the most prosperous area of Israel. The blue lake was covered with fishing and trading vessels. One of the great trade routes ran near the city, linking the Mediterranean, as well as the trade routes from north to south. Josephus said there were approximately 250,000 people in Galilee at that time.

Of all the miracles performed by Christ, it was here where He, no doubt, performed the most, even to the raising of the dead.

EXALTED TO HEAVEN

The phrase, *"Which are* (is) *exalted to heaven,"* refers to the Holy Spirit choosing this place as the headquarters of Christ. Of all the places in Israel, this was the chosen spot and, consequently, blessed immeasurably so. But yet, it seemed not to know Who was in its midst. Even though the citizenry of Capernaum did not turn on Christ as His hometown of Nazareth did, still, they little accepted Him either.

While thousands flocked to His side when He was actually in the city, still, most of the religious leaders, with the exception of a few, rejected Him. They would have been swayed heavily by Jerusalem; consequently, they had a choice! They could accept the Son of God, or they could kowtow to the religious hierarchy. They could not do both!

Regrettably, this situation has little changed. Religious hierarchies are almost always opposed to Christ even though they tout His name in one way or the other. They seek to exert great control over those under them, and if that control seems to be threatened in any way, they will then seek to destroy, using any means at their disposal.

As it was then, so it is now. The laity little knows or understands these things, and yet, the signs are so obvious. However, sheep generally follow whatever type of shepherd is leading them, irrespective that he may be a wolf in sheep's clothing.

THRUST DOWN TO HELL

The phrase, *"Shall be thrust down to hell,"* constitutes the severest pronounced punishment.

Much light was given, actually, the greatest light of all, but firmly rejected. They accepted Jesus as a teacher, or maybe even a prophet, but not as the Messiah, the Promised One of the prophets.

Josephus tells us that some 30 years after this *"woe"* had been uttered by Jesus, Rome ravaged this garden of Gennesaret and changed it into a ruin-covered solitude.

He said every town and village, including Capernaum, was completely destroyed, with the shores of the Sea of Galilee strewn with wrecks and putrefying bodies.

However, that judgment was only the beginning. The religious leaders of Capernaum will stand one day at the great white throne judgment and give account for the greatest light of all, which they rejected. Actually, the very one they stand before will be the same Jesus who had originally been in their midst, and they rejected. He was then their Saviour, and pleaded to be so, but now will be their judge.

Actually, the only city left standing on the shore of the Sea of Galilee is the city of Tiberias. It was built about 10 years before the ministry of Christ and was inhabited mostly by Gentiles. There is no record that Christ ever visited it.

From all of this, we realize that the acceptance of the gospel brings blessings of unprecedented proportions; however, the rejection of the gospel brings destitution and ruin.

(16) "HE WHO HEARS YOU HEARS

NOTES

ME; AND HE WHO DESPISES YOU DESPISES ME; AND HE WHO DESPISES ME DESPISES HIM WHO SENT ME."

HEARING PREACHERS SENT BY THE LORD JESUS CHRIST

The phrase, *"He who hears you hears Me,"* proclaims spiritual authority given to the messenger of the Lord; consequently, great is the dignity of the gospel messenger, though he be poor or even uneducated. In effect, Jesus is saying that when a God-called man or woman stands before people to deliver a message given by the Lord, it is the same as Jesus standing before those people and delivering it Himself. Such is a solemn statement and is meant to be so.

REJECTING GOD-CALLED PREACHERS

The phrase, *"And he who despises you despises Me,"* is fearsome indeed! There is no way that one could overstate this case. This means, and is properly stated, that the manner in which the man or woman of God is treated will ensure either blessing or judgment; consequently, no hand must be lifted against the one called of the Lord.

This in no way means that wrongdoing should be condoned in any manner. However, it also means that no fellow believer, irrespective of whom he thinks he may be, must take it upon himself to hinder, chastise, or punish the anointed of the Lord. That right is reserved by God alone. At one point in David's life, he did terribly wrong and paid for it severely; however, that did not give Absalom and Israel the right to rebel against him and attempt to destroy him. They had taken upon themselves a task that they could not hope to win, irrespective of their seeming strength. Their efforts were doomed to failure because this was God's man, irrespective of what had transpired.

To be sure, the actions of Absalom and those with him were not actions of righteousness, but rather of rebellious self-will. The statement is plain. When you strike God's messenger, you strike God. When you despise the one sent by the Lord, in effect, you are despising the Lord Himself. According to the words of Christ, it is impossible to separate the two.

As well, I think it would be obvious that if one blesses the messenger sent by the Lord, God will greatly bless such a person because as they bless His messenger, they are blessing Him.

IF WE DESPISE CHRIST, WE DESPISE GOD

The phrase, *"And he who despises Me despises Him who sent Me,"* refers to God the Father.

This statement pertains to the entirety of the plan of God. In other words, Jesus is saying that when His messenger is despised, in effect, one is despising the entirety of the plan of God and attempting to hinder it, thereby, in league with Satan.

As well, let us remember that these statements little concern the world, but rather religious leaders. The Lord will have patience with the world who rejects His messengers much longer than He will the church. All of what He is saying is directed at the religious leaders of Israel proper and little directed toward Rome. This tells us that the greatest hindrance to the true work of God on earth is seldom the world, but rather the church. It was then, and it is now. It must always be remembered that it was not the hated publicans who put Jesus on the Cross, but rather the church of that day.

Satan is a religious being and functions best in that realm. He does his work best by using religious men who wrest control of the body away from Christ and maliciously usurp authority. We might quickly add that it is all done in the name of the Lord.

RELIGION

As an example, the Assemblies of God, the largest Pentecostal denomination in the world, would have once bridled if anyone had referred to it as a denomination, and rightly so! It was originally formed in 1914 as a fellowship of churches with a like purpose of doctrine and a driving ambition to touch the world with the gospel of Jesus Christ. Consequently, its thrust was the salvation of mankind, which referred to the entirety of the world.

In that mode, God blessed it abundantly in that it did touch the world. However, this

NOTES

was not because of its constitution and by-laws, or any hierarchical structure, because it did not have such, at least regarding hierarchy. God blessed it as He always blesses by touching particular individuals, who, in this movement (and a movement it was) had the freedom to follow the call of God within their lives.

However, as time passed and the blessings of God became more and more pronounced, little by little religious men began to gain control until the fellowship gradually became a denomination. Then denominationalism crept in, with a religious hierarchy being formed and unscriptural control being exerted over churches and preachers. Today, it is bloated and big but, at the same time, weak and sickly, at least in a spiritual sense.

PENTECOSTAL?

Once it was truly Pentecostal, but now, it is Pentecostal in name only. Of course, there are still some godly preachers and godly laity in its confines; however, as a whole, it has by and large ceased to be of any benefit to the cause of Christ.

Now, if any person associated with the Assemblies of God reads this statement and grows angry, this is a sign that little spiritual discernment is present, and that their eyes are on this religious denomination instead of Christ. One of the first signs of denominationalism is acute anger expressed toward constructive criticism. For one to constructively criticize does not mean that one is bitter or that one seeks to destroy that being addressed. It is actually the other way around, with the strong desire that this terrible wrong direction be recognized and corrected.

Jesus is plainly saying in these statements that when men fight God, they cannot win, irrespective of how weak the messenger may seem and how strong the opposition may be. It is actually God they are fighting and not the poor messenger.

(17) "AND THE SEVENTY RETURNED AGAIN WITH JOY, SAYING, LORD, EVEN THE DEVILS ARE SUBJECT UNTO US THROUGH YOUR NAME."

THE SEVENTY

The phrase, *"And the seventy returned*

again with joy," speaks of the mission from which they had just returned and the joy they had because of the great victories that had been won.

"Saying, Lord, even the devils (demons) *are subject unto us through Your name,"* concerns the power that had been given unto them by Christ.

To be sure, this was only the beginning, and it continues unto this hour. Even as Jesus was about to ascend to the Father, He said, *"And these signs shall follow them who believe; in My name shall they cast out devils* (demons)*"* (Mk. 16:17). This power was not meant just for the *"Twelve"* or the *"seventy,"* but actually for all believers and for all time.

This means that the religion of ceremony, as beautiful as it may be, is of no consequence and, in fact, is not of God. It also means that religious intellectualism serves no purpose, at least as far as delivering people is concerned. As well, this strikes down humanistic psychology, which has no part, nor can it have a part in the work of God.

As should be obvious, this eliminates almost all Catholic and Protestant churches, for most fall into one or more of these categories.

THE DREAM

This which is commissioned by Jesus Christ and empowered by the Holy Spirit will set the captive free. It alone can perform this task, but sadly, very little deliverance is being presently performed because there are very few true believers. There are many professors but few believers!

Even though I have given the following in one of the previous volumes, I feel it would be proper to relate it again, and hopefully, it will be of help to Bible students.

In 1953, the Lord gave me a dream, which I believe was a portrayal of certain things that would happen to me in the future, which involved the work of God and the victory given. Frances and I had married in 1952, and Donnie would be born in 1954. I had just begun to preach. Even in those beginning years of preaching the gospel, it seemed that the powers of darkness opposed my efforts in an inordinate way. Maybe the way was actually no more difficult than

NOTES

others; however, it seemed to be so intense that at times I could hardly stand it. To be sure, that opposition has not stopped unto this day; however, I face it now in an entirely different manner, understanding somewhat more about the Word of God and my position in Christ.

The dream that was given to me, I definitely believe and actually know was from the Lord. As well, after the passing of much time and the seeking of His face incessantly regarding its meaning, I believe my interpretation (as will here be given) is from the Lord.

THE HOUSE

In the dream I found myself in a particular house with which I was not familiar. I remember standing in the middle of a large room with very high walls. I looked around, wondering why I was there, especially considering that I recognized nothing. Actually, the room was completely barren, with no furniture of any kind, not even a picture on the wall.

A terrible fear gripped me as I stood there, and the thought immediately came to me, "I must get out of this place."

There was one door that led into the room, with no other exit, not even any windows. In other words, except for that one door, I was trapped.

I now know that this which the Lord was showing me that night of so long ago was the trap that Satan had set for me. As I proceed with the dream, it will become quickly obvious that there was absolutely no way out of this trap, at least as far as human ingenuity, power, or ability were concerned. Satan had planned it well.

THE POWER OF DARKNESS

In the dream, as I stood in the room looking at the door and immediately making a start to leave, there suddenly appeared in the door, and even walking into the room, the most hideous looking man/beast that the mind could ever begin to comprehend. It seemed to stand eight or 10 feet tall and had the body of a bear and the face of a man. It had a huge bulk, which, in the natural, would have weighed as much as 300 or 400 pounds or more.

However, it was the face that I will never forget. It seemed that all the evil in the world was incorporated on the face of this beast, and above all, in its eyes. I have never seen such evil, or even anything that came close.

It looked at me with a hatred that words cannot express and with the intent written on that evil countenance, "I have you now."

As it began to descend on me, such fear gripped me as I had never known before. Actually, my legs buckled under me, and I fell to the floor. I was so weak that I could hardly move.

As that thing began to slowly walk toward me, my first thought was, "I must defend myself." Lying on the floor, I reached out with my hand, trying to find some type of club, but there was nothing. There was absolutely nothing I could do, at least in the natural. By this, the Lord was telling me, *"The weapons of our warfare are not carnal, but mighty through God"* (II Cor. 10:4).

THE NAME OF JESUS

While lying on the floor with this beast descending on me, and even coming to the place that he was directly over me, without any premeditation on my part, I shouted as loud as I could, "In the name of Jesus!"

Even though I shouted as loud as possible, still, due to weakness, my voice was no more than a whisper. I simply had no strength left. However, despite that, I found that the use of that mighty name was so powerful that the moment it was uttered, it wreaked instant havoc upon this power of darkness, i.e., demon spirit. This was in spite of my voice coming from me in my weakened condition.

I also learned that the use of the name of Jesus and the power of that great name were not predicated at all on my personal strength.

The moment I uttered that name, this beast began to scream, clutch its head, and stagger back. I know now that it was clutching its head because that is where the damage was done at Calvary. The Lord had said a long time before, *"And I will put enmity* (hatred) *between you* (Satan) *and the woman, and between your seed* (children of Satan) *and her seed* (Jesus Christ); *it shall bruise your head"* (Gen. 3:15).

NOTES

THE NAME OF JESUS THE SECOND TIME

Immediately upon uttering that name the first time, I began to gather strength and began to arise. At about that time, I said it the second time, "In the name of Jesus!" This time my voice was much stronger.

With my uttering that name the second time, this thing fell to the floor, still clutching its head and writhing like a snake that had just received a death blow. Now I was standing over him instead of him standing over me.

THE NAME OF JESUS THE THIRD TIME

Standing above this beast as it writhed on the floor, for the third time I said, "In the name of Jesus!" Even though I barely exerted any effort at all, it seemed as if a hundred loudspeakers were attached to my voice. It fairly boomed off the walls, with a strength that was absolutely supernatural.

THE MIGHTY RUSHING WIND

Immediately upon uttering the name of Jesus the third time, and with the tremendous strength given to me by the Lord, I heard the sound of a *"mighty rushing wind."* I did not see anything, but I distinctly heard it. I knew it was the Holy Spirit.

It hit that man/beast, i.e., demon spirit, with a force of power that literally picked it up and flung it out the door like a piece of tissue paper. In other words, what would have been impossible for me was no trouble at all for the Holy Spirit.

I learned in this dream how powerful the name of Jesus actually is and, as well, the almighty power registered in the Holy Spirit.

Every believer should understand that we are facing the powers of darkness in the spirit world that are far beyond our own strength and ability, but yet, not beyond the strength and ability of the Lord, not at all.

To try to face these things by natural means, one is doomed to failure. However, if we face them according to the Word of God, victory will be ours.

I AWAKENED FROM THE DREAM

When the dream concluded that night, I woke myself up praising the Lord in other tongues. In fact, the power of God was all over me to such an extent that it would be difficult even to describe.

As stated, I knew the dream was from the Lord; however, it was quite some time before I realized that it had a far greater meaning than I at first realized.

That night so long ago, the Lord was showing me what I would face in the future and the answer to the dilemma.

As I dictate these notes, I'm glad that I can say at this present time that by the grace of God, I am victorious over the world, the flesh, and the Devil. I give the Lord all the praise and all the glory for that. It was none of me and all of Him. The Evil One hit me with his best, but he did not succeed, as he cannot succeed. All I can say is, "Look what the Lord has done!"

(18) "AND HE SAID UNTO THEM, I BEHELD SATAN AS LIGHTNING FALL FROM HEAVEN."

SATAN

By the power of the Holy Spirit, Jesus saw into the future and observed Satan as he will be cast out of heaven at the approximate midpoint of the coming great tribulation.

Satan now has access to heaven and appears there regularly (Job, Chpts. 1 and 2). As is obvious from the statements in Job, he appears there for a variety of reasons, not the least being the accusation of the saints. His appearances continue up unto this moment and will do so until the coming time.

Many have asked why the Lord has allowed the Evil One to continue in this fashion. Why didn't He cast him out immediately?

This is called a mystery and is referred to in Revelation 10:7, *"But in the days of the voice of the seventh angel, when he shall begin to sound, the mystery of God should be finished, as He has declared to His servants the prophets."*

This is the seventh trumpet judgment that will take place in the coming great tribulation, and it serves as the announcement for the casting out of Satan, which will take place a short time later.

Revelation 10:6 tells us that this has long been delayed but will ultimately be brought to pass.

NOTES

This is necessary, the casting out of Satan, before the kingdoms of this world can become the kingdoms of God and of His Christ and our Saviour. It is announced in Revelation 11:15.

WHY THE DELAY?

As to why this has been delayed unto that coming time, we are not told; however, we do know everything done by the Lord, such as the delay of casting out Satan, is for a purpose and reason. God's ways are perfect. This much we do know:

Even though it has been the business of Satan to steal, kill, and destroy, still, at the same time, the Lord has used the Evil One to help in the perfecting of the saints. That men serve God and overcome Satan is a requirement respecting the finished product being developed by the Holy Spirit. Before man can make a choice, he must be tested. Satan and his minions of darkness are the testing agents. Even though Satan means to destroy, the Lord means to perfect.

Out of this span of time (approximately some 6,000 years at present) has come, and shall come, a body of overcomers who serve God with a willing mind and an obedient heart. Therefore, despite the damage, the finished product in Christ will be worth it all.

After Satan is cast from the earth, his time will then be very limited, approximately three and a half years (Rev. 12:10-12). During the last three and a half years of the coming great tribulation, the world will know sorrow and heartache as never before (Mat. 24:21).

This period will end with the second coming of Christ when Satan will then be cast *"into the bottomless pit"* (Rev. 20:2-3). All his demons and fallen angels will be with him.

He will be loosed for a short time after the thousand year kingdom age but will make little headway (Rev. 20:7-9).

Satan will then be cast into the *"lake of fire and brimstone,"* and *"tormented day and night forever and ever"* (Rev. 20:10).

(19) "BEHOLD, I GIVE UNTO YOU POWER TO TREAD ON SERPENTS AND SCORPIONS, AND OVER ALL THE POWER OF THE ENEMY: AND NOTHING SHALL BY ANY MEANS HURT YOU."

BEHOLD

The word *behold* signifies something about to be said, which is of vital significance. Actually, the announcement that Jesus would now make included not only the 70 but, as well, all who would follow in their train. It speaks of the coming of the Holy Spirit on the day of Pentecost, who would fill the hearts and lives of believers. In effect, it would give all believers, at least those who fully believe the Word of God, the same anointing power possessed by Christ, but yet, not fully to the degree. This would be possible because Jesus would satisfy the claims of heavenly justice by dying on Calvary and being raised from the dead, hence, glorified, which meant that the work was accomplished in totality (Jn. 7:39). As well, it is meant to continue through the entirety of the dispensation of grace, which includes the present, until the second coming.

POWER

The phrase, *"I give unto you power to tread on serpents and scorpions,"* refers to several things:

• The word *power* in the Greek is *exousia* and means "delegated authority." It is that delegated by Jesus Christ to believers (Mk. 16:17). This is the power and privilege of acting in His name.

• The word *tread* speaks of the child of God being victorious. On the body of Christ are the feet, which places Satan underfoot, literally stomping him. Christ is the head with all believers constituting His body. This is what Paul was speaking of when He said, *"And has put all things under His feet, and gave Him to be the head over all things to the church, Which is His body, the fullness of Him that fills all in all"* (Eph. 1:22-23).

This victory is to come about in two ways: first of all, a personal victory over every power of darkness; and secondly, victory over satanic forces that seek to hinder the work of God.

SERPENTS AND SCORPIONS

• The *"serpents and scorpions"* speak of evil spirits and are not to be taken literally. This is that to which Jesus was referring when He said, *"They shall take up serpents"* (Mk. 16:18). The Greek word for "take up" is *airo* and means to "do away with or kill" and should never have been translated "take up." Actually, Satan is referred to as *"that old serpent, called the Devil, and Satan"* (Rev. 12:9).

As stated, this power refers to the Holy Spirit but is given by Jesus Christ (Mat. 3:11; Acts 1:8).

The phrase, *"And over all the power of the enemy,"* means that there will be no part of Satan's kingdom that will not be affected by Spirit-filled believers.

This phrase tells us that while Satan definitely does have power, his power cannot match the power of the Holy Spirit resident in the Spirit-filled believer (I Jn. 4:4).

NO HARM

The phrase, *"And nothing shall by any means hurt you,"* does not speak of freedom from all physical or material injury. Actually, multiple tens of thousands over the centuries have died for the cause of Christ. It speaks of hurt in the spiritual realm. If, in fact, the believer is hurt in this manner, it means that he is not properly utilizing that which is made available to us. I speak of the Cross of Christ. I speak of the Cross of Christ, the name of Jesus, and the power of the Holy Spirit resident in every believer's life.

In a Campmeeting at Family Worship Center sometime back, in the Saturday night service, I made mention of the fact that Satan will tell the believer anything he can get him to believe. He will tell him that he (Satan) is going to destroy him (destroy the believer), his family, etc.

I then made the statement, "Satan is lying! If he could do such a thing, he would have already done it long ago."

When I made that statement, or words similar, the power of God fell in the place until I was unable to continue ministering. It seemed as if this great truth sank into the ears and hearts of all who were there that night. In just a moment, the light flashed as to Satan's lies and his inability to carry out his threats.

For over an hour, the people worshiped God in a manner that I have seldom seen.

This is the type of power held by every believer, although seldom realized, at least according to its full potential, by even the most spiritual.

(20) "NOTWITHSTANDING IN THIS REJOICE NOT, THAT THE SPIRITS ARE SUBJECT UNTO YOU; BUT RATHER REJOICE, BECAUSE YOUR NAMES ARE WRITTEN IN HEAVEN."

SPIRITS

The phrase, *"Notwithstanding in this rejoice not, that the spirits are subject unto you,"* means that this should not actually be the occasion for our joy. A tremendous lesson is taught in this statement.

The idea is of believers getting their eyes on the gift instead of the giver. The modern faith teaching, which in reality is no faith at all, leans in this direction. Everything is geared toward what the person receives, with every encouragement for the believer to use his or her faith to get things from God, etc. While God truly is a giver, still, the purpose of all that He does is not to draw people to what He can give, but rather as to who He is.

Back in 1991 when the Lord instructed me to begin two prayer meetings a day, He told me, "Seek Me for who I am, rather than for what I can do!" The occasion for rejoicing must not be the gift, whatever that may be, even to the casting out of demons as here outlined, or any other great thing for that matter, but rather something else entirely. The next phrase tells us what.

REJOICE

The phrase, *"But rather rejoice, because your names are written in heaven,"* tells us that the salvation of the soul must always be the occasion for rejoicing. Jesus is saying this:

• The Lord makes it personal by stating that we are to ever thank Him that He has saved us, and that this ever be the occasion for our rejoicing. Whatever else happens, our salvation eclipses all else.

• This means that priority for the church must always be the salvation of souls rather than the gifts of the Spirit, etc. It does not mean that these other things are insignificant, for in reality, they are very important.

However, it does mean that our priorities must never be confused.

The moment the church places its emphasis on things other than this all-important task of winning souls, that is the moment the church begins to lose its way.

This is what troubles me about some modern phenomenon that claims to be a moving and operation of the Holy Spirit. While anything the Holy Spirit does is truly important, that is, if it is actually and truly the Holy Spirit doing it, still, our priority must always be souls.

THE CHURCH

So, the church may be greatly boasting of its power to cast out demons, and it may be being done legitimately in the name of Jesus, just as the disciples. However, if it is ignoring the priority of the salvation of souls, then its rejoicing is coming from a wrong premise and will ultimately lead to spiritual anemia.

When Christians show tremendous interest in anything other than souls being saved and believers being baptized with the Holy Spirit, this shows that they are quickly getting their priorities wrong. That's what Jesus meant when He said, *"Rather rejoice, because your names are written in heaven."* This should be a lesson that we should learn.

THE LAMB'S BOOK OF LIFE

The phrase, *"Names are written in heaven,"* speaks of the *"Lamb's Book of Life"* (Rev. 21:27).

The qualification for entry into this book is to be *"born again"* (Jn. 3:3). Being a member of the Catholic Church, the Baptist church, the Pentecostal church, or any other church has nothing to do with entry into this book. But yet, tragically, millions think it does!

(21) "IN THAT HOUR JESUS REJOICED IN SPIRIT, AND SAID, I THANK YOU, O FATHER, LORD OF HEAVEN AND EARTH, THAT YOU HAVE HID THESE THINGS FROM THE WISE AND PRUDENT, AND HAVE REVEALED THEM UNTO BABES: EVEN SO, FATHER; FOR SO IT SEEMED GOOD IN YOUR SIGHT."

JESUS REJOICED IN SPIRIT

The phrase, *"In that hour Jesus rejoiced*

in Spirit," actually means in the Greek that Jesus greatly exulted in the Holy Spirit. This spoke of a great joy like a fountain springing up, which came from the depths of His soul. It is more, much more, than mere happiness or joy as we think of such, but rather the Holy Spirit moving upon Him so mightily that the word even had the connotation of jumping for joy. It is an exultation that knows no bounds. Whether Jesus literally leaped for joy is not known, but it is a certainty that He did this in His Spirit, even though it may possibly not have been done outwardly.

Why?

The sending out of the 70 and their returning with such testimonies of victory over the powers of darkness constituted the beginning of the church, which would later fill the earth. Even though His ministry to the Jews had failed because of their rebellion, still, the founding of the church was a resounding success (Mat. 16:18). In His Spirit and through the person and agency of the Holy Spirit, Jesus saw that the church would carry on that which He had begun and would fill the earth with that which the Spirit of God could do.

Even though we spoke of failure on the part of Jesus' ministry to the Jews, still, it would not be failure respecting the total conclusion. The failure was only in the temporary sense. Actually, the Jews will ultimately accept Christ as their Lord and Saviour, which will take place at the second coming. Regarding the total picture, God has never failed and, in reality, cannot fail.

THANKFULNESS

The phrase, *"And said, I thank You, O Father, Lord of heaven and earth,"* proclaims to us several things:

• Jesus referred to God as His Father in a unique special way that no one else can claim. To be sure, every believer can and, in fact, must refer to God as our Father, but we are adopted sons (Rom. 8:15), whereas Jesus is the only begotten Son of the Father (Jn. 3:16). However, the Lord has allowed us (His adopted sons and daughters) to share the same rights and privileges as one born into the family. We are made *"joint-heirs*

NOTES

with Christ," receiving by the grace of God the same portion received by the true Son (Rom. 8:17).

THE BENEFACTOR OF ALL

• Jesus rendered thanks to Him, showing Him to be the benefactor of all. Consequently, the pattern is laid down for all that we should constantly thank God for His abundant goodness to us, and to all for that matter! Thanksgiving and praise should be the hallmark of every child of God.

• Jesus proclaims the Father as the Lord of heaven and earth, and not Satan. Actually, this is the source of conflict.

Satan has laid an illegitimate claim to that which belongs to God. As such, he has tried through force to destroy that which God has made; however, Jesus sees His church treading *"on serpents and scorpions, and over all the power of the enemy."* This speaks of victory. The *"gates of hell shall not prevail against the church"* of the living God (Mat. 16:18).

The entirety of these passages tells us that Satan will not win in this conflict but is even now defeated.

• Inasmuch as Jesus rejoiced in the Holy Spirit, as well, every believer ought to constantly rejoice in this great victory. It is not something that will happen but, in fact, something that has already happened. In other words, in the mind of God, the supremacy of the body of Christ and the ultimate destruction of Satan and all his minions of darkness are an accomplished fact. In modern street terminology, "You can take it to the bank."

Hallelujah!

UNTO BABES

The phrase, *"That You have hid these things from the wise and prudent, and have revealed them unto babes,"* has reference to several things:

• Israel judicially refused their Messiah and, consequently, God's way; therefore, God judicially hid from them that which He would do.

• God does not reveal Himself to unbelievers. Actually, He purposely hides His will and way from such.

In fact, Israel was wise and prudent in the ways of God, having been given the law and the prophets; however, they did not use this wisdom and prudence properly, squandering what was given to them. They were supposed to be bearers of the light, but instead, extinguished that light in their own hearts. They did it deliberately and, therefore, their judgment was deliberate.

• The babes spoken of here concerned these people of humble occupations, such as fishermen, tax collectors, etc., who were mightily used of God, versus the religious aristocracy of Israel, who were not used at all.

As an example, when the angels appeared to announce the birth of the Saviour, they appeared to lowly shepherds rather than to the religious aristocracy (Lk. 2:8-12). Likewise, when Jesus arose from the dead, He did not appear to the unbelieving religious aristocracy, but rather to those of humble comportment, such as Mary Magdalene, from whom He had cast out seven demons.

What a mighty God we serve!

In fact, this scriptural law continues to be carried out in that God uses the lowly (poor in spirit) while ignoring the haughty and the puffed up. He exalts the humble while humbling the exalted (Lk. 14:11).

GOOD IN GOD'S SIGHT

The phrase, *"Even so, Father; for so it seemed good in Your sight,"* actually means that the conversion of souls was the cause of the Lord's joy, and the sovereignty of God in saving sinners was the secret of His exultation. He gloried in the just judgment that hid salvation from those who were *"wise in their own eyes, and prudent in their own sight"* (Isa. 5:21) and revealed it unto babes. The self-righteous are judicially blinded, but to the repenting sinner, light is granted.

The doctrine of the sovereignty of God is most offensive to moralists, for it belittles man and the majesty of his will, but that it is a fundamental doctrine of the Bible is absolutely certain.

However, that sovereignty is not arbitrarily based, but rather exercised on God's choice respecting man's acceptance or rejection of God's way.

(22) "ALL THINGS ARE DELIVERED

NOTES

TO ME OF MY FATHER: AND NO MAN KNOWS WHO THE SON IS, BUT THE FATHER; AND WHO THE FATHER IS, BUT THE SON, AND HE TO WHOM THE SON WILL REVEAL HIM."

EVERYTHING DELIVERED TO THE SON

The phrase, *"All things are delivered to Me of My Father,"* refers to Jesus being given the responsibility by the Father for defeating Satan and putting down his evil revolution. When this is done, and for a certainty it shall be (I Cor. 15:28), then the Lord will in turn deliver *"up the kingdom to God, even the Father; when He shall have put down all rule and all authority and power"* (I Cor. 15:24).

These *"all things"* constitute salvation for the soul, the baptism with the Holy Spirit, deliverance from the powers of darkness, and the total subjugation of satanic usurpation. That is the reason there is salvation in no other name (Acts 4:12).

So, any claim of salvation other than through Jesus Christ is spurious and, therefore, unacceptable to God. Man has to deal with Jesus Christ. The hope of salvation in any other manner is a fool's hope!

WHAT THE NAME MEANS

However, the mere believing in Jesus' name as some type of magic potion, consequently, saving the soul, is unscriptural. It is not in the way the name is used in water baptism, or any other endeavor, no matter how holy, but rather what the name means, which is Saviour. *"You shall call His name JESUS: for He shall save His people from their sins"* (Mat. 1:21).

The phrase, *"And no man knows who the Son is, but the Father,"* means that Jesus is of the Father and not of man. He was the gift of God and had no part with man respecting His incarnation, with the exception of Mary supplying a house or womb for His birth. He was not conceived by man but by God.

WHO THE FATHER IS

The phrase, *"And who the Father is, but the Son,"* means that no man can reach the Father or even know who the Father is except through the Son, i.e., the Lord Jesus Christ. Jesus alone is the door (Jn. 10:9).

This means that no Muslim, irrespective of praying five times a day and calling God *"Allah,"* actually knows who God is, for no one can know God except through Jesus. This means that no Mormon knows God, for they try to know Him through their false prophet and the church (Mormon church). Such cannot be done!

The same can be said for Catholicism, that is, if one is trying to know God through the Church, as most Catholics do, with Jesus merely being a part of the mix.

The same holds for any Protestant who places anything or anyone on a par with Jesus, attempting to reach God in that false manner.

The phrase, *"And he to whom the Son will reveal Him,"* refers to salvation being not of education or association, but rather by revelation.

Williams said, "All the elaborate machinery of man's religious ceremony, and all his self-determination to be a Christian are useless, for only those to whom the Son wills to reveal the Father possesses a saving knowledge of God, and He wills to reveal Himself to the sinful and guilty, in other words, those who know they are in this condition, and desire help from the Lord."

(23) "AND HE TURNED HIM UNTO HIS DISCIPLES, AND SAID PRIVATELY, BLESSED ARE THE EYES WHICH SEE THE THINGS THAT YOU SEE."

The overview is:

1. The phrase, *"And He turned Him unto His disciples, and said privately,"* refers to not only the Twelve but, as well, the 70, etc.

2. Even now He continues to do so accordingly, i.e., privately. He does not reveal Himself to the scornful, prideful, doubtful, or unbelievers, but only to those who truly believe.

3. Faith is the criterion, not education, environment, culture, race, or personal wealth. In fact, joining churches and being religious in no way brings revelation. Actually, most of the people who belong to churches, thinking this brings them salvation, do not really know the Lord because they have not sought Him through the Son.

4. The phrase, *"Blessed are the eyes which see the things that you see,"* means

much more than mere physical observation. In fact, tens of thousands saw the miracles Jesus performed just as His personal disciples did, but it did them little good. The religious leaders saw these miracles, as well, but they were not helped. So, mere observation is not what is being said here.

He is speaking of *"seeing"* with the eye of faith and believing what is seen.

5. Unbelief blinds spiritual eyes while faith opens them!

(24) "FOR I TELL YOU, THAT MANY PROPHETS AND KINGS HAVE DESIRED TO SEE THOSE THINGS WHICH YOU SEE, AND HAVE NOT SEEN THEM; AND TO HEAR THOSE THINGS WHICH YOU HEAR, AND HAVE NOT HEARD THEM."

The exegesis is:

1. The phrase, *"For I tell you, that many prophets and kings have desired to see those things which you see, and have not seen them,"* referred to those in the past who believed these things even though they had not seen them and, in fact, would not see them. This speaks of Christ and all He did!

2. *"And to hear those things which you hear, and have not heard them,"* as well, means that they believed all that Jesus said even though they did not personally hear Him say it.

3. Many thousands actually saw and actually heard all that Jesus did and said, but yet, still would not believe. This shows that faith is not in the senses, but rather in the heart.

(25) "AND, BEHOLD, A CERTAIN LAWYER STOOD UP, AND TEMPTED HIM, SAYING, MASTER, WHAT SHALL I DO TO INHERIT ETERNAL LIFE?"

THE LAWYER

The phrase, *"And, behold, a certain lawyer stood up,"* did not pertain to the time that Jesus was speaking privately with His disciples, but rather at a later time.

The word *behold* tells us that a tremendously important subject is about to be broached, which, in fact, tells us what true salvation will effect in a person's life.

The phrase, *"And tempted Him,"* means that he would test His knowledge of the law. A lawyer in Israel at that time was the same as a scribe and was one who devoted himself to the study of the law of Moses.

In fact, for the first time in his life, this lawyer had come to the right One. Jesus not only knew the law as no other man, but, in fact, He was the law.

Did this lawyer realize who Jesus actually was as he stood before Him that day?

No, he did not!

While this is probably the same individual in Matthew 22:35, he is probably not the same as the one in Mark 12:28. Consequently, he was one of those who saw, but he did not *"see,"* and heard, but did not *"hear."*

ETERNAL LIFE

The question, *"Saying, Master, what shall I do to inherit eternal life?"* was really posed wrongly because inheritance is by birth.

So, his question portrays to us that even though he was a scribe, or lawyer, and, therefore, supposed to be expert in the law of Moses, the very phrasing of his question reveals that he really did not know or understand that in which he was supposed to be expert. How so like most modern preachers!

Wrongfully interpreting the law as he was, he should have used the word *merit* instead of *inherit.*

Eternal life is man's greatest interest, and no more tremendous question could be asked than that of this verse.

WHAT IS ETERNAL LIFE?

That of which the lawyer spoke is a life lived in God and will, consequently, be with God forever (Rev. 22:5).

However, eternal life is not only that of endless duration, but the Holy Spirit, as well, places the emphasis on the quality or character of that life.

Eternal life stands in contrast to biological life. Biological life is derived and fleeting; it has no shaping impact on the personality. Eternal life is God's own life burning brightly not only with His vitality but with His own character. The wonderful message of the Scripture is that God has chosen to share this life—to share Himself—with human beings. You have been born again, Peter wrote, capturing the wonder of it, not of corruptible seed, but of incorruptible,

through the living and enduring Word of God (I Pet. 1:23).

God's life alone is able to break the grip of death on humanity. God's life alone can provide a basis for a warm, personal relationship with the Lord. God's life alone can lift humanity to the destiny for which we were originally intended.

As the Bible presents the stunning possibility of eternal life now, that possibility is always linked with Jesus. It is only through faith in the Son of God that a person receives eternal life. It is only through faith that a close fellowship develops, and it is through this that God's life is released to find expression through us.

THE SOURCE OF ETERNAL LIFE

To understand something about life, we must first of all look at death. Sin is the cause of death.

The Lord told Adam and Eve, *"Of every tree of the garden you may freely eat: But of the Tree of the Knowledge of Good and Evil, you shall not eat of it."*

He then said, *"For in the day that you eat thereof you shall surely die"* (Gen. 2:16-17).

The Lord was speaking of spiritual death, which is separation from God. It is to be understood that the Tree of the Knowledge of Good and Evil was not the cause of Adam's fall. It was a failure to heed and obey the Word of God, which is the cause of every single failure. Spiritual death ultimately brought on physical death and has, in fact, filled the world with death, all because of the fall.

Even then, man was so marvelously created, actually created to live forever by virtue of the Tree of Life, that, still, it took well over a thousand years for the physical body of man to wear down. In Chapter 5 of Genesis, we read of an astounding number of years that men lived, and that is no fable. They actually lived that long. For instance, Abraham, who lived about 2,000 years after Adam and Eve, died at 175 years old. Moses, some 400 years later, lived to be 120. By the time of David, the great king died at 70 years of age. That number on a worldwide basis has held true pretty much from then until now—and all of that despite the wonder drugs and the advancement of modern medicine, etc. It is original sin that kills, and continued sin that wreaks havoc on this earth.

JESUS, THE SOURCE OF ALL LIFE

We must understand that sin was no trivial matter. It is so powerful and so awful that it took God to rectify the situation with a horrid price that had to be paid, and we speak of the Cross.

Concerning Jesus Christ, the Scripture says, *"In the beginning was the Word, and the Word was with God, and the Word was God.*

"The same was in the beginning with God.

"All things were made by Him; and without Him was not anything made that was made.

"In Him was life; and the life was the light of men.

"And the light shines in darkness; and the darkness comprehended it not" (Jn. 1:1-5).

Jesus said of Himself, *"Verily, verily, I say unto you, He who hears My Word, and believes on Him who sent Me, has everlasting life, and shall not come into condemnation; but is passed from death unto life.*

"Verily, verily, I say unto you, The hour is coming, and now is, when the dead shall hear the voice of the Son of God: and they who hear shall live.

"For as the Father has life in Himself; so has He given to the Son to have life in Himself" (Jn. 5:24-26).

Then Paul says: *"I am crucified with Christ: nevertheless I live; yet not I, but Christ lives in me: and the life which I now live in the flesh I live by the faith of the Son of God, who loved me, and gave Himself for me"* (Gal. 2:20).

In totality, the Word of God points to Jesus as the source of all life.

WHAT DEATH MEANS TO THE BELIEVER

When Jesus gave Himself on the Cross of Calvary, He not only made it possible for mankind to have eternal life, which could be had and can be had by simple faith in Christ and what He has done for us at the Cross, but, as well, He took away the sting of death.

To every believer is the expectation of resurrection. When Lazarus died, Jesus soon went to where he was.

NOTES

Martha came to meet Jesus and said to Him, *"Lord, if You had been here, my brother had not died.*

"But I know, that even now, whatsoever You will ask of God, God will give it (to) *You.*

"Jesus said unto her, Your brother shall rise again.

"Martha said unto Him, I know that he shall rise again in the resurrection at the last day.

"Jesus said unto her, I am the resurrection, and the life: he who believes in Me, though he were dead, yet shall he live" (Jn. 11:21-25).

So, the resurrection is more than a mere philosophy; it is a person, the Lord Jesus Christ. When He died on the Cross of Calvary, He atoned for all sin (Col. 2:13-15) and, thereby, took away the sting of death.

BEFORE THE CROSS

Before the Cross, when believers died, their souls and spirits did not go to heaven, but rather down into paradise where they were actually held captive by Satan. He could not harm them, but still, they were his captives. They were there awaiting the Cross. If Jesus had not gone to the Cross, all believers would still be in the underworld and still held captive by Satan.

However, when Jesus died on the Cross, this atoned for all sin, past, present, and future, at least for all who will believe (Jn. 3:16). Actually, just before Jesus rose from the dead, He went down into paradise and *"led captivity captive,"* meaning that He made all those believers there His captives, and there was nothing that Satan could do about it. He sent them to the portals of glory. Now, when believers die, their souls and their spirits immediately go to be with the Lord in glory, all because of the Cross.

Death is an enemy, the enemy of all life. However, what Jesus did at the Cross will ultimately do away with all death, with nothing but *"life"* prevailing, and will prevail forever and forever.

The Scripture tells us that the day is going to come when *"there shall be no more death, neither sorrow, nor crying, neither shall there be any more pain: for the former things are passed away"* (Rev. 21:4).

(26) "HE SAID UNTO HIM, WHAT IS WRITTEN IN THE LAW? HOW READEST THOU?"

The exposition is:

1. The question, *"He said unto him, What is written in the law?"* presents Jesus immediately pointing to the Bible as the infallible authority.

2. If the Bible is not the authority, what is?

3. Regrettably, too many believers allow other things to dictate what they believe, such as their church denomination, etc. This is tragic inasmuch as such thinking has caused millions to be eternally lost. The criterion must ever be the Word of God. Jesus, as stated, set this example, and dogmatically so.

4. If the policy of a religious denomination, or local church for that matter, is contrary to the Word of God, that denomination or church must be abandoned in favor of the Word. When the believer stands before the Lord, he will not be judged according to what his denomination or local church taught or believed, but rather what the Word says. With that in mind, it is incumbent upon all to know the Word and to adhere to the Word. Men change, but the Word does not change!

5. The question, *"How readest thou* (How do you read it)?" is extremely important! Jesus was speaking not only of knowing the Word, but properly understanding it as well.

6. Many people simply read it wrongly. Too often it is read with the idea of making it conform to one's beliefs instead of allowing it to rather form our beliefs. The Bible is meant to prove our beliefs rather than our beliefs proving the Bible.

7. This Pharisee, as so many others, was not reading the Bible correctly.

(27) "AND HE ANSWERING SAID, YOU SHALL LOVE THE LORD YOUR GOD WITH ALL YOUR HEART, AND WITH ALL YOUR SOUL, AND WITH ALL YOUR STRENGTH, AND WITH ALL YOUR MIND; AND YOUR NEIGHBOR AS YOURSELF."

THE ANSWER GIVEN BY THE LAWYER

The phrase, *"And he answering said,"* proves that he did know the Bible, even though he did not properly understand it because he did not read it correctly.

NOTES

In his answer is revealed the clear knowledge of God and of truth that men at that time possessed in Israel. It was knowledge, we might quickly add, that was immeasurably in advance of that of the East and of Greece and Rome. It is the same presently.

Knowledge of the Bible is considered by most presently to be no knowledge at all because most simply do not know the Bible. To have a Bible education only is claimed not to be educated at all; however, a Bible education is the greatest education of all by far. The reason is simple: The Bible alone holds the answer regarding how men ought to live. The great questions of life are answered in the confines of its pages, and the solutions are given to every spiritual problem. To forsake it is to forsake the true way to life, irrespective of how much education one may possess otherwise. It is so valuable simply because it is the Word of God, which means it's not the word of man. Inasmuch as it is the Word of God, this means that it is error free and that it is also without contradiction. As well, this means that it holds the answer and the solution to every problem of life.

A BIBLE EDUCATION

As one great philosopher of the past said, "Irrespective as to how much education one may possess, if he does not truly have a Bible education, as well, he is not truly educated."

The phrase, *"You shall love the Lord your God with all your heart, and with all your soul, and with all your strength, and with all your mind,"* is quoted from Deuteronomy 6:5 and Leviticus 19:18.

Actually, Jesus would say that the entirety of the law was wrapped up in these two commandments (Mat. 22:36-40).

The idea is that one cannot love his *"neighbor"* as he should unless he loves God supremely. The reason for all the war, racism, hatred, and man's inhumanity to man is simply because man does not love God. In fact, many profess to do so while their actions prove otherwise.

What does it mean to love God as this passage proclaims?

To love God with all the heart is first and of necessity. As goes the heart, so goes all else.

The heart is the seat of emotions, feelings, and desires. When the Bible speaks of the heart, it is actually not speaking of the physical orb beating in the breast of the human being. One might sum up the heart by saying it is the soul and the spirit of the individual. So, God is to occupy the heart totally and not merely given first place.

The soul is the part of man that feels and, consequently, that which carries out the emotions of the heart.

The strength concerns one's ability and refers to active participation. While many claim to love God supremely, there is no effort put forth, leaving their claims suspect.

This means that if you truly love the Lord with all your strength, you will at the same time love His Word. Also, you will have an active prayer life, which guarantees relationship.

The mind is listed last but is definitely not least regarding significance.

The mind is the gateway to the spirit of man, which is the part of man that knows. Paul said, *"But be you transformed by the renewing of your mind, that you may prove (know) what is that good, and acceptable, and perfect, will of God"* (Rom. 12:2).

LOVE YOUR NEIGHBOR AS YOURSELF

The phrase, *"And your neighbor as yourself,"* places love for our fellowman on the same par as love for ourselves. As we have stated, if these two commandments were kept, this would eliminate all war, hatred, racism, etc.

So, the answer to that which constantly plagues the human family, and which society will never be able to solve, is found as close as Verse 27 of Chapter 10 of Luke. However, none of this can be done (loving one's neighbor) unless one has a proper relationship with Christ, which cannot be had unless one understands the Cross of Christ. Much of modern Christendom merely accepts a Christian philosophy. In other words, it attempts to keep the Golden Rule without Christ. Such is not to be! The key to all of this is Christ. He alone can change the human heart and make it possible to love God and one's neighbor as one should. Without Him, it is an impossible task!

(28) "AND HE SAID UNTO HIM, YOU HAVE ANSWERED RIGHT: THIS DO, AND YOU SHALL LIVE."

The construction is:

1. The phrase, *"And He said unto him, You have answered right,"* proclaims Christ, in effect, saying, "You know it, but you are not doing it."

2. *"This do, and you shall live,"* means that he was not doing what he knew to do. It must have come as a shock, even as the next verse portrays, for this man to have Jesus read him so astutely.

3. While he knew the correct answer it seems, the facts are, he wasn't doing what he knew he should do.

(29) "BUT HE, WILLING TO JUSTIFY HIMSELF, SAID TO JESUS, AND WHO IS MY NEIGHBOR?"

The synopsis is:

1. The phrase, *"But he, willing to justify himself,"* proclaims this man, as many, who may have very great religious knowledge, but yet, presume to criticize the Lord Jesus Christ.

2. Self-justification is the product of self-righteousness. In fact, much of the world seeks to justify themselves. It is very difficult for a person to admit he is a sinner and, thereby, unable to rid himself of his sin, at least within himself. Consequently, his righteousness is such as is measured among men. In other words, whatever wrong things he does, they are not nearly as wrong as some others are doing. As well, the so-called good he is doing is above what many others do. Consequently, in whatever capacity, most attempt to justify themselves.

3. Actually, this is what religion is all about. It is a method of self-justification. Of course, God will accept none of this.

4. The question, *"Said to Jesus, And who is my neighbor?"* proclaims this man attempting to escape his conviction.

5. By his question, he was insinuating to Christ that he was properly keeping the Word of God even though Christ had, in essence, said that he wasn't. He was attempting to divert the sting of his conscience by asking the question, *"Who is my neighbour?"*

6. He knew in his heart that he had approached Christ with every intent of causing

Him harm. He sought to entangle Him in His talk, which would dishonor Him in the sight of the people. So, his very conduct toward Christ showed what he was, and that he was not really attempting to obey the Word of God, despite his claims.

(30) "AND JESUS ANSWERING SAID, A CERTAIN MAN WENT DOWN FROM JERUSALEM TO JERICHO, AND FELL AMONG THIEVES, WHICH STRIPPED HIM OF HIS RAIMENT, AND WOUNDED HIM, AND DEPARTED, LEAVING HIM HALF DEAD."

The composition is:

1. The phrase, *"And Jesus answering said,"* proclaims to the world the parable of that which is called *"the good Samaritan."* However, even though it is a parable, without a doubt, it is an event that actually transpired.

2. *"A certain man went down from Jerusalem to Jericho, and fell among thieves,"* presents a common occurrence at that time. Jericho is about 18 miles from Jerusalem and was called *"the bloody way"* because of robbers infesting the country.

3. It does not say exactly who this traveler was, but from the description given, he was, no doubt, a Jew.

4. *"Which stripped him of his raiment, and wounded him, and departed, leaving him half dead,"* proclaims what happened to him, but it has a far greater meaning than is at first assumed.

5. The parables of the good Samaritan and of the prodigal son are peculiar to Luke. Grace is the theme of one and love of the other. Grace seeks misery, and love desires company—so the father's arm was thrown around the child's neck as he exclaimed, *"Let us eat and be merry!"* Grace goes forth alone; love returns accompanied.

6. Man chose the death road and the thieves. Unbelief and disobedience at once stripped him of his innocence and wounded Him to death with the poison dagger of sin.

7. It is possible that the thieves of this verse were two in number, were symbolic, and reappear in Luke 23:39.

(31) "AND BY CHANCE THERE CAME DOWN A CERTAIN PRIEST THAT WAY: AND WHEN HE SAW HIM, HE PASSED BY ON THE OTHER SIDE."

A CERTAIN PRIEST

The phrase, *"And by chance there came down a certain priest that way,"* actually proclaims this road heavily traveled by priests. Jericho was a priestly city, having approximately 12,000 priests who lived there at that particular time. As it fell their lot to minister in the temple in Jerusalem, they would of necessity make this journey. Actually, priests were allowed to live anywhere in Israel, but Jericho seemed to be a favorite place for many.

Even though Jesus heavily censured the Pharisees and scribes (Mat., Chpt. 23), this passage is the only negative remark He made about priests and Levites. As is obvious, even it was mild. This does not mean that they were without severe fault, especially considering that many of the priests were Sadducees, who were very similar to present-day modernists. However, it seems that most priests little opposed Him, with the exception of the chief priests. Actually, many priests accepted Christ after His ascension (Acts 6:7).

About 37 years from this time, Jerusalem, along with the temple, would be completely destroyed by the Romans, not to be raised again, at least at that time. Consequently, the very reason for the existence of priests and Levites would cease to exist.

PASS BY ON THE OTHER SIDE

Jewish priests will make one more appearance before the second coming when they will occupy the rebuilt temple in Jerusalem. This will begin at approximately the beginning of the coming great tribulation, or even before.

It is said presently that certain Jewish young men, who are thought to be of the tribe of Levi, are now training in Jerusalem in order to be ready to carry out these duties upon construction of the temple. That's how close we actually are!

"And when he saw him, he passed by on the other side," probably seemed perfectly logical at the moment.

The priest may have thought that the man's condition was contrived and a mere ploy to lure him over where he would be pounced upon by robbers, as was often done; or maybe he just did not want to be bothered by this stranger.

There is every evidence that the man was crying out for help, but the very one, a priest, who he thought surely would come to his aid, hurriedly passed by without even stopping.

To be sure, there are always problems and difficulties attached to helping anyone. It is never as simple as it seems! However, love is meant to bear those difficulties, whatever they may be.

(32) "AND LIKEWISE A LEVITE, WHEN HE WAS AT THE PLACE, CAME AND LOOKED ON HIM, AND PASSED BY ON THE OTHER SIDE."

THE LEVITE

The phrase, *"And likewise a Levite,"* spoke of those who were of the tribe of Levi. All priests were Levites, but all Levites were not priests. Some Levites had duties at the temple because only those of that tribe could function in the temple in any capacity.

"When he was at the place," refers to where the wounded man was lying half dead on the road. To be frank, millions of believers come to this particular *"place"* every day but do little or nothing to help fallen humanity. As we read this, Jesus demands that we put ourselves in the same place as the priest and the Levite. Is our response presently any better?

"Came and looked on him, and passed by on the other side," proclaims this man at least looking on, while the priest did not even bother with that.

In fact, much of the modern church world, falling in line with the psychological way, has become expert at looking on in order to diagnose the problem while never doing anything about it. In fact, the psychological way is expert at cataloging symptoms but does not know the cause or the cure. However, due to their expert knowledge of symptoms, and in that they are experts, millions are deceived into believing that the world of psychology also knows the cause and the cure. They don't!

SYMPTOMS

However, the observation and delineating of symptoms present little difficulty. Pavlov's dogs will always respond in similar, if not identical, fashion.

Even though that masquerade greatly fools many people, most have little regard as to how they act, of which they are already painfully aware, but rather why they do it and the cure for such aberrant action. However, the cause and cure are far beyond the realm of psychology, with it only able to do what the priest and Levite did of so long ago—pass by on the other side.

Leaving the realm of the natural and coming to the spiritual, dispensationally speaking, it was impossible for the priest and the Levite to succor the meritless misery of the traveler; for under the first covenant, the sinner had to cooperate with God in order for recovery. Such cooperation demanded outlay and activity. This man could contribute neither.

Under the first covenant the question is: "What can man do for God?" Under the second covenant, the question: "What has God done for man?"

The answer to the first question is: "Nothing!" The answer to the second is: "Everything."

(33) "BUT A CERTAIN SAMARITAN, AS HE JOURNEYED, CAME WHERE HE WAS: AND WHEN HE SAW HIM, HE HAD COMPASSION ON HIM."

The overview is:

1. The phrase, *"But a certain Samaritan, as he journeyed, came where he was,"* presents a man who was hated by the Jews. Even though the Samaritans had little love for the Jews, the hatred of the Jews for these people knew no bounds.

This Samaritan was travelling in Judaea, whereas most Jews would not even think of travelling through Samaria. If they had need to go to Galilee, which lay above Samaria, most would go the long route on the east side of Jordan, thereby, not setting foot on the soil of Samaria. That is how deep their hatred was.

2. *"And when he saw him, he had compassion on him,"* proclaims him doing the very opposite of what the others (though of the same nationality) had done, even though this man was a hated enemy. How so Christlike!

(34) "AND WENT TO HIM, AND BOUND UP HIS WOUNDS, POURING IN OIL AND WINE, AND SET HIM ON HIS OWN BEAST, AND BROUGHT HIM TO AN INN, AND TOOK CARE OF HIM."

BOUND UP HIS WOUNDS

The phrase, *"And went to him,"* was far more than merely observing, but rather would help, and help greatly!

The phrase, *"And bound up his wounds, pouring in oil and wine,"* as well, typifies Christ. Jesus did not merely look at fallen humanity. He came and touched our grievous sore and did whatever was necessary, even dying on the Cross of Calvary, in order to save the lost sons of Adam's fallen race. There was no other way it could be done! The song says:

"He poured in the oil and the wine,
"The kind that restores my soul,
"He found me bleeding and dying
"On the Jericho road,
"And He poured in the oil and the wine."

TOOK CARE OF HIM

The phrase, *"And set him on his own beast, and brought him to an inn, and took care of him,"* tells us that this wounded traveler was not rich and, therefore, could not possibly repay the kindness extended to him.

Likewise, humanity was a fallen wreckage when Jesus came to lift man out of the terrible bondage of darkness. There was nothing man could do to repay Christ, and, in fact, even though converted, he is still helpless to repay his benefactor. What the Samaritan did was out of pure love, which is a type of what the Lord has done for us.

As this man went to the wounded traveler, likewise, Jesus came to us. For all who will believe, He likewise binds up our wounds and gives us the Holy Spirit, typified by the oil, and great joy, typified by the wine. As well, by the transport of grace, He brought us to the *"inn"* of justification. There, He took care of us.

It was the custom in those days to first pour wine in a wound to cleanse it and then oil for healing purposes.

(35) "AND ON THE MORROW WHEN HE DEPARTED, HE TOOK OUT TWO PENCE, AND GAVE THEM TO THE HOST, AND SAID UNTO HIM, TAKE CARE OF HIM; AND WHATSOEVER YOU SPEND MORE, WHEN I COME AGAIN, I WILL REPAY YOU."

The synopsis is:

1. The phrase, *"And on the morrow when he departed,"* tells us that he stayed all night in the inn to make certain that the man was well cared for.

2. *"He took out two pence, and gave them to the host, and said unto him, Take care of him,"* was the equivalent of approximately $125 in today's value.

3. However, in the spiritual sense, Jesus Christ, the absolute Good Samaritan, has paid the price to satisfy the claims of heavenly justice regarding our care.

4. *"And whatsoever you spend more, when I come again, I will repay you,"* ensured not only the present care, but anything that would arise. Commensurately, the blood of Jesus Christ cleanses from all sin.

5. The man now helped was not told to make his way as best he could but was carried by the same living power that carried his deliverer. Christ imparts His own nature to the believer (Eph. 1:13).

An inn is a temporary home. It and its host are the church and the Holy Spirit. The *"two pence"* are the Old and New Testaments—a sufficient provision up to the return of the Divine Samaritan. When leaving, He confided His people to the Holy Spirit and to the Scriptures (Jn. 14:16; Acts 20:32). When He returns, He will receive His people from the Holy Spirit with not one missing.

(36) "WHICH NOW OF THESE THREE, DO YOU THINK, WAS NEIGHBOR UNTO HIM WHO FELL AMONG THE THIEVES?"

The exegesis is:

Several things are said in this question asked by Christ. Some of them are as follows:

1. Everything Jesus taught was amazingly simple. In fact, He took extremely complex questions about the most complex subjects and reduced them to their simplest form so that even a child could understand His answer. Consequently, this is a lesson

for all preachers of the gospel that we must follow accordingly.

The Pharisees and scribes oftentimes sought to make their answers very complex in order that the listener might think of them as very intelligent. In other words, they actively sought to always be over the heads of the people intellectually. In their minds, this set them apart from the masses.

Conversely, Jesus wanted the people to understand what He was saying. Consequently, His answers were simple to the point of simplicity.

2. In this answer as given by Christ through the story of the Good Samaritan, Christ portrays the true works that will follow one who is truly born again.

It is ironic that in those days men professed great love for God but little loved their neighbor. Now, men profess great love for their neighbor but express little love for God!

3. Jesus showed that if we really love God, it will be expressed by loving one's neighbor. Consequently, a great lesson is given to us in this illustration.

4. As well, the lesson that Jesus was portraying also concerned the thieves of a man's soul. Satan steals, kills, and destroys (Jn. 10:10). Consequently, it is the responsibility of every believer to help bring the more abundant life to every person so wounded, which includes the entirety of the world. Therefore, Jesus was speaking here not only of humanitarian provision, which is definitely necessary at times, but also in the taking of the gospel to the world.

(37) "AND HE SAID, HE WHO SHOWED MERCY ON HIM. THEN SAID JESUS UNTO HIM, GO, AND DO THOU LIKEWISE."

The form is:

1. The phrase, *"And he said, He who showed mercy on him,"* is the requirement of Christ concerning those who would follow the Lord.

2. *"Who is my neighbor?"* is the question asked by this man!

3. The answer is, "Anyone who needs help, and whom I, as a believer, have power and opportunity to help, no matter what his rank, race, or religion may be."

4. Mercy is a complement of grace. If one

is to notice, the question was not asked at all if the wounded traveler deserved mercy, but that it was automatically given. In other words, the believer is to conduct himself toward others as God has conducted Himself toward us.

5. The phrase, *"Then said Jesus unto him, Go, and do thou* (you do) *likewise,"* proclaims that not a single believer deserved the mercy and grace of God at conversion and thereafter, and fully understanding this, we are to conduct ourselves likewise toward all others.

6. Trench says, "In this parable two kinds of holiness are set before us—the one spurious, the other genuine. The spurious holiness is that of the priest and Levite, two officially holy persons—spurious holiness is sanctity divorced from charity. In the person of the Samaritan the nature of true sanctity is exhibited."

In this allegory, Spence goes on to say, "The wounded traveler represents mankind at large, stopped by the Devil and his angels. He is left by them grievously wounded, yet not dead outright. Priest and Levite were alike powerless to help. 'Many passed by,' once wrote a devout writer, 'and there was none to save.' Moses and his law, Aaron and his sacrifices, patriarch, prophet, and priest—these were powerless. Only the True Samaritan (Christ), beholding, was moved with compassion and poured oil into the wounds."

Another lesson taught in this parable is that some need to be placed in the position of the wounded traveler in order that they may be willing to receive help from anyone, even a hated Samaritan.

(38) "NOW IT CAME TO PASS, AS THEY WENT, THAT HE ENTERED INTO A CERTAIN VILLAGE: AND A CERTAIN WOMAN NAMED MARTHA RECEIVED HIM INTO HER HOUSE."

The composition is:

1. The phrase, *"Now it came to pass, as they went, that He entered into a certain village,"* speaks of Bethany (Jn. 11:1; 12:1-3), a suburb of Jerusalem.

2. The phrase, *"And a certain woman named Martha received Him into her house,"* referred to the home of Mary, her

sister, Martha, and their brother, Lazarus.

3. This section opens with the action of one woman (Mary) and closes with the exclamation of another (Martha). Thus, the lesson is taught that the closest physical relationship to Jesus, though it be that even of a mother, does not, and cannot, secure spiritual life. Martha had a physical relationship with Christ in serving Him, while Mary had a spiritual relationship by hearing and worshipping Him.

4. The word, *received* has the idea of Martha having planned and, consequently, preparing a meal for Christ and possibly some of His disciples. This was probably about four months before the crucifixion.

(39) "AND SHE HAD A SISTER CALLED MARY, WHICH ALSO SAT AT JESUS' FEET, AND HEARD HIS WORD."

The order is:

1. In the Christian life, the daily study of the Word of God must have first place. All other duties must give way to it. These passages proclaim that to us.

2. Sitting at Jesus' feet is a safe refuge from assaults upon the authority and inspiration of the Scriptures.

3. The word *also* shows that Mary took a fitting share in the household duties; however, inasmuch as Jesus was personally present, she felt that she must glean from Him all that was humanly possible. Consequently, in this scenario, we will learn a valuable lesson.

(40) "BUT MARTHA WAS CUMBERED ABOUT MUCH SERVING, AND CAME TO HIM, AND SAID, LORD, DO YOU NOT CARE THAT MY SISTER HAS LEFT ME TO SERVE ALONE? BID HER THEREFORE THAT SHE HELP ME."

MARTHA

The phrase, *"But Martha was cumbered about much serving,"* tells us several things:

• Martha was doing a good thing, but it was not the best thing. Basically, the great choice with the child of God is the choice between the good and the best. Satan would desire that one do nothing; however, if he cannot succeed in that fashion, he will attempt to keep us from the best, as he did Martha.

• In this scenario, we will learn God's priorities in these matters. We should learn them well!

• We learn that one can be very much involved in the work of the Lord and little involved in worship of the Lord; however, the Lord is much more concerned about the worker than the work. If the worker is right, the work will be right as well.

LORD

The question, *"And said, Lord, do You not care that my sister has left me to serve alone?"* tells us that Martha, at that time, did not truly realize that Jesus was Jehovah, or else, she never would have spoken so petulantly to Him.

"Bid her therefore that she help me," proclaims her telling the Lord what He should do, which characterizes so many believers.

Evidently, the Lord was teaching, with Mary and others eagerly listening. Quite possibly she had previously been helping her sister but had stopped due to listening to what Jesus had to say and, consequently, being greatly blessed. Martha, who desired to prepare a good meal for the Master, which is certainly commendable, had become somewhat exasperated that Mary had ceased to help. However, Martha, while certainly to be commended for her concern and industry, still failed in the most important part of all. While bread was important, it alone would not suffice. The Word of God, which Jesus was giving here, was even more important, much more!

From these passages, we learn that the church world is by and large divided respecting two directions:

1. Those who are working in some capacity for the Lord but have little if any relationship with Him.

2. Those who work for the Lord but, as well, like Mary, have a deep relationship. It is only this group who will accomplish anything for Jesus, even though they are little regarded by the world or even by much of the church.

(41) "AND JESUS ANSWERED AND SAID UNTO HER, MARTHA, MARTHA, YOU ARE CAREFUL AND TROUBLED ABOUT MANY THINGS."

JESUS ANSWERED

The phrase, *"And Jesus answered and said unto her, Martha, Martha,"* is said in pitying love. The same type of love was evidenced toward Peter when Jesus said to him, *"Simon, Simon,"* (Lk. 22:31), and *"Saul, Saul,"* speaking to Paul in Acts 9:4.

"You are careful and troubled about many things," concerned things which were important, but not the most important! This is the message conveyed by Jesus. As stated, if Satan can maneuver a believer into this position, sooner or later he will effect *"burn-out"* on that person, hence, the great number of nervous breakdowns among preachers, etc.

The church has by and large attempted to use secular psychology to address this problem (burn-out) when the reason is found in these very passages, and placed there accordingly by the Holy Spirit.

The basic problem is that we are trying to do by the means of the flesh what can only be done by the means of the Holy Spirit. This is the cause of burn-out. Please remember that there are two places where a person can be—the flesh or the Spirit. Paul said:

"There is therefore now no condemnation to them which are in Christ Jesus, who walk not after the flesh but after the Spirit" (Rom. 8:1).

The apostle then said, *"That the righteousness of the law might be fulfilled in us, who walk not after the flesh, but after the Spirit"* (Rom. 8:4).

And then, *"For they who are after the flesh do mind the things of the flesh; but they who are after the Spirit the things of the Spirit"* (Rom. 8:5).

WHAT CONSTITUTES WALKING AFTER THE FLESH

Anytime we place our faith in anything except Christ and the Cross, irrespective of what it might be, even if it's scriptural in its own right (such as fasting, etc.), this constitutes walking after the flesh. Incidentally, the word *walk*, as Paul used it here, has to do with the way one orders one's behavior. In other words, it is how we try to live this life for the Lord.

This direction, the direction of the flesh,

NOTES

without fail, will lead to nervous breakdowns, physical and spiritual burn-out, emotional disturbances, and even many types of illnesses. The simple fact is, due to the fall in the garden of Eden, man has been rendered ineffective as far as his own strength and ability are concerned. In other words, what needs to be done, we simply cannot do within ourselves.

So, when Paul spoke of the flesh, he was speaking of our own personal motivation, education, ability, strength, talent, etc. While those things within themselves are not wrong, we simply cannot live for God by those means. The great apostle also said:

Though I live in the flesh, I do not war after the flesh, for the weapons of my warfare are not carnal, but mighty through God to the pulling down of strongholds and every high thing and imagination that exalts itself against the knowledge of God (II Cor. 10:3-5).

WHAT DOES IT MEAN TO WALK AFTER THE SPIRIT

Walking after the Spirit speaks of the Holy Spirit. We know that the Holy Spirit is God. Of course, we know that God can do anything. What we are about to give is God's prescribed order of victory.

Walking after the Spirit means that we place our faith exclusively in Christ and the Cross, not allowing it to be moved elsewhere. Please remember, while Jesus Christ is the source of all things we receive from God, it is the Cross that is the means by which all of these wonderful things are given to us. Considering that Jesus Christ and Him crucified is actually the story of the Bible, this means that when we place our faith exclusively in Christ and the Cross, we are actually placing it totally and completely in the Word of God.

When the individual places his or her faith exclusively in Christ and the Cross, and maintains it exclusively in Christ and the Cross, then the Holy Spirit, who works exclusively in the Cross of Christ, will greatly and grandly help us in our living for God. Remembering that He can do anything, we quickly begin to understand that this is the key to victory.

Listen again to Paul:

"For the law of the Spirit of life in Christ Jesus has made me free from the law of sin and death" (Rom. 8:2). Now, let's give this same passage including the notes from THE EXPOSITOR'S STUDY BIBLE.

"For the law (that which we are about to give is a law of God, devised by the Godhead in eternity past [I Pet. 1:18-20]; this law, in fact, is 'God's prescribed order of victory') *of the Spirit* (Holy Spirit, i.e., 'the way the Spirit works') *of life* (all life comes from Christ but through the Holy Spirit [Jn. 16:13-14]) *in Christ Jesus* (anytime Paul uses this term or one of its derivatives, he is, without fail, referring to what Christ did at the Cross, which makes this 'life' possible) *has made me free* (given me total victory) *from the law of sin and death* (these are the two most powerful laws in the universe; the 'law of the Spirit of life in Christ Jesus' alone is stronger than the 'law of sin and death'; this means that if the believer attempts to live for God by any manner other than faith in Christ and the Cross, he is doomed to failure)*"* (Rom. 8:2).

This is God's way, and please understand that He has no other way because no other way is needed.

(42) "BUT ONE THING IS NEEDFUL: AND MARY HAS CHOSEN THAT GOOD PART, WHICH SHALL NOT BE TAKEN AWAY FROM HER."

The pattern is:

1. The phrase, *"But one thing is needful,"* proclaims to us the mind of God and tells us exactly where all victory is.

2. What is that *"one thing?"*

3. It is that which Mary was doing—sitting at the feet of Jesus and hearing Him speak. This can only be done presently by the method of prayer, study of His Word, and ardently seeking His face. Tragically, much, if not most of the church world, specializes in and makes other things priority that are not needful. Notice, He did not say, "Two, four, or ten," but only *"one!"* Therefore, He makes it very easy for the Christian to understand and leaves no excuse for our failing in this area.

4. The phrase, *"And Mary has chosen that good part,"* means that this is a

"choice," a choice, incidentally, that every believer must make. Regrettably, most choose that which Martha chose, hence, the spiritual leanness.

5. *"Which shall not be taken away from her,"* proclaims that if the believer will choose this *"good part,"* the Holy Spirit will guard this sacred choice. This is the very place to which the Holy Spirit desires to bring the child of God. This is the Holy of Holies! These are the people who touch the world. It would have been far better that day for cold leftovers to have been placed on the table, with everyone hearing eagerly the words of Jesus, rather than a nicely prepared hot meal and not hearing His words.

6. Once again, let's hear what Christ is saying:

"And He said to them all, If any man will come after Me (the criteria for discipleship), *let him deny himself* (not asceticism as many think, but rather that one denies one's own willpower, self-will, strength, and ability, depending totally on Christ), *and take up his cross* (the benefits of the Cross, looking exclusively to what Jesus did there to meet our every need) *daily* (this is so important, our looking to the Cross; that we must renew our faith in what Christ has done for us, even on a daily basis, for Satan will ever try to move us away from the Cross as the object of our faith, which always spells disaster), *and follow Me* (Christ can be followed only by the believer looking to the Cross, understanding what it accomplished, and by that means alone [Rom. 6:3-5, 11, 14; 8:1-11; I Cor. 1:17-18, 21, 23; 2:2; Gal. 6:14; Eph. 2:13-18; Col. 2:10-15]).

"For whosoever will save his life shall lose it (try to live one's life outside of Christ and the Cross)*: but whosoever will lose his life for My sake, the same shall save it* (when we place our faith entirely in Christ and the Cross, looking exclusively to Him, we have just found 'more abundant life')*"* (Lk. 9:23-24).

"Come, every soul by sin oppressed,
"There's mercy with the Lord,
"And He will surely give you rest,
"By trusting in His Word."

"For Jesus shed His precious blood,

"Rich blessings to bestow;
"Plunge now into the crimson flood
"That washes white as snow."

"Yes, Jesus is the truth, the way,
"That leads you into rest;
"Believe in Him without delay,
"And you are fully blest."

"Come, then, and join this holy band,
"And on to glory go,
"To dwell in that celestial land,
"Where joys immortal flow."

CHAPTER 11

(1) "AND IT CAME TO PASS, THAT, AS HE WAS PRAYING IN A CERTAIN PLACE, WHEN HE CEASED, ONE OF HIS DISCIPLES SAID UNTO HIM, LORD, TEACH US TO PRAY, AS JOHN ALSO TAUGHT HIS DISCIPLES."

The pattern is:

1. The phrase, *"And it came to pass, that, as He was praying in a certain place,"* is peculiar to Luke, with him mentioning Jesus praying some seven times (Lk. 3:21; 5:16; 6:12; 9:18, 28; 11:1; 22:41-44).

2. It is not without purpose that the Holy Spirit had this incident placed immediately following the incident with Mary and Martha. Jesus here does what He had admonished Martha to do—have fellowship with the Father, which Mary did.

3. *"When He ceased, one of His disciples said unto Him,"* means they had been studiously listening to Him, quietly observing the manner in which He had fellowship with His heavenly Father. They evidently noted the ease in which He prayed and the conversation that seemed to be so normal to Him; consequently, they wanted to pray, or rather to know how to pray, as He did.

4. *"Lord, teach us to pray, as John also taught his disciples,"* presented a notable request; however, it is not recorded that they ever asked to be taught how to preach. To be frank, when the Holy Spirit came on the day of Pentecost, all of these things were addressed. Actually, it is not really possible to properly pray or preach, or do anything for the Lord for that matter, without the aid and

NOTES

help of the Holy Spirit (Acts 1:8). And yet, the foundation that Jesus would lay down respecting that which we refer to as *"the Lord's Prayer"* should always serve as the model prayer.

(2) "AND HE SAID UNTO THEM, WHEN YOU PRAY, SAY, OUR FATHER WHICH ART IN HEAVEN, HALLOWED BE YOUR NAME. YOUR KINGDOM COME. YOUR WILL BE DONE, AS IN HEAVEN, SO IN EARTH.

(3) "GIVE US DAY BY DAY OUR DAILY BREAD.

(4) "AND FORGIVE US OUR SINS; FOR WE ALSO FORGIVE EVERY ONE WHO IS INDEBTED TO US. AND LEAD US NOT INTO TEMPTATION; BUT DELIVER US FROM EVIL."

The form is:

1. No believer can have a proper prayer life unless such believer understands the Cross of Christ.

2. By understanding the Cross, we are referring to the Cross respecting sanctification.

3. In fact, if one doesn't understand the Cross relative to sanctification, this means that one really does not understand the Cross as it regards justification, etc.

THREE DIVISIONS

This prayer contains three divisions:
1. God's interests (Lk. 11:2).
2. The believer's wants (Lk. 11:3).
3. The believer's daily dangers (Lk. 11:4).

The phrase, *"And He said unto them, When you pray, say,"* is not meant to be taken literally word for word but is meant to serve as leading and direction.

We will attempt to take these verses apart bit by bit:

OUR FATHER

This speaks of relationship. The Pharisees grew incensed with Jesus simply because He referred to God as His own unique personal Father. They were incensed at the familiarity. Of course, they had basically made God untouchable, with Jesus opening the door to Him that all who will may come.

In fact, any and all believers can and should always refer to God as their Father

NOTES

simply because all believers are born again, and as such, are born into the kingdom of God (Jn. 3:3).

If a person is truly born again and grows at all in the Lord, he will soon note the Spirit of God within him familiarizing the Father to him.

As well, all believers are now to pray to the Father in the name of Jesus (Jn. 16:23). Actually, even though not speaking of this presently, Jesus would relate this shortly before the crucifixion.

So, it is not proper to pray directly to Jesus or the Holy Spirit, but to pray directly to the Father in the name of Jesus (Jn. 16:23). However, if one properly prays, the entirety of the triune Godhead will be engaged, with the Father being spoken to in the name of Jesus and by the power of the Holy Spirit.

WHO IS IN HEAVEN

This means in contradistinction to our earthly fathers. As well, it speaks of the highest authority and the privilege of engaging in prayer to One who is the highest of the high. What a privilege!

In other words, the saint of God has the privilege of going straight to the throne of God in our supplication, and one cannot get higher than that. Unfortunately, so few take advantage of this distinct privilege. To be able to go to someone who is all-powerful, meaning that He can do anything and that He knows all things, past, present, and future, and, in fact, is everywhere, is a privilege indeed!

Saint of God, whatever we do, the Lord is inviting us to take full advantage of this glorious, wonderful opportunity. There is not a problem that cannot be turned around if one will truly seek the Lord, and do so habitually.

HALLOWED BE YOUR NAME

We are told to begin our prayer to the Father by praising His name. This properly distinguishes between the Creator and the created. God is to be praised more so for who He is rather than what He can do, even as wonderful as that is.

In other words, one must not launch into prayer by immediately engaging in a string of petitions, but rather by exalting and praising the name of our Lord.

The psalmist long ago said, *"Enter into His gates with thanksgiving, and into His courts with praise: be thankful unto Him, and bless His name"* (Ps. 100:4).

I can sense the presence of the Lord even as I dictate these notes.

The psalmist then was speaking of the earthly tabernacle or temple, whereas now, we are speaking of the original throne of glory, made possible for us by the Cross of Christ. In other words, it is the Cross that has opened up the way to the very throne of God that we may enter boldly into the throne of God, that we may obtain mercy, and find grace to help in time of need (Heb. 4:16). At any rate, praises to God must be paramount at the moment of the inception of prayer.

YOUR KINGDOM COME

This speaks of the kingdom of God, which the Lord ultimately must set upon earth. Jesus offered the kingdom to Israel at His first advent but was refused. Consequently, the *"times of the Gentiles"* were increased from that day until the present and will continue unto the second coming. At that time, the kingdom will come (Ezek., Chpts. 40-48; Rev., Chpt. 19).

When the kingdom comes, the world will know prosperity and peace as it has never known before. During that time, Satan will be locked away, along with all demon spirits and fallen angels, consequently, with the world free of this horrifying evil influence (Rev. 20:1-3).

As well, our Lord will rule and reign personally from Jerusalem, in effect, being the president of the entirety of the world—King of Kings and Lord of Lords.

So, the believer is to pray for this kingdom to come, and for all the obvious reasons.

YOUR WILL BE DONE, AS IN HEAVEN, SO IN EARTH

As is obvious, God's will is little being done at present and neither was it done in the past. God is not willing that any should perish, but we all know that most are perishing.

In heaven the will of God is being carried out, but on earth, not much at all!

What is the will of God?

One can say, and I think be totally correct, "The will of God is the Word of God." All other things, irrespective of how religious they may be, are not the will of God. Everything must coincide with His Word.

GIVE US DAY BY DAY OUR DAILY BREAD

This *"bread"* speaks of physical sustenance as well as spiritual sustenance, who is Jesus.

He said, *"I am the Bread of Life"* (Jn. 6:35).

The idea is that whenever the person comes to Christ, he enters into God's economy. This means that he looks exclusively to the Lord for leading, for guidance, and for all that we need in order to be what we need to be. If the believer will honor the Lord, develop a proper prayer life, and have his faith anchored in the Cross of Christ, and maintained in the Cross of Christ, he will find the Lord blessing him abundantly so. That means not only spiritually but financially and physically as well. God wants to bless His children. He wants to give us good things, and if we do it God's way, which is the way of the Cross, those blessings will be ours for the asking and for the taking.

AND FORGIVE US OUR SINS

This proclaims that there are no perfect believers, only a perfect God. The best of us, whomever that may be, still live in a house of flawed flesh. As such, according to the first beatitude, we must understand that we are flawed morally and spiritually (Mat. 5:3). Consequently, we must constantly look to Christ.

While the Bible does not teach sinless perfection, it most definitely does teach that the sin nature is not to have dominion over us (Rom. 6:14).

Sad to say, due to the far greater majority of the modern church little understanding the Cross of Christ as it refers to our sanctification, it is, in fact, being dominated by the sin nature. That for the believer is a miserable way to live. To be sure, it's not God's way. He intends for us to have victory over the sin nature that we do not habitually sin. However, that can only be done in one way, and that is by the believer placing his or her faith exclusively in Christ and what Christ has done for us at the Cross. As we have repeatedly stated, while Jesus Christ is the source of all things that we receive from God, the Cross of Christ is the means, and the only means, by which these good things can be given to us. When we speak of the Cross, we aren't speaking of the wooden beam on which Jesus died, but rather what He accomplished at that terrible place of death.

What did He accomplish?

For openers, He atoned for all sin, past, present, and future, at least for all who will believe (Jn. 3:16). For the believer, it is called *"justification by faith."* In other words, the believing sinner is to express faith in Christ and what He did at the Cross, and at that moment, every sin is totally and completely washed and cleansed, with the individual now looked at as totally perfect in the eyes of God. Please understand, God cannot accept anything less than perfection. So, how can He bring that about, considering that we aren't perfect.

While we aren't perfect, at least in the natural sense, due to the fact that our faith is exclusively in Christ and what He did at the Cross, which means that Satan is totally and completely defeated, in the eyes of God, He looks at us exactly as He looks at His Son. We died with Christ, we were buried with Him, and we were raised with Him in newness of life (Rom. 6:3-5). The Cross is God's answer for sin, and His only answer for sin. No other is needed!

FOR WE ALSO FORGIVE EVERY ONE WHO IS INDEBTED TO US

Actually, the forgiveness of our sins by the Lord is predicated on us forgiving others. The two are interchangeably linked together. This is the reason that many churches are dead, and many ministries are lifeless. Individuals refuse to forgive, which automatically stops all forgiveness of their sins, which is desperately needed by all.

It's not hard to forgive others, irrespective of what they have done, if we will stop and think for a moment of all the Lord has forgiven us. When we properly understand that, then it becomes much easier to forgive those who trespass against us.

AND LEAD US NOT INTO TEMPTATION

This, in effect, states, "Help me in my weakness not to be led into temptation." The idea is this:

God controls all, even how far Satan can go respecting the temptation of the saints. This is evident and obvious from Job, Chapters 1 and 2. In that the Lord sets the boundaries, the petition is that those boundaries be very restrictive on Satan.

In fact, Satan cannot do a single thing to the child of God unless the Lord allows him to do so. Now, the truth is, Christians can do terrible things to themselves, live a life of habitually sinning and following one failure after the other, because they do not avail themselves of all that we are promised in the Word. They do not understand the Cross of Christ as it refers to our sanctification, in other words, how we live for God. They have a modicum of understanding concerning the Cross and salvation, but sanctification, no! As a result of such life and living, even though they are saved and even used by God, still, such a person cannot live a victorious life. Satan takes full advantage of that, and of that one can be certain.

So, it's not so much that God allows Satan to do certain things under such circumstances, but that the believer is allowing Satan to do certain things that are very negative, which causes us all types of problems and situations. This is the biggest problem with the modern Christian. Not knowing or understanding God's prescribed order of life and living and, thereby, walking after the flesh, to be sure, Satan is going to take full advantage of that and, thereby, cause the believer untold problems. However, that's not so much God allowing such to happen as it is us who are allowing such to happen.

BUT DELIVER US FROM EVIL

There is only one deliverer, and that is the Lord. Man cannot deliver man despite the claims of humanistic psychology. This is the domain of God alone! This pertains to every power of darkness in whatever capacity it may be engaged, such as alcohol, drugs, religion, hate, greed, etc. The Lord alone can deliver from sin and its effects.

NOTES

Even as I dictate these notes, at this very moment, due to the fact of not understanding the Cross of Christ relative to our life and living, the far greater majority of Christians are living in a bondage of some nature. It may be one of the vices, or it may be that of pride and religion, but it is still bondage.

In fact, the Lord spoke to my heart some years ago and related to me just exactly the condition of the modern church.

Satan had almost gotten me to believe that most Christians are doing pretty well. The Evil One suggested that only a few are having problems and may need the Message of the Cross that we preach, but not many. I did not say anything to anyone about this, but it was in my heart.

Then, one Sunday night, Donnie was preaching at Family Worship Center. He wasn't addressing himself to the bondage of the children of Israel in Egypt, but in the course of his message, he made the statement that God had given to Moses, which had to be spoken to Pharaoh: *"Let My people go."*

The moment he said that, the presence of the Lord came over me greatly. I literally began to sob as the Lord spoke to my heart. He said to me:

"My people are in the same condition presently as the children of Israel were in Egyptian bondage. In other words, as My people were slaves to Pharaoh, My people presently are slaves to evil passions. It's all because of not understanding the means of life, living, and victory, which is the Cross of Christ."

If one is to notice, Jesus said that we are to *"preach deliverance to the captives"* (Lk. 4:18). That's what I am doing right here to you. I am preaching deliverance to you. In other words, I'm telling you how that we can be delivered and the only way and means in which we can be delivered, which is always by Christ and the Cross. Jesus Christ alone can deliver, and without exception, He always does so by the means of the Cross. That's where Satan was totally defeated (Col. 2:10-15; I Cor. 1:17-18, 23, 2:2).

(5) "AND HE SAID UNTO THEM, WHICH OF YOU SHALL HAVE A FRIEND, AND SHALL GO UNTO HIM AT MIDNIGHT, AND SAY UNTO HIM, FRIEND, LEND ME THREE LOAVES."

THE ANSWER AS GIVEN BY OUR LORD

The phrase, *"And He said unto them,"* presents at this time that which I refer to as "the parable of the three loaves." It is actually a continuance of His answer to the disciples respecting how they should pray. This parable is especially dear to me in a personal sense, which I will elaborate more fully momentarily.

Please understand that our Lord always has the answer, and that answer is always found somewhere in His Word.

A FRIEND

The phrase, *"Which of You shall have a friend,"* presents Jesus using illustrations that were readily understood by the people, and which graphically explained what He was saying. He drew things from everyday life that were easily recognizable and, therefore, simplified a very profound subject.

The *"friend"* here spoken of is none other than God. As is obvious, the Lord is speaking to and for believers. What a delight and honor to have God as one's friend! Consequently, we have one Who can meet any and every need.

MIDNIGHT

The phrase, *"And shall go unto him at midnight,"* is meant to portray the picture of a most inopportune time, as will quickly become obvious.

Most commentaries claim that much, if not most, traveling was done at night in those days; hence, the appearance of the seeker at midnight was not uncommon. However, from my investigation, such does not appear to be the case.

In fact, not much traveling was done at night at that time due to the infestation of robbers and bandits. So, if, in fact, that is the case, the appearance of this seeker at this time denotes extreme urgency. Consequently, the believer is taught that despite the difficulties and problems, one is to go to the Lord at any time, even at midnight so to speak! Even though this is the personal meaning, the parable, as well, has a much wider scope.

At this particular time, it is midnight

NOTES

respecting the world's situation; consequently, what we do, we must do quickly!

LEND ME THREE LOAVES

The phrase, *"And say unto him, Friend, lend me three loaves,"* actually presents a meager request. Three loaves were the daily bread ration for a Roman soldier. The loaf, incidentally, was very small.

I do not personally think the Lord is placing any type of emphasis on the smallness of the request. The emphasis is on the need itself, irrespective of its size or quantity. So, rather than point to a lack of faith on the part of the seeker, the Lord is rather portraying to the believer the necessity of coming to God for everything, irrespective of how small or large it may be. In fact, the smallness of the request emphasizes the greater population of the world that is poverty stricken. This is their answer! As well, what may be small to one may not be small to another.

(6) "FOR A FRIEND OF MINE IN HIS JOURNEY IS COME TO ME, AND I HAVE NOTHING TO SET BEFORE HIM?"

THE JOURNEY

The phrase, *"For a friend of mine in his journey is come to me,"* represents the one truly in need. In the first place, his traveling at night showed desperation.

Secondly, his stopping at this man's house was done so from a position of need. This represents the various vicissitudes of life that come our way, and with which we are unable to cope.

Even though we are believers, still, within ourselves, we have nothing to give to that needy soul, whomever and wherever he or she might be. If we aren't careful, we will attempt to give such a person things that will really not help them. In fact, if we don't understand the Cross of Christ, our help will be meager to say the least.

I HAVE NOTHING TO SET BEFORE HIM

The question, *"And I have nothing to set before him?"* represents a need that we are unable within ourselves to meet. In actual fact, it could be anything and in any capacity. I will give an example:

In 1992 (I believe it was), several

government officials came from the African country of Zaire and asked if they could have an audience with me. They were actually in service with us that Sunday morning at Family Worship Center in Baton Rouge, Louisiana, and were very colorful in their long, flowing African robes.

Frances and I, along with one of our associates, took them out to lunch after the service. They related how their country was experiencing great difficulties and stated that they had come for the express purpose of asking us to place our telecast on their network in their country. They felt the only answer to their problem was the gospel of Jesus Christ, and, of that, they were correct. They stated how they believed that our telecast would help respecting their dire circumstances. I immediately told them we would be glad to do so.

HOW?

However, even as I was telling them that we certainly would do this thing, immediately, I began wondering in my heart how we could carry it out. It would require the program each week being translated from English to French, which is quite costly. As well, it was an expense that we would have to bear. Actually, at least at that time, due to the shortage of funds, I did not know where the money would come from.

Exactly as this man in the parable as given by Jesus, I did what I had always done. I took it to the Lord, in essence, telling Him that these friends had come, and "I had nothing to set before them."

Frances and I discussed the situation several times after our African friends had left, not knowing how in the world this could be brought about, but yet, having felt led of the Lord to acquiesce to their request.

I went ahead and engaged our translator to come from France and begin translation programs, even though at the time no money was available. I did this because I knew it was the will of God, and God will always honor faith in accordance with His will.

We took this thing to the Lord in prayer, and did so repeatedly. Then, miracle of miracles, a piece of land that the ministry owned sold. Because of its location, we had

NOTES

thought that it would never sell; however, to our surprise, it sold for quite a sum of money over and above its original cost. Please allow me to say something else in respect to this.

GOD HAS A PLAN

As we have stated elsewhere, God has a plan for the human family, and He has given believers the privilege of entering into that plan, and by their faith, helping to carry it out. To be sure, the plan is modified more or less along the way according to the faith, or lack of such, among believers.

Some Christians have the misplaced idea that if God is going to do something, it will be done, irrespective of what people think or believe. That is not correct! While there are some things that do fall into that category, still, most things do not. For instance, the Lord knows the exact time each person is going to die. At times He will speak to a believer to witness to such an individual about his soul's salvation. If that person fails to obey the Lord, there is a good possibility that the individual will die without God. So, we must never take our place and position in the kingdom of God lightly. The Lord has allowed much to hinge upon our faith, which will result in great harm if such faith is not exercised.

So, the idea that God will do what He wants to do irrespective of the actions of His children is patently untrue. While some things may be done irrespective, much will not unless faith is exercised on the part of the believer.

(7) "AND HE FROM WITHIN SHALL ANSWER AND SAY, TROUBLE ME NOT: THE DOOR IS NOW SHUT, AND MY CHILDREN ARE WITH ME IN BED; I CANNOT RISE AND GIVE TO YOU."

The structure is:

1. The phrase, *"And he from within shall answer and say, Trouble me not: the door is now shut,"* presents an inopportune time. Let us explain it this way:

a. There are occasions, presented exactly as here, that are less conducive for faith. In other words, conditions are not right! However, as the text will show, we are not to allow this to stop us.

b. As well, and on a much broader scope, there are times when God's Spirit is moving greatly and times when it is not. It is somewhat like the waves of an ocean coming upon the beach. They ebb and flow. Nevertheless, this passage tells us that faith in God will move God to honor His Word irrespective of the circumstances. In other words, we are not to give up!

2. The phrase, *"And my children are with me in bed; I cannot rise and give to you,"* is about as clear a denial as one could ever hear.

3. If one is to notice carefully, this incident is not a matter of the will of God, but rather the particular circumstances. The idea is that this man in bed had the resources, actually, whatever was required, even though it was an inconvenient time. As well, in seeking God, most believers will find similar circumstances respecting difficulties and hindrances regarding their request. They are not to allow these things to stop them irrespective of their nature.

4. The following is the answer given to the man:

a. *"Trouble me not"*:

b. *"The door is now shut"*:

c. *"I cannot rise and give to you"*:

To say the least, such answers are not encouraging, especially considering that the Lord is likening His heavenly Father to the man in bed.

(8) "I SAY UNTO YOU, THOUGH HE WILL NOT RISE AND GIVE HIM, BECAUSE HE IS HIS FRIEND, YET BECAUSE OF HIS IMPORTUNITY HE WILL RISE AND GIVE HIM AS MANY AS HE NEEDS."

IMPORTUNITY

The phrase, *"I say unto you,"* is meant to address these denials and their seeming refusals. In other words, the Lord is telling us how to overcome every obstacle, even the greatest obstacle of all—that of God seemingly refusing us.

"Though he will not rise and give to him, because he is his friend," is meant to point out something very important.

God does not answer prayer for the simple reason that we are His children. He does not answer prayer simply because we are

recipients of His great salvation. Neither does He answer prayer for any one of a thousand reasons that one may name; however, He will respond to faith, and faith alone!

The phrase, *"Yet because of his importunity he will rise and give him as many as he needs,"* tells us something about faith that many have overlooked.

It tells us that importunity (persistence) will ultimately be completely successful. The borrower had only need to keep on knocking to get all he wanted.

The word *importunity* in the Greek text is *anaideia* and means "to be shameless." This means to keep knocking, irrespective of how obnoxious it may be to others, and irrespective of circumstances. I suppose it could mean even to the place of becoming a nuisance.

Faith is always tested, and great faith is always tested greatly. Contrary to much modern teaching, faith does not always reap results immediately, as Jesus here portrays. Faith has to stay the course irrespective of how long it takes. In other words, keep knocking!

TRUE FAITH AND MERE WISHFUL THINKING

Solomon said, *"Cast your bread upon the waters: for you shall find it after many days"* (Eccl. 11:1). While God does answer immediately at times, at others times, as here portrayed in the parable of the three loaves, the answer is not so easily or quickly obtained. This is what separates true faith from mere wishful thinking.

Too often and too much, many believers importune the Lord for a brief period of time and then quickly lose heart and quit. This portrays that they really do not have faith because faith will not quit!

One can see this man at midnight standing at the door knocking and the answer finally coming from within, in essence, telling the individual to go away. However, the need is desperate, so irrespective of the denials, the man keeps knocking.

After a period of time, the man inside realizes that his friend is not going to leave, so he might as well get up and give him whatever he desires because he cannot sleep with this racket anyway. That is exactly what happened!

Because of his persistent knocking, the man gave him as many as he needed, whatever that was! What a beautiful illustration! However, it is sad when so many believers little heed this as given by Jesus.

(9) "AND I SAY UNTO YOU, ASK, AND IT SHALL BE GIVEN YOU; SEEK, AND YOU SHALL FIND; KNOCK, AND IT SHALL BE OPENED UNTO YOU."

EMPHASIS

The phrase, *"And I say unto you,"* once again is given to proclaim emphasis. Jesus will now add to what He has already said, giving the believer a triple promise and in a double manner. Consequently, it is ironclad in its guarantee.

The meaning from this statement is that those who pray to God shall surely be heard, and it rests absolutely on the authority of the Lord Jesus Christ. It is not given as a fact that is self-evident, but as a fact that He, the speaker, knows to be true. In other words, as the speaker, Jesus knows what He is talking about.

ASK, AND IT SHALL BE GIVEN UNTO YOU

The phrase, *"Ask, and it shall be given you,"* presents the first requirement. James said, *"You have not, because you ask not"* (James. 4:2). In other words, he is saying that many attempt to have their needs met by the means of the world, which will never suffice. The believer is to go to God.

As well, we are not to *"ask amiss, that ye may consume it upon your lusts"* (James 4:3).

How can a person ask amiss?

The word *lusts*, as James uses it, means that it is our will but not God's will.

For instance, the man who continued to knock at the door until it opened had a legitimate need. His request did not concern things that he really did not need, but things instead that he desperately needed. These statements as given by Christ speak of relationship. We are to be so close to the Lord that we are well enough acquainted with Him so as to know what He does or does not desire. At the same time, if we pray in the Spirit, we will never pray contrary to the will of God, and the same goes for asking.

SEEK, AND YOU SHALL FIND

The phrase, *"Seek, and you shall find,"* goes back again to the persistence of the individual knocking at the door. To seek means that something is not found quickly or easily! However, we keep seeking.

KNOCK, AND IT SHALL BE OPENED UNTO YOU

The phrase, *"Knock, and it shall be opened unto you,"* as well, implies continued knocking if the answer is not granted immediately, or even if it is a negative answer. In other words, if they say, "Go away," we are to continue knocking anyway, and that is on the authority of Jesus Christ.

We have His promise that it will be *"given,"* and we shall *"find,"* and it *"shall be opened."*

(10) "FOR EVERY ONE WHO ASKS RECEIVES; AND HE WHO SEEKS FINDS; AND TO HIM WHO KNOCKS IT SHALL BE OPENED."

The synopsis is:

1. The phrase, *"For every one who asks receives,"* means exactly what it says. Does *"every one"* include you?

2. Certainly it does; therefore, it is meant to be taken personally. If we ask, ultimately, we will receive.

3. The phrase, *"And he who seeks finds,"* means everyone as well! If we keep seeking, we will ultimately find.

4. *"And to him who knocks it shall be opened,"* once again refers to everyone. We have the assurance that it will open.

5. In Verse 9, the emphasis is on asking, seeking, and knocking.

6. In Verse 10, the emphasis is on receiving, finding, and being opened.

7. How wonderful these promises are! How glorious in their broad sweep and all-inclusive invitation. How so much we could have more of whatever we need if we would only dare to believe God, following the admonitions of Christ.

(11) "IF A SON SHALL ASK BREAD OF ANY OF YOU WHO IS A FATHER, WILL HE GIVE HIM A STONE? OR IF HE ASK A FISH, WILL HE FOR A FISH GIVE HIM A SERPENT?

(12) "OR IF HE SHALL ASK AN EGG,

WILL HE OFFER HIM A SCORPION?"

THE GOODNESS OF OUR HEAVENLY FATHER

Jesus now leaves the premise of the believer's petition and concentrates on the goodness of our heavenly Father. In other words, we are not to be retiring in our supplications to Him but must ask in faith believing.

The question, *"If a son shall ask bread of any of you who is a father, will he give him a stone?"* proclaims that an earthly father would not do such a thing, and neither will the heavenly Father.

The question, *"Or if he ask a fish, will he for a fish give him a serpent?"* proclaims something cruel beyond compare, that is, if such were done. Of course, no earthly father would sanely do such a thing!

The question, *"Or if he shall ask an egg, will he offer him a scorpion,"* actually means an egg with a scorpion in it.

Why did Jesus use this type of example?

Many people, even believers, think of God as being cruel. Jesus is merely stating that, instead, the opposite is the case.

God is here presented as a loving, kind, generous, and compassionate heavenly Father, who delights in doing good things for His children.

FORGIVE GOD?

Regrettably, the world of so-called Christian psychology suggests that people should "forgive God," implying that He has done something wrong or negative to particular individuals.

This is blasphemy pure and simple! God has never done anything bad or harmful to anyone. Accordingly, there is nothing in the Bible that even remotely suggests that anyone should forgive God.

They would counter by saying that they know God has not done such things, but that if it will make the person feel better, he should do it, etc.

In other words, they are promoting a lie under the guise of it being a help to someone. Such is facetious! Lies never helped anyone, and by encouraging someone to engage in a lie, especially considering that it

NOTES

is about God, only deepens his problem, as all psychology does anyway!

THREE

If it is to be noticed, the number three is repeatedly used in this scenario. Jesus spoke of three loaves, and He gave three methods of petition. He then spoke of three methods of receiving and gave three examples of false assumptions.

Why these threes?

"Three" represents the triune Godhead and symbolizes the involvement of all three in the answering of prayer and its guarantee. Jesus is the one giving this lesson on prayer, with the heavenly Father being the one who answers prayer, and doing so through the agency and person of the Holy Spirit (Lk. 11:13).

(13) "IF YOU THEN, BEING EVIL, KNOW HOW TO GIVE GOOD GIFTS UNTO YOUR CHILDREN: HOW MUCH MORE SHALL YOUR HEAVENLY FATHER GIVE THE HOLY SPIRIT TO THEM WHO ASK HIM?"

GOOD GIFTS

The phrase, *"If you then, being evil, know how to give good gifts unto your children,"* proclaims that an earthly father would not dare substitute a stone for bread, etc. The lesson is that earthly parents will tend to do good things for their children even though, within themselves (the parents), they may be evil.

The question, *"How much more shall your heavenly Father give the Holy Spirit to them who ask Him?"* places God far above the level of mere humanity. Actually, He is the Creator, while man is merely created. Several things are said here:

HOW MUCH MORE ...

The words, *"How much more,"* place the heavenly Father in His proper position as far above earthly mortals. In this case, it refers not merely to power and wisdom, but above all, to goodness. In other words, God is a good God!

The phrase, *"How much more shall your heavenly Father,"* speaks of relationship. He is not merely God but our heavenly

Father and, as well, conducts Himself as a father toward us. Jesus is saying that whatever earthly parents do toward their children that we constitute as good, one can rest assured that the Lord will do far more.

The conclusion of the question, *"Give the Holy Spirit to them who ask Him,"* is asked rather than stated inasmuch as the promise is open-ended. In other words, there is no limit to what God can do or will do!

The phrase, *"How much more,"* is meant to stretch the limit of our imagination, even to a level that is incomprehensible to the natural mind. In other words, the ability of God and His desire to give to His children so far exceeds our ability to even comprehend that Jesus posed this statement in the form of a question.

THE HOLY SPIRIT

The Holy Spirit is spoken of here simply because it is through His agency and person that all things are done. God gives it as we ask in Jesus' name, but it is the Holy Spirit who actually carries out the work, whatever it may be.

In a crude explanation, it is somewhat like the believer praying for finances in some respect, with God the Father giving instructions to the Holy Spirit to find the money.

As I stated at the beginning of this parable of the three loaves, this is very dear to me personally.

In the spring of 1992, in one of our nightly prayer meetings, the Lord revealed to me that this very parable was to be a foundation for what He was going to do with me and this ministry. That particular night, He made it very real to my heart. It was a deep moving of the Holy Spirit that left absolutely no room for doubt as to exactly what the Lord was telling me. Consequently, this parable has been, as stated, especially dear to me from that moment until now.

It has encouraged me when at times everything looked hopeless. Time and again the Holy Spirit would bring it back to me and help me to relive it in my mind, with the Lord continuing to say, "Keep knocking."

To be sure, the rebuffs have been many.

Almost all of the church world has stated, "The door is closed"; however, time and time again, I have heard the voice of the Holy Spirit saying, "Keep knocking." To be sure, the night has been long, even at *"midnight,"* but through it all, I am seeing the door now begin to open.

LOOK WHAT THE LORD HAS DONE

In 2010, I believe it was, while in prayer one afternoon, the Lord spoke to my heart, saying the following: "The Devil tried to close the door to this ministry in the 1990s, but I kept it open about 10 percent." The Lord went on to say, "But I am about to open that door wide." That He has done and is doing.

In 2010, the Sonlife Broadcasting Network was born so to speak. While it had been in existence through our radio stations, this was our first excursion into television 24 hours a day, 7 days a week, in other words, a network.

As I dictate these notes, and at the present time, we are covering approximately 90 million homes in the U.S.A. and nearly 300 million more on a worldwide basis by television, 24 hours a day, 7 days a week, with the effort growing almost daily. When the Lord said, "I'm going to open that door wide," He meant what He said, and did what He said.

Most people would look at the length of time (from 1992 unto 2010) and think that it's impossible to wait that long. However, I can assure all and sundry that the wait has been worth it all.

I believe the Lord is going to help us touch this world with the great Message of the Cross, which will result in the greatest harvest of souls that the world or the church has ever known. When the Lord said that everyone who asks receives, He meant that. He didn't say that we would receive whatever we were asking immediately, but He did say that the answer would ultimately come.

(14) "AND HE WAS CASTING OUT A DEVIL, AND IT WAS DUMB. AND IT CAME TO PASS, WHEN THE DEVIL WAS GONE OUT, THE DUMB SPOKE; AND THE PEOPLE WONDERED."

The exegesis is:

1. The phrase, *"And He was casting out a devil* (demon), *and it was dumb,"* proclaims the power of God through Christ setting the captive free.

2. There are implications in the Greek text that tell us in this terrible bondage of mute silence that this was a form of insanity. In other words, the situation was very bad.

3. The phrase, *"And it came to pass, when the devil* (demon) *was gone out, the dumb spoke,"* proclaims an instant miracle. The man's mind was instantly cleared, and he was able to speak coherently. No longer did demon spirits control him. He had been set free by Jesus Christ. Wondrously and gloriously, millions have followed in his train.

4. This experience portrays to us that the condition that plagues humanity is far worse than is at first realized. Man's problem is not a mere lack of education, improper environment, or financial impoverishment. Man's problem is sin and Satan. In this terrible mix, demon spirits influence, sway, and even possess human beings.

5. Many would object to that, claiming were that so, the Devil, not the individual, is responsible; however, the individual is responsible because Jesus has come to set the captive free. Consequently, man remains bound in his darkness and spiritual ignorance simply because he refuses to go to the giver of eternal life. Jesus alone is the answer and the only answer! All the religions in the world cannot set one captive free. The greatest universities in the land cannot educate the powers of darkness out of humanity. Even the church holds no answer. It is all found in Christ!

6. The song says: "When Jesus comes, the tempter's power is broken!"

7. The phrase, *"And the people wondered,"* refers to their astonishment concerning the wonder of such a miracle. One moment this man was a mute and possibly insane as well. The next moment, after the touch of Jesus, he was able to speak and in his right mind.

(15) "BUT SOME OF THEM SAID, HE CASTS OUT DEVILS THROUGH BEELZE-BUB THE CHIEF OF THE DEVILS."

THE RESPONSE OF SOME

The phrase, *"But some of them said,"* records those who had, no doubt, been sent from Jerusalem and were haters of Christ. They were of the religious aristocracy of Israel and, therefore, of rank and position.

It is almost inconceivable in the face of such grand and glorious power, and evident love and compassion, that these individuals would see none of it, but rather only hatred and a lie!

"He casts out devils (demons) *through Beelzebub the chief of the devils* (demons),"* concerns a startling accusation that probably constitutes the terrible sin of blaspheming the Holy Spirit.

This happening probably took place approximately three to four months prior to the crucifixion. Consequently, the hatred here exhibited would increase in intensity until they had done what in their hearts they wanted to do all along, which was to kill Him.

Spence says, "Learned and experienced members of the Pharisee party, scribes and doctors of the law, had been told to watch this dangerous and popular Galilean teacher, and whenever it was possible, to lessen His influence among the people."

POWER FROM GOD

They could not deny the power of Christ, nor could they deny the reality of the healings, miracles, and deliverances. Therefore, they were faced with one of two choices: They could admit that He is of God, or claim He is of Satan. There is no middle ground considering the tremendous amount of power He possessed and used in wonderful and gracious capacities.

If they admitted that His power was from God, they would have to admit that He was the Messiah, thereby, accepting Him, and this they would never do. In fact, most of that which presently calls itself *"church"* does not accept Christ and has never accepted Christ. One must remember that these individuals were the religious leaders of Israel. As well, they were and are similar to most so-called religious leaders presently! Those who stood that day watching Him

NOTES

as He performed this great miracle, and then hearing the accolades of the crowd, grew even more incensed and blurted out their accusation.

Beelzebub, incidentally, was the Philistine god of flies, II Kings 1:2. It means "the dung god" or "lord of the dung hill," a most contemptuous and vile idol. It was identified as prince of demons.

Matthew records this incident as the man being blind as well as dumb, etc. (Mat. 12:22-23); however, it could have been another case altogether.

BLASPHEMING THE HOLY SPIRIT

At any rate, if this was the same case, Jesus followed up His answer to their accusation by saying to these accusers, in effect, that they had blasphemed the Holy Spirit because they attributed the power and work of God to Satan (Mat. 12:31-32).

Luke does not mention it as Matthew; however, this terrible judgment was the occasion here as there.

How could religious leaders be so wrong?

Even though we have dealt with this subject repeatedly, its dire consequences demand that it continue to be addressed.

These religious leaders and those who preceded them had so twisted the Word of God, adding to it or taking away from it, that it no longer was the Word of God. Consequently, Israel at the time of Christ, at least as far as the worship of God was concerned, had been reduced to a mere religion. In other words, they were little better, if any at all, than the other religions of the world, which they looked at with such disdain, i.e., the false worship of the Canaanites, etc.

In modern terminology, it would mean that much of modern Christianity has been so compromised that it is little different than Islam, Buddhism, Hinduism, etc., at least as far as people being saved is concerned. Of course, the principles of Christianity are light years ahead of anything else in the world. Nevertheless, if Christ is divorced from these great principles, which He is in many, if not most, cases, as noble and wonderful as those principles are, they cannot save anyone. Such is no more than a mere religion.

CONTROL

As well, men love to lord it over other men, and religious men love to lord if over others most of all. Judaism degenerated into mere religion because of religious hierarchy, and Christianity too often does the same thing because of abrogating the headship of Christ.

In this mix, and especially the judicial and Christianized versions, self-righteousness becomes acute. Hence, the idea that someone such as Jesus, who was a mere peasant in the eyes of these religious leaders, could exercise the power that was obvious in His ministry, and without their seal of approval, obviously meant, at least in their thinking, that He was not of God but of Satan. Therefore, to explain His power, they attributed it to Satan.

By far, the greatest hindrance to God and His work is the world of religion, and in whatever variety.

(16) "AND OTHERS, TEMPTING HIM, SOUGHT OF HIM A SIGN FROM HEAVEN."

The form is:

1. The phrase, "And others," probably consisted exclusively of Pharisees and scribes.

2. The words, "Tempting Him," refer, in this case, to attempts to ensnare Christ in His speech or actions. So, their motives were sinister and dark.

3. The phrase, "Sought of Him a sign from heaven," is somewhat strange considering that demons were cast out before their very eyes, as well as the greatest miracles in other capacities that the world had ever known. What other type of sign did they want?

4. The truth is, they would not have accepted anything that would have happened, irrespective of its nature. They were not there to investigate, but rather to accuse and, hopefully, to bring something about that would demean Him in the eyes of the people.

5. Let the reader beware! That spirit did not die with the Pharisees and scribes. It is very much alive at present!

(17) "BUT HE, KNOWING THEIR THOUGHTS, SAID UNTO THEM, EVERY KINGDOM DIVIDED AGAINST ITSELF IS BROUGHT TO DESOLATION; AND A HOUSE DIVIDED AGAINST A HOUSE FALLS."

The construction is:

1. The phrase, *"But He, knowing their thoughts, said unto them,"* presents the Holy Spirit informing Him of what they were thinking concerning His power to cast out demons.

2. He knew they were not sincere in their question concerning His power, but rather that they had deliberately taken this tact, and had done so against all reason and evidence.

3. The phrase, *"Every kingdom divided against itself is brought to desolation; and a house divided against a house falls,"* presented a truth easily recognizable by all. Division based on dissension is the sure destroyer of all. This is Satan's favorite method in churches. He starts dissension, which causes division, and then the church is pulling against itself.

4. Concerning the day of Pentecost, the Holy Spirit did not say for nothing, *"They were all with one accord in one place"* (Acts 2:1). Had there been dissension and, thereby, division, the Holy Spirit could not have functioned, as He cannot function anytime in such atmosphere.

(18) "IF SATAN ALSO BE DIVIDED AGAINST HIMSELF, HOW SHALL HIS KINGDOM STAND? BECAUSE YOU SAY THAT I CAST OUT DEVILS THROUGH BEELZEBUB."

SATAN

The question, *"If Satan also be divided against himself, how shall his kingdom stand,"* among other things, tells us of the existence of such a kingdom of evil, all armed and thoroughly organized to carry out its dread purposes. As well, Satan is held up as the chief of this evil confederacy.

Jesus appealed to the common sense of all who were there in that they easily recognized that such division would cause instant destruction, and, therefore, the claims of the Pharisees and scribes must be preposterous.

"Because you say that I cast out devils (demons) *through Beelzebub,"* presents the absurdity of such an accusation.

However, it should be quickly noted that if Satan has put something on someone, he, at least if it suits his purposes, can easily

remove it, i.e. sickness, etc. He does this at times to deceive people respecting false religions.

IS IT OF THE LORD?

There are some in Mormonism who claim to have received healings from the Lord while, at the same time, repudiating Christ and holding up Joseph Smith.

No, these people have not received healings from the Lord. If the Lord did such a thing, His kingdom would be divided, as well, which it is not.

Satan will often do these things to deceive people into believing that this religion, which is actually sponsored by him, is of God, thereby, snaring the souls of many.

As well, some people claim healings from the Lord respecting such places as Lourdes, where Mary is held up as the principal instead of Christ. Again, such healings are not from the Lord, but only Satan removing something he has placed on someone to start with in order to deceive people into believing that this religion of Catholicism is of God, which it is not!

Actually, even though this type of deception has been prevalent from the beginning, in the last days, it will exacerbate, thus, deceiving men by such power (Mat. 24:24; II Thess. 2:8-12; Rev. 13:4; 16:13-16; 19:20).

(19) "AND IF I BY BEELZEBUB CAST OUT DEVILS, BY WHOM DO YOUR SONS CAST THEM OUT? THEREFORE SHALL THEY BE YOUR JUDGES."

The structure is:

1. The question, *"And if I by Beelzebub cast out devils* (demons), *by whom do your sons cast them out?"* means that by condemning Him, accordingly, they were condemning themselves.

2. At that particular time, a certain sect of the Pharisees claimed to have power to cast out demons. Jesus was not actually saying they had this power, only that they claimed it. Actually, there was no proof that they did such.

3. At any rate, their claims placed them in juxtaposition. In all of their lives they had never seen anyone cast out demons by the power of Satan. Therefore, how could they in all honesty accuse Jesus of doing such?

NOTES

4. The phrase, *"Therefore shall they be your judges,"* seals the argument.

As the crowd heard Him that day, they were forced to reason that He was correct in His statement because they knew they had never heard of anyone casting out demons by the power of Satan. Therefore, the tables were turned on the Pharisees.

(20) "BUT IF I WITH THE FINGER OF GOD CAST OUT DEVILS, NO DOUBT THE KINGDOM OF GOD IS COME UPON YOU."

The form is:

1. The phrase, *"But if I with the finger of God cast out devils (demons),"* is a phrase often used among the Jews. The Ten Commandments were described as written on two tables of stone with the *"finger of God"* (Ex. 31:18).

The idea is that God has done whatever it is in question by His mighty power.

2. Even the most strident enemies of Jesus could not deny His power. The worst cases of insanity and demon possession had been instantly delivered by the power of God. They could not question the healings, miracles, or deliverances. Therefore, in an attempt to discredit Him, they were accusing Him of doing these mighty things by the powers of darkness. What a lame excuse!

3. *"No doubt the kingdom of God is come unto you,"* placed these individuals in an untenable position. As stated, the proof was so incontrovertible concerning who He was that they were on the horns of a dilemma. Every evidence said that He was of God. His power was undeniable! So, what recourse did they have?

4. In the face of such evidence, they chose to deny Him and as an excuse, credited what He was doing to Satan. The truth was, the kingdom of God had come unto them, but they had rejected it. As a result, they would lose their nation, and above all, their souls. As well, the *"times of the Gentiles"* would continue, subjecting the world to continued violence, war, sickness, and heartache, which has continued now for nearly 2,000 years up to the present. So, in a sense, their rejection was for the entirety of mankind.

(21) "WHEN A STRONG MAN ARMED KEEPS HIS PALACE, HIS GOODS ARE IN PEACE."

The order is:

1. The *"strong man"* is Satan.

2. He is *"armed"* with the powers of darkness, which are evil, wickedness, deception, and rebellion, all the product of sin.

3. *"His palace"* is the world, with all its attendant suffering, sorrow, and heartache.

4. *"His goods"* represent the far greater majority of mankind possessed by his evil.

5. His *"peace"* represents freedom from hostile action, which he enjoyed until the first advent of Christ. It certainly did not represent any peace for his victims.

(22) "BUT WHEN A STRONGER THAN HE SHALL COME UPON HIM, AND OVERCOME HIM, HE TAKES FROM HIM ALL HIS ARMOR WHEREIN HE TRUSTED, AND DIVIDES HIS SPOILS."

The order is:

1. The phrase, *"But when a stronger than he,"* speaks of Jesus Christ as being the *"stronger."* It might be quickly added that He alone is stronger. Education, money, power, culture, race, place, or position affect Satan not at all. Only Jesus Christ has any effect!

2. *"And overcome him,"* referred to what Jesus did at Calvary and the resurrection. There He defeated Satan and destroyed the power of his *"goods."*

3. The phrase, *"He takes from him all his armor wherein he trusted,"* concerns several things.

4. Considering the way and manner that man was created, Satan had successfully imprisoned the entirety of the human family merely by destroying Adam. Adam and Eve were given the power of procreation (the bringing of offspring into the world); however, the seed was with Adam alone. Consequently, when Adam fell, the entirety of the human family fell.

5. In Satan's mind, man could not be redeemed because of the nature of his creation and fall. The penalty for failure in the garden of Eden was death, which referred to spiritual death, and meant separation from God. This would result in physical and, ultimately, eternal death.

6. The price for redemption was life and, in effect, the death or sacrifice of a perfect life. In this manner, God could not redeem man, for God cannot die. As well, angels

could not redeem man because they were of another creation. Man could not redeem man because all men were sinners due to Adam's fall. So, in Satan's mind, the *"armor wherein he trusted"* was secure.

7. However, God did something that Satan did not expect. He became man, i.e., the incarnation (Isa. 7:14).

8. So, Jesus took from Satan everything in which he trusted, thereby, spoiling him.

9. The phrase, *"And divides his spoils,"* means that multiple millions have been redeemed from Satan's clutches, and instead of being captives of Satan, they are now captives of Jesus Christ (Eph. 4:8-9).

(23) "HE WHO IS NOT WITH ME IS AGAINST ME: AND HE WHO GATHERS NOT WITH ME SCATTERS."

The order is:

1. The phrase, *"He who is not with Me is against Me,"* places all on one side or the other. In effect, Jesus was saying that all who do not accept Him as Lord, Messiah, Saviour, and, in effect, God, are against Him and on the side of Satan. There can be no middle ground.

2. *"And he who gathers not with Me scatters,"* means that it will quickly become obvious as to who is of the Lord and who isn't!

3. He who is for Christ *"gathers"* or works to promote His person and His kingdom.

4. He who is not of Christ *"scatters,"* which means attempts to destroy the work of the Lord. This is an extremely somber statement and should be heeded carefully.

5. The believer must be very, very careful that through self-will, he does not find himself opposing the Lord. There are many and varied excuses that one may use in order to do wrong, while there is only one reason to do right, and that's because it is right!

6. Believers can easily find themselves in the position of Simon Peter when Jesus spoke of His coming crucifixion. Peter said, *"Be it far from You, Lord: this shall not be unto You."*

Jesus said to Peter, *"Get thee* (You get) *behind Me, Satan: you are an offence unto* (against) *Me: for you savor not the things that be of God, but those that be of men"* (Mat. 16:22-23).

7. Far too many believers *"savor not the*

things that be of God, but those that be of men." Consequently, they scatter instead of gather!

8. In fact, entire religious denominations find themselves scattering instead of gathering simply because they, as Peter, have their own agenda instead of God's.

(24) "WHEN THE UNCLEAN SPIRIT IS GONE OUT OF A MAN, HE WALKS THROUGH DRY PLACES, SEEKING REST; AND FINDING NONE, HE SAYS, I WILL RETURN UNTO MY HOUSE WHENCE I CAME OUT."

THE UNCLEAN SPIRIT

The phrase, *"When the unclean spirit is gone out of a man,"* concerns the efforts of man, whatever they may be, such as education, ability, culture, wealth, environment, etc., to save himself.

The phrase, *"He walks through dry places, seeking rest; and finding none,"* concerns the unclean spirit that has gone out.

"He says, I will return unto my house whence (from where) *I came out,"* concerns the demon spirit returning, even with more spirits, as the following verses proclaim.

Exactly what was Jesus saying?

As alluded to, the world is ever seeking to ameliorate its situation by its own methods. However, even though it may partially succeed for a period of time, ultimately, it will conclude worse than when it began.

As an example, America has tried to fill the void in man's soul with education. It has claimed that education is the answer. Just yesterday, the president said, "We must spend more money on education." This, they think, will solve the problem of the inner city gangs, high crime rate, man's inhumanity to man, etc.

A FALSE HOPE

It is amazing that men will continue to cling to this false hope when the evidence all about him speaks otherwise. The nation is woefully finding out that education is not the answer to the ills of man. Even though it may ameliorate the situation for a period of time, ultimately, Satan will return, even in a greater evil than before.

Another excellent example is Germany

and Japan. The evil that propelled them was destroyed by allied might and power in World War II. They have now quickly come back to prosperity as two of the mightiest nations in the world. Their defeated totalitarian governments were replaced by democracy; however, democracy, as desirable as it may be, is not the answer either!

These two nations now, despite their great prosperity, are beginning the terrible slide into apostasy because Jesus Christ is not allowed to fill the void.

As well, our excursions into Iraq and Afghanistan constitute another case in point. It is impossible to meld democracy with Islam, a fact that our leaders do not seem to understand. If one tries to introduce democracy without Bible Christianity, it, too, is a wasted effort. We spent over $1 trillion in Iraq, with over 4,000 American lives snuffed out and untold thousands wounded, and for what?

It is the religion of Islam that's killing these people in Iraq, Afghanistan, and other such countries in the world. On the other side of the coin, it is Bible Christianity that has made America the envy of the world. However, we do not seem to understand that and are quickly leaving that which has made us great. It is not the separation of church and state, which is biblical, but rather the separation of God and state. We are trying to figure God out of everything that we do, and when that happens, we are left with nothing but murder, crime, rape, criminal activity, etc.

(25) "AND WHEN HE COMES, HE FINDS IT SWEPT AND GARNISHED."

The structure is:

1. The phrase, "And when he comes," concerns evil spirits most certainly returning if Jesus Christ is not allowed to come in. This tells us that all of the world and even all of mankind, at least those without God, are controlled by demon spirits. This means that every country in the world that is controlled by various religions is controlled by demon spirits.

2. The phrase, "He finds it swept and garnished," means that while it was emptied of unclean spirits, it was adorned with things other than Christ. To be sure, it is an

adornment that Satan will not recognize.

3. This is why psychology cannot succeed in alleviating the problems of mankind. How foolish it is to think that such can be when it is obvious that humanistic psychology has no power. Satan does not respect methods, schemes, education, ability, wealth, ceremonies, or anything else. He respects Christ alone because of Christ's almighty power. This is plainly evidenced in Verse 22.

(26) "THEN GOES HE, AND TAKES TO HIM SEVEN OTHER SPIRITS MORE WICKED THAN HIMSELF; AND THEY ENTER IN, AND DWELL THERE: AND THE LAST STATE OF THAT MAN IS WORSE THAN THE FIRST."

SEVEN OTHER SPIRITS

The phrase, "Then goes he, and takes to him seven other spirits more wicked than himself," concerns the reoccupation by demon spirits.

The declaration of Verse 23 interrupts the argument respecting Satan's kingdom (Vss. 15-26) as opposed to Christ's. It is here introduced to show that there can be no neutrality in that war, for in such a campaign, everything takes its true place and must be either of Satan or of Christ.

The phrase, "And they enter in, and dwell there," proclaims these spirits able to do so simply because nothing is there, such as Christ, stronger than they are. Consequently, they are able to do whatever they desire with impunity, with no fear of expulsion.

As we have repeatedly stated, such shoots down the hypothesis of men, and even the church, who would replace Christ with their own inventions, be they ever so clever.

ALL TRUTH IS GOD'S TRUTH?

Just yesterday, Donnie brought to my desk one of the latest issues of the *Pentecostal Evangel*, the official publication of the Assemblies of God. In this recent publication was an article entitled, "All Truth Is God's Truth." The writer, a noted Christian psychologist in that particular denomination, was touting the likes of Freud, Maslow, Rogers, etc. He was claiming that their hypothesis of humanistic psychology, which, at its roots denies the Bible, is actually truth and, therefore, from God. Such is scriptural and spiritual ignorance to say the least, and blasphemy at worst.

Psychology is man's efforts to deliver or rehabilitate himself. If such were possible, then Jesus needlessly suffered the terrible expense of His life at Calvary.

No! Truth is not a philosophy, but rather a person, the Man, Christ Jesus (Jn. 14:6). Consequently, to attempt to have truth without Christ, which psychology does, is an impossibility and leads to a worse condition than ever.

"And the last state of that man is worse than the first," proclaims not only the failure of all of man's efforts to save himself but, as well, his sure destruction.

The only hope against the strong man, Satan, is the stronger man, the Lord Jesus Christ. Anything, be it education, money, talent, ability, or philosophy, that attempts to usurp authority over Him is doomed to failure.

(27) "AND IT CAME TO PASS, AS HE SPOKE THESE THINGS, A CERTAIN WOMAN OF THE COMPANY LIFTED UP HER VOICE, AND SAID UNTO HIM, BLESSED IS THE WOMB THAT BEAR YOU, AND THE PAPS WHICH YOU HAVE SUCKED."

The synopsis is:

1. The phrase, *"And it came to pass, as He spoke these things,"* expressed things of utmost importance. How wise were His words, and rightly so, because they were the words of God. As well, every believer must do everything within his power and ability, and above all, by the revelation of the Holy Spirit, to fully learn what *"these things"* mean. Nothing else is remotely of like significance.

2. It is a shame when many believers know the statistics of sports figures far more than they do the Word of God. The results are a great leanness of soul.

3. *"A certain woman of the company lifted up her voice, and said unto Him,"* is a perfect example of one who, while very religious, is at the same time very wrong.

4. *"Blessed is the womb that bear You, and the paps which You have sucked,"* is a belief that was, no doubt, shared by the listeners, that the exclamation was befitting

and truly religious. However, the Lord rebuked the exclamation, for it was of the flesh.

(28) "BUT HE SAID, YEA RATHER, BLESSED ARE THEY WHO HEAR THE WORD OF GOD, AND KEEP IT."

The synopsis is:

1. The phrase, *"But He said, Yea,"* means that it certainly was true that Mary was blessed of the Lord in being chosen to furnish the womb for the Messiah. As well, when she breast-fed Him, she was helping to prepare His growth into manhood, where and when He would overcome the strong man, Satan.

2. The one word *rather,* however, proclaims that having said that, something else was of far greater importance.

3. The phrase, *"Blessed are they who hear the Word of God, and keep it,"* means that the Lord greatly blesses those more who do this than even Mary. This would include all.

4. The modern worship of Mary by the Catholic Church proves that only man places her above others. Jesus, the Son of God, did not, and He spoke whatever God gave Him to speak. He said that they who hear the Word of God and keep it are the real blessed ones. Thus, both God and Christ are not in harmony with modern Mariolatry and all exaltation of Mary as being better than other Christians.

(29) "AND WHEN THE PEOPLE WERE GATHERED THICK TOGETHER, HE BEGAN TO SAY, THIS IS AN EVIL GENERATION: THEY SEEK A SIGN; AND THERE SHALL NO SIGN BE GIVEN IT, BUT THE SIGN OF JONAH THE PROPHET."

THE GREAT CROWD

The phrase, *"And when the people were gathered thick together,"* proclaims the occasion of a statement that would be made by Christ, which would testify to the truthfulness of the Scriptures respecting the queen of the South and Jonah and the men of Nineveh.

Further, He affirmed the fact of the resurrection and the judgment to come, declaring that all those persons will rise from the dead. This supplemental statement established the historic truth of the book of Jonah.

We will find that the Ninevites and the queen of Sheba believed without even the working of one miracle, but the greater than Jonah and Solomon was rejected though He had wrought many miracles.

THE EVIL GENERATION

"He began to say, This is an evil genera-tion," proclaims the unbelief of Israel. They were extremely religious, and yet, did not know God whom they spoke of constantly.

How is it possible to be so deceived?

If one ceases to make the Word of God the standard of all things, deception quickly ensues, be it Israel of old or the modern church. Any and all who will not hear the Word of God and keep it are evil.

The phrase, *"They seek a sign,"* records the inevitable result of unbelief. It is ironic, but signs were all around them in Jesus heal-ing the sick, casting out demons, and per-forming the greatest miracles ever known to man, even to the raising of the dead, but this was not recognized as signs. If men reject the Word of God, which Israel did, they will not accept that which is of God and, thereby, seek that which is not of God.

THE SIGN OF THE PROPHET JONAH

The phrase, *"And there shall no sign be given it, but the sign of Jonah the prophet,"* concerned the coming resurrection of Christ, which was symbolized by Jonah being three days and three nights in the belly of the whale. However, Israel would not believe the resurrection even though it was the greatest sign in the history of man.

Why?

When people depart from the Word of God, they simply cannot believe. It is the Word that gives faith, and if the Word is rejected, there remains no proper soil for faith to be nurtured. Consequently, unbelief reigns!

(30) "FOR AS JONAH WAS A SIGN UNTO THE NINEVITES, SO SHALL ALSO THE SON OF MAN BE TO THIS GENERATION."

The exegesis is:

1. The phrase, *"For as Jonah was a sign unto the Ninevites,"* means that the Ninevites must have heard of his deliverance from the great fish. He was entombed in

the monster for three days and three nights, and so was a type of Him who was three days and three nights in the heart of the earth, namely our Lord.

2. *"So shall also the Son of Man be to this generation,"* refers to the great sign of the coming resurrection.

3. Nineveh was given 40 days in which to repent. Jerusalem was given about 40 years. Repentance in the one case averted the judg-ment. Unbelief in the other determined the judgment.

4. As the resurrection was a sign to *"this generation,"* referring to the generation alive when it happened, likewise, our Lord's res-urrection continues to be a sign to any and all generations. That generation is not the only one culpable, but each and every one following must answer to this sign as well!

(31) "THE QUEEN OF THE SOUTH SHALL RISE UP IN THE JUDGMENT WITH THE MEN OF THIS GENERATION, AND CONDEMN THEM: FOR SHE CAME FROM THE UTMOST PARTS OF THE EARTH TO HEAR THE WISDOM OF SOLOMON; AND, BEHOLD, A GREATER THAN SOLOMON IS HERE."

THE JUDGMENT

The phrase, *"The queen of the South shall rise up in the judgment with the men of this generation, and condemn them,"* speaks of the queen of Sheba. The *"men of this generation"* spoke of the generation that Jesus ministered to. A great truth is here presented.

First of all, the judgment spoken of here by Jesus speaks of the coming great white throne judgment (Rev. 20:11-15).

As the Bible repeatedly affirms, a judg-ment is coming, irrespective that most peo-ple do not believe it, or even most of the so-called church. However, the unbelief reg-istered here in no way negates the happening of this coming time. This is one of the *givens* in the Word of God that will happen irre-spective of what man does or does not do. In other words, his obedience or disobedience has no effect on this coming time.

The basic reason that most do not believe in a coming judgment is because the world has been so psychologized. Psychology teaches that man is not to blame, but rather his environment, abuse as a child, etc. The Bible states the very opposite, proclaiming the fact that man is responsible for his actions and his sins. The world doesn't like to hear that. They would rather listen to the pap of psychology. Irrespective, the great white throne judgment is a given. In other words, irrespective as to what man thinks or does, every human being who has ever lived will face the Lord Jesus Christ. You can face Him now, as it regards the Cross, by giving your heart to Him, or you will face Him at the judgment, but face Him you will.

THE WISDOM OF SOLOMON

The phrase, *"For she came from the utmost parts of the earth to hear the wisdom of Solomon,"* speaks of her great journey, even taken at great expense; however, she was not disappointed!

What she saw and heard caused her to exclaim, *"Behold, the half was not told me"* (I Ki. 10:7).

According to this very statement by Christ, not only was she greatly impressed by the prosperity of Solomon's kingdom, but more than all, she accepted Christ as her Saviour. In other words, she made the God of Israel her God. It would be a trip for her that would repay itself millions of times over. The greatest thing that can ever happen to anyone is the privilege of hearing and accepting the gospel. Everything else pales by comparison!

THE GREATER THAN SOLOMON

The phrase, *"And, behold, a greater than Solomon is here,"* speaks of Jesus.

The idea is that a woman would travel a distance of over a thousand miles (from Ethiopia to Jerusalem) to see but a man, although a man touched by God, while Jesus, the Son of God, the Creator of all things, was in the very midst of Israel, and most would not accept Him.

Consequently, as Spence said, "The great queen, when at the day of judgment she will arise and will condemn Israel for their blind folly."

(32) "THE MEN OF NINEVEH SHALL RISE UP IN THE JUDGMENT WITH THIS

NOTES

GENERATION, AND SHALL CONDEMN IT: FOR THEY REPENTED AT THE PREACHING OF JONAH; AND, BEHOLD, A GREATER THAN JONAH IS HERE."

The overview is:

1. In Verses 29 through 32, the Lord Jesus testifies to the truthfulness of the Scriptures respecting the queen of the South and Jonah and the men of Nineveh. Further, Jesus affirms the fact of the resurrection and the judgment to come, declaring that all those persons will rise from the dead. This supplemental statement establishes the historic truth of the book of Jonah.

2. The phrase, *"The men of Nineveh shall rise up in the judgment with this generation, and shall condemn it,"* places another testimony before Israel.

3. *"For they repented at the preaching of Jonah; and, behold, a greater than Jonah is here,"* proclaims the fact that Israel would not repent at the preaching of Jesus. It especially speaks of the religious hierarchy.

4. As we have alluded, the judgment in question will be far more severe and pronounced than one may be led to believe. There will be absolutely no doubt as to the justness of the levied sentence.

5. As well, if those who accepted Christ, even though of little opportunity, will justly condemn those who have had great opportunity but would not accept, will it be possible that many generations, who had little or no opportunity to hear the gospel, will rightly condemn the church who grossly failed in this respect?

It is a sober thought!

This does not mean that those responsible will be lost, inasmuch as they are saved, but it does mean they will lose reward, and great reward at that!

(33) "NO MAN, WHEN HE HAS LIT A CANDLE, PUTS IT IN A SECRET PLACE, NEITHER UNDER A BUSHEL, BUT ON A CANDLESTICK, THAT THEY WHICH COME IN MAY SEE THE LIGHT."

THE LIGHT

The phrase, *"No man, when he has lit a candle, puts it in a secret place, neither under a bushel,"* proclaims exactly that of which I have just spoken.

Christ was the light of the world. He did not hide that light; it shone fully on every man. However, few accepted it, for the majority was so willfully blind that they remained unilluminated.

Jesus was speaking to those who clamored for a visible sign from heaven. Spence paraphrased his statement by saying, "Do not think for a moment that the sign I speak about, and which was prefigured in the story of the prophet Jonah, will be an obscure or secret thing. No man lights a lamp to hide: So will it be with that sign which will be given to you." He was speaking of the mighty sign of the resurrection of our Lord.

However, this statement by Christ has a side issue, to which we have alluded.

The gospel is meant to be given to others. It is not a light that should be hidden, and if the church does not give it to the world, it is the same as hiding the light. The only cure for darkness is light, and by that, we speak of the gospel of Jesus Christ.

THE LAMPSTAND

The phrase, *"But on a candlestick, that they which come in may see the light,"* proclaims that His resurrection, which will be the sign for which they were asking, will be visible to all. However, above all, it means that everyone must have the opportunity to *"see the light."* The sadness is, many have little or no opportunity at all.

In fact, the greatest hindrance to the gospel of Jesus Christ is the apostate church; however, to be sure, it does not have *"apostate"* written on it, but rather the very opposite. Nevertheless, by its actions, it is easy to determine what it really is.

I have had preachers go into television stations and endeavor to get our television program removed from the air. We have had it to happen here in America and, actually, all over the world for that matter.

Why?

Their denominational hierarchy had proclaimed that they desired this to be done, so this is what they would do. This shows preachers who were not led by the Holy Spirit, but rather by men. Sadly, those are not isolated cases but, actually, constitute the majority.

Why would these denominational hierarchies act as such?

HIERARCHY

A hierarchy is somewhat like a pyramid. That which is at the top rules everything below, which means that everything below answers to the one above. You won't find anything like this in the early church.

The book of Acts and the Epistles, which proclaim the early church, in other words, that which the Holy Spirit designed, does not mention such because such is not scriptural. In fact, it is woefully unscriptural.

Denominational hierarchies must control all preachers under them, and for those whom they cannot control, they seek to destroy. They will use any means at their disposal.

This was the same thing that happened to Christ. The religious hierarchy of Israel could not control Him, therefore, they must destroy Him, which they did, or thought they did!

The book of Acts and the Epistles give to us that which the Holy Spirit desires. Whatever it is that He wants, that is what I want. If it's not in the Bible, whatever men may say or think, of that, I have no interest.

(34) "THE LIGHT OF THE BODY IS THE EYE: THEREFORE WHEN YOUR EYE IS SINGLE, YOUR WHOLE BODY ALSO IS FULL OF LIGHT; BUT WHEN YOUR EYE IS EVIL, YOUR BODY ALSO IS FULL OF DARKNESS."

THE LIGHT

The phrase, *"The light of the body is the eye,"* presents two things: the gospel (Lk. 11:33), and the moral condition of those who heard it (Lk. 11:34-36).

What a lamp is to a room, the eye is to the body. If the lamp be broken, the room is full of darkness, and if the *"eye"* be diseased, the body is full of darkness.

The light is the gospel and the lamp is the eye, i.e., the heart. If it be morally healthy, it receives and diffuses the light so that the whole body is illuminated. However, if the eye, i.e., the heart, be diseased, it cannot receive the light, and, consequently, the whole body is full of darkness.

In the one case, the whole moral case is illuminated with truth. In the other case, there is moral darkness. Where the true light shines fully into the heart, there remains no darkness in it. When it does not shine, there is nothing but darkness.

SINGLE

The phrase, *"Therefore when your eye is single, your whole body also is full of light,"* concentrates on the one word *single*.

The Greek word is *Haplous* and means "singleness of purpose, which keeps us from the snare of having a double treasure and, consequently, a divided heart." It is used in a moral sense; however, the word *moral* has a wide range of coverage.

It speaks not only of those things that we know to be immoral, such as unlawful lusts, adultery, fornication, lasciviousness, etc., but, as well, stealing, cheating, profanity, pride, envy, malice, jealously, uncontrollable temper, etc. In other words, the word *moral* covers the waterfront so to speak.

The only way the eye can be *"single"* is for it to be fixed on Christ and what He did for us at the Cross. Any other effort is bound for failure.

The light spoken of here concerns the light of the Word of God and, once again, speaks of Jesus. It is absolutely impossible to separate Jesus, the living Word, with Jesus, the written Word. They are indivisible.

THE EYE

The phrase, *"But when your eye is evil, your body also is full of darkness,"* speaks of the eye that is not on Jesus and, therefore, on evil. There is no middle ground. It either is or isn't!

The darkness spoken of here concerns moral and spiritual darkness.

It must be quickly said that for one's eye to be single does not necessarily mean that there never will be a problem, but it does mean that it will ultimately come out right.

As well, for the eye to be evil does not necessarily mean that the moral darkness is always observable. In fact, it may not be observable at all, but ultimately, it will become noticeable.

(35) "TAKE HEED THEREFORE THAT THE LIGHT WHICH IS IN YOU BE NOT DARKNESS."

ARTIFICIAL LIGHT

Verse 35 is a foreboding statement as given by Christ and actually pertains to most of the religious world.

The Greek word is *phos* and in this instance means "something that is artificial." As well, it means something that "is not what is seems to be."

The verse could be translated accordingly: *"Take heed therefore that the light that is in you be not artificial light and, therefore, darkness."* As we have stated, millions fall under this deception. They think they have the gospel when, in reality, they don't!

Paul mentioned *"another Jesus," "another spirit,"* and *"another gospel"* (II Cor. 11:4). Consequently, it looked bright, and actually was, because it was given by *"an angel of light"* and, therefore, was a false light (II Cor. 11:14).

LIGHT AND DARKNESS

So, multiple millions call themselves Christian, actually thinking they are saved, but, in reality, they have never been born again and, therefore, have a false salvation. It is actually darkness.

At the time of Christ, Israel was affected and corrupted accordingly. They talked about God constantly and, in fact, were the people to whom God had given the law and the prophets. In reality, they were the only people on the face of the earth who had the light of the gospel. However, they twisted and subverted that light until it was no longer light, but rather darkness. Sadly, much of the modern church falls into the same category.

Millions attend churches that basically deny the baptism with the Holy Spirit. Others claim to believe in the Holy Spirit but conveniently ignore Him. In other words, what is done, irrespective of the name on the door, is done by man and not God. Consequently, all is darkness.

As well, one of the greatest dangers of all is that which is part true light and part darkness. The true light legitimizes the darkness and, therefore, deceives the person.

(36) "IF YOUR WHOLE BODY THEREFORE BE FULL OF LIGHT, HAVING NO PART DARK, THE WHOLE SHALL BE

FULL OF LIGHT, AS WHEN THE BRIGHT SHINING OF A CANDLE DOES GIVE YOU LIGHT."

The synopsis is:

1. The phrase, *"If your whole body therefore be full of light, having no part dark, the whole shall be full of light,"* speaks of that which I have just stated, that which is part dark and part light.

2. The business of the Holy Spirit is to get out all darkness and replace it with nothing but light. If He is allowed His way, this He shall do. There is nothing greater than having the whole body full of light.

3. The only way the whole body can be full of light is for the believer to place his or her faith exclusively in Christ and the Cross, and maintain it exclusively in Christ and the Cross. In essence, Jesus said so (Lk. 9:23; 14:27).

4. The phrase, *"As when the bright shining of a candle does give you light,"* presents a comparison.

5. The Pharisees had no *"candle,"* and, consequently, the light they claimed to have with them was actually darkness.

6. One of the major problems in the modern church is preachers who do not preach the Word. Some give book reports, with many, if not almost all, slanting their sermons toward the psychological way. There is no light from that source. The pulpit must shine as a bright shining candle, the candle of the gospel of Jesus Christ. As such, it will bring light to the entirety of the room. Those who are thus illuminated become lamps whose brilliance shines upon others to give them light. This is the gist of Verse 36.

(37) "AND AS HE SPOKE, A CERTAIN PHARISEE BESOUGHT HIM TO DINE WITH HIM: AND HE WENT IN, AND SAT DOWN TO MEAT."

The form is:

1. The phrase, *"And as He spoke, a certain Pharisee besought Him to dine with him,"* concerns the man evidently hearing what Jesus was saying.

2. By now the Pharisees were beginning to plot in earnest to stop the Master. They would try in many ways to ensnare Him in His speech or get him to say something that would lessen His influence among the people. They would not succeed, but it was not for lack of trying. So, as we shall soon see, this meal will not turn out to be too relaxing.

3. In the phrase, *"And He went in, and sat down to meat,"* we find the Lord accepting some invitations at times, but then, He would speak so faithfully to both hosts and guests on such occasions that He was, without a doubt, never invited again. His servants should imitate Him.

(38) "AND WHEN THE PHARISEE SAW IT, HE MARVELLED THAT HE HAD NOT FIRST WASHED BEFORE DINNER."

The pattern is:

1. The washing spoken of here had nothing to do with the washing of hands for cleanliness.

2. The Pharisees taught that a demon sat on unwashed hands, and unless a certain ritual was performed, the demon could be imbibed while eating, with the individual becoming demon possessed.

3. The hands and forearms had to be washed a certain way, with the knuckles rubbing a certain direction, with even the number of strokes prescribed. Then the hands had to be dried in a particularly prescribed manner as well!

4. It was a senseless, meaningless ritual, which had absolutely no scriptural foundation. This is what the Pharisee marvelled at. What little things religious people marvel at! They are straining at gnats!

5. As it quickly becomes obvious, Jesus had no interest whatsoever in outward ceremony, which plagued Israel of that day. This is at least one of the things that made the Pharisees so angry with Him. He preached that it was the condition of the heart that really mattered, not some outward ceremony that really changed nothing.

6. It is the same with modern churches. Multiple millions join churches, thinking somehow this effects some type of redemption. Others take the Lord's Supper or trust in water baptism, which are both proper scriptural ordinances. However, none of these things are essential to salvation, which comes only through grace by faith (Eph. 2:8-9).

(39) "AND THE LORD SAID UNTO HIM, NOW DO YOU PHARISEES MAKE CLEAN

THE OUTSIDE OF THE CUP AND THE PLATTER; BUT YOUR INWARD PART IS FULL OF RAVENING AND WICKEDNESS."

THE ANSWER AS GIVEN BY OUR LORD

The phrase, *"And the Lord said unto him,"* will not constitute something pleasant to hear. Jesus will be forthright, straight to the point, and even blunt. In other words, He will pull no punches and mince no words. When He is through, everyone will know exactly what He has said and exactly what is meant.

Evidently, quite a scene had been made by all who were there over the fact of Jesus not performing this ceremonial ritual of the washing of hands. I think one could say, as well, that what was done angered Him, and His response would be accordingly.

Much of the modern church would take umbrage at such action; however, they are quarreling with the giver of eternal life when they do. As well, false teachers, proclaiming a false message, are the bane of the church and the plague of society.

THE PHARISEES

The phrase, *"Now do you Pharisees make clean the outside of the cup and the platter,"* spoke of ceremonial cleanliness brought about by religious rituals of the washing of hands, cups, and dishes in a certain way. They were so hypocritical and showy in religion that they brought it into all details of life, which could and would be seen of men. That which was not seen of men mattered little (Mat. 23:1-33). In fact, theirs was an *outside religion* that dealt with outward appearance—of style, ornaments, rituals, forms, and what the eye could see.

RAVENING AND WICKEDNESS

"But your inward part is full of ravening and wickedness," presents a scathing denunciation!

The word *ravening* has to do with wicked greed and plunder. In other words, money and control were behind the entirety of their façade. They held the religious life of Israel in an iron grip. If the people did not do exactly what they told them to do, they were excommunicated from the synagogue, which, in effect, was a banishment of the worst kind. It meant all education was denied to their children because the synagogue was where teaching was done. In effect, it was the school of their day.

As well, employment was terminated, with few doors remaining open for gainful labor. The excommunicated individual was said to be *"cursed of God"* and, therefore, incapable of being saved; consequently, whatever vileness anyone desired to do to this type of person was encouraged and even applauded. So, one can see just how much control and authority this stranglehold had on the people.

When Jesus came, He, as we shall see, pulled no punches and minced no words. He cut into this hypocrisy like a hot knife through butter.

To be sure, they would have long since killed Him were it not for the massive crowds that flocked to Him because of His healing and miracle ministry.

It really has not changed presently because religion is a sordid business, and most religious denominations are little more than a sordid business. They are controlled pretty much by the same spirit that controlled the Pharisees; consequently, the same words of Jesus come down to them, whomever they may be.

I do not have that much knowledge about denominations in countries other than the U.S.A. and Canada.

(40) "YOU FOOLS, DID NOT HE WHO MADE THAT WHICH IS WITHOUT MAKE THAT WHICH IS WITHIN ALSO?"

The composition is:

1. The words, *"You fools,"* proclaim a caustic response on the part of Jesus as He told them exactly what they were. Unfortunately, most preachers seem to never read these words, therefore, claiming that love should be preached instead. They say that love unites while doctrine divides.

2. However, what kind of love would it be for Jesus to have placed a seal of approval upon the false doctrine of these people, which was causing so many people to be lost? In truth, it would be no love at all!

3. He called them *"fools"* because that is exactly what they were!

4. The question, *"Did not He who made*

that which is without make that which is within also?" refers to the whole man and that God desires the heart to be changed and the body to be cleansed.

It must also be understood that Jesus made these statements, not to the backs of these individuals, but to their faces. One can imagine the anger it caused.

(41) "BUT RATHER GIVE ALMS OF SUCH THINGS AS YOU HAVE; AND, BEHOLD, ALL THINGS ARE CLEAN UNTO YOU."

The structure is:

1. The phrase, *"But rather give alms of such things as you have,"* in the Greek reads, *"But rather give the things that are within an alms."*

That is, the heart, the will, and the affections, and then all other actions proceeding from a heart truly given to God will be acceptable to Him. Otherwise, such actions will be dead works. Thus, the Lord perpetually taught the necessity of the new birth.

2. *"And, behold, all things are clean unto you,"* has the idea that if the heart is right, everything else will be alright as well. Conversely, if the heart is not right, all the ceremonial cleansings will not do any good either.

3. This flies in the face of most church religion presently. Multiple millions of Catholics go through all the rituals and ceremonies but experience no heart change whatsoever. Sadly, the same can be said for many Protestants as well!

4. Jesus' heart was clean and pure; consequently, He had no fear of any demon crouching on His hand and it being accidentally imbibed while eating. Such was foolishness! His followers are to be the same as He.

(42) "BUT WOE UNTO YOU, PHARISEES! FOR YOU TITHE MINT AND RUE AND ALL MANNER OF HERBS, AND PASS OVER JUDGMENT AND THE LOVE OF GOD: THESE OUGHT YOU TO HAVE DONE, AND NOT TO LEAVE THE OTHER UNDONE."

WOE

The phrase, *"But woe unto you, Pharisees,"* constitutes the first of six *"woes."* Matthew mentioned eight (Mat., Chpt. 23). Whether these two incidents spoke of the

NOTES

same message or not is not known, with the likelihood being that they were two different messages altogether, hence, Luke's abbreviated version.

"For you tithe mint and rue and all manner of herbs," spoke of the minute care taken by the Pharisees to make certain that one little mint leaf was given out of every 10. The same would go for the rue, which was a bushy herb with bitter leaves used in stimulants.

As well, they would make a great show of selecting even this little inexpensive plant, which would make people think of them as being very religious.

JUDGMENT AND THE LOVE OF GOD

The phrase, *"And pass over judgment and the love of God,"* proclaims the things that are really important.

As well, it tells us what God is seeking. He has little or no interest in religious ritual or minute duties such as this. While the paying of tithe certainly is important, as Jesus would say, still, there were other things far more important.

The word *judgment* speaks of "justice." In other words, the Pharisees would make a great show of their religion while, at the same time, taking the money and even the livelihood of the poor and the deprived. There was no love of God, which would have shown itself in the fair and loving treatment of others; however, the Pharisees had glossed that over as well.

They claimed that all the rich were blessed by God while all the poor were cursed by God. Consequently, the poor in that deprived state were fair game for anything anyone desired to do. Religion is an awful thing, which I think these passages adequately portray. There is no sense of justice in it or a semblance of the love of God. In other words, these things are passed over as if they do not exist.

The phrase, *"These ought you to have done, and not to leave the other undone,"* refers to Jesus placing His seal of approval on the giving of tithes.

THE DOCTRINE OF TITHING

We must come to the conclusion that the doctrine of tithing is foundational in the Bible. In other words, it was before the law of Moses, continued during the law, and continues after the law in this day of grace. It is basically the foundation for giving to the work of God.

However, it is never to be looked at as though paying a tax or making an investment, and neither must we allow tithing to become a law. It should be looked at as only the foundation or minimum of that which we give to God, with the Holy Spirit continuing to lead us regarding how much more we should give.

The idea that one has satisfied his obligations to the Lord when he gives his tithe is facetious indeed. Many act as if 10 percent belongs to the Lord, while the balance belongs to them. In truth, all belongs to the Lord, with the ideal being that believers are to be led by the Spirit regarding that which they do in reference to giving.

Even though we will not go into a detailed account of giving as described in the New Testament, still, we will look at tithing as it is taught altogether in the Word of God.

TITHING BEFORE THE LAW OF MOSES

The Bible says that *"Abel ... brought of the firstlings of his flock,"* respecting sacrifice (Gen. 4:4).

The word *firstlings* actually means the firstborn of each sheep and constituted several, and, as well, referred to Christ as the *"firstborn."*

Also, there seems to be some idea, although not proven, that the word *firstling* had to do with a tithe. However, this we do know: Abraham paid tithe to Melchizedek, king of Salem (Jerusalem) (Gen. 14:18-20).

It is spoken of in this passage as a settled fact and something that had been carried on for quite some time. It very well could have begun with Abel some 2,000 years before Abraham.

TITHING UNDER THE LAW

It seems that under the law of Moses, 23 and one-third percent was required of all the people. It was broken up as follows:

• The priests were to be supported: Leviticus 27:30-33 says: A tithe (tenth) of every thing from the land, whether grain

from the soil or fruit from the trees, belongs to the LORD; it is holy unto the LORD. If a man redeems any of his tithe, he must add a fifth of the value to it. The entire tithe of the herd and flock—every tenth animal that passes under the shepherd's rod—will be holy to the LORD. He must not pick out the good from the bad or make any substitution. As well, 10 percent of everything the land produced was to be set aside to be used as God commanded.

• The care of the Levites: Numbers 18:21-32 instructs that tithes were to be used to maintain the Levites. That tribe was set apart to serve God, and its members were not given a district when Israel possessed the Promised Land. Deuteronomy 12:5-14 and 14:22-26 indicate that the tithes are to be brought to the central sanctuary, later established at Jerusalem.

Even though all priests were Levites, all Levites were not priests. The Levites were the only ones who could account for the many duties around the sanctuary and temple. Consequently, they were to be cared for with a second tithe.

• A third tithe was to be collected every third year for local distribution to the needy. Consequently, all three tithes constituted approximately 23 and one-third percent a year.

TITHING IN THE NEW TESTAMENT

Christ taught it: (Mat. 23:23; Lk. 11:42). We can conclude that this was teaching for the kingdom of heaven and, therefore, it included the New Testament church.

Paul taught it respecting the new covenant: he mentioned that teachers were to be paid (Gal. 6:6), and that ministers were to be supported (I Cor. 9:7-14; I Tim. 6:17-18). He also stated that Christians were to give as God prospered them (I Cor. 16:2). He, as well, taught that tithing is proof of obedience and appreciation of God's blessings (I Cor. 9:7-14; I Tim. 6:17-18; Heb. 7:6-10).

However, his greatest treatment of this was in Hebrews.

He said, *"But he* (Melchisedec) *whose descent is not counted from them received tithes of Abraham, and blessed him who had the promises"* (Heb. 7:6).

This proves that the Melchisedec

priesthood had commandment to take tithes of Abraham, as the Levites were commanded to take tithes of all Israel.

If Abraham paid tithes to Melchisedec, his natural and spiritual seed should continue to pay tithes to this priesthood since it has now replaced the Aaronic priesthood (Heb. 7:9-21).

Is the first priest of this order the only one to receive tithes? Should God require tithing under this priesthood at the first and then discontinue it when Christ became a priest after this order?

DOES GRACE LESSEN THE OBLIGATION OF MAN OR INCREASE IT?

Has this priesthood come to a self-supporting place where it needs nothing from those under its benefits?

Was it right that Abraham paid tithe to this priesthood and for Melchisedec to receive them for his support?

If it was right then, could it be wrong now to continue this same program?

Should a mere typical priesthood be supported and not the eternal priesthood itself?

Consequently, Abraham was the representative tithe-payer for all his seed to come, which includes the church. The Scripture says that we New Testament believers are children of Abraham. As such, we must carry on that which the Holy Spirit began in this man (Gal. 3:7; Heb. 7:2).

Jesus was saying that tithing should be practiced exactly as the Pharisees were doing it, but, as well, judgment and the love of God were not to be left off. If the latter is done, the first will be done also.

(43) "WOE UNTO YOU, PHARISEES! FOR YOU LOVE THE UPPERMOST SEATS IN THE SYNAGOGUES, AND GREETINGS IN THE MARKETS."

WOE UNTO YOU, PHARISEES

The phrase, *"Woe unto you, Pharisees!"* actually refers to the religious leaders of Israel.

If Jesus addressed present religious leaders, would He exclaim the same? With some exceptions, I know He would. The greatest hindrance to the work of God has always been those who profess but really do not possess.

As an example, one of my associates was relating to me just today how he taught a class in a major Pentecostal Bible college some years ago, and that a majority of the students in that class claimed to believe in some form of evolution, which is totally contrary to the Bible. As well, the professor who headed up that particular department believed accordingly. This is amazing when one considers that this particular denomination claims to believe the entirety of the Word of God. To be so wrong about something of this nature means that their entire understanding of the Word of God, such as it is, is skewed. Consequently, the churches these Bible college students will ultimately pastor will have little foundation in the Word of God at all simply because it (the Bible) is not believed!

THAT WHICH JESUS PREACHED

As Jesus preached this message that particular day, it must have aroused great anger in the hearts of His listeners because what He was saying was said directly to their faces. To be frank, this type of preaching would be frowned upon greatly in the modern church. In fact, were it happening now, it would not be accepted at all, and Jesus would be labeled a fanatic exactly as He was then.

Why did Jesus take this strong position against the religious leaders of Israel and very seldom, if ever, say anything derogatory at all concerning the worst type of sinners in Israel?

Evil is insidious in any form, but religious evil is the worst evil of all. As a point of reference, it was very obvious what the sinners were who professed nothing. However, these religious leaders of Israel professed to know God and were actually the spiritual leaders of the people. Consequently, they were leading people astray, to which Jesus alluded constantly (Mk. 6:34).

Sadly, most laymen are not versed enough in the Word of God to make competent spiritual decisions for themselves. To be sure, it is a deficiency that has caused hundreds of millions to die eternally lost; consequently, the majority of believers attend a particular church for all the wrong reasons. They do so because it is the denomination with which they have always been associated, the church has good social programs, etc. Precious few attend a church simply because the Word of God is preached uncompromisingly behind its pulpit, and the Spirit of God is prevalent within the services.

What made it so remarkable is this:

During Jesus' day, the Pharisees had impeccable reputations over Israel. As we have stated, their every waking hour was spent in trying to impress people with their religiosity, even down to the fine details. Consequently, most of the people believed that they were genuine; however, Christ came along and pronounced a terrible curse upon them, and in no uncertain terms. He did so because He knew their hearts, and their hearts were evil!

THE UPPERMOST SEATS

The phrase, *"For you love the uppermost seats in the synagogues, and greetings in the markets,"* concerned their love for attention and the praises of men. These uppermost seats were in a semicircle around the pulpit or lectern of the reader and faced the congregation in synagogues.

In essence, the Pharisees would occupy these seats, and would do so with great pomp and ceremony. They were the spiritual leaders of the people and demanded such recognition. This would coincide presently with those who strive for particular offices in modern religious denominations, offices which, in reality, have no scriptural authority.

In other words, they are man-made, and yet, these modern counterparts claim them to be spiritual offices even though they have no authority from the Word of God for such. They, as the Pharisees of old, demand obedience, which, in effect, is the cause of the far greater spiritual declension in the world today. As the laymen were little aware of the situation in Israel of Jesus' day, likewise, most are little aware presently as well!

THE LOVING OF PRAISE

As the Pharisees mingled among the crowds in their daily activities, they loved praise and, consequently, exaggerated their titles, etc. Sadly, this problem is no less

paramount in modern Pentecostal and Charismatic denominations and churches.

This is a spirit that Christ opposed so greatly because He knew how destructive it was and would be.

Does the reader realize that it is well nigh impossible for a person to be saved presently in most churches?

Do you realize that the majority of priests and preachers in that which is called Christendom little believes that Jesus is the Son of God? Do you realize that the majority does not believe that He actually rose from the dead?

And then, many who claim to believe all the Bible show by their actions that they, in fact, little do.

I realize that this sounds very negative, still, unbelieving religious leaders have always been the bane of the Word of God, and continue to be so unto this hour.

(44) "WOE UNTO YOU, SCRIBES AND PHARISEES, HYPOCRITES! FOR YOU ARE AS GRAVES WHICH APPEAR NOT, AND THE MEN WHO WALK OVER THEM ARE NOT AWARE OF THEM."

HYPOCRITES

The exclamation, *"Woe unto you, scribes and Pharisees, hypocrites!"* now adds the scribes, who were actually the pastors of the people, to the Pharisees, calling them both *"hypocrites."*

"For you are as graves which appear not, and the men who walk over them are not aware of them," spoke of the defilement that was attached to death.

According to the Mosaic law, anyone who touched a dead body, a tomb, or anything that pertained to death was ceremonially unclean and had to go through the ritual of purification, which pertained to the law of the red heifer. Death, being the ultimate result of sin, was symbolized by these commands. This is actually the reason that most Jews would not live in Tiberias. It was believed to be built, at least in part, on the site of an old, unsuspected cemetery.

In Matthew, Chapter 23, Jesus compared the Pharisees to *"whited sepulchres"* and, on this occasion, to unseen graves. There is a remarkable similarity.

WHITED SEPULCHRES

Some cunningly concealed their inward corruption so men were unaware of it. Others gilded a false profession with a semblance of religion. However, they were both alike, for they were both corrupt—the whited sepulchres and the concealed graves were totally depraved.

At any rate, Jesus was saying that as much as death defiled, likewise, the Pharisees and scribes were defiling Israel. It is quite a denunciation, to say the least!

The idea was that Jews, at times, walked over graves they did not know were there but, at any rate, were defiled, while, as well, they were being defiled by the Pharisees and scribes, of which they were not aware.

Can it presently be said that much of the church world is being defiled accordingly, of which they are not aware?

How could one be so defiled and not be aware of such?

Were it sins of the flesh and labeled as such, the recognition would be easy; however, inasmuch as it is religion and, thereby, claiming to be righteous and holy, it very easily deceives its followers.

FALSE DOCTRINE

False doctrine always appeals to a sinister motive in the hearts and lives of its devotees. With the doctrine of unconditional eternal security, it is the idea of continuing in sin, in other words, practicing sin, and still being saved.

In the greed message, it is the greed factor. Most everyone wants to be rich, and if they can find a way to do it under a cloak of religion, it is justified, or so they think.

Once again, Satan is very subtle. There is no harm in being rich, that is, if God blesses one accordingly; however, making that the thrust of one's spiritual activity makes it wrong. Jesus Christ did not die on Calvary to lift man out of poverty. He died and rose again the third day in order that man may be delivered from sin, his real problem. To be sure, this will lift people out of poverty, but that is not the general thrust of the gospel.

These religious leaders in Jesus' day enjoyed what they had because it made them

NOTES

rich and caused people to shower them with accolades. As well, they controlled the hearts and minds of the people. Therefore, the far greater majority had no desire to change.

(45) "THEN ANSWERED ONE OF THE LAWYERS, AND SAID UNTO HIM, MASTER, THUS SAYING YOU REPROACH US ALSO."

The overview is:

1. The phrase, *"Then answered one of the lawyers, and said unto Him,"* portrayed another group in Israel who were also scribes. Actually, all those associated with the law of Moses in any capacity, such as copyists, lecturers, teachers, etc., were called scribes. However, the lawyers were a group especially devoted to the difficult and disputed questions of the law. In other words, they were the elite of the scribes, i.e., pastors of the people.

2. *"Master, thus saying You reproach us also,"* proclaims the words of Jesus hitting home. There must have been quite an assemblage there that day, including Pharisees, scribes, and lawyers, all supposed masters of the law. So, Jesus was denouncing the very leaders of the people.

3. The title *"Master,"* as given to Him, was not really one of respect as we would think presently, but actually meant "teacher" or "Rabbi."

4. Those who held such positions in Israel were granted such by the Sanhedrin, with the laying on of hands. They were also given a key, which many wore around their necks until they died, with some even being buried with it. However, Jesus was not ordained by the Sanhedrin.

5. If one is to notice, Jesus was never referred to by His name or by the title *"Christ."* The former meant "Saviour," while the latter meant "anointed," both denoting Messiahship. The religious leaders felt, undoubtedly, that they must not refer to Him by any title that would lend any credence toward Messiah. However, they had to call Him something, therefore, they settled on *"Master"* or one of its derivatives.

(46) "AND HE SAID, WOE UNTO YOU ALSO, YOU LAWYERS! FOR YOU LADEN MEN WITH BURDENS GRIEVOUS TO BE BORNE, AND YOU YOURSELVES TOUCH NOT THE BURDENS WITH ONE OF YOUR FINGERS."

WOE UNTO YOU LAWYERS

The exclamation, *"And He said, Woe unto you also, you lawyers!"* presented a scathing denunciation of this group, as well. Whether or not the man expected such is not known. At any rate, Jesus' denunciation of all these various segments of religious leadership had the effect of uniting all of them against Him, irrespective of their personal animosity toward each other. In other words, their hatred for Jesus was greater than their hatred for each other, which was fairly pronounced in many cases, such as the Pharisees and the Sadducees. Jesus said what He said because it was true.

BURDENS GRIEVOUS TO BE BORNE

The phrase, *"For you laden men with burdens grievous to be borne,"* pertained to the oral tradition of the law, which was actually an addition by men.

There were 613 commandments added, broken into two divisions.

Scribes divided them into 248 affirmative ones to correspond with the number of the members of the body, and 365 negative ones to correspond with the days of the year, making a total of 613, which happened to be the number of letters in the Decalogue (Ten Commandments).

These were called *"fence laws,"* which were devised in order to keep people from breaking the original law of Moses. These fence laws came to be considered binding, and even more so than the original.

For the most part, these laws were silly, having to do with the washing of demons off the hands before eating, as stated, or the prohibition of a woman combing her hair on the Sabbath because there may be a speck of dust in her hair, and it would be considered plowing, which the law prohibited on the Sabbath.

So, it is understandable how the law of Moses had slowly been turned into a law of man and had become a burden *"grievous to be borne."*

RELIGION

The phrase, *"And you yourselves touch not the burdens with one of your fingers,"* proclaims the fact that these religious leaders made it very hard for the people. They did absolutely nothing to make their load easier, but rather to make it harder.

Such is religion!

When one sets out on the course of trying to earn one's salvation by keeping the law, whether it's the law of God or a law of one's making, he finds that he must do more and more, constantly adding to the law, because it never seems quite enough.

Such is law!

Some may read these words, thinking that the law of God as originally given to Moses was grievous as well! However, that is not correct.

The law was given that man might know what sin is (Rom 7:7). It was never meant to save the soul. People were saved then, as now, by looking to Calvary, which the sacrifices represented.

However, the Jews attempted to turn the law into an instrument of salvation, which it was not. Consequently, they felt that if the law contained salvation, more law would contain more salvation. Hence, they added the oral laws to the original, making a bad matter even worse.

(47) "WOE UNTO YOU! FOR YOU BUILD THE SEPULCHRES OF THE PROPHETS, AND YOUR FATHERS KILLED THEM."

The pattern is:

1. The exclamation, *"Woe unto you!"* is actually intended as a curse. In other words, Jesus was pronouncing the curse of God on these recalcitrant individuals.

2. *"For you build the sepulchres of the prophets, and your fathers killed them,"* in effect, says they were identical to their fathers who were murderers.

3. They were pretending to make amends for the crimes of past generations by this show of ostentatious piety.

4. In effect, Jesus was saying, "But if you really differed from your wicked fathers in spirit, if you indeed honored, as you profess to do by this gorgeous tomb-building, the holy men of God whom they killed, would you be acting as you now are doing—trying, as you know you are, to take My life?"

5. Jesus was saying, "Is not My life like

the lives of those murdered prophets? Are not My words resembling theirs?"

What an indictment!

(48) "TRULY YOU BEAR WITNESS THAT YOU ALLOW THE DEEDS OF YOUR FATHERS: FOR THEY INDEED KILLED THEM, AND YOU BUILD THEIR SEPULCHRES."

The form is:

1. The phrase, *"Truly you bear witness that you allow the deeds of your fathers,"* means they were following in the same train.

2. *"For they indeed killed them, and you build their sepulchres,"* means that it is far easier to admire dead saints than to identify oneself with living ones.

3. A man's life is the best proof of his opinions. It is hypocritical to pretend to admire dead saints and to make no effort to walk in their steps.

(49) "THEREFORE ALSO SAID THE WISDOM OF GOD, I WILL SEND THEM PROPHETS AND APOSTLES, AND SOME OF THEM THEY SHALL SLAY AND PERSECUTE."

The synopsis is:

1. The phrase, *"Therefore also said the wisdom of God,"* actually refers to Christ Himself!

2. He is the wisdom of God!

3. *"I will send them prophets and apostles,"* proclaims the *"I"* as emphatic and speaks of the divine self-consciousness of Jesus. The Redeemer identified Himself with God, and actually as God.

4. The prophets and apostles cover both the Old and New Testaments. Actually, apostles were not known in the Old Testament economy, with both prophets and apostles known in the New Testament. Jesus is pictured as the one who sends them, in effect, giving them a commission, hence, the words of the apostle Paul:

5. *"And are built upon the foundation of the apostles and prophets, Jesus Christ Himself being the chief corner stone"* (Eph. 2:20).

6. Consequently, in veiled form, He was announcing the formation of the church.

7. *"And some of them they shall slay* (kill) *and persecute,"* presents that which happened and does happen.

8. In effect, He was saying, "You will kill Me, and you will kill those I send!"

9. Remember, as we have repeatedly stated, this dire persecution seldom comes from the state but mostly from the church, i.e., apostate or false church.

(50) "THAT THE BLOOD OF ALL THE PROPHETS, WHICH WAS SHED FROM THE FOUNDATION OF THE WORLD, MAY BE REQUIRED OF THIS GENERATION."

The exegesis is:

1. The phrase, *"That the blood of all the prophets, which was shed from the foundation of the world,"* was pretty much shed exclusively by Israel.

2. Actually, the prophets seldom ventured outside the domain of Israel, even though they did have extensive messages for other nations and governments. Jonah is the exception, and he was accepted by Nineveh.

3. So Israel, the people of the prophets, in other words, the people from which the prophets sprang, were, as well, the one's who killed the prophets. This made their sin a double sin.

4. *"May be required of this generation,"* was a solemn announcement indeed, and yet, not recognized or believed by the religious leaders.

5. Why did the Lord demand so much of this generation (the generation to which He was ministering)?

6. It was a just judgment. The first advent of Christ as the Messiah was the culmination of all the prophecies of the past. Consequently, His ministry was of such magnitude that it far eclipsed all the others put together. Not only was there no reason for Israel to refuse, there was every reason for them to accept. However, they persisted in their rebellion. Consequently, grace refused is always judgment pronounced. The greater the grace, the greater the judgment!

7. In less than 40 years, this terrible prediction came true in all its awful finality. Jerusalem was completely destroyed by the Roman 10th Legion under Titus. Over 1 million Jews died in that carnage, with hundreds of thousands of others sold as slaves all over the world, so much so that the slave markets were glutted.

8. At that moment, these men could have repented and possibly averted that

slaughter. However, they were too sophisticated, at least in their own minds, to heed the appeal of this peasant. Therefore, they went to their doom!

(51) "FROM THE BLOOD OF ABEL UNTO THE BLOOD OF ZACHARIAH, WHICH PERISHED BETWEEN THE ALTAR AND THE TEMPLE: VERILY I SAY UNTO YOU, IT SHALL BE REQUIRED OF THIS GENERATION."

The structure is:

1. The phrase, *"From the blood of Abel unto the blood of Zachariah,"* speaks of the murder of Abel by his brother Cain and all in between, up to and including Zechariah, the prophet (Zech. 1:1).

2. Some have claimed that this was Zechariah, the son of Jehoiada, the high priest (II Chron. 24:20-22). However, the evidence points to Zechariah the prophet, who wrote the book that bears his name, and who was one of the last prophets of Israel.

3. If this is correct, the Jews did this terrible thing even after the dispersion, which means that they had learned little during their time of suffering.

4. The phrase, *"Which perished between the altar and the temple,"* presents several things:

a. God keeps an account of every injustice done.

b. Judgment is ultimately required for every injustice. Someone has said, "The mills of God grind slowly, but they grind exceedingly fine," meaning that they miss nothing!

c. They murdered the prophet in the face of God, in other words, very close to the altar, which prefigured Jesus dying on Calvary. Consequently, their sin was multifold and their judgment, as Jesus here proclaims, will be multifold.

5. The phrase, *"Verily I say unto you, It shall be required of this generation,"* is the second of a double pronouncement, guaranteeing its certitude.

6. When Jesus says something once, it is, as should be understood, of profound significance. However, when He says it twice, it is done for purpose and reason, denoting the seriousness, the utter seriousness of the occasion.

(52) "WOE UNTO YOU, LAWYERS!

FOR YOU HAVE TAKEN AWAY THE KEY OF KNOWLEDGE: YOU ENTERED NOT IN YOURSELVES, AND THEM WHO WERE ENTERING IN YOU HINDERED."

THE KEY OF KNOWLEDGE

The exclamation, *"Woe unto you, lawyers! for you have taken away the key of knowledge,"* basically proclaims why this *"woe"* is pronounced.

What is the *"key of knowledge?"*

In Matthew 23:13, Jesus denounced them for shutting up the kingdom of heaven; here, He charged them with taking possession of the key.

Such is the action of those who forbid the Bible to all. Israel substituted the Talmud for the Scriptures; the Roman church, the Missal, which it calls *"The Key of Heaven."*

Someone has said that the Talmud, in the form we now possess it, well represents the teaching of these schools so bitterly censured by the Lord (the Jewish Talmud *"explained"* the law).

In other words, they closed up the true Word of God to the people, for it alone is the true key of knowledge.

As one philosopher had said, "Irrespective of the degree of education one may possess, if he is not educated as well in the Bible, simply put, he is not educated." In truth, the Bible is the only revealed truth in the world and, in fact, ever has been.

Whenever preachers stand behind their pulpits and deliver a mishmash of psychological claptrap, they are denying the key of knowledge to their people, and instead, giving them that which contains no true knowledge and, in fact, a lie. That's the reason Paul said, *"Preach the Word"* (II Tim. 4:2).

HINDRANCE

The phrase, *"Entered not in yourselves, and them who were entering in you hindered,"* means that all who twist the Word, as did these lawyers, keep others from going in. They will not go in themselves, and they hinder all who would try. It means that some truly were trying to enter the kingdom of God but were diverted by these hypocrites.

The lesson here, as taught by Christ, is somber indeed! It tells us that those who hinder others from coming in, either by twisting the Word or attempting to stop the true Word, are, in effect, in league with Satan.

How can one oppose that which belongs to God and, at the same time, be serving God?

I think the answer to that is obvious. Jesus said, *"For he who is not against us is for us,"* (Lk. 9:50).

It as well means, *"For he who is against us is not for us."*

(53) "AND AS HE SAID THESE THINGS UNTO THEM, THE SCRIBES AND THE PHARISEES BEGAN TO URGE HIM VEHEMENTLY, AND TO PROVOKE HIM TO SPEAK OF MANY THINGS."

The order is:

1. The phrase, *"And as He said these things unto them,"* is said by some of the older texts to have said instead, *"And when He was gone out from thence,"* meaning that after uttering the last *"woe,"* He appeared to have risen and abruptly left the house of His Pharisee host.

2. *"The scribes and the Pharisees began to urge Him vehemently, and to provoke Him to speak of many things,"* probably has reference to these angry men following Jesus, attempting to get Him to say something in which they could accuse Him.

3. The word *provoke* is a peculiar Greek verb found only here in the New Testament. It conveys the idea of an angry school master overwhelming a pupil with questions so as to force the scholar to give wrong answers.

(54) "LAYING WAIT FOR HIM, AND SEEKING TO CATCH SOMETHING OUT OF HIS MOUTH, THAT THEY MIGHT ACCUSE HIM."

LAYING WAIT FOR HIM

The phrase, *"Laying wait for Him,"* has reference to the fact that this message preached by Christ and announcing the woes must be opposed at all costs. Jesus must be stopped! Consequently, their scheming would now begin in earnest.

By this message, Jesus had shown publicly His estimation in which He held the great schools of religious thought, which, then, in great measure, guided public Jewish opinion. In other words, He held it in utter contempt.

ENTRAPMENT?

The phrase, *"And seeking to catch something out of His mouth, that they might accuse Him,"* spoke of all types of traps they laid for Him, but to no avail!

Almost always the spirituality of Christ is held up as the great example, as it should be; however, His intelligence, as well, so far exceeded his contemporaries until it was actually no contest. Well did He say, *"A greater than Solomon is here"* (Lk. 11:31).

Solomon was the wisest man who ever lived, but Jesus was wiser, much wiser. Consequently, for anyone to think he could best Him by the matching of wits was facetious indeed! Even though the brightest minds, although evil, attempted to twist Him in His words, or to ask Him questions which seemed to constitute a trap any way He answered, He always answered perfectly. This alone was enough for them to know and understand who He actually was, but still, they would not believe! They gave Him no credit for His intelligence, and actually, it was the greatest they had ever experienced, miracles or claims, even though all were obvious and none with fault.

THE QUESTIONS OF THE AGES!

It is so tragic! They could have asked Him the questions of the ages and would have received the answers of the ages. Instead, they busied their time attempting to trap Him with riddles. Such shows the incurable heart of man, twisted in all its evil.

It has not changed presently! The gospel of Jesus Christ can be preached and proclaimed in all of its fullness under the anointing of the Holy Spirit, with it holding the answer to every single problem, but most pass it by, opting instead for the foolishness of this world.

Sadder still, the modern church, at least for the most part, seems to do the same.

"I've wandered far away from God,
"Now I'm coming home;
"The paths of sin too long I've trod,
"Lord, I'm coming home."

"I've wasted many precious years,
"Now I'm coming home;

"I now repent with bitter tears,
"Lord, I'm coming home."

"I'm tired of sin and straying, Lord,
"Now I'm coming home;
"I'll trust Your love, believe Your Word,
"Lord, I'm coming home."

"My soul is sick, my heart is sore,
"Now I'm coming home;
"My strength renew, my hope restore,
"Lord, I'm coming home."

CHAPTER 12

(1) "IN THE MEANTIME, WHEN THERE WERE GATHERED TOGETHER AN INNUMERABLE MULTITUDE OF PEOPLE, INSOMUCH THAT THEY TRODE ONE UPON ANOTHER, HE BEGAN TO SAY UNTO HIS DISCIPLES FIRST OF ALL, BEWARE YE OF THE LEAVEN OF THE PHARISEES, WHICH IS HYPOCRISY."

THE MULTITUDE

The phrase, *"In the meantime, when there were gathered together an innumerable multitude of people,"* concerns the great crowd that had come to Jesus in order to be healed or to hear Him speak.

It is sweet to the Christian heart to read of Jesus and *"multitudes," "great multitudes," "a very great multitude,"* and *"an innumerable multitude,"* for these statements show how attractive He was to the common people.

In heaven, *"a great multitude, which no man could* (can) *number"* will surround the throne of God with worship and praise (Rev. 7:9).

The phrase, *"Insomuch that they trode one upon another,"* concerns hundreds, if not thousands, attempting to get closer to Him.

THE DISCIPLES

The phrase, *"He began to say unto His disciples first of all,"* proclaims that the Messiah and His testimony were both rejected by Israel; therefore, the Lord here committed that testimony to the disciples and promised them the power of the Holy Spirit to enable them to render it (Lk. 12:12).

THE LEAVEN OF THE PHARISEES

The phrase, *"Beware ye of the leaven of the Pharisees, which is hypocrisy,"* constitutes a strong statement indeed!

What is a hypocrite?

This word pertains to the acting out of the part of a character, which is something other than what one really is.

• A hypocrite does not act spontaneously from the heart but with calculation to impress observers (Mat. 6:1-3).

• A hypocrite thinks only of the external trappings of religion while ignoring the central heart issues of love for God and others (Mat. 15:1-21).

• A hypocrite uses spiritual talk to hide base motives (Mat. 22:18-22).

Jesus gave the warning to hypocrites of every age: *"Woe unto you"* (Mat. 23:13; 15-16, 23, 25, 27, 29).

By and large, Christ was the only one who called the Pharisees and scribes *"hypocrites."* Actually, they had the confidence of the mass of the people.

Looking externally, it is easy to add blindness to their faults (Mat. 7:5), to God's workings (Lk. 12:56), to a true sense of values (Lk. 13:15), an over-valuation of human tradition (Mat. 15:7; Mk. 7:6), sheer ignorance of God's demands (Mat. 23:14-15, 25, 29), and love of display (Mat. 6:2, 5, 16). However, it was only Christ, the sole perfect reader of inward realities (Mat. 23:27-28), who dared pass this judgment. In other words, no one else would have called them hypocrites, but Christ did because He knew their hearts.

HYPOCRISY

As well, this verse tells us that a great part of church leadership, as here, is given over to hypocrisy. As it was the far greater majority in Jesus' day, it holds true presently as well. It is not what people say, but rather what God knows.

Also, very few, if any, of the Pharisees and scribes would have labeled themselves as hypocrites. In their minds, they were following the Lord, obeying His Word, and serving as examples for the people. As stated, many, if not most of the people, would have agreed with that assessment. However, that is not what Jesus said; consequently, He was flying in the face of most public opinion.

The first sign of their hypocrisy was their bitter opposition to Christ. It is impossible to be for God and against that which is of God. If one is truly following the Lord, one will truly know that which is of the Lord.

They did not know that Jesus was from God, and, in reality, was God, simply because they were not truly following the Word of God, but rather a religion of their own making. This is what constituted the *"leaven."*

This leaven was the interpretations and traditions of men, which they substituted for the Word of God (Mat. 15:1-9; 16:6-12; 23:1-33; Lk. 11:37-52).

Some Bible expositors claim that the Pharisees knew that what they were doing was wrong concerning these traditions of men; however, I think not!

By its very nature, deception causes one to hide the real truth, even from oneself. In other words, if a person tells a lie long enough, he begins to believe the lie. I think the Pharisees and scribes believed their own lie; however, this did not make it any less wrong.

(2) "FOR THERE IS NOTHING COVERED, THAT SHALL NOT BE REVEALED; NEITHER HID, THAT SHALL NOT BE KNOWN."

The exegesis is:

1. The idea of this verse is that everything covered over by hypocrisy will ultimately be revealed. What truly is or isn't will ultimately come out!

2. The wrong direction of hypocrisy will be handled in one of two ways:

a. Repentance will bring one to the right ways of the Lord and insure salvation. Actually, repentance to God is the only true cure for hypocrisy.

b. If hypocrisy is not handled by repentance, it will come out at the great white throne judgment (Rev. 20:11-15). For the Pharisees who repented, they found eternal life. For those who did not, they died eternally lost, despite their great claims and show of religion.

3. As well, the text tells us that God has decreed this, and it will come to pass.

4. Hypocrites are overly concerned about what men think instead of what God knows;

consequently, their entire life style is directed toward impressing men. Naturally, all would desire for people to think well of them; however, whether people do or do not really makes little difference. As stated, it's what God knows that really counts, and He alone is the one whom the individual must please.

5. The Scripture says, *"Enoch ... Had this testimony, that he pleased God"* (Heb. 11:5). There was nothing said about him having a testimony that pleased man. In fact, it probably did not please man.

6. So, if it is false, the Lord says that it will ultimately be revealed. Likewise, if it is real, that will ultimately be revealed.

(3) "THEREFORE WHATSOEVER YOU HAVE SPOKEN IN DARKNESS SHALL BE HEARD IN THE LIGHT; AND THAT WHICH YOU HAVE SPOKEN IN THE EAR IN CLOSETS SHALL BE PROCLAIMED UPON THE HOUSETOPS."

The structure is:

1. The phrase, *"Therefore whatsoever you have spoken in darkness shall be heard in the light,"* once again, but in a slightly different way, proclaims that sin will ultimately be brought out.

2. As well, it means that these things spoken in darkness, i.e., wrong doings, are always heard by God, who dwells in light.

3. *"And that which you have spoken in the ear in closets shall be proclaimed upon the housetops,"* concerns the plotting of the Pharisees behind closed doors. He was letting them know that He knew what they were doing.

4. As we now see, the whole world, and for all time, knows of these dastardly plots by these men, with nothing being hidden. What a warning! In other words, what they really were, despite what they said or what the people thought, would ultimately be revealed for all to know, and we mean all!

5. In the light of eternity, that goes not only for the Pharisees and scribes, but for every single person, irrespective of whom they may be. Once again, all such activity can be handled by repentance unto God, but if not, it will ultimately be heralded far and wide. In other words, eventually, the whole world, and for all time, is going to know exactly what was right and what was wrong.

(4) "AND I SAY UNTO YOU MY FRIENDS, BE NOT AFRAID OF THEM WHO KILL THE BODY, AND AFTER THAT HAVE NO MORE THAT THEY CAN DO."

The composition is:

1. The phrase, *"And I say unto you My friends, Be not afraid of them who kill the body,"* tells us two things:

a. The believer is not to fear man in any capacity. While common sense should be used in any and all things, still, no work for God should be predicated on what man will or will not do. The believer is to obey the Lord irrespective of what man may do.

To be sure, this hits at the very heart of every single individual. Tragically, most believers, and especially preachers, follow not God but man. While the laity mostly does so for different reasons, most of the time preachers do what they do out of fear of their denomination. In other words, if they do not abide strictly by the policy of that denomination, no matter how unscriptural, they fear the consequences; therefore, their decisions are made on that basis.

b. From this passage we know that persecution will follow those who truly follow Christ. Man, and more particularly religious man, is going to greatly oppose the true believer. As the Pharisees opposed Christ, likewise, their modern counterparts will oppose all true followers of Christ.

2. In these statements Jesus will not conceal the earthly price that His chosen servants must pay in their following of Him.

3. *"And after that have no more that they can do,"* proclaims the fact that there is a point beyond which human malice is utterly powerless. In other words, the most they can do is kill the body; they cannot take the soul.

4. So, man fear is not to be prevalent in the heart of the believer.

(5) "BUT I WILL FOREWARN YOU WHOM YOU SHALL FEAR: FEAR HIM, WHICH AFTER HE HAS KILLED HAS POWER TO CAST INTO HELL; YEA, I SAY UNTO YOU, FEAR HIM."

The synopsis is:

1. The phrase, *"But I will forewarn you whom you shall fear,"* tells us in no uncertain terms Who and what we should fear. It is God and God alone!

2. God is the one we are to please; God is the one to whom we are to look; and God is the one we must fear.

3. Consequently, to fear anything or anyone else is a direct contradiction of the Word of God.

4. The phrase, *"Fear Him, which after He has killed has power to cast into hell,"* tells us several things:

a. As stated, we are to fear God alone!

b. God has the power not only to kill but to place one in hell. Man can only kill; he has no authority thereafter.

c. This passage tells us in no uncertain terms that there is a hell.

d. This tells us that God actually places the person in hell. Many have claimed that Satan is the one who does such; however, this tells us differently. There is no domain in which He is not Lord, even hell itself.

5. The phrase, *"Yea, I say unto you, Fear Him,"* presents the second time this is stated and, therefore, is meant to be clearly understood.

6. The idea is that the greater fear of God will banish the lesser fear of man.

(6) "ARE NOT FIVE SPARROWS SOLD FOR TWO FARTHINGS, AND NOT ONE OF THEM IS FORGOTTEN BEFORE GOD?"

The composition is:

1. Every incident and transaction, no matter how small or seemingly insignificant, is known and recorded by God. He is omnipotent (all-powerful), omniscient (all-knowing), and omnipresent (everywhere at the same time).

2. Though persecution and bitter suffering (even death) may be the lot of the Lord's true servants, none of these things can happen, however, without the consent of God.

3. To be in the hands of such an all-wise and all-loving God provides a sense of security and well being unobtainable anywhere else.

(7) "BUT EVEN THE VERY HAIRS OF YOUR HEAD ARE ALL NUMBERED. FEAR NOT THEREFORE: YOU ARE OF MORE VALUE THAN MANY SPARROWS."

The composition is:

1. The phrase, *"But even the very hairs of your head are all numbered,"* presents

a degree of knowledge that, up to this very moment, is beyond the ability of any human being to comprehend.

2. So, this tells us that not only does God superintend every happening that takes place in the world, but He does so to such detail that it is beyond the scope of human imagination.

3. *"Fear not therefore: you are of more value than many sparrows,"* proclaims the fact that if God will superintend such care for a little sparrow, which is very nearly worthless, surely, we cannot doubt His knowledge of, or His caring for, the life or death of one of His proven and gallant followers.

4. To those who truly love and follow the Lord, such minute inspection and total knowledge are welcomed with open arms. However, to those who would desire to do wrong, which constitutes most of the world, they must understand, as well, that nothing can be hidden from the Lord. All are open and obvious to His eyes.

5. As well, we learn from this passage of the value of man above other parts of God's creation.

(8) "ALSO I SAY UNTO YOU, WHO-SOEVER SHALL CONFESS ME BEFORE MEN, HIM SHALL THE SON OF MAN ALSO CONFESS BEFORE THE ANGELS OF GOD."

CONFESSING CHRIST

The phrase, *"Also I say unto you, Whosoever shall confess Me before men,"* proclaims several things:

• Confessing Christ will not be easy and will be done in some cases in the face of persecution, even death.

• Confession before men is absolutely necessary if one is to truly serve the Lord.

• The word *whosoever* applies to all and means that none are excluded.

What does it mean to confess the Lord?

Confession means to declare publicly a personal relationship with, and allegiance to, Christ. It is an act of open, joyful commitment made to God in the presence of the world, by which a congregation or individuals bind themselves in loyalty to God through Jesus Christ.

As well, it implies a decision to pledge

oneself in loyalty to Jesus Christ as Lord in response to the work of the Holy Spirit.

To confess Jesus Christ is to acknowledge Him as the Messiah (Mat. 16:16; Mk. 4:29; Jn. 1:41; 9:22), as the Son of God (Mat. 8:29; Jn. 1:34, 49; II Jn. 4:15), that He came in the flesh (I Jn. 4:2; II Jn. 7), and that He is Lord, primarily on the grounds of the Cross, the resurrection, and ascension (Rom. 10:9; I Cor. 12:3; Phil. 2:11).

THE ANGELS OF GOD

As well, confession of Jesus Christ is linked intimately with the confession of sins. To confess Christ is to confess that He died for our sins, and, as well, to confess one's sins in real repentance is to look to Christ for forgiveness (I Jn. 1:5-10).

Although confession of sins is addressed to God, confession of faith in Jesus Christ must be made openly *"before men"* (Mat. 10:32; Lk. 12:8; I Tim. 6:12), by word of mouth (Rom. 10:9; Phil. 2:11), and as Jesus implies, it may be costly (Mat. 10:32-39; Jn. 9:22; 12:42).

Confessing Jesus Christ is the very opposite of denying Jesus Christ.

The phrase, *"Him shall the Son of Man also confess before the angels of God,"* has an eschatological perspective.

It means that Jesus will confess those who confess Him before the glorious throng of heavenly beings, both presently and in the coming day. This will be done before the mighty angels, as well as the awful seraphim, before that countless crowd of winged and burning ones who assisted at the awful mysteries of Sinai. Those who have confessed Him, witnessed for Him, and suffered because of Him shall be acknowledged in the most grand and glorious way by Him.

The grandeur of this confession before the angels and all the host of heaven shall so far eclipse our mild confession of Him before men that the reward is all out of proportion to the mere act itself.

(9) BUT HE WHO DENIES ME BEFORE MEN SHALL BE DENIED BEFORE THE ANGELS OF GOD."

The exegesis is:

1. As glorious and wonderful the recompense to the faithful and loyal, as equally

shameful will be that meted out to the cowardly and faint-hearted.

2. In other words, before this same glorious throng will the King detail the failure, which is because of man fear, of those whom He had spoken to for royal service. Now He is the Saviour; then He will be the judge.

3. As well, these passages declare to all that Jesus Christ, the poor Galilee Rabbi, is in truth King of Kings and Lord of Lords!

(10) "AND WHOSOEVER SHALL SPEAK A WORD AGAINST THE SON OF MAN, IT SHALL BE FORGIVEN HIM: BUT UNTO HIM WHO BLASPHEMES AGAINST THE HOLY SPIRIT IT SHALL NOT BE FORGIVEN."

TWO DIFFERENT TYPES OF SINS

Verse 10 proclaims two different types of sins and who can commit these sins.

1. *"And whosoever shall speak a word against the Son of Man, it shall be forgiven him"*: This statement says that for all people in the world and for whatever they might say against Jesus, they will be forgiven if they ask and seek such forgiveness. However, the forgiveness is not automatic, it must be sought (I Jn. 1:9).

2. *"But unto him who blasphemes against the Holy Spirit it shall not be forgiven"*: This blasphemy cannot be committed by those who make no profession of the Lord. The only contact these individuals have with the Holy Spirit is His convicting power. They are not called upon to make judgments concerning the work of God because they are not a part of that work, and they have no knowledge of it. Consequently, it is impossible for such a one to blaspheme the Holy Spirit.

This sin is committed by professors of religion. They claim to know God, as the Pharisees did, and among other things, attribute to Satan that which is of God, as the Pharisees did Jesus.

In fact, the Pharisees blasphemed the Holy Spirit when they claimed Jesus was casting out demons by the power of Satan instead of God. As such, and from that moment, they were doomed to eternal perdition.

I think many modern professors of religion fall into the same category as well.

NOTES

They have denied the Holy Spirit and attributed His work to Satan.

SOME QUESTIONS CONCERNING BLASPHEMING THE HOLY SPIRIT

• WILL SUCH A PERSON KNOW HE HAS BLASPHEMED THE HOLY SPIRIT?

No, he will not! The Pharisees did not know and neither will their modern counterparts. When the individual reaches this stage, he has long since left the Lord, that is, if he ever truly knew Him. Consequently, there is no witness of the Spirit to such adverse action simply because the Spirit is not there.

• WILL SUCH A PERSON CRY TO GOD FOR MERCY AND BE DENIED?

No! If he does not know he has blasphemed the Holy Spirit, there would be no desire for forgiveness simply because he does not think he's done anything wrong.

As well, the scriptural evidence is that for anyone who cries to God for mercy, such is always granted, and without exception. There is no such thing in the Word of God of anyone truly asking God for mercy but that it is granted.

• IS IT POSSIBLE THAT SOME HAVE BLASPHEMED THE HOLY SPIRIT AND CONTINUE TO PREACH?

Yes! There are some, if not many preachers, who continue to preach after blaspheming the Holy Spirit. In truth, the Pharisees and scribes continued right on even though having committed this terrible sin.

(11) "AND WHEN THEY BRING YOU UNTO THE SYNAGOGUES, AND UNTO MAGISTRATES, AND POWERS, TAKE YOU NO THOUGHT HOW OR WHAT THING YOU SHALL ANSWER, OR WHAT YOU SHALL SAY."

The order is:

1. The phrase, *"And when they bring you unto the synagogues, and unto magistrates, and powers,"* doesn't say "if," but rather *"when."* An example is Stephen before the Sanhedrin, as well as Peter's message before the same tribunal, and Paul's before Felix and Festus. Tens of thousands have followed in that train.

2. The world's system is opposed to Christ. However, in comparison to the apostate

church, the opposition is mild. Most of the persecution down through the ages has come about through man-made religion.

3. *"Take you* (You must take) *no thought how or what thing you shall answer, or what you shall say,"* simply means to not be full of anxiety.

4. It does not mean that no preparation should be made, but only that trust must be placed in the Lord to provide suitable answers.

(12) "FOR THE HOLY SPIRIT SHALL TEACH YOU IN THE SAME HOUR WHAT YOU OUGHT TO SAY."

The composition is:

1. This teaches us that the Lord has impressed upon the conscience and heart of His followers that whatever might be the trials, He will protect them, at least in the way He desires.

2. He has promised to so watch over them that the very hairs of their heads are numbered, and in heaven He acknowledges their faithfulness before the angels. As well, their mission is so important that its rejection will be more fatal than the rejection of Christ Himself. He has promised to all who truly follow Christ an active participation by the Holy Spirit in their efforts. The Holy Spirit is to be the teacher.

3. However, if one is to notice, He did not say that He would deliver every time, but that the Spirit would tell them what to say.

4. Paul was delivered several times, but there came a time that he was not delivered and actually paid with his life. The same could be said for all the apostles and millions of others down through the many centuries.

5. Once we start to follow Christ, our lives belong to Him. If He chooses to deliver, He shall; if not, He won't!

(13) "AND ONE OF THE COMPANY SAID UNTO HIM, MASTER, SPEAK TO MY BROTHER, THAT HE DIVIDE THE INHERITANCE WITH ME."

The pattern is:

1. The phrase, *"And one of the company said unto him,"* presents an individual making a request of the Lord. As we soon shall see, the request was selfish, as are so many of our requests.

2. *"Master, speak to my brother, that he divide the inheritance with me,"* proclaims the utter selfish worldliness of the man, who, after hearing the solemn and impressive words just spoken, could intrude such a request.

3. His mind was on mundane things, while Jesus was speaking of eternal things. How so like most in the modern church.

4. Much of the modern so-called faith ministry is, in fact, busily attempting to get their *"inheritance,"* while they ignore the things that really matter. The man could have asked Jesus any question he so desired, but he chose to present this secular matter; consequently, the insensibility and rudeness of the natural heart is here exhibited.

(14) "AND HE SAID UNTO HIM, MAN, WHO MADE ME A JUDGE OR A DIVIDER OVER YOU?"

The diagram is:

1. Had the Lord interfered in civil government, He would have placed Himself in the power of His enemies. That was not His place. He dealt with souls and directed men's attention to another life that lies beyond the grave.

2. At the same time, He unmasked the heart of the interrupter, and in His parable of the rich man, raised the question of the soul in comparison to worldly goods.

(15) "AND HE SAID UNTO THEM, TAKE HEED, AND BEWARE OF COVETOUSNESS: FOR A MAN'S LIFE CONSISTETH NOT IN THE ABUNDANCE OF THE THINGS WHICH HE POSSESSETH."

TAKE HEED

The phrase, *"And He said unto them, Take heed,"* concerns Jesus directing His answer not only to the man but now to the entirety of the crowd.

Jesus, as the reader of hearts, saw what was at the bottom of the man's question, which was greed, rather than a fiery indignation at a wrong endured.

The phrase, *"And beware of covetousness,"* presents one of the besetting sins of the human race.

WHAT IS COVETOUSNESS?

Someone has said that covetousness is

desire running riot. The commandment makes it clear that it is wrong to desire the wrong things: *"You shall not covet your neighbor's house, you shall not covet your neighbor's wife, nor his manservant, nor his maidservant, nor his ox, nor his ass, nor anything that is your neighbor's"* (Ex. 20:17). However, it is not wrong, and rather right, to desire and take pleasure in one's house, wife, possessions, etc.

Romans, Chapter 7, argues that there is a fault within, which is the real origin of covetousness.

It is a fault that transforms pleasure in good things into a passionate longing for what we do not have.

Actually, the tenth commandment, rather than making us less covetous, in reality, stimulates every kind of covetous desire (Rom. 7:8).

To say "don't" makes us aware of desire; it does not quench it. It takes a work of God's Spirit to redirect our passions and to give us contentment in those things that God intends us to have.

A MAN'S LIFE

The phrase, *"For a man's life consisteth* (consists) *not in the abundance of the things which he possesseth* (possesses)," is a truth of unparalleled proportions.

In fact, most of the world tries to find life in possessions. However, there is no *"life"* in these things.

Were man only a physical being, perhaps these things would satisfy; however, inasmuch as man is, as well, a spiritual being, material things do not satisfy. In fact, man is a spiritual being to a far greater degree than otherwise. The physical part dies and will go back to dust, while the spiritual, consisting of the soul and spirit, lives forever.

Someone has said, "The soul of man is so big that only God can fill it up."

When the Lord comes into the heart and life, He brings with Him a satisfaction that cannot be found any other place. This is the reason that many who live on a small fixed income and have little but the necessities of life still enjoy a fulfilled life in Christ that even a billionaire cannot have if he does not know God.

In fact, Jesus can take the place of anything, but nothing can take the place of Jesus.

JESUS

Let us say it again: Jesus can take the place of anything, but nothing can take the place of Jesus.

I had the occasion to visit the Soviet Union before it fell and to observe first hand the world's largest materialistic state. Claiming there was no God, its government attempted to satisfy the longing of the people with mere *"things."* However, even that was in short supply, very short supply!

In their quest for things and with the government enjoying total control, they somehow felt that big was better; consequently, they built huge buildings of every sort. For instance, the hotel, if one would call it that, in which we were staying, had 5,000 rooms; however, a godless, materialistic state will ultimately come to corruption, for in the ignoring of God, one ignores life.

Consequently, it fell, as fall it must! Tragically, America and Canada are more and more leaning in that direction. It is called the separation of church and state, which is biblical if done correctly; however, it is rather becoming the separation of God and state.

This is why Hollywood is so empty. It attempts to fill the void in man's life with things. Even though the world follows suit, still, there is no fulfillment, with only an emptiness remaining.

(16) "AND HE SPOKE A PARABLE UNTO THEM, SAYING, THE GROUND OF A CERTAIN RICH MAN BROUGHT FORTH PLENTIFULLY."

The order is:

1. The phrase, *"And He spoke a parable unto them, saying,"* proclaims the beginning of the eighteenth parable in this book.

2. *"The ground of a certain rich man brought forth plentifully,"* proclaims no wrongdoing thus far!

(17) "AND HE THOUGHT WITHIN HIMSELF, SAYING, WHAT SHALL I DO, BECAUSE I HAVE NO ROOM WHERE TO BESTOW MY FRUITS?"

The pattern is:

1. The phrase, *"And he thought within*

himself, saying," proclaims a mind-set that does not have God in all its thoughts.

2. The question, *"What shall I do, because I have no room where to bestow my fruits?"* could be answered in the words of Ambrose: "You have barns—the bosoms of the needy, the houses of the widows, the mouths of orphan and of infants."

3. Some have deducted from this story that God looks with disfavor on riches as riches; however, Augustine said in answer to such a mistaken deduction, "God desires not that you should lose your riches, but you should change their place."

(18) "AND HE SAID, THIS WILL I DO: I WILL PULL DOWN MY BARNS, AND BUILD GREATER; AND THERE WILL I BESTOW ALL MY FRUITS AND MY GOODS."

The form is:

1. The phrase, *"And he said, This will I do,"* proclaims plans being made without God. Millions have followed this path and have come to the same conclusion.

2. *"I will pull down my barns, and build greater,"* proclaims this man making preparation for his goods but nothing for his soul.

3. The phrase, *"And there will I bestow all my fruits and my goods,"* proclaims no care or thought for anything except his loved possessions. As such, most of the world follows in his train.

4. This man did get an abundance of riches, although there is little evidence that it was enjoyed, while most of the world doesn't even have that.

(19) "AND I WILL SAY TO MY SOUL, SOUL, YOU HAVE MUCH GOODS LAID UP FOR MANY YEARS; TAKE YOUR EASE, EAT, DRINK, AND BE MERRY."

The order is:

1. The phrase, *"And I will say to my soul,"* proclaims this man knowing that he had a soul and, as well, that he would live only for a time and not forever.

2. Yet, he talked of nothing except himself and what he should do, and of his fruits, his barns, and his goods.

3. *"Soul, you have much goods laid up for many years,"* proclaims him making provisions for the near future but nothing for the long future. The things he had laid up were of no consequence for that journey.

4. *"Take your ease, eat, drink, and be merry,"* proclaims him making a conscious decision to ignore his soul, and rather sow to the flesh.

5. Such characterizes most of the world!

(20) "BUT GOD SAID UNTO HIM, YOU FOOL, THIS NIGHT YOUR SOUL SHALL BE REQUIRED OF YOU: THEN WHOSE SHALL THOSE THINGS BE, WHICH YOU HAVE PROVIDED?"

The pattern is:

1. The phrase, *"But God said unto him, You fool,"* proclaims him being called the opposite by the Lord as he was, no doubt, called by the world.

2. The world would have lauded him, giving him write-ups in the major business magazines, as well as being interviewed over the major television business programs. He would have been the toast of Wall Street and the one whom millions would have sought to emulate. But yet, God said of him, *"You fool!"*

3. *"This night your soul shall be required of you,"* tells us that God ultimately makes all decisions, especially the final one. But yet, this man lived as though God had no say in his life whatsoever when, in reality, God had every say, as this fact was amply proven.

4. The man was a fool because he made no preparations for that which really counted, the moment of having to stand before God.

5. The question, *"Then whose shall those things be, which you have provided?"* tells us that he left his fruit ungathered, his corn unreaped, his barns unbuilt, and his soul unsaved.

6. As well, as Jesus here brings out, what would happen to all of his goods after he was gone? Solomon answered that:

7. He said, *"Yes, I hated all my labor which I had taken under the sun: because I should leave it unto the man who shall be after me.*

"And who knows whether he shall be a wise man or a fool?" (Eccl. 2:18-19).

8. It is best to take care of one's family and then give the remainder to the work of God.

(21) "SO IS HE WHO LAYS UP TREASURE FOR HIMSELF, AND IS NOT RICH TOWARD GOD."

The composition is:

1. The phrase, *"So is he who lays up treasure for himself,"* does not condemn riches or even growing richer. It does condemn the wrong manner of their use. They were hoarded and used for selfish purposes, while they could have done much good for the work of God.

2. The phrase, *"And is not rich toward God,"* proclaims the true riches.

3. Consequently, in this parable, we see that God labels all as fools who are not rich toward Him, irrespective of how much of this world's goods they may have.

4. This would mean that in the eyes of God, all in the Fortune 500 are fools, that is, if they do not know the Lord.

(22) "AND HE SAID UNTO HIS DISCIPLES, THEREFORE I SAY UNTO YOU, TAKE NO THOUGHT FOR YOUR LIFE, WHAT YOU SHALL EAT; NEITHER FOR THE BODY, WHAT YOU SHALL PUT ON."

THE WORD OF THE LORD

The phrase, *"And He said unto His disciples,"* points this message directly to the chosen Twelve, or even part or all of the 70. As well, this could have been delivered a little bit later when they were alone.

"Therefore I say unto you, Take no thought for your life," referred not only to His disciples but, as well, to all His followers, then and now.

In fact, our lives are not to be held too dear, but instead, are to be hidden in Christ. He has already made it abundantly clear that nothing can happen to us without His express approval. Would not it stand to reason that if He numbers the very hairs of our heads, He, likewise, watches every step?

I get somewhat amused at people, especially believers, who express a fear of flying. Why?

While our faith is not to be foolhardy, still, a normal amount of precaution is all that is necessary, with God promising to watch over us at all times.

OUR STATE IN LIFE

The phrase, *"What you shall eat,"* does not necessarily speak of a kind of food, but rather its supply.

At the same time, this does not mean

that God will reward laziness. Paul said, *"If any would not work, neither should he eat"* (II Thess. 3:10).

The phrase, *"Neither for the body, what you shall put on,"* refers to clothing.

The Jewish mind, and most others for that matter, was primarily occupied with the amassing of wealth. Actually, they linked wealth and the favor of God together, while thinking of poverty as a curse from God. So, the words of Jesus were indeed revolutionary, actually, the very opposite of what they believed.

To launch out into His work, even though called, and trusting Him totally for sustenance and supply was a new venture for these disciples. However, it was to teach them trust and faith. They would find God abundantly true to His Word, as all have found it so.

(23) "THE LIFE IS MORE THAN MEAT, AND THE BODY IS MORE THAN RAIMENT."

The overview is:

1. The phrase, *"The life is more than meat,"* refers to the fact that God has given life, and if He has provided something so infinitely precious, He certainly will provide sustenance, i.e., meat, for that life.

2. *"And the body is more than raiment,"* points, as well, to the body, which is a temple of the Holy Spirit, or at least is supposed to be, and for such a precious temple, He has certainly provided clothing.

3. Such speaks to the order of God's creation. It, as well, speaks of the economy of God. When the believer enters into God's economy, he takes unto himself God's provision, which is always bountiful. It is the most wonderful life there is!

4. The world, operating on its own economy, in its greed grasps after these *"things,"* when the Lord promises that all who trust Him will be adequately supplied according to need. As well, it can be done without greed and grasping.

(24) "CONSIDER THE RAVENS: FOR THEY NEITHER SOW NOR REAP; WHICH NEITHER HAVE STOREHOUSE NOR BARN; AND GOD FEEDS THEM: HOW MUCH MORE ARE YOU BETTER THAN THE FOWLS?"

The structure is:

1. The phrase, *"Consider the ravens,"* is meant to point to a bird that the law of Moses labeled as unclean. And yet, this little fowl, which was not even considered good enough to be used in sacrifice or food for the table, still enjoys God's ample provision.

2. The phrase, *"For they neither sow nor reap; which neither have storehouse nor barn,"* once again, is not meant to encourage laziness. It merely means to portray provision as supplied by God and built into His economy.

3. *"And God feeds them,"* specifies provision made at the outset of creation.

4. The question, *"How much more are you better than the fowls?"* proclaims a truth that some Christians find hard to believe.

5. The Lord is speaking of those who love and trust Him. They are His children and, consequently, enjoy His bounty.

6. No provision is made for those who do not belong to Him. While some may certainly provide wealth for themselves, the truth is, most don't! The majority of the world goes to bed hungry each night, wondering where their next meal is coming from. In effect, they are children of Satan and, as such, have no provision whatsoever. It is sad but true!

7. Also, Jesus was drawing our attention to His care of the lesser of His creation. If that is attended to so minutely, how much more will He attend His greatest creation, i.e., man.

(25) "AND WHICH OF YOU WITH TAKING THOUGHT CAN ADD TO HIS STATURE ONE CUBIT?"

WHAT THE BIBLE TEACHES ABOUT WORRY

Of all creation, man alone is given to worry, fear, rebellion, sin, and unbelief.

According to the Bible, a certain amount of anxiety is often legitimate. The very word *anxiety* indicates a sense of concern for self and/or for others. Paul spoke of the daily pressure of concern for all the churches (II Cor. 11:28), and stated that God's purpose in the body is that each part have equal concern for each other in that if one part suffers,

every part suffers with it (I Cor. 12:25-26).

The fact is, we are living in this present world, which, in actuality, is in opposition to God, and there are necessary concerns that each individual must attend to.

However, while it is legitimate to have concerns that we will at times experience as demanding pressures, there is a limit to their legitimacy. In fact, the worries of this life may so dominate our attention that they make God's work unfruitful in our lives (Mat. 13:22; Mk. 4:19). The pressures of legitimate concerns can cause us to so focus on worldly matters that we forget to relate our needs and our worries to the Lord.

JESUS' TEACHING ON ANXIETY

Jesus dealt directly, as we see here, with the subject of legitimate concern.

His teaching tells us not to worry about life or what we will eat, as we have already alluded. Jesus was speaking about necessities, not luxuries. They are thus objects of legitimate concern for one living in the material universe, but Jesus releases believers from the bondage of anxiety over necessities. God is a heavenly Father whose care extends even to vegetation and to animal life. We human beings are much more valuable to God than those other parts of His creation. Worry over what we will eat, drink, or wear— all these things the pagans pursue—is unnecessary because we have a heavenly Father who knows our needs and loves us dearly.

LINKING TO GOD

By linking legitimate concerns to God, believers are freed from anxiety and worry. This freedom allows us to concentrate on seeking God's kingdom and His righteousness, knowing that all these things will be given to us as well. So Jesus concludes, *"Do not worry about tomorrow, for tomorrow will worry about itself."*

What the pagan Greeks experienced as anxious concern over a tomorrow they could not control, the believer who knows God as a loving Father can experience in calm confidence. Released from fears about tomorrow, we can concentrate on doing God's will today as obedient subjects of a kingdom over which the Almighty rules.

BELIEVERS MUST ORIENT LIFE TO GOD

The Gospels recognize the tendency of legitimate human concerns to lead to a loss of perspective; we can forget God and adopt a pagan materialism that looks ahead anxiously and concentrates on running after the material things that seem to offer security. In order to avoid this tendency, believers must orient life to God and realize that life's meaning is to be found in living as subjects who are responsive to their loving, wise, and powerful king, the Lord Jesus Christ.

The Epistles recognize that human beings must live with and under some degree of pressure (I Cor. 12:25; II Cor. 11:28; Phil. 2:20). However, we must learn how to handle pressure so that anxiety does not become a dominating or distracting concern.

In Philippians 4:6, Paul uses the present imperative: *"Be careful for nothing* (Do not be anxious about anything)." Instead of letting our concerns nag at us, we are *"in everything by prayer and supplication* (petition), *with thanksgiving,* (to) *let your requests be made known unto God* (present our requests to God)."

THE ALTERNATIVE TO BEING ANXIOUS

The alternative is to bring to God those things that trouble us and then to leave them in His hands. We do this with thanksgiving for the release from worry that prayer provides, and we do it with confidence because we know that God hears and will act for us. Paul goes on to promise, *"The peace of God, which passes* (transcends) *all understanding, shall keep* (will guard) *your hearts and* (your) *minds through* (in) *Christ Jesus"* (Phil. 4:7).

The same prescription is repeated in I Peter 5:7, *"Casting all your care upon Him; for* (because) *He cares for you."*

THE AWARENESS OF GOD

Both anxiety and worry spring from natural and legitimate concerns, as we have stated, that are a part of life in this world. However, legitimate concerns are handled wrongly when they do one or more of the following:

• Become dominating concerns of our life and lead to fear.
• Destroy our perspective on life and cause us to forget that God exists and cares.
• Move us to drift into an attitude of constant worry and concern over a future that we cannot control.

Jesus deals with anxiety by calling us to an awareness of God. God does exist, and He cares. He is aware of our needs and is committed to meeting our needs. Remaining aware of God frees us from the tyranny of things. It enables us to focus our lives on our relationship with God and go on living a righteous and productive life.

USING ANXIETY CREATIVELY

The Epistles add to our understanding by pointing out that areas of legitimate anxiety exist even for the strongest of believers. However, the pressures of even legitimate concerns are not to dominate us or to make us habitually anxious, worried people. We escape by using anxiety creatively. This means that we must recognize the feelings of pressure and concern as a call to prayer. We should immediately turn to God to lay our needs and the needs of others before Him. We then turn back to live our lives encompassed by His peace. Anxiety, then, rather than pulling us away from God, instead, draws us to Him and thus fulfills His purpose for it in our lives.

(The thoughts on anxiety were derived from Lawrence Richards.)

(26) "IF YOU THEN BE NOT ABLE TO DO THAT THING WHICH IS LEAST, WHY TAKE YOU THOUGHT FOR THE REST?"

The pattern is:

1. The phrase, *"If you then be not able to do that thing which is least,"* concerns adding height to our physical being, which man, within himself, is unable to do.

2. *"Why take you* (do you take) *thought for the rest?"* means that if we cannot do even that, we should then realize our inadequacy and rely on God.

3. The idea is that God created all things, and in that creation, He made provision for its welfare.

4. As we have alluded, the only part of God's creation that has rebelled against Him and, consequently, taken themselves out from

His constant care is rebellious man. Therefore, the Lord does not provide for them because they have shunned His provision by their sinful, rebellious, obstinate lifestyle. However, to those who have accepted Him as Lord and Saviour, the Lord has promised, as given here, His watchful provision.

5. We are to simply trust Him, believing that He has provided and that all of our worry (thought) is not necessary.

6. Actually, such *"thought"* shows a lack of faith and at some degree, if continued, is sin (Rom. 14:23).

A PRAYER LIFE

Sadly and regrettably, most believers have no prayer life at all. Therefore, they have no relationship with the Lord, or at least very little, and that's a shame. When we understand that we can talk to one Who has made all things, who can do anything, and loves us even far more than a parent loves his children, then we should realize that the Lord wants to meet our every need, wants to bless us, desires to lift us up and strengthen us, and actually desires to give us good things, and in abundance. Sadly, most Christians treat the Lord as a stranger.

If you as a believer will set aside a few minutes each day, even as little as 15 minutes, and be habitual with this every day, things will begin to get better. This means that you will take everything to the Lord in prayer and will actually spend most of the time thanking Him for His grace. As stated, you will find that if you will keep this up and not stop, things will begin to improve, and in a bountiful way.

THE CROSS OF CHRIST

As well, the believer must also understand that it is the Cross of Christ that provides the means, in fact, the only means, through which the Lord gives us all of these good things. You as a believer must understand this. While Jesus Christ is the source of all things that we receive from God, the Cross of Christ is the means by which all of these wonderful things are given to us. When we accordingly place our faith in Christ and the Cross, and keep it in Christ and the Cross, we will find the Holy Spirit, who

NOTES

works exclusively within the parameters of the finished work of Christ, will then work mightily on our behalf. The Holy Spirit is God, which means that He can do anything. However, oftentimes we tie His hands, so to speak, by placing our faith in anything and everything else except the Cross of Christ.

Anytime we place our faith in other things, regardless of what they might be or how right they might be in their own way, such brings glory to self and not to Christ. It is the believer's faith in Christ and the Cross that always brings glory to God and never to ourselves.

When the believer begins to function accordingly, then you should expect God to bless you, to help you, and to strengthen you in whatever is necessary. You should anticipate and expect His blessings, and to be sure, He most definitely will come through. He has for untold millions of others, and He most definitely will for you.

(27) "CONSIDER THE LILIES HOW THEY GROW: THEY TOIL NOT, THEY SPIN NOT; AND YET I SAY UNTO YOU, THAT SOLOMON IN ALL HIS GLORY WAS NOT ARRAYED LIKE ONE OF THESE."

The diagram is:

1. The phrase, *"Consider the lilies how they grow,"* refers to their beauty and God's provision in His creation for this flower.

2. *"They toil not, they spin not,"* refers to two things:

a. *"They toil not"*: This does not refer to the growth process, but rather effort on their part to bring about beauty. The beauty will come.

As well, in applying this to the human family, it has no reference to one living idle, but rather laboring in the context, even as the lily that grows, of the thought that if we trust God and what He did for us through His Son Jesus Christ, and what Christ did for us at the Cross, we then surely begin to realize that He is going to provide for us. It is that simple!

b. *"They spin not"*: The word *spin* refers to "whirling around in a state of mental confusion," which, of course, the lily does not do. Naturally, it has no mind to do such because it is a very lower form of creation. Correspondingly, believers are to have no mind in that capacity as well. Our minds, at least as far as mental confusion is concerned, are to be exactly as the lily, which has no mind at all! Jesus chose this comparison for a reason, and we are to learn its lesson. In other words, we are not to worry about anything but commit all our care unto the Lord.

3. The phrase, *"And yet I say unto you, that Solomon in all his glory was not arrayed like one of these,"* tells us several things:

a. We learn from this exactly how far man has fallen. It tells us that the coming glorified state of believers will be far and away greater than the glory of Solomon.

b. No man has ever had the glory that Solomon had because it was given to him by God for a specific purpose. He was a type of Christ. And yet, the mere lily, which has not suffered a fall, has a glory or beauty greater than that of Solomon.

c. The lily abides by God's creation, and if the believer will do the same, he will enjoy the provision of that creation.

(28) "IF THEN GOD SO CLOTHE THE GRASS, WHICH IS TODAY IN THE FIELD, AND TOMORROW IS CAST INTO THE OVEN; HOW MUCH MORE WILL HE CLOTHE YOU, O YE OF LITTLE FAITH?"

PROVISION

The phrase, *"If then God so clothe the grass, which is today in the field, and tomorrow is cast into the oven,"* assures us of the fact that God even provides for that which is of short duration. As we have already stated, it means that this is a part of His creation, and in that creation, He has provided care and sustenance, regardless of the short lifespan.

LITTLE FAITH

The conclusion of the question, *"How much more will He clothe you, O ye of little faith?"* speaks, as should be obvious, to believers that they are eternal and, consequently, of untold value.

As stated, He is speaking here to and of believers and not unbelievers. The animal kingdom, along with the flowers and other parts of God's creation, are not in rebellion against Him; consequently, they enjoy His care and sustenance.

NOTES

By contrast, much of mankind is in rebellion against Him and, in effect, has said that they do not need God's care and sustenance. They can provide for themselves, hence, the starvation, poverty, sickness, suffering, and heartache in the world presently. God does not clothe these, nor is He obligated to do so.

However, once those in rebellion come to Christ and, thereby, cease their rebellion, becoming a child of God, they once again enter into God's creative care, in other words, His economy. He will take care of you!

The *"little faith"* means that the disciples fell into that category, at least at that time.

Why?

The mind-set of Israel was such that they erroneously thought that all rich people were rich because they were honored by God. As well, they believed all, or at least most rich people, to be saved.

Conversely, Israel at that time also believed that those who were poverty stricken were under the curse of God and, therefore, lost. In other words, Israel equated riches in the realm of money with salvation. Therefore, most all strived to be rich.

FOLLOW ME

When Jesus called His disciples to follow Him, which meant the leaving of their present occupations, this was revolutionary in the thinking of Israel. To be sure, the disciples did what our Lord demanded, but it was with the idea that such would ultimately hold great fortune for them. This certainly was true, but it was not in the way they thought.

Now, Jesus not only pulled them away from their occupations, but He, as well, told them not to be concerned about the things over which they had previously been so very concerned. So, His teaching was completely revolutionary, actually, 180 degrees from the present belief of Israel.

Whereas they had once placed great stock in worldly possessions, now they were told to give them little concern. All of this would teach them faith and trust and, as well, would pull them away from the error in which Israel was presently occupied. They were now coming into the true ways of God, and so should we.

The pulling away from occupations pertained only to those He had called and presently calls to the labor of ministry.

(29) "AND SEEK NOT YE WHAT YOU SHALL EAT, OR WHAT YOU SHALL DRINK, NEITHER BE YE OF DOUBTFUL MIND."

The promise is:

1. The phrase, *"And seek not ye* (do not seek) *what you shall eat, or what you shall drink,"* means that we definitely are to seek things but not that. Jesus is saying that these things are a given in His creation and kingdom.

2. It is not improper or unscriptural for a person to ask the Lord for things that are needed, such as clothing, automobiles, housing, etc. However, it is wrong to make these things our life's quest, even as some do.

3. The phrase, *"Neither be ye* (Do not be) *of doubtful mind,"* has great meanings:

a. The word *doubtful* in the Greek text is *meteorizo* and means "a distracted state of mind, wavering between hope and fear." It means to be carried about as meteors moved about with occurrence, tossed up and down. This is the only time this word is used in the New Testament.

b. It has the idea of the heathen who superstitiously seeks guidance by signs of the zodiac, witchcraft, etc. It means a believer is never to conduct himself accordingly, actually saying that if we do so, we are treating God as though He is a demon spirit who responds to incantations, spells, etc.

c. This has to do with the mind, which is the gateway to the spirit. If, in fact, the mind is of this disposition, it shows that the person does not know the Word of God, or else, does not believe the Word of God.

Believers who do not know the Word are at the whim of Satan's suggestions, which the word *doubtful* implies.

d. As well, as long as the believer has as the object of his or her faith something other than the Cross of Christ (whatever it might be), such an individual will be of a doubtful mind. In effect, the Cross of Christ is the story of the entirety of the Bible. Let it be understood that while Jesus Christ is the source of all things we receive from God, the Cross of Christ is the means, and

the only means, by which we receive all of these things from God. In fact, the Cross is the means for everything, excluding nothing. So, it behooves the believer to ever make the Cross of Christ the object of his faith because in doing so, this means that he is actually having faith in the Word of God. If the Cross of Christ is eliminated, then this means that the great theme of the Bible is totally eliminated, which means that such a person is going to have little success in the Spirit realm.

(30) "FOR ALL THESE THINGS DO THE NATIONS OF THE WORLD SEEK AFTER: AND YOUR FATHER KNOWS THAT YOU HAVE NEED OF THESE THINGS."

The promise is:

1. The phrase, *"For all these things do the nations of the world seek after,"* speaks of the world's economy and not God's economy.

2. They seek after these things because they have purposely taken themselves out from under God's watchful care and must, therefore, provide for themselves. As we have stated, that's the reason for the poverty, heartache, starvation, and want in the world.

3. The phrase, *"Your Father knows that you have need of these things,"* means that we are now in His kingdom care; therefore, we are, as well, into His creative care. Consequently, He will care for us just as much, and, actually, to a far greater degree than He does the ravens, lilies, etc.

(31) "BUT RATHER SEEK YE THE KINGDOM OF GOD; AND ALL THESE THINGS SHALL BE ADDED UNTO YOU."

The overview is:

1. The phrase, *"But rather seek ye* (you should seek) *the kingdom of God,"* tells us what we are to seek.

2. It also tells us that inasmuch as we are now in the kingdom of God, these things will automatically be provided.

3. *"And all these things shall be added unto you,"* tells us so, and in no uncertain terms.

4. Jesus was saying that those who are properly in this kingdom automatically are entitled to its benefits.

5. For instance, as a citizen of the United States of America, I am entitled to certain benefits, such as freedom of speech, freedom to worship God, etc.

6. Likewise, as I am now in God's kingdom, one of the benefits is His constant care and provision. I am to believe this, and it will come without fail. Jesus said so!

(32) "FEAR NOT, LITTLE FLOCK; FOR IT IS YOUR FATHER'S GOOD PLEASURE TO GIVE YOU THE KINGDOM."

The exegesis is:

1. The words, *"Fear not,"* are not a suggestion, but rather a command. If we fear, we do not properly love God and do not trust His love for us. Such shows that we do not trust God to keep His promises. John said, *"Perfect love casts out fear"* (I Jn. 4:18).

2. The words *little flock* in the Greek text are expressed by a double diminutive (meaning, to be small and greatly loved), so effectively expressing the Great Shepherd's tender care for His sheep.

3. To be sure, despite the great number of born-again people in the world, considering the entirety of the population, it is a little flock.

4. *"For it is your Father's good pleasure to give you the kingdom,"* presents a far greater promise than even the earthly kingdom they (the disciples) were anticipating.

5. They were expecting an earthly kingdom and foremost positions in it immediately, but He pointed them to another and more glorious kingdom.

6. This kingdom had far greater benefits than anything the kingdom of this world had to offer.

7. In the first place, it is eternal; consequently, all in it have eternal life.

8. Secondly, Jesus Christ is its head and not worldly dictators or incompetent politicians.

9. Thirdly, when it is finally realized in totality, it will cover the earth and be absent of sickness, suffering, sorrow, and death.

10. Fourthly, in this kingdom there will be no sin, rebellion, or disobedience, which causes the heartache of the present system.

11. As well, it is a kingdom that He gives us, which we in no way can earn. Entrance into it is by the born-again experience (Jn. 3:3).

(33) "SELL THAT YOU HAVE, AND GIVE ALMS; PROVIDE YOURSELVES BAGS WHICH WAX NOT OLD, A TREASURE IN THE HEAVENS THAT FAILS NOT, WHERE NO THIEF APPROACHES, NEITHER MOTH CORRUPTS."

NO HOARDING OR COVETOUSNESS

The phrase, *"Sell that you have, and give alms,"* does not refer to ordinary homes and necessities of life, for other passages make men responsible to provide for their own (I Tim. 5:8). The idea is not to hoard and covet such as the world does.

However, Jesus' statement is not without great purpose. He also said, *"It is more blessed to give than to receive"* (Acts 20:35); consequently, when one begins to *"give alms"* (offerings to support the work of God), in turn, this brings the blessings of God, which will provide even more than we can give.

BAGS WITHOUT HOLES

The phrase, *"Provide yourselves bags which wax not old,"* had to do with the custom of that day.

Money was kept in royal treasuries in bags, with the value marked on each one and then sealed. Private bankers also followed this plan.

Jesus is telling us that our trust must not be treasures here, but rather treasure there!

Once again, He is not meaning that we are to sell everything that we have and give it all away, and neither is it wrong to have bank accounts or saving accounts. That is not the idea. The idea pertains to priority, which must be the kingdom of God, and at all times.

AN ETERNAL TREASURE

The phrase, *"A treasure in the heavens that fails not, where no thief approaches, neither moth corrupts,"* proclaims the priority.

This is a great truth that all believers should take very seriously because it has to do with what really counts, as should be obvious.

Every believer, irrespective of who or where they may be, is in the kingdom and, consequently, should live a kingdom life. That life is expounded in these passages, that is, to a degree.

KINGDOM LIFE

The kingdom life demands that we put

God and His work first. While it may be true that the believer works at any number of occupations, with some even possibly becoming wealthy, still, all of that must be incidental to their promotion of the kingdom. That's what Jesus meant by saying, *"Seek ye first the kingdom"* (Vs. 31).

The care of that kingdom, concerning the taking of the gospel to the world, must be paramount. The believer must be involved prayerfully, personally, and financially. As well, it must not be incidental.

Every believer should know, at least as far as possible, through their support what is being done in any country of the world respecting the gospel of Jesus Christ. They should be concerned enough to investigate.

However, so few believers truly live the kingdom life. Living for God is too often a one-hour experience on Sunday morning, with the balance of the week (concerning the Lord and His work) being out of sight and out of mind. That is not only tragic, it is catastrophic!

(34) "FOR WHERE YOUR TREASURE IS, THERE WILL YOUR HEART BE ALSO."

The exposition is:

1. Jesus was talking about treasure.

2. He has plainly told us that treasure here will fail because of thieves and corruption. However, treasure there (referring to heaven) will never fail.

3. More important still, the heart is going to be where the treasure is, irrespective of whether the person is a believer or not.

4. As stated previously, the disciples were expecting an earthly kingdom and foremost positions in it immediately, but He pointed them to another and more glorious kingdom. He enthused them by that knowledge to set loose to the treasures of earth and be givers rather than getters.

5. As well, and as should be obvious, the language of these verses is figurative. This is clear from the words *"provide yourselves bags"* in Verse 33, for it is evident that Christian people are not commanded here to carry material bags.

(35) "LET YOUR LOINS BE GIRDED ABOUT, AND YOUR LIGHTS BURNING."

The structure is:

1. The phrase, *"Let your loins be girded*

about," refers to the hem of the robe being pulled up between the legs of the man and tied off at the waist. This gave him freedom of movement and denotes that every believer must be busy for the Lord.

2. *"And your lights burning,"* concerns watchfulness, and more perfectly, watchfulness of the coming of the Lord; therefore, working and waiting should characterize the Christian.

3. The idea, at least as far as the believer is concerned, pertains to the rapture of the church. It does not necessarily pertain to the time of His coming, but that the believer be ready at all times, consequently, watching.

(36) "AND YOU YOURSELVES LIKE UNTO MEN WHO WAIT FOR THEIR LORD, WHEN HE WILL RETURN FROM THE WEDDING; THAT WHEN HE COMES AND KNOCKS, THEY MAY OPEN UNTO HIM IMMEDIATELY."

The construction is:

1. The phrase, *"And you yourselves like unto men who wait for their Lord,"* refers, as stated, to the rapture of the church.

2. Some have claimed this refers to the second coming; however, very few are going to be waiting or watching for the second coming. Every indication is that it will be a total surprise to almost all the earth at that time (Rev., Chpt. 19).

3. However, while it definitely could apply to Israel at the time of the second coming, there is little indication that many will heed these words at that time. So, the spirit of the text can point to either the church or Israel.

4. *"When He will return from the wedding,"* in essence, means to "return from preparations for the wedding." If, in fact, that is correct, it refers to preparations for the *"marriage supper of the Lamb"* (Rev. 19:9), which will take place immediately before the second coming.

5. The phrase, *"That when he comes and knocks, they may open unto him immediately,"* speaks of readiness at all times.

6. All the time He was absent, they were to be busy preparing for this time and, as well, have their lamps trimmed and burning in order to receive Him. Is this what the modern church is doing? I think not!

(37) "BLESSED ARE THOSE SERVANTS,

WHOM THE LORD WHEN HE COMES SHALL FIND WATCHING: VERILY I SAY UNTO YOU, THAT HE SHALL GIRD HIMSELF, AND MAKE THEM TO SIT DOWN TO MEAT, AND WILL COME FORTH AND SERVE THEM."

WATCHING AND WAITING

The phrase, *"Blessed are those servants, whom the Lord when He comes shall find watching,"* proclaims those ready for the rapture.

There are millions in churches presently, while very religious, still are unsaved. Of course, these people will not go in the rapture.

WHO WILL BE READY FOR THE RAPTURE?

There is only one requirement, and that is to be born again. There is no such thing as a partial justification. One is either justified fully or not justified at all.

While many Christians are closer to the Lord than others, as would be obvious, still, all who are truly born again, which means they are truly justified, will go in the rapture.

I realize that it is taught that some Christians will not go because of certain things, but that is incorrect. Let us say it again:

If one is truly born again, then one is completely and totally justified. There is no such thing as a partial justification, in other words, half justified and the other half not justified. That does not happen and cannot happen.

It is claimed that there are approximately 1 billion Protestants in the world, as well as 1 billion Catholics. However, the number who are truly born again is far, far smaller than the large number given.

The way at which those numbers are arrived speaks of entire nations being counted as Christian, or whatever it may be; however, that does not mean that all of these people are born again. Actually, only a tiny percentage is truly born again. Jesus said: *"Because strait is the gate, and narrow is the way, which leads unto life, and few there be that find it"* (Mat. 7:14).

THE MARRIAGE SUPPER OF THE LAMB

The phrase, *"Verily I say unto you, that*

He shall gird Himself, and make them to sit down to meat, and will come forth and serve them," speaks of the marriage supper of the Lamb, with Jesus as the host, as here described. This will take place in heaven almost immediately before the second coming when all the saints at that time will come with Him (Rev., Chpt. 19).

(38) "AND IF HE SHALL COME IN THE SECOND WATCH, OR COME IN THE THIRD WATCH, AND FIND THEM SO, BLESSED ARE THOSE SERVANTS."

Several things are said in this verse:

• By the statements given by Christ, we know that date setting is valueless and unscriptural, at least pertaining to the rapture. The idea is *"watchfulness!"*

• The Jews divided the night into four watches, with the first watch beginning at 6 p.m. and extending to 9 p.m., and correspondingly through the night, implying that He could come at any time or watch. Of course, it is obvious that He has not come as of yet, respecting the rapture. As well, according to the signs of the times, we are living now in the last watch. Therefore, the rapture must be even at the door.

• The servants who are watching and, therefore, ready will be blessed, i.e., raptured. Those who aren't won't!

(39) "AND THIS KNOW, THAT IF THE GOODMAN OF THE HOUSE HAD KNOWN WHAT HOUR THE THIEF WOULD COME, HE WOULD HAVE WATCHED, AND NOT HAVE SUFFERED HIS HOUSE TO BE BROKEN THROUGH."

The composition is:

1. The idea of this verse is that the goodman of the house did not properly set a watch.

2. Consequently, the thief came and broke in without difficulty.

3. Therefore, the watching has to do not only with the coming of the Lord respecting the rapture of the saints but, as well, that Satan, who is the thief, not be allowed to steal our victory and walk with God (Jn. 10:10).

(40) "BE YOU THEREFORE READY ALSO: FOR THE SON OF MAN COMES AT AN HOUR WHEN YOU THINK NOT."

The pattern is:

1. The phrase, *"Be you therefore ready*

also," implies by the very sentence structure that some will not be ready even though warned; consequently, this means they are not born again, and it also means that they will not make the rapture, irrespective of how religious they might be.

2. *"For the Son of Man comes at an hour when you think not,"* refers to the one who is not ready. Their very spiritual disposition portrays that they are not expecting Him. How many so-called believers in America today, and the world for that matter, are expecting the rapture of the church? I'm afraid the answer is, "Not many."

3. The church, at least as far as America and Canada are concerned, has probably never looked for Jesus less than now as it regards the rapture. Even though a goodly percentage still hold to the second coming, fewer today are anticipating the rapture than possibly ever before, at least in modern times. The focus has become more and more on earth and its prosperity, rather than heaven and the kingdom of God. As we have stated, untold millions occupy churches all around the world, and while very religious, they still have never been born again. So, even though they are religious, these people, whomever they might be, are not seriously looking for the rapture of the church. Most know nothing about it and, furthermore, couldn't care less!

4. Nevertheless, He is coming, and it will be when many *"think not!"*

(41) "THEN PETER SAID UNTO HIM, LORD, DO YOU SPEAK THIS PARABLE UNTO US, OR EVEN TO ALL?"

The order is:

1. Peter was not quite certain as to whom the Lord was speaking, the Twelve, or all who follow Jesus, and for all time.

2. Peter's belief that Jesus was going to set up an earthly kingdom didn't relate at all to the things that Jesus was saying; therefore, he asked the question.

3. The disciples were reading Christ wrong, at least at that time, and untold millions are doing the same thing today.

(42) "AND THE LORD SAID, WHO THEN IS THAT FAITHFUL AND WISE STEWARD, WHOM HIS LORD SHALL MAKE RULER OVER HIS HOUSEHOLD,

TO GIVE THEM THEIR PORTION OF MEAT IN DUE SEASON?"

THE QUESTION

The beginning of the question, *"And the Lord said, Who then is that faithful and wise steward?"* proclaims Jesus as seemingly ignoring Peter's question, but actually answering it, even though it may not have been so clear to Peter at the outset.

Some have claimed that the *"steward"* refers to ministers only; however, the very nature of the word pertains not to position but to responsibility, which applies to all. Consequently, every believer, preacher and layman alike, is to be a good steward, hence, good stewardship.

This goes back to the *"treasure"* and just exactly what is to be concluded as treasure!

The two traits of a good steward are faithfulness and wisdom.

The conclusion of the question, *"Whom his lord shall make ruler over his household, to give them their portion of meat in due season,"* proclaims the responsibility of the steward.

This parable of the unfaithful servant is the same as the parable in Matthew 24:45-51, and similar to the parable of the talents (Mat. 25:14-30).

THE WORK OF GOD

When one sees how few really take the work of God seriously, the implications become very fearful. Many believers know the stats of sports figures far more than they do the Word of God. Others are immersed in business, with God getting the leftovers, if anything. Others feel that if they show up on Sunday morning, they have satisfied their duty and obligation for the week. Many of these have very little relationship with Christ and actually constitute the far greater majority of the church.

When they stand before God someday, they will realize how important all of this was, but then it will be too late.

A short time ago, I said to a very successful businessman, who owned vast holdings and has, as well, been very gracious and kind to this ministry, that all of his holdings would be mentioned little, if at all, at the judgment seat of Christ, with only his work done for God of any import at all!

Every single believer is given the position and responsibility of steward, with an account to be taken one day. That *"due season"* will come.

(43) "BLESSED IS THAT SERVANT, WHOM HIS LORD WHEN HE COMES SHALL FIND SO DOING."

The form is:

1. The phrase, *"Blessed is that servant,"* refers to the great reward that is coming; however, at the same time, the inference is that some servants will not be good stewards and, in effect, could lose their souls. So, we're talking about not only missing the rapture, but maybe even the ultimate loss of all! As we have stated, millions are in the church and, therefore, are very religious but have never been born again. Sadly and regrettably, they are just as lost as the brigand or the morally corrupt.

2. *"Whom his lord when He comes shall find so doing,"* tells us for a certainty that the Lord is coming.

3. As well, it tells us that faithfulness and wisdom must be evident at the time of that coming and not at some time in the past. The victory we had last month will not suffice for the present.

(44) "OF A TRUTH I SAY UNTO YOU, THAT HE WILL MAKE HIM RULER OVER ALL THAT HE HAS."

The diagram is:

1. The phrase, *"Of a truth I say unto you,"* proclaims that which is cast in iron and cannot be changed.

2. *"That He will make him ruler over all that He has,"* concerns the reward.

3. To be sure, the Lord making one ruler far surpasses anything the world may have to offer and of any magnitude. This is position, honor, greatness, and glory—all that one could ever think, and far beyond. So, Peter was being answered, if he only understood what was being said. No doubt, he did understand sometime later.

(45) "BUT AND IF THAT SERVANT SAY IN HIS HEART, MY LORD DELAYS HIS COMING; AND SHALL BEGIN TO BEAT THE MENSERVANTS AND MAIDENS, AND TO EAT AND DRINK, AND TO BE DRUNK."

The overview is:

1. The phrase, *"But and if that servant say in his heart, My lord delays his coming,"* at the same time tells us that the rapture of the church must be kept in the heart as a living hope (Titus 2:13; I Jn. 3:1-3).

2. All of these were servants and, therefore, stewards, at least as Jesus used this in the illustration. But still, some would be lost, as we shall see. This completely refutes the unscriptural doctrine of unconditional eternal security.

3. The idea is that there are many so-called believers who once were truly saved but now have ceased to trust the Lord and, in fact, have lost their way. They continue to be religious after a fashion, but there is no faith left in the Lord or His Word. They keep up the religious front to make individuals think one thing, but in their hearts, they have long since forsaken the Lord. In other words, they aren't saved!

4. As we have alluded, this passage, as well, tells us that the work of God and our relationship with Christ must be paramount at all times within our hearts. If this passage does not mean that, it means nothing.

5. *"And shall begin to beat the menservants and maidens, and to eat and drink, and to be drunk,"* too much describes the modern church.

6. The implication is that if the coming of the Lord is not expected and paramount in one's heart, this sinful action is the obvious result.

7. The beating of the menservants and maidens refers to an unloving, unchristlike attitude toward others.

8. *"To eat and drink,"* refers to the things of the world, which become paramount instead of the coming of the Lord.

9. *"To be drunken,"* speaks of joining the world outright. All pretense is now thrown aside, with the individual a Christian in name only, if that.

(46) "THE LORD OF THAT SERVANT WILL COME IN A DAY WHEN HE LOOKS NOT FOR HIM, AND AT AN HOUR WHEN HE IS NOT AWARE, AND WILL CUT HIM IN SUNDER, AND WILL APPOINT HIM HIS PORTION WITH THE UNBELIEVERS."

The exegesis is:

1. The phrase, *"The lord of that servant will come in a day when he looks not for Him, and at an hour when he is not aware,"* proclaims the obviousness of the situation.

2. This servant has long since ceased to look for the coming of the Lord. Actually, it is no longer on his mind, with him no longer being aware of the signs of the times or the moving of the Holy Spirit.

3. If it is to be noticed, this individual, whomever he or she might be, considers himself a believer. However, the Lord plainly said that such people will be appointed his portion with the unbelievers. That is a fearful statement!

4. The phrase, *"And will cut him in sunder, and will appoint him his portion with the unbelievers,"* pertains to losing far more than one's reward, but instead, his soul. Revelation 21:8 tells us what the portion of unbelievers is.

5. The implication is that he had formerly been a believer; however, he forsook that glorious and wonderful path of righteousness and began to conduct himself as an unbeliever; therefore, that became his eternal portion.

6. Consequently, this shoots down the fallacious idea that millions have respecting their salvation. They belong to a church and may even be involved in that church; however, their experience is superficial, with little, if any, relationship with Christ. Consequently, they have actually lost their salvation, that is, if they ever had it.

7. Regrettably, millions of these people are made to feel safe and secure by preachers who do not know the Word of God, or if they do know it, they have long since abandoned its great truths in favor of modern fads. To be sure, their portion will be the same!

(47) "AND THAT SERVANT, WHICH KNEW HIS LORD'S WILL, AND PREPARED NOT HIMSELF, NEITHER DID ACCORDING TO HIS WILL, SHALL BE BEATEN WITH MANY STRIPES."

The diagram is:

1. The phrase, *"And that servant, which knew his Lord's will,"* proclaims this individual not being able to plead ignorance, as many will, no doubt, do, at the great white throne judgment. This person, who characterizes

multitudes and perhaps the greater majority of those who claim to be Christian, will have no excuse whatsoever. He knew the right way but failed to walk therein.

2. *"And prepared not himself, neither did according to His will,"* proclaims apathy and self-will. As stated, this characterizes much of the modern church. It becomes somewhat scary when one realizes that despite all the miracles, Jesus said, *"Few there be that find it"* (Mat. 7:14).

3. As well, Jesus said, *"Not every one who says unto Me, Lord, Lord, shall enter into the kingdom of heaven; but he who does the will of My Father which is in heaven"* (Mat. 7:21).

4. *"Shall be beaten with many stripes,"* pertains to punishment, and not the mere loss of reward while retaining salvation. It simply means their punishment in hell will be greater because they had greater opportunity. Yes, this signifies these individuals as being eternally lost.

(48) "BUT HE WHO KNEW NOT, AND DID COMMIT THINGS WORTHY OF STRIPES, SHALL BE BEATEN WITH FEW STRIPES. FOR UNTO WHOMSOEVER MUCH IS GIVEN, OF HIM SHALL BE MUCH REQUIRED: AND TO WHOM MEN HAVE COMMITTED MUCH, OF HIM THEY WILL ASK THE MORE."

GREATER PUNISHMENT

The phrase, *"But he who knew not, and did commit things worthy of stripes, shall be beaten with few stripes,"* pertains to those who had little opportunity to accept Christ, if any at all.

This is not meant to put a premium on ignorance, as some do.

Some claim that those who have never had the opportunity to hear the gospel will be saved because of their ignorance. To do otherwise, they claim, is not fair!

Such thinking is unscriptural.

Were that true, we should close all churches, burn all Bibles, and stop all preaching of the gospel, consequently, ensuring the salvation of all by ignorance.

In respect to the fairness of such action, one must know that fairness is not the criterion. Neither is it sound logic. In fact, people die somewhere in the world every day from starvation, even though there is plenty of food elsewhere. As well, many die with diseases, which one dose of certain antibiotics would save. While it may not be fair, still, they die. Disease does not go away because of unfairness, and neither does sin go away because of ignorance.

The Lord told Ezekiel to warn the people; however, if he did not warn them, such lack of warning would not save them. In fact, the Lord said, *"The same wicked man shall die in his iniquity."* The Lord also said, *"But his blood will I require at your hand"* (Ezek. 3:18).

MUCH GIVEN AND MUCH REQUIRED

No! Respecting this verse, the idea is that the one who had little or no opportunity to accept Christ and live for Him will still be lost but will be punished far less, i.e., *"few stripes,"* than his counterpart who had every opportunity.

The phrase, *"For unto whomsoever much is given, of him shall be much required: and to whom men have committed much, of him they will ask the more,"* says the same thing in two ways.

People in certain countries of the world, such as America and Canada for instance, where the gospel has been widely proliferated, will have much to answer for if they reject Jesus Christ. Being able to hear the gospel at most any time, they are without excuse; consequently, inasmuch as they know better, or at least can know better, their sin is far blacker.

In other words, any sin committed in these areas is much darker in the eyes of God than the same sin would be in parts of the world where the gospel is not so well known.

It is not so much that the sin itself is any different, but that the person committing it must be judged according to opportunity to know the Lord, or lack thereof.

Some have claimed that these two Scriptures teach the Catholic doctrine of purgatory.

LET US LOOK AT THE
DOCTRINE OF PURGATORY

The Catholic Church has defined the

NOTES

existence of purgatory in the "Decree of Union" drawn at the Council of Florence in A.D. 1439, and again at the Council of Trent, which says:

"The Catholic Church, instructed by the Holy Spirit, has from sacred Scriptures and the ancient traditions of the fathers taught in sacred council and very recently in the ecumenical synod that there is a purgatory, and that the souls therein detained are helped by the suffrages of the faithful, but principally by the acceptable sacrifice of the altar."

The Catholic Church also teaches that Christians can indulge in two types of sin—*"mortal sins,"* which will damn the soul, and *"venial sins,"* which will not damn the soul but will consign one to purgatory. All, therefore, who die in venial sins, or with the temporal punishment of their sins still unpaid, must atone for them, the Catholics say, in purgatory.

The Catholic Church gets some of her beliefs from apocryphal writings (II Macc. 12:43-46).

Of course, these writings were considered by the Jewish rabbis as unworthy of being included in the Word of God, and for any number of reasons.

THE CATHOLIC CHURCH

The Catholic Church goes on to say that because she is the infallible teacher of divine revelation in the name of Bible and tradition, she has the authority to declare the Apocrypha an article of faith in her creeds (the apostles, the Nicene, and the Athanasian) and in her councils—namely, the Council of Constantinople and the Fourth Lateran Council in A.D. 1215.

The Catholic Church further believes that the faithful on earth, the saints in heaven, and the souls in purgatory are united together in love and prayer. According to her doctrine, the faithful on earth—still struggling to win the victory of salvation—form the *"Church Militant,"* while the saints in heaven are the *"Church Triumphant,"* and the souls in purgatory—still suffering in order to be completely purified from the effects of sin—constitute the *"Church Suffering."*

To sum it all up, the Catholic Church states

NOTES

that purgatory is the state or condition in which those who have died in a state of grace, which means to be faithful to the Catholic Church, but with some attachment to sin, suffer for a time before they are admitted to the glory and happiness of heaven. In this state and period of passive suffering, they are purified, they say, of repented venial sins. This satisfies the demands of divine justice for temporal punishment due for sins, and they are thus converted to a state of worthiness of the beatific vision.

THE CROSS OF CHRIST

All of this teaching of purgatory, in essence, is saying that what Christ did at the Cross is insufficient; consequently, there must be something added to His work in order for salvation to be procured.

This has to be one of the greatest insults to Christ that could ever be perpetrated by any individual or so-called church doctrine.

As well, and which we will deal with to a greater extent directly, money enters into all of this, for it takes money to get the people out of purgatory.

The idea is that the Catholic Church, at least in the thoughts of Catholics, is the Saviour. Jesus and what He did at the Cross is inconsequential, at least as it regards the Catholic Church.

WHAT DOES THE BIBLE SAY ABOUT PURGATORY?

The Bible says nothing about purgatory!

All the teaching on purgatory as a doctrine is a fabrication made up solely by the Catholic Church. It has no validation in Scripture whatsoever, and for all the obvious reasons, of which we have just noted the principle reason of all, the Cross.

Actually, these particular teachings are contradicted by the New Testament. We are told:

"Having therefore ... Boldness to enter into the Holiest by the blood of Jesus, By a new and living way" (Heb. 10:19-20).

Assuming that Paul wrote the book of Hebrews, as we believe he did, he taught that where sins are remitted, there is no further need of an offering for sins. Thus Paul concluded his argument on the priesthood of

Christ. Christ's offering is efficacious (effective) for all past, present, and future sins—but on the condition of proper confession of sin and meeting the terms of continued grace.

The Scripture just quoted (Heb. 10:19-20) gives the child of God full access to heaven when he or she dies. It is a grand conclusion to the doctrinal argument of the worthiness of every child of God to enter the portals of glory. In other words, by accepting the blood sacrifice paid for by our Saviour on the Cross, all have instant citizenship in heaven when God calls us home to be with Him.

It can perhaps be understood how the heathen can teach the doctrine of purgatory as it was taught in Egypt; however, no such excuse can be made for the cardinals, bishops, monsignors, and priests of the Roman Catholic Church.

Prayers for the dead go hand in hand with purgatory. In Catholic doctrine, prayer cannot be completely efficacious without the priests as intermediaries, and no priestly function can be rendered unless there is a special payment of money for them.

Therefore, in every land we find the priesthood of the Catholic Church devouring widow's houses and making merchandise of the tender emotions of sorrowing relatives sensitive to the immortal destiny of their beloved dead.

MONEY

One oppression under which people in Roman Catholic countries groan is the periodic nature of special devotions, which they are required to pay when death invades a Catholic family. Not only are there funeral services and funeral dues for the purpose of the departed at the time of the burial, but the priest pays repeated visits afterward to the family for the same purpose, and this entails seemingly endless heavy expenses.

The following is an advertisement that appeared in the August 2, 1946, "Our Sunday Visitor," a popular weekly Catholic newspaper.

ARE YOU INSURED?

"Write and ask about our plan to offer the Gregorian Masses after your death. This is real insurance for your soul.

"The Gregorian Masses for a soul in

purgatory are 30 in number and must be offered consecutively." At that time (1946), the minimum price was $30. It would be pretty near $400 presently, that is, if it continued according to inflation.

It was believed and taught by the Catholics that Christ appeared to St. Gregory and promised He would release souls from purgatory on payment of the money.

I remember years ago in south Louisiana, which is predominantly Catholic, turning on the radio and hearing a particular program hosted by a Catholic priest. He was telling the people to send so much money concerning individuals who had died. He stated that all of the body was out of purgatory except an arm, a leg, or some other body member.

This is one of the reasons the Roman Catholic Church is so rich: the tremendous amount of money pouring into its coffers each day by poor individual Catholics thinking they can retrieve the souls of departed loved ones from a place called purgatory; a place, incidentally, that, in fact, does not exist.

PAGAN

The Roman Catholic doctrine of purgatory is purely pagan and cannot for a moment stand in the light of Scripture. The Bible tells us: *"The blood of Jesus Christ His Son cleanses us from all sin"* (I Jn. 1:7).

On the other hand, for those who die without personal union with Christ and, consequently, are unwashed, unjustified, and unsaved, there can be no other cleansing.

"He who has the Son has life; and he who has not the Son of God has not life" (I Jn. 5:12).

As this Scripture, plus many others, proclaim, there is no halfway regarding salvation. One is saved, or one is not saved!

Thus, the whole doctrine of purgatory is a system of purely pagan imposture, dishonoring God and deluding men with a hope of atoning for it after death, thus cheating them out of their property and their salvation.

AN ARTICLE BY SANDY CARSON, A FORMER CATHOLIC PRIEST

He says:

"I am very happy to share with you

concerning the subject of purgatory from both historical and biblical perspectives. Let me begin by saying that I was a Catholic priest for seventeen years, serving in the Diocese of Alexandria, LA., from 1955 to 1972. I left the Catholic Church and priesthood solely because I came to realize certain contradictions between the Scriptures and Catholic theology. I do not have any bitterness, anger, or resentment toward the Catholic Church; however, I do have the conviction that my life and ministry must be squarely based upon the Scriptures, the supreme rule of faith and conduct."

SOLELY A TEACHING OF THE ROMAN CATHOLIC CHURCH

The doctrine of purgatory is a teaching exclusively of the Roman Catholic Church. It may be defined as an intermediate place or state after death where souls who die in God's grace make atonement, or satisfaction, for past sins and, thereby, become fit for heaven. This satisfaction is in the form of a temporary punishment which afflicts the soul until the demands of God's justice are fully met. This is in regard to unforgiven venial sins and the punishment still required by divine justice for forgiven sins, whether mortal (sins requiring eternal punishment) or venial sins (requiring some temporary punishment).

Catholics readily admit the term *"purgatory"* is not found in the Bible, but they claim that the factuality of this temporary and intermediate state of cleansing or purgation is found in both Scripture and tradition; thus they claim it as a matter of revelation. Because this place is one of spiritual cleansing, it is theologically called *"purgatory"*: that is, a place of purgation, i.e., to be purged.

FAITHFUL CATHOLICS?

In general, faithful Catholics expect to go to purgatory when they die, as it is believed that almost none die holy enough to enter immediately into heaven. There are exceptions, however. A plenary indulgence (full remission of all temporal punishment due to forgiven sin) can be granted by the Church to one who has repented of all sin. It is taught that either a plenary indulgence or martyrdom will take away all punishment otherwise due. In such a case, one would enter heaven immediately upon death.

Once a soul, the Catholics teach, is actually in purgatory, it has absolute assurance of entering heaven—eventually. When, no one knows. In the meantime, the faithful on earth may shorten the time a loved one spends in purgatory by obtaining indulgences for them, by having Masses said or offered for them, and by praying for them, to which we have already noted. Catholics have no assurance that their loved ones are really in heaven after death, but they trust they are at least in purgatory. Some Catholics are content to just get to purgatory, as they believe very few are really good enough to go immediately to heaven.

PRAYER FOR THE DEAD

The subject of purgatory is very much related to that of prayer for the dead. Dealing with one is, in effect, equivalent to dealing with the other. I believe it is best to begin our investigation with official Roman Catholic teaching on the subject. The basic Catholic teaching will be followed by commentary on it, as well as commentary on the church fathers and Scripture used by the Catholic Church to support these doctrines. Finally, I will present a view of these doctrines from the revelation of Scriptures.

OFFICIAL CATHOLIC TEACHING ON PRAYER FOR THE DEAD AND PURGATORY

General Council of Trent, Sixth Section, Decree on Justification, A.D. 1547, Cannon 30:

"If anyone says that after the grace of justification has been received, the guilt is so remitted and the debt of eternal punishment so blotted out for any repented sinner, that no debt of temporal punishment remains to be paid, either in this world or the other, in Purgatory, before access can be open to the kingdom of heaven, Anathema Sit."

(*"Anathema Sit"* is a Latin phrase meaning "let him be cursed." Such a curse is accompanied by excommunication.)

General Council of Trent, Twenty-fifth Session, Decree on Purgatory, A.D. 1563:

"The Catholic Church, instructed by the

NOTES

Holy Spirit and in accordance with Sacred Scripture and the ancient tradition of the fathers, has taught in the holy councils and most recently in this ecumenical council that there is a Purgatory and that souls detained there are helped by the acts of intercession of the faithful and especially by the acceptable sacrifice of the altar ..."

Letter of the Sacred Congregation for the Doctrine of the Faith on Certain Questions Concerning Eschatology, May 1979:

"She (Roman Catholic Church) believes in the possibility of a purification for the elect before they see God, a purification all together different from the punishment of the damned. This is what the Church means when speaking of hell and Purgatory."

SCRIPTURE VERSUS TRADITION: A COMMENTARY

Cannon 30 of the Sixth Session of the Council of Trent is, in fact, a condemnation of biblical truth, as will be shown. Cannon 30 also levels a curse against and proclaims the excommunication of those who accept such biblical truth. The Council of Trent's Decree on Purgatory established *"there is a Purgatory"* on the basis of the instruction of the Holy Spirit, on Scripture, and on the tradition of the fathers.

This alleged *"fact"* is indeed found in the *"tradition of the fathers,"* but nowhere in the Scriptures or in the instructions of the Holy Spirit. Certainly, the Holy Spirit could not violate the very Scriptures He Himself inspired.

Also, the Scriptures are not to be judged or added to by the teachings of the church fathers—regardless of their personal reputations for learning and holiness. On the contrary, the writings of the fathers are to be judged by the Scriptures.

The Catholic Church falsely claims that the writings of the fathers bear witness to the divine revelations not contained in Sacred Scripture. Thus, their writings are allegedly a source of *"oral tradition,"* a source of revelation equal to the Bible. However, the Scriptures themselves bear record (inspired as well as historical) that it has been a principle of God from the time of Moses that God's revelation to man is always permanently recorded in written form. This is evident from the following Scriptures: (Ex. 17:14; 24:4, 7-8; Josh. 1:8; 23:6; II Chron. 34:21, 29-33; Mk. 7:5-13; Rom. 15:4; I Cor. 4:6; II Tim. 3:16-17; 4:1-4).

THE BIBLE

There are many New Testament references to *"what is written,"* showing that the New Testament writers were aware of this principle. Except in II Thessalonians 2:15, the New Testament writers and persons (such as Jesus) never referred to tradition as a source of divine revelation. It is always the written Word that is upheld.

The Catholic Church uses II Thessalonians 2:15 as scriptural proof that tradition is a source of divine revelation (Vatican Council the II, Dogmatic Constitution on Divine Revelation, Chpt. 2, No. 8). However, it should be realized that all Scripture was not yet written when Paul exhorted the Thessalonians:

"Therefore, brethren, stand fast, and hold the traditions which you have been taught, whether by word, or our epistle."

All Scripture was not yet written. Likewise, the apostles were channels of revelation, so their oral teaching (tradition) would in no way contradict future New Testament writings. Also, the New Testament revelation ended with the death of the apostle John, and with his death, the written record became finalized and complete. That is to say, with the death of John, we have the completion of New Testament revelation as recorded in what is come to be accepted as the New Testament Scriptures.

CONTRADICTIONS

It must be admitted that the writings of the church fathers (learned leaders in the church of the first seven centuries), at times, contradict the plain teaching of Scripture (prayer for the dead and purgatory being cases in point). Therefore, *"the tradition of the fathers,"* mentioned by the Council of Trent, cannot be accepted as a source of divine revelation.

Finally, Jesus recognized the traditions of the Jews for what they were. To Jews they were equal to the commands of God, but, in reality, they were rules taught by men,

NOTES

which served to nullify the Word of God (Mk. 7:7-13). The Christian church fell into the same error as the Jewish church, that of embracing tradition as equal to the written Word and authority. The Scriptures, we might quickly say, are the sole rule of faith and practice. Actually, man cannot originate anything that God can use. Everything that is of God is always originated by the Lord, inspired by the Lord, and instituted by the Lord, whether the Scriptures or present illumination. Please understand that all illumination or revelation at the present time must coincide perfectly and totally with the Word of God in every respect, or it will have to be deemed as spurious.

A FREE LOOK AT THIS TRADITION

The following information is taken from the Dictionary of the Christian Church, pages 797 and 814.

• Tertullian (A.D. 160-215) was the earliest father to refer to prayer for the dead. He admitted there is no direct biblical basis for praying for the dead.

• Clement of Alexandria (A.D. 150-220) speaks of the sanctification of deathbed patients by purifying fire in the next life. In the early third century, there was much debate over the consequences of post-baptismal sin. A suggested solution was the idea of a purgatorial discipline after death. This concept was discussed at Alexandria, Egypt, at the time of Clement.

• Augustine (A.D. 354-430) taught purification through suffering in the afterlife. The concept of purgatory spread to the west— that is, to Italy and West Africa—through the powerful influence of Augustine and Gregory the Great.

• Gregory the Great (A.D. 540-604) was bishop of Rome. He popularized and developed the doctrine of purgatory, aiding its spread to the West.

• Thomas Aquinas (A.D. 1224-1274) also helped to popularize and develop the doctrine of purgatory.

COMMENTARY ON THE TRADITION OF THE FATHERS

The Roman Catholic Church assumes that the writings, opinions, and theologies

NOTES

of early Christian writers often expressed divine revelation handed down to them. That is, their writings include teachings of Christ and the apostles, which were always a part of revelation, but which were never written down under the inspiration of the Holy Spirit as Scripture. Such *"truths"* make up what is known as *"oral tradition"* (considered equal to Scripture as divine revelation).

There is no historical or scriptural basis for such an assumption. This is not to say their writings do not express any Christian truth at all, but it is to say that they are not the vehicles of revelation—the historical witnesses to revelation—that Roman Catholicism purports them to be. All of their writings must be judged by Scripture, the only bona fide record of actual revealed truth.

The fact is, error began to invade the church at a very early age (the first century, according to Chapter 15 of Acts and the book of Galatians). This error came in by way of the backgrounds, or religious heritage (heathen and Jewish), of those who were becoming Christian.

As people embraced Christianity, the church unfortunately embraced and *"baptized,"* or *"Christianized,"* some of their false practices (such as praying to the dead, that is, to saints). Maccabees is a record of false practice among the Jews of the second century B.C., the practice of praying for the dead *"that they may be loosed from their sins"* (II Macc. 12:45). I say this is a record of false practice because it plainly contradicts revelation, as we shall see.

It should be noted that II Maccabees (considered as Scripture in the Catholic Church, but not considered inspired by Protestants or Jews) is much less historically reliable than I Maccabees, though it covers roughly the same period, 175-134 B.C.

JUDAISM, ISLAM, AND CATHOLICS

It is interesting to note that Judaism and Islam both embrace the concept of purgatory in addition to such a concept found in Catholicism. Because it does contradict Christian revelation as determined by the Scriptures, we understand that purgatory is certainly not a Christian concept.

The concept of purgatory, therefore, possibly came into the church from a false practice in Judaism (Islam, beginning in the seventh century A.D., may have adopted it from Judaism or corrupt Christianity). Likewise, it could have entered Christian doctrine as a theological solution to the ultimate resolution of the punishment to be endured for them.

This, undoubtedly, had a lot to do with this since the problem and the solution were discussed at Alexandria in the third century. This makes it clear that the doctrine of purgatory does, in fact, represent man's idea of justice being fulfilled before God. However, this is not God's idea or wisdom.

THE SCRIPTURE

Scripture clearly reveals that all the demands of divine justice on the sinner have been completely fulfilled in Jesus Christ and what He did for us at the Cross. It also reveals that Christ has totally redeemed or purchased back that which was lost. The advocates of a purgatory (and the necessity of prayer for the dead) say, in effect, that the redemption of Christ is incomplete, which is blasphemy!

"Neither by the blood of goats and calves, but by His own blood He entered in once into the Holy Place, having obtained eternal redemption for us.

"For by one offering He has perfected forever them who are sanctified" (Heb. 9:12; 10:14).

It has all been done for us by Jesus Christ; there is nothing to be added or done by man.

The doctrines of Purgatory and prayer for the dead came into the church by way of human teachings and not by the revelation of Christ. Deception is a malady the church has had to contend with even in the first century. Paul was concerned that the church at Colossi might somehow be deceived by fine-sounding arguments (Col. 2:4). Consequently, he warned that church:

"Beware lest any man spoil you through philosophy and vain deceit, after the tradition of men, after the rudiments of the world, and not after Christ" (Col. 2:8).

ANTIQUITY AND RESPECTABILITY

Often, in Catholic circles, doctrine is

validated by tracing it to the *"early days"* or *"earliest centuries"* of the church. It is implied that antiquity is proof of revelation. That is fallacious! We have noted that error crept into the church even in the first century and had to be dealt with.

Note that even Peter (Vicar of Christ, head of the church on earth, supreme theologian of the church; i.e., pope—all by Catholic definition) was for a time walking in hypocrisy and outwardly conforming to error until Paul confronted him with the truth (Gal. 2:11-14).

"I personally believe," Sandy says, "that the promotion of certain doctrines by respected and learned men of early centuries (fathers of the church) gave those doctrines the aura of divine revelation. In short, respectable teachers gave false teaching respectability."

It is true that in the mid-fourth century, the Mass was offered for the dead, and intercessions for the departed were inserted in the canon of the Mass. This was simply the amplification of error. Speaking of error, the church knew no concept of ordained priesthood and holy sacrifice of the Mass until the third century. Likewise, such concepts were not universally accepted in the church until the fifth century.

COMMENT ON SCRIPTURES

II Maccabees 12:43-46 (The Apocrypha): The books of Maccabees are not considered as inspired outside the Roman Catholic and Greek churches. The inspiration and canonicity of these and other books were in dispute from the time of the African Councils of the late fourth century to the Reformation in the sixteenth century.

Accepted by the Jews of Alexandria, Egypt, these books were never accepted by the Jewish scholars of Israel as belonging to the Jewish Scriptures. Eventually, all Jews, including the Alexandrian Jews, accepted a list of canonical books (inspired Scriptures) that excluded the books of Maccabees. The Protestant reformers accepted this Old Testament canon of the Palestinian (and Alexandrian) Jews.

THE WORD OF GOD

The Council of Trent (A.D. 1545-1563)

NOTES

retained certain books (Maccabees included) in the Old Testament canon that had been approved by the late fourth century African Councils, but disputed by such notables as Jerome, Cyril of Jerusalem, John Demascene, and Gregory the Great.

This demonstrates a long-standing disagreement about these books within the Catholic Church. Therefore, II Maccabees 12:43-46 is not considered a scriptural basis for the doctrine of purgatory and prayer for the dead.

I Corinthians 3:11-15: the Catholics maintain that this passage pertains to purgatory.

The last verse says, *"If any man's work shall be burned, he shall suffer loss: but he himself shall be saved; yet so as by fire"* (I Cor. 3:15).

The *"fire"* here is figurative and is not meant to be taken literally.

It means that the fire of God's truth will burn up all false doctrine, false work, and false motives, figuratively speaking, thereby, leaving the person pure because of the blood of Jesus.

It is revealing that Paul said that all this will happen on the judgment day (judgment seat of Christ), and not before, thus eliminating any reference to a preceding day of purification between death and *"the day."*

In conclusion, I Corinthians 3:11-15 in no way can be accepted as a scriptural passage substantiating a place called purgatory. It only speaks of a person's works being judged by Christ, which will happen to all at the judgment seat of Christ (II Cor. 5:10).

A SUMMATION OF THE BIBLICAL TEACHING ON THE COMPLETE AND FINISHED WORK OF JESUS CHRIST

The Bible teaches clearly that Jesus Christ, as our substitute, endured the total punishment required to satisfy divine justice on account of our sins. The cost of our salvation was totally paid by Him. Therefore, purgatory and consequent practice of praying for the dead are not only unnecessary, but such theology is a denial that Christ completely redeemed us. Such a theology says that we, too, must suffer as payment for our sins. The Word says this:

Isaiah, Chapter 53: this passage (prophetic) shows that the passion of Christ culminating on the Cross was much more than simply a matter of the eternal Son of God infinitely meriting forgiveness of the world's disobedience by His obedience unto death, a death which had infinite value before the bar of divine justice. Redemption (to purchase back that which is lost) involved the price of purchase whereby righteousness is restored to men.

So, Jesus is described as our *"ransom"* (I Tim. 2:6; Heb. 9:15). He paid full price. He was and is the full price, so that by Him, we are set free. If that is true, and we are set free, then we are set free from all punishment as well as all guilt. One is not free if he still owes a debt of punishment.

How did Jesus qualify as our ransom? He qualified by His sinless perfection, by His obedience, and by the torturous punishment that He endured because of it. He endured divine wrath on the Cross as our substitute because He was the perfect substitute. This is prophetically affirmed and described in Isaiah, Chapter 53: He had no beauty, was disfigured; He was despised and rejected; He experienced sorrows (pains) and infirmities; He was smitten and afflicted by God, pierced, crushed, wounded, and punished; He bore the iniquity of us all. He was oppressed, stricken, cut off, and killed (assigned a grave); He poured out His life. Isaiah prophesied it.

THE PRICE PAID BY OUR LORD

"He shall see of the travail of His soul, and shall be satisfied: by His knowledge shall My righteous servant justify many; for He shall bear their iniquities" (Isa. 53:11).

One justified is also righteous; that is, he has right standing with God. This could not be true if such a one had to personally endure some additional punishment. Again, only Jesus is the ransom; He paid our total debt.

"For He has made Him to be sin for us, who knew no sin; that we might be made the righteousness of God in Him" (II Cor. 5:21).

Our right standing (righteousness) with God is a gift He imputes to us as a result of faith. We became righteous in Him and in

NOTES

Him alone, not through our own sufferings, penances, or merits.

"But to him who works not, but believes on Him who justifies the ungodly, his faith is counted for righteousness.

"Even as David also describes the blessedness of the man, unto whom God imputes righteousness without works" (Rom. 4:5-6).

It is all in Christ and all a gift, one not merited or achieved by any work, not even by enduring some supposed purgatory.

THE SACRIFICE OF CHRIST

Romans 3:21-26: this passage clearly says righteousness is totally from God as a gift, not as a result of any of our works (including suffering in an imagined purgatory). One would not have right standing (righteousness) before God if he still owed Him some debt of punishment. Again, righteousness is the result of faith in Jesus Christ alone, and never the result of works on our part of any nature. There is no place or necessity for any purgatory.

Paul said that Jesus is a *"propitiation through faith in His blood"* (Rom. 3:25), that is: Christ through His expiatory death is the personal means by whom God shows the mercy of His justifying grace to the sinner who believes.

This sacrifice also releases the believer from the infliction of any punishment because it is said the sacrifice met all the demands of divine justice: He did it to demonstrate His justice. This reveals that divine justice was completely fulfilled on Calvary's Cross. This fulfillment of divine justice is personally realized for the sinner when he has faith in Jesus and becomes a believer.

"There is therefore now no condemnation to them which are in Christ Jesus, who walk not after the flesh, but after the Spirit" (Rom. 8:1).

There is no judgment against the believer. Scripture nowhere supports the teaching that a sinner can be forgiven guilt and still be held responsible for enduring certain punishment to completely satisfy divine justice. Punishment is eliminated when guilt is forgiven because Jesus Christ endured it all on our behalf.

COMPLETE FORGIVENESS

Scripture makes it clear that when God forgives, our sins are blotted out. When something is blotted out, there is no remaining evidence of it (Ps. 51:9); they are as far away as the east is from the west (Ps. 103:12); they are behind God's back (Isa. 38:17); and they are remembered no more (Isa. 43:25). Forgiveness renders one innocent because he is just.

The Catholic theology on sin, forgiveness, penances, and purgatory represent a perversion of justice because it advocates the punishment of the innocent and, as well, denies the finished work of Christ.

(49) "I AM COME TO SEND FIRE ON THE EARTH; AND WHAT WILL I, IF IT BE ALREADY KINDLED?"

The pattern is:

1. The phrase, *"I am come to send fire on the earth,"* is used in a figurative sense. The fire of which He speaks is that of persecution.

2. Some have claimed this fire as the fire of Pentecost; however, the following verse abrogates that.

3. The apostles expected to enter immediately into an earthly kingdom of great splendor under the kingship of their Master. However, He told them that the effect of His presence upon earth would be His own death and their entrance upon a life of suffering. His object in coming to earth was to be distinguished from the effect of His coming. His object was to bring peace, but the effect was fire and sword (Mat. 10:34).

4. This effect was caused through the corruption of man's nature, for the presence of Jesus brought to surface the evil of the human heart. The depths of that evil and the hatred of the heart for God were manifested in the Cross.

5. The question, *"And what will I, if it be already kindled?"* spoke of the terrible opposition of the Pharisees and scribes against Him, which would mark the position of the apostate church, even as it continues unto this hour.

6. The early church saw that persecution continuing, even with the apostle Paul outlining it graphically in his epistles.

(50) "BUT I HAVE A BAPTISM TO BE

NOTES

BAPTIZED WITH; AND HOW AM I STRAITENED TILL IT BE ACCOMPLISHED!"

The order is:

1. The phrase, *"But I have a baptism to be baptized with,"* spoke of a baptism of suffering (Lk. 24:26; Acts 3:18; I Pet. 3:18). This baptism spoke of the terrible opposition of the Pharisees and scribes, of Calvary, and in a sense, even the opposition that continues against the true believer unto this moment.

2. The exclamation, *"And how am I straitened till it be accomplished,"* in effect, has a double meaning:

a. It is translated *"pressed"* in Acts 18:5, and in this sense, it may mean the ever present painful consciousness in the Lord's heart of the fearful baptism of Golgotha that awaited Him. This anguish reached its climax in Gethsemane.

b. Thus, He Himself felt the *"fire"* and *"sword"* of human hatred, which was the effect of His appearance among men, though his object in coming was to bless and to save them.

c. Or, the expression may have the force of II Corinthians 5:14 and its import. In that case, it would be that His burning desire to accomplish redemption continually constrained Him, for He could not, until after He had made an atonement for sin, give full liberty to the love, which dwelt in unfathomable depths in His bosom, to flow out to the guilty and lost.

(51) "SUPPOSE YE THAT I AM COME TO GIVE PEACE ON EARTH? I TELL YOU, NO; BUT RATHER DIVISION."

The form is:

1. The question, *"Suppose ye* (Do you suppose) *that I am come to give peace on earth?"* was actually His intention and, in fact, would come to the repentant heart. However, as a whole, it could not be because of the terrible wickedness of the human heart respecting the unconverted.

2. The phrase, *"I tell you, No; but rather division,"* refers to Christ not as the actual cause of division, but the occasion of it. Division is caused by rebellion of men against the gospel (II Cor. 2:14-17).

(52) "FOR FROM HENCEFORTH THERE SHALL BE FIVE IN ONE HOUSE

DIVIDED, THREE AGAINST TWO, AND TWO AGAINST THREE."

The overview is:

1. Because of Christ, the division in families has been obvious from that time until the present.

2. It is caused by one or more members of the family accepting Christ, while other members rebel against Him.

3. On the part of those in rebellion, oftentimes, a hatred literally builds up in their hearts, totally unlike anything else known to humanity. This within itself shows the tremendous power of Bible Christianity, which far eclipses any religion in the world.

(53) "THE FATHER SHALL BE DIVIDED AGAINST THE SON, AND THE SON AGAINST THE FATHER; THE MOTHER AGAINST THE DAUGHTER, AND THE DAUGHTER AGAINST THE MOTHER; THE MOTHER-IN-LAW AGAINST HER DAUGHTER-IN-LAW, AND THE DAUGHTER-IN-LAW AGAINST HER MOTHER-IN-LAW."

The exegesis is:

1. This is meant to proclaim the fact that blood ties are not strong enough to assuage this hatred. In effect, the moment a person comes to Christ, entering into the family of God, he is actually at that time closer to other believers than even to members of his own family who do not know Jesus Christ. That's how powerful the born-again experience really is.

2. To be sure, the division is not caused by the believing one, but by the unbelieving one. The true believer continues to love the unbelieving member, even in a greater way than ever before.

3. Therefore, they are not the cause, but only the occasion.

4. Why does such hatred often arise in unbelieving hearts, even as here projected?

5. To be sure, even the unbeliever cannot satisfactorily explain the reason for his hatred, often blaming something else, which probably doesn't even exist. The actual reason is far larger than even the individual knows.

6. The real reason is the constant battle between light and darkness, between righteousness and unrighteousness, and

between God and Satan. As well, it portrays the actual evil of the human heart, which cannot abide such righteousness in its presence, hence, the animosity.

7. Jesus used family members as an example because this is the closest tie; however, this animosity extends to all walks of life, whether in the work place, community, etc.

8. It is strange, even though the believer is the direct or indirect cause of all blessing upon a household, community, or nation, still, he is bitterly opposed.

(54) "AND HE SAID ALSO TO THE PEOPLE, WHEN YOU SEE A CLOUD RISE OUT OF THE WEST, STRAIGHTWAY YOU SAY, THERE COMES A SHOWER; AND SO IT IS."

The composition is:

1. The phrase, *"And He said also to the people,"* seems to imply that the previous had been to the disciples only.

2. *"When you see a cloud rise out of the west, straightway you say, There comes a shower; and so it is,"* proclaims the ability of the people to successfully read the sky concerning the weather, but unable to make spiritual judgments. So it is presently.

(55) "AND WHEN YOU SEE THE SOUTH WIND BLOW, YOU SAY, THERE WILL BE HEAT; AND IT COMES TO PASS."

The synopsis is:

1. In effect, Jesus was saying, "As easy as it is to predict the weather because of the habitual signs, it is likewise as easy to see spiritual signs and predict the outcome."

2. So, why were they so intelligent in one and lacking in the other?

(56) "YOU HYPOCRITES, YOU CAN DISCERN THE FACE OF THE SKY AND OF THE EARTH; BUT HOW IS IT THAT YOU DO NOT DISCERN THIS TIME?"

The synopsis is:

1. The words, *"You hypocrites,"* let us know why they were so spiritually deficient.

2. They really did not know God. They were supposed to be the people of the Book, but, in fact, they had so twisted and turned the Word of God until it no longer applied. They talked about God constantly, but, in reality, they did not know Him.

3. Jesus was actually saying that if they had shown as much diligence in spiritual

things as they did in natural things, such as the weather, etc., they would not be blind. However, then, as now, the Word of God is given little credence, while other things demand full attention.

4. The phrase, *"You can discern the face of the sky and of the earth,"* proclaims man investing all his time and attention in things that are of little consequence.

5. The question, *"But how is it that you do not discern this time?"* is, in effect, a warning of approaching judgment. He based this warning upon two factors:

a. Signs

b. Their own moral consciousness

6. He accused them of willful blindness to the prophecies of Daniel (Dan. 9:24-25), which define the actual appearing of the Messiah. This blindness was the more inexcusable because of their intelligence in other things. However, the truth is, they were not honest in their inquiries and in their profession of faith in the promised Messiah. He could read their hearts, and so He justly called them *"hypocrites."*

(57) "YEA, AND WHY EVEN OF YOURSELVES JUDGE YOU NOT WHAT IS RIGHT?"

The exegesis is:

1. This question posed to them by Christ proclaimed that not only was their judgment of Him unjust, but they were unrighteous in their judgment respecting any moral question as well!

2. This one question posed by Christ, concerning the moral judgment of men, then answers the questions presently of a corrupt judicial system, an ignorant educational system, the inadequacy of Congress, and the embracing of the humanistic psychological way by the modern church.

3. There is a Bible way, which, of course, Jesus espoused because He is the living way. As well, there is a way of the world. The problem of the modern church is that she attempts to pull the way of the world into the Bible way. They do so because they simply cannot judge what is right because they do not know the Bible and, in effect, have no desire to follow its leading. They do not understand that God cannot use anything that is devised by man, irrespective of how

NOTES

holy or godly the man might be, much less those who little know the Lord.

Whatever God uses, it is that which is conceived by Him, birthed by Him, instituted by Him, and carried out by Him. Yes, He uses men and women to do so, but it's always His plan, that is, if it's something that He uses.

4. Church government presently is, for the most part, the government of the world and not of the Bible. It is very similar with the Israel of Jesus' day. Hence, at least for the most part, it will crucify (spiritually) the followers of Christ exactly as Israel crucified Christ. It is all the same spirit!

(58) "WHEN YOU GO WITH YOUR ADVERSARY TO THE MAGISTRATE, AS YOU ARE IN THE WAY, GIVE DILIGENCE THAT YOU MAY BE DELIVERED FROM HIM; LEST HE HALE YOU TO THE JUDGE, AND THE JUDGE DELIVER YOU TO THE OFFICER, AND THE OFFICER CAST YOU INTO PRISON."

THE ILLUSTRATION

The phrase, *"When you go with your adversary to the magistrate,"* illustrates that which was common to the people. Jesus was using an earthly magistrate as an example, but He was actually speaking of the heavenly magistrate, God Almighty.

The adversary in this case is the law of Moses. All it could do was to bring them before the judge, the God of glory, and their doom would be terrible and eternal.

The phrase, *"As you are in the way, give diligence that you may be delivered from Him,"* even though using an illustration that all understood, still spoke of spiritual matters. In simple terms, Jesus was telling the people to get right with God before it was too late.

By Roman law, once litigants entered the court, an agreement was forbidden; hence, the wisdom of settling a dispute on the way to the court.

In effect, Jesus was telling these people, and all for that matter, that if they have to stand before God and give an account, they will automatically be found guilty. There is no way they can save themselves. Hence, this terrible thing must be settled and, in fact, can be settled by their acceptance of Jesus Christ. Otherwise, they will be lost, and lost eternally.

LOST

The phrase, *"Lest he hale you to the judge, and the judge deliver you to the officer, and the officer cast you into prison,"* proclaims that which will be if Jesus is refused.

The adversary, as we have stated, is the law of Moses. The judge is the Son of Man. The prison is hell. The sinner is urged to seek deliverance from the claim of the law while there is yet time.

In effect, Jesus was telling Israel that the law of Moses contained no salvation; it could only condemn. Consequently, if they insisted on standing before God with their claims of having kept the law, they would be sadly disappointed. Instead of being commended for their supposed righteousness, and supposed it was, they instead would be convicted.

(59) "I TELL YOU, YOU SHALL NOT DEPART THENCE, TILL YOU HAVE PAID THE VERY LAST MITE."

THE LAW CANNOT SAVE ANYONE

Jesus was saying that as the condition of release laid down in this verse is impossible to the sinner, for he could never discharge his indebtedness to a perfect obedience to God's law, so is it manifest that the law cannot save anyone. If they lived by the law of Moses and thought it brought salvation, which it did not do and, in fact, never could do, nor was it meant to do, they would be sadly and eternally disappointed. They would have to pay to the very last mite, which means having the curse of the law brought upon them, which was eternal death.

Jesus had come to fulfill the law, which God demanded, and which man could never do. Upon His fulfilling the law, and because it was perfectly kept by Him, all who have faith in His name are judged as perfect law keepers as well. This is what Jesus was saying to these people.

THE LAW IS AN ADVERSARY

However, sadly, they refused Him and continued to depend upon their own

NOTES

supposed righteousness, which did not exist, because they were not keeping the law and, in fact, could not keep the law. Consequently, they would be haled before the judge, i.e., the Lord Jesus Christ, and find out that the law was not really a savior, but rather an adversary.

The same can be said for all other efforts of false salvation, be it church membership, church ordinances, good works, moralism, etc. All fall down before God and are unacceptable to Him. Therefore, all who depend on these things, as most of the world does, will one day stand before God and find out that their homemade salvation was, in fact, no salvation at all. As well, with their sin still against them, they will have to pay to the very last mite, which they will find is impossible to do. Consequently, they will be cast into the debtor's prison, which is eternal hell.

The only answer is Jesus. He paid all the price that we may go free. Simple trust in Him discharges all of our spiritual debt; however, as He is today the Saviour, tomorrow He will be the judge and will demand exactness of all, which none can pay. It is so sad inasmuch as He has paid it all, that is, if men will only believe (Jn. 3:16).

"If you are tired of the load of your sin,
"Let Jesus come into your heart;
"If you desire a new life to begin,
"Let Jesus come into your heart."

"If it is for purity now that you sigh,
"Let Jesus come into your heart;
"Fountains for cleansing are flowing nearby,
"Let Jesus come into your heart."

"If there's a tempest your voice cannot still,
"Let Jesus come into your heart;
"If there's a void this world never can fill,
"Let Jesus come into your heart."

"If you would join the glad songs of the blest,
"Let Jesus come into your heart;
"If you would enter the mansions of rest,
"Let Jesus come into your heart."

CHAPTER 13

(1) "THERE WERE PRESENT AT THAT SEASON SOME WHO TOLD HIM OF THE GALILAEANS, WHOSE BLOOD PILATE HAD MINGLED WITH THEIR SACRIFICES."

The diagram is:

1. The phrase, *"There were present at that season,"* probably referred to the previous Passover when this particular event took place.

2. *"Some who told Him of the Galilaeans, whose blood Pilate had mingled with their sacrifices,"* is peculiar to Luke and is the only account given, unless that mentioned by Josephus was the same happening.

3. Evidently, something had gotten out of hand at the temple, and Pilate had dispatched soldiers to quell the disturbance. Whatever it was, some had been killed while they were offering up sacrifices at the great altar immediately in front of the temple. As stated, their blood *"had mingled with their sacrifices,"* i.e., with the blood of their sacrifices.

4. There was a fierce hatred that burned in the hearts of Jews toward the Romans, which occasioned clashes of this nature constantly. Israel felt that she should be the blessed nation in the world because she was the people of the Book and the prophets, hence, her hatred for Rome. Actually, Rome had more difficulties with this tiny country than possibly any other area of her far-flung empire.

5. Josephus related how at one Passover, some 3,000 Jews were butchered, with the temple courts filled with dead corpses. In another of these feasts, 2,000 people perished in similar manner.

(2) "AND JESUS ANSWERING SAID UNTO THEM, DO YOU SUPPOSE THAT THESE GALILAEANS WERE SINNERS ABOVE ALL THE GALILAEANS, BECAUSE THEY SUFFERED SUCH THINGS?"

The overview is:

1. The phrase, *"And Jesus answering said unto them,"* presents a message of somber note. Israel was facing a doom of unparalleled proportions, and yet, she little knew or understood that her situation was perilous, or why it was perilous!

2. Religious error so deceives and blinds its victims that they lose all sense of proper direction. As well, grace refused is judgment determined! The only cure is repentance, whether then or now.

3. The question posed by Jesus, *"Do you suppose that these Galilaeans were sinners above all the Galilaeans, because they suffered such things?"* was exactly what they thought. The flavor of the text suggests that these were Jerusalem Jews who were speaking to Jesus. Evidently they had assumed in their minds that the judgment suffered by the Galilaeans was because of their great sins. Conversely, they reasoned that they (the Jerusalem Jews) were much more righteous and would not suffer such.

(3) "I TELL YOU, NO: BUT, EXCEPT YOU REPENT, YOU SHALL ALL LIKEWISE PERISH."

NO!

The phrase, *"I tell you, No,"* proclaims a great truth.

One is not to judge others by the bad things that happen to them. While at times judgment definitely does come upon some because of evil they have committed, still, no one else has the right to judge them simply because in the eyes of God, there is very little difference between the one judged and the one judging (James 4:12).

"But, except you repent, you shall all likewise perish," presents a startling statement, which, no doubt, hit the listeners as a bombshell.

Williams said, "The Lord Jesus having come to earth to save men's souls, utilized every interruption to address the heart and conscience of the interrupters." What exactly was he saying:

• He placed all in the same category, making no difference in the ones having suffered judgment and the listeners who had posed the question.

• Repentance was demanded of all.

• Without repentance, all would perish, which is exactly what happened in A.D. 70.

The Greek word for *repent* is *metanoeo*

and means "to change one's mind for the better." It is not merely the forsaking of sin, but the changing of one's attitude toward it and his love for it. Hence, it is demanded by God as a condition of forgiveness and grace (Lk. 15:7; 24:47; Acts 2:38; 3:19; 17:30).

REPENTANCE AS A BIBLE DOCTRINE

The word that expresses the biblical concept of repentance in the Old Testament is *sub*. It is found over 1,000 times and has a wide range of meanings; however, its greatest thrust indicates turning from evil to God, from evil ways to God's ways. It is a commitment to a faith and way of life that involves turning from a previous way, and this is to *"repent."*

The Greek word in the New Testament, as we have stated, is *metanoeo* and means the same as the Old Testament word. It emphasizes a change of mind and attitude.

Repentance is demanded of both the believer and unbeliever.

Regarding the unbeliever, Paul said, *"Testifying both to the Jews, and also to the Greeks, repentance toward God, and faith toward our Lord Jesus Christ"* (Acts 20:21).

FAITH

Consequently, the repentant sinner owes such to God because it is God against whom he has sinned. As well, he must exhibit faith toward Christ in order to appropriate to himself the benefits of that which Christ has done on his behalf.

Actually, repentance demands faith and is exhibited by an expression of sorrow from one's heart over one's sins and the desire to change. Faith is belief in Christ as the only one who can bring about that change.

While the sinner may understand little of this, still, it is the heart that God judges, rather than particular words or actions.

So, every single person who has ever been born again engaged in repentance toward God and faith toward the Lord Jesus Christ. There are no exceptions!

Believers are called on to repent as well. Actually, almost all the admonishment for repentance in the Old Testament, as well as the New, is toward believers. To five of the seven churches of Asia, Jesus demanded

NOTES

repentance, and these, as is obvious, were believers (Rev., Chpts. 2-3).

MORE EVIL

When man removes himself by his self-will from God's direction and care, he finds that the God-willed consequence of his evil is more evil (I Sam. 15:11, 35; II Sam. 24:16; Jer. 18:10). However, whoever repents, even at the eleventh hour, finds a God of mercy and love, not of judgment (Jer. 18:8; 26:3, 13, 19; Jn. 3:9).

RETURN TO DEPENDENCE ON GOD

The call for repentance on the part of man is a call for him to return to his creaturely (and covenant) dependence on God. Such calls make it clear that the evil that God intends as a consequence of one's sin is not malicious or vindictive, but rather is intended to bring the person to repentance. As we have stated, he who commits evil finds further evil willed by God, but he who repents of his evil finds a God who repents of His judgment.

TURNING AROUND

Repentance is not just a feeling of being sorry or even the changing of one's mind, even though those things are employed, but it actually means a turning around, a complete alteration of the basic motivation and direction of one's life. In truth, one cannot do this on his own but must depend on God concerning His life-changing power. This is what is meant by repentance toward God and faith toward Jesus Christ.

Many need to repent of their *"good"* as well as their *"bad."* It is not that the good is wrong, but that dependence on such is wrong. Consequently, John the Baptist demanded repentance not just for obvious *"sinners"* but for *"righteous"* Jews as well. It was a decisive act of turning from the old way of life, especially their dependence on good works, and a throwing of oneself on the mercy of the coming One (Mat. 3:2, 11; Mk. 1:4; Lk. 3:3, 8; Acts 13:24; 19:4).

SEEING OURSELVES AS GOD SEES US

Repentance is the act of our seeing ourselves exactly as God sees us. This means to look past the façade of self-righteousness and recognize ourselves as what we really are, those who desperately need the Lord.

WE MUST SAY OF OURSELVES WHAT GOD SAYS OF US

We must not only see ourselves as God sees us but, as well, say of ourselves what God says of us. That's what John was speaking of when he said of believers, *"If we confess our sins"* (I Jn. 1:9).

It is regrettable that many modern Pentecostals and Charismatics little believe in repentance if at all, calling it an Old Testament doctrine, which has no validity in the New Testament. As we have already stated, repentance is a concept in both Testaments, actually providing the basic foundation of our relationship with God.

If it is to be remembered, concerning the seven messages given by Christ regarding the seven churches of Asia, which, in fact, span the entirety of the church age, we find that our Lord demanded repentance concerning five of these churches.

Actually, as we have already alluded, anytime the believer confesses his sin to the Lord, he is, in effect, repenting of that sin. Also, every sinner who comes to Christ, as stated, must repent, or else, he cannot be saved. So, the idea that repentance is not presently required shows a gross ignorance of the Word of God and a basic misunderstanding of the principle of faith. All repentance requires faith, and all faith requires repentance, at least where sin is involved, whether with the unbeliever or believer. The unbeliever repents of the very fact of being a sinner, while the believer repents of individual sins.

APATHY

The believer oftentimes must repent not only of sins committed but of attitudes, such as apathy, complacency, lack of burden or concern, etc.

In the Lord's Prayer, Jesus said that we must say, *"Forgive us our trespasses, as we forgive those who trespass against us."* As well, Jesus is making intercession for us 24 hours a day, seven days a week. So, if He is doing that, there must be some problem that needs intercession on our behalf (Heb. 7:25).

NOTES

We have come to believe that only the big five constitute sin, and I speak of nicotine, drugs, alcohol, pornography, and gambling. However, concerning sin, the Word of God says, *"An high look, and a proud heart, and the plowing of the wicked, is sin"* (Prov. 21:4). Solomon also said under the inspiration of the Holy Spirit, *"The thought of foolishness is sin"* (Prov. 24:9). The foolishness addressed here speaks of that which is perverse. James said, *"But if you have respect to persons, you commit sin"* (James 2:9). Paul said, *"For whatsoever is not of faith is sin"* (Rom. 14:23). The type of faith addressed here is faith in Jesus Christ and Him crucified. Any other type of faith is sin.

These reasons given constitute our dire need for the constant intercession of Christ, as should be overly obvious. Sin covers a wide swatch so to speak.

(4) "OR THOSE EIGHTEEN, UPON WHOM THE TOWER IN SILOAM FELL, AND SLEW THEM, THINK YE THAT THEY WERE SINNERS ABOVE ALL MEN WHO DWELT IN JERUSALEM?"

The exegesis is:

1. The phrase, *"Or those eighteen, upon whom the tower in Siloam fell, and slew (killed) them,"* portrays an event evidently known by all, which had been readily discussed.

2. Jesus' question, *"Think ye (Do you think) that they were sinners above all men who dwelt in Jerusalem?"* addresses the major topic of this discussion.

3. The Lord used these occasions as a great national lesson. Spence said, "Men are too ready, now as then, to give way to the unloving error of looking at individual misfortune as the consequence of individual evil. Such human uncharitable judgments," Spence went on to say, "the Lord bitterly condemns."

4. It is said that the Jews looked on this catastrophe as a judgment on the workmen who perished because they were paid by Pilate out of temple money. It had to do with the pool of Siloam located in Jerusalem.

(5) "I TELL YOU, NO: BUT, EXCEPT YOU REPENT, YOU SHALL LIKEWISE PERISH."

The synopsis is:

1. This verse is identical to Verse 3, and by it being given twice, it portrays the certitude of the prediction.

2. As stated, it was fulfilled in A.D. 70 with the destruction of Jerusalem by Titus the Roman general.

(6) "HE SPOKE ALSO THIS PARABLE; A CERTAIN MAN HAD A FIG TREE PLANTED IN HIS VINEYARD; AND HE CAME AND SOUGHT FRUIT THEREON, AND FOUND NONE."

THE PARABLE

The phrase, *"He spoke also this parable,"* refers to it being said immediately after the demand for repentance. Now, He will tell why!

"A certain man had a fig tree planted in his vineyard," is meant to use the fig tree as a symbolism for Israel.

As well, the image of the fig tree would not have set too well with the Pharisees and scribes, especially considering their exalted opinion of themselves and Israel as a whole. They, in essence, thought they were the entirety of the vineyard, and now to hear themselves described as only one tree in that vineyard, and a fig tree at that, they, no doubt, considered to be an insult.

Self-righteousness always has an exalted opinion of self while thinking very lowly of others. However, here we are seeing what God actually thought of Israel.

In fact, they were about to be destroyed, with the church taking their place and covering the entirety of the vineyard in one form or the other. Whereas Israel was national, the church is international.

FRUIT

The phrase, *"And he came and sought fruit thereon, and found none,"* proclaimed the present state of Israel. They had brought forth no fruit whatsoever!

The emphasis is clear. It wasn't that it was little fruit, or even sickly fruit, but actually none at all. What a dire circumstance!

What would He say about the modern church?

More particularly, what does He say about each believer individually?

To be sure, each believer is so judged, and the judgment rendered on Israel is declared,

in one way or the other, on individual believers presently.

We either bring forth fruit, or else, we are taken away and cast into the fire and burned (Jn. 15:2, 6).

So, let not the modern believer think that Israel under law was to suffer such with believers being exempted.

What kind of fruit?

A dissertation on this all-important subject is needed, but presently, we say that righteousness is the fruit required, which can only be given by Christ (II Cor. 5:21).

(7) "THEN SAID HE UNTO THE DRESSER OF HIS VINEYARD, BEHOLD, THESE THREE YEARS I COME SEEKING FRUIT ON THIS FIG TREE, AND FIND NONE: CUT IT DOWN; WHY CUMBERETH IT THE GROUND?"

The exegesis is:

1. The phrase, *"Then said He unto the dresser of His Vineyard,"* portrays the owner as God and the dresser as Jesus. As well, we must remember that as the vineyard, i.e., Israel, belonged to Him, likewise, the church belongs to Him (Mat. 16:18).

2. The Pharisees acted as though Israel belonged to them, while many so-called religious leaders in the modern church seem to think the same concerning the body of Christ.

3. In truth, despite what men think or say, there is no such thing, at least in the eyes of God, as a religious or so-called spiritual leader because Jesus is the sole head of the church (Col. 1:18).

4. *"Behold, these three years I come seeking fruit on this fig tree, and find none,"* illustrates the three years of our Lord's ministry up to now. Despite the greatest miracles by far the world had ever seen, with the Son of God ministering to the people, Israel remained spiritually blind, spiritually deaf, and spiritually dumb. There was no fruit!

5. The statement and question, *"Cut it down; why cumbereth it the ground* (why do you allow it to cumber the ground)?" represents a startling truth.

6. The popular belief that the unconverted person who leads a moral life does no harm to humanity is a man-made delusion. All who are not Spirit-born and who do not

bear spiritual fruit, however fair their lives may be, are comparable to the leaves of a fig tree; they shall surely perish.

(8) "AND HE ANSWERING SAID UNTO HIM, LORD, LET IT ALONE THIS YEAR ALSO, TILL I SHALL DIG ABOUT IT, AND DUNG IT."

The structure is:

1. The phrase, *"And He answering said unto Him,"* presents the Lord as the dresser speaking to His heavenly Father, the owner of the vineyard, i.e., Israel.

2. *"Lord, let it alone this year also, till I shall dig about it, and dung it,"* represents the last months of the last year of the Master's ministry, for it is thought that His ministry lasted for about three and one-half years.

3. Despite Israel's rebellion in the murdering of the *"dresser,"* still, the Holy Spirit was sent on the day of Pentecost, which produced the mighty miracle-working power of God in the ministries of the apostles and others exactly as it had been with Jesus.

(9) "AND IF IT BEAR FRUIT, WELL: AND IF NOT, THEN AFTER THAT YOU SHALL CUT IT DOWN."

CUT IT DOWN

The phrase, *"And if it bear fruit, well,"* proclaims the opportunity and, as well, an opportunity such as no people or nation had ever known. However, there was to be no fruit.

"And if not, then after that You shall cut it down," proclaims exactly what happened.

It did not bear fruit; consequently, it was *"cut down"* in A.D. 70.

Even after the destruction, which saw over a million Jews slaughtered, Israel continued, but without a temple, to attempt to have some semblance of a nation. However, in A.D. 135, they were totally destroyed and scattered all over the world, where they wandered as outcasts until 1948 when they once again became a nation, with the Star of David flying above Jerusalem for the first time in about 1,900 years.

JEWISH LEADERS

Sometime back, I had the occasion to speak with an assemblage of Jewish leaders in Washington D.C. The other speaker was Benjamin Netanyahu. If I remember

NOTES

correctly, this was in 1987, some nine years before he was elected the prime minister of Israel.

I had the occasion to speak with him a few moments after the meeting. Even though I had the privilege of meeting a number of Jewish leaders, still, there was something about this man that impressed me. While the Lord did not specifically relate anything to me concerning his future, still, I did feel the Holy Spirit impress upon me that he was unusual. Consequently, in a distant sort of way, I have followed his career and was not at all surprised when he was elected to the highest office in Israel.

His election, I think, has proven to be very good for Israel in that he understands many things that some of the other prime ministers seemingly did not understand. I do believe his election was the will of God and will steadily usher Israel toward its destiny with the Antichrist, and ultimately to their acceptance of the Lord Jesus Christ, which will take place at the second coming.

(10) "AND HE WAS TEACHING IN ONE OF THE SYNAGOGUES ON THE SABBATH."

The form is:

1. His ministering in a synagogue this late in His ministry was unusual. In the first two years, and especially the first year, the record seems to be that He taught and healed most every Sabbath in a synagogue. However, owing to the persistent enmity of the hierarchy in Jerusalem, He was little welcomed in all but a few synagogues.

2. This is a tragedy considering that the Son of God was not welcome in that which could be constituted as His own house. However, He is not welcome in most churches presently. The next verses tell us why.

(11) "AND, BEHOLD, THERE WAS A WOMAN WHICH HAD A SPIRIT OF INFIRMITY EIGHTEEN YEARS, AND WAS BOWED TOGETHER, AND COULD IN NO WISE LIFT UP HERSELF."

A SPIRIT OF INFIRMITY

The phrase, *"And, behold, there was a woman which had a spirit of infirmity eighteen years,"* means that a demon spirit had caused this sickness.

No! This did not mean the woman was demon possessed, for she was not. Jesus did not cast any demon from her but merely broke its hold, which caused her to be instantly healed, and to which the demon spirit had no more access.

In fact, many believers are likewise troubled by demon spirits, whether in the realm of sickness, poverty, or other types of problems. It is what one might call demonic oppression (Acts 10:38).

ONLY THE CROSS

This is not a matter to be taken lightly. Neither is it something that can be easily thrown off. To be sure, each and every believer can have total victory in this area, but oftentimes, it does not come as simply or easily as some would have us believe. Satan does not give ground easily and, in fact, will do so only in response to the power of God (Mk. 16:18).

"And was bowed together, and could in no wise lift up herself," constituted, some think, a curvature of the spine. At any rate, she was a perfect example of what Satan has done to the whole of humanity.

Mankind in general, at least in one way or the other, has *"a spirit of infirmity,"* brought on by Satan, and is *"bowed together."* As well, man in no wise, at least by his own strength and power, can lift up himself. He has repeatedly attempted to do so with education, psychology, or a host of other efforts or philosophies, but always has failed, as fail he must. Man simply does not have the power or ability to do so! Only one who is stronger can do such a thing, and that one is Jesus, and, in fact, He is the only one (Lk. 11:20-22).

Demonic oppression can affect a person in varied ways. It can cause nervous disorders, emotional disturbances, some types of sickness, even as here portrayed, and can cause depression. So, from these things, we can see how this is no laughing matter.

There is only one way of victory, and that is the Cross of Christ.

We must understand that Jesus atoned for all sin at the Cross, past, present, and future, at least for all who will believe (Jn. 3:16). This means that He broke the bondage of

sin that holds humanity in its terrible grip and that the captive can be set free.

As well, due to the fact of having atoned for all sin, Satan and all of his cohorts of darkness were defeated at the Cross. In fact, there is only one answer for sin and only one answer for demon powers, and that is the Cross of Christ.

To have victory, the victory for which Jesus has already paid such a price, the believer must understand the following:

GOD'S PRESCRIBED ORDER OF LIFE AND LIVING

• The believer must understand that everything we receive from God comes to us exclusively by Jesus Christ as the source. In other words, He alone is the source of all blessings (Jn. 1:1, 14, 29; 14:6, 20; Col. 2:10-15).

• The Cross of Christ is the means, and the only means, by which all of these wonderful things are given unto us (I Cor. 1:17-18, 23; 2:2).

• Considering that, the Cross of Christ must be the object of our faith, and the only object of our faith. When one has faith in Christ and the Cross, one is at the same time having faith in the Word of God. The reason is, the Bible is the story of Christ and Him crucified (Rom. 6:1-14; Gal. 6:14; Col. 2:10-15).

• With Christ as the source and the Cross of Christ as the means, and with our faith anchored squarely in the Cross, then the Holy Spirit will grandly and gloriously help us. This means that our faith must be in what Jesus did at the Cross. The Holy Spirit works exclusively within the parameters of the finished work of Christ and, in fact, will not work outside of those parameters (Rom. 8:1-11; Eph. 2:13-18).

(12) "AND WHEN JESUS SAW HER, HE CALLED HER TO HIM, AND SAID UNTO HER, WOMAN, YOU ARE LOOSED FROM YOUR INFIRMITY."

The synopsis is:

1. The phrase, *"And when Jesus saw her, He called her to Him,"* means that this miracle, like that of Nain, was unsolicited.

2. On entering the synagogue, His loving eye was attracted to this poor woman and

not to the beauty of the building or the rich clothing of the wealthy who may have been present. Such is the God of the Bible!

3. *"And said unto her, Woman, you are loosed from your infirmity,"* proclaims Him knowing exactly what was wrong with her, demon oppression, along with His command to be loosed.

4. What a statement! *"Woman, you are loosed from your infirmity,"* is a declaration of deliverance that is needed at one time or the other by every single human being who has ever lived. Only Jesus can effect such a deliverance.

(13) "AND HE LAID HIS HANDS ON HER: AND IMMEDIATELY SHE WAS MADE STRAIGHT, AND GLORIFIED GOD."

The composition is:

1. The phrase, *"And He laid His hands on her,"* represented the end for Satan. There was no way the Evil One could remain in the face of the word and way of Christ.

2. *"And immediately she was made straight,"* in essence, proclaims a miracle. One can well imagine the feelings of the bystanders and the joy of this woman when her back was made instantly straight. What a disconcerting and extremely hurtful posture she had been in for some 18 years. And now, she was instantly free!

3. As immediately this woman was made straight, as immediately Jesus can do the same for anyone. Morally, He is the only Saviour. Other things may change around the disfigurement, but nothing can make straight but Christ.

4. *"And glorified God,"* proclaims her immediately beginning to praise God for the miraculous change that was instantly wrought in her poor, formerly diseased frame. The healing was instant, and the praise was uninhibited.

5. This portrays that she was a woman who knew God, but yet, she was bound by this spirit of infirmity but was now loosed by the power of God.

(14) "AND THE RULER OF THE SYNAGOGUE ANSWERED WITH INDIGNATION, BECAUSE THAT JESUS HAD HEALED ON THE SABBATH DAY, AND SAID UNTO THE PEOPLE, THERE ARE SIX DAYS IN WHICH MEN OUGHT TO WORK: IN THEM

NOTES

THEREFORE COME AND BE HEALED, AND NOT ON THE SABBATH DAY."

THE HOSTILITY AND CORRUPTION OF THE HUMAN HEART

The phrase, *"And the ruler of the synagogue answered with indignation,"* proves that this glorious demonstration of grace, pity, and power, which proved that Jesus was the Messiah, as well, brought out the hostility and corruption of the ruler's heart.

So it is still! The nearer Christ comes to the Pharisees and the greater demonstration He makes of His grace toward the victims of sin and Satan, the more violent is the anger excited.

HEALING ON THE SABBATH DAY?

The phrase, *"Because that Jesus had healed on the Sabbath day,"* proclaims several things:

a. There was nothing in the law of Moses that said that a person could not be healed on the Sabbath day. This was an invention purely of man.

b. In the law of Moses, the Sabbath was made for man and not man for the Sabbath, opening the door for any good thing to be done on this particular day.

c. When men leave the Word of God and make up their own rules, such always breeds self-righteousness.

4. The phrase, *"And said unto the people, There are six days in which men ought to work: in them therefore come and be healed, and not on the Sabbath day,"* proclaims this self-righteous bigot rebuking Christ. If the truth be known, the Sabbath was only an excuse. They hated Jesus, irrespective of what day He performed a miracle. These Pharisees claimed to be of God but, in reality, were of Satan.

5. Religious evil is the highest form of evil! And yet, it is looked upon by most of the world as devout and pious when, in reality, it is the very opposite.

(15) "THE LORD THEN ANSWERED HIM, AND SAID, YOU HYPOCRITE, DOES NOT EACH ONE OF YOU ON THE SABBATH LOOSE HIS OX OR HIS ASS FROM THE STALL, AND LEAD HIM AWAY TO WATERING?"

The form is:

1. Seiss said, "Every where, even in our holiest moods and most sacred doings, there still flashes out the stern and humiliating accusation, 'O man, you are a sinner!'

2. "All your goodness is but abomination apart from Christ!

3. "Your only hope is in Him whose body was broken, and whose blood was shed for the remission of sins!"

HYPOCRITE

The phrase, *"The Lord then answered him, and said, You hypocrite,"* is said by the older manuscripts to have said *"hypocrites,"* and thus included all the Pharisees, at least those present who were of this spirit.

Jesus answering this man portrays righteous indignation, and rightly so! To be frank, this type of spirit stirred anger in Jesus as nothing else did; consequently, what He called him in front of all of the people was the highest insult of all. However, it was meant to be more than an insult; it was the proclamation of what this man and all like him really were.

This is at least one of the reasons they hated Him so malignantly. He gave them no credence, showed them no respect, and, in fact, publicly labeled them for what they actually were. Modern preachers should follow such an example and be prepared to pay the price.

RELIGIOUS LEADERS

If one is to notice, Jesus seldom, if ever, referred to anyone other than religious leaders after this fashion. In fact, He dealt with the three basic classes of people in three different ways.

1. To the common people, with many of them being what might be referred to as *"sinners,"* He addressed them unfailingly with mercy and compassion but never with condemnation.

2. With the ruling elite, if He addressed them at all, it was with a touch of sarcasm. For instance, as we shall see, when Herod was mentioned to Him, He referred to Herod as a *"fox"* (Lk. 13:32).

3. To the religious leaders of Israel, He addressed them with scathing denunciation,

NOTES

and in no uncertain terms. He left absolutely no doubt as to what they were. He pulled no punches, asked no quarter, and gave none (Mat., Chpt. 23).

He did this, no doubt, because they were leading the people astray; consequently, their guilt was by far the greater.

ANIMALS AND HUMAN BEINGS

The question, *"Does not each one of you on the Sabbath loose his ox or his ass from the stall, and lead him away to watering?"* hits at the very heart of the matter. He vividly drew a contrast between animals and human beings. The ox and the ass were personal property; the afflicted daughter of Abraham was but a woman, friendless and poor.

This means that every possible indulgence was to be shown in cases where their own interests were involved; however, no mercy or indulgence was to be thought of, though, where the poor and the sick only were concerned.

In other words, the Pharisees had no regard or concern for people, as most religions, with them simply being used to attain the desired end, in this instance, place and position.

Religious hierarchy within itself is grossly unscriptural because it abrogates the headship of Christ. They are not content to allow the Lord to serve as the Head but must fill this position themselves. They do so because, in effect, what they head up does not belong to God. It is man-made and, consequently, man-directed. It is my personal thought that any religious denomination, or local church for that matter, that maintains an unscriptural form of church government must be abandoned by all who truly love God, whether preacher or layman. A little leaven will ultimately leaven the whole lump.

Many preachers keep thinking the situation will improve; however, it is impossible for such to improve, barring total repentance, which is not usually the case.

When one observes the animosity between this hypocrite, who was a ruler of the synagogue, and Christ, one is observing that which continues unto this hour. The presence of Christ automatically draws this response.

(16) "AND OUGHT NOT THIS WOMAN,

BEING A DAUGHTER OF ABRAHAM, WHOM SATAN HAS BOUND, LO, THESE EIGHTEEN YEARS, BE LOOSED FROM THIS BOND ON THE SABBATH DAY?"

The diagram is:

1. The phrase, *"And ought not this woman, being a daughter of Abraham,"* is further evidence that she was a believer.

2. *"Daughter of Abraham,"* actually proclaims covenant relationship, which should have kept her free from this malady of darkness; however, her condition was, in fact, a statement proclaiming that the religious hierarchy of Israel had not lived up to the covenant. Thus, they had opened the door for admittance by Satan, with this woman, and thousands more like her, being the result. In effect, Jesus was telling this hypocrite that the fault was his alone. So, not only did He rebuke him for his faked religious piety but, as well, laid the blame at his feet and all others like him.

3. *Whom Satan has bound, lo, these eighteen years,"* proclaims the direct cause of her malady, but the door had been opened by the religious leadership of Israel.

4. The conclusion of the question, *"Be loosed from this bond on the Sabbath day?"* proclaims the deliverance of this woman as more important than keeping some silly man-made rule.

(17) "AND WHEN HE HAD SAID THESE THINGS, ALL HIS ADVERSARIES WERE ASHAMED: AND ALL THE PEOPLE REJOICED FOR ALL THE GLORIOUS THINGS THAT WERE DONE BY HIM."

The overview is:

1. The phrase, *"And when He had said these things, all His adversaries were ashamed,"* proclaims them being shown up in front of the people. They were ashamed, and rightly so, but they did not repent. So, they were ashamed but not changed.

2. *"And all the people rejoiced for all the glorious things that were done by Him,"* presents them doing exactly what they should have done, but this incensed these hypocrites even more!

3. From the flavor of the text, Jesus evidently healed many others at that particular time as well.

(18) "THEN SAID HE, UNTO WHAT

IS THE KINGDOM OF GOD LIKE? AND WHEREUNTO SHALL I RESEMBLE IT?"

THEN SAID HE

The phrase, *"Then said He,"* is an extremely important statement. The Greek word makes this clear.

The word *then* probably would have been better translated *therefore*, for it connects the two parables that follow with the two facts that precede respecting the bound woman and the blind ruler.

These parables are given to explain how it could be that Satan's power and teaching could have such a place in what professes to be the kingdom of God, i.e., the synagogue and the modern church. That kingdom was begun with one man, Abraham, and committed to the sons of Jacob. It had become a great worldly system in which Satan made his home, just as the unclean vultures in the air nested in the boughs of the abnormal mustard tree. So, in the very synagogue itself, Satan had bound a woman for 18 years, and she could in no wise lift up herself. How so much Satan has taken over great parts of the kingdom of God.

THE KINGDOM OF GOD

At the same time, Satan had so leavened the mind of the ruler of the synagogue with traditional corruption that his soul was hopelessly blinded.

This little word *then* or *therefore* makes it plain that the popular interpretation of these parables as predicting the triumph of the gospel is mistaken. Actually, they predict the very opposite!

The question, *"Unto what is the kingdom of god like?"* is meant to portray what Satan and religious men had done to the great plan of God as given to Abraham and Moses, as well as the prophets. It would apply presently to the church, also!

The question, *"And whereunto shall I resemble it?"* presents God Himself revealing His judgment about that which professed to be His kingdom.

Just as the Hebrew church became thoroughly leavened with sacerdotal evil, as well as the evil of false doctrine, so has the Christian church.

(19) "IT IS LIKE A GRAIN OF MUS-TARD SEED, WHICH A MAN TOOK, AND CAST INTO HIS GARDEN; AND IT GREW, AND WAXED A GREAT TREE; AND THE FOWLS OF THE AIR LODGED IN THE BRANCHES OF IT."

A GRAIN OF MUSTARD SEED

The phrase, *"It is like a grain of mustard seed, which a man took, and cast into his garden,"* has to do with the humble beginnings of the kingdom of God on earth, going as far back as Abel. In fact, its beginnings were so small that the Bible only records two conversions up to Noah: Abel and Enoch. There may well have been more, but only these two are recorded. At the time of the flood, only Noah and his family entered the ark. After that, the family of Abraham was the only people on earth who knew the Lord, other than Melchizedek and those who were with him, at least that is now known (Gen. 12:1-3; 14:18-20).

The phrase, *"And it grew, and waxed a great tree,"* speaks of the nation of Israel growing into millions of people, in fact, the only people on earth who had the Word of God.

Sometime ago while in Israel, our guide showed me a mustard tree and then took one of the tiny pods from its flowers and crushed it, causing the many seeds to fall into my hand. Truly, its seed is very small, especially considering the quite large tree it brings forth.

THE FOWLS OF THE AIR

The phrase, *"And the fowls of the air lodged in the branches of it,"* proclaims demon spirits spoken of as fowls making their home in this kingdom. Hence, this explains the spiritual corruption of the ruler of the synagogue who became incensed when Jesus delivered the woman who had been bound by Satan for some 18 years. Actually, almost the entirety of the religious leadership of Israel was bitterly opposed to Christ, with the kingdom of God almost totally corrupted. Even though it was rich, big, and powerful, still, it had no spiritual strength and, in fact, did not know God even though it was called *"the kingdom of God."*

PRESENT TIMES

It is basically the same at present. I will use my own person as an example.

Entire denominations would rather see people eternally lost, meaning that they would go to hell forever and forever, rather than be saved under this ministry. In fact, one preacher stated that rather than the people under our ministry giving their hearts to God, "Let them go to hell." That's the same spirit that nailed Christ to the Cross. There could be nothing more demonic than that. So, little or nothing has actually changed. It means that all who claim to be of God aren't of God. Their religious effort, and religion it is, is guided by Satan exactly as it was at the time of Christ.

(20) "AND AGAIN HE SAID, WHERE-UNTO SHALL I LIKEN THE KINGDOM OF GOD?"

The exegesis is:

1. The phrase, *"And again He said,"* is meant to proclaim a new era, namely the church, which the disciples at that time hardly understood at all.

2. The question, *"Whereunto shall I liken the kingdom of God?"* pertains, as stated, to the church, which is separate and apart from Israel, proven by the word *again.*

3. Israel failed, with the church raised up to take its place. As well, it had small beginnings, composed only of Jesus and His few wavering followers.

4. Spence said, "To the eye of sense it seemed impossible that this little movement could ever stir the world, and could ever become a society of mighty dimensions." In fact, counting both Catholics and Protestants, Christianity numbers nearly 2 billion adherents; however, the way that is counted refers to entire nations coming under the banner of Christianity. For instance, America is described as Christian and, thereby, numbered as some 310 million people. Of course, it is doubtful that one-half of one percent of that number is truly born again. Jesus said:

"Strait is the gate, and narrow is the way, which leads unto life, and few there be that find it" (Mat. 7:14).

(21) "IT IS LIKE LEAVEN, WHICH A WOMAN TOOK AND HID IN THREE

MEASURES OF MEAL, TILL THE WHOLE WAS LEAVENED."

LEAVEN

The phrase, *"It is like leaven,"* is meant to portray rot and corruption.

"Which a woman took," is used figuratively of the woman in an evil sense, representing wickedness, fallacy, uncleanness, unfaithfulness, and false religion (Lam. 1:17; Ezek. 16:15, 22, 26, 28-59; 23:1-49; 36:17; Hos. 1:2; 2:2-17; 3:1; Rev., Chpt. 17).

When used in a good sense, women represent Israel (Gen. 37:9-10; Ezek., Chpt. 16; Rev., Chpt. 12).

MEAL

The phrase, *"And hid in three measures of meal,"* symbolizes the Word of God (Mat. 4:4; Jn. 6:47-63).

"Three measures" represents a bushel, heaped up and running over, portraying the largeness of the church, exactly as the mustard tree of Verse 19.

The phrase, *"Till the whole was leavened,"* portrays the church at the end and exactly the same condition as Israel at its conclusion. As Israel was taken over by demon spirits, the church is, likewise, corrupted by false doctrine.

When Jesus came the first time, only a few truly knew God, and when He comes the second time, it will be the same, at least in comparison with the huge number who profess.

As Israel of old had become man-led, the modern church is man-led as well! As Israel of old had spiritually deteriorated until the law of Moses was polluted and corrupted, likewise, the mighty outpouring of the Holy Spirit in the modern church has, with some exceptions, followed suit.

FALSE DOCTRINE

Catholicism, which makes up nearly 1 billion of the adherents of Christianity, is idolatry pure and simple. However, Protestantism fares little better, with many in its ranks claiming that they will no longer attempt to evangelize Catholics because they claim that Catholic doctrine is scripturally satisfactory.

Tragically, most of the old line churches

NOTES

have so denied the Holy Spirit until there is little within their ranks that truly compares with New Testament Christianity. Regrettably, most of the Pentecostal denominations, as well as Charismatics, have pretty well denied who the Holy Spirit really is and what He really does, even though loudly trumpeting the manifestations of the Spirit. For the most part, they have accepted humanistic psychology and have become thoroughly psychologized, exactly as the world.

Counting both priests and preachers, well over 50 percent don't even believe that Jesus Christ is the Son of God. They, as well, deny His resurrection.

I think one could say without any fear of contradiction that a majority of priests and preachers deny the born-again experience by claiming that the church saves or by espousing false doctrine. Truly, the whole is leavened.

THE TRUE GOSPEL?

In many, if not most old-line churches, there is not enough true gospel preached for one to truly find Christ. There's almost no moving and operation of the Holy Spirit.

Sadder still, there was a day that certain Pentecostal denominations could be looked at with confidence, knowing that most preached the gospel, but sadly and regrettably, that is no longer true. One presently has to pick and choose regarding churches, and very carefully at that.

As well, false doctrine is rampant in Charismatic churches, especially considering the greed message and dominion teaching.

Yes, there are some good churches, but not as many as one would think, fulfilling exactly what Jesus said, *"Till the whole was leavened."*

The *"I"* of Verses 18 and 20 is most solemn. It is God Himself revealing His judgment about that which professed to be His kingdom.

Just as the Hebrew church became thoroughly leavened with sacerdotal evil, so has the Christian church been leavened with false doctrine.

(22) "AND HE WENT THROUGH THE CITIES AND VILLAGES, TEACHING, AND JOURNEYING TOWARD JERUSALEM."

TEACHING

The phrase, *"And He went through the cities and villages, teaching,"* implies that He was no longer welcome in any synagogue. Actually, during the last year of Jesus' public ministry, He was welcome in few synagogues.

In John 16:2, He said, *"They shall put you out of the synagogues: yes, the time comes, that whosoever kills you will think that he does God service."*

Several statements need to be made concerning this spoken by Christ in John 16:2:

THE ANOINTING OF THE HOLY SPIRIT?

As the church becomes more and more leavened and, consequently, thoroughly corrupt, it will become harder and harder to find a church where the gospel of Jesus Christ is preached under the power and anointing of the Holy Spirit. We must remember that the Holy Spirit will never anoint sin or false doctrine. In truth, most preachers presently have little knowledge of what the anointing of the Holy Spirit actually is. If the anointing of the Holy Spirit is upon a person's ministry, the fruit will be obvious. People will be saved, sick bodies will be healed, believers will be baptized with the Holy Spirit, and sinful bondages will be broken, with the fruit of the Spirit more and more evident in hearts and lives. That is the criteria given in the early church, in which the Holy Spirit was the Divine Teacher. To be sure, it says nothing concerning some of the fads presently sweeping the modern church.

OPPOSITION

The opposition and persecution toward true believers will become more and more intense, with these deceived followers of Satan excommunicating anyone who truly follows Christ. They did it to the Lord, and they will do it to His followers. In fact, they will be and are so deceived that they will actually think they're doing God, as Jesus said, a service.

ORGANIZED RELIGION?

The time is coming, if it has not already arrived, that if one truly wants to follow the Lord, he is going to have to disassociate himself from any and all organized religion. The facts are these:

While there are some godly preachers and laity in organized religion, more and more they're going to have to compromise their ministries in order to be accepted. Consequently, there will be less and less moving and operation of the Holy Spirit in these particular ministries, whomever and wherever they might be.

Organized religion refers not only to denominationalism but even to many so-called independent ministries because this spirit of man-led organization is just as prevalent in these particular churches as others.

A short time ago while returning from Egypt, we missed our flight in New York and found ourselves with a layover of about five or six hours in Atlanta, immediately after midnight.

Frances and I, along with others, were sitting in a little open restaurant in the terminal of the airport. During those hours, about the only people present were the airport personnel. After hearing that I was there, quite a few came up to me with some very kind words, etc. However, one particular testimony stands out.

A PERSONAL TESTIMONY

A dear black brother walked up to our table and said this to me:

"Brother Swaggart, I was saved under your television ministry about 10 years ago."

He then went on to say, "When you had your problem, I was shaken; however, I took it to the Lord, asking Him what I should do? He said to me, 'You stay true to Brother Swaggart's ministry, for I have called him, and he is preaching the truth."

I looked at this dear brother for a few moments, realizing that he had very little education and was actually working for menial wages. But yet, he had more of the leading of the Holy Spirit than most of the so-called religious leaders of this present time.

The phrase, *"And journeying toward Jerusalem,"* as stated by the Holy Spirit, has a great sadness.

This was the Lord's last journey to Jerusalem. He was finishing His ministry and heading toward His final conflict with Satan in order to redeem men (Col. 2:14-17; I Pet. 2:24).

All of this immediately preceded the last Passover where Jesus would actually become the sacrifice, which all the Passover lambs had represented in the many past centuries.

(23) "THEN SAID ONE UNTO HIM, LORD, ARE THERE FEW THAT BE SAVED? AND HE SAID UNTO THEM."

The overview is:

1. The phrase, *"Then said one unto Him,"* presents a question that is the kernel of what Jesus was saying concerning salvation.

2. The question, *"Lord, are there few that be saved?"* was asked, no doubt, because of the statements just made by Christ concerning the mustard tree and the three measures of meal. Hearing these statements, the man had come to the conclusion that all who profess Christ do not actually have Christ. In fact, only a few really and truly know the Lord.

3. The phrase, *"And He said unto them,"* concerns the answer to the man's question and directs itself to both the Hebrew church, which was then fast dying, and to the coming Christian church, which was just beginning to be born.

4. Even though these two churches were somewhat dissimilar, still, admission into each was the same: the confession of Jesus Christ, God's only Son, as Lord and Saviour.

(24) "STRIVE TO ENTER IN AT THE STRAIT GATE: FOR MANY, I SAY UNTO YOU, WILL SEEK TO ENTER IN, AND SHALL NOT BE ABLE."

THE STRAIT GATE

The phrase, *"Strive to enter in at the strait gate,"* automatically narrows the opening for admittance to salvation. It is not that God refuses people, but people refuse God, or at least God's way. Frances made a statement over our daily radio program the other day, which I think is worth repeating.

As it concerns involvement of the modern church in the political system and, consequently, endeavoring to change America by this process, she said:

"The Christian way is too narrow for

the modern political process to fit, that is, unless the narrow way is compromised."

The word *strive* in the Greek text is *agonizomai* and is used four ways:

1. To enter a contest; to contend in gymnastic games (I Cor. 9:27).

2. To contend with adversaries; to fight (Jn. 18:36; I Tim. 6:12; II Tim. 4:7).

3. To struggle with difficulties and dangers antagonistic to the gospel (Col. 1:29).

4. To endeavor with strenuous zeal to obtain something; to labor fervently (Lk. 13:24; Col. 4:12).

STRIVE

The word *strive* is kin to the *agony* of the garden (Lk. 22:44), and certainly teaches that one must put forth more personal effort than is shown in the far greater majority of claims upon Christ.

While it certainly does not refer to one earning salvation, which is impossible, it instead means that if one truly accepts Christ, one is going to have to follow Christ and not some man-made religious organization. This is actually what all of this means.

Even though in a limited way, it certainly has reference to the personal conflict with sin, still, the far greater majority of the meaning pertains to false religion and false ways, which have damned, and are damning, more people to hell than all the sins of the flesh combined a million times over.

A CLOSED DOOR

The phrase, *"For many, I say unto you, will seek to enter in, and shall not be able,"* proclaims that these had no life of stern self-surrender or painful self-sacrifice.

The word *many* in this phrase illuminates most of the professors of religion.

The *seeking* of which Jesus here speaks, along with the lack of being *able* to enter in, pertains to it being too late.

When is it too late?

It is too late after this life has ended. These verses (24-28) destroy the theory of repentance and salvation after death as taught by some.

Men may ask religious questions and so flatter themselves that they are religious. Further, they may have an ecclesiastical relationship to Christ, and yet, be shut out from heaven.

(25) "WHEN ONCE THE MASTER OF THE HOUSE IS RISEN UP, AND HAS SHUT TO THE DOOR, AND YOU BEGIN TO STAND WITHOUT, AND TO KNOCK AT THE DOOR, SAYING, LORD, LORD, OPEN UNTO US; AND HE SHALL ANSWER AND SAY UNTO YOU, I KNOW YOU NOT WHENCE YE ARE."

THE SHUT DOOR

The phrase, *"When once the master of the house is risen up, and has shut to the door,"* pertains to death. This is the period in time when the door of salvation is shut to the children of men. It has no reference to anything else.

In this life, anyone who truly comes to Christ, irrespective of what he has been, will find a glorious, wonderful welcome. Jesus epitomizes this in the parable of the prodigal son (Lk. 15:11-24).

"And you begin to stand without," refers to the great multitudes who thought they were within but, in reality, were without. To be truly in the kingdom of God, of which Jesus spoke, requires that one be truly *"born again"* (Jn. 3:3).

PLEASE OPEN THE DOOR

The phrase, *"And to knock at the door, saying, Lord, Lord, open unto us,"* tells us several things.

• They thought they were in, hence, the urgent knocking at the door when they find themselves without.

• They refer to Jesus as *"Lord,"* proclaiming that they knew the *talk* but did not have the *walk*.

When that door is shut, multitudes will repent, but it will be too late, believe too late, sorrow for sin too late, and begin to pray too late. Earth is the only place in creation where there is infidelity. There is no unbelief in hell.

The pronoun *us* signals a large multitude and, as well, those of a certain class. It speaks of those who fell under the sway of the *"fowls of the air,"* i.e., demon spirits, and leaven, i.e., false doctrine.

NOTES

I DO NOT KNOW YOU

The phrase, *"And He shall answer and say unto you, I know you not whence ye (where you) are,"* refers to the day of judgment when the dread award will be pronounced upon the unbelieving, the evil life, and the professors of religion. It is called *"the great white throne judgment"* (Rev. 20:11-15).

Jesus Christ is the master of the house and not religious men, religious denominations, or anyone or anything else! He alone is the Saviour and the one to whom men must answer. Actually, men cannot even know God unless they know Him through Christ. While much of the world glibly speaks of God, most have absolutely no idea about what they're speaking because they do not recognize His Son, the Lord Jesus Christ, and, in fact, the only *"door"* to God and to heaven (Jn. 10:7-18).

Let it ever be known that the master is not Mary or Muhammad; it is Jesus Christ!

The phrase, *"I know you not whence ye (where you) are,"* specifies that where they are, which speaks of religious activity, is not where Jesus is.

(26) "THEN SHALL YOU BEGIN TO SAY, WE HAVE EATEN AND DRUNK IN YOUR PRESENCE, AND YOU HAVE TAUGHT IN OUR STREETS."

The structure is:

1. The phrase, *"Then shall you begin to say,"* concerns itself with reaction when it is found out that the house was built upon sand and not rock.

2. *"We have eaten and drunk in Your presence,"* pertains to the vast multitude, even the far greater majority, who are religious but lost. They went to church but for all the wrong reasons, or else, the wrong kind of church, or both. They handled the Bible, i.e., His presence, but little knew what it actually said and looked even less to it as a rule of life and conduct. This represents the millions, as Israel of old, who talk about the Lord but really do not know the Lord. They involve themselves in religious things but are not really born again. As stated several times, it makes up the majority of that which calls itself the church.

3. The phrase, *"And You have taught in our streets,"* proclaims the great opportunity given but lost!

4. More particularly, this speaks of Israel and its response to the ministry and person of Christ; however, even in a greater way, and because of the fullness of the Spirit, it pertains to the church.

(27) "BUT HE SHALL SAY, I TELL YOU, I KNOW YOU NOT WHENCE YOU ARE; DEPART FROM ME, ALL YE WORKERS OF INIQUITY."

The overview is:

1. The phrase, *"But He shall say, I tell you, I know you not whence* (from where) *you are,"* proclaims Jesus Christ alone as the judge.

2. The question must be asked again, "Is one truly following Christ, or rather a particular church, doctrine, or religious denomination?" The consequences are so awful and eternal that one must be certain to make his salvation sure.

3. *"Depart from Me, all ye* (you) *workers of iniquity,"* proclaims Christ calling these professors of religion that which they would never dream, *"workers of iniquity."*

4. When most think of such, they think of sins of the flesh, which certainly do fall into that category. However, precious few would consider religious profession, irrespective of how sincere it might be, and all who engage in it as workers of iniquity. Consequently, this labels all false prophets and false doctrine as iniquity.

5. This means that God labels as iniquity all false worship, embracing of false doctrine, and occupation with man-made religion. Regrettably and sadly, this would incorporate all of Catholicism and most Protestantism as well! Once again, we get back to the few who will truly be saved.

6. One might say that if one has one's faith in anything other than Christ and the Cross, this is looked at by the Lord as iniquity. I pray that's not the case because if it is, this means that 99 percent of modern Christianity falls into the category of iniquity.

(28) THERE SHALL BE WEEPING AND GNASHING OF TEETH, WHEN YOU SHALL SEE ABRAHAM, AND ISAAC, AND JACOB, AND ALL THE PROPHETS, IN

THE KINGDOM OF GOD, AND YOU YOURSELVES THRUST OUT."

The composition is:

1. The phrase, *"There shall be weeping and gnashing of teeth,"* places the professors of religion on the same par as the atheist and Christ rejecter. They all go to the same hell and suffer the same just punishment.

2. Even as Jesus unflinchingly outlined and described this so very serious situation, I am doing my best to impress upon the reader that the mere saying of *"Lord, Lord"* is not enough. Millions are going to find to their dismay that neither their church membership nor all their religious works holds any validity. However, the sadness is, when the door is shut, i.e., death has come, the opportunity for salvation is ended once for all. This means that the purgatory of the Catholics does not exist. It also means that all self-devised ways of salvation are to no avail. It says, as well, that millions of good church members are going to be eternally lost! As stated, their hell will be identical to the unrepentant murderer, child molester, etc.

3. *"When you shall see Abraham, and Isaac, and Jacob, and all the prophets, in the kingdom of God,"* in effect, proclaims the way of salvation. It speaks of the Bible, Jesus Christ and Him crucified, of which these either lived or wrote. The Word of God is the criterion and nothing else!

4. *"And you yourselves thrust out,"* is very pointed and direct. It means that the judgment will be on an individual basis, as all such judgments must be!

5. To be shut out from heaven is to be shut into hell, with its hopeless weeping of remorse and its hopeless gnashing of despair. Here, as everywhere, Christ's teaching conflicts with modern thought.

(29) "AND THEY SHALL COME FROM THE EAST, AND FROM THE WEST, AND FROM THE NORTH, AND FROM THE SOUTH, AND SHALL SIT DOWN IN THE KINGDOM OF GOD."

THE GOSPEL FOR THE WORLD

The phrase, *"And they shall come from the east, and from the west, and from the north, and from the south,"* proclaims an end of any type of exclusivity of the gospel as practiced by the Jews in Jesus' day. Exactly as here stated, the gospel began in the East and then spread to the rest of the world. Civilization began in the East, probably in modern day Iraq where the garden of Eden may have been located. Man being God's highest creation pertained to God's total involvement. To lay the foundation for the gospel, the Lord called Abraham out of Ur of the Chaldees. From his loins sprang the Jews, who were to be a chosen people in order to give the world the Word of God and the Messiah, which they did. However, they became very exclusive in their beliefs, shutting out all others except themselves. Jesus said of them, *"Woe unto you, scribes and Pharisees, hypocrites! for you compass sea and land to make one proselyte, and when he is made, you make him twofold more the child of hell than yourselves"* (Mat. 23:15).

Consequently, not only would Israel not give the plan of salvation to the world, but they would instead give only their own brand, thereby, failing in this task, and even losing the way themselves. In its place, the church, which is made up of men, women, boys, and girls from all over the world, was raised up.

THE KINGDOM OF GOD

The phrase, *"And shall sit down in the kingdom of God,"* has reference to the composure and rest found in Christ where believers cease from their own works, hence, sitting down. Israel came to believe totally in their works and, consequently, missed God's plan of salvation, which is justification by faith. Sadly and regrettably, this is as most of the modern church, which depends on its church membership or religious activity. As stated, Jesus refers to all such as *"iniquity,"* and those who practice it, *"workers of iniquity."*

(30) "AND, BEHOLD, THERE ARE LAST WHICH SHALL BE FIRST, AND THERE ARE FIRST WHICH SHALL BE LAST."

The structure is:

1. The words, *"And, behold,"* are actually an exclamation and pertain to a very important statement about to be given.

2. The phrase, *"There are last which shall be first,"* refers basically to the church,

which is last i.e., after Israel, but will come in first because of being the first to accept Christ.

3. *"And there are first which shall be last,"* refers to Israel, which was first in line to receive Christ, but instead, rejected Him, and will, consequently, be the last to accept Him, which they will do at the second coming.

4. However, this statement as given by Christ is of far greater portent than mere place and position in the kingdom. It refers most of all to the kingdom of God in Israel being completely taken over by demon spirits, i.e., *"fowls of the air,"* and, thereby, totally losing their way. Regrettably, most in the church will do the same because of the leaven, i.e., false doctrine as preached and taught by the false prophets and false apostles. Consequently, He not only tells what will happen, but why it will happen!

(31) "THE SAME DAY THERE CAME CERTAIN OF THE PHARISEES, SAYING UNTO HIM, GET THEE OUT, AND DEPART HENCE: FOR HEROD WILL KILL YOU."

The synopsis is:

1. The phrase, *"The same day there came certain of the Pharisees, saying unto Him,"* proclaims a pretense on their part at friendliness and concern when their only true object was to stop Jesus in His Work and silence His Preaching.

2. Spence said, "The Pharisees, who as a party hated the Master, willingly entered into the design, and under the mask of pretended friendship warned him of Herod's intentions."

3. Inasmuch as the Lord was at this time in Galilee, which was in Herod's jurisdiction, it is likely enough that the enemies of the Lord were now anxious for Him to go to Jerusalem and its neighborhood. There he would be in the power of the Sadducean hierarchy and away from the protection of the Galilean multitudes, with whom His influence was still very great.

4. The phrase, *"Get Thee out* (You had better leave), *and depart hence: for Herod will kill You,"* was, as stated, only a pretended concern. In reality, they would have been happy if Herod had killed Him.

5. As well, the admonition of the

Pharisees may not have been pretended concern, but rather a sarcastic proclamation, which, in effect, said that the teaching of Jesus was so off the wall, so to speak, that He was going to bring the authority of Herod down on His head.

6. To be sure, many preachers have trimmed their messages in order that they may accommodate the powers that be, but not Jesus.

(32) "AND HE SAID UNTO THEM, YOU GO, AND TELL THAT FOX, BEHOLD, I CAST OUT DEVILS, AND I DO CURES TODAY AND TOMORROW, AND THE THIRD DAY I SHALL BE PERFECTED."

THE ANSWER AS GIVEN BY CHRIST

The phrase, *"And He said unto them,"* proclaims Him saying to them, irrespective of whether their warning was of pretended concern or sarcasm, that what He said and did was not subject to any man, be it Pharisee or Herod.

The highest authority in any land is the gospel of Jesus Christ. It bows to no man, or even angel. In fact, Paul said *"But though we, or an angel from heaven, preach any other gospel unto you than that which we have preached unto you, let him be accursed (damned)"* (Gal. 1:8).

The phrase, *"You go, and tell that fox,"* literally reads in the Greek text, *"she-fox,"* which was the most contemptuous name ever given to anyone by Jesus. Spence said, "It is possible it might have been intended not only for Herod but, as well, the Herodians, whose influence at that time was very powerful at court."

This was the man who had murdered John the Baptist and was referred to as *"Herod the tetrarch"* (Lk. 3:19). The city of Tiberias on the lake of Galilee was built by him in A.D. 22 and named in honor of the emperor Tiberius.

In A.D. 39, he was denounced to the emperor Gaius by his nephew, Agrippa, as a plotter and was summarily deposed and ended his days in exile.

THE WORKS OF THE LORD

The phrase, *"Behold, I cast out devils* (demons), *and I do cures today and*

NOTES

tomorrow," in effect, says that Herod is of the devil, i.e., controlled by demon spirits, and that the hour was coming when there would be no more demons such as him ruling among the sons of men. In other words, it was a declaration of war by Jesus, with His followers to take up the conflict against the powers of darkness.

The *"cures"* of which He spoke concerned the only true cure that man could ever have, which can come about only by and through the Lord Jesus Christ. Everything else, irrespective of how ingenious it may be, is a mere Band-Aid over cancer. Men attempt to rehabilitate while Jesus makes anew.

The *"today and tomorrow"* spoke of His personal ministry, i.e., today, and this ministry that would continue through His followers, i.e., tomorrow.

It was actually saying, that is, if these Pharisees desired to relate such to Herod, which they likely did not, that Herod and all such ilk were going to ultimately be deposed, while that which He was doing would ultimately reign triumphant.

The phrase, *"And the third day I shall be perfected,"* spoke of His death and being in the tomb for three days and three nights and then being resurrected, i.e., perfected. However, it is unlikely that anyone understood exactly at that time what He was saying.

(33) "NEVERTHELESS I MUST WALK TODAY, AND TOMORROW, AND THE DAY FOLLOWING: FOR IT CANNOT BE THAT A PROPHET PERISH OUT OF JERUSALEM."

NEVERTHELESS

The phrase, *"Nevertheless I must walk today, and tomorrow, and the day following,"* simply meant that He was on His way to Jerusalem, which would take some three days. Consequently, the mixing of this statement, which had a physical and present meaning, with the previous statement in Verse 32, which had a spiritual meaning, probably intentionally confused the issue to such an extent that the Pharisees had no idea as to that of which He was speaking. They were not sincere; therefore, His answer to them would be shaded, as it is to all of that caliber.

JERUSALEM

The phrase, *"For it cannot be that a prophet perish out of Jerusalem,"* predicted His demise on Calvary, while the previous verse depicted His resurrection. The resurrection being placed first proclaims to any and all, especially the demon powers of hell, that their murdering of Him would have an entirely different effect than that supposed and desired.

Jerusalem had become, as one expositor put it "the slaughterhouse of the prophets." With the exception of John the Baptist, and perhaps a few others, all had been killed there.

Why was there such hatred against Him and the prophets before Him, especially considering that God had said, *"I have chosen Jerusalem, that My name might be there?"* (II Chron. 6:6).

That which God has chosen is always opposed by Satan in a greater measure than all else. The reasons are obvious!

Jerusalem, even though originally chosen by God, had now become, exactly as Jesus had stated, a spiritual roost for the fowls of the air, i.e., demon spirits, i.e., religious hierarchy.

In fact, the hatred against Christ was so strong from this sector that even though Jesus attended the feast during His public ministry, there is no record that He ever spent a night in that city, other than the night He was arrested and crucified. He rather went to Bethany.

This speaks only of His three and a half years of public ministry, and not the previous time when He was a child.

(34) "O JERUSALEM, JERUSALEM, WHICH KILLS THE PROPHETS, AND STONES THEM WHO ARE SENT UNTO YOU; HOW OFTEN WOULD I HAVE GATHERED THY CHILDREN TOGETHER, AS A HEN DOES GATHER HER BROOD UNDER HER WINGS, AND YOU WOULD NOT!"

THE CITY OF JERUSALEM

The phrase, *"O Jerusalem, Jerusalem,"* is said as a cry of anguish and of love, but yet, with deep foreboding!

Little did the city realize at this time what He was saying and actually would not have believed it if they had known. They were quickly passing the point of no return, and I speak of the religious hierarchy.

Of course, it can be argued that the people were not responsible for this religious hierarchy, and consequently, it was unfair of God to judge them accordingly. However, the record is clear that the people pretty much had the type of spiritual leadership that they desired.

As we have stated, Jerusalem was the city that God had chosen (II Chron. 6:6). As such, He was to rule His people Israel from between the mercy seat and cherubim where the Holy Spirit was supposed to reside. Consequently, it was meant to be the Holiest place on the face of the Earth. However, it had gradually deteriorated until it was anything but that.

In fact, the Spirit of God had left the first temple shortly before it was destroyed, and it was observed by the prophet Ezekiel (Ezek. 11:23). This was approximately 600 years before Christ.

THE TEMPLE

In the second temple built on the same spot in Jerusalem by Zerubbabel after the dispersion, there is no record that the ark of the covenant was in the Holy of Holies because it had seemingly been lost or destroyed. Consequently, God really did not reside there at that time, at least in the fashion He had in the first temple.

The same could be said for this present temple built by Herod at the time of Christ. In fact, about the only time it could be said that God was truly in this temple was when Jesus came into its confines. However, He was rejected, and consequently, the spiritual deterioration was now complete. As the temple was, so was the city.

MURDER

The phrase, *"Which kills the prophets, and stones them who are sent unto you,"* proclaims the charge and, therefore, the indictment of the city. Its implications were of far greater import than meets the eye. It was not to be merely the destruction of another city but was, in effect, to affect the entirety of the world.

The rejection of Jesus by His own people, the Jews, would cause the times of the Gentiles to be continued, with the government of God (concerning this planet) delayed, hence, the continued war, strife, man's inhumanity to man, crime, sickness, disease, and injustice.

The Jews had rebelled against God's way; consequently, they rebelled against His prophets. This was the case with Israel of old and, sadly, is the case with the modern church, fulfilling the words of Jesus in that the *"whole is leavened."*

MERCY OFFERED

The phrase, *"How often would I have gathered thy* (your) *children together, as a hen does gather her brood under her wings,"* proclaims the countless opportunities given for repentance, but to no avail. Such speaks of great blessings eternally lost as God's way is repudiated in favor of man's way.

What the Lord desired to do with Israel was to give them total protection, and He would have done so upon proper obedience, which would have meant that no nation in the world could have overcome them. While some nations and armies are powerful, they are not all-powerful as God. However, Israel resorted to leaning on the frail arm of Egypt or other Gentile powers, thereby, forsaking God.

Is the modern church doing the same?

The modern church by and large forsakes God and the Scripture in two distinct ways, with both pointing to unbelief of the Word of God exactly as Israel of old:

1. HUMANISTIC PSYCHOLOGY

The embracing of humanistic psychology by the church is an open admission that God cannot, or will not, deliver man from sinful aberrations. As well, whether it is realized or not, the very embracing of psychology is of far greater import than just mentioned. It actually makes a statement that man can solve his own problems, which is a total repudiation of the entirety of the Word of God. If psychology is right, then man can rehabilitate himself, and Jesus went through a needless death. So, the implications are far greater than merely the embracing of a humanistic philosophy, but rather a denial of the very Word of God.

2. THE HEADSHIP OF CHRIST

The headship of Christ has been abrogated in favor of the headship of man over the church, which is a logical conclusion to the embracing of humanistic psychology. If man can cure himself, then man should govern himself. Consequently, Christ is no longer needed and, in fact, is no longer the head of the church, at least where man has abrogated that headship.

These two Christless directions were the bane of Israel and continue to this present hour with the modern church.

The phrase, *"And you would not,"* proclaims a conscious rejection of God in favor of man. Consequently, inasmuch as it was a conscious rejection, it will be a conscious judgment. Israel was not in this condition because of ignorance, but rather because of rebellion, which stemmed from unbelief.

(35) "BEHOLD, YOUR HOUSE IS LEFT UNTO YOU DESOLATE: AND VERILY I SAY UNTO YOU, YOU SHALL NOT SEE ME, UNTIL THE TIME COME WHEN YOU SHALL SAY, BLESSED IS HE WHO COMES IN THE NAME OF THE LORD."

DESOLATE

The word, *"Behold,"* proclaims an announcement of startling significance and clarity.

The phrase, *"Your house is left unto you desolate,"* in effect, speaks of the temple, which, with the rejection of Jesus, will now be rejected by God. Without Him, it was desolate, as any church, or person for that matter, is desolate.

As Israel, the modern church loses sight of what and who God is all about. The answer wasn't in the temple but in the One to whom the temple pointed.

It is not church denominations, but it is the One to whom they are supposed to proclaim. All is Christ, or nothing is Christ! He will not, nor can He, be a mere part of the mix. Salvation comes from Jesus alone and what He did for us at the Cross, and not the temple or the church!

As a result, the Lord has, no doubt, said to some religious denominations, just as He said of Israel of old, *"Behold, your house is left unto you desolate."*

IN THE NAME OF THE LORD

The phrase, *"And verily I say unto you, You shall not see Me,"* refers to Him not being where He is not wanted. However, not seeing Him meant they would see Caesar because they would say, *"We have no king but Caesar"* (Jn. 19:15). Hitler's gas ovens, plus a thousand other similar situations, have proven the fallacy of their choice.

The phrase, *"Until the time come when you shall say, Blessed is He who comes in the name of the Lord,"* is quoted from Psalms 118:26. It speaks of the coming kingdom age, which will immediately follow the second coming. Then Israel will finally accept Christ as Lord and Saviour; however, the one word *until* has held such sorrow and heartache as no people has ever seen on the face of the earth.

When He came the first time, they cursed Him and reviled Him, calling Him an impostor who performed His miracles by the power of Satan.

However, on that coming glad day, after much sorrow and heartache, they will finally say concerning Jesus, *"Blessed!"*

Back to the phrase, *"You shall not see Me,"* it means exactly what it says; they cannot see Jesus at all! They are spiritually blind, and as such, it is a judicial blindness ordered upon them by God because they willfully chose that direction against all evidence.

The Jews alone do not fall into this terrible blindness, as most of humanity follows suit.

The Muslims see Jesus as a prophet but not the Son of God, which, in effect, makes Him out a liar.

The Buddhists see Him as a historical figure, good, but not God.

The Hindus see Him merely as another one of their pantheon of many gods.

The modernists see Him as deceived and deluded.

The Catholics see Him as subservient to Mary inasmuch as they deny Him as the sole mediator between God and man, with Mary taking His place.

Many Protestants see Him as a mere figurehead, with their particular church denomination being paramount.

HOW DO YOU SEE HIM?

Jesus Christ is God (Jn. 1:1). He is the author and finisher of our faith (Heb. 12:2). He alone is our Saviour, *"Neither is there salvation in any other: for there is none other name under heaven given among men, whereby we must be saved"* (Acts 4:12). As well, He is the one to whom the Father has given all power (Mat. 28:18). Also, He is the judge (Rev. 20:12).

To believe anything less of Christ is a denial of His purpose and person and will forfeit one's salvation.

"I can see far down the mountain
"Where I wandered weary years
"Often hindered in my journey
"By the ghosts of doubts and fears
"Broken vows and disappointments
"Thickly strewn along the way
"But the Spirit led unerring
"To the land I hold today."

CHAPTER 14

(1) "AND IT CAME TO PASS, AS HE WENT INTO THE HOUSE OF ONE OF THE CHIEF PHARISEES TO EAT BREAD ON THE SABBATH DAY, THAT THEY WATCHED HIM."

THE PHARISEES

The phrase, *"And it came to pass, as He went into the house of one of the chief Pharisees,"* concerns a very influential rabbi, or even possibly a member of the vaunted Sanhedrin. Exactly where this was is not stated, but the incident seems to have happened on the way from Galilee to Jerusalem. Evidently He was invited, but as it will unfold, for sinister reasons.

Why would He have accepted such an invitation?

It was not to be said that Jesus did not take every single opportunity to proclaim the gospel to any and all, even the Pharisees who hated Him! Consequently, when standing at the judgment, they will have no excuse. The truth is, they invited Him, and He came, but His invitation extended to them was refused.

THE SABBATH DAY

"To eat bread on the Sabbath day," was said to be elaborate affairs, especially by one of wealth as this Pharisee, with only one rule observed, "That all food had been cooked the previous day so as not to violate the Sabbath."

"That they watched Him," means that they maliciously watched Him, with the idea in mind of trapping Him into breaking some man-made rule, etc. They hated Him while, at the same time, they greatly feared Him. His power was undeniable, even as we shall soon see.

They watched Him, attempting to find something wrong; therefore, because of willful blindness, they could not see what was right. In effect, all was right with Him, which could not be said of any other human being who has ever lived. Actually, it was His right that was a constant rebuke to their wrong!

On a personal basis, I have sorely grieved in my heart at the attitude of some modern religious leaders respecting my own ministry. For a long while, in my naiveté, I felt that if they could only see the operation and moving of the Holy Spirit, with people being saved and lives changed, they would surely change their minds. However, I finally came to realize that this was the very thing they despised—the operation and moving of the Holy Spirit. In fact, as the Pharisees of old, all religious professors despise any and all operations of the Holy Spirit. It is a rebuke to their vapid emptiness and stark powerlessness. So, they bitterly oppose the very thing that the true work of God is all about—the moving and operation of the Holy Spirit. By this alone can anything be done for God.

(2) "AND, BEHOLD, THERE WAS A CERTAIN MAN BEFORE HIM WHICH HAD THE DROPSY."

The overview is:

1. The two words, *"And, behold,"* proclaim the entrance of a scenario that is beyond the norm.

2. The phrase, *"There was a certain man*

before Him which had the dropsy," has reference to a disease, causing swelling due to excess water.

3. The words *"before Him,"* coupled with *"they watched Him,"* suggest that this man was not a guest but was brought there purposely by the Pharisees in order to set a trap for Jesus. Consequently, the man was stationed in a prominent position where the eyes of Jesus could not help but fall on him. Knowing his predisposition to heal the sick and destroy all the works of the Devil, they felt confident of the success of their plan. It was the Sabbath day, and consequently, they considered healing to be work and, therefore, improper on that day.

Whether the sick man was a party to their scheme or just their dupe is not known. At any rate, grace would reach out beyond the evil of the moment and meet the need of this poor soul, irrespective of his culpability or the lack thereof.

(3) "AND JESUS ANSWERING SPOKE UNTO THE LAWYERS AND PHARISEES, SAYING, IS IT LAWFUL TO HEAL ON THE SABBATH DAY?"

The exegesis is:

1. The phrase, *"And Jesus answering spoke unto the lawyers and Pharisees,"* proclaims Jesus instantly recognizing the situation and immediately judging the hypocrisy that broke the Sabbath when their own interests were involved. At the same time, He vindicated the rights of grace in connection with that which was the seal of the first covenant.

2. Irrespective of who was present, Jesus addressed His statement to the culprits, in this case, *"the lawyers and Pharisees."* Lawyers were the same as scribes, who were supposed to be experts in the law of Moses and teachers of the people, in effect, their pastors.

3. The question, *"Saying, Is it lawful to heal on the Sabbath day?"* drives right to the heart of the matter, with Jesus stealing their thunder before they could spring the trap. He would answer their question for them momentarily.

(4) "AND THEY HELD THEIR PEACE. AND HE TOOK HIM, AND HEALED HIM, AND LET HIM GO."

THE ACTION OF CHRIST

The phrase, *"And they held their peace,"* actually means they did not know what to say, especially considering that the ball was now in their court, so to speak.

They had expected Him to heal this man, and then they would pose this very question to Him, with a plan in mind of showing him up before the people as a Sabbath-breaker. However, He posed their own question to their own hearts, demanding an answer. Even though they might be wicked, still, they were not stupid.

There was no way they could best Him on scriptural grounds, and they knew it. His reputation, concerning His quick answers, had preceded Him.

HEALING

The phrase, *"And He took him,"* means that He zeroed in on the man so there would be absolutely no doubt what was being done. In other words, He would take their scheme and show it up in crystal clarity for what it was, an ugly display of religion. They had no concern for this man, only their petty rules. Jesus showed concern for the man, which put these lawyers and Pharisees on the spot in front of the onlookers. In other words, they lost face.

Religious men are concerned about rules while God is concerned about people. No, Jesus never at one single time, even momentarily, came close to abrogating the Scripture in any form; however, He did show contempt, as here, for man-made rules and regulations that had no validity in the Word of God.

The phrase, *"And healed him, and let him go,"* means that his healing was instantaneous and easily observable by all. In other words, even miraculously, the excess fluid in his body disappeared. As well, He did not *"let him go"* until the effects of this healing were obvious to all.

Their silence was deafening because they didn't know what to say. Whatever scheme they had, it had now fallen to the floor.

(5) "AND ANSWERED THEM, SAYING, WHICH OF YOU SHALL HAVE AN ASS OR AN OX FALLEN INTO A PIT, AND WILL NOT STRAIGHTWAY PULL HIM OUT ON THE SABBATH DAY?"

The structure is:

1. The phrase, *"And answered them,"* means He answered their silence and, as well, addressed Himself to the total error of their argument, showing them up greatly before the crowd, in fact, what they had intended to do to Him.

2. The beginning of the question, *"Which of you shall have an ass or an ox fallen into a pit,"* places their hypocrisy in its proper context. In effect, the Lord would tell them that they broke their own rules concerning the Sabbath constantly, and for much less reason than the healing of a man.

3. Self-interest is one of the strongest emotions of the natural heart. The Lord rebuked it in Verses 5, 8, 14, 18, and 26.

4. The conclusion of the question, *"And will not straightway pull him out on the Sabbath day,"* refers to that which should be obvious to all.

5. To be sure, the Lord was not criticizing them for doing such a thing, but rather their hypocrisy in condemning Him for a far greater and more noble act.

6. Religion is always after this fashion. It places a heavy burden on the people with its tedious rules and regulations, which are all man-devised, and cares little for the person involved. In truth, every single line in the Bible is given by God to make man's life better, in effect, serving man instead of man serving it.

7. The Jews, as many, turned it around and by their subtractions and additions, made it what it really was not, therefore, becoming a burden too heavy for any to bear. Paul said, *"For the kingdom of God is not meat and drink* (rules and regulations)*; but righteousness, and peace, and joy in the Holy Spirit"* (Rom. 14:17).

(6) "AND THEY COULD NOT ANSWER HIM AGAIN TO THESE THINGS."

The structure is:

1. Their silence was the better part of wisdom. To have answered at all would have shown them up even worse than they already looked. They now were placed in the position of favoring an animal over a man, and more particularly, the salvage of personal

property as more important than the salvage of a human heart and life, which is covetousness to the extreme.

2. The reader may weary of my constant reminders and even sharp barbs directed at religion, but I must remind all that I'm only commenting on that which happened, attempting to make it understood, and that it is just as much a problem now as then. The spirit of Phariseeism did not die with the extinction of this sect but, regrettably, is alive and well at the present. Satan is very successful at drawing the eyes and attention of the Christian laity, and even many of its preachers, away from that which is really the great destroyer of the work of God. I speak of man-devised religion, which is the greatest culprit of all.

3. They did not answer because they could not answer.

4. A pastor friend of mine wrote a so-called religious leader, asking for scriptural foundation regarding some of the rules and regulations of that particular denomination. Even though he wrote several letters, no scriptural basis was given because there was none; consequently, their position became glaringly obvious as being unscriptural. If the Bible is not to be our foundation for all things done, then what is to be the foundation? Of course, men can make and break rules as they will and, in fact, constantly do!

(7) "AND HE PUT FORTH A PARABLE TO THOSE WHICH WERE BIDDEN, WHEN HE MARKED HOW THEY CHOSE OUT THE CHIEF ROOMS; SAYING UNTO THEM."

The composition is:

1. The phrase, *"And He put forth a parable to those which were bidden,"* refers to the invited guests, which, as obvious, were of the wealthy class.

2. *"When He marked how they chose out the chief rooms; saying unto them,"* refers to the episode of the healing of the man being completed, with invited guests called to be seated for the banquet. Evidently, there was an obvious scurrying for the chief seats.

3. Israel was very class conscious at that time; consequently, most every gathering was marked by this vulgar display of clamor

for position, which was abhorred by Christ.

4. The idea pertained to the host or very special invited guests. Whoever sat next to these was shown to be individuals of importance.

5. It should be obvious that these hypocrites worked far more at this, consequently, breaking their own Sabbath rules, than Jesus did by healing a person with a mere word.

6. How gross!

(8) "WHEN YOU ARE BIDDEN OF ANY MAN TO A WEDDING, SIT NOT DOWN IN THE HIGHEST ROOM; LEST A MORE HONORABLE MAN THAN YOU BE BIDDEN OF HIM."

THE HIGHEST ROOM?

The phrase, *"When you are bidden of any man to a wedding, sit not down in the highest room,"* actually strikes at the very heart of these hypocrites, which was a love of praise, as well as place and position. This is what produces self-righteousness and what self-righteousness produces. This is also the reason that religion is so political, which characterizes almost all of that which presently calls itself Christian, and I especially speak of organized religion.

If one is to notice, much, if not most of Jesus' teaching, was directed, as here, toward the religious leaders of Israel; consequently, when one begins to understand the reason behind this, one then begins to unravel Satan's greatest effort to destroy the body of Christ.

The masses of people, who Jesus attended lovingly and graciously, represented a totally different approach on His part. Actually, the Pharisees and scribes had no regard for the common people, merely suffering them, and worst of all, using them. Consequently, if the laity takes the position of little interest in this all-important aspect of the ministry of Christ, they will play perfectly into Satan's hand, with that desire by the Evil One being carried out in totality. I speak of that very seriously inasmuch as it involves the loss of one's soul.

SCRIPTURAL?

What is not scriptural must be repudiated. So, the believer must know the Word of

God and allow it to lead him, which will be done by the power of the Holy spirit At the same time, he must take advantage, as God has ordained, of true spiritual leadership provided. I speak of apostles, prophets, evangelists, pastors, and teachers given by the Holy Spirit, *"For the perfecting of the saints, for the work of the ministry, for the edifying of the body of Christ"* (Eph. 4:11-12).

Consequently, at least one of the reasons Jesus directed so much attention toward leadership is that the believer may be helped and strengthened by those who are truly God-called, and not by some denominational hierarchy or preacher of conceit.

Regrettably, the number that falls into the former is very small, with the latter being very large.

GOD'S HANDS

How so unlike the self-surrender and self-sacrifice, as taught by the Lord, is this self-seeking grasping of these Pharisees and lawyers.

The phrase, *"Lest a more honorable man than you be bidden of him,"* positions the believer in God's hands instead of the hand of self-seeking. What others think is not that important anyway! It's what God knows that really counts. The believer, be he laity or leader, must be careful to place his life into the hands of God, allowing Him to guide and direct and to give promotion, that is, if such be His will.

However, far too many believers ask the Lord for certain things, and then, instead of leaving it in His hands, they immediately set out to manipulate the situation. Such proclaims no trust in God, but rather the greedy grasping of self-will. This is what the Lord here condemns.

(9) "AND HE WHO BADE YOU AND HIM COME AND SAY TO YOU, GIVE THIS MAN PLACE; AND YOU BEGIN WITH SHAME TO TAKE THE LOWEST ROOM."

THE LORD

The phrase, *"And He who bade you and him come and say unto you,"* places the Lord as the one who gave the invitation and, consequently, the one who gives the seating arrangements, i.e., place and position. After all, He is the host, with the banquet being His and, therefore, the right to choose as He so desires.

This affects everything from the least layman to the structure of organized religion, which too often takes such authority from the hands of God, making their own selections.

In the religious denomination with which I was formerly associated, through the years Frances and I observed this same type of action.

We saw how the mostly man-led leadership of that organization made the seating arrangements, so to speak, out of their own carnal minds instead of being led by the Holy Spirit. Not a single one whom they promoted and touted ever amounted to anything for God. In truth, sadly, they greatly opposed those whom God had truly chosen, and for all the obvious reasons.

SELF-PROMOTION

It is the same in the local church. Too often, there is a greedy grab inspired by self-promotion, with the consequences being a church that is man-led and man-directed, with the pastor far too often a mere figurehead. This is because many religious leaders have brought the government of the world over into the church, which, in effect, is an abomination in the eyes of God.

The Lord truly has a government for His church; however, it in no way resembles the government of the world. His government is not led by men but by the Holy Spirit and is according to His Word.

Consequently, the true believer is to allow the Lord to decide place and position, being pliable in His sight, which will always bring spiritual harmony, with God giving the increase. Anytime the headship of Christ is abrogated, which, sadly, is done in almost all of organized religion, and even that which is unorganized, so to speak, the conclusion is a man-directed affair. This, by its very nature, is not God-directed and, as a consequence, will perform no service whatsoever for the kingdom of God.

This does not mean that organization is wrong but does mean that it must be God's organization instead of man's.

GOD'S MAN

The phrase, *"Give this man place,"* is a statement, or rather a command, which must be taken very seriously.

The idea is that if *"this man,"* who, in effect, is God's man, is not given *"place,"* the Lord as the host will do whatever is necessary to ultimately insure His will.

In the modern church, this is at least one of Satan's greatest efforts, which is to block *this man's place* and insert his own choice, who will then be led by him and not God.

There is no way I can overemphasize the significance of this parable as given by Christ. The truth is that almost all of the church world not only refuses to *"give this man place,"* but rather will do anything in its power to destroy him. This is replete in much of church history.

SHAME

The phrase, *"And you begin with shame to take the lowest room,"* proclaims that which God will ultimately do to those who refuse His choice and rather insert their own.

Every single advancement in the kingdom of God through the ages has come about by those whom He has called, with Him ultimately bringing shame to the opposers. Saul and David are an excellent example!

David, within himself, sought no place and position, leaving the matter entirely in the hands of God; however, even as it became obviously apparent that David was God's choice, Saul, as well as the majority of Israel, refused to *"give this man place."* Saul, as a work of the flesh, wanted and promoted his government while refusing that of God, and most of the people, regrettably, followed suit. However, ultimately, the Lord brought down the house of Saul, and with great shame. He has done countless others the same way and will continue to do so.

To be sure, during the 15 or so years that David was hunted and hounded, precious few, to use a modern proverb, would have bought stock in David's company. However, God's choice ultimately prevails, irrespective of how strong, rich, or powerful the opposing force may be.

(10) "BUT WHEN YOU ARE BIDDEN,

GO AND SIT DOWN IN THE LOWEST ROOM; THAT WHEN HE WHO BADE YOU COMES, HE MAY SAY UNTO YOU, FRIEND, GO UP HIGHER: THEN SHALL YOU HAVE WORSHIP IN THE PRESENCE OF THEM WHO SIT AT MEAT WITH YOU."

THE CALL OF GOD

The phrase, *"But when you are bidden,"* respects the call of God, just as David and countless others have been called.

Isn't it beautiful the manner used by Jesus in teaching this all-important subject?

"Go and sit down in the lowest room," is the place and position that the truly God-called must take. One must never promote oneself. One must stay in the background and allow the Lord to chart the course.

Thankfully, the true call of God will always produce humility in the heart and life of the one called, that is, if one continues to allow the Holy Spirit to lead and guide. Sadly, some truly called have become lifted up in themselves and of their own volition, have failed to obey the Lord in taking *"the lowest room."* The results in such a case are always hurtful.

GO UP HIGHER

The phrase, *"That when He who bade you comes, He may say unto you, Friend, go up higher,"* places the Lord in the position of leader and guide. Unfortunately, some of us attempt by our own means to *"go up higher,"* with leadership taken out of the hands of God. This is why the truly God-called one must wait on the Lord.

Even though God has truly called someone, "bidden to come" does not necessarily mean he is presently ready for the task. The call does not equate maturity and development. That can only come about with time, consecration, and yes, some suffering!

"Then shall you have worship in the presence of them who sit at meat with you," is wrapped up in the one word *then!* This is God's time, which will then bring forth the intended results. *"Worship"* means honor and respect.

I look back with embarrassment and shame to the 1970s. God had called me for a particular task, and of that I was certain.

However, I foolishly equated the call with development and maturity and summarily announced to the Lord in prayer one particular day that I was now *ready*. To be sure, if I had only known how *unready* I actually was, I would have trembled in His presence accordingly; however, immaturity will do many brash things. Nevertheless, how patient, loving, and kind our heavenly Father is!

(11) "FOR WHOSOEVER EXALTETH HIMSELF SHALL BE ABASED; AND HE WHO HUMBLES HIMSELF SHALL BE EXALTED."

The composition is:

1. This Scripture is the cardinal principle of true Bible Christianity. It is the very opposite of the spirit of the world, which is greedy and grasping and is obvious to all. It is distinct and unique among all the religions of the world. Sadly, it is followed all too little.

2. As is obvious, the phrase, *"For whosoever exalteth himself shall be abased,"* speaks of self-exaltation. Its end result, irrespective of the present performance, will be abasement, i.e., "to make low, bring low."

3. Self-exaltation always puffs one up, and for the simple reason that one has brought about such position by his own scheming and ability. Consequently, an extremely un-Christlike attitude and spirit are developed in the heart. God has no choice in Christians but to abase such. If allowed to continue, it would wreak destruction and wreckage, compounding itself with each passing day.

4. *"And he who humbles himself shall be exalted,"* has the idea of one purposely placing himself in the *"lowest room,"* exactly as demanded by Christ. The idea is, if we do not voluntarily do this on our own, the Lord will do it for us, but it will be accompanied by great shame and disconsolation.

5. We have His promise that the exaltation will come if we conduct ourselves properly and allow Him to do that which only He can do.

(12) "THEN SAID HE ALSO TO HIM WHO BADE HIM, WHEN YOU MAKE A DINNER OR A SUPPER, CALL NOT YOUR FRIENDS, NOR YOUR BRETHREN,

NEITHER YOUR KINSMEN, NOR YOUR RICH NEIGHBORS; LEST THEY ALSO BID YOU AGAIN, AND A RECOMPENSE BE MADE TO YOU."

The synopsis is:

1. The phrase, *"Then said He also to him who bade Him,"* addressed the Pharisee who had invited Him to this feast. The previous parable had been spoken to the guests, while this is spoken to the host.

2. *"When you make a dinner or a supper,"* proclaims the action and the motive. It is not the activity that is condemned, but rather its purpose.

3. Tragically, much, if not most of that in Christendom that is purported to be for God, has instead a very selfish motive, which means it is not for God at all.

4. Money given for personal recognition has no approval by the Lord. As well, all work done and carried out with an agenda in mind, other than that devised by the Holy Spirit, can never be sanctioned by God. Regrettably, as stated, this characterizes much, if not most, of that which calls itself Christian!

5. *"Call not your friends, nor your brethren, neither your kinsmen, nor your rich neighbors,"* proclaims before all the heart attitude of this Pharisee. Even though this banquet was conducted on a Sabbath and, therefore, purported to be for the worship of God, at least in some manner, there were other motives in mind altogether.

6. *"Lest they also bid you again, and a recompense be made to you,"* proclaims what the motive really was.

7. It was a case of "I'll do good things for you, and you do good things for me." This is what Jesus was saying, which proclaimed the fact that even though it was religious, it was not right. Such attitude was of the spirit of "What's in it for me?" Such has no resemblance to that which is Christlike.

(13) "BUT WHEN YOU MAKE A FEAST, CALL THE POOR, THE MAIMED, THE LAME, THE BLIND."

THE POOR, THE MAIMED,
THE LAME, THE BLIND

The phrase, *"But when you make a feast,"* applies not only to that which the Pharisee was doing, but incorporates every other work that purports to be of God as well!

"Call the poor, the maimed, the lame, the blind," proclaims the Christlike spirit. This epitomizes God who sent His only Son down to this world, not because of what the world could do for Him, but because of what He could do for this world. The poor, maimed, lame, and blind adequately portray the human family to which Jesus came. This is love that asks nothing in return.

In this parable of the feast, we see two kinds of love:

1. EROS

The *"eros"* kind of love: This type of love is not mentioned by name in the Bible but is given by example in this very parable. The word means "love that is directed toward self-realization." In other words, this Pharisee wanted people to attend his feasts who made him look good in one way or the other. There was no real love exhibited, only the grasping for self-gratification.

Many churches fall into the same category. The pastor and many other members want people to attend their church who are rich, talented, important, etc., which will in turn make them look good. Actually, the entirety of the world operates on this very basis. It is satanic, evil, wicked, and wrong but, regrettably, pandemic in the world and, sadly, much of the church.

2. AGAPE

The *"agape"* kind of love: This is the type of love that invites the poor and the maimed, expecting nothing in return. It seeks to give and not receive. The idea of agape love is not to make the individual look good, but to do good to others who cannot do for themselves and can in no way repay it. Such is Christ!

This type of love, which actually means the God kind of love, who would give His only Son to a world who did not love Him, expresses ideas previously unknown in the world before the birth of Christ. The Greeks spoke of agape love but did not have it and did not know how it could be obtained. In fact, only God can give such love.

That's one reason a true church will invite all and make all welcome. That's one reason true Christianity seeks not to help

NOTES

those who in turn can repay that help, but rather those who have no way to repay and are unloved by the rest of the world.

(14) "AND YOU SHALL BE BLESSED; FOR THEY CANNOT RECOMPENSE YOU: FOR YOU SHALL BE RECOMPENSED AT THE RESURRECTION OF THE JUST."

The exegesis is:

1. The phrase, *"And you shall be blessed,"* is a signal promise given by God, with His Word standing as surety. In other words, the Lord proclaims that the blessing will come from Him and not people. Even looking at it in the vernacular of the world, it is hands down greater than the selfish grasping. To have the blessings of God is to have everything. To have the blessings of man, which the selfish method produces, in reality guarantees nothing because man cannot be trusted, while God can always be trusted.

2. *"For they cannot recompense you,"* means that while the poor, blind, etc., cannot do so, God will step in and bless on their behalf.

3. *"For you shall be recompensed at the resurrection of the just,"* proclaims the second blessing, which will come at the judgment seat of Christ.

4. The resurrection speaks of the rapture of the church when it will then be changed (I Thess. 4:16-17).

5. There will also be a resurrection of the unjust, which will take place about a thousand years after the resurrection of the just (Rev. 20:4-6). Whereas the resurrection of the just will place one with the Lord forever, the resurrection of the unjust will experience the *"second death,"* which is incarceration in the lake of fire forever and ever (Rev. 20:10-15).

(15) "AND WHEN ONE OF THEM WHO SAT AT MEAT WITH HIM HEARD THESE THINGS, HE SAID UNTO HIM, BLESSED IS HE WHO SHALL EAT BREAD IN THE KINGDOM OF GOD."

The exposition is:

1. The phrase, *"When one of them who sat at meat with Him heard these things, he said unto Him,"* proclaims a total lack of knowledge about what the Lord was saying.

2. *"Blessed is he who shall eat bread in the kingdom of God,"* proclaims a sectarian,

elitist attitude held by most Pharisees of that time.

3. By using the word *blessed* and directing it toward himself, this Pharisee loudly trumpeted his self-righteousness. In a sense, he was bringing forth a doctrine of national predestination. In other words, because he was a Jew, and especially a Pharisee, he thought that he would surely be accorded a great place in the kingdom of God.

4. The Lord's answer was revealing to say the least, as we shall see.

5. Millions sit in the same seat as this man, thinking surely they have a bountiful place in the coming kingdom of God because of their church membership, religious works, or self-induced morality, when, in reality, they have no place at all!

(16) "THEN SAID HE UNTO HIM, A CERTAIN MAN MADE A GREAT SUPPER, AND BADE MANY."

The synopsis is:

1. The phrase, *"Then said He unto him,"* presents the parable of the great supper. It is something these Pharisees readily understood but would be shocked at the conclusion!

2. *"A certain man made a great supper, and bade many,"* begins the parable with an illustration that was well known to the Jews of that age.

3. They recognized instantly that the *"certain man"* was God, and the *"great supper"* was the kingdom of God. As well, the *"many"* invited most certainly were the Jews, and included the long list of prophets and patriarchs, as well as the many of their nation from the time of Abraham. Truly, it was many!

4. Most of Israel at that particular time possessed a sectarian spirit, consequently, believing that being born a Jew guaranteed salvation. The only ones who would be excluded, at least in their thinking, were those who denied their Jewish heritage in some way, such as the publicans.

(17) "AND SENT HIS SERVANT AT SUPPER TIME TO SAY TO THEM WHO WERE BIDDEN, COME; FOR ALL THINGS ARE NOW READY."

The pattern is:

1. The phrase, *"And sent his servant at*

supper time to say to them who were bidden," refers to Jesus Himself as the servant.

2. *"Come; for all things are now ready,"* was the message of both John the Baptist and Christ, concerning entrance into the kingdom of God.

3. The two words *"now ready"* meant that the time had now come for the kingdom of God to be introduced. As such, the rejection or acceptance would have far reaching consequences, affecting every human being on the face of the earth, and for all time from that moment forward.

(18) "AND THEY ALL WITH ONE CONSENT BEGAN TO MAKE EXCUSE. THE FIRST SAID UNTO HIM, I HAVE BOUGHT A PIECE OF GROUND, AND I MUST NEEDS GO AND SEE IT: I PRAY YOU HAVE ME EXCUSED.

(19) "AND ANOTHER SAID, I HAVE BOUGHT FIVE YOKE OF OXEN, AND I GO TO PROVE THEM: I PRAY YOU HAVE ME EXCUSED.

(20) "AND ANOTHER SAID, I HAVE MARRIED A WIFE, AND THEREFORE I CANNOT COME."

I HAVE BOUGHT A PIECE OF GROUND

The phrase, *"And they all with one consent began to make excuse,"* proclaimed Israel then and most of the church now!

The entirety of this scenario is addressed to those who make a profession of faith, not necessarily the world.

Three different types of excuses are presented, which characterize the entirety of one's relationship with God or the lack thereof. They are as follows:

1. *"I have bought a piece of ground"*: The purchase of the ground constituted no wrong, but the desire to see it, even though the call was being given, proclaims unsuitable priority. This excuse speaks of the activity of commerce and self-interest, which will keep millions out of the kingdom of God.

If one is to notice, of the three excuses given, none of the activities involved, at least within themselves, constitute any wrongdoing. They are all perfectly legitimate activities; however, the stress is placed on priority. These individuals were supposed to be children of the kingdom and, consequently, made a profession of faith. However, their interest, as is obvious, was elsewhere, which characterizes much, if not most of the modern church, just as it characterized Israel of old.

As well, it was at night, so how could one inspect ground at that particular time? Consequently, they are called *"excuses!"*

I HAVE BOUGHT FIVE YOKE OF OXEN

2. *"And another said, I have bought five yoke of oxen"*: As well, this one claims the necessity of proving the oxen, which, once again, would be very difficult to do at night. This speaks of one's love for money and self-will, with little thought for the soul.

The idea is that the individual in question didn't want to answer the call so would manufacture any type of excuse that was at hand. As stated, the complaint was merely another excuse.

I HAVE MARRIED A WIFE

3. *"And another said, I have married a wife"*: this spoke of one's life and self-love being placed in Christ, but instead, charts its own course.

There was no harm in the marrying of a wife, but there was harm in putting this activity ahead of God.

The analogy should be well taken respecting all of these scenarios. It is the care and concern taken up with the things of the world, which, within themselves, are not necessarily wrong. However, it does show the self life, which is wrong, and consequently, the heart from which all of this proceeds.

To be sure, as the invitation was given to Israel, it is being given presently to the modern church. Regrettably, the excuses have not changed one whit! God is given an hour on Sunday morning, if that, with little thought given otherwise.

Many, if not most believers, know more about athletes and particular teams than they do about the Bible. Many, if not most Christians, read the Bible only casually, and even then, with little studious intent. God is just a part of the mix, with them congratulating themselves on their dedication when, in truth, they have no dedication at all.

(21) "SO THAT SERVANT CAME, AND

SHOWED HIS LORD THESE THINGS. THEN THE MASTER OF THE HOUSE BEING ANGRY SAID TO HIS SERVANT, GO OUT QUICKLY INTO THE STREETS AND LANES OF THE CITY, AND BRING IN HITHER THE POOR, AND THE MAIMED, AND THE HALT, AND THE BLIND."

THE SERVANT

The phrase, *"So that servant came, and showed his Lord these things,"* speaks of Jesus as the servant and the Lord as the heavenly Father.

It is ironic that the Lord was here telling the religious leaders of Israel what He was going to relate to the Father in a matter of days. As they listened to these words, little did they realize their importance. Evidently, they dismissed them out of hand as not worthy of consideration, continuing to think of themselves as *"blessed"* (Lk. 14:15).

THE MASTER OF THE HOUSE

"Then the Master of the house being angry said to His servant," proclaims the just anger of God over the rejection by Israel to the great invitation to enter the kingdom of God.

The phrase, *"Go out quickly into the streets and lanes of the city, and bring in hither the poor, and the maimed, and the halt, and the blind,"* represents the founding of the true church. It began, at least for the most part, with the poorest of the poor, and continues unto this hour to be the greatest harbor known to man for these whom the world cares little about.

In the 1980s, we were conducting city-wide (even nationwide) crusades in various Central and South American countries, as well as the Philippines and Africa. The largest stadiums in these respective countries were jammed to capacity, with many thousands responding to the invitation to come to Christ. As well, we were airing the gospel over television throughout all of these countries.

When the Lord first began to use us in this capacity, in prayer the Lord spoke to my heart and told me to preach Jesus Christ as the great centerpiece of my message. I was to make the messages simple and, above all, to lift up Jesus to the exclusion of all else.

Most of the people in our meetings were very poor. Consequently, the Lord spoke to my heart, saying that He was their only hope, and really, the only One who truly cared for them. I was to tell them to look to Him, and to Him exclusively, and not to governments, America, or any other supposed help, only Jesus.

This I attempted to do, and God blessed it abundantly so, with hundreds of thousands responding to the altar calls.

JESUS ALONE

In obeying the Lord in this endeavor, as I would speak the words extolling Jesus, with the interpreter repeating what had been said, you could feel a swell rise throughout those vast stadiums as the Holy Spirit took the message home to the hearts of these people. For the first time in their lives, many of them had found hope. In reality, there is no hope, whether rich or poor, other than Jesus. To look in any other direction is a fruitless exercise. To place one's hopes in other areas will always leave one unfulfilled.

(22) "AND THE SERVANT SAID, LORD, IT IS DONE AS YOU HAVE COMMANDED, AND YET THERE IS ROOM."

The synopsis is:

1. The phrase, "And the servant said, Lord, it is done as You have commanded," proclaims that this was already a settled fact in the mind of God at the time Jesus gave this parable. Of course, with God being omniscient, He knew these things from the beginning.

2. "And yet there is room," presents the vastness of the gospel promise and its ability to succor the entirety of the populations of the world. What Jesus did at Calvary and the resurrection was sufficient to cleanse the stain of every sin of every man, woman, boy, and girl in the entirety of the world, and for all time. As well, no terrible debauchery of the worst bondages of darkness can stand against the onslaught of the shed blood of the Lamb when faith arises to claim its vast benefits.

3. Let all who struggle in the sea of despond know and realize that irrespective of how many have already come, and irrespective of the degree of Satan's bondage, "Yet there is room!"

(23) "AND THE LORD SAID UNTO THE SERVANT, GO OUT INTO THE HIGHWAYS AND HEDGES, AND COMPEL THEM TO COME IN, THAT MY HOUSE MAY BE FILLED."

JESUS, THE LIGHT OF THE WORLD

The phrase, "And the Lord said unto the servant," proclaims Jesus being lifted up as the light of the world, and not Israel as a nation.

The command, "Go out into the highways and hedges," is the same as that said in Mark 16:15, but in a little different way.

The "highways" speak of the great cities of the world, with the "hedges" speaking of the hinterlands. No place is to be left untouched by the gospel.

The phrase, "And compel them to come in," speaks of the gospel message being preached with such power and force, as the Holy Spirit anoints it, that it becomes almost impossible to resist.

As an evangelist, countless times I have experienced this anointing in such a manner that in appealing to the lost, the word compel is the only way it can be adequately described. I have seen countless thousands respond to altar calls all over the world, trembling and shaking as they would come to Christ, corresponding to this very passage.

At this particular time (2013), I believe we are in the preparation stages of the greatest move of God the world has ever known as it regards souls being saved, believers filled with the Spirit, the sick healed, and bondages of darkness broken. I personally believe the anointing of the Holy Spirit is going to be so powerful that it will do exactly what Jesus here said, "Compel them to come in."

THE POWER OF GOD

This is not something new but that which has happened at times through the ages past. As an example, history records the preaching of Jonathan Edwards in New England when God so anointed him that grown men held to the pillars that held up the roof of the church in order that they may not topple into hell. Likewise, under Whitefield, hundreds, or even thousands, would fall on their faces, literally smitten by the convicting power of the Holy Spirit as they were *"compelled!"*

Actually, this is exactly what happened on the day of Pentecost when Peter, freshly baptized with the Holy Spirit, preached with such an anointing that the great crowd was *"pricked in their heart, and said unto Peter and to the rest of the apostles, Men and brethren, what shall we do?"* (Acts 2:37). Some 3,000 were saved that day.

This is what Jesus was talking about, and it is the only type of preaching (empowered by the Holy Spirit) that will tear down the defensive battlements of Satan, penetrate the shell, and, thereby, set the captive free. God deliver us from dead preachers preaching dead sermons to dead congregations!

The phrase, *"That My house may be filled,"* simply says that the plan of God, irrespective of the fall of Israel, will not be thwarted but will reap that which was originally intended. To be sure, His house will be filled, i.e., the kingdom of God.

(24) "FOR I SAY UNTO YOU, THAT NONE OF THOSE MEN WHICH WERE BIDDEN SHALL TASTE OF MY SUPPER."

The composition is:

1. The phrase, *"For I say unto you,"* presents Jesus speaking directly to Israel as He faced those Pharisees and scribes that day.

2. *"That none of those men which were bidden shall taste of My supper,"* speaks of Israel shut out because they rejected God's greatest gift to humanity, His only Son. So it was, and so it is!

(25) "AND THERE WENT GREAT MULTITUDES WITH HIM: AND HE TURNED, AND SAID UNTO THEM."

The pattern is:

1. The phrase, *"And there went great multitudes with Him,"* proclaims Him having left the home of this Pharisee and now continuing His journey toward Jerusalem.

2. With all knowing Jesus and their going to the Passover, as well, they seemed, at least at intervals, to crowd close to Him. This was, no doubt, respecting healing and also to hear Him teach.

3. *"And He turned, and said unto them,"* proclaims Him about to tell these multitudes exactly what it meant to truly follow Him.

NOTES

4. Spence said, "He was anxious now, at the end, clearly to make it known to all these multitudes what serving Him really signified—entire self-renunciation; a real, not a poetic or sentimental, taking up the Cross."

5. Spence went on to say, "Even His own chosen disciples were yet a long way from apprehending the terrible meaning of this Cross He spoke of, and which to Him now bore so ghastly a significance."

(26) "IF ANY MAN COME TO ME, AND HATE NOT HIS FATHER, AND MOTHER, AND WIFE, AND CHILDREN, AND BRETHREN, AND SISTERS, YEA, AND HIS OWN LIFE ALSO, HE CANNOT BE MY DISCIPLE."

The overview is:

1. *"Christ sent me not to baptize, but to preach the gospel: not with wisdom of words, lest the Cross of Christ should be made of none effect"* (I Cor. 1:17).

2. *"For the preaching of the Cross is to them who perish foolishness; but unto us who are saved it is the power of God"* (I Cor. 1:18).

3. *"For after that in the wisdom of God the world by wisdom knew not God, it pleased God by the foolishness of preaching* (preaching the Cross) *to save them who believe"* (I Cor. 1:21).

THOSE WHO COME TO JESUS

The phrase, *"If any man come to Me,"* addresses itself to the multitudes who were following and, as well, to men of all time.

What is going to be said is a far cry from most modern appeals. Men are encouraged today to come to Christ in order that He might make them rich and famous, etc. To cut to the chase, such is blasphemy!

"And hate not his father, and mother, and wife, and children, and brethren, and sisters, yea," speaks to the dearest affections of the human heart. It speaks of proper relationship with Christ.

The word *hate* here simply means "an idiom of preference." It means to love less.

HE CANNOT BE MY DISCIPLE

The nearest affections are the strongest, but no affection, however strong, must be permitted to compete with or displace Christ.

NOTES

To be sure, if one truly follows this command by the Lord, making Christ all in all, the love for one's nearest relatives will be even greater and stronger than previously, but in its proper place.

"And his own life also," means that everything must be laid on the line. The true believer loves his life in a lesser degree than he loves his Lord. The nearer anything (other than Christ) is to the heart, the more dangerous it is; and cost what it may, Christ must be followed, even to death itself. The world hates Him, and all that binds us to it must be subjected to His interests.

The cost must be counted, for salvation, eternal life, and heaven are all in question. There is but one way to the life that is life indeed, and that is to share Christ's rejection and walk His path of shame and death.

The phrase, *"He cannot be My disciple,"* proclaims the reason so may show such spiritual apathy, seeming to have no relationship at all with the Lord, even though professing Christ. If the truth be known, most of these are not and, actually, have never been His disciples because of not wanting to pay the price He demands.

(27) "AND WHOSOEVER DOES NOT BEAR HIS CROSS, AND COME AFTER ME, CANNOT BE MY DISCIPLE."

BEARING THE CROSS

The two words, *"And whosoever,"* proclaim that the price is the same for all. There is no such thing as a Western gospel, an Eastern gospel, etc. As well, there is no such thing as a white man's gospel or a black man's gospel. All must come the same way or come not at all.

The phrase, *"Does not bear his Cross,"* must have been an unparalleled shock to His listeners, including the disciples.

The cross was a well known instrument of torture in Jesus' day, being used by Rome in a very liberal way. As one entered most villages or cities, it was quite common to see individuals hanging on a cross outside the city and near the main road. It was meant by Rome to serve as a warning to all who would oppose Roman peace. It served its purpose well. The victims died slowly, at times, taking days, until they would literally go out of their minds with pain, thirst, and the breakdown of their nervous system. So, when Jesus spoke of bearing the Cross and proclaimed such as the criterion for following Him, many must have been repulsed then as now!

CANNOT BE MY DISCIPLE

The phrase, *"And come after Me, cannot be My disciple,"* proclaims that if He is truly followed, with the idea in mind of being His disciple, the bearing of the Cross is an absolute necessity.

What does it mean to bear the Cross?

The Cross, in the New Testament, is a symbol of shame and humiliation, as well as God's wisdom and glory revealed through it.

Further, the Cross is the symbol of our union with Christ, not simply in virtue of our following His example, but in virtue of what He has done for us and in us. In His substitutionary death for us on the Cross, we died in Him (II Cor. 5:14), and our old man is crucified with Him that by His indwelling Spirit, we might walk in newness of life, abiding in Him (Rom. 6:4; Gal. 2:20; 5:24; 6:14).

While it is certainly true that the Cross was a horrible place of shame and humiliation as it regards our Lord, and is that to a degree regarding His followers, yet, it is the Cross of Christ that has made everything possible. By that, we mean that every good thing that God gives to us, and I mean everything, the Cross of Christ is the means by which all of this is done. In other words, it is the Cross that has made it all possible. It was there that Jesus atoned for all sin. It was there that He broke the back of sin. It was there that our Lord defeated every power of darkness, from Satan on down. In other words, the Cross of Christ was a total victory for the human race and a total victory in the spirit world. That's why Satan hates the Cross to such an extent. It was there that he was defeated, there that his teeth were pulled, so to speak, and there that every blessing was made possible to the child of God.

In fact, taking up the Cross daily to follow Jesus (Lk. 9:23) presents itself as the greatest blessing, the most stupendous blessing, and the most all-encompassing blessing that any person could ever have. True, the Cross was a horrible thing for our Lord. The suffering that He endured, the shame that He endured, and the humiliation that He endured were actually beyond our comprehension. However, all of that made all of this possible.

THE CROSS AND SELF-RIGHTEOUSNESS

Most Christians have at least a modicum of understanding as it respects the Cross referring to salvation. "Jesus died for me," no doubt, is the greatest statement that a person could ever make; however, that's about as far as most believers ever get as it regards the Cross. In other words, they have no idea whatsoever as to the part the Cross plays in our every day life and living. With justification, they have some understanding. With sanctification, they have none at all! Please note the following:

• Jesus Christ is the source of everything we receive from God (Jn. 1:1-3, 14, 29; Col. 2:10-15).

• The Cross of Christ is the means, and the only means, by which all of these wonderful things are given to us (I Cor. 1:17-18, 21, 23; 2:2).

• Understanding that Jesus is the source, and the Cross is the means, the object of our faith must ever be Christ and the Cross (Rom. 6:1-14; Col. 2:10-15; Gal. 6:14).

• Making the Cross of Christ the object of our faith, the Holy Spirit, who is God, and who can do anything, will then work mightily on our behalf. He doesn't demand much of us, but He does demand that our faith be anchored strictly in Christ and the Cross. Faith anchored in anything other than the Cross of Christ always and without exception concludes in self-righteousness.

The hardest thing for the believer to come to the conclusion and understand it as he or she should is that within ourselves, we simply cannot live this life. We cannot do what God wants us to do. The law of Moses is a perfect example.

THE LAW OF MOSES

While the law of Moses was originated by God and, in fact, was God's standard of righteousness, still, the major purpose and reason for the law was to show man that due to

the fall, he, within himself, is unable to keep even the simplest commandments. The law portrayed that in glaring detail. But yet, man is loath to admit such. We like to think that we are our own man, and we can get the job done. Paul bluntly told us, *"And if Christ be in you, the body is dead because of sin; but the Spirit is life because of righteousness"* (Rom. 8:10).

By the use of the phrase, *"The body is dead because of sin,"* he is meaning that due to the fall, the physical body, which includes the mind of the individual, is woefully inadequate to do what must be done. In other words, if we are to have done in our hearts and lives what must be done, it's the Holy Spirit alone who can carry it out. Please understand that the Holy Spirit works entirely within the framework, so to speak, of the Cross of Christ. In other words, what Jesus did at the Cross gives the Holy Spirit the legal means to do all that He does for the believer. Paul also said:

"For the law of the Spirit of life in Christ Jesus has made me free from the law of sin and death" (Rom. 8:2). This passage plainly tells us that the Holy Spirit works totally within the parameters, so to speak, of the finished work of Christ, i.e., the Cross.

WHY IS THE CROSS OF CHRIST AN OFFENSE?

Paul plainly said it was. He said:
"And I, brethren, if I yet preach circumcision, why do I yet suffer persecution? then is the offence of the Cross ceased" (Gal. 5:11).

In other words, the apostle was saying that if he preached *"works,"* there would be no opposition or persecution, but inasmuch as he preached the Cross, then the opposition came against him. Why?

The Cross of Christ lays bare all of man's efforts, which are futile as it regards the Lord. In other words, man doesn't like to be told that all the efforts that he makes will not bring about victory over sin. It doesn't matter if it's fasting, prayer, money, witnessing, or whatever. Irrespective of what it is, and though it may be scriptural and proper in its own right, it will not bring about victory. To be told that none of these things work doesn't set too well with most Christians.

The only way the believer can properly live for the Lord, and I mean walk in victory over the world, the flesh, and the Devil, is by placing his or her faith exclusively in Christ and what Christ did for us at the Cross, and maintain it there exclusively. That is the secret for all life and living and the secret for all victory. This is God's way and His only way (Col. 2:10-15).

IS THE MODERN CHURCH PREACHING THE CROSS?

No!

It is impossible for the church to embrace humanistic psychology and the Cross of Christ at the same time. Either one cancels out the other. Regrettably, the modern church has embraced humanistic psychology in totality.

Peter said, *"According as His divine power has given unto us all things that pertain unto life and godliness, through the knowledge of Him who has called us to glory and virtue:"*

The great apostle went on to say, *"Whereby are given unto us exceeding great and precious promises: that by these you might be partakers of the divine nature, having escaped the corruption that is in the world through lust"* (II Pet. 1:3-4).

Now, either the Lord gave us all things that pertain unto life and godliness, or else, Peter lied. I choose to believe that Peter told the truth.

To embrace the Cross of Christ is to eliminate everything else (every other type of religious crutch) and to depend totally on Christ and what He did for us at the Cross.

Listen again to Paul:

ENEMIES OF THE CROSS

The great apostle said, *"Brethren, be followers together of me, and mark them which walk so as you have us for an example.*

"(For many walk, of whom I have told you often, and now tell you even weeping, that they are the enemies of the Cross of Christ."

The great apostle went on to say, *"Whose end is destruction, whose god is their belly, and whose glory is in their shame, who mind earthly things)"* (Phil. 3:17-19).

NOTES

God's way is the Cross of Christ. As stated, that's where all sin was atoned, all victory was won, and all of the powers of darkness were defeated. If we try to live for God by any means other than simple faith in Christ and the Cross, the end result is spiritual adultery (Rom. 7:1-4). The church presently, and I take no pleasure in saying this, is in worse condition than it has been anytime since the Reformation.

In fact, the modern church is spiritually in the same condition that the children of Israel were in, as it regards Egypt, as they were made to serve Pharaoh. I realize it's difficult for believers to come to that conclusion. However, due to the fact that the church has its faith in anything and everything except the Cross of Christ, spiritual slavery is the end result, one way or the other, every time.

VICTORY

As it regards sins and problems that invade the heart and life of the believer, thereby, causing tremendous problems, there's only one way over this, and that is by the Cross.

However, the believer must understand that he, within himself, cannot overcome the problem, whatever the problem is. I don't care how strong that you are or how determined you are, within yourself, you cannot overcome. As well, many of you would say, "But with God's help, I can do it." No, you can't!

That means that it's part you and part the Lord. It's got to be all of the Lord and none of you.

You as a believer must tell the Lord in no uncertain terms that within yourself, you do not have the strength or the ability to cease the activity that is causing you so much problem. To be sure, that activity is getting worse and worse, whatever it might be. You must unequivocally relate to the Lord your inability within yourself to overcome. Thereby, you are asking Him for His help, and under those circumstances, He will always respond favorably.

The truth is, most believers are loath to admit that within themselves, they cannot do at least something. Many Christians say,

"Oh, I believe in the Cross, but I believe we must do something ourselves as well!"

There is only one thing that the believer can do, and that is to exhibit faith in Christ and His finished work. If you are thinking of something else that you must do, what is that other thing? This is where the problem arises. Millions think that we've got to do something or the other in order to have victory, when no matter what we do, we cannot bring about victory. In truth, our efforts in this respect are not only not bringing us victory, but they're bringing us total defeat, and, as stated, the problem is getting worse and worse and will continue to get worse, whatever the problem is.

Paul also said: *"I am crucified with Christ: nevertheless I live; yet not I, but Christ lives in me: and the life which I now live in the flesh I live by the faith of the Son of God, who loved me, and gave Himself for me"* (Gal. 2:20).

In this short verse, the Holy Spirit through the great apostle literally tells us how to live for God. He begins with the Cross, *"I am crucified with Christ,"* and he ends with the Cross by saying, *"Who loved me, and gave Himself for me."*

So, taking up the Cross daily and following Christ is the greatest, most profitable thing that any believer can ever do. The Cross of Christ was definitely horrific as it regards our Lord, for there He died. However, as it regards us, the Cross has been turned into the most beautiful thing that a person could ever know. It is the source of all victory, all power over Satan, and all abundant life. It's all found in the Cross of Christ and what He did there.

WAS IT WHO HE WAS OR WHAT HE DID?

It was both!

No one could have done this thing, and we speak of the Cross, except the Lord Jesus Christ. God can only accept a perfect sacrifice, and His Son alone fulfilled that demand. No other human being could have, and no other human being even claimed to have been able to do so.

However, the reader should understand that while Jesus Christ was God, always had been God, and always will be God, still, He

did not redeem the fallen sons of Adam's lost race by being God. As stated, our Lord has always been God, but that fact alone did not save anyone. Now, think about that statement for a moment! If being God alone would solve the problem, then He didn't have to come down here and die on a cruel Cross. However, we know for God to be true to His nature, He had to address sin in totality, which could only be done with a perfect sacrifice, and that perfect sacrifice was God manifest in the flesh. In other words, God had to become man (the incarnation) in order to go to the Cross. God cannot die because He is Spirit, so in order to die, He had to become a human being (Jn. 1:14).

So, it was who He was and what He did, which refers to the Cross, that brought about the great redemption plan. In fact, the Cross of Christ was the greatest display of the wisdom of God that has ever been evidenced in human history.

(28) "FOR WHICH OF YOU, INTENDING TO BUILD A TOWER, SITS NOT DOWN FIRST, AND COUNTS THE COST, WHETHER HE HAVE SUFFICIENT TO FINISH IT?"

COUNTING THE COST

The phrase, *"For which of you, intending to build a tower,"* was the example that Jesus would use in order to explain the Cross-bearing of Christ regarding this life.

"Sits not down first (but that you sit down first), *and counts the cost,"* proclaims that which was common and well understood by the listeners.

However, He was speaking of something far more important than the mere construction of a building. He was speaking of the construction of a life, and above all, the soul of man. Consequently, there is nothing more valuable.

He was telling His listeners then and listeners now that before they embark upon this unending journey of following Him, they must fist count the cost. Above all, are they willing to pay the price?

SUFFICIENCY TO FINISH

This does not speak of the price of one's redemption, for that was paid solely and exclusively by Jesus Christ. To receive that, one only has to believe (Jn. 3:16).

However, to begin is not enough; one must finish this race if one is to win eternal life. To do so, the Cross of Christ must be carried constantly. To quit anywhere along the journey forfeits the eternal life at the conclusion of the journey. As well, as should be obvious, these statements by Christ completely refute the unscriptural doctrine of unconditional eternal security, which teaches that if one is truly born again, thereafter, they can never be lost, irrespective of what they do.

Such is an idle fancy of man and has no validity in Scripture.

The conclusion of the question, *"Whether he have sufficient to finish it?"* proclaims that the race must be finished before it can be said to have been run.

Were it impossible for one not to finish, then these statements by Christ make no sense and have no validity. In fact, many, if not most, do not *"finish it,"* hence, Jesus saying, *"Few there be that find it"* (Mat. 7:14).

CARRYING THE CROSS

In fact, the only way one can finish this race, and do so in victory, is by taking up the Cross daily (Lk. 9:23).

One must understand that every single thing we receive from the Lord, and I mean everything, all and without exception is made possible by the Cross of Christ, in other words, what Jesus there did. Now, the believer must come to that conclusion and must understand that and base his past, present, and future on that.

Understanding that, the believer's faith must ever be in Christ and what He has done for us at the Cross. In fact, in the way that Jesus put it, we must examine ourselves every morning and make certain that our faith is properly placed, hence, Him saying to *"take up his Cross daily"* (Lk. 9:23).

With our faith properly placed and, thereby, properly maintained, the Holy Spirit, who works exclusively within the parameters, so to speak, of the finished work of Christ, will then work mightily on our behalf. The Holy Spirit doesn't demand much of us, but He most definitely does demand

NOTES

that our faith be exclusively in Christ and the Cross. This pertains to our daily living.

Unfortunately, the church is very prone to placing its faith in all types of other things. I speak of fasting, the memorizing of Scriptures and quoting them over and over, the giving of money to the work of God, witnessing to souls, etc. All of these things, which we refer to as *"Christian disciplines,"* are most definitely biblical, at least in their own right. However, when we try to use them out of the place that God ordained them, this means we have taken our faith away from Christ and the Cross and placed our faith in something else altogether. That the Lord can never bless and can never help.

When a person does that, and I mean place his faith in something other than the Cross, this means that he really does not rightly understand the Cross, or else, he does understand it, and he is rebelling against that which God demands. Remember this:

No one rejects the Cross on theological grounds, meaning that it's too difficult to understand, but rather always on moral grounds. To be sure, it is the highest form of rebellion against God, and we speak of rebelling against the plan of God. For the believer, the Cross enables us to live a victorious life. And yet, sadly enough, I have to admit that most of the church is rebelling against the Cross of Christ. So as not to be misunderstood, let me say it again:

GOD'S PRESCRIBED ORDER OF LIFE AND LIVING

It is absolutely impossible for a believer to properly live for God, to have victory over the world, the flesh, and the Devil, and to grow in grace and the knowledge of the Lord without properly understanding the Cross of Christ as it refers to sanctification. While a person can be saved in this state, he cannot be victorious. That's why Paul bluntly said:

"As we said before, so say I now again, If any man preach any other gospel unto you than that you have received, let him be accursed" (Gal. 1:9).

The great apostle also said, *"Christ is become of no effect unto you, whosoever of you are justified by the law; you are fallen from grace"* (Gal. 5:4).

So, some might say, "If we do not subscribe to this that you are teaching about the Cross, you are then saying that we cannot live an overcoming life."

That's exactly what I'm saying! The Lord has one way, and that way is the Cross of Christ. That's why the great apostle also said, *"For I determined not to know anything among you, save Jesus Christ, and Him crucified"* (I Cor. 2:2).

(29) "LEST HAPLY, AFTER HE HAS LAID THE FOUNDATION, AND IS NOT ABLE TO FINISH IT, ALL WHO BEHOLD IT BEGIN TO MOCK HIM."

The synopsis is:

1. The phrase, *"Lest haply, after he has laid the foundation, and is not able to finish it,"* proclaims that since the price has not been suitably accounted for, he is unable to finish.

2. The truth is, many, if not millions, have already quit while still continuing to profess. They are no longer bearing the Cross of Christ, that is, if they ever did, with the results being that the flesh is now supreme. Consequently, they are no longer a disciple of the Lord.

3. *"All who behold it begin to mock him,"* is obvious concerning the story Jesus was relating, but that which it represented and which He intended spoke of demon spirits who will mock such a one. While some in the world may do such a thing, the far greater majority of mocking will come from the spirit world.

AN OLD TESTAMENT EXAMPLE

Immediately when David was anointed to be the king over all of Israel, he went against the fortress of Jebus, which actually was Jerusalem. It was inhabited by the Jebusites, who were a fierce warlike tribe that had never been defeated by Israel, with the exception of when Joshua came against them several hundreds of years previously. So, right in the heart of Israel, they had remained a stronghold against the people of God. In all of Saul's reign of some 40 years, he never did defeat the Jebusites.

And now, David said that this heathen

tribe must be defeated first of all, that is, if Israel was to be what it ought to be. The Scripture says:

"And the king and his men went to Jerusalem unto the Jebusites, the inhabitants of the land: which spoke unto David, saying, Except you take away the blind and the lame, you shall not come in hither, thinking, David cannot come in hither" (II Sam. 5:6).

In other words, the Jebusites were mocking David, saying to him that they could defend the city with only their lame and blind and defeat David. They were to find out otherwise!

So, Satan will mock you, as well, especially in your defeats; however, that stronghold can be pulled down. Paul said:

"For though we walk in the flesh, we do not war after the flesh:

"(For the weapons of our warfare are not carnal, but mighty through God to the pulling down of strongholds;)

"Casting down imaginations (philosophic strongholds; every effort man makes outside of the Cross of Christ), *and every high thing that exalteth itself against the knowledge of God* (all the pride of the human heart), *and bringing into captivity every thought to the obedience of Christ* (can be done only by the believer looking exclusively to the Cross, where all victory is found; the Holy Spirit will then perform the task)" (II Cor. 10:3-5).

PULLING DOWN THE STRONGHOLD IN YOUR LIFE

There are some people, actually even many, who, upon hearing the Message of the Cross, embrace it whole heartedly and definitely begin to see victory within their hearts and lives. However, sometimes there is one thing that hangs on over which they seemingly cannot obtain the victory. What is wrong?

If they were to be questioned, they would say, "Brother Swaggart, I believe the Message of the Cross with all of my heart, but I'm still not free."

Let me give you the solution to that problem.

The Lord intends that no sin dominate you in any manner. While that does not teach sinless perfection, it most definitely does teach that sin is not to have dominion over us (Rom. 6:14).

You, as a believer, must go before the Lord and tell Him in no uncertain terms that you, within yourself, are totally unable to get this problem out of your life. Tell Him that He must do this. Please understand that what we are facing in the spirit world as it regards demon spirits and fallen angels, and even Satan himself, is far ahead of our own personal strength and ability.

In other words, within ourselves, we cannot rid ourselves of the problem. The only thing we can do is furnish the Lord a willing mind and an obedient heart. Once you begin to rely totally on the Lord and cease the thinking that you somehow can get it out of your life, whatever it is, then the Lord will take over. We must remember that what is impossible for us is no problem with Him whatsoever.

So, get it out of your mind that you have the ability within yourself to overcome the problem. Even get it out of your mind that you can provide a little help when, in truth, you cannot provide anything except what we've already stated—a willing mind, and an obedient heart.

If you will do this and mean it with all of your heart, placing your faith exclusively in Christ and the Cross, and continue to do this, you'll wake up one morning with that problem gone, and there will never even be another desire for it in any capacity.

You see, we try to do in the flesh what can only be done by the power of the Holy Spirit.

Paul said, *"So then they that are in the flesh cannot please God"* (Rom. 8:8). Victory is yours, but only as long as you understand your place and position, and the place and position of Christ and what He has done for us at the Cross. You must understand that you can't live it yourself and cannot overcome this problem within your own ability and strength. It is impossible for you to do such in that capacity. So, you must tell the Lord that you can't do it, and you should mean it with all of your heart. Then, the Holy Spirit will take over.

(30) "SAYING, THIS MAN BEGAN TO BUILD, AND WAS NOT ABLE TO FINISH.

(31) "OR WHAT KING, GOING TO MAKE WAR AGAINST ANOTHER KING, SITS NOT DOWN FIRST, AND CONSULTS WHETHER HE BE ABLE WITH TEN THOUSAND TO MEET HIM WHO COMES AGAINST HIM WITH TWENTY THOUSAND?"

The pattern is:

1. In these scenarios as outlined by Christ, the tremendously important position of heralding Christ as one's Saviour is held up as an example. It is totally unlike the joining of organizations, or anything else for that matter. Following Christ involves the spirit world. As such, one must understand the opposition that will be brought to bear against the true believer.

2. However, it is to be understood that Jesus was not speaking of ability, talent, or even effort, but rather determination against all odds. God requires little of anyone, with the exception of a determination of faith to stay the course.

3. The Christian walk is not a problem free walk, as many would have us to believe. *Pilgrim's Progress*, a book written by John Bunyan, is an excellent example of what I say and should be read by all believers.

4. Regrettably, there will be many failures along the way. We do not enjoy speaking in this manner, but the truth is the truth. There will be times of acute discouragement, along with misunderstanding, and times when it seems that no one cares but Christ.

5. So, the idea is that irrespective of the opposition, difficulties, hindrances, or failures, the individual must make up his or her mind that whatever happens, he is going to stay the course. With that being the case, the Lord has promised that the course will be completed.

(32) "OR ELSE, WHILE THE OTHER IS YET A GREAT WAY OFF, HE SENDS AN AMBASSADOR, AND DESIRES CONDITIONS OF PEACE."

The form is:

1. The idea of this verse is that the believer is facing war, and war we might quickly add, until the very end.

2. Unfortunately, great segments of the modern body of Christ attempt to get people to believe that if they properly confess all

things, they can escape the war. However, such is not to be!

3. Unfortunately, many of God's people have made peace with Satan. The battle between the flesh and the Spirit has ended, and the Spirit has lost simply because the flesh was weak. So, while it is true that they have no more war, it is also true that they have no more victory. Satan is the master, for it can be no other way. Either Jesus is Lord, or Satan is lord!

4. That's the reason that when observing many believers who seem to never have any type of conflict, everything seemingly always goes well. If the spirit world could be looked into, one would see that they have quit fighting, thereby, losing the battle, and even the war. As such, they are no longer a disciple of the Lord.

(33) "SO LIKEWISE, WHOSOEVER HE BE OF YOU WHO FORSAKES NOT ALL THAT HE HAS, HE CANNOT BE MY DISCIPLE."

The overview is:

1. The key to victory in all other battles is the gathering of great resources to oneself; however, the key to this spiritual conflict is the very opposite—the forsaking all that one has.

2. Then the Lord can step in and give the victory, but if not allowed to do so, the verdict is clear, *"He cannot be My disciple."*

(34) "SALT IS GOOD: BUT IF THE SALT HAVE LOST HIS SAVOUR, WHERE-WITH SHALL IT BE SEASONED?"

SALT IS GOOD

The phrase, *"Salt is good,"* begins another parable and refers to the godly Christian life. Salt seasons and preserves, and so does the believer.

Actually, the only true light that is in the world is that which comes from the child of God. That is the secret of America's prosperity and freedoms, not its higher institutions of learning or its gross national product. It is the great number of true believers in this country, plus any other country that may be so blessed.

That is at least one of the reasons the coming great tribulation is going to be so awful—the salt will be removed, i.e., the body of Christ will be raptured away (I Thess. 4:16-17).

NOTES

As well, if the reader is the only member of your family that's saved, instead of looking at it in the negative, turn it into a positive. You as the *"salt"* in that family can be instrumental in bringing them to Christ. Actually, you may be their only hope.

LOSING ITS SAVOUR

The phrase, *"But if the salt have lost his savour,"* refers to salt no longer being salty and, consequently, good for nothing.

This is the problem presently in America. The church has lost its saltiness, i.e., the true purpose of life in Christ.

Actually, the modern church has come to the place that it is now popular to be born again. Of course, the reason it is popular in the world is because the salt has lost its savour, meaning that nothing is required of anyone anymore. People can claim to be born again while continuing in their old lifestyle, with no visible change whatsoever, while true salvation always produces righteousness, and without fail.

No! If the *salt* is present, it will be just as unpopular to be born again as it once was.

During Jesus' day, Israel had seen the *"savour"* lost in its salt. Consequently, they would be totally destroyed, exactly as the next verse proclaims.

SEASONED?

The question, *"Wherewith shall it be seasoned?"* means that there is no alternative to Christ. He and the Word are the saltiness of the salt. If that is removed, and it was removed from Israel, there was absolutely nothing that could take its place then or now.

The gospel of Jesus Christ is not one of several solutions but, in reality, the only solution. So, if the gospel (saltiness) is lost in any heart and life, city, community, or nation, there is nothing that can take its place. Universities, political parties, and philosophies all fall short.

(35) "IT IS NEITHER FIT FOR THE LAND, NOR YET FOR THE DUNGHILL; BUT MEN CAST IT OUT. HE WHO HAS EARS TO HEAR, LET HIM HEAR."

NOT FIT

The phrase, *"It is neither fit for the*

NOTES

land," means that it can no longer serve its intended purpose because it no longer has that which gives it purpose.

Consequently, Israel was thrust out from the land in A.D. 70 as Titus destroyed the city, temple, and nationhood of the people.

This is what makes some of the present doctrines being promoted, such as the greed message, so dangerous. Such false teaching abrogates the true purpose of the cause of Christ. The true believer gives to others constantly, while this false message turns everything inward.

As a result, the salt has lost its savor, no longer performing its intended purpose. In effect, one could say that it becomes sugar, which tastes good for the moment but has absolutely no similarity to salt, except in appearance.

CAST IT OUT

The phrase, *"Nor yet for the dunghill,"* is used by Jesus to proclaim that the wayward Christian is actually good for nothing. Many things, if not used for their intended purpose, can be used elsewhere; however, the savorless Christian does not fall into that category, actually becoming totally worthless.

"But men cast it out," has to do with its total worthlessness, as well, and beyond the shadow of a doubt, the same will be done for those who profess Christ but do not possess Christ. The implication is clear!

EARS TO HEAR

The phrase, *He who has ears to hear, let him hear,"* in effect, means that there is no way that Jesus can make it any plainer or clearer, and that if men do not legitimately hear what He is saying, it is because they do not desire to hear. They have ears but simply will not use them.

So, these statements by Christ completely refute the idea that everyone who begins the journey will finish the journey. The record is clear that some will be *"cast out"* along the way. In another way, He said the same thing, *"Not everyone who says unto Me, Lord, Lord, shall enter into the kingdom of heaven; but he who does the will of My Father which is in heaven"* (Mat. 7:21).

"Jesus is tenderly calling you home,
"Calling today, calling today;
"Why from the sunshine of love will
*　you roam,*
"Further and further away?"

"Jesus is calling the weary to rest,
"Calling today, calling today
"Bring Him your burden and you
*　shall be blest;*
"He will not turn you away."

"Jesus is waiting: O come to Him now,
"Waiting today, waiting today;
"Come with your sins, at His feet
*　lowly bow;*
"Come, and no longer delay."

"Jesus is pleading: O list to His voice,
"Hear Him today, hear Him today;
"They who believe on His name shall
*　rejoice;*
"Quickly arise and away."

CHAPTER 15

(1) "THEN DREW NEAR UNTO HIM ALL THE PUBLICANS AND SINNERS FOR TO HEAR HIM."

PUBLICANS

"Publicans" were tax collectors and looked at as traitors by the religious hierarchy of Israel. They were afforded no opportunity for salvation whatsoever and, consequently, were thoroughly condemned by the Pharisees.

As a result, the publicans and sinners as a class, who, of course, made up the great majority of the population, were by and large ignored by the religious hierarchy of Israel. If they were addressed at all, it was in a condescending manner, with the lofty pomp of the Pharisees and scribes plainly obvious.

However, Jesus dealt with them as equals and spoke to them kindly and with loving attention. Actually, this was something that had never happened in Israel; consequently, the publicans and sinners flocked to His side. To be sure, He met their every need, whether physical or spiritual.

GOD'S JOY OVER REPENTANT SINNERS

The point of the three parables presented in this chapter is God's joy over repenting sinners. They unveil the sentiments of His heart and not those of the repentant sinner, as is usually taught.

He did not sit still in heaven pitying sinners, just as the shepherd, the woman, and the father did not idly bewail the lost sheep, the lost silver, and the lost son. Instead, Christ left the starry crown of heaven for the thorny crown of earth in the activity of the love that seeks the lost till it is found.

The shepherd rejoiced, the woman rejoiced, and the father rejoiced. Such is the joy of God when sinners come to Jesus. This grace is a grace that seeks and a grace that receives. The first two parables, as we shall see, describe the former; the third parable, the latter. Grace convicts the conscience but attracts the heart. To be sure, the measure of that grace is the measure of the love that begets it.

As well, the stupidity of the sinner, his insensibility, and his depravity are expressed in these three parables. If the doubling of the dream to Pharaoh (Gen. 41:32) assured its certitude, how much more does the trebling of this parable make certain the attitude of God's heart to lost man.

(2) "AND THE PHARISEES AND SCRIBES MURMURED, SAYING, THIS MAN RECEIVES SINNERS, AND EATS WITH THEM."

THE PHARISEES AND THE SCRIBES

The phrase, *"And the Pharisees and scribes murmured,"* presents them conducting themselves exactly as their fathers in the wilderness, which brought plagues then and will bring the greatest plague of all now—the destruction of themselves and their country (Ex. 16:7-12; Num. 14:27; 17:5-10).

What was the cause of the murmuring of the Pharisees?

They were jealous of the vast crowds that gathered around Christ and the enthusiasm with which they received His message; consequently, they proceeded to find fault.

The phrase, *"This man receives sinners, and eats with them,"* proclaims their total

lack of knowledge of who Jesus was and what was His mission. He came to save sinners and, consequently, placed Himself on their level, but without their sin; thus, *"the common people heard Him gladly"* (Mk. 12:37).

SCATHING DENUNCIATION

If one is to notice, Jesus gave the Pharisees and scribes of Israel no place or position at all. In other words, He did what He did strictly according to the leading of the Holy Spirit, consequently, ignoring the religious hierarchy of Israel. He did not ask their permission, seek their approval, or play to their grandstand whatsoever. He did preach to them and answered their questions, but it was not at all what they desired to hear. Actually, He spoke of them and to them with scathing denunciation. Consequently, they hated Him.

Two things are said here:

1. No true man of God will submit his ministry to denominational heads or religious hierarchy. The moment he does, he has compromised his stand, his convictions, and the leading of the Holy Spirit. He cannot be led by God and man at the same time.

While he at all times will be courteous, kind, and thoughtful, he will never ask their permission or seek their approval. If he does, the salt has lost its savour (Lk. 14:34).

2. As a result, these Pharisees and scribes hated Jesus, as they will hate His modern followers as well! There is no way the two can come to terms.

So, if the man is looking for fame and fortune in the ministry, he will not find it in truly following the Lord, but rather hatred, opposition, and persecution.

Satan's spirit of opposition to the true work of God did not die with the Pharisees and scribes, but is alive and well presently and functions in the same manner. Nothing has changed except the date on the calendar.

(3) "AND HE SPOKE THIS PARABLE UNTO THEM, SAYING."

The overview is:

1. These particular parables were not designed to shade the meaning, as some were, but were open, obvious, revealing, and beautiful.

2. When Jesus wanted to convey a truth,

He oftentimes used a parable to do so. If He wanted to shade the reality, to cause the people to dig a little deeper, He would use a certain type of parable that would do what He desired.

(4) "WHAT MAN OF YOU, HAVING AN HUNDRED SHEEP, IF HE LOSE ONE OF THEM, DOES NOT LEAVE THE NINETY AND NINE IN THE WILDERNESS, BUT GO AFTER THAT WHICH IS LOST, UNTIL HE FIND IT?"

The exegesis is:

1. The phrase, "What man of you, having an hundred sheep," proclaims to these Pharisees and scribes a scenario that they readily understood.

2. "If he lose one of them," proclaims the value the Lord places on just one soul.

3. As well, the phrase could speak of the entirety of this world, which was lost at the fall. Of all God's creation, Earth is the only planet that is in rebellion against Him.

4. However, if this phrase does speak of this Earth at the fall, it does not of necessity mean that the remaining 99 speak of other planets, etc. Such would be taking the parable further than Jesus intended. Actually, He was merely speaking of the worth of the sinner and the effort that should be made to find him and bring him home.

5. "Does not leave the ninety and nine in the wilderness," does not mean that they are left alone, but rather that every effort is to be made to retrieve the one that is lost.

6. His leaving them does not show a lack of care, but rather the opposite. If He will go to this much trouble to secure the one, how much more to ensure the entirety of the flock!

7. In other words, if God loves sinners as much as He does, how much must He love those who have not strayed! This truth should not be lost in any of these three parables.

8. The conclusion of the question, "But go after that which is lost, until he find it?" proclaims the Lord coming down to this world to seek sinners.

9. Many say, "I found the Lord," when in reality, He found us!

(5) "AND WHEN HE HAS FOUND IT, HE LAYS IT ON HIS SHOULDERS, REJOICING."

NOTES

THE PARABLE OF THE LOST SHEEP

The parable of the lost sheep is also found in Matthew 18:12. There, it expresses love that seeks; here, the joy that finds.

The phrase, "Lays it on his shoulders," contains the possibility of the depth of meaning in Psalm 23:3, "He restores my soul: He leads me in the paths of righteousness for His name's sake."

The paths here mentioned speak of the appointed path, i.e., appointed by God.

THE ILLUSTRATION

At times, a recalcitrant sheep will leave that path, and because of acute dumbness, will quickly find itself lost, possibly caught in a rocky defile, and unable to extricate itself.

All it can do is bleat, which will have the desired effect. The shepherd, seeing that it is missing, will search for it and find it by its cries.

The shepherd will then take his crook, tenderly lift the wayward one up, and restore it to the path.

In fact, regrettably, this can happen several times, with the scene being repeated; however, if the little creature persists in leaving the appointed path, there will come a time when the shepherd will react differently.

Whereas he had always come immediately, now, he will not come so quickly. He will allow the lamb to bleat until it has no voice left. Stark fear then begins to set in with the little animal, with it not knowing that the shepherd is watching it all the time.

After a lapse, the shepherd will finally come to the lost sheep. He will take his crook as always and lift the sheep out, but then, he will do something he has not done previously.

After picking up the lamb, he will extend one of his front forepaws and, taking the heavy end of his crook, will bring it down smartly on the leg, breaking the bone.

He will then carefully set the break and carry the sheep on his shoulder until the leg is healed, exactly as is described here by Jesus.

Then the lamb will be much more prone to remain on the appointed path.

(6) "AND WHEN HE COMES HOME, HE CALLS TOGETHER HIS FRIENDS

AND NEIGHBORS, SAYING UNTO THEM, REJOICE WITH ME; FOR I HAVE FOUND MY SHEEP WHICH WAS LOST."

The composition is:

1. The phrase, *"And when he comes home, he calls together his friends and neighbors,"* should have been the religious leaders of Israel, but they coldly refused.

2. *"Saying unto them, Rejoice with me,"* is really the highest occasion for rejoicing in heaven, at least that is outlined in the Word of God.

3. Actually, the spiritual temperature of the church can be gauged by what occasions its joy. Is it buildings? Is it educational degrees? Is it money? Is it certain types of phenomena, which are erroneously at times called revival?

6. The true occasion for joy and rejoicing should be the salvation of souls; however, when such elicits little concern, as Israel at the time of Christ, such portrays the actual prevailing spiritual temperature.

7. The phrase, *"For I have found my sheep which was lost,"* according to heaven, is the greatest statement that could ever be made.

(7) "I SAY UNTO YOU, THAT LIKEWISE JOY SHALL BE IN HEAVEN OVER ONE SINNER WHO REPENTS, MORE THAN OVER NINETY AND NINE JUST PERSONS, WHICH NEED NO REPENTANCE."

The synopsis is:

1. The phrase, *"I say unto you,"* represents a pronouncement of urgent proportions. The church would do well to heed it carefully.

2. *"That likewise joy shall be in heaven over one sinner who repents,"* proclaims, as stated, that which makes heaven rejoice.

3. It should be obvious that this is why Jesus came. This is the sum total of the plan of God for the human family. While other things are certainly important, still, nothing can match a soul being saved.

4. *"More than over ninety and nine just persons, which need no repentance,"* must be properly understood.

5. The *"ninety and nine just persons,"* were rejoiced over greatly in heaven when they originally repented; consequently, it is the same for all.

(8) "EITHER WHAT WOMAN HAVING TEN PIECES OF SILVER, IF SHE LOSE

NOTES

ONE PIECE, DOES NOT LIGHT A CANDLE, AND SWEEP THE HOUSE, AND SEEK DILIGENTLY TILL SHE FIND IT?"

The overview is:

1. As the previous was the parable of the lost sheep, this is the parable of the lost coin.

2. The phrase, *"Either what woman having ten pieces of silver, if she lose one piece,"* merely points to something of value. The sheep was valuable, and the coin is valuable. Both are likened to a lost soul.

3. The conclusion of the question, *"Does not light a candle, and sweep the house, and seek diligently till she find it?"* even though obvious as to its meaning in the illustration, still, could speak of the light of the gospel. That alone, the gospel of Jesus Christ, will find that which is lost.

(9) "AND WHEN SHE HAS FOUND IT, SHE CALLS HER FRIENDS AND HER NEIGHBORS TOGETHER, SAYING, REJOICE WITH ME; FOR I HAVE FOUND THE PIECE WHICH I HAD LOST."

The pattern is:

1. Basically, the intent of Verse 9 is the same as Verse 6.

2. Godet said, "In these statements, we get a glimpse of God Himself rejoicing with His elect and His angels over the salvation of a single sinner!"

(10) "LIKEWISE, I SAY UNTO YOU, THERE IS JOY IN THE PRESENCE OF THE ANGELS OF GOD OVER ONE SINNER WHO REPENTS."

The exegesis is:

1. Even though this verse is very similar to Verse 7, still, there is some difference.

2. This statement by Christ tells us that not only does God rejoice over one sinner who repents but, as well, in the very presence of the angels of God, which speaks of the very throne of God.

3. When something is repeated, as these passages, the Holy Spirit is signifying the great importance of what is being said; consequently, please allow me to say it again:

The spiritual temperature of the church can be gauged by that which causes the greatest amount of rejoicing. According to Christ, if the church is where it ought to be, its greatest rejoicing will be reserved for the salvation of lost souls.

(11) "AND HE SAID, A CERTAIN MAN HAD TWO SONS."

The exegesis is:

1. This is the third and by far longest parable of the three and is called the parable of the prodigal son!

2. Some have said that this is the most beautiful story ever told. Considering what it represents—the seeking and the retrieving of the lost soul—there can be no doubt as to the sublime aspect of this beautiful illustration as given by Christ.

3. Whereas the two previous parables illustrated a sheep and coin, which were not capable of moral choices and action, this parable is different in that the sons did have these capabilities. Consequently, this parable is related by Jesus in greater detail.

4. Is it possible that the sheep and coin represented the Gentiles, who were eagerly sought after because they were almost helpless?

5. As well, is it possible that the prodigal represents the Jew who was not so much sought after but had to come of his own accord, as will happen at the second coming?

(12) "AND THE YOUNGER OF THEM SAID TO HIS FATHER, FATHER, GIVE ME THE PORTION OF GOODS THAT FALLS TO ME. AND HE DIVIDED UNTO THEM HIS LIVING."

The synopsis is:

1. The phrase, *"And the younger of them said to his Father,"* will be treated by this writer as the Jewish people, even though it definitely can apply to any and all.

2. *"Father, give me the portion of goods that falls to me,"* was typical at that time of Roman law. Whereas the son in modern times cannot receive an inheritance until the death of the father, then, it could be demanded by and large at any time.

3. What caused the young man to desire these goods at this time? Did he not have a good home with ample provisions? Was it not secure with every want provided?

4. As Jesus related the story, it shows that this young man left his home for all the wrong reasons, exactly as Israel left the Lord. The young man wanted the things of the world, and Israel wanted to be like other nations.

5. The phrase, *"And he divided unto them*

his living," seems to indicate by the pronoun *them* that a certain amount was guaranteed by law to each. The younger one took his and left.

6. It had to be a time of great sorrow for the Father, and it would seem that he must have done everything he could to talk him out of this tragedy, but to no avail. The prophets were sent to Israel, but they had no more success than the Father.

(13) "AND NOT MANY DAYS AFTER THE YOUNGER SON GATHERED ALL TOGETHER, AND TOOK HIS JOURNEY INTO A FAR COUNTRY, AND THERE WASTED HIS SUBSTANCE WITH RIOTOUS LIVING."

THE YOUNGER SON

The phrase, *"And not many days after the younger son gathered all together,"* concerned an inheritance that he really had not earned but had been freely given to him because of his relationship with his Father.

Williams said, "The son fell while yet in the father's house. He fell from the moment he desired the father's goods without the father's company; and it only needed a few days to find him in the far country. Backsliding begins in the heart, and very soon places the feet with the swine."

A FAR COUNTRY

The phrase, *"And took his journey into a far country,"* is *"far"* in more ways than one. There is an eternity between the house of God and the far country of sin. It speaks of being a long distance from the Father.

Someone has said, "Sin will take you further than you want to go and cost you more than you can afford to pay."

"And there wasted his substance with riotous living," speaks of that which was precious being thrown away. It was wasted not on abundant living, as that is given by Christ (Jn. 10:10), but on riotous living, which speaks of excess and, therefore, waste.

"Riotous living" speaks of that which is fast paced, excessive, tumultuous, and even ruinous. It characterizes the world. The noise, clamor, and inebriation makes one feel that he is really living when, in reality, there is no life about it, only ruin, which is waste.

Because of deception, the world refers to

a life lived for God and money given to God's work as waste when, in reality, it is the very opposite. The truth is, anything and everything done outside of Christ, irrespective of the present power or glamour, will come out at the conclusion only as waste. Conversely, everything done for God is the very opposite. In fact, we are only able to keep that which we give to the Lord.

(14) "AND WHEN HE HAD SPENT ALL, THERE AROSE A MIGHTY FAMINE IN THAT LAND; AND HE BEGAN TO BE IN WANT."

The composition is:

1. The phrase, *"And when he had spent all,"* refers to the squandering of the inheritance, which was done in short order. Satan does not replenish; he only uses. So, after awhile, whether it is beauty, money, power, or whatever else, one finds it spent. The lights are bright for awhile, but they soon dim.

2. The phrase, *"There arose a mighty famine in that land,"* is that which comes with the territory. Satan makes the individual believe, as Israel of old, that there will always be plenty, but ultimately, the famine comes.

3. *"And he began to be in want,"* represents the first time in his life he had ever experienced such a malady. He always had plenty at his Father's house but now experienced the very opposite. To be sure, as it happened to him, it has happened to all.

4. Lord Byron wrote:

My days are in the yellow leaf:
The flowers and fruits of love are gone;
The worm, the canker, and the grief,
Are mine alone.
The fire that on my bosom preys
Is lone as some volcanic isle;
No torch is kindled at its blaze
A funeral pile!

(15) "AND HE WENT AND JOINED HIMSELF TO A CITIZEN OF THAT COUNTRY; AND HE SENT HIM INTO HIS FIELDS TO FEED SWINE."

The order is:

1. The phrase, *"And he went and joined himself to a citizen of that country,"* speaks of desperation, for the word *joined* translated into forcing himself upon an unwilling employer. In short, he had been reduced to begging.

2. *"And he sent him into his fields to feed swine,"* represented the most degrading occupation in which any Jew could engage.

3. To a Jew, and especially one of such noble birth, a pig was so loathsome that it was very seldom spoken of by its name, but rather as *"that thing."*

(16) "AND HE WOULD FAIN HAVE FILLED HIS BELLY WITH THE HUSKS THAT THE SWINE DID EAT: AND NO MAN GAVE UNTO HIM."

The structure is:

1. The phrase, *"And he would fain have filled his belly with the husks that the swine did eat,"* means that he not only fed the swine but was forced to eat their swill as well! From so high, he had fallen so low!

2. *"And no man gave unto him,"* means that in the Devil's country, nothing is given, but everything must be bought, and it must be bought at a terrible price.

3. His father had given unto him constantly, but now he found that grace had no place in this far country.

(17) "AND WHEN HE CAME TO HIMSELF, HE SAID, HOW MANY HIRED SERVANTS OF MY FATHER'S HAVE BREAD ENOUGH AND TO SPARE, AND I PERISH WITH HUNGER!"

WHEN HE CAME TO HIMSELF

The phrase, *"And when he came to himself,"* is an interesting statement. It implies several things:

Outside of God, no person thinks right, acts right, walks right, talks right, or is right. The mental process is somewhat skewed, plus the very nature of the individual. Sin has a terrible debilitating effect on every part of the individual, be it mental, physical, or spiritual. Actually, this is the reason for the terrible problems in the earth, man's inhumanity to man, stealing, killing, injustice, etc.

The only thing keeping the world on a halfway even keel is the fact and presence of the body of Christ, even as small as it actually is. This is the reason Jesus likened the believer to *"salt"* and *"light"* (Mat. 5:13-14).

Nothing brought him to himself but absolute bodily suffering and cruel hunger. This tells us that men do not bend easily;

consequently, it is not common sense that drives most people to God, but rather the extremity of their situations.

ONLY IN CHRIST

No individual can realize his full potential except in Christ. Irrespective of the finest educational programs in the nation, or the world for that matter, until man attends to the spiritual, he can never be what he ought to be, and that can be done only in Christ.

The phrase, *"How many hired servants of my father's have bread enough and to spare,"* proclaims that the father was a man of means.

In other words, he was saying that even the lowliest servant in his Father's house was far better off than he was in this pig pen.

Men have bought Satan's lie that living for God deprives one of so many good things. Nothing could be further from the truth.

In Christ is everything that the heart desires. God blesses in every way that one could begin to imagine, be it physical, material, or above all, spiritual. Satan can only give things in the material sense, and even then, he does so seldom, as proven by the prodigal son. He cannot give anything physically, and above all, he cannot give anything spiritually.

PERISHING WITH HUNGER

Man's basic problem is that he is taught by modern education that he is a physical and mental person only. The spiritual is totally ignored as though it does not exist; however, the truth is, while man is physical and mental, he is, as well, spiritual. He was created by God with the breath of God placed within him, which meant God's image (Gen. 1:26; 2:7).

Unless the spiritual man is nourished, which can only be done by Christ, by the power of the Holy Spirit, and through the Word of God, man cannot be whole.

The phrase, *"And I perish with hunger,"* in a sense describes the entirety of the human family. The hunger, while physical, also transcends into the spiritual. Jesus spoke of those who *"hunger and thirst after righteousness"* (Mat. 5:6).

In a sense, the hunger for righteousness

NOTES

is the true hunger of the human heart, even though the human heart is so twisted and warped by sin that it does not realize this truth. Only when the person is spiritually awakened through the born-again experience does he realize that what he had been craving all along could only be found in Christ.

(18) "I WILL ARISE AND GO TO MY FATHER, AND WILL SAY UNTO HIM, FATHER, I HAVE SINNED AGAINST HEAVEN, AND BEFORE YOU."

The synopsis is:

1. The phrase, *"I will arise and go to my Father,"* is the first step for the penitent soul. Until the realization of need comes, nothing can be done. As stated, many have to come to a sad lot, even as this young man, before they will finally arise.

2. The word *arise* tells us that the journey to God is always upward, while that with Satan is always downward.

3. The phrase, *"And will say unto Him, Father, I have sinned against heaven, and before You,"* proclaims the admittance of wrongdoing, which is a necessity if one is to come to God.

4. Notice that the young man did not plead extenuating circumstances, lay the blame on others, or plead wrongs done to him. He placed the blame squarely where it belonged—upon himself.

5. He said, *"I have sinned,"* which is what God demands. He then said it was *"against heaven,"* which is correct concerning all sin.

6. Likewise, the words *"before You"* mean that he sinned against God, in effect, rebelling against God's way.

(19) "AND AM NO MORE WORTHY TO BE CALLED YOUR SON: MAKE ME AS ONE OF YOUR HIRED SERVANTS."

The exegesis is:

1. The phrase, *"And am no more worthy to be called Your son,"* proclaims his unworthiness, which is another requirement.

2. The owning up to one's sin and, therefore, one's responsibility is the first step, with the understanding of one's unworthiness being the second.

3. *"Make me as one of Your hired servants,"* is the position of humility that one must take; nevertheless, God has never received one as such, nor will He ever.

4. Whenever an individual returns to Christ, he is, without exception, restored to full privileges and rights. This we shall see in the coming verses; however, at the same time, this young man's willingness to take anything in the Father's house, no matter how lowly, proclaims the spirit and attitude that one must have in coming to Christ. To be frank, the sinner is in no condition to demand anything. In fact, if he does, it negates all salvation because salvation is a free gift. If it is approached from any other angle, the person is automatically disqualified.

(20) "AND HE AROSE, AND CAME TO HIS FATHER. BUT WHEN HE WAS YET A GREAT WAY OFF, HIS FATHER SAW HIM, AND HAD COMPASSION, AND RAN, AND FELL ON HIS NECK, AND KISSED HIM."

HE AROSE

The phrase, *"And he arose, and came to his Father,"* proclaims the willingness and obedience which must characterize the individual before one can be saved.

If one is to notice, as stated, the lamb and the coin were eagerly sought because they did not have the power to make moral choices. However, even though the young man definitely was sought, as was proven by his reception, still, he had to initiate the return from his own heart, as dealt with by the Holy Spirit. Otherwise, it is not true repentance!

HIS FATHER SAW HIM

The phrase, *"But when he was yet a great way off, his Father saw him,"* tells us something very special.

Even though the Father did not make any attempt to force the young man back, the very moment he showed a willingness to come back, a warm reception was initiated. In fact, the phrase shows that the Father was earnestly looking for him, which enabled Him to see him while a great way off.

This great way off may well have included, and no doubt did, that the Father knew exactly where the boy was at all times; however, the sinner must of his own free will take the initial step toward God, and when that is done, the Father sets in motion everything else that is needed.

NOTES

COMPASSION

The phrase, *"And had compassion,"* shows the heart of God. To be sure, the world had no compassion on him, as is obvious. The love or compassion of God is so absolutely heavenly that it is difficult for the individual to grasp its implications. It is love that loves when it is not loved in return. It is love that never stops. It is love that has or holds no condemnation. It is love that reaches out.

The two words, *"and ran,"* portray the only time in the Bible that God is shown as running. As well, that which occasions the running is that of a sinner coming home to Christ. Consequently, we are made to realize where the heart of God actually is, which is the salvation of souls.

"And fell on his neck, and kissed him," proclaims the first act that was done upon the return of the prodigal. One can only shout *"hallelujah!"*

(21) "AND THE SON SAID UNTO HIM, FATHER, I HAVE SINNED AGAINST HEAVEN, AND IN YOUR SIGHT, AND AM NO MORE WORTHY TO BE CALLED YOUR SON."

The exegesis is:

1. The phrase, *"And the son said unto him,"* shows the intent of the heart and the responsibility personally taken. If one is to notice, the Holy Spirit is careful to catalog these statements even though, as we shall see, they are of little import, at least as far as the Father is concerned. The record will show that He is more interested in the state of the heart than anything else.

2. *"I have sinned against heaven, and in Your sight, and am no more worthy to be called Your son,"* is as far as the young man got. He had intended to continue, as Verse 19 proclaims, *"Make me as one of Your hired servants,"* when the Father interrupted him, proving it was the state of the heart he was more interested in than anything else.

(22) "BUT THE FATHER SAID TO HIS SERVANTS, BRING FORTH THE BEST ROBE, AND PUT IT ON HIM; AND PUT A RING ON HIS HAND, AND SHOES ON HIS FEET."

The overview is:

1. The sacrifice of the Cross is the same to every member of the Israel of God, whatever be his status in the assembly.

2. This means that grace meets the needy one just where he is and as he is.

3. One might say, "To the poor, the gospel is preached." None can say, "The blood of Jesus is beyond me."

THE FATHER

The phrase, *"But the Father said to His servants,"* proclaims the interruption, as we have just said. The boy would have been satisfied to have been accepted as a servant, and even a hired servant, which was the lowest rung on the social ladder.

Hired servants, as Verse 19 proclaims, were those who had no steady employment but worked only when there was something for them to do; consequently, they did not have the protection or security provided regular servants. The young man was willing to become just a hired servant, which would be so much better than that to which he had been reduced.

THE BEST ROBE

The phrase, *"Bring forth the best robe,"* is a far cry from what he expected. He would be restored to full rights and privileges, which he never expected.

What must have gone through his mind when he was about ready to request the status of a hired servant when, all of a sudden, his Father interrupted him and demanded that the servants bring forth the best robe? What a wonderful God we serve!

The robe was that of II Corinthians 5:21.

As well, it should be noted that all of these wonderful things were done for the young man, it seems, even before he was brought to the house. The Father did not want people to see him in the rags and swill to which he had been reduced. How mindful He is of our feelings, when most of the time, we seem to have little concern for His.

To be sure, the boy had embarrassed his Father extensively on the previous demanding of his inheritance. Such showed a lack of trust and confidence. As well, it must have humiliated the Father even more when the boy left, which in itself was a statement

saying to one and all that he was not satisfied with what he had. Nevertheless, the Father would not repay in like kind, but rather the very opposite.

Williams said, "Grace ran to kiss the prodigal in his rags, and righteousness hasted to dress him in its robe; for he could not sit in his rags at the Father's board."

The phrase, *"And put it on him,"* signified, as stated, the righteousness of God supplied.

This is a perfect illustration, exactly as Jesus intended, to portray the righteousness of God freely given. As is obvious, this young man did not earn this, nor did he deserve it. The robe was given to him freely upon proper repentance, as it always is to any and everyone who comes God's way.

THE RING AND THE SHOES

The phrase, *"And put a ring on his hand,"* signified far more than meets the eye.

At that time a ring denoted freedom and pretty much served in the same capacity as a modern credit card. Such was a signet ring, which bore the crest of his Father's house. When items were purchased, the one who wore such a ring could simply press its top into clay, which would leave the impression of the crest, and would be honored by the merchant. As stated, it was about the same as a modern credit card.

The phrase, *"And shoes on his feet,"* denoted ownership, for slaves did not wear shoes.

All of these things were provided for him and declared his sonship; for servants were not thus arrayed and feasted.

All of these things proclaim that which love provides. There were no reproaches, rebukes, reproofs for the past, or irritating admonitions for the future, because the Father and His joy is the subject of the story more than the moral condition of the son.

(23) "AND BRING HITHER THE FATTED CALF, AND KILL IT; AND LET US EAT, AND BE MERRY."

The overview is:

1. In a sense, this signifies the Lord's Supper, thereby, proclaiming the validity of the covenant.

2. *"And be merry,"* signifies the joy at being able to be part of such a covenant.

3. The law of Moses was based on

performance, which placed man in a terrible position of not being able to measure up.

4. However, grace is based on promise, which is an entirely different matter all together.

5. The covenant of law, as we have stated, depended on performance, and even though God always performed perfectly, man performed poorly as always and, consequently, broke the covenant.

6. However, under grace, the new covenant has nothing to do with performance, but rather promise. Even though it is a covenant like all others and, of necessity, requires two or more parties, still, the Lord did something in this covenant that is totally unlike any other covenant.

7. Inasmuch as Jesus Christ is both God and man, He could meet the requirements, which He did by being both. As He sealed it with His own precious blood, the covenant cannot be broken. As God, He cannot fail, and as man, the perfect man, He kept the law perfectly, which no other man was able to do.

Consequently, by faith in what He did, we are allowed to become a part of the covenant through Jesus Christ, who was and is the perfect man. In other words, He, as the representative man, did and does for us that which we could not do for ourselves. Consequently, it is truly something to be merry about!

(24) "FOR THIS MY SON WAS DEAD, AND IS ALIVE AGAIN; HE WAS LOST, AND IS FOUND. AND THEY BEGAN TO BE MERRY."

The pattern is:

1. The phrase, *"For this My son was dead, and is alive again,"* so beautifully portrays the redemption process.

Men are dead in trespasses and sins and, consequently, can only be made alive again in Christ Jesus.

2. *"He was lost, and is found,"* signifies being without God and, thereby, lost, and then upon redemption, being, in effect, found.

3. *"And they began to be merry,"* signifies the greatest cause of joy ever known to humanity—the salvation of a soul.

4. The entirety of this beautiful parable can be summed up in three ways:

a. It signifies man who fell in the garden and, in effect, had to vacate its premises, as the prodigal. The return signifies that all who will may come.

b. The parable signifies Israel, also. She left that which God had designed for her, went her way, and has come to ruin, exactly as portrayed through the centuries. Nevertheless, she will return just as the prodigal. It will take place at the second coming.

c. It also pertains to backsliders. I speak of those who have left the safety, comfort, and protection of the Father's house, which always concludes as the waywardness of the prodigal. Nevertheless, they too can come home if they only desire to do so.

(25) "NOW HIS ELDER SON WAS IN THE FIELD: AND AS HE CAME AND DREW NEAR TO THE HOUSE, HE HEARD MUSIC AND DANCING."

The pattern is:

1. The phrase, *"Now His elder son was in the field,"* presents the second part of the parable, which most people little study, and which addressees itself to the Pharisees of all ages.

2. While this man was in the field, i.e., performing some type of service, the record will show, as given by Jesus, that He was of little true service to the betterment of this house. His attitude and spirit portray all too often those found in the work of God. His view was wrong! His attitude was wrong! Consequently, his service was wrong! Unfortunately, his breed is still alive and very prominent in Christian circles.

3. *"And as he came and drew near to the house, he heard music and dancing,"* signaled the celebration then taking place respecting the return of the prodigal.

(26) "AND HE CALLED ONE OF THE SERVANTS, AND ASKED WHAT THESE THINGS MEANT."

The order is:

1. The phrase, *"And he called one of the servants,"* proclaims the servant knowing more about the Father's business than even he, the elder son, knew. If his business had been the Father's business as it should have been, he would have been in the midst of the celebration.

2. *"And asked what these things meant,"*

proclaims him not knowing that which was dearest to the Father's heart.

3. How so much he signifies the far greater majority of the Christian world, which is in the work of God but not of the work of God. In other words, they have their own agenda, which is not the agenda of the Holy Spirit; consequently, they have absolutely no knowledge (as the elder son) concerning that which is truly happening and which gladdens the heart of the Father. As the elder son did not know, they, as well, do not know.

4. The thing dearest to the heart of the Father was the restoration of His son, i.e., salvation of souls. The elder son should have had the same concern because his business should have been to do the Father's will. However, doing his own thing, he had no knowledge of what was taking place.

5. I wonder how much this characterizes the balance of the Christian world. They are laboring, but to what effect? They are involved in the work, but what work?

(27) "AND HE SAID UNTO HIM, YOUR BROTHER IS COME; AND YOUR FATHER HAS KILLED THE FATTED CALF, BECAUSE HE HAS RECEIVED HIM SAFE AND SOUND."

The order is:

1. The phrase, "And he said unto him, Your brother is come," proclaims, as stated, the servant knowing more than the elder son. It is astounding that an event of this magnitude was happening, and he knew nothing of it.

2. "And your Father has killed the fatted calf," proclaims the celebration that takes place in heaven upon the salvation of souls, and should, as well, take place on earth among believers; however, much of the time, the joy and energy are spent on other pursuits.

3. The phrase, "Because he has received him safe and sound," proclaims a victory of unimagined proportions. And yet, the elder brother did not know!

(28) "AND HE WAS ANGRY, AND WOULD NOT GO IN: THEREFORE CAME HIS FATHER OUT, AND ENTREATED HIM."

The pattern is:

1. The phrase, "And he was angry," shows the true nature of his heart.

2. There is little doubt that the Pharisees

NOTES

and scribes, who were bitterly incensed with Jesus being the friend of publicans and sinners, knew this was spoken to them.

3. The last couple of years that I was with a particular Pentecostal denomination, I noticed this same reaction (anger) on their part, as some of the largest stadiums in the world were filled to capacity, with multiple tens of thousands responding to the altar calls. I was totally nonplussed at first! I did not understand how anger could be the response when such activity should elicit unparalleled joy.

4. Of course, as one analyzes this parable, at least its latter part, the reason becomes obvious. As stated, they are in the work but not of it. They really do not know the heart of God, so consequently, the thing Jesus died for, the salvation of souls, was not where their efforts were.

5. I do not mean to imply that all the missionaries were that way, for they were not. Some few were godly. Nevertheless, almost all the leadership did fall into that category. They were angry, and for the same reason as the elder brother.

6. The phrase, "And would not go in," proclaims rebellion of the highest order. Jesus spoke of this when He said, "But woe unto you, scribes and Pharisees, hypocrites! for you shut up the kingdom of heaven against men: for you neither go in yourselves, neither suffer ye them who are entering to go in" (Mat. 23:13).

7. "Therefore came his Father out, and entreated him," proclaims Jesus making every appeal to the scribes and Pharisees but, as here, to no avail. The patience he had shown with the prodigal, he shows, as well, with the rebellious. Such is our heavenly Father!

(29) "AND HE ANSWERING SAID TO HIS FATHER, LO, THESE MANY YEARS DO I SERVE YOU, NEITHER TRANSGRESSED I AT ANY TIME YOUR COMMANDMENT: AND YET YOU NEVER GAVE ME A KID, THAT I MIGHT MAKE MERRY WITH MY FRIENDS."

THE SELF-RIGHTEOUS ELDER BROTHER

The phrase, "And he answering said to

his Father," will be an answer totally different than that given by his younger brother.

This is what Jesus constantly reproached. All sin is bad! Consequently, what the prodigal did was terribly wrong. But yet, he repented and was instantly accepted.

On the other hand, his self-righteous elder brother would not repent because he saw no need for repentance, but rather to extol his own righteousness. Such is much of the modern church!

"Lo, these many years do I serve You," is said in the realm of merit. The reason he thought this way was because he had no relationship with the Father; consequently, it was just a job to him instead of it being his very own, as it actually was. While he did serve his Father, he did so for all the wrong reasons. How so much he characterizes so many in the modern church.

FALSE CLAIMS

The phrase, *"Neither transgressed I at any time Your commandment,"* proclaims his self-righteousness. Such is the so-called good church member or moralist. Their salvation is wrapped up in what they do or don't do.

While all the time he was claiming to never having transgressed, in truth, the entirety of his life was a transgression.

The way he said, *"Your commandment,"* proclaims that whatever he did was not out of love but was done grudgingly. In other words, he chaffed at these commandments, which is obvious from his terminology. In fact, he had no proper relationship with the Father.

"And yet You never gave me a kid, that I might make merry with my friends," portrays that while he was claiming a perfect obedience, his secret desire all the time had been to make merry with his friends. This showed that morally he was as much lost to his Father as was his brother.

(30) "BUT AS SOON AS THIS YOUR SON WAS COME, WHICH HAS DEVOURED YOUR LIVING WITH HARLOTS, YOU HAVE KILLED FOR HIM THE FATTED CALF."

The pattern is:

1. The phrase, *"But as soon as this Your son was come,"* now portrays him disowning

NOTES

any relationship with his younger brother. Of course, self-righteousness would have to feel this way! How could he associate with someone who had sunk so low?

2. In fact, he placed himself on a far higher pedestal regarding holiness than even his Father. His Father might own this prodigal son, but he, the elder brother, would not! So, by his own words, he has disassociated himself from the family.

3. *"Which has devoured Your living with harlots,"* shows the hatred of his heart to his Father and to his brother. He felt free to speak glibly of a sin that had already been washed, cleansed, and forgiven by the Father. In fact, self-righteousness enjoys parading other people's sins while conveniently overlooking its own.

4. Does the reader realize, as Jesus here portrays, how wicked and wrong it is to refer to something that has been washed by the blood of Jesus and forgiven by the grace of God? To do so shows, as the elder brother of old, that such a one does not understand what forgiveness or true salvation really is. In other words, they have not really been forgiven themselves so, consequently, refuse to forgive others.

5. *"You have killed for him the fatted calf,"* is a proclamation of self-righteousness, which cannot conceive of such a thing.

6. Instead of making merry, this man should be severely punished, at least in the mind of this self-righteous one.

(31) "AND HE SAID UNTO HIM, SON, YOU ARE EVER WITH ME, AND ALL THAT I HAVE IS YOURS."

The overview is:

1. The phrase, *"And He said unto him,"* proclaims the remonstrance of the Father. As his words were kind to the returning prodigal, likewise, they would be kind to the elder brother as well.

2. *"Son, you are ever with Me, and all that I have is yours,"* in effect, says that he really had not partaken of these riches, even though they were his for the asking.

3. He had tried to earn them, which was unnecessary, and actually unacceptable; consequently, he missed the entirety of the point of what salvation really is.

(32) "IT WAS MEET THAT WE SHOULD

MAKE MERRY, AND BE GLAD: FOR THIS YOUR BROTHER WAS DEAD, AND IS ALIVE AGAIN; AND WAS LOST, AND IS FOUND."

A GLADNESS

The phrase, *"It was meet that we should make merry, and be glad,"* proclaims a beautiful truth.

John 14:6 and Luke 15:20 are not contradictory but complementary. The one reveals the way to the Father's house; the other assures the reception there.

The one discloses the activities of the mind of God in redemption; the other, the emotions of the heart of God in reception.

Further, Christ as *"the way"* is symbolized in the robe, the ring, the sandals, and the fatted calf, for He is righteousness (II Cor. 5:21), eternal life (Jn. 11:25), sonship (Jn. 1:12), and peace (I Cor. 5:7-8).

The death of the sinless calf was a necessity ere the feast could be enjoyed. Had the prodigal refused this raiment and claimed the right to enter the Father's house in his rags and nakedness, he, like Cain, would have been rejected.

However, his was true repentance, and so it accepted these gifts, assuring purity, perpetuity, position, and provision. Consequently, these three parables, therefore, destroy the argument that no atoning and mediating Saviour is needed between God and the sinner, and they rest on the unseen foundation of I John 1:7.

LOST AND FOUND

"For this your brother was dead, and is alive again; and was lost, and is found," proclaims the end of the parable, as obvious, and that which is dearest to the heart of God—the salvation of lost souls.

While the church should certainly rejoice over many things, the greatest rejoicing should be reserved for the salvation of the lost. If that ever ceases to be primary and paramount, this is a sure sign the church has lost its way.

When this happens, it degenerates into the surly attitude of the self-righteous Pharisee. He had no concern for the lost and even less concern for their salvation. In fact, the

entirety of the relationship with the Father, such as it was, was built on a wrong premise. He felt that by merit, he had earned a place and position in the Father's house. Now he was extremely upset that one could claim this place and position through no merit whatsoever.

Consequently, he missed the entirety of the plan of salvation, not understanding that salvation must be a gift, or else, it is no salvation at all, and certainly cannot be earned by merit. In fact, the moment one attempts to earn such, one is automatically disqualified, even as the elder son.

The story ends; however, even though Jesus did not plainly say it, the way the parable concludes tells us that the returning prodigal was saved while the elder son was not.

Consequently, many of these publicans and sinners who came to Jesus were saved, which the parable is meant to illustrate, while the Pharisees were eternally lost, as represented by the elder brother.

As well, the scenario did not die with the time of Jesus but persists unto this very day.

"Why do you wait, dear brother
"Oh, why do you tarry so long?
"Your Saviour is waiting to give you
"A place in His sanctified throng."

"What do you hope, dear brother,
"To gain by a further delay?
"There's no one to save you but Jesus,
"There's no other way but His way."

"Do you not feel, dear brother,
"His Spirit now striving within?
"Oh, why not accept His salvation,
"And throw off your burden of sin?"

"Why do you wait, dear brother?
"The harvest is passing away;
"Your Saviour is longing to bless you,
"There's danger and death in delay."

CHAPTER 16

(1) "AND HE SAID ALSO UNTO HIS DISCIPLES, THERE WAS A CERTAIN RICH MAN, WHICH HAD A STEWARD; AND THE SAME WAS ACCUSED UNTO HIM THAT HE HAD WASTED HIS GOODS."

THE PARABLE OF
THE UNJUST STEWARD

"And He said also unto His disciples," could very well have been given soon after the parables of the previous chapter given to the Pharisees.

Someone said that Chapter 15 was addressed to the Pharisees in the hearing of the disciples, and Chapter 16 to the disciples in the hearing of the Pharisees.

The Word of the Lord is a two-edged sword. The parable of the steward may, therefore, judge the Pharisee as well as the publican. If so, then the elder brother, the unjust steward, and the rich man all portray the Pharisee in his three relationships to God— as a son, as a steward, and as a subject. As a son, he was loveless, for he had no affection for either his father or brother. As a steward, he was faithless, for the Word of God (the true riches) was entrusted to him, and he corrupted it. As a subject, he was lawless, for he refused to observe the Great Commandments of the law. Thus, Chapter 15 revealed his heart, and Chapter 16 revealed his conduct and his end.

A CERTAIN RICH MAN

The phrase, *"There was a certain rich man, which* (who) *had a steward,"* sets the stage for this parable.

The moral of this parable seems to be found in Verse 8. The idea presents itself of the unjust steward conniving and scheming to provide for himself, which the child of God ought to heed, at least regarding the lesson given concerning attention to spiritual matters. It seems that greater diligence is practiced by the world, as here presented, than by most believers concerning the things of God.

"And the same was accused unto him that he had wasted his goods," proclaims the setting of the story. The man had not acquitted himself very well, and now his employer called him to account.

(2) "AND HE CALLED HIM, AND SAID UNTO HIM, HOW IS IT THAT I HEAR THIS OF YOU? GIVE AN ACCOUNT OF YOUR STEWARDSHIP; FOR YOU MAY BE NO LONGER STEWARD."

CALLED TO GIVE ACCOUNT

The phrase, *"And he called him,"* has to do with this unjust steward. However, even though the gist of this parable is not in that direction, still, one day the Lord will call us, as well, to stand before Him at the judgment seat of Christ, where we will have to give account just as this man.

Last night in our prayer meeting, I related the thought that if all of us fully understood how important all of this is, and how that one day we will answer to Christ at the judgment seat of Christ, quite possibly we would do things far differently.

There, most of the things we think of on earth as being so important will not even be mentioned. Our work, life, ministry, attitude, motivation, and true heart purposes will be the only things that matter. We will answer for faithfulness, consecration, diligence, motives, zeal, purposes, and reasons. In other words, why did we do what we did? Was our real purpose for God or for self-aggrandizement?

THE JUDGMENT SEAT OF CHRIST

At the judgment seat of Christ where every believer shall stand, no sins will be judged there because that has already been done at Calvary. This judgment, which will take place immediately preceding the second coming and will include every believer who has ever lived, will pertain totally to the stewardship of our consecration to Christ.

The question, *"And said unto him, How is it that I hear this of you?"* concerns an earthly employer regarding an unjust steward. Being human, this employer's knowledge was limited. However, when we stand before Christ, *"He shall not judge after the sight of His eyes, neither reprove after the hearing of His ears: But with righteousness shall He judge"* (Isa. 11:3-4).

WE MUST GIVE ACCOUNT

The phrase, *"Give an account of your stewardship,"* will be the very words, or similar, which will be spoken to every believer at the judgment seat of Christ.

Then it will not matter what type of house we lived in, what type of clothing we wore, what type of car we drove, or how popular or unpopular we were. Business operations that take all of our time will hardly be mentioned there, if at all! Sporting activities, hobbies, and mundane things that rob us of much of our proposed effort for the Lord will be of no consequence. Only what's done for Christ will last.

YOU ARE OUT

The phrase, *"For you may be no longer steward,"* although spoken in an entirely different setting, will apply, as well, to every believer, although under different circumstances. Whereas this steward stood before his employer because he had wasted his goods and would summarily be dismissed, the believer will stand before Christ because his life's work is finished. However, will it not also be true that many believers have simply wasted his goods, i.e., wasted the life given by Christ?

We are stewards now; however, this probationary time comes to an end for all believers at death. It is for this life that we must give account.

(3) "THEN THE STEWARD SAID WITHIN HIMSELF, WHAT SHALL I DO? FOR MY LORD TAKES AWAY FROM ME THE STEWARDSHIP: I CANNOT DIG; TO BEG I AM ASHAMED."

The order is:

1. The question, *"Then the steward said within himself, What shall I do?"* applies not only to this man who wasted his master's goods, but it will apply, as well, to every believer. I personally think that many Christians are going to stand at that judgment and hear the words of Christ and will ask the same question, "What shall I do?" They will know His words are irrefutable and will realize that they have lost their reward, or at least most of it, because of unfaithfulness.

2. *"For my lord takes away from me the stewardship,"* pertains, as is obvious, to this man's malfeasance, but will pertain to the end of our lives regarding believers.

3. *"I cannot dig; to beg I am ashamed,"* has reference to digging out stores of goods from stockpiles to replace what was lost. The idea is that the goods that he was

charged with have been wasted, and there is no more stockpile.

4. Even though this is a very simple statement and, consequently, looked over by most believers, still, it holds a truth that we should heed.

5. Many people do not give to God as they should, always thinking they will make it up at some future time; however, when that time comes, as here, there is no reserve remaining. Therefore, God is the one who was cheated. How many have used their tithes for things other than God's work? As well, and possibly even far more important, how many have used the ability that God has given them exclusively for their own affairs with the Lord's work suffering lack? Consequently, the little phrase, *"I cannot dig"* turns out to be very important.

6. This man had used his master's goods in a lackadaisical, irresponsible manner exactly the same as many believers use that which God has given them. As he was ashamed to beg, many believers will be ashamed at the judgment seat of Christ.

(4) "I AM RESOLVED WHAT TO DO, THAT, WHEN I AM PUT OUT OF THE STEWARDSHIP, THEY MAY RECEIVE ME INTO THEIR HOUSES."

The form is:

1. The phrase, *"I am resolved what to do,"* proclaims the beginning of a plan or scheme to provide for himself.

2. The idea is that the believer should resolve, as well, that even though he cannot change the past, he can change the present and the future by the help of God. By that, we mean to make his or her life count for God.

3. *"That, when I am put out of the stewardship, they may receive me into their houses,"* proclaims this man, a worldling if you will, scheming as to how he can protect himself. While Jesus does not commend his dishonesty at all, He does direct attention to the plans being made to protect himself.

4. In effect, the Lord was saying that believers should give at least as much attention and time to their lives for Christ as this worldling did for his own welfare. Actually, this is the reason the Lord has given this parable.

5. Most believers give precious little

NOTES

attention to the Lord's work, thinking that attending church once a week (or whatever) satisfies their obligation to the Lord. Nothing could be further from the truth.

6. The primary occupation of every believer, be he preacher or layman, must be his service for the Lord Jesus Christ. While all laymen may do certain things to make a living, still, their primary focus must be their lives lived for God. To relegate Christ to one hour a week is tantamount to blasphemy. It shows a total misunderstanding of the great plan of salvation that one has. It shows a lack of understanding as to what we are to be as salt and light.

(5) "SO HE CALLED EVERY ONE OF HIS LORD'S DEBTORS UNTO HIM, AND SAID UNTO THE FIRST, HOW MUCH DO YOU OWE UNTO MY LORD?"

The exegesis is:

1. The phrase, "So he called every one of his lord's debtors unto him," institutes the beginning of his scheme.

2. It should be obvious that this man spent quite a considerable amount of time in coming up with this ingenious idea; consequently, the question must be asked as to exactly how much time and energy is put forth by the believer in attempting to make his life count for God. Tragically, most believers give little, if any, thought at all. They just sort of exist in a spiritual limbo, seemingly not recognizing the precious commodity of salvation they possess, or how the Lord desires to use them.

3. The question, "How much do you owe my lord?" which institutes his plan, is typical of that which is happening all over the world each and every day, and millions of times over. The scheming and planning are the ordinary course of events in the world, and as Paul said, "They do it to obtain a corruptible crown" (I Cor. 9:25).

(6) "AND HE SAID, AN HUNDRED MEASURES OF OIL. AND HE SAID UNTO HIM, TAKE YOUR BILL, AND SIT DOWN QUICKLY, AND WRITE FIFTY.

(7) "THEN SAID HE TO ANOTHER, AND HOW MUCH DO YOU OWE? AND HE SAID, AN HUNDRED MEASURES OF WHEAT. AND HE SAID UNTO HIM, TAKE YOUR BILL, AND WRITE FOURSCORE."

THE STEWARD

The steward actually had the right, as given to him by his employer, to set the price of certain commodities; however, as the text shows, he misused that right in order to ingratiate himself with these debtors. Since they would be indebted to him, one or more would take him into their employ inasmuch as he was now losing his present position. Two things are here said:

1. THE EMPLOYER

The employer could not do a single thing about the excellent deal his steward had given to these debtors, in effect, wiping out a great part of their debt. As stated, the man had the right to set the prices, but not in this fashion, as should be obvious. Nevertheless, Christ was portraying how the scheming and the planning that went into this showed diligence, forethought, and attention to detail, even though it was dishonest, actually, very dishonest. The believer must give as much forethought to the work of God but, of course, minus the dishonesty, as should be obvious.

Many have blanched at Jesus using an example of dishonesty to portray diligence, etc. However, the reader must understand that the entirety of the spirit of the world is made up of dishonesty in one form or the other. If the world is to be described, there is no other way for it to be portrayed. It is unscrupulous, dishonest, and even ungodly.

Jesus was simply pointing to the thought, labor, and planning that wicked men go through in order to further their own nefarious schemes. He was not commending the dishonesty, but rather the diligence for that which was wrong. It should be a lesson to believers that if wicked men can do such for personal gain, how much more should the believer labor and be faithful to the work of the Lord!

2. DISHONESTY

As this man was dishonest, many believers are dishonest with this great salvation that God has given them. It is not used properly, and neither is the will of God often sought. Salvation is too often dishonestly used on oneself, while the Lord intends for us to be a blessing to others.

A case in point is the modern greed message. This is, at least for the most part, a dishonest use of the plan of God and the Word of God. While the culpability is different with some due to lack of scriptural knowledge, still, dishonesty is the only way it can be rightly described.

(8) "AND THE LORD COMMENDED THE UNJUST STEWARD, BECAUSE HE HAD DONE WISELY: FOR THE CHILDREN OF THIS WORLD ARE IN THEIR GENERATION WISER THAN THE CHILDREN OF LIGHT."

THE UNJUST STEWARD

The phrase, *"And the lord commended the unjust steward, because he had done wisely,"* is not speaking of the Lord of Glory, but rather the steward's employer.

As well, the commendation is not meant to point to a proper way of doing things, but rather the clever way in which this was done in that the employer could do nothing about it. He merely acknowledged that the steward had made quite a plan to provide for himself.

THE CHILDREN OF LIGHT

The phrase, *"For the children of this world are in their generation wiser than the children of light,"* is the entirety of the moral of this parable as given by Christ.

They are wiser because the diligence given, crooked or otherwise, is the very best effort they have. And yet, even though possessing that which is far and away more important than anything the world has, still, most of the time, the children of light pay precious little attention or diligence to this all-important task.

In any given church, be it ever so godly, the pastor can probably easily count the number of those who are totally diligent for the work of God. Considering most, to show up on some of the service nights is about the depth of their consecration. And yet, the dishonest ways of the world will ultimately perish, while that done by the believer will have eternal consequences.

One noted philosopher said, or words to this effect, "If I truly believed, as you Christians say you believe, that Jesus is the Son of God, and that He died to set humanity free,

and that if men do not accept Him, they will die eternally lost, and if they do accept Him, they will have eternal life, I would sell everything I had, devoting my total time and attention to the telling of this story."

He went on to say, "But your apathy tells me that you really do not believe it, or else, you are not that concerned. Either way, you leave me with no choice but to reject what you say."

Tragically, what this man said is by and large true. Most believers, even as Jesus brought out in this parable, little believe what they really have, or else, have little concern. Either way is disastrous!

(9) "AND I SAY UNTO YOU, MAKE TO YOURSELVES FRIENDS OF THE MAMMON OF UNRIGHTEOUSNESS; THAT, WHEN YE FAIL, THEY MAY RECEIVE YOU INTO EVERLASTING HABITATIONS."

The synopsis is:

1. The phrase, *"And I say unto you,"* presents the custom of Christ respecting a strong point He desired to make; however, it was the urging of the Holy Spirit within Christ who desired that individuals pay close attention.

2. The people were accustomed to hearing the vacillation of the Pharisees; however, Christ always directed the listeners to Scripture, or else, used this form of salutation.

3. *"Make to yourselves friends of the mammon of unrighteousness,"* simply means that believers must learn to be faithful with money regarding others and the work of God.

4. Money is here called the *"mammon of unrighteousness"* simply because the love of such is the root of all forms of evil (I Tim. 6:10). What the Lord was saying is strong indeed.

5. The handling of money will prove very quickly the consecration of the Christian or lack thereof. Actually, Verse 11 tells us that Jesus actually judges the faithfulness of a believer, at least in part, as to how he handles that which is called the mammon of unrighteousness.

6. *"That, when you fail, they may receive you into everlasting habitations,"* actually refers to the time the believer dies. When that happens, Verse 22 tells us that the angels carry the soul and the spirit of the person into everlasting habitations, i.e., heaven.

(10) "HE WHO IS FAITHFUL IN THAT WHICH IS LEAST IS FAITHFUL ALSO IN MUCH: AND HE WHO IS UNJUST IN THE LEAST IS UNJUST ALSO IN MUCH."

The exegesis is:

1. The phrase, *"He who is faithful in that which is least is faithful also in much,"* implies that if a believer is faithful with his tithes and giving to God, it is an excellent sign that he will more than likely be faithful in all other aspects of his Christian endeavor.

2. *"He who is unjust in the least is unjust also in much,"* says the same thing as the previous phrase but in the opposite direction.

3. If an individual will not allow the Lord to have first place respecting money, in other words, he will not give to God, the Lord labels it as *"unjust,"* and plainly states that he will continue to be unjust in spiritual matters.

4. In this passage, money is referred to as *"least,"* with spiritual things labeled as *"much."*

(11) "IF THEREFORE YOU HAVE NOT BEEN FAITHFUL IN THE UNRIGHTEOUS MAMMON, WHO WILL COMMIT TO YOUR TRUST THE TRUE RICHES?"

UNFAITHFULNESS

The beginning of the question, *"If therefore you have not been faithful in the unrighteous mammon,"* places the responsibility squarely on the believer respecting money.

As we have already mentioned, with money being the cause of so many problems respecting dishonesty and unfaithfulness, Jesus referred to it as unrighteous mammon. Inasmuch as money, at least to some degree, is a part of all we do, with the love of it being the cause of so much evil in the world, it makes an excellent barometer concerning faithfulness of any believer.

Years ago when Frances and I were in meetings in the state of California, she sent me to the laundromat one particular Saturday morning. Needing change, I placed a dollar bill in a changer on the wall, which promptly gave me all the change in the machine, amounting to $30 or more.

There was a number that one was to call should there be problems. I rang the number, and a man answered.

I told him I had had a problem with his

money changing machine, with him answering somewhat surly. I then explained that I had put a dollar in the machine, and it had emptied out all the change it had, evidently malfunctioning.

I'll never forget it. There was a long silence, and then he asked, "And you are calling me to tell me about it?" He told me he would be right there.

If I remember correctly, he said that he had had people call him many times for various problems but never to report a problem of this nature, and he thanked me profusely.

Honesty with money in all circumstances is what the Lord is speaking of as well! This would pertain to the I.R.S. as well as the Lord. We must render to Caesar what belongs to Caesar and to God what belongs to God (Mat. 22:21).

PLACED IN TRUST

The conclusion of the question, *"Who will commit to your trust the true riches?"* is so to the point that it needs very little explanation.

This plainly tells us, at least as I read it, that if a person is unfaithful with money, respecting honesty and giving to God, he simply is not saved, irrespective of his profession.

This also means that a believer pays his debts. While some may be forced into a position to where they cannot pay the bill immediately, at least they can call the individual or company in question and let them know the circumstances. To ignore an obligation simply will not be done by a true believer.

As well, the true Christian will be generous with his money, being fair with the entirety of his family, and yet, teaching them its value.

Considering what Jesus has said here, I think it would be difficult to overstate the significance of this down to earth, practical teaching that applies to everyone. If a person cannot be trusted with money in any capacity, Jesus plainly says that he cannot be trusted with salvation, i.e., true riches. In view of the seriousness of what is being said, we would do well to heed it carefully.

(12) "AND IF YE HAVE NOT BEEN FAITHFUL IN THAT WHICH IS ANOTHER MAN'S, WHO SHALL GIVE YOU THAT WHICH IS YOUR OWN?"

The structure is:

1. The phrase, *"And if ye (you) have not been faithful in that which is another man's,"* strikes at our practical everyday living. Among other things, it speaks of our employment.

2. When we're working for another man, do we give him a fair day's work? Is his equipment or goods handled with care and responsibility? The unjust steward wasted his employer's goods (Lk. 16:1).

3. Over a period of years, we have employed many hundreds and even thousands of people at the ministry. These jobs range from heads of departments to driving trucks, or whatever it may be. Sadly, it is a rarity to find those who will look at their jobs and take them with responsibility, conducting themselves accordingly. Many of them will work only if someone is standing over them keeping them working.

Regrettably, if left on their own, most would do little or nothing, even though the work that they must do is very obvious. And yet, almost all of these people call themselves Christians. In this passage, the Lord plainly tells us that He expects faithfulness regarding the discharging of our tasks in the employment of another.

4. The conclusion of the question, *"Who shall give you that which is your own?"* tells us that the Lord will not bless someone who does not discharge his responsibilities as he should.

5. Verses 9 through 13 give us the reason most Christians never grow in the Lord and are not blessed. They can't be trusted with money, and they show little responsibility in working for someone else. Consequently, the Lord plainly said that He will not bless them in that which requires responsibility. If they have not conducted themselves as they should with the property of others, they will not conduct themselves as they should with that which God gives. Consequently, He simply does not bless.

(13) "NO SERVANT CAN SERVE TWO MASTERS: FOR EITHER HE WILL HATE THE ONE, AND LOVE THE OTHER; OR ELSE HE WILL HOLD TO THE ONE, AND DESPISE THE OTHER. YE CANNOT SERVE GOD AND MAMMON."

TWO MASTERS

The phrase, *"No servant can serve two masters,"* proclaims that which is obvious, and yet, that's what many believers attempt to do.

If we are truly serving God, we will seek to do what He desires to be done. We will handle money with honesty, responsibility, and generosity because that is God's way, and not with selfishness and irresponsibility, which is man's way.

Likewise, we will properly handle the property of others, as well as give them a fair day's work, that is, if we are in their employ, because that is God's way. We will not serve ourselves concerning slovenly attitude and irresponsibility.

Jesus likened the scenario to two masters. We are either serving God or ourselves, with the simple truth being that we cannot serve both.

The phrase, *"For either he will hate the one, and love the other; or else he will hold to the one, and despise the other,"* tells us exactly who and what the person is.

The implication is that if one acquits himself responsibly in these matters, this shows his love for God. If not, it shows that despite his profession, he actually despises the Lord.

GOD AND MAMMON

The phrase, *"Ye (You) cannot serve God and mammon,"* places God and money side by side, for this is what *mammon* means, at least in this case.

Money within itself is not here demeaned by Jesus, but rather the manner in which we hold or handle it. Neither is the amount in question, but rather our faithfulness.

In these passages, Jesus was saying that irrespective of how loudly and how often we profess our godliness, if it does not show up in our practical, everyday living, especially in the matters of money and our responsibility toward others, our profession is vain. This statement is plain and clear: if we are unfaithful in these things, who will commit to our trust the true riches?

If I understand these passages correctly, Jesus was not necessarily speaking of salvation, but rather of His blessing poured out upon an individual. The meaning is that He simply cannot trust most professing believers with any responsibility; hence, they are little blessed, if at all!

(14) "AND THE PHARISEES ALSO, WHO WERE COVETOUS, HEARD ALL THESE THINGS: AND THEY DERIDED HIM."

THE PHARISEES

The phrase, *"And the Pharisees also, who were covetous, heard all these things,"* proclaims the crowning sin, not only of the Pharisees but, as well, of many believers.

This is what makes the modern greed message so wrong! Under the cloak of godliness, it breeds covetousness. Regrettably, there is a certain amount of greed, one could possibly say, in the hearts of us all. Consequently, for one to be unfaithful in money or the things money can buy, as Verses 9 through 13 proclaim, is bad enough; however, to attempt to make God a part of these schemes, as the greed message does, makes the sin far worse.

For a man to steal people's money is one thing; however, to fraudulently take it away from them by claiming that if they give so much, God will give so much in return, makes God a part of the lie and is, therefore, much more evil. While God surely does bless those who give to His work, still, if that is the only reason for our giving, it is actually no longer giving, but rather a bad investment or a gamble.

THE PHARISEES MADE FUN OF JESUS

The phrase, *"They derided Him,"* means they sneered at Him, actually making fun of Him.

The Pharisees murmured at Him in their character as the elder brother (15:25-32), and in their character as the rich man (Vss. 19-31), they derided Him.

Israel had come to believe that riches equaled godliness, and poverty equaled the curse of God; consequently, a person who was rich, as were many of the Pharisees, was automatically labeled as godly. So, that which Jesus said about money completely burst their theological balloon. The doctrine of the modern greed message is pretty much the same, claiming that if a person

doesn't have a lot of money, he has no faith.

Regarding the deriding by the Pharisees, Spence says, "It is all very well," they would say, "for one springing from the ranks of the people, landless, moneyless, to rail at wealth and the possessors of wealth; we can understand such teaching from one such as you."

(15) "AND HE SAID UNTO THEM, YOU ARE THEY WHICH JUSTIFY YOURSELVES BEFORE MEN; BUT GOD KNOWS YOUR HEARTS: FOR THAT WHICH IS HIGHLY ESTEEMED AMONG MEN IS ABOMINATION IN THE SIGHT OF GOD."

HUMAN JUSTIFICATION

The phrase, *"And He said unto them, You are they which justify yourselves before men,"* characterizes much of the modern church as well!

In fact, the Pharisees exerted great influence upon the people, which generated great respect for them, because of their strict and religious lives. In other words, they had an impeccable reputation throughout Israel. This was because they did everything to be seen of men and to be thought highly of them. They gained the respect of Israel because most people based their beliefs on what they could see outwardly. Most of the time, as here, it is totally wrong.

As is obvious, Jesus was extremely hard on these individuals, even calling them hypocrites. This is the worst thing anyone could be labeled, even though their hypocrisy was probably in many cases an unconscious hypocrisy.

Hypocrisy is always the result of self-righteousness even though the individual, as the Pharisees, very little recognizes it as such.

So, the people probably little understood Jesus' opposition to the most powerful religious group in Israel. Actually, had His ministry not been accompanied by the greatest miracles the world had ever known, He would have been dismissed outright as little more than a crank. It is little different presently.

HYPOCRISY

Many, if not most of the religious heads of major denominations, or even in independent circles, fall into the same category, with the people, as Israel of old, little knowing at all of this deep hypocrisy and ungodliness.

To be frank, there is little record that the people actually believed Jesus regarding the Pharisees even though His statements were bold, to the point, and very public. If they did not believe Christ, it is little likely that they will believe His true prophets, at least what few there truly are in these modern times.

Most of the religious leadership of modern times seek to justify themselves before men. They do this in two ways:

1. They set out to please men instead of God and, therefore, conduct themselves accordingly. Very few preachers will stand up for what they know to be right, especially if it means bucking the system.

2. Their messages are trimmed in order that they never oppose popular opinion. In other words, their messages are little given by the Spirit, if at all, but are rather political. In a spiritual sense, they hold up their fingers to see which way the wind is blowing and trim their sails accordingly. They will very seldom, if ever, say anything that is unpopular. They will not oppose false doctrine, and they will be quick to label anyone as a destroyer of unity who stands up for the Bible and what it teaches.

Even though the Pharisees despised most of the people, especially those referred to as the "unwashed masses," still, they sought to appear very religious before them, which they were successful in doing.

Likewise, modern professors of religion little care for people, but rather their denomination or group, and their place and position in it.

GOD KNOWS THE HEART

The phrase, *"But God knows your hearts,"* signifies what is all important.

All other matters not at all. Naturally, it is desirable to have others think well of us; still, whether they do or don't really doesn't matter that much. It's what God knows that really counts and, in fact, is the only thing that counts. If the whole world is shouting my praises, and God says "No," their praises will amount to little, if anything. Conversely, if all the world hates me, and God

NOTES

says otherwise, while I may be grieved at their response, still, in the long run, it will have little effect on me personally, although it definitely could have a negative effect on the work of God in general.

One day every believer will stand before Christ to give account. Then it really will not matter what others thought but only what He knows.

ABOMINATION IN THE SIGHT OF GOD

The phrase, *"For that which is highly esteemed among men is abomination in the sight of God,"* presents a startling statement!

The idea is that men, even religious men, are so ungodly that whatever is esteemed highly by a great number is usually an abomination in the sight of God.

This means that while a godly ministry may have the plaudits of the crowd for awhile, the plaudits will soon be lost, that is, if the Word of God continues to be obeyed by that particular ministry. This was true with John the Baptist and even with Christ.

That which is not of God, Satan does not oppose. That which is of God is greatly opposed by the Evil One; consequently, inasmuch as most believers do not know their Bibles, they will soon lose interest and go after that which is more popular. Thankfully, a few do not follow the crowd, but most do!

One can pretty much observe that whoever is popular with the church is seldom popular with God. Conversely, if the individual is truly touched by God, he or she is seldom popular with the church.

One must ever know that it is the sight of God that really matters and not that of man.

(16) "THE LAW AND THE PROPHETS WERE UNTIL JOHN: SINCE THAT TIME THE KINGDOM OF GOD IS PREACHED, AND EVERY MAN PRESSES INTO IT."

The overview is:

1. The phrase, *"The law and the prophets were until John,"* actually meant, "As far as John," which included that prophet. In other words, John ministered under the law, but as the last prophet of that era.

2. *"Since that time the kingdom of God is preached, and every man presses into it,"* proclaims the new covenant and its differences. They are as follows:

a. The new covenant began with Jesus, *"For the law was given by Moses, but grace and truth came by Jesus Christ"* (Jn. 1:17).

b. The law was strictly for Israel, with all Gentiles who came in forced, in effect, to become a proselyte Jew. Conversely, the new covenant opened the door to all, with *"every man pressing into it."*

c. The kingdom of God is obtained by being born again and is done by faith, and we are speaking of faith in Christ and the Cross. It does not involve the law, which was actually fulfilled by Christ and abolished because it had fulfilled its task (Jn. 3:3; Col. 2:14-17).

(17) "AND IT IS EASIER FOR HEAVEN AND EARTH TO PASS, THAN ONE TITTLE OF THE LAW TO FAIL."

THE LAW

By making the statement He made, Jesus was not saying that the law would fail, but rather that it would be fulfilled, even down to the smallest *"tittle."* Actually, He would fulfill the law in every capacity and, in fact, would be the only one who ever did. The Pharisees, even though they loudly trumpeted their religion, did not keep the law at all. The next verse will give us one way that they broke it constantly.

WHY WAS THE LAW OF MOSES GIVEN?

• The law of Moses, given to Moses by God, was the only law on the face of the earth given by God. There were many other laws that were man-made, but they were totally unfair, inequitable, and contained precious little justice. Above all, all of those man-made laws left God out of the equation.

• God's law was the only law in the world that told man how to live in every capacity. It was totally just, fair, equal, and showing no partiality. It addressed itself to every facet of man's life, even down to the smallest detail.

• In addition to showing man how to live, it also pointed to a coming Redeemer and made provision for salvation through the sacrifices, which pointed to the coming Christ.

The sacrifices could not save but only served as a symbol of the One who was to come, who could save and, in fact, did save, providing there was faith exhibited.

• The law within itself contained no

NOTES

salvation, but rather served as a schoolmaster to bring men to Christ. In other words, the law was given to man by God, at least in one respect, to show man that he was incapable of living up to this law, even though it was totally fair and impartial. It was meant to show man how incapable and weak he really was. As stated, no one except Jesus ever kept the law fully, not even Moses.

THE INADEQUACY OF MAN

Men were supposed to see their inadequacy in attempting to keep the law and then throw themselves, consequently, on the mercy and grace of God. Unfortunately, Israel made a god out of the law, even as men make a god out of almost everything.

By the time of Christ, the Pharisees trumpeted loudly as to how perfect their law keeping actually was. They were experts at pointing fingers at others, even Jesus, claiming that He broke the law constantly, which meant He was not the Messiah.

In truth, Christ never broke the law at all, keeping it perfectly. He only broke the man-made laws, which had originated with the Pharisees and others. Regrettably, men are still making laws today in the church and love to point fingers at others who do not keep them.

(18) "WHOSOEVER PUTS AWAY HIS WIFE, AND MARRIES ANOTHER, COMMITS ADULTERY: AND WHOSOEVER MARRIES HER THAT IS PUT AWAY FROM HER HUSBAND COMMITS ADULTERY."

DIVORCE

It may seem strange and out of place that this verse is inserted here. The enemies of inspiration have even claimed that Verses 16 through 18 were not supposed to be here, but were introduced by some copyist, thus, they display their ignorance.

Jesus was addressing Himself to the Pharisees who were deriding Him, in effect, claiming His teaching was wrong and opposed to the law of Moses, with them even claiming that they kept the law while He did not. This is found in Verse 15.

The argument is this:

The Pharisees justified themselves before men, but God read their hearts. They professed to admire the prophets while they painted their sepulchres white, therefore, claiming to be rigid observers of the law.

However, John was one of the prophets, actually the greatest of them. Under his ministry, all kinds of men heard his message gladly and pressed into the kingdom, with the Pharisees alone refusing to listen and repent.

As to the law, it commanded: *"You shall not covet,"* and *"you shall not commit adultery."* Both of these commandments, the Pharisees disobeyed, and this is the reason that Jesus here spoke of marriage, adultery, and divorce, because the Pharisees treated divorce lightly and were secretly covetous and immoral. This is why, when exposed to the Lord, they derided Him.

THE PHARISEES

Jesus was pointing out that it was useless for the Pharisees to hope to escape the judgment of the law, hence, His quoting Verse 17. Accordingly, the great Lawgiver Himself, who Jesus actually was, drew aside the veil that hides the abyss of eternal judgment, as we shall see in the balance of this chapter, and revealed the doom of the self-righteous and self-indulgent transgressor.

In the time of our Lord, the teaching of the rabbis on the question of marriage was exceedingly lax and tended toward grave immorality in the family life.

To be sure, when Herod Antipas unlawfully married Herodias, his brother's wife, no rabbi or doctor in Israel but one raised his voice in indignant protest, and that one was the friend in connection with Jesus of Nazareth, the prophet John the Baptist.

Divorce for the most trivial causes was sanctioned by the rabbis and even such men as Hillel, the grandfather of Gamaliel. Tradition speaks of him as the rabbi whose lectures were listened to by the boy Jesus. He taught that a man might divorce his wife even for the most trivial offenses, such as putting too much salt in the soup, that is, if he so desired.

In other words, if for whatever reason he did not like his wife, even for trivial offenses, he could use such as grounds for divorce.

The Pharisees, while trumpeting loudly

their keeping of the law, in effect, were not keeping it at all, even committing adultery.

So, Jesus showed up these hypocrites, and in the illustration given of the rich man and Lazarus, actually told them that they were going to hell.

(19) "THERE WAS A CERTAIN RICH MAN, WHO WAS CLOTHED IN PURPLE AND FINE LINEN, AND FARED SUMPTUOUSLY EVERY DAY."

The structure is:

1. Many have claimed this illustration to be a parable and, consequently, not to be taken literally; however, Jesus here gave the name of Lazarus, with such not occurring in any other parable. Consequently, this is not a parable but an illustration of an actual happening, and told exactly as it took place.

2. Without going into detail, the rich man described here was very rich and, therefore, concluded by the Pharisees to be godly, for they equated riches with godliness and poverty with the curse of God; consequently, this illustration would blow to pieces their erroneous hypothesis concerning their standard for righteousness.

3. As we have already stated, many in the modern greed gospel conclude that the rich man had great faith while Lazarus had none. The Bible says otherwise!

(20) "AND THERE WAS A CERTAIN BEGGAR NAMED LAZARUS, WHICH WAS LAID AT HIS GATE, FULL OF SORES."

The composition is:

1. As Jesus said, *"There was a certain rich man,"* He now said, *"There was a certain beggar named Lazarus."*

2. Men can claim that these men did not exist in reality if they so desire, while Jesus said they did, but they will answer to God in the judgment.

3. This we know about the two: the rich man refused to allow his riches to bring him to God, while the poor man did not allow his poverty to keep him from God.

4. Riches have a tendency to boost one's ego, while poverty has a tendency to do otherwise. Consequently, it's much more difficult to reach the rich man for God than it is the poor man.

5. The phrase, *"Which was laid at his gate, full of sores,"* proclaims this rich man

seeing Lazarus constantly but offering little or no help whatsoever.

6. As well, these two descriptions perfectly describe the Pharisees and their approach to the poor people of Israel. In fact, the poor were looked upon with disdain. It was claimed that they must not be pleasing God very well, hence, their poverty. So, at least in their thinking, if it was God's will for them to be in this condition, they would be abrogating the will of God by helping these poor, unfortunate souls. Consequently, the rich man could pass Lazarus each day, offer no help whatsoever, and suffer no twinge of conscious.

7. It is amazing how many men will twist the Scriptures to make them fit their own theology. Unfortunately, this is not the exception, but rather the rule!

(21) "AND DESIRING TO BE FED WITH THE CRUMBS WHICH FELL FROM THE RICH MAN'S TABLE: MOREOVER THE DOGS CAME AND LICKED HIS SORES."

The pattern is:

1. The phrase, *"And desiring to be fed with the crumbs which fell from the rich man's table,"* probably means that this rich man felt very good with himself in even allowing crumbs to be given to this beggar.

2. How so similar to the modern greed message, which, in actuality, is little faith at all. They look down upon those such as Lazarus, claiming that if they had the proper faith, they wouldn't be in that condition and are, consequently, dismissed exactly as the rich man dismissed Lazarus.

3. One particular church was brought to my attention, whose pastor would not allow people to put bumper stickers on their cars advertising the church unless the cars were of a certain late year and model.

4. I do not doubt that this stinks in the nostrils of God. My only thought is to how bad the stench actually is.

5. The phrase, *"Moreover the dogs came and licked his sores,"* proclaims that this man was not only poverty stricken, even down to the level of a beggar, but, as well, was sick. As stated, he would not fit the mold, as many modern, so-called faith Christians are described, but would definitely fit God's mold, enough, we might quickly add, to be praised by Christ for time and eternity.

So, I guess we have a choice! We can be lauded by the Pharisees or lauded by Christ; we cannot be lauded by both!

(22) "AND IT CAME TO PASS, THAT THE BEGGAR DIED, AND WAS CARRIED BY THE ANGELS INTO ABRAHAM'S BOSOM: THE RICH MAN ALSO DIED, AND WAS BURIED."

THE DEATH OF THE BEGGAR

The phrase, *"And it came to pass, that the beggar died,"* proclaims the conclusion of this mortal coil with all its pain, suffering, privation, and want—at least for this beggar, because he knew the Lord as his personal Saviour.

The phrase, *"And was carried by the angels into Abraham's bosom,"* proclaims several startling truths:

• The moment this believer closed his eyes in death, they were opened immediately in paradise.

• This tells us that regarding the saint of God, upon the death of the body, the soul and the spirit are carried or escorted by angels into heaven. What a wonderful and beautiful thought!

• At that time, all righteous souls went to paradise, which was in the heart of the earth, while now, due to the Cross, they go to heaven.

Until Jesus died on Calvary, thereby paying heaven's claims and redeeming man, and rose from the dead, all righteous souls were still held captive by Satan to a certain degree. Even though angels transported the soul and the spirit to paradise, in fact, it was next door to the place called hell and, in a sense, was even a part of hell, with only a great gulf separating the two.

Because of the Cross of Christ, which settled the terrible sin debt for humanity, at least for all who will believe, all of these souls were liberated by the Lord and taken to heaven, whereto all righteous now ascend upon death, and all because of the Cross (Eph. 4:8-10; Phil. 1:23).

THE RICH MAN ALSO DIED

The phrase, *"The rich man also died, and was buried,"* proclaims an entirely different story.

While, no doubt, a great funeral oration was held for him, while the body of Lazarus was probably thrown into a pauper's grave, still, irrespective of what was said or done on earth concerning the rich man, the moment he died, he opened his eyes in hell.

To be sure, every human being on earth faces either heaven or hell at death, according to one thing—their having accepted Jesus Christ as Lord and Saviour or having refused Him.

Many of the rich think they are saved because they give to some noble cause and charitable work; however, good works do not save anyone. Being a good citizen or even a church member effects no salvation. It is alone the acceptance of Christ and what He did at Calvary that effects one's eternal destiny (Jn. 3:3, 16).

AN ILLUSTRATION

As I dictate these words, we have just returned from Egypt where we saw the pyramids. These were built at tremendous expense in order to house the bodies of particular Pharaohs, which were to equip them, or so it was thought, for the afterlife. However, irrespective of the expense involved, and it was staggering to say the least, such had no effect whatsoever on the eternal souls and spirits of these individuals.

It is dreadful that the entirety of the human family speeds toward this eternal destiny with so few making preparations. Let it be known that first, second, and third opportunities are on this side of the grave. There is no such thing as a purgatory or another chance after death.

As well, there aren't two, four, or 10 ways to provide for this time but, in fact, only one. That one way is the Lord Jesus Christ. This means that Muhammad is not the way, or Joseph Smith, or any other false luminary. It is only Jesus! (Jn. 10:10).

It also means that every single person in this world is either on his way to heaven or hell. There is no other place or intermediate state, only heaven or hell!

(23) "AND IN HELL HE LIFTED UP HIS EYES, BEING IN TORMENTS, AND SEETH ABRAHAM AFAR OFF, AND LAZARUS IN HIS BOSOM."

NOTES

THE BIBLICAL DOCTRINE OF HELL

The phrase, "And in hell he lifted up his eyes," means that as he closed his eyes in death on earth, he opened them immediately in hell.

Hell is mentioned some 53 times in the Bible. It begins in Deuteronomy 32:22, "For a fire is kindled in My anger, and shall burn unto the lowest hell." It closes with Revelation 20:14, "And death and hell were cast into the lake of fire. This is the second death."

To not believe that there is a literal place called hell is to not believe the Bible. So, one has a choice. He can believe what the Bible says about this place, or he can disbelieve it; however, failing to believe what the Bible says about hell in no way negates the soul from going there upon death of the body.

Actually, almost all disbelieve the entirety of the Bible, or some part; however, unbelief does not delay the action or truth of its solemn statements. In fact, the Bible does not merely contain truth, it is truth (Jn. 17:17).

Some misguided preacher said that hell should not be mentioned because it frightens people. In that case, someone should have told Jesus because He illustrated the fact and horror of this place as no other. It would be far better for people to be frightened here than frightened there when it is too late.

ALL UNSAVED GO TO HELL IMMEDIATELY UPON DEATH

At physical death the soul and spirit leave the body (James 2:26). If one is saved by the blood of Jesus, his soul and spirit go to heaven immediately at death to await the resurrection of the body (Lk. 20:38; Jn. 11:25-26; II Cor. 5:8; Eph. 3:15; 4:8-10; Phil. 1:21-24; Heb. 12:22-23; Rev. 6:9-11).

If the person is unsaved, his soul and spirit immediately go to hell at death to await the resurrection of the body, which will take place immediately after the thousand year kingdom age (Isa. 14:9; Lk. 16:19-31; II Pet. 2:9; Rev. 20:11-15).

HELL IS LOCATED IN THE HEART OF THE EARTH

At His death on Calvary, Paul said that

Jesus *"descended first into the lower parts of the earth"* (Eph. 4:9). He did this to liberate those in paradise.

Jesus Himself said, *"So shall the Son of Man be three days and three nights in the heart of the earth,"* which spoke of going down into hell and not only liberating the righteous who were in paradise but, as well, preaching to the spirits (fallen angels) in prison (Mat. 12:40).

Once again, these are not idle fairy tales but an actual truth as stipulated by the Bible.

Could not God make such a place? Seeing that the soul and spirit are immortal (cannot physically die) and that matter proves no obstruction, would it not be logical for this place to be in the heart of the earth?

THERE ARE FIVE DEPARTMENTS IN THE UNDERWORLD OF DEPARTED SPIRITS

1. Tartarus (I Pet. 3:19; II Pet. 2:4; Jude 6-7): This prison is a special one for fallen angels who sinned before the flood. No human beings or demons ever go to this underworld prison.

2. Paradise (Lk. 16:19-31; 23:43): this was the abode of the righteous after physical death where they were held captive by Satan against their will until Christ conquered death, hell, and the grave.

This place is now empty of the righteous who go to heaven at death since Christ rescued the captives in paradise and took them to heaven with Him when He ascended on high.

3. Hell (Mat. 16:18; Lk. 16:19-31): this is the torment compartment of Sheol-Hades where wicked souls have always gone and will always go until the end of the millennium.

Then the wicked will be brought out of hell to be reunited with their resurrected and immortal bodies and then be cast into the lake of fire forever (Rev. 20:11-15).

4. The Abyss or bottomless pit (Lk. 8:26-31; Rom. 10:7; Rev. 9:1-3, 11; 11:7; 17:8; 20:1-10): This is the abode of demons and some fallen angelic beings. No human soul and spirit ever goes to the Abyss.

5. The lake of fire: This is the eternal hell and perdition of all fallen angels, demons, and wicked men (Rev. 20:6, 11-15; 21:8; 22:15).

NOTES

It is the final hell prepared for the devil and his angels (Mat. 25:41) and is eternal in duration (Isa. 66:22-24; Mat. 25:46; Rev. 14:9-14; 19:20; 20:10-15).

THE FIRE OF HELL IS LITERAL FIRE

The word *fire* is found in Scripture 542 times and is used figuratively only a few times. It is always clear when it is used figuratively, as of *"anger"* (Ps. 89:46), *"jealousy"* (Ps. 79:5), or *"zeal"* (Ps. 104:4; Jn. 2:17). All the other times it means a literal fire.

Some false cults claim that while hell is a real place, the soul will be immediately burned up. They derive this from a misinterpretation of Malachi 4:1. However, this passage in Malachi does not refer to hell at all, but to the battle of Armageddon when the fire will fall from heaven, devouring the bodies of the wicked and killing them (Ezek. 38:17-21; Zech. 14:1-15; II Thess. 1:7-10; Rev. 19:11-21).

Just a casual reading of Malachi will show that it refers to the second advent of Christ and not to hell. Actually, not one word is said about hell in Malachi.

There is no Scripture that teaches the annihilation of the soul and spirit in any capacity. All passages teach the soul is now immortal, and the body will also be immortal in the resurrection, whether saved or unsaved.

THE PUNISHMENT OF HELL IS ETERNAL

The Scripture speaks of eternal damnation (Mk. 3:29), eternal judgment (Heb. 6:2), everlasting fire (Mat. 18:8; 25:41), and everlasting punishment (Mat. 25:46).

In the book of Revelation, it tells that the wicked will be *"tormented day and night forever and ever"* (Rev. 20:10).

The same words translated "eternal, everlasting, and forever and ever," used to state the eternity of God, Christ, the Holy Spirit, life, etc., are also used of hell and punishment. Therefore, if these persons and things are eternal, then hell and punishment are eternal.

Some erroneously teach that *forever* means "age-long." This may be true when used in a limited and qualified sense of temporary things, as in Exodus 21:6, but when used literally of God's plan, it always means eternal, which is forever.

HELL IS NOT THE GRAVE
AS TAUGHT BY SOME

In Scripture, hell is never the place of the body, and the grave is never the place of the soul (Ps. 16:10; Acts 2:25-29).

Hell is a place of full consciousness (Isa. 14:9-15; Ezek. 32:27-31; Lk. 16:19-31), whereas the grave is not.

As well, hell is a place of conversations (Isa. 14:9-16; Ezek 32:21; Lk. 16:19-31), whereas the grave is not.

It is a place where men are conscious of life on earth but cannot visit earth to warn men of its real torments (Lk. 16:26-31), with, of course, nothing like this taking place in the grave.

Since the soul is immortal and the body mortal (Gen. 3:19l Eccl. 3:19-21), then it is clear that the body only goes into the grave to see corruption until its resurrection to immortality, when, if wicked, it will be punished in hell with the soul, or if righteous, it will be permitted to enjoy eternal bliss in heaven.

No, the grave is not hell, and even a simple investigation of Scripture will prove such.

SOUL SLEEP IS NOT
TAUGHT IN SCRIPTURE

Some cults teach that the soul and spirit sleep after death and, therefore, do not immediately go to heaven or hell, dependent on their spiritual state. Such is false!

All Scriptures used to teach soul sleep clearly refer to the body, which does sleep in the dust of the earth until the resurrection of the body (Dan. 12:2; Jn. 5:28-29). The body is the only part of man that dies at physical death (James 2:26). The reason it dies is because the inner man, the life of the body, leaves the body. It then goes back to dust and is spoken of as being asleep (Gen. 3:19; Eccl. 3:19-21; Mat. 9:24; Jn. 11:11; I Cor. 11:30; 15:6, 18, 20, 51; I Thess. 4:13-17).

THERE IS FULL
CONSCIOUSNESS IN HELL

This is amply illustrated to us by the minute detail that Jesus gave respecting the rich man in hell and the conversations conducted. It is obvious from this text in Luke, Chapter 16, that the memory is very sharp

NOTES

concerning past events on earth and opportunities wasted. The following are some sources of torment to the lost in the eternal regions of hell:

• Remorse and despair in seeing the righteous and godly, whom they have despised, now clothed in glory, immortality, eternal life, and all the bliss of God (Lk. 16:23).

• Abhorrence of the very evil that they know has damned their souls and put them in torment (Lk. 16:25).

• Eternal desire for the good that would have freed them from torment (Lk. 16:25).

• Memory of lost opportunities in life that could have caused them to be with the redeemed (Lk. 16:25).

• Regret over deeds committed, which can never be recalled (Lk. 16:25).

• Absolute hopelessness of escape from eternal misery or alleviation from the least degree of suffering (Lk. 16:26).

• Eternal separation from loved ones or from the redeemed whom they can see beyond an impassable gulf (Lk. 16:26). This was true concerning the impassable gulf when souls were in paradise, but is not true since the righteous souls were delivered by Jesus from that place. It is now empty. There is no scriptural evidence that lost souls can now see loved ones in heaven.

• Regret over their bad examples in life that have caused friends and loved ones to be damned (Lk. 16:27-31).

• Ever deepening remorse for not listening to the Word of God and for not spending their time, talents, and money to propagate the Word of God, so that many others could escape torment (Lk. 16:29-31).

• Last of all, the fire and brimstone, which they will suffer forever and forever (Isa. 66:22-24; Mat. 25:41, 46; Lk. 16:23-31; Rev. 14:9-11; 20:11-15; 21:8).

TORMENTS

The phrase, *"Being in torments,"* proclaims that which was true then continues to be true to the present, and will be true forever. Among all the awful things about hell, no doubt, the worst is that it will never end.

The Greek word for *"torments"* is *basanos,* which means "the state of grief, sorrow, and torment." If one is to notice, the word is plural, meaning many and varied types of torments.

"And seeth Abraham afar off, and Lazarus in his bosom," pertains to the abode, at that time, of both the righteous and unrighteous dead.

Paradise is referred to in Verse 22 as *"Abraham's bosom,"* and partially so in this verse.

Abraham was the first man to be given the full plan of God regarding the redemption process, and consequently, in a sense, every single believer, even under the new covenant, is a child of Abraham (Gen. 12:3; 15:6; Mat. 1:1).

However, men were saved before Abraham on the same principles of faith in Christ, even though their information was scant, such as Abel, Enoch, and Noah.

Of course, where righteous souls go to at present upon death is not referred to as Abraham's bosom.

Until Jesus died and rose from the dead, all righteous souls, as we have repeatedly stated, went to paradise upon death. This was located in the heart of the earth and was separated from the burning side called hell only by an impassable gulf. Consequently, it seems that people in hell could then look over into paradise and observe the bliss and protection afforded these dear saints. Thus did the rich man concerning Lazarus.

(24) "AND HE CRIED AND SAID, FATHER ABRAHAM, HAVE MERCY ON ME, AND SEND LAZARUS, THAT HE MAY DIP THE TIP OF HIS FINGER IN WATER, AND COOL MY TONGUE; FOR I AM TORMENTED IN THIS FLAME."

A CRY OF DESPAIR

The phrase, *"And he cried and said,"* speaks of a cry of pain, despair, and desperation.

No one ever spoke so clearly about hell as the Lord Jesus, and yet, men in high positions in the church are not afraid to say that His statements about it are untrue. God help us!

"Father Abraham, have mercy on me," proclaims a petition, which, no doubt, has come from the voices of everyone who has gone to this horrible place, and sadly, most have! However, all such petitions for mercy

can be granted only on this side of the grave and, in fact, will be granted readily to anyone who cries to the Lord. However, as stated, all second, third, etc. opportunities are on this side of the grave. After death, the opportunities for salvation are ended.

From these passages, we know and understand that the inner man, made up of the soul and the spirit, which cannot die, has the same consciousness, understanding, and even appearance as the outer man. This is proven by the appearance of Moses and Elijah to Christ and the disciples on the Mount of Transfiguration (Lk. 9:27-36).

LITERAL PAIN

The phrase, *"And send Lazarus, that he may dip the tip of his finger in water, and cool my tongue,"* proclaims the hurting of his conscious, as well as the literal pain.

Lazarus sat at his gate for quite some time, with the rich man seeing him on a daily basis, no doubt, and doing nothing for him. Now his conscience hurt greatly, so he would ask for Lazarus.

The phrase, *"For I am tormented in this flame,"* proclaims the literalness of the fire along with the unending torment it brings, as well as other torments of lost opportunities.

This tells us, as well, that the soul and spirit are indestructible. In other words, they never die.

Many misunderstand the Scripture, *"The soul that sins, it shall die,"* as referring to physical death (Ezek. 18:20). However, the death spoken of here pertains to spiritual death, which is separation from God and not physical death. As stated, the soul and spirit cannot die.

At the resurrection of the unjust, which will take place about a thousand years after the resurrection of the just, an indestructible body will be given to the unjust, which, as well, cannot be destroyed. It is called the second death (Rev. 20:4-6, 11-15).

(25) "BUT ABRAHAM SAID, SON, REMEMBER THAT YOU IN YOUR LIFETIME RECEIVED YOUR GOOD THINGS, AND LIKEWISE LAZARUS EVIL THINGS: BUT NOW HE IS COMFORTED, AND YOU ARE TORMENTED."

The synopsis is:

1. The only way that a person can escape hell is by accepting Jesus Christ and what He did for us at the Cross.

2. Jesus Christ is the way, the truth, and the life (Jn. 14:6).

3. Upon simple faith in Christ, salvation is instantly given to the believing sinner (Jn. 3:16).

ABRAHAM

The phrase, *"But Abraham said,"* refers, as is obvious, to consciousness after death with the ability to converse, etc. Actually, not a lot has changed about the individual, with the exception of location. This is what Jesus was speaking of when He said to the Sadducees, who claimed there was no resurrection, *"God is not the God of the dead, but of the living"* (Mat. 22:32). He meant that people do not pass out of existence when they die, but actually continue to live, but in another state.

Understanding this, every person should surely understand the seriousness of this life lived without God. At death, it is all over, at least respecting opportunities to be saved. However, at death, respecting eternity, it has just begun and will never end, whether in heaven or hell. It is a sober thought!

REMEMBER

The phrase, *"Son, remember that you in your lifetime received your good things,"* in no way means that this was the cause of him being lost. It merely means that he was treated very well but showed no thankfulness for his blessings and ignored others, as Lazarus, who he could have helped but did not.

It should be noticed that this man's record was not one of vice, crime, or folly, and neither had he been a monster of wickedness, but rather a Jew who, no doubt, thought he was right with God and probably was very religious. However, his lack of compassion for the less fortunate showed that he really had no true walk with God and, consequently, died lost. More than likely, this man would have been a welcome member of most modern churches, but, in fact, he had never been born again and, thereby, died eternally lost.

On the other hand, even if he had been generous with his money, this in no way would have purchased him salvation. All of these good things are a result of salvation and not the cause. Unfortunately, many think that such generosity procures salvation. It does not!

FAITH

One is saved by faith, which means to trust Christ, having faith in what He did at Calvary (Jn. 3:3, 16). To be sure, one may have very little understanding of what the Lord actually did at Calvary upon coming to Christ. However, as the Holy Spirit moves upon the heart, bringing conviction, if the person will only yield according to what little faith he has, salvation will instantly be afforded, irrespective of what the individual has done in the past.

Abraham was just merely letting the man know that irrespective of what he claimed in the spiritual sense, there were no tangible results of any salvation, for, in fact, there was no salvation.

LAZARUS

"And likewise Lazarus evil things," proclaims in stark clarity that which the rich man knew to be true.

There is no way that a man can truly be saved and pass someone daily, as Lazarus, seeing him in his condition, and offer no help whatsoever! I wonder if this extends to professing believers, who seem to have no concern whatsoever for the lost, and will do little, if anything, to help take the gospel to these poor lost souls.

If we are to take this literally, as Jesus gave it, I think it would give us pause for reflection. Multiple millions are in the state of Lazarus, with only one great difference: They do not know Christ as Lazarus knew Christ. Consequently, they are not only suffering terrible despair, but above all, they are spiritually lost without God. Of course, God is the final judge; however, this illustration, as given by Christ, means that quite a number of people who claim to be saved really have no fruit whatsoever to back up their claims. I think the record is clear that many professors, who do not actually possess, will be eternally lost.

COMFORT AND TORMENT

The phrase, *"But now he is comforted, and you are tormented,"* proclaims the tables as having now turned.

The word *now* is that which is all-important. It speaks of the time after death. What will the status of the reader be at that time? Will it be one of comfort or torment?

In fact, and sadly so, most of the rich people of the world will come to a terrible conclusion exactly as this rich man of Jesus' story. As well, and thankfully so, many of the poor and dispossessed of this world, because they have made Jesus their eternal Saviour, will have the privilege of living with Him forever and forever and experiencing the comfort that only He can bring.

The lesson should be learned well from this illustration that in comparison to eternity, this life is very short. Whatever our status presently respecting riches, fame, power, and popularity are of no consequence after death. The only thing, and I mean the only thing that really matters, is our knowledge and acceptance of the Lord Jesus Christ as our Lord and Saviour.

What good did this man's money do him at this time? What good did all the beautiful and nice things he possessed do him now? The truth is, none at all! The one thing he needed, he did not have, and that was salvation.

Men die, even important men, and their obituaries attempt to spell out their achievements on earth; however, irrespective of the flowing prose, it is always exactly as a certain billionaire who died. One man asked how much he left. The other answered and said, "He left it all!" The only thing that one can take with him into eternity is his faith in God. We must never forget that.

Lazarus had nothing on earth, as is obvious, except one thing, and that was the one thing that really mattered—the Lord Jesus Christ. And beautifully so, that was the only coin that was spendable at the bank of heaven. It was all he needed!

(26) "AND BESIDE ALL THIS, BETWEEN US AND YOU THERE IS A GREAT GULF FIXED: SO THAT THEY WHICH WOULD PASS FROM HENCE TO YOU CANNOT; NEITHER CAN THEY PASS TO US, THAT WHICH WOULD COME FROM THENCE."

The exegesis is:

1. The phrase, *"And beside all this, between us and you there is a great gulf fixed,"* spoke of that which existed at the time. Paradise was then separated from the burning side of hell by this impassable gulf. As we have stated, since the resurrection of Christ, the paradise side is empty, with all righteous souls now being taken immediately to heaven upon death of the body.

2. *"So that they which would pass from hence to you* (pass from us to you) *cannot; neither can they pass to us,"* proclaims, whether then or now, that all opportunities for salvation are on this side of the grave. The fool's hope of the Catholic doctrine of purgatory, which actually does not even exist, is just that, a fool's hope.

3. As well, the heathenistic doctrine of reincarnation is another fool's hope that does not exist.

4. Man is created by God as an eternal soul and, as such, will never die, spending an eternity in either heaven or hell according to the acceptance or rejection of Christ. It is just that simple!

5. This present life is the probationary time, and when it ends, either earlier or later, there is no more opportunity for salvation. That is the reason the Holy Spirit constantly moves upon the individual respecting his soul's salvation, at least those to whom the gospel is preached. Consequently, it is the task of the church, even the most important thing in the eyes of God, that every individual upon the face of the earth have an opportunity to either accept Christ or reject Christ. In fact, the Holy Spirit places great stock in each individual having an opportunity whether they accept or not.

(27) "THEN HE SAID, I PRAY THEE THEREFORE, FATHER, THAT YOU WOULD SEND HIM TO MY FATHER'S HOUSE."

The composition is:

1. The phrase, *"Then he said, I pray thee* (you) *therefore, father,"* proclaims that before he died, he had a working knowledge of God and, more than likely, even professed

salvation. His terminology proclaims that. And yet, one of the great truths among men, brought out in this illustration by Jesus, is the fact that true salvation will result in a certain lifestyle. Part of that lifestyle will certainly concern compassion for others, which this man did not have, even though provided an excellent opportunity regarding Lazarus.

2. As well, it should be understood that this is the only example of praying to a dead saint in Scripture. Let those who do so remember that prayer to all others will avail just as much as this prayer did—nothing.

3. *"That you would send him to my father's house,"* concerns the earnest regard that people in hell have respecting their loved ones on earth who do not know God. In other words, they don't want them to come where they are.

(28) "FOR I HAVE FIVE BRETHREN; THAT HE MAY TESTIFY UNTO THEM, LEST THEY ALSO COME INTO THIS PLACE OF TORMENT."

The form is:

1. The phrase, *"For I have five brethren* (brothers),*"* proclaims a concern for their souls' salvation now but, regrettably, had no concern when he was on earth. Everything else demanded his time with, it seems, making money the chief priority. Things of God were seldom regarded, if at all.

2. Such describes almost all of the human family. For one thing that really counts, the eternal destiny of the soul, most have no regard or concern. One communications baron made the statement a short time ago, "I want to go to hell because that's where all the fun is going to be."

3. Despite his ability to make large sums of money, the man, in the eyes of God and all who know Christ, is a fool. To be sure, there will be no fun in hell, only torment.

4. *"That he may testify unto them,"* now proclaims the only thing that really matters, but sadly and regrettably, it is too late!

5. If one is to notice, he had no interest in Lazarus telling his brothers how to make more money, or to do a host of other things. Only one thing was of prime significance, and that was, as stated, their souls' salvation.

6. *"Lest they also come into this place of torment,"* concerns the burden every

person in hell has, which the church presently should have. Regrettably, it seems that it little does!

7. Hell is a place of torment, not a state or a condition of life.

(29) "ABRAHAM SAID UNTO HIM, THEY HAVE MOSES AND THE PROPHETS; LET THEM HEAR THEM."

The pattern is:

1. As Abraham answered the rich man, such represents God's answer to all of mankind and for all time.

2. This statement, *"They have Moses and the prophets,"* did not mean that this event happened during the time of Moses, but that Abraham is referring to the Word of God.

3. The Bible is God's revelation to man. As such, it contains everything that needs to be known and understood concerning God's plan for man.

4. There are no unbelievers in hell, and neither is there any salvation there. The rich man repented, but it was too late. His concern that his brothers would perish shows effectually how his conscience was aroused, but he remained a prisoner in that dread dungeon.

5. Many believe in salvation after death. The Lord Jesus destroys that doctrine here. There is no salvation in the lower world if the testimony of the Scriptures to the conscience be rejected in this present world.

6. The Scriptures contain all that is necessary for salvation.

(30) "AND HE SAID, NAY, FATHER ABRAHAM: BUT IF ONE WENT UNTO THEM FROM THE DEAD, THEY WILL REPENT."

The overview is:

1. In this Scripture, we see in glaring detail just how much concern is registered in hell over the lost condition of loved ones on earth.

2. His thinking was, as most, that surely such a spectacle as one coming from the dead would cause men to repent; however, unbelief will accept no proof, irrespective of its source. To be frank, other than the Bible, there are all types of proof respecting the claims of Christ. It is obvious in changed lives, as well as answered prayer; however, men do not see because they refuse to see.

NOTES

3. In fact, just days from this particular time, another Lazarus did come back from the dead and did so by the power of Christ. Though some true, faithful hearts welcomed the mighty sign with joy, still, it did not serve to touch the cold and calculating spirit of the Pharisees, scribes, and Sadducees. They were thirsting for the blood of the Master, whom they feared and hated, and whose word had summoned the dead back into their midst.

4. The mighty wonder wrought no change there. One went unto them from the dead, and yet, their hard hearts only took counsel together how they might put Lazarus to death again.

(31) "AND HE SAID UNTO HIM, IF THEY HEAR NOT MOSES AND THE PROPHETS, NEITHER WILL THEY BE PERSUADED, THOUGH ONE ROSE FROM THE DEAD."

The composition is:

1. Abraham was saying to him, as stated, that the Scriptures contain all that is necessary for salvation. A returned spirit could add nothing to them, and a man who will not listen to the Bible will not listen to a multitude if raised from the dead.

2. To further prove the point, Christ has been raised from the dead with irrefutable proof to substantiate that happening, and still, men are not persuaded about the reality of hell and life after death.

3. This illustration as given by Jesus, concerning eternity and man's place in it, certainly represents the most clear-cut teaching found in the Bible, and it is so simple that a child can understand it. There is no reason for anyone to misunderstand what He said.

4. As well, we are not to draw the inference that riches equate to ungodliness and poverty to godliness. This just happened to be the case respecting these two individuals. In truth, Abraham had been very wealthy, possibly to a far greater extent than this particular rich man, and yet, he was one of the godliest men who ever lived.

5. We also learn from this example as given by Christ that riches do not equate to salvation as then thought by the Jews, and neither does poverty equate to being lost as believed by them also. As well, the state of each does not point to faith or the lack of it, for the rich man had no faith at all, although rich, and Lazarus had great faith, although extremely poor.

6. We also learn in glaring, stark reality that the only thing that really matters in life is being right with God. All else, no matter how seemingly important, is of little consequence.

"Amazing grace how sweet the sound,
"That saved a wretch like me!
"I once was lost, but now am found,
"Was blind, but now I see."

CHAPTER 17

(1) "THEN SAID HE UNTO THE DISCIPLES, IT IS IMPOSSIBLE BUT THAT OFFENSES WILL COME: BUT WOE UNTO HIM, THROUGH WHOM THEY COME!"

THE WORD OF JESUS CHRIST

The phrase, *"Then said He unto the disciples,"* represents the teaching here given by Christ as immediately following the illustration given concerning the rich man in hell.

Some have claimed that Chapter 17 has no proper chronological order and was just placed here by Luke, and represented things said and done by Christ at another time. However, a proper division of the Word proclaims that the happenings of Chapter 17 are in chronological order.

OFFENSE

The phrase, *"It is impossible but that offenses will come,"* refers to the fact of the opposition against the child of God and from whom it will mostly come.

Paul said the following concerning offenses: *"And I, brethren, if I yet preach circumcision, why do I yet suffer persecution? then is the offense of the Cross ceased"* (Gal. 5:11).

This comes in two ways.

First of all, there is an animosity in the world against the Lord Jesus Christ and all who follow Him. Why?

One man said the other day over worldwide news, "Islam is the most intolerant religion on the face of the earth, while Christianity is the most tolerant."

What made this so startling was that this man is a liberal, but he has enough knowledge to see that which is obvious, which many do not seem to be able to see, especially those in our government.

Why this animosity against the Lord Jesus Christ? What has He done to hurt anyone? The truth is, He has never hurt anyone but has given life to untold millions. So, why the animosity?

The animosity is there because of the fall in the garden of Eden. Jesus Christ is real. God the Father is real. In other words, it's not some made-up figment of one's imagination. Unfortunately, due to the fall, every human being, unless born again, carries within himself or herself the seed of rebellion against God, which fosters hatred against the Lord Jesus Christ. In fact, they don't even understand it themselves.

I remember hearing a woman over television, who is the host of a particular program (she is an open lesbian), as she began a tirade against Christianity. She was stating how evil and wicked Christianity is and how wonderful that Islam is.

I wondered if the dear lady understood that she would be summarily executed for being a lesbian if she lived in any country ruled and controlled by the religion of Islam. No, because of the fall, this hatred and animosity is there against the Lord Jesus Christ and all who follow Him.

THE CROSS

Second, as it regards the church itself, there is an animosity in all religion against Jesus Christ and the Cross. Why?

Faith in anything other than the Cross of Christ always brings glory to the individual and none at all to the Lord. Besides that, it doesn't help one iota. Faith in Christ and the Cross, in other words, what He did for us at the Cross, brings glory totally and completely to the Lord and none at all to man. Religious man doesn't like that. So, if we preach the Cross as we should, there is going to be animosity that arises against us coming from the direction of the church per se.

Paul's greatest adversaries in the early

church were that segment of the church that desired to add law to grace, hence, opposing Paul at every turn. To be sure, it has not changed even unto this hour.

(2) "IT WERE BETTER FOR HIM THAT A MILLSTONE WERE HANGED ABOUT HIS NECK, AND HE CAST INTO THE SEA, THAN THAT HE SHOULD OFFEND ONE OF THESE LITTLE ONES."

The exegesis is:

1. The phrase, *"It were better for him that a millstone were hanged about his neck,"* respects that which the Lord thinks of such and the judgment He will ultimately bring upon these offenders, whomever they might be.

2. No Christian can oppose the Cross without suffering the judgment of God.

3. The Cross of Christ is God's prescribed order of life and living, and there is no other. To oppose that in any capacity is to oppose the plan of God for the entirety of the human race, whether salvation or sanctification.

4. *"And he cast into the sea,"* means this would be a lesser doom than to be cast into the lake of fire and suffer its torments and companionship with the rich man, whom Jesus had just mentioned. Barring repentance, this will actually be the eternal destination.

5. The phrase, *"Than that he should offend one of these little ones,"* says three things:

a. God constantly watches over His children and notes each and every offense.

b. He takes every offense very seriously, carefully noting the offender.

c. The little ones mentioned here have nothing to do with children, but rather believers who are clothed with humility, consequently, allowing the Lord to defend them. They are little in their own eyes and judged to be the same by the offenders, but they are held very dear by the Lord and watched over minutely by Him.

(3) "TAKE HEED TO YOURSELVES: IF YOUR BROTHER TRESPASS AGAINST YOU, REBUKE HIM; AND IF HE REPENT, FORGIVE HIM."

The composition is:

1. The phrase, *"Take heed to yourselves,"* is spoken directly to the disciples.

2. They were not to think that the Pharisees were the only ones who could commit

NOTES

sin, but they were to take special care that they did not fall into the same spirit. Consequently, this is a warning given to all believers, and for all time.

3. *"If your brother trespass against you, rebuke him,"* has to do with Matthew 18:15-17.

4. This tells us that the offended party should first go to the individual who has committed the wrong and attempt to satisfy the situation.

5. If that fails, the offended party is to take one or two witnesses with him and go again to the offender and attempt to assuage the situation.

6. If that fails, it is to be taken to the leaders of the local church.

7. If the situation is still not brought to a satisfactory conclusion, the offended party must withdraw all fellowship from the offender but continue to pray for him. In the future, if he actually does repent, he is to be instantly forgiven and fellowship restored respecting the two parties.

8. The phrase, *"And if he repent, forgive him,"* is simple and needs very little explanation. If the person truly repents, we are to truly forgive, and that means with the same type of forgiveness extended to us by the Lord. In other words, the offense is to be put behind us and not brought up anymore. We are to look at the offender as though he never committed any type of offense. The Lord conducts Himself toward us in this manner; consequently, He demands the same of us toward others.

(4) "AND IF HE TRESPASS AGAINST YOU SEVEN TIMES IN A DAY, AND SEVEN TIMES IN A DAY TURN AGAIN TO YOU, SAYING, I REPENT; YOU SHALL FORGIVE HIM."

The diagram is:

1. In Verse 3, the Lord warned His disciples not to think only of the sins of the Pharisees but of their own, as well, especially the sin of an unforgiving spirit.

2. A repentant brother was to be forgiven seven times in a day. When Peter asked Him on another occasion if he were to stop at seven times (Mat. 18:21), Jesus said *"Not ... Until seventy times seven,"* i.e., 490 times. It actually means endless forgiving.

3. Once again, the Lord calls upon us

to do the same to others as He does for us. Furthermore, how can we expect the Lord to forgive us, as He must do many times, if we have an unforgiving spirit toward others? Consequently, these are very serious admonitions and should be taken very seriously, as should be obvious!

4. So, here, Jesus told them—the future teachers of His church—how they must act. While ever the bold, untiring, and fearless rebukers of all vice and of every phase of selfishness, at the same time, they were never to be tired of exercising forgiveness the moment the offender was sorry. The repentant sinner was to never be repelled by them.

5. Even if the person does not repent, the offended party should forgive that person in his heart even though there can be no fellowship. It must be remembered that Joseph, who was a type of Christ, did not run and embrace his brothers when he first saw them as they came into Egypt to buy grain. He recognized them even though they did not recognize him. Before fellowship could be restored, he had to make certain that these were changed men, and thank God, they were.

(5) "AND THE APOSTLES SAID UNTO THE LORD, INCREASE OUR FAITH."

The overview is:

1. This request to *"increase our faith"* was probably asked on the premise of what He had just told them to do regarding repentance and forgiveness. In their minds, they, no doubt, wondered if they were equal to such a task. In fact, they were not, and neither are we.

2. And yet, the Lord will give grace to the humble in order that we may be able to perform this excellent and beautiful attribute (James 4:6).

3. So, the apostles asked for great faith in the realm of forgiving others, despite their offenses, instead of great faith for healing the sick, etc. What a lesson for us!

(6) "AND THE LORD SAID, IF YOU HAD FAITH AS A GRAIN OF MUSTARD SEED, YOU MIGHT SAY UNTO THIS SYCAMINE TREE, BE THOU PLUCKED UP BY THE ROOT, AND BE THOU PLANTED IN THE SEA; AND IT SHOULD OBEY YOU."

The exposition is:

1. The phrase, *"And the Lord said, If you had faith as a grain of mustard seed,"* proclaims small, but yet, real faith, and would produce the powers sufficient to accomplish what seemed to them impossible. According to Spence, He says, "If you have any real faith at all, you will be able to win the victory over yourselves necessary for a perpetual loving judgment of others."

2. *"You might say unto this sycamine tree, Be thou plucked up by the root,* concerns a formidable task, but one which an unforgiving spirit will grow into if not plucked up.

3. *"And be thou planted in the sea,"* concerns us throwing the offenses of others into the sea, symbolically speaking, at least upon proper repentance, exactly as Jesus does with our sins (Mic. 7:19). Once again, what He did for us, we are expected to do for others.

4. *"And it should obey you,"* means that if one believes God for the faith to carry out the type of Christlike life demanded, the Lord will see to it that our human nature has the strength, as well, to carry out the task.

5. Consequently, the searching doctrine of Verses 1 through 4 made the apostles conscious that something higher than fallen human nature alone could obey such teaching.

6. The Lord replied that faith was a power so real that its smallest provision could remove the greatest moral obstacles.

7. Once again allow us to mention that Jesus called for the greatest faith to be exercised respecting our heart condition toward Him and others. If we do not properly forgive, at the same time, we cannot be forgiven; consequently, He was addressing Himself to the most important aspect of the Christian experience. If we fail in this, we fail in everything. Conversely, if we succeed in this, by the help of the Lord I might quickly add, everything else will fall into place.

(7) "BUT WHICH OF YOU, HAVING A SERVANT PLOWING OR FEEDING CATTLE, WILL SAY UNTO HIM BY AND BY, WHEN HE IS COME FROM THE FIELD, GO AND SIT DOWN TO MEAT?

(8) "AND WILL NOT RATHER SAY UNTO HIM, MAKE READY WHEREWITH I MAY SUP, AND GIRD YOURSELF, AND

SERVE ME, TILL I HAVE EATEN AND DRANK; AND AFTERWARD YOU SHALL EAT AND DRINK?"

The exegesis is:

1. The Lord would now proceed to teach the disciples, and all others of His followers, a very valuable lesson. He spoke of duty, and as was His custom, he used a short story to illustrate this all-important truth.

2. He used the illustration of an ordinary servant who is hired to do particular things.

3. His tasks are to work in the fields, feeding cattle, and, as well, to help serve the table.

4. The essence of the story is that the servant serves his master first and himself last. I'm afraid that the modern greed message is the very opposite of what Jesus was here teaching.

5. For Christianity and the promises of God to be used in order to make men financially rich is a perversion of the gospel and a total denial of this which Jesus spoke. This is actually what Jesus was warning against (I Tim. 6:3-11).

6. While the Lord definitely does bless His people, and blesses abundantly, that is to never be the motive for service.

7. The believer is to give his life for the cause of Christ because the Lord has done so much for us in redeeming us and giving us eternal life. Consequently, if we give our very lives, we will only be doing our duty and will merit nothing extra, even though the Lord, in His grace and mercy, may well bless us with extra things, which He always does.

(9) "DOES HE THANK THAT SERVANT BECAUSE HE DID THE THINGS THAT WERE COMMANDED HIM? I THINK NOT."

The exposition is:

1. The question, *"Does he thank that servant because he does the things that were commanded him?"* plainly tells us that no extra blessing is promised for the doing of our duty and living for God.

2. Actually, the blessing of salvation coupled with the leading of the Holy Spirit produces untold blessings within themselves. In other words, the performing of our duty to God, which we know we must perform, within itself is a blessing of unparalleled proportions, that is, if we properly understand who we are and who He is.

3. The entire scenario speaks of humility and a proper evaluation of oneself.

(10) "SO LIKEWISE, WHEN YOU SHALL HAVE DONE ALL THOSE THINGS WHICH ARE COMMANDED YOU, SAY, WE ARE UNPROFITABLE SERVANTS: WE HAVE DONE THAT WHICH WAS OUR DUTY TO DO."

The structure is:

1. The phrase, *"So likewise, when you shall have done all those things which are commanded you,"* proclaims things such as faithfulness, consecration, dedication, zeal, love, prayer, study of the Word of God, and any task He requires of us.

2. *"Say, We are unprofitable servants: we have done that which was our duty to do,"* strikes a fatal blow to the doctrine of salvation by works.

3. Jesus was forewarning the apostles against flattering themselves by thinking that they would be entitled to admiration if they lived without injuring others, if they practiced perpetual forgiveness, and if they worked wonderful miracles. He now added that having fulfilled all of these conditions, they would be no better than unprofitable servants. That is, they would in no way have benefited their Master but actually themselves.

4. So, the attitude of the believer is to be, "I am an unprofitable servant," to which the Master will respond, *"Well done, thou* (you) *good and faithful servant"* (Mat. 25:21).

5. This probably ties in with the salvation afforded the woman in the house of Simon the Pharisee. Jesus said, *"Her sins, which are many, are forgiven; for she loved much: but to whom little is forgiven, the same loves little"* (Lk. 7:47).

(11) "AND IT CAME TO PASS, AS HE WENT TO JERUSALEM, THAT HE PASSED THROUGH THE MIDST OF SAMARIA AND GALILEE."

The construction is:

1. The phrase, *"And it came to pass, as He went to Jerusalem,"* proclaims the conclusion of an event that began in the mind of God before there was ever a world (I Pet. 1:19-20). It would conclude at Calvary and the resurrection, which would effect the redemption of mankind. This was just days before that momentous event.

2. *"That He passed through the midst of Samaria and Galilee,"* proclaims the last time these regions would see Him, at least before the resurrection.

3. These had been the most blessed areas on the face of the earth. They had had the privilege of entertaining the ministry of the Son of God, which resulted in the greatest demonstration of healing and miracle-working power that the world has ever known. But yet, due to the opposition of the religious hierarchy, no satisfactory penetration was made into the hearts of most of the people. In fact, if the leadership of any church or denomination is opposed to the moving of the Holy Spirit, it is highly unlikely that the Spirit of God will be allowed to function in any capacity. Consequently, those in that particular church or churches had best find some place else to go instead of trying to reform the thing from within, which cannot be done.

4. As an aside, Jesus passing through the midst of Samaria and Galilee means that He was traveling eastward in order to cross the Jordan River, where He would then turn south and go toward Jericho.

(12) "AND AS HE ENTERED INTO A CERTAIN VILLAGE, THERE MET HIM TEN MEN WHO WERE LEPERS, WHICH STOOD AFAR OFF."

The diagram is:

1. The phrase, *"And as He entered into a certain village,"* no doubt, proclaimed this village being in Galilee. It was to be the greatest day these 10 lepers would ever know.

2. *"There met Him ten men who were lepers, which stood afar off,"* was done with purpose. Levitical law stated that they had to remain approximately a hundred feet or so away from other people (Lev. 13:21, 45-46; 14:2).

3. However, now their world, and the entirety thereof, was about to change. They would meet Jesus.

(13) "AND THEY LIFTED UP THEIR VOICES, AND SAID, JESUS, MASTER, HAVE MERCY ON US."

DESPERATION

The phrase, *"And they lifted up their voices,"* proclaims them doing this because they could not come closer to Jesus. No doubt, they had heard of His miracle-working power. They had heard that He had even cleansed lepers; consequently, they, no doubt, oftentimes discussed between themselves the possibility of Jesus coming their way, and what they would do should this great event happen.

Quite possibly, the news of His arrival preceded His coming, as it, no doubt, did, with people shouting the glad message from person to person, which fell upon the ears of these hapless lepers. What must they have thought when they were told, "Yes, it is Jesus of Nazareth!"

MERCY

The phrase, *"And said, Jesus, Master, have mercy on us,"* was a cry not too unlike that of blind Bartimaeus, who would have his blind eyes opened very shortly upon the arrival of Jesus in Jericho.

Having no idea exactly what happened when they called to the Master, but yet, surmising what could have taken place, I can hear the word as it spread among the 10, "It is Jesus of Nazareth."

When they cried to Him, not at all sure what He would do, the most critical ones must have thought that if He did not do something for them, they couldn't make it much longer.

As they cried out across the distance, there is some indication in the next verse that He may not have heard them on the first cry, with them continuing to attempt to attract His attention.

As they stood waiting, with each moment seeming like an eternity, someone may have spoken out loud, as much to himself as to others, saying, "What do you think He will do?"

It is my personal thought that wherever Jesus was, the power of God could be instantly felt. If, in fact, that was the case, these lepers could feel it as well; consequently, one may have lifted up his voice and began to sing:

"I just feel like something good is about to happen,
"I just feel like something good is on its way.
"He has promised that He'd open all of heaven,

"And brother, it could happen any day.
"When God's people humble themselves and call on Jesus,
"And they look to heaven expecting as they pray,
"I just feel like something good is about to happen,
"And brother, this could be that very day."

(14) "AND WHEN HE SAW THEM, HE SAID UNTO THEM, GO SHOW YOURSELVES UNTO THE PRIESTS. AND IT CAME TO PASS, THAT, AS THEY WENT, THEY WERE CLEANSED."

The overview is:

1. The phrase, *"And when He saw them, He said unto them,"* proclaims them finally getting His attention.

2. *"Go show yourselves unto the priests,"* proclaims this as all that He said. There is no record that He prayed, but rather gave them this instruction.

3. This command assured cleansing, for only a cleansed leper was to show himself to the priests (Lev., Chpts. 13-14; Deut. 24:8). It was as much as to say, "You are clean." They knew they were unclean, but they believed Christ's word, went away with the conviction that it was true, and were immediately healed on the way.

4. Their appearing before priests as cleansed lepers would demonstrate that Jesus was both Messiah and Jehovah, for God alone could heal leprosy after this manner.

5. *"And it came to pass, that, as they went, they were cleansed,"* proclaims the miracle taking place as they turned to obey the command respecting the priests.

6. The cleansing of the leper is, in effect, a type of salvation, for leprosy at that time was a type of sin and uncleanness. With a word, Jesus healed this worst of diseases, and with a word, He will accept all who come to Him for salvation.

7. As God alone could heal leprosy, likewise, it is God alone who can save from sin.

(15) "AND ONE OF THEM, WHEN HE SAW THAT HE WAS HEALED, TURNED BACK, AND WITH A LOUD VOICE GLORIFIED GOD."

The exegesis is:

1. The phrase, *"And one of them, when he saw that he was healed,"* concerned the Samaritan.

2. Only heaven will reveal the gladness of his heart upon seeing this dread malady leave his body and health instantly return.

3. The phrase, *"Turned back, and with a loud voice glorified God,"* proclaims such a gladness of heart at his newfound state that he could not keep silent. As well, he must turn back and thank the One who brought him this deliverance.

4. As he glorified God with a loud voice, it is obvious that the Holy Spirit sanctioned this display of praise.

5. To be sure, there will come a day that the entirety of the world will glorify God with a loud voice, even as they are doing it at this moment in heaven (Rev. 5:12).

(16) "AND FELL DOWN ON HIS FACE AT HIS FEET, GIVING HIM THANKS: AND HE WAS A SAMARITAN."

The structure is:

1. The phrase, *"And fell down on his face at His Feet, giving Him thanks,"* proclaims that which hundreds of millions will desire to do when at long last they stand before Him.

2. He could now come close to Jesus, even touching His feet, because he was no longer a leper but now cleansed by the spoken word of Jesus of Galilee.

3. *"Oh happy day, oh happy day, "When Jesus washed my sins away."*

4. *"And he was a Samaritan,"* is delineated by the Holy Spirit for purpose. The Jews hated the Samaritans, with whom he would never have been allowed to associate, except they were all lepers.

5. Being a member of a despised people, no doubt, made him more humble than the others and, as well, more thankful for what Jesus had done for him.

6. Even though the Jews hated the Samaritans, still, Jesus ministered there often and showed no partiality whatsoever.

(17) "AND JESUS ANSWERING SAID, WERE THERE NOT TEN CLEANSED? BUT WHERE ARE THE NINE?"

The pattern is:

1. The phrase, *"And Jesus answering said,"* proclaims questions that will probe the hearts of men.

NOTES

2. The question, *"Were there not ten cleansed,"* proclaims some displeasure at the others not returning to give thanks.

3. The question, *"But where are the nine?"* proclaims, in essence, the attitude of Israel as a whole.

4. Perhaps one could say that Jesus performed 10 times the miracles in Israel as He did in Samaria, but Israel showed no thanksgiving whatsoever, while this Samaritan did.

5. The idea seems to be that while Jesus did want them to go to the priests as originally commanded, still, they could do that after expressing their thanksgiving to Him. However, despite a miracle of unprecedented proportions, which, in effect, gave them back their lives, there seemed to be little or no thanksgiving or thoughtfulness on their part in this regard. Such proclaims the ingratitude of men as a whole.

6. And yet, there is one more thing. For this man who returned, who was a Samaritan, it is doubtful that the priests, who, of course, were Jewish, would have given him any shift at all.

(18) "THERE ARE NOT FOUND WHO RETURNED TO GIVE GLORY TO GOD, SAVE THIS STRANGER."

GLORY TO GOD

The phrase, *"There are not found who returned to give glory to God,"* proclaims in the words of Christ the rightness of the former leper in his returning to give glory to God. I think it would be difficult to overdo that of which the leper did.

How important is it really in giving glory to God?

I think it would be very difficult to overdo this, at least if we're truly giving glory to God and not trying to call attention to ourselves. Most of mankind, and even the church, gives God little glory. In fact, in most churches, there is no glory given to God at all, with any type of praises being frowned upon. To be frank, that type of church is not even really a church in the eyes of God.

The very purpose of mankind is to truly praise the Lord. The book of Psalms, which is actually earth's first songbook, is by and large praise to God. The last five psalms open with praise.

NOTES

THE PSALMS

- *"Praise ye the LORD. Praise the LORD, O my soul"* (Ps. 146:1).
- *"Praise ye the LORD: for it is good to sing praises unto our God"* (Ps. 147:1).
- *"Praise ye the LORD. Praise ye the LORD from the heavens"* (Ps. 148:1).
- *"Praise ye the LORD. Sing unto the LORD a new song, and His praise in the congregation of saints"* (Ps. 149:1).
- *"Praise ye the LORD. Praise God in His sanctuary"* (Ps. 150:1).

So, coming from the heart of the redeemed one should be a constant flow of praise to God.

God has done so much for us, and continues to do so much for us, that we could never adequately thank Him even if we spent all eternity praising Him. So, if we truly understand who He is and what He has done for us, we will truly praise Him continually.

Coming up from the earth and going into the spirit world is a constant spewing of blasphemy, profanity, doubt, and unbelief, which, in effect, praises Satan. How much this must gladden the heart of the Evil One, and how much he must call attention to such, actually throwing it in the face of God. In effect, he says, "They are praising me," which he wanted all along (Job, Chpt. 1).

THE PRAISES OF THE SAINTS

When believers praise the Lord, several things happen:

- Praises make a statement saying that God is victorious in all things, having defeated the Evil One.
- Moses said, *"And five of you shall chase an hundred, and an hundred of you shall put ten thousand to flight"* (Lev. 26:8).

This simply means that the praises of five believers cancel out the blasphemy of a hundred unbelievers, and the praises of a hundred believers cancels out the blasphemy of 10,000 unbelievers. Consequently, it should be well understood exactly how powerful that praises to God are, and how they overcome the spirit world of darkness.

So, if God's people truly praise Him, the host of angels hears only praises to God instead of the blasphemy that praises Satan.

THE CROSS OF CHRIST

Coupled with our praises, when the believer's faith is anchored squarely in the Cross of Christ, this affects the spirit world as nothing else. It is because it was there that Jesus defeated the powers of darkness in every capacity (Col. 2:14-15). That's why Paul said:

"Christ sent me not to baptize, but to preach the gospel: not with wisdom of words, lest the Cross of Christ should be made of none effect" (I Cor. 1:17).

That's why he also said, *"For the preaching of the Cross is to them who perish foolishness; but unto us who are saved it is the power of God"* (I Cor. 1:18).

That's why he said, as well, *"I determined not to know anything among you, save Jesus Christ, and Him crucified"* (I Cor. 2:2).

Satan hates the Cross as he does simply because it was there that he and all his cohorts of darkness were totally defeated. So, when the believer places his or her faith exclusively in Christ and the Cross, and couples that with praises to God on a continuing basis, this is the perfect blueprint for victory in every capacity.

THE STRANGER?

The words, *"There are not found,"* as used by Jesus, means that God is actively seeking those who will praise His name.

"Save this stranger," actually addresses itself to that which would shortly come.

Israel would not praise Him; therefore, the Lord would turn to the Gentiles, i.e., strangers, who would praise Him and, in fact, do so unto this day the world over.

As well, this tells us that if a church, or a major denomination for that matter, refuses to praise the Lord, He will raise up others who will do so. The same goes for the individual. God is going to have people who will praise Him irrespective of whom they may be.

(19) "AND HE SAID UNTO HIM, ARISE, GO YOUR WAY: YOUR FAITH HAS MADE YOU WHOLE."

The exegesis is:

1. The phrase, *"And He said unto him, Arise, go your way,"* proclaims that which Jesus ever does—He lifts people up, i.e., arise.

2. *"Your faith has made you whole,"* proclaims that not only was he healed but saved as well!

3. All of them showed faith by asking Jesus for healing, which they received; however, only one, it seems, was also given eternal life, and that was because He glorified God.

4. In fact, millions receive from the Lord every day but do not allow themselves, for whatever reason, to go deeper with the Lord and, therefore, miss out on so much.

5. This is what makes the greed message so wrong! Its devotees seek only what they can get from God instead of what God can give them. There is a vast difference.

(20) "AND WHEN HE WAS DEMANDED OF THE PHARISEES, WHEN THE KINGDOM OF GOD SHOULD COME, HE ANSWERED THEM AND SAID, THE KINGDOM OF GOD COMETH NOT WITH OBSERVATION."

THE KINGDOM OF GOD

The phrase, *"And when He was demanded of the Pharisees, when the kingdom of God should come,"* proclaims a mindset of Israel of that day and, as well, of the person and ministry of Christ.

The messages of Christ, coupled with His miracles, left absolutely no doubt as to what Jesus was, or more particularly, who He was, i.e., the Messiah. They knew He claimed this position, the culmination of all Jewish hopes; however, all the great rabbinical schools of that day, in which the Pharisees had received their training, connected the coming of the Messiah with a grand revival of Jewish power. In other words, the yoke of Rome would be thrown off, with Israel once again becoming the premier nation in the world, and all of this by the might and power of the Messiah.

A MISINTERPRETATION OF THE WORD OF GOD

They believed this error because of a misinterpretation of the Word of God. While it was true that prophecies had been given claiming this very thing, still, there were great conditions involved. Israel had not met those conditions but, in fact, had gone in the other direction. They were extremely

religious but, as well, extremely self-righteous; consequently, their self-righteousness would not allow them to accept Christ even though He obviously fulfilled all the prophecies.

For instance, Isaiah, Chapter 53, graphically portrayed what the suffering Messiah would be like. A proper interpretation of that chapter, which, in fact, was very easy to do, fit Jesus perfectly.

They read into the Word of God what they wanted to see and ignored that which they did not delight in hearing. So, the type of Messiah they were waiting for, who would be politically triumphant, was not the type promised in the Word.

NOT WITH OBSERVATION

The phrase, *"He answered them and said, The kingdom of God cometh not with observation,"* has to do with hostility and concerned various outward externals, such as Rome being overthrown with violence and power, etc.

The Jews had held up all of these external happenings as a sign that the person who brought them about would be the Messiah. So, their observations were wrong.

To be frank, most believers presently fall into the same trap as the Jews of old in that they base their beliefs on outward observations. As such, they mostly miss that which God is doing!

(21) "NEITHER SHALL THEY SAY, LO HERE! OR, LO THERE! FOR, BEHOLD, THE KINGDOM OF GOD IS WITHIN YOU."

The order is:

1. The phrase, *"Neither shall they say, Lo here! or, lo there!"* refers to these externals. In other words, He was saying that all of these outward signs they were talking about were not scriptural and really had no bearing on the kingdom of God.

2. The phrase, *"For, behold, the kingdom of God is within you,"* actually has two meanings:

a. It would have been better translated, "The kingdom of God is within your midst." This referred to Jesus! In effect, He is the kingdom of God, but Israel would not recognize Him.

b. The kingdom of God begins within the

heart, and must begin there before it can affect the externals.

3. This is what Israel was missing. They wanted all the material, social, and physical aspects of the kingdom of God, but they did not want the spiritual aspects, which had to do with a changed heart and life. They simply did not believe they needed changing because self-righteousness never sees its own need.

4. All who have Jesus have the kingdom of God. However, the physical, social, and material aspects of that kingdom will not come about until Israel actually accepts Christ, which they will do at the second coming. When Israel accepts Christ, they will begin these aspects of the kingdom, which will last for a thousand years, with Jesus ruling personally from Jerusalem (Ezek., Chpts. 40-48; Zech., Chpt. 14; Rev., Chpt. 20).

(22) "AND HE SAID UNTO THE DISCIPLES, THE DAYS WILL COME, WHEN YOU SHALL DESIRE TO SEE ONE OF THE DAYS OF THE SON OF MAN, AND YOU SHALL NOT SEE IT."

The diagram is:

1. The phrase, "And He said unto the disciples," presents Him turning away from the Pharisees, who would not believe anything He said anyway, and turning to His disciples.

2. "The days will come, when you shall desire to see one of the days of the Son of Man, and you shall not see it," has a double meaning:

a. It speaks of the disciples personally, who, after the ascension of Christ and the day of Pentecost, would have a far greater understanding of all the things Jesus said and did, and would long to have the opportunity to relive those former days.

Such are many believers! Some few have excellent churches with God-anointed pastors, with many not realizing what they really have.

b. The seeing of the "days of the Son of Man" is a desire of all believers. This cannot be brought to pass until the end of the church age, which has now lasted for nearly 2,000 years. However, even as Verse 30 proclaims, the day is coming when the Son of Man will be revealed.

(23) "AND THEY SHALL SAY TO YOU,

NOTES

SEE HERE; OR, SEE THERE: GO NOT AFTER THEM, NOR FOLLOW THEM."

The structure is:

1. The phrase, "And they shall say to you, See here; or, see there," proclaims various happenings in the world, and Bible expositors who point to these things, claiming they fulfill Bible prophecy. While some few are definitely correct, many are not.

2. For instance, many have attempted to set dates for the rapture of the church. During World War II, some Bible teachers claimed that Mussolini was the Antichrist. Others, as well, have been pointed to as a fulfillment of this end-time prophecy.

3. It should be obvious that all of these things are wrong, and it's because of an improper interpretation of Scripture.

4. As an example, the Scripture tells us that the man of sin will not be revealed until after the rapture of the church (II Thess. 2:6-8).

5. However, the greatest concentration of false representations will take place in the coming great tribulation, to which this verse more than all alludes.

6. Many at that time will claim to be the Messiah, or else, of God, with the Antichrist being the chief impersonator, at least at the beginning. In fact, he will claim to be the long awaited Messiah, and Israel will believe him, at least for a period of time (Jn. 5:43).

7. "Go not after them, nor follow them," has reference to whatever sign these false messiahs point to as not being the real thing. Jesus then explained what the real thing is going to be, which leaves absolutely no doubt as to what is being done, or Who it is.

(24) "FOR AS THE LIGHTNING, THAT LIGHTENETH OUT OF THE ONE PART UNDER HEAVEN, SHINETH UNTO THE OTHER PART UNDER HEAVEN; SO SHALL ALSO THE SON OF MAN BE IN HIS DAY."

The composition is:

1. The phrase, "For as the lightning," has reference to two things:

a. As a flash of lightning is sudden, the Coming of Jesus Christ, referred to as the second coming, will be sudden as well. It will take place in the midst of the battle of Armageddon.

b. As lightning has great power and glory, likewise, Jesus' second coming will have the same.

2. Actually, His second advent will contrast with His first. II Thessalonians, Chapter 1, describes it. It will not be local, obscure, and with humiliation, but universal, powerful, and glorious.

3. *"That lighteneth* (lightens) *out of the one part under heaven, shineth* (shines) *unto the other part under heaven,"* proclaims the universal nature of His coming.

4. In other words, the heavens will be illuminated with such a display at that time that the entirety of the nations of the world will know and realize that something overly magnificent has happened. Actually, it will be so magnificent that it will be unique in the history of mankind.

5. No doubt, the heavens will be showered with meteorites, with the planetary bodies adding their display to this grand moment, actually, the grandest in all of history. It is the second coming of the Lord, which will be the most cataclysmic event the world has ever known.

6. *"So shall also the Son of Man be in His day,"* represents a day as the world has never known before. The other days of history have mostly been for Satan, but the second coming will signal the end of Satan's days and the beginning of the day of the Son of Man.

(25) "BUT FIRST MUST HE SUFFER MANY THINGS, AND BE REJECTED OF THIS GENERATION."

The form is:

1. This Scripture tells us that the suffering Messiah must precede the glorified Messiah.

2. Actually, the glories of that coming day of triumph will have a relation to, and will be the result of, His atoning sufferings at Calvary.

3. In other words, it is the Cross that has made and will make all of this possible.

(26) "AND AS IT WAS IN THE DAYS OF NOAH, SO SHALL IT BE ALSO IN THE DAYS OF THE SON OF MAN."

The pattern is:

1. The phrase, *"And as it was in the days of Noah,"* means that the world at the time of the second coming will be as indifferent and corrupt as in the days of Noah, and Lot for that matter.

2. In other words, despite the information given in the Word of God, the world at that time will not be looking at all for the coming of the Son of Man.

3. When He comes back the second time, He will not come back to be beaten, spit upon, and crucified, but rather will come back as King of Kings and Lord of Lords.

(27) "THEY DID EAT, THEY DRANK, THEY MARRIED WIVES, THEY WERE GIVEN IN MARRIAGE, UNTIL THE DAY THAT NOAH ENTERED INTO THE ARK, AND THE FLOOD CAME, AND DESTROYED THEM ALL."

The construction is:

1. The phrase, *"They did eat, they drank, they married wives, they were given in marriage,"* proclaims business as usual. In other words, as the world did not expect the predictions of Noah to come to pass respecting the flood, neither will the world expect the second coming, which is proclaimed in the Bible.

2. *"Until the day that Noah entered into the ark,"* means that up to that very moment, they laughed at his predictions.

3. The entering into the ark actually means that many saw him do that, which was met with derision.

4. In fact, one could say, at least in a spiritual sense, that Noah, i.e., the body of Christ, is about ready to enter the ark, i.e., the rapture, at which the world, as well as much of the church, continues to laugh.

5. *"And the flood came, and destroyed them all,"* proclaims that the negative response in no way altered the judgment that was coming.

6. The second coming of Christ will not only bring life and glory to this planet but, as well, will bring death and destruction to those who blaspheme the name of the Lord. Such will include the Antichrist and all of his armies. As well, it will include a smashing of modern governmental systems, which Jesus referred to as *"the times of the Gentiles"* (Lk. 21:24).

7. So, the second coming will bring destruction to all haters of God, and life to those who look for Him.

(28) "LIKEWISE ALSO AS IT WAS IN THE DAYS OF LOT; THEY DID EAT, THEY DRANK, THEY BOUGHT, THEY SOLD, THEY PLANTED, THEY BUILT."

The synopsis is:

1. The phrase, *"Likewise also as it was in the days of Lot,"* pertained to the destruction of Sodom and Gomorrah.

2. *"They did eat, they drank, they bought, they sold, they planted, they built,"* proclaims once again that it was business as usual, exactly as the days of Noah; however, there was a difference:

3. Noah did preach to the people of his generation; however, there is no record that the twin cities received any warning.

4. There were two angels sent to Sodom to retrieve Lot and his family, but it is not known if they were commissioned to warn them. When it was known that they were in the city, the homosexuals—*"Both old and young, all the people from every quarter"*—would have beaten down the door to take the two angels by force had they not been smitten with blindness by the angels (Gen. 19:4-11). So there was little opportunity to warn anyone!

(29) "BUT THE SAME DAY THAT LOT WENT OUT OF SODOM IT RAINED FIRE AND BRIMSTONE FROM HEAVEN, AND DESTROYED THEM ALL."

The synopsis is:

1. The phrase, *"But the same day that Lot went out of Sodom,"* even as *"Noah entered into the ark,"* could very well be symbolic of the rapture. In fact, the angels said to Lot, *"I cannot do anything till you come out of Sodom (outside the city),"* speaking of the coming judgment and the absolute necessity for Lot and his family to be brought out first (Gen. 19:22).

2. In both cases, judgment did not come until the righteous were taken out. Likewise, during the coming great tribulation, judgment will not come until the righteous are taken away. The wrath of God is to be poured out upon the unrighteous, not the righteous. Actually, Paul said, *"For God has not appointed us to wrath, but to obtain salvation (be raptured) by our Lord Jesus Christ"* (I Thess. 5:9).

3. *"It rained fire and brimstone from heaven, and destroyed them all,"* proclaims, like the flood, the destruction of the twin cities, but not until Lot had been removed.

(30) "EVEN THUS SHALL IT BE IN THE DAY WHEN THE SON OF MAN IS REVEALED."

The synopsis is:

1. This is the second coming!

2. As stated, this will be the time that the Antichrist and his mighty armies are destroyed, which is recorded in Ezekiel, Chapters 38 and 39.

3. There will be at least a seven year period of time between the rapture and the second coming, and quite possibly even more. Actually, the rapture should not literally be referred to as a coming because Christ will not really come to earth at that particular time. It seems that He will come part way, with the saints going to meet Him (I Thess. 4:16-17).

(31) "IN THAT DAY, HE WHICH SHALL BE UPON THE HOUSETOP, AND HIS STUFF IN THE HOUSE, LET HIM NOT COME DOWN TO TAKE IT AWAY: AND HE WHO IS IN THE FIELD, LET HIM LIKEWISE NOT RETURN BACK."

IN THAT DAY

The phrase, *"In that day,"* refers to the second coming and not the rapture (Mat. 24:27-31; 25:31-46; Rev. 19:11-21).

"He which shall be upon the housetop, and his stuff in the house, let him not come down to take it away: and he who is in the field, let him likewise not return back," has nothing to do with the rapture, as some have believed, for that event will be sudden *"in the twinkling of an eye"* (I Cor. 15:51-58).

This event, as described by Christ, in no way resembles the rapture, for the individuals here mentioned will have time to do certain things, even though warned otherwise!

Verses 31 through 37 pertain to the mobilization of Israel against the Antichrist. As stated, Ezekiel describes it in Chapters 38 and 39.

It will be the time that the Antichrist will attempt to annihilate Israel because in so doing, that is, if he could so succeed, he would abrogate the prophecies concerning these ancient people, thereby, making void the plan of God. So, at that time (the battle of Armageddon), Israel will fight for her life and existence and, in fact, will lose some two-thirds of her people (Zech. 13:8). Were it not for the second coming, the Antichrist would accomplish his task and annihilate Israel. However, to be sure, Jesus will come!

ATTEMPTS TO DESTROY ISRAEL

Of course, this is not the first time Satan has attempted to destroy these ancient people, but he will come closer to succeeding at this time (the battle of Armageddon) than ever before.

In 1940, Adolph Hitler began his persecution of the Jews, which continued through much of 1945. During that time, he ruthlessly slaughtered some 6 million, with every intention of killing all, at least, those he could get to. Satan had placed this in his mind even though Satan's reasons were different from Hitler's.

Satan knew that the time had now come, even after some 1,900 years, for Israel to once again become a nation, thereby, beginning the fulfillment of the prophecies concerning her restoration and ultimate acceptance of Jesus Christ. Consequently, if they could be destroyed, God's promises would fall to the ground.

However, he did not succeed, and in 1948, Israel, for the first time in 1,900 years, became a sovereign state. It is within her ancient borders and, as well, is referred to as *"Israel."* To be sure, this was not by chance but predestined by the Lord. In fact, Israel is God's prophetic time clock.

At the present time, Israel, completely void of spiritual power we may quickly add, but yet, watched over by the Lord, is attempting to solve the Arab problem with the Palestinian Accords. However, this has not worked, with terrorist activity continuing even unto this very hour.

THE ANTICHRIST

Very shortly, the Antichrist will come upon the scene, posing as a man of peace and exhibiting extraordinary wisdom, actually given to him by Satan (Dan. 11:36-39). Israel will think he is the Messiah and will accept him as such (Jn. 5:43).

NOTES

In 1987, I had the privilege of being one of the speakers at a particular assembly in Washington, D.C., with most attending being Jewish. The other speaker was Benjamin Netanyahu, the present prime minister of Israel.

I had the occasion to spend a little time with him (a very short time) after the meeting had ended. I sensed in my spirit, and believe I was told so by the Lord, that this man would play a very important part in Israel's future. Consequently, I have followed his career with great interest and was not surprised at all at his election as the prime minister of Israel, which came as a shock to most.

Exactly what part he will play remains to be seen. It may even be negative, but whatever it is, it is according to the plan of God respecting these people.

At the beginning, the whole world will tout the Antichrist as the savior of mankind. In fact, he will not show his true colors then, and with his extraordinary wisdom, will be able to solve problems, such as those that presently exist between the Muslims and Israel, and will, therefore, gain the plaudits of the world.

To what degree the world will accept him as the Messiah of Israel is not known; however, Israel definitely will accept him as such at that time.

THE SEVEN YEAR COVENANT

He will then draw up a seven year covenant, guaranteeing Israel's safety, which will include other nations, even possibly the United Nations. At that time, Israel will completely trust him, in effect, letting down their guard. As stated, they will praise him and accept him as their Messiah (Dan. 9:27).

However, at the midpoint, he will break his covenant with Israel and actually invade the country and take over the newly built temple, thereby, showing his true colors (Dan. 8:9-14; 9:27; 11:45; Mat. 24:15; II Thess. 2:4; Rev., Chpt. 13). Israel will then suffer her first military defeat since becoming a nation in 1948.

Israel will then flee to Petra, which is in present day Jordan, where the Lord will give her protection for about three and one-half years (Rev. 12:13-14).

At that time, the Antichrist could easily defeat Israel but for two things:

THE TWO THINGS

First of all, a great earthquake will cause havoc in the pursuing army of the Antichrist (Rev. 12:15-16). Secondly, the Antichrist will hear tidings out of the east and the north and will take his armies in that direction to consolidate his empire, thereby, leaving Israel for another day (Dan. 11:44).

Israel will then begin to filter back into Jerusalem, especially considering that the Antichrist has gone on to attend to larger things. They will furiously rearm but with precious little help from other nations. Having won his battles, the Antichrist will now consolidate his forces and will come down once and for all to totally annihilate Israel. It is the battle of Armageddon and, as stated, is described in Ezekiel, Chapters 38 and 39.

When he comes down upon Israel, the swift mobilization, which shall occur by Israel, is addressed by Jesus in Luke 17:31-37.

Every man is going to be needed to fight the Antichrist, and will be needed hurriedly, hence, the admonition given in Verse 31.

(32) "REMEMBER LOTS WIFE."

The structure is:

1. In this one passage, Jesus recognized the historical fact of Lot's wife being turned to salt. The Gospels and the Pentateuch, therefore, must stand or fall together (Gen. 19:26).

2. Lot's wife, against the command of the angels, looked back and, consequently, turned to a pillar of salt. Jesus used her as an example, in effect, saying that if there is hesitation on the part of Israel at the beginning of the battle of Armageddon, they will be destroyed just as Lot's wife. As is obvious, the Lord was emphasizing haste without hesitation.

(33) "WHOSOEVER SHALL SEEK TO SAVE HIS LIFE SHALL LOSE IT; AND WHOSOEVER SHALL LOSE HIS LIFE SHALL PRESERVE IT."

The construction is:

1. The phrase, *"Whosoever shall seek to save his life shall lose it,"* refers to the Jews who will think that by fleeing in other directions, they will preserve themselves,

NOTES

which, in reality, will have the opposite effect.

2. *"And whosoever shall lose his life shall preserve it,"* refers to those who go forward to the battle and, as a result, will have the protection of the Lord. Actually, to those who defend Jerusalem, the Lord said, *"And he who is feeble among them at that day shall be as David; and the house of David shall be as God, as the angel of the LORD before them"* (Zech. 12:8).

3. This simply means that as David was anointed by the Holy Spirit to fight, so will those be who defend Israel, with the army of Israel at that time having the power of God. They will fight as no men and women have ever fought.

4. Consequently, it seems that the far greater majority, which will number several million who will lose their lives at this time among the Jews, will pertain mostly to those who refuse to defend Jerusalem.

5. It must be understood that at this time, Israel still has not accepted Jesus as the Messiah and, in effect, is away form God. Nevertheless, she will have the help of God as possibly she has never had that help before. Actually, at this time she will begin to call upon the Messiah, which will precipitate the second coming.

(34) "I TELL YOU, IN THAT NIGHT THERE SHALL BE TWO MEN IN ONE BED; THE ONE SHALL BE TAKEN, AND THE OTHER SHALL BE LEFT.

(35) "TWO WOMEN SHALL BE GRINDING TOGETHER; THE ONE SHALL BE TAKEN, AND THE OTHER LEFT.

(36) "TWO MEN SHALL BE IN THE FIELD; THE ONE SHALL BE TAKEN, AND THE OTHER LEFT."

The order is:

1. These passages refer to the mobilization of Israel regarding the battle of Armageddon.

2. As well, it speaks of great haste in that it must be done quickly, and it pertains to both men and women.

3. The idea is that while some are taken to stand in the front lines, others will be left to protect the rear. In fact, all will be used in the conflict, with the exception of those who attempt to flee, which many, no doubt, shall do, and lose their lives in the process.

(37) "AND THEY ANSWERED AND SAID UNTO HIM, WHERE, LORD? AND HE SAID UNTO THEM, WHERESOEVER THE BODY IS, THITHER WILL THE EAGLES BE GATHERED TOGETHER."

The pattern is:

1. The question, *"And they answered and said unto him, Where, Lord?"* proclaims the lack of knowledge of the disciples as to exactly what Jesus was talking about.

2. In effect, they were asking, "Where are these people going to be taken?"

3. *"And He said unto them, Wheresoever the body is, thither* (there) *will the eagles be gathered together,"* refers directly to the battle of Armageddon. This is what he was actually saying:

a. At the battle of Armageddon, the arrival of Christ will destroy many people, actually, five-sixths of the armies of the Antichrist (Ezek. 39:2), which will, no doubt, number millions.

b. At that time, the Lord through Ezekiel said, *"Speak unto every feathered fowl, and to every beast of the field, Assemble yourselves, and come; gather yourselves on every side to My sacrifice that I do sacrifice for you, even a great sacrifice upon the mountains of Israel, that you may eat flesh, and drink blood"* (Ezek. 39:17).

4. This is what Jesus was meaning when He spoke of the eagles being gathered together.

"While Jesus whispers to you,
"Come, sinner, come!
"While we are praying for you,
"Come, sinner, come!"
"Now is the time to own Him,
"Come, sinner, come!
"Now is the time to know Him,
"Come, sinner, come!

"Are you too heavy laden?
"Come, sinner, come!
"Jesus will bear your burden,
"Come, sinner, come!"
"Jesus will not deceive you,
"Come, sinner, come!
"Jesus can now redeem you,
"Come, sinner, come!"

"Oh, hear His tender pleading,

"Come, sinner, come!
"Come and receive the blessing,
"Come, sinner, come!
"While Jesus whispers to you,
"Come, sinner, come!
"While we are praying for you,
"Come, sinner, come!"

CHAPTER 18

(1) "AND HE SPOKE A PARABLE UNTO THEM TO THIS END, THAT MEN OUGHT ALWAYS TO PRAY AND NOT TO FAINT."

THE PARABLE

The phrase, *"And He spoke a parable unto them to this end,"* has to do with prayer and faith, the two most powerful ingredients in the Christian experience. As well, this parable and the one to follow, which speaks of humility and self-righteousness, are actually a part of the teaching of the preceding chapter.

Inasmuch as He spoke of the end time in that chapter and the acute deepening apostasy that will then prevail, He now gives the ingredients for spiritual survival. They must be heeded at all costs.

PRAYER

The phrase, *"That men ought always to pray,"* actually proclaims to us that prayer is the resource of faith as the Word of God is its ingredient. In other words, without a proper prayer life, faith cannot be truly exercised, irrespective of how much it is claimed. What is He telling us here?

He is telling the believer that prayer must be a constant resource and, as well, engaged constantly. That doesn't mean a person must stay on his knees constantly, but it does mean that we are to have a spirit of prayer constantly.

However, I think it is an absolute necessity for a believer to have a set time each day to get alone with God, irrespective of the length of time. While one should constantly breathe a prayer to the Lord regarding all things, still, that will not take the place of one shutting out all other duties and getting alone with the Lord. So, both must be engaged.

RELATIONSHIP WITH CHRIST

Prayer deepens and strengthens relationship, and I speak of relationship with Christ. It is impossible to have a proper relationship with the Lord without having a proper prayer life. The two go hand in hand.

A deep, abiding relationship with the Lord causes the believer to learn who the Lord rightly is and what He has rightly done for us, and I speak of the Cross.

The greatest relationship there has ever been is that which was entertained between the incarnated Christ and His heavenly Father. He sought the will of the Father constantly and did nothing unless that will was ascertained. That must be our example.

The phrase, *"And not to faint,"* means "not to lose heart."

This implies the very thing the Lord will teach in this parable, which is importunity. This means to be persistent, even overly so in our requests.

The idea is that the answer may not come immediately and, in fact, seldom does. However, if we have ascertained that the needs or desires are according to the Word of God, nothing must stand in the way of the believer in receiving an answer to his prayer, irrespective of how long he must knock at that door. In fact, this very thought comes from the lips of the Master Himself and must be heeded.

Satan does not want the believer to have his prayers answered, and to be sure, the more that petition pertains to the carrying out of the will of God, the more that Satan will hinder. So, the believer must persist and not lose heart.

In truth, most believers pray little at all. Consequently, they have little or no relationship with Christ. Then, when a crisis arises, which it shall sooner or later, they go to the Lord and if the answer does not come immediately, they quit. This shows a lack of faith, and it shows no relationship at all!

A PERSONAL EXPERIENCE

In October 1991, we reached a crisis point in the ministry, and the fault was mine and mine alone. I was being given advice from all quarters, telling me I had to quit

preaching or start to do this or that, all of which was unscriptural.

One particular night (it must have been about October 18 or something close to that), about eight or 10 of us went to prayer. That night the Lord moved so mightily that it would be difficult for me to explain the tremendous moment given to us by the Holy Spirit.

The Lord spoke that night, saying, "I'm not a man that I should lie, neither the son of man that I should repent; what I have blessed nothing can curse."

He was telling me by that, that I must continue to preach the gospel. He is the one who called me, and as He said, He is not a man that I should go back on that which He has ordained.

Earlier that day, I laid my Bible on the coffee table in front of the couch where I, along with others, was sitting and made this statement, "I don't know the answer to victory over the world, the flesh, and the Devil, but I know the answer is contained in the Word of God, and by the grace of God, I'm going to find that answer."

The next morning I asked the Lord if He wanted me to stay on television. Once again, we were in a prayer meeting. The Lord told me emphatically that I was to most definitely stay on television. The first reaction I had was, "How in the world will we be able to finance it?"

In answer to my prayer, the Lord took me to Chapter 17 of Matthew.

Peter had come to the Master and stated that they had been demanded to pay taxes. Jesus actually said that they did not owe the taxes but to keep from offending the people, He would pay them anyway.

Peter then answered that they had no money.

The Lord told him to go down to the Sea of Galilee, cast in a hook, and the first fish he caught, look in its mouth, and he would find a piece of money. He was to take it and go pay the taxes. Evidently, it would be some type of coin, whether gold, silver, etc.

This Peter did and paid the taxes.

The Lord spoke to me saying, "As I met the need that day regarding taxes, I will meet the need of the television ministry."

I knew it was the Lord who spoke to me,

but I also reasoned in my heart that this was the most unorthodox means of raising money that I had ever heard in my life.

However, as I look back now to those many years ago, the Lord did exactly what He said He would do. In ways I never dreamed, funds were raised to pay for the television ministry.

TWO PRAYER MEETINGS A DAY

If I remember correctly, it was that same morning when I was going to the office that the Lord gave me the word regarding television. At that time He told me that I was to begin two prayer meetings a day. One was to be at 10 o'clock each morning for whoever would like to join me and one at 6:30 each evening.

He did not tell me exactly that for which I was to seek. He merely told me, "Do not seek Me so much for what I can do, but rather for who I am."

Looking back at those many years, I know that He was telling me that my relationship with Him must deepen.

Time and time again, I grew very weary and at times discouraged, but over and over the Lord would give me a moving of the Spirit in one of these prayer meetings. They lasted a little bit over 10 years, and I never missed a single prayer meeting during that time, except the few times that we were out of town. Then it happened!

THE MESSAGE OF THE CROSS

If I remember correctly, it was in 1997. I don't recall what month it was. I had come to my office early, as I always did. I would spend some time with the Lord in prayer and study before the 10 o'clock prayer meeting.

That morning the Lord began to open up to me the Message of the Cross. I had preached the Cross strongly all over the world and had seen untold thousands brought to a saving knowledge of Jesus Christ. Because of that, had you mentioned the Cross to me before that, I would have thought I knew everything about the Cross. I was to find out that I actually knew very little.

While I did understand the Cross relative to salvation, I had no understanding whatsoever of the Cross regarding sanctification,

in other words, how we live for God on a daily basis. I had made the statement that I knew the answer to my problem was found in the Bible, but this morning, the Lord was to answer me and show me that the answer definitely was to be found in the Bible.

THE SIN NATURE

As it regards the Message of the Cross, the first thing the Lord showed me was the sin nature. He took me to Chapter 6 of Romans to give me this great truth.

To fail when you're trying so hard not to fail is the most debilitating thing in which one could ever engage. As the Holy Spirit taught me some things about the sin nature, I learned that if we do not understand what the sin nature is, we're going to fail, no matter how hard we try otherwise. Sadly, most believers presently understand precious little about the sin nature, if anything at all.

In further study, I learned that this was the first thing the Lord showed the apostle Paul. We find that in Chapters 6 and 7 of Romans.

Then, a few days later, the Lord showed me the solution to the sin nature problem.

THE CROSS!

In prayer that morning, the Holy Spirit said the following to me:
• "The answer for which you seek is found in the Cross."
• "The solution for which you seek is found in the Cross."
• "The answer for which you seek is found only in the Cross."

I can't even begin to relate how I felt when the Lord gave me that great word. He took me once again to Chapter 6 of Romans, along with Chapters 7 and 8.

And yet, there was one thing about it I didn't understand.

What part did the Holy Spirit play in all of this?

The Lord had said, "The answer is found only in the Cross," and if it is only in the Cross, again I ask, "Where does that leave the Holy Spirit?"

It was about a month later that the Lord gave me the final part of this tremendous revelation, which He had already given to the apostle Paul nearly 2,000 years ago, and, no doubt, many others, as well, down through the centuries.

The Lord was to show me how the Holy Spirit works, which is a tremendous revelation.

THE HOLY SPIRIT

In 1988, at a time of acute crisis, it seemed that the powers of darkness were so strong that I would not be able to stand it. While in prayer that morning, I even spoke to the Lord and reminded Him of the great promise that He had given. He had said that He would not allow anything to come upon us any harder than we could bear, but He would always make a way of escape. It seemed as though there were 500 pounds on my shoulders crushing me down. Then it happened!

Immediately and instantly, the presence of the Lord came all over me. Instead of being crushed, it was as though I was floating on thin air. I've never taken a drink of any type of alcohol in my life, and neither have I taken any drugs; however, I do know what the power of God is like, and I am positive that Satan doesn't have anything that is even remotely close.

Then the Lord spoke this to my heart:

"I'M GOING TO SHOW YOU THINGS ABOUT THE HOLY SPIRIT YOU DO NOT NOW KNOW"

Nine years passed, and there was nothing that I could put my finger on that was a fulfillment of what the Lord had told me that morning in 1988. I knew the Lord had spoken that word to me, but yet, there was nothing that had taken place that I could say, "This is it." Then it happened!

Loren Larson and I were in the radio studio. Inasmuch as the Lord had just begun to open up the great Message of the Cross to me, we were doing our best to teach it to our audience, respecting the several stations we then had.

The program was almost over. Then something came out of my mouth that was unrehearsed, something I did not previously know, and something I had never heard or read. I made the following statement:

"The Holy Spirit works exclusively

NOTES

within the parameters of the finished work of Christ, and He will not work outside of those parameters."

I knew it was right, but I didn't understand where it had come from. I had never had anything like that happen to me before, and I've had nothing to happen like that since.

The room grew silent for a moment, and Loren said, "Brother Swaggart, can you give me Scripture for that?"

How could I give him Scripture when it was something that 10 minutes before, or even five minutes before, I did not know and had never heard? Then I looked down at my Bible that was open, and my eyes fell on Romans 8:2. It read:

"For the law of the Spirit of life in Christ Jesus has made me free from the law of sin and death." I knew that was the word that provided the foundation for what I had just said, which is how the Holy Spirit works.

HOW THE HOLY SPIRIT WORKS

If one will think about it a few moments, how the Holy Spirit works is one of the greatest truths in the entirety of the Word of God.

It is the Cross of Christ that gives the Holy Spirit the legal means to do all that He does. Before the Cross, due to the fact that the blood of bulls and goats could not take away sins, the Old Testament saints lived under that terrible dread of original sin. In other words, animal blood was insufficient to settle anything.

So, when believers in Old Testament times died, they did not go to heaven because they could not go to heaven. The stain of sin was still there, which could not gain admittance to heaven. Instead, they were taken down into paradise where they were actually captives of Satan. He could not hurt them, but nevertheless, they were his captives, hence, Paul saying, *"When He ascended up on high, He led captivity captive, and gave gifts unto men"* (Eph. 4:8).

The phrase, *"He led captivity captive,"* is a strange phrase. It means that all of these believers in paradise were captives of Satan, but when Jesus died on the Cross, that settled the sin debt, and settled it forever. Then He went down into paradise, and He led captivity captive, which means that

He made all of these souls in paradise His captives, and there was nothing that Satan could do about it.

Please understand, when Jesus died on Calvary and said, *"It is finished,"* that meant exactly what it said. What is it about that statement that you do not understand? It meant the plan of redemption was totally and completely finished. Nothing else remained to be done.

So, when Jesus went down into paradise, He did not go down into that nether region with demons beating up on him, as is said by some preachers, but rather He went down into that place totally and completely victorious. He was victorious over the world, the flesh, and the Devil due to what He had done at Calvary's Cross. There He atoned for all sin, and actually broke the back of sin, and totally and completely defeated every principality and power of darkness, which included Satan and all the demon spirits of the darkened spirit world. It was done! It was finished!

Some said, "No, He had to first be resurrected." Naturally, He had to be resurrected, but due to the fact that He had atoned for all sin, this meant that Satan could not do anything as it regarded His resurrection. Conversely, had He failed to atone for even one sin, He could not have risen from the dead. However, due to the fact that He atoned for all sin, past, present, and future, at least for all who will believe, His resurrection was a given.

Now, since the Cross, when believers die, their souls and their spirits instantly go to heaven because the sin debt has been settled.

I HAVE KEPT MY PROMISE TO YOU

The program ended, and I stood up to walk out the door when the Spirit of God came all over me. I stopped! The Lord spoke to me and said, "Do you remember that morning in March 1988 when I told you that I would tell you things about the Holy Spirit you then did not know?"

Of course, I remembered. Then the Lord said:

"I have just kept My promise to you in showing you a tremendous truth as to how the Holy Spirit works."

As stated, it is the Cross that gives the Holy Spirit the legal means to do all that He does, hence, it being referred to as a *"law"* (Rom. 8:2).

No, it's not the law of Moses, but rather a law devised by the Godhead in eternity past.

All of this means that we must understand what I've just said, further understanding that the Cross of Christ must ever be the object of our faith. That speaks of what Jesus there did and the victory He there won, which was done altogether for you and me. To know how the Holy Spirit works is to know how to have victory, and I'm speaking of victory over the world, the flesh, and the Devil. While the Bible does not teach sinless perfection, it most definitely does teach that sin is not to have dominion over us (Rom. 6:14). The only way that one can properly address the sin nature is by placing one's faith exclusively in Christ and the Cross.

• Our Lord is the source of all things we receive from God. He is the one who paid the price, which He did at Calvary's Cross (Jn. 1:1-3, 14, 29; Col. 2:10-15).

• The Cross of Christ is the means by which all of these wonderful things are given unto us (I Cor. 1:17-18, 23; 2:2; Gal. 6:14).

• With our Lord as the source and the Cross as the means, and the only means, our faith must be anchored and maintained in Christ and the Cross exclusively. When we do that, that is actually having faith in the Word. In fact, the only thing the child of God can glory about is the Cross of Christ (Gal. 6:14; Rom. 6:1-14; Col. 2:10-15).

• With our faith anchored completely in Christ and the Cross, then the Holy Spirit, who works exclusively within the parameters of the Cross of Christ, will work grandly on our behalf. The Holy Spirit is God. This means that there is nothing He cannot do. This is the way it is meant that we are to live for God. What is demanded of us, we cannot do; however, to be sure, the Holy Spirit will do it. So, how do I get Him to do all these wonderful things in my life?

We place our faith exclusively in Christ and the Cross, and then the Holy Spirit will work mightily on our behalf (Rom. 8:1-11; Eph. 2:13-18; I Cor. 1:18).

From that moment until now, the Holy

Spirit has led me deeper and deeper into the magnificence of the Cross.

However, to go back to the original thought, I firmly believe that my obeying the Lord when He told me to start two prayer meetings a day is that which served as a trigger to open the storehouse of heaven. This is not meaning that one can pray one's way through to victory, etc, for one cannot, but it does mean that it opens the door to the Word of God where we can find the answers. Without a proper prayer life, it's not possible.

Incidentally, while I do not meet now with people on a daily basis in prayer, I do reserve two to three times each day for a period of time to get alone with the Lord simply because I have much to pray about.

(2) "SAYING, THERE WAS IN A CITY A JUDGE, WHICH FEARED NOT GOD, NEITHER REGARDED MAN."

The order is:

1. The phrase, *"Saying, There was in a city a judge,"* proclaims Jesus selecting someone to use as an example who was as much unlike God as could possibly be. In other words, if one can get a petition answered from such a man as this by using the method Jesus proclaims, one can surely get a petition answered by God, who is the very opposite of this unjust judge.

2. *"Which feared not God, neither regarded man,"* proclaims exactly what type of individual this man was. He did not care what God or man thought, and yet, a poor woman without influence was able to bend him to her will.

(3) "AND THERE WAS A WIDOW IN THAT CITY; AND SHE CAME UNTO HIM, SAYING, AVENGE ME OF MY ADVERSARY."

The form is:

1. The phrase, *"And there was a widow in that city,"* pictures a woman, as stated, who has no influence and, therefore, no reason, at least in that society, for anyone to do anything to help her. And yet, she was able to have her petition favorably addressed.

2. *"And she came unto him,"* concerned the only place she could go respecting her particular need.

3. *"Saying, Avenge me of my adversary,"* actually says, "Do me justice."

(4) "AND HE WOULD NOT FOR A

WHILE: BUT AFTERWARD HE SAID WITHIN HIMSELF, THOUGH I FEAR NOT GOD, NOR REGARD MAN."

The pattern is:

1. *"And he would not for a while,"* means simply that he paid her no mind. As stated, she was a person with no influence, and especially considering that he had no regard for justice or fairness, there was no reason to heed her, at least in his mind. So, she was ignored, at least at the beginning.

2. *"But afterward he said within himself, Though I fear not God, nor regard man,"* proclaims something that had happened, which caused him to change his mind. The next verse tells us what that was.

(5) "YET BECAUSE THIS WIDOW TROUBLES ME, I WILL AVENGE HER, LEST BY HER CONTINUAL COMING SHE WEARY ME."

The overview is:

1. The phrase, *"Yet because this widow troubles me, I will avenge her,"* simply means that she wouldn't leave the judge alone.

2. *"Lest by her continual coming she weary me,"* means that every time the judge looked up she was there. At first, as stated, he ignored her, but after awhile, it became impossible to do so.

3. So, it was either answer her petition, or else, be driven to the point of total distraction.

4. Considering the power of this judge, and especially his lack of regard for God or man, it tells us that this woman took her life into her hands with her persistence. In fact, this man had the power to do with her, or to her, whatever he desired. He could have imprisoned her or even killed her. So her role was exceedingly dangerous. And yet, she felt her petition was significant enough to take her life in her hands in order to obtain justice. It seems that she felt that if justice was not given, there was no point in her existence; consequently, she threw into her quest a determination that must get results.

5. Jesus is telling us that our petition must be on the same basis, especially concerning extremely important requests, such as the salvation of a loved one, or any number of things.

(6) "AND THE LORD SAID, HEAR WHAT THE UNJUST JUDGE SAYS."

The overview is:

1. The argument that lies on the surface of the parable teaching is obvious.

2. If such a judge will in the end listen to the prayer of a supplicant for whom he cares nothing, will not God surely listen to the repeated prayer of a supplicant whom He loves with a deep, enduring love?

3. The Lord is telling us something extremely important here that if we will heed, it can change our life and living.

(7) "AND SHALL NOT GOD AVENGE HIS OWN ELECT, WHICH CRY DAY AND NIGHT UNTO HIM, THOUGH HE BEAR LONG WITH THEM?"

ELECT

The beginning of the question, *"And shall not God avenge His own elect?"* simply means that one surely must have as much faith in God as this woman did an unjust judge!

The word *elect*, which has to do with election, must be looked at as well.

AN ERRONEOUS UNDERSTANDING OF ELECTION

In simple terminology, some claim that the Bible teaches that some people are elected by God to be eternally lost, with others being elected to be eternally saved, and there's nothing that they have to say about it. In other words, the individual has no choice in the matter, with God arbitrarily choosing.

In truth, this doctrine is instigated by Satan and has no place in Scripture.

CALLING AND ELECTION (ROM. 8:33)

The doctrine of calling and election has been surrounded by many traditional theories and mysteries down through the centuries, but there is no excuse for this as the term simply means "chosen." Any person or group of persons selected or chosen of God for any particular purpose is the elect of God. Christ is called God's elect, which should be obvious (Isa. 42:1; I Pet. 2:6).

A particular woman in a local church is called an *"elect lady"* (II Jn. 1, 13). Israel as

a nation is spoken of as the elect of God (Isa. 45:4; 65:9, 22; Mat. 24:22-31; Mk. 13:20-27; Rom. 11:7, 28; I Pet. 1:2).

The church, made up of both Jews and Gentiles, is called the elect of God (Rom. 8:33; Col. 3:12; I Thess. 1:4; Titus 1:1). Angels are also called the elect of God (I Tim. 5:21). Anyone called to be saved and chosen for any particular mission is elected of God for that work (Jn. 6:70; 13:18; 15:16; Acts 1:2; 9:15; 15:7). Every person saved is the elect or chosen of God to salvation (Jn. 15:19; II Thess. 2:13; James 2:5; Rev. 17:14).

FINAL ELECTION TO SALVATION IS MAN'S RESPONSIBILITY

We can say with all assurance that any calling and election of God is based upon the free moral agency of those called and chosen. God offers the same mercies and blessings to all alike, but all do not accept these benefits alike, therefore, there naturally are different consequences.

THE BIBLE

It says that God's ways are always righteous (Ps. 145:17). He is no respecter of persons (Rom. 2:11; James 2:9). His will is for all to be saved (I Tim. 2:4-5; II Pet. 3:9). God's will and ways are made plain in His Word, and all who conform to them are loved on an equal basis according to the degree of obedience. This is how God will be able to judge all men according to His ways (Prov. 24:12; Jer. 17:10; Ezek. 18:30; 33:20; Hos. 12:2; Mat. 16:27; I Cor. 3:11-15; II Cor. 10:9-10; II Tim. 4:4; Rev. 20:11-15).

God repeatedly declares that He demands wholehearted service from every man (Deut. 11:13; Josh. 22:5; I Sam. 12:20; Mat. 22:37). God constantly searches the hearts of men and deals with them in order to bring them to righteousness (Job 33:14-30; Ps. 139:23; Jer. 11:20; 17:9-10; 20:12; Heb. 4:12). Therefore, God does not choose some to be saved and others to be lost, and He is not responsible for those who will be lost.

NO DIRECT STATEMENTS

"As many as were ordained to eternal life believed" (Acts 13:48).

The ones who rejected the gospel on this

occasion were the Jews, God's own elect who were first offered the gospel, thus proving that after men are chosen to be saved, they can reject truth and be lost (Acts 13:45-49). That the Jews were the elect of God and first chosen to carry the gospel is one of the most clearly stated facts in Scripture (Mat. 10:5; 15:21-28; 21:33-46; Jn. 1:11; Rom. 1:16; 3:1-6; 9:4-5).

Israel rejected the gospel and even killed their own Messiah. They murdered the saints and hardened against God until it was no wonder Paul waxed bold and said, *"It was necessary that the Word of God should first have been spoken to you: but seeing you put it from you, and judge yourselves unworthy of everlasting life, lo, we turn to the Gentiles"* (Acts 13:46).

Paul continued by saying that God had called him to bring the Light of the gospel to the Gentiles and unto the ends of the earth, showing that it is God's purpose to save all who believe in all nations (Acts 10:34-35). When the Gentiles heard this, many of them were glad and believed the gospel and glorified the Word of the Lord. This is why they were ordained to eternal life.

ORDAINED

The Greek word for *"ordained"* is *tasso* and means "to appoint, to arrange, to assign a place." It is translated *"ordained"* (Acts 13:48; Rom. 13:1); *"set"* (Lk. 7:8); *"appointed"* (Mat. 28:16; Acts 22:10; 28:23); *"determined"* (Acts 15:2); and *"addicted"* (I Cor. 16:15).

Not one statement in all these passages teaches that God or man's will is arbitrary in any plan for others who were appointed. God has ordained that all who believe will receive eternal life.

He has ordained that there be human governments, but he does not force man to have them, nor does He directly impose His will in every detail of human governments (Rom. 13:1-8).

Actually, no Scripture uses the word *ordained* to lead us to believe that any person referred to was forced to do anything contrary to his will.

To teach according to Acts 13:48 that God ordained some to be saved and some to be lost, disregarding all other Scriptures to the

NOTES

contrary, does not show honesty with truth. This verse really means, as in other translations, "As many as were ordained to *(set for)* eternal life believed"; that is, those who set themselves to believe the gospel, therefore, received eternal life and glorified the Word of the Lord.

ISRAEL, JACOB, AND ESAU

Another passage in the Bible used to prove (or attempt to do so) that God elects some to be saved on the basis of His own choice alone, regardless of the wills of the free moral agents, is Romans 9:1-24. In these passages, Paul is showing how the Jews, who were chosen of God to evangelize the world and to whom God gave the promises, were failing God despite their election, and that they would be cut off because of their rebellion. Any Bible statement must be understood in connection with the subject of the passage.

Regarding Jacob and Esau, Paul wrote, pertaining to the Lord, *"Jacob have I loved, but Esau have I hated"* (Rom. 9:13).

It is shown in these passages why Jacob was chosen in preference to Esau. It was not simply because of God's will only, or because He was a respecter of persons, for He is not. It was because of the nature, traits, and disposition of the boys.

Esau was devoid of spiritual things, and he freely chose to be this way (Heb. 12:16). Jacob was a man who loved God and had a disposition to choose spiritual things. God saw the difference in the makeup of the two boys before they were born and made His choice on these grounds. God can see and know the type of people from the very beginning. Before Ishmael was born, God predicted that he would be a wild man and that his hand would be against all other men (Gen. 16:11-12).

THE LORD PREFERRED
JACOB TO ESAU

If God could see the different persons that both Jacob and Esau were going to be, then He had plenty of grounds for His choice of Jacob over Esau. When God said He loved Jacob and hated Esau, He simply meant that He preferred Jacob to Esau. To *hate* is a Hebrew and Greek idiom meaning "preference."

This is what Jesus meant in Luke 14:26 when He said that unless a man *"hate not his father, and mother, and wife, and children, and brethren, and sisters, yea, and his own life also, he cannot be My disciple."* This simply means that one must prefer Christ to his relatives and his own life and put God first. So it was in the case of Jacob and Esau (Mal. 1:2-3; Rom. 9:10-13).

GOD'S CHOICE

God preferred Jacob to Esau, and this preference was naturally based upon what God could see in them. God, who can see the innermost traits of each person, also naturally prefers the ones who desire spiritual things and who choose to do His will; whether they do His will or not is another question. All can do His will if they choose to do so because the means of grace is for all alike (Jn. 3:16-20; Rev. 22:17).

God's choice is always made upon the basis of the submission or rebellion of the persons involved. No man is forced to resist the will of God, but those who do resist receive damnation, and this is what Paul teaches in Romans, Chapter 9.

This is why there is no unrighteousness with God. He gives all men the free choice of their actions to submit to His will or rebel against it, and the final responsibility is upon them, not upon God. God will have mercy upon whom He will have mercy, and He has promised to have mercy upon all who submit to Him. Mercy and compassion are not shown because of men's works, but they come through grace when men choose and submit to the will of God.

EPHESIANS 1:4-11

These passages are used to prove that God chooses from eternity past certain people to be saved. However, this passage only reveals that God's plan is that all who are to be saved were chosen to be holy, and that this purpose of God was made before the disruption of the world.

God predestinated that the saved should be holy before God forever, but who and which ones will be saved and be holy is left

entirely to the choice of each individual to conform to the plan of God and enjoy, consequently, the predestinated blessings of God.

The lost were likewise predestinated to be lost but who or which persons will be lost is left entirely to the choice of the individual. He can refuse to the end of his life, if he so desires, to conform to the plan of God. The plan itself is the thing that is predestined, not the individual conformity of one single person to that plan.

NO CONCRETE EXAMPLES

It is true that no man can be saved except God deals with him (Jn. 6:47, 44) and that God's people are called His own possession (Eph. 1:14). However, this does not mean that God does not deal with all men, or that all men who desire cannot become the people of God.

The Holy Spirit is faithful to deal with all men as they hear the gospel (Jn. 16:7-15; Rom. 10:9-17). The Bible speaks of Christ being the light that lights every man who comes into the world (Jn. 1:9). No man has been saved or has been forced to stay saved against his will. Because men are born of God's will and not their own (Jn. 1:13) is no proof that they are saved only because of God's will.

It simply means that salvation has not been provided by the will of man, but it is also true that God cannot and will not save one man if he himself (the man) does not will it (Jn. 3:16-20; 22:17; Mk. 16:15-16; I Tim. 4:10). It is God's will to save all, but all are not saved, so, it must also take the will of man in accepting the gospel for him to be saved.

GOD'S BLESSINGS

The blessing of God upon every person is conditional upon personal faith and conformity to the gospel, not upon predetermined choices of God. Meeting gospel conditions, such as repentance and faith, are not works that purchase salvation, but are necessary requirements to be saved if one wants the salvation purchased by the blood of Christ. Choosing to eat a meal prepared by someone does not earn the meal, but it is necessary to eat it if one wants the benefits of the food provided for him.

If God should seek to save and keep individuals contrary to their wills, He would break His own laws and fail to carry out His own plan. God could not be guilty of such unlawful dealings, so, if men are finally lost, it is not because God has failed, His plan has failed, the sacrifice of Christ has failed, or that God did not have power to keep them contrary to His plan. If God's promises and covenants were made on the condition that man must fulfill righteousness, then God cannot do otherwise than to cut off all who refuse to conform to His demands.

If God failed to hold men to the terms of the contracts He has made with them, He would be a liar, and all men with free wills would lose respect for Him. The following are a few of the many passages that plainly teach that God's dealings have always been on the condition of obedience (Ex. 15:26; 19:5-6; 22:23-24; 23:30-33; 32:33; Lev. 26:3-46; Deut. 7:12-14; 8:10-20; Josh. 23:16; 24:20; I Sam. 12:14-15, 24; Jn. 15:1-6; I Cor. 15:1-5; Col. 1:23; Heb. 3:6, 12-14; 4:11; 6:4-12; II Pet. 2:20-22).

CONTRARY TO THEIR FREE CHOICE

Nothing is hard to understand about election, foreknowledge, or predestination when we realize that it is God's plan itself, and not personal conformity to that plan, that has been foreknown and predestinated. God decrees that all who do conform will be saved, and all who do not will be lost, and this is the sum and substance of these doctrines. God's decrees were never made to determine the choices of free moral agents as to whether some will be saved or others will be lost.

The decrees of God are those parts of His plan to which all must conform in order to be saved, and those who refuse will be lost. Men have made the great mistake of making the doctrine of decrees, to which all must conform to be saved, the same as the free acts of men and conforming to those laws.

God does not determine our willing and doing, but He does decree the basis of the action for free moral agents that will save or damn them accordingly. This does not mean that the initiative of man's salvation

is with man. It is with God, who chooses to make a way of salvation for all men, especially of them who believe and that conform to His plan of their own free choice.

MAN'S CHOICE

The reason God saves only a few is because only a few choose the way of God, and therefore, God is free from the final responsibility of the salvation or damnation of anyone.

If God offers pardon to all, then all can accept alike, or the offer of pardon is a fraud. If all can accept, then He is fair to all regarding salvation and damnation; therefore, it rests with the individual and not with God.

To argue that God offers a pardon to all alike and then to contradict this by saying that He offers it to only a few special one's whom He has chosen to save does not make sound logic and is not scriptural. God does not force one to become willing and another to become unwilling to be saved. He deals with all men, seeking to persuade them to be saved, and because some become willing and others do not is no sign that God is responsible for the choice made.

The phrase, *"Which cry day and night unto Him,"* proclaims two things:

1. God answers prayer and, in fact, delights in answering prayer, but will do so only in His way.

2. Believers are strongly encouraged to bring every petition to the Lord, and do so, at least if it is according to His Word, until the answer comes.

The conclusion of the question, *"Though he bear long with them?"* has reference to the fact that even though the judge delayed from selfish indifference, God at times delays from an all-wise purpose, depending on what is asked or whether one has faith or not (Heb. 11:6; James 1:5-8).

If it is something that is promised only for the next life, then the delay is clear from Scripture. If it is something promised in this life, then refuse to give up until it is received, at least after one determines that it is God's will (Mat. 17:20; 21:22; Mk. 9:23; 11:22-24; Heb. 11:6; James 1:5-8).

(8) "I TELL YOU THAT HE WILL AVENGE THEM SPEEDILY. NEVERTHELESS WHEN THE SON OF MAN COMES,

SHALL HE FIND FAITH ON THE EARTH?"

The overview is:

1. The phrase, *"I tell you that He will avenge them speedily,"* is simply the assurance that God will answer prayer and that in comparison to man, He will answer speedily.

2. Most of the things asked of God are impossible with man, and even if possible, take an inordinate length of time. So, if God does not answer immediately, and as stated, He does see fit to delay, still, what He does is much quicker than anything man could do, if at all.

3. The question, *"Nevertheless when the Son of Man comes, shall He find faith on the earth?"* pertains to the second coming.

4. In fact, by the time of the second coming, the true church will already have been raptured away (I Thess. 4:16; II Thess. 2:7-8).

5. As well, many, if not most of those saved during the great tribulation, will be assassinated by the Antichrist (Rev. 6:9-11; 7:9-17; 13:16-18; 15:2-4; 20:4-6).

6. Consequently, there won't be much faith in God on the earth at the time of the second coming.

7. As well as the great lesson on prayer taught by Christ in this parable, He is also telling believers that the condition of the earth will steadily deteriorate, spiritually speaking, instead of the opposite as taught by some.

8. Actually, the question of Verse 8 shows the uselessness of expecting the conversion of the world before Christ comes, and makes evident the foolishness of supposing that all people are good at heart despite their outward conduct, and so will all ultimately be in heaven.

(9) "AND HE SPOKE THIS PARABLE UNTO CERTAIN WHICH TRUSTED IN THEMSELVES THAT THEY WERE RIGHTEOUS, AND DESPISED OTHERS."

The structure is:

1. The phrase, *"And He spoke this parable unto certain which trusted in themselves,"* refers to the Pharisees and all like them, even to this present hour.

2. The Pharisees claimed salvation as a right on two grounds:

a. Because they belonged to the chosen race, namely Israel.

b. Because they rigidly and minutely claimed to obey the precepts of a singular code of laws, many of them devised by themselves and their fathers. Upon these two grounds, they claimed salvation.

3. *"That they were righteous, and despised others,"* proclaims the twin curse of self-righteousness.

4. Self-righteousness is that which is produced as the result of a works religion. As well, the self-righteous despise all others who depend on the grace of God alone; consequently, religion, which is always man-devised, is the most destructive element in the world and, in fact, ever has been.

5. This parable is so graphic and so absolutely clear as to its meaning that even a child can understand it. It outlines so perfectly God's plan of salvation and, as well, delineates man's pitiful efforts to save himself by a religion of his own making. There is no room or reason for misinterpretation.

(10) "TWO MEN WENT UP INTO THE TEMPLE TO PRAY; THE ONE A PHARISEE, AND THE OTHER A PUBLICAN."

TWO MEN

The phrase, *"Two men went up into the temple to pray,"* starkly contrasts the two. Both were going to the temple to pray, but only one would be heard by God, who would probably be the very opposite of the one most men would choose.

So, this tells us that all types of people go to church to pray on Sundays, or whatever day, but for many, the effort is a fruitless exercise.

THE PHARISEE

The phrase, *"The one a Pharisee,"* pertained to the ruling religious party in Israel at the time of Christ. Inasmuch as they claimed to believe the entire Bible, they would have been called the fundamentalists of their time.

While it is certainly not wrong to believe all of the Bible, but actually right, still, one must not allow one's beliefs of this nature to breed self-righteousness as, sadly, it does in many cases.

It is regrettable, but these individuals who claimed to believe all of the Bible and to uphold it rigidly, in fact, hated Christ, who was the living Word (Jn. 1:1).

NOTES

HOW COULD SOMEONE WHO CLAIMED TO BELIEVE ALL THE BIBLE BE SO FAR OFF BASE?

To be sure, it was not the believing of the Bible that caused this problem, but rather the very opposite, actually, not believing it. In other words, despite their claims, they really did not believe the Bible, nor did they follow it, but rather followed rules and regulations of their own manufacture. They had actually added over 600 commands to the original law of Moses, even claiming that they were more important than the Bible itself. Such is the deception of man, and more importantly, the deception of religious man.

THE PUBLICAN

"And the other a publican," refers to mostly tax collectors. These were Jews who, at least in the eyes of other Jews, had sold out to Rome. In other words, they were traitors and deemed as the lowest of the low and, consequently, unable to be saved; however, that's not what the Lord said!

(11) "THE PHARISEE STOOD AND PRAYED THUS WITH HIMSELF, GOD, I THANK YOU, THAT I AM NOT AS OTHER MEN ARE, EXTORTIONERS, UNJUST, ADULTERERS, OR EVEN AS THIS PUBLICAN."

A PRAYER THAT WAS NOT HEARD

The phrase, *"The Pharisee stood and prayed thus with himself,"* proclaims the prayer of this man, and actually many, if not most! Even though his prayer was directed to God, still, it was actually *"with himself,"* meaning "to himself."

The phrase, *"God, I thank You, that I am not as other men are,"* proclaims the beginning of this prayer as obvious proof that this man did not know who he was or what or who God was? He was a self-righteous, conceited, bragging example of what religion will do to a person.

THE SELF-RIGHTEOUSNESS OF RELIGION

Here is the basic reason religion is antithetical to a real relationship with God. Religion always contains an element of

self-righteousness. By the term *self-righteousness,* we mean the central tendency of humans to try to earn their own salvation or to retain their own salvation, either totally or partially.

Probably no one ever understood self-righteousness any better than the apostle Paul, mainly because he practiced it for nearly half of his earthly life. He probably was in his early to mid-thirties when he was converted to Christ, and he lived as a legalistic Pharisee until that time. His own testimony is expressed in many locations in his writings, but it probably is as clear in the following verses as it is in any other place:

"Though I might also have confidence in the flesh. If any other man thinks that he has whereof he might trust in the flesh, I more" (Phil. 3:4).

These are not just empty words because this man could back up his claim to self-righteousness. To prove his point he drew back the curtain of his past life when he was known as Saul of Tarsus. By doing so, he showed that no religious person ever had more of which to boast than he did. His inventory of personal attainments included seven items. He probably could have listed more, but these seven put him far ahead of most others. And yet, this man would later write and say to us, *"God forbid that I should glory* (boast), *save in the Cross of our Lord Jesus Christ, by whom the world is crucified unto me, and I unto the world"* (Gal. 6:14).

THE RELIGION OF THE APOSTLE PAUL

The great apostle now gives his credentials for self-righteousness:

"Circumcised the eighth day, of the stock of Israel, of the tribe of Benjamin, an Hebrew of the Hebrews; as touching the law, a Pharisee;

"Concerning zeal, persecuting the church; touching the righteousness which is in the law, blameless" (Phil. 3:5-6). Please notice that the first four items in this catalog of merits have to do with involuntary benefits that were his because of heredity and environment.

• First, he was circumcised on the eighth day in accordance with the requirements of the Mosaic law (Lev. 12:3). By way of contrast, Jewish proselytes were circumcised as adults, and Ishmael was 13 when he was circumcised (Gen. 17:25).

• Second, Saul was a true Israelite, a term utilized in the Bible for the people chosen by God to be His witnesses on the earth (Isa. 43:1-10; Rom. 11:1; II Cor. 11:22).

• Third, he was a member of the tribe of Benjamin, the only tribe that remained faithful to Judah when the other ten tribes rebelled (I Ki. 12:21). After the Babylonian captivity, this tribe actually merged with Judah (Ezra 4:1). Saul himself probably was named after the first king of Israel, who was also a member of the tribe of Benjamin.

• Fourth, the apostle Paul was *"an Hebrew of the Hebrews,"* a title that indicates that he was born into a family where both Hebrew and Aramaic were spoken (Acts 21:40; 22:2). Most Jews of the day were Hellenists who spoke the Greek language and accepted Greek customs (Acts 6:1). As one can see, Paul's involuntary merits could not be matched.

• Neither could his voluntary merits. He chose to be a Pharisee, the strictest Jewish religious sect of his day.

• He decided to be more zealous than any of his fellow Pharisees. He was so consumed with his own zeal that he attempted to waste the New Testament church because he honestly believed it was a threat to Judaism (Acts 7:58; 9:1-2).

• Lastly, Paul attempted to be the most blameless (self-righteous) Pharisee who ever lived and in his own eyes, he was. However, he received a rousing revelation of Christ (Acts 9:3-8), which literally revolutionized his life.

THE REVELATION OF CHRIST

Paul expressed his climactic conversion to Christ with the word *but* in Philippians 3:7, *"But what things were gain to me, those I counted loss for Christ."* Suddenly, all the precious possessions of his former life meant nothing in comparison with his newly-found relationship with Jesus. In fact, all these former merits suddenly seemed as dung or rubbish. He said, *"Yea doubtless, and I count all things but loss for the excellency of the*

NOTES

knowledge of Christ Jesus my Lord: for whom I have suffered the loss of all things, and do count them but dung, that I may win Christ" (Phil. 3:8).

The Greek term for *knowledge* refers to an experiential knowledge. In other words, Paul's knowledge of God was not just a matter of mental assent; it was based on a personal relationship with Christ.

THE RIGHTEOUSNESS OF CHRIST

Paul exchanged his own righteousness for the righteousness of Jesus. He knew that the latter type of righteousness would be the only kind of righteousness that would suffice in the future day of judgment. *"And be found in Him, not having my own righteousness, which is of the law, but that which is through the faith of Christ* (faith related to Christ), *the righteousness which is of God by faith"* (Phil. 3:9).

His own personal deliverance from the bondage of self-righteousness made it easy for Paul to understand the religious bondage of his fellow Jews. *"Brethren, my heart's desire and prayer to God for Israel is, that they might be saved.*

"For I bear them record that they have a zeal of (for) *God, but not according to knowledge"* (Rom. 10:1-2).

The apostle certainly could empathize with his fellow Jews who were pursuing a religion of self-righteousness with a zeal that was not based on an experiential knowledge of God.

GOD'S RIGHTEOUSNESS

The word *zeal* contains the idea of possessing an all-consuming desire for something. Paul's fellow Israelites were extremely sincere, just like he was before he became a Christian, but their sincerity involved the self-righteousness of religion, not the true righteousness of God.

In fact, Paul said, *"For they being ignorant of God's righteousness, and going about to establish their own righteousness, have not submitted themselves unto the righteousness of God"* (Rom. 10:3). This verse gets to the heart of the real problem with self-righteousness. Whatever form it takes, and a multitude of types exist, it will always be involved in some way with erecting a monument to self.

The Greek infinitive for *"to establish"* literally carries the idea of erecting a monument to one's own efforts. This invariably happens to a degree when people abandon God's righteousness. *"Have not submitted"* stems from a military term, which portrays the orderly lineup of a military detachment under a commanding officer.

DEGREES OF SELF-RIGHTEOUSNESS

This kind of discussion automatically makes many believers defensive because they argue that they have not totally abandoned God's righteousness like Israel did. The problem is that many Christians drift by degrees from the righteousness of Christ to self-righteousness. Hence, they get bound in the self-righteousness of religion to the degree that they depart from God's righteousness. I mean by this that God will accept no righteousness except the righteousness of God, which the believer can receive, and receive instantly upon faith evidenced in Christ and what Christ did for us at the Cross.

The great prophet Isaiah said, *"But we are all as an unclean thing, and all our righteousnesses* (righteous acts) *are as filthy rags; and we all do fade as a leaf; and our iniquities, like the wind, have taken us away"* (Isa. 64:6). The only real righteousness that we have is the righteousness of God; anything else is the self-righteousness of religion.

Paul said the same thing when he penned, *"For Christ is the end of the law for righteousness to everyone who believes"* (Rom. 10:4). The Greek noun for *end* means "purpose," and this word occupies the position of emphasis in the Greek text. In other words, the entire purpose of the Mosaic law is to point people to the righteousness of God who can deliver them from sin. *"Wherefore the law was our schoolmaster to bring us unto Christ, that we might be justified by faith"* (Gal. 3:24).

RELIGION SPECIALIZES IN SELF-RIGHTEOUSNESS

In conclusion, the apostle Paul decried his former self-righteousness, and he

NOTES

decried this self-righteousness of his fellow Israelites. We forget that religion specializes in self-righteousness or human attempts to bring us to God or to keep us close to God.

The latter is the area in which multitudes of sincere believers allow themselves to be co-opted into the self-righteousness of religion. That is, they began their Christian experience with total dependence on the righteousness of God, but later drift into a mindset of feeling that they have developed personal righteousness.

Again, the only real righteousness that a human has is the righteousness of God, that is, if he has any at all. It is all of Christ and none of us. In other words, we are not righteous because we do certain things, but we're righteous only because of the righteousness of God in our lives, which is obtained by the believer placing his faith exclusively in Christ and what Christ has done for us at the Cross.

FAITH

Allowing ourselves to be gradually assimilated into the self-righteousness of religion will cause us to believe that our good works somehow contribute to our righteousness. Of course, we should manifest good works! James said, *"Even so faith, if it has not works, is dead, being alone.*

"Yes, a man may say, You have faith, and I have works: show me your faith without your works, and I will show you my faith by my works" (James 2:17-18). When Christ truly lives in and through us, good works will be manifested, but we must be careful that we do not take credit for these good works. They result from Christ living in and through us, not because of any righteousness of our own.

Let us make it crystal clear that the righteousness of God is afforded us only on the basis of our faith; however, for the faith to be genuine, it must have as its correct object *"Jesus Christ, and Him crucified"* (I Cor. 1:17-18, 23; 2:2; Col. 2:10-15).

In fact, the Cross of Christ makes everything possible that we receive from God. While our Lord Jesus Christ is the source of all things we receive from God, it is the Cross of Christ that is the means by which these things are given to us. Simple faith in Christ and what He did for us at the Cross will instantly cause God to impute to us a perfect, pure, and spotless righteousness— the righteousness of God. If this righteousness is attempted to be attained in any other way, that way is automatically rejected by the Lord (II Cor. 11:1-4).

(Most of the portion on the self-righteousness of religions was derived from the notes of Dr. Bernard Rossier, former professor at Jimmy Swaggart Bible College.)

RELATIVE RIGHTEOUSNESS

The phrase, *"Extortioners, unjust, adulterers, or even as this publican,"* points to the faults that self-righteousness gleefully points out in others. This is what one might call "relative righteousness," which God can never accept. In other words, they judge their righteousness by the righteousness of others, or the lack thereof, at least as seen through their eyes.

Much of the church operates in this fashion. Somehow it makes one feel superior to point out the problems of others, or else, one's sin does not seem so bad if he can find worse sins in others, whether real or imagined.

From the inference given by Christ, I think it is obvious that none of us have any right to point at someone else, as this Pharisee did. The Lord must be terribly displeased with such action.

As well, at the very moment the Pharisee was berating this publican in prayer, the Lord was forgiving the man of whatever sins he had actually committed. Consequently, the accusations as tendered by the Pharisee regarding the publican were, in fact, a slap in the face of God, as well as a denial of God's grace. When one does that, one is shutting himself off, as well, from the grace of God!

Does the reader fully understand the terrible wickedness committed when the sins of someone else are brought up, which, in truth, God has already washed, cleansed, and forgotten?

In other words, by bringing up such, God, in effect, is called a liar. And yet, many believers seem to have no compunction whatsoever about dragging out things that

God has forgiven. To do such proclaims that the Pharisee did not know or understand the grace of God, or else, had chosen to ignore it, which compounds the sin. But yet, this is something that relative righteousness will always do.

(12) "I FAST TWICE IN THE WEEK, I GIVE TITHES OF ALL THAT I POSSESS."

The construction is:

1. The phrase, *"I fast twice in the week,"* proclaims self-righteousness adding to or taking away from the Word of God.

2. The Lord had commanded only one annual fast (Lev. 16:29; Num. 29:7). In the days of the prophet Zechariah, three more fasts had been added by man, which meant they were not from God (Zech. 8:19). By the time of Christ, two fasts a week were commanded by the rabbis.

WORKS RIGHTEOUSNESS

3. The phrase, *"I give tithes of all that I possess,"* seemingly makes him feel very good about himself, especially considering that the publican had probably given little or nothing to God.

4. As the previous verse portrayed relative righteousness, this verse portrays works righteousness, which translated into individuals attempting to earn their salvation by their good works.

Millions fill modern churches and, sadly, follow in the train of this Pharisee of old. They think that attending church and involving themselves in all types of community projects earn them salvation.

Millions of others think that by belonging to a certain church, their salvation is guaranteed or at least enhanced. Irrespective of what it may be or how good it may be, all constitutes works and can never be accepted by God in the realm of righteousness. It is the same old story of Cain offering his vegetables, which God would not accept (Gen. 4:3-5).

(13) "AND THE PUBLICAN, STANDING AFAR OFF, WOULD NOT LIFT UP SO MUCH AS HIS EYES UNTO HEAVEN, BUT SMOTE UPON HIS BREAST, SAYING, GOD BE MERCIFUL TO ME A SINNER."

The structure is:

1. The phrase, *"And the publican,*

standing afar off," means that he did not feel free to come close to the temple appointments as had the Pharisee, and for the obvious reasons. He felt, and actually knew, that he was a moral leper. Consequently, there was no self-worthiness.

2. This is the first thing that God demands in a person, at least for that person to be accepted. The individual must know and realize that there is no moral good in him. As well, even the best of us, whomever that may be, fall into the same category. Believe it or not, Romans 3:9-18 applies to all.

3. Fully understanding this, as the Pharisee obviously did not, we can never feel free to speak harshly of others.

4. *"Would not lift up so much as his eyes unto heaven,"* refers to him realizing just how unclean he actually was.

5. Justification by faith is a declaration by God that the respected party is not guilty by virtue of faith in Christ and what Christ has done for us at the Cross. Consequently, when one is declared *"not guilty,"* one can look God in the eye and not blink.

6. This publican was in the process of being justified, and then he would be able to lift up his eyes unto heaven and look God full in the face, so to speak, without guilt or condemnation. As stated, such is justification by faith.

7. *"But smote upon his breast, saying, God be merciful to me a sinner,"* brought instant results because his plea was based upon atonement and not on self-righteousness.

8. Every afternoon at 3 p.m., the evening lamb was offered as a propitiation for the sins of that day. The publican pleaded forgiveness and acceptance because of the merit of that atoning blood. It foreshadowed the atoning death of the Lamb of God, who was Himself the propitiation, i.e., the mercy seat.

(14) "I TELL YOU, THIS MAN WENT DOWN TO HIS HOUSE JUSTIFIED RATHER THAN THE OTHER: FOR EVERY ONE WHO EXALTS HIMSELF SHALL BE ABASED; AND HE WHO HUMBLES HIMSELF SHALL BE EXALTED."

The pattern is:

1. It is the Cross of Christ that has made justification possible (Rom. 6:1-14).

NOTES

2. Everything the believer receives from God comes exclusively by the means of the Cross.

3. That's the reason Paul said, *"I determined not to know anything among you save Jesus Christ, and Him crucified"* (I Cor. 2:2).

WHAT IS JUSTIFICATION BY FAITH?

The phrase, *"I tell you, this man went down to his house justified rather than the other,"* tells us much about God and the human heart.

This passage by Christ announces, even under the old law of Moses, the principle of justification by faith, which is the only foundation on which God can cleanse and sanctify a sinner.

In the Old Testament, the concept of justification by faith began with the fall of Adam and Eve in the garden of Eden. It said, *"The Lord God made coats of skins, and clothed them,"* which implied sacrifice (Gen. 3:21).

From this concept as outlined in Genesis 4:1-7, man was taught that the sacrifice of a clean animal looked forward to the promised Redeemer (Heb. 9:22). To be sure, the sacrifice of a clean animal could not save anyone simply because the blood of bulls and goats could not take away sins. However, what it represented, namely the coming Redeemer and faith in what He would do, served as an atonement for sin and, in effect, justification by faith.

COVERED OR CLEANSED?

However, it must be understood that justification by faith in Old Testament times, although complete in the mind of God, still fell short respecting benefits, although granting total salvation.

For instance, before Jesus died on Calvary, men's sins were not taken away literally but only covered, hence, the *atonement*, which actually means "to cover or conceal." Now that Jesus has died on Calvary, our sin is not merely covered but, in effect, totally and completely taken away (Jn. 1:29).

As well, before Calvary, which paid for man's redemption, and the resurrection, which ratified that redemption, men could not be baptized with the Holy Spirit (Jn. 7:37-39). Now, any believer can be baptized with the Holy Spirit (Acts 2:4; 19:1-7).

Also, before Jesus came, righteous souls were taken to paradise, which was very close to hell, with both being located in the heart of the earth, and there, they were actually held captive by Satan (Lk. 16:19-31; Eph. 4:8-9). Since the resurrection, believers no longer go to paradise when they die, but rather to heaven itself.

Justification by faith is a legal concept entered into by God strictly on His initiative, which declares a guilty person, in effect, not guilty. As stated, it is done by faith and not by works.

THE CONCEPT AS GIVEN TO ABRAHAM WAS ENLARGED

The Scripture says, *"And he believed in the LORD; and He counted it to him for righteousness"* (Gen. 15:6).

This was the basis for justification in the Old Testament and is the basis in the New Testament.

It simply means that Abraham had faith in what God told him concerning the coming Redeemer. Accordingly, on this basis alone (faith in the promise), God instantly accounted Abraham as righteous.

The theological meaning of justification rests heavily on the judicial concept. God is the ultimate judge of all beings in the universe. He will evaluate their actions and will not clear the guilty. Yet, David in Psalm 51, appealed to God for forgiveness. David relied on God's mercy, despite the fact that a sentence of condemnation would have been completely justified by the fact of David's sin.

David faced this dilemma and expressed his conviction that it was God's saving action alone that could free him from guilt and restore his joy. Thus, David called on God to justify (to declare him innocent) despite his sin and his guilt. He did this despite what the law of Moses said, which clearly condemned him, and all others who had sinned as well.

In fact, there was no salvation in the law; consequently, David could not appeal to that source; however, he appealed to the blood

that was applied to the doorpost in Egypt, which was a type of the coming shed blood of Jesus Christ. God had said, *"And the blood shall be to you for a token upon the houses where you are* (irrespective of who you are)*: and when I see the blood, I will pass over you"* (Ex. 12:13).

THE BLOOD

Consequently, David said, *"Purge me with hyssop, and I shall be clean: wash me, and I shall be whiter than snow"* (Ps. 51:7).

The blood was applied by hyssop to the doorposts in Egypt.

Therefore, David was not allowed to escape the penalty of the law just because he was king, as some people think. The penalty of the broken law held for him as it did all others. David did what all others at that time did, at least who had faith in God. He appealed to the promise of God that if faith and trust were offered in what the sacrifices represented, washing and cleansing from sin would be the result, with forgiveness granted, which made null and void the penalty of the broken law.

When David said, in Psalm 51:16, *"For You desire not sacrifice; else would I give it: You delight not in burnt offering,"* he simply meant that the blood of bulls and goats could not take away sins (Heb. 10:4). However, what these sacrifices foreshadowed (the shed blood of Jesus Christ) definitely could take away sin.

Irrespective, the sacrifice must be offered with the understanding of what it represented. The death of the clean animal was a figure of what should happen to the sinner, but instead, would be borne by Christ. Consequently, the Lord told David, *"The sacrifices of God are a broken spirit,"* which means not a hint of self-righteousness, but *"a broken and contrite heart,"* which God *"will not despise"* (Ps. 51:16-17).

ISAIAH, CHAPTER 53

Passages like Psalm 51 prefigure the doctrine of justification as it is developed in the New Testament, but already in Isaiah, Chapter 53, the Old Testament gives a clear picture of that developed doctrine. Isaiah looked ahead to the suffering of Jesus. In

Isaiah 53:6, he saw, at least in some measure, Christ's sacrificial death, in which *"the LORD has laid on Him the iniquity of us all,"* and described some of the events of Calvary in graphic detail. Then the prophet concluded:

"He (God the Father) *shall see of the travail of His soul* (the soul of Christ), *and shall be satisfied: by His knowledge* (that of Christ) *shall My righteous servant* (Jesus Christ) *justify many: for He* (Jesus) *shall bear their iniquities.*

"Therefore will I divide Him a portion with the great, and He (the Lord Jesus) *shall divide the spoil with the strong; because He has poured out His soul unto death: and He was numbered with the transgressors; and He bore the sin of many, and made intercession for the transgressors"* (Isa. 53:11-12).

On the basis of faith in that poured-out life, God will declare many righteous, despite their sins and failures.

JUSTIFICATION IN THE NEW TESTAMENT

Even though justification by faith has been the manner in which God has saved believing sinners from the very beginning, it was the apostle Paul who developed this great doctrine.

Paul began his argument in Romans by showing that no human being is righteous in God's sight (Rom., Chpts. 1-3). Since all are sinners, with no exceptions, God at the same time can save all on the basis of a pronounced faith in Christ. Romans 3:21-31 announces a righteousness from God that is given freely if received by faith in Christ Jesus. Paul shows that the substitutionary death of Jesus provided a basis on which God can make this judicial pronouncement.

As human beings always fall far short of the divine standard of righteousness, which is the only standard God will recognize, humanity's only hope is a righteousness that is separate and distinct from human actions.

PAUL GOES BACK TO ABRAHAM

With Romans 4:3, Paul goes back in history and shows that his presentation of justification by faith is in harmony with the Old Testament. *"Abraham believed*

God," Paul quotes from Genesis, *"and it was counted unto* (credited to) *him for* (as) *righteousness."*

Moving on through history, Paul shows later in Romans, Chapter 4, that justification has always come through faith and not through human efforts to live by the law.

In Romans, Chapter 5, the apostle returns to the death of Christ and says, *"Therefore being* (since we have been) *justified by* (through) *faith, we have peace with God through our Lord Jesus Christ"* (Rom. 5:1).

JUSTIFICATION IS ALWAYS IN THE PAST TENSE

Please note that in Romans 5:1, Paul says that *we have been.* God, the judge, has already announced His verdict. The person who has faith in Jesus stands acquitted now. The divine judge has spoken, and no one can annul the divine decision. Through faith, we are declared righteous and stand acquitted of every charge that might be brought against us.

Consequently, one might say the following:

• Justification declares the believing sinner as not guilty, but it goes further than that.

• It declares the believing sinner innocent of all charges. The verdict of "innocent" is far different than the verdict of "not guilty."

• Justification also means that not only is a person not guilty and, as well, declared innocent, he also is perfect. That is because our perfection is totally and solely in Christ. In other words, our faith in Him and what He did at Calvary automatically gives us His perfection. Paul proclaims that performance or one's behavior is not the basis on which righteousness is given. In effect, no one's performance can win a verdict of "righteous" in the sight of God. This is nailed down by saying, "By observing the law no one will be justified," or in other words, it does not come by works or performance (Gal. 2:16). Here Paul introduces another dimension of divine justification.

CHRIST WHO LIVES IN THE BELIEVER

Through the person and agency of the

Holy Spirit, Christ now actually lives in the believer. Jesus said: *"At that day you shall know that I am in My Father, and you in Me, and I in you"* (Jn. 14:20).

And then in Romans, Paul said, *"Know you not, that so many of us as were baptized into Jesus Christ* (plainly says that this baptism is into Christ and not water [I Cor. 1:17; 12:13; Gal. 3:27; Eph. 4:5; Col. 2:10-15]) *were baptized into His death?* (When Christ died on the Cross, in the mind of God, we died with Him; in other words, He became our substitute, and our identification with Him in His death gives us all the benefits for which He died; the idea is that He did it all for us!)

"Therefore we are buried with Him by baptism into death (not only did we die with Him, but we were buried with Him, as well, which means that all the sin and transgression of the past were buried; when they put Him in the tomb, they put all of our sins into that tomb also): *that like as Christ was raised up from the dead by the glory of the Father, even so we also should walk in newness of life* (we died with Him, we were buried with Him, and His resurrection was our resurrection to a "newness of life").

"For if we have been planted together (with Christ) *in the likeness of His death* (Paul proclaims the Cross as the instrument through which all blessings come; consequently, the Cross must ever be the object of our faith, which gives the Holy Spirit latitude to work within our lives), *we shall be also in the likeness of His resurrection* (we can have the 'likeness of His resurrection,' i.e., 'live this resurrection life,' only as long as we understand the 'likeness of His death,' which refers to the Cross as the means by which all of this is done)" (Rom. 6:3-5).

THE PRINCIPLE OF FAITH

In Galatians, Chapter 3, Paul argues that the principle of faith, which operates in justification, must also be applied as the believer seeks to live a righteous life: all who rely on observing the law are under a curse (Gal. 3:10) and the righteous will live by faith (Gal. 3:11).

NOTES

Paul then shows, as we have attempted to bring out, how the principle of faith infuses the entire Old Testament as well as the New Testament. Only by misunderstanding the message of the Old Testament could God's people have imagined that righteousness could be won by their efforts to conform to the law or by any other manner of works.

Only by misunderstanding the doctrine of justification can believers today imagine that they may become righteous by a struggle to live by a law, whether the Old Testament law or a law of their own devising. Reliance on God both for salvation and for power to live a righteous life is the only option the believer has, or needs for that matter!

To be sure, justification by faith includes much more than merely a pardon: It includes also a transformation. God will declare, as stated, the sinner righteous, and then God will act to make the sinner what God has declared him to be.

JUSTIFICATION IS ALWAYS TOTAL AND NEVER PARTIAL

This is very important to understand. *"The blood of Jesus Christ ... Cleanses us from all sin,"* and not just some sin (I Jn. 1:7).

John again emphasizes such by saying, *"To cleanse us from all unrighteousness"* (I Jn. 1:9).

And yet, we have many religious denominations and preachers who attempt to add something to this finished work. In other words, they add some type of penance, etc. Such does despite to the Spirit of grace and is actually an insult to what Christ did at Calvary and the resurrection. Either He cleanses from all sin, or He doesn't. If He doesn't, then our faith is vain (I Cor. 15:14).

To emphasize what I am saying: If many modern preachers had their way, Peter would not have been able to preach on the day of Pentecost because of his past failure. In their eyes, he was unworthy; however, the Lord didn't see it that way, and His way is the only way that matters.

As well, David would have been deposed as king, which is what an apostate church attempted to do, but God did not depose him because of the very thing of which we speak. David was justified by faith.

ABRAHAM

According to most modern doctrines of works religion, Abraham would have forfeited his right to the promised child, Isaac, because he lied about his wife, subsequently, submitting her to a possible defilement, which could have destroyed the entirety of the plan of God. Consequently, this sin was far more grievous than one realizes. Regrettably, Abraham did the same identical thing all over again a short time before Isaac was born (Gen., Chpt. 20). However, Abraham did not forfeit God's call or plan because of justification by faith.

If these detractors of the grace of God would think for a moment, they would realize that according to their doctrine, no one is saved, not even themselves. The reason is glaringly obvious. There has never been a believer who has not had to go to God time and time again and seek mercy, grace, and forgiveness for wrongs committed. While it is certainly awful for any believer to sin, which will always bring extremely negative results, still, as John said, *"And if any man sin, we have an advocate with the Father, Jesus Christ the righteous:*

"And He is the propitiation for our sins: and not for ours only, but also for the sins of the whole world" (I Jn. 2:1-2).

CAN JUSTIFICATION BE LOST

Yes, it can!

Paul said, *"Stand fast therefore in the liberty* (justification by faith) *wherewith Christ has made us free, and be not entangled again with the yoke of bondage* (works religion)*"* (Gal. 5:1).

The words *"entangled again"* refer to leaving justification by faith and going back to personal efforts and the attempt to justify oneself. Paul said that if this happens, as it has happened many times, *"Christ is become of no effect unto you, whosoever of you are justified by the law* (attempt to be justified by law or personal efforts)*; you are fallen from grace* (fallen from justification by faith)*"* (Gal. 5:4).

The idea is that it is faith in Christ and

what He did for us at the Cross that justifies one. If the person, as stated, leaves faith and resorts to works, then he nullifies his place and position in Christ. It's faith that got us in, and that is the only source of entrance, and faith moved to something else other than Christ and the Cross can take one out of grace, i.e., justification.

HOW CAN ONE BE JUSTIFIED?

Millions attempt to justify themselves by their efforts, which God will not and, in fact, cannot accept.

Others come to Christ, truly being justified by faith in Christ, but then, little by little, as Paul here declared, begin to think that their religious works, whatever they may be, bring about some type of righteousness. In other words, it becomes a mixture of works and faith. Under these circumstances, faith in Christ is nullified, with the person falling from grace.

Justification by faith is not just the principle of faith alone; it must be faith in Christ and Christ alone, which includes what He did for us at the Cross as well. If we try to eliminate the Cross from Christ, we are left with *"another Jesus,"* which God can never accept (II Cor. 11:4).

If an individual believes that his salvation consists of having faith in Christ plus belonging to a certain church, keeping a certain set of rules, or doing certain other things, he has then nullified the grace of God. In effect, he is saying that what Jesus did at Calvary is not quite sufficient and needs other things added to complete the process.

However, it should be quickly stated that while no good deeds of any nature can contribute toward one's justification in Christ, still, one must ever understand that justification by faith never gives a person license to sin (Rom. 6:1-2). In fact, justification by faith is the only way to overcome sin.

SIN

Some of the believers in Paul's day, as now, were arguing that if salvation is free and separate from works, likewise, they reasoned, one could not lose his justification by committing sin because grace would instantly pardon him. However, Paul addressed that very dogmatically by saying, *"God forbid. How shall we, who are dead to sin, live any longer therein?"* (Rom. 6:2).

Consequently, if an individual desires to continue in sin after justification by faith, he will forfeit his justification. *"Continue in sin"* means continuing the practice of sin, in other words, living a sinful life and making no effort to overcome the problem. It stands to reason that as a result, at a point in time, which is left up to God, he will forfeit his justification.

In other words, the publican, who went to his house justified, could not and would not desire to continue his extortion, unrighteousness, adultery, etc. He had been set free from that bondage of darkness, and he would continue to be free by his trust in Christ.

SELF EXALTATION

The phrase, *"For every one who exalts himself shall be abased; and he who humbles himself shall be exalted,"* proclaims the basis for acceptance by God.

Those who exalt themselves do so as the Pharisee by thinking the things they do or don't do in the realm of personal acts make them righteous. In God's eyes, they are abased, i.e., humiliated.

The lack of humility here mentioned has far more to do than the mere action of the individual. It speaks of a denial of what one really is—a sinner who cannot save himself—and a denial of what Jesus has done at Calvary. If man could save himself by his works, Christ died needlessly, and we know that He most definitely did not die needlessly.

Conversely, the person who humbles himself is, in effect, saying that he realizes he is a sinner, deserving of eternal damnation, and in no way can save himself. Consequently, he throws himself on the mercy and grace of God, with God exalting him by granting salvation.

As a result of this teaching by Christ respecting the Pharisee and publican, we learn that there are no degrees in justification. Verse 14 does not teach that the Pharisee was partly justified and the publican fully, but it means that the one was wholly justified and the other not at all.

Had man originated these two parables, the first on faith and the second on justification, he would probably have set them in an opposite order. However, the order in the Scripture is divine.

First, the fruit of faith is shown and then its root, which is justification, the greatest gift that God ever gave humanity.

(15) "AND THEY BROUGHT UNTO HIM ALSO INFANTS, THAT HE WOULD TOUCH THEM: BUT WHEN HIS DISCIPLES SAW IT, THEY REBUKED THEM."

The form is:

1. The phrase, *"And they brought unto Him also infants, that He would touch them,"* will now be used as an object lesson to teach what He has just said—the humbling of oneself.

2. The parents, and rightly so, desired that Jesus touch their children, i.e., bless them. Such desire shows that they concluded that Jesus was from God, with some even believing, no doubt, He was the Messiah.

3. What happened to these children whom Christ touched is not known; however, inasmuch as He greatly sanctioned such, it should be obvious that they were affected greatly in a positive sense. It could not be otherwise!

4. *"But when His disciples saw it, they rebuked them,"* proclaims them thinking, no doubt, they were doing the right thing. Jesus was always very busy, and they reasoned that He did not have time for mere children, especially just to touch them; however, they reasoned wrong!

(16) "BUT JESUS CALLED THEM UNTO HIM, AND SAID, SUFFER LITTLE CHILDREN TO COME UNTO ME, AND FORBID THEM NOT: FOR OF SUCH IS THE KINGDOM OF GOD."

The composition is:

1. The phrase, *"But Jesus called them unto Him,"* proclaims the Master countermanding that done by the disciples, and doing so publicly.

2. *"And said, Suffer little children to come unto Me, and forbid them not,"* simply means to allow children to come to Him and, as well, not to do anything that would hinder them.

3. *"For of such is the kingdom of God,"* tells us two things:

a. Jesus was presenting an object lesson by using these children to reinforce that of what He was speaking, respecting the humbling of oneself concerning entrance into the kingdom of God.

b. All children below the age of accountability, irrespective of their race, are protected by the grace of God because they are innocent. In other words, no child has ever died lost, with all who died in a state of childhood now in heaven.

4. What is the age of accountability?

5. There is no standard age. It would have to do with environment, influence, upbringing, and opportunity to learn about the gospel. Many children have little opportunity, if any at all. Consequently, they would come to the age of accountability later than those who had ample opportunity and upbringing.

6. However, at some point, the child is then responsible for his soul's salvation and will be judged accordingly.

(17) "VERILY I SAY UNTO YOU, WHOSOEVER SHALL NOT RECEIVE THE KINGDOM OF GOD AS A LITTLE CHILD SHALL IN NO WISE ENTER THEREIN."

The exegesis is:

1. The phrase, *"Verily I say unto you,"* is used often by Jesus, especially when a statement of great significance is to be given.

2. *"Whosoever shall not receive the kingdom of God as a little child shall in no wise enter therein,"* gives us the requirement on the part of the sinner for salvation.

3. Why did Jesus use a child as an example of the single most important thing there is—the receiving of Christ as one's Saviour?

4. First of all, a child is unpretentious. As well, a child has no pride but, actually, an innate humility, which remains with him as long as he is in the state of innocency.

5. As a result, children in this state do not know if they are rich or poor or if their parents are educated or uneducated. As well, they have no predisposition toward other children, regarding their color, race, or status; consequently, they have no prejudice or bias.

6. By Jesus giving this example, we are told, in essence, that the greatest hindrance

to the entering of the kingdom of God is the refusal of many to humble themselves before God. It is the pride factor.

(18) "AND A CERTAIN RULER ASKED HIM, SAYING, GOOD MASTER, WHAT SHALL I DO TO INHERIT ETERNAL LIFE?"

The synopsis is:

1. The phrase, *"And a certain ruler asked Him,"* presents the same one mentioned in Matthew and Mark (Mat. 19:16; Mk. 10:17). Inasmuch as it is detailed three times, it tells us that the Holy Spirit strongly desires that the message be heeded.

2. *"Good Master, what shall I do to inherit eternal life?"* tells us several things about this man, to which Jesus will address Himself.

3. By the use of *"Good Master"* as a salutation, the man was addressing Jesus not as the Messiah but as a good teacher, in other words, a man, and no more than a man. He was asking for instructions respecting salvation exactly as he would address any other man, not recognizing Jesus as the one who could give salvation.

4. As millions of others, he thought that he could do certain things in order to bring about salvation, which is the mistake of most of humanity. A religion of works, which characterizes most of the world, is wrapped up in the word *do*. Salvation is wrapped up in the word *done*, referring to what Christ did at Calvary.

5. He used the word *inherit*, which Mark also used, whereas the ruler probably meant *merit*. Matthew records him saying, *"That I may have eternal life?"*

6. As well, even though he was a ruler and wealthy, still, these did not satisfy the longing of his heart, as they do not satisfy the spiritual cry in any heart.

7. He knew and believed in the great biblical doctrine of eternal life, which tells us much about him. Being an Israelite, he had access to the Word of God; however, like so many others, he appears to have little studied the contents. He is similar to others who have access to the Bible but little know what it says.

WHAT IS ETERNAL LIFE?

In short, it is the life of God incorporated

in the heart and life, or one should say, the soul and the spirit of an individual. It means that such a person will live forever, but it is much, much more than a continuance of being. It is a bliss unparalleled, the description of which is given in the Word of God.

When Adam and Eve fell in the garden, they lost eternal life and went into eternal death, for the wages of sin is death (Rom. 6:33). Even though given every opportunity to come back to the Lord and regain eternal life, sadly and regrettably, there is no record that our first parents made this move toward God. As far as we know, they died eternally lost and are in hell today, and will be there forever and forever.

Eternal life is not merely an existence of being, but it carries with it, and is, in fact, the life of God, which is a pulsating factor that guarantees all that God is. While it is true that all believers will live with the Lord Jesus Christ in the New Jerusalem forever and forever, the description of which is given to us in the last two chapters of the book of Revelation, still, that is really only the fruit of the results of eternal life as given by God. The very being of God rests and resides in the heart and life of every believer, but it will receive its full expression only when the trump of God sounds. The Scripture says concerning that time:

THE ULTIMATE VICTORY

"Behold, I show you a mystery (a new revelation given by the Holy Spirit to Paul concerning the resurrection, i.e., rapture)*; We shall not all sleep* (at the time of the resurrection [rapture], many Christians will be alive), *but we shall all be changed* (both those who are dead and those who are alive),

"In a moment, in the twinkling of an eye (proclaims how long it will take for this change to take place), *at the last trump* (does not denote by the use of the word 'last' that there will be successive trumpet blasts, but rather denotes that this is the close of things, referring to the church age)*: for the trumpet shall sound* (it is the 'trump of God' [I Thess. 4:16]), *and the dead shall be raised incorruptible* (the sainted dead, with no sin nature), *and we shall be changed* (put on the glorified body).

"For this corruptible (sin nature) *must put on incorruption* (a glorified body with no sin nature), *and this mortal* (subject to death) *must put on immortality* (will never die).

"So when this corruptible (sin nature) *shall have put on incorruption* (the divine nature in total control by the Holy Spirit), *and this mortal* (subject to death) *shall have put on immortality* (will never die), *then shall be brought to pass the saying that is written, Death is swallowed up in victory* ([Isa. 25:8], the full benefits of the Cross will then be ours, of which we now have only the firstfruits [Rom. 8:23]).

"O death, where is your sting? (This presents the apostle looking ahead and exulting in this great coming victory. Sin was forever atoned at the Cross, which took away the sting of death.) *O grave, where is your victory?* (Due to death being conquered, the 'grave' is no more and, once again, all because of what Christ did at the Cross [Col. 2:10-15])" (I Cor. 15:51-55).

It must never be forgotten that all life is wrapped up in God. He is the source of life, the embodiment of life, and the antithesis of death, and we must remember, spiritual death refers to separation from God, and separated forever.

THE ACCEPTANCE OF JESUS CHRIST

The way to eternal life, and the only way, is Jesus Christ. He said:

"I am the way, the truth, and the life: no man comes unto the Father, but by Me" (Jn. 14:6). In other words, this means that Muhammad is not the way to God, or Buddha, or anyone or anything else, only Jesus. He is the one who paid the price at Calvary's Cross, making it possible for all who will to have eternal life. He gave Himself as a sacrifice on the Cross, which satisfied the terrible sin debt that man owed to God and could not pay. He paid it for us by the giving of Himself. It was a sacrifice that was perfect and, thereby, a sacrifice totally accepted by God. To gain this eternal life, which is the grandest thing by far that could ever happen to a human being, all one has to do is accept Jesus Christ. John the Beloved wrote:

"For God so loved the world, that He gave His only begotten Son, that whosoever

believes in Him should not perish, but have everlasting life" (Jn. 3:16).

Believing in Him means that we believe that Jesus Christ is the Son of God, and that He died on Calvary's Cross to pay the debt we could not pay. We accept Him as the Saviour of our souls and, thereby, make Him the Lord of our lives. It is all done by simple faith, believing in Him and what He did for us. It's that simple!

The very moment that one does this, eternal life is instantly given to such a soul, irrespective of who he is or what sins he committed in the past. All sins are cleansed and forgiven, with new life becoming a part of the individual, whomever he might be.

(19) "AND JESUS SAID UNTO HIM, WHY DO YOU CALL ME GOOD? NONE IS GOOD, SAVE ONE, THAT IS, GOD."

WHAT IS GOOD?

The phrase, *"And Jesus said unto him,"* presents Christ addressing something the man has really not asked, but which is the underlying problem respecting his question.

The question, *"Why do you call Me good?"* goes to the heart of the matter.

He really did not conclude Jesus to be the Messiah, which is what the word *good* denotes.

In fact, the word good was never used, even of the most famous rabbis, by their pupils. So, by him using the word good, he was saying, in essence, "I do not believe You are the Messiah, but I will pay you the greatest tribute I possibly can!" Irrespective, he was looking on Jesus only as an earthly teacher.

WHO IS GOOD?

The phrase, *"None is good, save One, that is, God,"* destroys the entire myth of his belief system. Actually, he thought of himself as good because of doing certain things, as did much of Israel of that day. It characterizes the majority of the present as well!

To do some good things does not necessarily denote goodness. Many do these things from an ulterior motive, to gain acceptance by others, to appease the conscious, or to try to earn salvation, as do hundreds of millions of Catholics, Protestants, etc.

Man is capable of doing some good things, despite the fall, because he was originally made in the image of God; however, as here noted, this in no way equips him for salvation. Unless he is born again, he is *"desperately wicked"* (Jer. 17:9).

In the ultimate sense, only God is good, exactly as Jesus said! Although human beings may be good in comparison to one another (Lk. 6:45; 19:17), nothing in any human action can be beneficial to God in the sense that it will merit salvation. However, all true believers are called by God to do good works enthusiastically and so to glorify the Lord.

(20) "YOU KNOW THE COMMANDMENTS, DO NOT COMMIT ADULTERY, DO NOT KILL, DO NOT STEAL, DO NOT BEAR FALSE WITNESS, HONOUR YOUR FATHER AND YOUR MOTHER."

The synopsis is:

1. The phrase, *"You know the commandments,"* refers him to the Bible.

2. And yet, why did Jesus take this tact, knowing that even if he could keep the commandments, they would not save him?

3. Jesus did this because this is where the young man was. He thought he could earn or merit eternal life by doing these things; consequently, Jesus would show him that he had failed even that in which he thought he had excelled.

4. *"Do not commit adultery, Do not kill, Do not steal, Do not bear false witness, Honour your father and your mother,"* omits the first four, which relate to God, and the last one, which really sums up the entirety of all commandments.

5. It seems that this man, as Paul (Phil. 3:6), had kept the letter of the law. However, the tenth commandment, *"You shall not covet,"* showed that, in reality, he had broken the first two commandments, which pertain to God, as we shall see.

(21) "AND HE SAID, ALL THESE HAVE I KEPT FROM MY YOUTH UP."

The exegesis is:

1. There is a definite possibly that he was looking for commendation instead of actually wanting to know the answer to his question. He was rich, which in the eyes of Jews constituted a form of righteousness.

He was a ruler, which again, in their eyes constituted favor with God. He was a devout student of the law, so quite possibly he was congratulating himself and thought that, surely, Christ would do the same.

2. By the use of the word *all*, he was insinuating that he had not only kept the commandments named by Jesus but, as well, the other six.

3. To tell God how good we are is never a wise course to take, as should be overly obvious.

4. He was serving as his own judge, which is always a sure sign of self-righteousness. And yet, as recorded by Mark, Jesus *"loved him,"* denoting a feeling beyond the normal love that God has for all men.

(22) "NOW WHEN JESUS HEARD THESE THINGS, HE SAID UNTO HIM, YET YOU LACK ONE THING: SELL ALL THAT YOU HAVE, AND DISTRIBUTE UNTO THE POOR, AND YOU SHALL HAVE TREASURE IN HEAVEN: AND COME, FOLLOW ME."

THE ANSWER AS GIVEN BY CHRIST

The phrase, *"Now when Jesus heard these things, He said unto him,"* proclaims Christ patiently listening. He would answer him, but it would not be the answer the young man desired.

"Yet you lack one thing," proclaims an extremely big thing.

Anyone who attempts to justify himself by his own performance, even as this young man, will always find, and without exception, *"yet you lack one thing,"* or many things for that matter!

THE WORD OF THE LORD

"Sell all that you have, and distribute unto the poor, and you shall have treasure in heaven: and come, follow Me," is actually saying several things:

• This statement by Jesus is not meant to institute a charity program for the poor. The poor, as needy as they may be, are not the subject of this conversation.

• Actually, eternal life is not really the subject, even though this is what the young man asked, but rather following Jesus.

This is the secret of the Christian experience and the obtaining of eternal life. The whole Christian program from Matthew to Revelation is summed up in these two words. No man can have eternal life who does not do this (Jn. 10:27-29). This literally means to obey all things in the New Testament that Christians are supposed to do (James 1:18-27; 2:8-26; I Jn. 1:7; 2:3-6, 15-17; 3:5-10; 5:1-5, 18).

His great possessions stood in between him and obeying the Lord; consequently, that proved a hindrance, and whatever they may have been had to be laid aside.

One thing is certain, at death he was going to lay it aside irrespective! As well, what he would have gained by following Jesus would have so far eclipsed that which he gave up that it would have been no comparison.

However, the price seemed too high for him, as it seems to millions of others.

(23) "AND WHEN HE HEARD THIS, HE WAS VERY SORROWFUL: FOR HE WAS VERY RICH."

The form is:

1. The phrase, *"And when he heard this,"* proclaims the opposite of what he possibly thought he would hear. As stated, he probably expected commendation but was now jolted to reality by what Jesus said and was, consequently, very disturbed.

2. *"He was very sorrowful,"* proclaims the heart attitude of multiple millions. They want the Lord, but they do not desire to pay the price the Lord demands.

3. The answer as given by Jesus is a far cry from the modern health and wealth gospel. This erroneous gospel (another gospel) tells men how to get more and more wealthy in the realm of money, while Jesus says the very opposite.

4. *"For he was very rich,"* proved to be his obstacle, although it did not have to be. Many things can come between a person and God, proving to be as great a hindrance as this; however, I think the money problem probably presents the greatest obstacle of all. As stated, it doesn't have to, but often it does, as here!

(24) "AND WHEN JESUS SAW THAT HE WAS VERY SORROWFUL, HE SAID,

HOW HARDLY SHALL THEY WHO HAVE RICHES ENTER INTO THE KINGDOM OF GOD!"

The pattern is:

1. The phrase, *"And when Jesus saw that he was very sorrowful,"* means that Jesus intently looked at this young man during the time of his deep consternation.

2. *"He said, How hardly shall they who have riches enter into the kingdom of God,"* presents a total shock to all who heard Jesus, even the disciples. As we have repeatedly stated, Israel believed at this time that money and wealth, in whatever capacity, constituted great blessings from God and, consequently, great spirituality as well!

3. So, they would have thought that this young man had an *"in"* with God.

4. So now, Jesus added to the illustration of the rich man dying and going to hell this blanket statement concerning those who seek after riches. In their minds, this was inconceivable; consequently, their theology was turned upside down.

(25) "FOR IT IS EASIER FOR A CAMEL TO GO THROUGH A NEEDLE'S EYE, THAN FOR A RICH MAN TO ENTER INTO THE KINGDOM OF GOD."

The overview is:

1. The phrase, *"For it is easier for a camel to go through a needle's eye,"* is said by Wuest, the Greek scholar, to be a literal needle.

2. *"Than for a rich man to enter into the kingdom of God,"* proclaims an impossibility with man, but not with God.

3. Why is it harder for the rich to accept Christ?

a. Many rich have gained their riches by oppressing the poor and do not desire to stop (Neh. 5:1-13; Prov. 18:23; Jer. 22:13-19; James 2:6-7; 5:1-7).

b. Normally, their lack of trust in God (Job 21:7-15; Ps. 52:1-6).

c. Their trust in riches (Job 31:24-28; Ps. 52:1-6; Prov. 18:11; I Tim. 6:17).

d. Their pride over success (Ps. 52:1-6; 73:3-9; Prov. 28:11; Ezek. 28:5; I Tim. 6:4-19).

e. Sinful pleasures afforded because of their riches (Jer. 5:7-9, 27-31; Amos 6:1-6).

f. Boasting of their abilities (Deut. 8:17-18; Jer. 9:23; I Tim. 6:4-19).

NOTES

g. Their unwillingness (for many) to share with the destitute (Mk. 10:17-27; Lk. 18:22-26; I Tim. 6:17-19; I Jn. 3:17).

h. Their covetousness for more riches (Lk. 12:15-21; 16:13-31).

i. Their high-mindedness (Deut. 8:17; I Tim. 6:17-18; James 1:10).

j. Their refusal to obey God (Prov. 23:4; Mat. 6:19-21; Mk. 10:21; Lk. 12:15; I Tim. 6:17-18).

(26) "AND THEY WHO HEARD IT SAID, WHO THEN CAN BE SAVED?"

The exegesis is:

1. This question emphasizes the startled response of those who heard Jesus because most Jews believed that riches were a sign of God's favor and blessing.

2. So, at least in their minds, if the rich found it difficult to be saved, whom they thought were nearer to God than all others, who then could be saved?

3. Actually, Jesus also said, *"Strait is the gate, and narrow is the way, which leads unto life, and few there be that find it"* (Mat. 7:14).

(27) "AND HE SAID, THE THINGS WHICH ARE IMPOSSIBLE WITH MEN ARE POSSIBLE WITH GOD."

The exegesis is:

1. The idea is that the rich cannot get salvation on the same basis as they get everything else, for salvation is on a different basis.

2. God does not respect them any more than the poor. They have to meet the same conditions as others, and this is why it is hard for them, and why so few pay the price to get saved.

3. Actually, salvation in any case, and for anyone, rich or poor, is impossible with men, i.e., meaning there is nothing man can do to save himself. However, it is possible with God, whether he is rich or poor. He only has to meet God's conditions, which are to humble himself before the Lord and accept Jesus Christ as the Saviour of his soul and, thereby, make Him the Lord of his life. That is the same requirement for all, rich or poor, great or small!

(28) "THEN PETER SAID, LO, WE HAVE LEFT ALL, AND FOLLOWED YOU."

The diagram is:

1. This statement by Peter lets us in on some of Peter's thoughts, as well as all the disciples.

2. In fact, Peter and the others had left all in order to follow Jesus; consequently, what would be their reward?

3. His question does not seem to denote covetousness on his part or for the disciples as he was their spokesman. It probably pertained more so to what eternal life meant than anything else, although temporal things may have been in his mind as well!

(29) "AND HE SAID UNTO THEM, VERILY I SAY UNTO YOU, THERE IS NO MAN WHO HAS LEFT HOUSE, OR PARENTS, OR BRETHREN, OR WIFE, OR CHILDREN, FOR THE KINGDOM OF GOD'S SAKE,

(30) "WHO SHALL NOT RECEIVE MANIFOLD MORE IN THIS PRESENT TIME, AND IN THE WORLD TO COME LIFE EVERLASTING."

The overview is:

The phrase, "And He said unto them, Verily I say unto you," is meant to point directly to the Twelve, but yet, includes all.

"There is no man who has left house, or parents, or brethren, or wife, or children, for the kingdom of God's sake," has a double meaning:

1. To truly follow Christ, men will have to leave all these things, at least in the sense of making them subservient to the will of God. Nothing must come between the person and Christ.

However, if this is properly done, there will be even a greater love for one's parents, brethren, wife, children, etc.

2. If this is done, great reward will be forthcoming, both presently and eternally.

MANIFOLD MORE IN THIS PRESENT TIME

The phrase, "Who shall not receive manifold more in this present time," means exactly what it says.

The word manifold means "many times over." In other words, living for God returns the greatest benefits that one could ever imagine, not only in eternal life, which is a far greater value than all else, but, as well, even in this present world.

The phrase, "And in the world to come life everlasting," as stated, is the greatest of all. So, the rewards are great to say the least, and they actually constitute a gross understatement.

The blessings of living for God are absolutely impossible to relate. They are so abundant, so manifold, and so everlasting that one is hard put to comprehend it all.

The only thing that one truly gives up to live for Jesus is a load of sin, while gaining everything. So, the terms He demands are not hard or grievous at all. They are things anyone can do, which will guarantee eternal dividends.

(31) "THEN HE TOOK UNTO HIM THE TWELVE, AND SAID UNTO THEM, BEHOLD, WE GO UP TO JERUSALEM, AND ALL THINGS THAT ARE WRITTEN BY THE PROPHETS CONCERNING THE SON OF MAN SHALL BE ACCOMPLISHED."

The composition is:

1. The phrase, "Then He took unto Him the Twelve, and said unto them," no doubt, noted a very solemn occasion. The disciples had their minds on the great reward they would be getting, while Jesus was facing the Cross. How so unspiritual and carnal most of us are, even at times that call for the opposite, as here. And yet, He patiently explained to them their coming reward, which, in fact, would be purchased at such great price, all by Him.

2. "Behold, we go up to Jerusalem," which would bring Him to the end of His earthly ministry. It was a ministry that by and large failed among His own people but, nevertheless, would succeed greatly respecting the planting of the church. His own, the Jews, would reject Him, while the Gentiles would accept Him!

3. "And all things that are written by the prophets concerning the Son of Man shall be accomplished," involved a number of predictions:

a. Delivered to Gentiles (Ps. 2:1-3; Mat. 27:2; Acts 4:27).

b. Mocked (Ps. 22:13, 16, 18; 69:21-26; 109:25; Mat. 27:27-32, 41).

c. Spitefully entreated (Ps. 22:13, 16, 18; Isa., Chpts. 52-53; Mat. 27:27-32).

d. Spit upon (Isa. 50:6; Mat. 26:67; 27:30; Mk. 14:65; 15;19).

e. Scourged (Isa. 52:14; 53:1-12; Mat. 27:26; Mk. 15:15; Jn. 19:1).

f. Put to death by crucifixion (Ps. 22:1, 16; Zech. 13:6; Mat. 26:2; 27:22-24; Acts 2:23; 3:15).

(32) "FOR HE SHALL BE DELIVERED UNTO THE GENTILES, AND SHALL BE MOCKED, AND SPITEFULLY ENTREATED, AND SPIT ON."

The exposition is:

1. The phrase, *"For He shall be delivered unto the Gentiles,"* referred to the fact that Jews, inasmuch as they were ruled by Rome, had no power to carry out a sentence of execution. That must be done by Rome, hence, the Gentiles.

2. *"And shall be mocked, and spitefully entreated, and spit on,"* was Bible prophecy, as stated.

3. How is it possible that they could hate Him so much? He had done nothing but good, but yet, they hated Him.

4. They hated Him because their hearts were evil, despite their profession of religion, and because His righteousness was a constant rebuke to their unrighteousness.

5. As well, they looked at Him as a threat to their lifestyle and riches. The crowds by the tens of thousands flocked to Him, and, as well, He had such power that He was able to perform any type of miracle. He fulfilled all the prophecies concerning the Messiah, and in their hearts they knew He was the Messiah. Nevertheless, they killed Him because they were wicked, and even more so, they were religiously wicked, which is the greatest wickedness of all!

(33) "AND THEY SHALL SCOURGE HIM, AND PUT HIM TO DEATH: AND THE THIRD DAY HE SHALL RISE AGAIN."

The composition is:

1. The phrase, *"And they shall scourge Him,"* coupled with the other forms of torture, meant they were not content to merely kill Him, they had to make Him suffer every indignity that was possible to heap upon a helpless individual, or at least one who would not defend himself.

2. *"And put Him to death,"* refers to that which they lusted after—His life.

3. *"And the third day He shall rise again,"* naturally pertained to the resurrection,

the greatest event to date in the annals of human history, and possibly the greatest event of all time.

(34) "AND THEY UNDERSTOOD NONE OF THESE THINGS: AND THIS SAYING WAS HID FROM THEM, NEITHER KNEW THEY THE THINGS WHICH WERE SPOKEN."

The exegesis is:

1. The phrase, *"And they understood none of these things,"* means that Jesus' words fell upon deaf ears.

2. Why?

3. Knowing and seeing the miracles that He constantly performed, thus, hearing the wonderful words that came out of His mouth, they were not ready to give up the hopes of an earthly messianic glory, which they would share. Someone said, "We must learn to love divine truths before we can understand them."

4. There was no reason whatsoever to misunderstand what Jesus was saying. Actually, He had related this same message to them several times. Nevertheless, they were so taken up with their own ambition that they little knew or understood the will of God at that moment.

5. *"And this saying was hid from them,"* does not speak of the Lord blinding their eyes and minds, but that their own selfish desires accomplished that task. Sadly, the far greater percentage of the modern church world falls into the same category. The things of God are hidden from most who claim Jesus as their Saviour simply because carnal minds cannot grasp or understand spiritual things. Consequently, the true purpose of God that He is carrying out in this world presently is lost upon these individuals.

6. *"Neither knew they the things which were spoken,"* constitutes the results of their stubborn self-will. They had a plan of God worked out in their minds, which was contrary to the Word of God, as well as what Jesus had been telling them. They were so tuned to this wave length that they could not see, hear, or think anything else.

(35) "AND IT CAME TO PASS, THAT AS HE WAS COME NEAR UNTO JERICHO, A CERTAIN BLIND MAN SAT BY THE WAY SIDE BEGGING."

JERICHO

The phrase, *"And it came to pass, that as He was come near unto Jericho,"* is claimed by some to be a contradiction inasmuch as both Matthew and Mark speak of Jesus going out of Jerusalem when this healing took place (Mat. 20:29; Mk. 210:46). However, there is no discrepancy or contradiction.

Luke is simply saying that as Jesus was coming into Jericho at that particular time, a blind man was sitting by the side of the highway begging. That is to say, as Jesus was approaching the city on this one side, Bartimaeus was sitting in his usual place on the other side, unconscious that the wonderful Saviour was drawing near and would presently heal Him.

BARTIMAEUS

The phrase, *"A certain blind man sat by the way side begging,"* is said by Mark to be Bartimaeus (Mk. 10:46).

As well, Matthew mentions *"two blind men,"* while Mark and Luke only speak of one. Some have claimed these, as well, to be two different incidents; however, every indication is that all were referring to the same happening.

For whatever reason, Mark and Luke did not mention the second blind man, with the main reason being that the Spirit of God desired it that way.

TRADITION

Tradition says that Bartimaeus became quite prominent in the early church in Jerusalem, with this possibly being the reason that he was singled out, with the other one ignored, except in the account given by Matthew. Just because the second one is not mentioned by Mark and Luke, it does not mean that it did not happen or that there is a contradiction.

At any rate, the miracle of the healing of Bartimaeus is one of the most beautiful and graphic in Scripture. As well, this is the only time the Bible records that Jesus was in the city of Jericho. As Jesus was going to the Cross, this was probably the only time that Bartimaeus would have to be healed. Bartimaeus fits the stereotype of the world.

He was blind, exactly as the world is spiritually blind. As well, he was a beggar, at least when compared with what God originally intended. As Jesus was the only answer for Bartimaeus, Jesus is the only answer for the world.

Inasmuch as Mark spoke of him as *"Bartimaeus, the son of Timaeus,"* some believe that he may have come from a good family but somehow fell on hard times and then went blind. However, that is only speculation.

(36) "AND HEARING THE MULTITUDE PASS BY, HE ASKED WHAT IT MEANT."

BARTIMAEUS COULD HEAR, BUT HE COULD NOT SEE

The phrase, *"And hearing the multitude pass by,"* refers to a later time after Jesus had already entered the city and was now actually departing.

"He asked what it meant," concerns the commotion that took place when the news spread that Jesus was near.

It must have been quite a moment, considering that Jesus had not previously been to Jericho, or at least that is recorded. Nevertheless, everyone there knew of Him with, no doubt, the excitement running high.

At this time Jericho, which was about 18 miles from Jerusalem, was a popular resort. Its palm groves and balsam gardens were a present from Antony to Cleopatra. It is said that Herod the Great bought them from her and made Jericho one of his royal cities, and adorned it with many stately buildings. He died there as well!

Jericho was the first city taken by Joshua upon the entrance of the children of Israel into the Promised Land. It was a very unusual victory, with the Lord using miraculous means to accomplish His will (Josh., Chpt. 6). About 600 years later, it was the sight of another miracle—the Lord healing the waters of Jericho through the prophet Elisha (II Ki., Chpt. 2).

THE SPRING OF WATER

Beautifully and wondrously enough, the spring of water still flows in Jericho, with the water continuing to be pure and clean. I have personally seen the well that is located a very short distance from the ruins of ancient Jericho, which Joshua marched around. Actually, the city of Jericho that existed at the time of Christ was a little bit west of ancient Jericho, in which nothing but ruins remain at this time. (The city is now in the hands of the Palestinians as a part, so to speak, of the peace accord with Israel.)

The last time I was in the city of Jericho, at least as I dictate this account, was in June 1996. We took the old road out of Jericho toward Jerusalem, which is seldom traveled by modern tourists. Actually, this would have been the road taken by Jesus, which intersects the modern road after a few miles.

The road winds its way westward over the mountains of Judaea. One particular spot is extremely interesting in that a very narrow valley runs between two tall mountains. It is called *"the valley of the shadow of death,"* after David's 23rd Psalm. It was one of the most remarkable and beautiful sights I think I have ever seen.

(37) "AND THEY TOLD HIM, THAT JESUS OF NAZARETH PASSES BY."

The synopsis is:

1. This would have been the greatest news that had ever fallen upon his ears. Every indication is that he had heard much about Jesus and had, no doubt, sought God earnestly that Jesus would pass his way. As the months passed and lengthened into years, he may have grown very weary in waiting, wondering if his prayer would ever be answered and if Jesus would ever come this way? Being a beggar, there was little way that he could get to Jesus, so Jesus must come to him.

Likewise, the world, in its awful, sinful state, could not go to Christ, so Christ came to us.

2. It would be difficult to imagine what his thoughts were when they told him, *"Jesus of Nazareth passes by!"* However, feeling that this may be his one and only opportunity, he was determined somehow to get to Jesus.

(38) "AND HE CRIED, SAYING, JESUS, THOU SON OF DAVID, HAVE MERCY ON ME."

The diagram is:

1. The phrase, *"And he cried, saying,"* points to his desperation and determination. He was not to be denied!

2. The phrase, *"Jesus, Thou Son of David,"* is a messianic salutation, which meant that irrespective of what others might have said, Bartimaeus believed that Jesus Christ was the Messiah.

3. By this time, the name of *"Jesus of Nazareth"* was a household word. His fame had spread abroad to the entirety of the country. No doubt, the argument was very heated respecting His being the Messiah, an argument so widespread that it had, no doubt, fallen on the ears of this blind beggar.

4. Hearing of the great miracles that Jesus was performing, even to the raising of the dead, every indication is that Bartimaeus had reasoned in his mind that irrespective of what others said, he believed that Jesus was truly the long awaited one, *the Son of David,* the Messiah. Consequently, he addressed Him accordingly.

5. The phrase, *"Have mercy on me,"* seems to be a request he had studiously thought out. He would ask for mercy because he had, no doubt, heard that Jesus was very merciful, placing no distinction between the rich or the poor, the old or the young, beggars or beautiful.

6. If, in fact, that's what Bartimaeus thought, he was exactly right!

(39) "AND THEY WHICH WENT BEFORE REBUKED HIM, THAT HE SHOULD HOLD HIS PEACE: BUT HE CRIED SO MUCH THE MORE, THOU SON OF DAVID, HAVE MERCY ON ME."

The overview is:

1. The phrase, *""And they which went before rebuked him,"* probably spoke of the large Passover crowd on the way to Jerusalem, possibly even traveling with Jesus because of the same destination. At any rate, some of them attempted to hush the beggar.

2. This is a prime example of what normally happens when a person attempts to come to the Lord. There will always be some who will try to stop the petition, claiming all sorts of things.

Consequently, the seeking soul is going to have to learn that in his quest to find the Lord, he is going to have to sidestep and overlook the detractors, which always seem to be many. As they tried to hush

Bartimaeus, they will attempt to hush the modern Bartimaeus as well!

3. The phrase, *"That he should hold his peace,"* proclaims exactly that which the Devil wanted. However, it is sad when people who claim to be believers, even as these Passover pilgrims, aid Satan in his work. However, let it ever be known that the Lord never censures anyone for coming to Him. Actually, the exact opposite is the case. He bids all to come! (Mat. 11:28-30).

4. *"But he cried so much the more, Thou Son of David, have mercy on me,"* proclaims him doubling his efforts, if possible. He would not be denied! Consequently, he would become a tremendous encouragement to all who seek the Lord, which is at least one of the reasons the Holy Spirit had his story given in three of the Gospels.

(40) "AND JESUS STOOD, AND COMMANDED HIM TO BE BROUGHT UNTO HIM: AND WHEN HE WAS COME NEAR, HE ASKED HIM."

JESUS STOPPED

The phrase, *"And Jesus stood,"* simply means He stopped. Even though only a short phrase, this is an extremely important statement.

First of all, Bartimaeus maybe sensed that this was the only time Jesus would pass this way. He would have had no knowledge of the coming crucifixion, which would actually take place in a matter of hours, but he probably felt that this would be his only opportunity, hence, his persistence.

As well, spiritually speaking, the tide rises and ebbs in every life. That doesn't mean that one can reach God only at certain times, but that it is definitely easier at particular times than others. Consequently, if the day of visitation is not heeded, more than likely, it will never be heeded.

One must understand that Jesus was in the final hours of that which had been planned since before the foundation of the world. Consequently, the significance of this moment cannot be properly comprehended, even by the most spiritual of individuals.

FAITH

And yet, even though Jesus was on His

NOTES

way to redeem the whole of humanity, still, because of a man's faith, He would stop. This should show us how strong and powerful that faith in God actually is. Without faith, it is impossible to please God (Heb. 11:6). So, the journey of the ages would be halted for a little while in order to meet the needs of a blind beggar. What a wonderful Lord we serve!

At this time, if one could have seen into the Spirit world, one would have, no doubt, witnessed a myriad of angels as they hovered around Christ as He came to the last leg of His journey to Jerusalem. This is what all of heaven had pointed toward—the redemption of humanity. And yet, that mighty host must stand and wait as Jesus answered the faith of this poor wretched soul. To be sure, if He did it for him, and He most certainly did, He will, as well, for any and all who will cry out to Him. He has never turned His back on the earnest cry of a seeking soul.

BRING HIM TO ME

So, *"Jesus stood!"* As He stood, so did all of heaven, including the mighty angelic hosts.

"And commanded him to be brought unto Him," proclaims Jesus answering faith and overriding the condemnation of those who had tried to stop Bartimaeus.

The word *commanded* means that He had become aware of the hindrance of those who had tried to hush the beggar; consequently, he would not tolerate such action. The beggar's cry would be answered.

"And when he was come near, He asked him," means that willing hands, at the command of Christ, quietly and quickly guided the blind beggar to Jesus. Mark recorded that the former detractors said, *"Be of good comfort, rise; He calls you"* (Mk. 10:49).

Mark also stated, *"And he, casting away his garment, rose, and came to Jesus."*

As well, this was a gesture of faith on his part because this *"garment"* was the badge of the beggar. At night he covered himself with it, and during the day, it was laid in front of him so that passersby could throw money on it if they would. He had such faith that Christ would heal him that as he came toward Jesus, he realized he would not need the beggars garment any longer; consequently, he cast it away.

(41) "SAYING, WHAT WILL YOU THAT I SHALL DO UNTO YOU? AND HE SAID, LORD, THAT I MAY RECEIVE MY SIGHT."

The synopsis is:

1. The question, *"Saying, What will you that I shall do unto you?"* constituted the greatest words that had ever fallen upon his ears. What a question! Considering that it came from the Lord of Glory who can do anything, it is even more astounding.

2. Godet said, "Jesus seems to open up to the beggar the treasures of divine power in 'What will you that I shall do unto you?' and to give him, as it were, carte blanche."

3. The phrase, *"And he said, Lord, that I may receive my sight,"* constituted the words he had, no doubt, wanted to say for a long, long time.

One of the versions, *The Curetonian,* has him saying in the account of Matthew, *"That our eyes might be opened and we might see You."*

(42) "AND JESUS SAID UNTO HIM, RECEIVE YOUR SIGHT: YOUR FAITH HAS SAVED YOU."

The construction is:

1. The phrase, *"And Jesus said unto him, Receive your sight,"* proclaims Matthew giving the account that Jesus *'touched their eyes,"* speaking of the two (Mat. 20:34).

2. *"Your faith has saved you,"* concerns not only his remarkable healing, even a miracle, but, as well, and even greater, the salvation of his soul.

3. Jesus here commended his faith, which included his persistence, as faith always does. Conversely, the people would have stopped him if they had had their way.

4. Our prayer should be that instead of being a hindrance to any seeking soul, we should rather provide a helping hand.

(43) "AND IMMEDIATELY HE RECEIVED HIS SIGHT, AND FOLLOWED HIM, GLORIFYING GOD: AND ALL THE PEOPLE, WHEN THEY SAW IT, GAVE PRAISE UNTO GOD."

THE MIRACLE OF SIGHT

The phrase, *"And immediately he received his sight,"* must have occasioned a time of tremendous joy. What must it be like to be blind and, all of a sudden, to be able to see? How does it feel to come instantly from stygian darkness to instant light?

There is no way that one could grasp or even partially understand the feelings that must have been in the heart of Bartimaeus.

"And followed Him," is very short and cryptic, but with some indications that he not only followed Jesus at the moment but, in fact, all the way to Jerusalem.

This I do know: Had that been me, I would definitely have followed Him as long as it was earthly possible. As stated, tradition says he did exactly that, becoming prominent in the early church.

GLORIFYING GOD

The two words, *glorifying God,* proclaim two things:

1. Such healings and miracles always glorify God. A person being sick or, as here, blind, does not bring glory to God, as claimed by some.

What glory was it to the Lord with Bartimaeus sitting by the roadside begging? The answer is quick, "None at all!"

That which brought God glory, and continues to bring Him glory unto this moment, is the powers of darkness being totally and completely defeated in one's life, whether the physical, financial, domestic, mental, or spiritual. Jesus came to destroy the works of Satan, and as such, it brings God glory.

2. Not only did this miracle bring glory to God, as well, Bartimaeus, seemingly with a loud voice, expressed that glory. Why not? He had just experienced one of the greatest miracles ever recorded in human history. Consequently, he was not timid or shy but began to glorify God.

The phrase, *"And all the people, when they saw it, gave praise unto God,"* records the entirety of this crowd of people joining in, and probably even the ones who had attempted to hush the former beggar.

Why is it that most churches at present little glorify God, if at all? Possibly, it is because nothing happens in these churches that occasions such glory.

However, where the Spirit of God is, things will happen, and true believers will, as Bartimaeus of old, glorify God.

"Pass me not, O gentle Saviour,
"Hear my humble cry;
"While on others You are calling,
"Do not pass me by."

"Let me at Your throne of mercy
"Find a sweet relief;
"Kneeling there in deep contrition,
"Help my unbelief."

"Trusting only in Your merit,
"Would I seek Your face:
"Heal my wounded, broken spirit,
"Save me by Your grace."

"You, the spring of all my comfort,
"More than life to me,
"Whom have I on earth beside Thee?
"Whom in heaven but Thee?"

CHAPTER 19

(1) "AND JESUS ENTERED AND PASSED THROUGH JERICHO.

(2) "AND, BEHOLD, THERE WAS A MAN NAMED ZACCHAEUS, WHICH WAS THE CHIEF AMONG THE PUBLICANS, AND HE WAS RICH."

JERICHO

The phrase, *"And Jesus entered and passed through Jericho,"* proclaims this town, as well as other places visited by Jesus, as greatly honored. Wherever He went was blessed, and whoever He touched was blessed abundantly so.

He never left a place in a worse state than when He found it but always immeasurably better; likewise, with every person.

Just last night, I heard George Foreman, the former heavyweight champion of the world, interviewed over television concerning his life. He spoke of having made millions of dollars but of a life that was wasted and spent. Then he met Jesus.

When he met Him, everything changed for the better. It is identical with any and all. To meet Him is to meet life, and to have

His life is to have eternal life. So, Jericho would never be the same again.

ZACCHAEUS

"And, behold, there was a man named Zacchaeus, which was the chief among the publicans," meant he was a tax collector and, consequently, hated by his fellow Jews.

If one is to notice, the blind beggar, at least as the Holy Spirit proclaims it, is here preferred before the rich tax collector. Bartimaeus was last but is put first. He was told *"to rise"* but Zacchaeus was told *"to come down."* Thus, rich and poor meet on the one level as sinners before God.

Incidentally, had the Twelve learned the lesson taught by the healing of the blind beggar, they would have prayed as he did, and Jesus would have given them spiritual sight.

Zacchaeus, being *"chief among the publicans,"* means that he was the head of the tax office at Jericho and perhaps over a whole district.

"And he was rich," proclaims the only type of rich people that the religious hierarchy of Israel believed not to be saved. They claimed that he was a traitor, having sold out to Rome as a tax collector.

Jericho, under the Herods, had again become an important center of trade. It lay on the road from Peraea to Judaea and Egypt, and of necessity, had an important custom house, of which Zacchaeus was its head.

The balm, which came especially from the Gilead district, was sent through there and to all parts of the world. Consequently, Zacchaeus would have had great opportunity to enrich himself, which he evidently did.

(3) "AND HE SOUGHT TO SEE JESUS WHO HE WAS; AND COULD NOT FOR THE PRESS, BECAUSE HE WAS LITTLE OF STATURE."

The pattern is:

1. The phrase, *"And he sought to see Jesus who He was,"* proclaims a need that was similar to that of Bartimaeus. One was a beggar, and yet, woefully lacking, which would be obvious. The other was rich but still lacking because money never satisfies the spiritual thirst of the human heart. So, at the conclusion of the matter, as stated, both were beggars.

2. Zacchaeus would see who Jesus was, but yet, there is not the least bit of information in Scripture concerning His (Jesus') appearance. His stature, complexion, color of hair or eyes, His voice, expression, manner, or general appearance is not recorded for the painter or the historian. We shall know nothing about these things until we shall see Him face to face.

3. *"And could not for the press,"* refers to the tremendous crowd around Jesus, with many probably desiring healing, etc.

4. Using a play on words, as the *"press"* hindered Zacchaeus from seeing Jesus of that day so long ago, likewise, the *"press"* has kept many from seeing Him in this day and time.

5. *"Because he was little of stature,"* evidently means that he was head and shoulders shorter than most other men.

(4) "AND HE RAN BEFORE, AND CLIMBED UP INTO A SYCOMORE TREE TO SEE HIM: FOR HE WAS TO PASS THAT WAY."

The pattern is:

1. The phrase, *"And he ran before,"* means that he ascertained the direction Jesus was going and sought to find a vantage point, which he did. It would be the greatest thing he ever did.

2. *"And climbed up into a sycomore tree to see Him,"* is said to have been a fig-mulberry, which grew to a considerable height, with low, spreading branches that were easy to climb.

3. One can well imagine this rich, prosperous man submitting himself to this indignity, but yet, it turned out to be the greatest thing he ever did.

4. The phrase, *"For He was to pass that way,"* is a statement of monumental proportions.

5. As stated, wherever Jesus went, beautiful and gracious things happened. He was and is the only one who can change people's lives. The kings, dictators, and despots of that, and any age, could bring a cosmetic change to the area but never in the heart and life of an individual. Only Jesus could do that. It is the same presently, despite great technological advancement.

(5) "AND WHEN JESUS CAME TO THE PLACE, HE LOOKED UP, AND SAW

HIM, AND SAID UNTO HIM, ZACCHAEUS, MAKE HASTE, AND COME DOWN; FOR TODAY I MUST ABIDE AT YOUR HOUSE."

The form is:

1. *"And when Jesus came to the place, He looked up, and saw him,"* seems to have been orchestrated by the Holy Spirit. A hungry, seeking heart will always find the Lord.

2. *"And said unto him, Zacchaeus, make haste, and come down,"* seemingly proclaims Jesus as not having to seek information regarding who this man was but already knowing because, evidently, the Holy Spirit had informed Him.

3. *"For today I must abide at your house,"* proclaims the deity and kingship of Jesus, although little used. He did not ask for lodging but, as a king, commanded such.

4. Jericho was known as a city of priests, with perhaps as many as 20,000 residing in the city, and yet, our Lord, ignoring public opinion, passed over their houses and announced His intention of lodging for the night with one whose life's occupation was so hateful to the Jewish religious world.

5. This would be the greatest day this *"house"* had ever seen or known.

(6) "AND HE MADE HASTE, AND CAME DOWN, AND RECEIVED HIM JOYFULLY."

The overview is:

1. As Bartimaeus, it seems that this man had heard much about Jesus, and even that Jesus had chosen a publican (Matthew) to be one of His disciples. Inasmuch as Zacchaeus was an outcast and looked at by his fellow Jews as a moral leper, he, no doubt, took heart, feeling that Jesus might possibly satisfy the longing of his soul.

2. Being wealthy, he could have easily sought out Jesus, whereas Bartimaeus did not have that privilege, but yet, he did not do so until this moment.

3. Perhaps he was afraid of rejection; however, at any rate, his wildest dreams were about to come true.

(7) "AND WHEN THEY SAW IT, THEY ALL MURMURED, SAYING, THAT HE WAS GONE TO BE A GUEST WITH A MAN WHO IS A SINNER."

MURMURING

The phrase, *"And when they saw it, they*

all murmured," probably spoke of the citizens of Jericho and may have included some of the pilgrims on their way to the Passover.

The words, *"They all,"* show the spirit of the age that gripped Israel at that particular time. It was narrow, sectarian, cold, aloof, and above all, self-righteous. And yet, Jesus seemed to take no notice whatsoever of the general feeling, but did what He knew to be right, irrespective of what people thought.

Actually, He never catered whatsoever to public whim, prevailing opinion, conventional wisdom, or any other public or political opinion, but charted His own course as outlined by His heavenly Father.

How so much preachers should take a clue from Jesus in respect to their ministries. To preach what people want to hear is, and always has been, at least to a certain degree, the norm for the ministry; however, such ministry changes no lives because God cannot sanction such.

The true minister of the gospel must, under all circumstances, deliver the message given to him by the Lord without adding to or taking away from its content. It must be delivered without fear or favor. Above all, it must not be compromised whatsoever.

WHAT THE LORD WANTS

It is not the business of the messenger to be concerned as to the possible negative response of the hearers, but only that the message be faithfully delivered.

Back in the 1980s, I was a member of the National Religious Broadcasters Association. A request was sent out from that organization asking all media preachers to do a survey of their audience, thereby, ascertaining what they desired respecting ministry.

I wrote them back, and as kindly as I could, I told them that I had no interest in what the people wanted. I was only interested in delivering to them what I believed the Lord had given unto me. I felt that way then, and I feel that way now.

"Saying, That He was gone to be guest with a man who is a sinner," proclaims, as Jerusalem, Jericho being a city of many priests in which this stern exclusive spirit was especially dominant.

What I'm about to say will be strong, but I believe it to be the truth.

RELIGION

Having preached crusades all over the world, I have generally found, with a few exceptions, that the cities in which the headquarters of religious organizations are located have been the hardest of all to reach with the gospel. Actually, I have sensed the demon forces of darkness, mainly religious spirits, more highly operative in these areas than any place else. Such was Jerusalem and Jericho.

As we have previously stated, quite possibly, this is the reason that it seems Jesus took no delight in going to Jerusalem. When He did go in order to keep the respective feasts, there is no record that He ever spent a night in that city during His public ministry, with the exception of the night that He was arrested. As well, perhaps with Jericho being a city of many priests, this is the reason that He never visited the place before now.

It is very difficult, if not impossible, for religious denominations not to be ultimately taken over by man, irrespective of how noble and holy may have been their beginnings. When this happens, the Holy Spirit does not and, in fact, cannot function with demon spirits, i.e., religious spirits, taking His place. Consequently, if the ministry of Christ is to be an example, which it certainly must be, the greatest evil is found in that which is called church.

Yes, in the midst of all of this, there are some who truly love the Lord and are doing their very best to serve Him. This is the true church, or remnant, but as Jesus stated, *"Few there be that find it"* (Mat. 7:14).

(8) "AND ZACCHAEUS STOOD, AND SAID UNTO THE LORD; BEHOLD, LORD, THE HALF OF MY GOODS I GIVE TO THE POOR; AND IF I HAVE TAKEN ANYTHING FROM ANY MAN BY FALSE ACCUSATION, I RESTORE HIM FOURFOLD."

ZACCHAEUS

The phrase, *"And Zacchaeus stood, and said unto the Lord,"* records the moral effect of his conversion—he took his stand alongside Jesus in public and declared that from that moment, the half of his goods he would give to the poor, and he would restore fourfold all overcharges of taxation.

"Behold, Lord, the half of my goods I give to the poor," proclaims his salvation affecting the entirety of his lifestyle.

Without Jesus saying anything concerning this, at least that is recorded, Zacchaeus, unlike the rich young ruler, immediately volunteered such.

"And if I have taken any thing from any man by false accusation, I restore him fourfold," further gives evidence of his conversion.

Roman law required a fourfold restitution, but Levitical law only demanded the principle and one-fifth part added (Num. 5:7). However, he imposed upon himself the severe measure of Exodus 22:1. Thus he judged himself and, as well, true repentance will always act as he did.

TRUE CONVERSION

Zacchaeus felt that he could not begin too soon to obey the promptings of the new life that had come into his heart. Faith that does not purify the heart and life is not a divine faith, and grace that cannot be seen like light and tasted like salt is vain.

True conversion to Christ will always have a positive effect on any and every facet of one's life. Debts are paid. Wrongs are righted, at least as far as possible. Forgiveness is sought, etc.

Just the other day, a dear brother related to me how he came to Christ by watching our telecast. Having previously known very little, if anything, about the Lord, he did not say anything to his wife at first. I asked him, "How did she find out?"

His answer was very interesting: "When I quit stopping at the bars on the way home at night, she knew there was a change."

Salvation that doesn't change a life for the good in every way mentioned, and many ways not mentioned, is not true salvation. Actually, this is the bane of the modern church. I speak of people joining the church but never truly being born again and, consequently, not changing at all. Such is not true salvation!

NOTES

(9) "AND JESUS SAID UNTO HIM, THIS DAY IS SALVATION COME TO THIS HOUSE, FORSOMUCH AS HE ALSO IS A SON OF ABRAHAM."

SALVATION

The phrase, *"And Jesus said unto him,"* will be the very opposite of what He said to the rich young ruler (Lk. 18:22).

"This day is salvation come to this house," is the greatest thing that could be said respecting any house.

This is the answer for the inner city and the gang problem, the education problem, marriage and divorce, the crime rate, and any other problem that besets humanity. Actually, it is the only answer.

"Forsomuch as he also is a son of Abraham," proclaims Jesus declaring this man to be the very opposite of what his holier-than-thou critics had said.

In truth, the Word of God was not violated respecting the position of tax collector, that is, if the person was honest. There was no wrongdoing or sin in any part of this occupation. Jesus had said as much when He said, *"Render to Caesar the things that are Caesar's"* (Mk. 12:17).

SELF-RIGHTEOUSNESS

The hatred the Pharisees had for such people stemmed from their self-righteousness. As well, it had root in their sectarian attitude that they were so holy they could not have any dealings with Gentiles. Inasmuch as Rome had subjugated Israel and ruled them, anyone who would willingly serve Rome was looked at as a traitor and, consequently, beyond salvation.

However, all of that was of their making and had nothing to do with the Bible. In fact, self-righteousness makes up its own rules and ignores the Word of God. This was the major problem between the Pharisees and Christ, and continues to be the major problem presently.

One religious leader accused me of not believing in church government.

Quite the contrary; everything I stand for, espouse, preach, and proclaim is the government of God, which rules, or at least should rule, in the hearts and lives of believers. Actually, this is the very essence of Christianity. The government of Christ, expressed in the *"kingdom of God,"* becomes the ruling force in all that the saint does and is.

THE GOVERNMENT OF THE LORD

However, I do not believe in the government of many of these religious denominations, which is unscriptural, and grossly so. If the Bible is not going to be the criterion, what is? The truth is, man has usurped authority over God in almost everything and, especially, church government. Anytime this is done, ruin is the result.

Sometime ago, one preacher said that the modern church is far advanced over the book of Acts and, consequently, has found much better ways to do things.

Such a statement is silly, to say the least. Actually, this preacher seems to be ignorant of the fact that the Holy Spirit, who is God, and, therefore, omniscient (all-knowing), is the author of the book of Acts, as well as the entirety of the Bible.

As a result, He gave the outline respecting church government, as well as everything else that pertains to our lives and what God expects of us. To proclaim that modern man knows more than the Holy Spirit is ignorance gone to seed, so to speak. However, this is exactly what many modern preachers believe, even though such would probably be denied, but their actions prove otherwise. If it is not God's way, then it becomes man's way and, therefore, of Satan. I'll ask it again, "If the Bible is not to be the criterion, what is?"

A SON OF ABRAHAM

Jesus was saying that Zacchaeus had as much right to salvation as any other person in Israel. He was just as much a son of Abraham as any other. Even though man had denied him these rights, this did not mean that God had denied him. In fact, the Lord saved Zacchaeus, and he is now in heaven, whereas the Pharisees, who looked down their noses at him and strutted in their self-righteousness, sadly and regrettably, died and went to hell. So, it's not what man says, but what God says!

(10) "FOR THE SON OF MAN IS COME TO SEEK AND TO SAVE THAT WHICH WAS LOST."

The pattern is:

1. We must understand that the Cross was not an incident and not an accident; it was a sacrifice.

2. Actually, no person could have killed Christ. He had to lay down His life of His own accord (Jn. 10:17-18).

3. In reality, the Cross was planned from before the foundation of the world (I Pet. 1:18-20).

SAVED?

Someone has said that salvation cleanses the sinner's house as well as the sinner's heart. Therefore, the house was such that Jesus might enter, and so He disposed of the Pharisaic objection of Verse 7.

Jesus was not ashamed to sup with sinners, for His purpose in coming to earth was to seek and save them.

This statement by Christ not only points toward those poor wandering souls who are lost and know it but, as well, to the Pharisees, and all like them, who will not admit their need of a Saviour and, thereby, will not allow Him to save them. A person must admit he is lost before Christ can save him, and this seems to be a difficult admittance for most.

In talking to many people about their souls through the years, I remember distinctly one man who I questioned on an airplane, asking him, "Are you saved?" His answer was typical!

"Saved from what?" he asked!

He did not believe the Bible was the Word of God, that Jesus was the Son of God, or that he was a fallen being and, therefore, in desperate need of redemption.

RELIGIOUS BUT LOST

Even more so, and worse than this of which I have mentioned, are the millions upon millions ensconced in churches who are very religious but, at the same time, very lost. As the Pharisees of old, they cloak themselves in a covering of religion and, thereby, deceive themselves into believing that all is well when in reality, they have never been born again. They are the hardest of all to reach.

As well, the word *seek* implies that man was not necessarily seeking God, but rather the contrary. In fact, when Adam and Eve sinned, they immediately began to run from the Lord, and man has been running ever since (Gen. 3:9-10).

The seeking of the lost, at least on the part of God, involves far more than a mere quest, but rather an extremely active participation, even to the extent that it is beyond the pale of human comprehension. That God would lower Himself to the level of a mere human being, taking upon Himself the *"form of a servant,"* is beyond understanding. However, the fact that He would die *"even the death of the Cross"* in order to save man takes it even further into the incomprehensible (Phil. 2:5-8).

Even though Jesus mixed with sinners, to which the Pharisees objected strenuously, He most definitely never mixed with their sin. Their sin never touched His purity, but most definitely, His purity touched their sin.

(11) "AND AS THEY HEARD THESE THINGS, HE ADDED AND SPOKE A PARABLE, BECAUSE HE WAS NEAR TO JERUSALEM, BECAUSE THEY THOUGHT THAT THE KINGDOM OF GOD SHOULD IMMEDIATELY APPEAR."

THE PARABLE

The phrase, *"And as they heard these things, He added and spoke a parable, because He was near to Jerusalem,"* basically had to do with Bartimaeus declaring Jesus as the Son of David, and Zacchaeus conducting himself toward Jesus as the King of Israel, even though he did not use the term. In effect, Christ accepted both titles. He did not rebuke them for acclaiming Him in this manner.

The deity and kingship of Jesus appear in the words, *"Zacchaeus ... I must abide at your house."*

The phrase, *"Because they thought that the kingdom of God should immediately appear,"* probably has reference not only to that deep settled thought of the disciples, but was, as well, exacerbated concerning

NOTES

the recent happenings of Bartimaeus and Zacchaeus.

Recognizing this, His disciples thought that upon entering His royal city, He would at once establish His kingdom, but the Lord, by the parable of the pounds, taught them that the day was yet far distant. This parable, incidentally, is peculiar to Luke.

THE MISINTERPRETATION OF THE MISSION OF CHRIST

It was common at that time for a prince or nobleman to proceed to Rome, there to receive a kingdom from Caesar, and to return and govern it. History records that Archelaus, the son of Herod, had just done so; consequently, the framework of the parable was, therefore, familiar to the people who heard it.

Before we deal with this parable, let us look at the situation of the disciples respecting their erroneous interpretation of the mission of Christ, despite the fact that He had repeatedly told them what would soon happen respecting His crucifixion, etc. (Lk. 18:31-33).

We have to understand that these men loved God. In fact, they were some of, if not the most, choice believers on the earth at that time. So, how could they misinterpret what He was saying?

It is Satan's business to get the believer off track in that he not know or understand what the will of God is, and especially to misinterpret the Word of God. It could probably be said that every believer has faced this problem at one time or the other. When it happens, the Holy Spirit automatically begins the attempt to pull the person back to the correct position. Sometimes He is successful and sometimes not. Most definitely, He was successful with the disciples.

All, even the disciples, will go astray because of the problem of self-will. The Word of God is interpreted in these situations as we desire it to be instead of how it actually is. In other words, we try to mold the Bible into our thinking instead of allowing the Bible to mold our thinking. If this happens, the error will only compound itself. If the believer is humble before the

Lord, the Holy Spirit will be able to pull the believer back to the correct path. If there is no humility, self-will shall prevail, with the person bringing upon himself untold difficulties, even the potential loss of the soul.

So, we should allow the experience of the disciples to be a lesson to us, understanding how easy it is to be led astray. As stated, self-will is the culprit; however, the greatest problem of all in such a situation is the believer placing his or her faith in something other than the Cross of Christ. In fact, the only way we can be brought into total conformity to the will of God is that our faith be anchored and maintained in Christ and the Cross. This is imperative (I Cor. 1:17-18, 23; 2:2).

(12) "HE SAID THEREFORE, A CERTAIN NOBLEMAN WENT INTO A FAR COUNTRY TO RECEIVE FOR HIMSELF A KINGDOM, AND TO RETURN."

The form is:

1. Even though this parable is very similar to the parable of the talents (Mat. 25:14), still, they are totally different in that the parable of the talents presents the sovereignty of the Master, with that of the pounds, the responsibility of the servants. The latter, therefore, contemplates the joy of the servants; the former, the joy of the Lord.

2. Thus we find that what is gained spiritually in this world will not be lost but enlarged in the world to come.

3. "He said therefore, A certain nobleman," refers to Jesus Himself.

4. "Went into a far country to receive for Himself a kingdom," concerns the time from the ascension forward, with Jesus in heaven where He is being vested with royalty (Ps. 2:6). Then He will come back crowned "KING OF KINGS, AND LORD OF LORDS" (Rev. 19:16), and He will receive the kingdom of the earth, therefore, exercising His government with great authority (Isa. 9:7; 11:1-5; Rev. 11:15).

The phrase, "And to return," proclaims the second coming, of which we have just spoken.

(13) "AND HE CALLED HIS TEN SERVANTS, AND DELIVERED THEM TEN POUNDS, AND SAID UNTO THEM, OCCUPY TILL I COME."

NOTES

The pattern is:

1. The phrase, "And He called His ten servants," refers to all who follow Him. The number 10 in Jewish ideology pertains to an indefinite number and, therefore, all who follow Him, irrespective of the number.

2. "And delivered them ten pounds," as well, refers to the responsibility given to all His servants in whatever time period they may have lived. This refers to all who are truly born again and, consequently, make up the church, even from its beginning to the second coming. In other words, every single believer has a responsibility in the kingdom, and we must quickly add, a responsibility given to him by the Lord at conversion.

3. "Occupy till I come," refers to the discharge of that responsibility on the part of each and all to the second coming.

(14) "BUT HIS CITIZENS HATED HIM, AND SENT A MESSAGE AFTER HIM, SAYING, WE WILL NOT HAVE THIS MAN TO REIGN OVER US."

The structure is:

1. The phrase, "But His citizens hated Him," refers to the Jews at His first coming. Their hatred resulted in His crucifixion.

2. "And sent a message after Him, saying, We will not have this man to reign over us," concerns the rejection of Jesus by the Jews. They would basically say these very words not too many hours after Jesus gave this parable. Pilate would ask the mob, "Shall I crucify your king?"

3. Their answer from the chief priests was, "We have no king but Caesar" (Jn. 19:15).

(15) "AND IT CAME TO PASS, THAT WHEN HE WAS RETURNED, HAVING RECEIVED THE KINGDOM, THEN HE COMMANDED THESE SERVANTS TO BE CALLED UNTO HIM, TO WHOM HE HAD GIVEN THE MONEY, THAT HE MIGHT KNOW HOW MUCH EVERY MAN HAD GAINED BY TRADING."

The exegesis is:

1. The phrase, "And it came to pass, that when He was returned," pertains to the second coming.

2. "Having received the kingdom," pertains to Revelation 11:15, "The kingdoms of this world are become the kingdoms of our Lord, and of His Christ; and He shall reign

forever and ever." Jesus Christ will then be King of Kings and Lord of Lords over the entirety of the earth.

3. *"Then He commanded these servants to be called unto Him, to whom He had given the money,"* actually refers to the *"judgment seat of Christ"* (II Cor. 5:10), and refers to an action already completed. In other words, this information will have been learned at the judgment seat of Christ, which will take place immediately before the second coming, and will take place in heaven. However, the action of that learned will not be put into motion until after the second coming.

4. *"That He might know how much every man had gained by trading,"* places this all important responsibility in terminology easily understood by all.

5. The idea is that every believer (servant) is going to have to give account to Christ for his life lived for Him. He expects us to bear fruit (Jn. 15:1-8). Regrettably, many believers think they are saved only so they can miss hell. In truth, there is much more to salvation than that. All believers have a responsibility of faithfulness, proper motivation, dedication, and consecration. We are His representatives and, as such, are looked at equally, even though some have different callings.

6. In other words, while the Lord may not expect as much from one of Paul's converts as He does Paul himself, regarding the winning of souls, etc., He will expect as much regarding faithfulness, proper motivation, and responsibility, respecting whatever task He has assigned.

(16) "THEN CAME THE FIRST, SAYING, LORD, YOUR POUND HAS GAINED TEN POUNDS."

The synopsis is:

1. As stated, this has to do with the judgment seat of Christ, where all motives and actions of believers will be judged pertaining to reward.

2. However, it will not be a judgment of the believers' sins, for those were judged at Calvary and can never be judged again.

3. It appears that this one called *"the first"* had done well with that which the Lord had given him.

(17) "AND HE SAID UNTO HIM, WELL, THOU GOOD SERVANT: BECAUSE YOU HAVE BEEN FAITHFUL IN A VERY LITTLE, HAVE THOU AUTHORITY OVER TEN CITIES."

The diagram is:

1. The phrase, *"And He said unto him, Well, thou good servant,"* proclaims that which I have just stated and concerns the Lord being very pleased with the results. All believers must assuredly know that all must stand before Christ one day to give account. What will His answer be toward us respecting the responsibility given?

2. *"Because you have been faithful in a very little,"* proclaims the basis of all judgment, which is faithfulness.

3. *"Have thou authority over ten cities,"* concerns reward, as stated, according to our faithfulness.

4. Some have claimed that these cities are to be taken literally, and that they represent the reward given to believers in the coming kingdom age. However, there would not be that many cities in the world, respecting all the believers who have ever lived. Consequently, it must pertain to reward only, whatever that might be!

5. All reward is to be judged basically according to faithfulness. In other words, the Lord has given me as a person responsibility for world evangelism. On the other hand, He may have delegated you or someone else to pray 20 to 30 minutes a day for us, or whatever the Holy Spirit desires. The reward will not be according to the size of the responsibility but to the faithfulness as to how we carry it out, whatever it might be.

(18) "AND THE SECOND CAME, SAYING, LORD, YOUR POUND HAS GAINED FIVE FOUNDS."

The exegesis is:

1. This tells us that while the second servant had done well, still, he had not been as faithful as the first servant.

2. Consequently, his reward was less.

3. As is obvious, as stated, the Lord here is stressing faithfulness.

(19) "AND HE SAID LIKEWISE TO HIM, BE THOU ALSO OVER FIVE CITIES."

The structure is:

1. If it is to be noticed, there were no

complaints respecting the rewards, with the exception of the one who did nothing.

2. In fact, there was no reward for him whatsoever, only eternal damnation, as the record will show.

(20) "AND ANOTHER CAME, SAYING, LORD, BEHOLD, HERE IS YOUR POUND, WHICH I HAVE KEPT LAID UP IN A NAPKIN."

The synopsis is:

1. The phrase, *"And another came, saying,"* represents the one who did nothing.

2. In effect, and if our interpretation is right, this one will not even be at the judgment seat of Christ because he did not truly know the Lord.

3. *"Lord, behold, here is Your pound,"* proclaims that he once knew the Lord but brought forth no fruit whatsoever! In that case, *"Every branch in Me that bears not fruit He takes away"* (Jn. 15:2).

4. So, this man would not have been in the first resurrection, but instead, was eternally lost and will ultimately stand at the *"great white throne"* judgment (Rev. 20:11-15).

5. *"Which I have kept laid up in a napkin,"* means that he did absolutely nothing with his life given him by the Lord, consequently, bearing no fruit, which will not be looked at too kindly.

6. Sadly and regrettably, this fits the lives of too many who call themselves Christians. While they once truly gave their hearts to the Lord, as the *"pound"* represents, still, there was no faithfulness to the Lord. It did not seem to be so much a life of sin and failure as a life of spiritual apathy. Every church has this type of people, and most are easily recognized.

(21) "FOR I FEARED YOU, BECAUSE YOU ARE AN AUSTERE MAN: YOU TAKE UP THAT YOU LAID NOT DOWN, AND REAP THAT WHICH YOU DID NOT SOW."

The construction is:

1. The phrase, *"For I feared You,"* represents a glaring untruth. If he had truly feared the Lord, he would have conducted himself otherwise. No! His alleged fear was only an excuse.

2. *"Because You are an austere man,"* once again, presents a falsehood. In truth, the Lord is merciful, gracious, long-suffering,

and not willing that any should perish; however, He does expect faithfulness, which is the criterion here.

3. *"You take up that you laid not down, and reap that which You did not sow,"* is once again a false description. In fact, the wicked servant was a liar.

(22) "AND HE SAID UNTO HIM, OUT OF YOUR OWN MOUTH WILL I JUDGE YOU, YOU WICKED SERVANT. YOU KNEW THAT I WAS AN AUSTERE MAN, TAKING UP THAT I LAID NOT DOWN, AND REAPING THAT I DID NOT SOW."

The pattern is:

1. The phrase, *"And He said unto him, Out of your own mouth will I judge you,"* in effect, proclaims the man passing sentence upon himself. If that's what he claimed the Lord to be, that's what the Lord would be!

2. *"You wicked servant,"* tells us that this man had lost his salvation, for the Lord would never call His true servant *"wicked."*

3. In other words, it seems he had once been a true servant of the Lord but had lost his way through apathy, or for whatever reason. At any rate, Jesus now labeled him as wicked!

4. *"You knew that I was an austere man, taking up that I laid not down, and reaping that I did not sow,"* means that if he truly believed that, he would have done something with his life.

5. The truth is, he thought he could get by with his excuse being accepted.

6. While we must not read more into this than we should, still, inasmuch as Jesus mentioned three individuals, with one of them being judged as wicked, I wonder how close this one-third ratio will actually come respecting those in the church but Christian in name only?

(23) "WHEREFORE THEN GAVE NOT YOU MY MONEY INTO THE BANK, THAT AT MY COMING I MIGHT HAVE RECEIVED MY OWN WITH USURY?"

The composition is:

1. The question, as asked here by the Lord, proclaims that no believer is excused to inactivity or uselessness, but that there will be opportunity afforded to everyone who is willing to use his talent in a humble and obscure way, if not in a heroic and conspicuous way.

NOTES

2. So, regarding the least among God's children, whomever that may be, faithfulness is required.

3. Because faithfulness is the criterion, a commodity that anyone can exhibit, no excuse will be tolerated.

(24) "AND HE SAID UNTO THEM WHO STOOD BY, TAKE FROM HIM THE POUND, AND GIVE IT TO HIM WHO HAS TEN POUNDS."

The composition is:

1. The phrase, *"And He said unto them who stood by,"* probably refers to the angels, with the place being the great white throne judgment.

2. *"Take from him the pound, and give it to him who has ten pounds,"* as concerns the indolent servant, has something in common with the foolish virgins (Mat. 25:12) and the unrighteous (Mat. 25:41). They were all judged, not because of what they did, but because of what they failed to do.

3. *"Be sure your sin will find you out"* (Num. 32:23), was uttered as a warning against failure and wrongdoing. Preachers usually use these words in reference to secret sins, but this is not the original meaning.

4. The idea of taking the single pound away from this wicked servant and giving it to him who has ten pounds presents a law within itself. Whatever reward the one pound salvation has, so to speak, cannot be kept by the wicked servant, proclaiming the loss of his soul, with any reward, whatever it might be, given to the one who had the most reward.

(25) "(AND THEY SAID UNTO HIM, LORD, HE HAS TEN POUNDS.)"

The overview is:

1. This sentence was not uttered by the Lord but by those who were listening to Him as He related this parable.

2. They were aghast that the pound taken from the man would be given to the one who already had 10 pounds.

3. Consequently, they failed to understand the reward of great faithfulness. It will reap not only the fruit of its own labor but, as well, even that of others who have forfeited their rights through unfaithfulness.

(26) "FOR I SAY UNTO YOU, THAT UNTO EVERY ONE WHICH HAS SHALL BE GIVEN; AND FROM HIM WHO HAS NOT, EVEN THAT HE HAS SHALL BE TAKEN AWAY FROM HIM."

The construction is:

1. The phrase, *"For I say unto you,"* is in response to the exclamation by the crowd.

2. *"That unto every one which has shall be given,"* is the iron law of reward guaranteed to the faithful.

3. *"And from him who has not, even that he has shall be taken away from him,"* proclaims the loss of everything.

4. Some claim that this does not refer to salvation but merely to reward. However, as stated, it cannot be imagined that Jesus would refer to someone who is saved, even though all reward is lost (as certainly shall be with some), as a wicked servant!

(27) "BUT THOSE MY ENEMIES, WHICH WOULD NOT THAT I SHOULD REIGN OVER THEM, BRING HITHER, AND SLAY THEM BEFORE ME."

The exegesis is:

1. The phrase, *"But those My enemies,"* is claimed by some to refer to other than this parable; however, that is incorrect.

2. These who are placed in the category of the wicked servant are labeled now as *"enemies,"* and more particularly, *"My enemies,"* referring to enemies of Christ.

3. *"Which would not that I should reign over them,"* pertains to all who fall into the category, including the entirety of the earth for all time, as well as Israel who rejected Him.

4. *"Bring hither* (here), *and slay* (kill) *them before Me,"* has reference to the great white throne judgment and the angels at that time, who will cast all these into the furnace of fire (Mat. 13:41-42).

5. Every believer must understand from this parable, and others similar, that the Lord expects fruit of all those who serve Him. In order that all may be able to participate, faithfulness is presented as the criterion, which has to do with one's motives and consecration. We should heed it well!

(28) "AND WHEN HE HAD THUS SPOKEN, HE WENT BEFORE, ASCENDING UP TO JERUSALEM."

The diagram is:

1. The phrase, *"And when He had thus spoken,"* probably was given to His disciples

on the road from Jericho to Bethany, a distance of about 12 miles.

2. *"He went before, ascending up to Jerusalem,"* is literally correct, for Jerusalem is approximately 3,500 feet higher than Jericho due to the terrain.

3. The main body of pilgrims going to the feast in Jerusalem would have parted with Jesus when He stopped at Bethany.

4. The indication seems to be that the next night Jesus was in the house of Simon the leper where Lazarus was recently raised from the dead. Mary and Martha were there, as well, when Lazarus was risen. Also, this is where Mary anointed Him for His burial (Mat. 26:6-13; Mk. 14:3-9; Jn. 11:1-9).

(29) "AND IT CAME TO PASS, WHEN HE WAS COME NIGH TO BETHPHAGE AND BETHANY, AT THE MOUNT CALLED THE MOUNT OF OLIVES, HE SENT TWO OF HIS DISCIPLES."

The exegesis is:

1. The phrase, *"And it came to pass, when He was come nigh* (near) *to Bethphage and Bethany, at the mount called the Mount of Olives,"* proclaims the time that He will set in motion the preparations for the triumphant entry. Bethany was the home of Mary, Martha, and Lazarus. However, it is undoubtedly true that Jesus knew about this great entry a long time before now, possibly even years.

2. Every evidence is that He had begun studying the Word of God long before He was 12 years old. Even at that tender age, He exhibited a profound knowledge of the Scriptures (Lk. 2:40-49).

3. Inasmuch as the Holy Spirit taught Him the Scriptures (Ps. 119:102), He positively knew all the prophecies pertaining to Himself, even at a young age, and most certainly the prophecy of Zechariah demanding this public presentation of Jesus as the King of Israel (Zech. 9:9).

4. *"He sent two of His disciples,"* concerned something that would, no doubt, be a mystery to them, which the following verses proclaim. Actually, Jesus was always doing mysterious things, which the disciples little understood at the time, because the Holy Spirit would have instructed Him to do so.

NOTES

(30) "SAYING, GO YE INTO THE VILLAGE OVER AGAINST YOU; IN THE WHICH AT YOUR ENTERING YOU SHALL FIND A COLT TIED, WHEREON YET NEVER MAN SAT: LOOSE HIM, AND BRING HIM HITHER."

KING OF KINGS, AND LORD OF LORDS

The phrase, *"Saying, Go ye into the village over against you,"* was either Bethany or Bethphage, which were located very near each other.

"In the which at your entering you shall find a colt tied," was at the entrance to the village. There is no evidence that preparations had been made for this, and actually, the reaction of the owners will show that fact. The Holy Spirit had informed Him exactly what to do and where the colt would be tied.

Matthew mentioned two animals, while Mark and Luke, as well as John, only mentioned one.

Inasmuch as Matthew proclaimed Jesus as the King, He spoke of two animals, representing both Jews and Gentiles. Jesus will be King not only over the Jews in that coming glad day, but the Gentile nations, as well, hence, *"KING OF KINGS, AND LORD OF LORDS"* (Rev. 19:16).

THE TRIUMPHANT ENTRY

Mark, Luke, and John did not mention the two animals because Jesus was presented in a different light by the three evangelists than what he was presented by Matthew. The three would have presented Him more to Israel, hence, the one animal, than to the entirety of the world as did Matthew.

As well, Zechariah had prophesied that two animals would be used, with, it seems, Jesus riding one first and then the other (Zech. 9:9).

The phrase, *"Whereon yet never man sat,"* concerns Jesus as King as no other; consequently, it must be an animal not ridden previously.

As well, there has never been a man as this man, the incarnate Son of God. So, this animal was fitting.

The phrase, *"Loose him, and bring him hither* (here),*"* proclaims that the triumphant entry would begin now.

As stated, the prophecy of Zechariah demanded this public presentation of Jesus as the King of Israel. The publicity of this entrance at a time when Jerusalem was crowded because of the Passover, the publicity of His trial, and the publicity of His death was most important for establishing beyond refutation the fact of His claim as the fact of His crucifixion.

Had He been stoned to death in some popular tumult or secretly murdered like John the Baptist, unbelievers might have denied that He ever died at all. However, there is no fact in history as undeniable as the crucifixion.

His death was the cornerstone and crowning act of His ministry. It was the death for sinners in order to atone for their sins. His death was the life of the world, and it was witnessed by a multitude of people.

(31) "AND IF ANY MAN ASK YOU, WHY DO YE LOOSE HIM? THUS SHALL YOU SAY UNTO HIM, BECAUSE THE LORD HAS NEED OF HIM."

The synopsis is:

1. The question, *"And if any man ask you, Why do ye loose Him?"* portrays that no previous preparation had been made for the borrowing of the animal.

2. Why?

3. Jesus as King (this is what He represented in the triumphant entry) does not and, in fact, must not ask permission. He is sovereign; consequently, He demands what He needs, and it is instantly done.

4. *"Thus shall you say unto him, Because the Lord has need of him,"* presents the manner of a king.

5. It should always be realized that Jesus Christ is not only the Redeemer of our lives, but He is also King. As such, whatever He has need of is to be given instantly. This means that we belong to Him in totality.

6. All of our finances belong to Him, not just 10 percent as some erroneously believe. Our occupation is His as well! Our families are dedicated to Him, plus the very desires of our hearts.

7. This means that whatever our occupation, our main profession is the service of the Lord Jesus Christ, and because He is King, we are His subjects.

(32) "AND THEY WHO WERE SENT WENT THEIR WAY, AND FOUND EVEN AS HE HAD SAID UNTO THEM."

The structure is:

1. The phrase, *"And they who were sent went their way,"* probably refers to Peter and John.

2. *"And found even as He had said unto them,"* proclaims them minutely following His directions and finding things exactly as He had said.

3. This is the way it always is when we follow the Lord. We are to receive direction from Him and then follow exactly as He has said. This is the secret of all victory in the church.

4. Regrettably, much, if not most of that done by the Lord, is that which is devised by men, which God cannot bless. He strongly demands as King that we hear Him and then follow His directions. Victory is then assured.

(33) "AND AS THEY WERE LOOSING THE COLT, THE OWNERS THEREOF SAID UNTO THEM, WHY DO LOOSE YE THE COLT?"

The composition is:

1. The phrase, *"And as they were loosing the colt,"* proclaims them doing exactly what Jesus had said do, which was to take the animal without saying anything to anyone.

2. Of course, the Lord knew the owners would confront them, with them being told what to say.

3. As stated, a king does not ask permission!

4. The question, *"The owners thereof said unto them, Why loose ye* (do you loose) *the colt?"* was a normal response to what was happening.

(34) "AND THEY SAID, THE LORD HAS NEED OF HIM."

The overview is:

1. They repeated exactly what the Lord told them to say, and it seems that no more questions were asked.

2. There must have been a finality, an authority, or even a power associated with what the two disciples were doing, which was instantly recognized by the owners of the animals.

3. As well, when they used the words, *"The Lord,"* the owners, whomever they

may have been, evidently understood immediately to whom they were referring. What an honor it was to have Jesus use the property of these men regarding the triumphant entry! I wonder if they fully realized in their minds just exactly how special this moment was.

4. As well, I wonder if we realize how privileged we are to have a part in that which God is doing.

5. I constantly tell people, especially when we ask for their help regarding the airing of SonLife television in remote places of the world, how privileged they are to have a part in this. And yet, I'm afraid that so many of us do not realize how blessed we are to be able to participate in something that will have eternal dividends.

6. God help us to be more spiritually minded in order that we may know and understand that the work of God is the single most important thing in the world. As well, we must understand that any part we may be able to play in that work, be it seemingly so menial, is a privilege beyond comprehension.

(35) "AND THEY BROUGHT HIM TO JESUS: AND THEY CAST THEIR GARMENTS UPON THE COLT, AND THEY SET JESUS THEREON."

The overview is:

1. The phrase, *"And they brought him to Jesus,"* concerned the one He would ride, with the other trotting alongside, as Matthew proclaims.

2. At this moment, it is not certain if they knew exactly what Jesus was going to do; however, they would very soon find out.

3. *"And they cast their garments upon the colt, and they set Jesus thereon,"* proclaims the disciples providing extra garments to cushion the ride.

(36) "AND AS HE WENT, THEY SPREAD THEIR CLOTHES IN THE WAY."

The synopsis is:

1. The phrase, *"And as He went,"* records the beginning of the triumphant entry. Every possibility exists that the Spirit of God, even in great joy, began to saturate the mountainside, and especially the people. All could sense this was something special.

2. *"They spread their clothes in the way,"* concerns the vast number of pilgrims

who had come from all over Israel, and even other places, for the Passover. This road would have been filled with people.

3. As they saw Him riding this animal, even many who had been healed by Him, they somehow recognized the significance of the moment, even though they did not comprehend it. They began to pull off their outer garments and lay them on the road in front of the animal as Jesus led the procession.

(37) "AND WHEN HE WAS COME NEAR, EVEN NOW AT THE DESCENT OF THE MOUNT OF OLIVES, THE WHOLE MULTITUDE OF THE DISCIPLES BEGAN TO REJOICE AND PRAISE GOD WITH A LOUD VOICE FOR ALL THE MIGHTY WORKS THAT THEY HAD SEEN."

The exegesis is:

1. The phrase, *"And when He was come near, even now at the descent of the Mount of Olives,"* means that He had reached the top of the mountain, coming from the other side, with Jerusalem bursting into full view. He would descend the mountain, cross the brook Kidron, ascend Mount Moriah on the other side, and go through the eastern gate to the temple site.

2. Incidentally, that gate is now closed and sealed by the Jews. They claim that it will be opened when their Messiah comes, fulfilling Zechariah 9:9. Of course, they're right on one point—it will be opened, and the Messiah, no doubt, will enter once again, fulfilling the prophecy of Zechariah. However, it will be Jesus, the one who made the first entry, who will make the second entry at the second coming. Actually, at His second coming He will return to this very mountain, the Mount of Olives (Zech. 14:4), from which He will undoubtedly make His entry.

3. *"The whole multitude of the disciples began to rejoice and praise God with a loud voice for all the mighty works that they had seen,"* no doubt, referred to scores, if not hundreds or even thousands, who had seen His healing power, or even had been healed by Him. At any rate, the whole multitude began to praise God with a loud voice, which, no doubt, caused the mountain to ring with the shouts of exclamation heard even in Jerusalem.

4. In fact, it could have been Israel's

finest hour, which it was intended to be, but Israel did not want her King; therefore, they lost the kingdom! However, in a coming glad day, it will be regained. Ezekiel records this triumphant moment in Chapter 43 of his book, but that entrance refers to the millennial temple after it is already built.

(38) "SAYING, BLESSED BE THE KING WHO COMES IN THE NAME OF THE LORD: PEACE IN HEAVEN, AND GLORY IN THE HIGHEST."

BLESSED BE THE KING

The phrase, *"Saying, Blessed be the King who comes in the name of the Lord,"* is taken from Psalm 118:26; however, it must be noted that there is no record of any of the religious leadership of Israel shouting this acclamation. In fact, the doing of this by the crowd only caused their hatred for Jesus to be intensified, if possible! To be frank, the coming of the Lord, in whatever capacity, as by visitation of the Holy Spirit, is seldom, if ever, greeted by religious hierarchy with favorable light.

As it was then, so it is now! Almost all so-called religious leadership, respecting denominations and denominationalism, is opposed to any genuine moving of the Holy Spirit because such always threatens their control. Anyone who fights anything that is of God, whether overtly or covertly, is, in effect, doing the work of Satan. As well, for those who place themselves in a neutral position, they, in fact, are not neutral. The parable of the pound emphasizes that. This individual did not lose the pound that was given him, but neither did he add to it. Consequently, the Lord referred to him as a wicked servant.

PEACE IN HEAVEN

The phrase, *"Peace in heaven,"* is of far greater magnitude than at first believed.

Jesus was to suffer and die in a few hours to bring peace to heaven as well as earth. He completely defeated Satan, and did so at the Cross (Col. 2:14-17; Heb. 2:14-15), making it possible to reconcile all things in heaven and in earth and make them one again as before rebellion was begun by Lucifer (I Cor. 15:24-28; Eph. 1:10).

The phrase, *"And glory in the highest,"* is

said a little differently than Matthew, Mark, and John, as they used the word *Hosanna!* Luke's book was addressed more so to Gentiles. Consequently, the word *Hosanna* would have had little meaning to them.

(Hosanna is an exclamation of adoration, meaning *"Oh, save!"* or *"Oh, save us now!"*)

To Israel's rejection of her King, the kingdom of God would have to be postponed. As a result of this, there were certain things that Israel did not know:

THINGS THAT ISRAEL DID NOT KNOW

• Due to their rejection of Him, this was not the time for the kingdom of God to appear (Lk. 19:11-27).

• That the Messiah had to suffer first and die to redeem mankind (Lk. 17:20-25).

• That the greatest of all conquerors was in their midst, but that His conquests had to be in the spirit realm before it could be in the natural kingdoms of the world (Col. 2:14-17; Heb. 2:14-15).

• That the greatest battle of all ages, and we speak of demon spirits and fallen angels who opposed Christ while He was on the Cross, would be fought in their midst in a few more hours (Jn. 12:31; Col. 2:14-15; Heb. 2:14-15).

• That all satanic powers would be defeated and spoiled by the death of Jesus on the Cross (Col. 2:10-15; I Pet. 2:24).

• That the guarantee of the restoration of man's dominion would be accomplished at that time (Jn. 19:30; I Cor. 15:24-28; Gal. 3:13; Heb. 2:9-15; 10:10-13).

• That the church must be built and the church age run its course before the kingdom could come in totality (Acts 15:13-18; Eph. 3:1-6; 5:25-31; II Thess. 2:7).

• That the many prophecies of the dispersion and regathering of Israel, the reign of Antichrist, the future tribulation period as outlined in Revelation, Chapters 6 through 19, and other prophecies have to be first fulfilled before the second advent and the coming kingdom age (Ezek., Chpt. 37; Zech., Chpt. 14; Rev., Chpts. 19-20).

(39) "AND SOME OF THE PHARISEES FROM AMONG THE MULTITUDE SAID UNTO HIM, MASTER, REBUKE YOUR DISCIPLES."

The pattern is:

1. The phrase, *"And some of the Pharisees from among the multitude said unto Him,"* proclaims these people watching but in no way joining into the exclamations of joy. As stated, they were bitterly opposed to Him, and above all, to the messianic claims. They were looking for a conquering Messiah and not a suffering Messiah, which Isaiah, Chapter 53, foretold.

2. In fact, Jesus was a conquering Messiah, actually, the greatest conqueror of all time. He conquered sin, Satan, and death; however, in their self-righteousness, the Pharisees and others of their ilk felt they had no need of such a conqueror.

3. They wanted a conqueror who would overthrow Rome, and above all, one whom they had chosen. However, it was not possible that God would, or even could, accept that chosen by them.

4. *"Master, rebuke Your disciples,"* in no way constitutes the last time this demand has been made.

5. Satan will do all he can to stop God's people from praising the Lord. Most of the time, he uses religion to carry out his evil design. Consequently, in the far greater majority of churches, praise of, and unto, the Lord is conspicuously absent. The truth is, they do not praise Him because, as the Pharisees of old, they do not know Him.

(40) "AND HE ANSWERED AND SAID UNTO THEM, I TELL YOU THAT, IF THESE SHOULD HOLD THEIR PEACE, THE STONES WOULD IMMEDIATELY CRY OUT."

The form is:

1. The phrase, *"And He answered and said unto them,"* concerns an answer they did not desire or even fully understand.

2. *"I tell you that, if these should hold their peace,"* refers to those who were praising the Lord, and that God would always have a people to praise Him.

3. *"The stones would immediately cry out,"* has to do with several things:

a. God demands praise because praise glorifies Him and, as well, proclaims to the spirit world that God's plan will succeed, and Satan will ultimately be overthrown.

b. It is impossible for true praise and

doubt to be entertained at the same time. Actually, praise is the exclamation of faith.

c. In a way, all of God's creation praises Him. It does so through functioning as it was originally created.

d. In a sense, modern recording tape fulfills these exact words of Jesus. It is made up of sand and other ingredients, which make up stones.

e. Worship is what we are, and praise is what we do.

(41) "AND WHEN HE WAS COME NEAR, HE BEHELD THE CITY, AND WEPT OVER IT."

The composition is:

1. The phrase, *"And when He was come near, He beheld the city,"* proclaims a scene of unparalleled beauty.

2. It is said that the temple was gleaming white, with most of it of comparatively new construction. As well, the estates of the rich and powerful surrounded the temple on the north, west, and south. With it being Passover season and, therefore, spring, the gardens surrounding the palatial homes boasted every type of beautiful flower in full bloom. It was undoubtedly one of the most beautiful scenes in the world. All of this was as a result of the blessings of God, but the religious leaders little appreciated it, if at all.

3. *"And wept over it,"* refers to loud crying, lamentations, and even wailing. In this case, the Greek word for *wept* is *klaio* and means all the things we have stated.

4. I wonder what the reaction was of the great crowd, and even the Pharisees, when in the very midst of this extravagant celebration of the triumphant entry, Jesus began to weep uncontrollably.

5. Many things look right with man, as this scene here boasted, but to the spiritual eye, nothing was right.

6. This outcry of sorrow is peculiar to Luke. As man, He wept, and as God, He spoke.

7. His compassion here appeared most vividly. As God, He knew the cruelty, the self-righteousness, the rebellion, the pride, the hypocrisy, and the sins of this people. He knew, as well, that in just a few days, He would die, and yet, He wept over them!

(42) "SAYING, IF YOU HAD KNOWN, EVEN YOU, AT LEAST IN THIS YOUR DAY, THE THINGS WHICH BELONG UNTO YOUR PEACE! BUT NOW THEY ARE HID FROM YOUR EYES."

IF YOU HAD KNOWN

The phrase, *"Saying, If you had known,"* concerns all the things they should have known and, in fact, could have known had they only studied and obeyed the Word of God.

The word *known* has to do with Jesus and the recognition of Him as the Messiah. There was no excuse for them not to know who He was.

In fact, the religious leaders did know or could have known. When men might know truth but refuse to know it, a just judgment blinds them, and they perish.

In fact, the same can be said not only of the Jews of old, but every human being on the face of the earth.

There are not many places on earth where a person cannot find out about Jesus Christ if he will only put forth the effort. This especially goes for America, Canada, and many other nations of the world.

Just yesterday we were discussing over our daily radio program the statement of Jesus, *"And this gospel of the kingdom shall be preached in all the world for a witness unto all nations; and then shall the end come"* (Mat. 24:14).

UNTO ALL NATIONS

Looking at our own ministry, I think we can say without fear of exaggeration that through television, we have preached basically to every nation of the world. Counting many other preachers, one can say, I think, that this Scripture has been fulfilled, making it possible for billions to know, that is, if they desire to know.

However, due to His personal presence, the Israel of Jesus' day had the opportunity to know as no other nation or people has ever known. But yet, despite the greatest miracles ever known by man, even to the raising of the dead, Jesus was rejected and murdered.

The phrase, *"Even you, at least in this your day,"* refers to the very time of visitation of which we have just spoken. This was

their day, and to be sure, it was a day as no one has ever had.

As well, anytime the gospel is preached under the anointing of the Holy Spirit by whatever method, this becomes the day of salvation for all who hear, and even those who have the opportunity to hear but refuse to do so.

The phrase, *"The things which belong unto your peace!"* refers to that which they could have had, such as salvation, the baptism with the Holy Spirit, and great blessings from God, and on a scale absolutely beyond comprehension.

As well, this holds true for any and all who accept Christ as their Saviour. Untold blessings await them. Jesus called it more abundant life (Jn. 10:10).

HIDDEN

The phrase, *"But now they are hid from your eyes,"* refers to judicial blindness.

In other words, when the evidence is freely shown, and the people have opportunity to see, but refuse to see, then God wills further spiritual blindness on them. In fact, that which is hidden from their eyes is hidden unto this day. The Jews did not see and, in fact, cannot see, because of willful blindness, which brought on judicial blindness. In other words, due to their own actions, God judged them accordingly.

The gospel of Jesus Christ has a peculiar different effect than any philosophy in the world.

If men accept a false religion, such as Hinduism, Islam, Catholicism, etc., they are always worsened by the experience, and terribly so, but if they reject these religions, they are none the worse.

However, with the gospel of Jesus Christ, if men accept it, they are immeasurably bettered. Conversely, if they reject it, they do not remain static but sink to a lower level, and in every capacity.

REJECTION OF THE GOSPEL

This is one of the reasons that America is steadily losing her way. She has been exposed to the gospel, possibly as no other nation on earth, and has by and large rejected it. The consequences are obvious!

When the gospel is rejected, whether by a person or a people, immorality, perversion, and injustice greatly accelerate. In fact, three things have characterized the fall of every civilization and empire in the past:

1. Homosexuality
2. Incest
3. Pedophilia

These three sins are pandemic in America at this time.

The only defense against such is the gospel preached under the anointing of the Holy Spirit. Regrettably, this is in short supply, with the energy of most of the church being spent in fruitless endeavors.

And yet, the Word of God screams at us the solution. It says:

"If My people, who are called by My name, shall humble themselves, and pray, and seek My face, and turn from their wicked ways; then will I hear from heaven, and will forgive their sin, and will heal their land" (II Chron. 7:14).

(43) "FOR THE DAYS SHALL COME UPON YOU, THAT YOUR ENEMIES SHALL CAST A TRENCH ABOUT YOU, AND COMPASS YOU ROUND, AND KEEP YOU IN ON EVERY SIDE."

The pattern is:

1. The phrase, *"For the days shall come upon you, that your enemies shall cast a trench about you,"* was fulfilled in totality in A.D. 70.

2. Titus, the Roman general, thinking it a waste of man power to attempt to take Jerusalem by frontal assault, surrounded it by a line of fortifications in order to cut off the city from all supplies and, thereby, to reduce it to famine.

3. *"And compass you round, and keep you in on every side,"* was fulfilled literally as well.

4. The Romans actually surrounded Jerusalem with a stone wall, making escape impossible. The inhabitants were kept in on every side, thus fulfilling this prophecy given by Jesus some 37 years earlier.

(44) "AND SHALL LAY YOU EVEN WITH THE GROUND, AND YOUR CHILDREN WITHIN YOU; AND THEY SHALL NOT LEAVE IN YOU ONE STONE UPON ANOTHER; BECAUSE YOU KNEW

NOTES

NOT THE TIME OF YOUR VISITATION."

UTTER DESTRUCTION

The phrase, *"And shall lay you even with the ground,"* concerns the utter destruction carried out by the Roman 10th Legion under Titus. The city was reduced to rubble.

"And your children within you," concerns the terrible loss of life among the Jews. Approximately 1.1 million people were killed. Actually, the people died in every conceivable way possible (by starvation, killed in battle, etc.); however, tens, if not hundreds of thousands, were crucified. In fact, so many were crucified that it is said that there simply were no more places to put crosses in the ground. They demanded crucifixion of the Son of God and, in turn, were crucified.

"And they shall not leave in you one stone upon another," was, as well, fulfilled in totality.

Josephus said that some stones were up to 94 feet long, 10 and one-half feet high, and 13 feet wide. One hundred and sixty-two marble columns held up the porches, which were 52 feet high.

Every stone was removed and a plow run over the place where it stood, fulfilling Micah 3:12.

YOU KNEW NOT THE TIME OF YOUR VISITATION

The phrase, *"Because you knew not the time of your visitation,"* refers to the life and ministry of Jesus, which constituted the greatest visitation ever experienced by any people anywhere for all time. In effect, the One they had spoken of since the days of Abraham, and even unto the beginning, literally came down to live with them and took upon Himself human flesh and frailty. However, they were so taken up in their self-righteousness that they did not recognize Him for who He was.

In truth, the religious leaders knew, but no recognition was given, simply making the situation worse. Great will be the doom of those who steel their hearts against a visitation of grace.

This is what makes America's position so precarious. It could probably be said that no nation in the world has had such a visitation of the grace of God, except possibly Israel of old. Grace refused is judgment pronounced!

In fact, the entirety of the world has experienced grace for the last nearly 2,000 years. Even though multiple millions have accepted Christ, still, the far greater majority has done otherwise. Therefore, the judgments of Revelation, Chapters 6 through 19, must come.

WHEN JESUS CAME

Jesus was crucified at the end of the sixty-ninth week of Daniel 9:24-27, or 483 years after the commandment at the end of the Babylonian captivity to restore Jerusalem and the temple (Dan. 9:25). Consequently, the religious leaders of Israel knew approximately when the Messiah was coming due to Daniel's prophecies, which meant that their horrible sin was not the sin of ignorance.

The Scriptures were replete concerning this time of visitation, speaking not only of the time, as stated, but exactly what kind of Messiah He would be (Isa., Chpt. 53).

From the prophecies, they knew that He would be born of a virgin (Isa. 7:14; Lk. 1:26-38); He was to be born in Beth-lehem (Mic. 5:2; Mat. 2:1); as a child, He would be taken into Egypt and then return (Hos. 11:1; Mat. 2:13-15); He would be called a Nazarene, meaning an inhabitant of Nazareth (Mat. 2:23—no prophet of old wrote this, but rather *"spoke"* it); His ministry would primarily be in Galilee (Isa. 9:1-2; Lk. 4:14); He would have a miracle ministry (Isa. 61:1-2; Lk. 4:21); He would come from the tribe of Judah (Gen. 49:10; Mat. 1:1; Lk. 2:1-4); He would be sold for 30 pieces of silver (Zech. 11:13; Mat. 27:9); He would be disfigured, which took place immediately before the crucifixion (Isa. 52:14; Mat. 27:29-31); and He would be buried among the rich (Isa. 53:9; Mat. 27:57). Consequently, there was no excuse for the religious leaders of Israel to not know who and what He was. They were spiritually deaf because they desired to be deaf; they were spiritually blind because they desired to be blind. He alluded strongly to this when He said:

"And in them is fulfilled the prophecy of Isaiah, which says, By hearing ye shall hear, and shall not understand; and seeing ye shall see, and shall not perceive:

"For this people's heart is waxed gross,

NOTES

and their ears are dull of hearing, and their eyes they have closed; lest at any time they should see with their eyes, and hear with their ears, and should understand with their heart, and should be converted, and I should heal them" (Mat. 13:14-15).

This means, as stated, that they purposely closed their ears and their eyes and, consequently, reaped a just judgment.

(45) "AND HE WENT INTO THE TEMPLE, AND BEGAN TO CAST OUT THEM WHO SOLD THEREIN, AND THEM WHO BOUGHT."

The pattern is:

1. The phrase, *"And He went into the temple,"* actually refers to the next day.

2. While He did go into the temple immediately after the triumphant entry, according to Mark, He simply surveyed the situation and then returned to His lodging at Bethany with the Twelve (Mk. 11:11). This that Luke proclaims took place on the following day.

3. *"And began to cast out them who sold therein, and them who bought,"* probably took place in the court of the Gentiles. This was an area reserved for the Gentiles where they could come and pray and seek God and be converted to the God of Israel. In this area money changers had set up their tables, and stalls were built. Lambs were brought in, along with clean birds, to be used in sacrifice.

Roman coins were not allowed in the temple because they pictured the head of Caesar, who the Romans claimed to be a deity; consequently, money had to be exchanged when, oftentimes, the people were cheated. As well, there was an awful din and racket, with the sellers of various animals shouting out their "good deals," until the entirety of the scene had become one of noise and tumult, which was the very opposite of that intended.

4. This is the second purification of the temple, with the first being earlier in His ministry (Jn. 2:15).

(46) "SAYING UNTO THEM, IT IS WRITTEN, MY HOUSE IS THE HOUSE OF PRAYER: BUT YOU HAVE MADE IT A DEN OF THIEVES."

IT IS WRITTEN

The phrase, *"Saying unto them, It is written,"* refers to Isaiah 56:7 and Jeremiah 7:11.

"My house is the house of prayer," is extended by Mark, which is, no doubt, the complete rendering. *"My house shall be called of all nations the house of prayer"* (Mk. 11:17). The *"all nations"* would definitely refer to the court of the Gentiles.

The court of the Gentiles was a huge expanse on the south side of the temple where, as stated, Gentiles could come and pray. They were not allowed beyond the middle wall of partition, which was reserved for Jews only.

There were actually four courts, with the first being the innermost court, where only the priests were allowed, except during the time of the Feast of Tabernacles. Then other men could come close to the altar.

Next to the court of the priests was the court of Israel where men could enter. The women's court was next to that, and the last court was that of the Gentiles.

As well, each court was elevated to a certain degree, with the court of Gentiles being the lowest of all.

Incidentally, as Paul wrote, Jesus *"has broken down the middle wall of partition between us,"* meaning the wall that separated Jews and Gentiles at the temple (Eph. 2:14).

THE WALL

This wall of stone was about 6 feet high. To cross it meant death to any Gentile.

Christ fulfilled all the law of Moses with all of its commandments, ordinances, and rituals, and provided a new covenant entirely for both Jews and Gentiles, making them one and on the same level in all things.

To emphasize this, the literal veil in the temple was rent from top to bottom when on the Cross, Jesus cried, *"It is finished."* This indicated that the way into the Holiest had been made for all men, that the old law was at an end (all fulfilled in Christ), and a new covenant ratified.

Incidentally, the Cross of Christ was not dependent on the resurrection of Christ, but rather the resurrection of Christ was dependent on the Cross of Christ. What do we mean by that?

If Jesus had not done what He set out to do at the Cross, which was to atone for all sin, past, present, and future, then He could not

have been risen from the dead (Rom. 6:23).

In other words, had He failed to atone for even one sin, the smallest of sins, He could not have risen, but the fact that He arose tells us that the work was completed at Calvary's Cross. Some want to argue that the victory is in the resurrection. No it isn't! You won't find anywhere in the Bible where our salvation was wrapped up in the resurrection, as important as that was.

However, the proof is abundant in the Word of God that it was wrapped up and finished at the Cross of Christ, hence, the veil being rent from top to bottom at that particular moment. In other words, the Lord did not await the resurrection of Christ to rend the veil, but He did it at the moment that Jesus expired.

The Cross of Christ is the foundation of everything we believe. Jesus Christ is the new covenant, meaning that this covenant is not merely on paper but is in a person—the person of the Lord Jesus Christ. However, the meaning of this covenant is the Cross of Christ, the meaning of which was given exclusively to the apostle Paul, which he gave to us in his 14 epistles. It's the Cross! The Cross! The Cross!

THE HOUSE OF PRAYER

The phrase, *"My house is the house of prayer,"* proclaims what the old temple was to become and what the new temple is to be, namely, the heart and life of the believer (I Cor. 3:16).

Prayer is the greatest privilege of the believer, but yet, engaged so seldom. In truth, the believer is to *"pray without ceasing,"* which means to be in an attitude of prayer at all times (I Thess. 5:17).

At the direction of the Lord, we had two prayer meetings a day for over 10 years (I personally still engage in this prayer time). We were seeking the Lord. In fact, had it not been for that prayer time, I do not believe that I would now have the great Message of the Cross. I do not believe there would be an Expositor's Study Bible.

In fact, when it began, the Lord told me, "Don't seek Me so much for what I can do, but rather seek Me for who I am." In other words, I was to seek for relationship with Him.

A DEN OF THIEVES

The phrase, *"But you have made it a den of thieves,"* means, as is obvious, that it was being used for the exact opposite of that intended by the Lord.

Incidentally, under the old law, God dwelt in a literal building, actually, between the mercy seat and cherubim (Ex. 25:8-9, 22).

At that time, the Lord could not dwell directly in the hearts and lives of believers simply because the price for man's redemption and, therefore, cleansing and sanctification, had not been paid, which Jesus would do at Calvary (Jn. 7:39). Consequently, the Lord dwelt in a building made by hands.

However, since Calvary, access to God is made possible *"by a new and living way,"* which is actually Jesus. Now the Holy Spirit can dwell directly in the heart and life of the believer. This is all *"by the blood of Jesus"* (Heb. 10:19-20), meaning the price that Jesus paid on Calvary's Cross by the giving of Himself as a sacrifice.

THE HOUSE OF GOD?

Some people mistake church buildings for the house of God, which they are not. While they certainly may be dedicated to God, as actually all things should be that pertain to the believer, still, the only house on this earth where God dwells is the human heart and life of those who have been washed in the blood of the Lamb.

Of course, it is to be understood that God is omnipresent and, therefore, everywhere; however, He dwells spiritually only in believers.

As a result of having a false understanding of what the house of God actually is, some believers have thought it wrong for a church to have a kitchen, a bookstore, etc. In trying to equate the ancient temple, as we are discussing here, with modern church buildings, which actually have no relationship whatsoever, many have a false understanding of what the true temple really is (I Cor. 3:16).

(47) "AND HE TAUGHT DAILY IN THE TEMPLE. BUT THE CHIEF PRIESTS AND THE SCRIBES AND THE CHIEF OF THE PEOPLE SOUGHT TO DESTROY HIM."

JESUS TEACHING

The phrase, *"And He taught daily in the temple,"* pertained to the approximate five days before His arrest and trial on the sixth day. This is derived from John 12:1 and Matthew 21:1-17. As well, Christ showed by His action that a house of praying should be equally a house of preaching.

"But the chief priests and the scribes and the chief of the people sought to destroy Him," concerns, as is obvious, the religious hierarchy of Israel.

Religion, which is man-devised and, consequently, man-made, always opposes God. As it did then, it continues to do so unto this very hour.

In truth, until Jesus came, it was not too easy for Israel to ascertain just how evil and corrupt their religious leaders were. Everything these leaders did was cloaked with a heavy covering of religious activity, with them talking about God constantly; however, when Jesus came, portraying the true way, it was glaringly different from this hierarchy. Even then, it was not easy for many to see. It has not changed presently; consequently, many may ask how they may know for certain that who they follow is correct.

THE CRITERION IS THE WORD OF GOD

The criterion is always the Word of God. If the believer will follow the Word, and that means that one must know the Word of God well enough to follow it, one will forever be safe. However, truly following the Word will always cause one to have to make some hard decisions. If the church or denomination that one is following is not adhering to the Word, and that means in all things, then the Word must take preference over everything else. That means that the Word must come first at the expense of friends, denominational affiliation, relatives, and all else. That's what Jesus meant when He said, *"Come follow Me!"*

As well, as should be glaringly obvious, one cannot oppose that which belongs to God and at the same time be serving God. The religious leaders of Israel opposed Christ greatly. Despite the fact that they claimed loudly and often how close to God

NOTES

they were, the fact remains that they did not truly know God. Had they known Him, they would have known His Son.

So, if religious men fight or oppose in any way that which is truly of God, this means one of two things:

1. The believer does not have all the light on the subject but will soon see the light and, consequently, stop the opposition, as many have.

2. Despite the claims, the individual does not know the Lord at all and, consequently, greatly opposes that which is of God.

To be sure, much of Christianity falls into one of the two categories.

That which is not of God will always seek to destroy that which is truly of God. It stems back to Cain killing his brother Abel.

However, irrespective of how big, rich, or powerful that religious hierarchy may be, as Israel of old, if it seeks to destroy the true work of God, it will only succeed in destroying itself. Israel is a perfect example of that. God's true way will ultimately prevail.

(48) "AND COULD NOT FIND WHAT THEY MIGHT DO: FOR ALL THE PEOPLE WERE VERY ATTENTIVE TO HEAR HIM."

The composition is:

1. The phrase, *"And could not find what they might do,"* means they eagerly sought any and every way possible to destroy Him.

2. It was not as easy as it might seem simply because great crowds followed Him, and He had the ear of the people. So, they were in somewhat of a quandary as to exactly what to do in order to carry out their evil schemes. Their lack of harm was not because of lack of desire, but rather the means to carry it out. Sin originates in the heart and is there long before the act itself is committed.

"For all the people were very attentive to hear Him," actually means, "They hung on His lips," or, "They hung onto every Word."

They could little know that this would be the last messages He would bring, at least in person. As well, the anointing of the Holy Spirit was upon Him as it had been on no other before or since.

Consequently, what He said opened up the Word of God as they had never heard it before. It was not dead and dry as the Pharisees or these religious leaders, but rather full of life. Such is the Holy Spirit, and such is the Word of God (Lk. 4:18-19).

"Patiently, tenderly pleading,
"Jesus is standing today;
"At your heart's door,
"He knocks as before,
"O turn Him no longer away."

"Gracious, compassionate mercy,
"Brought Him from mansions above;
"Caused Him to wait just outside your
   gate,
"O yield to His wonderful love."

"Can you not now hear Him calling?
"Do not ill treat such a Friend:
"Give up your sin, O, let Him come in,
"Lo! He will be true to the end."

"Now is the time to receive Him,
"Grant Him admission today;
"Grieve Him no more, but open your
   door,
"And turn Him no longer away."

CHAPTER 20

(1) "AND IT CAME TO PASS, THAT ON ONE OF THOSE DAYS, AS HE TAUGHT THE PEOPLE IN THE TEMPLE, AND PREACHED THE GOSPEL, THE CHIEF PRIESTS AND THE SCRIBES CAME UPON HIM WITH THE ELDERS."

JESUS TAUGHT AND PREACHED

The phrase, *"And it came to pass, that on one of those days,"* probably spoke of Monday. He would be arrested Tuesday night, or as they reckoned it, on Wednesday, for the new day began at the going down of the sun rather than at midnight as we now reckon time.

"As He taught the people in the temple, and preached the gospel," proclaims teaching and preaching as the means of proclaiming the Word of God. Regrettably, millions ignore this, which is God's way as evidenced by Christ, and substitute in its place religious ceremony, such as water baptism, the Lord's Supper, and other religious rites.

As important as some or all of these things may be, they are all the result of salvation and not the cause. Nothing can take the place of God's tried and proven method of teaching and preaching the gospel.

When a church, or entire religious denomination for that matter, begins to lose its way, it is because the teaching and preaching of the Word of God become lax until they pretty well cease altogether. So, there are really two problems:

1. A lack of teaching and preaching.

2. A lack of teaching and preaching the true Word of God.

THE CHIEF PRIESTS, THE SCRIBES, AND THE ELDERS

The phrase, *"The chief priests and the scribes came upon Him with the elders,"* appears to present a formal deputation from the supreme council of the Sanhedrin, the ruling body of Israel. They were upset with Him for several reasons:

• The triumphant entry: This was a bold move that incorporated thousands of people and, in effect, was a proclamation of Him as the Messiah of Israel. They were angry not only at this move but, as well, at the tremendous outbursts of acclamation on the part of the people toward Him.

• The cleansing of the temple: This had angered them greatly, perhaps even more so than the triumphant entry, simply because it was a direct affront to their authority. As well, it struck at their financial base simply because they received a rake-off from all the exchange of money, plus buying an selling of animals for sacrifice, etc.

• The allowing of the children in the temple to praise Him: Matthew gives this account (Mat. 21:15-16). Their crying, *"Hosanna to the Son of David"* was a proclamation of Him as the Messiah.

In this confrontation we are allowed to observe the age-old conflict of God's way versus man's way. I speak of man's religion. Regrettably, almost the entirety of the world for all time is immersed in man's religion, with very few actually following Christ. For the true followers of Christ, the anger expressed against Christ will be expressed against believers as well. Satan, who is a very religious figure, cannot abide God's way in any form; therefore, he must oppose

it greatly, and he uses religion most of all to do so.

(2) "AND SPOKE UNTO HIM, SAYING, TELL US, BY WHAT AUTHORITY DO YOU THESE THINGS? OR WHO IS HE WHO GAVE YOU THIS AUTHORITY?"

The synopsis is:

1. The phrase, *"And spoke unto Him, saying,"* presents them having no desire whatsoever to hear the wonderful things He was teaching and preaching. These, in fact, were the greatest words that man had ever heard, but they would rather try to stop Him. Satan must ever seek to stop the teaching and the preaching of any and all who are called of God. As stated, he will use religious men and women to carry out this evil design more than anyone or anything else.

2. The question, *"Tell us, by what authority do You these things?"* is a trap designed to force Him to openly claim a divine commission.

3. In fact, He had claimed such a divine commission many times, even in the temple a few hours earlier when He said, *"My house is the house of prayer."* This signified that the house was His, which it could only be were He God; however, if challenged, He could always claim He was only quoting Scripture (Isa. 56:7).

4. As they now posed the question to Him, if He answered as they thought He should, they would have grounds to call Him before the Sanhedrin.

5. The question, *"Or who is He who gave You this authority?"* is their second question, actually pinpointing the source of authority. They knew He claimed God as His sole authority, but they wanted Him to say it publicly in the temple, especially in answer to their pointed questions.

6. Of course, they did not believe His source was God, but yet, it was very difficult to explain the miracles; therefore, they attributed these to Satan, which, in fact, was blasphemy of the Holy Spirit (Mat. 12:24-32).

7. Of course, if they recognized His authority as God, that would mean He was from God. This they would not do! So, the more they weaved their web, the more they got caught in it themselves.

(3) "AND HE ANSWERED AND SAID

UNTO THEM, I WILL ALSO ASK YOU ONE THING; AND ANSWER ME."

The synopsis is:

1. The phrase, *"And He answered and said unto them,"* presents a totally different response than they had expected.

2. Once again, they attempted to match wits with Him, which would cause them, as always, to lose face. It is amazing that they failed each time, but yet, continued in their efforts to trap Him.

3. The phrase, *"I will also ask you one thing; and answer Me,"* is said with some force.

4. In demanding an answer from them, the Lord was claiming an answer from authorized teachers, which they claimed to be, who were acquainted with the facts. So, the tables were now turned, with Him putting them on the spot.

(4) "THE BAPTISM OF JOHN, WAS IT FROM HEAVEN, OR OF MEN?"

The synopsis is:

1. They had not anticipated such a response, and above all, this question.

2. However, that which He asked was not a trick question as theirs had been, but rather a legitimate question with a legitimate and obvious answer pointing to the source of His authority.

3. Consequently, they were on the horns of a dilemma!

(5) "AND THEY REASONED WITH THEMSELVES, SAYING, IF WE SHALL SAY, FROM HEAVEN; HE WILL SAY, WHY THEN BELIEVED YOU HIM NOT?"

The pattern is:

1. The phrase, *"And they reasoned with themselves,"* proclaims that as they went into a huddle, they well understood the horns of their dilemma.

2. While we marvel at the manner in which Jesus handled this situation, as He handled all, still, we must understand that the religious leaders of Israel were sealing their doom and the doom of their nation. This would cause untold suffering to millions of people. So, it is not a matter of mere wits, but rather a rebellion of darkness, which would plunge Israel into a stygian night from which she has not yet recovered.

3. The question, *"If we shall say, From*

heaven; He shall say, Why then believed you Him not?" only deepens their dilemma.

4. John the Baptist was a divinely accredited messenger who, among other things, was raised up for the sole purpose of paving the way for the Messiah and introducing Him. So, if they acknowledged that John was a true prophet of God, then they would have to acknowledge his message, and more importantly, the one he introduced, the Lord Jesus Christ.

5. As an aside, it should be obvious that while the people, for the most part, did receive and accept John and, consequently, his message, the religious hierarchy, with some few exceptions, did not!

(6) "BUT AND IF WE SAY, OF MEN; ALL THE PEOPLE WILL STONE US: FOR THEY BE PERSUADED THAT JOHN WAS A PROPHET."

The exegesis is:

1. The phrase, *"But and if we say, Of men,"* does not actually tell us what they truly believed, but only their casting about for an answer that would buttress their case.

2. What people do is not always a sign of what they actually believe in their hearts. In the case of John the Baptist, and especially Jesus, religious hierarchy based its position not on an honest investigation, but rather self-will. They formed a conclusion based on what they wanted and not what the Scripture said, to which they had easy access. However, once self-will is given priority, one will soon begin to believe what is done.

3. The Word of God is to be the criterion for all things, and not self-will, personal desires, or outside influence of any nature.

4. *"All the people will stone us: for they be persuaded that John was a prophet,"* concerns the people being far ahead of their so-called spiritual leaders.

5. Actually, the popularity of John had risen greatly since his death. Regrettably, that is sad but true in most cases respecting those whom God has chosen. Most of the church world, even of Paul's day, did not really realize who and what he actually was until he was gone. Such is the same presently and, in fact, always has been.

6. Now the people would stone others,

it was thought, who claimed a disbelief in John, while they were not nearly as zealous for his ministry when he was alive. Such is human nature!

(7) "AND THEY ANSWERED, THAT THEY COULD NOT TELL WHENCE IT WAS."

The composition is:

1. This answer caused them to lose face greatly in front of the people. As a religious hierarchy, they claimed the right of deciding all momentous questions. Therefore, to decline to pronounce judgment on so grave a question as the position of John, that mighty preacher who had so stirred and roused Israel, and who paid with his life for rebuking crime in high places, showed them to have no spirituality at all.

2. Consequently, they came up with a lame answer, *"That they could not tell whence it was."*

3. What a cop out!

(8) "AND JESUS SAID UNTO THEM, NEITHER TELL I YOU BY WHAT AUTHORITY I DO THESE THINGS."

The form is:

1. Even though Jesus would not answer them directly, the following parable of the householder, which He immediately gave, unmistakably gave them the answer.

2. By claiming to be the spiritual leaders of Israel and, as stated, by claiming to be the authority on all religious subjects, when they refused to answer concerning John, Jesus, by refusing to answer them, in effect, publicly denied their authority.

3. As well, His statement was given with some sarcasm, which, no doubt, was very obvious to the large crowd of people who had gathered.

(9) "THEN BEGAN HE TO SPEAK TO THE PEOPLE THIS PARABLE; A CERTAIN MAN PLANTED A VINEYARD, AND LET IT FORTH TO HUSBANDMEN, AND WENT INTO A FAR COUNTRY FOR A LONG TIME."

The pattern is:

1. The phrase, *"Then began He to speak to the people this parable,"* will, as stated, outline in graphic detail the answer to the question these religious leaders had asked. In this parable He would describe Himself

as the one sent from heaven, and in such clarity that all surely understood exactly what He was saying and, as well, exactly what they would do to Him.

2. *"A certain man planted a vineyard,"* alludes to God as the man and Israel as the vineyard.

3. *"And let it forth to husbandmen,"* actually referred to the religious leaders of Israel, whomever they were, and who served in this capacity from the very beginning to the present hour. There were some few godly ones among this group down through the many years, but not many. This present group, as outlined in Verse 1, was some of, if not the most wicked, of all.

4. *"And went into a far country for a long time,"* pertains to the time of Abraham up to Christ.

(10) "AND AT THE SEASON HE SENT A SERVANT TO THE HUSBANDMEN, THAT THEY SHOULD GIVE HIM OF THE FRUIT OF THE VINEYARD: BUT THE HUSBANDMEN BEAT HIM, AND SENT HIM AWAY EMPTY."

The diagram is:

1. The phrase, *"And at the season He sent a servant to the husbandmen,"* speaks of the prophets who were sent at intervals.

2. *"That they should give Him of the fruit of the vineyard,"* has to do with growth in the Lord that should have taken place and would have been brought about had the people obeyed God. As John, Chapter 15, brings out, the bearing of spiritual fruit is demanded of all believers. There are no exceptions! As well, a truly Spirit-filled life will bring forth fruit, and without exception.

3. *"But the husbandmen beat him, and sent him away empty,"* concerns the treatment of the prophets. They were not favorably attended and, for the most part, totally rejected. To be frank, at least one of the notorious Gentile nations, the Assyrians, heeded the voice of the prophet Jonah when there is little record of Israel or Judah heeding any prophet.

4. So, whatever angels were in attendance, and even the Holy Spirit, would have to report that no fruit was available—empty.

(11) "AND AGAIN HE SENT ANOTHER SERVANT: AND THEY BEAT HIM ALSO,

AND ENTREATED HIM SHAMEFULLY, AND SENT HIM AWAY EMPTY.

(12) "AND AGAIN HE SENT A THIRD: AND THEY WOUNDED HIM ALSO, AND CAST HIM OUT."

The overview is:

1. The repetition concerning the sending of the servant, i.e., prophets, is meant to outline the continued efforts by the Lord to bring about a successful and profitable conclusion.

2. However, such was not to be!

3. Without exception, the prophets were shamefully handled, maltreated, and rejected, with some even being killed; consequently, to whom much light is given, much is required, and much light was given to Israel, as should be obvious.

(13) "THEN SAID THE LORD OF THE VINEYARD, WHAT SHALL I DO? I WILL SEND MY BELOVED SON: IT MAY BE THEY WILL REVERENCE HIM WHEN THEY SEE HIM."

THE LORD OF THE VINEYARD

The question, *"Then said the Lord of the vineyard, What shall I do?"* is, no doubt, not at all being lost upon the hearers of the parable.

The question does not constitute a lack of knowledge on the part of God as to what He will do but, in effect, actually states what will be done.

"I will send My beloved Son," constitutes the greatest act in the annals of human history. This speaks of the Lord Jesus Christ Himself.

"It may be they will reverence Him when they see Him," concerns two things:

Using the last as first, they did see Him and, in fact, were looking at Him even as He spoke this parable. What did they see?

Even though He was accused of having an illegitimate birth, the truth is, His birth actually was the only legitimate birth that has ever been. All others were born in original sin, but not Jesus. Inasmuch as He was not fathered by normal means, the corrupt seed of man did not incorporate itself in Him.

THE BELOVED SON OF GOD

As well, His life was perfect. There was

absolutely nothing that any person could lay a hand on as being unscriptural or wrong in the sight of God. He obeyed the heavenly Father perfectly and, consequently, perfectly obeyed the law.

Also, His ministry was perfect in that it contained no class consciousness whatsoever, and neither did it exclude anyone who would come in humble contrition.

So, for the first time in human history, Israel, among all the people of the world, was privileged to see perfection.

Inasmuch as He was the beloved Son of God and, in effect, an heir, the vineyard belonged to Him, with Him having the right to demand fruit; however, irrespective of who He was, the sovereign Lord of Glory, they showed Him no reverence at all! Instead, they claimed that He was born of fornication (Jn. 8:41) and cast out demons by the power of Satan instead of the power of God (Mat. 12:24). They never once referred to Him by the name of *Jesus*, which means "Saviour" or "Christ," which means "anointed," proclaiming to all that they did not recognize Him as such.

(14) "BUT WHEN THE HUSBANDMEN SAW HIM, THEY REASONED AMONG THEMSELVES, SAYING, THIS IS THE HEIR: COME, LET US KILL HIM, THAT THE INHERITANCE MAY BE OURS."

The structure is:

1. The phrase, *"But when the husbandmen saw Him,"* proclaims the greatest visitation they had ever had, but to no avail!

2. *"They reasoned among themselves, saying, This is the Heir,"* proclaims in no uncertain terms that the scribes and Pharisees knew exactly who Jesus really was.

3. *"Come, let us kill Him, that the inheritance may be ours,"* proclaims that even though they knew who He was, the Son of God, their response was one of murder, for they killed Him!

4. By doing so and by claiming the inheritance would then be theirs, they were, in effect, saying that they would abort God's plan and purpose for their existence. They would then determine their own course, hence, *"The inheritance may be ours."*

5. Actually, millions of others follow in their footsteps by refusing God's plan for

their lives. In essence, this is what happened at the fall of man in the garden of Eden. Adam and Eve literally took that which belonged to God (their lives) and claimed them as their own and, thereby, pushed God out of the picture. History is replete as to what that choice has brought upon the world.

(15) "SO THEY CAST HIM OUT OF THE VINEYARD, AND KILLED HIM. WHAT THEREFORE SHALL THE LORD OF THE VINEYARD DO UNTO THEM?"

The composition is:

1. The phrase, *"So they cast Him out of the vineyard, and killed Him,"* says in no uncertain terms exactly what they would do and, in fact, did do!

2. The question, *"What therefore shall the Lord of the vineyard do unto them?"* now proclaimed to these hearers exactly what God was going to do to the nation of Israel; however, as they did not listen to the prophets, they would not now listen to God's only Son.

3. Israel then placed themselves into a position in which no sane people would desire to be.

(16) "HE SHALL COME AND DESTROY THESE HUSBANDMEN, AND SHALL GIVE THE VINEYARD TO OTHERS. AND WHEN THEY HEARD IT, THEY SAID, GOD FORBID."

DESTRUCTION

The phrase, *"He shall come and destroy these husbandmen,"* constitutes that which happened, and exactly as Jesus said.

It took place about 37 years later when Titus laid siege to Jerusalem because of their constant rebellion against Rome and in a period of time, reduced the city to total destruction. Over 1 million Jews were killed in this carnage, with other parts of Israel suffering the same fate. There is a lesson we must here learn.

Whenever the Word of God is given to a person, area, or nation, that to which it is given is never the same again. It is either immeasurably better because of the acceptance of Christ or immeasurably worse if Christ is rejected. It is not that God orders judgment upon those who reject Christ, but rather that the heart becomes harder because of that rejection. This is because the person or people in such circumstances go deeper into sin and all manner of evil. Actually, this is what is happening to America at present.

AMERICA

I think one will have to admit that this nation has gone deeper into sin, and continues to do so unto this hour, even at an alarming rate. Despite technological advancements, economic power, and America being the world's only superpower, still, the educational structure is falling apart, and the family unit is being attacked as never before, with homosexuality and lesbianism on the increase, and with crime exploding. In other words, America cannot build prisons fast enough to house the inmates. And now, same-sex marriage is slapping God in the face. To be sure, even though the Lord is long-suffering, He will put up with such only so long. In other words, America, sad to say, is ripe for judgment.

If the truth be known, all of this is because of the rejection of God and His Son, the Lord Jesus Christ. Unless there is revival, the deteriorating situation will only continue. At the same time, one can say that the church is to blame for all of this. Even though I do not like to say it, if the truth is known, the church presently is in worse spiritual condition than at any time since the Reformation. That's how bad that it really is.

Concerning Israel of which Jesus spoke, it was not that God shook His fists at Israel because of their rejection of His Son and thus pronounced judgment, but rather that He no longer protected them from their enemies, and it was by their own desires.

At their rejection of Jesus Christ, they said, *"We have no king but Caesar"* (Jn. 19:15); consequently, the Lord allowed them to have Caesar, which has proven to be a hard taskmaster.

THE VINEYARD

The phrase, *"And shall give the vineyard to others,"* actually has reference to the church.

It was the intention of the Lord that Israel accept her Messiah, the Lord Jesus Christ, and evangelize the world, i.e., the Gentiles. Now, because of Israel rejecting Christ, the church is the vineyard.

"And when they heard it, they said, God forbid," proclaims that they knew exactly what Jesus was saying and exactly what He meant.

The parable (story) within itself was an improbable one. The conduct of the husbandmen, the long patience of the owner of the vineyard, and his last act in sending his beloved and only son all make up a history without parallel in human experience. Yet, this is an exact sketch of what did actually take place in the eventful story of Israel!

In other words, it was a prophetic picture of the future of the Jewish people fulfilled with terrible exactness. The words, *"God forbid,"* portray that they had little idea, if any at all, of the serious danger that now confronted them, and neither does America for that matter! As well, most individuals and even entire religious denominations are blind to the dangers they face.

Jesus had already told them, *"Oh ye hypocrites, you can discern the face of the sky; but can you not discern the signs of the times?"* (Mat. 16:3).

Their exclamation of *"God forbid!"* should have been "God have mercy on us!" However, they did not see that which was happening in their very midst because their spiritual eyes were dim, if not blind. As well, their spiritual ears were dull, if not deaf. Such is much of the modern church!

(17) "AND HE BEHELD THEM, AND SAID, WHAT IS THIS THEN THAT IS WRITTEN, THE STONE WHICH THE BUILDERS REJECTED, THE SAME IS BECOME THE HEAD OF THE CORNER?"

BEHELD THEM

The phrase, *"And He beheld them, and said,"* portrays far more than meets the eye.

In the Greek there is a hint of anger in the expression *"beheld them."* This pertained to hundreds of people listening, as well as the religious leaders, as Verse 19 proclaims that they were still present.

The beginning of the question, *"What is this then that is written?"* points to Psalm 118:22.

Jesus took the people and the religious leaders back to the Word, which, in fact, they should have known. They would have known had they truly studied the Word of God; however, then, as now, the Word is too often given credence only when it corresponds with something we believe. In other words, it is used only to buttress, or at least attempt to do so, an erroneous belief.

Someone has said, "The Word of God interprets itself if it will be allowed to do so." By this, we mean that for a doctrine to be correct, it must be the same from Genesis through the book of Revelation. So, one Scripture will be interpreted by many other Scriptures, basically saying the same thing, i.e., interpreting itself.

THE STONE

The conclusion of the question, *"The stone which the builders rejected, the same is become the head of the corner,"* points to Jesus Himself. He is here represented as the stone, and above all, *"the head of the corner,"* or in other words, *"the cornerstone."*

As such, it is that which holds up the entirety of the building, i.e., that which held up Israel.

Israel's power and strength were not in the law of Moses, their temple, or anything else for that matter, other than Jesus. He was everything, but regrettably, they recognized Him as nothing. He was, in effect, telling them, "If the cornerstone is removed, the entire building will fall," which is exactly what happened.

The same must be said for the modern church! When Jesus ceases to be all in all, with other things taking His place instead, the building will then fall, irrespective of how great, rich, or powerful it may seem to be.

(18) "WHOSOEVER SHALL FALL UPON THAT STONE SHALL BE BROKEN; BUT ON WHOMSOEVER IT SHALL FALL, IT WILL GRIND HIM TO POWDER."

The construction is:

1. The phrase, *"Whosoever shall fall upon that stone shall be broken,"* speaks of Israel, which fell upon Him to destroy Him, but instead, they were broken themselves. In other words, the effort to destroy Christ is a battle that no one can win.

2. *"But on whomsoever it shall fall, it will grind him to powder,"* actually has reference to Daniel 2:45, where Jesus is represented as the stone, which smashes the kingdoms of this world at the second coming and becomes *"a great mountain, and fills the whole earth"* (Dan. 2:35).

3. So, Jesus presented Himself here as the principle figure of the entirety of humanity and the world, and proclaimed the rise or fall of all based on their acceptance or rejection of Him. It is a lesson that should be carefully heeded because He meant exactly what He said.

(19) "AND THE CHIEF PRIESTS AND THE SCRIBES THE SAME HOUR SOUGHT TO LAY HANDS ON HIM; AND THEY FEARED THE PEOPLE: FOR THEY PERCEIVED THAT HE HAD SPOKEN THIS PARABLE AGAINST THEM."

THE STONE THE BUILDERS REJECTED

The phrase, *"And the chief priests and the scribes the same hour sought to lay hands on Him,"* proclaims the fact that they became extremely angry at Him because of the parable and His portrayal of Himself as *"the stone which the builders rejected."*

Religion always seeks to kill Christ, and by a variety of means. It does it through ignoring Him, relegating Him to a minor position, or adding to or taking away from that which He has said. Not very many are willing to allow Him to be Lord of their lives.

In fact, most present-day religious leaders have forsaken the Word of God in favor of their own constitution and bylaws. That is a rejection of Christ pure and simple, irrespective of what the claims may be otherwise.

Oftentimes, individual believers make their church equal with Christ by believing that association with it in some manner constitutes one's salvation, or at least a part thereof. Millions offer God their good works, none of which He will accept. It is Christ and Christ alone!

Consequently, according to the very words of Jesus, there are few indeed who truly make Him the Lord of their lives (Mat. 7:13-14).

THEY FEARED THE PEOPLE

The phrase, *"And they feared the people,"* proclaims the gist of religion. It caters to the people as to what they want and not what God wants.

While it is certainly true that the people were right in this instance, with these religious leaders totally wrong, still, whatever is done must be done not because of what the people want, but because of what the Word of God says.

"For they perceived that He had spoken this parable against them," portrays Jesus doing two things:

1. In effect, the parable was against them, but only because they made it against them. The greater thrust was that they would know exactly what was going to happen and, thereby, repent. So, it was meant to draw them to God instead of merely being in opposition to them.

2. Jesus preached that which should be preached and, most of the time, that which antagonized and even greatly angered the religious leaders, irrespective of what they thought. Actually, there has never been any preacher in history whose message was so opposed to the conventional wisdom. And yet, He preached it fearlessly and without compromise at all.

HYPOCRITES

Every true preacher of the gospel must look to Jesus as the example. However, at the same time, we must understand that His heart was pure at all times respecting all things. Can we say the same for ourselves?

To say it another way: He had no personal animosity against these religious leaders, or anyone else for that matter, even though He called them to their face hypocrites, snakes, vipers, etc. (Mat., Chpt. 23).

The moral of this statement is: The harder one preaches, the purer the heart must be. Such preaching must not be done out of personal animosity, self-gratification, or self-will.

The end result is going to be the same in both cases, with religion greatly opposing the message of the Lord; however, heart purity on the part of the messenger causes the message to be straight and, thereby, given with the anointing of the Holy Spirit. The Lord cannot anoint the message, irrespective of how correct it is, if He cannot anoint the messenger. The idea that the message only is important, irrespective of who delivers it, is false. Ideally, both are to be intertwined, the message and messenger, hence, the absolute necessity of the heart of the messenger being right with God.

(20) "AND THEY WATCHED HIM, AND SENT FORTH SPIES, WHICH SHOULD FEIGN THEMSELVES JUST MEN, THAT THEY MIGHT TAKE HOLD OF HIS WORDS, THAT SO THEY MIGHT DELIVER HIM UNTO THE POWER AND AUTHORITY OF THE GOVERNOR."

The exegesis is:

1. The phrase, *"And they watched Him,"* referred to the religious leaders who intently sought to catch Him in His words in order to level a charge of treason against Him.

2. These were troublesome times, with plots being hatched constantly against the hated Roman dominion. So, it would not be difficult, they thought, to lay a charge against Jesus to the Roman authorities, hence, the question concerning the tribute money, which followed almost immediately.

3. It is a shame, they watched Him in order to hurt Him but not to hear the gracious words that came from His mouth or the miracles performed by His hand.

4. The phrase, *"And sent forth spies, which should feign themselves just men, that they might take hold of His words,"* pertained to those who attempted to trap Jesus with the question concerning the tribute money.

5. *"That so they might deliver Him unto the power and authority of the governor,"* was, in effect, their plan.

6. For them to lay hold on Him in the temple would have excited the anger of the people, which could have caused a riot, etc. So, they were hard put to find a way to stop Him, consequently, attempting to pit Him against Rome and Rome against Him. Then, they thought, Rome would do their dirty work for them.

(21) "AND THEY ASKED HIM, SAYING, MASTER, WE KNOW THAT YOU SAY AND

TEACH RIGHTLY, NEITHER DO YOU ACCEPT THE PERSON OF ANY, BUT TEACH THE WAY OF GOD TRULY."

The exegesis is:

1. The phrase, *"And they asked Him,"* pertained to these spies.

2. *"Saying, Master, we know that You say and teach rightly,"* was certainly true, but yet, a lie on their part because they did not believe that at all.

3. *"Neither do You accept the person of any, but teach the way of God truly,"* was exactly right but with evil design on their part. They had laid their little trap carefully in order to get Him to say something of which they could charge Him with treason. They were not praising Christ, only insulting Him, or at least attempting to do so.

(22) "IS IT LAWFUL FOR US TO GIVE TRIBUTE UNTO CAESAR, OR NO?"

The synopsis is:

1. Matthew and Mark both tell us that the Herodians and Pharisees, who normally hated each other, along with the Sanhedrin, were united in this plot to ensnare Jesus. He was equally hated by all of these hostile parties in Israel, who were supposed to be the leaders of the church of that day. They hated Him because His righteousness was a constant rebuke to their unrighteousness and hypocrisy.

2. This tribute was a tax levied by Rome on every person in Israel at a denarius a head.

3. Trying to equate it with the purchasing power of today is not easy. Taking everything into consideration, it was probably worth about $300 in today's purchasing power. On top of all the other taxes, one could well see how this could be economically hurtful, especially considering several members of a family, with each obligated to pay this tax.

4. However, it was probably opposed by the scrupulous legalists and the more zealous Jews because of it involving a great humiliation rather than the payment of money.

5. The denarius, or coins of that time, had on one side the laureate head of the Emperor Tiberius, with his mother, Livia, in the role of Pax (a Roman god), holding a branch and scepter, which to some of these zealous Jews was idolatry.

6. This very tax occasioned quite a number of uprisings, as in the case of Judas of Galilee (Acts 5:37).

7. The question was designed in order to trap Jesus any way He answered it, or so they thought!

8. If He said, "Yes, it is lawful for the Jews to give this tribute to Caesar," then the Pharisees could use this as a means of undermining His popularity with the people, for this tax was very unpopular. They would label Him as a traitor, pawning Himself off as the King Messiah, and then paying tribute to the hated Gentiles.

9. On the other hand, if He said that such payment of tribute was unlawful, then the Herodians, who also hated Him but were in favor of the tax or anything Rome did, would have denounced Him as one who taught the people treason against Rome. With the vast following He had, this would have probably caused Rome to act immediately.

10. So, in their thinking, this question was so designed and of such interest to the whole of Israel that first of all, He must answer, and secondly, either way He answered, or so they thought, would play right into their hands, which was their aim.

(23) "BUT HE PERCEIVED THEIR CRAFTINESS, AND SAID UNTO THEM, WHY DO YOU TEMPT ME?"

The structure is:

1. The phrase, "But He perceived their craftiness," means that He saw through their treachery and trickery. The Spirit of the Lord instantly told Him exactly what they were up to, and what the question was designed to do. In truth, they had little interest in what His thoughts were regarding this very important question.

2. The question, "And said unto them, Why do you tempt Me?" in effect, let them know that He knew exactly what they were doing and their hypocrisy.

3. It is amazing at the means and ways they used to snare or trap Him, and how easily He pushed aside their barbs and spoke words of great wisdom. Of course, everything He said was in that category, but sadly, Israel little heard or saw.

4. To tempt God, for that is what they were doing, is a serious offense indeed!

WHAT DOES IT MEAN TO TEMPT GOD?

They were not testing God, which in itself is bad enough because it speaks of unbelief, but rather tempting Him, which couples unbelief with sarcasm. It is the same thing Satan did in the temptation when he tempted or dared Jesus to turn the stones to bread, leap from the pinnacle of the temple, etc.

In Exodus 17:7, Israel tempted the Lord by asking, "Is the LORD among us, or not?"

Concerning Israel's failure to go into the Promised Land, the Lord said of them, "And have tempted Me now these ten times, and have not hearkened to My voice" (Num. 14:22).

Psalm 78 speaks some three times of Israel tempting the Lord, all during the 40 years of wandering in the wilderness, and all because of unbelief.

And yet, it showed an unbelief far greater than normal, which had actually deepened into hostile revolt against God. As such, it insulted Him by calling His word into question and daring Him to do anything about it.

This resulted in that entire generation being left to die in the wilderness. It also resulted in the generation of Jesus' day being so totally destroyed by the Romans that they were left unable to pay any tribute to God at all, and were forced to give everything to Rome, even their very lives.

So, I think it is obvious that tempting God is not a desirous occupation at all!

(24) "SHOW ME A PENNY. WHOSE IMAGE AND SUPERSCRIPTION HAS IT? THEY ANSWERED AND SAID, CAESAR'S."

The exegesis is:

1. The phrase, "Show Me a penny," was, as stated, the Roman denarius.

2. Matthew and Mark imply that no one in the group had such a coin simply because such was not normally brought into the temple, for this is where this confrontation took place. While they were obtaining the coin, it is easy to imagine the tension that built while they waited.

When it was brought, Jesus answered, "Whose image and superscription has it?"

3. His question should have jarred within the fact that they were in this condition, subjugated by Rome, because of their rebellion

against God. God intended for Judah, and more importantly, David's son who sat upon the throne, to be the guiding light of the world. However, when they rebelled in the days of Jeremiah, the light was extinguished, with the scepter of power passing from the faltering hands of the kings of Judah to Gentile powers, where it has remained ever since and is called *"the times of the Gentiles"* (Lk. 21:24).

Due to their continued rebellion, it is obvious that they did not at all catch the full meaning of His question.

4. The phrase, *"They answered and said, Caesar's,"* was them, in effect, admitting that Caesar now controlled them, irrespective of their chaffing under Gentile rule.

(25) "AND HE SAID UNTO THEM, RENDER THEREFORE UNTO CAESAR THE THINGS WHICH BE CAESAR'S, AND UNTO GOD THE THINGS WHICH BE GOD'S."

THE RESPONSE OF OUR LORD

The phrase, *"And He said unto them,"* would actually answer two questions.

"Render therefore unto Caesar the things which be Caesar's," portrays Jesus using a different word than they had used.

In Verse 22, they asked, *"Is it lawful for us to 'give',"* while in Jesus' answer, He used the word *"render,"* which spoke of paying something as a debt.

Swete says, "The coin is Caesar's; let him have his own. The fact that it circulates in Judaea shows that it is in the ordering of God's providence. Judaea is now under Roman rule; recognize facts, so long as they exist, as interpreting to you the Divine will, and submit."

UNTO GOD THE THINGS WHICH BE GOD'S

The phrase, *"And unto God the things which be God's,"* presents the same obligation to God that must be discharged exactly as to Caesar.

The question rested on an implied incompatibility of the payment of tribute with the requirements of the law of God. Jesus replied that there was no such incompatibility. Debts to man and debts to God are

both to be discharged, and the two spheres of duty are at once distinct and reconcilable.

As well, in this Jesus taught the turbulent Jewish people that the way to regain their independence from Caesar was not to violate the duty of submission to Caesar by a revolutionary shaking off his yoke, but to return to the faithful fulfillment of all duties toward God. To render to God what is God's is the way for the people of God to obtain a new David instead of Caesar as their Lord.

Regrettably, even though they marvelled at His answer, they still ignored what He said and failed in both duties—obligation to Caesar and submission unto God.

As well, in this answer the Lord placed His approval on the separation of church and state, which Israel, and no other nation in the world at that time, enjoyed. Actually, it would see little fruition until the forming of the United States as a nation in 1776. As such, it has set the standard for the world, guaranteeing freedom to discharge one's submission to the Lord without interference from the state and, as well, to pay one's obligations to the state.

Regrettably and sadly, under the Obama Administration, the freedom to worship God as one sees fit is becoming more and more contested.

(26) "AND THEY COULD NOT TAKE HOLD OF HIS WORDS BEFORE THE PEOPLE: AND THEY MARVELLED AT HIS ANSWER, AND HELD THEIR PEACE."

The pattern is:

1. The phrase, *"And they could not take hold of His words before the people,"* means that He had so answered that there was nothing they could lay hold on in order to charge Him before the people or before Rome.

2. *"And they marvelled at His answer, and held their peace,"* means they literally stood amazed at Him at the way He answered the question, which left them speechless.

3. In their trickery, they were positive that His answer would serve their purpose, but to their amazement, it served no purpose at all for their evil designs.

(27) "THEN CAME TO HIM CERTAIN OF THE SADDUCEES, WHICH DENY THAT THERE IS ANY RESURRECTION; AND THEY ASKED HIM."

The form is:

1. The phrase, *"Then came to Him certain of the Sadducees,"* presents the only occasion in the gospels, at least that is recorded, where Jesus came in direct conflict with the Sadducees.

2. This group was not nearly as large as the Pharisees, but yet, controlled the office of the high priest at this period, and would have been labeled as the modernists of their day.

3. *"Which deny that there is any resurrection,"* means that their interpretation of the Word of God ruled out an afterlife, consequently, reducing the plan of God to mere window dressing.

4. Spence says of them, "Supercilious worldliness, and a quiet indifference to all spiritual things, characterized them at this period."

5. Actually, they had little contact with Jesus during His earthly ministry, and while the Pharisees hated Jesus intensely, the Sadducees professed to look on Him rather with contempt.

6. *"And they asked Him,"* has reference to scorn. In other words, even though the Pharisees had not been able to silence Him, they were confident that their little tricky question on the resurrection would put Him to shame. However, they would, as well, portray their utter ignorance of the things of God.

(28) "SAYING, MASTER, MOSES WROTE UNTO US, IF ANY MAN'S BROTHER DIE, HAVING A WIFE, AND HE DIE WITHOUT CHILDREN, THAT HIS BROTHER SHOULD TAKE HIS WIFE, AND RAISE UP SEED UNTO HIS BROTHER."

The form is:

1. The phrase, *"Saying, Master, Moses wrote unto us,"* means they acknowledged as divine the books of Moses, which spanned Genesis through Deuteronomy. They (the Sadducees) placed no credence in the balance of the Bible of that day (Joshua through Malachi); however, their question would portray the glaring fact that their knowledge of the Pentateuch was also extremely faulty.

2. *"If any man's brother die, having a wife, and he die without children, that his brother should take his wife, and raise up*

NOTES

seed unto his brother," was taken from Deuteronomy 25:5.

3. God's enemies are always able to quote the passages they have studied in order to oppose a doctrine in which they do not believe. They are good at memorizing certain chosen verses, but they misapply and misinterpret the Scriptures to suit their own purposes. As stated in II Peter 3:16, they wrest them *"unto their own destruction."* False religions thrive on this refusal to make an honest investigation of truth for truth's sake.

(29) "THERE WERE THEREFORE SEVEN BRETHREN: AND THE FIRST TOOK A WIFE, AND DIED WITHOUT CHILDREN.

(30) "AND THE SECOND TOOK HER TO WIFE, AND HE DIED CHILDLESS.

(31) "AND THE THIRD TOOK HER; AND IN LIKE MANNER THE SEVEN ALSO: AND THEY LEFT NO CHILDREN, AND DIED.

(32) "LAST OF ALL THE WOMAN DIED ALSO."

The pattern is:

1. Deuteronomy 25:5-9 does not contain this illustration, at least in this fashion. This is a hypothetical situation conjured up by the Sadducees, which they thought sealed their argument that there was no such thing as a resurrection.

2. Some Jews had the mistaken idea that in the future life men would have their wives as in this world. The Sadducees took advantage of this error to disprove, they thought, the doctrine of the resurrection.

3. Of course, all of this showed their lack of knowledge of the Word of God. In fact, they openly admitted they didn't believe any part of the Bible with the exception of the books of Moses.

(33) "THEREFORE IN THE RESURRECTION WHOSE WIFE OF THEM IS SHE? FOR SEVEN HAD HER TO WIFE."

The construction is:

1. The rabbis in Jesus' day taught that if a woman had two husbands in this life due to the death of the first, she will have the first only in the next life. However, they had no scriptural foundation whatsoever for such a doctrine, which was false, as Jesus would here portray. Once again, their

foolish thinking was derived from not knowing the Scriptures.

2. The truth is, they studied the Bible constantly but only with an attempt to make it fit their own speculative ideas. In other words, they did not allow it to mold their thinking but tried to make it conform to their thinking. Consequently, they came up with all types of foolish ideas.

3. This tells us that the written Word cannot be properly understood without a proper relationship with the living Word.

4. In posing this question, the Sadducees, no doubt, offered it with a little smile of smug satisfaction, especially considering that the Pharisees could not answer it and, therefore, felt that Jesus could not either.

(34) "AND JESUS ANSWERING SAID UNTO THEM, THE CHILDREN OF THIS WORLD MARRY, AND ARE GIVEN IN MARRIAGE."

The order is:

1. The phrase, *"And Jesus answering said unto them,"* proclaims Him, as usual, using the sarcastic trick questions posed by His enemies to portray great biblical foundational truths. As well, as usual, He would do so in few words.

2. The phrase, *"The children of this world marry, and are given in marriage,"* places the institution of marriage solely in this present world and not in the world to come. Consequently, the foolishness of Mormonism is fully exposed.

3. As well, in this world beyond the grave, while He told us of a continuing existence of varied and ever-increasing activity, He threw to the ground the foolishness of the nirvana of the Buddhist, as well as the so-called sensual paradise of the Muslims.

4. He explained that marriage is but a temporary expedient to preserve the human race through the bringing of children into the world, without which, death would soon put an end.

5. As well, marriage is meant to portray ideally, that is, through the role of husband and wife, the portrayal of Christ and His church (Eph. 5:22-33).

(35) "BUT THEY WHICH SHALL BE ACCOUNTED WORTHY TO OBTAIN THAT WORLD, AND THE RESURRECTION

NOTES

FROM THE DEAD, NEITHER MARRY, NOR ARE GIVEN IN MARRIAGE."

THE RESURRECTION OF THE DEAD

The phrase, *"But they which shall be accounted worthy to obtain that world,"* speaks of the *"blessed and holy"* of the first resurrection (Lk. 21:34; Jn. 5:28-29; 14:1-3; I Cor. 15:23, 51-58; Eph. 5:26-28; Phil. 3:20-21; I Thess. 4:13-17; II Thess. 2:7; Rev. 20:4-6).

As well, these are made worthy *"by the blood of the Lamb, and by the word of their testimony"* (Rev. 12:11).

"That world" speaks of the eternal age, or the age of the ages, when Jesus rules forever on this earth (Isa. 9:6-7; Dan. 2:44-45; 7:13-14, 27; Zech., Chpt. 14; Mat. 13:42, 50; 25:31-46; Lk. 1:31-33; Rev. 11:15; 20:1-15; 22:4-5).

"And the resurrection from the dead," proclaims unequivocally that there will be a resurrection.

Here, Jesus was speaking of the first resurrection of life. This will include only the sainted dead, along with saints who are alive at that time, and not the ungodly dead, who will not be resurrected until the conclusion of the kingdom age. That will be a thousand years later than the first resurrection of life (Rev. 20:11-15).

MARRIAGE

The phrase, *"Neither marry, nor are given in marriage,"* pertains to the saints of all past ages, at least through the first resurrection to the second coming (Rev., Chpt. 19).

However, this only includes those mentioned and not those who come to Christ during the millennium, who will continue to marry and have children (Isa. 65:20-25; Rev., Chpt. 20). Actually, it seems this will continue on into the new earth, which will last forever (Rev., Chpts. 21-22).

At that time, and forever, there will be two classes of people on the earth—those with glorified bodies and then the natural people. Those with glorified bodies will have had part in the first resurrection mentioned here by Jesus and will help Him administer the affairs of His creation forever. Those considered natural people will continue to marry and have children, etc., while faithfully serving the Lord (Rev. 21:24)

These will be the natural earthly people, constituting nations as now, who accepted Christ during the millennium, and they will, thereby, remain alive forever by partaking of the *"Tree of Life"* (Rev. 22:1-2). They will multiply and replenish the earth and carry out the original program of God on earth as Adam and others would have done if man had not sinned (Gen. 1:26-28; 8:22; 9:12, 16; 17:1-9, 19).

As well, after the kingdom age, which will constitute Satan's last short-lived effort (Rev. 20:7-10), there will never again be any sin or rebellion against God (Rev. 22:3-5).

(36) "NEITHER CAN THEY DIE ANY MORE: FOR THEY ARE EQUAL UNTO THE ANGELS; AND ARE THE CHILDREN OF GOD, BEING THE CHILDREN OF THE RESURRECTION."

DEATH IS ENDED

The phrase, *"Neither can they die any more,"* has to do with the first resurrection of life. At that time all saints of God will put on glorified bodies, which will be like Jesus after His resurrection (I Jn. 3:2).

This is what God intended in the very beginning. If Adam and Eve had not sinned, and their offspring did not sin, they would not have died. It was sin that brought death into the world, which was separation from God (Gen. 2:17). This separation, which was spiritual death, ultimately brought on physical death.

When one looks in the book of Genesis and notes the extreme longevity, one must be assured that these are not fables but the actual time these people lived (Gen. 5:8, 11, 14, 17, 20, 27). The truth is that they were so wondrously made that it took that long for death to ultimately wear them down and then finally die. It was somewhat after the time of Abraham that the lifespan degenerated into an approximate 70 to 80 years, with a few living longer, and many living a much shorter time.

Mortality presently reigns in the human body, but immortality will reign in the resurrected body. Paul said it will be a body that God will give the resurrected saints (I Cor. 15:38).

"For they are equal unto the angels," is only speaking of immortality. Actually, there

is every evidence that when God originally made man, He made him higher than the angels (Ps. 8:4-9). The word *angels* in Psalm 8:4-9 should have been translated "God" or "the Godhead," for the Hebrew word is *Elohim,* which is a singular noun and is never translated "angels."

THE CREATION OF MAN

We're told that God originally formed man out of the *"dust of the ground, and breathed into his nostrils the breath of life; and man became a living soul"* (Gen. 2:7).

As well, the Lord made man in His own image bodily. *"So God created man in His own image, in the image of God created He him; male and female created He them"* (Gen. 1:27).

The Hebrew word for *image* is *tselem* and means, "Shape, figure, and bodily form" (Gen. 1:7; 5:3; 9:6; Ex. 20:4; Lev. 26:1; Ps. 73:20; 106:19; Isa. 40:19-20; 44:9-17; 45:20; 48:5; Jer. 10:14; 51:17).

Even though there is a likeness, still, the difference is staggering in that God's body is spirit while man's is physical.

Neither Deuteronomy 4:15 nor any other Scripture does away with the bodily form of God (spirit body). Just because Israel at this time did not see any form when God spoke is no proof that He is bodiless and without form any more than someone else who might be heard and whose body is not seen. Many in Israel, in fact, did see God's body (Gen., Chpt. 18; 32:24-30; Ex. 24:9-11; Josh. 5:13-15; Judg. 6:11-23; 13:3-23; I Chron. 21:16-17; Job 42:5; Isa., Chpt. 6; Ezek. 1:26; Dan. 7:9-14; 10:5-6; Acts 7:56-59; Rev. 4:2-5; 5:1-7).

THE SPIRIT WORLD

There is no question but what man was made in the likeness of God in soul and spirit (Eph. 4:22-24; Col. 3:10), but this does not do away with a body image and likeness of God as well. All angels and spirit beings have bodies as well as souls and spirits. Even resurrected human bodies are called spiritual (I Cor. 15:42-44), yet, they will also be material (Lk. 24:39; Phil. 3:21).

Misunderstanding of this subject comes from not knowing what spirits are like.

SPIRIT, SOUL, AND BODY

• Man's soul is the seat of the emotions, passions, desires, appetites, and all feelings (Job 14:22).

Consequently, one can say that one's soul is that which feels, while the spirit of man is that which knows (I Cor. 2:11).

• The inner man, consisting of soul and spirit, is eternal (I Pet. 3:4).

• Man was made a little lower than God originally but fell from that lofty state (Ps. 8:3; Heb. 2:7).

• Man was created sinless, but capable of sin, due to the free moral agency of man (Gen. 2:17; Rom. 5:12-21; I Jn. 3:4).

Man was made a threefold being—spirit, soul, and body (I Thess. 5:23; Heb. 4:12).

MAN'S DOMINION

Psalm 8:6 places man at the head of all God's works—the heavens, including the sun, moon, and stars, and the earth, including all living things. It makes him next to God in position and power over all creation.

Thus, Adam was originally made higher than the angels, but by sin, he was brought very low and made subject to death. Now, man, in his lessened state (short of God's glory, Rom. 3:23), is below angels.

Christ Himself was made lower for a time to take man's low place and to raise him again higher than angels, as he originally was. Christ has been exalted to a place higher than angels, or any other being except the Father (Eph. 1:21-23; Phil. 2:9-11; I Pet. 3:22).

Redeemed man is to be raised up to that exalted position with the Lord (Rom. 8:17-18; Eph. 2:6-7; 3:8-11; II Tim. 2:12; Heb. 2:5-11; Rev. 1:6; 5:10; 22:4-6).

Even though man was given such dominion at the beginning, he never exercised it due to the fall; however, such dominion over all God's creation will be realized and carried out in the resurrection and forever thereafter.

The phrase, *"And are the children of God, being the children of the resurrection,"* simply means that all believers will be children of the resurrection simply because they are children of God through the born-again experience (Jn. 3:3).

The angels are here introduced because Jesus was speaking to Sadducees, who (Acts 23:8) denied the existence of these glorious beings.

(37) "NOW THAT THE DEAD ARE RAISED, EVEN MOSES SHOWED AT THE BUSH, WHEN HE CALLED THE LORD THE GOD OF ABRAHAM, AND THE GOD OF ISAAC, AND THE GOD OF JACOB."

The exegesis is:

1. The phrase, *"Now that the dead are raised, even Moses showed at the bush,"* took these Sadducees to the very part of the Bible they claimed to believe, the Pentateuch, called the five books of Moses, Genesis through Deuteronomy.

2. So, Jesus would meet them on their own ground and show them how empty their so-called belief really was. Jesus was referring to Exodus 3:1-6.

3. The phrase, *"When he called the Lord the God of Abraham, and the God of Isaac, and the God of Jacob,"* presents a solid truth concerning life after death. The next verse tells us how.

(38) "FOR HE IS NOT A GOD OF THE DEAD, BUT OF THE LIVING: FOR ALL LIVE UNTO HIM."

The synopsis is:

1. The phrase, *"For He is not a God of the dead,"* refers to dead bodies gone back to dust.

2. *"But of the living,"* refers to the living, immortal souls of all men.

3. *"For all live unto Him,"* proves that the souls and spirits of all human beings are immortal (I Pet. 3:4).

4. This Scripture could be more accurately translated, "Not a God of dead beings but of living beings."

The simple meaning is: God would never have called Himself the God of Abraham, Isaac, and Jacob if these patriarchs, after their short lives, had become mere crumbling dust. God cannot be the God of a being who does not exist.

5. So this means that every person who has ever lived is alive at this very moment, regarding their souls and spirits, whether in hell or heaven.

6. This does away with the lie of reincarnation, for such does not exist. It also does

NOTES

away with the nirvana of Buddhism, which is a place or state of oblivion to care, pain, or external reality.

(39) "THEN CERTAIN OF THE SCRIBES ANSWERING SAID, MASTER, YOU HAVE WELL SAID."

The construction is:

1. The phrase, *"Then certain of the scribes answering said,"* refers to Pharisees who did believe in the resurrection and also believed in angels, etc.

2. *"Master, You have well said,"* obviously means that during all the arguments between the Pharisees and Sadducees respecting these great questions, no Pharisee had thought of using Exodus 3:3-6.

3. Exodus completely answered the question, and did so from the very book the Sadducees claimed to believe; consequently, they were left speechless.

(40) "AND AFTER THAT THEY DO NOT ASK HIM ANY QUESTION AT ALL."

The structure is:

1. Godet said, "Aware from this time forth that every snare laid for Him will be the occasion for a glorious manifestation of His wisdom, they give up this method of attack," including both Pharisees and Sadducees.

2. And yet, they did not give Him any credit for His great wisdom.

3. It was a case of the blind leading the blind, and they all fell in the ditch.

(41) "AND HE SAID UNTO THEM, HOW SAY THEY THAT CHRIST IS DAVID'S SON?"

HOW SAY THEY THAT CHRIST IS DAVID'S SON?

The phrase, *"And He said unto them,"* concerns Him turning the tables and asking them a question. Actually, it would be the most important question the Pharisees and Sadducees had ever been asked, for it dealt with the divinity of Christ.

The question, *"How say they that Christ is David's Son?"* speaks of the anointed One, for this is what the word *Christ* actually means and is actually transliterated into the word *Messiah.*

From II Samuel, Chapter 7, most Jews knew that the Promised One, the Messiah, would come from the royal line of David. David was human, and so would the Messiah be human. Thus, He would be David's Son because He would come through that family.

This had to do with the incarnation and went all the way back to Genesis 3:15. From this passage, as well as what the Lord said to David, they knew that the Messiah would be human.

They also knew from Genesis 12:1-3 that the Messiah would come through the seed of Abraham, which meant the Jewish people. They, as well, knew from the prophecy of Jacob in Genesis 49:10 that the Messiah would come from the tribe of Judah. Due to what the Lord told David, they even knew what family in that tribe would bring forth the Messiah, hence, Jesus speaking of David's Son.

A LACK OF KNOWLEDGE CONCERNING THE WORD

So, they should have been well acquainted with that of which He was speaking, but sadly, they were not because they had little knowledge of the Word of God even though it was readily available.

We find Jesus constantly quoting Scripture to the religious leaders of Israel, thereby, proclaiming great doctrines, which they should have been very familiar with. But yet, like so many today, they had so added to or subtracted from the Word of God that they little knew its real meaning.

So now, Jesus established that the Messiah would be David's Son, and that He was, in fact, David's Son, as his lineage went back to David through both Solomon and Nathan, both sons of David. (Joseph, the foster father of Jesus, went back to David through Solomon, and Mary traced her lineage back to David through Nathan, another son, with David, as all Jews, going back to Abraham) (Mat. 1:1).

(42) "AND DAVID HIMSELF SAID IN THE BOOK OF PSALMS, THE LORD SAID UNTO MY LORD, SIT THOU ON MY RIGHT HAND."

THE BOOK OF PSALMS

The phrase, *"And David himself said in the book of Psalms,"* refers to Psalm 110:1.

"The LORD said unto My Lord," proclaims deity on the part of the Messiah, which struck at the heart of the false belief of the Jews of Jesus' day, who expected their Messiah to be merely a beloved man.

This is one of the most remarkable sayings of Jesus in that He distinctly claims for Himself divinity, in other words, a participation in omnipotence. However, under the thin veil of some parables, He had repeatedly told them that He was the Messiah.

When He cleansed the temple and allowed the children to welcome Him with messianic salutation, all clearly stated that He was the Messiah.

In truth, a large portion of the population believed Him to be the Messiah, hence, the religious leaders having difficulty finding a way to take Him for fear of the people.

In this passage, He showed that whoever was the Messiah must be divine, as here stated. He spoke over and over again as the Messiah and acted with the power and authority of the Messiah. So, the proof was undeniable.

LORD

The first *"LORD"* in David's statement that was quoted by Christ refers in the Hebrew to *"Jehovah"* and is said to be David's Lord.

The second *"Lord"* is translated *"Adonai"* but should have been translated *"Jehovah"* as well.

One manuscript reads, *"Jehovah said unto My Jehovah,"* and should have been translated accordingly in all cases of this nature. Actually, the title *"Lord"* in Psalm 110:5 is translated *"Jehovah"* in the Hebrew and is the same as the second Lord in Verse 1.

This tells us that there are two divine persons called Jehovah. Actually, there are three such divine persons—the Father, the Son, and the Holy Spirit. All of them are God, Adonai, Jehovah, and everything else that God is.

In Genesis 19:24, we read of Jehovah on earth (who was visible to Abraham) as raining fire on Sodom from Jehovah in heaven.

The phrase, *"Sit Thou* (You sit) *on My right hand,"* refers to the ascension, where Jesus is presently (Mk. 16:19). He is sitting at the right hand of the Father (Eph. 1:20).

NOTES

(43) "TILL I MAKE YOUR ENEMIES YOUR FOOTSTOOL."

The composition is:

1. This is happening now, will be extended further in the coming great tribulation, and will be concluded at the end of the coming kingdom age when Satan and all his minions of darkness will be locked away in the lake of fire forever (Rev. 20:10).

2. Paul said, *"Then comes the end, when He shall have delivered up the kingdom to God, even the Father; when He shall have put down all rule and all authority and power.*

"For He must reign, till He has put all enemies under His feet.

"The last enemy that shall be destroyed is death" (I Cor. 15:24-26).

(44) "DAVID THEREFORE CALLED HIM LORD, HOW IS HE THEN HIS SON?"

The form is:

1. With this question, Jesus placed the incarnation squarely before the Pharisees.

2. The difficulty the Lord put before His listeners, and at the same time tossed into the lap of the Pharisees, was the question of how can Messiah also be human since He is Jehovah—deity? At once, as stated, the incarnation was brought before them.

3. One of the charges brought against Christ was that He called God His private and unique Father, *"making Himself equal with God,"* thus deity (Jn. 5:18). Therefore, the Jewish leaders rejected the teaching and fact of the incarnation and Jesus' claim to deity.

4. Also, it is well to notice our Lord's testimony to the divine inspiration of David, which pertains to the Holy Spirit, and also the recognition by David of the two other persons of the Trinity—the Father saying to the Son, *"You sit on My right hand, till I make Your enemies Your footstool."* Thus, we have the Trinity mentioned in an Old Testament setting.

5. David called Jehovah (the Messiah) *"Lord"* because He is God.

6. He is also his (David's) Son through the incarnation—God becoming flesh and dwelling among men (Isa. 7:14; Jn. 14:12).

(45) "THEN IN THE AUDIENCE OF ALL THE PEOPLE HE SAID UNTO HIS DISCIPLES."

The structure is:

1. What He would say, compressed in Verses 46 and 47, actually pertained to the terrible message of Matthew, Chapter 23.

2. The Holy Spirit moved upon Matthew to write the first gospel primarily for Israel and, therefore, freely exposed its hypocrisy.

3. He caused Luke to write the third gospel to be more applicable to the entirety of the world. Consequently, He made prominent Christ's attitude toward sinners. Hence, Luke alone mentioned the sinner of Luke 7:37, the prodigal son, Zacchaeus, and the dying thief. The narrative of His grace to these occupies much space, but His denunciation of the Pharisees only two verses, as we shall see.

(46) "BEWARE OF THE SCRIBES, WHICH DESIRE TO WALK IN LONG ROBES, AND LOVE GREETINGS IN THE MARKETS, AND THE HIGHEST SEATS IN THE SYNAGOGUES, AND THE CHIEF ROOMS AT FEASTS."

The pattern is:

1. The phrase, *"Beware of the scribes,"* spoken to His disciples, nevertheless, was spoken in the hearing of all the people plus the scribes. So, everyone heard Him say this.

2. As stated previously, the scribes were supposed to be masters of the law of Moses and, consequently, the spiritual leaders or pastors of the people.

3. Most all of the scribes were Pharisees.

4. *"Which desire to walk in long robes,"* had to do with the conspicuousness of the fringes, with the longer than usual tassels (Num. 15:38-40). Although commanded by the law of Moses, the scribes and Pharisees took it to excess, attempting to make themselves appear what they truly were not.

5. *"And love greetings in the markets,"* had to do with the long greetings especially tailored for these individuals, which spoke of their supposed piety, righteousness, etc.

6. *"And the highest seats in the synagogues,"* spoke of the seats next to the speaker, which faced the congregation. The spiritual leaders sat in these seats, etc.

7. *"And the chief rooms at feasts,"* spoke of the chief place beside the host.

8. So, it becomes obvious that they desired to be seen of men, and their religion was a *show,* but containing no substance.

NOTES

(47) "WHICH DEVOUR WIDOWS' HOUSES, AND FOR A SHOW MAKE LONG PRAYERS: THE SAME SHALL RECEIVE GREATER DAMNATION."

The order is:

1. The phrase, *"Which devour widows' houses, and for a show make long prayers,"* spoke of prayers prayed in the presence of these women in order to get their money. They talked these women into giving all their money to the temple, that is, upon their deaths, but had the contract so worded that, in fact, much, if not most of the money, came to them personally.

2. Actually, the Pharisees were placed in several different categories, even by their own. Some were called "stumblers," and so referred to them being so humble that they shuffled along, not raising their feet from the ground. In truth, this was a mock humility. How they thought that doing such could make them humble is anyone's guess.

3. Another group was called "bleeders," which was meant to insinuate that they were so modest that they would not raise their eyes when walking, thereby, running against walls, etc. This was done primarily because they might see a woman and think impure thoughts, etc.

4. Of course, the shuffling and the walking into walls were meant to make a great show outwardly and, thereby, to receive the praises of men. In truth, as stated, there was no humility or modesty.

5. The phrase, *"The same shall receive greater damnation,"* refers to judgment.

6. It should become obvious that Christ detests show, which always produces hypocrisy.

7. So, these would be judged far more harshly even than those who were in deep sin and made no pretense otherwise.

"Almost persuaded, now to believe;
"Almost persuaded, Christ to receive;
"Seems now some soul to say,
"Go Spirit, go Your way,
"Some more convenient day on You I'll call."

"Almost persuaded, come, come today;
"Almost persuaded, turn not away;
"Jesus invites you here,

"Angels are lingering near,
"Prayers rise from hearts so dear,
"O wanderer, come."

"Almost persuaded, harvest is past!
"Almost persuaded, doom comes at
    last!
"Almost cannot avail; almost is but to
    fail!
"Sad, sad, that bitter wail, almost but
    lost!"

CHAPTER 21

(1) "AND HE LOOKED UP, AND SAW THE RICH MEN CASTING THEIR GIFTS INTO THE TREASURY."

The diagram is:

1. The phrase, *"And He looked up,"* could well mean that He was sitting, even resting, after the clash with the scribes and Sadducees.

2. He was in the covered colonnade of that part of the temple that was open to Jewish women. Here was the treasury, with its 13 boxes on the wall, where people could give offerings, all according to their tribe.

3. These boxes were called shopheroth, or trumpets, because they were shaped like trumpets. It is said that some of these were marked with special inscriptions denoting the destination of the gifts. Only Mark and Luke mention this.

4. *"And saw the rich men casting their gifts into the treasury,"* implies that they were making a show of their gifts, desiring to impress the people by the amount, etc. It seems that almost all of Israel had become one big show of religion, with almost no substance in fact.

(2) "AND HE SAW ALSO A CERTAIN POOR WIDOW CASTING IN THITHER TWO MITES."

The overview is:

1. As this woman would never have made a show out of putting in such a small amount, evidently the Holy Spirit informed Jesus of all these proceedings: her poverty, the amount given, and that she had nothing left.

2. The *"two mites"* were probably worth something less than a dollar in 2013 purchasing power.

3. In this scenario, the Lord will make abundantly clear the motive of the heart respecting giving. He will tell us, as well, how God looks at what we give, and to be sure, that is the only thing that is really important.

4. As a result, this illustration has been of tremendous comfort to millions down through the centuries, who long to give to God but have precious little to give. The Lord shows here that He judges the amount given by many and different factors. Hopefully, we will look at some of these factors.

(3) "AND HE SAID, OF A TRUTH I SAY UNTO YOU, THAT THIS POOR WIDOW HAS CAST IN MORE THAN THEY ALL."

TRUTH

The phrase, *"And He said, Of a truth I say unto you,"* present a new concept of giving. As will be obvious, giving had degenerated into a *show* to impress people, which, of course, eliminated most people, who had no such large gifts to give. The Lord will teach that whatever is done is judged rather by the motives than by other particulars, such as the amount, etc.

THIS POOR WIDOW

The phrase, *"That this poor widow has cast in more than they all,"* no doubt, came as a shock to the listeners, as well as His disciples.

The words *"poor widow"* means that she worked hard for what little bit she did have.

Israel had deteriorated into this showy religion because of wrong thinking, which resulted from a wrong interpretation of the Scripture or the ignoring of it altogether.

THE KINGDOM OF GOD

The Jews in Jesus' day had long since come to the conclusion that wealth equated to the blessing of God, with poverty the very opposite. Consequently, the richer one was, the closer to God one was, at least in their thinking.

If that was so, then the showy method of giving followed suit. It probably was carried out under the auspices that God had blessed them abundantly, and consequently, they were giving abundantly. All was done with a great show and under a great panoply of religion, and maybe even praises to God, etc.

However, it was not God who had blessed these individuals who were rich, but rather their own cunning, etc. (Not to mean that all rich fell into this category, for some few did not).

Of course, Jesus blew this thinking out of the water by stating, *"How hardly shall they who have riches enter into the kingdom of God!"* (Lk. 18:24).

The moral of this is that false doctrine does not have a stopping place; instead, it continues to go more and more astray if not corrected. In other words, a small amount of leaven ultimately corrupts the whole, and such was Israel.

In the eyes of God, this woman had given more, not only than the giver of the richest gift, but actually all combined. At least this is what the Lord said, which is the only conclusion that matters.

(4) "FOR ALL THESE HAVE OF THEIR ABUNDANCE CAST IN UNTO THE OFFERINGS OF GOD: BUT SHE OF HER PENURY HAS CAST IN ALL THE LIVING THAT SHE HAD."

GIVING

The phrase, *"For all these have of their abundance cast in unto the offerings of God,"* means that they had much left, constituting very little given, at least in the eyes of God.

"But she of her penury hast cast in all the living that she had," spoke of her gift, as small as it was, being larger than all others combined because she gave all.

What do we learn from this?

• God doesn't judge the quality of the gift by its size but by the motivation of the heart.

• Her consecration was such that she longed to give to God, even though it was such a small amount and, above all, that it was all that she had. This shows that she put God first in all things.

• Many others may get the credit here because of large gifts, while many, like this dear lady, will get the credit there. Actually, Jesus is giving us a portrayal of how God keeps score. We should heed it carefully!

THE POOR WIDOW

If we take the attitude that our gift is small and, consequently, of no use, we have completely misunderstood the reason for giving. We learn that the Lord delighted in what this woman did and made such obvious to all.

LARGE GIFTS

The large gifts, just because they were large, did not bring about censure from Christ, but only the showy method by which they were given. It is obvious that $50,000 will do much more for the work of the Lord than $20. However, if God has so blessed an individual that he can give large amounts, and He definitely has with some, it must be given with the thought and motivation that God, who knows all as well sees all, will bless us accordingly, at least in respect to our motives. Not too many people giving small amounts will be lifted up in pride with such, but large gifts can cause pride to be generated if we're not careful and properly motivated by Christ. Actually, the Lord judges all things according to our motives. This *"poor widow"* was motivated to give to God because she loved Him, despite the smallness of her gift. The rich men (at least these) were motivated to give to God in order that they might make a big show and impress others. Such does not always hold true in these situations and categories, but it does many times.

As far as we know, that which Jesus said about the widow's alms was the last word of public teaching. If, in fact, that is the case, it is significant that this last word would be on the subject of money!

(5) "AND AS SOME SPOKE OF THE TEMPLE, HOW IT WAS ADORNED WITH GOODLY STONES AND GIFTS, HE SAID."

The structure is:

1. The phrase, *"And as some spoke of the temple,"* was said on the way up the Mount of Olivet as Jesus and His disciples left the city.

2. *"How it was adorned with goodly stones and gifts, He said,"* according to Matthew, was spoken by the disciples (Mat. 24:1).

3. Actually, the temple was one of the

most beautiful buildings in the world. It was covered with white marble or white sandstone, in either case, brilliant as the sun reflected off its adornments.

(6) "AS FOR THESE THINGS WHICH YOU BEHOLD, THE DAYS WILL COME, IN THE WHICH THERE SHALL NOT BE LEFT ONE STONE UPON ANOTHER, THAT SHALL NOT BE THROWN DOWN."

THE BEAUTY OF THE TEMPLE

The phrase, *"As for these things which you behold,"* referred to the beauty of the temple, which the disciples were even then admiring.

The temple was the very center of Jewish worship of God; however, sadly, the worship had deteriorated, at least for the most part, to mere ritual and ceremony. It is said that the temple was rich in particular things, such as crowns, shields, and vessels of gold and silver, presented by princes and others who visited this holy house on Zion. The historian, Tacitus, for instance, calls it "a temple of vast wealth."

The disciples were very impressed with it, as were all others who visited Jerusalem.

"The days will come, in the which there shall not be left one stone upon another, that shall not be thrown down," must have come as a startling shock to the disciples as it was spoken by Jesus.

Some of the stones and blocks of marble with which the temple had been built were so enormous that it surprised even Titus, the Roman general, when the city fell.

Josephus says that some of the great stones were as much as 60 feet long and 15 feet high. Without the aid of modern equipment, how they were able to maneuver stones of such vast size and weight is a mystery even to the present. (Others have said that some of the stones were even larger and longer than these just mentioned.)

THE FULFILLMENT OF THE PREDICTIONS OF CHRIST

According to Matthew, when Jesus said these words, the disciples, becoming fearful that He would be overheard and even accused of treason, pulled Him into a private place so they could ply Him with other

questions concerning that which He had just said (Mat. 24:3).

About 37 years later, the Lord's words were fulfilled in totality, with the attack by the Romans actually beginning at approximately the very place on the side of Olivet where Jesus had made this prediction.

Actually, Titus had given instructions that the temple was to be spared because of its wealth and beauty; however, he did not have the respect and loyalty of the troops that his father Vespasian had demanded.

(Vespasian had been called to Rome where he had now become Caesar, with his son Titus taking his place as commander in chief of the Roman 10th Legion.)

The soldiers had heard that gold was mixed in the mortar between the great stones, which resulted in them hooking oxen to these great blocks and pulling them down. There was no gold in the mortar.

Josephus, writing upon the utter demolition of the city and temple, says that, with the exception of Herod's three great towers and part of the western wall, the whole circuit of the city was so thoroughly leveled and dug up that no one visiting it would believe that it had ever been inhabited. Total was its destruction, fulfilling exactly what Jesus had said.

(7) "AND THEY ASKED HIM, SAYING, MASTER, BUT WHEN SHALL THESE THINGS BE? AND WHAT SIGN WILL THERE BE WHEN THESE THINGS SHALL COME TO PASS?"

QUESTIONS DIRECTED AT CHRIST

The phrase, *"And they asked Him, saying,"* is by and large similar to that reported by Matthew, with some exceptions.

Luke deals with the coming destruction by Titus that we have just mentioned, while Matthew does not allude to it at all, except maybe in passing.

Actually, Jesus, no doubt, said many things in all of these discourses that were not reported, or else, reported only in part. To be sure, in the relating of each instance, the Holy Spirit, no doubt, guided the writer to give that which He (the Holy Spirit) desired.

The question, *"Master, but when shall these things be?"* is the same as reported by

Matthew (Mat. 24:3). They desired to know the time of this coming destruction, hence, the word *when*.

The question, *"And what sign will there be when these things shall come to pass?"* is somewhat different than the question recorded by Matthew, *"And what shall be the sign of Your coming, and of the end of the age?"*

Actually, they asked all three of these questions, which were promptly answered by Christ, but with both accounts of Matthew and Luke needed in order to make up the whole statement.

So, they wanted to know when these things will happen and the signs that will appear when they are about to be fulfilled.

THE PROPHECIES

Matthew and Luke record in graphic detail the words of Jesus respecting the plan of God from that time forward.

Even though the church is not mentioned by name, still, it is referred to in Verses 4 through 14 of Matthew's account in Chapter 24. Luke only slightly refers to it in Chapter 21:8-11.

Matthew does not mention the soon coming destruction of Jerusalem, except only in passing, with Luke dealing with it extensively. Most of that given by Matthew concerns the destruction of Jerusalem by the Antichrist, which has not even yet come to pass, while Luke mentions this (Vss. 25-28), but only in passing.

Coupled with the prophecies of Daniel and John in the book of Revelation, along with references by other prophets and apostles, these are the only accounts in the world of that which is to happen in the future, even the near future. And yet, precious few take advantage of its wealth of information, rather seeking the foolish prognostications of man, which change by the hour.

Sadder still, even most of the modern church little knows or understands what is said here, either ignoring it all together, or else, relegating it to history.

(8) "AND HE SAID, TAKE HEED THAT YOU BE NOT DECEIVED: FOR MANY SHALL COME IN MY NAME, SAYING, I AM CHRIST; AND THE TIME DRAWS NEAR: GO YE NOT THEREFORE AFTER THEM."

DECEPTION

The phrase, *"And He said, Take heed that you be not deceived,"* is the exact manner in which Matthew also begins his account—the warning of deception.

This deception, as we shall see, is mainly in the realm of religion.

The phrase, *"For many shall come in My name, saying, I am Christ,"* actually means they will carry out their perfidious work in the name of Jesus, while all the time claiming to be anointed, for that is what the name *"Christ"* actually means. The idea is that all of these claiming such do not, in fact, have it and are not from God.

Even though this problem had persisted from the very beginning, still, in these last days, it will exacerbate.

The tragedy is that much of the modern church, even the Pentecostal and Charismatic varieties, who claim to know better, little know any more what the true anointing of the Holy Spirit actually is.

Remember this! The criterion must always be the Word of God. If what is done does not measure up by the Word, it should be rejected out of hand.

THE WORD OF GOD

As I dictate these words, the leaders of popular so-called faith ministries speak constantly of the anointing of the Holy Spirit, but sadly, without much true knowledge of what it really is.

How do I know that?

Many place money before anything else, and I speak of attempting to tell the people how to use the Word of God in order to get rich. While there is some truth in what is said, such only makes their lie even greater. Actually, a lie without some truth is hardly acceptable, even as this warning by Christ portrays.

There is almost no biblical fruit to their ministry, such as souls being saved, lives being changed, bondages being broken, sick bodies truly being healed (not mere claims), or believers being baptized with the Holy Spirit. So, it is deception, pure and simple.

Regrettably, that will not be the only example, with more and more deceivers filling the land and claiming great things in the name of Jesus, and claiming great anointing when, in reality, it is false.

Jesus warned against this by speaking of false prophets. He said, *"Wherefore by their fruits you shall know them"* (Mat. 7:15-20).

THE TIME OF FULFILLMENT

The phrase, *"And the time draws near,"* refers to the coming rapture of the church, immediately followed by the great tribulation, which will end with the second coming of the Lord (Rev., Chpt. 19). In other words, the Lord is telling us that the closer the church gets to this particular time, the more prolific will be the deceivers.

"Go ye not therefore (Do not go) *after them,"* is blunt and leaves no room for further interpretation.

However, unless the individual knows the Word of God, which can only come about by diligence and attention given to it, deception will be easy.

Even those who know the Word, or think they do, can be deceived, as well, if they have an improper relationship with Christ, meaning that their faith is placed in something other than Christ and the Cross.

(9) "BUT WHEN YOU SHALL HEAR OF WARS AND COMMOTIONS, BE NOT TERRIFIED: FOR THESE THINGS MUST FIRST COME TO PASS; BUT THE END IS NOT BY AND BY."

The overview is:

1. The phrase, *"But when you shall hear of wars and commotions, be not terrified,"* means that this is the lot that Israel has brought upon herself, as well as the entirety of the world, by their rejection and refusal of Christ as Messiah. They subjected the world to continued rule by the Gentiles, called, *"the times of the Gentiles,"* and is addressed in the latter part of this chapter.

2. God intended for Israel to be the premier nation, thereby, guiding the Gentile world to the light of the gospel, but Israel forfeited that position because of sin. Consequently, the scepter of power was passed to the Gentiles, which took place about 600 years before the first advent of Christ, and, as stated, continues unto this hour due to Israel's rejection of Christ.

NOTES

3. *"For these things must first come to pass,"* in effect, have characterized the world from then until now.

4. The phrase, *"But the end is not by and by,"* means that the end is not immediate.

5. In a veiled way, Jesus is referring to the soon coming destruction of Jerusalem, but telling the disciples and all others that this does not signify the end but really only the beginning.

(10) "THEN SAID HE UNTO THEM, NATION SHALL RISE AGAINST NATION, AND KINGDOM AGAINST KINGDOM."

The synopsis is:

1. The phrase, *"Then said He unto them,"* refers to the time immediately preceding the coming great tribulation, including that period.

2. This refers to the wars that will form the 10 kingdoms of Daniel 7:23-24 and Revelation 17:12, and to the wars between the 10 kingdoms under the Antichrist, and the many nations north and east of the old Roman Empire (Dan. 11:40-45).

3. *"Nation shall rise against nation, and kingdom against kingdom,"* proclaims the very opposite of that taught by the majority of the modern church.

4. Many teach that these things are all past, with things in the world getting better and better until finally, Christianity will cover the entirety of the globe, with everything brought into unity. Then Christ will come back to begin the millennium.

5. Jesus says the very opposite!

(11) "AND GREAT EARTHQUAKES SHALL BE IN DIVERS PLACES, AND FAMINES, AND PESTILENCES; AND FEARFUL SIGHTS AND GREAT SIGNS SHALL THERE BE FROM HEAVEN."

The pattern is:

1. The phrase, *"And great earthquakes shall be in divers places,"* speaks of such happening all over the world, and greatly increasing in these last days.

2. *"And famines, and pestilences,"* speaks of intensification greater, far greater, than normal. Actually, great famines will be brought about when the Antichrist makes his bid for world dominion, as outlined in Revelation 6:2-6.

3. *"And fearful sights and great signs*

shall there be from heaven," has to do with the seal, trumpet, and vial judgments (Rev. Chpts., 6-18).

4. Even though Verses 8 through 11 can allude in some small way to the time of the church, its greatest interpretation belongs to the coming great tribulation.

(12) "BUT BEFORE ALL THESE, THEY SHALL LAY THEIR HANDS ON YOU, AND PERSECUTE YOU, DELIVERING YOU UP TO THE SYNAGOGUES, AND INTO PRISONS, BEING BROUGHT BEFORE KINGS AND RULERS FOR MY NAME'S SAKE."

The exposition is:

1. The phrase, *"But before all these,"* refers to Verses 8 through 11, and now speaks of the soon destruction of Jerusalem in A.D. 70, and that which follows.

2. *"They shall lay their hands on you,"* concerns the early church, even up to the present. It speaks of persecution.

3. *"And persecute you, delivering you up to the synagogues,"* has reference to the apostles, who were subject to these persecutions in the times of the early church.

4. *"And into prisons, being brought before kings and rulers for My name's sake,"* is found replete in the book of Acts and has often been the case from then until now.

5. The true way of Christ has always been tolerated, if at all, while the religions of the world are accepted eagerly.

(13) "AND IT SHALL TURN TO YOU FOR A TESTIMONY."

The exposition is:

1. This means that believers must not allow their testimony to be hindered by persecution, but rather allow it to be strengthened.

2. As Jesus spoke these words, He was the testimony, but when He left, which He soon would, believers were to be the testimony.

3. That testimony now must be *"Jesus Christ, and Him crucified"* (I Cor. 1:23; 2:2).

(14) "SETTLE IT THEREFORE IN YOUR HEARTS, NOT TO MEDITATE BEFORE WHAT YOU SHALL ANSWER."

The synopsis is:

1. The phrase, *"Settle it therefore in your hearts,"* simply means to have faith in God that He would supply that which was necessary when the time came.

NOTES

2. *"Not to meditate before what you shall answer,"* means not to be in fear, anxiety, and agitation.

3. In other words, the Lord is saying that perilous times are going to come before His second advent.

(15) "FOR I WILL GIVE YOU A MOUTH AND WISDOM, WHICH ALL YOUR ADVERSARIES SHALL NOT BE ABLE TO GAINSAY NOR RESIST."

The exegesis is:

1. The phrase, *"For I will give you a mouth and wisdom,"* simply speaks of the unction of the Holy Spirit in the heart and life of the believer giving the help that is needed.

2. *"Which all your adversaries shall not be able to gainsay nor resist,"* does not mean that the believer will be accepted, but rather that the testimony cannot be refuted. An example is in the way Jesus handled the Pharisees, scribes, and Sadducees.

3. The book of Acts is replete with this, as well as the thousands, if not millions of times, it has happened up to now all over the world, and by believers of every nationality.

(16) "AND YOU SHALL BE BETRAYED BOTH BY PARENTS, AND BRETHREN, AND KINSFOLKS, AND FRIENDS; AND SOME OF YOU SHALL THEY CAUSE TO BE PUT TO DEATH."

This passage tells us that many believers will not be delivered, but rather will pay with their lives, i.e., *be put to death.* Fox's Book of Martyrs is just one account of the hundreds of thousands who have died down through the ages for the cause of Christ.

(17) "AND YOU SHALL BE HATED OF ALL MEN FOR MY NAME'S SAKE."

FOR MY NAME'S SAKE

This one verse is ample proof of the validity of Christianity. Anything that can survive such opposition and even grow until it is now the largest in the world proves the integrity of its founder, the Lord Jesus Christ, and the sincerity of its converts. The fact of its success in the face of such difficulties is proof of its divine origin.

The opposition is *"for My name's sake."*

It is Jesus who stands at the intersection of all humanity, which includes nations, kingdoms, and empires. To most people, God is an abstract being and, therefore, not offensive. However, the person of Jesus is very offensive to the unregenerate heart simply because of the claims He has made.

In other words, He has said that if one is to deal with God, he will have to do so through Him, the Lord Jesus Christ (Jn. 10:9). Inasmuch as the Father has committed all judgment unto the Son (Jn. 5:22), because He is the one who paid the price for man's redemption at Calvary's Cross, men will either trust Him as Saviour or face Him as judge. One way or the other, the entirety of mankind will face Jesus Christ.

THE LORD JESUS CHRIST

The Jews hate Christ because they branded Him as an impostor, and did so despite a mountain of evidence to the contrary. As well, most of the Gentile world follows suit because His righteousness given to those who believe in Him is an affront to the unrighteousness of evil hearts.

Even though Islam is the most violent religion in the world, having spilled rivers of blood, still, it draws little opposition in comparison to Bible Christianity, even though true Christianity has no violence.

Why?

The spirit of the world, which is of Satan, and the spirit of Islam, as well as all other religions, are identical, with all coming from the same source. Consequently, there is little animosity, if any, aroused against these religions, even though they are terribly detrimental to mankind.

Even at the present, much of America little knows or understands the terrible danger of Islam, at least if they ever gained an upper hand. Despite the terrorist activities, which have resulted in the loss of thousands of American lives, there is still little animosity in the United States against this vile work of Satan. As we have said, the reason is that the spirit of most in America and Islam, and the world for that matter, is basically all the same.

For instance, the policy of the United States is that most Muslims are wonderful peace-loving people, with only a few who are radicals causing all the problems, etc.

NOTES

Nothing could be further from the truth.

While all Muslims aren't murderers, the truth is, all Muslims are in sympathy with the murderers. We must understand that. In other words, all Muslims, at least if they are true to the Koran (and most are) hate America and Israel. The hatred for Israel goes all the way back to Abraham, a time frame of some 4,000 years. The hatred for the United States is because of our support of Israel. They are called the little Satan while we are called the big Satan. What one has to understand is the following:

The Muslims do not lack the will; they lack only the way. In other words, if they had the upper hand, they would turn this nation in a few hours' time into a river of blood. Every person in it would be forced to become a Muslim, or else, be killed or become a slave. That is Islam. However, precious few Americans seem to understand that.

DECEPTION

Sometime back over television, I heard a comedian, who is an open avowed lesbian, state how that she hated Christianity and how that Islam was so much better than Christianity.

What the foolish woman did not seem to know is that if she lived in a Muslim country, due to the fact that she is a lesbian, they would cut her head off. No, I am not exaggerating. That is exactly what they would do—cut her head off. Evidently, she has not taken the time or the trouble to look a little bit into Islam to see what it actually is. But, of course, most in America, or the world for that matter, haven't done their homework as it regards this subject.

There is nothing in the world more evil than the religion of Islam. There is a spirit of murder that's in this particular religion, and if they cannot kill the infidel, and incidentally, an infidel is anyone who is not a Muslim, they will in turn kill each other. It's the spirit of murder.

For instance, when the uprising began in Egypt and then spread to Libya, etc., it was heralded as the *"Arab spring."* In other words, our governmental officials were so foolish as to believe that you could pair democracy with Islam. The two aren't on the same planet.

I told Frances when it began that the dictators running these countries, no doubt, were corrupt. However, if the uprising succeeded, the people of Egypt and other Muslim countries would not come out the better, but rather the worse. That's exactly what has happened. There is no such thing as an Arab spring, just as there has never been a golden age of Islam. America is flirting with disaster by opening our borders to these people and refusing to understand that they have but one thing in mind, and that is to destroy our way of life. They do not lack the will, as stated, only the way, and it looks as though we here in America are giving them the way.

(18) "BUT THERE SHALL NOT AN HAIR OF YOUR HEAD PERISH."

The exegesis is:

1. How can Jesus say this when He has just spoken of being *"put to death"* (Vs. 16).

2. He was speaking in general regarding Verses 12 through 17, but now He directs His remarks toward the coming destruction of Jerusalem in A.D. 70.

In the carnage that developed, which saw over 1 million Jews killed, not a single Christian lost his or her life because they read these very verses and did exactly what Jesus said to do.

(19) "IN YOUR PATIENCE POSSESS YE YOUR SOULS."

PATIENCE

The idea is that despite the trouble, problems, and even tragedies that seem to happen all around the believer, he is to confidently look to the Lord for strength, leading, guidance, and help. If the situation does not seem to improve, he is to be patient, knowing that God has all things under control, and that everything He does is for the benefit of the believer and not his hurt.

WHAT IS PATIENCE?

Patience, it is said, is the capacity for self-control despite circumstances that might arouse the passions or cause agitation.

Paul said that love is patient (I Cor. 13:4). Of course, it would have to be patient in order to be love.

In personal relationships, patience is forbearance. This is not so much a trait as a

way of life. We keep on loving or forgiving despite provocation, as illustrated in Jesus' appointed stories in Matthew, Chapter 18. Patience also has to do with our reaction to the troubles we experience in life.

PATIENCE IS CONTINUING TO BELIEVE

It means to believe when the answer does not come immediately.

Actually, this is what Jesus is talking about. Even though believers are constituted as *"salt"* and *"light,"* and such presence definitely has a positive effect on all situations at hand, still, oftentimes, great problems and troubles come anyway, just as they did in Jerusalem of the very time Jesus is speaking.

When this happens, as it sometimes does, the believer is to be patient, knowing that God is causing or allowing something to be brought about, even though seemingly hurtful at the present, that will ultimately bring forth good. This is a matter of faith, which also demands patience.

THE PATIENCE OF JOB?

The Holy Spirit through James caused this apostle to write, *"You have heard of the patience of Job"* (James 5:11).

Even though Job little understood any of the things happening to him, his patience was such that even the Holy Spirit makes mention of this attribute, and speaks of Job allowing the Lord to work His perfect work within his life. Without patience, it could not have been done. That's the reason Paul said, *"But we glory in tribulations also: knowing that tribulation works patience"* (Rom. 5:3).

(20) "AND WHEN YOU SHALL SEE JERUSALEM COMPASSED WITH ARMIES, THEN KNOW THAT THE DESOLATION THEREOF IS NEAR."

The pattern is:

1. The phrase, *"And when you shall see Jerusalem compassed with armies,"* spoke of the invasion by Titus in A.D. 70. We know that Jesus is not speaking of the Antichrist, at least here, because of what He said in Verse 24.

2. While He did use similar terminology (Mat. 24:16-20) concerning the yet to come invasion of Jerusalem by the Antichrist, still, they are two separate events altogether,

separated by at least 2,000 years or more.

3. As we have stated, the Holy Spirit had Matthew report the far-off judgment, while He had Luke report the judgment soon to come, even though all was from the same address given by Christ on the Mount of Olives.

4. In this manner, the believers of the early church, which numbered many thousands, would not get them confused, and according to the instructions recorded by Luke, would be spared this horror. Actually, as stated, not a single believer was killed in the carnage of Jerusalem by Titus, which saw over 1 million Jews slaughtered. They heeded the words of Christ as given here and so left the city according to these instructions.

5. The phrase, *"Then know that the desolation thereof is near,"* speaks of the moment that Titus would begin to surround the city, which would be the signal that they were to leave, which they did!

(21) "THEN LET THEM WHICH ARE IN JUDAEA FLEE TO THE MOUNTAINS; AND LET THEM WHICH ARE IN THE MIDST OF IT DEPART OUT; AND LET NOT THEM WHO ARE IN THE COUNTRIES ENTER THEREINTO."

The form is:

1. The phrase, *"Then let them which are in Judaea flee to the mountains,"* spoke of all those who believed this word, which all Christians did. Consequently, they left not only Jerusalem, but the entirety of Judaea as well.

2. *"And let them which are in the midst of it depart out,"* means that no part of Judaea would be safe from the Roman armies.

3. *"And let not them who are in the countries enter thereinto,"* speaks of the Christians who lived in surrounding countries, but they were not to come to Judaea or Jerusalem at that time. As stated, these words were heeded in totality by the many thousands of the early church, with not one single Christian losing his or her life in this carnage. What a testimony to the overriding action of the hand of God in the protection of His people.

(22) "FOR THESE BE THE DAYS OF VENGEANCE, THAT ALL THINGS WHICH ARE WRITTEN MAY BE FULFILLED."

DAYS OF VENGEANCE

The phrase, *"For these be the days of vengeance,"* refers, as is obvious, to judgment. Mercy and peace were offered to Israel, but to no avail (Lk. 19:41-44).

If they had accepted that visitation, which would have meant to accept Christ, these horrible days of vengeance would never have come (Mat. 23:37-39; Lk. 13:33-35).

Paul would later write as the Holy Spirit spoke through him, *"Vengeance is Mine; I will repay, saith the Lord"* (Rom. 12:19). So, God exacts vengeance on those who spurn His call, especially when they do violence to the messenger, with Jesus being the greatest messenger of all, whom they crucified.

THE FULFILLED WORD

Every war that comes to a nation is, in effect, vengeance from the Lord. This means even the nation that is in the right, such as America and certain others in World War II. The terrible witness of Nazi Germany was obvious to all; however, America and other allied nations were not without sin as well! Consequently, at least some judgment came to America, along with others, which resulted in much sorrow and heartache.

That is the reason that the Lord said through Solomon, *"Rejoice not when your enemy falls, and let not your heart be glad when he stumbles:*

"Lest the LORD see it, and it displease Him, and He turn away His wrath from him" (Prov. 24:17-18).

"That all things which are written may be fulfilled," pertains only to those things written concerning the destruction of Jerusalem, such as Hosea 9:7. It also speaks of that which Jesus prophesied and predicted, such as Matthew, Chapter 24, and Luke, Chapter 21, as well as Mark, Chapter 13, which were written not long after this was predicted.

However, even though this of which Jesus speaks only pertains to Jerusalem, etc., still, everything written in the Word of God concerning prophecy will ultimately be fulfilled according to its appointed time exactly as this was fulfilled.

(23) "BUT WOE UNTO THEM WHO

ARE WITH CHILD, AND TO THEM WHO GIVE SUCK, IN THOSE DAYS! FOR THERE SHALL BE GREAT DISTRESS IN THE LAND, AND WRATH UPON THIS PEOPLE."

WOE

The phrase, *"But woe unto them who are with child, and to them who give suck, in those days!"* speaks of the haste required at that time.

As well, the *"woe"* uttered here by Christ is one of love and pity for people who sealed their own doom. If one is to notice, very similar instructions are given concerning the coming battle of Armageddon when the Antichrist will attempt to destroy Jerusalem (Mat. 24:15-22). At that time, also, Jerusalem will be surrounded by the armies of the Antichrist, and half of the city will be taken (Zech. 14:1-5). So, similar events as to the punishment of women and children will happen at both times. In fact, concerning the battle of Armageddon, Zechariah, Chapter 14, states that the women will be ravished exactly as they were by the armies of Titus.

The phrase, *"For there shall be great distress in the land, and wrath upon this people,"* came to pass exactly as stated.

THE JUDGMENT OF GOD

It is said that the Jews were crucified in such numbers before the walls during the siege that the Romans wanted more room for crosses. Multitudes in the cities died of famine until the valleys outside were filled with rotting corpses.

Titus, himself, groaned and threw up his hands in horror and called God to witness that he was not responsible for this carnage.

No fewer than 600,000, who were thrown out of the gates, were counted by the Romans. Altogether, 1.1 million Jews died; 97,000 were sold as slaves for trifling prices; 40,000 were freed because no one bought them; and 347,490 more, plus multitudes not counted, perished in many other ways. Truly, there was *"great distress!"*

Once again allow us to state that it was not God who did this thing, but that He withdrew His hand of protection, which left Israel defenseless.

NOTES

He did this because that's what they said they wanted (Jn. 19:15).

(24) "AND THEY SHALL FALL BY THE EDGE OF THE SWORD, AND SHALL BE LED AWAY CAPTIVE INTO ALL NATIONS: AND JERUSALEM SHALL BE TRODDEN DOWN OF THE GENTILES, UNTIL THE TIMES OF THE GENTILES BE FULFILLED."

THE SWORD

The phrase, *"And they shall fall by the edge of the sword,"* is, as we have stated, exactly what happened, and on a horrifying scale.

Renan said of this awful slaughter, "That it would seem as the whole Jewish people had determined upon a rendezvous for extermination."

Because of the Jews' resistance and attitude, Titus, the son of Emperor Vespasian, commanded the Roman armies to raze the city of Jerusalem so completely as to look like a spot that had never been inhabited.

CAPTIVE INTO ALL NATIONS

The phrase, *"And shall be led away captive into all nations,"* is exactly what happened. Even though the Jews had pretty much stuck together, forming Jewish ghettos in whatever city they were in, still, sooner or later, they have suffered terrible persecution.

Since the crucifixion of Christ, the Jews have suffered a twofold hatred:

1. The world has blamed them, calling them "Christ killers," which has given vent to evil hearts and using this as an excuse. So, such animosity rages unto this hour, although wrong, and has exacerbated an already acute problem.

2. Satan hates the Jewish people with a ferocious intensity that has inspired the terrible bloodletting, such as the Holocaust of World War II. Satan knows that many of the Bible prophecies yet to be fulfilled pertain to the Jews. He knows their salvation and restoration are predicted, which will, as well, occasion the second coming of the Lord, with Him ruling and reigning forever.

Consequently, he has tried more than once to exterminate these people, with his greatest attempt just ahead in the coming great tribulation; however, he will not be successful, but not for lack of trying.

JERUSALEM

The phrase, *"And Jerusalem shall be trodden down of the Gentiles,"* has actually proven the case since Jerusalem was destroyed by the Babylonians some 600 years before Christ.

They were followed by the Medes and the Persians, then the Greeks, and then Rome, which controlled Israel when Christ was born.

After that, the Saracen, Norsemen, and Turks, along with the Arabs, have fulfilled this prediction through the centuries. Even though some Jews have continued to live in Jerusalem all through the centuries, still, it has pretty much been controlled by Gentiles until 1948 when they once again, according to Bible prophecy, became a nation. Actually, this was the reason for the Holocaust of World War II, with Satan using Hitler in an attempt to exterminate them as a people so that the prophecies could not be fulfilled concerning their regathering. However, Satan did not succeed, as he will not succeed in the coming great tribulation.

The following Scriptures proclaim Israel's regathering, which began in 1948: "... *Again the second time to recover the remnant of His people, which shall be left ... And He shall set up an ensign for the nations, and shall assemble the outcasts of Israel, and gather together the dispersed of Judah from the four corners of the earth"* (Isa. 11:11-12).

The prediction here is that the Lord will gather Israel again a second time. This indicates a previous gathering.

When?

THE FIRST AND SECOND GATHERING

All members of the 13 tribes who wanted to return to their own land after the Babylonian captivity gathered together. This was about 500 years before the birth of Christ.

This was the first gathering of Israel from among the nations as pictured in Ezra, Nehemiah, Haggai, Zechariah, and Malachi. They kept coming back in great numbers until they were a great nation again in the days of Christ, though ruled by Rome.

Jesus then predicted their defeat by the Romans, and the complete destruction of their city and temple again as in the days of Nebuchadnezzar over 600 years before, as given in Luke 21:24 and elsewhere. Through Luke, He predicted the captivity of Israel (the Jews) among all nations again (Lk. 21:20-24), declaring their house would be left desolate until the latter days (Mat. 2:37-39).

The statement, *"Again the second time,"* could not have been fulfilled until the first gathering from Babylon and other nations had been accomplished and their second dispersion had come to pass, which was in A.D. 70 when the Romans took them captive among all nations, fulfilling Luke 21:20-24.

God never regathered them since this dispersion until 1948, when they once again became a nation after some 1,900 years of being scattered all over the world. This regathering, which began in 1948, will continue until the beginning of the coming kingdom age. This will immediately follow the second coming and will gather most, if not all Jews, from around the world and bring them to Israel. There they will serve as the leading nation in the world under Christ, actually, the priestly nation.

THE WORD OF GOD

The following are just a few of the Scriptures proclaiming this grand event:

• The Lord will yet choose Israel and Jacob, and will set them in their own land (not in a new land never promised) (Isa. 14:1).

• The people (Gentiles) shall bring them to their own place, and the house of Israel shall possess their oppressors (Isa. 14:2).

• *"You shall be gathered one by one, O you children of Israel ... And shall worship the* Lord *in the Holy Mount at Jerusalem"* (Isa. 27:12-13).

• *"I will bring your seed* (Israel–Jacob) *from the east,"* west, north, and south, *"from the ends of the earth; Even everyone who is called by My name"* (Isa. 43:5-7).

• *"At that time they shall call Jerusalem the throne of the* Lord *... In those days the house of Judah shall walk with the house of Israel, and they* (both houses of Israel) *shall* come together out of the land of the north to the land that I have given for an inheritance unto your fathers" (Jer. 3:17-18).

• The day is come that the Lord lives, who brought the children of Israel from all lands where He had given them: *"and I will bring them again into their own land that I gave unto their fathers"* (Jer. 16:14-16; 23:5-8).

• *"I will gather the remnant of My flock out of all countries whither* (where) *I have driven them, and will bring them again to their folds ... They shall fear no more"* (Jer. 23:3-4).

PROMISES MADE

• *"I will bring again the captivity of My people Israel and Judah ... I will cause them to return to the land that I gave to their fathers, and they shall possess it ... These are the words that the LORD spoke concerning Israel and concerning Judah ... In the latter days you shall consider it ... At the same time, says the LORD, will I be the God of all the families of Israel, and they shall be My people ... I will ... Gather them from the coasts of the earth ... He who scatters Israel will gather him* (them)." They shall come to Zion and *"I will make a new covenant with the house of Israel, and with the house of Judah ... They shall be My people"* (Jer. 30:3-31:4; 32:37-44).

• *"I will even gather you ... Out of the* (all) *countries where you have been scattered, and I will give you the land of Israel ... I will give them one* (a new) *heart and I will put a new spirit within you ... And they shall be My people, and I will be their God"* (Ezek. 11:17-20; 16:60-63).

• *"When I shall have gathered the house of Israel from the people among whom they are scattered, and shall be sanctified in them in the sight of the heathen, then shall they dwell in their* (own) *land that I have given to* (My servant) *Jacob ... They shall dwell safely ... With confidence"* (Ezek. 28:25-26).

• *"The children of Israel shall abide many days without a king ... Prince ... Sacrifice ... Image ... Ephod, and without Teraphim. Afterward shall the children of Israel return* (to their land), *and seek the LORD ... And David their king; and shall fear the LORD and His goodness in the latter days"* (Hos. 3:4-5).

THE TABERNACLE OF DAVID

• *"I will sift the house of Israel among all nations, like as corn is sifted in a sieve ... In that day will I raise up the tabernacle of David that is fallen ... I will raise up his ruins, and I will build it as in the days of old ... And I will bring again the captivity of My people of Israel, and they shall build the waste cities, and inhabit them ... And I will plant them upon* (in) *their* (own) *land, and they shall no more be pulled up out of their land which I have given them"* (Amos 9:9-15).

The apostle James, the half-brother of Jesus Christ, said that this prophecy of Amos would be fulfilled after the church age and said that all the prophets agreed with this (Acts 15:13-18).

• *"He shall send His angels with a great sound of a trumpet, and they shall gather together His elect from the four winds, from one end of heaven to the other"* (Mat. 24:31).

This tells us that angels will help regather Israel after the second coming.

As should be obvious, these Scriptures concerning the regathering of Israel will not be completely fulfilled until after the second coming; however, Israel becoming a nation in 1948 was the beginning of this fulfillment.

The regathering has steadily continued since 1948, with not the least being the immigration of nearly 1 million Jews from the former Soviet Union upon the fall of that empire.

However, the completion of this gathering, which began in 1948, will not take place until the Jews accept Christ as their Saviour, which they will immediately do after the second coming. Then will be the conclusion of that gathering, which began in 1948, and will affect, as stated, every Jew in the world, with even angels helping in this final gathering.

THE TIMES OF THE GENTILES

The phrase, *"Until the times of the Gentiles be fulfilled,"* proclaims by Jesus an extremely important intersection in the history of mankind.

God intended for Israel to be the premier nation in the world, in fact, leading the world to the Lord. As the first God-called king of

Israel, David was given this task. (Saul was not God-called.) David's sons were to rule in succession down through the centuries, in righteousness and holiness we might add, until the Son of David, the Lord Jesus Christ, would come. He would usher in the kingdom of God, consequently, setting right that which Satan had done in the garden of Eden. That's what the disciples were talking about after the resurrection of Jesus when they asked Him, *"Lord, will You at this time restore again the kingdom to Israel?"*

"And He said unto them, It is not for you to know the times or the seasons, which the Father has put in His own power" (Acts 1:6-7).

However, the sons of David proved unfaithful, with that house being thrown down because of sin. When this happened, the scepter of world power was taken from the faltering hands of the kings of Judah and given to the Gentiles, the first being Nebuchadnezzar, beginning the times of the Gentiles, which continues even up to this present time.

When Jesus came, as we have stated elsewhere in these volumes, He offered Israel the kingdom of God rather than the kingdom of man, which they then had through the Romans (Mat. 4:17), but they rejected it, saying, *"We have no king but Caesar"* (Jn. 19:15).

Consequently, the times of the Gentiles continued and, as stated, has done so unto the present hour. In fact, it will continue until the second coming.

Today, Israel occupies a great portion of the land, but still, the West Bank, the Gaza Strip, and even East Jerusalem are occupied by the Gentiles (Arabs), as well as the temple mount.

THE LAST OF THE LAST DAYS

Very soon the rapture of the church will take place (I Thess. 4:16-17), after which the Antichrist will be revealed (II Thess. 2:6-8).

By his machinations, or somehow, Israel will gain control of the temple mount, or at least some part of it, thereby, rebuilding their temple. They will also sign a seven-year agreement with the Antichrist, who they will actually think is their Messiah.

However, he will break his seven-year

NOTES

covenant with them, take over Jerusalem and the future Jewish temple as his religious capital building, and begin beast worship (Dan. 9:27; 11:4-45; 12:7; Mat. 24:15-21; II Thess. 2:1-12; Rev., Chpt. 13; 14:9-11; 15:2-4; 20:4-6).

Jerusalem will then be in Gentile hands, or at least partly so, for 42 months, finally being liberated at the second coming of Christ (Zech., Chpt. 14; II Thess. 2:8-12; Rev. 11:1-3; 12:6, 14; 13:5; 19:11-21). The times of the Gentiles will then end, ushering in the kingdom age, with Jesus ruling personally from Jerusalem, and Israel being fully restored (Ezek., Chpts. 40-48).

The times of the Gentiles, which began about 600 years before Christ and continues unto this hour, were ushered in for two reasons:

1. Israel's sin caused her to forfeit her position, with power being given to the Babylonians.

2. Given a second opportunity, Israel failed again, even crucifying their Messiah, with the risen Lord turning to the Gentiles, in a sense, it being their time, i.e., times of the Gentiles, i.e., the church age, which, incidentally, is about over.

(25) "AND THERE SHALL BE SIGNS IN THE SUN, AND IN THE MOON, AND IN THE STARS; AND UPON THE EARTH DISTRESS OF NATIONS, WITH PERPLEXITY; THE SEA AND THE WAVES ROARING."

SIGNS

The phrase, *"And there shall be signs in the sun, and in the moon, and in the stars,"* now proclaims the Lord returning to His former subject of signs concerning His second coming, which was first broached in Verses 8 through 11.

The signs given, which will include the greatest sign of all—the coming of the Lord—make it clear and plain that these passages have not yet been fulfilled, as claimed by some.

These signs, concerning the planetary bodies, will have their fulfillment in the coming great tribulation, as recorded in Revelation, Chapters 6 through 19.

The phrase, *"And upon the earth distress*

of nations," proclaims a distress far greater than any previous times. This pertains to the coming great tribulation when the Antichrist will seek to take over the world. He would succeed were it not for the coming of the Lord (Rev., Chpt. 19).

PERPLEXITY

The words *"With perplexity,"* refer to "problems without a solution."

So, these predictions tell us that the demise of the Soviet Union, leaving America as the only superpower, the position of which we are fastly losing, will not usher in the new age of understanding and prosperity as believed by some. Actually, at this very moment, the seeds are already being sown for coming world trouble and the advent of the Antichrist. However, that which will greatly exacerbate the trouble of the nations will be the rapture of the church, which means that all salt and light are removed.

At this time America thinks that her universities, Congress, and the Supreme Court, along with her high gross national product, are the secret of her success. She, as well as every other nation of the world, will find out then that it was really the blood-bought church that was responsible for the freedoms and prosperity, but it will be too late.

THE TRUE CHURCH

Without this restraining factor of the church (the true church), evil will accelerate alarmingly. Paul addressed this when he said, *"For the mystery of iniquity does already work: only he* (the church) *who now lets* (hinders) *will let* (continue to hinder), *until he* (the church) *be taken out of the way* (raptured).

"And then shall that wicked (the Antichrist) *be revealed, whom* (the Antichrist) *the Lord shall consume with the spirit of His mouth, and shall destroy with the brightness of His coming"* (II Thess. 2:7-8).

The phrase, *"The sea and the waves roaring,"* does not pertain to bodies of water, but rather to nations roaring in discontent, anger, rebellion, and war (Rev. 17:15).

So, attempting to understand these predictions concerning the nations of the world in light of the present situation is wrong. It

is only when the true church is taken out, which will leave precious little restraint against iniquity, that these predictions will be fulfilled.

(26) "MEN'S HEARTS FAILING THEM FOR FEAR, AND FOR LOOKING AFTER THOSE THINGS WHICH ARE COMING ON THE EARTH: FOR THE POWERS OF HEAVEN SHALL BE SHAKEN."

FAILING THEM FOR FEAR

The phrase, *"Men's hearts failing them for fear,"* has nothing to do with heart disease, but rather men losing heart, i.e., having no more courage to continue.

"And for looking after those things which are coming on the earth," gives the reason for men losing heart. Revelation, Chapters 6 through 19, give us in graphic detail an account of that which will happen. There is a possibility that over half of the population of the world, totaling now (2013) approximately 7.5 billion people, could die during the seven-year tribulation period as a result of war and plagues. The words, as stated here by Jesus, do not present a very pretty picture.

POWERS

The phrase, *"For the powers of heaven shall be shaken,"* proclaims a judgment of God that will fall upon unbelieving Israel and the Gentile nations, which will have no precedent in all past history and no counterpart in all succeeding history.

The functional disturbances in the sun, moon, and stars occur during the great tribulation period and are literal. These are spoken in the sixth seal judgment (Rev. 6:12-14).

As well, these *"powers"* refer to the satanic hosts that now rule the air above the earth (Eph. 2:1-3; 6:12).

As stated, they are now above us but will not be at the coming of Christ, for they will be cast down to earth three and a half years before then (Rev. 12:7-12).

Isaiah spoke of them being defeated at the end of this age (Isa. 24:21-22; 34:4). Both Isaiah and Jesus made predictions of them while they were powers in the heavenlies.

At Christ's coming, they not only will be shaken and completely defeated, but they will be cast into prison for 1,000 years (Isa. 24:21-22; Rev. 20:1-10).

The planets and the hosts of heaven are distinguished in II Kings 23:4-5. The hosts of heaven are intelligent beings and have been worshipped and served by men in past ages (II Ki. 17:16; 21:3, 5; II Chron. 33:3-5; Jer. 8:2; 19:13; Zeph. 1:5; Acts 7:42).

(27) "AND THEN SHALL THEY SEE THE SON OF MAN COMING IN A CLOUD WITH POWER AND GREAT GLORY."

THE SECOND COMING

The two words, *"And then,"* refer to the conclusion of the great tribulation when these terrible things will have happened.

The phrase, *"Shall they see the Son of Man coming,"* could very well refer to television transmission all over the world. At the battle of Armageddon, in which Jesus will come back (Ezek., Chpts. 38-39; Rev., Chpt. 19), the Antichrist, bearing down on Jerusalem, with half of the city falling, will, no doubt, have every television network in the world represented. He will desire that the world see his great victory over Israel and will, without a doubt, be transmitting every happening on the battlefield to most of the world.

To be sure, at least if the disturbances in the heavens caused by the planetary bodies do not disturb television transmission, every camera will, without a doubt, turn toward the heavens as Jesus comes back with every saint who has ever lived. It will be in splendor and glory such as the world has never seen or known. In this context, the world will *"see the Son of Man."*

The phrase, *"Coming in a cloud,"* does not speak of the clouds of the heavens that can be easily observed, but rather clouds of saints, which will include every believer who has ever lived, even from the first page of human history (Acts 1:9).

POWER AND GREAT GLORY

The phrase, *"With power and great glory,"* as stated, refers to all the heavenly bodies that the Lord created accompanying His return with a display of such magnitude that there is no way it could be described with mere words. The very creation, which has groaned for deliverance since the fall in the

garden of Eden (Rom. 8:19-23), will at long last be delivered.

As stated, every saint of God who has ever lived, all the way from Abel to the moment of His coming, will be with Him, which will, within itself, form a splendor indescribable. In conjunction with this, an angelic host will accompany the Lord and all the saints.

When He came the first time, it was with great humiliation, with Him actually being raised as a peasant. As He began His ministry, it was with great opposition, even from His own family.

During this humiliation, He was ill-treated, despised, and rejected of men. At His crucifixion, He was spit upon, beaten, and had His beard pulled from His face, with a crown of thorns placed upon His brow. He died in a horrible manner, forsaken by all.

However, when He comes back the second time, it will not be to undergo the indignities that He suffered the first time, but rather the very opposite. His coming will be of such splendor and glory that it will defy description. No superlatives or adjectives will be enough to fully explain this coming time.

This we do know: It will be totally unlike anything that has ever happened in human history. By the grace of God and because of His love, and through nothing I have done that would merit such, I will be with Him, along with every other saint of God who has ever lived. I can only shout *"Hallelujah!"*

(28) "AND WHEN THESE THINGS BEGIN TO COME TO PASS, THEN LOOK UP, AND LIFT UP YOUR HEADS; FOR YOUR REDEMPTION DRAWS NIGH."

BEGINNING TO COME TO PASS

The phrase, *"And when these things begin to come to pass,"* refers to the signs of Verses 8 through 11, as well as Verses 25 and 26.

Paul would somewhat address himself to this, respecting the church of the Thessalonians (II Thess. 1:1).

Some thought that Jesus was going to come immediately, but Paul told them that certain things must happen first before the day of Christ would be at hand (II Thess. 2:2).

In Verse 3 of Chapter 2, he warned them of deception exactly as Jesus had done (Lk. 21:8).

He then told them that the rapture of the church must take place before the man of sin could be revealed (II Thess. 2:7-8). Actually, all of these things will take place during the coming great tribulation. But yet, many preliminary things are now taking place, which will lead up to these momentous events.

For instance, Israel becoming a nation in 1948 is one of these preliminary events. As well, the terrible deception that is going to grip this world when the Antichrist makes his debut is already in the church, and increasing in intensity almost on a daily basis. So, the seedbed of all of this is taking place presently and will only increase in intensity the closer we get to that particular time.

LOOK UP

The phrase, *"Then look up, and lift up your heads,"* is actually addressed to Israel immediately preceding the second coming. It really does not pertain to the church because the church has been raptured by this time.

Actually, the whole of Matthew, Chapter 24; Mark, Chapter 13; and Luke, Chapter 21, is addressed to Israel, with the church mentioned only in passing.

How many in Israel will read these words at that particular time is not known. However, due to the 144,000 accepting Christ and actually being raptured during the great tribulation (Rev. 7:1-8; 12:5), plus the ministry of the two witnesses (Rev. 11:3-12), the possibility definitely exists that many Jews will read these very words of Jesus.

This will be a terrible time for Israel, actually, the worst that has ever been. Satan will pull out all the stops in order to completely annihilate these people in order to foil the plan of God for the human family. As well, many false messiahs will make their appearance at this time simply because Israel will now realize, with the whole world turning against her, that the coming of the Messiah will be, and is, their only hope.

So, it certainly stands to reason that many in Israel at that particular time will peruse these very words. Exactly what inference they will draw from them is not known. We do know that after the second coming, most of Israel will not really know that the Messiah

NOTES

is actually Jesus, whom they crucified, until they ask, *"What are these wounds in Your hands? Then He shall answer, Those with which I was wounded in the house of My friends"* (Zech. 13:6).

REDEMPTION

In 1990 (I believe it was), a book was written by an academic in Israel concerning the Messiah. In the book he stated that the Messiah definitely was coming, and He probably would be Jesus Christ, the one they crucified nearly 2,000 years ago. The book was immediately taken off the market and banned, but this does show us that some of these people are investigating the birth, life, and ministry of Christ, plus His crucifixion and resurrection. Actually, it is impossible for any Jew, or anyone, to read Isaiah, Chapter 53, and fail to understand that it speaks of Jesus. However, despite that, the blindness that fills Israel continues unto this hour (Rom. 11:25).

The phrase, *"For your redemption draws nigh* (near)*,"* speaks not of the rapture of the church, as many have been led to believe, but the deliverance of Israel at the second coming when Christ comes with the raptured saints (Isa. 11:10-12; 66:7-8; Zech., Chpt. 14; Mat. 24:29-31; Rom. 11:25-29; Rev., Chpt. 19).

The word *redemption* has a twofold meaning in this passage:

1. It refers to Israel being saved from the Antichrist by the second coming,

2. And then it also refers to the literal redemption of Israel as they accept Christ as their Messiah, their Saviour, and their Lord, which will immediately follow the second coming (Zech. 12:10-14; 13:1).

(29) "AND HE SPOKE TO THEM A PARABLE; BEHOLD THE FIG TREE, AND ALL THE TREES."

The diagram is:

1. The phrase, *"And He spoke to them a parable,"* has to do with the second coming and the beginning of the kingdom age.

2. *"Behold the fig tree, and all the trees,"* should not present a mystery. Jesus is using a simple illustration that is meant to point to the second coming.

3. Actually, the fig tree represents Israel in the last days.

(30) "WHEN THEY NOW SHOOT FORTH, YOU SEE AND KNOW OF YOUR OWN SELVES THAT SUMMER IS NOW NIGH AT HAND."

The overview is:

1. The idea is that the interpreters of prophecies concerning the second coming are to allow trees to serve as an example.

2. *"When they now shoot forth,"* is, as everyone knows, the time of spring.

3. *"You see and know of your own selves that summer is now nigh* (near) *at hand,"* presents that which should be obvious to all. Summer follows spring.

(31) "SO LIKEWISE YE, WHEN YOU SEE THESE THINGS COME TO PASS, KNOW YE THAT THE KINGDOM OF GOD IS NEAR AT HAND."

WHEN YOU SEE THESE THINGS COME TO PASS

The phrase, *"So likewise ye* (you)*,"* is meant to say that when the budding of trees begins, it is easy to know that spring has arrived, which will be followed shortly by summer. Likewise, it should be just as easy to see the appointed signs concerning the second coming.

"When you see these things come to pass," once again speaks of the happenings of Verses 8 through 11, as well as 25 and 26. And yet, as we have already stated, preliminary happenings are already taking place pointing to these things, which should be a lesson for the church.

Sadly, much of the modern church world is teaching and believing the very opposite of that taught by Christ; it is called "dominion theology," or words to that affect.

In an abbreviated form, it teaches that there will be no rapture of the church. First of all, the rapture points to the great tribulation, which will take place immediately after the rapture, and which these teachers claim will not happen. Actually, they teach that the books of Daniel and Revelation have by and large been fulfilled and are now ancient history.

So, the rapture is repudiated because such is not needed, they say, due to the fact that conditions in the world are getting better and better, with the world being Christianized, which will shortly usher in the kingdom age.

As should be overly obvious to anyone who seriously studies the Word of God, such foolishness is not even hinted at in the Bible, but rather the very opposite.

THE RAPTURE OF THE CHURCH

The rapture of the church (I Thess. 4:16-17) will happen simply because of the great tribulation coming upon this world, as spoken by Jesus in Matthew 24:21. As well, Jesus would hardly come back, as Paul described it, *"In flaming fire taking vengeance on them who know not God,"* referring to the Antichrist and his armies, etc., if the world was gradually getting better, with the church ushering in the kingdom age (II Thess. 1:7-10).

The teaching that the church is going to usher in this glorious age is brought about by spiritual pride, which the greed gospel and the political message fit into very easily. It's a heady thing to teach and to believe that Christians are so high and mighty that we will change the world. Of course, it is covered by a veneer of twisted Scriptures, with a type of false glory given to Christ. However, once the cover is pulled off, it is man elevating man instead of elevating Christ.

THE RAPTURE COULD TAKE PLACE AT ANY TIME

The Bible teaches that the rapture of the church could take place at any moment (I Thess. 4:16-18; II Thess. 2:7; Rev. 4:1). It teaches that the Antichrist will make his debut immediately following the rapture, or at the most, several years until that time (II Thess. 2:7-12). At the conclusion of the great tribulation, the battle of Armageddon will be fought, with the Antichrist attempting to completely destroy Israel in order to stop prophecy from being fulfilled (Ezek., Chpts. 38-39). During the battle of Armageddon, Jesus will come back, which is referred to as the second coming, and will have all the saints of God with Him (Rev., Chpt. 19).

The phrase, *"Know ye (You know) that the kingdom of God is near at hand,"* means that all of these things will point to the second coming, which will usher in the kingdom of God.

To be sure, as Jesus said in Verse 25 and Revelation, Chapters 6 through 19, the entrance of the kingdom of God will not be peaceful, prosperous, or placid, as these false teachers proclaim, but rather the very opposite. It will come in with great destruction, with the Antichrist and five-sixths of his vast armies being killed (Ezek. 39:1-8).

THE KINGDOM OF GOD

The kingdom of God, which Jesus will head up personally, is that which Israel refused at the first advent (Mk. 1:15). Now Israel will accept it because they will accept Him.

It is impossible to divorce the King, who is Jesus Christ, from the kingdom. Even though multiple millions of born-again believers have had the kingdom of God in their hearts due to their acceptance of Jesus Christ, still, it is only the spiritual part that is now obtained, and not the physical and material. Then, the kingdom of God will come about in totality, affecting the entirety of the world with prosperity and freedom such as mankind has never known before, and in every capacity.

The curse that now covers the earth, causing inclement weather, earthquakes, drought, hurricanes, and famine will be lifted. Then, even the deserts shall blossom like the rose. The very nature of the animal kingdom will be changed as well! In effect, *"The earth shall be filled with the knowledge of the glory of the LORD, as the waters cover the sea"* (Hab. 2:14).

(32) "VERILY I SAY UNTO YOU, THIS GENERATION SHALL NOT PASS AWAY, TILL ALL BE FULFILLED."

The form is:

1. This verse is simple in its meaning.

2. It refers to the generation alive at the time of these happenings of Verses 8 through 11 and 25 through 26.

3. The Lord is simply saying that all these things will take place in the span of that generation. In other words, it will not be dragged out over a long period of time, hundreds of years, etc.

(33) "HEAVEN AND EARTH SHALL PASS AWAY: BUT MY WORDS SHALL NOT PASS AWAY."

The order is:

NOTES

1. The meaning of this statement is that irrespective of what is taking place in the world or what some may say, these things predicted by Jesus are going to come to pass in totality and exactly as He said. In other words, these are not conditional prophecies. These events are set in concrete, so to speak, and will come to fruition.

2. The trouble with the world, and even much of the modern church, is that it does not believe the Word of God. Such is understandable concerning the world but not so understandable concerning the church. And yet, this is where Satan makes his greatest inroads.

3. Doubt and unbelief regulate great portions of the Word of God to a false or improper interpretation. When men fail to rightly divide the Word of Truth, they arrive at erroneous conclusions. Hence, people are told by false teachers that certain portions of the Word of God passed away with the apostles, or else, do not apply to the present, etc. However, regarding prophecy, or anything else in the Word of God for that matter, one can rest assured that it will come to pass exactly as stated.

4. First of all, Jesus said it, and secondly, He says it is surer of fulfillment even than the stability of heaven and earth.

(34) "AND TAKE HEED TO YOURSELVES, LEST AT ANY TIME YOUR HEARTS BE OVERCHARGED WITH SURFEITING, AND DRUNKENNESS, AND CARES OF THIS LIFE, AND SO THAT DAY COME UPON YOU UNAWARES."

The exegesis is:

1. The phrase, *"And take heed to yourselves,"* begins a portion of teaching that applies to the entirety of the body of Christ for all time, even though it is pointed to those who are living on the earth after the rapture, enduring the great tribulation (Mat. 24:15-22; Rev., Chpts. 6-19).

2. *"Lest at any time your hearts be overcharged with surfeiting, and drunkenness, and cares of this life,"* points to the things that are not spiritual. The idea pertains to the believer's constant struggle with the flesh, the world, and Satan.

3. Concerning worldliness, which this portrays, someone explained it as a ship,

representing believers, floating in the ocean, which represents the world. As long as it is merely in the water and the water not in it, it can be of valuable service in the hauling of cargo, people, etc. However, the moment the water, which represents the world, gets in the ship, which represents believers, then the ship is lost, or else, severely damaged.

4. The word *overcharged* means "to be weighed down" with things which are not spiritual.

5. *"And so that day come upon you unawares,"* actually points to the coming of the Lord, but can point to other things also:

  a. The rapture

  b. Death

6. The implication is, at least in its ultimate meaning, that the world will not be expecting the second coming. It will look as though the Antichrist is going to take the day, annihilate Israel, and conquer the entirety of the world, thereby, throwing it into a spasm of sorrow and hurt. However, at the moment it seems that all is lost, Jesus Christ will come back with such power and glory that it defies all description.

(35) "FOR AS A SNARE SHALL IT COME ON ALL THEM WHO DWELL ON THE FACE OF THE WHOLE EARTH."

The form is:

1. The phrase, *"For as a snare shall it come on all them,"* refers to the manner in which Jesus will carry out the second coming.

2. The Antichrist and his armies will gather in Israel. They are there for the purpose of destroying these people, however, the Lord has *"gathered them together into a place called in the Hebrew tongue Armageddon,"* for the sole purpose of their destruction (Rev. 16:16). Therefore, that which they think is their victory suddenly becomes a snare.

3. *"Who dwell on the face of the whole earth,"* has reference to the entirety of the world, as is obvious.

4. At that time, the world will not anticipate the coming of Christ and will, therefore, be making plans concerning the reign of the Antichrist. So, not only will the Middle East be affected but, actually, the entirety of the planet. Jesus Christ will come back according to the prophecies of Daniel symbolized

NOTES

by a *"stone* (which) *was cut out without hands, which smote the image upon his feet that were of iron and clay, and broke them to pieces."*

5. Daniel went on to say, *"And the stone* (the Lord Jesus Christ) *that smote the image* (the Antichrist) *became a great mountain, and filled the whole earth* (Jesus Christ will reign as King of Kings and Lord of Lords over the entirety of the earth)" (Dan. 2:34-35).

(36) "WATCH YE THEREFORE, AND PRAY ALWAYS, THAT YOU MAY BE ACCOUNTED WORTHY TO ESCAPE ALL THESE THINGS THAT SHALL COME TO PASS, AND TO STAND BEFORE THE SON OF MAN."

WATCH AND PRAY

Verse 36 is the first plain reference in Scripture to the coming rapture of the church.

"Watch ye therefore, and pray always," proclaims the two requirements for proper preparation:

1. *"Watch ye therefore"*: This speaks of the spirituality of the believer in being able to discern that which is truly of the Lord. It speaks of one who truly knows the Word of God and, consequently, watches events that transpire and equates them in whatever capacity with the Word.

As well, it speaks of a watchman who watches against false doctrine and false teachers. The church is greatly blessed to have such but oftentimes conducts itself in the very opposite by opposing those who point out error, claiming they are destroying the unity. Paul said, *"They watch for your souls, as they that must give account"* (Heb. 13:17).

PRAY ALWAYS

2. *"And pray always"*: It is impossible to have a proper relationship with Christ without a proper prayer life. Such portrays communion with the Father and, consequently, has proper leading and direction. Without prayer, such relationship cannot be maintained. Regrettably, the modern church is not a praying church, which will make it very susceptible to the coming deception, which, in reality, has already begun.

"That you may be accounted worthy to

escape all these things that shall come to pass," refers, as stated, to the rapture.

The Greek word for *"worthy"* is *axioo* and means "To think or count worthy," and pertains to what God thinks of us.

The idea is that the Lord may count us worthy, which is suggestive of grace.

The word *accounted* in the Greek is *kataxioo* and means "to account worthy" or "to judge worthy."

This pertains to righteousness, which is granted exclusively by God on condition of faith (Rom. 4:3).

So, the *worthiness* spoken of here by Jesus has nothing to do with self-righteousness or that which one does attempting to make one righteous, but rather righteousness that is granted freely by Christ upon faith in God by the believer. It is the only type of righteousness that God will recognize, and it is that which must be had by the believer.

TO STAND BEFORE THE SON OF MAN

The phrase, *"And to stand before the Son of Man,"* refers to being taken to be with the Lord before the coming great tribulation (I Thess. 4:16-17).

This Scripture plainly tells us that all the things coming upon the earth in the great tribulation will not be undergone by believers, for God, Paul said, *"Has not appointed us to wrath, but to obtain salvation by our Lord Jesus Christ"* (I Thess. 5:9).

Some preachers erroneously teach that the church will have to go through the great tribulation, or else, part of it; however, Jesus said, *"To escape all these things that shall come to pass."* Consequently, that refers to the entirety of the great tribulation and not just a part, as some teach.

(37) "AND IN THE DAYTIME HE WAS TEACHING IN THE TEMPLE; AND AT NIGHT HE WENT OUT, AND ABODE IN THE MOUNT THAT IS CALLED THE MOUNT OF OLIVES."

The exposition is:

1. The phrase, *"And in the daytime He was teaching in the temple,"* concerned His last hours before the crucifixion. Knowing what would befall Him, still, He continued to open the Word of God to the throngs who filled the temple at that Passover time.

What an honor to have had the privilege to hear Him and what gracious words proceeded out of His mouth. And yet, they little understood who He really was.

2. By now, the religious hierarchy had already made their decision concerning His removal, which would be carried out any way they could. They hated Him, and even though they little realized it, their hatred would seal their own doom. As we have repeatedly stated, an encounter with Christ never leaves one static, but rather immeasurably better or worse, according to one's acceptance or rejection.

3. The phrase, *"And at night He went out, and abode in the mount that is called the Mount of Olives,"* presents an ironic bit of knowledge.

4. There is no record that Jesus spent a single night in Jerusalem during His public ministry, other than the night He was arrested. Every time He would leave out of the city at night and retire to either Bethany or the Mount of Olives.

5. When one considers where and how He spent the night, one is aghast that the Son of God, the one who created all things, the maker of heaven and earth, would actually have no place to lay His head, with the exception of a rock. The humiliation He suffered has no comparison in the annals of human history, especially considering who He really was.

(38) "AND ALL THE PEOPLE CAME EARLY IN THE MORNING TO HIM IN THE TEMPLE, FOR TO HEAR HIM."

ALL THE PEOPLE

The phrase, *"And all the people,"* concerns the many thousands who filled Jerusalem at that time in order to keep the Passover. Without a doubt, Jesus was the topic of conversation by all, with most wanting to see Him and, above all, hear Him.

The temple mount is a large place, with the outer court of the temple surrounded by a portico inside the walls. As described by Josephus, the south porch had four rows of columns and was called the Royal Porch. The porticoes of the other sides each had two rows.

Solomon's porch stretched along the east side (Jn. 10:23; Acts 3:11; 5:12). In these colonnades the scribes held their schools and debates (Mk. 11:27; Lk. 2:46; 19:47), and the merchants and moneychangers had their stalls (Lk. 19:45-46; Jn. 2:14-16), which Jesus had cleansed a little earlier.

This was probably the place where Jesus was teaching, due to its large size. There were, no doubt, hundreds of people gathered, possibly even several thousands. (This well could have been the place where Peter preached on the day of Pentecost, which resulted in *"about three thousand"* people being saved) (Acts 2:40-41).

THE PEOPLE

The phrase, *"Came early in the morning to Him in the temple,"* speaks of the time immediately after daylight. One can easily see the hunger that was in the hearts of the people, in their getting up that early in order to secure a place to where they could hopefully hear Him without difficulty. From the previous verse, it seems that in those days immediately before the crucifixion, He basically spent the entirety of each day in the temple teaching the people. Even though this text does not say, quite possibly, there were great healings as well!

"For to hear Him," proclaims that this was the major purpose and desire.

What must it have been like to hear Him?

To hear a message preached by anyone under a heavy anointing of the Holy Spirit is totally unlike anything else in the world. Due to the unction of the Holy Spirit upon the effort, the Word of God literally comes alive. As it goes forth, needs are met, questions are answered, longings are fulfilled, and great strength given—all of this through the unction of the Holy Spirit upon the Word of God and by an obedient instrument, i.e., preacher of the gospel.

GOD WITH US

However, inasmuch as Jesus had an anointing such as no man has ever had before or since, and that He knew the Word of God as no other, what He said must have been of such magnitude that it defies description. In my mind's eye, I can well see the hundreds or thousands standing there with tears rolling down their faces, transfixed as

NOTES

the words came out of His mouth. I can imagine that hardly a sound was being made except a muffled sob here and there, due to the heavy presence of the Holy Spirit. As well, they hung on every word, not desiring to miss one syllable. They were hearing the Son of God, the one who Isaiah called *"Immanuel,"* i.e., God with us (Isa. 7:14).

To *"hear Him"* was to hear the giver of life presenting the words of life.

It has not changed from then unto now. He alone holds the answer, for He is the answer. He alone knows the way because He is the way. He alone gives salvation because He is salvation.

"And this is life eternal, that they might know You the only true God, and Jesus Christ, whom You have sent" (Jn. 17:3).

"Out of my bondage, sorrow, and night,
"Jesus, I come, Jesus, I come;
"Into Your freedom, gladness, and light,
"Jesus, I come to Thee;
"Out of my sickness, into Your health,
"Out of my want and into Your wealth,
"Out of my sin and into Yourself,
"Jesus, I come to Thee."

"Out of my shameful failure and loss,
"Jesus, I come, Jesus, I come;
"Into the glorious gain of Your Cross,
"Jesus, I come to Thee;
"Out of earth's sorrows into Your balm,
"Out of life's storms and into Your calm,
"Out of distress to jubilant psalm,
"Jesus, I come to Thee."

"Out of unrest and arrogant pride,
"Jesus, I come, Jesus, I come;
"Into Your blessed will to abide,
"Jesus I come to Thee;
"Out of myself to dwell in Your love,
"Out of despair into raptures above,
"Upward for aye on wings like a dove,
"Jesus, I come to Thee."

"Out of the fear and dread of the tomb,
"Jesus, I come, Jesus, I come;
"Into the joy and light of Your home,
"Jesus, I come to Thee;
"Out of the depths of ruin untold,
"Into the peace of Your sheltering fold,
"Ever Your glorious face to behold,
"Jesus, I come to Thee."

CHAPTER 22

(1) "NOW THE FEAST OF UNLEAVENED BREAD DREW NIGH, WHICH IS CALLED THE PASSOVER."

The order is:

1. At this time each year, three feasts were observed by Israel.

2. The first feast was Passover, which was held on April 14. (Due to the way that the Jewish months fell, some claim that Passover could have come on the last day or so of our March.) This was a type of the crucifixion of Christ at Calvary (Lev. 23:5).

3. This was followed immediately by the Feast of Unleavened Bread, which lasted for seven days. This was a type of Christ as a spotless life that was without sin and His body without blemish. So, the sacrifice offered on Calvary was a perfect sacrifice (Lev. 23:6).

4. The last feast, which immediately followed the Feast of Unleavened Bread, was the Feast of Firstfruits, which took place on the first day of the week and typified the resurrection of Christ (Lev. 23:9-14).

5. On that day a priest was to wave a sheaf of barley before the Lord, for it was the time of barley harvest and represented the first of the grain harvest. Likewise, Jesus was *"the firstfruits of them who slept"* (I Cor. 15:20).

6. Exodus, Chapter 12, records the first Passover, which brought about the deliverance of the children of Israel from Egyptian bondage. This was about 1,600 years before Christ. So, that first lamb and all the millions that followed were types of Christ, who, in effect, was the Passover. As the innocent lambs spilled their blood, likewise, Jesus would spill His blood.

(2) "AND THE CHIEF PRIESTS AND SCRIBES SOUGHT HOW THEY MIGHT KILL HIM; FOR THEY FEARED THE PEOPLE."

THE CHIEF PRIESTS AND SCRIBES

The phrase, *"And the chief priests and scribes,"* represented the religious hierarchy of Israel. It is ironic: the world did not crucify Him, but the church did!

It is sad but true, but the church continues to crucify Him unto this hour.

The great plan of God concerning the redemption of humanity was given through the law of Moses to the Jewish people. As such, they were the most privileged on the face of the earth and were referred to as "God's chosen!" Regrettably and sadly, they little by little apostatized by adding to or subtracting from the Word of God, or ignoring it altogether. By the time Jesus came, which was about 2,000 years after Abraham, they had *"made the commandment of God of none effect by your* (their) *tradition"* (Mat. 15:6).

THEY FEARED THE PEOPLE

Jesus called these chief priests and scribes *"hypocrites"* (Mat. 15:7).

The phrase, *"Sought how they might kill Him,"* corresponds perfectly with Verse 7 where it says, *"The Passover must be killed."* Jesus was the Passover, so He must be killed because the Scriptures predicted it, and because only His atoning death could expiate man's sin.

All four gospels record at great length His death while only two briefly record His birth. Modern popular theology reverses this; it magnifies His birth and belittles His death.

The phrase, *"For they feared the people,"* concerned most of Israel, who thought of Him as the Messiah, or at least a great prophet. Considering that He had healed multiple thousands, He was known far and wide.

As we have just stated, hundreds, if not thousands, were flocking to the temple each day to hear Him speak. Consequently, these religious leaders were in a quandary as to how to go about killing Him, considering His popularity. Judas had not yet come along to solve their problem for them. This would happen shortly, as the next verse proclaims.

(3) "THEN ENTERED SATAN INTO JUDAS SURNAMED ISCARIOT, BEING OF THE NUMBER OF THE TWELVE."

The exegesis is:

1. Satan entered into Judas just hours before the Master was crucified.

2. Why? How?

3. Chapter 6 of St. John proclaims the

fact that Judas rebelled at the idea of the Cross. He was looking for money and fame, not a Cross (Jn. 6:70-71).

SATAN ENTERS INTO JUDAS

The phrase, *"Then entered Satan into Judas surnamed Iscariot,"* pertained to the present time, even though Satan had been working on Judas for quite some time. About six months earlier, Jesus had said of Judas, *"Have not I chosen you Twelve, and one of you is a devil?"* (Jn. 6:70).

The word *devil,* as Jesus used it, simply means "adversary" or "false accuser." Here it reveals Judas as an adversary of Christ, not that Satan had entered into him at that particular time.

Many argue that Judas was never saved; however, the Scripture says differently.

Speaking of the Twelve, it says that Jesus *"Called His twelve disciples together, and gave them power and authority over all devils* (demons), *and to cure diseases."* It then said, *"And He sent them to preach the kingdom of God, and to heal the sick"* (Lk. 9:1-2).

Jesus would not have given such power and anointing to one who was not a believer.

As well, shortly before the day of Pentecost, Peter said, *"Concerning Judas ... For he was numbered with us, and had obtained part of this ministry."*

He also said, *"This ministry and apostleship from which Judas by transgression fell, that he might go to his own place"* (Acts 1:16-25).

For one to fall as Judas did, one must have something from which to fall. He fell from the ministry and apostleship, which one certainly would have to be saved in order to have.

ASSOCIATION, ENVIRONMENT, PARTICIPATION

It is clear that the betrayal was no sudden impulse. It was a seed that had been germinating for some time, but probably not in the form it ultimately took.

Losing one's way with God, as Judas did, is not a matter that happens overnight. As well, I think one can say that these things always begin because of a weakening of relationship. Even though Judas rubbed shoulders

with Jesus every day, observing the mighty miracles and hearing Him speak words of life, still, that within itself is not enough.

Consequently, we know that association, environment, and participation, within themselves, guarantee nothing. Judas certainly had an association with Jesus, and his environment was the best there could ever be. As well, he certainly did participate with the things of Jesus.

In other words, a believer, as Judas, can be in the godliest church in the world and sitting under the godliest preaching and still lose his or her way with God. In fact, many have done so. Asaph, David's worship leader, is a prime example. He of all people was honored with the privilege of being in the presence of the Lord almost constantly, and yet, he said of himself, *"But as for me, my feet were almost gone; my steps had well nigh slipped"* (Ps. 73:2).

So, association, environment, and participation are no guarantee against the losing of one's way. Thankfully, Asaph made his way back, saying, *"Until I went into the sanctuary of God; then understood I their end"* (Ps. 73:17).

We learn from Asaph's experience that looking outside the sanctuary distracts the mind and foments the heart, but looking up strengthens and comforts.

WAS JUDAS PREDESTINED TO DO WHAT HE DID?

Instead of looking to Jesus, who is the true sanctuary, Judas looked out and away from the Lord as a result of self-will because of denying the Cross, which ultimately destroyed his relationship with Christ.

Judas saw Christ in a different role than was His actual purpose in coming to this earth, even as did the other disciples. However, he followed that through to an ultimate destruction, whereas the other disciples turned back from that pursuit and got their eyes exclusively on Jesus.

To maintain relationship with Christ, one must have constant communion with Christ, which can only be done through prayer, worship, and the study of the Word of God.

Was Judas predestined to do what he did?

No! Psalm 109, in type, deals with two individuals—Ahithophel, who betrayed David, who served as a type of Judas, who betrayed Jesus.

This was given about a thousand years before Christ and perfectly portrayed what Judas did and what he was and became.

However, such prediction does not speak of predestination, but rather foreknowledge, which God has the power to do.

Some things are definitely predestined by God, such as Him sending His Son into the world, His being born of the Virgin Mary, dying on Calvary to save lost humanity, and being raised from the dead. As well, the rapture of the church is predestined, along with the great tribulation, the battle of Armageddon, and the second coming of the Lord, plus the coming kingdom age. Of course, many other things are predestined as well. That means these things will happen irrespective of what man does.

WHOSOEVER WILL

However, the salvation or loss of souls is never predestined by God. The invitation of salvation is given to the whole world in that Jesus Christ died for the whole world (Jn. 3:16). To accept or reject salvation is based on the premise of free moral agency and *"whosoever will"* (Rev. 22:17).

The expression that Satan entered in Judas is strong and shows that a person, in this case a fallen angel, rules over the powers of evil. This has to do with the kingdom of darkness and speaks of Satan, as stated, who heads up that kingdom, along with myriads of other fallen angels and demon spirits. It also includes all of mankind who rejects Christ. Such are automatically placed in the kingdom of darkness with Satan as their head, whether they believe it or not. The only way for one to escape this kingdom of darkness, which one is actually born into as a result of original sin, is to be born again. This takes one out of the kingdom of darkness and puts one into the kingdom of God (Jn. 3:3).

Paul said, speaking of the heavenly Father, *"Who has delivered us from the power of darkness, and has translated us into the kingdom of His dear Son"* (Col. 1:13).

NOTES

WHAT DID LUKE MEAN WHEN HE SPOKE OF SATAN ENTERING INTO JUDAS?

It does not mean a bodily entrance into Judas, for that is impossible.

It does mean "union with, and consecration to the same end—one in mind, purpose, and life."

It is the same way with the Holy Spirit and Him dwelling in us (I Cor. 3:16).

It perhaps may be best understood by the example of a man and woman through marriage becoming one in life together, to be in each other's plans, life, etc.

However, whether being filled with Satan or the Holy Spirit, and definitely including the things we have just stated, there is, as well, the literal entering into the spirit of a person by either the spirit of Satan or the Lord, whichever is the case.

Satan is limited in that he is not omnipresent as God and can only be extended through demon spirits and fallen angels such as himself. Of course, at times, as here stated, he will attend to the task, as with Judas, by becoming personally involved.

However, the Holy Spirit, being God, is omnipotent (all-powerful), omniscient (all-knowing), and omnipresent (everywhere), and as such, He can personally fill the heart and life of any and all.

So, Satan would now help Judas do this thing by his personal evil presence. At the same time, the Holy Spirit would help Jesus do that which He had to do in order to overcome the Evil One by going to the Cross to redeem mankind.

"Being of the number of the Twelve," is delineated, especially by the Holy Spirit, that all may know the opportunity and privilege Judas had in being included in this group, but now despised.

Actually, this very statement means that Judas was definitely saved when he was originally chosen by the Lord. However, he would now forfeit his salvation, which had probably happened sometime before, and will be eternally lost.

(4) "AND HE WENT HIS WAY, AND COMMUNED WITH THE CHIEF PRIESTS AND CAPTAINS, HOW HE MIGHT BETRAY HIM UNTO THEM."

The exegesis is:

1. The phrase, *"And he went his way,"* although pertaining to his liaison with the religious hierarchy, has a far greater meaning in that he was no longer going God's way. There is no middle ground. We either go God's way, or else, we go our way, which, in reality, is Satan's way.

2. *"And communed with the chief priests and captains, how he might betray Him unto them,"* proclaims the most evil deed ever carried out by a human being. And yet, it is being carried out each and every day by most of the world and most of the church.

3. Why did Judas want to betray Jesus?

4. It is clear that the betrayal was no sudden impulse. At some point, he set up self as the one object of all his thoughts. He followed Jesus from then on because he believed in doing so, he could best serve his own interests. His ambition was cruelly disappointed by his Master's gradual unfolding of His views respecting His kingdom, which was not to be of this world.

5. He was still further shocked by the undisguised announcement on the part of Jesus, whose greatness and power he recognized from the first, that He would be rejected by the nation and even put to death.

6. Some have even suggested that he seems to have fancied that he could force the manifestation of Christ's power by placing Him in the hands of His enemies.

Of course, if that was his thought, it was the old trap of trying to bring good out of evil, which cannot be done, at least by man.

7. It seems that he completely misunderstood Christ, as did all the other disciples at the beginning! However, he took it further than the others by remaining in that misunderstanding simply because he desired to do so. As self-will became more and more prominent in his life, with his relationship with Christ weakening by the day, he became fertile territory for Satan, who always takes advantage of such attitude and direction. Satan cannot force a believer to do such things, but he can take advantage of self-will, which he always does. That self-will did not include the Cross, and when He heard Jesus say, *"Except you eat the flesh of the Son of Man, and drink His blood, you*

have no life in you" (Jn. 6:53), that's when the rejection began.

That's when many of the people began to leave Jesus with even His personal disciples wavering. How much they knew and understood that Jesus was speaking of the Cross, at least at that time, is not clear. At any rate, this is what caused Judas to turn aside! It was to accept the Cross or reject the Cross. Sadly and regrettably, Judas rejected it, even as do millions.

(5) "AND THEY WERE GLAD, AND COVENANTED TO GIVE HIM MONEY."

The synopsis is:

1. The phrase, *"And they were glad,"* portrays evil beyond belief. It is more tragic still when one realizes that this was the church of that particular day. If one thinks it has changed presently, then one is sadly wrong. The same religious spirit that hated Christ then hates His true followers presently because it is the same spirit that the religious leaders then had, which is of Satan. In other words, they were all in league with Satan despite their profession of some kind of faith.

2. In this scenario, it becomes easy to observe the workings of religion, which characterize much of the modern church, i.e., apostate church.

3. By the words *apostate church*, we are referring to anything that is man-led instead of Holy Spirit-led. That which is man-led has the Cain and Absalom spirit, which are one and the same.

4. Instead of these religious leaders being glad that Jesus had come to redeem humanity, they were glad that they now had an opportunity to kill Him.

5. *"And covenanted to give him money,"* simply means they sweetened the pot.

6. It is obvious that Judas' greed for money entered into this. But yet, it seems this was not the real reason for his betrayal, but rather a side issue. The 30 pieces of silver he received was simply not enough money to satisfy an overwhelming greed.

7. When a person is taken over by Satan, he begins to do ridiculous things. Thus, Judas would do the most ridiculous thing of all.

(6) "AND HE PROMISED, AND SOUGHT OPPORTUNITY TO BETRAY

HIM UNTO THEM IN THE ABSENCE OF THE MULTITUDE."

The synopsis is:

1. They were fearful of arresting Jesus in the presence of the multitude for fear they would create a riot, which it, no doubt, would.

2. Therefore, they had to carry out this act when He was alone, or at least in the presence of His disciples only.

3. Judas promised to provide this opportunity, which, in fact, would take place that very night.

(7) "THEN CAME THE DAY OF UNLEAVENED BREAD, WHEN THE PASSOVER MUST BE KILLED."

The order is:

1. This statement simply means that the time of the eating of the Passover was quickly approaching, which would be on a Thursday. It would be killed and prepared on Wednesday.

2. As Jesus spoke these words, it was Tuesday, meaning that He ate the Passover a day early in order to be the true Passover on the Cross.

3. In the manner in which Jews then reckoned time, Tuesday would end at sundown, with Wednesday beginning, which was the day Jesus was crucified, and not Friday as many believe.

(8) "AND HE SENT PETER AND JOHN, SAYING, GO AND PREPARE US THE PASSOVER, THAT WE MAY EAT."

The composition is:

1. The phrase, *"And He sent Peter and John,"* had to do with the preparation of the Passover, which constituted the Last Supper.

2. *"Go and prepare us the Passover, that we may eat,"* means that Peter and John, representing the apostolic band, took a lamb to the temple, where it was killed.

3. The priest caught the blood and passed it to the one nearest the altar, who instantly sprinkled it toward the base of the altar.

4. The carcass of the little lamb was then taken to the appointed place where the supper was held, roasted, and with unleavened bread, wine, and bitter herbs, the feast was eaten (Ex. 12:8).

(9) "AND THEY SAID UNTO HIM, WHERE WILL YOU THAT WE PREPARE?"

NOTES

The composition is:

1. At this time, they probably thought that Jesus was going to eat the Passover at the regular time on Thursday, not realizing that He, as they, would eat it a day early.

2. At this stage, they did not even know where it was to be prepared.

3. They were engaging in one of the most poignant moments in history, the Last Supper, and yet, they were totally desolate of comprehension.

(10) "AND HE SAID UNTO THEM, BEHOLD, WHEN YOU ARE ENTERED INTO THE CITY, THERE SHALL A MAN MEET YOU, BEARING A PITCHER OF WATER; FOLLOW HIM INTO THE HOUSE WHERE HE ENTERS IN."

The form is:

1. The phrase, *"And He said unto them, Behold, when you are entered into the city,"* presents the first of their directions. As usual, the directions will be detailed in one sense of the word and the very opposite in the other.

2. *"There shall a man meet you, bearing a pitcher of water,"* would seem at first glance not to be too informative, considering that the city was filled with men; however, in those days, men did not carry pitchers of water, with that being reserved for women. Consequently, such would be easy to spot simply because a man carrying a pitcher of water was unusual.

3. *"Follow him into the house where he enters in,"* would be the place where the Passover would be eaten.

4. Did Jesus make these preparations before now?

5. If He did, the disciples were not informed, which would be highly unlikely.

6. It is speculative as to whose house this was, but some think it may have been the house of John Mark who wrote the gospel that bears his name.

(11) "AND YOU SHALL SAY UNTO THE GOODMAN OF THE HOUSE, THE MASTER SAYS UNTO YOU, WHERE IS THE GUESTCHAMBER, WHERE I SHALL EAT THE PASSOVER WITH MY DISCIPLES?"

The diagram is:

1. The phrase, *"And you shall say unto the goodman of the house, The Master says*

unto you," portrays Jesus in a far different light than asking permission.

2. He spoke as a king and, consequently, told instead of asked.

3. The question, *"Where is the guestchamber, where I shall eat the Passover with My disciples?"* is not asking if there is, in fact, a guestchamber, but rather, "Where is it?"

(12) "AND HE SHALL SHOW YOU A LARGE UPPER ROOM FURNISHED: THERE MAKE READY."

The overview is:

1. This could well be the same *"upper room"* as in Acts 1:13, as it most probably was.

2. The word *"furnished"* refers to the cushions and such things needed for the many guests to recline on while eating.

3. If one follows the Holy Spirit, He will lead one to a *"large* (upper) *room furnished: there made ready."*

(13) "AND THEY WENT, AND FOUND AS HE HAD SAID UNTO THEM: AND THEY MADE READY THE PASSOVER."

The exegesis is:

1. The phrase, *"And they went, and found as He had said unto them,"* will always be the case regarding anything in His Word.

2. *"And they made ready the Passover,"* means that they prepared the lamb for roasting, along with the making of the unleavened bread, etc.

3. In this scenario concerning the preparation for the Passover, there is a beautiful symbolism respecting the Christian experience. It is as follows:

a. Jesus calls us exactly as He called Peter and John. As He sent them, He always sends us on a mission, and in whatever capacity.

b. The man bearing the pitcher of water, as stated, is a type of the Holy Spirit. We are to follow Him. To follow anything or anyone else will lead to other than that which is prepared for the believer. The Holy Spirit must be followed.

c. He will always lead us to a large upper room furnished with all the things of the Spirit, which alone can satisfy the cravings of the human heart.

d. There we will sit down and eat with Jesus, portraying communion, fellowship, and great blessing, for the Holy Spirit always leads to Jesus.

(14) "AND WHEN THE HOUR WAS COME, HE SAT DOWN, AND THE TWELVE APOSTLES WITH HIM."

The overview is:

1. The phrase, *"And when the hour was come,"* referred to the Passover, which was now ready, possibly being a little after sundown, which was their Wednesday. As well, the hour had come for Him to fulfill the Passover type, which had originally been given to Moses in Egypt some 1,600 years before (Ex., Chpt. 12). The great price that had to be paid in order to redeem man and to set aside the curse of the law, which had been planned through the ages, was now on the threshold of fulfillment. Although of such a price that it defies description, still, coupled with the resurrection, it would be the greatest three days in human history, and for all time.

2. The phrase, *"He sat down,"* is tremendously significant within itself.

3. In Egypt they were told to eat the Passover standing (Ex. 12:11) simply because the work of deliverance from Egypt had not yet been carried out, which was a type of victory over the world, the flesh, and the Devil. Upon arriving in the Promised Land, they were to eat sitting and resting simply because the Promised Land was a type of salvation already given. Actually, it pointed to justification by faith, hence, sitting and resting, and not by works, by which salvation and victory over sin cannot be obtained (Eph. 2:9; I Cor. 2:2).

4. *"And the twelve apostles with Him,"* included Judas, as is obvious.

5. Even though the terrible plans for the betrayal of Jesus had already begun to foment, Jesus would make one last effort to bring Judas to repentance, but sadly, to no avail (Lk. 22:21).

(15) "AND HE SAID UNTO THEM, WITH DESIRE I HAVE DESIRED TO EAT THIS PASSOVER WITH YOU BEFORE I SUFFER."

The exegesis is:

1. The phrase, *"And He said unto them,"* concerns itself with the act of the ages, which the apostles could not comprehend at that time.

2. The phrase, *"With desire I have desired*

to eat this Passover with you," presents a strong passion on the part of Jesus. The word *desire* in this case in the Greek is *epithumia* and means "a craving, or longing." There were several reasons for that:

a. This would be the last Passover, at least that God would recognize, which had begun some 1,600 years earlier. It would be the last because Jesus would now fulfill the type.

b. In the fulfilling of this type, man would be redeemed from the horrible grip of sin, Satan, and death, at least all who will believe (Jn. 3:16).

c. In effect, at this Passover Jesus would present the symbolism of the new covenant. Even in actuality, as it would be cut at Calvary a few hours later, still, its symbolism would here be introduced and would continue through the church age.

d. The symbolism would pertain to His body given and blood shed, typified in the Lord's Supper.

e. It was here that the church was founded, with the outpouring of the Holy Spirit on the day of Pentecost, ratifying that which was done.

3. The phrase, *"Before I suffer,"* spoke of the next morning when He would be crucified at the time of the morning sacrifice, which was at 9 a.m.

4. Little did Israel know that this Passover was the greatest of all Passovers because all that which had been symbolized through the many centuries would now be fulfilled. Consequently, there is no way the mind of man can fully comprehend the significance of this time, even though Israel realized it not at all, not even His chosen disciples.

(16) "FOR I SAY UNTO YOU, I WILL NOT ANY MORE EAT THEREOF, UNTIL IT BE FULFILLED IN THE KINGDOM OF GOD."

The synopsis is:

1. The phrase, *"For I say unto you, I will not any more eat thereof,"* referred to two things:

a. Jesus would ascend to the Father a few days later and would not physically be here anymore, at least at that time.

b. That which the Passover represented was now fulfilled and would require its continuance no longer. There would be no

NOTES

point in continuing to offer up lambs, which symbolized the coming Christ, when the Lamb of God had been offered up Himself, therefore, fulfilling all the types (Jn. 1:29).

2. *"Until it be fulfilled in the kingdom of God,"* has to do with the entirety of the church age, the second coming, and the beginning of the kingdom age. The key is in the word *fulfilled.*

3. Even though the total price was paid at Calvary for man's redemption, still, all that redemption affords has not yet been received.

4. The believer is presently sanctified and justified, but he is not yet glorified. That will happen at the resurrection, or as referred to, the rapture (I Cor. 15:51-57; I Thess. 4:16-17). Then at the second coming, all will be fulfilled, with Jesus reigning personally in Jerusalem over the entirety of the earth. Every saint of God in glorified bodies will help Him to administer the affairs of His dominion, now given back to man (Gen. 1:28; Ps. 8:3-9).

5. In the coming kingdom age, the Passover, as well as the sacrifices, will be reinstituted, but strictly as a memorial of what Jesus has done for humanity (Ezek., Chpts. 40-48).

(17) "AND HE TOOK THE CUP, AND GAVE THANKS, AND SAID, TAKE THIS, AND DIVIDE IT AMONG YOURSELVES."

The diagram is:

1. The phrase, *"And He took the cup,"* constituted the beginning of the Passover meal.

2. The usual custom was that a cup was filled with wine (grape juice) for everyone. A blessing was pronounced, after which, the wine was drunk. Then, unleavened bread, bitter herbs, and the lamb were brought in. Thanksgiving was offered for the many blessings of life and the food handed around to each guest.

3. The second cup of wine was drunk, after which, an explanation of the feasts was given with Exodus 12:26-27. The company then sang Psalms 113 and 114, followed by another blessing.

4. Then the food was eaten. After this, a third cup of wine was drunk, and Psalms 115 and 118 were sung.

5. *"And gave thanks,"* pertained then to deliverance from Egypt, but now must be offered for what Christ did at Calvary and the resurrection.

6. *"And said, Take this, and divide it among yourselves,"* probably represented a large cup or container filled with grape juice, which was passed around and a portion given to each one.

(18) "FOR I SAY UNTO YOU, I WILL NOT DRINK OF THE FRUIT OF THE VINE, UNTIL THE KINGDOM OF GOD SHALL COME."

THE LORD'S SUPPER

Verse 18 is the same as Verse 16.

Even though the Passover is no longer continued, and for the obvious reasons, the Lord's Supper, which actually began that day, does continue, but without the physical presence of Christ.

The Lord's Supper is different than the Passover, although it has its roots in that ritual, simply because a lamb roasted and eaten is no longer needed because Christ became that lamb. As well, the grape juice is to represent His shed blood, with the bread representing His broken body.

The phrase, *"For I say unto you, I will not drink of the fruit of the vine,"* represents grape juice and not fermented wine as some would have us believe.

The very meaning of fermented wine makes it unsatisfactory to represent the blood of the Lord Jesus Christ. As is known, fermented wine is grape juice in which decay (or rot) has taken place. In other words, the process of fermentation is the breakdown of large molecules caused by the influence of bacteria or fungi. Wine then results from the degenerative action of germs on pure substances.

WINE?

Fermented wine used in Communion would actually symbolize tainted, sinful blood, and not the pure and perfect blood of Jesus Christ. We must remember that the symbolism here is extremely important. The perfect blood of Jesus had to be made evident for it to be a perfect cleansing for our sins.

NOTES

Pure, fresh grape juice tends toward life, but fermented wine tends toward sin and death. Alcohol used for drinking purposes is both a narcotic and a poison. It could hardly be used as a symbol for the blood of the Lord Jesus Christ.

As well, the Jews were required to use unleavened bread with the Passover Feasts, and they were commanded that during that time, *"There shall no leavened bread be seen with you, neither shall there be leaven seen with you in all your quarters"* (Ex. 13:7).

As early as this, bread that had been tainted with bacteria or yeast was considered unsuitable at this event celebrated by the Jews. Jesus also used unleavened bread in initiating the Lord's Supper.

Consequently, the point is this: If the Lord specifically chose bread that had no bacteria and no fungus spores in it to picture His broken body, does one honestly think He would choose alcoholic wine, fermented wine, which is directly the product of fungi or bacteria, to represent His blood? I hardly think so! The pure blood of Jesus Christ would be best represented by pure grape juice.

THE KINGDOM OF GOD

Under the Mosaic law, the high priests were commanded, *"Do not drink wine nor strong drink ... When you go into the tabernacle of the congregation, lest you die: it shall be a statute for ever throughout your generations"* (Lev. 10:9).

One must remember that these priests entering into the tabernacle were types of the Lord Jesus Christ, who is our Great High Priest; therefore, the question must be asked:

Would Jesus, the night He was betrayed, drink intoxicating wine before going to the crucifixion and entering into His high priestly work? I think not! It would have been a rejection and a contradiction of His own word given in Leviticus.

"Until the kingdom of God shall come," refers to the beginning of the kingdom age when Jesus will reign in Jerusalem, and Israel will have accepted Him as Saviour, Lord, and Messiah.

Whereas each and every believer presently has the kingdom of God in the heart, referring to a spiritual rebirth, the physical and material aspect of the kingdom of God has not yet been realized. It will be realized in totality in the coming kingdom age. Then, Jesus will *"drink of the fruit of the vine,"* as He will then eat of the Passover lamb.

Incidentally, the kingdom of God is coming, and without a doubt.

(19) "AND HE TOOK BREAD, AND GAVE THANKS, AND BROKE IT, AND GAVE UNTO THEM, SAYING, THIS IS MY BODY WHICH IS GIVEN FOR YOU: THIS DO IN REMEMBRANCE OF ME.

(20) "LIKEWISE ALSO THE CUP AFTER SUPPER, SAYING, THIS CUP IS THE NEW TESTAMENT IN MY BLOOD, WHICH IS SHED FOR YOU."

THE DOCTRINE OF THE LORD'S SUPPER

• It was instituted at the time of the Passover meal. Actually, it is a continuation of the Passover in a sense, but yet, corresponding with the fulfillment of the Old Testament type and the incorporation of the new, which it is actually meant to portray (Lk. 22:14-20).

• It is *"the Lord's Supper"* (I Cor. 11:20), *"the Communion of the blood of Christ,"* and *"the Communion of the body of Christ,"* and what it means to the believer (I Cor. 10:16).

• The elements used were *"the fruit of the vine"* (grape juice, Mk. 14:25; Lk. 22:18), and *"unleavened bread"* (Mat. 26:17, 26; Mk. 14:12, 22; Lk. 22:7, 19).

• The bread was broken, symbolizing the marred and striped body of Christ for our healing (Isa. 52:14; 53:4-5; Mat. 26:26; Lk. 22:19; I Cor. 10:16; 11:24-29; I Pet. 2:24).

• The grape juice symbolized the blood of Christ shed for the remission of sins (Mat. 26:28; Mk. 14:24; Lk. 22:20; I Cor. 10:16; 11:25-29; Eph. 1:7; Col. 1:14, 20).

• Each believer is to partake of this supper (Mat. 26:26-27; Mk. 14:22; Lk. 22:17; I Cor. 10:16-17; 11:28).

• Thanksgivings and blessings were offered for it in that which Christ has done for all who will believe (Mat. 26:26-27; Mk. 14:22-23; Lk. 22:17-19; I Cor. 10:16; 11:24).

• It is a remembrance of the death of Christ until He comes again (Lk. 22:19; I Cor. 11:24-26).

NOTES

• It can be partaken daily (Acts 2:42, 46), weekly (Acts 20:7; I Cor. 10:17), or as *"often"* as desired (I Cor. 11:26). It seems that early disciples observed it daily until they began to have weekly meetings, and then it was observed every Sunday, according to history, Acts 20:7, and I Corinthians 16:2. However, there is no scriptural set time.

• It will be observed forever by Christ and all believers in the *"kingdom of God,"* i.e., the coming kingdom age (Mat. 26:29; Mk. 14:25; Lk. 22:18, 30).

• It is an ordinance that should bring unity and love among believers and not division and strife (I Cor. 10:16-17; 11:16-30).

• It should be partaken in faith and proper examination of self, with the repenting of any sins before it is taken, or condemnation, sickness, and even death may result (I Cor. 11:17-30).

• While the Lord does not demand perfection for the Lord's Supper to be taken, He does demand faith in Christ and the Cross, and that exclusively. Otherwise, sickness could occur, and the believer could die prematurely. While such a one's soul will not be lost, still, his service on earth could be cut short (I Cor. 11:27-30).

A SYMBOLISM OF THE CUTTING OF THE COVENANT

As well, the Lord's Supper is a symbolism of the cutting of the covenant, which took place at Calvary, and which actually portrays the new covenant that took the place of the old.

The cutting of the covenant in Old Testament times meant the death of an innocent victim, with its body actually split in half. The two parties making the covenant would walk between the two halves, with the understanding that if either one broke the covenant, he would suffer the same fate as the sacrificed animal. As well, many times, a small amount of blood was drawn from the finger of each participant, with cut finger touching cut finger, therefore, mixing the blood, thereby saying that now both were one.

Even though God made many covenants with man in Old Testament times, all the covenants were broken by man, in other words, man never lived up to his part of the covenant even though made with God (Gen. 3:21; 8:21-22; 12:1-3; 15:1-17; 22:15-18; 26:1-5; 28:10-19; Ex. 19:3-6; Deut., Chpts. 27-29; II Sam. 7:1-17).

THE NEW COVENANT

The new covenant, however, which the Lord's Supper portrays, cannot be broken. The following is the reason:

In effect, the new covenant, which cannot fail, was made in Jesus and Jesus alone, for He was both God and man. When He died on the Cross, *"God was in Christ, reconciling the world unto Himself"* (II Cor. 5:19). As well, Jesus was the representative man. As such, He cut the covenant on our behalf, and consequently, it cannot fail, for *"He abides faithful: He cannot deny Himself"* (II Tim. 2:13). In effect, Jesus is both God and man, so He fulfills both parties.

So, whenever the believer partakes of the Lord's Supper, he is celebrating the covenant that cannot fail. Hallelujah!

THE DOCTRINE OF TRANSUBSTANTIATION

As well, we must mention the erroneous doctrine of transubstantiation believed by the Catholics, and consubstantiation believed by the Lutherans, with that of the Catholics teaching that the grape juice and bread, when partaken, turn into the literal blood and flesh of Jesus Christ. The doctrine of consubstantiation teaches that it turns into the body and blood of Jesus in spirit, but not literally, as the Catholics believe.

Leviticus 3:17 and 7:26 forbid the eating of blood. Jesus and the apostles, being godly Jews, would have refused to drink of such a cup. Hence, the language as used by Jesus, *"This cup is the New Testament in My blood,"* is figurative and not literal.

(For an extended dissertation on the error of the Catholic Mass, please see our commentary on Matthew.)

(21) "BUT, BEHOLD, THE HAND OF HIM WHO BETRAYS ME IS WITH ME ON THE TABLE."

The overview is:

1. John goes into much greater detail respecting Jesus' dealing with Judas, and the evidence seems clear that Jesus, even

NOTES

unto the last moment, attempted to bring Judas out of this quagmire of spiritual darkness, but to no avail (Jn., Chpt. 13).

2. It seems clear that Judas partook of the Last Supper and, as well, had his feet washed by Christ.

3. Also, Judas is a representation of all in the church who are with Christ but not of Christ. However, where the percentage then was only one out of 12, it is now far higher, with the percentages possibly being reversed, fulfilling Matthew 13:33, where the whole of the kingdom of heaven is leavened, i.e., corrupted.

(22) "AND TRULY THE SON OF MAN GOES, AS IT WAS DETERMINED: BUT WOE UNTO THAT MAN BY WHOM HE IS BETRAYED!"

The exposition is:

1. The phrase, *"And truly the Son of Man goes, as it was determined,"* speaks of predestination, at least as far as the act is concerned, but not the person.

2. In other words, it was predetermined (predestined) that Jesus would be given over for crucifixion.

3. *"But woe unto that man by whom He is betrayed,"* tells us that it was not predetermined who the man would be, even though it was predetermined that some man would do such a thing. While it is true that it was predicted that Judas would do this thing, still, as stated, this was through the foreknowledge of God and not predestination. The act was predestined, not the one who would carry out the act.

4. Judas did what he did out of his own choice, even with Jesus making attempts to bring him to his senses up unto the very last moment.

5. The word *woe* had already been expressed in prophecy about a thousand years earlier in Psalms 109.

(23) "AND THEY BEGAN TO ENQUIRE AMONG THEMSELVES, WHICH OF THEM IT WAS THAT SHOULD DO THIS THING."

The form is:

1. The phrase, *"And they began to enquire among themselves,"* is deepened by the extended treatment given by Matthew, with the disciples questioning their own hearts with, *"Is it I?"* This shows us that

none of the disciples knew of Judas' disposition. He had kept it well concealed, and considering the attitude of all, this was not difficult.

2. It seems that all the disciples felt that Jesus was going to restore the kingdom again to Israel, consequently, throwing off the Roman yoke. Of course, they would be chief lieutenants in this new order of things; consequently, when Jesus spoke of being crucified and then being raised from the dead, even though it was clearly stated, their unbelief caused them to be blinded to what He was really saying.

3. So, inasmuch as they all felt the same way, including Judas, he was really not out of step at the last concerning this false ideal. The difference seems to have been that he would force the issue, with the others not going that far.

4. By the phrase, *"Which of them it was that should do this thing,"* it appears that they discussed the betrayal in detail.

5. When this conversation was taking place, what were the thoughts of Judas during this time? As well, this was another opportunity for him to abandon this way of darkness, but sadly, it was an opportunity lost.

(24) "AND THERE WAS ALSO A STRIFE AMONG THEM, WHICH OF THEM SHOULD BE ACCOUNTED THE GREATEST."

STRIFE

The phrase, *"And there was also a strife among them,"* took place almost immediately after the supper, and seems to have been only one of several of this nature (Mat. 20:24; Mk. 10:41).

It is almost inconceivable to think that this would be going on just hours before the crucifixion.

The Greek word for *"strife"* in this instance is *philoneikia* and means "contention." Consequently, the argument seems to have been fairly heated.

The phrase, *"Which of them should be accounted the greatest,"* once again lends credence to the thought of who would have the place of preeminence in this kingdom soon to be brought about by Jesus, or so they thought! It is amazing that they could

not see what He had so plainly shown them or hear what He had so clearly told them! This shows that environment, association, and even participation do not necessarily guarantee a correct way. In fact, it is clear that it doesn't.

And yet, I wonder if we would have done any better had we been there instead.

A HUNGER AND DESIRE FOR CHRIST

Many are in good churches, at least what few there are, where the gospel is faithfully preached behind the pulpit, and the Spirit of God moves constantly among the people, but still, they have their own agenda, which is not of God and if allowed to have its way, will, in fact, destroy that which God is truly doing.

In the heart of the believer, there must be a hunger and a desire for Christlikeness, and a Christlikeness that is attempted in the right way. Adam and Eve wanted to be like God, which in itself is noble, but tried to be like Him in an ungodly, selfish, and disobedient manner. Consequently, they became totally unlike Him, as do many modern believers.

Many desire to heal the sick and cast out demons and have people think highly of them respecting their Christlikeness when, in reality, with some, there is no Christlikeness at all!

In fact, this nearness to Christ, which is the greatest position to which a person could attain, cannot be had unless the believer's faith is expressed entirely in Christ and what He has done for us at the Cross. The Cross alone is the answer for self-righteousness, the answer for self-will, and the direction we must go. There is no other, only the Cross.

In the following verses, Jesus carefully outlines what true greatness and Christlikeness really is, and how it can be obtained.

(25) "AND HE SAID UNTO THEM, THE KINGS OF THE GENTILES EXERCISE LORDSHIP OVER THEM; AND THEY THAT EXERCISE AUTHORITY UPON THEM ARE CALLED BENEFACTORS."

THE LORDSHIP PROBLEM

The phrase, *"And He said unto them, The kings of the Gentiles exercise lordship over them,"* proclaims the way of the world, which the believer is not to emulate.

After the initial outpouring of the Spirit on the early church, which resulted in most of the known world of that day being evangelized, slowly but surely the church began to apostatize. It did so because man's ways gradually pushed out God's ways, which are outlined in the Word of God. The Catholic Church was the result! As such, and because it had forsaken God's ways and adopted the ways of the world, it began to exercise lordship over the people. The results were the Dark Ages because God will not work and function when man insists on having his way.

Regrettably, the lordship problem has continued even after the Reformation in many denominational hierarchies. The word *lordship,* means "have or take dominion over."

In truth, at this present time, this problem of lordship is acute in some Pentecostal denominations, as well as Charismatic associations.

I do not speak of organization, which is necessary and needful, but rather a suppressing of the leading and direction of the Holy Spirit, with man exercising that authority.

As an example, in a major Pentecostal denomination, which once eagerly sought the leading, guidance, and direction of the Holy Spirit, now, for the most part, does the very opposite.

GOD'S METHOD

God's method is to deal with a particular person concerning His will about all things, and then for that person to carry out that will. However, this particular denomination greatly frowns on such activity, demanding that their committees, counsels, or presbytery boards make all such decisions, consequently, telling where and what should be done, etc. Most of these boards do not even seek the face of the Lord regarding direction anymore, but rather have the misconceived idea that whatever they decide is automatically God's will.

In effect, they have abrogated the headship of Christ, taking over that position themselves. Clearly and simply, the Holy

NOTES

Spirit will not work in such an arrangement because it is totally in opposition to the Word of God (Jn. 16:12-15).

God does not work through committees, boards, etc. He deals directly with an individual, which the Bible clearly delineates. For instance, when Jesus addressed the churches in Chapters 2 and 3 of Revelation, He did not address a headquarters church in Jerusalem, or anyone else for that matter. He addressed each particular church, and more specifically, the pastor of each church (Rev. 2:1, 8, 12, 18; 3:1, 7, 14). As well, when the Lord gave the new covenant to the church, He did not give it to a group, board, or denominational hierarchy. He instead gave it to one man, Paul (Gal. 1:1; 2:5-7).

BIBLE GOVERNMENT

Whenever the Lord desired to deliver Israel from Egyptian bondage, He did not speak to a group or committee, but rather to a single man, Moses. Actually, this is found from Genesis to Revelation and is so clearly delineated that only evil hearts would even think of abrogating that which is the true government of the Spirit.

One religious leader accused me of not believing in church government. Oh yes, I believe in church government even more, much more, than He does, but I believe in the kind the Bible proclaims and not the kind he espouses. The Word of God is the government of God.

RELIGIOUS DENOMINATIONS?

To be brief, there is no such thing in the New Testament as a religious denomination. There is definitely organization and fellowship. If the Holy Spirit had desired denominations or denominationalism, the early church would have been an excellent time for such instigation. However, none were formed because none were desired!

As a case in point, when the Assemblies of God was formed in 1914, it was formed as an organization and a fellowship. In that capacity, even though in time it did adopt some unscriptural government, it touched the world for Jesus Christ. Over a period of time, it has abandoned the role of "fellowship among churches with a common

not demean the desire for greatness, only in obtaining it in the wrong manner. And yet, the Lord's definition of *greatness* will never be accepted by the world, while He will never accept the world's standard.

So, the believer has one or the other as a choice. He cannot have both!

The word *younger* refers to one who is a "listener, learner, and a servant."

"And he who is chief, as he who does serve," is, as stated, the total opposite of the world.

The world's standard of greatness pertains to the one being served, and the more he has serving him, the greater his greatness, etc. With the Lord, it is the exact opposite.

And yet, to fully understand what Jesus is really saying is to understand the spirit of the action that He presents. No matter who the person may be or how much he is used by God, he is to keep a kind, gracious, and serving spirit. That is the idea!

GREATNESS!

What a person really is pertains to how he treats someone, whom he considers to be far beneath his own station in life, when no one else is looking.

That's what a person really is, and that's what Jesus was proclaiming. The puffed up, prideful, egotistical, and self-willed braggart can never be accepted by the Lord.

Consequently, their strife among themselves, with aspirations of greatness and who would fill that spot is shown up for what it really is—a greedy grasping after personal recognition and position. If this spirit had continued, it would have destroyed the early church before it even began. As well, it will destroy the modern church, although long established.

To aspire to the Lord's standard of greatness should be the aspiration of every believer, and yet, to do such will never exalt one, but rather humble one. Actually, I think that's what the Spirit is attempting to do!

The way that one begins on this road to greatness is to understand that the Cross of Christ is the means by which all of these wonderful things are given to us. As well, the Cross of Christ is the way and means in which the Holy Spirit works within our

lives, demanding that our faith be exclusively in Christ and what He did for us at the Cross (Rom. 6:1-14; 8:1-11; I Cor. 1:17-18, 23; 2:2).

(27) "FOR WHETHER IS GREATER, HE WHO SITS AT MEAT, OR HE WHO SERVES? IS NOT HE WHO SITS AT MEAT? BUT I AM AMONG YOU AS HE WHO SERVES."

WHO IS GREATER?

The question, *"For whether is greater, he who sits at meat, or he who serves?"* as asked by Jesus, is meant to point out the total contrast between the ways of the world and the ways of God. They are total opposites and, consequently, opposed to each other.

It is possible, judging from Peter's permitted fall, that he desired to be the greatest.

The question, *"Is not he who sits at meat?"* is meant to point to the thinking of the world.

As is obvious, the more that a person is being served, at least in the eyes of the world, such signifies his station, place, and position. Regrettably, this was what the strife was all about in Verse 24, *"Which of them should be accounted the greatest."* Unfortunately, this spirit of personal greatness, acquired according to the ways of the world, continues to be pandemic in the church. The desire to be looked up to and to be thought great by others is the spirit of the world and not of Christ. The believer must come to the place that his entire life is given over to pleasing God, consequently, for everything done to be for His eyes only. This is the place the Holy Spirit is attempting to bring us.

HE WHO SERVES

The phrase, *"But I am among you as He who serves,"* portrays, as is obvious, the way of the Lord and, consequently, the way and attitude that must be developed by the child of God. Actually, the believer can only provide a willing mind and obedient heart as such a task is impossible within one's capabilities. However, if the believer properly yields to the Holy Spirit, this beautiful work of *"he who serves"* can be brought about.

The expositor said, "Man's standard of

greatness is to be served; God's is to serve. Man's standard is to receive; God's is to give. Man's standard is to humble others; God's is to humble oneself. Failure to obey God's principles of life caused both Lucifer (Isa. 14:12-14; Ezek. 28:11-17; I Tim. 3:6) and Adam to exalt themselves" (Gen., Chpt. 3).

That of which Jesus was speaking, *"But I among you as He who serves,"* probably refers to His action in washing their feet, which characterized His entire life and ministry, which was not mentioned by Luke but by John (13:3-17).

In preaching the gospel for over a half century, I have had the privilege of meeting a few people in these many years who were such examples of Christ. I personally felt that it left a positive marked impression upon my life. Without exception, there was one principle that stood out in their lives, and it was this of which Jesus mentioned, *"He who serves."* In their lives, there was no pretension, self-will, solicitation for personal glory, or aspiration for greatness in the eyes of others, at least that I saw.

Consequently, I left their presence desiring to be more like Christ rather than to have some personal attribute of talent and ability that they may have possessed. That's the point I'm trying to make, and which I believe Jesus was making.

CHRISTLIKE

All of us at times have the occasion to meet individuals who impress us with talent, ability, or other complements or attributes. That is good; however, to have the privilege to meet someone who is so Christlike that one leaves his presence with the desire to be like Christ instead of possessing equal talent or ability, etc., is that of which I speak. Regrettably, such people are rare, but that is the place and position to which the Holy Spirit attempts to bring all believers.

Sadly, I think He doesn't have much success most of the time because of our lack of cooperation.

(28) "YOU ARE THEY WHICH HAVE CONTINUED WITH ME IN MY TEMPTATIONS."

The exegesis is:

1. After the mild rebuke given, Jesus now

warmly commended His disciples. This tells us that every good deed and every noble thought, with each bit of generosity and self-forgetfulness on our part, is at once recognized and rewarded a hundredfold now as then.

2. What a wonderful Lord we serve!

3. The three and one-half years of public ministry of Christ proclaimed, as should be obvious, the greatest expression and moving of the Holy Spirit that has ever been seen or known. The miracles performed were literally beyond human comprehension. There is no way that mere words could adequately describe all that Christ did and said. But yet, the opposition by the Pharisees and others was fierce.

4. He was truly *"despised and rejected of men"* (Isa. 53:3). Actually, virtually all of the religious hierarchy hated Him and sought with every means at their disposal to stop His ministry, which they ultimately did by murdering Him on the Cross.

5. Even though the spiritual direction of the disciples may have been misplaced at times, as is here evident, still, with the exception of Judas, they loved Jesus and stood with Him and for Him, despite the attitude or opinions of others. While they would have some difficulty, as we shall see, at the crucifixion, still, they would climb out over this time of terrible spiritual darkness, with the day of Pentecost bringing an infilling of the Holy Spirit, which would make them veritable giants for Christ.

6. So, the moral of this statement by Christ, among other things, is that we must continue with Him, not only in His miracles, blessings, and good things but, as well, in the reproach. Actually, it is impossible to have the redemption without the reproach. Unfortunately, many want the positive but not the negative. Such is not to be!

7. So, even though Jesus foreknew that they would all forsake Him, yet, in His most wonderful and tender love, He praised their fidelity and courage and promised them a recompense all out of proportion to their service, as we shall see.

(29) "AND I APPOINT UNTO YOU A KINGDOM, AS MY FATHER HAS APPOINTED UNTO ME."

THE KINGDOM

The phrase, *"And I appoint unto you a kingdom,"* is actually twofold:

1. The kingdom of God was already in their hearts due to their being *"born again"* (Jn. 3:3). However, the total fulfillment of this passage has to do with the coming kingdom age, which will commence at the second coming, and will join the material and physical with the spiritual. Then the kingdom of God will cover the world in every sense.

2. As well, this pertains not only to the disciples but to every believer. All resurrected saints will have part in the coming kingdom of God (Dan. 7:18, 27; Rom. 8:17; I Cor. 4:8; 6:2-3; II Tim. 2:12; Rev. 5:10; 20:4-6).

The phrase, *"As My Father has appointed unto Me,"* is at least one of the greatest statements ever uttered.

THE KINGDOM AT THE BEGINNING

At that particular time, there were probably only a few hundred, or at the most, a few thousand in this kingdom, but now can be numbered by the hundreds of millions, not counting the vast number who have already gone on to be with the Lord. As well, the story of the civilized world has been the story of this kingdom. It alone is the source of all blessing, improvement, technological advancement, and above all, freedoms afforded mankind. The hinge is on this kingdom alone.

In extending this kingdom, Paul, *"Assayed to go into Bithynia"* which was toward the east, *"but the Spirit suffered them not"* (Acts 16:7).

Instead, the Lord *"in a vision"* called them to Macedonia, which was due west (Acts 16:9-10). As a result, the gospel went to Spain and then to England and other parts of Europe. From England it ultimately came to North America, with pilgrims coming to this new land, looking for freedom to worship God as they chose.

CIVILIZATION AND THE GOSPEL

In looking at civilization and its spread around the world, if one is to be honest, one must conclude that civilization followed the gospel, and not that the gospel followed civilization.

If honesty continues to be entertained, it would have to be said that England and America, as nations, have contributed more toward the advancement of civilization and the freedoms of mankind than any other nations in the world. This is solely because of the gospel of Jesus Christ, i.e., the kingdom of God.

Of course, the struggle has been long and hard. Catholicism, which is not a part of the kingdom of God, fought long and hard for supremacy in England and was finally overthrown only by the Church of England, which was little better than Catholicism, if any at all, only that it gave no allegiance to the pope in Rome or elsewhere.

However, through the ministry and preaching of men such as John Wesley, etc., a great move of God came to England, despite the state church, which ushered England into a force for the betterment of humanity all over the world. This does not mean that wrongs and ill guided direction were not taken, but that overall, greater good was brought about.

OUTPOURING OF THE HOLY SPIRIT

The great advancement of the kingdom of God in America saw mighty revivals almost from its beginning as a nation. Along with that, the mighty outpouring of the Holy Spirit, which actually began at the turn of the 20th century, catapulted America, and above all the kingdom of God, into an even greater development. Regrettably, England did not accept the outpouring of the Holy Spirit as readily as America and has, consequently, deteriorated in power and influence from that time.

With the outpouring of the Holy Spirit came, as well, an advancement in technology unparalleled in history. Yes, this scientific advancement, as predicted by Daniel the prophet, is directly tied to the pouring out of the Holy Spirit (Dan. 12:4).

If one is to notice, almost all technological advancement has taken place in the 20th century going into the 21st, with almost all scientific achievement taking place in America and England, the two nations which most experienced and embraced this outpouring at the beginning, although, as stated, England not nearly as much as America.

It must ever be understood that Jesus Christ is the head of this kingdom, with such granted to Him by the Father; consequently, everything is tied to Him in one way or the other.

(30) "THAT YOU MAY EAT AND DRINK AT MY TABLE IN MY KINGDOM, AND SIT ON THRONES JUDGING THE TWELVE TRIBES OF ISRAEL."

The construction is:

1. The phrase, *"That you may eat and drink at My table in My kingdom,"* proclaims that the glory of the royal table and the kingly throne should effectually destroy the petty ambition of the childish attempts to be chiefs and greatest.

2. To be sure, they were very poor servants, but no servants ever had such an admiring, compassionate, and tender Master.

3. The eating and drinking at His table has reference to the coming kingdom age, as mentioned in Verse 18. This tells us that it will be a literal kingdom and not one in Spirit only. Then, as now, it is Spirit only but, ultimately, as stated, will be realized in totality.

4. *"And sit on thrones judging the twelve tribes of Israel,"* is a privilege which will be enjoyed only by the twelve apostles, with Matthias having taken the place of Judas. Other duties all around the world relating to the government of Christ will be relegated to all other believers.

5. The twelve tribes are mentioned four times in the New Testament (here and in Mat. 19:28; Acts 26:7; and James 1:1). They still exist.

6. During the coming kingdom age when Jesus will rule supreme over the entirety of the world from Jerusalem, Israel will once again be the predominant nation in the world under Christ. She will, in effect, serve the Lord as originally intended as a nation of priests, with certain duties ascribed to each of the twelve tribes (Ezek., Chpts. 40-48). At that time, the twelve apostles will serve as the supreme judges of the twelve tribes, with David as king and Jesus as King of Kings and Lord of Lords of the

entirety of the world (Ezek. 37:24; Hos. 3:5; Rev. 19:16).

7. During the coming kingdom age, this rule and authority will be literal, respecting an eternal earthly kingdom, and not just a spiritual rule over the church.

(31) "AND THE LORD SAID, SIMON, SIMON, BEHOLD, SATAN HAS DESIRED TO HAVE YOU, THAT HE MAY SIFT YOU AS WHEAT."

SATAN

The phrase, *"And the Lord said, Simon, Simon,"* is the same voice that said, *"Abraham, Abraham,"* (Gen. 22:11).

"Behold, Satan has desired to have you," portrays to us a glimpse into the spirit world, which was very similar to the same request made by Satan concerning Job (1:12). Consequently, we should understand that these are examples of what is constantly going on in that world so close to us, but yet, unknown to most individuals unless revealed by the Lord.

SATAN'S DESIRES

The word *desired* in the Greek text is *ex-aiteo* and means "to demand" or "to obtain by asking."

Satan asked that he may tempt and try the apostles. He had already tempted Judas, and he had won him. Possibly this signal victory encouraged him to make this request.

We may imagine the Evil One arguing thus before the Eternal:

"These chosen ones who are appointed to work in the future so tremendous a work in Your name are utterly unworthy. Let me try to lure them away with my lures. Lo, they will surely fall. See, one has already fallen."

The phrase, *"That he may sift you as wheat,"* tells us that the Lord drew the parameters, beyond which, Satan could not go.

Satan sifts to get rid of the corn; God winnows to get rid of the chaff (Mat. 3:12; I Pet. 5:8-9).

It seems that this attack upon Peter by Satan, and granted by the Lord, was possibly in respect to his desire for greatness.

Satan tempts in order to bring out the bad, while God tests to bring out the good.

Of course, one wonders why the Lord

would allow Satan such latitude, especially considering the damage done and the spiritual frailty of believers in general.

THE SPIRIT WORLD

From what little we know about the spirit world, especially considering this type of situation, it seems that Satan does have some latitude, but with parameters drawn by the Lord. Such latitude seems to rest with the type of call on a person's life. In other words, if God places a certain call of tremendous significance on a person's life, consequently, giving him the anointing of the Spirit to carry out that call, it seems that Satan, as with Job and Peter, is allowed greater freedom of action regarding such an individual.

Sometime ago in addressing a group of preachers, I made a statement concerning the jealousy and envy that seems to persist among some preachers regarding other preachers who are called for particular tasks, which seems to attract a certain amount of popularity, etc.

I told them of how such a call of God makes one a target for the powers of darkness, and from what we see here, it is allowed by the Lord. Much, if not most of the time, it results in tremendous suffering. I stated that if they only knew this, there would be precious little jealousy or envy. If one is truly called of God for a particular task of great significance to the kingdom of God, to be sure, Satan, as here, will level all his forces at that individual in order to stop him or her. Of that, one can be certain.

THE REASON?

Of course, the stock answer is that God gives enough power that no thrust by Satan, irrespective of its strength, can prevail. While that is true, it is also the ideal. The truth is that within every armor, one might say, there is a flaw.

Actually, unless the individual, no matter who he or she might be, understands the Cross of Christ as it regards victorious living, such a person is doomed to failure, irrespective of the call of God on his heart and life. God has one way of salvation, which is Christ and the Cross, and one way of victory

regarding our life and living, and that is Christ and the Cross. Unfortunately, precious few individuals understand the Cross of Christ as it regards everyday living for the Lord. Consequently, the failures are absolutely mind boggling.

As someone has said, "Desperation always precedes revelation." This means that the Lord, at times, allows Satan certain latitude in order that pressure may be applied to the individual so that the flaw can be found and cured in no other manner. It must be understood that such temptations and testing are not allowed by the Lord in order that He may know the extent of our faith, for He already knows, but, in effect, that we may know. Jesus knew the weaknesses of Peter, but Peter did not know. As well, it seems from the text that irrespective of what Jesus said, Peter still would not know until he was made to face the powers of darkness in his own frail strength. Then he realized how weak he really was and how far from true greatness.

However, on the other hand, there is no evidence that Satan was allowed latitude with Job, respecting personal weakness, as Peter. Some may argue that when he finally saw the Lord, he exclaimed, *"Behold, I am vile"* (Job 40:4), proving such weakness.

However, there is no one, irrespective of how holy one may be, who, upon seeing the Lord as Job did, would not exclaim the same.

THE WORTHLESSNESS OF SELF

Job was made to discover the worthlessness of self, irrespective of his perfection concerning his efforts to obey God (Job 1:1). Actually, this is the first step in the Christian experience, with the Song of Solomon proclaiming the worthiness of Christ as the last step. However, the Song of Solomon can never be reached until Job has been first passed through.

It is evident that the unconverted man needs to be brought to the end of himself, but that a man who feared God, who was perfect in his efforts and who hated evil, should also need this is not so clear, even to many mature Christians.

The simple truth is that God, at times, uses Satan as His instrument in addressing the character, causing men to seek God's holiness rather than their own. Such is described with Job and Peter. Satan was the instrument, but the hand that used him was God's. The fact of these experiences with men such as Job and Peter is to explain to believers, who, like these two, are conscious of personal integrity, why calamities and sorrows are permitted to afflict them.

For instance, the creed of both Job and Peter was orthodox, for Job approached God through sacrifice, and Peter followed Christ from obedience, devotion, and dedication.

From outward appearances, it seems that the conduct of both Job and Peter was faultless; however, the sharp trials that came to both revealed to them unknown depths of moral ugliness. Job's challenge to measure himself with God and Peter's challenge to measure up to his own boasts made both conscious that in their flesh, there dwelt no good thing. This is a deep and painful experience that all believers have not reached and, in fact, cannot reach without being subjected to similar tests as Job and Peter.

THE VISION OF THE BURNING OF THE CHAFF

In 1982 (I believe it was), while in Guatemala City, Guatemala, in a crusade, the Lord gave me a vision concerning the sifting of the wheat and, more particularly, the burning of the chaff. It was sometime after midnight, and I had arisen to go into the adjoining room to pray about the coming meeting and other things.

As the Lord brought this vision of the threshingfloor before my eyes, I plainly saw the chaff completely separated from the wheat as it piled up somewhat on the ground around the threshingfloor. As well, I saw the flames hungrily lick at the chaff and burning it, exactly as described in the Scripture (Mat. 3:12).

As the Spirit of God moved upon me mightily that night, and with the vision of the burning chaff in stark relief before my eyes, I asked the Lord as to the necessity of the burning of this refuse, especially considering that it had been fully separated from the wheat and was not actually even on the threshingfloor any longer.

NO TRACE LEFT

The Lord answered me in beautiful simplicity by saying, "There must be no trace left of the flesh, of which the chaff is a type."

At that particular time, little did I realize exactly what that vision meant and how it would pertain to me personally.

As with Job and Peter and, no doubt, millions of others, I felt the terrible pain, although an absolute necessity of the burning of the chaff with unquenchable fire. But yet, it has served to draw me closer to God than I have ever been in my life.

In the spring of 1988, with my ministry in pieces, with a thousand questions unanswered, and with my name a joke over the entirety of the world, I remember awaking early one morning before daylight, that is, if I had ever been to sleep, and asking the Lord why such had to be, and more particularly, why in this manner.

Public humiliation is of such portent that most do not survive it, especially on a worldwide scale. Actually, without the grace of God, I don't think such would be survivable.

Realizing that Job's friends are abundant, and with their recriminations, they seem to have all the answers, still, to those few who truly know God, the answers, if any at all, are not that simple.

That early morning hour as the hot tears burned my cheeks, and when death would have seemed pleasant, the Lord, I believe, gently spoke to me.

He said, "You have asked Me why? I will answer you in this manner.

"As I crippled Jacob, I had to cripple you, and whatever I do with you in the future, you will always be reminded by the limp."

(32) "BUT I HAVE PRAYED FOR YOU, THAT YOUR FAITH FAIL NOT: AND WHEN YOU ARE CONVERTED, STRENGTHEN YOUR BRETHREN."

THE LORD PRAYED FOR PETER

The phrase, *"But I have prayed for you,"* tells us two things:

1. Satan was granted his request but with parameters.

2. Jesus had interceded on Peter's behalf, which guaranteed a positive result.

As well, as Jesus prayed for Peter, one can feel certain that He has prayed for all of us at times. The Scripture says, *"Wherefore He is able also to save them to the uttermost who come unto God by Him, seeing He ever lives to make intercession for them"* (Heb. 7:25). The pronoun *"them"* includes you and me.

"That your faith fail not," tells us that Satan's attack is always delivered against faith, for if faith fails, all fails.

THE DARK MOMENT OF DESPAIR

Someone has said that the appointed time contemplated in this prayer was not the moment of Peter's denial, but the dark moment of despair when the dark deed was already done, with him going out and weeping bitterly. Then Satan must have whispered to him: "You have committed spiritual suicide; now you are mine"; but the Lord's look, as evidenced in Verse 61, was that which upheld his faith and will uphold ours as well.

IF A PERSON'S FAITH DOES NOT FALL, HAVE THEY IN FACT FALLEN?

Of course, one can judge failure in many ways. However, the type of failure pointed to here is that of which we speak.

The answer has to be a resounding "no!" While Peter did fail, he did not fall! While he denied the Lord three times, which, within itself, is certainly failure, still, that speaks only of the battle and not the war. While he lost the battle, he did not lose the war. Judas lost not only the battle but the war, as well; consequently, his failure was the ultimate failure.

No believer is judged fallen by God who continues to trust Christ. Were that not so, the entirety of the Christian family would have to be judged as fallen. While it is true that all of us, at one time or the other, lose battles, that does not mean we lose the war. We only fall when we quit. Peter did not quit; Judas did!

What did Jesus mean by Peter's faith failing?

He was speaking of that which Judas did in refusing to trust Christ any longer by not coming to Him, asking for forgiveness. The faith of Judas failed when he turned

NOTES

away from the Lord instead of unto the Lord.

Peter did not fail in the ultimate test, even though he did fail in the primary test, because he turned to the Lord instead of away from the Lord.

As we say often at Family Worship Center, "If you don't quit, God won't quit!"

When remembering the time that Abraham was seeking the Lord about sparing Lot, knowing that Sodom and Gomorrah where Lot was, was going to be destroyed, we must remember that Abraham quit asking before God quit giving.

THE CALL OF GOD

"And when you are converted," does not pertain to conversion, i.e., to be born again, as many think. The word *conversion* in the Greek text is *epistrepho* and means "to turn towards," and in this case, to turn toward Christ exactly as Peter did, but Judas would not.

"Strengthen your brethren," should be obvious as to its meaning.

It has to do with the statement of Jesus to Peter after the resurrection, *"Feed My sheep"* (Jn. 21:15-17).

He was, in fact, telling Peter, and all others in similar circumstances, that the call of God had not been abrogated by that which had happened. Of course, it should be obvious because if such were true—the call rescinded—no one called of God would be able to continue. All have failed in some respect, and while possibly not known by others, is definitely known by God.

As well, Peter was called to be a leader, hence, the word *"strengthen your brethren."* That position was not abrogated either!

If one does not understand this, then one does not understand the grace of God. Either the blood of Jesus cleanses from all sin as the Word says (I Jn. 1:7), or else, it doesn't, and the Bible is a lie. I know it does, and everyone who claims to know the same thing should conduct themselves accordingly.

As well, and last, Peter was still a brother, as other believers were to him *"brethren."*

MODERN ERROR

And yet, if Peter had been an ordained minister with many modern denominations, it would have been demanded of him that he not preach for a period of two years, or some such period of time, and that he undergo several months, if not years, of psychological counseling, with a sign-off from a psychologist before any ministry could be engaged at any time, at least with that denomination.

Consequently, Simon Peter would not have been allowed to be in the temple on the day of Pentecost because he would not have been worthy to associate with the others, especially considering what he did. Therefore, he, as well, would not have preached the inaugural message on that great day, which resulted in *"about three thousand"* being saved (Acts 2:41).

Also, Peter could not have been with John when the lame man was healed at the gate called Beautiful simply because, for a probationary period of time, Peter would not have been worthy to associate with John, at least according to some modern denominations.

The sermon he preached after the healing of the lame man, which resulted in about 5,000 men being saved, besides the women and children (Acts 4:4), could not have been preached, at least by Peter. Actually, Peter would have had to be removed, at least according to these denominations, for much of the happenings of the book of Acts.

THE BIBLE MUST BE THE CRITERION

Such foolishness, and foolishness it is, is a blatant denial of the grace of God, the precious blood of Jesus, and faith in that atoning work. The idea that one must subscribe to some silly rules of men, which have no scriptural foundation whatsoever, proclaims a total misunderstanding respecting justification by faith, which is the bedrock of all that is Christian.

In the idea of punishment, they seem to forget that Jesus was punished for our sins on the Cross of Calvary. For us to administer more punishment is, in effect, saying that what Jesus suffered was not enough, and we have to add more to what He has already done. This is an insult of unprecedented proportions to our Lord and must anger the Lord greatly. To repudiate what He did at the Cross, and such activity is most definitely a repudiation of His finished

NOTES

work, is a sin far worse than anyone realizes.

In truth, if one adds anything to the finished work of Christ, Paul emphatically stated, *"Christ is become of no effect unto you, whosoever of you are justified by the law* (or works of your own making)*; you are fallen from grace"* (Gal. 5:4).

Either the Word of God is the criterion for all that we do and believe, or else, we can ignore the Bible, consequently, making up our own rules as we go along, exactly as do many religious denominations, which, in effect, is no faith at all. The moment one takes away or adds to the finished work of Christ, one has abrogated all that Christ did. Either the blood of Jesus cleanses from all sin, or it doesn't. I know it does (I Jn. 1:7).

There is no such thing as probation with God, which, within itself, crassly states that what Jesus did was not sufficient and needs certain things added, which is blasphemy.

Thank the Lord that Peter was not a member of some of these modern denominations, but was rather a follower of Christ. As such, he received that which only Christ could give, and continues to give we might quickly add.

(33) "AND HE SAID UNTO HIM, LORD, I AM READY TO GO WITH YOU, BOTH INTO PRISON, AND TO DEATH."

The synopsis is:

1. The phrase, *"And he said unto Him,"* represents Peter, no doubt, sincere but totally unable within himself to carry out his boasts.

2. *"Lord, I am ready to go with You, both into prison, and to death,"* I think constituted Peter's true feelings, at least at the time; however, the actual event, which would come very soon, would prove to be far more than he could ever think of handling within his own strength.

3. Many love to paint Peter as a loud-mouthed braggart, who could little back up his boasts. That is not the case.

4. He was a man who truly loved Christ, and, as stated, I believe he meant what he said. Nevertheless, his spiritual strength, because it was woefully misplaced, was not nearly as strong as he thought. Consequently, he not only would not go to prison, much less die for the Lord, but would not

even make it past the first little girl who pointed him out. To be sure, that which he would learn the hard way would ultimately come to fruition exactly as he had stated. Tradition says that at the end of his ministry, Peter died on a cross, crucified upside down, because he felt he was not worthy to die as his master had died.

5. The statement as rendered by Jesus to Peter is very brief. As such, Peter, no doubt, did not understand what Jesus was actually saying. After the fact, it is very easy for us to presently point out Peter's foibles; however, had we been in his shoes, I wonder if we would have done any better, and probably not even as well!

(34) "AND HE SAID, I TELL YOU, PETER, THE COCK SHALL NOT CROW THIS DAY, BEFORE THAT YOU SHALL THRICE DENY THAT YOU KNOW ME."

THE LORD'S ANSWER TO PETER

The phrase, "And He said, I tell you, Peter," constitutes the words of Christ and comes from the one Who truly knows all.

What must Peter have thought when he heard the prediction concerning his denial of Christ, and even "this day"?

Luke did not mention it, but Matthew stated that Peter answered Christ, exclaiming that he would die before he would deny the Master. As well, all the disciples said the same thing (Mat. 26:34-35).

So, if Peter little understood what Jesus had said respecting Satan sifting him as wheat, he surely had no problem whatsoever in understanding what Jesus said about the denials.

The phrase, "The cock (rooster) shall not crow this day, before that you shall thrice (three times) deny that you know Me," pinpoints the time and exactly the number of times this would happen.

If one is to notice, Jesus had been addressing Peter as "Simon," while now addressing him as "Peter."

Why?

PETER

The name Peter means "rock or stone" so, in effect, Jesus was telling him that even though he was not now Peter, i.e., a rock, as his new name implies, nevertheless, despite the coming denials, he would ultimately become Peter, the rock.

I know the use of this name by Jesus meant nothing to Peter at this moment, but later, upon recalling this incident, which he, no doubt, did many times, it had to be a source of great encouragement.

If a person truly loves the Lord, as Peter surely did, failure in any capacity is a terrible thing. All have failed, and sadly, this is not a rare occurrence. Still, for one who has been given a greater responsibility by the Lord, which Peter certainly enjoyed, any type of failure, especially one so severe as denying the Saviour, quickly becomes a weight that is unbearable. Were it not for the grace of God, an individual under such circumstances could not understand the spiritual results of such an action.

THE SYMPTOM

Actually, Peter's failure was more a symptom than anything else. It is the same with us presently. Unfortunately, the modern church little knows or understands what causes the problem; therefore, it treats the symptom, which does no good at all.

Failure always results in the believer in some way minimizing the Cross or forsaking it altogether. The only answer for sin, temptation, etc., is the Cross of Christ. Paul said:

"But this man (this priest, Christ Jesus), after He had offered one sacrifice for sins forever (speaks of the Cross), sat down on the right hand of God (refers to the great contrast with the priests under the Levitical system, who never sat down because their work was never completed; the work of Christ on the Cross was a 'finished work' and needed no repetition)" (Heb. 10:12). Let me say it again:

The only answer for sin is the Cross of Christ. In other words, the believer must understand that Jesus addressed all sin at the Cross, past, present, and future, at least for all who will believe, and, as well, defeated every power of darkness from Satan down (Col. 2:10-15). So, the believer will never get victory over sin unless his or her faith is exclusively in Christ and the Cross.

Unfortunately, many think they can fast so many days and that will take care of sin, or they can quote certain Scriptures and that will defeat sin, but they will find to their dismay that the only answer for sin is the Cross of Christ. As long as we are treating the symptoms, we will never get to the root of the problem. It is only when we understand the Cross of Christ relative to the sin question, and we realize that there is no victory outside of the Cross, that we will then begin to find victory within our hearts and lives. Otherwise, it will be one failure after the other.

(35) "AND HE SAID UNTO THEM, WHEN I SENT YOU WITHOUT PURSE, AND SCRIP, AND SHOES, LACKED YOU ANY THING? AND THEY SAID, NOTHING."

The composition is:

1. The phrase, *"And He said unto them,"* presents a complete change of subject matter.

2. Even though His own crucifixion was looming just ahead, His thoughts were centered more so on the future of His disciples than even His own tragic destiny.

3. The question, *"When I sent you without purse, and scrip, and shoes, lacked you (did you lack) any thing?"* speaks of the last three and one-half years of their public ministry. These were the halcyon days when they had the favor of the people; consequently, they were greeted with applause and, no doubt, due to the many healings and miracles, money and necessities were thrust upon them, etc.

4. *"And they said, Nothing,"* speaks of every need being abundantly met. Even though the needs will continue to be met, still, *He will send them forth as lambs in the midst of wolves* (Lk. 10:3). As such, they would meet with much hostility and opposition.

(36) "THEN SAID HE UNTO THEM, BUT NOW, HE WHO HAS A PURSE, LET HIM TAKE IT, AND LIKEWISE HIS SCRIP: AND HE WHO HAS NO SWORD, LET HIM SELL HIS GARMENT, AND BUY ONE."

A DIFFERENT SET OF RULES

The phrase, *"Then said He unto them,"* would now present a different set of rules.

"But now, he who has a purse, let him

take it, and likewise his scrip," simply meant that their needs, although supplied, would not be done nearly as easily as in the past. Paul exampled this from time to time, earning his daily bread as a tentmaker.

When Paul went into new areas to plant churches, he was dealing mostly with pagans, and naturally, they would have no thought whatsoever before their conversion to give money to the work of the Lord. Even after many were saved, with the church being planted, especially when it came to his own personal upkeep, Paul made little effort in some places to receive funds for himself. However, he did make strong appeals for things other than his own (II Cor., Chpts. 8-9).

PROVERBIAL AND SYMBOLIC EXPRESSIONS

As well, the words of Jesus tell us that those who are truly called by Him must not be afraid to labor with their own hands if necessary. If any man thinks himself too good to do the type of things even that Paul did to earn a living in order that he may preach the gospel, then he is not needed and, in fact, cannot be used in the kingdom of God. A person who is truly called of God must be willing to do anything, irrespective of how menial it may be. If the man or woman does not have that type of attitude, then they might as well forget working for God because the Lord simply cannot use them.

"And he who has no sword, let him sell his garment, and buy one," presents this as a symbolism.

Actually, *"the purse," "the scrip," "the sword,"* and *"the garment"* are proverbial and symbolic expressions. They mean that during Christ's absence, if necessary, they were to perform manual labor to earn their daily bread and, as well, were to accept the protection of an ordered government. The term *"sword"* means the power of the magistrate (Rom. 13:4).

Paul accepted and claimed the protection of the sword in Acts 16:37; 21:39; and 25:11.

When the Lord was with them as king, He demonstrated His ability to supply all their needs. While He certainly would continue to do this, still, during the time of His rejection, they were to be rejected with Him, as has been the case from then until now.

(37) "FOR I SAY UNTO YOU, THAT THIS THAT IS WRITTEN MUST YET BE ACCOMPLISHED IN ME, AND HE WAS RECKONED AMONG THE TRANSGRESSORS: FOR THE THINGS CONCERNING ME HAVE AN END."

The structure is:

1. The phrase, *"For I say unto you, that this that is written must yet be accomplished in Me,"* refers to Isaiah, Chapter 53, and is the first time the Lord refers to that text, which is the most complete and preeminent of all the predictions concerning His passion.

2. The great price that Jesus would pay for the redemption of humanity had begun in the mind of God even before the *"foundation of the world"* (I Pet. 1:20). It was now mere days from being accomplished.

3. The pronoun *"Me"* proclaims that He was the only one who could do such a thing, hence, the reason for God becoming man, i.e., the incarnation.

4. *"And He was reckoned among the transgressors,"* is taken from Isaiah 53:12.

5. This does not mean that He was a transgressor, for He was not. Actually, He would be crucified not for His own sins, for He had none, but as Isaiah said, *"For the transgression of my people was He stricken"* (Isa. 53:8).

6. The word *"numbered,"* as used by Isaiah, or *"reckoned,"* as used by Jesus, means that Israel considered Him a transgressor even though they could find no wrongdoing for which He could be charged. So, their accusation was, *"Because He made Himself the Son of God"* (Jn. 19:7).

7. In this there was no transgression because He actually was the Son of God!

8. *"For the things concerning Me have an end,"* concerned that which He would do very shortly—die on Calvary and be raised from the dead. The plan and prediction of the ages were now about to be satisfied. The promise had been given immediately after the fall in the garden of Eden. The seed of the woman would bruise the head of Satan, even though Satan would *"bruise His* (Jesus') *heel,"* i.e., the crucifixion (Gen. 3:15).

NOTES

(38) "AND THEY SAID, LORD, BEHOLD, HERE ARE TWO SWORDS. AND HE SAID UNTO THEM, IT IS ENOUGH."

THE SWORD

The phrase, *"And they said, Lord, behold, here are two swords,"* proclaims that they did not understand that to which He referred concerning the purchasing of a sword. They took it literally whereas He was speaking symbolically respecting the authority of Gentile nations, etc. As we have stated, He was referring to the protection of an ordered government. Consequently, as stated, when the Jews attempted to kill Paul, he claimed the protection of the sword, as recorded in Acts 16:37; 21:39; and 25:11. The following is extreme, but I believe it to be true.

That sword protects the gospel, at least to a certain extent, all over the world. For instance, even in America, many of those in positions of religious leadership would stop any and all proclamations of the gospel, at least that which did not agree with their brand, except for the power of the sword, i.e., the law of the land. As well, if the sword did not protect such freedoms in any country, Catholicism, at least where it rules, would stop by force any and all who were opposed to that religion, as they did for centuries. So, in Verse 36, He was speaking of the power of the magistrate.

And yet, in many places, this sword has not been for the benefit of the believer, but rather his harm.

THE GOSPEL OF JESUS CHRIST

The phrase, *"And He said unto them, It is enough,"* proclaims Him making no attempt to correct their false assumption in the securing of two swords, knowing that the meaning would become abundantly clear after the day of Pentecost.

In twisting these passages, the Catholic Church perverted its intent in the famous Bull of Pope Boniface VIII, which he claimed gave him both secular and spiritual power that resulted in indescribable torture and death for untold thousands of believers for several hundreds of years.

The gospel of Jesus Christ is never to be propagated by the sword, or any type of force. It is to be done solely through the power, person, and agency of the Holy Spirit, and all strictly on spiritual terms. While the power of the magistrate is definitely given to secular government (Rom. 13:1-6), it is never given in any form to the church. Such action, or the spirit of such action, which characterizes many religious denominations, is an abrogation of our Lord's position as the head of the church.

(39) "AND HE CAME OUT, AND WENT, AS HE WAS WONT, TO THE MOUNT OF OLIVES; AND HIS DISCIPLES ALSO FOLLOWED HIM."

The exposition is:

1. The phrase, *"And He came out, and went, as He was wont* (accustomed), *to the Mount of Olives,"* constitutes the beginning of the agony in the garden. This was a place that Jesus often frequented when He was in the Jerusalem area. Evidently, it afforded a place of solitude and privacy.

2. I have been to the garden of Gethsemane several times. It faces the eastern wall of Jerusalem, with the brook Kidron running between the Mount of Olives, where the garden is located, and the wall.

3. An olive grove is still situated on the side of the mountain, with some of the trees claimed to be 2,000 years old or older. If, in fact, that is the case, that would mean that a few of these trees would have been there at the time of Jesus.

4. On our last trip to this sacred place, upon observing one of the trees that definitely looked to be of antiquity, it is very difficult to properly explain exactly how I felt, knowing that the possibility did exist that the agony of Christ could have taken place near this very same tree, and most definitely in the vicinity.

5. The phrase, *"And His disciples also followed Him,"* proclaims, it seems, them not quite knowing what He was going to do and what the occasion would present. The very word *"Gethsemane"* signifies "oil-press," and is a fitting symbol for that which He would endure.

(40) "AND WHEN HE WAS AT THE PLACE, HE SAID UNTO THEM, PRAY THAT YOU ENTER NOT INTO TEMPTATION."

THE PLACE OF SURRENDER

The phrase, *"And when He was at the place,"* spoke of far more than mere location. It was to be the place of surrender and spoke of surrender to the will of God.

This place of surrender is that to which every believer must come. For millions of Christians, Jesus is Saviour, but He is not Lord. Many have claimed that this cannot be; however, for anyone to think that Jesus is Lord, and completely so, in the hearts and lives of all believers is simply not facing facts. In reality, this struggle between the flesh and the Spirit is an ongoing process, which literally wrestles for supremacy of the soul. James said, *"The Spirit who dwells in us lusts to envy"* (James 4:5). This simply means that the Spirit of God, who dwells in the believer (I Cor. 3:16), is envious of any control held by the world, i.e., Satan. If Jesus were Lord in every aspect of every believer's life, such Scriptures would make no sense.

So, the battle rages constantly for this supremacy, even as evidenced by Christ in His passion as Satan attempted to pull Him away from the will of God. However, Satan did not succeed in any capacity. Nevertheless, millions of believers have come to this place and have refused to surrender to the will of God. Consequently, their spiritual growth stopped, with no fruit being brought forth, which will have dire spiritual consequences if continued.

TEMPTATION

The phrase, *"He said unto them, Pray that you enter not into temptation,"* tells us several things:

• As we have already stated, this temptation to subvert the will of God is ever present, even as it was with Christ. This is, no doubt, the believer's greatest area of conflict and the soil on which Satan spends his greatest efforts.

One could probably say that every single temptation, irrespective of its direction, is for the purpose of subverting the will of God in the life of the believer. The believer is to follow the Word of God, which is the will of God.

• There is only one defense against this type of attack, and that is that the believer make certain that his faith is anchored squarely in Christ and what Christ has done for us at the Cross, and with that followed by prayer. Jesus said *"pray!"*

It is sad that many in the modern church presently recommend other things. I speak of modern psychology. As well, I speak of pastoral counseling, which uses the methods of psychology. I speak also of the confession principle, which claims that we do not really have to pray because prayer is an admission of need, and the new creation man, they say, has need of nothing.

• The entire episode, as presented by Jesus, speaks of a trap or snare laid by Satan, which has a very powerful lure by the suggestion of another way other than God's way. If one leaves the prescribed way of the Cross and of prayer, which almost all do, the results will not and, in fact, cannot be victory.

(41) "AND HE WAS WITHDRAWN FROM THEM ABOUT A STONE'S CAST, AND KNEELED DOWN, AND PRAYED."

The synopsis is:

1. The phrase, "And He was withdrawn from them about a stone's cast," is only mentioned by Luke.

2. Peter, James, and John went with Him that extra distance (Mat. 26:37; Mk. 14:33).

3. *"And kneeled down, and prayed,"* tells us that if Jesus had to do this, and we speak of prayer, His servants should imitate Him.

(42) "SAYING, FATHER, IF YOU BE WILLING, REMOVE THIS CUP FROM ME: NEVERTHELESS NOT MY WILL, BUT THINE, BE DONE."

THE WILL OF GOD

The phrase, *"Saying, Father, if You be willing, remove this cup from Me,"* spoke of that which He would have to drink in the spiritual sense.

The ancients assigned to each guest at a feast a cup of wine, which, by its quality, expressed the respect given to the recipient. So, the word *"cup,"* came to signify a portion either of pleasure or of pain.

The Lord's agony in Gethsemane cannot have been that which is proper to a mere

NOTES

man, for multitudes of martyrs have gone joyfully and courageously to the most fearful deaths.

Hebrews 5:7 shows the wrath of God that was to judge Him as if He, and He alone, was the only sinner that ever existed, and this caused that agony. So, His death was not just a great example of resignation and self-sacrifice, as multitudes vainly think.

THE PRICE OF SURRENDER

The phrase, *"Nevertheless not My will, but Thine* (Yours), *be done,"* suggests to us the price of surrender.

We had the place, and now we have the price.

What is the price?

It is the willingness to obey the will of God, irrespective of its direction.

Mark recorded that Jesus said, *"Abba, Father, all things are possible unto You,"* meaning that His Father, being able to do all things, could effect salvation in another way (Mk. 14:36).

However, even though another way may have been more satisfactory to the flesh, it would not have been the will of God because as grievous as this way was, it was the best way and, therefore, the will of God.

As we have stated, this is ever the battleground of the soul. It is our will versus God's will. To be sure, God has only one will, which is His perfect will, which rules out that commonly referred to as a permissive will. Paul said, *"That you may prove what is that good, and acceptable, and perfect, will of God"* (Rom. 12:2).

(43) "AND THERE APPEARED AN ANGEL UNTO HIM FROM HEAVEN, STRENGTHENING HIM."

The form is:

1. Several things are told us in this passage:

THE PEACE OF SURRENDER

We had the place of surrender and the price of surrender, and now we have the peace of surrender. However, it was not the taking away of the agony, i.e., *the cup,* but rather strengthening Him to stand the agony. This tells us that it was so awful, even as we have stated, such as no human being has ever suffered, that if it had not been for this extra strength, He would have died, as Satan, no doubt, was attempting to do.

2. This shows us that angels at times are dispatched by the Father from heaven in order to help. Such is evidenced by an angel opening the prison doors in order that Peter and the other apostles might go free (Acts 5:17-20).

3. How often this is done would depend on the need and is always at the discretion of the heavenly Father. I suspect that such is done more often than one realizes, with such incidents not visible to the eye most of the time.

4. From this we learn that the Lord has not promised to remove all difficulties from us but will give us the strength to bear whatever is required. This is evidenced by Paul praying three times for the thorn in the flesh to be removed but was denied such and given the answer by the Lord, *"My grace is sufficient for you: for My strength is made perfect in weakness"* (II Cor. 12:7-9).

(44) "AND BEING IN AN AGONY HE PRAYED MORE EARNESTLY: AND HIS SWEAT WAS AS IT WERE GREAT DROPS OF BLOOD FALLING DOWN TO THE GROUND."

The diagram is:

1. The phrase, *"And being in an agony He prayed more earnestly,"* concerns the terrible conflict and its struggle.

2. This also tells us that as the struggle intensified, His praying, as well, intensified. Surely, this should portray to us the power of prayer.

3. The praying more earnestly does not mean that He was less earnest or sincere previously, but that He cried to His heavenly Father even in a greater agony of soul, if possible, knowing that this was the only means by which He could attain victory. Prayer was and is the only recourse. And yet, the modern church little believes in such, rather advocating the foolish prattle of Freudian psychology.

4. God help us!

5. *"And His sweat was as it were great drops of blood falling down to the ground,"* proclaims and portrays a recognized fact that under extreme mental pressure, the

pores may become so dilated that blood may issue from them so that there may be bloody sweat. A number of cases are on record of such agony. So, it is not parabolic, but rather literal.

(45) "AND WHEN HE ROSE UP FROM PRAYER, AND WAS COME TO HIS DISCIPLES, HE FOUND THEM SLEEPING FOR SORROW."

VICTORY WON

The phrase, *"And when He rose up from prayer, and was come to His disciples,"* signals the victory won, at least in this great struggle concerning the will of God.

It was not that Jesus did not want or desire to do the will of His Father, for doing such epitomized His very life. That was never in question. The agony consisted of what that will meant.

The cup He had to drink, symbolically speaking, consisted of all the vile sin of humanity heaped and dumped upon Him, and in a way that is absolutely incomprehensible to the heart of man. *"For He has made Him to be sin* ('a sin-offering') *for us, Who knew no sin"* (II Cor. 5:21).

To explain such, one cannot! As stated, it is beyond the comprehension of mere mortals.

SLEEP FOR SORROW

The degree of vileness that one could imagine would not even begin to scratch the surface of what this horror meant as He hung on Cavalry. Perhaps Psalm 22 expresses it to a greater degree than anything else, and yet, it takes one beyond what one can even begin to imagine.

"My God, My God, why have You forsaken Me? why are You so far from helping Me, and from the words of My roaring?" (Ps. 22:1).

At this horrible hour on Calvary, God had to forsake Him because God could not look upon sin, even though borne by His spotless, pure, perfect, and only Son.

The phrase, *"He found them sleeping for sorrow,"* is a statement that proclaims the agony of the time, which affected all who were around Jesus.

What did it mean exactly to sleep for sorrow?

The only answer that could be given is that the terrible weight of this oppression was of such severity that they simply did not have the strength to fight it off. Perhaps it is easy to criticize them, thinking that we would have done better; however, such is doubtful, very doubtful!

(46) "AND SAID UNTO THEM, WHY SLEEP YE? RISE AND PRAY, LEST YOU ENTER INTO TEMPTATION."

WHY DO YOU SLEEP?

The question, *"And said unto them, Why sleep ye (Why do you sleep)?"* presents the moment He awakened them. He did not expect an answer.

This particular time with the apostles, as with Jesus, was the hardest and most difficult of the past three and a half years. They were facing three things:

1. They were in error in interpreting the Scripture concerning the suffering Messiah, thinking He would use His power to forcibly install the kingdom at that time. Their mind-set was so much in this direction that they little understood His statements respecting the crucifixion and resurrection. Self-will was their problem.

2. The events, as they were now unfolding, made them realize that the situation was not as they had formerly thought. There was a foreboding in the air, which had begun sometime earlier, and had clouded the trip to Jerusalem from Galilee. The signs were ominous!

3. The oppression of Satan, the same oppression that attempted to kill Jesus prematurely, was now so strong that it mightily affected Peter, James, and John as well. They simply did not have the spiritual strength at the time to fight off this effort by hell itself and, accordingly, would ultimately fail.

RISE AND PRAY

The phrase, *"Rise and pray, lest you enter into temptation,"* once again emphasizes the only defense against the powers of darkness.

Perhaps it would have been better translated, *"Lest you succumb to temptation."*

I think the original text will bear it out

that the temptation within itself was unavoidable. It was their power to resist that was in question.

What kind of temptation?

It was the temptation to forsake Him and run, leaving Him to the merciless hatred of His enemies, which portrayed them as cowards woefully lacking in responsibility.

Regrettably, we know how grievously they all felt.

If Jesus was telling His disciples, as well as all others, that prayer is the only defense against this onslaught of Satan, and He definitely was, then we must come to the conclusion that almost all of the modern church is constantly succumbing to temptation simply because the modern church is precious little a people of prayer. Thankfully, the events of this time, coupled with the infilling of the Holy Spirit on the day of Pentecost, would drastically change these men for the better. Regrettably, most of the church world is not changed primarily because there is no Pentecost or prayer in their lives.

These men would become prayer giants in the very near future (Acts 6:4).

(47) "AND WHILE HE YET SPOKE, BEHOLD A MULTITUDE, AND HE WHO WAS CALLED JUDAS, ONE OF THE TWELVE, WENT BEFORE THEM, AND DREW NEAR UNTO JESUS TO KISS HIM."

The structure is:

1. The phrase, *"And while He yet spoke, behold a multitude,"* concerned itself with the group coming to arrest Jesus, consisting of Roman legionnaires detailed for this duty from the cohort of guard in the Antonia Fort, and of Levitical guards belonging to the temple. There were officials from the Sanhedrin also in the group.

2. *"And He who was called Judas, one of the Twelve, went before them,"* proclaims the Holy Spirit purposely explaining who Judas was so as not to confuse him with others of the same name.

3. The words, *"One of the Twelve,"* constituted that group being the most signally honored of all mankind in the annals of human history. They had been selected by God the Father for the singular most important task on the face of the earth,

personal association with the Son of God, and then the proclamation of this great message to the entirety of the world. And yet, Judas would trample underfoot this high and noble honor, this select place and position, and this status, the envy of all the prophets of old.

4. Is Judas the only one to have done such a thing? I think not! Any and all who repudiate Christ fall into the same category.

5. Judas led the way in this garden of Gethsemane simply because he had spent many nights there with the Master and the fellow disciples in the past three and a half years. He was leader at this time, but of the most ignoble and perfidious act ever carried out by a human being.

6. *"And drew near unto Jesus to kiss Him,"* was evidently the prearranged sign to show which one was Jesus, to make His arrest easy for this multitude.

(48) "BUT JESUS SAID UNTO HIM, JUDAS, YOU BETRAYEST THOU THE SON OF MAN WITH A KISS?"

The exposition is:

1. The phrase, *"But Jesus said unto him,"* portrays the carrying out of the act that He had predicted at the Last Supper (Lk. 22:21-22).

2. The question, *"Judas, you betrayest thou* (do you betray) *the Son of Man with a kiss?"* must have struck deep into the heart of the traitor.

3. This was the most infamous kiss in history.

(49) "WHEN THEY WHICH WERE ABOUT HIM SAW WHAT WOULD FOLLOW, THEY SAID UNTO HIM, LORD, SHALL WE SMITE WITH THE SWORD?"

The structure is:

1. The phrase, *"When they which were about Him saw what would follow,"* speaks of the imminent arrest of Jesus.

2. The question, *"They said unto Him, Lord, shall we smite with the sword?"* is the very opposite of what He wanted them to do.

3. As stated, at that time they did not understand what He was talking about when He mentioned the purchasing of a sword (Lk. 22:36-38).

(50) "AND ONE OF THEM SMOTE

THE SERVANT OF THE HIGH PRIEST, AND CUT OFF HIS RIGHT EAR."

The construction is:

1. This was Peter (Jn. 18:10). As well, John gives the servant's name as Malchus.

2. Also, John mentioned that before Simon cut off the servant's ear, Jesus asked the question of the group coming to arrest Him, *"Whom do you seek?"*

3. They answered Him, *"Jesus of Nazareth."*

4. Jesus said unto them, *"I am He."*

5. When He said this, John recorded, *"They went backward, and fell to the ground"* (Jn. 18:4-6).

6. This proclaims the fact of the tremendous power that resided in Christ, and that they took Him only because He freely gave Himself to them. Actually, had He the spirit that characterized Peter at this time, He could have easily killed them all; however, He never once in all of His ministry used His power for anything destructive or to better Himself in any capacity. It was always used for the healing and help of others. What a lesson for all of us.

7. I think it is obvious that Peter was trying to kill the man. I doubt seriously that he meant only to sever his right ear, but was rather aiming at severing his head. Thankfully, he did not succeed.

(51) "AND JESUS ANSWERED AND SAID, SUFFER YOU THUS FAR. AND HE TOUCHED HIS EAR, AND HEALED HIM."

The synopsis is:

1. The phrase, *"And Jesus answered and said, Suffer you thus far,"* probably means, although it has been debated, "Bear with My disciples." If that is the meaning, and it probably is, He was actually apologizing to them for Peter's action. Once again, what an example!

2. *"And He touched his ear, and healed him,"* presents the last miracle of healing He performed before the crucifixion, at least that is recorded; consequently, this miracle was exceptional. It was the healing of a wound caused by violence; it was worked on an enemy; it was not requested; there was no faith expressed, and sadder still, no thankfulness on the part, or so it seems, of the one healed.

3. How so much the Lord lived exactly that which He preached, *"Love your enemies, bless them who curse you, do good to them who hate you"* (Mat. 5:44).

(52) "THEN JESUS SAID UNTO THE CHIEF PRIESTS, AND CAPTAINS OF THE TEMPLE, AND THE ELDERS, WHICH WERE COME TO HIM, BE YE COME OUT, AS AGAINST A THIEF, WITH SWORDS AND STAVES?"

The composition is:

1. The phrase, *"Then Jesus said unto the chief priests, and captains of the temple, and the elders, which were come to Him,"* represented the religious hierarchy of Israel, the very ones who, instead, should have welcomed Him.

2. The Holy Spirit is careful to delineate that these religious leaders were present. This presents two things to us:

a. All religions that do not have Christ at the head, which none do, are false and, thereby, always oppose the true work of God.

b. Even that which begins right, as Judaism did, is ultimately corrupted by the insistence of men inserting their own ways and, thereby, replacing the ways of the Lord. So was Israel of old, as here presented, and so is the modern church (Mat. 13:31-33).

3. The question, *"Be ye (Do you) come out, as against a thief, with swords and staves?"* actually presents two thoughts:

a. "If I wanted to use My power against you, your swords and staves would do you no good at all."

b. "I am not a thief, as should be obvious, so why do you treat Me as one?"

(53) "WHEN I WAS DAILY WITH YOU IN THE TEMPLE, YOU STRETCHED FORTH NO HANDS AGAINST ME: BUT THIS IS YOUR HOUR, AND THE POWER OF DARKNESS."

THE DEAD OF NIGHT

The phrase, *"When I was daily with you in the temple, you stretched forth no hands against Me,"* presents the truth of His position and the fallacy of theirs.

If they were so determined to arrest Him, why did they not do it in the temple instead of waiting until the dead of night?

• They had no legitimate charge they could bring against Him, despite every effort being made by their brightest minds to find something.

• They feared the great crowds of people that filled Jerusalem, especially at this Passover season. Jesus had healed many of these people, and many of them believed Him to be at least a great prophet and possibly even the Messiah!

So, to arrest Him publicly in the temple would have possibly instigated a riot, with maybe even some of these religious leaders being stoned.

• They were crooks and thieves themselves, consequently, they conducted themselves accordingly by arresting Him at night when they would not be detected.

THE POWER OF DARKNESS

The phrase, *"But this is your hour, and the power of darkness,"* is a chilling statement!

The first portion, *"This is your hour,"* refers to God allowing the religious leaders of Israel to do this dastardly thing. That does not mean they were predestined to do such, and it certainly was not the will of God. However, inasmuch as their hatred spewing from their own hearts spurred them on, God would allow them to carry out this terrible thing, which would fulfill prophecy and effect the redemption of mankind. So, He would take their perfidious, evil, and wicked action and use it for His ultimate glory in the redemption of man without violating their free moral agency whatsoever.

The latter part of the phrase, *"And the power of darkness,"* means that the energy by which they were doing this thing was the energy of the power of darkness, i.e., Satan himself!

It is possible that Satan knew that Jesus was going to die and actually inspired these religious leaders to cooperate with him (with Satan) in carrying it out; however, it doesn't mean that he fully understood, if at all, what the death of Jesus would accomplish in the redemption of mankind. Or else, he did understand it but thought that death was so powerful, which he, at least to a certain extent, controlled, that Jesus would not be able to rise from the dead.

SATAN

As God, Satan knew that Jesus could do anything. However, he also knew that in becoming man, even though He never ceased to be God, still, He never used the attributes of deity during this time but functioned only as a man filled with the Holy Spirit. Quite possibly, he thought that Jesus, in His humanity, would not be able to overcome death. This much we do know:

Satan's mind, although much more brilliant than any human being who has ever lived, is so twisted by sin and rebellion against God that he does not believe the truth. It would stand to reason that inasmuch as deception is the tool by which he has destroyed much of the human family, he, at the same time, is deceived himself. Even though Satan greatly fears God, even so much that he trembles, still, he exists in deception, consequently, functioning accordingly and, therefore, thinks he is able to do things that he really cannot do (James 2:19).

So, he would inspire these religious leaders to carry out this deadly act of crucifixion on the Son of God, not realizing that the death of Christ would redeem man, at least those who believe, and will, as well, destroy him, i.e., destroy Satan.

(54) "THEN TOOK THEY HIM, AND LED HIM, AND BROUGHT HIM INTO THE HIGH PRIEST'S HOUSE. AND PETER FOLLOWED AFAR OFF."

THE ARREST OF JESUS

The phrase, *"Then took they Him, and led Him, and brought Him into the high priest's house,"* proclaims they were able to do so only with His permission.

The high priest at this time was Caiaphas, son-in-law to Annas, who was the legal high priest but had been deposed by the Roman power sometime before. Annas, however, although prevented by the Roman government from using the high priestly insignia, was apparently looked upon by the people as the rightful possessor of this high religious office. Evidently, he exercised the chief authority in the Jewish councils. It seems that he and Caiaphas shared the palace of the high priest.

There were three trials of a sort of the Lord by the Jews that night and during the early morning.

1. The first was before Annas as recorded in John 18:12-18.

2. The second was before Caiaphas and what has been termed a committee of the Sanhedrin (Mat. 26:59-68; Mk. 14:55-65; Jn. 18:24).

3. And then, the third was formally before the whole Sanhedrin at dawn (Mat. 27:1; Mk. 15:1; Lk. 22:66-71).

PETER FOLLOWED AFAR OFF

The phrase, *"And Peter followed afar off,"* does not record, as many believe, the reason for Peter's failure.

Peter's failure began a long time before this moment. It wasn't that he followed afar off, warmed himself by the fire, etc.

Peter's problem began, as did all the disciples, when he assumed the Word taught something it did not teach, or that he simply did not know what it taught.

Worse yet, he would not believe Jesus regarding His true mission but placed a gloss on it of his own choosing.

The culprit in all of this is self-will. Instead of Jesus using Peter, Peter was desiring to use Jesus. How many of us have done the same?

Consequently, when Peter arrived at the time of this great test, it was already a foregone conclusion as to what he would do, which, as stated, included, to a lesser extent, the other disciples as well. However, despite all of this, they would become some of the greatest men of God who ever lived. The lives they led after the ascension of Christ and Pentecost was a testimony to the fact that they had been with Jesus, and that the Holy Spirit now filled their hearts.

We can look at this incident in the life of Peter, which we certainly should do, and, thereby, learn from it; however, our gaze should not remain there. We should further look to Acts 4:8, where it says, *"Then Peter, filled with the Holy Spirit."*

As someone has beautifully said, "The true believer has no past while Satan has no future."

(55) "AND WHEN THEY HAD KINDLED

A FIRE IN THE MIDST OF THE HALL, AND WERE SET DOWN TOGETHER, PETER SAT DOWN AMONG THEM."

The diagram is:

1. The phrase, *"And when they had kindled a fire in the midst of the hall, and were set down together,"* speaks of those who had arrested Jesus bringing Him to the high priest's house.

2. It may seem strange to some for a fire to be needed at the Passover season inasmuch as it falls in the month of April; however, Jerusalem, situated approximately a half mile above sea level, can get quite chilly at this time of the year, hence, the fire.

3. *"Peter sat down among them,"* proclaims him arriving at the palace with John, who was able to procure admission for the both of them due to being known to the high priest.

4. It is easy to see into this as another reason for his failure—his warming himself at the fire of the enemies of Christ—but I think that little mattered.

5. I doubt seriously that Peter, at least at this stage, knew what he was doing. He simply did not know what to do, fearing the worst, and yet, simply unable to do much of anything. However, the moment was very close when he would do exactly what Jesus said he would do—deny that he even knew his master.

(56) "BUT A CERTAIN MAID BEHELD HIM AS HE SAT BY THE FIRE, AND EARNESTLY LOOKED UPON HIM, AND SAID, THIS MAN WAS ALSO WITH HIM."

The form is:

1. The phrase, *"But a certain maid beheld him as he sat by the fire, and earnestly looked upon him,"* provides the first occasion of the terrible denial.

2. Peter had boasted that he would die or go to prison for Jesus, but even though his intentions may have been good, his strength and reserve were such that he could not even manage a weak confession of Christ to this young girl. How much less would he die or go to prison for Jesus, even though he probably meant what he said at the time it was uttered.

3. He was now operating on his own strength because of his disobedience and

self-will, which he found, as we all do, woefully inadequate.

4. *"And said, This man was also with Him,"* probably came as a surprise to Peter.

5. It is doubtful that he noticed the girl staring at him as he was probably locked in his own thoughts, especially considering the heartache of the moment. Consequently, when she pointed a finger at him, thereby, pointing him out, it must have startled him greatly. He evidently did not think anyone would recognize him here, or quite possibly, such had not entered his mind.

(57) "AND HE DENIED HIM, SAYING, WOMAN, I KNOW HIM NOT."

The order is:

1. This is the first of three denials that Jesus predicted.

2. Peter's sin was of a far more grievous nature than most realize.

3. Jesus had plainly said in one of His messages, *"Whosoever shall deny Me before men, him will I also deny before My Father"* (Mat. 10:33). Consequently, what was done was extremely serious, and even above that, it was done when Jesus needed him most.

(58) "AND AFTER A LITTLE WHILE ANOTHER SAW HIM, AND SAID, YOU ARE ALSO OF THEM. AND PETER SAID, MAN, I AM NOT."

The overview is:

1. The phrase, *"And after a little while another saw him, and said, You are also of them,"* presents the occasion for the second denial.

2. I wonder what Peter thought after the first denial. Did it come to his mind what Jesus had said? Did he remember his boasts?

3. *"And Peter said, Man, I am not,"* represents the second denial.

4. Even though we are given this account in cold, jarring black and white, and by the Holy Spirit at that, still, this is not the Simon Peter that we know. Despite what he did, this is not who he was or what he was, even though he did this dastardly thing.

(59) "AND ABOUT THE SPACE OF ONE HOUR AFTER ANOTHER CONFIDENTLY AFFIRMED, SAYING, OF A TRUTH THIS FELLOW ALSO WAS WITH HIM: FOR HE IS A GALILAEAN."

The exegesis is:

1. The phrase, *"And about the space of one hour after another confidently affirmed,"* represents the occasion for the third and final denial.

2. As well, what must that hour have been to Simon Peter? For a believer to fail the Lord is a terrible thing in any case; however, to fail in this manner, as stated, brings a despair that is beyond comprehension. To be sure, the closer one is to the Lord, even as Peter, the worse the agony and condemnation. As many believers can testify, at least if they will be honest, it is so severe that were it not for the grace of God, it is doubtful that one could live through such an ordeal.

3. Sin is a horrid business, and it carries such a penalty that it is no wonder the Holy Spirit through Paul would say, *"The wages of sin is death"* (Rom. 6:23).

4. *"Saying, Of a truth this fellow also was with Him: for he is a Galilaean,"* probably represents someone nearby who overheard Peter speak, recognized the accent, and then figured out who he was.

(60) "AND PETER SAID, MAN, I KNOW NOT WHAT YOU SAY. AND IMMEDIATELY, WHILE HE YET SPOKE, THE ROOSTER CROWED."

THE CROWING OF THE ROOSTER

The phrase, *"And Peter said, Man, I know not what you say,"* is the third denial and exactly the number that Jesus predicted.

Jesus was speaking the Word of God. Consequently, it, which includes the entirety of the Bible, cannot fail in any capacity. Therefore, this scenario should be a lesson to us:

• The Word of God is infallible and, thereby, will come to pass exactly according to what is said.

• It and it alone is the rule of life. There is no light other than the Word of God. It is the only revealed truth in the world today and, in fact, ever has been.

• Every believer should study it diligently and make it a daily habit for the spiritual man exactly as food and water are taken for the physical man.

The truth will set a person free.

And yet, on the other hand, the judgment pronounced upon sin, unrighteousness, and disobedience of the Word will be brought about whether the individual knows the Word of God or not.

THE WORD OF THE LORD

It is somewhat like a manual telling a person how to derive so many miles to the gallon respecting his automobile. To achieve these results, the individual must know what the manual says and then do what the manual says.

However, if the person is ignorant of what the manual says about this subject, his ignorance will not stop the lesser mileage from being brought about.

Peter knew what Jesus said but seemingly did little or nothing to forestall such. Jesus had told him to pray, as well as all the other disciples, but evidently this admonition was not heeded. Consequently, he did exactly what Jesus said he would do.

"And immediately, while he yet spoke, the rooster crowed," happened exactly as Jesus predicted in Verse 34.

It is said that ever after, Peter could not hear a rooster crow but that he would fall on his knees in sorrow at the memory of what happened at this time.

(61) "AND THE LORD TURNED, AND LOOKED UPON PETER. AND PETER REMEMBERED THE WORD OF THE LORD, HOW HE HAD SAID UNTO HIM, BEFORE THE ROOSTER CROWS, YOU SHALL DENY ME THREE TIMES."

The pattern is:

1. The phrase, *"And the Lord turned, and looked upon Peter,"* probably refers to the moment that Jesus was being led from the interrogation before Caiaphas to be examined before the Sanhedrin. It seems that the third denial took place at that moment, with Peter answering the man with oaths and curses (Mk. 14:71), with Jesus, no doubt, overhearing him. He was attempting to assure the bystanders that he had no connection with and knew nothing of Jesus of Nazareth. About that time Jesus looked upon Peter, not with anger but only the most tender pity and sorrow.

2. *"And Peter remembered the word of*

the Lord," implies that he seemingly had forgotten what Jesus had said.

3. Due to the dramatic events, it is somewhat understandable; however, nothing must take precedence over *"thus saith the Lord."* We would do well to forget everything else, as seemingly important as it may be, and remember only that which the Lord has said.

4. *"Before the rooster crows, you shall deny Me three times,"* presents this coming back to Peter in full force, with all its attendant implications.

(62) "AND PETER WENT OUT, AND WEPT BITTERLY."

WEEPING BITTERLY

One look from Jesus brought Peter to his senses.

This type of weeping bitterly always signals repentance. David had said about a thousand years earlier, *"The sacrifices of God are a broken spirit: a broken and a contrite heart, O God, You will not despise"* (Ps. 51:17).

Let the reader always remember that the Lord will always forgive, irrespective of what is done, if we will come to Him in such brokenness (I Jn. 1:9). As well, no conditions are attached to such forgiveness, and neither is the individual placed on some type of probation. He is always, as Peter, restored immediately to full rights and privileges as though the terrible thing was never done. It is called justification by faith.

The account of Peter's denial is carried by all four evangelists.

There are a couple of things in these accounts that seem to be contradictions but really aren't.

For instance, Matthew, Luke, and John only mention the rooster crowing one time, while Mark mentions it crowing twice— after the first denial and the last (Mk. 14:68-72). There is no discrepancy. Three of the evangelists failed to mention the first crowing, but that in no way means that it did not happen.

NO DISCREPANCY

As well, Luke mentions a maid accusing Peter first, followed by two men (Lk. 22:56-60).

NOTES

Matthew, Mark, and John speak of two maids and one man, or else, simply used for the last the pronoun *"they."*

Once again, there is no discrepancy. More than likely, from the way the text describes it, quite a number accused Peter, with a maid the second time making the formal accusation, and then a man standing nearby evidently joining in. Peter answered the man and not the maid, hence, the account of Luke.

It is the same as several people giving an account of anything that has happened, with one or more mentioning things that the others did not mention. However, that doesn't mean there is a discrepancy just because one gives a little more detailed information than the other.

Instead of being a flaw, as the skeptic enjoys proclaiming, it is rather proof that these things happened exactly as they were told. Were it a fabrication, every account would be word for word identical.

(63) "AND THE MEN WHO HELD JESUS MOCKED HIM, AND SMOTE HIM."

The pattern is:

1. The phrase, *"And the men who held Jesus mocked Him,"* referred to them goading Jesus that He use His power to stop them, that is, if He had any power.

2. Quite possibly, some of these men had seen Jesus heal in the temple as recently as the last few days, and even had witnessed Him healing the severed ear of Malchus. However, they were so hardened and godless that nothing of righteousness registered on them anymore. Is it any wonder that God abandoned the nation to destruction?

3. *"And smote Him,"* fulfilled the prophecies of Isaiah where he said, *"As many were astonished at You; His visage was so marred more than any man, and His form more than the sons of men"* (Isa. 52:14).

4. The word *marred* in the Hebrew is *mishchath* and means "to disfigure."

5. The idea is that in His sufferings, the Messiah was so bruised, beaten, marred, disfigured, striped, mutilated, injured, spit upon, and torn that His outward appearance was awful to behold.

6. He suffered so much that even the most wicked of hard-hearted men shuddered

with shock at such treatment heaped upon Him by enemies, and yet, enemies who called themselves servants of God.

7. He became so disfigured and destitute of His natural beauty and handsomeness that men were stricken with amazement, disgust, and heart-sickness at what they saw. The more perfect His body, which it was, the more marred He seemed in suffering.

(64) "AND WHEN THEY HAD BLIND-FOLDED HIM, THEY STRUCK HIM ON THE FACE, AND ASKED HIM, SAYING, PROPH-ESY, WHO IS IT WHO SMOTE YOU?"

RELIGIOUS EVIL

The phrase, *"And when they had blind-folded Him, they struck Him on the face,"* portrays a scene far more horrible than these mere words are able to convey.

It must be remembered that this trial was being conducted at night, which was in violation of Levitical law. As well, at this stage, He had been formally charged with nothing. And yet, they beat Him unmercifully.

Why?

Their hatred of Him was so intense, and I speak of the high priests, chief priests, members of the Sanhedrin, and elders, that the moment they had an opportunity to do such, as illegal as it was, they struck out at Him with a vengeance. It was something they had wanted to do all along but simply lacked the opportunity. Now they would take full advantage of Him being in their hands and would vent their hatred.

Why did they hate Him so much?

Self-righteousness always hates imputed righteousness. Religion always hates relationship.

PERSONAL EXPERIENCE

Little understanding this, when I first went on nationwide radio with our daily program, *The Campmeeting Hour,* and then a little later, with our telecast (this was in the early 1970s), I was met by this same spirit. Being somewhat naïve, I could not understand why certain individuals were opposed to me to such an extent, especially considering that I really did not even know them. And yet, they would go to any lengths to attempt to destroy me, especially considering they

were claiming, and strongly so, to serve the same God I was serving.

Even though I disagreed with many of them respecting their doctrine, there was no animosity in my heart and no ill feelings or ill will toward any of them. For a long while, I could not understand why they had such hatred for me. To be frank, I was still lacking somewhat in understanding even when my own denomination, of which I had been part since I was a child, made every effort that was humanly possible to destroy me and this ministry.

Had there been misunderstandings or disagreements, possibly it would have made more sense; however, none of that had happened. But yet, I found a hatred so intense that when the opportunity presented itself, as with Jesus, they took every advantage of that opportunity, sparing no expense, and doing anything that was humanly possible to further their destructive purposes.

The simple fact is, these people did not know God, irrespective of the loudness of their profession. As the religious leaders of Israel of old, their self-righteous hatred built up against me, not because of something I had done to them, for I had done nothing. They were angry because of the move of God within my life and that which the Lord was doing all around the world. As the Pharisees and religious leaders of old, they saw themselves losing control of the people, or at least they thought they were, and as religion always does, it will go to any lengths to protect control.

While all the time claiming to be of God, they would do everything humanly possible to destroy that which was really of God. The same spirit I faced, and so many others down through the centuries have faced, is the same spirit that Christ faced. Of course, there is some difference.

RELIGION

Christ was perfect while none of us are. However, the Holy Spirit, who works within me and all others who truly follow the Lord, is the same Holy Spirit who worked in Christ. To get to the bottom line, this is what this religious spirit of darkness actually opposes. They are opposing the working, manifestation, and operation of the Holy Spirit while all the time mouthing religious phraseology and claiming to be of God.

Actually, their claims in this realm must at the same time destroy all else that is not a part of that claim.

Religion is a frightful business and is not, nor ever has been, of God! It is Satan's greatest effort among all his efforts in opposing the true work of God.

So, the same spirit that mocked and beat Christ and ultimately hung Him on a Cross is the same spirit that has opposed all of His followers, and with the same intensity, at least wherever possible.

THE SPIRIT OF DARKNESS

The only thing that stops this hatred from manifesting itself in the same manner now is the law of the land, at least in countries that guarantee religious freedom. Where law is absent, religious men, as the Pharisees and religious leaders of old, will resort to any measure, even physical violence, to stop any and all who do not promote their brand of religion. That hatred burns no less at present and does not manifest itself, at least in totality, only because of lack of opportunity.

This is the spirit that caused Cain to murder Abel, Joseph's brothers to sell him into slavery, Korah to oppose Moses, and Saul to oppose David. It is the same spirit that opposed Paul greatly in the early church, which continues unto this hour.

As is obvious, and as we have repeatedly stated, these men who were mocking and beating Jesus claimed to be of God and actually were carrying out this perfidious action in the temple itself. Likewise, Jesus claimed to be of God and truly was. So, as should be obvious, both could not be correct; consequently, the people had to make a choice. They could follow those who controlled the temple and were, in fact, very religious, or they could follow Jesus. They could not follow both!

CLAIMING TO BE OF GOD

It is the same presently. Many who head up religious denominations, be they Catholic or otherwise, and even many who call

themselves independent, etc., fall into the same category as these mockers of Christ. There are exceptions, but not many.

This one thing is certain: Nearly always, if not always, that which claims to be of God but really isn't will oppose strongly that which is really of God. One cannot be of God and fight God at the same time. While one may be momentarily sidetracked, if the individual is sincere before the Lord, he will soon be led back to the path of righteousness. However, the evil heart of unbelief, although acutely religious, will always oppose faith. That common thread runs throughout the entirety of the Word of God. Consequently, religion would crucify the Lord in the name of the Lord.

The question, *"And asked Him, saying, Prophesy, who is it who smote You?"* will one day be answered in totality.

These mockers will one day stand before God, with each name being called out and exactly the number of blows that they delivered to the face of Jesus.

Once again, allow me to state that all of this was carried out, not by cruel Rome, but rather by the religious leaders of Israel of that day.

(65) "AND MANY OTHER THINGS BLASPHEMOUSLY SPOKE THEY AGAINST HIM."

JESUS THE SON OF GOD

And yet Jesus said, *"All manner of sin and blasphemy shall be forgiven unto men ... And whosoever speaks a word against the Son of Man, it shall be forgiven him"* (Mat. 12:31-32). It is forgiven if the person asks for forgiveness.

In other words, as hateful, wicked, and blasphemous as this was, if any of them had asked Jesus to forgive them, it would have instantly been done.

The lackeys of these religious leaders knew much about Jesus. They knew that He claimed to be the Messiah, or else, that many people thought He was. Of course, His healings and miracles were known far and wide. So, now they taunted Him, no doubt, demanding that if He really was such, He should now use His power.

They little knew or realized that the one

Who had created all things was standing before them. They little knew that this was the same one Who gave the law to Moses on Mount Sinai. They little understood that this was the one Who said, *"Let there be light: and there was light"* (Gen. 1:3).

Paul said that these religious leaders did not know the *"wisdom of God"* (which, in reality, is the Word of God) … *For had they known it, they would not have crucified the Lord of Glory"* (I Cor. 2:7-8).

THE TRIAL OF CHRIST

The occasion of these happenings probably took place after the hearing before Caiaphas and a committee of the Sanhedrin when Caiaphas arose, and with awful solemnity, adjured Jesus to say whether He was the Christ, the Son of God.

Jesus answered definitely in the affirmative, which occasioned Caiaphas to rent his robe, to which the assembly cried, *"He is guilty of death."* They considered His claim to be blasphemy.

He would now be taken to the full meeting of the Sanhedrin in order to legalize what had already been done. It was probably as Jesus was being led across the court that Jesus looked at Peter, and Peter looked at Jesus and saw the horror of what had happened. We might quickly state that His face and body were so disfigured and torn that He actually ceased to look human, but rather like an animal.

Knowing that he had denied his Lord, especially at a time such as this, was actually more than Peter could stand. If God had not lifted the burden and condemnation through forgiveness, which He did, this would have ultimately destroyed the fisherman. As stated, as bad as the denial was, the aftereffects, with Satan taking full advantage, was even a greater crisis. Satan must have taunted Peter with his great failure, telling him how hopeless now all was; however, and gloriously so, Peter turned toward Jesus instead of away from Him, as Judas. He lost the battle, but he did not lose the war. While he experienced failure, he did not fall because, as stated, a fall is not possible as long as one continues to trust Christ, which Peter did. He did not lose his faith!

NOTES

(66) "AND AS SOON AS IT WAS DAY, THE ELDERS OF THE PEOPLE AND THE CHIEF PRIESTS AND THE SCRIBES CAME TOGETHER, AND LED HIM INTO THEIR COUNCIL, SAYING."

THE RELIGIOUS HIERARCHY OF ISRAEL

The phrase, *"And as soon as it was day,"* proclaims the fact that the Sanhedrin as a council could only meet by day.

Even though Jesus had already been questioned by Caiaphas and had admitted to being divinity, it all must be done again, for those proceedings took place at night, which was illegal.

"The elders of the people and the chief priests and the scribes came together," proclaims the religious hierarchy of Israel.

This constituted the Sanhedrin, which consisted of some 70 members, and according to Josephus, the high priest at this particular time was president. Thus, Caiaphas was president at the trial of Jesus and Ananias at the trial of Paul (Acts 23:2).

The jurisdiction of this court, which was the highest court in Israel and would have been similar to the United States Supreme Court, exercised not only civil jurisdiction according to Jewish law but also criminal jurisdiction to some degree. It had an administrative authority and could order arrests by its own officers of justice (Mat. 26:47; Mk. 14:43; Acts 4:1).

It was empowered to judge cases that did not involve capital punishment. Capital cases required the confirmation of the Roman procurator, in this case, Pontius Pilate.

The Sanhedrin generally sat in a semicircle and had two clerks of court, one to record votes of acquittal and the other votes of condemnation. There were normally many others at these sessions, as well, such as witnesses or those who were interested in the procedure.

THE SANHEDRIN

In capital cases, such as that of Jesus, the arguments for acquittal were presented and then those for conviction. If one spoke for acquittal, he could not reverse his opinion, but if he spoke for condemnation, he could later change his vote, if so desired.

The law was that acquittal might be declared on the day of the trial, but condemnation must wait until the day following, which was not carried out with Jesus.

In voting, members stood, beginning with the youngest. For acquittal, a simple majority sufficed; for condemnation, a two-thirds majority was required. If 12 of the 23 judges necessary for a quorum voted for acquittal and 11 for conviction, the prisoner was discharged. If 12 voted for conviction and 11 against, the number of judges had to be increased by two, and this was repeated up to a total of 71, or until an acquittal was achieved.

The benefit of the doubt was allowed to persons where the case was as doubtful as this. Indeed, always, the benefit lay with the accused, except in the case of Jesus.

THE LEGALITY OF THE TRIAL OF JESUS

In this regard, the legality of the trial of Jesus has been discussed by many writers, and it is fairly clear that His trial was a gross miscarriage of justice.

The history of the Sanhedrin is not too clear. Traditionally, it originated with the 70 elders who assisted Moses (Num. 11:16-24). Ezra is supposed to have reorganized this body after the exile.

After A.D. 70, the Sanhedrin was abolished and replaced by a Court of Judgment.

At this meeting it seems that at least two members of the Sanhedrin who were loyal to Jesus were not present, or if they were present, they did not vote for His condemnation. These two members were Joseph and Nicodemus.

The phrase, *"And led Him into their council, saying,"* was to constitute, they thought, His trial, but in reality, it was their trial.

Here, they destroyed themselves. At their request and by their actions, the Lord would lift His hand from these formerly called His chosen people, leaving them, even at their own request, to the mercy of Caesar, who would exact a heavy toll.

In fact, some 37 years later, this very hall where they tried Jesus would be torn to pieces, with not one stone left upon another. There were over 1 million Jews who died

NOTES

in that carnage as Jerusalem was totally destroyed and their nation, for all practical purposes, dissolved. Caesar proved to be a hard taskmaster.

(67) "ARE YOU THE CHRIST? TELL US. AND HE SAID UNTO THEM, IF I TELL YOU, YOU WILL NOT BELIEVE."

ARE YOU THE CHRIST?

The question, *"Are You the Christ?"* seems to have dispensed with all previous formalities.

Evidently, all who were present were aware that Jesus had admitted to this while before Caiaphas, which Luke, incidentally, passed over, but is recounted by both Matthew and Mark.

However, whatever He said in the previous meeting was looked at by them as more spiritual than political. They were now desiring a political answer in order that they may charge Him before Pilate. The other meeting was not legal, while this one was; therefore, they would have to go through the procedure again.

He stood there a forlorn sight, having been beaten and mocked, with His face, no doubt, grotesquely swollen, and with blood staining His garment and possibly even dripping from open wounds. Even in this condition, His accusers showed no sympathy. Their hatred was such that they would have killed Him then and there, or even long before, had it been legal for them to have done so.

The short two words, *"tell us,"* are said with anger and determination.

YOU WILL NOT BELIEVE

In effect, they greatly demanded of Jesus, claiming the supremacy of their royal court. In that political body, for it had long since ceased to be spiritual, they would demand, and He must answer.

The phrase, *"And He said unto them, If I tell you, you will not believe,"* constitutes an answer far broader than they had asked.

No! They did not believe that He was the Messiah even though He fulfilled every single Scripture, even down to the minutest detail. As well, He had performed miracles to such a degree that it was well nigh impossible not to understand that such originated with God. And yet, they accused Him of performing these miracles by the power of Satan. When they did this, they blasphemed the Holy Spirit!

All they desired was an answer in the affirmative so they could charge Him before Pilate, knowing that Rome did not allow the claims of any kings or rulers of any nature, except those officially appointed by Rome. So, a claim of being the Messiah, in effect, the Jewish king, was a claim to the throne of David.

Actually, Jesus ignored their question in this realm, in effect, placing the emphasis totally on their unbelief. It must have given them room for pause.

If He really was the Messiah, the Son of God, what had they done?

But yet, their hatred completely overrode the obvious truth.

(68) "AND IF I ALSO ASK YOU, YOU WILL NOT ANSWER ME, NOR LET ME GO."

THEY WOULD NOT ANSWER

The phrase, *"And if I also ask you,"* refers to the particular parables and questions the Lord had recently put to these religious leaders, such as Matthew 22:45. Their efforts to trap him with theological questions had not only proved unsuccessful, but had rather fallen out according to His answers to prove His case.

"You will not answer Me," refers to the fact that they were not looking for truth.

On a personal basis, it took me quite some time to understand this respecting a particular modern Pentecostal denomination to which I had once belonged. I watched them set about to keep people from coming to our meetings. They even stationed preachers outside the auditoriums to attempt to spot church members who were attending, or more particularly, preachers of that denomination who were attending our meetings. They would in turn be censored in some way, that is, if they attended our meetings. For quite some time, I grieved over this, wondering why. Had I been opposing these people, saying something derogatory or preaching some type of false doctrine, it

NOTES

would have been understandable. However, the only thing we were doing was attempting to preach the Word of God and, thereby, seeking God day and night that the anointing and convicting power of the Holy Spirit would be present in the services. Oftentimes it was and is in great ways resulting in many people being saved, etc.

Many times I would muse in my mind or in conversations with others that if these so-called leaders would only come and see for themselves, they would surely understand that what they were doing was wrong, even to the place of attempting to stop the work of God.

THE OPERATION OF THE HOLY SPIRIT

However, I finally came to the place that I had to admit to myself their real reason. Despite claiming to be Pentecostal, they actually did not want or desire a moving and operation of the Holy Spirit in any capacity. Instead of being convinced by that, it was actually the very thing they did not want or desire.

To be truthful, that was the reason for their animosity and position all along. They had long since opted for the ways of the world, i.e., humanistic psychology, etc. As a result, the operation of the Holy Spirit was a throwback to what they once were but no longer wanted. So, as the Pharisees and religious leaders of Jesus' day, they must oppose the messenger. If they opposed the message outright, some few of the people of this denomination, who still longed for the moving of the Holy Spirit, would be greatly offended, and these individuals would be exposed for what they really were.

Therefore, they would attack the messenger exactly as they did Jesus of long ago. Other excuses would be used and so-called reasons given, but what I have said is the truth. The same spirit that murdered Christ is the same spirit that is alive and well today in most religious circles. As stated, there are a few exceptions here and there, but precious few!

I wish I could say that the present situation will change, which I certainly pray that it shall; however, every indication in the Word of God is that it not only will not change, but will actually grow worse.

TILL THE WHOLE WAS LEAVENED

Jesus said, *"Another parable spoke He unto them; The kingdom of heaven is like unto leaven, which a woman took, and hid in three measures of meal, till the whole was leavened"* (Mat. 13:33).

This passage tells us that the church in the last days before the second coming of Christ will be totally corrupted except for a small remnant, just as Israel was totally corrupted immediately before the first advent of Christ except for a small remnant. It is an identical parallel.

The Pharisees were the fundamentalists in that day and the very group who was supposed to believe all of the Word of God, including miracles, etc. They would correspond with the modern Pentecostals and others of the present. They were bitterly opposed to Christ exactly as their modern counterparts.

Of course, Christ is not here personally at this particular time as He was 2,000 years ago, but the same Spirit that was in His life and ministry (Lk. 4:17-18) is in His true followers, and is opposed now by religious hierarchy exactly as it was then.

So, as the Pharisees and religious leaders would not answer Jesus, neither will they answer now.

The phrase, *"Nor let Me go,"* refers to the ceasing of opposition.

These religious leaders who claimed so much of God but, in reality, were operating by the powers of darkness, as we have stated, had no interest in truth. They were only interested in one thing, and that was to stop Jesus, and they would even resort to murder to do so. Such is the spirit of religion.

(69) "HEREAFTER SHALL THE SON OF MAN SIT ON THE RIGHT HAND OF THE POWER OF GOD."

The pattern is:

1. The phrase, *"Hereafter shall the Son of Man,"* presents the last time that Jesus would refer to Himself as the Son of Man. In effect, this did answer their question, but not pointedly.

2. *"Sit on the right hand of the power of God,"* refers to the judgment seat and, in

NOTES

effect, says to these people who call themselves judges:

"Today you are judging Me, but tomorrow I will judge you. Now I am your Saviour, or at least would be if you would only allow Me, but tomorrow I will be your judge."

3. The Holy Spirit through Paul affirmed this prediction of Christ by saying, *"And what is the exceeding greatness of His power to us-ward who believe, according to the working of His mighty power.*

"Which He wrought in Christ, when He raised Him from the dead, and set Him at His own right hand in the heavenly places."

He then said, *"Far above all principality, and power, and might, and dominion, and every name that is named, not only in this world, but also in that which is to come:*

"And has put all things under His feet, and gave Him to be the Head over all things to the church."

"Which is His body, the fulness of Him that fills all in all" (Eph. 1:19-23).

(70) "THEN SAID THEY ALL, ARE YOU THEN THE SON OF GOD? AND HE SAID UNTO THEM, YOU SAY THAT I AM."

The diagram is:

1. The question, *"Then said they all, Are You then the Son of God?"* is resident in the word *"You,"* the form of an insult.

2. According to Spence, they meant, "And are You, then, do You, poor man, vain in your imagining, and Your deception, do You assert Yourself to be the Son of God?"

3. *"And He said unto them, You say that I am,"* even though not resident in the Greek, but in the Hebrew, denotes a strong affirmation. In other words, in the clearest possible language, He said, *"I am!"*

4. As stated, this question had already been asked at the previous mockery and had received the same definitive answer. However, it was now said in the daylight hours in front of the Sanhedrin, which made these proceedings legal and gave these devils the answer for which they were looking.

5. Below outlines 10 reasons the Jews killed Jesus:

a. Kingship (Mat. 2:2-3, 16; Jn. 18:33-40; 19:12-22).

b. Telling the truth (Lk. 4:21-29; Jn. 8:40).

c. Healing on the Sabbath (Mat. 12:9-14; Mk. 3:1-6; Jn. 5:16; 9:16).

d. Jealousy (Mat. 26:3-4; 27:18; Mk. 14:1; 15:10; Lk. 22:2; Jn. 11:48).

e. Ignorance (Mat. 26:64-66; Mk. 14:63-64; Jn. 12:40; Acts 3:17).

f. Fulfilling of prophecy (Lk. 13:33-35; Jn. 12:38-40; 18:31-32; 19:11, 28, 36-37; Acts 2:22-36; 3:18).

g. Claiming Sonship (Jn. 5:18; 10:24, 39; 19:7).

h. Unbelief (Jn. 5:38-47; 6:36; 9:40-41; 12:36-38).

i. Claiming to be God (Jn. 8:53-59; 10:33).

j. Fear of losing their authority (Jn. 11:46-53; 12:10-11, 19).

(71) "AND THEY SAID, WHAT NEED WE ANY FURTHER WITNESS? FOR WE OURSELVES HAVE HEARD OF HIS OWN MOUTH."

The overview is:

1. The question, *"And they said, What need we any further witness?"* proclaims exactly what they wanted.

2. First of all, as stated, they had no authority within themselves to carry out a death sentence on Christ. That had to be done by the Roman governor, Pontius Pilate. As well, Pilate would have been little interested in their theological accusations, irrespective of what they may have been; consequently, they had to have a political reason in order to carry weight with Pilate.

3. For Jesus to claim to be the Son of God also meant that He was claiming the throne of David as king.

4. It didn't matter that He had stated by example that His kingdom was not of this world. Pilate would have no interest in these spiritual questions, only that someone was claiming to be king, consequently, meaning a usurpation of the authority of Rome. So, those were the grounds on which they would charge Him.

5. *"For we ourselves have heard of His own mouth,"* simply meant they would all witness against Him to Pilate that He had made this claim. Consequently, it would be very difficult for Pilate to ignore the charge of the highest Jewish court in the land, a court, incidentally, that Rome had sanctioned.

NOTES

6. This was Wednesday morning shortly after daylight. Having the charge they desired, which was also trumped up and false, at least in the way they presented it, they would now present Him to Pilate.

7. Pilate then sent Him to Herod who mocked Him and sent Him back to Pilate who gave Him up to be crucified, which took place Wednesday morning at 9 a.m., the time of the morning sacrifice.

Jesus was crucified on Wednesday and not Friday as presumed in order to fulfill His own prediction of being *"three days and three nights in the heart of the earth"* (Mat. 12:40).

"Have your affections been nailed to the Cross?
"Is your heart right with God?
"Do you count all things for Jesus but loss?
"Is your heart right with God?"

"Have you dominion over self and over sin?
"Is your heart right with God?
"Over all evil without and within?
"Is your heart right with God?"

"Is there no more condemnation for sin?
"Is your heart right with God?
"Does Jesus rule in the temple within?
"Is your heart right with God?"

"Are all your powers under Jesus' control?
"Is your heart right with God?
"Does He each moment abide in your soul?
"Is your heart right with God?"

"Are you now walking in heaven's pure light?
"Is your heart right with God?
"Is your soul wearing the garment of white?
"Is your heart right with God?"

CHAPTER 23

(1) "AND THE WHOLE MULTITUDE OF THEM AROSE, AND LED HIM UNTO PILATE."

THE MULTITUDE

The phrase, *"And the whole multitude of them arose,"* included the entirety of the Sanhedrin, with the possible exception of Joseph of Arimathaea and Nicodemus, who may or may not have been present.

There were, no doubt, many hangers-on, along with the officers of the temple, who Jesus had probably angered by the cleansing of the temple, as well as other onlookers.

They had now formally condemned Him to death, but with the sentence unable to be carried out unless Pilate agreed with their assessment and, thereby, performed the foul deed.

The Sanhedrin condemnation to death was, however, from the Jewish standpoint, illegal. In capital cases judgment could not be legally pronounced on the day of trial, but in the case of Jesus, the accused was condemned on the same day, with the sentence carried out.

It should be noted that the Pharisees, who were members of the Sanhedrin and who claimed to be sticklers for the law of Moses, made no protest whatsoever against this illegality to the Sadducees, who held the majority in this high court. They hated Christ so much that the violation of the law of Moses meant nothing to them, as the abrogation of the Word of God means nothing to their modern counterparts.

PILATE

The phrase, *"And led Him unto Pilate,"* presents the second step that had to be carried out if, in fact, they were to rid themselves of Jesus once and for all. However, they would find to their bitter dismay that even though they were successful in executing Him, they would not be successful in ridding themselves of Him. Their perfidious deeds have hung around their necks from that day until this.

A short time ago on our daily telecast, *A Study in the Word,* which airs over the Sonlife Broadcasting Network, we taught a series on the book of Acts.

At a given point in the series, I spoke of Paul's difficulties with his fellow countrymen and casually made mention that they would

have killed him had the opportunity presented itself. I did not elaborate on it whatsoever, only making mention of that fact, and only one time if I remember correctly.

Almost immediately, we received a telephone call from the Jewish Defamation Society. The man who called and talked to my secretary was nice enough but made mention that they had spent nearly 2,000 years trying to live down the crucifixion of Christ, and they did not desire to be thought of as wanting to have killed Paul as well! Even though this thing with Paul, as Christ, happened nearly 2,000 years ago and in no way involved this present generation, as would be obvious, still, their present response shows the guilt that still hangs over their heads even though nearly 20 centuries removed. What they did is one thing; who He is and was presents something else altogether!

THE JEWISH PEOPLE

Over the years I have been a strong friend to the Jewish people, as all true Christians must be. The roots of Christianity, of course, are embedded in Judaism and are a natural outgrowth. Their Bible, the Old Testament, is our Bible, as well, including the New Testament, which they reject. So, it would be impossible for any true Christian to understand this and not have an abiding love for the Jewish people.

However, it is virtually impossible to preach the New Testament without recognizing the fact of what Israel did to their Messiah and our Saviour.

In speaking with many Jewish leaders through the years, they bridle at the stigma that continues to be attached to them because of this act. Their complaint is that this is something that happened nearly 2,000 years ago, and this present generation is in no way responsible, which, of course, is true. And yet, the truth is that the present generation of Jewish people, at least for the most part, loves Christ no more than that generation of so long ago. So, in that capacity, they continue to be guilty, as is most of the world for that matter.

A PERSONAL EXPERIENCE

Sometime back, as I have related elsewhere

in these volumes, I had the occasion to spend some time with the Jewish liaison to Congress. By and large the Jews had always promoted liberals in America, thinking that benefitted them the most. Consequently, they were somewhat lacking in understanding as to why the Reagan Administration, which was then in power, had been kinder to the state of Israel than any previous administration, liberal or otherwise. Thinking that conservatives, which Reagan was, were their enemies, the man asked me how this could be.

I patiently explained to him that the Christian community had played a strong part in the election of President Reagan, and that Christians, at least true Christians, strongly espoused the Jewish cause and position, at least in certain things, and especially the state of Israel.

He could not understand that either, thinking that Christians were actually the cause of all their problems.

Again I explained to him that all who claim to be Christian actually are not, but that all true Christians love Israel, and for the obvious reasons.

I'm not certain if he really understood what I was saying inasmuch as everything I was saying was totally contradictory to all the things he and other Jews had always been taught.

Pontius Pilate owed his high position as procurator of Judea to his friendship with a man by the name of Sejanus, the powerful minister of the Emperor Tiberius.

PONTIUS PILATE

When Judea became subject to the Roman Empire, it seems that Pilate, through the interest of Sejanus, was appointed to govern it with the title of procurator, or collector of the revenue. He was also invested with judicial power. This was in A.D. 26, and he held the post for 10 years.

He was deposed from his office in disgrace at the end of his tenure, and about the only mention of him in history is his connection with the Lord Jesus Christ on this momentous occasion.

His behavior in the one great event of his life—when Jesus was brought before

NOTES

his tribunal—would illustrate his character. Biblical history records that he was superstitious and yet cruel; afraid of the people he effected to despise; faithless to the spirit of the authority with which he was lawfully invested.

Spence said of him, "In the great crisis of his history, from the miserably selfish motive of securing his own petty interests, we watch him deliberately giving up a man, Whom he knew to be innocent, and felt to be noble and pure, to torture, shame, and death."

There are several stories concerning his death, with one being that he walked out into a lake and did not stop, thereby, drowning himself, committing suicide.

(2) "AND THEY BEGAN TO ACCUSE HIM, SAYING, WE FOUND THIS FELLOW PERVERTING THE NATION, AND FORBIDDING TO GIVE TRIBUTE TO CAESAR, SAYING THAT HE HIMSELF IS CHRIST A KING."

ACCUSATIONS

The phrase, *"And they began to accuse Him, saying,"* presents their response to Christ from the very beginning of His ministry.

Despite the fact that He had healed literally thousands and had set untold numbers free from terrible bondages of sin, in effect, giving their lives back to them, these religious leaders had not one kind word to say about Him. Their hatred was total; consequently, all they could do was accuse.

In this, they followed the spirit of their father, Satan, who accuses the brethren (Rev. 12:10).

In fact, all believers should think very carefully about this very important subject. To accuse that which is of the Lord is the same as accusing the Lord.

The phrase, *"We found this fellow perverting the nation,"* presents their first accusation.

They were meaning that Christ was attempting to agitate the nation of Israel to enter into rebellion against Caesar. This was a total fabrication, with Him doing the very opposite (Isa. 42:1; Mat. 12:19).

In fact, there were zealots in Israel at that time who were advocating that very thing;

however, Jesus was never a party, even in the slightest way, to their efforts.

If one is to notice, the Pharisees and others of similar stripe never called Jesus by His name. They instead referred to Him as teacher, or some such appellative. Here they just used the word *this*, with the word *fellow* being inserted by the translators. By such a manner, they were insulting Him to the very limit of their ability.

"And forbidding to give tribute to Caesar," constituted their second accusation and was, as well, a lie.

Actually, He had taught the very opposite, demanding that Caesar be given his due (Lk. 20:25).

CHRIST A KING

The phrase, *"Saying that He Himself is Christ a king,"* presented their third accusation and was a lie, at least in the way it was presented.

They were claiming that He was telling Israel that He was king instead of Caesar.

While He definitely was a king, He plainly said that His kingdom was not of this world (Jn. 18:36). As well, He had refused the offer to be king and taught that this was not the time of His kingdom (Lk. 19:11-27; Jn. 6:15; Acts 1:6-7).

As stated, He did not deny that He was born to be the King of the Jews, but He made it clear that this was not the time to establish His kingdom.

If one is to notice, all of these accusations were couched in political terms, attempting to pit Jesus against Caesar, which was their aim. They had no regard for the truth and, in fact, did not know truth or have truth in any measure. Had they known truth, they would have known the Old Testament and known that Jesus was the Messiah and, in fact, truth personified. In other words, Jesus did not merely have truth, He was and is truth (Jn. 14:6).

Conversely, and despite their claims of knowing God and being His representatives on this earth, the Pharisees and Sadducees did not know God and were actually children of the Devil, who is a liar and the father of it (Jn. 8:44). Consequently, they could only do what their father, Satan, did, and that was

to lie, for the entirety of their lives was lies.

A man is not a liar because he lies, but lies because he is a liar. These people were not merely telling a lie but were, in fact, liars!

(3) "AND PILATE ASKED HIM, SAYING, ARE YOU THE KING OF THE JEWS? AND HE ANSWERED HIM AND SAID, YOU SAY IT."

ARE YOU THE KING OF THE JEWS?

The question, *"And Pilate asked Him, saying, Are You the King of the Jews?"* presents Pilate completely ignoring the first two accusations, seeing clearly that they were baseless.

As well, Luke seems to give only a bare summary of the examination, with John going into much greater detail. Some even feel that John may have been present at this interrogation.

According to John, Jesus was left standing in the hall of judgment, into which the Jews would not enter.

The Passover was drawing near; consequently, they could not enter any dwelling that had not been cleansed of all leaven, which, of course, was not the case respecting the palace of Pilate.

Pilate knew from past experience how fiercely these fanatics resented any slight offered to their religious feelings (Jn. 18:28). Therefore, he walked out on the porch and addressed them while leaving Jesus inside.

In observing this, the picture becomes crystal clear as to what religion really is. It must keep its rules while at the same time murdering the Lord of Glory. What a contradiction! They would not walk into Pilate's judgment hall because they would defile themselves, while at the same time, they would murder their Messiah, and do so in cold blood, and suffer no twinge of conscience whatsoever. Regrettably, that spirit continues to strive unto this present time.

MY KINGDOM IS NOT OF THIS WORLD

The phrase, *"And He answered him and said, You say it,"* gives us only a preliminary sketch of what was actually said. John records that before this incident, Pilate had told the Jewish Sanhedrin, *"Take you Him* (You take Him), *and judge Him according to your law."*

The Jews answered by saying, *"It is not lawful for us to put any man to death,"* clearly proclaiming what they were after. They wanted the death of Jesus Christ and would be satisfied with nothing else (Jn. 18:31).

While Pilate posed this question to Jesus concerning Him being king, among other things, Jesus answered, *"My kingdom is not of this world"* (Jn. 18:36).

In truth, Jesus Christ is King, actually, *"KING OF KINGS, AND LORD OF LORDS"* (Rev. 19:16). Because of being rejected, He did not assume that role then but one day will. This will happen at the second coming when He will take over the authority and rulership of the world (Ezek., Chpts. 38-48; Dan. 2:35-35; Rev., Chpt. 19).

When Pilate looked at this pitiful, forlorn figure standing before him, His garment stained with blood and His face and head grotesquely swollen from the beatings and the crown of thorns, his question concerning Jesus being a king was probably as much in the spirit of sarcasm as the desire for information.

(4) "THEN SAID PILATE TO THE CHIEF PRIESTS AND TO THE PEOPLE, I FIND NO FAULT IN THIS MAN."

PONTIUS PILATE

The phrase, *"Then said Pilate to the chief priests and to the people,"* proclaimed his greatest fear. Little did he realize it, but he was facing God and man. His fear of God, even though at the time he did not really know that Jesus was God, was of far less magnitude than his fear of men.

He could seek to please men, or he could seek to please God, but he could not please both.

This scenario, as borne out by Pilate, is portrayed every day millions of times over in altogether different circumstances, but yet, with the same results. Man-fear keeps many people from God and many believers from being their best for the Lord.

While the believer should do everything within his power to be kind and gracious to all men, his foremost responsibility by far is to the Lord. The Lord must be obeyed and pleased above all else and all others.

As well, it must be remembered that if we let down in the slightest regarding this all-important principle, such leaven will ultimately spread until we are pleasing God not at all!

As an example, among preachers, and even laymen for that matter, if the church or denomination demands something that is unscriptural, even in the slightest, such must not under any circumstances be obeyed, even to the point of withdrawing from that church or denomination if necessary. If we compromise at all regarding the Word of God, we will ultimately compromise all.

I FIND NO FAULT IN THIS MAN

The phrase, *"I find no fault in this man,"* is the truth in its entirety. There was no fault in Jesus whatsoever! Neither has any human being ever found any fault in Him, at least a fault that is true and right. And yet, most of the world does find fault with Him, although dishonestly.

The Muslims claim that while Jesus was a great prophet, He was not the Son of God, and above that, would have to be subservient to Muhammad.

The modernists claim that He was a good man but deceived and, consequently, not the Son of God. The Buddhists claim that while Jesus may, in fact, have been God, anyone can become god by practicing a certain regimen, consequently, denying the true divinity of Christ.

If one attempts to understand Christ in any capacity except as God manifest in the flesh, he will understand Him not at all. As such, He took the place of man, actually becoming the representative man for all men and, thereby, suffered the penalty of the broken law at Calvary's Cross. He did it all for us and as the perfect sacrifice, He was accepted by God on behalf of all who will believe. Consequently, in Him alone is salvation. It resides in no other!

SACRIFICE

Jesus did for us what we could not do for ourselves. He lived a perfect life, keeping the law in every respect, not failing even one time, and, as stated, He did it all for mankind but not at all for Himself. As well, He went to the Cross in order to address the broken law by giving Himself as a sacrifice, which pleased God. In other words, His sacrifice of Himself on the Cross of Calvary was accepted by God in totality as price paid and penalty suffered in totality for every sin and for the entirety of mankind, past, present, and future, at least for all who will believe (Jn. 3:16).

All a man has to do, any man, irrespective of what he has done or what he has been in the past, is recognize himself as a sinner and recognize Jesus Christ as the Son of God, and exhibit faith in Him and what He did for us at Calvary. That person instantly will have a perfect righteousness, the righteousness of God, imputed to him. It only takes faith.

As all men died, spiritually speaking, in Adam, all men can be saved in Christ by simply exhibiting faith. It's just that simple!

One of the greatest theologians of the 19th century stated that, "The Cross of Christ was the greatest display of the wisdom of God, of anything and everything that God has done for the human race, even greater than all of creation." The Cross was a way that God could honestly justify an obviously guilty person and at the same time justify Himself in doing so. It's the Cross! The Cross! The Cross!

So, the verdict from God concerning Christ is that He was *"well-pleased"* with Him (Lk. 3:22). With impartial man, it was, *"I find no fault"* in Him.

(5) "AND THEY WERE THE MORE FIERCE, SAYING, HE STIRS UP THE PEOPLE, TEACHING THROUGHOUT ALL JEWRY, BEGINNING FROM GALILEE TO THIS PLACE."

The synopsis is:

1. The phrase, *"And they were the more fierce,"* proclaims that Pilate's position came somewhat as a surprise to these fanatics; consequently, their anger knew no bounds.

2. *"Saying, He stirs up the people,"* is a stronger accusation than the first. The Greek word for *"stirs"* is *anaseio* and means "to instigate." It is somewhat like inciting a mob to riot. Of course, what they were saying was basely false.

3. The phrase, *"Teaching throughout all Jewry, beginning from Galilee to this place,"* was true concerning His teaching,

NOTES

but not true respecting the subject matter.

In all His teaching, He never one time referred to Rome or anything that even resembled any type of sedition. As well, all of His teaching was done in public with nothing done in secret. Consequently, they could not bring anyone forth as a witness to substantiate their claims. People knew what He had said, and it had nothing to do with sedition.

(6) "WHEN PILATE HEARD OF GALILEE, HE ASKED WHETHER THE MAN WERE A GALILAEAN."

The synopsis is:

1. The fact that Jesus was a Galilaean aroused Pilate's interest strongly simply because he felt he could now shift the responsibility to Herod.

2. Herod's district included Galilee.

3. He was using every tactic he could to force someone else to make a decision concerning Christ. The reason was simple: he knew that Christ was innocent.

(7) "AND AS SOON AS HE KNEW THAT HE BELONGED UNTO HEROD'S JURISDICTION, HE SENT HIM TO HEROD, WHO HIMSELF ALSO WAS AT JERUSALEM AT THAT TIME."

The structure is:

1. The phrase, *"And as soon as He knew that He belonged unto Herod's jurisdiction, he sent Him to Herod,"* proclaims him thinking he could wash his hands of the affair.

2. Pilate was very fearful of this situation because he had powerful enemies in Rome. As well, history records that his once powerful patron Sejanus had just fallen from favor, which placed him (Pilate) in even greater jeopardy.

3. In his heart, he knew that he should release Jesus because it was obvious this man had done nothing wrong. But yet, he would attempt to shift the responsibility to another, an effort that would prove unsuccessful.

4. *"Who himself also was at Jerusalem at that time,"* constituted the Passover season, which brought Herod to the city. His usual residence was Capernaum, which had been the headquarters of Jesus, as well, but yet, seemingly without much impact upon this murderer.

(8) "AND WHEN HEROD SAW JESUS, HE WAS EXCEEDING GLAD: FOR HE

WAS DESIROUS TO SEE HIM OF A LONG SEASON, BECAUSE HE HAD HEARD MANY THINGS OF HIM; AND HE HOPED TO HAVE SEEN SOME MIRACLE DONE BY HIM."

HEROD

The next time he sees Jesus, he will be exceedingly sad and in eternal remorse over his many sins. He will especially remember that this very man whom he mocked could have saved his soul from eternal hell. Herod and all others will be forced to bow the knee to Him (Phil. 2:9-11).

This was Herod Antipas, the murderer of John the Baptist. He was at that time living in open incest with Herodias, who was his niece and, as well, had been the wife of Phillip, his brother.

Herodias was the daughter of Aristobulus, son of Herod the Great, and, therefore, the niece of both Herod and Philip. She first married Phillip, her uncle, by whom she had Salome. Later, she left him to live publicly with her brother-in-law, Herod.

JOHN THE BAPTIST

John the Baptist had spoken out against this crime of nature, with Herod summarily executing him.

"For He was desirous to see him of a long season, because he had heard many things of Him," had to do somewhat with both of them being headquartered in Capernaum.

Jesus probably performed more miracles in Capernaum than any place else. Consequently, He was the talk of this small city, and rightly so. As is obvious, these many things had come to the ears of Herod.

"And he hoped to have seen some miracle done by Him," was, as Godet summed up the situation, "Jesus was to Herod Antipas as a juggler is to a sated court—an object of curiosity." It seems he had very little interest in Him otherwise!

I wonder if this man knew that Jesus was the very one whom his father, Herod the Great, had attempted to murder as a little baby boy (Mat., Chpt. 2).

(9) "THEN HE QUESTIONED WITH HIM IN MANY WORDS; BUT HE ANSWERED HIM NOTHING."

NOTES

The diagram is:

1. The phrase, *"Then he questioned with Him in many words,"* presents a picture of some importance to say the least.

2. What type of questions he asked, we are not told; however, whatever they were, Jesus completely ignored him and them.

3. *"But He answered him nothing,"* tells us that the questions were trivial. This pompous egomaniac did not for a moment realize that the Lord of Glory, the Creator of the ages, was standing before him. To Herod, He was just another curiosity.

4. And yet, he had previously thought that Jesus was John the Baptist risen form the dead, proclaiming that he was plagued by conscience and superstition. Today he is in hell and will be there forever and forever.

(10) "AND THE CHIEF PRIESTS AND SCRIBES STOOD AND VEHEMENTLY ACCUSED HIM."

The overview is:

1. In this passage, along with the next, we find the church joining with the world, i.e., Herod, in accusing Jesus. The word *vehemently* is used, which in the Greek is *eutonos* and means "forcibly."

2. One can see Jesus standing in the mist of these devils, both secular and religious, and the sight is chilling to say the least.

3. If one is to notice, neither Herod nor Pilate, as evil as they were, demanded the death of Jesus, with even Pilate attempting to release Him. However, the church of that day proved to be far crueler than the world, where they did demand His death.

4. No! This is not meant to be a diatribe against the true church, but only that which is apostate, which, in fact, includes the far greater majority.

5. Jesus said, *"Few there be that find it,"* speaking of the straight and narrow way (Mat. 7:13-14). So, this means that most of the people who call themselves Christian, in fact, do not know the Lord, and are actually a part of the same spirit of darkness to which Herod and Pilate belonged, as well as these chief priests and scribes.

6. Deception is probably Satan's most powerful weapon, especially when one considers that almost all the world is deceived and always has been. Those who like Herod

and Pilate give little or no thought to the things of God, pinning their hopes on this present world, are certainly deceived. As stated, most of the modern church, as always, falls into the same category.

(11) "AND HEROD WITH HIS MEN OF WAR SET HIM AT NOUGHT, AND MOCKED HIM, AND ARRAYED HIM IN A GORGEOUS ROBE, AND SENT HIM AGAIN TO PILATE."

The construction is:

1. The phrase, *"And Herod with his men of war set Him at nought, and mocked Him,"* records the attitude and thinking of this despot.

2. Inasmuch as Jesus would not perform a miracle for the entertainment of Herod, or even answer him, he had now come to the conclusion that the stories he had heard concerning these miracles were a hoax. Consequently, he would treat Jesus accordingly—not as a criminal but as a religious fanatic worthy only of contempt and scorn.

3. *"And arrayed Him in a gorgeous robe,"* probably refers to a cast off robe, which had once been luxurious and beautiful. It was intended to mock Jesus as a claimant of the kingdom.

4. As well, it was this Herod with whom the Lord had spoken so recently, for Him, a rare bitterness, *"You go, and tell that fox (literally 'she-fox')"*—Herod (Lk. 13:32).

5. *"And sent Him again to Pilate,"* means that Herod, as well, found no cause for death in Him. Consequently, we have a second record and public attestation of His innocence.

6. Thus, the civil rulers of both Galilee and Judaea were in accord that He was innocent and should not be put to death. However, divine providence had already decreed that He should die for the sins of the people—the very people who kept demanding His life until Pilate finally gave in and turned Him over to be crucified.

7. So, Pilate's ploy did not work. He now found himself once again facing Jesus.

8. As we have previously stated, this will not be the last time that Pilate or Herod will face Jesus, for they will face Him at the *"great white throne"* judgment (Rev. 20:11-15).

(12) "AND THE SAME DAY PILATE

NOTES

AND HEROD WERE MADE FRIENDS TOGETHER: FOR BEFORE THEY WERE AT ENMITY BETWEEN THEMSELVES."

The exegesis is:

1. *"And the same day Pilate and Herod were made friends together,"* was included in what some referred to as the first hymn of the early church (Acts 4:27).

2. *"For before they were at enmity between themselves,"* proclaims not only this scene but, as well, countless others ever since, where worldly men, apparently irreconcilable, meet together in friendship when opportunity offers itself for wounding Christ!

(13) "AND PILATE, WHEN HE HAD CALLED TOGETHER THE CHIEF PRIESTS AND THE RULERS AND THE PEOPLE."

The exegesis is:

1. As stated, Pilate once again found himself with Jesus standing before him.

2. The gathering of most, if not all of the religious leaders of Israel, together at this time, and for the purpose of murdering the Messiah, would be a meeting bringing more sorrow and heartache than any meeting that has ever been conducted in the history of mankind. As we have stated, wherever Jesus is involved, there are always consequences of the highest order. They are positive or negative according to acceptance or rejection. No other person in history effects this type of outcome. As well, it holds true for a single individual, a nation, or for the entirety of the world for that matter.

3. Jesus Christ is God! As such, He is the maker of humanity and, in fact, the Creator of all things (Jn. 1:3). As well, He paid the price for man's redemption, in effect, the greatest sacrifice by far ever offered. It was so great, in fact, that no other sacrifice will ever be needed. Considering that the Father has committed all judgment unto the Son, our response to Him in any capacity has eternal consequences, whether good or bad.

4. In A.D. 39, Herod Antipas was denounced to the Emperor Gaius by his nephew Agrippa as a plotter. He was deposed from his tetrarchy and ended his days in exile.

5. As stated, it is supposed that Pilate committed suicide.

6. In A.D. 70, those of this group of religious leaders who were left alive were

NOTES

ruthlessly murdered by the Roman general Titus, along with over 1 million other Jews, with the temple being completely destroyed and Israel, in effect, ceasing to be a nation.

(14) "SAID UNTO THEM, YOU HAVE BROUGHT THIS MAN UNTO ME, AS ONE WHO PERVERTS THE PEOPLE: AND, BEHOLD, I, HAVING EXAMINED HIM BEFORE YOU, HAVE FOUND NO FAULT IN THIS MAN TOUCHING THOSE THINGS WHEREOF YOU ACCUSE HIM."

The exposition is:

1. The phrase, "Said unto them, You have brought this man unto me, as one who perverts the people," presents Pilate now more than ever seeing through their scam.

2. The statement seems that he had thought hard on this accusation while Jesus was in the presence of Herod. It was a trumped up charge, and he knew it.

3. "And, behold, I, having examined Him before you," presents a strong statement indeed!

4. The Greek word for examine in this case is anakrino and means "to examine forensically, i.e., public discussion, and even as examining by torture."

5. So, the examination of Jesus by Pilate had reached a conclusion predicated on the following:

a. The accusations against Christ had been public and, therefore, subject to the minutest scrutiny. Even from a public forum, which is the most exact forum of all, no witnesses could be found to corroborate the accusation of Jesus perverting the people.

b. Jesus had been tortured severely at this point, which has a tendency to make men confess to the truth if, in fact, they have lied. Under torture, Jesus said nothing because there was nothing to be said.

6. The phrase, "Have found no fault in this man touching those things whereof you accuse Him," presents the second public confession of Pilate, who also publicly acknowledged that the civil rulers of Galilee had found no fault in Him.

7. Pilate, his wife, Herod, Judas Iscariot, the dying thief, and the centurion all testified to Christ's innocence. This is extremely revealing, for had He been guilty of even one sin, He could not have atoned for sin.

(15) "NO, NOR YET HEROD: FOR I SENT YOU TO HIM; AND, LO, NOTHING WORTHY OF DEATH IS DONE UNTO HIM."

The composition is:

1. The phrase, "No, nor yet Herod," means that this despot found Him innocent but, nevertheless, took the opportunity to mock Him.

2. To be sure, when we consider that the religious hierarchy of Israel was clamoring for His blood, it would have been very easy for Herod to ingratiate himself to these devils by yielding to their demands. However, this he did not do, and for reasons we will never know.

3. "For I sent you to him," refers to the Sanhedrin being sent to Herod, along with Jesus.

4. "And, lo, nothing worthy of death is done unto Him," should have been translated "by Him."

5. However, even using such terms of Jesus as "nothing worthy of death," etc., is a crass insult of the highest order. This would go for His arrest and the accusations. In fact, He was the only perfect human being who ever lived, with no flaw, fault, or blemish. By this, and above all, we speak of the moral sense, as well as the physical.

(16) "I WILL THEREFORE CHASTISE HIM, AND RELEASE HIM."

The form is:

1. Chastisement (scourging) within itself was singularly unjust and cruel.

2. Spence said, "Pilate positively subjected a man whom he had pronounced innocent to the horrible punishment of scourging, just to satisfy the clamor of the Sanhedrists, because he was fearful of what they might accuse him of at Rome, where he knew he had enemies."

3. He thought perhaps that such brutal torture would surely satisfy the blood lust of these people, but he was to be dreadfully mistaken.

4. The short phrase, "And release Him," was said concerning the release of one prisoner each year at the Passover.

(17) "(FOR OF NECESSITY HE MUST RELEASE ONE UNTO THEM AT THE FEAST.)"

The order is:

1. This custom was probably introduced at Jerusalem by the Roman power. There is no evidence of such in Levitical law, even though some expositors attempt to link it with one of the oral commandments added by the Pharisees, claiming that it typified the release of the children of Israel from Egyptian bondage.

2. Such a release was a common occurrence at some of the Latin feasts in honor of the gods.

3. The Greeks had a similar custom, which was probably adopted by Rome. If so, it was a method to appease subjugated people on certain of their feast days. Evidently, Pilate thought that he could solve his problem concerning Jesus by this method; however, he was to find that this ploy did not work either. These devils would prefer a robber to the Son of God. I might quickly add that they chose a robber, and they have been robbed ever since.

(18) "AND THEY CRIED OUT ALL AT ONCE, SAYING, AWAY WITH THIS MAN, AND RELEASE UNTO US BARABBAS."

The pattern is:

1. The phrase, *"And they cried out all at once,"* proclaims their strong opposition to his decision to release Jesus.

2. *"Saying, Away with this man, and release unto us Barabbas,"* is exactly what they got and have had ever since.

3. They preferred a robber, as John styled him, to the Son of God. So, they got the robber.

4. The nations of the world have robbed them of their dignity, pride, and lives for nearly 2,000 years.

5. They claim to have suffered because they have been forced to bear the stigma of Christ; however, it is not the stigma of Christ they bear but their decision concerning Christ.

6. This man Barabbas seemed to be a bandit chief, who carried on his lawless career under the veil of patriotism, and was supported and protected in consequence by many of the people.

7. Some have thought that the name of Barabbas was prefixed by the name of Jesus as well. In fact, it was a common name at that particular time.

8. It is possible that when Barabbas was selected, Pilate, with some scorn, asked the

populace whom they preferred, Jesus Barabbas or Jesus Christ!

(19) "(WHO FOR A CERTAIN SEDITION MADE IN THE CITY, AND FOR MURDER, WAS CAST INTO PRISON.)"

The pattern is:

1. It was bad enough to prefer a robber over Jesus, but to prefer a murderer, which Barabbas also was, presented itself as a horror that would be perpetrated upon them from that day forward.

2. As a result, Titus murdered over 1 million Jews in cold blood about 37 years later. Adolf Hitler murdered 6 million Jews in World War II. Untold millions of others have been murdered between Titus and Hitler.

3. Barabbas was also guilty of sedition, which refers to rebellion against lawful authority.

4. As well, down through the centuries, many civil rulers have broken the law in regard to their dealing with Jews. It is as though sedition, robbery, and murder have followed them for nearly 2,000 years, which it definitely has.

5. Sadly and regrettably, if the past has not been enough, the future Antichrist will practice these three crimes against Israel as none before him. So, whatever measure we mete, it is measured to us again (Mat. 7:2).

(20) "PILATE THEREFORE, WILLING TO RELEASE JESUS, SPOKE AGAIN TO THEM."

The exegesis is:

1. This presents Pilate for the fourth time as recorded by Luke, attempting to release Jesus, but to no avail!

2. This man, Pilate, seemed to be a very intelligent man but, at the same time, did not have the strength and fortitude to stand up for what was right.

3. This made it even worse when one considers that Pilate knew very well what was right but was not strong enough to carry it out.

(21) "BUT THEY CRIED, SAYING, CRUCIFY HIM, CRUCIFY HIM."

The overview is:

1. The phrase, *"But they cried,"* means they shouted aloud and kept shouting.

2. *"Saying, Crucify Him, crucify Him,"* presented the type of execution they demanded.

3. Their scheme was threefold:

a. They had to arrest Him at night for fear of the people. In fact, the whole thing had to be rushed through before the people even knew what happened, which it was.

b. Even though they could condemn Him, they had no power to carry out the death sentence; therefore, they must persuade Pilate to carry out this act, and so the charges were political in nature.

c. They demanded His death by crucifixion because the law of Moses said that, *"If a man have committed a sin worthy of death … And you hang him on a tree … (He) is accursed of God"* (Deut. 21:22-23).

4. So, His death by crucifixion would seem to the people that He must at least be guilty of some of these charges, or Pilate would not have ordered His death, and above all, by crucifixion.

(22) "AND HE SAID UNTO THEM THE THIRD TIME, WHY, WHAT EVIL HAS HE DONE? I HAVE FOUND NO CAUSE OF DEATH IN HIM: I WILL THEREFORE CHASTISE HIM, AND LET HIM GO."

The composition is:

1. The phrase, *"And he said unto them the third time,"* refers to the times he had attempted to free Jesus on the premise of the custom of releasing a prisoner at the Passover each year. Actually, this was about the fifth time he had made such an attempt overall.

2. The question, *"Why, what evil has He done?"* was a question they could not answer because, in fact, He had done no evil.

3. *"I have found no cause of death in Him: I will therefore chastise Him, and let Him go,"* sounds a note of desperation.

4. A very short time before this, Matthew records that Pilate's *"wife sent unto him, saying, Have thou (You have) nothing to do with that just man: for I have suffered many things this day in a dream because of Him"* (Mat. 27:19).

5. This was another attempt by the Holy Spirit to reach the governor, but Pilate did not have the courage to do what was right. He kept trying to find ways to release Jesus that would satisfy the religious leaders. Such was not to be done.

6. One must always remember that while there are a thousand excuses one may use

to do nothing or to do wrong, there's only one reason to do right, and that is because it is right.

(23) "AND THEY WERE INSTANT WITH LOUD VOICES, REQUIRING THAT HE MIGHT BE CRUCIFIED. AND THE VOICES OF THEM AND OF THE CHIEF PRIESTS PREVAILED."

The overview is:

1. The phrase, *"And they were instant with loud voices, requiring that He might be crucified,"* tells us two things:

a. Many have said that the same crowd who was crying *"Hosanna to the highest"* at the triumphant entry was now crying *"crucify Him!"* However, that is incorrect.

These happenings took place not too long after daylight, which saw most of the people who were present at the triumphant entry in bed. No! The rabble who joined the religious leaders that early morning hour was for the most part the night people, or else lackeys of the Sanhedrin.

b. While this mob, clamoring for the release of Barabbas in the place of Jesus, had ceased, the terrible cry, *"Crucify Him!"* was raised in its place.

2. The phrase, *"And the voices of them and of the chief priests prevailed,"* presents their success, but a success they would ever rue.

3. Little did they realize it, but their prevailing sealed their own doom.

(24) "AND PILATE GAVE SENTENCE THAT IT SHOULD BE AS THEY REQUIRED."

IT SHOULD BE AS THEY REQUIRED

The phrase, *"And Pilate gave sentence,"* would prove to be the worst day of his life but could have been the best. However, as he now knows, the next time he stands before the Son of God, which will most assuredly happen, then the roles will be reversed. Jesus will then hand down the sentence, and it will be at the great white throne judgment (Rev. 20:11-15).

"That it should be as they required," speaks of them prevailing, as the previous verse said, and Pilate, through cowardice and the fear of man, acquiescing to their demands.

Let it ever be known that in its wickedness, religious hierarchy must be resisted irrespective of the demands. To fail to do so places one in the same position as Pilate of old. To be sure, this scene is played out one way or the other each day, and possibly thousands of times. We should take a lesson from this.

Most of the demands for the abrogation of the Word of God, as here, will not come from the world, but rather the world of religion. Thousands of preachers demand that if a person speaks in tongues, such actions must cease, or else he (the speaker) is no longer welcome at that church.

Religious denominational heads, in effect, have replaced Christ. They demand, as the religious hierarchy of old, certain things of their preachers, which some preachers know to be wrong. Sadly, most give in to such demands, *"That it should be as they required."* It is the same spirit that crucified Christ.

WHAT THE RELIGIOUS LEADERS REQUIRED CONCERNING JESUS

To do right, almost all of the time, a person has to stand against the crowd. Much of the time, he has to stand against the church as well! So, it is never going to be easy. It is impossible to please the Devil and the Lord at the same time. And yet, many preachers compromise their message, attempting to do so.

Luke omits the scourging of Jesus, along with the mocking of the soldiers and the crown of thorns.

This was a horrible punishment and took place at about this juncture in Luke's account.

The condemned person was usually stripped and fastened to a pillar or stake and then scourged with leather thongs tipped with leaden balls or sharp spikes.

The effects, as described by the Romans, were terrible to say the least. Not only the muscles of the back, but the breast, the face, and the eyes were torn as well. The very entrails at times were laid bare, the anatomy was exposed, and the sufferer, convulsed with torture, was often thrown down in a bloody heap at the feet of the judge.

In our Lord's case, this punishment must have been very severe, especially considering

NOTES

that Pilate probably hoped that the sight of this lacerated, torn body would elicit some type of pity from these devils, but it was to no avail!

THE KING OF THE JEWS

As well, the Jewish law allowed only 40 stripes, which was usually stopped at 39, so the law would not be broken; however, the Romans had no such law. They could whip a man until he died, which many did.

In June, 1996, Frances and I, Donnie and Debbie and the grandchildren, and nearly 100 other friends stood where it is believed to be the very place where Jesus was condemned—Pilate's judgment hall.

There is even a possibility that a particular truncated column still standing was the pillar used for victims to be scourged, and where Jesus may well have suffered this horrible punishment.

As we stood there that day singing "Amazing Grace," it is very difficult to properly relate exactly how I felt. And yet, He suffered all of this for a world who did not love Him.

After this came the crown of thorns, imitating what they had probably seen the emperor wear in the form of a laurel wreath. The crown was made, it is believed, from a thorn bush, which grows exceedingly large thorns called "victor's thorns." Some of them, it is said, are up to six inches in length.

In His right hand, they placed a reed to simulate a scepter and before this sad, woe-begone figure, *"They bowed the knee ... Saying, Hail, King of the Jews!"* (Mat. 27:29).

Spence said, "There is some comfort in the fact that even in the midst of the mockery, the truth made itself felt, for He was indeed 'The King of the Jews!'"

(25) "AND HE RELEASED UNTO THEM HIM WHO FOR SEDITION AND MURDER WAS CAST INTO PRISON, WHOM THEY HAD DESIRED; BUT HE DELIVERED JESUS TO THEIR WILL."

The pattern is:

1. The phrase, *"And he released unto them him who for sedition and murder was cast into prison, whom they had desired,"* portrayed, as stated, them getting exactly that for which they asked—sedition, robbery,

and murder. It has plagued them from that day until this.

2. *"But he delivered Jesus to their will,"* was the very worst thing he had ever done in all his life.

3. He was not man enough to stand up to this crowd, thinking possibly that if he did so, Rome would take a dim view. So, he saved his own life and lost it, exactly as Jesus said (Mat. 10:39).

(26) "AND AS THEY LED HIM AWAY, THEY LAID HOLD UPON ONE SIMON, A CYRENIAN, COMING OUT OF THE COUNTRY, AND ON HIM THEY LAID THE CROSS, THAT HE MIGHT BEAR IT AFTER JESUS."

SIMON A CYRENIAN

The phrase, *"And as they led Him away,"* presents the horrifying trip to the place of crucifixion, with Jesus carrying the Cross.

There were several different types of instruments of this nature, but the Roman Cross was undoubtedly the one on which Jesus died. Generally, the condemned carried the horizontal beam, which could have weighed from 50 to 100 pounds, with the vertical beam normally left in the ground at the place of execution.

"They laid hold upon one Simon, a Cyrenian," who was, as Mark tells us, the father of *"Alexander and Rufus,"* seemingly notable persons in the early church (Mk. 15:21).

Rufus was greeted by Paul in his letter to the Romans. He was described as a choice Christian. It seems his mother, the wife of Simon of Cyrene, had shown herself a mother to Paul as well (Rom. 16:13).

Also, some think the Simeon of Antioch of Acts 13:1 was the Simon of the Cross.

Very likely their connection with Jesus dated from this incident on the road to Calvary.

Cyrene was an important city in North Africa, with a large colony of resident Jews. As well, the Cyrenian Jews had a synagogue of their own in Jerusalem, which they frequented on the trips to Jerusalem to keep the feasts.

ON HIM THEY LAID THE CROSS

The phrase, *"Coming out of the country,"* either meant that Simon was just arriving

in Jerusalem in order to keep the feasts, or else he was lodging in one of the villages nearby and was coming into Jerusalem to the temple. At any rate, it would be the greatest day of his life, and yet, at great price to Jesus. However, every good thing that any believer has was purchased at great price, which is the price of which Simon had the distinct privilege to be a part.

"And on Him they laid the Cross," probably means, even though the Bible does not specifically say, that Jesus ultimately became too weak to bear the weight of the Cross. He had been beaten so severely that it, no doubt, resulted in a great loss of blood. So, Simon was compelled, *"That he might bear it after Jesus."* Whatever he saw that day would forever change his life, as well as that of his entire family.

The horror of this scene was incomprehensible, especially considering that Jesus was to be the sacrifice of the ages, thereby, purchasing redemption for humanity. Still, Simon of Cyrene was, without a doubt, the most privileged man who ever lived. While so many were attempting to hurt Christ at this moment, he was one of the few who tried to help Him.

Matthew used the word *compelled,* respecting the Romans pressing Simon into this service (Mat. 27:32). It implies that he did not at first desire this horrifying duty, especially considering that he probably didn't even know who it was at first that was being crucified. Judaea was not his home so he may not have known Jesus at all; however, in a few moments' time, he would realize this man was different than any he had ever known. Thus, whatever took place thereafter would, it seems, make him a stalwart for Christ.

To be sure, the bearing of the Cross after Jesus continues to be demanded of every follower of Christ. Even though we do not presently have the gruesome task as that of Simon of Cyrene, still, the principle is the same.

The Cross is a place to die, and more particularly, the death of the flesh, until the Spirit rules (Lk. 9:23-26).

(27) "AND THERE FOLLOWED HIM A GREAT COMPANY OF PEOPLE, AND OF

WOMEN, WHICH ALSO BEWAILED AND LAMENTED HIM."

A GREAT COMPANY OF PEOPLE

The phrase, *"And there followed Him a great company of people,"* probably referred to two classes of people.

The first group would have been made up of the usual concourse of curious onlookers, with the remainder consisting of those who had just heard the news of Jesus being crucified, which probably was unbelievable to them. As stated, Jerusalem was filled with Passover pilgrims, probably numbering as many as 1 million people. Almost all of these people, and especially the ones who lived in Israel proper, were very acquainted with Jesus, with many of them having experienced great healings at His hands.

What must have been their thoughts when they heard that Jesus was being crucified? They could not imagine such a thing happening, especially to someone who was so good and even perfect! Consequently, upon hearing the rumor, which they would find out to be all too true, they would have hurried toward the temple site, with many of them coming upon the procession that witnessed this awful scene. No doubt, hundreds, if not thousands, slowly walked beside Jesus with sobs filling their throats, hearts breaking, and not understanding why or even how this thing could have happened. However, it was happening before their very eyes. They could thank their religious leaders for this! As stated, it continues to happen every day.

GREAT SORROW

The phrase, *"And of women, which also bewailed and lamented Him,"* uses the word *also,* which tells us that many people were weeping and crying as a result of what their eyes were seeing.

The Holy Spirit purposely mentioned these particular women for a reason.

No woman is mentioned in the Gospels as having spoken against the Lord or as having a share in His death. On the contrary, He was anointed by a woman for His burial, and women were last at His grave and first at His sepulchre. They ministered to His wants, and they bewailed and lamented Him, as

here recorded. Pilate's wife interceded for Him. He first appeared to a woman after His resurrection, and of a woman, He was born.

(28) "BUT JESUS TURNING UNTO THEM SAID, DAUGHTERS OF JERUSALEM, WEEP NOT FOR ME, BUT WEEP FOR YOURSELVES, AND FOR YOUR CHILDREN."

The form is:

1. The phrase, *"But Jesus turning unto them said,"* represents the first time He spoke since His last interrogation before Pilate.

2. *"Daughters of Jerusalem,"* is a fixture of the Song of Solomon. That particular book has a bearing on why Jesus used this phrase.

3. Among other things, the book consists of Solomon, the great king of Israel, and a lowly shepherd both vying for the hand of the beautiful Shulamite damsel.

4. Even though as a secondary meaning, the damsel can stand for the church, her primary focus is Israel. As well, both the lowly shepherd and Solomon typify Christ.

5. The moral is that before Israel can have and know Jesus as the Great King, typified by Solomon, she must first accept Him as the lowly shepherd, which she at first refused to do, hence, the statement by Christ given to these daughters of Jerusalem.

6. When Israel finally accepts Jesus as the lowly shepherd, which they will do at the second coming, then and only then can they know Him as the Great King (Song of Solomon 1:5, 7; 3:5; 5:16; 8:4).

7. *"Weep not for Me, but weep for yourselves, and for your children,"* proclaims His rejection by the religious leaders of Israel and the subsequent judgment that would follow.

8. To be sure, this was said with great concern regarding what He knew would happen shortly. His thoughts were not on Himself, but others!

9. Many who would suffer this terrible judgment would include some of those, no doubt, standing there that day, and especially their children. He was speaking of the coming carnage that would be brought about by Titus when Jerusalem would be destroyed in A.D. 70. Over 1 million Jews died in that terrible conflict. Consequently, this tells us, and should have told them, approximately when this terrible judgment would take place.

(29) "FOR, BEHOLD, THE DAYS ARE COMING, IN THE WHICH THEY SHALL SAY, BLESSED ARE THE BARREN, AND THE WOMBS THAT NEVER BEAR, AND THE PAPS WHICH NEVER GAVE SUCK."

The diagram is:

1. The phrase, *"For, behold, the days are coming,"* would actually see fulfillment about 37 years from that time. It would be A.D. 70 when Titus would destroy Jerusalem, and this very street over which Jesus was carrying this Cross would run red with the blood of its citizens.

2. *"In the which they shall say, Blessed are the barren, and the wombs that never bear, and the paps which never gave suck,"* presents a strange beatitude.

3. Through all their checkered history, every woman of Israel so passionately longed that this barrenness might not be their position!

4. And yet, Jesus called these very ones (the barren) blessed!

5. He was speaking of the horror that was coming, which would be so bad that the dead would be the blessed, along with the children never born.

6. No doubt, these very words uttered by Jesus were said over and over by the women in the siege of Jerusalem when children died by the thousands because of the famine that resulted when Titus surrounded the city.

(30) "THEN SHALL THEY BEGIN TO SAY TO THE MOUNTAINS, FALL ON US; AND TO THE HILLS, COVER US."

The overview is:

1. The phrase, *"Then shall they begin to say to the mountains,"* tells us by the word *then* that this prophecy speaks of the destruction of Jerusalem in A.D. 70. Consequently, it could not refer to the sixth seal of Revelation 6:12-17, which will be fulfilled in the first half of the coming great tribulation, which will be after the rapture of the church.

2. The phrase, *"Fall on us; and to the hills, Cover us,"* presents a cry of despair, which has continued from that moment until now.

3. While a few times in the past nearly 2,000 years the Jews have experienced a measure of blessing and prosperity, even as now with the protection of America, still, this is sadly only the calm before the storm.

NOTES

4. Israel's darkest day, however, is yet to come. In the last half of the coming great tribulation, they will, no doubt, say these very words all over again, exactly as their forefathers and as Jesus predicted. Jesus said that, that time will be worse than anything that ever has been.

(31) "FOR IF THEY DO THESE THINGS IN A GREEN TREE, WHAT SHALL BE DONE IN THE DRY?"

THE GREEN TREE

The question, *"For if they do these things in a green tree"* actually refers to Jesus Himself.

He was the Lord of Glory and the incarnate Son of God and held no animosity against Rome, or anyone else for that matter. As well, He had only done good to all men, never creating sedition, strife, or spreading hatred.

As well, the green tree represented Him bringing the glory of God, with all its attendant blessings, prosperity, anointing of the Holy Spirit, healing, miracles, and goodness, which is a blessing unparalleled to any people.

The conclusion of the question, *"What shall be done in the dry?"* refers to the time when He would be gone, with the blessings of God gone, as well, due to Him being rejected by Israel.

So, if Rome would crucify Him, the epitome of all that is good, how much more would they do to Israel, which was not good, and was actually fomenting rebellion against Rome? Above all, Israel would be bereft of the blessings and protection of the Lord.

THE QUESTION ASKED BY JESUS

History is replete with the fulfillment of this question asked by Jesus. In the annals of human history, there has probably never been such a display of anger, cruelty, and rage leveled against any people as it was when Titus destroyed Jerusalem in A.D. 70 with the 10th Legion. Over 1.1 million Jews died in that horror, with hundreds of thousands of others being sold as slaves all over the world of that day.

The use of the term *"green tree"* is one of the many references to the humanity of Jesus. Below, a few are listed:

- Human names (Mat. 1:1, 21; 2:2; 8:20; 11:19; Jn. 1:29, 41; 4:25; 20:16; Rom. 1:3; I Cor. 15:45; Rev. 5:5; 22:16).
- Human mother (Gen. 3:15; Isa. 7:14, 9:6-7; 11:1; Mat. 1:18-23; Gal. 4:4).
- Human babyhood (Lk. 2:15), childhood (Lk. 2:40, 52), and manhood (I Tim. 2:5).
- Human flesh and blood body (Jn. 1:14; Heb. 2:4-18; I Jn. 4:1-6).
- Human in all things like men (Heb. 2:9-18; 4:14-16).
- Human in life on earth (Lk. 2:40, 52; Jn. 5:30-46; 6:57; 7:16; 8:27-29; Phil. 2:5-11; Heb. 2:9-18; 4:14-16; 5:7-9).
- Human in limitations and passions: grew in body and spirit (Lk. 2:40, 52), wept (Jn. 11:35), hungered (Mat. 4:1-11; Mk. 11:12), thirsted (Jn. 4:7; 19:28), slept (Mat. 8:24), grew weary (Jn. 4:6), sorrowed (Isa. 53:3-4), suffered bodily pain (Lk. 22:44; I Pet. 3:18, 41), craved sympathy (Mat. 26:36-40; Lk. 22:14-27), was tempted (Mat., Chpt. 4; Heb. 4:14-16), died physically (Jn. 19:30; Acts 1:3; 2:23; I Pet. 2:24), and was resurrected bodily to live in a glorified human body forever (Lk. 24:49; Jn. 20:27; I Cor., Chpt. 15; Zech. 13:6).

(32) "AND THERE WERE ALSO TWO OTHERS, MALEFACTORS, LED WITH HIM TO BE PUT TO DEATH."

The exposition is:

1. So, we learn from this passage that two other individuals—malefactors, i.e., criminals—made this horrifying trek with Him, carrying their crosses. Some think these were companions of Barabbas who had just been released.

2. Considering that Jesus would die for the sins of the world, it is fitting that He would be accompanied by two such as this. This was typified by the two mountains in Israel, side by side, called *"the mount of cursing and the mount of blessing."* They were named Mount Ebal and Mount Gerizim, located near Shechem. Ebal was the mount of cursing while Gerizim was the mount of blessing (Deut. 11:29; 27:9-13).

3. However, the altar was built on Mount Ebal, the one of cursing (Deut. 27:1-8), instead of Gerizim, that of blessing. This was because man's problem is the curse of sin, which can only be eradicated by the shed blood of Jesus Christ. This will then guarantee the blessings, i.e., Gerizim.

4. Unfortunately, many modern churches have attempted to erect the altar on the mount of blessing exclusively, that is, if they even believe in the Cross at all, which most don't. This is especially true of the faith movement, which is really no faith at all, at least that which God will recognize. By that, they are saying, whether they realize it or not, that man's problem is a lack of blessing, which, in their thinking, speaks of money, prosperity, etc. This is a serious abrogation of the gospel and everything the Bible teaches. Man's problem is sin, which has brought the curse that can only be eradicated by the altar, i.e., the death of Christ on the Cross.

So, Jesus would go to His death among criminals, taking the full penalty of the curse upon Himself, even though He had never sinned and was not personally subject to its penalty. He would suffer that penalty for all of mankind that upon faith in what He did, the blessings of justification by faith and all its attendant prosperity can be given freely to the believing sinner.

(33) "AND WHEN THEY WERE COME TO THE PLACE, WHICH IS CALLED CALVARY, WHERE THEY CRUCIFIED HIM, AND THE MALEFACTORS, ONE ON THE RIGHT HAND, AND THE OTHER ON THE LEFT."

CALVARY

The phrase, *"And when they were come to the place, which is called Calvary,"* refers to the place of a skull, called in the Hebrew Golgotha, which was a hill that looked like a skull.

On one of our trips to Israel sometime back, flying all night long, we arrived in Tel-Aviv sometime in the early afternoon. We drove from there to Jerusalem, arriving at approximately 5 p.m., the time of the rush hour traffic as people were going home from work.

Winding our way through the traffic and through the city to get to the hotel, the car stopped at a particular intersection, and I happened to look out the window to my right. As I did, I realized that I was basically at the foot of Golgotha as it loomed large above me.

I cannot tell you how I felt, especially considering the unexpected observation of the place where Jesus paid for the sins of humanity.

For a moment as tears filled my eyes, I felt this was wrong for all of this din of activity to take place around the most sacred spot on the face of the earth. A giant bus station is located at the very base of Calvary, with passengers coming and going, big buses belching black smoke, etc.

However, while sitting there waiting for the light to change and these thoughts filling my mind, it seemed the Lord spoke to me, saying words to this effect, "The activity you see is a sign of life, and that is why I came. So the activity that surrounds this place portrays more so what I did for the human family than if the place were a shrine."

WHERE THEY CRUCIFIED HIM

The phrase, *"Where they crucified Him,"* portrays the response of the world and the church of that day to God's greatest gift, His only Son. But yet, the Lord would cause even the wrath of man to praise Him (Ps. 76:10). The Cross, which was the most horrifying instrument of torture the world had ever known, became an emblem of beauty because of what Jesus did on that Cross.

As we have stated, most of the time the victims carried the cross beam of the cross instead of the entire cross, which would have been too heavy to carry. When they arrived at the place of crucifixion, the soldiers would have caused Jesus to lie on His back on the ground. They would have placed the cross beam under His shoulders and stretched out His hands on either side. They would have then taken two spikes and driven them through both wrists into the Cross.

Many think that the nails were driven into the palms of His hands; however, the weight of His body would have pulled the flesh loose if the nails had been driven in this fashion. They were driven in the wrists, so they would not pull out. As well, the Jews considered the wrist a part of the hand.

THE CROSS

After they had nailed His hands to the crossbar, they would have picked Him up,

along with the crossbar, and placed it on top of the upright part of the Cross protruding out of the ground, called the stipe. They would have either tied the crossbar to the upended portion, or else, nailed it in place. About middle ways of the perpendicular part of the Cross was fastened a piece of wood called a *sedile*, on which the condemned rested, if one could call it that. This was necessary, else during the long torture, the weight of the body could have pulled the wrists loose from the nails, with the body falling from the Cross.

The Cross was not very high, probably about 6 or 7 feet, if that.

At the bottom of the Cross, one foot would have been placed over the other, with a long spike driven through both feet into the Cross.

Due to the terrible torture the body had already experienced, coupled with the shock of what was now happening, burning fever would soon set in, producing a terrible thirst, hence, Jesus saying, *"I thirst"* (Jn. 19:28).

The increasing inflammation of the wounds in the back, hands, and feet, with the congestion of blood in the head, lungs, and heart, along with the swelling of every vein, produced pain that would be impossible to describe unless one had experienced such.

Some would hang there for days, actually dying of pain and starvation; however, Jesus would die in only six hours. He was placed on the Cross at the time of the morning sacrifice, 9 a.m., and died at the time of the evening sacrifice, 3 p.m., thus fulfilling the great biblical types.

The phrase, *"And the malefactors, one on the right hand, and the other on the left,"* may not have been the only ones crucified that day, but were the only ones in this particular position. As stated, both of these men on these other two crosses were criminals.

(34) "THEN SAID JESUS, FATHER, FORGIVE THEM; FOR THEY KNOW NOT WHAT THEY DO. AND THEY PARTED HIS RAIMENT, AND CAST LOTS."

THE PRAYER OF CHRIST

The phrase, *"Then said Jesus, Father, forgive them; for they know not what they do,"* proclaims three things:

1. In this first saying from the Cross, of which there were seven, Jesus, as always, thought of others before Himself, even in this horrifying condition.

2. One might say that this is the only prayer ever prayed by Jesus that was not answered. While it is true that the Lord certainly would have forgiven these devils who had done this thing if they had only repented, there is no evidence that they did such. The Lord will not and, in fact, cannot forgive those who will not repent, thereby, causing the prayer of Jesus not to be answered, at least in this case.

3. In His statement, *"For they know not what they do,"* He was saying that this act would bring untold judgment upon their heads, causing sorrow and heartache, which would actually destroy their nation.

THE GARMENTS OF CHRIST

The phrase, *"And they parted His raiment, and cast lots,"* referred to the soldiers.

Four soldiers were normally stationed at every cross, but it seems that a centurion was among these soldiers, which was not normally the case. Such an officer was one of substantial rank, actually in charge of a hundred men. Quite possibly Pilate appointed him this duty because of its implications. It was to be the greatest day of his life, for he would find salvation in Jesus.

Normally the clothing of the victims was awarded to the soldiers as a compensation for this extremely distasteful duty, to say the least.

Consequently, they would strip Jesus of His robe, which was without seam. Due to it not having a seam, which they could rip, they cast lots as to who would win the robe. As a result of their taking the clothing, Jesus was left completely naked, without even a loin cloth to cover Him.

This must have been of great glee to His enemies, as they desired not only to torture Him but to humiliate Him as much as possible. Such is religion!

Some have claimed that the robe was very simple, coarse, and of very little worth; however, since John mentioned that it was without seam, it is doubtful that he would have said it was worthless (Jn. 19:23).

NOTES

(35) "AND THE PEOPLE STOOD BEHOLDING. AND THE RULERS ALSO WITH THEM DERIDED HIM, SAYING, HE SAVED OTHERS; LET HIM SAVE HIMSELF, IF HE BE CHRIST, THE CHOSEN OF GOD."

The overview is:

1. The phrase, *"And the people stood beholding,"* has the connotation of an awed silence. Just who made up this crowd is not known. Quite possibly there were some, or even many, in this group whom He had healed and delivered.

2. *"And the rulers also with them derided Him,"* spoke of the leaders of the church. These animals were not content to have Him crucified; they must mock Him, even while He was dying. The irony of it all is that He also died for their sins even though they were so spiritually blind, they could not see.

3. The word *derided* meant that they "mocked Him."

4. *"Saying, He saved others; let Him save Himself, if He be Christ, the chosen of God,"* proclaims an utter ignorance of the mission of the Messiah and of the gospel. If He had saved His life, He could not have saved others (Mat. 16:25; Mk. 8:35; Lk. 9:24; 17:33).

5. The title *Christ* means "the Anointed" and was a description, as given by the prophets, of the coming Messiah.

6. If it is to be noticed, His detractors never referred to Him by the name of Jesus, which meant "Saviour" or "Christ," which meant, as stated, "the Anointed." These religious leaders refused to admit, even from the beginning, that Jesus was the Messiah. To be factual, anyone who came from God, they would have rejected.

7. It is basically the same presently. The church, for the most part, accepts Saul and rejects David.

(36) "AND THE SOLDIERS ALSO MOCKED HIM, COMING TO HIM, AND OFFERING HIM VINEGAR."

The structure is:

1. The phrase, *"And the soldiers also mocked Him,"* probably was carried out by these heathen simply because they heard these religious leaders mocking Him.

2. What an example!

3. *"Coming to Him, and offering Him vinegar,"* was in response to His plea for water (Jn. 19:28).

4. This vinegar was, it is said, a sour wine, a common drink of the soldiers and others. It was probably laced with narcotics and stupefying drugs.

5. However, Matthew records that He only tasted it and *"would not drink"* (Mat. 27:34). He would not dull the sense of pain or cloud the clearness of His mind; therefore, He refused it.

6. The Scriptures seem to indicate that such drink was offered three times, with Him taking some only at the very last in order that He may speak the last words (Jn. 19:28-30).

7. With the loss of so much blood and the burning fever that racked His body due to the torture and shock, He would have been terribly dehydrated, even to the place, at least at the last, of being unable to speak. Consequently, He would take a few drops in order to moisten His mouth and tongue that He may utter the last words, *"Into Your hands I commend My Spirit"* (Lk. 23:46).

8. It is probable that He uttered the words, *"It is finished,"* immediately before the final statement (Jn. 19:30).

(37) "AND SAYING, IF YOU BE THE KING OF THE JEWS, SAVE YOURSELF."

The exegesis is:

1. No doubt, the soldiers had heard these religious leaders mocking Jesus concerning Him being their king. They would have had little knowledge concerning these titles and relating them to Jesus.

2. So, overhearing them and knowing that kings were seldom, if ever, crucified, they would join in with the mockery.

3. What none of these knew was that He was not only the King of the Jews but the Creator of the heavens and earth, the maker of all things. And yet, as we shall see, there were certain things that happened that should have informed them of who He really was and, in fact, was understood by one of the thieves and the centurion.

(38) "AND A SUPERSCRIPTION ALSO WAS WRITTEN OVER HIM IN LETTERS OF GREEK, AND LATIN, AND HEBREW, THIS IS THE KING OF THE JEWS."

The synopsis is:

1. The phrase, *"And a superscription also was written over Him,"* constituted that written by Pilate.

2. He probably did it not so much to mock Jesus, but rather to mock His detractors. It showed his utter contempt for the Jewish people, and especially for those who had clamored for the crucifixion of Christ—the religious leaders of Israel.

3. And yet at the same time, even though He did not know, and neither did the enemies of Christ, Jesus really was the King of the Jews.

4. The phrase, *"In letters of Greek, and Latin, and Hebrew,"* presented a common practice of that day, due to the many nationalities normally represented in the major cities of the Roman Empire.

5. The title, *"THIS IS THE KING OF THE JEWS,"* differs a little from the other three gospels.

6. Matthew said, *"THIS IS JESUS THE KING OF THE JEWS"* (Mat. 27:37).

7. Mark said, *"THE KING OF THE JEWS"* (Mk. 15:26).

8. John said, *"JESUS OF NAZARETH THE KING OF THE JEWS"* (Jn. 19:19).

9. Once again, the slightly different wording in all accounts, instead of proving an inaccuracy, rather proves the opposite. Had it been a fabrication, each word would have been identical, as should be obvious.

10. As well, even though the four reports of the inscriptions slightly differ verbally, they do not differ substantially.

11. Also, inasmuch as the inscription was given in three languages, this could account for the slight variation, with all the evangelists possibly not quoting from the same language. Nevertheless, as stated, the meaning is the same in all four.

(39) "AND ONE OF THE MALEFACTORS WHICH WERE HANGED RAILED ON HIM, SAYING, IF YOU BE CHRIST, SAVE YOURSELF AND US."

The structure is:

1. The phrase, *"And one of the malefactors which were hanged railed on Him,"* is reported by Matthew and Mark as both doing this in the beginning; however, at a point, the other one, which we will read

about momentarily, changed completely.

2. The expositors tell us that the Greek word describing the insults of both is a much milder word meaning "reproach." However, as one began to turn toward Christ, asking for mercy, the word used here by Luke concerning the impenitent one is much stronger, which referred to injurious and insulting language.

3. So, one was angered at the acceptance of Christ by the other and, consequently, became more vile.

4. *"Saying, If you be Christ, save Yourself and us,"* in fact, would be partially answered. One of the thieves would be saved, and the other one could have, as well, had he only yielded.

(40) "BUT THE OTHER ANSWERING REBUKED HIM, SAYING, DO NOT YOU FEAR GOD, SEEING YOU ARE IN THE SAME CONDEMNATION?"

The exposition is:

1. The phrase, *"But the other answering rebuked Him,"* proclaims the spirit of true repentance.

2. The question, *"Saying, Do not you fear God, seeing you are in the same condemnation?"* simply means that he was owning up to his guilt, which is the first requirement of repentance.

3. It is a petition, at least if given in the spirit, which the Lord will never refuse, as exampled by this incident.

(41) "AND WE INDEED JUSTLY; FOR WE RECEIVE THE DUE REWARD OF OUR DEEDS: BUT THIS MAN HAS DONE NOTHING AMISS."

The order is:

1. The phrase, *"And we indeed justly; for we receive the due reward of our deeds,"* proclaims him making no excuses, admitting to his sin, and holding no enmity toward his executioners, which presents a powerful truth.

2. The human race is plagued with the problem of blaming others for failures.

3. A so-called religious leader said something very telling to me some years ago that concerned something very evil that had been done by some of his preachers against me.

4. I mentioned it to him, and he quickly retorted, "But it's your fault, you know!"

NOTES

5. No! It was not my fault.

6. Whatever wrong I do is my fault as whatever wrong you do is your fault; however, whatever I do gives you no excuse for wrongdoing, as whatever you do gives me no excuse for wrongdoing.

7. That crutch is as old as Adam and Eve, as both placed the blame elsewhere when confronted by the Lord.

8. Adam said, *"The woman whom You gave to be with me, she gave me of the tree, and I did eat"* (Gen. 3:12).

9. So, in effect, Adam was not only blaming Eve but God, also, for his failure.

10. When the Lord approached Eve, asking her what she had done, *"The woman said, The serpent beguiled me, and I did eat"* (Gen. 3:13).

11. At least, she did not blame God as her husband Adam did!

12. So, this dying thief conducted himself in true repentance by not blaming others for his misdeeds.

13. *"But this Man has done nothing amiss,"* presented the only one, other than the centurion, who gave Jesus a kind word at the crucifixion.

14. The religious leaders mocked him, along with the soldiers, as well as other people. Conversely, a thief spoke kindly to Him and gained eternal life, along with the centurion, who spoke kindly of Him, with tradition saying that He received the same.

(42) "AND HE SAID UNTO JESUS, LORD, REMEMBER ME WHEN YOU COME INTO YOUR KINGDOM."

WHEN YOU COME INTO YOUR KINGDOM

The phrase, *"And he said unto Jesus,"* speaks of kindness and recognition as to who Jesus really was, which was one of the few kind words Jesus heard during this horrible ordeal.

"Lord, remember me when You come into Your kingdom," presents the simple prayer of repentance.

The conversion of the thief is peculiar to Luke. It is one of the most remarkable conversions recorded in the Bible, or anywhere else for that matter.

In one flash of light, the Holy Spirit

revealed Christ to him and taught him of the Lord's future kingdom of glory, though at the moment, He was hanging in shame and agony on the tree. The thief did not ask for any physical relief for his pain, but only for a remembrance in the future kingdom.

They were in the same condemnation—he justly, but the Lord only as a perfect sacrifice bearing the sin of the world—consequently, a sinner by imputation and not by actual acts of sin.

He prayed that they might be together in the same glory. So, the precious blood then flowing for his sins cleansed him so effectually that at that moment, it made him as fit to enter paradise as Christ Himself. They both had the same title for entrance there (Heb. 9:12; 10:19).

THE DIVINE NATURE OF THE THIEF'S REPENTANCE IS EVIDENCED BY THE FOLLOWING:

• His concern about his companion (Vs. 40).
• His confession of his own sinfulness (Vs. 41).
• His confession of Christ's innocence (Vs. 41).
• His faith in Christ's power and willingness to save him—he called Him Lord and declared his belief, therefore, that He had a kingdom (Vs. 42).
• He prayed to Him (Vs. 42).
• He asked for no great thing but only to be remembered; this was humility (Vs. 42).

AS WELL, HIS SHORT PRAYER EMBODIED A GREAT CREED

He believed that:
• His soul lived after death.
• The world to come will be one of blessing or misery.
• A crucified Jew was the Lord of Glory.
• His future kingdom was better than this present world.
• Christ intended to have pardoned sinners in that kingdom.
• He would receive into it the truly penitent.
• The key of that kingdom was hanging at Christ's girdle, so to speak, though He Himself was hanging naked on the tree.

NOTES

• By resting his soul for eternal salvation upon this dying Saviour, he had that kingdom assured to him.

HIS PRAYER WAS TO THE LORD AND NOT TO MARY

Actually, it seems that his intelligence concerning spiritual things exceeded that of all the apostles prior to Pentecost.

As well, there is something else that should be acutely noticed:

Near the Cross of the dying thief stood the apostle John, Mary, the mother of our Lord, her sister, Mary the wife of Cleophas, Mary Magdalene, and John's own mother, but to none of these exalted saints did the malefactor turn for help.

He turned from them and prayed directly to Jesus, with nothing and nobody between his sin-stained soul and the sin-atoning Saviour.

He did not cry, "Oh, Holy Mother of God!—refuge of sinners, pray for me! I put my whole trust and confidence in the power of your intercession."

Neither did he appeal to her sister as being the holy aunt of God or to John as being the beloved apostle of the Lord. Had he trusted any one of these great saints, he would have perished, for salvation is in Christ and Christ alone. He alone is the one and the only refuge for sinners (Acts 4:12).

(43) "AND JESUS SAID UNTO HIM, VERILY I SAY UNTO YOU, TODAY SHALL YOU BE WITH ME IN PARADISE."

PARADISE

The phrase, *"And Jesus said unto him,"* concerns the response of what the dying thief had said to the Lord of Glory.

The Lord will always answer, as here, a sincere cry and appeal. He has never turned a single one away who came with such humility and petition.

So, if one wants to know how to reach God, the example set by this dying thief on the Cross cannot be, I think, improved upon.

"Verily I say unto you, Today shall you be with Me in paradise," is a statement of fact and not a question as some claim.

On the morning of that day, the malefactor walked the stone floor of his dark dungeon in a tumult of horror, and on the evening of that same day, he walked the golden street of the city of light in a tumult of joy!

The thief had asked Him to remember him concerning a kingdom, which he thought might be far off.

TODAY

However, Jesus let him know that he was entering into that kingdom on that very day. So, invariably, we always get far more from the Lord than that which we ask. This is the only instance we have of Jesus using the word *paradise.*

THE CROSS CLOSED UP PARADISE

Paradise was in the heart of the earth where all righteous souls went before the death, resurrection, ascension, and exaltation of Christ. There was only a great gulf that separated it from the burning side, which was referred to as *"hell."* For a description, please read Luke 16:19-31.

Paradise is now empty, for at His resurrection, Jesus liberated all these righteous souls out of that underground place. They were summarily taken to heaven.

Now, when a righteous soul goes home to be with the Lord, he is taken directly to heaven upon death (Phil. 1:21-24), which was made possible by what Jesus did at the Cross. In other words, our Lord atoned for all sin and upon the believing sinner evidencing faith in Christ, all sin is removed totally and completely from such a person and is replaced by imputed righteousness, the righteousness of God (Rom. 5:1).

THE MANNER IN WHICH THE DYING THIEF WAS SAVED

• He was not baptized in water, could not take the Lord's Supper, and neither did he belong to any church, and yet, he was instantly saved.

This tells us that while these things are possibly very important in their own rite, they have nothing to do with one's salvation.

Salvation is so exact that if any of these other things, or any part thereof, were a necessity, this man could not have been saved. Consequently, those who claim that one must undergo these rituals, or others not

named, in order to be saved are preaching a false gospel. Paul called it *"another gospel"* (Gal. 1:6).

• The record is clear that the only requirement on the part of this man was faith in Christ (Eph. 2:9).

For those who would claim that such is too easy, I would remind them that it is not easy at all, considering the terrible price paid by Christ at Calvary.

As well, to those who would add anything else to this one requirement, Paul said that they themselves, irrespective of whom they might be, are *"fallen from grace"* (Gal. 5:4).

• Also, his salvation was instant, with no mention of any probationary place, such as purgatory as taught by the Catholics.

The dying thief constituted the very first believer to come in on the finished work of Christ, for Jesus died before him, thereby, fulfilling the requirements.

As the song says:
"And there may we, though vile as he,
"Wash all our sins away."

As well, even though he was taken to paradise, his duration there was very short. Jesus immediately came back after liberating all of these precious souls, with this man included in that great number.

(44) "AND IT WAS ABOUT THE SIXTH HOUR, AND THERE WAS A DARKNESS OVER ALL THE EARTH UNTIL THE NINTH HOUR."

The synopsis is:

1. The phrase, *"And it was about the sixth hour,"* represented high noon in the manner in which we now reckon time.

Jesus had been on the Cross by now for about three hours, having been placed there at 9 a.m. our time, which was actually the time of the morning sacrifice.

2. *"And there was a darkness over all the earth until the ninth hour,"* represented 3 p.m., the time of the evening sacrifice, when Jesus actually died.

3. The darkness was not caused by an eclipse, for the moon was full, it being the Passover time. The moon cannot eclipse at that time.

4. The darkness that descended for that three-hour period was brought on by God the Father in order that Jesus may be hidden

at this crucial time when He was bearing the sin of the world, in effect, becoming the sin offering. As such, God could not look upon Him for that reason.

5. As well, we hear no more taunts and jeers from the religious leaders, with the darkness, no doubt, casting a pall over them. That should have been enough to tell them that Jesus was no ordinary man but, in fact, God who had become man in order to redeem humanity. As well, He was the Creator of all things.

6. However, they were so jaded and hardened that nothing could reach them. Once again, if one would not believe the Word of God, which spoke so abundantly of the coming Messiah, and saying exactly what He would be like (Isa., Chpt. 53), then one would not believe anything else either, no matter the drama of the moment.

7. In respect to the extent of this darkness, Tertullian claimed that a notice of this darkness was found in the archives of Rome pertaining to this particular time.

8. Even though God ordained this darkness, and for the obvious reasons, still, creation responded to its Creator; consequently, the One who made everything was dying, and above that, He was bearing the penalty of the curse, which was death. Therefore, creation would respond accordingly with darkness.

(45) "AND THE SUN WAS DARKENED, AND THE VEIL OF THE TEMPLE WAS RENT IN THE MIDST."

THE DARKNESS

The phrase, *"And the sun was darkened,"* means that the darkness was so deep that it literally blotted out the light of the sun.

Jesus suffered this darkness that you and I may not have to suffer its horror.

As well, what He experienced during this three-hour period, no one will ever know. This was the time that He bore the sin penalty of the world. It is proclaimed in Psalms 22:1-21.

"And the veil of the temple was rent in the midst," probably referred to the approximate time He died, about 3 p.m. The veil of which the passage speaks is the inner veil that hung between the Holy Place and the Holy of Holies.

Into the Holy of Holies, no ordinary priest,

NOTES

or anyone else for that matter, could enter, with the exception of the high priest, and that was once a year and with blood.

This was done on the Great Day of Atonement when the high priest would enter this place twice, once for Himself, offering the blood of the slain animal on the mercy seat, and then again, offering blood on the mercy seat for all of Israel.

At the time of Jesus, the Great Day of Atonement was not kept, at least according to Levitical law, because at that time, there was no ark of the covenant (Lev., Chpt. 16). In fact, there had not been one for approximately 600 years.

THE ARK OF THE COVENANT

The original ark as designed by the Lord, with the plans given to Moses, disappeared at about the time of the Babylonian invasion. Some claim that Jeremiah hid it in a cave, and with him going into Egypt and dying there, he left no one instructions as to how it could be found. Of course, that is speculation.

Others claim that it is now hidden in a subterranean vault beneath the present temple site, and it has actually been seen; however, it is supposed to be on the Arab side, consequently, controlled by the Muslims, who will not allow the Jews entrance.

Once again, all of this is speculation.

This one thing is known: Nebuchadnezzar took many of the holy utensils to Babylon, but there is no record of the ark being taken (II Chron. 36:18-19).

As well, there is no record of the ark of the covenant being either in the temple built by Zerubbabel after the dispersion or in Herod's temple during the time of Christ, as stated.

It is said that this heavy veil, which hid the Holy of Holies, weighed approximately 2,000 pounds and was about 4 inches thick. According to Josephus, it was so strong that four yoke of oxen could not pull it apart.

Matthew said it *"was rent in twain from the top to the bottom"* (Mat. 27:51), signifying that it was not done by human ingenuity but by God.

This meant that due to the death of Jesus Christ on Calvary, thereby, bearing the sin penalty of the world and consequently satisfying the claims of heavenly justice, the way was now open for all to come directly to the throne of God (Heb. 4:16).

THE BLOOD

The cumbersome manner of the Old Testament proclaimed that no one could approach God without the blood of an innocent victim, hence, the sacrifices. Even then, the sinner could go only so far. He needed a priest to serve as a mediator on his behalf, and above all, the high priest had to serve as the mediator for all of Israel on the Great Day of Atonement.

The reason that any believer can approach God at any time at present is because Jesus Christ was the sacrifice, with His blood now applied to the mercy seat of heaven (Heb. 9:12), thereby, opening the door to all. As well, inasmuch as He was the perfect sacrifice, there is no need for any other sacrifice to ever be offered, hence, the one sacrifice sufficing for all time (Heb. 9:11-12).

As well as Jesus having been the perfect sacrifice, which forever settled the sin question, He is also our mediator, not requiring the services of an earthly priest, or any one else for that matter (I Tim. 2:5; Heb. 8:6; 9:15; 12:24).

In view of what Jesus did at Calvary, the invitation is now given, *"And the Spirit and the bride say, Come. And let him who hears say, Come. And let him who is athirst come. And whosoever will, let him take the Water of Life freely"* (Rev. 22:17).

(46) "AND WHEN JESUS HAD CRIED WITH A LOUD VOICE, HE SAID, FATHER, INTO YOUR HANDS I COMMEND MY SPIRIT: AND HAVING SAID THUS, HE GAVE UP THE GHOST."

INTO YOUR HANDS I
COMMEND MY SPIRIT

The phrase, *"And when Jesus had cried with a loud voice,"* proclaims the fact that He had strength enough left to do this; therefore, they, in effect, did not take His life, but He gave it up freely. When the human body is weakened, the voice weakens most of all.

"He said, Father, into Your hands I

commend My Spirit," proclaims the last words He uttered. It was the dismissal of His Spirit which He commended to His Father.

This tells us that the soul and spirit, which together are indivisible, can be separated from the body, which they are at death. Regarding believers, upon death, the soul and the spirit instantly go to be with the Lord, with every indication that it is accompanied by angels (Lk. 16:22).

A short time earlier, it seems that Jesus cried, *"Eli, Eli, lama sabachthani? that is to say, My God, My God, why have You forsaken Me?"* (Mat. 27:46).

At that moment Jesus was bearing the sin penalty of the world, with all of its attendant penalty and curse, on which God could not look. However, His last words, the commending of His Spirit to His Father, proclaim that the Father had accepted the price paid, satisfying the claims of heavenly justice, and would now receive His Son and our Saviour.

AND THUS HE DIED

The phrase, *"And having said thus, He gave up the ghost,"* proclaims the fact that this was His own voluntary act. He had already told His disciples of His own independent power to lay down and take up His life (Jn. 10:17-18).

Dr. Westcott said, "It may not be fitting to speculate on the physical cause of the Lord's death, but it has been argued that the symptoms agree with a rupture of the heart, such as might be produced by intense mental agony."

Matthew also recorded that at the time of His death, *"the earth did quake, and the rocks rent,"* signifying an earthquake.

His creation convulsed when He died (Mat. 27:51).

Expositors attempt to properly describe that which He did at Calvary, but there is no way that the mind of man can portray such an event or even understand all that happened. It is beyond the pale of human comprehension. Such love, one could perhaps say, is not possible for mere mortals to grasp.

Considering what He did, one should never again doubt one's salvation, respecting the cleansing and washing of all sin.

The song says:

"Jesus paid it all, all to Him I owe,

"Sin has left a crimson stain,

"He washed it white as snow."

(47) "NOW WHEN THE CENTURION SAW WHAT WAS DONE, HE GLORIFIED GOD, SAYING, CERTAINLY THIS WAS A RIGHTEOUS MAN."

The construction is:

1. The phrase, *"Now when the centurion saw what was done, he glorified God,"* concerns all the things that happened, especially the last cry of Jesus at His death.

2. *"Saying, Certainly this was a righteous man,"* has Matthew recording him saying, *"Truly this was the Son of God"* (Mat. 27:54).

3. Mark has him saying, *"Truly this man was the Son of God"* (Mk. 15:39).

4. No doubt, the centurion said all these things, and even possibly much more, which are not recorded.

5. Every indication is that he recognized Jesus as the Son of God and not just one of many gods as believed by many Romans, as some claim.

6. Tradition affirms that this man's name was Longinus, that he became a devoted follower of Christ, preached the gospel, and ultimately died a martyr's death.

7. Also, the testimony of this centurion that Jesus really died is irrefutable, completely laying to rest the claim that Jesus only swooned and was revived in the tomb. The lengths to which unbelievers go in attempting to prove their assertions only make their unbelief more apparent and their story more ludicrous.

(48) "AND ALL THE PEOPLE WHO CAME TOGETHER TO THAT SIGHT, BEHOLDING THE THINGS WHICH WERE DONE, SMOTE THEIR BREASTS, AND RETURNED."

The composition is:

1. The phrase, *"And all the people who came together to that sight,"* speaks of quite a number who had heard that Jesus was being crucified, which probably spread over Jerusalem like a flash. They were most likely dumbfounded and stunned, not quite understanding how such a thing could happen.

2. It seems that the people, including

even the chosen apostles, did not fully understood how absolutely wicked the religious leaders were. They observed all the outward accoutrements and as such, probably looked at these men as having excellent reputations. Instead, their hearts were evil and black, thereby, totally opposed to God and His work.

3. It is really little, if any, different at present!

4. Upon hearing this dread news, many, no doubt, rushed to the *"sight,"* possibly even many who had been healed by Christ.

5. *"Beholding the things which were done,"* seems to indicate that quite a few were there when He died, standing in the darkness, hearing His last words, and, thereby, experiencing the earthquake.

6. The word *beholding* means they carefully observed all the details, realizing that what was happening was certainly not ordinary, but was rather extraordinary or even supernatural. In fact, no one had ever witnessed a scene of this nature, or would they ever again.

7. *"Smote their breasts, and returned,"* speaks of an agony of heart, knowing that something horrible had happened and that a great wrong had been done.

8. The next time that Israel sees Him, *"They shall look upon Me whom they have pierced, and they shall mourn for Him, as one mourns for his only son"* (Zech. 12:10).

(49) "AND ALL HIS ACQUAINTANCE, AND THE WOMEN WHO FOLLOWED HIM FROM GALILEE, STOOD AFAR OFF, BEHOLDING THESE THINGS."

The exegesis is:

1. The phrase, *"And all His acquaintance,"* concerned His chosen disciples and other chosen followers.

2. *"And the women who followed Him from Galilee, stood afar off, beholding these things,"* seems to indicate that they stood near the Cross for a time (Jn. 19:25-27) and then retired, for whatever reason, to a further distance (Mat. 27:55-56).

3. Many have claimed that this was because of a lack of courage and devotion, which caused them to fear to stand beside their master and friend at this awful time.

4. However, not knowing all the

circumstances, quite possibly, those accusations are without merit.

5. There is some small indication that Jesus wanted John to take His mother Mary a distance away from the Cross in order that she may not have to look upon this horrible scene any longer (Jn. 19:25-27).

6. This we do know, some 33 years before, Simeon had prophesied over Mary, *"Yes, a sword shall pierce through your own soul also"* (Lk. 2:35).

7. That day the sword pierced her soul to such an extent that she had probably stood about all that she could stand. Knowing that was true, it stands to reason that Jesus would seek to spare her greater suffering, hence, possibly telling them to take her some distance away where she would not be so close to the agony. If that happened, which it more than likely did, it is very understandable why the other women, as well as even some or all of the disciples, would have stood with her.

(50) "AND, BEHOLD, THERE WAS A MAN NAMED JOSEPH, A COUNSELLOR; AND HE WAS A GOOD MAN, AND A JUST."

The synopsis is:

1. The phrase, *"And, behold, there was a man named Joseph, a counsellor,"* speaks of Joseph of Arimathaea, a member of the Sanhedrin. This man was a person of high distinction in Jerusalem and evidently of great wealth.

2. *"And he was a good man, and a just,"* was said by Luke and sanctioned by the Holy Spirit.

3. Spence says, "Each evangelist speaks of Joseph in high terms, and each in his own way."

4. Matthew writes of him as *"a rich man"* (Mat. 27:57).

8. Mark called him *"an honorable counsellor"* (Mk. 15:43).

9. John used the title *"being a disciple of Jesus"* (Jn. 19:38).

(51) "(THE SAME HAD NOT CONSENTED TO THE COUNSEL AND DEED OF THEM;) HE WAS OF ARIMATHAEA, A CITY OF THE JEWS: WHO ALSO HIMSELF WAITED FOR THE KINGDOM OF GOD."

The construction is:

1. The phrase, *"The same had not*

consented to the counsel and deed of them," speaks of the illegal and unjust decision of the Sanhedrin, of which he was a part.

2. It is not quite certain if Joseph, who, along with Nicodemus, was a member of the Sanhedrin, and who loved Jesus, were actually present when the votes were cast. However, there is some indication that they may have been, with the words *not consenting* meaning that they deposited their votes for acquittal.

3. *"He was of Arimathaea, a city of the Jews,"* constituted a famous town in Jewish history as the home of the prophet Samuel; however, Joseph now lived in Jerusalem due to the fact of being a member of the Sanhedrin.

4. *"Who also himself waited for the kingdom of God,"* is a strong statement speaking of his consecration.

5. In Joseph of Arimathaea and Nicodemus, we have specimens of a class of earnest and devout Jews, even though small, who loved God and, consequently, loved and respected Jesus and somewhat believed in Him as the Messiah. And yet, from many mixed and various motives, they shrank from confessing Him before men until after the Cross had been endured.

6. As it was then, so it is now. There is always a price tag attached to an open and avowed following of Jesus. In truth, there is no such thing as a secret disciple of Christ, at least for any period of time. Ultimately, as here, there must be an open confession before all of one's acceptance of, and loyalty to, Christ as the Saviour of mankind and the Lord of Glory.

(52) "THIS MAN WENT UNTO PILATE, AND BEGGED THE BODY OF JESUS."

THE RELIGIOUS LEADERS OF ISRAEL

There is no way that one could adequately comprehend the feelings of these few who gathered around Jesus as He hung on the Cross, bearing the sin penalty of the world. This One, and this One alone, was totally good and had used His power only to better humanity. Because of Him, thousands had been gloriously and wondrously healed by the power of God. Hundreds, if not thousands, had been delivered from demon spirits, in effect, their lives given back to them. Untold thousands had heard Him teach the Word of God, which brought a lift to their hearts that none had ever before experienced, at least in this fashion.

And yet, the religious leaders of Israel killed Him!

In the minds of those who loved Him, their world had come to an inglorious end, for, at least as they thought at that moment, life thereafter was not worth living. The only One who really mattered was dead.

THE BODY OF JESUS

However, it seems that all of them had forgotten the words that He had uttered, even though they heard them plainly, that on the third day He would rise again. While now all was dark, on Sunday morning He would rise from the dead, but now they could not at all see how this was possible.

Joseph, being a member of the Sanhedrin and obviously very wealthy, was able to immediately secure an audience with Pilate where he would beg the body of Jesus.

There is an urgency about this because the High Sabbath of the Passover would begin at sundown. If Jesus was not taken down from the Cross before then and placed in a tomb, actually the personal tomb of Joseph, they would have to allow Him to remain on the Cross for another 24 hours.

Pilate marvelled that Jesus was so soon dead, as it generally took days for such victims to die (Mk. 15:44-45). However, Pilate could not understand that it was not really the crucifixion that killed Jesus, but rather Him giving up His own life (Jn. 10:18). Consequently, when the terrible task, the most horrible ever endured in history, was completed (the bearing of the sin penalty of the world), Jesus then expired of His own will. He was crucified at 9 a.m., the time of the morning sacrifice, and died at 3 p.m., the time of the evening sacrifice.

It seems that the centurion, who had testified at the death of Jesus, accompanied Joseph to an audience with Pilate. When the centurion verified that Jesus was indeed dead, Pilate then gave up His body (Mk. 15:45).

(53) "AND HE TOOK IT DOWN, AND WRAPPED IT IN LINEN, AND LAID IT

NOTES

IN A SEPULCHRE THAT WAS HEWN IN STONE, WHEREIN NEVER MAN BEFORE WAS LAID."

HE TOOK HIM DOWN

The short phrase, *"And He took it down,"* referring to the body of Jesus, says so very much while saying so very little.

John records that Nicodemus also aided in this process, with possibly even the centurion helping as well. It could have happened in this fashion:

First they would have loosed the crossbar from the upright post to which it was attached. In some cases it was nailed, while in other cases it was tied. At this time, they would have left His hands nailed to the crossbar.

After loosing the crossbar, they would have pulled the single nail, which had pierced both His feet, with one foot draped over the other. What instrument they used to do this is not known; however, as they handled His feet, what must their thoughts have been?

THE FEET OF CHRIST

These feet were the fulfillment of the prophecy of Isaiah, *"How beautiful upon the mountains are the feet of Him who brings good tidings, who publishes peace; who brings good tidings of good, who publishes salvation; who says unto Zion, Your God reigns"* (Isa. 52:7).

These feet that they now gently handled and were brutally scarred by gaping holes through the instep of each had fulfilled in totality that which the Divine Spirit had spoken through the ancient prophet.

Some feel that the Cross was not very high, with the legs somewhat pulled up and folded. If that were true, then they could have taken Him down, with the crossbar still attached to His hands, without resorting to any type of ladders. More than likely this is the way it was, with them gently lowering Him to the ground.

They would now take the same instrument that had pulled the nail from His feet and do the same with the nails in His hands. Those hands, which had never hurt a soul but had ministered healing, deliverance, and life to so many, now contained gaping holes where the nails had been—holes that will remain forever (Zech. 13:6).

They must have then taken cloths and attempted to wipe the blood from His body. As well, they would have taken the crown of thorns from off His head.

THE CHURCH?

There was not much they could have done with His face inasmuch as part, if not all His beard, had been pulled out by the roots. This would have left a grotesque sight, as Isaiah had predicted (Isa. 52:14). As well, they could have done very little with His back because it had basically been brutally lacerated with the lash.

They would have done the best they could to wipe the blood from the gaping wound in His side as well as His feet. It would have been a task that would have torn their hearts out by the roots. This was man's answer, and more particularly, the answer of the apostate church toward God's greatest gift, His only Son. When one sees this, one is seeing the result of religion.

As evil, wicked, and dastardly as the world is, it really did not carry out this grue-some deed, but rather those who claimed to name the name of the Lord. The world has never been the greatest hindrance to the work of God, but ever the church—always the church.

Thankfully, there is a remnant that serves God truthfully, and has in all ages, which makes up the true church. Nevertheless, it is small, as it always has been. The far greater percentage of that which calls itself church, however, is really not of God, but as the Pharisees of old, of their father the Devil. As such, they continue to crucify Christ, so to speak, unto this very hour.

THE SEPULCHRE

The phrase, *"And wrapped it in linen,"* pertained to a part of the burial process, which was done very hurriedly because the High Sabbath of the Passover would begin at sundown, which would necessitate all work coming to a halt. As well, according to John, it seems they must have mixed burial spices of myrrh and aloes in with the linen

NOTES

as they wrapped His body (Jn. 19:39-40). They would attempt to add more of these burial spices three days later but would find they were no longer needed.

"And laid it in a sepulchre that was hewn in stone, wherein never man before was laid," constituted the tomb that belonged to Joseph and the very kind predicted by Isaiah.

Isaiah said, *"And He made His grave with the wicked,"* which spoke of Him dying with the thieves on the Cross, *"And with the rich in His death,"* which spoke of Joseph, who was rich, with this tomb being that which belonged to Joseph (Isa. 53:9).

It is only a short distance from Calvary to the tomb, to which they could have easily carried the body of Jesus. It is even possible that they prepared His body there instead of the crucifixion site.

(54) "AND THAT DAY WAS THE PREPARATION, AND THE SABBATH DREW ON."

The structure is:

1. The phrase, *"And that day was the preparation,"* spoke of the preparation for the Passover, which was to be eaten the next day, which was Thursday. As stated, Jesus had eaten the Passover with His disciples a day early.

2. *"And the Sabbath drew on,"* was not speaking of the regular weekly Sabbath of Saturday, but rather the High Sabbath of the Passover, which was a Thursday.

3. This is what has confused so many people simply because they think it is speaking of the Saturday Sabbath; therefore, they claim erroneously that Jesus was crucified on Friday. He was crucified on Wednesday.

4. This special Sabbath, or the first day of the Feast of Unleavened Bread, which was also the day of the Passover, always came on the fifteenth of Nisan regardless of what day of the week it fell on. It was on Thursday, which was from our Wednesday sunset to Thursday sunset.

5. As well, the Jewish months did not correspond with our present months inasmuch as the first of their months began at approximately the middle of our months. So, this month of Nisan would have begun near the middle of our month of March, with the fifteenth corresponding with approximately

the first of our April.

(55) "AND THE WOMEN ALSO, WHICH CAME WITH HIM FROM GALILEE, FOLLOWED AFTER, AND BEHELD THE SEPULCHRE, AND HOW HIS BODY WAS LAID."

The pattern is:

1. The phrase, *"And the women also, which came with Him from Galilee,"* would have included *"Mary Magdalene, and Mary the mother of James and Joseph, and the mother of Zebedee's children"* (Mat. 27:56).

2. Actually, Matthew recorded that there were *"many women who were there."*

3. These were women whose lives, as Mary Magdalene, had been gloriously and wondrously changed by His life-giving power. While it was probably different with each one, still, they desired to do whatever they could to be of service (Mat. 27:55).

4. The phrase, *"Followed after, and beheld the sepulchre, and how His body was laid,"* does not exactly say that they participated in this which was done by Joseph and Nicodemus, but does proclaim that they were witnesses of all that was carried out. When they left, His body had been laid in the tomb.

5. As stated, it was a new tomb, which proclaims that the Lord's sacred body was not brought into contact with any type of corruption.

(56) "AND THEY RETURNED, AND PREPARED SPICES AND OINTMENTS; AND RESTED THE SABBATH DAY ACCORDING TO THE COMMANDMENT."

The exegesis is:

1. The phrase, *"And they returned, and prepared spices and ointments,"* means that they returned to the places where they were staying while in Jerusalem, and would have made these preparations on Friday.

2. *"And rested the Sabbath day according to the commandment,"* had to do, as stated, with the High Sabbath of the Passover, which began at sundown Wednesday. They could not have done any work on that day; therefore, they would have made these preparations, as stated, on the following day.

3. They would have also rested again on the regular weekly Sabbath of Saturday as required, which immediately preceded the resurrection, which happened on the first day of the week. So, there were two Sabbaths that took place in this three-day period—the High Sabbath of the Passover, which was a Thursday, of which we are now speaking, and the regular weekly Sabbath of Saturday.

*"There's a great day coming,
"A great day coming,
"There's a great day coming by and by;
"When the saints and the sinners
"Shall be parted right and left,
"Are you ready for that day to come?"*

*"There's a bright day coming,
"A bright day coming,
"There's a bright day coming by and by;
"But its brightness shall only come
"To them who love the Lord,
"Are you ready for that day to come?"*

*"There's a sad day coming,
"A sad day coming,
"There's a sad day coming by and by;
"When the sinner shall hear his doom,
"'Depart, I know you not,'
"Are you ready for that day to come?"*

CHAPTER 24

(1) "NOW UPON THE FIRST DAY OF THE WEEK, VERY EARLY IN THE MORNING, THEY CAME UNTO THE SEPULCHRE, BRINGING THE SPICES WHICH THEY HAD PREPARED, AND CERTAIN OTHERS WITH THEM."

THE FIRST DAY OF THE WEEK

The phrase, *"Now upon the first day of the week,"* in one sense of the word, represents the greatest day ever recorded.

Jesus satisfied the claims of heavenly justice against man by the giving of His own perfect body as a sacrifice in the shedding of His precious blood. He, thereby, satisfied the claims of the law and abrogated its curse. Still, had He not risen from the dead, all would have been in vain. Then again, if He carried out what He was supposed to do on the Cross, then the resurrection was a given. In a sense, one might say that His resurrection ratified what was done at Cavalry. In a strict sense, the Cross was not dependent on the resurrection, but rather the resurrection was dependent on the Cross.

The day before, which was Saturday, was the last Sabbath of the old covenant, and it was scrupulously respected. However, this first day of the week represented the first day of the new covenant and was celebrated by the greatest event of all, the resurrection of Christ from the dead.

"Very early in the morning" represents dawn, even before the rising of the sun. Consequently, the sun would rise this day on a risen Lord, constituting it as the greatest day, as stated, in the annals of human history.

As should by now be obvious, Jesus spent three full days and three full nights in the tomb (Mat. 12:40), having been crucified on Wednesday and having risen from the dead sometime after sunset on Saturday evening, which would have been the beginning of the Jewish Sunday.

The phrase, *"They came unto the sepulchre,"* speaks of the women in Verse 55 of the previous chapter.

THE RESURRECTION

The phrase, *"Bringing the spices which they had prepared, and certain others with them,"* proclaims that not a single one of these women, the disciples, or anyone else for that matter, believed that Jesus would rise from the dead.

He had plainly told them that He would be put to death and the third day rise again (Lk. 18:33). However, they simply did not believe Him! Having seen Him brutally treated, and then having watched Him die on the Cross before their very eyes, it was beyond them to believe or even comprehend the idea that He actually would rise from the dead. How they accounted for His predictions is anyone's guess. Quite possibly they thought these predictions had some type of spiritual meaning with which they were not acquainted. At any rate, they were in no way prepared for what was to actually happen.

Who the *"certain others"* were who came with the women to the tomb, we are not

told. However, whomever they were, it was to be a day to remember.

THE ACCOUNT OF THE RESURRECTION

All four evangelists give an account of the resurrection. None of the four, however, attempt to give a history of it simply from a human point of sight. Each writer simply relates his account, making no effort to correlate it with the other accounts. No, there is no discrepancy or contradiction. The Holy Spirit desired that it be given the way it was, and for particular reasons. Just because one person relates something that another does not mention concerning the same incident does not mean that there is a contradiction, error, or discrepancy.

Paul wrote, *"All Scripture is given by inspiration of God"* (II Tim. 3:16), which means that the Holy Spirit inspired the writers to say what they said and to give the account exactly as they did, which guarantees 100 percent accuracy.

The way the accounts of the resurrection are given proves their veracity. Had it been a fable, all four accounts would have been word for word identical.

Among other reasons, I am persuaded that the Holy Spirit designed the Scriptures in this fashion for a purpose. It is done to turn away the skeptical, while at the same time, drawing in the believer. Jesus' parables were much of the time given in the same manner. The merely curious would not understand and, thereby, turn away, while the hungry of heart would press in. This is exactly what the parable was designed to do and, thereby, the hungry heart would glean great truths.

So, the Word of God confuses the skeptics, and purposely so, while enlightening the seeker.

(2) "AND THEY FOUND THE STONE ROLLED AWAY FROM THE SEPULCHRE."

The synopsis is:

1. This stone weighed several hundred pounds, thereby, requiring at least two or three men to roll it away from the door, where it had been placed.

2. Actually, as these women were nearing the tomb, they were wondering how they would move this great stone in order to

finish the embalming process on the body of Jesus (Mk. 16:3). To their surprise, they found the stone rolled away.

3. Let it be said that the angel who rolled away the stone (Mat. 28:2) did not do so to let Jesus out, for He had already risen from the dead, but rather to let these women in so they might see that the tomb was empty. Stones or material walls presented no object whatsoever to the glorified Jesus, with Him able to pass through such without difficultly (Lk. 24:31; Jn. 20:19).

(3) "AND THEY ENTERED IN, AND FOUND NOT THE BODY OF THE LORD JESUS."

THE TOMB

The phrase, *"And they entered in,"* speaks of haste on their part, as would be obvious.

I have stood in this tomb several times, but the last time I was there proved to be the greatest experience of all.

As I looked down at the stone shaft where Joseph and Nicodemus, and possibly others, had laid Him, all of a sudden, the overwhelming glory of all that was done began to flow over me. The tears began to come, along with a sense of wonder mixed with joy. It is very difficult to explain!

As stated, I stood there looking at this very spot several times in years past but had not been affected thusly. For some reason, this time seemed to be different. It was as if a deeper realization came over me than I ever before had.

Since that resurrection morning, multiple tens of millions have entered into His resurrection life, whereas then, it was only a handful.

THE BODY OF THE LORD JESUS

The phrase, *"And found not the body of the Lord Jesus,"* proclaims His resurrection title, Lord Jesus, and occurs about 40 other times in the Epistles.

It should be stated that no evangelist described the resurrection simply because no earthly being was present at that momentous occasion. While they do mention particular signs, such as the earthquake, the appearance of angels, and the stark terror of the guards, none speak of the actual

resurrection itself. This again shows they did not believe He would actually rise from the dead.

They knew what He had said concerning being three days and three nights in the heart of the earth (Mat. 12:40), and, as stated, they had heard Him say that on the third day, He would rise again. So, if they had actually believed Him, they would have been standing near the tomb when the sun went down on Saturday evening, awaiting His resurrection the moment it became dark, which signaled the first day of the week. However, they simply did not believe and missed out on the greatest event in human history. They watched Him die, but they did not watch Him rise from the dead.

THE RESURRECTION

Let it be known that the founders of all the great religions of the world have long since turned to dust in their tombs. However, there is no memorial to the founder of Christianity simply because the others were mere men while Jesus Christ was and is God. As the song says, "We serve a risen Saviour!"

As these women did not find the body of the Lord Jesus, neither has anyone else. To be sure, if His resurrection was a fake, as claimed by the Jews, no stone would have been left unturned until His body was found. The finding of such would have proved Him an impostor; however, a corpse was not found because a corpse did not exist.

The resurrection of Jesus Christ is the greatest proof of all He had said and done. As well, that the Jews could not disprove His resurrection proves the veracity of the Bible account. Consequently, proof after proof piles up, which constitutes an undeniable, unassailable position. Jesus Christ rose from the dead!

(4) "AND IT CAME TO PASS, AS THEY WERE MUCH PERPLEXED THEREABOUT, BEHOLD, TWO MEN STOOD BY THEM IN SHINING GARMENTS."

The composition is:

1. The phrase, *"And it came to pass, as they were much perplexed thereabout,"* simply means they did not know what to make of the situation.

2. Who had rolled away the stone?

3. Where was the body of Jesus?

4. *"Behold, two men stood by them in shining garments,"* speaks of two angels.

5. Matthew and Mark both mention only one angel; however, these are not the same happenings. One angel was there a few minutes earlier, with two now present at this occasion. Actually, there were probably millions of angels around this tomb and city at this time.

6. The shining garments described here speak of a long, stately robe reaching to the feet, or even trainlike, sweeping the ground.

7. As well, the word *shining* means "to flash as lightning." Consequently, their appearance was unlike anything that is of this world. That's because it was not of this world but of another world.

8. The demons that surrounded the Cross as Jesus was dying, which Psalm 22 exclaims, were now totally defeated, with angels taking their place.

(5) "AND AS THEY WERE AFRAID, AND BOWED DOWN THEIR FACES TO THE EARTH, THEY SAID UNTO THEM, WHY SEEK YE THE LIVING AMONG THE DEAD?"

FEAR

The phrase, *"And as they were afraid,"* proclaims their reaction to the empty tomb, and more specifically, to the angels.

"And bowed down their faces to the earth," pertains to the women, and implies that the sight of these angels was so dazzling that it blinded their eyes, causing them to look downward.

The question, *"They said unto them, Why seek ye* (do you seek) *the living among the dead?"* presents not only a statement of fact but, as well, a rebuke to their unbelief. The question as presented by the angel has a touch of sarcasm.

Why is it so hard for man to believe God?

Actually, unbelief is the very first sin addressed and convicted by the Holy Spirit (Jn. 16:9).

Unbelief was a part of the great sin of pride that caused the fall in the garden of Eden. Adam and Eve simply did not believe what God had said, consequently, disobeying what He had said.

He told them not to eat *"of the Tree of the Knowledge of Good and Evil ... For in the day that you eat thereof you shall surely die"* (Gen. 2:17).

Their doing the very thing He said not to do, even with its dire consequences, shows that they did not believe Him. They heard what He said, and they understood what He said. Genesis 3:3 bears that out. However, they did believe Satan's lie when he told them the very opposite of what God had said, *"You shall not surely die"* (Gen. 3:4).

UNBELIEF AND DECEPTION

So, unbelief became a part of the deception and continues to plague man unto this very moment.

The Greek word for unbelief is *apistia*. It is a failure to respond to God with trust, but rather rejection.

"Unbeliever" is a general term that can be applied to anyone who has not yet put his trust in Christ. Such persons are characterized by unbelief, even as Christians are characterized by their believing attitude toward God. We are taught how to associate with unbelievers—even with the immoral at times (I Cor. 5:9-13). After all, God may open eyes blinded by Satan through our presentation of the gospel (II Cor. 4:4). In other words, we are in the world but never of the world.

We are always to remain spiritually sensitive and avoid compromising situations (I Cor. 10:27-33). We are also to avoid entering into *"yoked"* relationships with unbelievers (II Cor. 6:14).

Whereas *unbeliever* is simply a term that characterizes one who is not a Christian, *unbelief* has strong negative overtones. In one of the miracles of Jesus, the anxious father struggled between belief and unbelief (Mk. 9:24). Actually, believing is the action part of faith.

However, at heart, unbelief is staggering back from God's revelation of Himself and refusing to respond, as Abraham did, with trust (Rom. 4:20). Thus, unbelief exhibits a sinful heart that turns away from the living God (Heb. 3:12).

UNBELIEF AND THE CHRISTIAN

While unbelief is certainly the underlying

cause of all rejection of God and His plan of salvation among sinners, unbelief is also a problem among Christians. Paul addressed this readily, as we have just stated, saying, *"Take heed, brethren, lest there be in any of you an evil heart of unbelief, in departing from the living God"* (Heb. 3:12). As should be obvious, he was speaking to believers!

He also said, when speaking of the children of Israel and their failure to enter into the Promised Land, *"So we see that they could not enter in because of unbelief"* (Heb. 3:19). This is the reason the disciples, along with the others, did not see Jesus rise from the dead. They simply did not believe what He had said.

BELIEVERS?

Millions of believers are not baptized with the Holy Spirit, consequently, severely affecting their spiritual growth, and all because of unbelief. The same can be said for healing, at least in some cases. While failure to receive healing may not impair one's spiritual growth, still, it can affect one's physical well-being, as should be obvious.

Many, if not most Christians, little pray simply because they do not believe that God answers prayer.

The criterion is the Word of God. We are to rightly divide the Word (properly interpret) and believe what it says. The tragedy is that the Bible is not the foundation for most Christians but only a part. They base what they believe on what others say or what their denomination teaches, with the Bible given little place.

The disciples, along with others, had their own agenda, which speaks of pride; consequently, they did not properly hear or believe what Jesus said about His death and crucifixion. Millions of modern believers fall into the same category in one capacity or the other. Thankfully, this situation was cured with the disciples by the resurrection and the infilling of the Holy Spirit. However, it was not until the meaning of the new covenant, which is the Cross of Christ, was given to the apostle Paul that everything finally began to come into focus.

Unless one has a proper understanding of the Cross of Christ relative to salvation

NOTES

and sanctification, then one cannot properly understand the Word of God. The Cross ties everything together. It was the greatest display of the wisdom of God that creation has ever known, and the great sin of the church is that it makes too little, far too little, of the Cross of Christ. What Jesus there did is so stupendous, so remarkable, so miraculous, and so glorious that Paul referred to it as *"the everlasting covenant"* (Heb. 13:20). In other words, it will never have to be amended or replaced. It is perfect because it is all in Christ.

(6) "HE IS NOT HERE, BUT IS RISEN: REMEMBER HOW HE SPOKE UNTO YOU WHEN HE WAS YET IN GALILEE."

The synopsis is:

1. *"He is not here, but is risen,"* are, without a doubt, the greatest words ever spoken. This phrase, or a derivative of it, became the watchword of the early church—*"He is risen!"* No, in those first years of the early church, they did not preach the Cross simply because they didn't know anything about the Cross. It was not until this great revelation of the Cross, which is the meaning of the new covenant, was given to the apostle Paul that the full meaning of that glorious covenant began to be made available to all believers.

Some preachers claim that Jesus had to fight demons to be raised from the dead, etc. Nothing like that is in the Bible. Jesus defeated all demon spirits at the Cross (Col. 2:15). When Jesus died on the Cross, at that moment, Satan and all of his cohorts of darkness were totally and completely finished. The Scripture plainly says that Christ triumphed over them (Col. 2:15). So, when Jesus went down into paradise to deliver all of those souls who were there, He did not go down there as a defeated man, but He went down there totally and completely victorious. When He rose from the dead, demon spirits did not try to stop Him from that glorious moment because there was nothing they could do. They had been totally defeated at the Cross.

So, the Cross of Christ was not dependent on the resurrection, but rather the resurrection was dependent on the Cross. Jesus did everything that He set out to do at the Cross, which was to atone for all sin, past, present, and future, at least for all who will believe (Jn. 3:16). With sin being the sword held over the heads of men by Satan, so to speak, that is now gone. Since the Cross, anyone who remains under the domain of Satan, be it believer or unbeliever, does so simply because he does not know how to avail himself of the great victory won at Calvary. While demon spirits most definitely did everything they could to Christ while He was on the Cross, the moment He died, that satisfied the demands of a thrice-holy God, meaning that God accepted the sacrifice of His Son. With that being done, the victory was won, totally and completely.

In fact, if Jesus had failed to atone for even one small sin, He could not have risen from the dead because the Bible says *"the wages of sin is death"* (Rom. 6:23). So, the fact of His resurrection proved the veracity of His victory won over Satan at the Cross. Please understand that the salvation of every person, the baptism with the Holy Spirit, divine healing, answered prayer, and victory over the world, the flesh, and the Devil, all, and without exception, are made possible by the Cross of Christ. That means that every believer should make the Cross of Christ the object of His faith. In doing that, that is placing one's faith in the entirety of the Bible simply because the entirety of the Bible is the story of Jesus Christ and Him crucified.

2. The believer is now washed, sanctified, and justified (I Cor. 6:11), but no believer is yet glorified. This will take place at the rapture of the church (I Cor. 15:51-53; I Thess. 4:16-17).

3. Through what Jesus did at Calvary, the fear of death has been removed. The sting of death will then be taken away at the rapture (I Cor. 15:55).

4. Paul wrote that at the end of the kingdom age, *"The last enemy that shall be destroyed is death"* (I Cor. 15:26). This speaks of death in all its forms, be it physical or spiritual.

5. Jesus is the firstfruits of this, and *"afterward they who are Christ's at His coming"* (I Cor. 15:23).

6. *"Remember how He spoke unto you when He was yet in Galilee,"* proclaims the angels drawing these women back to the

NOTES

words of Jesus. They were being reminded of that failure to believe.

(7) "SAYING, THE SON OF MAN MUST BE DELIVERED INTO THE HANDS OF SINFUL MEN, AND BE CRUCIFIED, AND THE THIRD DAY RISE AGAIN."

The construction is:

1. The phrase, *"Saying, The Son of Man must be delivered into the hands of sinful men,"* is derived from Luke 18:32 and 33. The angels here called the religious leaders of Israel and the Gentiles, which spoke of Pilate, etc., sinful men.

2. *"And be crucified, and the third day rise again,"* proclaims the fact that Jesus had plainly told them exactly what would happen. As we have said several times, they did not believe Him simply because they had their own agenda.

(8) "AND THEY REMEMBERED HIS WORDS."

The exposition is:

1. Williams said, "Recollection is more important than information."

2. They remembered them now because they had come to pass exactly as Jesus had predicted.

3. His word should have been so precious to them that they would husband each statement and glean the full import of its meaning. However, that was not the case!

4. They had other plans, so they missed out on the greatest event in history—the resurrection of the Lord Jesus Christ; however, lest we be too hard on them, how much are we missing by taking lightly His Word or not believing it at all?

5. The Bible is *"His words."* As such, we should master its contents, or at least seek to do so. Inasmuch as the Word of God is alive, it would be impossible to exhaust its resources. However, we must empty our hearts of our own agenda and allow the Holy Spirit to subdue self-will until we know what the Word of God says. Then we must apply it to our lives in its totality.

(9) "AND RETURNED FROM THE SEPULCHRE, AND TOLD ALL THESE THINGS UNTO THE ELEVEN, AND TO ALL THE REST."

The overview is:

1. The phrase, *"And returned from the*

sepulchre," proclaims the connotation of their returning in a far different manner than they had originally supposed.

2. They had gone to finish the embalming process of adding more spices to the body of our Lord but, of course, did not find a body, but rather an empty tomb. Besides that, they had witnessed the appearance of two angels in such striking array that it defied description.

3. *"And told all these things unto the Eleven,"* evidently speaks of a place where they had all gathered at this early morning hour.

4. According to Matthew and John, Mary Magdalene had come to the tomb a little bit ahead of the other women. Mark mentions that Mary, the mother of James, and Salome, were with her, while Matthew and John did not mention this fact.

5. According to John, Mary Magdalene went and told Peter and John about the empty tomb, with the two disciples then going to investigate for themselves. This was before Mary had seen the Lord. Peter and John only saw an empty tomb without an angel appearing unto them. It seems that immediately after this, Jesus appeared to Mary Magdalene, who was alone at the time, and who was the first to see Him (Mk. 16:9; Jn. 20:11-17).

6. Almost immediately after Jesus appeared to Mary Magdalene, she was joined by Mary, the mother of James, with Jesus then appearing to the both of them (Mat. 28:8-10). Very soon after this appearance, both Mary Magdalene and the other Mary were joined by other women, with no record that the other women saw the Lord, and all of them going to tell the disciples what they had seen and heard.

7. As stated, Peter and John had already seen the empty tomb by now, but nothing else. Consequently, as we shall see, they would be somewhat skeptical of the message they were now about to hear.

(10) "IT WAS MARY MAGDALENE, AND JOANNA, AND MARY THE MOTHER OF JAMES, AND OTHER WOMEN WHO WERE WITH THEM, WHICH TOLD THESE THINGS UNTO THE APOSTLES."

The exegesis is:

1. It is beautifully amazing that the Holy

Spirit purposely delineates the fact that it was the women who first experienced all these grand happenings, and above all, with two of them witnessing the appearance of Jesus.

2. *"Which told these things unto the apostles,"* actually constitutes a reversal of what should have been, and it was because of unbelief on the part of the apostles.

3. The very title *apostle* means "one sent on a special mission, with a special message." Therefore, they should have been the ones telling the women and all others, and would have been had they not been so immersed in unbelief.

4. As the situation unfolded, even in our present society, this scenario would be humiliating enough, but in the society of that particular time, it was grossly humiliating. Women did not nearly have the status then as now. To be sure, it was Jesus, even as here illustrated, who gave them back the status lost in the garden of Eden, with Eve being the first to fall. What a rebuke to the faithlessness of the apostles! Because of their unbelief, women will forever have the distinction and honor of being the first to witness the resurrection of our Lord. There could be no higher or greater honor!

5. Even though the women, as well, were not expecting a resurrection (evidenced by their bringing the embalming spices for His body), still, their unbelief, as here is glaringly evident, was not nearly as acute as that of the apostles.

(11) "AND THEIR WORDS SEEMED TO THEM AS IDLE TALES, AND THEY BELIEVED THEM NOT."

IDLE TALES?

The phrase, *"And their words seemed to them as idle tales,"* actually means in the Greek "silly nonsense."

One can almost see Mary Magdalene, along with Mary, the mother of James, relating to the Eleven exactly how Jesus had appeared unto them, with the other women joining in speaking of the appearance of the angels. The words in exclamative bursts must have tumbled out of them as they hurriedly attempted to explain what they had seen. Matthew mentions their *"fear and great joy"* (Mat. 28:8).

The appearance of the angels, and especially Jesus, would have had such an effect on them that it would be difficult to describe. They had been witnesses of the greatest happening in human history. Jesus was alive!

UNBELIEF

The phrase, *"And they believed them not,"* (Lk. 24:11) presents the disciples' attitude of unbelief as extremely strong, meaning they dismissed these testimonies out of hand. They accepted nothing that was said. Why?

If there had been only one witness, perhaps one could understand their attitude; however, in keeping with Scripture (Deut. 17:6; Mat. 18:16), two witnesses to the appearance of Christ were present. In addition, the other women were lending their voices to the appearance of angels, with them saying, *"He is not here, He is risen."* So, there was no excuse for their unbelief inasmuch as the evidence was irrefutable.

• For instance, as stated, there were two witnesses to the resurrection of Christ.

• If Jesus did not rise from the dead, what happened to His body? The disciples knew they had not moved it.

• Above all of that, He had told them repeatedly that He would be killed by the religious leaders of Israel but would rise again on the third day.

Once a person sets a course of unbelief, it feeds upon itself, with the little leaven ultimately corrupting the whole. Unbelief never remains static. It always increases, with the person sinking deeper and deeper into the quagmire, which colors his or her thinking concerning everything. We are here observing an excellent case in point, and above all, among the Lord's own disciples. This tells us that no heart, irrespective of environment, participation, or association is immune from this deadly peril.

FAITH

The reason such is so acute, so dangerous, and so debilitating is because the entirety of one's life and work for God is anchored in the realm of faith. If faith is lacking in God's Word, unbelief is the automatic result, which, as stated, continues to get worse and

worse. Unbelief was so acute in the disciples that Thomas would shortly say, *"Except I shall see in His hands the print of the nails, and put my finger into the print of the nails, and thrust my hand into His side, I will not believe"* (Jn. 20:25).

This is how bad the situation had become! Unbelief, being a state of the heart, is not easily changed, even by incontestable proof. It actually would become so acute that Jesus, as we shall see, would refer to at least two of the disciples as fools!

The reason for their unbelief, resulting in their demeanor, attitude, and negative spirit, was a departure from the Word of God. The Word is always the criterion. If that is set aside, as it was in this case by the disciples, unbelief is the unchangeable result.

The only cure for unbelief is repentance and a return to the Word of God.

(12) "THEN AROSE PETER, AND RAN UNTO THE SEPULCHRE; AND STOOPING DOWN, HE BEHELD THE LINEN CLOTHES LAID BY THEMSELVES, AND DEPARTED, WONDERING IN HIMSELF AT THAT WHICH WAS COME TO PASS."

The structure is:

1. The phrase, *"Then arose Peter, and ran unto the sepulchre,"* should have been translated, *"Now Peter had arisen,"* speaking in the past tense something that happened before the second report of Verse 10.

2. When the first report was given by Mary Magdalene concerning the tomb being empty, there was no mention made of seeing Jesus, with every evidence being that there was no appearance of Christ up to this moment (Jn. 20:1-2).

3. At that time, Peter and John, as John records it, went to inspect the situation for themselves. They, too, saw the empty tomb, but nothing more.

4. The phrase, *"And stooping down, he beheld the linen clothes laid by themselves,"* tells us something very important.

The linen clothes laying there by themselves proved that His body had not been stolen. If such had been the case, the thieves certainly would not have stopped to take all the time to unwrap the linen from around the corpse.

5. When Jesus rose from the dead, this

linen wrapping either fell from Him of its own accord, He took it off Himself, or else, it was taken off by angels. However it was done, it was not removed from a corpse but one Who was alive.

6. *"And departed, wondering in himself at that which was come to pass,"* is the beginning of faith, but yet, very weak.

7. It should be noted that no appearance of either angels or Christ was forthcoming as yet to any of the disciples because of continued unbelief. However, that would soon change! Nevertheless, at His first appearance to them, He *"upbraided them with their unbelief and hardness of heart, because they believed not them which had seen Him after He was risen"* (Mk. 16:14).

(13) "AND, BEHOLD, TWO OF THEM WENT THAT SAME DAY TO A VILLAGE CALLED EMMAUS, WHICH WAS FROM JERUSALEM ABOUT THREESCORE FURLONGS."

The composition is:

1. The phrase, *"And, behold, two of them went that same day to a village called Emmaus,"* speaks of two of the followers of Christ. One was Cleopas, the father of James the Less and husband of Mary, the sister of Mary, the mother of Jesus (Jn. 19:25). Actually, Mary, the wife of Cleopas, should have been translated *"Maria,"* for that actually was her name.

2. The other follower of Jesus is not known, but may ancient and modern scholars hold that it was Luke himself who was one of the seventy (Lk., Chpt. 10), and the reason he did not mention himself was that he was the writer of this story.

3. The *"same day"* spoken of here refers to Sunday, the resurrection day. This was a startling and momentous day to say the least!

4. Luke goes into detail, giving us a beautiful account of this happening, while Mark only mentions it in passing, with Matthew and John not referring to it at all (Mk. 16:12-13).

5. Emmaus was a small village southeast of Jerusalem. What their business was there, we are not told.

6. *"Which was from Jerusalem about threescore furlongs,"* constituted approximately seven miles.

7. It is said that this village contained baths or wells, which were medicinal springs. If, in fact, Luke was the other disciple spoken of here, and with him being a physician, this may account for their short journey to this place.

(14) "AND THEY TALKED TOGETHER OF ALL THESE THINGS WHICH HAD HAPPENED."

The diagram is:

1. *"All these things,"* pertained to the crucifixion.

2. It, as well, addressed itself to the testimonies of the women concerning the appearance of angels, and even the appearance of Christ.

3. To be frank, it was not possible that the topic of conversation would be anything else other than the resurrection of Christ.

(15) "AND IT CAME TO PASS, THAT, WHILE THEY COMMUNED TOGETHER AND REASONED, JESUS HIMSELF DREW NEAR, AND WENT WITH THEM."

The overview is:

1. The phrase, *"And it came to pass, that, while they communed together and reasoned,"* has reference to the fact that they were deep in thought, totally taken up with their conversation, thereby, oblivious to their surroundings.

2. *"Jesus Himself drew near, and went with them,"* would not of itself have occasioned consternation or surprise. The roads in those days were heavily trafficked with pedestrians, and someone doing this would not have been out of the ordinary.

3. However, that the Lord would go to this length in order to show His disciples the right way graphically describes His grace and love and, as well, a position He has taken with all of us respecting true direction. If the heart is honest and sincere before God, the Lord will go to any length to bring the individual back to the path of righteousness (Ps. 23:3).

4. Since the day of Pentecost, He primarily uses the Holy Spirit, although there is nothing in the Word of God that precludes Him appearing personally, as here. As we shall see, whatever manner He uses, irrespective of the vessel, such as preachers of the gospel, etc., the purpose will always be

to take the individual, as here, back to the Word of God. Unbelief always comes about by not abiding by the Word, and unbelief can only be rooted out as the individual returns to the Word and, thereby, to faith.

5. Jesus *"went with them,"* because this was the only manner in which their terrible error could be corrected.

(16) "BUT THEIR EYES WERE HOLDEN THAT THEY SHOULD NOT KNOW HIM."

The exegesis is:

1. The phrase, *"But their eyes were holden,"* refers to the Lord personally in some manner keeping His true identity from them.

2. The Greek word for *"holden"* is *krateo* and means "to hold in check, restrain, or to retain."

3. So, the evidence is that He purposely desired that He be incognito, at least for a short while.

4. *"That they should not know Him,"* was for purpose and reason. Why?

5. Had he appeared to them immediately as Christ, while they would have known definitely that He indeed had risen from the dead, He desired that their knowledge be based not on appearances but on the Word of God. Therefore, as a stranger opening up the Word to them, He would teach them a valuable lesson that was not for them only but for all other followers of Christ, and for all time as well!

6. He wanted them to know and understand that His resurrection pertained to far more than just merely being raised from the dead. He would take them to the Word of God and show them the purpose for His coming into this world, His dying on Calvary, and His paying the price for man's redemption. In effect, He was saying that if they had known the Word as they should, they would have had far greater understanding of these events than proved to be the case.

7. It is sad, but the example of the disciples in not taking full advantage of the Word is prevalent, as well, in modern church circles, and always has been. Most believers simply do not know the Word as they should; consequently, they are easy prey for Satan's lies, distortions, and half-truths.

(17) "AND HE SAID UNTO THEM,

WHAT MANNER OF COMMUNICATIONS ARE THESE THAT YOU HAVE ONE TO ANOTHER, AS YOU WALK, AND ARE SAD?"

The pattern is:

1. The phrase, *"And He said unto them,"* will prove to instigate the greatest conversation they had ever been privileged to have with anyone.

2. The question, *"What manner of communications are these that you have one to another, as you walk, and are sad?"* was a question to which He already knew the answer. However, He wanted to draw them out and have them relate their feelings.

3. It is ironic, but they were sad simply because they did not know the Word and, consequently, did not believe what He had plainly said about His death and resurrection.

4. The manner of *"communications"* was the same manner that many believers have presently. Their conversation constituted communications of doubt, unbelief, and even despair, which brought about sadness and was the very opposite of what it should have been.

5. I suspect that the Lord has been asking the question of this very text of many believers from that time until this, and probably, at one time or the other, to every single believer. How so much we miss, as here, by our faithlessness.

(18) "AND THE ONE OF THEM, WHOSE NAME WAS CLEOPAS, ANSWERING SAID UNTO HIM, ARE YOU ONLY A STRANGER IN JERUSALEM, AND HAVE NOT KNOWN THE THINGS WHICH ARE COME TO PASS THEREIN THESE DAYS?"

The form is:

1. The phrase, *"And the one of them, whose name was Cleopas, answering said unto Him,"* reveals in the question to be asked some incredulity. Had he known this was Jesus, he would have conducted himself quite differently. This should be a lesson to us as well.

2. Paul said, *"Be not forgetful to entertain strangers: for thereby some have entertained angels unawares"* (Heb. 13:2).

3. The question, *"Are You only a stranger in Jerusalem, and have not known the things which are come to pass therein these days?"* is asked with some sarcasm.

4. Regrettably, Jesus was treated as a stranger in Jerusalem, even though it was the city He had originally chosen *"that My name might be there"* (II Chron. 6:6).

5. Regrettably, Israel did not want Him; therefore, the nation would serve no further purpose and would be destroyed totally in A.D. 70 by Titus and the Roman 10th Legion.

(19) "AND HE SAID UNTO THEM, WHAT THINGS? AND THEY SAID UNTO HIM, CONCERNING JESUS OF NAZARETH, WHICH WAS A PROPHET MIGHTY IN DEED AND WORD BEFORE GOD AND ALL THE PEOPLE."

The order is:

1. The question, *"And He said unto them, What things?"* is asked solely for the purpose of drawing them out.

2. *"And they said unto Him, Concerning Jesus of Nazareth,"* was used in this fashion to distinguish Jesus from all the others who bore the same name, for its use was common at that time. Consequently, the name Jesus of Nazareth was both hated and loved. It remains no less today.

3. *"Which was a prophet mighty in deed and word before God and all the people,"* if it is to be noticed, does not mention Jesus being the Messiah. Actually, the next verse will show that even though they once believed that He was, their faith had been so shaken by His death that they seemingly no longer held this view, even though continuing to believe that He was a great prophet.

4. How wrong they were!

(20) "AND HOW THE CHIEF PRIESTS AND OUR RULERS DELIVERED HIM TO BE CONDEMNED TO DEATH, AND HAVE CRUCIFIED HIM."

The overview is:

1. The apostate church did to Jesus what they have continued to do ever since. Regrettably, most of organized religion falls into the same category. Their business is not to preach Jesus, but rather to condemn Him to death by unbelief, doubt, and sarcasm respecting His Word.

2. As here, most, if not all religious efforts, are designed to stop the gospel instead of preaching the gospel. Regrettably, this runs the gamut in almost all religious leadership,

irrespective of the denomination. There are hopefully a few exceptions, but not many!

3. As this very Scripture proves, plus a score of others, the enemy of the Lord is not nearly so much the world as it is the apostate church. While Pilate did carry out this perfidious task of crucifixion, still, it was the religious leaders of Israel who demanded it and are charged with it.

(21) "BUT WE TRUSTED THAT IT HAD BEEN HE WHICH SHOULD HAVE REDEEMED ISRAEL: AND BESIDE ALL THIS, TODAY IS THE THIRD DAY SINCE THESE THINGS WERE DONE."

The composition is:

1. The phrase, *"But we trusted that it had been He which should have redeemed Israel,"* tells us two things:

a. This shows they no longer believed He was the Messiah.

b. They had confined their Bible reading to that which the Scriptures promised respecting the Messiah's glory and kingdom, but they had been blind to the multitude of types and prophecies foretelling His sufferings as an atoning Saviour.

2. *"And beside all this, today is the third day since these things were done,"* could read, *"This is three days since these things were done."*

3. Considering the information they would now give concerning the women, they seem to dwell on the third day, perhaps remembering what Jesus had said, *"And the third day He shall rise again"* (Lk. 18:33).

(22) "YEA, AND CERTAIN WOMEN ALSO OF OUR COMPANY MADE US ASTONISHED, WHICH WERE EARLY AT THE SEPULCHRE."

The pattern is:

1. The phrase, *"Yea, and certain women also of our company made us astonished"* refers to the accounts given by Mary Magdalene and the others.

2. So, this shows that these two were with the disciples, and possibly a number of others, when the women brought this information.

3. *"Which were early at the sepulchre,"* speaks of Verse 1. As stated, they had brought spices to the tomb for the embalming process.

(23) "AND WHEN THEY FOUND NOT

HIS BODY, THEY CAME, SAYING, THAT THEY HAD ALSO SEEN A VISION OF ANGELS, WHICH SAID THAT HE WAS ALIVE."

The order is:

1. The phrase, *"And when they found not His body,"* emphasizes the fact that they knew this much was true because two of their own, even Peter and John, had verified this.

2. This was extremely perplexing simply because they knew that none of their group had stolen the body. They also knew it was in the far greater interest of the religious leaders of Israel who had crucified Him that His body remain in the tomb. They had even impressed upon Pilate the necessity of stationing soldiers at the tomb around the clock in order that no one make away with the corpse (Mat. 27:62-66). So, what had happened to the body?

3. *"They came, saying, that they had also seen a vision of angels, which said that He was alive,"* proclaims, by the use of the word *also*, that these two men were not so sure of the veracity of the account of the angels and their message concerning His resurrection.

4. As of yet, Jesus had not appeared to any of the disciples, but only, it seems, to Mary Magdalene and Mary the mother of James (Mat. 28:1-10), with Mary Magdalene being the first of these two to see Him (Mk. 16:9).

5. Consequently, these two disciples, Cleopas and Luke, that is, if it was Luke, were possibly the first men to see Jesus after the resurrection. Actually, when these two would hurry back to Jerusalem after Jesus had revealed Himself to them, 10 of the Eleven still would little believe (Mk. 16:12-13).

6. As we shall see, it seems Peter had also now seen the Lord (Vs. 34).

(24) "AND CERTAIN OF THEM WHICH WERE WITH US WENT TO THE SEPULCHRE, AND FOUND IT EVEN SO AS THE WOMEN HAD SAID: BUT HIM THEY SAW NOT."

The pattern is:

1. The phrase, *"And certain of them which were with us went to the sepulchre,"* speaks of Peter and John (Jn. 20:1-10).

2. *"And found it even so as the women had said: but Him they saw not,"* means that they verified that the body was gone,

NOTES

but they did not see the angels or the Lord. Consequently, the words, *"But Him they saw not,"* contain doubt about the testimony of the women regarding His appearance.

3. As well, they used the word *vision* (Lk. 24:23) respecting the angels, insinuating that they believed that the women had seen angels and possibly even the Lord, but it was only a vision, hence, spiritual, instead of literal. So, they had attempted to explain away these glorious testimonies, which would cause Jesus to strongly upbraid the apostles (Mk. 16:14).

(25) "THEN HE SAID UNTO THEM, O FOOLS, AND SLOW OF HEART TO BELIEVE ALL THAT THE PROPHETS HAVE SPOKEN?"

The form is:

1. The phrase, *"Then He said unto them,"* portrays Him hearing them out and now answering. His beginning statement was strong!

2. The words *"O fools"* would have been better translated *"O foolish men!"*

3. This tells us that the Lord concludes all as very foolish, who do not make His Word the basis for all their actions and decisions. While this certainly applies to the world, even though they will not adhere to the Word, it applies more than all to the church. Regrettably, the modern church, with some few exceptions, is little of the Word. Of these, "foolish" is the label attached by the Lord.

4. *"And slow of heart to believe all that the prophets have spoken,"* pulls these two, as all others, back to the Bible. It alone is the criterion for all things done. It would be so no less concerning Jesus, His mission, purpose, and sufferings.

(26) "OUGHT NOT CHRIST TO HAVE SUFFERED THESE THINGS, AND TO ENTER INTO HIS GLORY?"

THE LORD JESUS CHRIST

The question, *"Ought not Christ to have suffered these things?"* means the Bible predicted His sufferings and should have been obvious to His followers, and would have been had they only devoted time and attention to the Word of God.

The first prophecy of the Bible concerns

His suffering and struggles with Satan (Gen. 3:15). Other whole chapters are devoted to this (Ex., Chpt. 12; Ps. 22; Isa., Chpt. 53).

Many separate passages reveal the sufferings of the Messiah (Isa. 50:4-7; 52:14; Dan. 9:26; Zech. 13:6-7).

As well, all the sacrifices and offerings from Abel forward picture these sufferings. So, beginning with Moses and continuing through all the prophets, He made it clear why these events had to take place before His coming in glory and the instigation of the kingdom.

THE GLORY OF GOD

The conclusion of the questions, *"And to enter into His glory?"* proclaims that the Bible does outline the coming kingdom of glory and power, hence, the triumphant Messiah. However, it must be preceded by the mission of the suffering Messiah.

Jesus was telling them that they must believe all the prophecies. Jews were good at believing the glory and the greatness of the kingdom that would make them great in the eyes of the Gentiles, but they would not believe those of His humility and sufferings. Consequently, they crucified Him because He did not fulfill their hopes and ambitions, or even sympathize with them under the Roman yoke.

The failure of Israel, and above all the disciples, to understand the purpose of the suffering Messiah is of far greater magnitude than a mere failure to understand these prophecies. To fail to understand them is to fail to understand the condition of man in his lostness, and above all, his inability in any capacity to save himself.

It is a failure to understand the magnitude of sin and just how lost that man really is. As well, it is a failure to understand the magnitude of what this terrible sinful condition has brought about in this world, i.e., the sufferings, heartache, war, death, and destruction.

So, to misunderstand this is to misunderstand the entirety of the plan of God for the human family and, as well, the key to the darkest problems that beset the fallen sons of Adam's lost race.

NOTES

THE SACRIFICES

This is amazing that they did not understand this, especially considering the sacrifices that Israel had been offering for nearly 1,600 years. The death of the innocent victim was a gruesome sight, with its blood poured out at the base of the great altar even worse. The death of these innocent victims (clean animals) pointed to the coming Redeemer and the horror of the judgment He would undergo in our place, typified by the fire on the great altar. This was meant by God to be a gruesome thing, which it was, and was meant to portray not only the price that would have to be paid, but the awfulness and horror of such sinful condition, which would require such an offering.

Regrettably, all of these rituals had been reduced to mere ceremony, with its true meaning seemingly lost upon Israel. This covered the entirety of the nation with a cloud of unbelief, including even the chosen of Christ.

If man fails to understand just how badly he is lost, then he will fail to understand the magnitude of the price that was paid for his redemption. No wonder Jesus said, *"O fools!"*

(27) "AND BEGINNING AT MOSES AND ALL THE PROPHETS, HE EXPOUNDED UNTO THEM IN ALL THE SCRIPTURES THE THINGS CONCERNING HIMSELF."

The exposition is:

1. The phrase, *"And beginning at Moses,"* tells us that Moses was the author of the Pentateuch, which is Genesis, Exodus, Leviticus, Numbers, and Deuteronomy. Consequently, he was the first one to write into a book that which was given to him by God.

2. *"And all the prophets,"* proclaims Jesus outlining two of the three divisions of the Old Testament. Those three divisions are the law (Pentateuch), prophets, and the Psalms, which included all the wisdom books.

3. *"He expounded unto them in all the Scriptures the things concerning Himself,"* meant that He took quite a bit of time, beginning, as stated, with Genesis 3:15.

4. The Lord told them, as well as us, that the Bible is the supreme authority as to faith and doctrine because it is inspired.

5. Its subject is the sufferings and glories of Christ—His sufferings as the sin-bearer

and His glories as sin-purger (Phil. 2:5-11; Heb. 1:3).

6. It may truly be said that Christ went into death, Bible in hand, and that He came out from among the dead, Bible in hand. He insisted that it predicted His death and resurrection in relation to sin and its judgment.

7. So, immediately prior to His death and immediately subsequent to His resurrection, He made more than 30 quotations from the inspired Word.

(28) "AND THEY DREW NIGH UNTO THE VILLAGE, WHITHER THEY WENT: AND HE MADE AS THOUGH HE WOULD HAVE GONE FURTHER."

The exegesis is:

1. The phrase, *"And they drew nigh* (near) *unto the village, whither* (where) *they went,"* presents the intersection of life that comes to all. They would now have to make a choice as to whether they wanted His presence to continue with them or allow the business at hand to interrupt.

2. There was certainly nothing illegitimate about their activity at this village, whatever it was, and they easily could have felt, as most, that it demanded immediate attention at the expense of having Jesus with them. However, for the last hour or so, they had experienced a manifestation of the Word of God, given to them by none other than Jesus Himself, even though at the time they were not aware it was Him. They did know that something great had happened, as they would later exclaim.

3. This is somewhat the same scenario as Mary and Martha. Mary wanted to sit at Jesus' feet and hear His word, while *"Martha was cumbered about much serving,"* and correspondingly complained about the lack of help concerning her sister.

4. Jesus would answer Martha's complaint by saying, *"Martha, Martha, you are careful and troubled about many things:*

"But one thing is needful: and Mary has chosen that good part, which shall not be taken away from her" (Lk. 10:38-42).

5. *"And He made as though He would have gone further,"* presents the normal manner of the Lord. He does not intrude Himself but must be invited.

6. Spence said, "This was no feint or deception. The Lord would have left them then to themselves had they not prayed Him with real earnestness to abide with them."

7. Stier said, "How many are there, to whom He has drawn near, but with whom He has not tarried, because they have suffered Him to go away again.

8. "How comparatively rare it is for men to reach the full blessing they might receive."

(29) "BUT THEY CONSTRAINED HIM, SAYING, ABIDE WITH US: FOR IT IS TOWARD EVENING, AND THE DAY IS FAR SPENT. AND HE WENT IN TO TARRY WITH THEM."

ABIDE WITH US

The phrase, *"But they constrained Him, saying, Abide with us,"* is the same heart-petition that must be entertained by all, that is, if Jesus is to abide.

The word *constrained* is strong, meaning in the Greek text "to compel as by force." In other words, they would not take "no" for an answer!

This is the attitude that faith must take and, in fact, will take, if it is true faith. An example is given by Jesus in Luke, Chapter 11, concerning the man who knocked at a friend's door at midnight, asking for *"three loaves."*

The response from inside the house at first was not positive; however, due to the *"importunity"* of the man, he was given as much as he needed (Lk. 11:5-13).

Many believers are content with a manifestation of the Lord but stop short of what He really desires to do in the heart and the life of the individual, namely abide! While the manifestation, as given on the road to Emmaus, was wonderful to say the least, due to their insistence that Jesus abide with them, they would receive a revelation of His resurrected person. Consequently, it seems as if God's way is laid out according to the following:

GOD'S WAY

• At particular times in our lives, the Lord takes up position with us without us really knowing exactly how important the visitation really is. Many, even most, regrettably, are content with this; however, a second step is always presented, which is basically left up to us respecting our hunger and thirst for the Lord, or lack thereof.

• The invitation must be extended, *"Abide with us,"* and done so forcibly if greater revelation is to be given. The Word is always given first, as it was here, but its purpose is to reveal Jesus in a greater and more glorified way.

At this particular time, we can allow other interests to come first, which, if done, will occasion Jesus going further without us.

This insistence can well be exampled by the account of Jacob wrestling with the Lord, and saying to Him, *"I will not let You go, except You bless me"* (Gen. 32:24-30).

As Jacob of old and the example given to us in the account by Luke, we can see *"God face to face,"* or not see Him at all!

At this stage in our walk with the Lord, all hinges on our hunger and thirst for the Lord and our faith.

• The biblical direction is that if we take full advantage of what has been afforded us, we will receive a revelation of Christ in His resurrection power. This is what Paul was speaking of when he said:

"That I may know Him, and the power of His resurrection, and the fellowship of His sufferings, being made conformable unto His death" (Phil. 3:10).

THE DAY IS FAR SPENT

Even though the first manifestation of Jesus presenting the Word to these two disciples was glorious indeed, it was meant to lead unto a fuller revelation of Christ Himself, which it did! However, to receive this, the individual must insist, *"Abide with us!"* This is the heartfelt desire of Christ, and that which He intends all along. However, as we have stated, He will not do so unless truly desired, and with a desire that will not be denied.

The phrase, *"For it is toward evening, and the day is far spent,"* was true in more ways than one.

No, had they not insisted that He come with them, they would not have lost their souls. However, they would have been denied a blessing unparalleled in human history—to be among, if not the first men, to whom He would reveal Himself after the resurrection. This is amazing considering

that He had not revealed Himself even to His chosen Eleven at this present time, with the exception possibly of Peter.

"Toward evening" is definitely referring to the time of day concerning this incident; however, in a spiritual sense, it has a far deeper meaning.

Jesus said, *"I must work the works of Him who sent Me, while it is day: the night comes, when no man can work"* (Jn. 9:4).

The Lord abiding with us and us abiding with Him in heaven, while certainly extremely important, nevertheless, is not what the Holy Spirit is now calling to account. Jesus wants to abide with us now! For Him to do the work within our lives that must be done, and for us to correspondingly do His work, we must go further than a mere presentation of the Word, even as wonderful as that may be. We must insist that He abide with us, which He desires that we do, and greatly so! With many, it is growing late, and the day is far spent. The urgency pertains to now, and with reason.

TO TARRY WITH THEM

Along with each individual response, the time for this world is advancing toward evening. The signs of the times are being speedily fulfilled. In truth, the next harvest may be the last!

The phrase, *"And He went in to tarry with them,"* constitutes, one might say, the greatest thing that ever happened to them. The day that had begun with such sorrow, at least as far as they were concerned, would end in the most glorious in the history of man. They may well have been the first men to witness this tremendous happening.

(30) "AND IT CAME TO PASS, AS HE SAT AT MEAT WITH THEM, HE TOOK BREAD, AND BLESSED IT, AND BREAK, AND GAVE TO THEM."

HE TOOK, HE BLESSED, HE BROKE, HE GAVE

The phrase, *"And it came to pass, as He sat at meat with them,"* presents a tremendously significant meaning. It is similar with, and refers to, the Passover He had recently eaten with them, what we now refer to as *"the Lord's Supper."*

"He took bread, and blessed it, and break (broke it), and gave to them," presents itself as a pattern and is done so for reason.

He did the same thing, and in that order, when He fed the thousands with five loaves and two fish, and again with seven loaves and a few little fish (Mat. 14:17; 15:34), as well as the partaking of the Passover, as stated. We must derive the lesson He is teaching us.

This order or manner, as stated, is not without design and refers to the manner in which Jesus was given to us, and the manner in which we are to be given to the world. The order is *took, blessed, broke,* and *gave.*

HE TOOK BREAD

This is symbolic of God taking His only Son and giving Him as the living Word to the world (Jn. 3:16).

In the same manner, God takes us, but with some difference, of course. Jesus was taken out of heaven, while we are taken out of the world. However, in a sense the purpose is the same. As Jesus was the living Word, typified by the bread, you and I are to be filled with the Word, i.e., bread, as well!

AND BLESSED IT

This refers to God's blessings upon Jesus. While believers constantly pray, as they should, for the blessings of God, still, God's true blessings cannot really come upon man as such, but only on Jesus in man. Of course, at the moment of conversion, Jesus is in the believer, with the believer experiencing great blessings (Jn. 14:20).

AND BROKE IT

This typifies the death of Jesus on the Cross in order that we may have salvation.

As well, the believer is to likewise take up his Cross, even on a daily basis, and follow Jesus. This speaks of the sacrificed life and the dying daily to the things of the world (Lk. 9:23; I Cor. 15:31).

Many believers seek to remain at the blessing stage, which, of course, is always appealing to the flesh; however, if the believer remains at that stage, ultimately, the believer will spiritually die. For believers to be rightly given to the world to where they will be a blessing to others, they first

must be broken, and that's not a pleasant experience, but it is a necessary experience. Unfortunately, many try to avoid the breaking experience; however, if we are to be rightly used of God, the breaking process must always take place.

AND HE GAVE TO THEM

The Lord cannot give self-will to a hurting world. He can only give that, as stated, which has been broken as the bread was here broken. Too many Christians are attempting to give themselves to the world, which can never save or help anyone. Jesus must be given to hurting mankind, and He can only be given if the believer is properly broken.

As we have also stated, the breaking process is not pleasant; consequently, that particular message is not popular.

One may ask how the breaking process is to be brought about.

If one truly knows the Lord and is truly following Him, such will be brought about by the Holy Spirit in His own time. Some, and perhaps all of us at one time or the other, have attempted to do such through our own efforts. However, irrespective of the religious garb, all such efforts constitute the flesh, in which God will have no part. This is a work that can only be done by the Holy Spirit and is a process that actually never ends. The battle now between the flesh and the Spirit is unending and will not really end until the trump sounds.

The disciples were about to find this out. They were now about to leave the blessing stage and go into the breaking stage when they could finally be given to the world.

(31) "AND THEIR EYES WERE OPENED, AND THEY KNEW HIM; AND HE VANISHED OUT OF THEIR SIGHT."

OPENED EYES

The phrase, *"And their eyes were opened,"* speaks more than all of their spiritual eyes. I think believers should pray constantly that their eyes be opened, and if opened, to remain so.

I am persuaded that many believers, exactly as these two disciples, are blind to many things. These men were believers, and as a result, they loved the Lord;

however, they were blind to great parts of the Scripture that told of His sufferings as well as what He had said concerning His resurrection.

Are we blind to certain aspects of the Word of God, consequently, missing out on many blessings? If these two disciples could have been, and they were, then many others are as well!

Millions of believers need to have their eyes opened concerning the baptism with the Holy Spirit, the leading of the Spirit, divine healing, or to properly divide the Word.

However, one might say that the greatest need of all is for the believer to have his or her eyes opened as it regards the Message of the Cross. The Cross of Christ is the foundation of the great redemption plan. Millions of Christians understand the Cross somewhat as it regards salvation but not at all as it regards sanctification. Consequently, it is impossible for such a believer to live a victorious life. One can be saved and not understand this, but one cannot walk in victory unless one properly understands the Cross of Christ.

THEY KNEW HIM

The phrase, *"And they knew Him,"* was possible only because He had opened their eyes. The object as always is to see Jesus; however, let it be stated that these men could not open their eyes themselves. It only came about because they had a hunger for the Lord. He has promised that if we *"hunger and thirst after righteousness,"* we *"shall be filled"* (Mat. 5:6).

The entirety of the purpose of the Holy Spirit is that we may know Him.

Millions know their doctrines, religious denominations, or a particular church, but they little know Him. However, the Holy Spirit will only reveal Him!

The phrase, *"And He vanished out of their sight,"* proclaims Him doing so, but only after He had accomplished His purpose. These two disciples would never be the same again.

As an aside, we are now witnessing His glorified body on which all natural laws are suspended. He could appear or disappear! As well, matter was of no hindrance to Him, with Him passing through such with ease.

As John said, this is what we will have at the first resurrection (I Jn. 3:2).

(32) "AND THEY SAID ONE TO ANOTHER, DID NOT OUR HEART BURN WITHIN US, WHILE HE TALKED WITH US BY THE WAY, AND WHILE HE OPENED TO US THE SCRIPTURES?"

The synopsis is:

1. The phrase, *"And they said one to another,"* now presents an entirely different type of conversation or communication than before. In a moment's time, their world had irrevocably changed. They had seen Jesus, and He was not dead, but alive!

2. The question *"Did not our heart burn within us, while He talked with us by the way?"* now calls to account what had happened to them on their short journey with Jesus.

3. When He spoke, it was unlike anything they had ever heard before. Every question was answered, with every fear being dissolved.

4. As an aside, the wife of Cleopas had already seen the Lord (Mat. 28:1-10), and now he had been privileged to see Jesus as well.

5. The conclusion of the question, *"And while He opened to us the Scriptures?"* proclaims the occasion for what happened to them.

6. The business of Christ through the Holy Spirit is to help us understand the Word of God. When He does, it becomes alive and has a consequent effect. Otherwise, it cannot be properly understood and leaves one unmoved.

(33) "AND THEY ROSE UP THE SAME HOUR, AND RETURNED TO JERUSALEM, AND FOUND THE ELEVEN GATHERED TOGETHER, AND THEM WHO WERE WITH THEM."

The order is:

1. The phrase, *"And they rose up the same hour, and returned to Jerusalem,"* presents a joy they could not contain and a message they could not keep. Jesus was not dead, but alive! Consequently, the day that had begun so dark would now conclude with such joy and light.

2. *"And found the Eleven gathered together, and them who were with them,"* presents a meeting that was quickly changing from despair to great joy.

3. Admittedly, they had to arrive at this place by stages, but they were on their way.

(34) "SAYING, THE LORD IS RISEN INDEED, AND HAS APPEARED TO SIMON."

The form is:

1. The phrase, *"Saying, The Lord is risen indeed,"* presents a conversation of victory, in fact, the greatest victory ever recorded in human history.

2. The evidence was now overwhelming. He was not dead, but alive! The doubt, at least for most, was beginning to vanish away.

3. What a delight it would have been to have overheard this conversation. Excitement must have filled the room; however, it was only beginning, with the balance of the night presenting even greater testimonies.

4. *"And has appeared to Simon,"* records something glorious and wonderful! The Scripture does not give us the account of this appearance but is only mentioned here. What was said, we do not know; however, it would convince Simon Peter.

5. It is open to debate as to whom Jesus first appeared among the disciples, whether the two at Emmaus or Simon Peter; however, that honor at this stage is of little consequence. That He has appeared is all that matters.

6. Considering Peter's terrible failure, one can well imagine the joy that sprang up in his heart concerning Jesus appearing to him. He now knew, and beyond the shadow of a doubt, that he was forgiven.

7. However, the record is clear that despite the testimony of the women, and even of Simon Peter, some of them still were not interpreting the resurrection correctly. Mark 16:13-14 proclaims this fact.

8. Perhaps they thought that these appearances were visions or something similar; nevertheless, in a few minutes' time, all would experience the greatest moment of their lives. Jesus would appear and even eat with them.

(35) "AND THEY TOLD WHAT THINGS WERE DONE IN THE WAY, AND HOW HE WAS KNOWN OF THEM IN BREAKING OF BREAD."

THE TESTIMONY

The phrase, *"And they told what things*

NOTES

were done in the way," concerned, no doubt, an excited presentation of one of the greatest events in human history—the appearance of Jesus Christ to these two after the resurrection.

"And how He was known of them in breaking of bread," has the idea that they freely told all who were gathered that at first, they did not recognize who Jesus was, but portrayed in detail how He was made known to them.

As I have already stated, this day would begin, at least to the disciples, as one of the blackest in history but would conclude as one of the most glorious in history. Jesus was alive!

The entirety of this scenario concerning these two disciples on the way to Emmaus and being joined by Jesus, and eventually Him being revealed to them, is very important to me personally.

In the latter part of 1993, I believe it was, we had gathered for one of our regular nightly prayer meetings. There must have been 25 or 30 present. I read an account of this very text, and I commented on it for a few minutes. Then we went to prayer.

About 10 or 15 minutes into this time of intercession, the Spirit of the Lord began to come upon me, bringing this very illustration of the two disciples into focus, especially pertaining to my own petitions.

He said this to me:

THE WORD OF THE LORD

"As no amount of argument or presentation could convince My disciples that I had been raised from the dead, likewise, the same holds true for your own particular ministry."

He went on to say, "There is nothing you or anyone else can do, at least in the natural sense, that will make people believe you concerning what I am doing in your life and ministry. In the minds of My disciples, I was dead and would not be resurrected. In the minds of the Christian public, you are dead and cannot be resurrected."

However, then He said, "I can change their minds! I can open their blinded eyes!"

And finally, "If I have to appear to them, even as I appeared to the two disciples on the road to Emmaus, I will do so."

From that moment I have seen the Lord begin to do this. It has been a little here and a little there, exactly as He told me He would do it, but it is happening.

A little later in one of the morning prayer meetings, the Lord began to deal with my heart concerning the true body of Christ.

The Holy Spirit began to impress upon me that morning that very few in the world or the apostate church would ever change, at least regarding this Ministry. However, the Lord told me, I believe, that those who truly love Him and, consequently, are led by Him, who make up the true body of Christ, will have the truth revealed to them about this ministry. I was to pray accordingly that this would be done, which we have done faithfully from then to now.

THE LORD IS DOING EXACTLY WHAT HE SAID HE WOULD DO

What most think is of little significance; however, I am very concerned about what true believers think about us. Even though it is only God who really matters, still, I know it is His will that all true believers think and believe right regarding all situations.

Consequently, this extended account as Luke presents it concerning the appearance of Christ to the two disciples, is very dear to me personally.

Nothing could open the eyes of these men to the resurrection of Christ but a revelation of Christ to them personally, which was done. In other matters, the Lord can do the same thing, and often does, exactly as I believe He has revealed to me.

If believers are always led by the Spirit, they will always have true guidance and direction. Regrettably, much of the body of Christ is not led by the Spirit but by prevailing opinion or personal bias and prejudice. Those who follow in that vein will never know the true blessings of God; however, those who are led by the Spirit will receive the rewards, which only the Spirit can give.

LOOK WHAT THE LORD HAS DONE

As I dictate these notes, I look back and marvel at what the Lord has done. Yes, it has been a long time when we look back to those years ago; however, the Lord has done exactly what He said He would do.

In 2010, He instructed me to begin the SonLife Broadcasting Network. This is television 24 hours a day, seven days a week. At the time of this writing, we cover approximately two-thirds of the nation of America, plus a hundred or so million homes in other countries of the world. In fact, the Lord has told us to place the programming in every city in the world that will accept it, and that we are attempting to do. That we must do and that we will do. Also, as it regards this network, the Lord has given us the message, the Message of the Cross. The early church began with the Cross, and the Holy Spirit is telling us that the church will go out with the Cross.

As well, the Lord has turned the hearts of untold thousands of people, and is continuing to do so unto this hour, that they see truthfully what this ministry actually is. As stated, only the Lord can do that, but that He has done and is doing.

I believe that the Lord has told me that the greatest harvest of souls the world has ever known is about to take place. I believe that He has also related to me that this ministry (Jimmy Swaggart Ministries) will play a great part in this harvest.

A DREAM

If I remember correctly, I was about 10 years of age. I dreamed I was standing in front of our home in the little backwater town of Ferriday, Louisiana. As I stood there that day, I looked to the right, and in the dream I saw a globe of the world about the size of a basketball, suspended in space. Then, all of a sudden, I saw a figure standing very nearby this globe, looking up at it, and I recognized him to be Satan.

For a period of time, he looked at the globe and then turned and looked at me and said, "You will not do it; I will stop you."

That was all that he said and then turned back and looked at the globe again and then, once again, turned and looked at me. He repeated the same thing again, "You will not do it; I will stop you."

I was just a child, and at that time I did not really know what the dream meant. I did not know what Satan was talking about, but I do know what I dreamed.

I now know exactly what He was addressing. He knew that the Lord had called me for world evangelism. He also knew that it would result in untold millions being saved by the precious blood of the Lord Jesus Christ. So, he would do everything within his power to stop us. However, he did not succeed, as he cannot succeed.

In the 1980s, we saw a tremendous part of this world touched with the gospel as we aired television programming, translated into the languages of the people, in many nations of the world. It was a tremendous harvest; however, this harvest that is coming will eclipse anything the world or the church has ever known. It is possible through television for millions of people to be saved. When the Spirit of God begins to move, anything can be done, and to be sure, He has moved, He is moving, and He shall move. It will be, I believe, the greatest moving and operation of the Holy Spirit that the world has ever seen, known, witnessed, or experienced.

THE BAPTISM WITH
THE HOLY SPIRIT

In the 1970s, the Lord spoke to my heart that I was to set aside a service in each of the meetings here in the U.S.A. in order for believers to be baptized with the Holy Spirit. He told me that I was also to air those services over television, which we did do. We saw thousands baptized with the Holy Spirit with the evidence of speaking with other tongues as the Spirit of God gave the utterance.

That day in prayer, the Lord also spoke to me, saying, "If you will believe Me, I will fill as many as a thousand people in a single service."

In the oncoming years, we saw many people filled with the Spirit but never as many as a thousand in a single service.

If I remember correctly, it was either 1986 or 1987. It was our third meeting in Madison Square Garden in New York City. It was a Sunday afternoon. The building was jammed to capacity, seating some 22,000.

As I preached that Sunday afternoon and

prayed for people who wanted to be saved, I then asked how many desired to be baptized with the Holy Spirit. A forest of hands went up all over that vast coliseum. I had them to come to the front and line up along the front, but I found quickly that the line would extend down each aisle all the way to the back, and then around the back, plus in the great balconies.

At any rate, the Lord moved magnificently. We had to go to London, England, that night, which, incidentally, is about five or six hours ahead of the U.S.A. After arriving in London, I told Frances that I was going to go to the park, which was right across the street from the hotel, and seek the Lord for awhile, which I did.

Hyde Park is probably 15 or 20 miles long and several miles wide. At any rate, as I began to pray, the Lord spoke to my heart, saying, "How many were baptized with the Holy Spirit yesterday afternoon?" All of a sudden, it dawned on me that we had seen over a thousand people baptized with the Holy Spirit, exactly as the Lord had told me years earlier. Then the Lord spoke this to me:

"If you will believe me, I will fill as many as 10,000 with the Holy Spirit in a single service."

With the events that followed, I wondered many times, "Did the Lord really say that to me or did it just come out of my own mind?" I thought about it many times, but I really could not come to any conclusion. I wondered, "If it was the Lord, how in the world could this happen?"

THE YEAR 2013

We have a prayer meeting every Saturday morning at the church, and I had just returned from that prayer meeting. A little bit after noon, I began to feel an unction by the Holy Spirit to go pray. This I did.

As I began to pray, the Lord brought back to me that time of prayer in Hyde Park back in 1986. He then said to me:

"Yes, I did speak to you, and I told you that if you would believe Me, I would fill as many as 10,000 people in a single service with the Holy Spirit. That was not out of your mind; that was Me speaking to you."

He then said to me, "When you go to your

service in the morning at Family Worship Center, take a look at the television cameras. When My Spirit begins to move, and considering that you are going out over a good part of the world by television, I can easily fill 10,000 and many more, and that's what I will do."

So, not only are we going to see untold hundreds of thousands brought to a saving knowledge of Jesus Christ but, as well, untold thousands baptized with the Holy Spirit with the evidence of speaking with other tongues, even as the Spirit of God gives the utterance (Acts 2:4).

Yes, the modern church is in terrible spiritual condition; however, there are still many who have not bowed the knee to Baal and who love the Lord with all of their hearts. To be sure, that which the Lord has said He will do, that He shall do.

Back to the dream, the Devil is a liar. He may try, but he has not stopped this ministry, and by the grace of God, he will not stop this ministry. We will accomplish what the Lord has called us to do.

(36) "AND AS THEY THUS SPOKE, JESUS HIMSELF STOOD IN THE MIDST OF THEM, AND SAID UNTO THEM, PEACE BE UNTO YOU."

JESUS

The phrase, *"And as they thus spoke,"* pertains to the account as given by the two disciples, as well as the appearance to Simon. This was a moment of such excitement and thrill that it defied description.

"Jesus Himself stood in the midst of them," refers to an instant appearance and revelation. John added that *"the doors were shut,"* meaning that there was some fear of the authorities that they may even try to arrest them (Jn. 20:19).

So, Jesus did not come through the door or a window but just miraculously appeared in their midst. As He miraculously *"vanished out of their sight,"* concerning the two disciples (Vs. 31), He now miraculously appeared to their sight.

"And said unto them, Peace be unto you," presents His first words to them. The last time He saw them, they were basely forsaking Him in the garden, but His first

words to them in resurrection were, *"Peace be unto you!"* Amazing grace!

Even though this is the ordinary Jewish greeting, on this occasion it possessed far more than the ordinary meaning. This peace was His solemn, comforting greeting to His own and proclaimed that all is well.

The word *peace,* as here used by Jesus, implied "prosperity" and refers to "quietness and rest" and means "to set at one again."

PEACE WITH GOD

Not withstanding the crucifixion, the purpose of the disciples was weakened, if not completely destroyed. Now, they were *one again,* and that speaks of purpose and mission.

This type of peace concerns our sanctification. It speaks of the peace of God.

When one comes to Christ, one obtains peace with God, which speaks of the enmity being removed between God and the sinner (Eph. 2:14-15). However, even though all believers have peace with God, all believers do not have the peace of God. When people come to the Lord, they are given justifying peace, and then they are to have sanctifying peace. This can only come about by the believer placing his or her faith exclusively in Christ and what Christ did for us at the Cross, and maintaining our faith in that finished work. So, as stated, all true believers have peace with God, but all believers do not have the peace of God. Let us say it again!

As justifying peace comes strictly from Christ by the means of the Cross, likewise, sanctifying peace comes in the same manner. Unfortunately, most Christians leave what got them in, namely the Cross. In other words, it's faith in Christ and what He did for us at the Cross that gives us salvation upon our faith. Unfortunately, after salvation, many believers, and I think one could say all believers, place their faith in something else that God constitutes as works, which cannot bring any victory to anyone. Anything other than the Cross of Christ is constituted by the Lord as works and flesh. Let's try to make it easier to understand.

GOD'S PRESCRIBED ORDER OF LIFE AND LIVING

• Jesus Christ is the source of all things

that we receive from God (Jn. 1:1-3, 14, 29; Col. 2:10-15).

• The Cross of Christ is the means, and the only means, by which all of these wonderful things are given to us (I Cor. 1:17-18, 23; 2:2; Gal. 6:14).

• Christ and what He did for us at the Cross must ever be the object of our faith. To place our faith in anything else constitutes spiritual adultery (Rom. 7:1-5; Rom. 6:1-14).

• We must understand that Jesus is the source, and the Cross is the means, and thereby place our faith and thereby maintain our faith. Then, the Holy Spirit, who works exclusively within the parameters of the finished work of Christ, will work mightily on our behalf, without which, we cannot walk in victory (Rom. 8:1-11; Eph. 2:13-18).

That in brief is God's prescribed order of victory. While the Bible does not teach sinless perfection, it most definitely does teach that sin is not to have dominion over us (Rom. 6:14). The way, and the only way to walk in victory on a daily basis before the Lord, victorious over the world, the flesh, and the Devil, is that we understand that which we have just given to you concerning the Cross. The problem is sin. A lot of Christians don't like to admit that, but it is the truth. The only answer for sin is the Cross of Christ (Heb. 10:12).

(37) "BUT THEY WERE TERRIFIED AND AFFRIGHTED, AND SUPPOSED THAT THEY HAD SEEN A SPIRIT."

The form is:

1. The phrase, *"But they were terrified and affrighted,"* speaks to the suddenness of the event and the manner in which it was done. They were speaking of Him constantly and the startling phenomenon of this day when, all of a sudden, He appeared. One moment He was not there, and the next moment He was!

2. *"And supposed that they had seen a spirit,"* explains to us their thinking concerning His resurrection, as mentioned in Verse 34.

3. It seems that they believed the two disciples, as well as Peter and the women; however, it also seems that they thought His appearance to these individuals had been

in spirit form, as the next few verses will prove. In other words, they still did not fully believe that Jesus Christ had risen from the dead and had a literal flesh and bone body. This was beyond their comprehension and, as is obvious, beyond their faith.

(38) "AND HE SAID UNTO THEM, WHY ARE YOU TROUBLED? AND WHY DO THOUGHTS ARISE IN YOUR HEARTS?"

The synopsis is:

1. The phrase, *"And He said unto them,"* presents the fact that not only were they terrified and affrighted but, as well, were speechless. All were standing and staring at Him in open-mouthed astonishment. It is as though, and, no doubt, was, their eyes were transfixed on Him, with the entirety of the room becoming suddenly silent and still.

2. The question, *"Why are you troubled?"* addresses itself to many things. It was addressed to them, but to us as well!

3. Why are we troubled, that is, if, in fact, we are?

4. All such attitude and activity is a result of a lack of trust, which robs us of the peace of God.

5. There was no reason for any of these disciples to be troubled, just as there is no reason for us to be troubled. Jesus had plainly told them exactly what would happen regarding His crucifixion, and even though it would be horrible to say the least, still, He had also told them He would rise on the third day. Had they believed that, while they certainly would have grieved for what was done to Him, still, their peace would not have been destroyed because they would have known, and should have known, that He would be raised from the dead. However, they did not believe that, as much of the church world presently does not believe the Bible. Consequently, there is little trust and little peace!

6. The question, *"And why do thoughts arise in your hearts?"* pertains to fear, doubt, discouragement, and even despair, all brought on by lack of faith in God's Word.

7. We would do well to carefully analyze these questions as asked by Jesus simply because all of us, at one time or the other, have fallen into the same trap. The thoughts fill our hearts, most especially at night. Satan

NOTES

paints a picture of failure, bankruptcy, sickness, death, rejection, and half a hundred other things of like nature. Such thoughts arise because of a lack of knowing the Word of God or a lack of believing the Word of God, hence, the questions of Jesus.

(39) "BEHOLD MY HANDS AND MY FEET, THAT IT IS I MYSELF: HANDLE ME, AND SEE; FOR A SPIRIT HAS NOT FLESH AND BONES, AS YOU SEE ME HAVE."

HANDLE ME AND SEE

The phrase, *"Behold My hands and My feet, that it is I Myself: handle Me, and see,"* tells us, as stated, that while they did believe He had been raised from the dead, they believed, at least at this stage, that He was merely in spirit form with no tangible body.

So, at first they did not believe in His resurrection at all, and now they had an erroneous concept of what His resurrection actually was. Such, regrettably, characterizes most modern believers. They fall into the category of total disbelief of great segments of the Word of God, or else, have an erroneous concept of what they actually do believe. Only a precious few truly view Jesus as He really is as proclaimed by the Word.

Man's problem is that he filters the Word of God through bias, prejudice, conventional wisdom, prevailing opinion, and denominational interpretations.

The grace of God is fully demonstrated here by Jesus in His condescension to their doubts and reasonings by His invitation to handle Him (I Jn. 1:1).

THE GLORIFIED BODY

The phrase, *"For a spirit has not flesh and bones, as you see Me have,"* presents a startling revelation:

• Jesus, in the resurrection, was not a spirit. This speaks of something disembodied.

• Jesus' glorified body had flesh and bones, but no blood. Presently, the life of the flesh is in the blood (Lev. 17:11). With Jesus, it was now the Spirit, which will be in all glorified bodies in the resurrection (I Cor. 15:45).

• As well, the glorified body, as portrayed by Christ, as we have stated, is not subject to natural laws.

Jesus' invitation to His disciples to *"handle Me, and see,"* evidently made a deep impression upon them.

As well, according to the words of John, it seems as if they did accept the invitation of Christ to touch Him, etc.

THE APOSTLE JOHN

John wrote, saying, *"And our hands have handled, of the Word of Life."*

He said as well, *"For the life was manifested, and we have seen it, and bear witness, and show unto you that eternal life, which was with the Father, and was manifested unto us"* (I Jn. 1:1-2).

This then was proof of the resurrection that admitted no shadow of doubt.

Spence said, "These words, this sight, changed their lives. What cared they afterwards for men and men's threatenings? Death, life, to them were all one. They had seen the Lord, they had handled with their hands that which was from the beginning."

Browning wrote the following poem, which speaks of the dying John dwelling on the thought that when he was gone, there would be no one left who saw and touched the Lord.

If I live yet, it is for good, more love
Through me to men: be nought but
*   ashes here*
That keep awhile my semblance, who
*   was John,—*
Still, when they scatter, there is left on
*   earth*
No one alive who knew (consider this!)
—Saw with his eyes and handled with
*   his hands*
That which was from the first, the
*   Word of Life.*
How will it be when none more saith,
*   'I saw'?"*

(40) "AND WHEN HE HAD THUS SPOKEN, HE SHOWED THEM HIS HANDS AND HIS FEET."

The construction is:

1. John also adds that He invited them, as well, to see the wound in His side.

2. It seems that He pointed to all the wounded members of His body to show that in the resurrection body, He retained these

marks of His wounds. We also know that He will retain these wounds forever because John also mentioned in the writing of the book of Revelation, *"And in the midst of the elders, stood a Lamb as it had been slain"* (Rev. 5:6).

3. As well, the prophet Zechariah proclaimed that Jesus will show at least His wounded hands to restored Israel immediately after the second coming (Zech. 13:6).

4. So, every evidence is that Christ will bear these wounds forever as a sign of the price He paid to redeem lost humanity.

5. It becomes more precious still when we realize that each and every redeemed saint will one day look upon these wounds exactly as did the disciples that memorable day so long ago.

(41) "AND WHILE THEY YET BELIEVED NOT FOR JOY, AND WONDERED, HE SAID UNTO THEM, HAVE YOU HERE ANY MEAT?"

The order is:

1. The phrase, *"And while they yet believed not for joy, and wondered,"* seems to mean that they were beginning to believe but still had some reservations and, therefore, their joy was not complete.

2. This seems to be indicated by the question now asked by Jesus.

3. The question, *"He said unto them, Have you here any meat?"* is meant to further portray to them the fact that He still retained a human body, albeit glorified, and that as such, He could partake of food. As a spirit does not have flesh and bones, likewise, it does not eat.

(42) "AND THEY GAVE HIM A PIECE OF A BROILED FISH, AND OF AN HONEYCOMB."

The pattern is:

1. Both fish and honey were staples in the Jewish diet.

2. Evidently, someone was preparing, or had prepared, an evening meal. As well, this gathering probably took place in the upper room where they had eaten the Passover.

3. It is only speculation, but some believe it may have been the home of John Mark, who wrote the book of Mark.

(43) "AND HE TOOK IT, AND DID EAT BEFORE THEM."

(44) "AND HE SAID UNTO THEM, THESE ARE THE WORDS WHICH I SPOKE UNTO YOU, WHILE I WAS YET WITH YOU, THAT ALL THINGS MUST BE FULFILLED, WHICH WERE WRITTEN IN THE LAW OF MOSES, AND IN THE PROPHETS, AND IN THE PSALMS, CONCERNING ME."

THESE OTHER WORDS

The phrase, *"And He said unto them, These are the words which I spoke unto you, while I was yet with you,"* spoke of the three and a half years of the incarnation.

"That all things must be fulfilled, which were written in the law of Moses, and in the prophets, and in the Psalms, concerning Me," tells us two things:

1. One cannot help but be struck by the weight Jesus attached to Old Testament words and types and prophecies by this repeated mention.

2. As we have previously stated, Jews divided the Old Testament into three parts:

a. *"The law of Moses"*: this consisted of the first five books of the Bible—Genesis through Deuteronomy.

b. *"The prophets"*: This consisted of all the books that made up the major prophets and the minor prophets. The minor prophets were referred to as such not because they were less significant, but only because their books were much shorter.

c. *"The Psalms"*: This consisted of the wisdom books, which included Job, Ecclesiastes, Song of Solomon, Proverbs, and Psalms. The Jews also included Daniel in this section, even though Jesus referred to Him as a prophet (Mat. 24:15).

THE OLD TESTAMENT

This we do know: All things concerning the suffering of Jesus were fulfilled in their entirety and with minute precision. As well, all things pertaining to His second coming and the setting up of the kingdom of God will come to pass exactly as the previous. Of that, one can be certain!

The indication is that Jesus was referring to the whole tenor of the Old Testament in its typical and symbolic character to Himself, rather than to isolated Scriptures. Actually, the whole of the Old Testament points to the coming Christ in one way or the other.

The law of Moses with its sacrifices pointed graphically to the price He would pay at Calvary.

The taking of the Land of Promise by the children of Israel is a portrayal of what Jesus would do through Calvary and the resurrection.

The kings of Israel, through the lineage of David, were meant to point to Christ in the incarnation and as the coming King of Israel.

So, instead of there being a paucity of material concerning who He was and what He was to do, He opened up to them a veritable river of information, which, in fact, they should have known.

(45) "THEN OPENED HE THEIR UNDERSTANDING, THAT THEY MIGHT UNDERSTAND THE SCRIPTURES."

The exegesis is:

1. John further elaborated on this by saying, *"He breathed on them, and said unto them, Receive ye the Holy Spirit"* (Jn. 20:22).

2. *"Then opened He their understanding,"* points to the day of Pentecost, as outlined in Verse 49. Their understanding did not really open until they were baptized with the Holy Spirit.

3. *That they might understand the Scriptures,"* proclaims the fact that among the many tasks of the Holy Spirit in the enlightenment He gives one is the understanding of the Word of God.

4. The book of Acts graphically illustrates the tremendous insight these men now had concerning the Scriptures of the Old Testament hitherto only partly understood.

5. Immediately after the infilling of the Holy Spirit, Peter preached a message that graphically outlined, even in its brevity, the person and place of Christ in the Old Testament Scriptures concerning the redemption of humanity (Acts, Chpt. 2). Without the aid of the Holy Spirit, it would have been impossible in this short length of time, or at all for that matter, for anyone, even Peter, to have accumulated such depth of understanding of the Word of God as portrayed.

6. So, I think it is clear in the Scriptures that the help of the Holy Spirit is absolutely

NOTES

necessary if one is to have a proper understanding of the Bible.

7. The Bible is the only book in existence that can close itself to the reader. He who wrote it can alone open it.

(46) "AND SAID UNTO THEM, THUS IT IS WRITTEN, AND THUS IT BEHOOVED CHRIST TO SUFFER, AND TO RISE FROM THE DEAD THE THIRD DAY."

IT IS WRITTEN

The phrase, *"And said unto them, Thus it is written,"* concerns all the things we have just mentioned respecting the sacrifices (Lev., Chpt. 16); the promise to Abraham (Gen. 22:18); the paschal lamb (Ex., Chpt. 12); the scapegoat (Lev. 16:1-34); the brazen serpent (Num. 21:9); the greater prophet (Deut. 18:15); the star and sceptre (Num. 24:17); the smitten rock (Num. 20:11; I Cor. 10:4); Immanuel (Isa. 7:14); He who bore our griefs (Isa., Chpt. 53); the branch (Jer. 23:5; 33:14-15); the heir of David (Ezek. 34:23); the ruler from Beth-lehem (Mic. 5:2); the lowly King (Zech. 9:9); the pierced victim (Zech. 12:10); the smitten shepherd (Zech. 13:7); the messenger of the covenant (Mal. 3:1); the sun of righteousness (Mal. 4:2), plus many other passages.

TO RISE FROM THE DEAD THE THIRD DAY

The phrase, *"And thus it behooved Christ to suffer, and to rise from the dead the third day,"* points to several things:

• Before there can be a triumphant Messiah, there had to be a suffering Messiah. The great price for man's redemption must be paid, and that's what Calvary did. As stated, the sacrifices pointed to this so graphically by the killing of the animal, with its blood being poured out at the base of the altar, and part or all of it being burned on the altar. Considering all of the Scriptures, and we have given some, there was no excuse for the disciples, or the whole of Israel for that matter, not knowing the correct description of the Messiah.

• What Christ did was predestined and was accordingly written in the Scriptures; however, the parties who carried out this evil deed, such as the Pharisees, etc., were not predestined, at least as to whom they would be, only that someone would do this thing.

• The phrase concerning Jesus being in the grave three days and nights, or rising on the third day, is used 13 times in the New Testament (Mat. 12:40; 16:21; 17:23; 20:19; Mk. 8:31; 9:31; 10:34; Lk. 9:22; 18:33; 24:7, 46; Acts 10:40; I Cor. 15:4).

Why three days?

It was the custom to mourn for the dead three full days and nights, called days of weeping. This was followed by four days of lamentation, thus making seven days (Gen. 27:41; 50:10; I Sam. 31:13; Job. 2:13).

According to rabbinical notion, the spirit wandered about the sepulchre for three days, hoping to reenter the body, but when corruption set in, the spirit left. The corruption was believed to begin on the fourth day.

There is no scriptural evidence to this idea, and, in fact, there is scriptural evidence to the contrary.

THE SOUL AND THE SPIRIT OF MAN

When Jesus died, He said, *"Father, into Your hands I commend My Spirit,"* proving that the Spirit leaves immediately upon death (Lk. 23:46).

However, due to this error of thinking among the Jews, it seems that three full days and three full nights were ordered by God so as to preclude all doubt that death had actually taken place as it regarded Christ. This lays to rest the suggestion that Christ might have been in a trance and correspondingly revived in the tomb.

After three full days and nights, the Jews then legally concluded that one was dead; therefore, there was no doubt concerning the death of Jesus because He was three full days and nights in the tomb. As well, the Roman guard was stationed there around the clock for three full days and nights (Mat. 27:62-66). Consequently, both Jews and Gentiles were forced to testify that He was indeed dead.

One must understand that this was before the time of modern embalming, therefore, the waiting period of three days.

Over and over again, Jesus testified to the authenticity and veracity of the Scriptures. Inasmuch as the Word of God (the Bible)

is the only revealed truth in the world and, in fact, ever has been, it stands to reason that it is, as well, the single most important thing there is. Consequently, every believer should master its contents, at least as far as is possible. It should be priority concerning our reading habits, study, and meditation. It alone holds the key to life because it presents Jesus.

(47) "AND THAT REPENTANCE AND REMISSION OF SINS SHOULD BE PREACHED IN HIS NAME AMONG ALL NATIONS, BEGINNING AT JERUSALEM."

REPENTANCE

The phrase, *"And that repentance and remission of sins should be preached in His name,"* proclaims God's method of proclaiming His Word and carrying out His work. Any other method is unscriptural.

As is obvious, Jesus proclaimed that His preachers must preach repentance, in other words, that all men must repent. This goes for believers and unbelievers.

The following outlines that which respects the doctrine of repentance:

• Its nature: contrition, confession, faith, restitution (II Cor. 7:8-11).
• Its necessity (Lk. 13:1-5).
• Its power (Lk. 18:14; Rom. 10:9-10).
• How produced (Jn. 16:8; Rom. 2:4; II Cor. 10:8-11; Heb. 4:12).
• Not expiatory or meritorious, but qualifies for pardon (Acts 2:38; 3:19; Rom. 10:9-10; I Jn. 1:9).
• Demanded of all men (Lk. 13:1-5; 24:47; Acts 10:35; 17:30).
• By whom preached (Mat. 28:19-20; Mk. 15:15-20; Lk. 24:48; Acts 1:8).
• How preached (Lk. 24:49; Acts 1:4-8; 5:31-32; Rom. 15:18-19, 29; I Cor. 2:1-5; 4:20; Heb. 2:1-4).
• Must not be delayed (II Cor. 6:2; Eph. 5:14; Heb. 4:7).
• How attested (Lk. 3:8; Acts 5:32; Rom. 1:5; 10:16; II Cor. 10:11).

Repentance is demanded of the unsaved, or else, they cannot be saved (Acts 2:38); however, repentance refers to the state of the heart far more than the actual verbiage used.

When the publican smote his breasts,

saying, *"God be merciful to me a sinner,"* he was functioning in the spirit of repentance, even though the word was never used. Jesus said, *"This man went down to his house justified"* (Lk. 18:13-14).

The simple, literal meaning of repentance is "to be sorry, to change one's mind, to turn back, return." To be sure, the sinner accepting Christ does all of this, even though he may not fully understand the meaning of all that has happened.

REPENTANCE INVOLVES THE FOLLOWING:

• Repentance simply means that one admits that he is wrong, and God is right.

• Repentance will always be honored by God, even at the eleventh hour. Whoever turns to God finds a God of mercy and love, not of judgment (Jer. 18:8; 26:3, 13, 19; Jn. 3:9).

• The call of repentance on the part of man is a call for him to return to dependence on God (Hos. 6:1-3; 14:1-2).

• Repentance is feeling sorry, but far more than that. It is a changing of one's mind, a turning around, and a complete alteration of the basic motivation and direction of one's life.

• One of the greatest examples of repentance is found in the story of the prodigal son (Lk. 15:11-24).

• Repentance means that one acknowledges that one has no possible claim upon God and, therefore, submits oneself to God without excuse or attempting to justify one's actions (Lk. 18:13).

• Repentance demands that one in some respect becomes like a little child, acknowledging one's immaturity before God and one's inability to live life apart from God.

• Repentance is God's gift, at least in respect to Him allowing us to do such, and it is man's responsibility.

THE PREACHING OF REPENTANCE

If believers stray from the Word of God, they are called upon to repent as well as unbelievers. When Jesus addressed the seven churches of Asia, five of these churches were ordered to repent (Rev., Chpts. 2-3).

It is sad that the modern church little preaches repentance or even believes in

this basic Bible doctrine. It is sadder still when those who claim to know and understand the baptism with the Holy Spirit, such as many Charismatics, as well, demean the doctrine of repentance, claiming it is an Old Testament doctrine and has no relativity to the new creation man. Such teaching flies in the face of Scripture and, therefore, is an abrogation of the Word of God.

When Jesus said that *"repentance and remission of sins should be preached,"* He was not speaking of Old Testament times, but rather that of the church respecting the new covenant.

Above all, the inference of this text is that sins cannot be remitted unless repentance is preached and practiced. In other words, one cannot confess away his sins or rid himself of this terrible malady in any way except by repentance.

AMONG ALL NATIONS

The phrase, *"Among all nations, beginning at Jerusalem,"* means that the standard is the same for all.

God's plan of salvation is identical for all, regarding race, color, and culture, i.e., all nations.

The taking of the gospel, which began at Jerusalem and as is outlined in the book of Acts, must be proclaimed to the entirety of mankind. Two things are here demanded:

1. *"Repentance and remission of sins should* (must) *be preached in His name,"* along with all the other rudiments of the gospel. The trouble is, many things are preached, with repentance little preached at all.

2. It must be preached over the entirety of the world, and it is the responsibility of every believer to help in this all-important endeavor. Paul would later say, *"How shall they hear without a preacher?*

"And how shall they preach, except they be sent?" (Rom. 10:14-15).

(48) "AND YOU ARE WITNESSES OF THESE THINGS."

The record is:

1. This statement, as given by Christ, proclaims that Christianity was not begun as the result of an enlightened philosophy, as with all religions. It was begun by men and women who literally witnessed the

incarnate Son of God in all His earthly ministry preaching the words of life, healings, miracles, and the fulfillment of all Bible prophecy, at least as it pertained to Him.

2. They also witnessed His death at Calvary and, above all, His resurrection. Consequently, they could say, *"We have seen, and do testify."*

3. Westcott said, "They had no labored process to go through; they saw. They had no constructive proof to develop; they bore witness. Their source of knowledge was direct, and His (Jesus') mode of bringing conviction was to affirm."

(49) "AND, BEHOLD, I SEND THE PROMISE OF MY FATHER UPON YOU: BUT TARRY YE IN THE CITY OF JERUSALEM, UNTIL YOU BE ENDUED WITH POWER FROM ON HIGH."

THE PROMISE OF MY FATHER

The phrase, *"And, behold, I send the promise of My Father upon you,"* refers to the baptism with the Holy Spirit. The fulfillment of that promise took place on the day of Pentecost, and the continuing of its action has not stopped from that moment until now.

"But tarry ye in the city of Jerusalem, until you be endued with power from on high," concerns direction and pertains to that which would be received, the baptism with the Holy Spirit.

Several things are here said:

TARRY

They were not to go build churches, preach revivals, witness to lost souls, or attempt to carry out the work of God in any fashion until they were first baptized with the Holy Spirit. In fact, Jesus also said:

"And, being assembled together with them, commanded them that they should not depart from Jerusalem, but wait for the promise of the Father" (Acts 1:4). In other words, this was not a suggestion, but rather a command. The truth is, precious little is going to be done for the Lord by those who have not heeded this command. There may be much religious activity, but there will be nothing substantial done for the cause of Christ. Everything done by God on this earth is done in the name of Jesus through the

person and agency of the Holy Spirit. Within oneself, nothing can be carried out or done for the Lord, irrespective of one's ability, talent, or education. The baptism with the Holy Spirit, which is always accompanied by the speaking with other tongues (no exception), is an absolute requirement for all that is done for the Lord, no matter how little or large. If the *"promise of the Father"* is not resident and prevalent in the heart and life of the believer, irrespective of all the religious machinery, nothing for God will be accomplished. Let us say it again, "This is not a suggestion, but rather a command."

THEY WERE TO WAIT

The reason that the followers of Christ were told to tarry or wait was because the Holy Spirit had not yet come in the new dimension, which would characterize the great dispensation of grace, all made possible by the Cross. They were not really waiting to be filled, but rather waiting for Him to come.

The Holy Spirit came on the day of Pentecost and has remained ever since, so there is no excuse for any believer not to be filled. All the person has to do is simply believe and yield.

As it regards being baptized with the Holy Spirit, if a person who is born again will simply ask the Lord to fill him, at that moment he will sense words that are not English or any other language learned as a child. This is the Holy Spirit giving the utterance. He will give the utterance, but He will not speak for you or force you to speak. In other words, you are to speak out the words that you hear down in your spirit, words which are not your natural language. As we have stated, that is the Holy Spirit giving the utterance, but you must do the speaking yourself.

Go ahead and speak out these words that you hear, and you will find the Spirit of God taking possession of you in a way that you never dreamed before.

THE BAPTISM WITH THE HOLY SPIRIT

It is true that every believing sinner receives the Holy Spirit at conversion. This is the work of the Spirit called regeneration.

NOTES

However, being born of the Spirit, which happens to every believing sinner at conversion, and being baptized with the Spirit constitutes two different things. The first one, as stated, is for regeneration, while the second is for power.

When preachers teach that one receives the Holy Spirit at conversion, in a sense they are correct; however, that is not the Holy Spirit baptism of which Jesus was here speaking. All of these people to whom he was speaking were already saved. They needed power, and that power could come only by and through the Holy Spirit baptism.

In other words, the baptism with the Holy Spirit with the evidence of speaking with other tongues is an experience separate and apart from salvation. While one may be baptized with the Holy Spirit moments after conversion, which has happened at times, it is not possible for one to be baptized with the Holy Spirit at conversion. While the believing sinner can receive salvation, he cannot receive the baptism with the Holy Spirit until he is born again. Jesus said so:

"And I will pray the Father, and He shall give you another Comforter, that He may abide with you forever; Even the Spirit of Truth; whom the world cannot receive, because it sees Him not, neither knows Him: but you know Him; for He dwells with you, and shall be in you" (Jn. 14:16-17).

Jesus plainly said here that the unredeemed cannot be baptized with the Holy Spirit. As well, before the Cross, the Holy Spirit was with believers but not in believers. The reason was, the blood of bulls and goats could not take away sins (Heb. 10:4). Since the Cross, due to the fact that all sin was atoned, which answered the question of original sin and, as well, of the broken law, now the Holy Spirit can come into the born-again believer to dwell forever.

JERUSALEM

Jesus said, "But tarry ye in the city of Jerusalem." Why Jerusalem?

Jerusalem was the city that God had chosen to place His name (II Chron. 6:6). Consequently, it was the city where the temple was constructed and where the Lord resided between the mercy seat and the cherubim in the Holy of Holies. It was where all the sacrifices were offered and where the feasts were kept.

As well, it was the place where Jesus died and rose from the dead. It would also be the place where the Holy Spirit would first fall, and rightly so!

However, after the Holy Spirit came on the day of Pentecost, we find in the Word of God that it was not localized anymore. It came to Samaria (Acts, Chpt. 8), to Damascus (Acts, Chpt. 9), then to Caesarea (Acts, Chpt. 10), and then to Ephesus (Acts, Chpt. 19). In truth, He filled the entirety of the world, at least where hungry hearts called out to Him. Peter said on the day of Pentecost, "For the promise is unto you, and to your children, and to all who are afar off, even as many as the Lord our God shall call" (Acts 2:39).

And then, concerning those the Lord has called, which includes all, Jesus said, "And the Spirit and the bride say, Come. And let him who hears say, Come. And let him who is athirst come. And whosoever will, let him take the Water of Life freely" (Rev. 22:17).

POWER

Jesus said, as well, "Until you be endued with power from on high": the Greek word for power is dunamis and means "inherent power, the power of reproducing itself."

In effect, the Lord changed His earthly domicile, so to speak, from the temple to the hearts of those who are regenerated (I Cor. 3:16). Consequently, the Spirit-filled believer does not have to look to an outside source, as all other things do, but has within him this reproducing dynamo, i.e., the Holy Spirit.

This power is given to the believer that he or she may carry on the works of Christ (Jn. 14:12-14).

To be sure, this is the power of the Holy Spirit and not human power or effort. The church is filled with human endeavor, which creates much activity but sees nothing done for the Lord. This power is from the Lord and enables the believer to do great and mighty things for the Lord Jesus Christ (Mk. 16:15-20).

And finally, this power is from on high, thereby, from God and not from man.

(50) "AND HE LED THEM OUT AS FAR AS TO BETHANY, AND HE LIFTED UP HIS HANDS, AND BLESSED THEM."

The synopsis is:

1. The phrase, *"And He led them out as far as to Bethany,"* ever proclaims this place as hallowed because of its tender associations. On this Ascension Day, it would be forever linked to heaven.

2. It is situated on the farther side of the Mount of Olives and is actually a suburb of Jerusalem. It was the home of Jesus' beloved friends, Mary, Martha, and Lazarus. As well, it was where Jesus was anointed for His burial (Mk. 14:3-9).

3. *"And He lifted up His hands, and blessed them,"* proclaims Him as Israel's High Priest having made atonement and, consequently, lifting up His hands and blessing the people.

4. So, when He was last seen, the picture would forever dwell in the hearts of those who were there of His hands outstretched in blessing. In a spiritual sense, they remain thusly to this hour, and ever shall be.

5. What a thrill to know that Jesus is a blesser and that He blesses all who come to Him and, in fact, never ceases to do so.

(51) "AND IT CAME TO PASS, WHILE HE BLESSED THEM, HE WAS PARTED FROM THEM, AND CARRIED UP INTO HEAVEN."

The exegesis is:

1. The phrase, *"And it came to pass, while He blessed them,"* implies continued blessing. As stated, it is continued unto this hour and, in fact, will continue forever.

2. *"He was parted from them, and carried up into heaven,"* pertains to the ascension.

3. He hastened to the Cross in order to atone for His people's sins, but He did not hasten to the glory, for He was reluctant to leave His beloved sheep.

(52) "AND THEY WORSHIPPED HIM, AND RETURNED TO JERUSALEM WITH GREAT JOY."

The record is:

1. The phrase, *"And they worshipped Him,"* means His presence was still with them even though He had already been

NOTES

carried up into heaven. They worshipped, and we are to continue to worship!

2. He ascended on the fortieth day after His crucifixion. In 10 more days, making 50 in all, He would send the promise of the Father.

3. *"And returned to Jerusalem with great joy,"* signaled a different group of people, at least regarding their faith, spirit, and emotions, than at the crucifixion. Then all was darkness; now all was light.

4. They had great joy because they knew that Jesus had risen from the dead. There was no doubt about that!

5. As well, He had given them instructions regarding Him sending the Holy Spirit. They were to go to Jerusalem and wait, with every anticipation of that which He would send being glorious beyond description or comprehension. They would not be disappointed.

(53) "AND WERE CONTINUALLY IN THE TEMPLE, PRAISING AND BLESSING GOD. AMEN."

The record is:

1. The word *continually* does not mean that they stayed in the temple the entirety of the next 10 days and nights because they actually did not. Some of this time was spent in the upper room (Acts 1:12-13).

2. It does mean that whatever time they spent in the temple, they were continually praising and blessing God.

3. This would serve as an example for us so that praise and worship will always be carried out by those who truly know the Lord. As it is impossible for the unconverted to worship and praise Him, it is also impossible for the true believer not to worship and praise Him.

"Have you been to Jesus for the cleansing power?
"Are you washed in the blood of the Lamb?
"Are you fully trusting in His grace this hour?
"Are you washed in the blood of the Lamb?"

"Are you walking daily by the Savior's side?

"Are you washed in the blood of the
Lamb?
"Do you rest each moment in the
Crucified?
"Are you washed in the blood of the
Lamb?"

"When the Bridegroom comes will
your robes be white?
"Are you washed in the blood of the
Lamb?
"Will your soul be ready for the man-
sions bright,
"And be washed in the blood of the
Lamb?"

"Lay aside the garments that are
stained with sin,
"And be washed in the blood of the
Lamb;
"There's a fountain flowing for the
soul unclean,
"O be washed in the blood of the
Lamb!"

BIBLIOGRAPHY

INTRODUCTION

George Williams, *William's Complete Bible
Commentary*, Grand Rapids, Kregel
Publications, 1994 , Pg. 742.

CHAPTER 1

H.D.M. Spence, *The Pulpit Commentary:
St. Luke Vol. I,* Grand Rapids, Eerdmans
Publishing Company, 1978.
Ibid.
Ibid.
Ibid.
Ibid.
Ibid.
Ibid.

CHAPTER 2

H.D.M. Spence, *The Pulpit Commentary:
St. Luke Vol. I,* Grand Rapids, Eerdmans
Publishing Company, 1978.
John Henry Cardinal Newman, *An Essay on
the Development of Christian Doctrine,*

New York, Longmans Green and Co., 1920,
Pg. 373.
H.D.M. Spence, *The Pulpit Commentary:
St. Luke Vol. I,* Grand Rapids, Eerdmans
Publishing Company, 1978.
George Williams, *William's Complete Bible
Commentary*, Grand Rapids, Kregel
Publications, 1994, pg. 744.
Kenneth S. Wuest, *Wuest's Word Studies
in the Greek New Testament: Colossians
1:15,* Grand Rapids, Eerdmans Publishing
Company, 1942.

CHAPTER 3

Frederic W. Farrar, *The Gospel According to
St. Luke,* Oxford, University Press, 1893,
Pg. 131.
H.D.M. Spence, *The Pulpit Commentary,*
Grand Rapids, Eerdmans Publishing
Company, 1978.
George Williams, *William's Complete Bible
Commentary*, Grand Rapids, Kregel
Publications, 1994.
H.D.M. Spence, *The Pulpit Commentary,*
Grand Rapids, Eerdmans Publishing
Company, 1978.
George Williams, *William's Complete Bible
Commentary*, Grand Rapids, Kregel
Publications, 1994.

CHAPTER 4

H.D.M. Spence, *The Pulpit Commentary:
St. Luke,* Grand Rapids, Eerdmans
Publishing Company, 1978.
Ibid.
R.H. Mounce, *The Essential Nature of New
Testament Preaching,* Grand Rapids,
Eerdmans Publishing Company, 1960,
Pg. 84.

CHAPTER 5

H.D.M. Spence, *The Pulpit Commentary:
St. Luke,* Grand Rapids, Eerdmans
Publishing Company, 1978.
Kenneth S. Wuest, *Wuest's Word Studies in
the Greek New Testament: Mark,* Grand
Rapids, Eerdmans Publishing Company,
1942, Pg. 41.
Kenneth S. Wuest, *Wuest's Word Studies in
the Greek New Testament: Mark 2:6-7,*

NOTES

Grand Rapids, Eerdmans Publishing Company, 1942.

Kenneth S. Wuest, *Wuest's Word Studies in the Greek New Testament: Mark 2:14*, Grand Rapids, Eerdmans Publishing Company, 1942.

C.H. Mackintosh, *Notes on the Book of Leviticus*, New York, Loizeaux Brothers, 1880, Pg. 97.

H.D.M. Spence, *The Pulpit Commentary: St. Luke 5:33*, Grand Rapids, Eerdmans Publishing Company, 1978.

Ibid.

C.H. Mackintosh, *Notes on the Book of Leviticus*, New York, Loizeaux Brothers, 1880, Pg. 128.

Ibid., Pg. 129.

H.D.M. Spence, *The Pulpit Commentary: St. Luke 5:37-38*, Grand Rapids, Eerdmans Publishing Company, 1978.

CHAPTER 6

Kenneth S. Wuest, *Wuest'sWord Studies in the Greek New Testament: Mark 2:28*, Grand Rapids, Eerdmans Publishing Company, 1942.

H.D.M. Spence, *The Pulpit Commentary: St. Luke 6:24*, Grand Rapids, Eerdmans Publishing Company, 1978.

H.D.M. Spence, *The Pulpit Commentary: St. Luke 6:37*, Grand Rapids, Eerdmans Publishing Company, 1978.

CHAPTER 7

H.D.M. Spence, *The Pulpit Commentary: St. Luke 7:1*, Grand Rapids, Eerdmans Publishing Company, 1978.

H.D.M. Spence, *The Pulpit Commentary: St. Luke 7:7*, Grand Rapids, Eerdmans Publishing Company, 1978.

George Williams, *William's Complete Bible Commentary*, Grand Rapids, Kregel Publications, 1994 , Pg. 750.

H.D.M. Spence, *The Pulpit Commentary: St. Luke 7:16*, Grand Rapids, Eerdmans Publishing Company, 1978.

H.D.M. Spence, *The Pulpit Commentary: St. Luke 7:19*, Grand Rapids, Eerdmans Publishing Company, 1978.

H.D.M. Spence, *The Pulpit Commentary:*

NOTES

St. Luke 7:30, Grand Rapids, Eerdmans Publishing Company, 1978.

H.D.M. Spence, *The Pulpit Commentary: St. Luke 7:31*, Grand Rapids, Eerdmans Publishing Company, 1978.

CHAPTER 8

H.D.M. Spence, *The Pulpit Commentary: St. Luke 8:10*, Grand Rapids, Eerdmans Publishing Company, 1978.

H.D.M. Spence, *The Pulpit Commentary: St. Luke*, Oxford University Press, 1893.

H.D.M. Spence, *The Pulpit Commentary: St. Luke 8:49*, Grand Rapids, Eerdmans Publishing Company, 1978.

Kenneth S. Wuest, *Wuest'sWord Studies in the Greek New Testament: Mark 5:40*, Grand Rapids, Eerdmans Publishing Company, 1942.

Ibid.

CHAPTER 9

H.D.M. Spence, *The Pulpit Commentary: St. Luke 9:7*, Grand Rapids, Eerdmans Publishing Company, 1978.

H.D.M. Spence, *The Pulpit Commentary: St. Luke 9:16*, Grand Rapids, Eerdmans Publishing Company, 1978.

H.D.M. Spence, *The Pulpit Commentary: St. Luke 9:18*, Grand Rapids, Eerdmans Publishing Company, 1978.

H.D.M. Spence, *The Pulpit Commentary: St. Luke 9:20*, Grand Rapids, Eerdmans Publishing Company, 1978.

H.D.M. Spence, *The Pulpit Commentary: St. Luke 9:23*, Grand Rapids, Eerdmans Publishing Company, 1978.

H.D.M. Spence, *The Pulpit Commentary: St. Luke 9:24*, Grand Rapids, Eerdmans Publishing Company, 1978.

Kenneth S. Wuest, *Wuest's Word Studies in the Greek New Testament: Mark 8:35-37*, Grand Rapids, Eerdmans Publishing Company, 1942.

Kenneth S. Wuest, *Wuest's Word Studies in the Greek New Testament: Mark 8:38*, Grand Rapids, Eerdmans Publishing Company, 1942.

Kenneth S. Wuest, *Wuest's Word Studies in the Greek New Testament: Mark 9:2*,

Grand Rapids, Eerdmans Publishing Company, 1942.

H.D.M. Spence, *The Pulpit Commentary: St. Luke 9:29*, Grand Rapids, Eerdmans Publishing Company, 1978.

George Williams, *William's Complete Bible Commentary*, Grand Rapids, Kregel Publications, 1994, Pg. 752.

Kenneth S. Wuest, *Wuest's Word Studies in the Greek New Testament: Mark 9:7*, Grand Rapids, Eerdmans Publishing Company, 1942.

Kenneth S. Wuest, *Wuest's Word Studies in the Greek New Testament: Mark 9:28*, Grand Rapids, Eerdmans Publishing Company, 1942.

H.D.M. Spence, *The Pulpit Commentary: St. Luke 9:42*, Grand Rapids, Eerdmans Publishing Company, 1978.

H.D.M. Spence, *The Pulpit Commentary: St. Luke 9:43*, Grand Rapids, Eerdmans Publishing Company, 1978.

H.D.M. Spence, *The Pulpit Commentary: St. Luke 9:46-47*, Grand Rapids, Eerdmans Publishing Company, 1978.

Kenneth S. Wuest, *Wuest's Word Studies in the Greek New Testament*, Grand Rapids, Eerdmans Publishing Company, 1942.

H.D.M. Spence, *The Pulpit Commentary: St. Luke 9:50*, Grand Rapids, Eerdmans Publishing Company, 1978.

H.D.M. Spence, *The Pulpit Commentary: St. Luke 9:50*, Grand Rapids, Eerdmans Publishing Company, 1978.

George Williams, *William's Complete Bible Commentary*, Grand Rapids, Kregel Publications, 1994, Pg. 752.

Ibid., Pg. 753.

CHAPTER 10

H.D.M. Spence, *The Pulpit Commentary: St. Luke 10:1*, Grand Rapids, Eerdmans Publishing Company, 1978.

George Williams, *William's Complete Bible Commentary*, Grand Rapids, Kregel Publications, 1994, Pg. 708.

H.D.M. Spence, *The Pulpit Commentary: St. Luke 10:36-37*, Grand Rapids, Eerdmans Publishing Company, 1978.

Ibid.

NOTES

CHAPTER 11

H.D.M. Spence, *The Pulpit Commentary: St. Luke 11:14-36*, Grand Rapids, Eerdmans Publishing Company, 1978.

H.D.M. Spence, *The Pulpit Commentary: St. Luke 11:31*, Grand Rapids, Eerdmans Publishing Company, 1978.

CHAPTER 13

George Williams, *William's Complete Bible Commentary*, Grand Rapids, Kregel Publications, Pg. 759, 1994.

H.D.M. Spence, *The Pulpit Commentary: St. Luke 13:4*, Grand Rapids, Eerdmans Publishing Company, 1978.

H.D.M. Spence, *The Pulpit Commentary: St. Luke 13:9*, Grand Rapids, Eerdmans Publishing Company, 1978.

H.D.M. Spence, *The Pulpit Commentary: St. Luke 13:31*, Grand Rapids, Eerdmans Publishing Company, 1978.

H.D.M. Spence, *The Pulpit Commentary: St. Luke 13:32*, Grand Rapids, Eerdmans Publishing Company, 1978.

CHAPTER 14

H.D.M. Spence, *The Pulpit Commentary: St. Luke 14:25*, Grand Rapids, Eerdmans Publishing Company, 1978.

Ibid.

CHAPTER 15

H.D.M. Spence, *The Pulpit Commentary: St. Luke 15:9-10*, Grand Rapids, Eerdmans Publishing Company, 1978.

George Williams, *William's Complete Bible Commentary*, Grand Rapids, Kregel Publications, Pg. 763, 1994.

H.D.M. Spence, *The Pulpit Commentary: St. Luke 15:14*, Grand Rapids, Eerdmans Publishing Company, 1978.

George Williams, *William's Complete Bible Commentary*, Grand Rapids, Kregel Publications, Pg. 763, 1994.

CHAPTER 16

H.D.M. Spence, *The Pulpit Commentary:*

St. Luke 16:14, Grand Rapids, Eerdmans Publishing Company, 1978.

CHAPTER 17

H.D.M. Spence, *The Pulpit Commentary: St. Luke 17:6*, Grand Rapids, Eerdmans Publishing Company, 1978.

CHAPTER 18

Kenneth S. Wuest, *Wuest'sWord Studies in the Greek New Testament: Mark 10:25*, Grand Rapids, Eerdmans Publishing Company, 1942.

H.D.M. Spence, *The Pulpit Commentary: St. Luke 18:40-41*, Grand Rapids, Eerdmans Publishing Company, 1978.

CHAPTER 20

Henry Barclay Swete, *The Gospel According to St. Mark: The Greek Text with Introduction, Notes and Indices*, Macmillan, New York, 1902, Pg. 276.

H.D.M. Spence, *The Pulpit Commentary: St. Luke 20:27-28*, Grand Rapids, Eerdmans Publishing Company, 1978.

H.D.M. Spence, *The Pulpit Commentary: St. Luke 20:39-40*, Grand Rapids, Eerdmans Publishing Company, 1978

CHAPTER 21

H.D.M. Spence, *The Pulpit Commentary: St. Luke 21:24*, Grand Rapids, Eerdmans Publishing Company, 1978.

CHAPTER 22

H.D.M. Spence, *The Pulpit Commentary: St. Luke 22:70*, Grand Rapids, Eerdmans Publishing Company, 1978.

CHAPTER 23

H.D.M. Spence, *The Pulpit Commentary: St. Luke 23:1*, Grand Rapids, Eerdmans Publishing Company, 1978.

H.D.M. Spence, *The Pulpit Commentary: St. Luke 23:8*, Grand Rapids, Eerdmans Publishing Company, 1978.

NOTES

H.D.M. Spence, *The Pulpit Commentary: St. Luke 23:23*, Grand Rapids, Eerdmans Publishing Company, 1978.

H.D.M. Spence, *The Pulpit Commentary: St. Luke 23:46*, Grand Rapids, Eerdmans Publishing Company, 1978.

H.D.M. Spence, *The Pulpit Commentary: St. Luke 23:50-51*, Grand Rapids, Eerdmans Publishing Company, 1978.

CHAPTER 24

George Williams, *William's Complete Bible Commentary*, Grand Rapids, Kregel Publications, 1994, Pg. 774.

H.D.M. Spence, *The Pulpit Commentary: St. Luke 24:28*, Grand Rapids, Eerdmans Publishing Company, 1978.

Ibid.

REFERENCE BOOKS

Atlas Of The Bible—Rogerson
Expository Dictionary of Bible Words—L. O. Richards
Matthew Henry Commentary On The Holy Bible—Matthew Henry
New Bible Dictionary—Tyndale
Strong's Exhaustive Concordance Of The Bible
The Complete Word Study Dictionary
The Essential Writings—Josephus
The Expositor's Study Bible—Jimmy Swaggart
The Interlinear Greek—English New Testament—George Ricker Berry
The International Standard Bible Encyclopedia
The Pulpit Commentary—H. D. M. Spence
The Student's Commentary On The Holy Scriptures—George Williams
The Zondervan Pictorial Encyclopedia Of The Bible
Vine's Expository Dictionary Of New Testament Words
Webster's New Collegiate Dictionary
Word Studies In The Greek New Testament, Volume I—Kenneth S. Wuest
Young's Literal Translation Of The Holy Bible

INDEX

The index is listed according to subjects. The treatment may include a complete dissertation or no more than a paragraph. But hopefully it will provide some help.

As well, even though extended treatment of a subject may not be carried in this Commentary, one of the other Commentaries may well include the desired material.

For information concerning the *Jimmy Swaggart Bible Commentary,* please request a Gift Catalog.

You may inquire by using Books of the Bible.

- Genesis (639 pages) (11-201)

- Exodus (639 pages) (11-202)

- Leviticus (435 pages) (11-203)

- Numbers
Deuteronomy (493 pages) (11-204)

- Joshua
Judges
Ruth (329 pages) (11-205)

- I Samuel
II Samuel (528 pages) (11-206)

- I Kings
II Kings (560 pages) (11-207)

- I Chronicles
II Chronicles (528 pages) (11-226)

- Ezra
Nehemiah
Esther (288 pages) (11-208)

- Job (320 pages) (11-225)

- Psalms (672 pages) (11-216)

- Proverbs (311 pages) (11-227)

- Ecclesiastes
Song Of Solomon (238 pages) (11-228)

- Isaiah (688 pages) (11-220)

- Jeremiah
Lamentations (456 pages) (11-070)

- Ezekiel (508 pages) (11-223)

- Daniel (403 pages) (11-224)

- Hosea
Joel
Amos (496 pages) (11-229)

- Obadiah
Jonah
Micah
Nahum
Habakkuk
Zephaniah (545 pages) (11-230)

- Haggai
Zechariah
Malachi (449 pages) (11-231)

- Matthew (888 pages) (11-073)

- Mark (606 pages) (11-074)

- Luke (736 pages) (11-075)

- John (532 pages) (11-076)

- Acts (697 pages) (11-077)

- Romans (536 pages) (11-078)

- I Corinthians (632 pages) (11-079)

- II Corinthians (589 pages) (11-080)

- Galatians (478 pages) (11-081)

- Ephesians (550 pages) (11-082)

- Philippians (476 pages) (11-083)

- Colossians (374 pages) (11-084)

- I Thessalonians
II Thessalonians (498 pages) (11-085)

- I Timothy
II Timothy
Titus
Philemon (687 pages) (11-086)

- Hebrews (831 pages) (11-087)

- James
I Peter
II Peter (730 pages) (11-088)

- I John
II John
III John
Jude (377 pages) (11-089)

- Revelation (602 pages) (11-090)

For telephone orders you may call 1-800-288-8350 with bankcard information. All Baton Rouge residents please use (225) 768-7000.

For mail orders send to:
Jimmy Swaggart Ministries
P.O. Box 262550
Baton Rouge, LA 70826-2550

Visit our website: www.jsm.org

NOTES